Fourth
Edition

Human Resources Management: Perspectives, Context, Functions, and Outcomes

Gerald R. Ferris
Department of Management
College of Business
Florida State University

M. Ronald Buckley
Division of Management
Michael F. Price College of Business
University of Oklahoma

Donald B. Fedor
Organizational Behavior Group
DuPree College of Management
Georgia Institute of Technology

Prentice
Hall

Upper Saddle River, New Jersey 07458

Library of Congress Cataloging-in-Publication Data

Human resources management : perspectives, context, functions, and outcomes / edited
by Gerald R. Ferris, M. Ronald Buckley, Donald B. Fedor.— 4th ed.
    p.   cm.
    Includes index.
    ISBN 0-13-060854-8 (pbk.)
    1. Personnel management.   I. Ferris, Gerald R.   II. Buckley, M. Ronald.
III. Fedor, Donald B.
HF5549.H8735   2002
658.3—dc21   2001053123

Acquisitions Editor: Melissa Steffens
Editor-in-Chief: Jeff Shelstad
Senior Managing Editor (Editorial): Jennifer Glennon
Assistant Editor: Jessica Sabloff
Editorial Assistant: Kevin Glynn
Media Project Manager: Michele Faranda
Marketing Manager: Shannon Moore
Marketing Assistant: Christine Genneken
Managing Editor (Production): John Roberts
Production Editor: Maureen Wilson
Production Assistant: Dianne Falcone

Permissions Coordinator: Suzanne Grappi
Associate Director, Manufacturing: Vincent Scelta
Production Manager: Arnold Vila
Manufacturing Buyer: Michelle Klein
Cover Design: Bruce Kenselaar
Cover Illustration/Photo: Grace Davies/Omni-Photo
    Communications, Inc.
Full-Service Project Management and Composition:
    BookMasters, Inc.
Printer/Binder: R.R. Donnelly

Credits and acknowledgments borrowed from other sources and reproduced, with permission, in this textbook are
as follows: p. 335 Jack Zenger, Dave Ulrich, & Norm Smallwood, The New Leadership Development, *Training &
Development*, March 2000, pp. 22–27. p. 563 Bob Nelson, The Care of the Un-Downsided, *Training & Development*,
April 1997, pp. 41–43. p. 370 David D. Dubois, The 7 Stages of One's Career, *Training & Development*, December
2000, pp. 45–50. p. 8 Copyright © 1995 by the American Psychological Association, Reprinted (or Adapted) with
permission. p. 398 Reprinted with Permission from the American Arbitration Association. p. 459 Elmer H. Burack.
(1999) 'Spirituality in the workplace', *Journal of Organisational Change Management*, Vol 12 No 4, pp. 280–291.
p. 547 James G. Clawson & Mark E. Haskin, Beating the Career Blues, *Academy of Management Executive*. p. 567
Harry Levinson & Jerry C. Wolford, Approaching Retirement as the Flexibility Phase, *Academy of Management
Executive*. p. 4 Bill Leonard, What Do CEO's Want from HR?, *HR Magazine*. p. 364 Michelle Martinez, Prepared
for the Future: Training Women, *HR Magazine*.

Pearson Education LTD.
Pearson Education Australia PTY, Limited
Pearson Education Singapore, Pte. Ltd
Pearson Education North Asia Ltd
Pearson Education, Canada, Ltd
Pearson Educación de Mexico, S.A. de C.V.
Pearson Education—Japan
Pearson Education Malaysia, Pte. Ltd

10 9 8 7 6 5 4 3 2 1
ISBN 0-13-060854-8

Brief Contents

Contents

Preface

Twenty-one years ago, we published the first edition of this book of readings in human resources management (HRM), then called *Current Issues in Personnel Management* (edited by Rowland, London, Ferris, and Sherman). The field was considerably different then, and beginning to undergo major change in status, importance, and perspective, and we tried our best to capture the key issues of importance in the field in the articles we selected for the book.

In many respects, our mission and objectives have not changed as we present our newest edition of this book, *Human Resources Management: Perspectives, Context, Functions, and Outcomes,* Fourth Edition. We continue to address the needs of undergraduate, professional, and graduate courses in HRM. We have retained the same structure used in the third edition of this book, which attempts to conceptualize, identify, and articulate what we consider to be the important contemporary perspectives and issues in the field today, and then to assemble a set of current readings that best address these perspectives and issues with a decidedly applied, rather than overly scientific, orientation. Once again, we have included a mix of recently published articles reprinted by permission from journals in the field, along with many articles written specifically for the book.

The fourth edition of *Human Resources Management* contains 47 articles, of which 35 were prepared especially for this volume. One of the goals we have had for this book, since the publication of the first edition, has been to increase the number of original articles written for the book in an effort to provide a more tailored fit of readings to our structure and perspectives for the book. The 35 original articles in this volume represent a 27 percent increase over the third edition in the number of specially prepared articles.

Whereas the fundamental structure we introduced in the third edition has been largely retained, this edition has been modified somewhat in both organization and content to reflect some new and different issues facing HRM in recent years. New chapters have been added to this edition that address such issues as corporate culture, values, employee rights and responsibilities, ethics, the nature of the changing employment relationship, mergers and acquisitions, and employee cynicism, and how such factors influence the practice of HRM. Following is an overview of the fourth edition's structure and contents.

Part I, *The Field of Human Resources Management*, offers an introduction to and overview of the field; the material is organized into two chapters. The first, *Overview of Human Resources Management*, provides a historical view of the field and its evolution, as well as a discussion of the meaning of this evolution for the development of future human resources professionals. Chapter 2, *Perspectives on Human Resources*

Management, treats three important perspectives on the field (i.e., strategic, political, and international) and demonstrates both the opportunities and challenges that these perspectives pose for human resources management.

Part II, *The External Context of Human Resources Management,* identifies certain features of the external environment or context that have impact on human resources activities. Chapter 3, *The Contemporary Legal Environment,* representatively reflects the strong influence of key aspects of federal legislation and case law on human resources issues in organizations. Chapter 4, *The Labor Market and the Changing Workforce,* deals with some important labor market characteristics and challenges and examines what diversity in the workforce means for organizations today.

Part III, *Functions of Human Resources Management,* provides thorough coverage of the various activities and functions of human resources management, although reorganized a bit since the previous edition of this book. Chapter 5, *Human Resources Planning and Staffing,* includes all of the material that is traditionally found in separate chapters devoted to human resources planning, recruitment and selection, career planning and development, and promotion and succession processes. The grouping of these various issues into a single chapter is intended to reflect their natural relatedness and the need to view them in an integrated way in organizations. Chapter 6, *Performance Evaluation and Management,* addresses the performance appraisal process, outlining some of the problems encountered and suggesting possible solutions. The articles in Chapter 7, *Compensation and Reward Systems,* are concerned with the importance of the compensation function in organizations; they include examinations of compensation strategy and executive pay. Chapter 8, *Human Resources Development,* addresses a number of issues related to the building of workforce skills at various levels and the need to link training and development efforts with business strategy.

Part IV, *The Internal Context of Human Resources Management,* examines features of the internal organizational environment or context that have impact on HRM. Chapter 9, *Labor Relations in Contemporary Work Environments,* discusses the critical issues surrounding unions and their future in organizations today, with reference to alternative forms of workforce governance, and alternative strategies and postures unions might take in efforts to be more influential in how organizations are run. Chapter 10, *Rights, Responsibilities, and Ethics,* is a new chapter in this edition and it examines issues including accountability, the new psychological contract and changing nature of the employment relationship, ethical issues in HRM, and the nature of empowerment and participation. Chapter 11, *Organizational Culture and Change,* is also a new chapter in this edition; it focuses on the influential and reciprocal role of organization culture in the formulation and implementation of HRM policies and practices. The chapter also examines the nature of change in organizations, including how culture and HRM are key components of such change processes. Furthermore, the chapter investigates some issues related to the relatively new topic of spirituality in the workplace, and its role in both organization culture and HRM. A number of issues are examined in Chapter 12, *Work Environment Stressors, Support, Safety, and Health.* Articles here investigate important stressors in the work environment including both work and family considerations, sexual harassment, and anger and violence at work. Other articles focus on stress-coping mechanisms or support systems like employee assistance programs, which can enhance health and well-being in the workplace.

The book concludes with Part V, *Outcomes of Human Resources Management*, which comprises three chapters. Chapter 13, *Employee Attitudes*, emphasizes the importance of the way employees view their work, management, and the organization; it stresses the potential dysfunctional consequences of negative attitudes, as well as the functional consequences of positive attitudes. Chapter 14, *Organizational Exit*, reflects the broad range of processes through which employees can depart from organizations. Retirement, downsizing, and other issues are examined in this chapter. Finally, Chapter 15, *Performance and Effectiveness*, treats what may well be the ultimate criteria for HRM. Topics examined include the influence and effectiveness of the human resources department, as well as performance management issues and how they impact on organizational performance. Also addressed are self-management issues, the increasing importance of customer service orientation and how it relates to HRM, and the implications of HRM for organizational reputation and image.

Thus, the fourth edition of *Human Resources Management: Perspectives, Context, Functions, and Outcomes* reflects some updating, expansion, and considerable coverage of the multitude of issues confronting human resources management today and in the future. With its organization and comprehensive coverage, this edition can serve as a stand-alone text for a course in HRM, or as an effective supplement to a conventional textbook that will allow the student to transcend the boundaries established by traditional treatments of the subject matter and explore some new issues.

ACKNOWLEDGMENTS

We gratefully acknowledge the assistance and support provided by our editors at Prentice Hall who helped make the fourth edition of *Human Resources Management* possible, and the following people for their helpful comments after reviewing the manuscript: Jai Ghorpade, PhD (San Diego State University), Professor Joseph F. Salamone (State University of New York at Buffalo), and Jonathan S. Monat, PhD (California State University, Long Beach).

We would like also to thank our colleagues who gave unselfishly of their time to contribute high quality original papers for this book: Jim Austin (Ohio State), Dharm Bhawuk (Hawaii), Philip Benson (New Mexico State), Nancy Napier (Boise State), Mike Harvey (Mississippi), John Veres (Auburn—Montgomery), Becky Thacker (Ohio), Pete Villanova (Appalachian State), Dwight Frink (Mississippi), Neal Mero (Mississippi), Bob Robinson (Mississippi), Matt Stollak (Mississippi State), Carmen Galang (Victoria), Suzanne Zivnuska (Florida State), Pam Perrewé (Florida State), Darren Treadway (Florida State), Randy Blass (Florida State), Kelly Zellars (North Carolina—Charlotte), Dave Gilmore (North Carolina—Charlotte), Angela Young (Cal State—LA), Jack Howard (Illinois State), Vic Devinatz (Illinois State), Ceasar Douglas (Florida State), Mike Bowen (South Florida), Wayne Hochwarter (Florida State), Christian Kiewitz (Alabama), Wendy Smith (Wittenberg), Jim Wilkerson (Southern Illinois), Bob Renn (Memphis), Bethany Himel (Memphis), John Keiser (Massachusetts—Amherst), Gloria Harrell-Cook (Mississippi State), Chris Shalley (Georgia Tech), Chuck Parsons (Georgia Tech), Harry Triandis (Illinois), David Allen (Memphis), Anthony Wheeler (Oklahoma), Chad Higgins (Washington), Danielle Beu (Louisiana

Tech), Grant Fenner (Memphis), Walter Davis (Mississippi), John Bernardin (Florida Atlantic), Jeff Hornsby (Ball State), Jonathon Halbesleben (Oklahoma), Greg Manley (Oklahoma), Mike Mumford (Oklahoma), Robin Salter (Auburn), Astrid Podsialowski (Hawaii), Jennifer Graf (Hawaii), Ronald Sims (William and Mary), Toni Locklear (Applied Psychological Techniques, Inc.), Katherine Jackson (Auburn—Montgomery), and Wesley Scroggins (Southwest Missouri State).

We appreciate all of our colleagues (and friends) very much!

PART

I

THE FIELD OF HUMAN RESOURCES MANAGEMENT

Our intention in Part I is to provide an introduction and overview of human resources management. This field is a dynamic discipline. Many of the truisms that were helpful in the past are no longer useful in facilitating the effective use of the human resources component of organizations. As all managers are managers of human resources, it is crucial that all managers have an accurate view of the human resources component. This overview will put the history and future of our field in proper perspective.

To accomplish this we have chosen, for Chapter 1, articles that are forward looking instead of historical. These articles confront the evolution of the field and the implications of this evolution for current practitioners. Further, these articles raise important implications for the development of future professionals in the field of human resources management. Lastly, they are intended to give us a glimpse of the future in human resources management, so we can plan accordingly.

The articles in Chapter 2 present a number of different perspectives (strategic, political, international) on human resources management. Significantly, these articles outline the challenges that face human resources professionals and, at the same time, demonstrate the opportunities that exist for those who see the importance of the human resources function. We have decided to place some emphasis on international issues as we believe they are an important component of the future of human resources management. By reading the articles in this chapter, you will gain an appreciation of the complexity of the field of human resources, along with optimism concerning the challenges and opportunities awaiting those who have as their goal effective use of human resources in organizations.

CHAPTER

1

OVERVIEW OF HUMAN RESOURCES MANAGEMENT

Although the history of human resources management has been relatively short, it has included a number of important advances. The field has developed greatly since the early stages of the Army Alpha and Beta Classification tests and the Hawthorne studies. Personnel clerks have been replaced by human resources professionals. Whereas personnel was once handled by clerical staff, human resources management is now handled by professionally educated and trained staff. We have realized that human resources are the spark that facilitates the organization engine. Because organizations have such a large investment in their human resources, it only makes sense that they exert a sincere effort to excel at human resources. Failure to do so can have a negative effect upon organizational profitability.

With respect to human resources management, two important questions need to be raised: Where have we been? and Where are we going? The answers to these questions are pivotal if we are to accept the challenge of international competition. Much research and practitioner thought go toward addressing these issues. Many questions concerning human resources have been satisfactorily resolved; many more remain. The challenge is to continue to develop novel approaches to the implementation of the science of human resources management.

The authors of the articles in this chapter confront a number of the aforementioned issues. Leonard has interviewed a number of CEOs in order to determine their perception of the appropriate role of human resources management in an environment of increasing complexity. In order to improve organizations, this survey reveals many potential areas of improvement and emphasis for the future. Cascio confronts an important issue, namely, the need for a redefinition of work itself. He outlines a research and thought agenda that will help us manage human resources effectively in the future.

READINGS

WHAT DO CEOS WANT FROM HR?

Bill Leonard

What do chief executive officers really think of the human resources profession? And how do CEOs think HR should change to meet the growing needs of their organizations?

To find out, *HRMagazine* recently interviewed five CEOs who represent a broad spectrum of industries, company sizes, and geographic locations. One CEO spent many years working in HR; the others have less experience with human resources management.

Despite these varied backgrounds, the comments from all five CEOs reveal common themes—and common areas where HR can stand to improve.

A UNIQUE RELATIONSHIP

As HR professionals increasingly strive to become strategic partners with top management, their relationship with CEOs takes on new significance. All the CEOs interviewed for this article agree that—of all the members of their management teams—their relationship with the top HR professional may be the most important.

The amount of time CEOs spend with HR executives underlines the importance of this relationship.

"I'm probably speaking with our senior vice president of human resources about 40 percent of my time at work," says Robert McDonald, CEO of the North American division of Standard Chartered Bank in New York. "It seems that I am always talking to her and seeking her advice and input."

Likewise, Mike R. Bowlin, chairman and CEO of ARCO, the Los Angeles–based oil and energy giant, constantly consults his top HR executive.

"I believe that I spend as much time with John Kelly (senior vice president of HR) as anyone else who works for me," he says. "There is no major decision that takes place in the company that John is not involved with, and I fully expect him to have an opinion on business decisions. As CEO, I use John as a personal consultant and sounding board for ideas and problem solving. Many times, he and I go to lunch and just bounce ideas off each other, which works well for us."

All five CEOs say that as HR has gained more access to their offices, the head of HR has assumed a unique relationship with the CEO. But how can HR make sure that relationship remains solid?

"The key to a good relationship between the CEO and the head of HR is honesty," believes Craig Sturken, chief executive officer of Farmer Jack Supermarkets in Detroit. "For the relationship to really work well, there has to be a trust, closeness, and almost intuitive understanding between the CEO and the head of HR. The last thing that you want to do as CEO is stifle that relationship; it's crucial to the success of your business."

Girard Miller, president and CEO of ICMA Retirement Corp. in Washington, D.C., says HR must relate well to both employees and top management. "It's a hard role to play, I believe. A good HR professional must have the ability to thoroughly develop a trusting relationship with the employees, while at the same time be something of a collaborator and serve as a confidant to the CEO."

Miller adds that HR must work closely with CEOs. "I'm a firm believer that the HR function must be a direct report to the CEO," he says. "I think that there are just too many opportunities for mischief, if it is not."

THE STRATEGIC ROLE OF HR

Why do these CEOs place such emphasis on the strategic role of HR in their organizations? The answer lies in the evolving and strategic role of the profession.

"HR has become a very important component in our strategic planning processes," says Mike Goodrich, president and CEO of BE&K Inc., an engineering and construction company based in Birmingham, Alabama. "We need to anticipate where our company is going to be five to six years down the road, and HR is crucial to understanding the changing demographics and expectations of our workforce."

The other CEOs agree that HR executives must understand and embrace their evolving strategic role, which includes helping track the skills of the workforce and matching them up with the organization's needs.

"HR management is one of the critical resources that we have to carry on our business plan," says Bowlin. "Our people are what will truly build a sustainable competitive advantage. In the long run, everyone has the same access to capital and technology, so a company's human resources is what makes the difference and makes it successful. It is the key resource."

McDonald fully expects "HR to be the guardian of information as to where your best people are in the organization and what their talents are."

Miller adds that "HR needs to know how the personnel talent of the organization can make a difference to the short-term business plans as well as the long-term strategy."

THE BOTTOM-LINE APPROACH

As HR's role as a strategic partner has evolved, the focus and knowledge necessary to be a successful HR executive have also changed. For example, the CEOs interviewed for this article emphasized that—although HR has improved its understanding of financial issues—more work needs to be done.

"When it comes to the bottom line, I would say that HR generally has been a bit out to lunch," says McDonald. "But their understanding of the bottom line has improved over the past few years, and I do believe most HR executives are striving to better understand how their decisions and actions can truly affect the bottom line."

Miller goes so far as to characterize HR's comprehension of financial issues as "soft." "HR professionals are not as far along as I, as a CEO, would like to see them," he says. "I believe they get the idea when it comes to their own budget but have a tough time understanding concepts such as variable costs versus fixed costs."

Miller says this is true with his current vice president of HR but adds that she has been a willing student. "And her willingness to learn is really the key here and clearly shows that she is interested and committed to improving the bottom line of this organization," he adds.

Sturken's experience mirrors that of McDonald and Miller; a solid financial orientation has not been a strength of most of the HR professionals he has worked with.

"I believe there has been a lack of concentration on the bottom line among many of the HR people I have known," Sturken says. But, like Miller, he sees improvement.

"I will hand it to my current vice president of HR," he says. "She is trying hard to learn and improve her knowledge and skills, and I believe that her efforts will pay off for both her and our company in the long run."

Sturken encourages HR professionals to strengthen their financial knowledge by taking advantage of educational opportunities. "I always advise my HR staff to take courses in business finance and financial planning," he says. "There are a lot of seminars and workshops on the fundamentals in accounting for nonfinancial managers. I have had managers come back from these courses and give suggestions and ideas to our accounting department on streamlining and improving some systems."

OTHER SKILLS

Besides a strong bottom-line orientation, several of the CEOs say their HR executives and managers need to be more aggressive and work on their powers of persuasion.

"At my company, we have a saying that you need to push the envelope," says Goodrich. "And HR has never really pushed the envelope with me. I have no problem saying 'no' if I think it's too much. I have said 'no' plenty of times to our information technology department. But HR has never pushed hard enough or far enough for me to say 'no' yet."

Bowlin says that HR has moved into the role of internal consultants at ARCO, but he is quick to point out that the term "consultants" does not mean he wants a bunch of "yes men or women" on his staff. He wants people who will challenge and question decisions that they believe are flawed.

"The people who acquiesce too quickly are usually gone quickly," he says. "But then if you have someone who tries to be too controlling, that's not good either. What we want is a team player who is knowledgeable, bright, and aggressive and has good consulting skills," Bowlin says.

Part of being a good consultant, says Bowlin, is being persuasive. "This is a skill that HR needs to work on, I believe," he says. "To succeed, you must have the ability to be persuasive and move the organization forward and to influence key business decisions."

To be more persuasive, however, many HR professionals need more education in business fundamentals.

"Clearly, HR professionals today are better trained than I was when I began my career 30 years ago [in HR]. But they do need sufficient and fundamental business training to participate and contribute to the company."

Miller goes a step further, saying that HR managers seem to lack some business training that is necessary to perform in today's workplace.

"I find generally that many HR professionals' business math skills and dimensions are fairly weak," Miller says. "I believe that the skill level is slowly improving and that's largely due, in part, to the fact that it is changing from the personnel function to the HR function."

Miller also believes that HR professionals have a "lack of vision" when it comes to the big picture of the organization.

"HR professionals have been getting by focusing on the day-to-day. They need to develop a broader and farther-reaching vision and understand where their organization is headed and how they can help steer the company in that direction," Miller adds.

McDonald says that HR is "being a bit insular." He says that one of the major problems with HR is that the profession's executives and managers have tended to focus solely on their HR departments.

"Their primary focus was HR, and the company was secondary to that. All the company did was provide them a paycheck, and that was the prevailing attitude 20 years ago," says McDonald. "It has improved, but I think because of that attitude, HR's reputation among other departments was a bit tainted. That reputation has improved vastly in recent years, but there's always room for improvement."

McDonald believes that improvement comes when HR sees itself as an internal consultant. "It really makes my job easier if I'm working with someone who sees themself as working with internal clients rather than seeing themself as just a part of the HR group," says McDonald. "Those who think outside the four dots and believe that they are serving internal clients get my vote."

BEYOND SKILLS

The CEOs interviewed for this article tend to agree that the best and most successful HR professionals have a real passion for their jobs.

"The better HR professionals that I have worked with have been compassionate and have deep feelings for our employees," says Goodrich. "They have a burning desire to see our employees succeed and build better lives for themselves. It's a trait that I have truly admired among most of the really good and successful HR professionals that I have known."

Bowlin agrees that true success comes from a passion for your job. "To really truly succeed, you have to be passionate about your work. You have to feel that you can make a difference," he says. "And if you are really good and passionate about your job, and you work in HR, you can really make one of the most positive impacts of any group within a company."

THE FUTURE OF HR

All five of the CEOs have to think strategically about the short- and long-term issues that confront their organizations. Two of the key issues they identified for their organizations—and, consequently, for HR—are recruiting and diversity.

Sturken says that the primary problem his company faces is a drastic labor shortage. The tight labor market has made recruiting and retention top priorities at his company.

"Retail is really tough right now," Sturken says. "It's a quality of life issue. The question that we face is, How can we improve our employees' lifestyle? People don't want to work weekends and evenings, and that's the lifeblood of retail. None of the old rules work when it comes to recruiting and hiring people. HR has to be very creative and market and merchandize our company and the advantages of working here. It's a very different ball game now."

Goodrich agrees that the labor market's rules have changed but attributes many of the changes to a dramatic shift in demographics.

"We really have been paying close attention to the changing demographics of our workforce," Goodrich says. "We have more women and more Latinos working in the construction industry today, and we must be prepared to respond to these changes."

He adds that the aging of the workforce will present some interesting challenges to the workplace. That is a trend that will also profoundly affect Miller's organization, which manages retirement funds for local governments.

"As the baby boom generation ages, we will have a powerful growth curve over the next five to six years in this organization," Miller says. "The demand for more retirement benefits and retiree medical care will be tremendous and will affect all businesses. We have to begin considering how we are going to pay for those benefits."

Bowlin believes that effectively managing multicultural diversity is the primary challenge that faces HR and corporate America.

"ARCO has to design HR systems that recognize cultural differences and help the company be more effective in those cultures. It's a high priority for us," Bowlin says. "As this company becomes more global, how we manage diversity will be key to our success."

The workplace challenges of multi-cultural diversity only emphasize the importance of developing a global focus when dealing with HR issues, according to McDonald.

"The challenge of HR is cross-cultural. It is a huge job to make that cultural bridge,"

he says. "HR professionals can prepare to meet these challenges by making themselves available for international assignments, and by that I mean living outside the country for three to four years. International mobility is key. Today's economy is a global economy, and HR has to be ready to accept the roles and challenges that the global marketplace brings." ■

WHITHER INDUSTRIAL AND ORGANIZATIONAL PSYCHOLOGY IN A CHANGING WORLD OF WORK?

Wayne F. Cascio

As citizens of the twentieth century, we have witnessed more change in our daily existence and in our environment than anyone else who ever walked the planet. But if you think the pace of change was fast in this century, expect it to accelerate in the next one. The twenty-first century will be even more complex, fast paced, and turbulent. It will also be very different. Industrial and organizational psychology potentially has much to contribute to this new world of work. It has the potential to lead change rather than to simply react to it, but to do so it must seize opportunities to provide research-based answers to pressing organizational problems. This article is organized into two parts. The first part describes some of the dramatic changes that are affecting the world of work; the second proposes a research agenda in six key areas in which applied psychologists often practice. I begin by considering the changing nature of economic competition.

CHANGING NATURE OF ECONOMIC COMPETITION

Just as wars—two World Wars, the Korean conflict, Vietnam, and Desert Storm—dominated the geopolitical map of the twentieth century, economics will rule over the 21st. The competition that is normal and inevitable among nations increasingly will be played out, not in aggression or war but in the economic sphere. The weapons used will be those of commerce: growth rates, investments, trade blocs, and imports and exports (Nelan, 1992).

These changes reflect the impact of globalized product and service markets, coupled with increased domestic competition (largely fueled by deregulation in telecommunications, airlines, and banking) and new business start-ups. By a wide margin, however, global competition is the single most powerful economic fact of life in the 1990s.

In the relatively sheltered era of the 1960s, only 7 percent of the U.S. economy was exposed to international competition. In the 1980s, that number zoomed past 70 percent, and it will keep climbing (Gwynne, 1992). Today, one in five American jobs is tied directly or indirectly to international trade. Merchandise exports are up more than 40 percent since 1986, and every $1 billion in U.S. merchandise exports generates approximately 20,000 new jobs. For the most part these are good jobs that pay about 22 percent more than average ("Investing in people," 1994).

The results of accelerated global competition have been almost beyond comprehension—free political debate throughout the former Soviet empire, democratic reforms in Central and South America, the integration of the European community, the North American Free Trade Agreement, and an explosion of free market entrepreneurship in Southern China. In short, the free markets and free labor markets that we in the United States have enjoyed throughout our national history have now become a global passion (Doyle, 1992).

There is no going back. Today, firms and workers in America must compete for business with firms and workers in the same industries in England, France, and Germany; in Poland, Hungary, and the former Russian republics; in Mexico, Brazil, Argentina, and Chile; and in Japan, Korea, Malaysia, Taiwan, Singapore, Hong Kong, and China, just to name a few of our competitors. However, it takes more than trade agreements, technology, capital investment, and infrastructure to deliver world-class products and services. It also takes the skills, ingenuity, and creativity of a competent, well-trained workforce. Our competitors know this, and they are spending unstintingly to create one.

The *World Competitiveness Report* (1994) provides a ranking of countries that combines the quality of public education, levels of secondary schooling and on-the-job training, computer literacy, and worker motivation. The United States ranks sixth, behind (in descending order) Singapore, Denmark, Germany, Japan, and Norway. Although none of the higher-ranking countries is as heterogeneous as the United States, the lesson for decision makers is clear: The race to create a broad, technically literate labor pool has no finish line!

Impact on Jobs in the United States

As nations around the world move from wartime to peacetime economies, from industrial societies to information societies, we are witnessing wrenching structural changes in our economy. These changes have impacted most profoundly in terms of jobs (Cascio, 1993). In the United States, more than seven million permanent layoffs have been announced since 1987. That number includes six million between 1987 and 1992 (Baumohl, 1993), 615,000 in 1993 (Byrne, 1994), and 516,000 in 1994 (Murray, 1995).

Companies are not downsizing because they are losing money. Fully 81 percent of companies that downsize in a given year were profitable in that year. Major reasons, according to the American Management Association's 1994 survey on downsizing, were strategic or structural in nature: to improve productivity, transfers of location, new technological processes, mergers and acquisitions, or plant obsolescence ("1994 AMA").

Laid-off workers who must return to the job market often must take huge pay cuts. Downward mobility is the rule rather than the exception ("Downside," 1994). Of roughly 2,000 workers let go by RJR Nabisco, for example, 72 percent found jobs subsequently but at wages that averaged only 47 percent of their previous pay ("Jobs," 1993). Surprisingly, older, higher-paid workers may fare better. A recent study of 311 workers (285 men and 26 women) whose average age and salary were 57 and $75,000, respectively, took an average of 5.6 months to land jobs that paid an average of $61,500 (Drake, Beam, Morin, Inc., 1994). Whether young or old, however, the bottom line for most reemployed workers is that both their spending power and their standards of living have dropped.

What's happening here? In a nutshell, as an executive in the pharmaceutical industry noted, we're moving from an economy where there are a lot of hard-working people to one where there are fewer, smarter-working people (Pilon, 1993). Jobs aren't being lost temporarily because of a recession; rather, they are being wiped out permanently as a result of new technology, improved machinery, and new ways of organizing work. In the following sections, I briefly examine the impact of these changes and then discuss how organizations are responding, particularly to the changes affecting managers and workers.

Effects of Technology on Organizations and People

Fifty million workers use computers every day along with other products of the digital age—faxes, modems, cellular phones, and e-mail. This is breaking down departmental barriers, enhancing the sharing of vast amounts of information, creating "virtual offices" for workers on the go, collapsing product development cycles, and changing the ways that organizations service customers and relate to their suppliers and to their employees. To succeed and prosper in the changing world of work, companies need motivated, technically literate workers.

A caveat is in order here, however. It relates to the common assumption that because production processes have become more sophisticated, high technology can substitute for skill in managing a workforce. Beware of such a "logic trap." On the contrary, high technology actually makes the workforce even more important for success, as Pfeffer (1994) has noted,

> This is because more skill may be necessary to operate the more sophisticated and advanced equipment, and with a higher level of investment per employee, interruptions in the process are increasingly expensive. This means that the ability to effectively operate, maintain, and repair equipment—tasks all done by first-line employees—become even more critical. (p. 8)

Ideally, therefore, technology will help workers make decisions in organizations that encourage them to do so ("Workplace of the Future," 1993). However, organizations of the future will look very different from organizations of the past, as the next section illustrates.

Changes in the Structure and Design of Organizations

In today's world of fast-moving global markets and fierce competition, the windows of opportunity are often frustratingly brief (Byrne, 1993). The features that dominated industrial society's approach to designing organizations throughout the nineteenth and twentieth centuries—mass production and large organizations—are disappearing. Trends such as the following are accelerating the shift toward new forms of organization for the twenty-first century (Kiechel, 1993): (a) smaller companies that employ fewer people; (b) the shift from vertically integrated hierarchies to networks of specialists; (c) technicians, ranging from computer repair persons to radiation therapists, replacing manufacturing operatives as the worker elite (see Barley, 1991); (d) pay tied less to a person's position or tenure in an organization and more to the market value of his or her skills; (e) the change in the paradigm of doing business from making a product to providing a service; and (f) the redefinition of work itself—growing disappearance of "the job" as a fixed bundle of tasks (see Bridges, 1994) and increased emphasis on constantly changing work required to fulfill the ever-increasing demands of customers. This will require constant learning, more higher order thinking, and the availability to work outside the standard hours of 9 A.M. to 5 P.M.

In this emerging world of work, more and more organizations will focus carefully on their core competencies and outsource everything else. They will be characterized by terms such as *virtual, boundary-less,* and *flexible,* with no guarantees to workers or managers. Hundreds of big companies have outsourced noncore operations: Continental Bank Corporation has contracted its legal, audit, cafeteria, and mailroom operations to outside companies. American Airlines is doing the same with customer service jobs at 30 airports.

This approach to organizing is no short-term fad. The fact is, organizations are becoming leaner and leaner, with better and better trained "multispecialists"—those who have in-depth knowledge about a number of different aspects of the business. Eschewing narrow specialists or broad generalists, organizations of the future will come to rely on cross-trained multispecialists to get things done. One such group whose roles are changing dramatically is that of managers.

The Changing Role of the Manager

In the traditional hierarchy that used to comprise most bureaucratic organizations, rules were simple. Managers ruled by command from the top (essentially one-way communication), used rigid controls to ensure that fragmented tasks (grouped into clearly defined jobs) could be coordinated effectively, and partitioned information into neat compartments—departments, units,

and functions. Information was (and is) power, and, at least in some cases, managers clung to power by hoarding information. This approach to organizing, that is, 3-C (command, control, and compartmentalization) logic, was geared to achieve three objectives: stability, predictability, and efficiency.

In today's reengineered, hypercompetitive work environments, the autocratic, top-down command-and-control approach is out of step with the competitive realities that many organizations face. To survive, organizations have to be able to respond quickly to shifting market conditions. In this kind of an environment, a key job for all managers, especially top managers, is to articulate a vision of what the organization stands for and what it is trying to accomplish. The next step is to translate that vision into everything that is done and to use the vision as a benchmark to assess progress over time.

A large and growing number of organizations now recognize that they need to emphasize workplace democracy to achieve the vision. This involves breaking down barriers, sharing information, using a collaborative approach to problem solving, and an orientation toward continuous learning and improvement. For many managers, these kinds of skills simply weren't needed in organizations designed and structured under 3-C logic.

Does this imply that we are moving toward a universal model of organizational and leadership effectiveness? Hardly. Contingency theories of leadership such as path-goal theory (House, 1971), normative decision theory (Vroom & Yetton, 1973), or least-preferred coworker (LPC) contingency theory (Fiedler, 1967) suggest that an autocratic style is appropriate in some situations. In recent years many organizations (e.g., Eaton Corporation and Levi Strauss & Co.) have instituted formal information-sharing and workplace education programs that reduce or eliminate a key condition that makes autocratic leadership appropriate—workers who lack the information or knowledge needed to make meaningful suggestions or decisions. More often, today's networked, interdependent, culturally diverse organizations require transformational leadership (Bass, 1985). The ability of leaders to transform followers to bring out their creativity, imagination, and best efforts requires well-developed interpersonal skills, founded on an understanding of human behavior in organizations. Industrial and organizational psychologists are well-positioned to help managers develop these kinds of skills.

In addition, although by no means universal, much of the work that results in a product, service, or decision is now done in teams—intact, identifiable social systems (even if small or temporary) whose members have the authority to manage their own task and interpersonal processes as they carry out their work. Such teams go by a variety of names—autonomous work groups, process teams, and self-managing work teams. All of this implies a radical reorientation from the traditional view of a manager's work.

In this kind of an environment, workers are acting more like managers, and managers more like workers. The managerial roles of controllers, planners, and inspectors are being replaced by coaches, facilitators, and mentors (Wellins, Byham, & Wilson, 1991). This doesn't just happen—it requires good interpersonal skills, continuous learning, and an organizational culture that supports and encourages both.

Flattened hierarchies also mean that there are fewer managers in the first place. The empowered worker will be a defining feature of such organizations.

The Empowered Worker— No Passing Fad

It should be clear by now that we are in the midst of a revolution—a revolution at work.

Change isn't coming only from large, high-profile companies doing high-technology work. It has also permeated unglamorous, low-tech work. As an example, consider Toronto-based Cadet Uniform Services, which outfits the employees of some of North America's leading corporations (Henkoff, 1994).

Cadet doesn't just hire people to drive trucks, deliver clean uniforms, and pick up dirty ones. Rather, its concept of customer service representatives (CSRs) extends much further. They are mini-entrepreneurs who design their own routes, manage their own accounts, and, to a large extent, determine the size of their paychecks.

Cadet ties compensation almost entirely to measures of customer satisfaction. Lose a customer on your watch and your salary sinks. CSR pay is about $40,000 a year, nearly twice the industry average. In practice, Cadet rarely loses a customer; its annual defection rate is less than 1 percent. Employees don't leave either; turnover is a low 7 percent. To a large extent this is because Cadet spends considerable time and effort on selecting employees—who take pride in their work, are exceedingly neat, and are outgoing. In all, 46 ethnic groups are represented at Cadet.

How has the company done? Its annual growth has averaged 22 percent for the past 20 years, and it boasts double-digit profit margins that exceed the industry norm. Says Quentin Wahl, chief executive officer, "The jobs we do aren't so special—the pay is good, but it's not great. The main thing we have to sell to employees is the culture of the organization" (Henkoff, 1994, p. 122).

Organizations of the 1990s, both large and small, differ dramatically in structure, design, and demographics from those of even a decade ago. Demographically, they are far more diverse. They comprise more women at all levels, more multiethnic, multicultural workers, more older workers, workers with disabilities, robots, and contingent workers. Paternalism is out; self-reliance is in. There's constant pressure to do more with less and steady emphasis on empowerment, cross-training, personal flexibility, self-managed work teams, and continuous learning. Workers today have to be able to adapt to changing circumstances and be prepared for multiple careers. Industrial and organizational psychologists are helping to educate prospective, current, and former workers to these new realities. In the future, they will be expected to do much more, as I describe later, but first I consider some organizational responses to these new realities.

Implications for Organizations and Their People

What do these trends imply for the ways that organizations will compete for business? In a world where virtually every factor that affects the production of goods or the delivery of services—capital, equipment, technology, and information—is available to every player in the global economy, the one factor that doesn't routinely move across national borders is a nation's workforce. In the years to come, the quality of the American workforce will be a crucial determinant of America's ability to compete and win in world markets.

Human resources can be sources of sustained competitive advantage as long as they meet three basic requirements: (a) They add positive economic benefits to the process of producing goods or delivering services; (b) the skills of the workforce are distinguishable from those of competitors (e.g., through education and workplace learning); and (c) such skills are not easily duplicated (Barney, 1991). Human resource systems (the set of interrelated processes designed to attract, develop, and maintain human resources) can either enhance or destroy this

potential competitive advantage (Lado & Wilson, 1994).

Perhaps a quote attributed to Albert Einstein, the famous physicist, best captures the position of this article. After the first atomic reaction in 1942, Einstein remarked, "Everything has changed, except our way of thinking" ("Workplace of the Future," 1993, p. 2). As psychology in general, and industrial and organizational psychology in particular, stands poised on the brink of the 21st century, I believe that our greatest challenge will be to change the way we as a field think about organizations and their people. The first part of this article addressed some key changes in the world of work; the remainder identifies some pressing research questions that must be addressed if our science is to remain relevant to twenty-first-century organizations.

A RESEARCH AGENDA FOR INDUSTRIAL AND ORGANIZATIONAL PSYCHOLOGISTS

Each of the following sections identifies traditional practices, new developments, and research questions that require attention if the field is to lead organizational change rather than react to it. These sections are job analysis, employee selection, training and development, performance appraisal, compensation (including incentives), and organization development. Admittedly, these areas represent only some of the broad range of activities that psychologists are engaged in and that relate to the management of people in work settings. In total, however, they comprise much of the work in this area.

Job Analysis: Identifying the Work to Be Done and the Personal Characteristics Necessary to Do the Work

Traditional task-based "jobs" were once packaged into clusters of similar tasks and assigned to specialist workers. Today, many firms have no reason to package work that way. Instead, they are unbundling tasks into broader chunks of work that change over time. Such shifting clusters of tasks make it difficult to define a job, at least in the traditional sense. Practices such as flex time, job sharing, and telecommuting, not to mention temporary workers, part-timers, and consultants, have compounded the definitional problem.

Job analysis is a common activity of industrial and organizational psychologists, and there exists a well-defined technology for doing such analysis (Gael, 1988; Harvey, 1991; Ilgen & Hollenbeck, 1991; McCormick, 1979). Terms such as *job element, task, duty, position, job, job description,* and *job family* are well-understood parts of the lexicon of industrial and organizational psychologists everywhere.

Today, however, there is a detectable shift away from a task-based toward a process-based organization of work. A *process* is a collection of activities (such as procurement, order fulfillment, product development, or credit issuance) that takes one or more kinds of input and creates an output that is of value to a customer (M. Hammer & Champy, 1993). Customers may be internal or external. Individual tasks are important parts of the process, but the process itself cuts across organizational boundaries and traditional functions, such as engineering, production, marketing, and finance.

Consider credit issuance as an example. Instead of the separate jobs of credit checker and pricer, the two may be combined into one "deal structure." Such integrated processes cut response time and increase efficiency and productivity. Bell Atlantic created a "case team"—a group of people who have among them all of the skills necessary to handle an installation order. Members of the team—who previously were located in different departments and in different geographical areas—were brought together into a single unit and given total responsibility for installing the equipment. Such a process operates, on average, ten times faster than the assembly line version it replaces. Bell Atlantic, for example, reduced the time it takes to install a high-speed digital service link from 30 days to 3 (M. Hammer & Champy, 1993).

Employees involved in the process are responsible for ensuring that customers' requirements are met on time and with no defects, and they are empowered to experiment in ways that will cut cycle time and reduce costs. Result: Less supervision is needed, while workers take on broader responsibilities and a wider purview of activities. Moreover, the kinds of activities that each worker does are likely to shift over time.

In terms of traditional job analysis, this leaves many unanswered questions and a number of challenges. Some of these questions follow.

What will be the future of traditional task-based descriptions of jobs and job activities? Should other types of descriptors replace task statements that describe what a worker does, to what or whom, why, and how? Will "task cluster" statements or "subprocess" statements become the basic building blocks for describing work? What does a job description look like in a process-based organization of work? Will job specifications (which identify the personal characteristics—knowledge, skills, abilities, and other characteristics—necessary to do the work) supersede job descriptions? Does identification of the environmental, contextual, and social dimensions of work become more important in a process-based structure? Will emphasis shift from describing jobs to describing roles?

Managers often look to industrial and organizational psychologists to help them analyze jobs and describe work processes as a foundation for other human resource management activities, such as employee selection, training, compensation, work and organization design, and performance appraisal. In the next section, I discuss the implications of the new organization of work for employee selection.

Selecting Employees

In the traditional paradigm, so-called "one-shot" selection–placement programs worked as follows: analyze the job, identify relevant job performance criteria, identify job-related predictors of performance, validate predictors, and then select candidates who score highest on the set of validated predictors. As with job analysis, the technology for working within this paradigm is also well developed (see, e.g., Cascio, 1991; Guion, 1991; Schmitt & Borman, 1993).

I just described the problems associated with analyzing jobs under a process-based organization of work. To compound those problems, consider that relatively few jobs in today's economy are performed independently of others and that most are interdependent or coordinate in nature—that is, they are a function of group efforts, not just the sum of individual talents. For example, both Xerox Corporation and General Electric (GE) now develop new products through multidisciplinary teams that work in a single process, instead of vertical functions or departments. At GE a senior team of 9–12 people oversees nearly 100 processes or programs worldwide, from new product design to improvement of the yield on production machinery. The senior team—consisting of managers with multiple competencies rather than narrow specialists—exists to allocate resources and ensure coordination of the processes and programs. "They stay away from the day-to-day activities, which are managed by the teams themselves," explains Harold Giles, manager of human resources in GE's lighting business ("The Horizontal Corporation," 1993, p. 79). That's quite a change from the traditional role of a supervisor.

Let us add just one more complicating factor to this mix: In some cases workers will join intact work teams that stay together to perform different kinds of work, such as assembly of different models of an automobile, or different products entirely, as under a flexible manufacturing system. In project-based work, such as research and development, consulting, legal defense, or movie production, "virtual" teams consisting of multidisciplinary players are created to work on a project and then are disbanded when the project is finished. In these cases, the nature of the work changes, as does the composition of the teams that do the work.

From the point of view of industrial and organizational psychology, the challenge is to move beyond valid, job-based predictors because the work to be done changes constantly. This raises a number of research issues relevant to the selection of employees (including managers): How does the selection process influence team effectiveness? As Klimosky and Jones (1995) noted, selecting the right mix of individuals to comprise a team implies attention to worker requirements on at least three dimensions: ability, values and personality, and politics (a team member's future role in making things happen once a decision is reached).

Will the role of tests of cognitive abilities focus on identifying candidates with general (as opposed to specific) abilities, such as basic verbal and numeracy skills, the ability to think critically, to reason logically, and to draw conclusions from a body of facts? If so, this would comport with recent findings that general cognitive ability is an efficient predictor in terms of job performance (Ree & Earles, 1992; Ree, Earles, & Teachout, 1994) and training performance (Ree & Earles, 1991).

How can psychology contribute to the optimal use of people with lower levels of cognitive abilities? Because not all jobs require high levels of cognitive ability (e.g., many types of service jobs), what other types of predictors of work performance will validly forecast success in such jobs?

Services, which now account for 74 percent of the gross domestic product, and 79 percent of all employment in the United States, are expected to account for all of the net growth in jobs in the next decade. Will measures of personality characteristics—for example, adaptability, empathy, and ability to work under stress—receive relatively more attention than cognitive ability tests in jobs whose primary objective is customer service? To be sure, the ability to select, train, and retain front-line, customer-contact workers will be a top priority for many organizations. Companies such as Marriott and Disney now require the same skills of workers that they once demanded of managers—"people who are resilient and resourceful, empathetic and enterprising, competent and creative" (Henkoff, 1994, p. 110).

There is no question that well-developed measures of personality characteristics can account for additional variance in the prediction of behavior on the job (Hogan, 1991; Ones, Mount, Barrick, & Hunter, 1994; Tett, Jackson, Rothstein, & Reddon, 1994). Although a wide variety of such measures exists, they have not been used routinely to select employees. However, given the emphasis on effective interpersonal interaction in the new forms of work organization, more and more managers insist that such characteristics be taken into account. This poses another question of interest to industrial and organizational psychologists, namely the following:

Do alternative modes of pre-hire personality assessment—paper-and-pencil measures, interactive video, computer-based, structured individual or group interviews, or situational tests, for example—provide equivalent psychometric properties? Do they measure the same constructs? As Campbell and Fiske (1959) noted, any test or other measurement procedure is really a trait–method unit—that is, a test measures a given trait by a single method. Hence if one wants to know the relative contribution of trait and method variance to test scores, one must study more than one trait (e.g., dominance and affiliation) and use more than one method (e.g., paper and pencil and interactive video). Second-order confirmatory factor analysis (Marsh & Hocevar, 1988) may be especially helpful in this context.

To probe personality characteristics, pre-hire assessment procedures, especially those used by large organizations, often include patterned behavior description interviews, in which candidates are asked to provide detailed accounts of actual situations (Alderman, 1995). For example, instead of asking, "How would you reprimand an employee?" now it's "Give me a specific example of a time you had to reprimand an employee. What action did you take, and what was the result?" Answers tend to be remarkably consistent with actual (i.e., subsequent) job behavior (Dipboye & Gaugler, 1993; Weekley & Gier, 1987).

Alternatively, interviewers may pose "What would you do if . . . ?" questions. Such questions compose the situational interview, which is based on the assumption that a person's expressed behavioral intentions are related to subsequent behavior. In the situational interview, candidates are asked to describe how they think they would respond in certain job-related situations. Validities for both types of interviews vary from about 0.22 to 0.28 (Motowidlo et al., 1992). This brings up the following questions. (a) Does it matter whether patterned behavior description interview questions or situational interview questions are administered face-to-face or by computer? (b) Do they (interview questions) measure the same constructs and yield equivalent validities? (c) Will work samples or situational tests be used more frequently to assess the compatibility of potential team members, especially members of self-managed work teams? Such procedures measure the ability to do, not just the ability to know. Group-based situational tests (e.g., the leaderless group discussion) have long been used in management selection (e.g., Bass, 1954). How should they be designed to fit the context of a self-managed team—whether intact or virtual?

"Why is it that I always get a whole person when what I really want is a pair of hands?" Henry Ford lamented (Labich, 1994, p. 64). In today's (and tomorrow's) world of work, characteristics of the whole person—cognitive as well as personality— are required to improve continuously the business processes that satisfy the needs of internal and external customers. Managers know this, and increasingly they are turning to industrial and organizational psychologists for answers.

Training and Development

The old Chinese proverb, "Give a man a fish and you feed him for a day; teach a man to fish and you feed him for life," fits neatly into today's emphasis on self-reliance and career resiliency. Career-resilient workers are dedicated to continuous learning. They stand ready to reinvent themselves to keep pace with change, they take responsibility for their own career management, and they are committed to their company's success (Waterman, Waterman, & Collard, 1994). This implies two things: (a) Companies must make it easy for employees to learn and to become flexible, and (b) workers should have the right to obtain ongoing training.

For example, at Sun Microsystems, a core value is "We acknowledge the essential link between company growth and the development of individuals" ("Career," 1994). To make this link a reality, Sun supports training and development activities in three areas: (a) assessment of interests, values, and temperament (to help employees understand who they are and where they are going); (b) assessment and development of technical and functional work skills (to help employees benchmark and improve their work performance); and (c) assessment and development of work strategies (to help employees understand and improve their performance in areas such as problem solving and conflict resolution).

Compelling as the idea of training may seem, there are strong disincentives for implementing it. To illustrate, consider just three macrolevel structural issues in the design and delivery of training (Cascio, 1994b):

1. Corporate commitment is lacking and uneven. Most companies spend nothing at all on training. Those that do spend tend to concentrate on managers, technicians, and professionals, not rank-and-file workers. Fully 89 percent of American workers never receive any formal training from their employers ("Labor Letter," 1991).

2. Poaching trained workers is a major problem for U.S. businesses and provides a strong disincentive for training. Unlike in Germany, where local business groups pressure companies not to steal one another's employees, there is no such system in the United States (Salwen, 1993). This has profound consequences for "selling" senior managers on the value of training in the United States.

3. Despite the rhetoric about training being viewed as an investment, current accounting rules require that it be treated as an expense. Business might spend more on training if accounting rules were revised. Unlike investments in plant and equipment, which show up on the books as an asset, training expenditures are seen merely as expenses to be deducted in the year they are incurred ("Labor Letter," 1991).

Industrial and organizational psychologists have little control over these macrolevel problems. However, there is much that they can contribute. For example, with respect to the poaching problem, it is important to point out the "training paradox," as described by Robert Waterman (Filipczak,

1995). The paradox runs both ways. That is, if employees take charge of their own employability by keeping their skills updated and varied so they can work for anyone, de facto they build more job security with their current employer—assuming the employer values highly skilled, motivated employees. Similarly, the company that provides lots of training and learning opportunities is more likely to retain workers because it creates an interesting and challenging environment. In theory, therefore, increasing an individual's employability outside a company simultaneously increases his or her job security and desire to stay with the current employer.

A related area in which psychologists can contribute on the basis of strong inferences from data is that of training evaluation. The literature on training evaluation shows that whereas the potential returns from well-conducted training programs can be substantial, there is often considerable variability in the effectiveness with which any given training method or content area is implemented (Cascio, 1994a). Considerable planning (through needs analysis) and follow-up program evaluation efforts are necessary to realize these returns. Both needs analysis and program evaluation are well-developed areas in industrial and organizational psychology (Goldstein, 1989, 1994; Kraiger, Ford, & Salas, 1993).

For example, one issue that often vexes employers is whether to spend money on reskilling programs for older workers with shorter payback periods. Another is whether to invest in training for the hard-core unemployed or for workers who lack basic literacy skills. In both cases, business sees lower payback probabilities. Utility analyses can play an important role in dispelling myths about the costs of training relative to its benefits. The technology is available now to do such analyses (Cascio, 1989), and a number of them already have been reported in the personnel psychology literature (Cascio, 1994a). However, what generally has not

been reported, and that will be essential in the future, is objective evidence of the extent to which the financial returns forecasted by utility analyses actually do materialize.

One area in which objective evidence does indicate positive payoffs for individual and organizational performance is that of high-performance work practices (HPWPs), of which training is an integral component. Such practices provide workers with the information, skills, incentives, and responsibility to make decisions essential for innovation, quality improvement, and rapid response to change (U.S. Department of Labor, 1993). A recent study based on a national sample of nearly 1,000 publicly-traded firms found that HPWPs have an economically and statistically significant impact both on employee turnover and productivity on short-term and long-term measures of corporate financial performance (Huselid, 1995).

Earlier I showed how the roles of workers and managers are changing dramatically, from controlled to empowered, from boss to mentor. Both groups will require extensive training and support to change entrenched attitudes and beliefs to function effectively in the new world of work. For example, empowered employees need to develop the kind of understanding of business and financial issues that no one but an owner or an executive used to be concerned with (Bridges, 1994). Moreover, several studies have supported the novel proposition that the "skills gap" is really about attitudes (Cappelli, 1992). Thus a 1989 employer survey by Towers Perrin found that the most common reasons for firing new employees were absenteeism and failure to adapt to the work environment; only 9 percent of the workers were dismissed because of difficulties in learning how to perform their jobs. A 1990 survey by the National Association of Manufacturers found that the belief that applicants would not have the work attitudes and behaviors needed to adapt to the work environment was almost twice as common a reason for rejecting applicants as the next most important factor. This raises several intriguing research questions:

If attitudes play such an important role in work performance, then constructs such as adaptability, consistency, and prosocial behavior become particularly important components of workplace learning programs. To what extent can such characteristics be taught? How should they be taught? To what extent can research findings in applied social psychology, cognitive psychology, and instructional technology inform training practice in these areas?

In designing training systems to promote team development and workplace learning, what are the most effective methods for developing skill, knowledge, and attitudinal competencies (Cannon-Bowers, Tannenbaum, Salas, & Volpe, 1995)? Do results hold up when teams must operate in stable as opposed to rapidly changing environments?

Senior managers are looking for evidence of the extent to which workers and managers can change their attitudes and behavior to fit new organizational designs. Research is needed to identify methods and activities that will facilitate and maintain such change. The relapse prevention model, a cognitive–behavioral model of self-control strategies designed to reduce the likelihood of relapse, is a good place to start (Marx, 1982).

Performance Appraisal

Performance appraisal refers to the systematic description of the job-relevant strengths and weaknesses of an individual or group. In recent years, one issue that has generated considerable debate is the relevance and appropriateness of performance appraisal in work contexts that emphasize total quality management (TQM).

TQM emphasizes the continuous improvement of products and processes to ensure long-term customer satisfaction. Its group problem-solving focus encourages employee empowerment by using the job-related expertise and ingenuity of the workforce. Cross-functional teams develop solutions to complex problems, often shortening the time taken to design, develop, or produce products and services. Because a team may not include a representative of management, the dividing line between labor and management often becomes blurred in practice, as workers themselves begin to solve organizational problems. Thus adoption of TQM generally requires cultural change within the organization as management reexamines its past methods and practices in light of the demands of the new philosophy (Wideman, 1993).

If the "father of TQM," W. Edwards Deming, had his way, appraisal systems that tie individual performance to salary adjustments would be eliminated. In his view, such systems hinder teamwork, create fear and mistrust, and discourage risk-taking behavior, thereby stifling innovation. Worse yet, Deming believes, most appraisal systems are based on the faulty assumption that individuals have significant control over their own performance—that is, that most individuals can improve if they choose to do so by putting forth the necessary effort (Deming, 1986).

Most industrial and organizational psychologists would agree that as a basis for implementing a "pay-for-performance" philosophy, performance appraisal is a meaningful tool only if workers have significant control over the variables that impact their individual performance. If not, then it is true, as Deming (1986) believes, that appraisals only measure random statistical variation within a particular system. Here are three suggestions for harmonizing these two processes (Wideman, 1993): Let customer expectations (a) generate individual or team performance expectations, (b) include results expectations that identify actions to meet or exceed those expectations, and (c) include behavioral skills that make the real difference in achieving quality performance and total customer satisfaction.

Here are several other pressing research issues in appraisal:

1. Traditionally, the immediate supervisor is responsible for rating subordinates (Bernardin & Beatty, 1984; Murphy & Cleveland, 1991). New organizational designs that incorporate self-managed work teams or manufacturing "cells" (small teams of workers) may not have an immediate supervisor. Research is needed to provide answers to questions such as Who should rate performance under these circumstances and on what criteria? What should be the relative role (if any) of customers or suppliers? McIntyre and Salas (1995) have identified a number of behavioral indicators of team performance, and their work can help guide future research in this area.

2. To create greater allegiance to a process, rather than to a boss, GE has begun to put in place so-called "360–degree appraisals" in which peers and others above and below the employee evaluate the performance of an individual in a process ("The Horizontal Corporation," 1993; see also Tornow, 1993). Research is needed to identify the relative weights of the various raters as well as optimal means for combining information. Moreover, given that multiple perspectives are represented (e.g., peers, subordinates, and supervisors), and that each is best able to rate different aspects of performance (Borman, 1974; Mabe & West, 1982), what should each rater rate?

3. In work that is highly coordinate in nature (e.g., grant proposal writing and process reengineering), it is simply not possible to disaggregate individual from team performance. Although individual behaviors can be rated (e.g., initiative,

flexibility, and effort), individual outcomes cannot. As McIntyre and Salas (1995) pointed out, teamwork and task work are distinct. Research is needed to identify the components and mechanics of team-based performance appraisal.

4. What is the most appropriate format and method for communicating performance feedback when multiple perspectives are represented? Should a single individual serve as the conduit for such feedback? Who is responsible for following up to ensure that goals are set and progress is monitored? What is the long-term impact of such feedback on behavior and work outcomes (Smither et al., 1995)?

Answers to these kinds of questions are particularly relevant to the changing world of work. Industrial and organizational psychologists have the tools and know-how to advance cumulative knowledge in this area while making genuine contributions to better management of human resources.

Compensation and Incentives

Traditionally, pay systems were job-based. That is, each job had an intrinsic worth (identified through the process of job evaluation) so that, in theory at least, pay stayed relatively constant regardless of who performed the job. Individual contributions were rewarded, as was position in the hierarchy and tenure on the job. Base salaries tended to increase year after year, as percentage increases yielded larger and larger amounts of money added to the base.

In today's flatter, less hierarchical organizations, the old assumptions about pay systems are being questioned. Some organizations are rewarding employees not just for individual performance but also for the development of their skills and for team or organizational performance (Ost, 1995). Others are asking employees to put more of their pay at risk. Consider each of these trends.

In a skill- or knowledge-based pay system, workers are not paid on the basis of the job they currently are doing but rather on the basis of the number of jobs they are capable of doing, or on their depth of knowledge. In such a "learning environment," the more workers learn, the more they earn. Workers at American Steel & Wire can boost their annual salaries by up to $12,480 by acquiring as many as 10 skills. Is there any impact on productivity or morale? A recent survey of 27 companies with such programs revealed that 70 percent to 88 percent reported higher job satisfaction, product quality, or productivity. Some 70 percent to 75 percent reported lower operating costs or reduced turnover ("Skill-Based Pay," 1992).

Such systems cannot work in all situations. They seem to work best when the following conditions exist (Gomez-Meija & Balkin, 1992): (a) A supportive human resource management (HRM) philosophy underpins all employment activities (such a philosophy is characterized by mutual trust and the conviction that employees have the ability and motivation to perform well); (b) HRM programs such as profit sharing, participative management, empowerment, and job enrichment complement the skill- or knowledge-based pay system; (c) technology and organization structure change frequently; (d) employee exchanges (i.e., assignment and rotation) are common; (e) there are opportunities to learn new skills; (f) employee turnover is relatively high; and (g) workers value teamwork and the opportunity to participate.

A second trend among many firms is to increase the proportion of pay that is at risk or variable, thereby reducing fixed costs. A third trend is to use team or organization-wide incentives, such as profit sharing or productivity gain sharing, to provide

broader motivation than is furnished by incentive plans geared to individual employees. Their aim is twofold: to increase productivity and to improve morale by giving employees a feeling of participation in and identification with the company (Florkowski, 1987).

It is important to distinguish *gain sharing* from *profit sharing*. The two approaches differ in three important ways (T. H. Hammer, 1988): (a) Gain sharing is based on a measure of productivity. Profit sharing is based on a global profitability measure. (b) Gain sharing productivity measurement, and bonus payments are frequent events, distributed monthly or quarterly, whereas the measures and rewards of profit-sharing plans are annual. (c) Gain-sharing plans are current distribution plans, in contrast to most profit-sharing plans, which have deferred payments. Hence gain-sharing plans are true incentive plans rather than employee benefits. As such they are more directly related to individual behavior and therefore can motivate worker productivity.

Does profit sharing improve productivity? One review of 27 econometric studies found that profit sharing was positively related to productivity in better than 9 of every 10 instances. Productivity was generally 3 to 5 percent higher in firms with profit-sharing plans than in those without plans (U.S. Department of Labor, 1993).

Does gain sharing improve productivity? Of 72 companies using Improshare (Fein, 1982)—production standards based on time-and-motion studies, plus a sharing of productivity gains 50–50 between employees and the company—38 companies were nonunion and 34 were represented by 18 international unions. The average gain in productivity over all companies using the plan after one year was 22.4 percent. Productivity gains tended to be larger if workers were provided with training and information; gains tended to be smaller, none, or negative (i.e., productivity deteriorated) if workers perceived that there was "nothing in it" for them.

Such changes in compensation and incentive systems raise several important research questions:

1. American culture emphasizes "rugged individualism" rather than a group orientation. What specific contextual issues are relevant when team or organization-wide incentives are applied in such a culture?
2. Empowerment emphasizes an active role for employees in determining outcomes. Yet employees sometimes feel powerless to influence profits, as under a profit-sharing program. How can firms deal with this inconsistency?
3. Logically, team-based performance appraisals should form the basis for team-based incentives. However, there is almost no extant research on team-based appraisals (an exception is Norman & Zawacki, 1991), with respect either to process or to format.
4. Although firms such as General Foods, General Motors, Procter and Gamble, and Anheuser-Busch have been experimenting with skill- or knowledge-based pay (Tosi & Tosi, 1987), job evaluation methods remain more popular. Why? What employee or work-related factors might enhance the applicability of such systems in a changing world of work?

Organizational Development

Organizational development (OD) can be described broadly as the use of planned, behavioral science-based interventions in work settings for the purpose of improving organizational functioning and individual development (Porras & Robertson, 1992). At its core, OD is about change, and in the future world of work, "the core competitive advantage for companies will be their capacity for mastering revolutionary change at all levels of the organization" (Tichy, 1994).

For many organizations, this will require a metamorphosis into a "learning organization." Yet as compelling a notion as that is, in-depth interviews with 350 executives in 14 industries found that in attempting to implement change, from work redesign to organization culture, many firms had not learned from their past mistakes, or else somehow felt doomed to repeat them (Arthur D. Little, Inc., 1994). As many as 70 to 80 percent of change initiatives had failed; 40 percent of the executives surveyed were very unhappy, finding change too slow or patchy; there were no significant benefits from the change initiatives; and 80 percent of the companies expected to be going through other major changes within a few years.

These results are not encouraging, but they certainly increase opportunities and raise some important research issues for industrial and organizational psychologists. These issues span two broad areas: planning for change (based on theory) and implementing change (based on practice). With respect to planning, the most pressing need is to develop a well-specified theory about the process of organizational change. Indeed, a comprehensive review of literature in the field of OD concluded, "It is a major weakness of the field that, as a group, the theories supposed to define the dynamics of the planned change process are so vague" (Porras & Robertson, 1992, p. 760). Specifically, two types of research are needed:

1. Identification and specification of alternative models of organizations on which to base change process theories. As has been shown, both the structure and variety of organizational forms are changing dramatically as organizations strive to meet the ever-changing demands of the marketplace. Change process theory is not keeping pace.

2. More comprehensive frameworks, categorization schemes, or models that will allow industrial and organizational psychologists to make sense of the theory and knowledge that already exists (Woodman, 1989).

In the Arthur D. Little (1994) survey, those who were successful in implementing change were able to help managers and employees fundamentally change the way they think about and approach change. This can be done in a number of ways. From the perspective of implementing change, a variety of OD intervention techniques exists, from simple to complex, from short term to long term, from affecting one individual to affecting an entire organization, and from affecting only one organizational variable (e.g., social factors) to affecting several (e.g., organizing arrangements, technology, and physical setting) (Porras & Robertson, 1992).

If OD interventions are to be maximally effective, however, practitioners must identify the best change technique or combination of techniques to apply to a given situation, while at the same time addressing fundamental characteristics such as underlying assumptions, beliefs, and attitudes. Unfortunately, present OD theory does not provide sufficient guidance for determining the best techniques to use in particular situations. As a result, practice is leading theory, instead of the other way around (Mirvis, 1988).

What Can Be Done?

Perhaps the greatest need in this area today, as in the past, is for methodologically sound evaluations of the relative impact of alternative OD interventions. Problems such as the unit of analysis and random assignment of individuals to groups make classic experimental designs difficult to implement in field settings. This should not be cause for abandonment of efforts to evaluate the relative impact of alternative interventions. Application of quasi-experimental designs, qualitative research methods (Van Maanen, 1979), and assessment of the agreement of laboratory and field results (Gersick, 1989) all can contribute to the advancement of knowledge and practice.

Thousands of change efforts are initiated every year. If the field is to maintain a scientific basis for its continued existence, then it is essential to evaluate change efforts to determine which interventions have the greatest impact on which organizational variables. The ultimate objective is to develop cumulative knowledge that can be translated into a science-based practice of OD that is directly useful to organizations. Such knowledge will be critical to mastering change at all levels and ensuring a sustained competitive advantage for organizations that rely on behavioral science-based change interventions to do so.

Summary and Conclusions

Dramatic changes are affecting the world of work. Some of these include increased global competition, the impact of information technology, the reengineering of business processes, the shift from vertically integrated hierarchies to networks of specialists, smaller companies that employ fewer people, and the change in the paradigm of doing business from making a product to providing a service. Beyond those, there is an emerging redefinition of work itself: growing disappearance of the job as a fixed bundle of tasks, along with an emphasis on constantly changing work required to fulfill the ever-increasing demands of customers.

There are great opportunities for industrial and organizational psychologists to contribute to the betterment of human welfare in the context of these changes. To lead change rather than to follow it, however, will require a break with traditional practices and a focus on rigorous research that addresses emerging trends. This article identified six key areas in which to start: job analysis, employee selection, training and development, performance appraisal, compensation (including incentives), and organizational development. These challenges provide an exciting agenda with large potential payoffs for individuals, organizations, and society as psychology moves into the twenty-first century. ∎

REFERENCES

Alderman, L. (1995, April). What you need to ace today's rough-and-tough job interviews. *Money, 35,* 36, 38.

Arthur D. Little, Inc. (1994). *Managing organizational change: How leading organizations are meeting the challenge.* Cambridge, MA: Author.

Barley, S. (1991). *The new crafts: The rise of the technical labor force and its implications for the organization of work.* Philadelphia: National Center on the Educational Quality of the Workforce, University of Pennsylvania.

Barney, J. (1991). Firm resources and sustained competitive advantage. *Journal of Management, 17,* 99–120.

Bass, B. M. (1954). The leaderless group discussion. *Psychological Bulletin, 51,* 465–492.

Bass, B. M. (1985). *Leadership and performance beyond expectations.* New York: Free Press.

Baumohl, B. (1993, March 15). When downsizing becomes "dumbsizing." *Time,* 55.

Bernardin, H. J., & Beatty, R. W. (1984). *Performance appraisal: Assessing human behavior at work.* Boston: Kent.

Borman, W. C. (1974). The rating of individuals in organizations: An alternative approach. *Organizational Behavior and Human Performance, 12,* 105–124.

Bridges, W. (1994, September 19). The end of the job. *Fortune,* 62–64, 68, 72, 74.

Byrne, J. A. (1993, February 8). The virtual corporation. *Business Week,* pp. 98–103.

Byrne, J. A. (1994, May 9). The pain of downsizing. *Business Week,* pp. 60–69.

Campbell, D. T., & Fiske, D. W. (1959). Convergent and discriminant validation by the multitrait-multimethod matrix. *Psychological Bulletin, 56,* 81–105.

Cannon-Bowers, J. A., Tannenbaum, S. I., Salas, E., & Volpe, C. E. (1995). Defining competencies and establishing team training requirements. In R. A. Guzzo & E. Salas (Eds.), *Team effectiveness and decision making in organizations* (333–380). San Francisco: Jossey-Bass.

Cappelli, P. (1992). *Is the "skills gap" really about attitudes?* Philadelphia: National Center on the Educational Quality of the Workforce. (Educational Quality of the Workforce Catalog No. WP01).

Career management services @ Sun. (1994). Milpitas, CA: Author.

Cascio, W. F. (1989). Using utility analysis to assess training outcomes. In I. Goldstein (Ed.), *Training and development in organizations* (63–88). San Francisco: Jossey-Bass.

Cascio, W. F. (1991). *Applied psychology in personnel management* (4th ed.). Upper Saddle River, NJ: Prentice Hall.

Cascio, W. F. (1993, February). Downsizing: What do we know? What have we learned? *Academy of Management Executive, 7* (1), 95–104.

Cascio, W. F. (1994a). *Documenting training effectiveness in terms of worker performance and adaptability* (Educational Quality of the Workforce Catalog No. WP23), Philadelphia: University of Pennsylvania, National Center for the Educational Quality of the Workforce.

Cascio, W. F. (1994b). *Public investments in training: Perspectives on macro-level structural issues and micro-level delivery systems* (Educational Quality of the Workforce Catalog No. WP24). Philadelphia: University of Pennsylvania, National Center for the Educational Quality of the Workforce.

Deming, W. E. (1986). *Out of the crisis.* Cambridge, MA: MIT Center for Advanced Engineering Study.

Dipboye, R. L., & Gaugler, B. B. (1993). Cognitive and behavioral processes in the selection interview. In N. Schmitt & W. C. Borman

(Eds.), *Personnel selection in organizations* (135–170). San Francisco: Jossey-Bass.

Downside to the jobs upturn. (1994, November 14). *Business Week*, 26.

Doyle, F. P. (1992, June). Unpublished keynote address, National Academy of Human Resources, Santa Fe, NM.

Drake, Beam, Morin, Inc. (1994). *Career transition study, November 1993 to August 1994.* Washington, DC: Author.

Fein, M. (1982, August). *Improved productivity through worker involvement.* Paper presented at the annual meeting of the Academy of Management, New York.

Fiedler, F. E. (1967). *A theory of leadership effectiveness.* New York: McGraw-Hill.

Filipczak, B. (1995, January). You're on your own: Training, employability, and the new employment contract. *Training*, 29–36.

Florkowski, G. W. (1987). The organizational impact of profit sharing. *Academy of Management Review, 12,* 622–636.

Gael, S. (Ed.). (1988). *The job analysis handbook for business, industry, and government.* New York: Wiley.

Gersick, C. J. G. (1989). Marking time: Predictable transitions in task groups. *Academy of Management Journal, 32,* 274–309.

Goldstein, I. L. (Ed.). (1989). *Training and development in work organizations.* San Francisco: Jossey-Bass.

Goldstein, I. L. (1994). *Training in organizations: Needs assessment, development, and evaluation* (4th ed.). Monterey, CA: Brooks/Cole.

Gomez-Mejia, L. R., & Balkin, D. B. (1992). *Compensation, organizational strategy, and firm performance.* Cincinnati, OH: Southwestern.

Guion, R. M. (1991). Personnel assessment, selection, and placement. In M. D. Dunnette & L. M. Hough (Eds.), *Handbook of industrial and organizational psychology*, 2nd ed., Vol. 2 (327–397). Palo Alto, CA: Consulting Psychologists Press.

Gwynne, S. C. (1992, September 28). The long haul. *Time*, 34–38.

Hammer, M., & Champy, J. (1993). Reengineering the corporation. New York: *Harper Business*, 90.

Hammer, T. H. (1988). New developments in profit sharing, gainsharing and employee ownership. In J. P. Campbell & R. J. Campbell (Eds.), *Productivity in organizations* (328–366). San Francisco: Jossey-Bass.

Harvey, R. J. (1991). Job analysis. In M. D. Dunnette & L. M. Hough (Eds.), *Handbook of industrial and organizational psychology* (2nd ed., Vol. 2, 71–163). Palo Alto, CA: Consulting Psychologists Press.

Henkoff, R. (1994, October 3). Finding, training, and keeping the best service workers. *Fortune*, 110–122.

Hogan, R. T. (1991) Personality and personality measurement. In M. D. Dunnette & L. M. Hough (Eds.), *Handbook of industrial and organizational psychology* (2nd ed., Vol. 2, 873–919). Palo Alto, CA: Consulting Psychologists Press.

House, R. J. (1971). A path-goal theory of leader effectiveness. *Administrative Science Quarterly, 16,* 321–339.

Huselid, M. A. (1995). The impact of human resource management practices on turnover, productivity, and corporate financial performance. *Academy of Management Journal, 38,* 635–672.

Ilgen, D. R., & Hollenbeck, J. R. (1991). The structure of work: Job design and roles. In M. D. Dunnette & L. M. Hough (Eds.), *Handbook of industrial and organizational psychology* (2nd ed., Vol. 2, 165–207). Palo Alto, CA: Consulting Psychologists Press.

Investing in people and prosperity. (1994, May). U.S. Department of Labor, Washington, DC, 7.

Jobs in an age of insecurity. (1993, November 22). *Time*, 35.

Kiechel, W., III. (1993, May 17). How we will work in the year 2000. *Fortune*, 38–52.

Klimoski, R., & Jones, R. G. (1995). Staffing for effective group decision making: Key issues in matching people and teams. In R. A. Guzzo & E. Salas (Eds.), *Team effectiveness and decision making in organizations* (291–332). San Francisco: Jossey-Bass.

Kraiger, K., Ford, J. K., & Salas, E. (1993). Application of cognitive, skill-based, and affective theories of learning outcomes to new methods of training evaluation. *Journal of Applied Psychology, 78,* 311–328.

Labich, K. (1994, November 14). Why companies fail. *Fortune,* 52–54, 58, 60, 64, 68.

Labor letter. (1991, October 22). *The Wall Street Journal,* A1.

Lado, A. A., & Wilson, M. C. (1994). Human resource systems and sustained competitive advantage: A competency-based perspective. *Academy of Management Review, 19,* 699–727.

Mabe, P. A., & West, S. G. (1982). Validity of self-evaluation of ability: A review and meta-analysis. *Journal of Applied Psychology, 67,* 280–296.

Marsh, H. W., & Hocevar, D. (1988). A new, more powerful approach to multitrait–multimethod analyses: Application of second-order confirmatory factor analysis. *Journal of Applied Psychology, 73,* 107–117.

Marx, R. D. (1982). Relapse prevention for managerial training: A model for maintenance of behavior change. *Academy of Management Review, 7,* 433–441.

McCormick, E. J. (1979). *Job analysis: Methods and applications.* New York: AMACOM.

McIntyre, R. M., & Salas, E. (1995). Measuring and managing for team performance: Emerging principles from complex environments. In R. A. Guzzo & E. Salas (Eds.), *Team effectiveness and decision making in organizations* (9–45). San Francisco: Jossey-Bass.

Mirvis, P. H. (1988). Organization development: Part I: An evolutionary perspective. In W. A. Passmore & R. W. Woodman (Eds.), *Research in organizational change and development* (Vol. 2). Greenwich, CT: JAI Press.

Motowidlo, S. J., Carter, G. W., Dunnette, M. D., Tippins, N., Werner, S., Burnett, J. R., & Vaughan, M. J. (1992). Studies of the structured behavioral interview. *Journal of Applied Psychology, 77,* 571–587.

Murphy, K. R., & Cleveland, J. N. (1991). *Performance appraisal: An organizational perspective.* Boston: Allyn & Bacon.

Murray, M. (1995, May 4). Thanks, goodbye: Amid record profits, companies continue to lay off employees. *The Wall Street Journal,* A1, A5.

Nelan, B. W. (1992, Fall). How the world will look in 50 years (Special issue: Beyond the Year 2000). *Time,* 36–38.

1994 AMA survey on downsizing and assistance to displaced workers. New York: American Management Association.

Norman, C. A., & Zawacki, R. A. (1991, September). Team appraisals—team approach. *Personnel Journal,* 101–104.

Ones, D. S., Mount, M. K., Barrick, M. R., & Hunter, J. E. (1994). Personality and job performance: A critique of the Tett, Jackson, and Rothstein (1991) meta-analysis. *Personnel Psychology, 47,* 147–156.

Ost, E. J. (1995). Team-based pay: New wave strategic initiatives. In J. B. Miner & D. P. Crane (Eds.). *Advances in the practice, theory, and research of strategic human resource management* (353–366). New York: Harper Collins.

Pfeffer, J. (1994). *Competitive advantage through people.* Boston: Harvard Business School Press, 8.

Pilon, L. J. (1993, February 22). Quoted in "Jobs, Jobs." *Business Week,* 74.

Porras, J. I., & Robertson, P. J. (1992). Organizational development: Theory, practice, and research. In M. D. Dunnette & L. M. Hough (Eds.), *Handbook of industrial and organizational psychology* (2nd ed., Vol. 3, 719–822). Palo Alto, CA: Consulting Psychologists Press.

Ree, M. J., & Earles, J. A. (1991). Predicting training success: Not much more than g. *Personnel Psychology, 44,* 321–332.

Ree, M. J., & Earles, J. A. (1992). Intelligence is the best predictor of job performance. *Current Directions in Psychological Science, 1,* 86–89.

Ree, M. J., Earles, J. A., & Teachout, M. S. (1994). Predicting job performance: Not much more than g. *Journal of Applied Psychology, 79,* 518–524.

Salwen, K. G. (1993, April 19). The cutting edge: German-owned maker of power tools finds job training pays off. *The Wall Street Journal,* A1, A7.

Schmitt, N., & Borman, W. C. (Eds.). (1993). *Personnel selection in organizations.* San Francisco: Jossey-Bass.

Skill-based pay boosts worker productivity and morale. (1992, April 18). *The Wall Street Journal,* A1.

Smither, J. W., London, M., Vasilopoulos, N. L., Reilly, R. R., Millsap, R. E., & Salvemini, N.

(1995). An examination of the effects of an upward feedback program over time. *Personnel Psychology, 48,* 1–34.

Tett, R. P., Jackson, D. N., Rothstein, M., & Reddon, J. R. (1994). Meta-analysis of personality–job performance relations: A reply to Ones, Mount, Barrick, & Hunter (1994). *Personnel Psychology, 47,* 157–172.

The horizontal corporation. (1993, December 20). *Business Week,* 77–81.

Tichy, N. (1994, May). The future of workplace learning and performance. *Training and Development,* S46.

Tornow, W. W. (1993). Perceptions or reality: Is multi-perspective measurement a means or an end? *Human Resource Management, 32,* 221–230.

Tosi, H., & Tosi, L. (1987). What managers need to know about knowledge-based pay. In D. A. Balkin & L. R. Gomez-Mejia (Eds.), *New perspectives on compensation* (43–48). Upper Saddle River, NJ: Prentice Hall.

U.S. Department of Labor. (1993, August). *High performance work practices and firm performance.* Washington, D.C.: U.S. Government Printing Office.

Van Maanen, J. (Ed.). (1979). Qualitative methodology [Special issue]. *Administrative Science Quarterly, 24* (4).

Vroom, V. H., & Yetton, P. W. (1973). *Leadership and decision making.* Pittsburgh, PA: University of Pittsburgh Press.

Waterman, R. H., Jr., Waterman, J. A., & Collard, B. A. (1994, July–August). Toward a career-resilient workforce. *Harvard Business Review,* 87–95.

Weekley, J. A., & Gier, J. A. (1987). Reliability and validity of the situational interview for a sales position. *Journal of Applied Psychology, 72,* 484–487.

Wellins, R. S., Byham, W. C., & Wilson, J. M. (1991). *Empowered teams: Creating self-directed work groups that improve quality, productivity, and participation.* San Francisco: Jossey-Bass.

Wideman, T. G. (1993, October). Performance appraisal in a total quality management environment. *The Industrial-Organizational Psychologist, 31* (2), 64–66.

Woodman, R. W. (1989). Organizational change and development: New arenas for inquiry and action. *Journal of Management, 15,* 205–228.

Workplace of the future: A Report of the Conference on the Future of the American Workplace. (1993). New York: U.S. Departments of Commerce and Labor.

World Competitiveness Report. (1994). Lausanne, Switzerland: World Economic Forum and Institute for Management Development.

C H A P T E R

2

PERSPECTIVES ON HUMAN RESOURCES MANAGEMENT

Although the field of human resources management has been with us for nearly 70 years, only recently has there been major redirection in thought concerning its importance to the effectiveness of organizations. For many years human resources management was viewed as a maintenance function for the organization, a repository of files and information but not a function that had any noticeable impact on the bottom line.

During the mid- to late-1960s and the 1970s, a different perspective began to emerge that elevated the importance and status of human resources management. A number of factors contributed to this changing perspective on the field and the practice of personnel/human resources management (PHRM) in organizations. Perhaps the most critical factor was the enactment of considerable federal legislation, particularly with respect to fair employment practices. As a result the personnel function gained more visibility and influence by acquiring responsibility for a variety of critical interactions with powerful federal regulatory agencies such as the Equal Employment Opportunity Commission, the Occupational Safety and Health Administration, and the Internal Revenue Service, which carefully monitored—and continue to monitor—the employment practices of organizations with respect to fairness, health and safety, and retirement income security.

Other factors that have led over the years to an increase in the importance and status of PHRM include the focus on productivity and the changing nature and demographics of the U.S. workforce. All of these factors, when placed in the context of significant economic and political changes in the rest of the world, have created the need for a newer, more business-focused perspective on the field.

The newer perspective is that of strategic human resources management. This perspective takes a broader, more integrated view of the personnel function; seeks to link the human resources function with the longer-term strategies of the organization; and asks how the human resources function can facilitate the implementation of those strategies. In this environment the importance and status of PHRM will continue to increase as the field responds to changing requirements and expectations.

We have divided this chapter into three areas dealing with strategic perspective, political perspective, and international perspective. Harrell-Cook represents the strategic perspective. She contends that human resources management is the optimal route an organization can follow in order to realize a competitive advantage over other organizations in the same industry. Hers is a cautionary note—she outlines how to do this and proceeds to explain why organizations fail to implement strategic human resources management. Harvey and Napier take a global perspective in their approach to human resources management. They recommend a global perspective—organizations exist in a global environment and this must be taken into account when developing human resources strategies. Smith and Salter have taken a specialized approach—they address the gender-based problems that may occur in the context of global organizations. They directly confront the issues with which women must be concerned when they are considering global assignments. The article by Treadway is an integration of the political perspective of human resources management. Politics occur in organizations. Human resources professionals need to ensure that politics have a positive impact upon human resource functions. This is difficult as organizations are increasing in ambiguity, which has been shown to be a variable associated with political behavior.

READINGS

HUMAN RESOURCES MANAGEMENT AND COMPETITIVE ADVANTAGE: A STRATEGIC PERSPECTIVE

Gloria Harrell-Cook

The strategic management of human resources is a much discussed issue in both organizational research and in the world of management practice. It is touted as the optimal route that firms should follow in order to recognize a competitive advantage over other businesses in their industry. Yet few firms have achieved the high levels of integration of human resources management with organizational strategy that is professed to result in those benefits. This article explores the concept of strategic human resources management (SHRM), its definition, its evolution, its relationship to competitive advantage, and reasons why firms fail to implement strategic human resources systems.

SHRM: WHAT IS IT?

A measure of success for any organization is the extent to which it effectively and efficiently moves toward the achievement of its strategic (or long-term) goals. Many factors affect that progress, including executive vision and leadership, availability of financial resources, appropriate and efficient technology, and adequacy of other capital assets, such as the building itself. All of these resources and assets are necessary, but they are not sufficient for organizational success. Without its employees and the value they provide through the contribution of their skills, knowledge, and abilities, the organiza-

tion is but a mere shell and can accomplish nothing.

The aforementioned resources must be managed in such a manner as to facilitate the outcomes that the organization wishes to achieve, and so it is with the human resources of the firm. In order to recognize their strategic aims, organizations must have in place the policies and practices that effectively and efficiently aquire and maintain employees with the skills, knowledge, and abilities necessary to the achievement of organizational goals. Further, these policies and practices must be such that they elicit the behaviors and contributions on the part of employees that will result in the desired types and levels of firm performance. Randall Schuler (1992) argued that managers see the purpose of SHRM as "getting the strategy of the business implemented effectively," and offered the following prescription for accomplishing that purpose:

> Strategic human resource management is largely about integration and adaptation. Its concern is to ensure that (1) human resources (HR) management is fully integrated with the strategy and the strategic needs of the firm; (2) HR policies cohere both across policy areas and across hierarchies; and (3) HR practices are adjusted, accepted, and used by line managers and employees as part of their everyday work. (p. 18)

In short, organizations must carefully construct and implement management practices that maximize the fit of employee performance with the overarching objectives of the firm. (The issue of "fit" is discussed at greater length in a following section of the article.)

The contributions of employees, then, are of critical importance to the strategic success of the firm, and managers are becoming increasingly aware of this importance. Human resources, as the term implies, are sources of value creation and, when managed strategically, are also a potential source of competitive advantage for the firm. However, this is a notion that is relatively new to both the science and practice of human resources management. In fact, it was not until 1981 that the idea of linking human resources management with strategy surfaced in literature (DeVanna, Fombrun, & Tichy, 1981). The next section examines the evolution of human resources management to its present state.

SHRM: HOW DID WE GET HERE?

In the preceding paragraphs, efficiency and effectiveness are noted as the two key ingredients to organizational success. Efficiency is defined as obtaining the most output, whether that output be goods or services, for the least input. The goal of efficency, therefore, is to minimize costs. Effectiveness, on the other hand, is concerned with successfully meeting organizational objectives and goals. That is, an effective organization is doing what it set out to do. While each of these ingredients is important in its own right, neither, alone, is sufficient to provide an organization with optimal outcomes. Both must be subjects of intensive management attention.

For much of American history, the focus of management and management scholars with regard to employee management has been on efficiency. Labor, just as any other input, was seen as a cost of production and such costs were to be minimized. Consequently, much effort was directed toward discovering the fastest and cheapest way to do a job. With the advent of industrialization in the nineteenth and early twentieth centuries came mass production and the emergence of assembly-line work. Work was subdivided into its simplest parts, so that it could be performed by unskilled workers, and work on the line was overseen by a hierarchy of supervisors and managers. The focus on efficiency was manifested through close supervisory monitoring of employee productivity and scientific management research as to the one "best" way to do the job. There was little concern or even need for worker input other than the physical exertion required to do the job. Rather, management's charge was to operate efficiently, keeping costs down and productivity up.

This mindset prevailed through the majority of the twentieth century, and research on employee or personnel management was focused primarily on improving productivity. Both managers and researchers operated on the assumption that workers were motivated primarily by money, and monetary incentives coupled with work engineering were the subjects of greatest interest. Worker dissatisfaction began to grow as working conditions and worker welfare continued to be ignored by management. Consequently, workers organized unions in an attempt to have some voice in bettering their plights. Management determinedly pursued their productivity objectives, however, and any attention paid to workers' thoughts, feelings, or welfare was in an attempt to quell labor unrest.

Some of the work conducted during this period had unexpected results that caught the attention of management. The Hawthorne experiments (Roethlisberger & Dickson, 1939), for example, studied the effects of illumination on productivity. Surprisingly, productivity increased whether lights were raised, lowered, or left unchanged. The effects on productivity, the researchers concluded, were not a result of the physical working environment, but rather a psychological response to the attention the workers received. For some period of time after the publication of these studies, managers and researchers concerned themselves with improving the psychological and social aspects of work. It is important to note, however, that the objective of this concern and research was still to improve efficiency. Therefore, when increases in productivity resulting from those efforts proved to be somewhat lackluster, this movement (known as the human relations movement) began to wain.

The concentration on worker efficiency served American organizations well for more than three quarters of the twentieth century. Throughout this time, the U.S. competitive market was fairly isolated against significant competition from foreign markets. Efficiency in resource utilization proved to be an effective mechanism for ensuring success when all organizations were playing on the same economic field. When productivity was high and costs were relatively low, organizational effectiveness seemed to follow.

However, in the mid-1980s, corporate America received a rude awakening: global competition. Domestic corporations were encountering not only an enlarged group of competitors, but their very viability was being threatened because of the superior quality of imported goods. The competitive arena had changed, and along with it, the competitive priorities of American firms were transformed. Quality goods were available, and both intermediate and end consumers were demanding quality.

Increasing globalization and rapidly changing customer demand over the next two decades only exacerbated the competitive problems of U.S. companies. Customer responsiveness, and the flexibility and agility required by that responsiveness, became imperatives. Organizations could no longer rely on worker and technological efficiency to remain competitive; employee contribution to effectiveness was requisite as well. The keys to address these new competitive issues lay with the employees of the firm. Competitive strategy became an increasingly important issue during this time period. And while senior management could formulate strategies, reaching those strategic goals depended on the employees.

It was beginning to be recognized that it is the employees who must create the value added of the products and/or services offered by the firm. Competitive pressures forced corporations toward a different perspective of labor. In addition to efficiency, management must now look to employees for value creation. Rather than viewing labor as a cost to be minimized, management came to the realization that employees of the firm were resources from which value could be derived. Faced with that reality, management and researchers began to think about managing their human resources strategically.

SHRM: A NEW PARADIGM

A common theme in the area of strategic human resources management (SHRM) is the effect of human resources (HR) policies and practices on organizational outcomes. Much of the early work examined the impact of individual practices on firm performance. These studies found that a number of HR practices had a positive effect on performance. Among the practices investigated were intensive selection practices (Terpstra & Rozell, 1993), goal setting (Terpstra & Rozell, 1994), training and organizational support (Russell, Terborg, & Power, 1985), and contingent and base pay (Gerhart & Milkovich, 1990). Outcomes examined were various measures of firm financial performance.

Of course, these practices are important in and of themselves, but practices do not exist in isolation. Rather, they exist together as a system of HR practices. Recognition of this fact provoked an interest in examining the entire system of HR practices, and the effect of that system (rather than individual practices) on firm performance. This type of work has become known as the "systems" approach to SHRM, and makes the argument that HR practices are most effective when they are bound together in a coherent system designed to facilitate the achievement of organizational goals. In other words, the various practices that compose the overall HR system must fit together, and must also "fit" with the strategic objectives of the organization. Three streams of work have emerged that take the systems approach to SHRM, with differing perspectives on the fit issue: the universalistic perspective, the configurational perspective, and the contingency or strategic-fit perspective.

Proponents of the universalistic perspective (e.g., Huselid, 1995; Pfeffer, 1994) contend that there is one "best" way to manage human resources in any and all firms. In this stream of work, SHRM is viewed as the implementation of a set of high performance work practices or innovative work practices. These innovative work practices are constructed to motivate and facilitate worker contribution to organizational success. As such, they stand in opposition to the more traditional "control" systems of HRM, and have a focus on effectiveness as well as efficiency. Practices argued to be indicative of innovative work systems have varied from study to study, and have included selection, performance appraisal, incentive compensation, job design, grievance procedures, training, recruiting intensity, criteria for promotion, information sharing, attitude assessment, employment security, and labor-management participation.

It is argued that the use of these HRM practices has a positive effect on the bottom line of the firm through increased worker motivation (and thereby increased productivity) and enhanced worker efficiency (Ichniowski, Kochan, Levine, Olson, & Strauss, 1996). Some advocates of high performance work practices have argued that these HR systems impact firm performance in that they incent employees to contribute "discretionary effort" (Appelbaum, Bailey, Berg, & Kalleberg, 2000). Bailey (1993) maintained that organizations may not be receiving the maximum benefit from employees because employees, in general, do not work to their fullest potential. Work systems that motivate workers to contribute this effort, above and beyond the norm, will result in higher levels of organizational performance relative to organizations where those systems do not exist.

Examinations of organizations utilizing high performance or innovative work practices have provided evidence that these systems are indeed associated with higher firm performance. Although it is not clear from the research that the HRM system "caused" better performance, there are examples that give credence to that assumption. Work transformation at the New United Motors Manufacturing, Inc. (NUMMI) facility in Fremont, California, is heralded as one of those examples (Ichniowski et al., 1996).

NUMMI, a joint venture between Toyota and General Motors (GM), reopened a closed GM facility in 1982, with 85 percent of their workforce composed of GM workers laid off at the time of the plant closing. These employees had worked under the traditional work systems of GM. Toyota introduced their production system, and its accompanying changes in work (or HRM) practices. Training in problem solving, teamwork, elimination of work rules, changes in wage structure, and an emphasis on communication (all included in high performance work systems literature) were part of the change. NUMMI, formerly one of GM's poorest performers, became one of the best-performing auto assembly plants in the United States within two years, ranking highest in both productivity and quality. Further, this improvement in performance was achieved with essentially the same technology utilized in the former GM plant, indicating that the human factor and worker contributions were largely responsible for the improvement.

In spite of the success at NUMMI, and other evidence of the effect of high performance work practices, the "one size fits all" model of HRM has its drawbacks. Many of the measures of high performance work practices are very generic in nature. For instance, while use of extensive recruiting and intensive selection processes indicate that a firm is carefully recruiting and selecting its employees, those terms are not very definitive. In other words, they don't tell us much about *exactly* what skills, knowledge, and abilities the organization is selecting nor *exactly* how those attributes are assessed. The case is similar with training. The amount of training tells how much attention the organization is paying to development, but it doesn't provide information as to what and how the organization is training.

It may be, then, that the universalistic perspective to SHRM provides a generic framework for organizations to follow and indicates that all facets of HRM should be carefully constructed. In the construction phase of the system, however, managers will have to fine-tune their HRM systems to "fit" with their organizational goals and objectives.

It is this concern with fit that differentiates the configurational and strategic-fit approach from the universalistic. The two perspectives are discussed together, but differ slightly from one another. The configurational approach suggests that there are certain bundles of HR practices that fit together, and are most appropriate given a certain industrial and business environment. That is, some bundles of practices are appropriate or fit with one industry, while another bundle of practices should be utilized in a different industry. The strategic-fit approach, on the other hand, does not identify what specific practices should be included in an HR system. In fact, some practices may be substitutes for others (Appelbaum et al., 2000). For instance, a company may hire for general intelligence and train the employees on the specifics of the job. Another company may gain an employee with the same skill, knowledge, and ability level by hiring a person with prior experience in the job, negating the need for job-specific training. In this case, hiring for experience substitutes for extensive job training. Either practice might fit equally well with the organization's strategy.

According to the configurational and strategic-fit perspectives of SHRM, fit of the HR system revolves around the extent to which that system meets two criteria (Wright & McMahan, 1992). First, the individual practices contained within the system must be those that are optimal for carrying out the strategy of the firm. This fit is referred to as "vertical" or "external" fit. In HR terms, this means that those individual practices must provide the organization with the ability to attract people with the skills, knowledge, and abilities required to carry out the organization's purpose, and must induce those people to contribute those skills, knowledge, and abilities at a maximal level.

The second type of fit required is "horizontal" or "internal" fit. That is, all HR practices and policies in a firm's HRM system must be consistent with one another. Ideally, the components of the system should be complementary and reinforcing to have the strongest effect on performance. If the practices reinforce one another, it is argued, synergy will be created so that the effect of the entire system will be greater than the effect of the sum of each of its parts. To illustrate, if the organization wants individuals who are capable of innovation, they will select for characteristics indicative of that ability. But innovation will be further enhanced if the organization also includes innovative endeavors in the performance appraisal system, rewards innovative behavior, and structures work so that the environment is conducive to innovation. These various factors reinforce each other, and serve to promote innovation above and beyond the level of each individual factor.

But fit is easier discussed than achieved. In an actual organization, the formulation of the HRM system may be systematic (i.e., planned together as a whole) or unmethodical (i.e., put together piecemeal, one practice at a time, without regard for how that practice interacts or fits with others already in existence). The consequential coherence of the various components of the system would be, therefore, high or low, respectively, as would the effect of the system on organizational performance. It has been argued that failure to achieve fit results in a competitive disadvantage to the organization (Barney & Wright, 1998). There is evidence to show that firms who have managed to obtain high congruence of their HRM systems with their organizational objectives have reaped the benefits.

One company has achieved this high level of fit is Nordstrom, who has enjoyed much success as one of America's leading retailers. Nordstrom's strategic focus is on gaining and maintaining customer loyalty through providing extremely high levels of individualized customer service. Stories abound with regard to the type of services expected by this employer and provided by employees. Very few retailers have sales personnel who are willing to change a customer's tire or organize a personal fashion show to allow a customer to choose her wardrobe for an upcoming cruise. Such service is not at all uncommon at Nordstrom, and their human resource system is all about ensuring that sales clerks will provide this level of attention.

Nordstrom invests its time, effort, and money in recruiting energetic, college-educated sales personnel. The focus of selection is, to some degree, on previous experience with customers. The strongest focus, however, is on attitude, energy, and the desire of the individual to make a career out of retailing: personality and motivation are key. Training is informal, and consists of frequently presented motivational programs designed to keep customer service at the top of every employee's priorities. Compensation is heavily commission-oriented, and sales clerks can earn sizable sums. Many Nordstrom employees earn up to twice the industry average. Performance appraisals consist of monthly rankings of employees in each department based on sales. These performance appraisals are also the basis of promotions. Practically all of Nordstrom's managers are promoted from within based on their prior sales performance. In the Nordstrom system, high performers advance, and poor performers are dismissed. In addition to these HR practices, Nordstrom allows their sales clerks high autonomy in how they do their job. Sales clerks operate their sales area as if they were their own private enterprises, using their imagination and creativity to serve the customer in the best way they possibly can. Nordstrom's one rule is "Use your best judgment at all times." Nordstrom's management of human resources obviously fits with their strategic objectives of highly differentiated customer service. The component practices and policies support those objectives, but also fit together and reinforce each other.

Has this strategic-fit of HR paid off for Nordstrom? The answer is a resounding yes. During the 1980s and 1990s, Nordstrom was an industry leader in both service and growth. Also during that time period, the company recorded the highest sales per square foot of any retailer in the nation. Strategic management of its human resources enabled Nordstrom to develop and sustain a competitive advantage in its industry.

It is important to note, however, that tight alignment of the human resources system with the strategy of the firm can be troublesome when the competitive environment begins to change. The competitive environment in the retail industry has seen some changes over the last few years, and Nordstrom has been confronted with the need to address those changes. When factors in the marketplace are in flux, the organization needs to pay close attention and be ready to adapt or fine-tune its strategy to keep the organization in alignment with the competitive environment and to recognize optimal firm performance. Naturally, if an organization is going to maintain fit of HRM with its strategy, any adjustment in strategic objectives may require some fine-tuning of the HR system. Thus a firm's HR systems and strategy must be tightly intertwined. This being the case, then, HR must play a far different role in modern organizations than in traditional firms of the past. HR has to become a highly involved member of the strategic processes of the firm.

HR AS A STRATEGIC PARTNER

Historically, the HR function has played a very small role in American organizations. In fact, in the early periods of industrialization, the HR function, per se, did not even exist. It was not until management was confronted with the labor unrest of the early twentieth century that they began to pay some attention to worker welfare in an attempt to reduce labor disruptions. It was during this period that the position of welfare secretary was established to oversee the employee welfare programs undertaken to pacify disgruntled employees. The welfare secretary was the forerunner of what later became known as the personnel manager. The personnel function was responsible for a number of tasks: recruitment; job analysis; administration of performance review systems, wages, benefits, and training; personnel record maintenance; and labor relations. Most personnel departments were staffed with individuals who were specialists in their given area of responsibility. The person responsible for recruiting and selection was a specialist in interviewing; the person responsible for training was a specialist in training, and so forth. There was little, if any, interaction and coordination between the various subdivisions of the personnel department or between the personnel function as a whole and other areas of the organization. Personnel in most traditional organizations was basically administrative in nature and isolated from the other functions of the organization, including strategic planning.

When faced with the competitive pressures of the 1980s and 1990s, organizational leaders began to recognize the importance of the contributions of its employees to the firm's overall performance. As noted earlier, managers began to see the employees of the organization as an asset or a resource from which value could be derived, as opposed to a cost to be minimized. The widespread adoption of the term *human resources* was evidence of this change in management mindset. With the increasing importance being placed on the human resources of the firm, the position of the human resource function was also enhanced. Today, the role of the HR function is increasingly recognized as a strategic one which is vital to the achievement of the goals of the firm. If HR is going to play a central role in aligning the organization's human resources capabilities with the strategic orientation of the firm, it must become a strategic partner. HR's shift in role and responsibility, however, requires some transformation of the function itself from its traditional "personnel"-oriented structuring.

Perhaps the most obvious element of that transformation process is the need for the full integration of the HR function into the strategic planning and implementation processes of the organization. To get a clear picture of exactly what full integration means, we might refer to Webster's definition of the word *integrate:* to make into a whole. Without high involvement of the HR function in the strategic processes, that whole is not complete. Rather, a very important part is missing.

Executives can spend as many hours as they like making strategic decisions in their corporate offices, but unless the capabilities exist (or can be readily acquired) to carry out those strategic directives, those hours are wasted. In order to arrive at a strategic plan that is workable, executives need information about the skills, knowledge, and abilities that are required by that plan, and whether or not the people of the organization possess those characteristics. Further achievement of strategic goals may require hiring new people, training current employees, changing compensation systems to encourage the behaviors needed, or even the restructuring of the work itself. All of these requirements fall under the umbrella of HR's responsibility, and therefore the planning process requires substantial input from HR with regard to these areas. Further, HR is in the best position to know how these various practices will "fit" together to attain the highest outcomes for the organization, so their input is crucial to obtaining horizontal fit and synergy.

Therefore, HR should have a significant role in the strategic planning process. This does not mean that other senior managers simply ask HR for information. If strategic alignment is going to be achieved, it is essential that HR managers not only have the opportunity for input, but that they also have the authority to influence the decisions that are made. If they are to have that authority, they must also demonstrate the ability to make sound business decisions: something not required of traditional personnel managers. In order to engage in SHRM and become a strategic partner in the firm, HR managers must possess good

business skills in addition to HR functional skills.

Janice Tomlinson (1993) outlined five factors that HR must accomplish in order to become a strategic partner. HR must

1. learn as much about the company's business as possible,
2. be more cognizant of and responsive to the organization's competitive needs and direction,
3. move away from a narrow concentration on the traditional HR functions,
4. become involved in developing cooperative relationships with managers, and assisting managers in finding solutions to their problems, and
5. illustrate the criticality of HR to organizational success.

In short, it requires good business acumen on the part of HR managers to fully participate as a strategic partner. They must know the business, if they are to align the HR system with the goals of that business. HR managers must demonstrate competence in their strategic role if their contributions to strategic planning and implementation are going to give the organization an edge over their competitors. It must be HR's goal to provide the organization with a source of sustainable competitive advantage.

SHRM AND SUSTAINABLE COMPETITIVE ADVANTAGE

As noted in a foregoing section, all three perspectives of SHRM include the notion that managing human resources strategically will result in higher levels of organizational performance. The contention is that SHRM can provide the firm with a competitive advantage, an edge over its rival firms, which results in higher profits and/or value of the firm. Further, it has been argued that the human resources of the firm may be the only source of *sustainable* advantage (i.e., a competitive advantage that may be held for a relatively long period of time) available to firms in the global marketplace of today. But why should this be the case?

Arguments about SHRM and sustainable competitive advantage derive from the resource-based view of competitive advantage (Barney, 1995, 1991; Barney & Wright, 1998). This view states that in order for a resource to be a source of sustainable competitive advantage, it must possess four characteristics. The resource must be valuable, rare, not easily imitated, and the firm must be organized in such a manner as to effectively and efficiently exploit the resource. If a resource is not valuable, it will not provide the organization with a competitive advantage of any sort. Further, if it does not possess the second and third characteristics, any competitor could easily gain access to the same resource and negate any competitive advantage which the resource provided to the original holder. The competitive advantage in that case, then, was not sustainable. Few of the resources traditionally thought of as sources of competitive advantage possess those four characteristics. Human resources, however, can possess those characteristics if they are managed strategically, and appropriate organizational structure and systems will ensure that they are.

Barney and Wright (1998) presented a convincing case for human resources as a source of sustainable competitive advantage. They argued that human resources are indeed valuable, rare, not easily imitated, and that appropriate organizational structures and systems will enable firms to fully realize the benefits of such resources. Human resources are valuable to the extent that they create value for the organization. Value can be created through reducing costs (concentrating on efficiency) or by differentiation of the product or the service so that the firm can charge higher prices for its product or service. Strategic management of human resources may actually accomplish both those goals simultaneously.

Appelbaum and her colleagues (2000), for example, examined the restructuring work and HR practices in the apparel industry. This restructuring involved the introduction of employee participation; the use of teams, training, and group-based pay; and was undertaken because of a change in the competitive environment necessitating higher levels of customer responsiveness. After the new system had been in place for a period of time, these companies recognized a significant reduction in costs due to reduced time to produce a garment, less inventory buildup, and substantially fewer reworks due to poor quality. In addition, these reductions in cost were realized even though labor costs (wages) increased. But cost reduction was not the only positive outcome of this initiative in SHRM. The companies also gained improved customer responsiveness, as intended, and significant improvements in product quality, both of which created value for the firms.

Does SHRM produce value through human resources who are rare? The answer is yes, to the extent that an organization has the capability to attract, retain, and develop employees who have the highest levels of skills, knowledge, and abilities necessary to achieve organizational goals, and who can induce the contribution of those attributes to the betterment of the firm. Barney and Wright (1998) used Nordstrom as an example of successful exploitation of the capabilities of its employees. In an industry where most retailers consider low skills and high turnover as a given, Nordstrom broke the mold. With close attention to its HR system, Nordstrom has acquired and gained a competitive advantage from the unique characteristics of its workforce.

The third criteria for sustainable competitive advantage is inimitability. Can't organizations copy what other competitors in their industries are doing? Don't organizations benchmark the leaders in the industry? The answer is yes. But the inimitability of the value created by the human resources of a firm lies in its embeddedness in the history and social culture of the firm (Barney & Wright, 1998). The HR system of the firm evolves over a period of time, and is reinforced and shaped by the organization's unique culture and history dating back to the founder. It is these factors that make it difficult to identify and copy exactly those policies and practices that are at the base of behaviors and performance in a successful firm. Further, while an organization may implement the same policies and practices as its more successful competitor, it cannot easily, if at all, duplicate the history and culture in which those practices are embedded. Nordstrom's culture, for example, was initiated by its founder when the first store was opened in 1901. John Nordstrom's business philosophy was to provide exceptional service, selection, quality, and value. While the company has grown extensively over the last 100 years, that philosphy has pervaded the entire organization, and has driven the value creation achieved by its employees.

Organization is the final criteria of sustainable competitive advantage. Barney and Wright (1998) argued that firms must be organized in a manner to take full advantage of the resource. More specifically, organizations must have systems of policies and practices that induce and facilitate the full contributions of employees who are capable of producing value that is rare and inimitable. The focus on systems brings attention again to the need for a highly integrated and cohesive set of practices that are best suited to achieve the organization's goals. SHRM, in its purest sense, satisfies that criteria.

As Barney and Wright (1998) contended, the management of human resources plays an integral role in the development of a sustainable competitive advantage. When human resource policies and practices are chosen with a clear vision of their suitability in terms of inducing the types and levels of performance necessary to achieve organiza-

tional goals, and when those systems of complementary and reinforcing practices are implemented effectively, competitive advantage will follow. In light of the attractiveness of this concept in theory, then, why do we not see SHRM in all firms?

SHRM: IMPEDIMENTS TO MAKING THE MOVE

There are a number of reasons why organizations may not undertake the transformation process necessary to move to SHRM. One of the more obvious reasons why firms don't link human resource systems to organizational strategy is that the firm has no clear formal strategy. If a firm does not engage in strategic planning, then HRM cannot be a part of a nonexistant process. While we would expect that a major proportion of larger firms do have an on-going program of strategic planning, this may not be the case for many small- to medium-sized firms. Quite often the only strategic goal of these organizations may be "to make money."

A less obvious impediment to making the move to SHRM is that the organizational philosphy may not be consistent with the underlying reasons for engaging in SHRM. That is, the senior management of the organization may not view the employees as resources from which value can be derived. Management may still adhere to the traditional view of labor as an input of production whose cost should be minimized. In this traditional view, labor is believed to be a commodity, an interchangeable product that can easily be bought in the marketplace. Employees are not recognized as assets. If employees are not believed to be a source of value creation, it is highly unlikely that management would feel the need to involve HR in the strategic planning process. It is unsettling to think that this philosophy might still exist in some corporations; however, it would be naïve to assume that it does not.

A third restraint on moving to SHRM may be the time, effort, and expense involved in making that change. Conducting the analyses necessary to arrive at a suitable strategy for the firm, given both its internal and external environments, is time-consuming in and of itself. When that process is compounded by the complexities of matching HR practices and policies to the strategy (and to each other), the process becomes even more cumbersome. Unless management sees some compelling reason for investing in such a process, it may fall by the wayside. This is especially likely to happen when a firm is experiencing business difficulties. Managers may feel overwhelmed simply trying to deal with the day-to-day problems that arise. They may focus on "putting out the hottest fires" so to speak, to the detriment of engaging in SHRM. Ironically, the failure to manage human resources strategically may be the very reason underlying the business difficulties with which they are faced.

Politics and threatened power may also prevent the transition to SHRM. If HR managers play an integral role in the strategic decision-making process, and have the power to influence strategic decisions, this is certain to reduce the decision-making latitude of those managers previously "in charge" of the process. These managers may feel that introduction of HR into the strategic planning process is an intrusion, and the HR manager as someone who is usurping their power. In this case, there is likely to be strong resistance on the part of the traditional decision makers to the inclusion of HR in the strategic processes. Similarly, unions may see SHRM as potentially diminishing their power. This is especially likely if the SHRM system includes participative decision making, a move to incentive pay, or revisions of the promotion system to base promotions on performance—all moves that are contrary to a traditional union con-

tract. Unions may oppose the move to SHRM in order to avoid the implementation of those practices that they feel to be contrary to union philosophy.

A final impediment to the SHRM transition is the nature of the investments required. Managing human resources strategically may require a number of financial investments for the development of more intensive selection devices, for training, for increased pay, and so forth. Management may see these investments as risky propositions for a number of reasons (Harrell-Cook & Ferris, 1997). First, there is no guarantee that the organization will see a return on those investments. Even though there is evidence that SHRM influences the firm's bottom line positively, there is no guaranteed rate of return as when investing in bonds, for instance. Second, even if there is a payoff to the investment, say in terms of improved employee performance or increased employee skills, management has no assurance that the firm will reap the full rewards. If employees leave the company, the skills go with them. So, essentially, the employee and the next employing firm will recognize a portion of the benefits from the organization's investment. Third, and finally, any payoff for investing in human resources takes time. When firms are faced with pressures for improved short-term performance, managers may be unwilling to wait as long as it may take to see the returns on the investments in human resources required to move to SHRM.

Is it worth all the effort and trouble to make the transition to SHRM? There is growing evidence from both real-world business turnarounds and academic research to suggest that the payoff is there. SHRM is still a relatively new concept in both business and research. Perhaps as more significant and substantial manifestations of its benefits accrue, more and more managers will be convinced of the value of SHRM.

SUMMARY AND CONCLUSION

The field and practice of SHRM is still in its infancy, having been born of the need of organizations to deal with competitive pressures that required more of employees than simple physical effort. There is substantial evidence that managing human resources strategically is beneficial to an organization. The goal of SHRM is to provide the organization with the capabilities that will ensure the effective and efficient achievement of their strategic objectives. By providing the mechanisms to acquire, retain, and develop the individuals who possess the highest levels of skills, knowledge, and abilities needed by the organization, and by inducing the full contribution of those assets toward the betterment of the firm, SHRM can provide the firm with a source of sustainable competitive advantage. While numerous firms have made the move and recognized the consequential benefits of SHRM, others remain unable or reluctant to make the transition from traditional, administrative HR. As more evidence accumulates that illustrates the impact of managing human resources strategically, it is likely that more and more firms will be convinced that SHRM is the way to manage their people. One thing is certain, SHRM is not a fad: It's good business that's here to stay. ■

REFERENCES

Appelbaum, E., Bailey, T., Berg, P., & Kalleberg, A. (2000). *Manufacturing advantage: Why high-performance work systems pay off.* Ithaca, NY: Cornell University Press.

Bailey, T. (1993). Organizational innovation in the apparel industry. *Industrial Relations, 32,* 30–48.

Barney, J. (1991). Firm resources and sustained competitive advantage. *Journal of Management, 17,* 99–120.

Barney, J. (1995). Looking inside for competitive advantage. *Academy of Management Executive, 9* (4), 49–61.

Barney, J., & Wright, P. (1998). On becoming a strategic parner: The role of human resources in gaining competitive advantage. *Human Resource Management, 37* (1), 31–46.

Devanna, M., Fombrun, C., & Tichy, N. (1981). Human resources management: A strategic perspective. *Organizational Dynamics, 10* (3), 51–67.

Gerhart, B., & Milkovich, G. R. (1990). Organizational differences in managerial compensation and financial performance. *Academy of Management Journal, 33* (4), 663–691.

Harrell-Cook, G., & Ferris, G. R. (1997). Competing pressures for human resource investment. *Human Resource Management Review, 1,* 317–340.

Huselid, M. A. (1995). The impact of human resource management on turnover, productivity, and corporate financial performance. *Academy of Management Journal, 38* (3), 635–672.

Ichniowski, C., Kochan, T. A., Levine, D., Olson, C., & Strauss, G. (1996). What works at work: An overview and assessment. *Industrial Relations, 35* (3), 299–333

Pfeffer, J. (1994). *Competitive advantage through people: Unleashing the power of the work force.* Boston: Harvard Business School Press.

Roethlisberger, F. J., & Dickson, W. J. (1939). *Management and the worker.* Cambridge, MA: Harvard University Press.

Russell, J. S., Terborg, J. R., & Power, M. L. (1985). Organizational productivity and organizational level training and support. *Personnel Psychology, 38,* 849–863.

Schuler, R. S. (1992). Strategic human resources management: Linking the people with the strategic needs of the business. *Organizational Dynamics, 21* (1), 18–32.

Terpstra, D. E., & Rozell, E. J. (1993). The relationship of staffing practices to organizational measures of performance. *Personnel Psychology, 46,* 27–48.

Terpstra, D. E., & Rozell, E. J. (1994). The relationship of goal setting to organizational profitability. *Group and Organization Management, 19* (3), 285–294.

Tomlinson, J. (1993). Human resources—partners in change. *Human Resource Management, 32* (4), 545–554.

Wright, P. M., & McMahan, G. C. (1992). Theoretical perspectives for strategic human resource management. *Journal of Management, 18* (2), 295–320.

STRATEGIC GLOBAL HUMAN RESOURCES MANAGEMENT IN THE TWENTY-FIRST CENTURY

Michael Harvey
Nancy K. Napier

> *"Successful global management will possess a complex amalgamation of technical, political, social, organizational, and cultural competencies, none of which will come from one pool of candidates that have been used to fill foreign assignments."*
>
> —(GHOSHAL & BARTLETT, 1997A)

To compete in a global marketplace, organizations must create an effective means to develop and maintain a global competitive advantage (Minehan, 1998). There is a growing consensus among top management that globally successful organizations will use the uniqueness of their human resources and their system of managing human resources to gain this competitive advantage (Bartlett & Ghoshal, 1992, 1995; Pfeffer, 1994; Ghoshal & Bartlett, 1997b). Identifying, attracting, and retaining an adequate supply of global managers who are capable of coordinating the global strategic efforts of the company is a daunting task. It is not clear that there are sufficient numbers of high-caliber managers to fill existing positions (Stroh & Caligiuri, 1998; Welch, 1994).

The effective global organization of the twenty-first century will have to become a repository of skills, competencies, routines, and dynamic capabilities that are managed by multicultural management teams in a manner difficult for global rivals to replicate (Barney, 1991; Prahalad & Hamel, 1990). The development of global management will have to be formed to effectively administer knowledge acquisition and dissemination in global organizations (Earley & Mosakowski, 2000; Millman, 1999; Napolitano, 1998). It is projected that global managers of the future must develop a pluralistic mindset (i.e., developing and maintaining multiple perspectives in order to solve complex global problems) and not be ethnocentric or "Westernized" when managing in the global competitive arena (Aguirre, 1997; Harvey, Novicevic, & Speier, 1999; Reynolds, 1997).

The rate of globalization of businesses headquartered in the United States and in other developed economies is increasingly becoming contingent on having a sufficient number of qualified global managers (Gregersen, Morrison, & Black, 1998; Ghoshal & Bartlett, 1997a). In a recent survey of the *Fortune* Global 500, by Authur Andersen and Bennett & Associates, 81 percent of the respondents to the survey indicated their companies intended to rapidly expand their overseas interests throughout the world (*Expatriate*, 1997). In another survey of *Fortune* 500 companies, researchers found that 85 percent of the human resources managers did not believe they would have an adequate number of global leaders (i.e., managers) to implement their company's global expansion plans (Gregersen et. al., 1998). This shortage of qualified global managers could put companies at a competitive disadvantage when dealing with global companies in Europe, Asia, and other developed countries.

There appears to be a trend among international human resources managers that their organizations' global competitiveness and ultimately their global core competencies will depend upon the uniqueness of their organizations' global managers. Therefore, the development of global human resources systems for selecting, training, and motivating global managers must be effective to gain and maintain global competitive advantage (Bartlett & Ghoshal, 1994, 1995; Ghoshal & Bartlett, 1997a; Minehan, 1998; Prahalad & Hamel, 1990, 1993). This increased importance of selecting and maintaining a high-quality global workforce accentuates the strategic impact that human resources management is going to have on the success and/or failure of companies in the twenty-first century.

Global managers will have to possess a complex amalgamation of technical, functional, cultural, social, and political skills to successfully navigate the intricacies of the new global manager responsibilities (Fish, 1999; Nohria & Ghoshal, 1997; Pucik & Saba, 1998). Amassing a sufficient number

of global managers for multicultural teams has been characterized as a "contest." The ultimate prize in this contest is providing an organization with the ability to compete by developing core competencies based upon an organization's global management team which would be difficult to match by global rivals (Heene, 1994; Hamel & Heene, 1994; Rumelt, 1994; Sanchez, Heene, & Thomas, 1997). Selecting managers for inclusion in the global management team and developing a global mindset become critical issues that have not been adequately addressed by many large multinational and global organizations (Montgomery & Yip, 1999; Napolitano, 1998; Yip & Madsen, 1996; Paul, 2000).

THE EVOLUTIONARY STAGES OF INTERNATIONAL BUSINESS

Organizations that have a domestic focus to their business strategy efforts have identified enough market potential to satisfy their growth/profit requirements for the future. Their only concern relative to the global marketplace is foreign competitors that may enter their domestic market. Therefore, even domestic organizations need to monitor global business trends and competition in order to develop a defensive mechanism to protect their home markets. The human resources function is not directly affected by international activities, but is affected indirectly, because domestic organizations must anticipate the future influence of selling internationally or addressing foreign organizations selling in their domestic markets. For many reasons (i.e., declining domestic demand, increased competition in home market, a desire to expand sales faster than can be accomplished by selling in the domestic market, increasing environmental regulations that force the company to move outside its own country, obsolescence of products or technology, or a myriad of other compelling reasons), companies may decide to enter into international sales.

The early stages of international sales may be in response to excess production capacity, or large inventories that need to be converted into incremental sales. Attention to the differences in the foreign markets is frequently overlooked at this stage of internationalization, and products are sold to reduce domestic prices (i.e., increasing production utilization) or decrease the cost of carrying too large or outdated final product inventories. A company in this preliminary stage of internationalization has very few employees that are selected or trained in international business; most frequently the responsibility for marketing/selling overseas is shifted to outside foreign sales agents or brokers. As sales and subsequently profits from the international sale of products grow, personnel are hired to manage the overseas sales of the company. These "international" managers are typically located in the home country of the organization, but can make frequent trips overseas as the international segment of the business continues to grow.

Once entrenched in "international business orientation," many organizations develop a multi-foci perspective leading to a "multinational orientation" (e.g., involved in overseas businesses across multiple nations) (Pucik & Katz, 1986). The evolution from international to multinational necessitates integrating each specific host country's environmental requirements into the general operating style of the multinational organization. The country-specific contextual adaptation to legal, cultural, social, and individual psychological dimensions of "doing business in" requires local managers with social knowledge of host countries' culture and institutions (Aguirre, 1997; Reynolds, 1997).

An overreliance on local managers, however, can result in other problems, as discovered by Tellabs, Inc., a Chicago-based designer and manufacturer of telecommunication products. When the company opened its facility in Ireland and staffed it with local managers, parent company management did not take the time to adequately communicate Tellab's corporate culture (i.e., informal, flexible, and entrepreneurial) to the Irish staff, which operated more formally and less entrepreneurial. As a result, when an American executive went to Ireland, the Irish managers would appear to agree with suggested changes, yet they would not always proceed in the anticipated manner. The problem was a major cultural and communication gap despite the use of the same language (Solomon, 1993a).

Multinational organizations face a series of challenges as they progress into a more global perspective, and as the challenge from global competitors intensifies. The evolution to a global orientation requires organizations to develop the ability to amass top management teams (TMTs) in both the headquarters and subsidiary locations with a multicultural strategic orientation (Sambharya, 1996). This multicultural orientation enables management to strategically act globally while addressing the competition in local markets effectively (Ghoshal & Bartlett, 1997a). Although this multicultural orientation facilitates effective global management, it also creates cognitive diversity across the TMTs that needs to be managed proactively. Managing this cognitive diversity of orientations, domains, and memberships necessitates the reevaluation of the centric strategic orientation present in the global management systems and practices of many multinational corporations (MNCs). What is needed is a global management staffing strategy that enables global consistency among various managerial talent pools and the foreign subsidiaries (Harvey, 1997; Harvey & Buckley, 1997).

DEVELOPING A GLOBAL HUMAN RESOURCES MANAGEMENT PERSPECTIVE

There is a growing group of international human resources managers that contend that selection and other human resources functions should not be viewed separately, but must be viewed as an integrated system of human resources functions (Becker & Gerhart, 1996; Huselid, 1995; Huselid, Jackson, & Schuler, 1997). International human resources management scholars appear to have adopted this systemic approach toward human resources functions by developing integrative international human resources management (IHRM) frameworks (e.g., Dowling, Welch, & Schuler, 1999; Taylor, Beechler, and Napier, 1996; Welch, 1994). These integrated systems should be attuned to the strategic position taken by the firm relative to its future global expectations.

By examining all human resources functions as a system, it is felt that better collective human resources decisions will be made, which will increase the consistency among the various operating units in a global network. However, it would be difficult at present to claim that the selection of expatriate managers is a systemic, well-articulated, and documented process. The complexity of selecting expatriates to fill changing assignments is becoming more vexing given the staffing requirements associated with global organizations entering emerging markets. Therefore, it would appear to be a propitious time to develop an expatriate selection process that is keyed to the multiple requirements of global organizations, the abilities of candidates, a better understanding of candidates' methods of learning, and the overall competence of managers across a broad spectrum of personal and professional skills. If organizations are going to be effective global competitors, the competence repertoire of expatriate managers will play an integral role in the effective development and implementation of the organizations' strategies.

Three strategic orientations have been espoused for addressing global strategic international human resources management (SIHRM)[1]: (1) adaptive or polycentric, (2) exportive or ethnocentric, and (3) integrative or regiocentric/geocentric (Ondrack, 1985; Taylor et al., 1996). First, an exportive or ethnocentric orientation to international HRM staffing (Welch, 1994) focuses on a full-scale transfer of the parent organization's HRM system to the subsidiary, and makes use of parent-country nationals (i.e., expatriates) for staffing key positions in an overseas subsidiary. From a SIHRM perspective, an exportive orientation facilitates organizational control while providing important international developmental experience for promising managers of the parent organization (Black, Gregersen, & Mendenhall, 1992b; Schuler, Dowling, & DeCieri, 1993; Tung, 1993).

Second, an adaptive or polycentric orientation has relied on recruiting primarily host-country nationals (HCNs) (e.g., individuals from within the country) to manage the subsidiary operation. The subsidiary adapts its human resources management (HRM) policies, philosophies, and personnel to the local environment with limited intervention or control from the parent organization (Taylor et al., 1996), and more adaptive local autonomy. Particularly in developing countries, where expatriates may be more reluctant to go, and where the countries themselves want to develop the competencies that training and work in global firms can offer, this approach has become more common.

Finally, an integrative orientation (Taylor et al., 1996) can be used where HRM policies and practices transfer from the parent to the subsidiary and from the subsidiary

---

[1]The three strategies have been given different labels by different authors. As noted in the Taylor et al. manuscript, the concepts espoused are comparable. We have chosen to use adaptive, exportive, and integrative and note in the text their relationships with prior research.

back to the parent organization. An assumption is that there are practices that the subsidiaries or regional groups may have developed that would be useful to transfer back to the headquarters—or eventually throughout the organization. This orientation extends prior research on geocentric approaches that focused on staffing subsidiary locations by using the most qualified personnel regardless of nationality (Heenan and Perlmutter, 1979; Schuler et al., 1993). The regio- and geocentric approach typically also includes the use of third-country nationals (TCNs); that is, experienced managers from neither the parent nor the host country, who have the skills to run subsidiary operations and often take on regional management responsibilities (Schuler et al., 1993).

These three approaches to staffing international organizations depend upon a company's stage of evolution in international business. The exportive human resources orientation is most frequently used in companies who have just entered the international marketplace or are in a transition period where management is attempting to gain an understanding of the potential in selling overseas. Firms that have recognized the future potential of international/multinational markets tend to use the adaptive human resources strategy. The rationale for using local managers and adapting human resources policies is to help ensure that there is a fit between the company's strategy and the requirements of the local market. The integrative strategy attempts to utilize the best ideas/policies from the home and host countries, and to meld them into a unique set of practices that will differentiate the company from global competitors. Regardless of the orientation, organizations face great difficulty in identifying and retaining an adequate number of quality managers to place in their overseas operations. Therefore, it becomes imperative to have a diversified and adequate pool of potential

candidates to select from when staffing overseas operations.

GLOBAL MANAGERS IN DEMAND: WHERE AND HOW TO SOURCE THEM?

The need for managers in the foreign operations of a MNC is growing due to the potential markets and the strategic intent of MNCs to become global competitors. By becoming global in scope, the MNC should be able to use the comparative advantage (i.e., unique stocks of resources such as raw materials, cost of labor, number of potential employees, and technology) to make it more competitive. As the demand for managers grows, the supply of qualified managers has not kept pace (Gregersen et al., 1998). Therefore, it becomes imperative to identify potential "pools" of candidates for overseas assignments.

Three categories of candidates constitute the bulk of the potential overseas managers: (1) *expatriates* (home country nationals)—managers transferred from the MNC's home country to serve on overseas assignments; (2) *local nationals* (host country nationals)—individuals in the host country where the MNC is conducting business; and (3) *inpatriate managers*—individuals hired by the MNC who are permanently/semipermanently transferred to the headquarters to serve as a "bridge" between the headquarters and the foreign operations of the organization (Harvey, 1997). A fourth group of potential overseas managers are third country nationals (i.e., employees who are from neither the home nor the host country but who work in the host country). This group is quite limited in number and thus is not discussed in this article.

Each of the three primary pools of potential overseas managers has positive and negative attributes as a group (as summarized in Table 2-1). It should not be construed that all managers in a category will

TABLE 2-1 Relative Advantages/Disadvantages of Labor Pools for Foreign Assignment

Consideration	Expatriate			Local National			Third Country National		
	High	*Moderate*	*Low*	*High*	*Moderate*	*Low*	*High*	*Moderate*	*Low*
Relative cost	X					X	X		
Past training	X					X		X	
Availability (number)		X		X					X
Loyalty		X				X			X
HQ. confidence	X					X		X	
Complexity of compensation package	X					X		X	
Cultural/political sensitivity			X	X			X		
Corporate culture/communication and understanding	X					X		X	
Family problems/issues	X					X		X	
Motivation to succeed in organization	X					X		X	
Probability of assignment fulfillment			X		X		X		
Target of competitor recruiting		X			X		X		
Willingness to extend/take additional foreign assignment			X	X			X		

have all the attributes discussed. Even so, a large percentage of the candidates from a category will exhibit these characteristics.

Expatriate Managers

Historically, expatriates have typically been the preferred choice in overseas staffing strategy for U.S.-based MNCs. Expatriates typically have advanced technical/business skills, experience, and informal knowledge in working within the parent organization (Black, Gregersen, & Mendenhall, 1992a; Dowling et al., 1999; Marquardt & Engel, 1993). The appeal of this group has been in the parent organization's ability to effectively exert control through expatriate as-

signments (Adler & Ghadar, 1990; Beamish & Inkpen, 1998; Birdseye & Hill, 1995; Black et al., 1992a; Edstrom & Galbraith, 1977; Feldman & Thompson, 1993; Schuler et al., 1993; Tung, 1993). By using expatriates, the company knows and controls more closely what occurs abroad. However, evidence suggests that expatriate managers experience a high rate of failure related to difficulties in adjusting and managing across cultural settings (Birdseye & Hill, 1995; Black, Mendenhall, & Oddou, 1991).

The selection of expatriate managers for overseas assignments has been examined by a number of researchers attempting to determine how to select managers who can be effective overseas (Fish, 1999; Ones & Viswesvaran, 1997; Ryan, McFarland, Baron, & Page, 1999; Spreitzer, McCall, & Mahoney, 1997). In practice, technical or functional expertise has been the dominant criteria for selecting managers for overseas assignments (Mendenhall, Dunbar, & Oddou, 1987; Tung, 1981, 1982). Early attempts at identifying an appropriate method for selecting expatriate managers frequently centered on a set of desired personal characteristics that could help improve the chances of expatriate managers' "survival" during overseas assignments (e.g., Baliga & Baker, 1985; Hays, 1971, 1974; Tucker, 1978; Tung, 1981).

Although different methods exist for selecting managers among various cultures, the core concepts have centered on functional capabilities and personal characteristics of potential candidates (see Levy-Leboyer, 1994, for a review of European selection methods). While these early studies identified a number of issues that could influence the success or failure of expatriate managers, initially very little was done to develop a more systemic approach to the expatriate selection process.

Table 2-2 illustrates the individual, organizational, environmental, and systemic issues that could have an impact on expatriate success/failure, as exemplified in research on expatriate selection. Past expatriate selection processes focused for the most part on characteristics of expatriate managers and on the factors impacting success or failure of these individuals during their assignments. This *ex post* assessment of characteristics has been modified to take into consideration an *ex ante* examination of personality characteristics of potential expatriate managers.

More recently, researchers have focused on the "Big Five" personality characteristics.

1. *Extroversion*—the ability of expatriates to successfully assert themselves and gain acceptance in the social environment through social relationships (Ones & Viswesvaran, 1997).

2. *Agreeableness*—being identified as a team player through the formation of reciprocal social alliances and the building of social capital in the organization (Caligiuri, 2000b).

3. *Conscientiousness*—being trustworthy, diligent colleagues who are productive and supportive of increased organizational performance (Hogan & Goodson 1990).

4. *Emotional stability*—the intrapersonal ability to adapt and cope with stress in professional and personal spheres of one's life (Buss, 1991).

5. *Openness and intellect*—having the ability to effectively complete a functional assignment being aware of the environment, and allowing for adaptation of behavior to changing conditions in that environment.

Research suggests that by better understanding the personal attributes of managers, MNCs could better assess managers' ability to adapt/adjust to foreign environments.

While these personality characteristics may have a predictive capability relative to the success of expatriate managers, the empirical research to fully support this position is somewhat lacking. A comprehensive review of 117 empirical studies using the Big Five personality characteristics (Barrick & Mount, 1991) found that conscientiousness was the best single predictor of overseas performance. Comparable research conducted in Europe resulted in similar, although weaker, results. In addition, the tie to organizational performance, using the Big Five personality characteristics as the primary selection means, is also somewhat tentative (for a review of the issues, see Wood, 1999). Use of the Big Five personality attributes as a selection tool for expatriate managers has led to the development of classifications or

TABLE 2-2	Predicting Success/Failure of Expatriate Managers			
Expatriate Performance	*Individual*	*Organizational*	*Environmental*	*Systemic*
SUCCESS	• "Big Five" personality characteristics • technical competence • cultural adaptability • previous cultural adjustments • extensive foreign travel	• cross-cultural training • repatriation program • knowledgeable IHRM managers • separate IHRM process/ procedures • mentoring program	• relocation to similar economy/culture • reduced government restriction • similarity of languages	• planning perspective • integrated IHRM system • increased use of technology • flexibility of IHRM system • consistency of systems globally
REPRESENTATIVE RESEARCH	Caligiuri, 2000a & b; Stroh & Caligiuri, 1998; Ones & Viswesvaran, 1997; Spreitzer, McCall, & Mahoney, 1997	Feldman & Bolino, 1999; Harvey et al., 1999; Katz & Seifer, 1996; Selmer et al., 1998	Bartlett & Ghoshal, 1995; Tung & Miller, 1990	Lado & Wilson, 1994; Harvey, 1996b; Becker et al., 1997; Harris & Brewster, 1999; Ferris et al., 1999; Fish & Wood, 1996
FAILURE	• family issues • unwillingness to be relocated • dual-career issues • commitment to assignment • lack of language capabilities • inadequate support for the employee/family	• lack of career planning • inadequate orientation • inadequate compensation programs • inadequate training programs	• emerging markets • restrictions on HR by government • hostility (climate, healthcare, etc.) of environment • cultural taboos (women, minorities)	• "centric" IHRM orientation • *ad hoc* case-by-case negotiations with candidates • inadequate career development process during foreign assignment • ineffective performance appraisal system
REPRESENTATIVE RESEARCH	Caligiuri et al., 1998; Harvey, 1998; Fish & Wood, 1997; DeCieri et al., 1991	Brewster & Pickard, 1994; Brewster, 1995; Chen, 1994; Florkowski & Fogel, 1999	Harvey et al., 1999; Dowling et al., 1999	Harris & Brewster, 1999; Pucik & Saba, 1998; Fish, 1999; Brewster & Scullion, 1997.

categories of social skills to be used for the selection of managers.

The equivocal research results also have forced practitioners to deal with the issue of manager selection in more concrete ways. Several classification schemes illustrate the intent of the practitioners to establish multiple means to predict success for expatriate managers. The Ashridge Management Research Center identified five categories with multiple items in each category: (1) strategic awareness and support, (2) adaptability in new/novel environmental situations, (3) sensitivity and openness to other cultures and social mores, (4) language capabilities, and (5) interpersonal communication skills (Harris & Brewster, 1999). Other studies also support "soft" skills (i.e., skills not directly tied to technical training and functional expertise) including global awareness, international strategy, cultural empathy, international or cross-cultural team building, international negotiation skills, ethical understanding of conducting business in foreign countries, and self-efficacy. Many practitioners feel that having multiple screening devices augments the more traditional personality characteristics selection tools.

The past several decades have seen numerous reports on the alarming rate of failure of expatriate managers. These failures have been attributed to lack of adequate cross-cultural training of expatriate managers, family-related issues, significant difficulty in adjusting to the host country/organization, lack of transition/adjustment support by the organization, and a myriad of other reasons (e.g., Searle & Ward, 1990; DeCieri, Dowling, & Taylor, 1991; Brewster & Pickard, 1994; Pucik & Saba, 1998; Caligiuri, Hyland, Joshi, & Bross, 1998; Florkowski & Fogel, 1999).

Expatriate failure rates continue to be high and costly, and have been blamed for a variety of issues including difficulties in adjusting to and managing across cultures and work-family conflict (e.g., dual-career conflicts) (Webb & Wright, 1996; Dowling, et al., 1999). For example, Motorola, Inc., an Illinois-based world-known exporter of telecommunication and semiconductor equipment, calculates that a mid-level foreign assignment of a $75,000-a-year expatriate runs $600,000 to $2.25 million for a three-year posting. Linda Kuna, Motorola's global assignment manager, has noted that by sending the wrong kind of individual you can damage your relationships with a host country, you can lose business opportunities, and you damage the career path for individuals who probably should not have been sent overseas.

A latent issue that has received less attention, but could have a major indirect impact on the dependence on expatriate managers, is the growing strategic importance of emerging markets (e.g., China, Russia, India, Indonesia, Malaysia, Turkey, Philippines, and select Eastern European countries) (Garten, 1996, 1997a, 1997b). These emerging markets will constitute over 87 percent of the world population in 2025, and are considered to be the prime targets for the growth of global organizations (*World*, 1996). The emerging markets are frequently culturally distant, normally have significantly lower levels of economic development and, for the most part, represent a potential hardship to expatriates coming from developed countries. The reluctance of expatriates to take assignments in these less attractive locations may limit global organizations' expansion opportunities and global managers' development. IHRM experts have begun to examine a number of alternatives to the exclusive use of expatriates to meet the management manpower needs for growth in emerging markets (Gregersen et al., 1998).

Local Nationals

MNCs can also use the indigenous inhabitants of the countries in which they are doing business as managers/employees in their organizations. Advantages to utilizing the local population in the operation of the company's foreign organization include: (1) tacit knowledge of local cultural, social, and economic characteristics, which may be difficult for expatriates to understand; (2) less expensive employment costs, due to the fact of not having to pay for living allowances or incentives to take positions in foreign operations; (3) willingness to work in foreign MNCs due to compensation, benefits, and prestige of working for these organizations; (4) a large potential pool of individuals who want to work for MNCs; (5) the ability to interface with local institutions because of professional and personal networks; (6) stability in the foreign operation, in that local employees are not being transferred into the organizations for a short-duration assignment like expatriate managers; (7) little to no adjustment time to the host country culture, in that they are inhabitants of the country; (8) acceptance by coworkers and the ability to be good role models for the local workforce; (9) the favorable attitude of local government to employment and training of indigenous workers; and (10) the availability of some top candidates (e.g., women) who may be shunned by local firms, as is common with blue chip Japanese firms (Moynihan, 1993; Rondinelli & Bigoness, 1997; Scullion, 1992; Tung, 1993).

Despite such compelling arguments for MNCs to hire foreign nationals in the host country, disadvantages exist as well, including (1) perceived possible lack of loyalty to the "foreign" organization or its management; (2) difficulty in retaining local nationals that have been trained and are successful in their current position (i.e., other foreign-owned MNCs often raid qualified and trained local nationals); (3) little to no formal business education; (4) reluctance to be employed by MNC in cultures where it may limit future employment by indigenous firms; (5) the "best and brightest" home country nationals work for family owned/operated companies or the government, therefore the remaining candidates are not the best talent available in the host country (i.e., employing "second string" candidates); (6) in some societies, age, and not competence, is the rule of order in the country, reducing the effectiveness of younger employees hired as managers; (7) some reluctance and difficulty in training local nationals to Western business practices and

the standard operating policies of the MNC; (8) strict cultural/social standards that make some potential candidates of less value due to restrictions on their potential influence in their own country (e.g., different tribal groups); (9) a distrust of foreign nationals by home country managers due to their lack of international experience or other innate biases held by key managers; and (10) a view by younger locals that MNCs are starting points for their careers, to be "used" as training grounds before moving back to the local firms (Ali, Krishnan, & Azim, 1997; Atkinson, 1994; Solomon, 1993a, 1995; Sue, 1997; Quelch & Dinh-Tan, 1998).

As the rate of globalization accelerates, it is inevitable that more host country nationals will be selected for key management positions in overseas operations. But even with the growing need for managers, many U.S. MNCs are reluctant to "give control" of their foreign subsidiaries to host country nationals. Thus an alternative pool of candidates has recently been identified: inpatriate managers.

Inpatriate Managers

Inpatriate managers are host country nationals transferred to the headquarters organization on a semipermanent or permanent basis to serve as "linking-pins" to global markets (Harvey, 1997). They are rapidly becoming an effective new pool and staffing strategy, especially for emerging markets, and they make particularly good "sense" for the United States where immigrants make up as much as 40 percent of the annual growth in the U.S. workforce (Solomon, 1995). Inpatriate managers have the local knowledge of the emerging market and reside long enough in the United States to establish credibility in the headquarters organization for control of emerging country subsidiaries (Harvey, Speier, & Novicevic, 2000; Harvey et al., 1999). The tacit knowledge of inpatriate managers makes them a value component in developing a sustainable core competency of local adapted strategies (effectiveness) while, at the same time, remaining aligned to global goals and strategies (efficiency) of the global organization. Such a distinctive corporate "signature" to act locally ensures local acceptance of products/services without reducing the efficiency necessary for global competition (Ghoshal & Bartlett, 1997b).

The inpatriate managers responsible for emerging markets will be expected to develop effective local control and coordination in terms of (1) an external focus on local government relations, (2) cultural leadership of indigenous employees and relational partners (i.e., channel-of-distribution members, suppliers, customers and the like), (3) social networking, (4) teamwork, (5) a keen sense of the dynamics of the local market in conjunction with the global perspective of the organization, and (6) a high level of local social knowledge of institutions and key functional counterparts (Bartlett & Ghoshal, 1992; Caligiuri & Stroh, 1995; Martinez & Quelch, 1996; Sohn, 1994). If the "soft" skills derived from the context-specific social knowledge of emerging markets are becoming the key determinants of successful country managers, it would appear that inpatriate managers would be a worthwhile complementary pool of candidates to expatriates (Harvey, 1997; Harvey, Speier, & Novicevic, 1999).

Table 2-3 shows a normative comparison of expatriates and inpatriates for both developed and emerging country markets. It becomes readily apparent that inpatriate managers have a distinct competitive advantage in social knowledge and the resulting "soft" skills necessary to be effective in emerging markets. Local country nationals are excluded from the comparison because of the limited potential candidate pool in emerging economies.

An additional contribution of inpatriate managers to the management team of global organizations is their diversity of background and pluralistic orientation to global competition. The sheer difference in education, training, and business experiences in emerging economies adds value to the strategic capabilities found in the management team of the global organization. The recognition of the need for cultural diversity in global management has recently become a topic in boardrooms throughout the world. Matsushita's president has told management, "to become a truly global company, we have to have diversity in top management" (Harvey & Buckley, 1997).

Sony sells approximately 80 percent of its products in foreign markets and recognizes the need to have a pluralistic strategic orientation. Sony's board of directors has appointed two non-Japanese members and has plans to hire host country nationals as top executives for functional positions in Japan and for many of its overseas subsidiaries. The European global organization Royal Dutch-Shell has 38 nationalities represented in its London headquarters, exemplifying multicultural globalism. This multiculturalism reinforces the development of a "global mindset" of managers throughout the organization (Kefalas, 1998; Kedia & Mukherji, 1999; Paul, 2000). The utilization of inpatriate managers could also be used to increase the economic, cultural, political, and social diversity in global organizations.

As global organizations move away from dependence on a single pool of potential candidates for global managers, an opportunity opens for inpatriate managers to serve as organizational boundary spanners between the domestic and foreign operations of a company. Functioning as organizational "go-betweens," inpatriate managers can provide the tacit knowledge necessary to effectively communicate and develop new perspectives on emerging markets (Harvey & Novicevic, 2000; Harvey et al., 1999). The diversity of perspectives is important throughout the global organization, but is of

TABLE 2-3   Expatriate/Inpatriate Appropriateness Analysis

| | Responsibility for Assignment | | | |
| | Expatriate | | Inpatriate | |
Candidate Characteristics	*Developed**	*Emerging*	*Developed*	*Emerging*
Renewable resource (extended assignments)	L**	L	H	H
Willingness to be responsible for overseas position	M	L	H	H
Motivation to participate in global assignments	M	L	H	H
Relative cost characteristics	H	H	L	L
Flexibility (social/cultural/family)	M	L	H	H
Organizational cultural "fit"	H	L	M	H
Level of peer acceptance	L	M	M	H
Headquarters confidence	H	M	M	H
Level of stress	M	H	M	L
Internal political understanding	H	L	M	H

 * = developed economies: emerging economies
 ** = *Level of Appropriateness of Pool of Candidates*
  H = High
  M = Moderate
  L = Low

Source: Adapted from Harvey, M., C. Speier, & M. Novicevic, 1999, "The Role of Inpatriation in Global Staffing," *International Journal of Human Resource Management*, vol. 10, no. 3.

particular value in the top management team (TMT). Without the in-house knowledge of the differences among markets and the significant discrepancies between the emerging and developed economies, the TMT is dependent on outsiders [i.e., local and third country nationals] to communicate strategic intent and maintain control of the subsidiary operations (Harvey et al., 1999; Miller, Burke, & Glick, 1998).

If inpatriate managers are a growing necessity for the globalization of the organization (i.e., due to shortage of other candidate pools and because of the need to acquire local knowledge of the emerging markets), the question becomes, "how can these inpatriate managers be selected? Can the same "recipe," traditionally used for the selection of expatriate managers, be used in the selection process for inpatriate man-

agers? Given the tacit knowledge that is necessary to compete in emerging markets, it appears that inpatriate managers should be selected based upon "multiple IQs" (e.g., intellectual, political, social/cultural, intuitive, network, emotional, creative, etc.) that indicate various skills as well as the learning capacity of inpatriates. If acquiring knowledge to effectively compete is a requirement in the new global competitive arena, then selection could be guided by the various learning capacities of the inpatriate manager.

SUMMARY AND CONCLUSIONS

One of the critical elements in the strategy to become more involved in international business is the need for an adequate number of managers to fill overseas positions. Typically, in U.S.-based organizations, expatriate managers (i.e., U.S. citizens) have filled these positions. These expatriated managers were typically assigned overseas for three to five years, and then were repatriated back to the United States. Significant problems have long existed—and continue—with expatriate managers: with the relocation and adjustment (resulting in higher failure rate) and with refusal to take foreign assignments (resulting in fewer qualified applicants).

To make up for the shortage of qualified managers to fill overseas positions, many organizations have begun to utilize local nationals and third country nationals, yet these groups have their own drawbacks. A new group of managers (i.e., inpatriates) has emerged who have a unique set of skills and cultural backgrounds that can be useful to organizations operating in many economic and culturally distant countries. The future of global organizations will be dependent on how effectively they can put together a complement of expatriates, host country nationals, and inpatriate managers to compete in the global marketplace. Therefore, there is a need for an international/global human resources management infrastructure that can address the complexities of managing personnel throughout the world.

Most firms go through an evolutionary process as they become more involved in international business. This evolution (i.e., international, multination, and global) has direct implications for the human resources function. Human resources management policies and processes become more complex and difficult to manage as organizations become more involved in business among different countries. Therefore, a systemic orientation to the human resources management function is required. This SIHRM framework initially addressed the differences that occur when managers are sent to foreign countries. These differences are pri-

marily examined in the light of how to help the transferred manager adapt and to fit into the foreign country and the overseas organization of the company. The focus of SIHRM is providing the ability to adapt to each country and for each manager.

As organizations become more involved in the global marketplace, however, the HR system must adapt to the growing complexity of the global operations of the company. A Strategic Global Human Resource Management (SGHRM) system has as its strategic goal "glocalization" (i.e., develop a global system with a local flexibility built in to allow for adaptation of HR policies and practices to fit the local market, but maintain consistency with the global HR principles and policies). The SGHRM system embodies a global network perspective that recognizes the need for internal consistency of HR policies but at the same time allows for development of variations of corporate HR policies to the needs of the local markets. As one might imagine, SGHRM systems are very complex by the very nature of the number of countries and the differences in the human resources requirements and practices found in these economically, culturally, and institutionally diverse countries.

Some academic researchers as well as HR management practitioners are forecasting that HRMs will be the key determinant of how successful global organizations will be in the twenty-first century. Without an adequate number of qualified managers to fill overseas positions, the future of the company will be constrained. Whether these experts are correct or not, one can not argue with the growing complexity of managing the HR function in organizations that are globalizing their business operations. The challenges for HR management will be matching the complexity of global business with a management system that can meet the needs of global organizations. ■

REFERENCES

Adler, N., & Ghadar, F. (1990). Strategic human resource management: A global perspective. In R. Reiperl (Ed.), *Human resource management: An international comparison* (235–260). New York, NY: Walter de Gruyter.

Aguirre, M. (1997). Multiculturalism in a labour market with integrated economies. *Management Decision, 35* (7), 489–496.

Ali, A., Krishnan, G., & Azim, A. (1997). Expatriate and indigenous managers' work loyalty and attitude toward risk. *The Journal of Psychology, 131* (3), 260–270.

Atkinson, D. (1994). Multinational training: A call for standards. *The Counseling Psychologist, 22*, 300–307.

Baliga, G. M., & Baker, J. C. (1985). Multinational corporate policies for expatriate managers: Selection, training, evaluation. *Advanced Management Journal, 50* (4), 31–38.

Barney, J. (1991). Firm resources and sustained competitive advantage. *Journal of Management, 17* (1), 99–120.

Barrick, M. R., & Mount, M. K. (1991). The big five personality dimensions and job performance. *Personnel Psychology, 44*, 1–26.

Bartlett, C., & Ghoshal, S. (1992). What is a global manager? *Harvard Business Review, 70*, 124–132.

Bartlett, C., & Ghoshal, S. (1994). Changing the role of top management: Beyond strategy to purpose. *Harvard Business Review, 72* (6), 79–88.

Bartlett, C., & Ghoshal, S. (1995, May–June). Changing the role of top management: Beyond systems to people (Part Three). *Harvard Business Review*, 132–143.

Beamish, P. W., & Inkpen, A. C. (1998). Japanese firms and the decline of the Japanese expatriate. *Journal of World Business, 33* (1), 35–50.

Becker, G., & Gerhart, B. (1996). The impact of human resource management on organizational performance: Program and prospects, *Academy of Management Journal, 39* (4), 779–801.

Birdseye, M., & Hill, J. (1995). Individual, organizational/work and environmental influences on expatriate turnover tendencies: An empirical study. *Journal of International Business Studies, 26* (4), 787–813.

Black, S., Gregersen, H., & Mendenhall, M. (1992a). *Global Assignments.* San Francisco: Jossey-Bass.

Black, S., Gregersen, H., & Mendenhall, M. (1992b). Toward a theoretical framework of repatriation adjustment. *Journal of International Business Studies, 23* (4), 737–760.

Black, S., Mendenhall, M., & Oddou, G. (1991). Toward a comprehensive model of international adjustment: An integration of multiple theoretical perspectives. *Academy of Management Review, 16*, 291–337.

Brewster, C., and Pickard, J. (1994). Evaluating expatriate training. *International Studies of Management & Organization, 24* (3), 18–29.

Buss, D. M. (1991). Evolutionary personality psychology. In M. Rosenzweig & L. W. Porter (Eds.), *Annual Review of Psychology, 42* (459–492). Palo Alto, CA: Annual Review Inc.

Caligiuri, P. (2000a). Selecting expatriates for personality characteristics: A moderating effect of personality on the relationship between host national contact and cross-cultural adjustment. *Management International Review, 40* (1), 61–80.

Caligiuri, P. (2000b). The big five personality characteristics on predictions of expatriates' desire to terminate the assignment and supervision-rate performance. *Personnel Psychology, 53*(1), 67–88.

Caligiuri, P., Hyland, M., Joshi, A., & Bross, A. (1998). A theoretical framework for examining the relationships between family adjustment and expatriate adjustment to working in the host country. *Journal of Applied Psychology, 83* (4), 598–614.

Caligiuri, P. & Stroh, L. (1995). Multinational corporate management strategies and international human resource practices: Bring SIHRM to the bottom line. *The International Journal of Human Resource Management, 6* (3), 494–507.

DeCieri, H., Dowling, P., & Taylor, K. (1991). The psychological impact of expatriate relocation on partners. *International Journal of Human Resource Management, 2*, 377–414.

Dowling, P., Welch, B., & Schuler, R. (1999). *Intention of human resource management: Managing people in a multinational context.* Cincinnati, OH: South-Western College Publication.

Early, C., & Mosakowski, E. (2000). Creating hybrid team cultures: An empirical test of transnational team functioning. *Academy of Management Journal, 43* (1), 26–49.

Edstrom, A., & Galbraith, J. (1977, June). Transfer of managers as a coordination and control strategy in multinational organizations. *Administration Science Quarterly,* 248–263.

Feldman, D., & Thompson, H. (1993). Expatriates, repatriate, and domestic geographic relocation: An empirical investigation of adjustment to new job assignments. *Journal of International Business Studies, 24* (3), 507–529.

Fish, A. (1999). Selecting managers for cross-border assignments: Building value into the process. *International Journal of Management Review, 1* (4), 461–483.

Florkowski, G., & Fogel, P. (1999). Expatriate adjustment and commitment: The role of host-unit treatment. *International Journal of Human Resource Management, 10* (5), 783–802.

Garten, J. (1996). The key emerging markets. *The Columbia Journal of World Business, 31* (2), 6–31.

Garten, J. (1997a). Trouble ahead in emerging markets. *Harvard Business Review, 75,* 38–49.

Garten, J. (1997b). *The big ten: The emerging markets and how they will change our lives.* New York: Basic Books.

Ghoshal, S., & Bartlett, C. (1997a). The myth of the generic manager: New resource competencies for management roles. *California Management Review, 40* (1), 92–107.

Ghoshal, S., & Bartlett, C. (1997b). The individualized corporation: A fundamentally new approach to management. New York: Harper Business.

Gregersen, H., Morrison, A., & Black, S. (1998). Developing leaders for the global frontier. *Sloan Management Review, 40* (1), 21–32.

Hamel, G., & Heene, A. (1994). Conclusions: Which theory of strategic management do we need for tomorrow? In G. Hamel & A. Heene (Eds.), *Competence-based competition* (15–19). New York: Wiley.

Harris, H., & Brewster, C. (1999). The coffee machine system: How international selection really works. *The International Journal of Human Resource Management, 10* (3), 488–504.

Harvey, M. (1997). Inpatriate training: The next challenge for global human resource management. *International Journal of Intercultural Relations, 21* (3), 393–428.

Harvey, M., & Buckley, M. (1997). Managing inpatriates: Building global core competency. *Journal of World Business, 32* (1), 35–52.

Harvey, M., Novicevic, M., & Speier, C. (1999). The impact of emerging markets on staffing the global organization. *Journal of International Management, 5* (2), 34–46.

Harvey, M., & Novicevic, M. (2000). Staffing global marketing positions: What we don't know can make a difference. *Journal of World Business, 35* (1), 80–94.

Harvey, M., Speier, C., & Novicevic, M. (1999). Inpatriate managers: How to increase the probability of success. *Human Resource Management Review, 9* (1), 51–82.

Harvey, M., Speier, C., & Novicevic, M. (2000). An innovative global management staffing system: A competency-based perspective. *Human Resource Management, 39* (4), 381–394.

Hays, R. D. (1971). Ascribed behavioral determinants of success—failure among U.S. expatriate managers. *Journal of International Business Studies, 2,* 40–46.

Hays, R. D. (1974). Expatriate selection: Insuring success and avoiding failure. *Journal of International Business Studies, 5* (1), 25–37.

Heenan, D. A., & Perlmutter, H. V. (1979). *Multinational organization development.* Reading, MA: Addison-Wesley.

Heene, A. (1994). Foreword. In G. Hamel & A. Heene (Eds.), *Competence-based competition* (25–27). New York: Wiley.

Hogan, G., & Goodson, J. (1990). The key to expatriate success. *Training and Development Journal,* January, 50–52.

Huselid, M. (1995). The impact of human resource management practices on turnover, productivity, and corporate financial performance.

Academy of Management Journal, 38 (3), 635–672.

Huselid, M., Jackson, S., & Schuler, R. (1997). Technical and strategic human resource management effectiveness as determinants of firm performance. *Academy of Management Journal, 40* (1), 171–188.

Kedia, B., & Mukherji, A. (1999). Global managers: Developing a mindset for global competitiveness. *Journal of World Business, 34* (3), 230–247.

Kefalas, A. G. (1998). Think globally, act locally. *Thunderbird International Business Review, 40* (6), 547–562.

Levy-Leboyer, C. (1994). Selection and assessment in Europe. In H. Triendis, M. Dunnette, & L. Hough (Eds.), *Handbook of Industrial and Organizational Psychology* (Vol. 4, 173–190). Palo Alto, CA: Consulting Psychologists Press.

Marquardt, M., & Engel, D. (1993). *Global human resource development.* Upper Saddle River, NJ: Prentice Hall.

Martinez, J., & Quelch, J. (1996). Country managers: The next generation. *International Marketing Review, 13* (3), 709–734.

Mendenhall, M., Dunbar, E., & Oddou, G. (1987). Expatriate selection, training and career-pathing: A review and critique. *Human Resources Management, 26* (3), 331–345.

Miller, C., Burke, L., & Glick, W. (1998). Cognitive diversity among upper-echelon executives: Implications for strategic decision processes. *Strategic Management Journal, 75*(4), 506–517.

Millman, T. (1999). From national account management to global account management in business-to-business markets. *Thexis, 4,* 2–9.

Minehan, M. (1998). Futurist task force. *HRM Magazine,* 188–192.

Montgomery, D., & Yip, G. (1999). Statistical evidence on global account management programs. *Thexis, 4,* 10–13.

Moynihan, M. (1993). *The economist intelligence unit global manager: Recruiting, developing and keeping world class executives.* New York: McGraw-Hill, Inc.

Napolitano, L. (1998). Global account management: The new frontier. *NAMA Journal, 34* (3), 21–33.

1996 *World Resources: A guide to the global environment 1996–1997,* joint publication of the World Resource Institute, the United Nations Environment Programme, the United Nations Development Programme, and the World Bank, Oxford University Press: New York, 173–176.

Nohria, N., & Ghoshal, S. (1997). *The differentiated network: Organizing multinational corporations for value creation.* San Francisco: Jossey-Bass.

Ondrack, D. (1985). International transfers of managers in North American and European MNCs. *Journal of International Business Studies,* 1–19.

Ones, D., & Viswesvaran, C. (1997). Personality determinants in the prediction of aspects of expatriate success. In Z. Aycan (Ed.), *New approaches to employee management: Expatriate management theory and research* (Vol. 4, 63–92). New York.

Paul, H. (2000). Creating a global mindset. *Thunderbird International Business Review, 42* (2), 187–200.

Pfeffer, J. (1994). *Competitive advantage through people.* Boston, MA: Harvard Business School Press.

Prahalad, C. K., & Hamel, G. (1990). The core competence of the corporation. *Harvard Business Review, 68,* 79–93.

Prahalad, C. K., & Hamel, G. (1993). Strategy as stretch and leverage. *Harvard Business Review, 71.*

Pucik, V., & Katz, J. (1986). Information, control, and human resource management in multinational firms. *Human Resource Management, 25,* 103–122.

Pucik, V., & Saba, T. (1998, December). Selecting and developing the global versus the expatriate manager: A review of the state-of-the-art. *Human Resource Planning, 21* (4), 40–51.

Quelch, D., & Dinh-Tan, C. (1998, July–August). Country managers in transitional economies: The case of Vietnam. *Business Horizons,* 34–40.

Reynolds, C. (1997). Strategic employment of third country nationals: Keys to sustaining the transformation of HR functions. *Human Resource Planning, 20* (1), 33–40.

Rondinelli, D., & Bigoness, W. (1997). Retaining Asian host-country managers in U.S. multinationals: The challenges in Thailand and Singapore. *Business and the Contemporary World, IX* (2), 277–298.

Rumelt, R. (1994). Foreword. In G. Hames & A. Heene (Eds.), *Competence-based competition* (XV–XIX). New York: Wiley.

Ryan, A., McFarland, L., Baron, H., & Page, R. (1999). An international look at selection practices: Nations and culture as explanations for variability in practice. *Personnel Psychology, 52,* 359–391.

Sanchez, R., Heene, A., & Thomas, H. (1997). *Dynamics of competence-based competition.* Oxford, U.K.: Pergamon.

Sambharya, R. (1996). Foreign experiences of top management teams and international diversification strategies of U.S. multinational corporations. *Strategic Management Journal, 17,* 739–746.

Schuler, R., Dowling, P., & DeCieri, H. (1993). An integrative framework of strategic international human resource management. *International Journal of Human Resource Management, 1,* 717–764.

Scullion, H. (1992, Winter). Creating international managers: Retirement and development issues, *Human Resources Management,* 67–75.

Searle, W., & Ward, C. (1990). The prediction of psychological and sociocultural adjustment during cross-cultural transitions. *Journal of Intercultural Relations, 14,* 449–464.

Sohn, J. (1994). Social knowledge as a control system: A proposition and evidence from Japanese FDI behavior. *Journal of International Business Studies, 25* (2), 295–324.

Solomon, C. (1993a). Learning to manage host-country nationals, *Personnel Journal, 74* (3), 60–65.

Solomon, C. (1993b). Managing today's immigrants. *Personnel Journal, 72* (2), 56–66.

Solomon, C. (1995). Helping hand pulls global inpatriates onboard. *Personnel Journal, 74* (1), 40–49.

Spreitzer, G. M., McCall, M. W., & Mahoney, J. P. (1997). Early identification of international executive potential. *Journal of Applied Psychology, 82* (1), 6–29.

Stroh, L. K., & Caligiuri, P. M. (1998). Strategic human resources: A new source for competitive advantage in the global arena. *The International Journal of Human Resource Management, 9,* 1–17.

Sue, D. (1997). Multicultural training. *International Journal of Intercultural Relations, 21* (2), 175–193.

Taylor, S., Beechler, S., & Napier, N. (1996). Toward an integrative model of strategic international human resource management. *Academy of Management Review, 21* (4), 959–985.

Tucker, M. (1978). *The measurement and prediction of overseas work assignments in the Navy (U.S. Navy Contract Number N00600b73-D-0780).* Denver, CO: Centre for Research and Education.

Tung, R. (1981). Selection and training of personnel overseas assignments. *Columbia Journal of World Business, 16* (1), 68–78.

Tung, R. (1982). Selection and training procedures of U.S., European, and Japanese multinationals. *California Management Review, 25,* 57–71.

Tung, R. (1993). Managing cross-national and intra-national diversity. *Human Resource Management, 32* (4), 461–477.

Webb, A., & Wright, C. (1996). The expatriate experience: Implications for career success. *Career Development Journal, 1* (5), 38–44.

Welch, D. (1994). HRM implications of globalization. *Journal of General Management, 19* (4), 52–68.

Wood, S. (1999). Human resource management and performance. *International Journal of Management Reviews, 1* (4), 367–413.

Yip, G., & Madsen, T. (1996). Global account management: The new frontier in relationship marketing. *International Marketing Review, 13* (3), 24–42.

THE INFLUENCE OF ORGANIZATIONAL POLITICS IN HUMAN RESOURCES MANAGEMENT PRACTICES

Darren C. Treadway

"One of the penalties for refusing to participate in politics is that you end up being governed by your inferiors."

— PLATO

One of the most pervasive and salient of all topics in organizations today, political behavior is capable of representing the extremes: all that we despise, and all that we aspire to be. Political behavior can be obvious and unseen, blatant and carefully concealed, deceitful and honorable, preemptive and reactive, a career builder and a career disaster, organizationally productive and self-serving. The political nature of individuals and organizations presents tremendous challenges and opportunities for the modern human resources professional. The failure to explicitly address the politics inherent in human resources (HR) decisions has, unfortunately, rendered the explanations by the traditional, rational perspective incomplete in today's dynamic environment.

The goal of this article is threefold. First, a brief discussion of the history of human resources management (HRM) demonstrates the need for synthesis of the political perspective. Second, we evaluate the effect that political activity has on the implementation of selection, performance management, safety, and organizational change initiatives in organizations. Third, we consider the forces that are driving change in the human resources field, and discuss their implications for political activity within the organization. Integrating these goals, we seek to answer the question, "How does political behavior affect an organization's HR practices?"

POLITICS AND HUMAN RESOURCES MANAGEMENT: THE CONVERGENCE OF TWO FIELDS

Organizational politics and HRM are two fields with similar histories. While the scholarly roots of both fields can be traced to the early twentieth century, it is the developments of the last three decades that have brought these fields into organizational prominence. This most recent era has witnessed two significant paradigm shifts: a shift away from exclusive focus on the rational perspective to the political perspective; and a shift away from the personnel function to HRM. Other articles in this book more thoroughly discuss the evolution of human resources management. For our purposes, we briefly address the recent history of each field, and acknowledge that the contemporary role of the HR function is highly integrated with the assumptions of the political perspective.

Organizational Politics: Emerging from the Machine

Organizational scholars have offered numerous perspectives of organizational decision making. The rational model has traditionally dominated conversation in both business schools and industry. The popularity of this model exists in part because of the clear-cut answers it provides.

From the perspective of rational decision making, organizations are simply extended machines in which a set of interchangeable parts, human and technological, can be inserted into a process for the purpose of accomplishing the universal objective of organizational survival.

While the rational model offers easy to understand prescriptions for organizational action, the value of those prescriptions rests on the degree to which one can accept the inherent assumptions of the model (i.e., universal interests, adequate resources, and clear objectives). Proponents of the political perspective argue that organizations are essentially human entities, with little or no resemblance to the well-oiled machine depicted by the rational model. At best, human interactions are complicated and messy. At worst, human interactions are conflicting and random. From the political perspective, organizations are political arenas characterized by divergent interests, scarce resources, and ambiguity.

Organizational decision makers have long understood the divergent nature of individual interests within the organization. Interventions addressing organizational mission, culture, and compensation are just a few of the many ways that organizations attempt to align the interests of the employee with the interests of the organization. Thus we can envision the role of HR as supporting and motivating the alignment of organizational and individual interests. The policies implemented by the HR department provide a behavioral blueprint that connects individual action, organizational benefit, and individual reward.

The Evolving Role of Human Resources Management

Much of twentieth-century management practice has evaluated human behavior as a simple mathematical equation. The traditional personnel function in most organizations has operated within this equation. Given certain incentives, working conditions, employee characteristics, and materials, we can project that employees will perform at an acceptable level. Global competition, workforce diversity, and rapidly advancing technology, however, have produced a complex environment for which simple equations are no longer adequate. HRM has evolved as a linking mechanism between the machine characteristics of organizational production and the turbulence of the human capital environment.

The 1970s represented a "coming of age" for the human resources field. As a result of the civil rights movement, U.S. organizations found themselves coping with not only new legislation, but also a new spirit of employee worth. These developments launched human resources as a function that emphasized proactive responses to the turbulent nature of employee behavior. Chief executive officers with an HR background were heralded as the "new corporate heroes" (Meyer, 1976), and were thus elevated to a previously unattainable status.

A prolonged recession, coupled with poor industry performance, generated a change in the basic psychological contracts of the American worker during the 1980s. Strategic HRM was born of this crisis and sought to connect HR activities to the overall organizational strategy. Gone were the days of the parental organization, individual job design, and lifetime employment. In their place, workers were presented with outsourcing, teams, and contingent working relationships. The emulation of Japanese business practices and the increase in team-based employment provided a key opportunity for the HR function to deliver bottom-line results. Ultimately, it was these bottom-line results that positioned human resources as a permanent and legitimate player in the executive boardroom.

The 1990s was a time of great change and even greater prosperity for American business. Organizations had to adjust quickly to changing technology, expanding markets, and labor shortages. Once again, human resources was at the forefront in addressing these challenges and shouldering the responsibility for acquiring, developing, and retaining employees with both the skills to meet the challenges of today's workplace and the flexibility to adapt to tomorrow's workplace.

Human resources has changed dramatically in the last three decades and there is little reason to believe that the environment within which HR practitioners operate will become less complex in the future. The new realities of the human resources field have moved beyond the explanations offered by the rational, personnel model of the past. Tight competition for human capital, increasing ambiguity in job design, and decreasing employee loyalty echo the assumptions of the political model. An understanding of the political nature of human behavior and its impact on HR practices is, therefore, likely to provide more accurate prescriptions for the challenges facing the human resources professional in the new millennium.

POLITICS IN THE EMPLOYEE SELECTION PROCESS

> *"Never hire anyone who is going to report directly to you who you do not intuitively just plain like from first impressions. If your instincts tell you you're going to have a hard time working with someone, pass."*
>
> —FRED CHARRETTE

The hiring process may be the ultimate arena for political behavior in organizations. Both parties involved in the exchange have much to gain, and even more to lose. It can be assumed that the applicant is participating in the interview because the position is desirable and because the position offers the opportunity for personal or financial betterment. The organization must hire an employee in order to improve production deficiencies caused by the underutilization of production potential or the strain caused by understaffed production units. Staffing a position with a "warm body" may be an improvement for the organization, but organizations ideally look for the candidate that best "fits" their organization.

During the interviewing process, most recruiters are not trying to evaluate the applicants' qualifications; they are attempting to assess "fit." "Fit" is an ambiguous term whose definition is debated among researchers, yet believed to be understood by practitioners. It might be said that if you have to ask what "fit" is you will never understand it. "Fit" can be defined as a unique bundle of qualifications that not only fulfills the occupational qualities of the job, but generates the proper chemistry during human interaction.

Despite its intuitive appeal, "fit" is problematic in that it is poorly defined. The bundle of attributes which signal "fit" to one interviewer may not be the same bundle another interviewer utilizes. Given specific direction in regard to the criteria of fit, these same two interviewers may perceive "fit" very differently. Further, neither of their attribute bundles may agree with that which the organization as a whole considers an adequate "fit." The interviewing process can be a very inaccurate science because organizations and individual interviewers have difficulty specifically identifying the indicators of organizational or job-specific "fit," yet they continue to place excessive weight on these indicators for hiring decisions

"Fit" as a Reciprocal Exchange

Most evaluations of "fit" in the interviewing process address the issue from the perspective of the interviewer. Assessment of person-job or person-organization "fit" is seen as a post-hiring decision issue. It would be remiss to ignore the significant role that the perceptions of these types of "fit" have on the candidate's assessment of the attractiveness of a job alternative. Therefore, the selection process must be considered a reciprocal exchange process, during which both parties simultaneously assess the "fit" and signal it to the other party. We suggest that, during this interaction, each party utilizes a collection of political behaviors that are designed to project an image congruent with the expectations of the other party.

Common interviewing strategies echo the political nature of the selection process on the part of the candidate. For example, well-prepared applicants are instructed to conduct research on the organization. They are also advised to make certain that they utilize the recruiting pamphlet buzzwords as a means of demonstrating to the interviewer that they are the right person for the job. The basic assumption is that style will at least complement, if not compensate for, substance in relation to the applicant's qualifications.

Another common strategy is for applicants to "talk themselves up" as a means of ensuring that the interviewer is presented with the best possible perception of their qualifications. While the overzealous candidate may be seen as pushy or egotistical, this type of behavior is expected within the interviewing context. In most cases, very few of us would hire a candidate who is so humble that he or she has difficulty discerning themselves from the other applicants. An interviewer expects a candidate to present himself or herself in the best possible light. Research has supported that candidates engaging in self-promotion tactics will be rated more favorably by their interviewer than candidates who do not promote themselves (Stevens & Kristof, 1995).

The reciprocal nature of the transaction is most evident after the interviewer determines that the candidate is the right person for the job. It is at this point that the interviewer begins to act as a recruiter and attempts to signal a person-organizational "fit" to the applicant. Interviewers will stress those qualities of the organization that best meet the specified needs of the individual, while often neglecting the organizational realities of the position. After sensing a growth need on the behalf of the applicant, for example, the interviewer may talk endlessly about rapid advancement potential. Citing story after story of similarly qualified employees who have advanced with lightning speed to the top of the company, the interviewer may fail to tell the applicant that company growth has been halted and an abundance of qualified candidates are already vying for the position. This common interviewing style maximizes the short-term self-interest of the interviewer at the long-term expense of the applicant. By traditional definition, this is an example of political behavior.

The Use of Networks in the Selection Process

The best way to get your foot in the door of a company is to have "connections." We might know someone, for example, who played golf with our father at the country club or went to college with the director of operations. In either case, the collection of acquaintances and friends that an individual acquires in their lifetime has a great deal to do with the career opportunities they are presented.

From the perspective of the applicant, a strong network connection within the organization can only be seen as increasing their likelihood of employment. The organization also benefits from networks. Organizations often ask their employees, ideally their best employees, to recruit individuals who are "just like them." Further, new hires who have strong network ties within the organizations are likely to be more committed to their jobs and more likely to receive support from their network member.

Leveraging networks in the selection process has many benefits to the organization, but is also a mechanism that has a great potential for discrimination. Individuals tend to associate with those who are like themselves. While this similarity may take the form of mutual interests, these interests often vary with demographic characteristics. These selection techniques have the potential to homogenize the organization and create the potential for discrimination. While this discrimination may be unintended, the consequences cannot be ignored.

Organizational Considerations in Selection

The decline in both organizational loyalty on behalf of employees and employee loyalty on behalf of the organization has made the use of political behavior more relevant than ever in the selection process. Acting on behalf of the organization and in competition for increasingly scarce human resources, interviewers are driven to political behavior. Employees are faced with a market situation in which their skills are in demand and they have ample opportunities to improve their financial situation. This competitive context provides the need for the organization to both leverage assets and reduce deficiencies in their selection process. Consequently, organizations should address operationalized "fit" and proper training of

interviewers in order to harness the potential of the political system.

Utilizing "fit" as a selection criterion can be a dangerous proposition for organizations. The implicit assumption of the "fit" criterion is that style complements or may even compensate for substance. The entire premise behind the "dress for success" concept is that interviewers are more likely to place undue weight on individuals who look, act, or have similar life experiences to themselves. Unfortunately, when the life experiences signaling "fit" to the interviewer also happen to vary with demographic traits, such that candidates with diverse backgrounds are underrepresented, the organization risks discrimination. For this reason, it is important for organizations to operationalize "fit" within their organization.

Researchers have utilized numerous qualitative and quantitative techniques to uncover a proper operationalization of the "fit" construct. The problem may lie in the fact that "fit" is, by definition, unique to a particular situation. Therefore, the organizational decision makers must accomplish the task of properly defining its boundaries. Organizational decision makers must exhaustively define those attributes upon which an employee will be evaluated. They must further support the use of those attributes in the hiring process, through training and candidate evaluation systems.

The second area of improvement in the selection process is to properly train interviewers. Interviewers should be trained in more than the newly defined "fit" criteria for the organization. They must be trained in interviewing techniques which, when properly utilized, increase the propensity for evaluating the candidate on substance rather than form. One such technique is behavioral-based interviewing which, through specifically designed questions and persistent probing, directs applicant responses to specific past experiences in which they have demonstrated the behavior indicating "fit."

POLITICS IN THE PERFORMANCE MANAGEMENT PROCESS

> *"The root of all politics is competition. Performance reviews usually judge people against their colleagues. All salespeople compete against each other. There are winners and losers in all companies. Playing politics is the way to stand out. So you must play to win."*
>
> — D. PARDOE

What is the behavior of your employees in the month before their annual review? Are there manners better and their attitude more upbeat? Do they complete all of tasks on time? Do they comment more often about your weight loss or your attractive attire? Perhaps your employees always interact this way. Most of us, however, might view this as political behavior designed to ensure that the employee gets the best review and, consequently, the highest pay increase. In this context, each of these behaviors are political in nature. Each has the potential to destroy employee morale and even undermine the performance appraisal process as a whole.

Managers spend the majority of their time assisting employees in conforming their work-related behaviors to organizational norms. Much has been made in the popular press about manager style in accomplishing these goals (i.e., empowerment, coaching). Yet in all instances, organizations establish performance management systems to assist the manager in obtaining acceptable performance and to protect the organi-

zation against frivolous litigation. The two most central components of these performance management systems are disciplinary procedures and performance evaluations.

Politics and Employee Disciplinary Actions

In an ideal world, subordinates who are underperforming would welcome guidance from their supervisors as a means of improving the quality of their work life. Employee counseling sessions would represent a significant opportunity to reinforce the covenant between the employee and the organization. To the contrary, most counseling sessions reek of conflict and distrust, creating a situation in which both the manager and the subordinate have much to lose. For the employee, the counseling session is often seen as the first step towards termination. For the supervisor, the subordinate's continued poor performance is a bad reflection on the supervisor and could affect their performance bonus or cause them to lose their job.

From the moment the employee is asked to speak with the supervisor, the atmosphere is full of tension and conflict. Each party views their own interests as being attained only if the other party's interests are defeated. During the counseling process, employees often attempt to manage the impression they present to their supervisor in order to reduce the consequences of the infraction that is being addressed. They may accomplish this by apologizing, justifying, or casting blame. Given a situation of repeated infractions, recent research suggests that employees who used justification as a means of accounting for their transgressions were offered a lesser punishment than those who simply apologized (Giacalone & Payne, 1995).

Politics and Performance Evaluation

The performance evaluation process is a complex and high-stakes exchange between supervisor and subordinate. From the employee's perspective, this process is usually less about performance than it is about pay increases. With this in mind, supervisors are forced to accomplish two tasks during this process. First, they must provide an allocation of pay increases that is perceived both as equitable and motivating by their employees. In addition to providing motivation for their employees, a second goal of the process is to remain within the limits of the organizational budget. Supervisors most often have benchmarks for yearly raises: "Make sure your unit is at 3 percent this year." This benchmark or fixed raise amount provides the supervisor with the choice of either an equitable or equal distribution of raises. The supervisor would be equitable in issuing good performers a 4 or 5 percent raise and giving lower performers a 1 or 2 percent raise. Alternatively, the supervisor may believe that if she equally distributes the raises to all employees, regardless of their performance, she will avoid conflict.

Neither allocation decision will present a situation devoid of conflict. In essence, employees are competing for what they believe is an equitable portion of a finite pie. It is obvious that the organizational realities of resource constraints and conflicting employee motivations present a situation in which political behavior flourishes. Further cultivating the potential for political behavior is the fact that an increasing number of positions in the new service economy do not have objective measures of performance. This performance ambiguity provides an opportunity for employees to create an impression of their performance, which may bear little resemblance to their actual performance. It should thus come as no surprise that some of the most extensive research on the influence of politics in HR practices addresses performance evaluation.

Research has demonstrated that political behavior on the part of the employee is an integral component of the performance evaluation exchange. The use of supervisor-directed influence tactics has been found to increase subordinates' overall performance ratings because it creates greater goodwill or liking in the supervisor (Wayne, Liden, Graf, & Ferris, 1997). Other studies have shown that individuals who utilize logic and reasoning in their influence attempts were given more favorable outcomes by their supervisor than were those who were assertive and forceful (Kipnis & Schmidt, 1988).

Politics in Promotion Decisions

One important aspect of the performance management process is the role it plays in assessing, and often recommending, employees for promotion. Surveys have found that employees perceive politics to be intricately involved in promotion decisions, and research has supported that politics are often an important aspect in determining which employees are promoted and which employees are not (Gandz & Murray, 1980). These findings support the intuitive notion that promotions are often as much a product of "who you know" as they are of "what you know."

Extending research on supervisory political behavior in performance evaluation allows articulation of three important facets defining the political nature of the promotion process (Longnecker, Sims, & Gioia, 1987). First, the participants in the process are highly aware of the impact performance appraisals have on promotion decisions. Second, they are further aware that because of the limited number of advancement opportunities and the need for continued employee productivity after the evaluation, the review must be a political process. Third, in contrast to other research on the impact of politics in promotion decisions, this research presents the rater as being engaged in political behavior, not just the individual being evaluated. Realizing that their written appraisal affects not only the employee's compensation, but also their future advancement opportunities, managers often inflate their evaluations of the employee. This once again demonstrates the reciprocal nature of political behavior in the exchange between manager and employee.

The majority of research evaluating the use of subordinate political behavior and supervisor's assessments of promotability has focused on the type and effectiveness of the subordinate's upward influence tactics. The use of favor rendering (Wayne et al., 1997) and assertiveness tactics (Thacker & Wayne, 1995) on the part of the subordinate have been found to increase the subsequent promotability assessments made by their supervisors. Interestingly, these same studies found that self-promotion and ingratiation, behaviors that benefit a job candidate during the interviewing process, actually have a detrimental impact on the supervisor's assessment of promotability. Although the selection and the promotion processes may seem similar on the surface, it appears that very different norms exist for the use of political behavior.

Organizational Considerations in Performance Management

From the organizational standpoint, the preceding discussion presents two avenues that may serve to reduce the effects of politics on the performance management process. First, employers must develop specific guidelines for accountability and sanctions within their organization. Specific guidelines will prevent managers from allowing the justifications of the employee to overly influence management decisions. This consistency should further assist the organization by reducing perceived injustices, which may lead to charges of discrimination against the organization.

In addressing the impact of political behavior on the performance management process, organizations also need to ensure that managers focus solely on the behavior, and not the person, during the disciplinary process. Justifications may work as an influence tactic in disciplinary cases because the supervisor is focused on the shortcomings of the individual within the process or context that did not allow them to perform, rather than focus on the substandard performance. The problem with this type of approach is that the natural human reaction is to show compassion for the individual's circumstances. Therefore, organizations must provide their managers with the training necessary to simulate this type of experience, in order that they may become adept at overcoming the tension involved in these exchanges.

POLITICS AND HUMAN RESOURCES MANAGEMENT: THE NEXT GENERATION

"There is nothing permanent except change."
—Heraclitus

The economic landscape of the corporation is changing on a daily basis. Two decades ago, few imagined the wealth of explanation provided by applying the political perspective to issues in the human resources field. As we begin the millennium, we must look to the opportunities presented by the new economy. Three forces are driving the human resources practices of organization: globalization, diversity, and organizational change. Future application of the political perspective to these forces should assist human resources practitioners and researchers in understanding the effects these forces have on the implementation of human resources practices.

Globalization and Politics

Human resources texts written in the last two decades seem to consistently identify globalization as a challenge for future research and practice. Yet in 20 years, little research has been conducted to address this issue. Even less has been accomplished toward developing an understanding of politics in global settings. Moreover, no work has attempted to simultaneously address the effects of political influence on global human resources practices. There is little doubt that organizational politics exist in some form in all cultures. As with other Western concepts, however, there is every reason to believe that the rules of the game may be very different. The redefinition of these rules is likely to render obsolete our current understanding of politics and HRM practices.

Feeding the rapid pace of our global expansion is the ever-changing face of technology. Technology has permeated every aspect of organizations and has fundamentally redefined the meaning of work. Technology has simultaneously shrunk the world and expanded the boundaries of the organization. Businesses are able to effectively manage local businesses at the global level, and employees are able to participate in team-based work environments without ever leaving home. As organizational structures change and whole job classes become obsolete, HR policies must change in order to support both the new environment and the communication norms of the emergent organization.

Technological advancements have made communicating around the world not only expedient, but also increasingly rich. Thus, we may envision a continuum of influence mediums ranging in communication richness from "snail mail" to e-mail to videoconferencing. As practitioners and researchers, we know little about the mechanics of politics in the cyber-age. However, we suggest that the richer the communication medium, the more closely our current understanding of political activity will explain the behaviors of the participants. Future investigation must seek to evaluate questions such as how individuals utilize e-mail to influence supervisor perceptions of their performance, or how videoconferencing influences the effectiveness of disciplinary counseling. The answers to queries of this type will effectively define the parameters of political behavior in the workplace of the future.

Diversity and Politics

A second force driving the HR field is the ever-diversifying nature of the workplace. The workforce of today is much different from the workforce of 50 years ago, or even the workforce of two decades ago. An increasing participation of females and workers of other ethnic/racial minorities in the workplace has effectively changed the type and tone of communication within the organization. The growing number of communication styles and expectations increases the potential for misunderstanding and conflict.

In relation to organizational politics, research supports that increasing diversity in the workplace will change the nature of, and reactions to, political behavior. Organizational politics research has found that differences exist between males and females in their propensity to use a particular type of political behavior. Further research supports that demographic minorities perceive different levels of politics within the organization (Ferris, Frink, Bhawuk, Zhou, & Gilmore, 1996) than do their majority counterparts. As these external pressures change organizational demography, will the game remain the same? Will females utilize political behaviors in a manner that is more similar to male preferences, or will the standard of what is appropriate resemble traditional feminine values and preferences? Will demographic minorities perceive less politics in their organization as they become dominant concerns?

The Politics of Organizational Change

In today's turbulent environment, organizational initiatives for change appear to be never-ending as organizations appear to continually reinvent themselves. To the degree that this reinvention affects the manner in which the employees' work is structured, the manner in which employees are compensated, or the knowledge and skills of employees, these change efforts must be considered HR initiatives.

Lewin's force field analysis is a technique often utilized by change agents in assessing both the forces for and against the change effort. Political behavior is the mechanism by which the change agent reduces the forces against change and thus generates the motivation necessary to implement the change effort. In this manner, organizational change is in essence a power play by an ideological out-group, seeking to influence the behavior and thought processes of the majority coalition. To that end, power and politics are most prevalent in critical, high-level decisions such as reorganizations (Pfeffer, 1992). To the degree that a change intervention affects the organization as a whole, the greater the political involvement must be of those individuals who are implementing the change (Kumar & Thibodeaux, 1990).

Congruent with this perspective, Bender, Urban, Galang, Frink, and Ferris (1996) identified change management skills as one of the core competencies of the "new" HR professional, along with business and functional knowledge. Further, change leadership is seen as the most critical of these competencies. Change leadership is difficult to define because, like other HR practices, it exists outside of the quantifiable, rational workings of the organization. The ambiguity inherent in the change process provides fertile ground for political activity. As such, we suggest that the HR professional's political skill, defined as the ability to effectively influence others through persuasion, manipulation, and negotiation (Mintzberg, 1983), is at the core of change leadership competency.

The ability to utilize political skill to influence the forces resisting change is a key dimension of the HR professional's role in the change process. Human resources professionals should therefore not only cultivate proactive political relationships, but should seek to hone their political skills through training and experience. Too often in the change process, human resources becomes a pawn played at the whim of the organizational change agent. Human resources can be a player in the long-term success of the change intervention only by establishing power and influence through their use of political behavior.

The Challenge for HR Professionals

The political perspective presents two fundamental challenges for HR professionals. First, awareness of the political nature of HR processes presents an obligation on the part of the HR practitioner to construct policies and train operators to reduce the degree of error involved in the implementation of organizational practices. This error reduction, while not eliminating politics, will help to ensure that HR decisions result in organizationally functional outcomes. Second, the increasing complexity and ambiguity of the workplace presents the opportunity for HR professionals to become leaders in the change process. By increasing both their knowledge of the political nature of organizations and their political skill, HR professionals can generate innovative solutions designed to leverage both personal and organizational assets.

Much has been written in the popular press about eliminating office politics, and thus ridding organizations of that which hinders their performance. The prescriptions offered in such writings are ultimately futile. Organizational politics has existed since the first human beings came together in groups for the purposes of survival. As we have evolved, so has our ability to recognize and navigate the political landscape. The continued evolution of HR practices lends even more legitimacy to the consideration of the political perspective in the implementation of HR initiatives. ■

REFERENCES

Bender, J. B., Urban, T. F., Galang, M. C., Frink, D. D., & Ferris, G. R. (1996). Developing human resources at ARCO oil and gas company. In G. R. Ferris & M. R. Buckley (Eds.), *Human resources management: Perspective, context, functions, and outcomes* (Third edition). Upper Saddle River, NJ: Prentice Hall.

Ferris, G. R., Frink, D. D., Bhawuk, D. P. S., Zhou, J., & Gilmore, D. C. (1996). Reactions of diverse groups to politics in the workplace. *Journal of Management, 22,* (1), 23–44.

Gandz, J., & Murray, V. V. (1980). The experience of workplace politics. *Academy of Management Journal, 23,* 191–213.

Giacalone, R. A., & Payne, S. L. (1995). Evaluation of employee rule violations: The impact of impression management effects in a historical context. *Journal of Business Ethics, 14,* 477–487.

Kipnis, D., & Schmidt, S. M. (1988). Upward-influence styles: Relationship with performance evaluation, salary, and stress. *Administrative Science Quarterly, 33,* 528–542.

Kumar, K., & Thibodeaux, M. (1990). Organizational politics and planned organizational change. *Group and Organizational Studies, 15,* (4), 357–365.

Longnecker, C. O., Sims, H. P., & Gioia, D. A. (1987). Behind the mask: The politics of employee appraisal. *Academy of Management Executive, 1,* 183–193.

Meyer, H. E. (1976). Personnel directors are the new corporate heroes. *Fortune, 93,* (2), 84–88.

Mintzberg, H. (1983). *Power in and around organizations.* Upper Saddle River, NJ: Prentice Hall.

Pfeffer, J. (1992). *Managing with power.* Boston, MA: Harvard Business School Press.

Stevens, C. K., & Kristof, A. L. (1995). Making the right impression: A field study of applicant impression management during job interviews. *Journal of Applied Psychology, 80,* (5), 587–606.

Thacker, R. A., & Wayne, S. J. (1995). An examination of the relationship between upward influence tactics and assessments of promotability. *Journal of Management, 21,* (4), 739–756.

Wayne, S. J., Liden, R. C., Graf, I. K., & Ferris, G. R. (1997). The role of upward influence tactics in human resource decisions. *Personnel Psychology, 50,* 979–1006.

WOMEN IN ANOTHER WORLD: EXPATRIATE MANAGERS

Wendy Gradwohl Smith
Robin S. Salter

The movement toward globalization of business has had a significant impact on human resources policies, especially when it comes to managerial development. As a result, there has been a steady increase in the number of managers who are deployed on international assignments (i.e., expatriate managers). Studies indicate that expatriates and executives perceive international assignments as developmental tools that can aid career advancement (e.g., Lyness & Thompson, 2000; Tung, 1998). For instance, at least 50 percent of the expatriates in Oddou and Mendenhall's (1991) study believed their international assignment improved their ability to plan, communicate with and motivate others, and understand business patterns. A 1996 study by Catalyst on "Women in Corporate Leadership" (reported in Solomon, 1998) found that approximately half of the Fortune 500/Service 500 CEOs endorsed the view that international experience is critical for advancing in an organization. Companies are also recognizing the value of foreign assignments, particularly because successful expatriate performance should be tied to organizational outcomes. In Stroh and Caligiuri's (1998) study, effective development of global leaders through international assignments was positively associated with financial success of the organization.

On the basis of these studies, it is evident that international assignments are important to both individual employees and organizations. Yet it seems that companies are not fully utilizing their resources when it comes to expatriation. Statistics show that women are highly underrepresented in these assignments (e.g., GMAC Global Relocation Services/Windham International, National Foreign Trade Council, & SHRM Global Forum, 2000). To the extent that women are not getting these experiences, women managers will be adversely affected in terms of career progression. This occurrence will only further exacerbate the "glass ceiling" effect—an invisible barrier that disadvantages women and minorities from reaching top-level management positions (The Glass Ceiling Commission, 1995).

The current article takes the perspective that increasing the number of female expatriate managers is an organizational impera-

tive for several reasons. First, disparate numbers of male as compared to female expatriate managers may be interpreted as blatant sex discrimination against women, which can have expensive legal ramifications. Second, in Catalyst's study "Passport to Opportunity: U.S. Women in Global Business" (reported in Miller, 2000), most of the surveyed HR executives believed that there is a shortage of expatriate managers. In fact, many stated that their organizations were or would soon be placing greater emphasis on the development of international managers. Because female expatriate managers are as effective as male expatriate managers (Adler, 1987; Caligiuri & Tung, 1999; Taylor & Napier, 1996), organizations would be wise to utilize previously untapped resources (e.g., women) for such assignments.

Although there is voluminous research on the expatriation process in general, there is limited research on female expatriation issues. The purpose of this article is to highlight female managers' experiences in international assignments. Due to space limitations, we selectively discuss expatriation topics that are more likely to affect female than male managers (see Selmer, 1995, for a comprehensive review of the expatriate process). It is organized into three stages of the expatriation process. First, issues related to appointing women to expatriate assignments will be discussed. In particular, we review the literature on whether women are interested in international assignments and reasons why women may be unsuccessful in gaining these positions. The second portion will cover performance issues in foreign assignments. Specifically, barriers to successful performance, job effectiveness, and cross-cultural adjustment will be explored. Finally, we turn to topics related to returning from the assignment, such as reduced autonomy. At the conclusion, we summarize the literature by providing suggestions for HR practice.

STAGE 1—APPOINTING WOMEN TO ASSIGNMENTS

The following section presents data on the percentage of expatriate assignments occupied by women. Next, we discuss whether female managers pursue expatriate positions and factors that influence their acceptance or rejection of such assignments. We then explore possible explanations for why women may not be getting the expatriate assignments they desire.

Female Managers' Willingness to Accept International Assignments

Almost 20 years ago, Adler (1984c) reported that only 3 percent of U.S. expatriates were women. Since that time, the percentage of female expatriates has inched upward with women currently representing 13 to 14 percent of the expatriate workforce (GMAC Global Relocation Services et al., 2000; Tung, 1998; Windham International, National Foreign Trade Council, & Institute for International Human Resources, 1999).

According to GMAC Global Relocation Services et al. (2000), human resources professionals predict that female expatriates will increase to 21 percent by the year 2005. However, given that the percentage of female expatriates has risen only 3 percent since 1993, GMAC analysts suggest that this prediction is not realistic (see Figure 2-1). One possible explanation for the relatively small percentage of women in expatriate positions is that female managers do not desire international assignments. Our review provides little evidence to indicate that women are not interested in acquiring international experience. However, research on women's attitudes toward both international and domestic relocation does indicate that issues related to dual-career relationships have a greater impact on women's willingness to relocate when compared to men.

General Attitudes Toward International Assignments Survey research on attitudes toward expatriate assignments has generally reported that women are at least

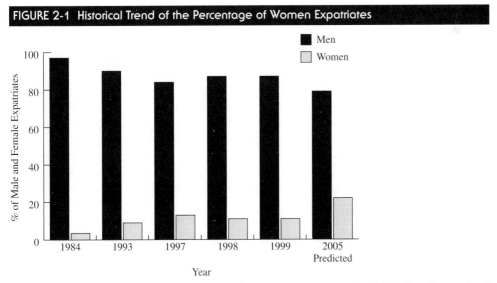

FIGURE 2-1 Historical Trend of the Percentage of Women Expatriates

Source: Data for 1984 was taken from Adler (1984b). All other percentages cited in Windham International et al. (1999) and GMAC Global Relocation Services et al. (2000).

as interested as men in foreign assignments (Adler, 1984b; Hill & Tillery, 1992; Lyness & Thompson, 1997; Stroh, Varma, & Valy-Durbin, 2000; Tung, 1998). In a study that explored predictors of willingness to accept an expatriate assignment, Aryee, Chay, and Chew (1996) found no significant effect for gender. Another indicator that women and men are equally interested in acquiring overseas experience is the comparatively high percentage of women who work for the American Foreign Service (AFS). Between 1975 and 1995, the percentage of women Foreign Service Officers (FSOs) rose from 9 to 25 percent (Jones, 1999). In a 1994 address, Rozanne L. Ridgway, former ambassador to Finland and Germany, remarked that women currently represent almost 50 percent of Americans entering the diplomatic class. This is a somewhat remarkable statistic given AFS's history of inequitable treatment of women (until 1970, AFS women were required to resign upon getting married). The increase in female foreign service officers may be partially attributable to the organization's efforts to assign husband-and-wife teams to foreign offices whenever possible (Jones, 1997).

Interest Among Women in Dual-Career Relationships   Survey research has also indicated that women are less likely to accept foreign assignments if they are in dual-career relationships (Lyness & Thompson, 1997; Stroh et al., 2000). This is consistent with studies of domestic relocation in which women were less likely to relocate than men (Markham & Pleck, 1985; Turban, Campion, & Eyring, 1992), and gender was most predictive of willingness to relocate among dual-career couples (Markham & Pleck, 1985).

For both male and female managers, the spouse's willingness to relocate has a significant effect on the manager's willingness to accept an overseas assignment (Brett & Stroh, 1995). A review by Harvey and Wiese

(1998) reported that 20 to 25 percent of primary expatriate candidates refuse assignments, while another 20 to 25 percent commute internationally due to dual-career concerns. For female managers, the issue of spouse employment during an overseas assignment presents added challenges. Being an unemployed male or male trailing spouse is a violation of the "male as primary breadwinner" social norm. Furthermore, men have traditionally been defined by their work and roles as providers (Brett & Stroh, 1995; Harvey, 1997; Harvey & Wiese, 1998; Punnett, Crocker, & Stevens, 1992).

Consistent with these views, a recent study of expatriate couples found that female expatriates and their husbands place equal importance on the husbands' career when considering an expatriate assignment (Harvey, 1997). However, male expatriates and their wives held discrepant views regarding the importance of the wives' career interruption. Female trailing spouses indicated their careers were of primary concern while their male expatriate husbands rated this factor as being significantly less important (Harvey, 1997).

Factors That Impede Women's Chances of Attaining Expatriate Assignments

Although much of the literature suggests that women do want international assignments, there is substantial evidence that they are not getting them. For instance, Lyness and Thompson (2000) found that female executives perceived difficulties in obtaining opportunities to move geographically. In support of their beliefs, these women had fewer international assignments, fewer years in international assignments, and were expatriated to fewer countries compared to male executives.

There are several possible explanations for the disparity between women's willingness to accept foreign assignments and their lack of international opportunities. One possible explanation may be that women lack the qualifications necessary for international appointments. However, there is compelling evidence against this reasoning. Stroh, Brett, and Reilly (1992) found that differences between male and female managers in geographic mobility could not be explained by human capital variables. Also, gender differences in managerial ability tend to be small and insignificant (e.g., Eagly, Karau, & Makhijani, 1995). Although statistics show that women are underrepresented at the middle- and upper-management levels from which expatriate managers are most frequently selected (Berthoin Antal & Izraeli, 1993), research suggests that female managers may not be moving into top management positions or getting expatriate assignments because of organizational and perceptual barriers.

Organizational Barriers Organizational barriers such as recruiting policies may explain the small percentage of female expatriate managers. In one study, 80 percent of female expatriates indicated that their organizations lacked explicit policies for sending women managers on foreign assignments (Westwood & Leung, 1994). Many also noted that their organizations were more likely to use informal means for recruiting expatriates (e.g., word of mouth). Because women have less access to informal communication networks (see Ibarra, 1993), women tend to be disadvantaged by such open recruiting policies (e.g., Hoover, 2000; Stroh et al., 2000).

Perceptual Barriers Perceptual barriers may also interfere with women's chances of being selected for foreign assignments. Biases (e.g., stereotypes, implicit theories) come into play when individuals base their perceptions of other people on the basis of a prototype, which are implicit theories of the characteristics, traits, and behaviors that represent the most typical member of a category. In turn, the degree of fit between a person's attributes and the prototype influences subsequent decision making. This prototype-matching process is likely to affect perceptions of women's potential management ability (e.g., Heilman, Block, Martell, & Simon, 1989) and willingness to relocate (e.g., Eby, Allen, & Douthitt, 1999).

Specifically, decision makers may be less likely to select females for international assignments because they *do not perceive women as managers.* Research consistently shows that the traits and behaviors associated with women are not congruent with traits and behaviors linked to managers; men, on the other hand, are perceived to possess characteristics that greatly overlap with the manager prototype (e.g., Schein, 1973, 1975). As a result, people are more likely to think of a man when a manager prototype is activated in memory. Consequently, women are less likely to come to mind when making selection decisions for international assignments. This seems to be consistent with reports by female expatriates that organizations may naively overlook, rather than consciously reject, sending women overseas (Adler, 1987).

Because leadership characteristics such as assertiveness and skill in business matters are more closely associated with male managers than female managers (e.g., Heilman et al., 1989), decision makers may *perceive women as ineffective* leaders or managers.[1] Although the effects are small, women tend to receive lower leadership evaluations compared to men (e.g., Eagly, Makhijani, & Klonsky, 1992). Yet it is important to note that male raters are more likely to devalue female leaders while women demonstrate

---

[1]In this article we use the terms *leader* and *manager* interchangeably. However, we recognize the two terms are not always considered to be synonymous.

less gender bias in leadership evaluations (e.g., Eagly et al., 1992).

Host country nationals' attitudes toward women may also lead decision makers to assume women will not be effective in expatriate assignments (e.g., Adler, 1984a). Interestingly, and consistent with the research, males assume women face more difficulties in an expatriate assignment due to prejudicial attitudes. For example, male supervisors in Stroh et al.'s (2000) study were more likely than female expatriates to believe that women's success would be affected by foreigners' prejudice while female supervisors and female expatriates were more inclined to say prejudice would not be a factor. Adler (1984b) found that males were more likely than females to blame women for their low occurrence in international assignments on the grounds that they are ineffective and unqualified, although neither explanation was extremely popular among either sex. Furthermore, males, as compared to females, consistently hold more negative views of women as managers (e.g., Burke, 1994; Cromie, 1981; Tomkiewicz & Adeyemi-Bello, 1995). Consequently, women may not be securing expatriate assignments because the individuals who are making selection decisions, mainly men, are allowing sex-role stereotypes to influence their decisions (Chusmir & Frontczak, 1990).

Finally, decision makers may perceive women as having more *negative attitudes about relocating.* Markham and Pleck (1985) note that while many women in their study were willing to relocate and many men were not, gender differences still emerged; overall, females were less willing to relocate. The authors suggest these gender differences might affect the perceptions of those responsible for offering positions that require relocation.

In addition, managers who relocate tend to be married, male, have a nonworking spouse and/or no children (e.g., Collie, 1989; Employee Relocation Council, 1991). Eby

and colleagues (1999) contend that individuals who do not fit this prototype (e.g., married women) are perceived as unwilling to relocate and are not offered the relocation position. In particular, decision makers may assume that married women will not want to relocate because the husband's job will (or should) take precedence. In support of their argument, Eby et al. (1999) found that married women were less likely to receive an offer to relocate than married men. Furthermore, individuals were less likely to recommend a married woman for a job that required relocation partly as a result of perceptions that she would be unwilling to move and unable to adjust to the new location. These findings are consistent with reports that organizations are reluctant to send women overseas because of perceived dual-career difficulties (Adler, 1984a).

STAGE 2—PERFORMING IN ASSIGNMENTS

Once selected, women managers' experiences in expatriate assignments may not parallel men's. In the following section, we discuss organizational, legal, and perceptual barriers that may impede women's performance overseas. Despite these barriers, we provide evidence that women expatriates are successful in these assignments. Factors that influence expatriate adjustment are also reviewed.

Barriers to Women's Performance in Expatriate Assignments

Organizational Barriers   Research suggests that men and women are treated differently by the home office in the terms and conditions of the expatriate assignment. For instance, many of the women expatriates in Westwood and Leung's (1994) study did not believe men and women were treated equally on international assignments by the home country organization even after they were selected for the position. Women tend to be offered shorter assignments that restrict travel within and outside the foreign country, and limit interactions to internal employees or customers (Adler, 1987). These restrictions undermine female expatriates' performance in several ways.

Limiting the duration of the assignment can impede female expatriate managers' adjustment to the new culture. While many women may be given expatriate assignments of less than one month in duration (Adler, 1984b), only a minority of expatriate managers report they feel comfortable working in a foreign environment within the first one to three months of an assignment (Tung, 1998). Other estimates suggest that, on average, it may take one year to adjust to a new culture (e.g., Westwood & Leung, 1994).

The amount of discretion associated with the female expatriate's role appears to be positively related to adjustment (Taylor & Napier, 1996). Organizations that limit where and with whom female expatriates can do business are inadvertently decreasing job breadth and depth. As such, female expatriates' skills and abilities will be underutilized, which is likely to have a negative effect on job attitudes (Beehr, 1981; Gavin & Axelrod, 1977; Terry, Nielsen, & Perchard, 1993), attendance (e.g., Kaufmann & Beehr, 1986), and intentions to stay with the organization (e.g., Gupta & Beehr, 1979). Because international assignments can be a critical developmental activity (e.g., Tung, 1998), the potential to develop new skills and abilities is compromised when the terms of the assignment are curbed.

Finally, restrictions on the types and terms of assignments send a clear message to female expatriates, host country employees, and clients that the organization questions women's ability to be effective in these situations. This, in concert with organizational reluctance to select women managers for foreign assignments, may result in a self-fulfilling prophecy. Women managers may form negative impressions of their qualifi-

cations, probability of being selected, and ability to be successful in an international assignment. Consequently, female managers may not even bother competing for these positions (Berthoin Antal & Izraeli, 1993; Chusmir & Frontczak, 1990) or may act in a way that confirms the organization's expectations (Adler, 1987). Furthermore, it will be more difficult for female expatriates to convince host country nationals that they possess power and authority if the home office appears to lack confidence in them. In fact, it has been recommended that companies publicize the level of authority possessed by female expatriate managers through such means as formal introductions by a top executive and dissemination of information about their credentials (Wah, 1998).

Legal Barriers   Under Title VII of the 1991 Civil Rights Act, U.S. citizens working overseas are granted the same equal employment opportunities and protection from discrimination as individuals working within the United States. These protections are in effect as long as the employer is a U.S.-owned or controlled company, and Title VII laws do not violate laws of the host country (Cava & Mayer, 1993; Feltes, Robinson, & Fink, 1993). As such, organizations should ensure that male and female expatriates are treated equally in terms of being selected for and setting conditions of assignments.

However, organizations operating within foreign countries that prohibit women from participating in certain activities may have no other choice than to discriminate against women. For example, Cava and Mayer (1993) describe a hypothetical scenario in which a company operating in Saudi Arabia would not be able to hire women to drive delivery vans. A thorny situation exists, however, when companies operate in an area in which gender discrimination is the norm, yet there are no gender-specific laws relevant to female employees. In this situation, companies are liable under Title VII if they engage in discriminatory behavior (such as requesting that women defer to male managers in the presence of clients who are host nationals), even if they do so only to save face with host nationals (Cava & Mayer, 1993).

Because failure to heed foreign restrictions can result in serious consequences, it is important that human resources managers and women expatriates be aware of local laws and enforced restrictions not written in the laws prior to beginning an assignment. From a review of U. S. Department of State Travel Sheets, Saudi Arabia appears to have the greatest number of laws restricting the conduct of women. For example, women in Saudi Arabia are not allowed to drive automobiles, publicly socialize with men who are not close relatives, or eat in restaurants that do not have a "family section" designated for them. For further information on country-specific travel information, visit the U. S. Department of State Web site at www.state.gov.

Feltes, Robinson, & Fink (1993) recommend hiring local consultants to help clarify local laws and customs and to work with the company in formulating an action plan to avoid problems in advance. It is also recommended that multinational corporations (MNCs) avoid sending one "token" female to any location in which multiple positions are available. The placement of several women in a location lessens perceptions among locals that female employees are there simply to satisfy legal requirements. As previously stated, providing women managers with position power and titles that convey authority should have a positive effect on perceptions of qualifications (Caligiuri & Cascio, 1998; Taylor & Napier, 1996). In addition, having multiple positions filled by women in a given location reduces the employer's risk of a gender-related lawsuit if a female employee is dismissed (Feltes et al., 1993).

Perceptual Barriers   Even if organizations have sex-blind policies in the terms and conditions of the assignment, women may lack influence and authority over both home and host country nationals because of the nature of leader prototypes. Lord and Maher (1991) purport that the amount of influence a leader has depends upon the extent to which a person is perceived to be a leader. As previously discussed, individuals may use a prototype to determine whether the target person is a leader. If there is a high degree of overlap between the two sets of characteristics, the person is "recognized" as a leader. Depending upon the contents of the prototype, this matching process has the potential to affect perceptions of female leaders in a positive or negative way.

On the one hand, men and women managers are likely to be initially perceived in terms of sex-role stereotypes or gender categories rather than job-related categories (e.g., Heilman, 1984; Heilman, Martell, & Simon, 1988). Because traits associated with males overlap a great deal with a leader prototype (e.g., Heilman et al., 1989), males are more likely to be perceived as leaders. In fact, both males and females from the United States (Brenner, Tomkiewicz, & Schein, 1989; Schein, 1973, 1975; Schein, Mueller, & Jacobson, 1989), Germany and Britain (Schein & Mueller, 1992), and China and Japan (Schein, Mueller, Lituchy, & Liu, 1996) perceive requisite management characteristics to be strongly associated with males in general. While males from different countries unanimously perceive few similarities between successful middle managers and females in general, cross-cultural differences are evident in the degree to which women perceived requisite management characteristics as being related to females in general (Schein & Mueller, 1992; Schein, Mueller, & Jacobson, 1989; Schein, Mueller, Lituchy, & Liu, 1996). Consistent with other research, female managers have a better chance of being perceived as leaders by other females as opposed to males.

Yet results from a large-scale research project (GLOBE) suggest women may be just as likely as men to be perceived as leaders. Participants from 62 countries identified traits that were perceived to enhance leadership, herein called universal positive traits (Den Hartog, House, Hanges, Ruiz-Quintanilla, & Dorfman, 1999). Many of these traits are congruent with female characteristics such as democratic leadership (e.g., communicative, coordinator, team builder) and sensitivity (e.g., honest, trustworthy). On the basis of prototype matching, these results suggest that female managers may be perceived as effective leaders because characteristics associated with females overlap with universal positive leadership traits. Consequently, women, as well as men, may benefit from cross-cultural training prior to departure that focuses on traits and behaviors that are associated with favorable leadership across countries. If training focuses on culture-specific traits and behaviors, some researchers suggest that women may be better equipped to adjust their leadership style to fit cultural demands (e.g., Westwood & Leung, 1994).

Most of the research presented to this point has assumed that gender information plays a significant role in perceptual processes. Yet several studies suggest that host country nationals pay more attention to female expatriates' foreign status rather than their gender (Adler, 1987; Taylor & Napier, 1996; Westwood & Leung, 1994). Consequently, female expatriates are treated differently than local women (Adler, 1987; Westwood & Leung, 1994). For instance, 50 to 75 percent of the female expatriates in Westwood and Leung's (1994) study did not feel they experienced any difficulties because of their gender. While many of the women perceived societal sexism in Hong Kong, few experienced sexism at work (Westwood & Leung, 1994). Ironically, female expatriate managers may have more problems with expatriate men than host country nationals (Adler, 1987; Westwood & Leung, 1994). It has been argued, however, that foreign female managers may not recognize sexist behavior among host country nationals due to cultural differences in verbal and nonverbal communication (e.g., Westwood & Leung, 1994). In addition, research suggests that women may deny personal discrimination due to information-processing limitations as well as motivational/emotional biases that minimize the likelihood that women would perceive themselves as victims (see Crosby, Cordova, & Jaskar, 1993).

Other research indicates that gender is less likely to affect perceptions when performance information is readily available (Heilman, 1984; Heilman et al., 1988; Tosi & Einbender, 1985). For instance, when men and women are labeled as "successful managers," both are equally likely to be viewed as possessing characteristics consistant with successful middle managers (Heilman et al., 1989) and successful upper-level managers (Dodge, Gilroy, & Fenzel, 1995). The descriptor "successful" may provide job-related information that diminishes the effect of sex-role stereotypes on leadership perceptions. In practical terms, job titles that clearly denote authority and power may alleviate host country nationals' confusion about female expatriates' role (Adler, 1987). In addition, providing clients and subordinates with performance information that emphasizes competence in the managerial role and making frequent references to past successes should counteract the negative effects of sex-role stereotypes in the leadership perception process. At any rate, it appears critical for women expatriates to manage initial impressions of host country nationals and for male expatriates to support women's efforts in the foreign assignment (Adler, 1987).

Women's Effectiveness in Expatriate Assignments

Despite the fact that women face some unique obstacles in foreign assignments, the majority of the studies find that female expatriate managers are just as effective as male expatriates, regardless of the cultural values held by the country to which the expatriate is deployed (Caligiuri & Tung, 1999). Subjective reports from female expatriate managers suggest women perform well in their assignments (Adler, 1987; Taylor & Napier, 1996) and are no more likely to desire terminating their assignment than men (Caligiuri & Tung, 1999). Supervisor-rated performance does not seem to differ for male and female expatriates either (Caligiuri & Tung, 1999), and objective data confirms these subjective ratings. For instance, Adler (1987) found that female expatriates were likely to be promoted or given another international assignment based on their success in the previous assignment.

When gender does play a role in performance, it tends to be related to positive consequences. For instance, female expatriates may place greater emphasis on interpersonal relationships (Taylor & Napier, 1996; Westwood & Leung, 1994). As a result, women may be better at getting others to open up to them (Adler, 1987; Westwood & Leung, 1994), showing interest in others by remembering personal information (Taylor & Napier, 1996), and noticing and responding to cultural differences (Westwood & Leung, 1994). Women are also less likely to be treated in an abrasive or aggressive way (Westwood & Leung, 1994). Moreover, host country nationals may be more willing to do business with female managers because they may not be perceived as a threat; yet this also implies that women may be perceived as lacking power, authority, and credibility (Westwood & Leung, 1994).

In addition, women expatriates tend to be noticed and remembered easily because of their infrequent occurrence in international assignments (Adler, 1987; Taylor & Napier, 1996; Westwood & Leung, 1994). Some researchers (e.g., Adler, 1987) have found that female expatriates experience a "halo effect," in which host country nationals infer female expatriates must be competent if the organization was willing to send them on such an unlikely assignment. However, other studies (e.g., Feltes et al., 1993) indicate that women's token status in expatriate assignments may be viewed negatively, especially when these women represent countries with well-known affirmative action laws. As the numbers of female expatriate managers increase, it is unclear whether women will continue to experience greater visibility or "halo effects." Yet with this change, the negative effects of women's token status in international assignments should diminish.

Adjustment in the Expatriate Assignment

Adjustment can be defined as the "degree of a person's psychological comfort with various aspects of a new setting" (Black & Gregersen, 1991, p. 498). The role of adjustment in the expatriation process has been widely noted in the literature (e.g., Black, Mendenhall, & Oddou, 1991). Past research indicates female expatriates experience similar levels of work adjustment as male expatriates (e.g., Taylor & Napier, 1996). Yet in a recent study by Caligiuri and Tung (1999), women reported lower adjustment when expatriated to countries where there were few working women and where cultural values emphasized assertiveness and maintenance of the status quo. Because adjustment tends to be positively correlated with job performance in the international assignment (e.g.,

Kraimer, Wayne, & Jaworski, 2001), it is important to discuss factors that may aid or hinder female expatriates' adjustment.

Job Expectations   Realistic expectations about the job should be positively related to expatriate adjustment (e.g., Stroh, Dennis, & Cramer, 1994), as well as other job-related outcomes such as job satisfaction and remaining in the assignment (e.g., Buckley, Fedor, Veres, Wiese, & Carraher, 1998; Wanous, Poland, Premack, & Davis, 1992). A recent study by Harvey (1997) found that female expatriates who had not yet departed on an international assignment held similar views about international relocation issues as female expatriates who had just returned from an assignment. Meanwhile, male expatriates who had not yet departed and those who had returned held incongruent views. The results suggest that women may seek more information or spend more time thinking about the international assignment prior to leaving and therefore have greater realistic expectations compared to men. This, in turn, should be associated with positive work outcomes, such as adjustment.

Family Adjustment   One factor that is associated with an expatriate's adjustment and success in an international assignment is family adjustment (e.g., Caligiuri, Hyland, Joshi, & Bross, 1998; Fukuda & Chu, 1994). A recent study (Caligiuri et al., 1998) found that family characteristics and attitudes about the global relocation indirectly affected expatriate adjustment through the family's adjustment to the new culture. Families who were able to effectively communicate, adapt to new situations, and provide emotional support experienced greater family adjustment than families lacking these characteristics. In addition, families with positive attitudes about the move adjusted to the new culture, regardless of family coping characteristics. This parallels research that has found that expatriates' attitudes

about the move significantly predict expatriate adjustment (e.g., Stroh et al., 1994).

Spousal Adjustment   Spousal adjustment, in particular, is positively related to expatriate success as defined by expatriate adjustment (e.g., Black & Stephens, 1989; Stroh et al., 1992; Stroh et al., 1994) and intentions to stay in the international assignment (e.g., Black & Stephens, 1989). Because the work environment provides some predictability and opportunities to interact with host country nationals on a day-to-day basis, expatriates tend to adjust more readily than their spouses (Harvey & Wiese, 1998). To complicate things further, recent statistics show that 57 percent of individuals who relocate for international assignments are involved in dual-career relationships (*Global,* 1997, as cited in Harvey & Wiese, 1998). Having a career spouse has been related to negative perceptions of the global relocation, which in turn is related to family adjustment and ultimately expatriate adjustment (e.g., Caligiuri et al., 1998).

Although the dual-career trend is likely to affect both male and female expatriates, female expatriates may have greater difficulties with spousal adjustment. Male spouses are likely to have difficulty accepting a homemaker role (Harvey & Wiese, 1998; Westwood & Leung, 1994) and/or traditional expatriate spouse activities (e.g., Punnett et al., 1992). Nonworking males may feel isolated and ignored because most social support networks are geared toward female trailing spouses. In addition, males are more likely to experience negative reactions within societies that devalue men who do not work outside the home (e.g., Punnett et al., 1992). For these reasons, there is greater pressure on male spouses to be employed during the foreign relocation. Unfortunately, work permit restrictions within the foreign country and male spouses' job selectivity (e.g., wanting jobs that will advance career and provide challenging opportunities) reduce the odds of finding suitable employment (Punnett et al., 1992).

Also related to dual-career issues, female expatriates may experience greater role strain as they attempt to balance work and family demands. Domestic research shows that women perform more child-care activities and are responsible for ensuring household chores get completed, even when both spouses hold jobs with similar financial and professional status (e.g., Biernat & Wortman, 1991). While the social support that husbands provide is beneficial to expatriate adjustment (Caligiuri, Joshi, & Lazarova, 1999), dual-career female expatriates may experience greater work-family conflict than dual-career male expatriates due to disproportionate responsibilities for housework and child care. In fact, several studies have found that working mothers experience greater family to work interference than their male counterparts (e.g., Crouter, 1984; Williams & Alliger, 1994).

STAGE 3—RETURNING FROM ASSIGNMENTS

The literature on expatriate assignments consistently emphasizes that it is important for the home office, expatriates, and spouses to prepare for repatriation. The return home, particularly after assignments lasting several years, requires adjustments similar to those experienced upon entry into the host country. Yet many multinational corporations (MNCs) do not address this stage due to a belief that the transition should be easy (Punnett, 1997). It is clear that repatriation difficulties can significantly impact managerial performance (Black, Gregersen, & Mendenhall, 1992), and the reported turnover rate among repatriates within one year of their return ranges from 20 to 50 percent (Black et al., 1992; Grove & Hallowell, 1997; Stoltz-Loike, 1998). Although we were unable to locate any empirical research that examines differences in the repatriation of men versus women, there are two widely discussed problems for which gender differences might be expected. Our discussion in this section is organized around problems associated with being out of touch with the home office (out of sight, out of mind) and being assigned to positions with decreased responsibility and autonomy upon return from the assignment.

Out of Sight, Out of Mind

One of the more critical issues for repatriates is the concern that they have been forgotten during their time overseas (Hauser, 1999). Thus, they may not have been considered when their departments were planning staffing budgets, reorganizing, or evaluating employees for promotions. Returnees may find themselves in a "holding pattern" for a period of time, in which they have no clearly defined functional role in the organization (Black et al., 1992). Periodic visits to the home office can help expatriates stay connected (Hauser, 1999).

Home country mentors can assist expatriates with a variety of issues that may surface at all stages of the assignment.[2] As liaisons, mentors keep expatriates informed about changes happening back home and can ensure expatriates are not forgotten during their time abroad. Bürgi (1999) has proposed three criteria that are essential for effective expatriate mentoring relationships. First, the mentor must be someone the expatriate trusts. Secondly, the mentor should be a senior level manager with the power to effectively champion the expatriate's ac-

---

[2]Although we emphasize the importance of home country mentors, women expatriates should also benefit from in-country mentors, especially during Stage 2 (e.g., Caligiuri & Cascio, 1998).

complishments and guard her interests while overseas. Finally, in order to empathize with issues faced by the expatriate, mentors should have expatriate experience themselves (Bürgi, 1999).

While mentors may be helpful in maintaining ties between expatriates and home country organizations, women tend to experience complications in obtaining mentors. Opportunities to develop mentoring relationships with senior-level women in the organization are limited because there are so few women in senior-level positions (Ruderman & Hughes-James, 1998). In the case of women expatriates, the availability of senior-level female managers who also have expatriate experience is likely to be extremely limited. Cross-gender mentoring relationships can also be problematic because women have limited access to senior-level male managers outside of the office, and both parties may be reluctant to pursue or cultivate a close mentoring relationship (Ragins, 1989; Ruderman & Hughes-James, 1998). Furthermore, male mentors may not be able to empathize with the issues faced by their female protégées (Lyness & Thompson, 2000).

For women expatriates to develop mentoring relationships with senior-level managers who have international experience, a formal mentoring program would be required. However, formally assigned mentors (in comparison to naturally occurring relationships) are less likely to fill the role of trusted confidant or guardian of expatriates' career interests (Bürgi, 1999). In addition, Grove and Hallowell (1997) suggest that mentors assigned to expatriates should be referred to as "investment managers," charged with the task of maximizing the company's return on its expatriate investment. Baughn (1995) has recommended that successful repatriation should be incorporated into the performance evaluations of mentors. In doing this, organizations com-

municate the importance of providing expatriates with the support required for success both during and after the assignment.

Demotions and Reduced Autonomy Upon Return

Because MNCs can afford to send only a limited number of managers abroad, expatriates may enjoy significantly higher levels of responsibility and autonomy during their assignments. However, upon their return they are often given assignments with less responsibility and autonomy (Black et al., 1992). Oftentimes these positions are demotions from the jobs they occupied before the assignment (Black et al., 1992). While rapid organizational change may prevent the home office from formally guaranteeing a specific return assignment (Solomon, 1995), the company should develop an informal career plan with the expatriate prior to departure (Stoltz-Loike, 1998). In addition, the appointment of a mentor may help ensure that the expatriate is well represented when decision makers implement strategic changes (Bürgi, 1999).

We were unable to identify any published research that addressed differences in the types of repatriation assignments received by men versus women. However, because women executives tend to be given less authority than men (Lyness & Thompson, 1997) (and also as a result of the mentoring and networking disparities mentioned previously), women expatriates may be more susceptible to reductions in responsibility and autonomy than men upon repatriation. This is unfortunate because women with international experience have reported greater personal development than men on dimensions such as leadership ability, emotional stability, sociability, and responsibility (Watts, Webster, Morley, & Cohen, 1992), as well as improved skills related to people management, communication, negotiation, political skills, tolerance, and patience (West-wood & Leung, 1994). However, among women, competency, hard work, and ambition are not believed to be sufficient to propel them above the glass ceiling and into senior management positions as long as they continue to remain outside male-dominated informal networks (Cannings & Montmarquette, 1991; Metzley Davies, 1998).

CONCLUSION

We have explored women managers' experiences in international assignments and the advantages and disadvantages they might encounter as a result of being female. Although few differences are found between male and female expatriates in their willingness to accept an international relocation or successful job performance, there still may be some reluctance from organizations to select women for foreign assignments. Once overseas and upon return, female expatriates may endure further complications. To ensure expatriate success, organizations should address these issues through HR policies and practices. The suggestions outlined in Table 2-3 should help global organizations fully utilize and benefit from their human resources. ∎

TABLE 2-3   Suggestions for HR Practice

Stage 1—Appointing Women to Assignments

To improve motivation to accept assignments

- For both female- and male-lead assignments, offer a variety of expatriate support services to accommodate the diverse needs of dual-career couples (Harvey & Wiese, 1998).
- Recruit qualified trailing spouses to fill overseas positions or establish networks with other organizations to advertise qualifications of trailing spouses (Taylor & Napier, 1996).

To increase assignment offers for women

- Establish formal and specific criteria for recruiting and selecting expatriates (Caligiuri & Cascio, 1998; Stroh et al., 2000).
- Provide training for decision makers on how to reduce biases in the expatriate selection process.

Stage 2—Performing in Assignments

To alleviate barriers to successful performance

- Be aware that it is illegal to consider gender when selecting expatriates or establishing the terms and conditions of assignments, except when foreign laws prohibit women from participating in certain activities (Caligiuri & Cascio, 1998; Cava & Mayer, 1993; Feltes et al., 1993).
- Educate women about foreign laws or enforced restrictions not written in the laws and provide them with realistic responses to situations in which they experience harassment or discrimination (Taylor & Napier, 1996; Cava & Mayer, 1993; Caligiuri & Tung, 1999; Caligiuri & Cascio, 1998).
- Train expatriates on behaviors that are associated with universal positive or culture-specific positive leadership traits.
- Provide expatriates with high position power, job titles that clearly communicate their level of authority, and introductions to host country nationals that emphasize their credentials (Caligiuri & Cascio, 1998; Taylor & Napier, 1996; Wah, 1998).
- Teach expatriates ways to manage initial impressions of host country nationals and provide ways in which employees (e.g., male expatriates) can promote and support women expatriates (Taylor & Napier, 1996; Caligiuri & Tung, 1999).
- When multiple positions are available in a given location, fill more than one of these positions with qualified women (Caligiuri & Cascio, 1998; Feltes et al., 1993).

TABLE 2-3 *(continued)*

Stage 2 — Performing in Assignments

- Take advantage of opportunities to expose host country nationals to successful women within the organization (Caligiuri & Cascio, 1998).
- Offer diversity training to all employees, including host nationals working within the organization (Caligiuri & Cascio, 1998), without imposing home country views.

To facilitate adjustment

- Prior to the assignment, implement expectation-lowering procedures (Buckley et al., 1998; Caligiuri & Tung, 1999) or realistic previews (Wanous et al., 1992) of the assignment and culture, which might include talking with other women who have held expatriate assignments in a particular country (Stroh et al., 2000; Caligiuri & Cascio, 1998).
- Create opportunities for expatriates (and their families) to interact with host country nationals (Selmer, 1995).
- Create or identify programs that will aid the adjustment of expatriates' children such as child care and language classes (Caligiuri & Cascio, 1998).
- Create or identify programs for trailing spouses that will facilitate their adjustment such as assistance in finding suitable employment (Caligiuri & Cascio, 1998).
- Provide support for daily life activities, which will be especially helpful for dual-career couples, such as housekeeping and child care services.

Stage 3 — Returning from Assignments

To prevent out of sight, out of mind

- Develop a formal mentoring program and hold mentors accountable for the management of expatriates (Baughn, 1995; Grove & Hallowell, 1997).

To address concerns of reduced autonomy

- Utilize the cross-cultural experience of repatriates soon after their return (e.g., through assignment of relevant projects, task forces, etc.) and avoid placing expatriates in return assignments with little authority or responsibility (Baughn, 1995; Grove & Hallowell, 1997).
- While it may not be possible to promise specific return assignments, generate a general career plan with assignees before the expatriate assignment begins (Stoltz-Loike, 1998).

REFERENCES

Adler, N. J. (1984a). Expecting international success: Female managers overseas. *Columbia Journal of World Business, 19,* 79–85.

Adler, N. J. (1984b). Women do not want international careers: And other myths about international management. *Organizational Dynamics, 13,* 66–79.

Adler, N. J. (1984c). Women in international management: Where are they? *California Management Review, 26,* 78–89.

Adler, N. J. (1987). Pacific basin managers: A gaijin, not a woman. *Human Resource Management, 26,* 169–191.

Aryee, S., Chay, Y. W., & Chew, J. (1996). An investigation of the willingness of managerial employees to accept an expatriate assignment. *Journal of Organizational Behavior, 17,* 267–283.

Baughn, C. (1995). Personal and organizational factors associated with effective repatriation. In J. Selmer (Ed.), *Expatriate Management:*

New Ideas for International Business (215–230). Westport, CT: Quorum Books.

Beehr, T. A. (1981). Work-role stress and attitudes toward co-workers. *Group and Organization Studies, 6*, 201–210.

Berthoin Antal, A., & Izraeli, D. N. (1993). A global comparison of women in management: Women managers in their homelands and as expatriates. In E. A. Fagenson (Ed.), *Women in management: Trends, issues, and challenges in managerial diversity. Women and work: A research and policy series* (Vol. 4, 52–96). Newbury Park, CA: Sage Publications.

Biernat, M., & Wortman, C. B. (1991). Sharing of home responsibilities between professionally employed women and their husbands. *Journal of Personality and Social Psychology, 60,* 844–860.

Black, J. S., & Gregersen, H. B. (1991). Antecedents to cross-cultural adjustment for expatriates in Pacific Rim assignments. *Human Relations, 44,* 497–515.

Black, J. S., Gregersen, H. B., & Mendenhall, M. E. (1992). Toward a theoretical framework of repatriation adjustment. *Journal of International Business Studies, 23,* 737–760.

Black, J. S., Mendenhall, M., & Oddou, G. (1991). Toward a comprehensive model of international adjustment: An integration of multiple theoretical perspectives. *Academy of Management Review, 16,* 291–317.

Black, J. S., & Stephens, G. K. (1989). The influence of the spouse on American expatriate adjustment and intent to stay in Pacific Rim overseas assignments. *Journal of Management, 15,* 529–544.

Brenner, O. C., Tomkiewicz, J., & Schein, V. E. (1989). The relationship between sex role stereotypes and requisite management characteristics revisited. *Academy of Management Journal, 32,* 662–669.

Brett, J. M., & Stroh, L. K. (1995). Willingness to relocate internationally. *Human Resource Management, 34,* 405–424.

Buckley, M. R., Fedor, D. B., Veres, J. B., Wiese, D. S., & Carraher, S. M. (1998). Investigating newcomer expectations and job-related outcomes. *Journal of Applied Psychology, 83,* 452–461.

Bürgi, P. T. (1999, Winter). Don't leave headquarters without a personal mentor. *Expatriate Observer* [Online serial]. Available online at www.shrmglobal.org/publications/orc/199xpat.htm.

Burke, R. J. (1994). Canadian business students' attitudes towards women as managers. *Psychological Reports, 75,* 1123–1129.

Caligiuri, P. M., & Cascio, W. F. (1998). Can we send her there? Maximizing the success of Western women on global assignments. *Journal of World Business, 33,* 394–416.

Caligiuri, P. M., Hyland, M. M., Joshi, A., & Bross, A. S. (1998). Testing a theoretical model for examining the relationship between family adjustment and expatriates' work adjustment. *Journal of Applied Psychology, 83,* 598–614.

Caligiuri, P. M., Joshi, A., & Lazarova, M. (1999). Factors influencing the adjustment of women on global assignments. *International Journal of Human Resource Management, 10,* 163–179.

Caligiuri, P. M., & Tung, R. L. (1999). Comparing the success of male and female expatriates from a U.S.-based multinational company. *International Journal of Human Resource Management, 10,* 763–782.

Cannings, K., & Montmarquette, C. (1991). Managerial momentum: A simultaneous model of the career progress of male and female managers. *Industrial and Labor Relations Review, 44,* 212–228.

Cava, A., & Mayer, D. (1993). Gender discrimination abroad. *Business and Economic Review, 40,* 13–16.

Chusmir, L. H., & Frontczak, N. T. (1990). International management opportunities for women: Women and men paint different pictures. *International Journal of Management, 7,* 295–301.

Collie, H. C. (1989). Two salaries, one relocation: What's a company to do? *Personnel Administrator, 34,* 54–57.

Cromie, S. (1981). Women as mangers in Northern Ireland. *Journal of Occupational Psychology, 54,* 87–91.

Crosby, F., Cordova, D., & Jaskar, K. (1993). On the failure to see oneself as disadvantaged: Cognitive and emotional components. In M. A. Hogg & D. Abrams (Eds.), *Group motivation: Social psychological perspectives* (87–104). New York: Harvester Wheatsheaf.

Crouter, A. C. (1984). Spillover from family to work: The neglected side of the work-family interface. *Human Relations, 37,* 425–442.

Den Hartog, D. N., House, R. J., Hanges, P. J., Ruiz-Quintanilla, S. A., & Dorfman, P. W. (1999). Culture specific and cross-culturally generalizable implicit leadership theories: Are attributes of charisma/transformational leadership universally endorsed? *Leadership Quarterly, 10,* 219–256.

Dodge, K. A., Gilroy, F. D., & Fenzel, L. M. (1995). Requisite management characteristics revisited: Two decades later. *Journal of Social Behavior and Personality, 10,* 253–264.

Eagly, A. H., Karau, S. J., Makhijani, M. G. (1995). Gender and the effectiveness of leaders: A meta-analysis. *Psychological Bulletin, 117,* 125–145.

Eagly, A. H., Makhijani, M. G., & Klonsky, B. G. (1992). Gender and evaluation of leaders: A meta-analysis. *Psychological Bulletin, 111,* 3–22.

Eby, L. T., Allen, T. D., & Douthitt, S. S. (1999). The role of nonperformance factors on job-related relocation opportunities: A field study and laboratory experiment. *Organizational Behavior and Human Decision Processes, 79,* 29–55.

Employee Relocation Council (1991). *Fact sheet.* (Available from Employee Relocation Council, 1720 N. Street N. W., Washington, D.C. 20036.)

Feltes, P., Robinson, R. K., & Fink, R. L. (1993). American female expatriates and the Civil Rights Act of 1991: Balancing legal and business interests. *Business Horizons, 36,* 82–85.

Fukuda, K. J., & Chu, P. (1994). Wrestling with expatriate family problems: Japanese experience in East Asia. *International Studies of Management and Organization, 24,* 36–47.

Gavin, J. F., & Axelrod, W. L. (1977). Managerial stress and strain in a mining organization. *Journal of Vocational Behavior, 11,* 66–74.

The Glass Ceiling Commission (1995, November). *A solid investment: Making full use of the nation's human capital. Recommendations of the Federal Glass Ceiling Commission.* Washington, D.C.

GMAC Global Relocation Services/Windham International, National Foreign Trade Council, & SHRM Global Forum (2000). *Global relocation trends 2000 survey report.*

Grove, C., & Hallowell, W. (1997, May). The dark side of repatriation. *Benefits & Compensation Solutions* [Online serial]. Available online at www.bcsolutionsmag.com.

Gupta, N., & Beehr, T. A. (1979). Job stress and employee behaviors. *Organizational Behavior and Human Performance, 23,* 373–387.

Harvey, M. (1997). Dual-career expatriates: Expectations, adjustment and satisfaction with international relocation. *Journal of International Business Studies, 28,* 627–658.

Harvey, M., & Wiese, D. (1998). The dual-career couple: Female expatriates and male trailing spouses. *Thunderbird International Business Review, 40,* 359–388.

Hauser, J. (1999). Managing expatriates' careers. *HR Focus, 76,* 11.

Heilman, M. E. (1984). Information as a deterrent against sex discrimination: The effects of applicant sex and information type of preliminary employment decisions. *Organizational Behavior and Human Performance, 33,* 174–186.

Heilman, M. E., Block, C. J., Martell, R. F., & Simon, M. C. (1989). Has anything changed? Current characterizations of men, women, and managers. *Journal of Applied Psychology, 74,* 935–942.

Heilman, M. E., Martell, R. F., & Simon, M. C. (1988). The vagaries of bias: Conditions regulating the undervaluation, equivaluation, and overvaluation of female job applicants. *Organizational Behavior and Human Decision Processes, 41,* 98–110.

Hill, C. J., & Tillery, K. R. (1992, *Autumn*). What do male/female perceptions of an international business career suggest about recruitment policies? *SAM Advanced Management Journal,* 10–14.

Hoover, J. (2000). Use women managers abroad. *Engineering News Record, 245,* 107.

Ibarra, H. (1993). Personal networks of women and minorities in management: A conceptual framework. *Academy of Management Review, 18,* 56–87.

Jones, D. T. (1999, December). You call this a career? *Foreign Service Journal* [Online serial].

Available online at www.afsa.org/fsj/Dec99/jones.htm.

Jones, M. (1997). Two for the road: When it comes to sending employees abroad, some companies are finding that a husband-and-wife team can be a winning combination. *Working Woman, 22* (11), 50–53.

Kaufmann, G. M., & Beehr, T. A. (1986). Interactions between job stressors and social support: Some counterintuitive results. *Journal of Applied Psychology, 71*, 522–526.

Kraimer, M. L., Wayne, S. J., & Jaworski, R. A. (2001). Sources of support and expatriate performance: The mediating role of expatriate adjustment. *Personnel Psychology, 54*, 71–99.

Lord, R. G., & Maher, K. J. (1991). *Leadership & information processing: Linking perceptions and performance.* London: Routledge.

Lyness, K. S., & Thompson, D. E. (1997). Above the glass ceiling? A comparison of matched samples of female and male executives. *Journal of Applied Psychology, 82*, 359–375.

Lyness, K. S., & Thompson, D. E. (2000). Climbing the corporate ladder: Do female and male executives follow the same route? *Journal of Applied Psychology, 85*, 86–101.

Markham, W. T., & Pleck, J. H. (1985). Gender and willingness to move for occupational advancement: Some national sample results. *Center for Research on Women, Wellesley College Working Paper No. 150.*

Metzley Davies, S. A. (1998). Women above the glass ceiling: Perceptions on corporate mobility and strategies for success. *Gender & Society, 12*, 339–355.

Miller, L. (2000, December). Misconceptions hamper foreign assignments for female managers. *HR Magazine,* 12.

Oddou, G., & Mendenhall, M. E. (1991). Succession planning for the 21st century: How well are we grooming our future business leaders? *Business Horizons, 34*, 26–34.

Punnett, B. J. (1997). Towards effective management of expatriate spouses. *Journal of World Business, 32*, 243–257.

Punnett, B. J., Crocker, O., & Stevens, M. A. (1992). The challenge for women expatriates and spouses: Some empirical evidence. *International Journal of Human Resource Management, 3*, 585–592.

Ragins, B. R. (1989). Barriers to mentoring: The female manager's dilemma. *Human Relations, 42*, 1–22.

Ridgway, R. L. (1994). *1994 George C. Marshall lecture.* Paper presented at the George C. Marshall lecture series, City of Vancouver, Canada.

Ruderman, M. N., & Hughes-James, M. W. (1998). Leadership development across race and gender. In C. D. McCauley, R. S. Moxley, & E. Van Velsor (Eds.) *The Center for Creative Leadership Handbook of Leadership Development* (291–335). San Francisco, CA: Jossey-Bass.

Schein, V. E. (1973). The relationship between sex role stereotypes and requisite management characteristics. *Journal of Applied Psychology, 57*, 95–100.

Schein, V. E. (1975). The relationship between sex role stereotypes and requisite management characteristics among female managers. *Journal of Applied Psychology, 60*, 340–344.

Schein, V. E., & Mueller, R. (1992). Sex role stereotyping and requisite management characteristics: A cross cultural look. *Journal of Organizational Behavior, 13*, 439–447.

Schein, V. E., Mueller, R., & Jacobson, C. (1989). The relationship between sex role stereotypes and requisite management characteristics among college students. *Sex Roles, 20*, 103–110.

Schein, V. E., Mueller, R., Lituchy, T., & Liu, J. (1996). Think manager—think male: A global phenomenon? *Journal of Organizational Behavior, 17*, 33–41.

Selmer, J. (Ed.). (1995). *Expatriate management: New ideas for international business.* Westport, CT: Quorum Books.

Solomon, C. M. (1995). Repatriation: Up, down or out? *Personnel Journal, 74*, 28–37.

Solomon, C. M. (1998, May). Women expats: Shattering the myths. *Global Workforce,* 10–14.

Stoltz-Loike, M. (1998). *Managing a global workforce: A cross-cultural guide.* New York, NY: Warren, Gorham, & Lamont.

Stroh, L. K., Brett, J. M., & Reilly, A. H. (1992, August). *What seems obvious may not be true: A non-recursive model predicting expatriate ad-*

justment. Paper presented to the Academy of Management Meeting, Las Vegas, NV.

Stroh, L. K., & Caligiuri, P. M. (1998). Strategic human resources: A new source for competitive advantage in the global arena. *International Journal of Human Resource Management, 9*, 1–17.

Stroh, L. K., Dennis, L. E., & Cramer, T. C. (1994). Predictors of expatriate adjustment. *International Journal of Organizational Analysis, 2*, 176–192.

Stroh, L. K., Varma, A., & Valy-Durbin, S. J. (2000). Why are women left at home: Are they unwilling to go on international assignments? *Journal of World Business, 35*, 241–255.

Taylor, S., & Napier, N. (1996). Working in Japan: Lessons from Western expatriates. *Sloan Management Review, 37*, 76–84.

Terry, D. J., Nielsen, M., & Perchard, L. (1993). Effects of work stress on psychological well-being and job satisfaction: The stress-buffering role of social support. *Australian Journal of Psychology, 45*, 168–175.

Tomkiewicz, J., & Adeyemi-Bello, T. (1995). A cross-sectional analysis of the attitudes of Nigerians and Americans toward women as managers. *Journal of Social Behavior and Personality, 10*, 189–198.

Tosi, H. L., & Einbender, S. W. (1985). The effects of the type and amount of information in sex discrimination research: A meta-analysis. *Academy of Management Journal, 28*, 712–723.

Tung, R. L. (1998). American expatriates abroad: From neophytes to cosmopolitans. *Journal of World Business, 33*, 125–144.

Turban, D. B., Campion, J. E., & Eyring, A. R. (1992). Factors relating to relocation decisions of research and development employees. *Journal of Vocational Behavior, 41*, 183–199.

Wah, L. (1998). Surfing the rough sea. *Management Review, 87* (8), 25–29.

Wanous, J. P., Poland, T. D., Premack, S. L., & Davis, K. S. (1992). The effects of met expectations on newcomer attitudes and behaviors: A review and meta-analysis. *Journal of Applied Psychology, 77*, 288–297.

Watts, F. N., Webster, S. M., Morley, C. J., & Cohen, J. (1992). Expedition stress and personality change. *British Journal of Psychology, 83*, 337–341.

Westwood, R. I., & Leung, S. M. (1994). The female expatriate manager experience. *International Studies of Management and Organization, 24*, 64–85.

Williams, K., & Alliger, G. (1994). Role stressors, mood spillover, and perceptions of work-family conflict in employed parents. *Academy of Management Journal, 37*, 837–868.

Windham International, National Foreign Trade Council, & Institute for International Human Resources. (1999). *Global relocation trends 1999 survey report.*

PART

II

THE EXTERNAL CONTEXT OF HUMAN RESOURCES MANAGEMENT

If organizations were insular entities and had little contact with the external environment, concern with external issues could be minimal. But organizations exist in dynamic, complex environments. Many activities concerning the management of human resources are directly related to addressing external constraints. The external environment in which an organization operates has a significant impact on human resources activities. Ignorance of these environmental constraints significantly dilutes the effectiveness of human resources management.

Part II of this text covers features of the external environment that have impact upon the human resources management function. The articles in Chapter 3 reflect the significant influence of the law on the successful operation of an organization. We have decided to emphasize issues in sexual harassment and the Americans with Disabilities Act (ADA). In this chapter the emphasis is on what a human resources manager can do to comply with the vast amount of case law and legislation affecting sexual harassment issues and the ADA.

The workforce is changing, and a successful human resources program must keep abreast of these demographic changes. The articles in Chapter 4 examine some of the key labor market characteristics that will pose a challenge for human resources. Creating diversity in the workplace is a goal of many organizations. What impact will this have on human resources? The articles in this chapter identify the challenges and opportunities that diversity will bring to the human resources function. Organizations must respond to changes in the external environment. So far, the 1990s and 2000s have seen environmental events dictating human resources policies in many organizations. When environments demand downsizing, redesign, or restructuring, or when mergers and acquisitions occur, human resources are significantly affected.

3

THE CONTEMPORARY LEGAL ENVIRONMENT

Federal legislation with respect to fair employment practices has had a major influence on personnel and human resources management over the past 25 years. To move toward a greater sense of fair treatment for all, Title VII of the Civil Rights Act of 1964 made it a violation to discriminate on the basis of race, color, religion, sex, or national origin in the employment relationship. Subsequent legislation and court decisions moved the pendulum away from unfair discrimination toward equity for all. Some would argue that, in recent years, the pendulum has swung too far to the other side and that we are seeing evidence of reverse discrimination, which clearly was not the intention of those working to promote civil rights. Additional legislation, such as the Age Discrimination in Employment Act of 1967 and a 1978 amendment that disallows mandatory retirement before age 70, expanded the application of fair employment practices to all activities in the processing of people *through* and *out of* organizations. Examples include promotion and transfer activities, training and development, compensation, and termination.

The use of personnel testing as an aid to employment decisions declined after the passage of the Civil Rights Act. It has since increased, however, as companies have begun to realize that it is not tests per se that are discriminatory but the ways and the situations in which the tests are used.

Although the last administrations did not make major cuts in the budgets of federal regulatory agencies that oversee compliance with the law in regard to the employment relationship, they relegated these agencies to a lower level of visibility and generally de-emphasized the issues they address. Counterforces to this federal posture are emerging, however. Many state and local governments are creating their own laws and ordinances to protect employee rights.

Legal issues pervade all that occurs in the human resources management function. For that reason many of the subsequent articles in this book are concerned with legal issues. Some of the writing concerns the legal defensibility of performance appraisal. We have decided to emphasize the contemporary issue of sexual harassment. Shalley and Parsons present a historical perspective on the issue of sexual harassment and discuss the evolution of this activity. They also present areas that may be next in terms of protection: psychological harassment and incivility at work. Robinson and Frink look at sexual harassment from the standpoint of what every practicing manager needs to know about this issue, along with the terminology that pervades this issue. Importantly, legal interpretations of this issue continue to evolve.

READINGS

HARASSMENT IN THE WORKPLACE: RECOGNIZING IT AND YOUR LEGAL LIABILITY

Christina E. Shalley
Charles K. Parsons

A supervisor discovers that an employee is HIV positive and becomes more critical of her work, verbally insults her, and begins to "write her up." The employee is eventually discharged. In another company, an employee who has been on disability leave several times because of back problems is subject to an onslaught of verbal harassment, assigned to inappropriate tasks, and given a desk that is much too small for him. In both of these examples the employees pursued disability harassment claims that were recognized by two appellate courts (Clark, 2001). These events demonstrate that employers are liable for more types of illegal harassment than simply those associated with sexual harassment.

Cases of harassment occur routinely in workplaces. The amount and frequency of lawsuits being filed concerning harassment can be quite alarming for most organizations. However, not all forms of harassment are illegal. Nonetheless, any type of harassment has many potential costs for an employer, including lost productivity; lower job satisfaction and organizational commitment; and increased absenteeism, turnover, and the use of medical benefits. For example, a 1987 study found that sexual harassment had cost the federal government $267 million in two years, from May 1985 through May 1987, for losses in productivity, sick leave costs, and employee replacement costs (MSPB, 1988). Harassment is a serious

problem, and there are different preventative steps that can be taken. In this article we will discuss exactly what constitutes different forms of workplace harassment, and when it is considered to be illegal. We will focus on both illegal forms of workplace harassment and other forms of harassment that are not necessarily illegal, but still highly undesirable and potentially quite costly for individuals and organizations.

In the workplace, generally, harassment is any form of repeated, unwanted behavior that causes an individual to feel persistently annoyed, worried, disturbed, mentally distressed, or tormented. Overall, if you are harassed because of the protected class that you belong to (i.e., race, sex, color, national origin, or religion) this falls under the legal protection of Title VII of the Civil Rights Act. The majority of the court decisions and employment guidelines on harassment that exist have dealt with the most prevalent form of harassment in the workplace, that of sexual harassment. Therefore, we will begin by focusing on sexual harassment. Later we will discuss other forms of harassment that are based on one's protected class (e.g., race, religion) and psychological harassment. This latter form of harassment is a broader type of behavior where an individual or individuals are treated in a psychologically abusive fashion at work (e.g., verbal abuse, derogatory comments) that does not necessarily have anything to do with their protected class status, but nonetheless causes them to experience severe psychological discomfort. This type of harassment typically is not legally actionable. Nonetheless, it is important for an organization to be aware of instances of psychological harassment, and ways to avoid their occurrence in the workplace.

SEXUAL HARASSMENT

Sex discrimination in the workplace has been prohibited since the passage of the Civil Rights Act of 1964. Although Title VII of this Act did not say anything explicitly about sexual harassment, it is considered to be illegal sex discrimination under Title VII of the Civil Rights Act of 1964/91. It wasn't until the mid to late 1970s that courts began to seriously recognize sexual harassment as a form of sex discrimination. In 1980, after the first few significant sexual harassment cases were decided, the Equal Employment Opportunities Commission (EEOC) issued guidelines to use to help determine when activity does and does not constitute illegal sexual harassment. According to the current EEOC Guidelines on Sexual Harassment, verbal or physical conduct of a sexual nature can be considered harassment if (1) submission to such conduct is made either explicitly or implicitly a term or condition of employment, (2) submission to or rejection of such conduct by an individual is used as a basis for determining employment decisions affecting the individual, or (3) such conduct has the purpose or effect of substantially interfering with an individual's work performance or creates an intimidating, hostile, or offensive work environment.

Sexual harassment represents a serious organizational problem that exacts tremendous costs in worker morale and potential. Victims of sexual harassment potentially suffer tangible costs of lost jobs, wages, and opportunities, and also intangible, emotional costs including physical and mental stress, anger, humiliation, frustration, guilt, withdrawal, and dysfunctional family life. In the past decade there has been a great deal of publicity surrounding some high profile cases of sexual harassment, from the EEOC's handling of sex discrimination cases with Hooter's restaurants to continuing revelations of sexual misconduct in the armed forces to Paula Jones's accusations of sexual harassment against President Bill Clinton. In 1991, the nation was glued to radios and televisions to hear the Senate Judiciary Committee's hearings on the confirmation of Clarence Thomas as a Supreme Court justice. Professor Anita Hill described her experience working for Thomas, her former boss and then head of the EEOC, in which she alleged that she was repeatedly subjected to sexual harassment. Since 1991 the number of claims of sexual harassment received by the EEOC has more than doubled. In 1991, 6,883 sexual harassment complaints were submitted to the EEOC. In recent years, the caseload had grown to over 15,000 per year. Through EEOC settlements with employers, monetary relief for victims of sexual harassment increased from $7 million in 1991 to $55 million in 2000. Court awards add substantially to this monetary sum. Although both males and females can be harassers or victims of sexual harassment, in recent years 80 percent or more of the sexual harassment cases brought before the EEOC and courts are by female employees against male harassers.

How common is sexual harassment across organizations? According to the American Psychological Association, sexual harassment is so widespread that it touches the lives of 40 to 60 percent of working women. This estimate is based on survey responses of those actually experiencing harassment rather than the actual reporting rates, which are far lower. In addition, a recent survey sponsored by the Society for Human Resource Management found that the frequency of formal harassment complaints to employers had increased from 1995 to 1998.

There are two legal theories on which an action for sexual harassment may be brought: (1) quid pro quo sexual harassment (covered under section 1 & 2 of the EEOC Guidelines definition) and (2) hostile environment sexual harassment (section 3 of the EEOC definition). The legal term of quid pro quo translates roughly to "something for something." In quid pro quo harassment, an employee perceives that he or she is required to engage in sexual activity in exchange for workplace benefits or entitlements such as raises, promotions, or continued employment. Essentially, in these cases the employee is claiming that a supervisor or someone in authority is offering workplace benefits in exchange for sexual favors or is threatening to take away benefits if the employee refuses to submit to their demands regarding sexual favors. This is considered to be sex discrimination because employees are being forced to decide whether they should comply with conditions that other employees do not have to face because of their sex.

One of the earlier, most influential cases in this area was *Barnes v. Costle* (561 F.2d 983 D. C. Cir. 1977). Paulette Barnes was repeatedly offered continued employment and potentially enhanced employment opportunities in exchange for sexual favors to her supervisor, the director of the Environmental Protection Agency's (EPA) equal employment opportunity division as his administrative assistant. Barnes alleged that after continually resisting these overtures, the director, alone and in concert with other agents of the EPA, began a conscious campaign to belittle and harass her. She was stripped her of job duties, removed from his department, and eventually suffered the loss of her job. Based on the facts of the case, the court decided this was actionable sexual harassment, because this would not have oc-

curred but for her sex. In other words, males in this department were not susceptible to such approaches by their supervisor.

Quid pro quo sexual harassment is a more obvious form of sexual harassment, thus it is easier for individuals to understand and recognize. Because it involves some power differential (i.e., the ability to give or remove workplace entitlements), organizations need to carefully monitor supervisors' behavior, particularly with regard to dating in the workplace. Dating between a supervisor and subordinate may be entirely consensual, which would not constitute sexual harassment, although this could cause conflict of interest issues at work. On the other hand, even if no direct promise or threat has been made, if the situation causes an employee to feel that he or she has no choice but to engage in certain activities with someone in a position of authority, this could be considered sexual harassment. Furthermore, even if a relationship is consensual at one point in time, there could be potential problems in the future with regard to raises, promotions, and so on once the relationship is over, or from other employees that feel the subordinate is gaining unfair advantages because of said relationship. The courts are divided on whether it is sex discrimination for an employer to favor an employee or applicant with whom he or she is having a romantic relationship (e.g., *King v. Palmer*, D.C. Cir. 1985; *DeCintio v. Westchester County Medical Center*, 2d. Cir. 1986). However, it is not considered sex discrimination to discharge an employee for having an affair with another employee, as long as the rule is applied gender neutrally.

Consensual relations are not forbidden in the workplace and employees are free to date whomever they please unless it is against company policy. Nonetheless, more and more companies are adopting polices to prohibit employee dating as a response to occurrences of sexual harassment. Some policies state that employers can ask managers and supervisors to inform them if they are involved in a relationship with another employee so that they can be separated in the workplace immediately. For example, one party can be moved to a different department. Where couples cannot be separated in the workplace, one of the pair may be asked to leave voluntarily or be terminated. Who goes should be the choice of the couple, presuming they both are in good standing in the company. Organizations should be careful not to terminate routinely the female or the person of lower status, since often the male is in a higher position and thus this could be construed as sex discrimination.

In *Meritor Savings Bank, FSB v. Vinson* (477 U.S. 57, 1986) the Supreme Court distinguished between the two concepts of quid pro quo and hostile environment sexual harassment. This was the Supreme Court's first time interpreting Title VII to cover sexual harassment. The Court's opinion was that sexual harassment that is so pervasive as to create a hostile or abusive work environment is a form of sex discrimination. A hostile environment claim of sexual harassment alleges that the employer maintains a work environment that denies equal opportunity to one sex. Hostile environment harassment can be more difficult to recognize than quid pro quo harassment, and employers and employees are often confused about what activities constitute this offense. The essential elements of a hostile environment claim are that (1) the alleged activities are gender based, (2) they affect a term or condition of employment, (3) they are unwelcome, (4) the activities are severe or pervasive enough to create an abusive working environment, and (5) the employer had actual or constructive knowledge of the hostile environment and took no prompt remedial action. Activities that can contribute to a hostile environment include lewd jokes; comments on physical attributes; displaying sexually suggestive materials, pictures, or computer graphics; comments of a sexual

nature directed to an individual; vulgar and offensive language or gestures; inappropriate touching; ostracizing workers of a particular gender; and so on.

Typically, in order to win in court the behaviors contributing to a hostile work environment have to be unwelcome, severe, and pervasive. A ribald work atmosphere in which the alleged victim fully and willingly participated is not considered to be in violation of the Act. On the other hand, "voluntary" participation does not establish that the employer's conduct was welcome. For example, although a coworker may tolerate hearing off-color jokes at work, the telling of them may be unwelcome. In court, the plaintiff's failure to object, his or her past conduct with others, as well as the plaintiff's sexual fantasies can be probed to determine whether the activity complained about was really unwelcome.

In terms of the second essential element, conditions of employment, the harassment must be more than trivial. It must be severe enough to alter the conditions of employment. Thus, usually one instance of any of the aforementioned behaviors would not be considered sexual harassment, unless this instance was unusually severe, but repeated instances could add up to sexual harassment. The severe and pervasive requirement to create an objectively hostile and abusive work environment in order to be considered discriminatory is intended to be sufficient to ensure that courts and juries do not mistake ordinary socializing in the workplace for discriminatory "conditions of employment." Courts tend to rely heavily on psychological or sociological testimony from experts about the effects of certain behaviors to help them in making a decision as to whether the conditions of employment have been affected. Furthermore, the harassing behavior need not involve sexual behavior. For instance, a woman entering a nontraditional workplace where the majority of employees are male and encountering verbal harassment because she is a woman in a predominately male environment is considered sexual harassment because she would not be harassed if it were not for her sex.

Severity is usually determined by using a reasonable person standard. This standard essentially involves asking, given the facts of a case, would a reasonable person find this to be harassing? A reasonable person standard is essentially gender neutral. However, psychologists report that men and women experience, view, and react to certain conduct or behaviors differently. For instance, women have been found to characterize more behavior as sexual harassment than men (Gutek, 1985). In many instances, there is agreement between men and women on what constitutes sexual harassment (Gutek & O'Connor, 1995), but in other cases, male and female definitions are inconsistent (Terpstra & Baker, 1987). Thus, if the same behavior is viewed from the perspective of a reasonable woman, the verdict may be quite different than if it is judged by using the perspective of a reasonable man. Because of this argument, some district courts seem to prefer the reasonable victim standard, which takes into account the sex of the victim in determining if sexual harassment has occurred (e.g., *Ellison v. Brady,* 924 F. 2d 872, 9th Cir. 1991). This is consistent with current EEOC compliance advice. The Supreme Court has not made it clear exactly what they consider a reasonable person standard to mean and currently the lower courts can decide whether they want to use a reasonable person or reasonable victim standard.

In two different decisions, the Supreme Court ruled on whether an employee has to suffer tangible effects—such as loss of benefits, lower job performance, or severe psychological harm—in order to constitute hostile environment sexual harassment. In *Meritor Savings Bank v. Vinson,* Mechelle Vinson alleged sexual harassment even though she suffered no loss of tangible job benefits. The Court decided that this claim constituted hostile environment sexual harassment. However, the Court's language in that decision was so general that it gave the lower courts relatively little guidance in how to apply it. In 1993 the court interpreted it more broadly in *Harris v. Forklift Systems, Inc.* (114 S. Ct. 1993). Teresa Harris worked as a manager for over two years at Forklift Systems, Inc. and during this time Hardy, the owner and president of the company, often insulted her because of her gender and often made her the target of unwanted sexual innuendoes. She subsequently quit and sued for sexual harassment. The Supreme Court had to decide whether suggestive comments by a boss must go beyond the mere offensive and deliver psychological damage to constitute sexual harassment. The Supreme Court ruled that the law as applied to sexual harassment was violated when, for any of a variety of reasons, "the environment would reasonably be perceived and is perceived as hostile and abusive." Thus the plaintiff does not have to prove that he or she was pushed to the edge of mental collapse. One of the most important parts of the Harris opinion was its rejection of a requirement that the plaintiff's job performance actually suffered, which some employer groups had argued for as a standard.

Does same-sex harassment constitute illegal sexual harassment under Title VII? Various district courts have ruled on same-sex sexual harassment, with the rulings varying drastically. In March 1998, the U.S. Supreme Court resolved this conflict by ruling in *Oncale v. Sundowner Offshore Service Inc.* (118 S. Ct. 1998) that employers may be held liable for same-sex harassment under Title VII. In the *Oncale* case, a male employee brought a sexual harassment suit against his former employer, male supervisors, and coworkers. Oncale was employed on an oil platform in the Gulf of Mexico, working on an eight-man crew. On several occasions, he alleges that he was subjected to sex-related, humiliating actions against him by three other workers, two of whom had supervisory authority, in the presence of the rest of the crew. There were physical assaults in a sexual manner and a threat of rape. No remedial action was taken following complaints to supervisory personnel. Eventually Oncale quit and filed a complaint against his employer and the Supreme Court found in Oncale's favor. Oncale originally filed suit in District Court, but the court found that Oncale had no cause of action under Title VII because he was a male being harassed by other males. The fifth Circuit of Appeals Court affirmed. The Supreme Court reversed and remanded the case. They stated that ". . . harassing conduct need not be motivated by sexual desire to support an inference of discrimination based on sex." The Court said that while preventing male on male harassment was not the principal evil that Congress had been concerned with in enacting Title VII, it does fall under the category of reasonably comparable evils.

According to the Oncale ruling by the Supreme Court, if claiming same-sex harassment, the plaintiff must show that they are harassed because of their sex (i.e., sexual desire cannot be an issue) rather than for some other nondiscriminatory reason. A critical issue is "whether members of one sex are exposed to disadvantageous terms or conditions of employment to which members of their other sex are not exposed" (*Harris v. Forklift*). This ruling seems to echo the earlier *Barnes v. Costle* ruling in which the circuit court decided sexual harassment was actionable if it would not have occurred but for the victim's sex.

EMPLOYER LIABILITY FOR SEXUAL HARASSMENT

Employers are not absolutely liable for workplace harassment. Liability is based on the application of common law rules of agency. In deciding whether an employer has vicarious liability in a case, the Court turns to agency law principles because Title VII defines the term "employer" to include "agents." The Court relies on the general common law of agency, rather than on the law of any particular state. In the first sexual harassment case decided by the Supreme Court (*Meritor Savings Bank v. Vinson*), the court decision did not discuss the distinction between quid pro quo and hostile environment sexual harassment with regard to the employer's liability for discrimination, but held that agency principles apply in terms of the employer having vicarious liability for its agent. Thus, in Meritor, a supervisor with no immediate superior at the establishment who has power regarding the hiring, pay, assignment, and firing of workers at the establishment is the "employer" for the purpose of establishing liability for the hostile environment created by that supervisor. When a court finds for the plaintiff in a case of quid pro quo sexual harassment, there is no adequate defense that an employer can raise. Even if the employer took all reasonable steps to prevent this from occurring, the law calls for strict liability, which is the application not based on fault or intentional or negligent behavior but because someone has to pay for the damages.

Recently, the Supreme Court in two separate decisions clarified the issue of liability by stating under what conditions employers may be held liable for misconduct by their supervisors. On June 26th, 1998, the court ruled 7–2 that employers always are potentially liable for supervisors' sexual misconduct toward an employee (*Faragher v. City of Boca Raton*, 118 S. Ct. 2275, 1998; *Burlington Industries v. Ellerth*, 118 S. Ct. 2257, 1998). In the first case the Supreme Court had to decide under what conditions employers are legally responsible and financially liable for a supervisor's harassment they were unaware of. Similarly, in the second case, Kimberly Ellerth sued her former employer, Burlington Industries, over the alleged sexual misconduct of her boss's boss, but she failed to use the internal complaint procedures in place and did not inform anyone in supervisory authority about the harassment. In both cases the Court ruled that an employer is liable for its supervisors' sexual harassment, even if they did not know about the misconduct. However, in some cases where the harassment does not culminate in a tangible employment action taken against the employee, an employer can defend itself by saying it had taken reasonable steps to prevent harassment on the job.

The Court created a two-part test to be used by employers in defending themselves against sexual harassment lawsuits. The Court found that employers are automatically liable for sexual harassment by supervisors of any employee who directly or indirectly reports to them. Employers will be automatically liable for sexual harassment by supervisors unless (1) the employer exercises reasonable care to prevent and correct promptly any sexual harassment, and (2) the victim unreasonably failed to take advantage of any preventive or corrective opportunities provided by the employer or to avoid harm otherwise. The Court stated that they believed that the usual sexual harassment case involved a misuse of power by supervisors. Thus, they felt that with this approach employers have the "opportunity and incentive" to, among other things, "screen, train, and monitor" supervisors.

With hostile environment, unlike quid pro quo sexual harassment, the standard is not strict liability. There are actually two different standards that apply depending on whether the harasser is an "agent" of the employer, such as a supervisor or manager, or if he or she is a coworker, subordinate, or customer. In determining liability, besides distinguishing between quid pro quo and hostile environment discrimination, who is harassing the alleged victim is an important point to consider. In the case of agents, the employer is deemed to know when any of its agents

knows about the behavior either through witnessing said action, because of a complaint, or being told by the victim or a third party, and they did not take immediate corrective action. Essentially the employer "should have known" when harassing behavior occurs and they are liable for their agents.

In the case of sexual harassment by coworkers, clients, or customers, the employer is liable if they knew or should have known and did not remedy the situation. Moreover, harassment is imputed to the "employer" if the employer does not have a clearly expressed policy against sexual harassment and clearly stated, reasonable avenues for making harassment complaints known to management. To further substantiate this point, a recent study by Juliano and Schwab (2001) found that employers lost over 70 percent of harassment lawsuits in district courts when they did not have a formal sexual harassment program or a generalized grievance procedure that covered sexual harassment. Therefore, when proper procedures are in place, the employer is not liable for harassment by lower-level employees if they are unaware of its occurrence.

To avoid liability, the employer that knew or should have known about the harassment must take prompt, effective, remedial action. Reprimands, reassignments, denials of scheduled pay increases, coupled with counseling for offending employees, may be adequate. Discharge of the offender is not always required. In all cases, severity of the entire situation is important in determining the appropriate discipline. Before the 1991 Civil Rights Act amended Title VII, a victim of harassment could secure no damages for pain, suffering, or even for medical expenses required to remedy any emotional trauma. Because of this, plaintiffs would often attach to their Title VII suit a pendent claim under state law for torts such as infliction of emotional distress, battery, and invasion of privacy for which damages can be collected under state law. Now under the Civil Rights Act of 1991, a plaintiff can sue for compensatory and/or punitive damages.

Harassment of an employee by a customer can occur in any occupation or industry, but is more common in occupations where there is a lot of one-on-one contact between the employee and the customer, such as in service occupations like sales, restaurant and bar serving positions, and customer service jobs. This type of harassment situation is potentially harder to deal with since the harasser is not an employee and employers might fear any discussion of the incident could yield a loss of business. Nonetheless, appropriate steps need to be taken to end the harassment of an employee. Sometimes simply telling the customer or client that such behavior will not be tolerated stops the offending action. If this does not work, one good approach may be to talk to a high-level person in the client company to try to cooperatively solve the problem. This can work well because the business relationship between the two companies can be preserved while directly addressing and eliminating the offensive behavior. Sometimes, merely assigning the employee that has complained to work with other equally desirable customers can solve the situation. However, a harasser typically will harass more than one person, so this may serve as only a short-term solution. Under no circumstances should the employee be removed from certain job assignments and given duties of lesser responsibilities or pay in order to get them away from the harasser. This would be considered a transfer that is to the victim's disadvantage and, as such, it would be considered retaliation by the employer for claiming sexual harassment, which is in further violation of the law.

Often an employee's immediate response to harassment is to quit his or her job, and thereafter possibly seek reinstatement with the employer coupled with a de-

mand for back pay for the period of unemployment. This is considered a case of constructive discharge, if the employee felt they had to involuntarily resign to escape intolerable and illegal employment requirements. "A constructive discharge exists if working conditions are such that a reasonable person in the plaintiff's shoes would feel compelled to resign" (*Bruhwiler v. University of Tenn.*, 6th Cir.1988; *Thompson v. Tracor Flight Systems, Inc.*, 2001, Cal App.). In order to establish constructive discharge, the plaintiff must establish three elements: (1) the defendant has engaged in the illegal conduct; (2) the illegal conduct was "intolerable" to a reasonable person—this requires circumstances such as assignment of demeaning or dangerous jobs, a dramatic demotion, or especially humiliating or unceasing harassment; and (3) the employee's action must be caused by, and in response to, the illegal conduct. Thus the employee's resignation is viewed as a reasonable and foreseeable response to the employer's illegal conduct (*Calhoun v. Acme Cleveland Corp.*, 1st Cir. 1986).

OTHER FORMS OF HARASSMENT

In theory, any form of harassing behavior that occurs primarily because of an individual's protected class status is illegal under equal employment opportunity laws such as the Civil Rights Act, Age Discrimination in Employment Act, or Americans with Disabilities Act. For example, racial harassment is when the employer imposes on the harassed employee different terms or conditions of employment based on race, by requiring an employee to work in an atmosphere in which severe or pervasive harassing activity is directed at the employee because of their race and/or color. A similar definition would apply to national origin harassment. The number of non-sex harassment claims are rising. In 1999 there were 8,338 race and national origin harassment claims filed with the EEOC, versus 4,424 in 1990. Typically, these claims allege that nonwhites are being subjected to slurs or a higher level of scrutiny than whites. The EEOC has recently revised its guidelines to say that the Supreme Court's sex-harassment standard applies to all types of harassment. Although most companies have begun to make sure that their sexual harassment policy is formal and well communicated in their organization, these same companies often neglect to make sure that their policies explicitly address all forms of harassment. Additionally, the 1998 rulings that expanded employer liability in sexual harassment lawsuits also apply to racial and other forms of illegal harassment. Thus companies will have a harder time persuading judges to dismiss racial harassment claims involving supervisors before trial, leading to more incidents of litigation.

Regarding racial harassment, in a landmark case, *Rogers v. EEOC* (454 F 2d 234, 1971), the Court of Appeals for the Fifth Circuit held that the practice of racially segregating patients in a doctor's office could amount to discrimination in "the terms, conditions, or privileges" of employment, thereby violating Title VII. The principal opinion in the case concluded that employment discrimination was not limited to the isolated and distinguishable events of "hiring, firing, and promoting." Rather, Title VII could also be violated by a work environment "heavily polluted with discrimination" because of the deleterious effects of such an atmosphere on an employee's well-being. Accordingly, after *Rogers,* a plaintiff claiming employment discrimination based upon race could assert a claim for a racially hostile work environment in addition to the classic claim of so-called "disparate treatment." A disparate treatment claim requires a plaintiff to prove an adverse employment consequence and discriminatory intent by the employer. A hostile environment claim requires the plaintiff to show that the work environment was so pervaded by racial harassment

as to alter the terms and conditions of his or her employment. Therefore, an employer is responsible for racial harassment if the employer is the one harassing employees, or if they permit this type of harassment to occur in the workplace. An individual who feels they have been racially harassed can sue under Title VII or the alternative statutes for race discrimination, such as the post-Civil War statute (e.g., 42 U.S.C. Section 1981). The statute was passed after the Civil War to, among other things, ensure that race is not used to make an adverse employment decision, and if so, the statute provides the right to sue for damages in a court of law. Thus a plaintiff in a racial discrimination case can establish a violation of Title VII or 42 U.S.C. Section 1981 by showing that the work environment is "so heavily polluted with discrimination as to destroy completely the emotional and psychological stability of minority group workers . . ."

In *Vance v. Southern Bell Telephone and Telegraph Company* (863 F.2d 1503, 11th Cir. 1989), Vance, a black woman, found what she thought was a noose hanging from the light fixture above her work station about a week after being transferred into the department. Two days later she found another noose. She did not report the incidents to any Southern Bell official at the time, but did so later. The employer did little or nothing after being told. The Court said that in order to determine whether a hostile environment is severe enough to adversely affect a reasonable employee, the law requires that the finder of fact examine not only the frequency of the incidents, but the gravity of the incidents as well. The court found that, by viewing all the evidence in context, Vance satisfied her burden of producing evidence sufficient to create a jury question on her section 1981 claim. Vance produced substantial evidence that Southern Bell failed to investigate the noose incidents even after they were brought to the company's attention. Vance produced evidence that a reasonable jury could conclude that in creating a hostile environment, her supervisor acted as an agent of Southern Bell under the standard outlined by the statute. Vance was awarded over one million dollars.

There have also been some cases of harassment because of color. For example, in *Walker v. Secretary of the Treasury, Internal Revenue Service* (742 F. Supp. 670, n.D.Ga., Atlanta Div. 1990), a light-skinned black employee alleged that her supervisor was discriminating against her because of her skin color. The supervisor was a brown-skinned black, and the employee alleged that the supervisor said and did derogatory things to her because the supervisor resented her lighter skin color. In this case, the court recognized that color could be a basis for discrimination under Title VII, but held that the employee failed to demonstrate that the employer had discriminated since there were legitimate nondiscriminatory reasons for the dismissal.

Ethnic slurs or other verbal or physical conduct because of an individual's nationality constitute harassment if they create an intimidating, hostile, or offensive working environment; unreasonably interfere with work performance; or negatively affect an individual's employment opportunities. Employers who enforce segregation by race or national origin inherently create an oppressive work environment, and thus discriminate in regard to a condition of employment. Thus segregating the work area, changing area, toilets, or eating areas according to race or national origin or sponsoring or organizing social or athletic events by racial or ethnic groups is illegal. However, an employer does not have to eliminate self segregation by employees during nonworking hours, such as in eating areas or at social events (*Domingo v. New England Fish Co.,* 9th Cir. 1984).

An oppressive environment is also created by employers if they direct customers of the same national origin to certain employees, for instance, Hispanic customers to Hispanic employees and Anglo customers to Anglo employees (*Rogers v. EEOC,* 5th Cir. 1971). If the work environment is charged with religious or ethnic hostility, this cannot be tolerated by management. Such a hostile environment occurs when workers of a particular religion or heritage are subjected to higher levels of supervision or criticism, regularly subjected to crude or practical jokes, or exposed to religious or ethnic insults, jokes, or graffiti. The plaintiff must prove that they were repetitive or debilitating incidents that would seriously affect the psychological welfare of a reasonable person. Rarely will one stray ethnic or religious insult or occasional practical joke rise to that level. As with sexual harassment, employers should maintain a workplace free from harassment and take immediate corrective action if necessary.

PSYCHOLOGICAL HARASSMENT

Another form of harassment that can occur in the workplace which is not considered illegal is psychological harassment. Psychological harassment includes any type of behavior that is verbally abusive to an employee, humiliates them, and makes them uncomfortable in the workplace. Although this type of harassment is not illegal, it exacts some of the same costs as illegal forms of harassment, including lower morale and productivity, increased absenteeism, and more frequent use of employee benefits (e.g., sick leave, medical problems). For instance, over a one-year period in 1993, an estimated 2.2 million U.S. workers were victims of physical attacks, 6.3 million were threatened, and 16.1 million were harassed (Northwestern National Life Insurance Company, 1993). Organizations' downsizing, reengineering, budget cuts, increased pressures for productivity, and so on have all been cited as catalysts for the increase in aggressive workplace behaviors and incivility (e.g., Baron & Neuman, 1996).

Why is psychological harassment not considered illegal? In this country we are employed at will, with the idea that you can choose to work for any employer and you can leave their employment at any time. Employees also have the option to try to set up or join a union, which would give them greater power in dealing with management. With the exception of antidiscrimination legislation (e.g., Civil Rights Act), there are few laws that specifically deal with how employees can be treated at work. Employee litigation against employers for any harassment that leads to personal injury requires evidence of harm and intent, whereas harassment laws have the broader scope of liability previously described and evidence of an offensive environment that affects a term or condition of the job.

There are different forms of psychological harassment, some more aggressive than others, with harassment taking the form of direct threats of violence to more indirect or subtle abuse (Baron & Neuman, 1996). For example, in one workplace survey it was found that 32 percent of the respondents had observed others being exposed to verbal harassment at work (Bjorkqvist, Osterman, & Hjelt-Back, 1994). Similarly, a survey of 327 first-line workers revealed that more than half reported experiencing acts of mistreatment at work over a three-year period (Ehrlich & Larcom, 1994). Mistreatment at work can take a variety of forms from physical aggression (e.g., Baron & Neuman, 1996) to verbal harassment (e.g., Bjorkqvist et al., 1994) to less intense forms such as incivility or rudeness (Andersson & Pearson, 1999).

Recently more attention has been focused on incivility because so many employees are victims of rudeness in the workplace (e.g., Andersson & Pearson, 1999; Pearson, Andersson, & Porath, 2000). Workplace incivility entails violating workplace norms for mutual respect, such that individuals feel less cooperative, connected, and motivated to interact. Thus, incivility disrupts work routines and can diminish performance. Instigators of incivility are three times as likely to be of higher status than their targets, are generally rude to their peers, disrespectful of their subordinates, and hard to get along with (Pearson, et al., 2000). Moreover, incivility can be the start of more overt acts of workplace aggression (Pearson, et al., 2000). For instance, research has shown a high correlation between incivilities and crime (e.g., Taylor & Gottfredson, 1986). Furthermore, Baron and Neuman (1996) suggested that violence in the workplace is rarely a spontaneous act but more of a culmination of an escalating pattern of negative interactions. Therefore, workplace incivility has been suggested to be the precursor to more directly aggressive acts in the workplace (Andersson & Pearson, 1999).

Given the above, what can be done? First, it is important for organizations to realize that all forms of harassment are potentially damaging to the target, as well as to their colleagues and other bystanders. Second, organizations should set and communicate clear expectations for what is considered to be appropriate and inappropriate behavior in the workplace. By fostering civil interactions and dealing with uncivil ones, harassment is less likely to occur. Furthermore, it is clear that those at higher levels of the organization need to be appropriate role models for desirable behavior. If managers' behavior and conduct is deemed to be civil, their employees are more likely to follow their lead. Finally, consideration of these issues when selecting, orienting, and training employees should increase the likelihood of a workplace free of harassment. ■

REFERENCES

Andersson, L. M., & Pearson, C. M. (1999). Tit for tat? The spiraling effect of incivility in the workplace. *Academy of Management Review, 24,* 452–471.

Baron, R. A., & Neuman, J. H. (1996). Workplace violence and workplace aggression: Evidence on their relative frequency and potential causes. *Aggressive Behavior, 22,* 161–173.

Bjorkqvist, K., Osterman, K., & Hjelt-Back, M. (1994). Aggression among university employees. *Aggressive Behavior, 20,* 173–184.

Clark, M. M. (2001). ADA outlaws disability-based harassment, two courts say. *HR News, 20* (1), 7.

Ehrlich, H. J., & Larcom, B. E. K. (1994). *Ethnoviolence in the workplace.* Baltimore: Center for the Applied Study of Ethnoviolence.

Gutek, B. A. (1985). *Sex and the workplace: The impact of sexual behavior and harassment on women, men and organizations.* San Francisco: Jossey-Bass.

Gutek, B. A., & O'Connor, M. (1995). The empirical-basis for the reasonable woman standard. *Journal of Social Issues, 51* (1), 151–166.

Juliano, A. & Schwab, S. J. (2001). The sweep of sexual harassment cases. *86 Cornell Law Review 548.*

Northwestern National Life Insurance Company. (1993). *Fear and violence in the workplace.* Research report, Minneapolis, MN.

Pearson, C. M., Andersson, L. M., & Porath, C. L. (2000). Assessing and attacking workplace incivility. *Organizational Dynamics, 29,* 123–137.

Taylor R. B., & Gottfredson, S. (1986). Environmental design, crime and prevention: An examination of community dynamics. In A. J. Reiss & M. Tonry (Eds.), *Communities and crime.* Chicago: University of Chicago Press.

Terpstra, D. E., & Baker, D. D. (1987). A hierarchy of sexual harassment. *Journal of Psychology, 121* (6), 599–605.

U.S. Merit Systems Protection Board (MSPB), 1988. *Sexual Harassment in the Federal Government: An Update.*

A MANAGER'S PRIMER FOR SEXUAL HARASSMENT IN THE WORKPLACE

Robert K. Robinson
Dwight D. Frink

It has been only a quarter of a century since sexual harassment became an actionable charge under Title VII of the Civil Rights Act of 1964 (*Williams v. Saxbe,* 1976). During that time, there have been significant developments in sexual harassment case law and litigation, including (1) nationwide legal recognition of same-sex sexual harassment, (2) equal opportunity harassment by bisexuals, (3) increased standards on employer liability for sexual harassment perpetrated by supervisory and managerial personnel, and (4) guidelines for mitigating damages when employers are found liable.

In this article, we examine these developments and the legal obligations that they impose on organizations. This article focuses only on the legal ramifications posed by sexual harassment under Title VII of the Civil Rights Act of 1964 and the subsequent actions managers must take in order to meet minimum legal compliance. Issues involving the ethical or social efficacy of anti-harassment policies and training are beyond the scope of this article. It is important that the reader understands the term "*actionable sexual harassment.*" This term merely means sexual harassment for which there are legal grounds for action in a court of law. Hence, this article focuses strictly on the human resources compliance aspect of sexual harassment rather than its behavioral facet.

If we are to understand the current developments in this evolving legal concept, it is first necessary to examine its origins. Prior to 1976, sexual harassment did not exist as a behavior that was actionable under Title VII. The first case granting it legal legitimacy, *Williams v. Saxbe* (1976), involved a female public information specialist who was discharged because she refused the sexual advances of her male supervisor. On April 20, 1976, a federal district court concluded that the retaliatory actions of the male supervisor were, in fact, retaliatory sex discrimination and were prohibited under Title VII (*Williams v. Saxbe,* 657, 1976). Within the year, at least two other district courts accorded sexual harassment actionable status (*Tomkins v. Public Service Electric & Gas,* 1976; *Capaci v. Katz Bestoff,* 1976). These courts had given impetus to the concept that retaliatory action by a supervisor against an employee who refused/rejected his sexual advances was a form of gender-based discrimination—this form eventually known as quid pro quo sexual harassment.

Initially, however, there was some disagreement among the federal courts. Several courts concluded the opposite, that sexual harassment was not the sort of activity that constituted unlawful discrimination within the scope of Title VII (*Corne v. Bausch and Lomb, Inc.,* 1975; *Miller v. Bank of America,* 1976). In fact, the federal district court for the Northern District of California concluded that:

it would not be difficult to foresee a federal challenge based on alleged sex motivated considerations of the complainant's superior in every case of a lost

promotion, transfer, demotion or dismissal. And who is to say what degree of sexual cooperation would found a Title VII claim? It is conceivable, under plaintiff's theory, that flirtations of the smallest order would give rise to liability. The attraction of males to females and females to males is a natural sex phenomenon and it is probable that this attraction plays at least a subtle part in most personnel decisions. Such being the case, it would seem wise for the Courts to refrain from delving into these matters short of specific factual allegations describing an employer policy which in its application imposes or permits a consistent, as distinguished from isolated, sex-based discrimination on a definable employee group. (*Miller,* 1976, p. 236)

However, by 1978 most federal courts had accepted sexual harassment as gender-based discrimination (*Mumford v. James T. Barnes & Co.,* 1977; *Barnes v. Costle,* 1977; *Heelan v. Johns-Manville Corp.,* 1978; *Hardin v. Carlson,* 1978). It must be noted that at this conjuncture, most courts saw sexual harassment as being limited strictly to retaliatory actions involving the employees' tangible job benefits. This invariably limited the potential to only those employees/agents of an employer who controlled tangible job benefits—supervisors and managers.

At first sexual harassment was also viewed as a phenomenon that involved only members of the opposite sex, usually male perpetrators with female victims. In fact, one federal circuit, the Fifth, would not recognize same-sex sexual harassment until 1996 (*Oncale v. Sundowner Offshore Services,* 1996); a topic addressed later in our discussion.

ESTABLISHING ACTIONABLE SEXUAL HARASSMENT

Thus far, we have used *actionable sexual harassment* to indicate its special legal status; now we intend to explain that term in detail.

As actionable sexual harassment developed, the federal courts began standardizing the means to establish grounds for litigation. A series of conditions, or legal proofs, were created. If the complaining party could satisfy these conditions (and the employer could not rebut them), the court would consider Title VII to have been violated. As a violation of the Civil Rights Act of 1964, the complaining party would have to demonstrate that the sexual harassment specifically violated those prohibitions of the Act dealing with equal employment opportunity. Title VII makes it unlawful "to fail or refuse to hire or to discharge any individual, or otherwise to discriminate against any individual with respect to his compensation, terms, conditions, or privileges of employment, because of such individual's race, color, religion, sex, or national origin" (42 U.S.C. § 2000e-2). In order to be "actionable" sexual harassment, it must be demonstrated that the conduct in question is indeed a form of discrimination on the basis of sex. In regard to all Title VII complaints, "sex" means a biological condition and not a behavior or a preference (*Ulane v. Eastern Airlines,* 1985).

In order to establish sexual harassment as actionable under Title VII, four conditions, or proofs, must be satisfied (see Table 3-1). If any of these four conditions are not established, there is no "actionable" sexual harassment. Again, Title VII applies only in those situations involving unlawful discrimination based on an individual's race, color, religion, sex, or national origin.

First, the alleged victim must belong to a class or group protected under Title VII. This may seem a moot point, but it precludes an individual from filing a sexual harassment complaint based on sexual orientation. An employee who is being harassed because he or she is gay, lesbian, or a transvestite is not protected under Title VII (*Voyles v. Ralph K. Davies Medical Center,* 1975, *aff'd mem.,* 1978; *DeSantis v. Pacific Telephone & Telegraph,* 1979). To establish the first proof, the object of the alleged harassment is either male or female.

Second, the alleged victim must be subjected to unwelcome sexual harassment.

TABLE 3-1 Sexual Harassment Proofs	
Proofs for Quid Pro Quo Sexual Harassment	***Proofs for Hostile Environment Sexual Harassment***
• The complaining party is a member of a protected class.	• The complaining party is a member of a protected class.
• The conduct of a sexual nature was unwelcomed. The complaining party did not encourage the conduct by word or deed.	• The conduct of a sexual nature was unwelcomed. The complaining party did not encourage the conduct by word or deed.
• But for the complaining party's sex, he or she would not have been subjected to the unwelcomed conduct.	• But for the complaining party's sex, he or she would not have been subjected to the unwelcomed conduct.
• The complaining party's acceptance or rejection of the unwelcomed conduct would affect tangible job benefits.	• The unwelcomed conduct was so severe or pervasive as to create an intimidating and adverse work environment.
• *Respondeat superior.* When the employer knew, or should have known, of the harassment and failed to take appropriate action.	• *Respondeat superior.* When the employer knew, or should have known, of the harassment and failed to take appropriate action.

This means that the alleged victim did nothing, by word or deed, to encourage the harassing behavior. If the victim has indicated that the behavior is unacceptable, this is usually sufficient to establish that it was unwelcome. In the event that the victim actively (and of his or her own volition) participated in the sexual behavior, it is questionable that the conduct was "unwelcome" (*Meritor Savings Bank FSB v. Vinson,* 1986, p. 68).

Third, the sexual harassment in question must be shown to have been based on the alleged victim's sex. The victim must prove that the conduct at issue was not merely tinged with offensive sexual connotations but actually constituted discrimination because of his or her sex (*Oncale,* 1998). The critical issue here is whether the members of one sex are exposed to disadvantageous conditions of employment (in this case unwelcomed behavior of a sexual nature) to which members of the other sex are not exposed (*Holman v. State of Indiana and Indiana DOT,* 2000). If this condition is not met, Title VII has not been violated. If Title VII has not been violated, then the case can proceed no further.

The fourth condition varies based on the type of sexual harassment involved—quid pro quo or hostile environment. Therefore, a discussion of these two types of sexual harassment is necessary.

Quid Pro Quo Sexual Harassment

Quid pro quo, the original form of sexual harassment, occurs when submission or rejection of sexual advances is made explicitly or implicitly a condition of the victim's employment. In essence, submission to requests for sexual favors or tolerance of unwelcomed behavior (i.e., bodily contact, sexist comments, etc.) by the employee becomes the basis for future employment decisions affecting that individual (U.S. Equal Employment Opportunity Commission, 2001). The effect of the employee's acceptance or rejection must be tangible. The employee risks loss of job, loss of a promotion, loss of a pay increase, or poor performance evaluations for rejecting this behavior. Conversely, the employee may enjoy these benefits for acquiescing. For example, a complaining party could establish a situation as being quid pro quo sexual harassment if he or she was denied a promotion for which he or she was qualified because he or she rejected the sexual advances of his or her supervisor. Quid pro quo could also be established if the complaining party received the promotion only after agreeing to the supervisor's advances. In either instance, a tangible job benefit was at stake.

Hostile Environment Sexual Harassment

It was not long after quid pro quo harassment gained legal recognition that another form of actionable sexual harassment emerged. Beginning in 1981, some federal courts began expanding the activities that would constitute actionable sexual harassment by including those behaviors that would create an abusive work environment (*Bundy v. Jackson,* 1981). Several Federal Circuit Courts of Appeal began applying the legal standards created for racial harassment to similarly motivated conduct directed at individuals because of sex. The intent of these courts was to eliminate situations by which supervisors and/or coworkers were attempting to drive female employees from traditionally male workplaces or jobs. Such practices had previously been encountered by blacks who had integrated previously segregated workplaces (*Rogers v. EEOC,* 1971). The underlying motivation for the harassment was simple. Make the undesired employee so miserable by purposefully creating an intimidating work environment that he or she would dread coming to work. In the end, a constructive discharge is accomplished. The working conditions become so intolerable that the victim quits. On the surface, this appears to be a voluntary action on the part of the victim. In actuality, it is the intended outcome, perpetrated by the harassers.

It was this premeditated conduct that hostile environment sexual harassment was intended to combat. However, by its very nature, hostile environment sexual harassment also greatly expanded the pool of potential harassers. Previously, under the quid pro quo form, only members of management could engage in the harassment. Now the victim's peers, coworkers, could also create an actionable situation. Because racial harassment was designed to cover an extensive range of abusive and intimidating behaviors, its modification to sexual harassment invariably cast an equally broad net. As potentially intimidating behaviors were expanded, so was the pool of potential harassers. In addition to courts finding that hostile work environments can be created by supervisors and coworkers, subordinates have also been identified as a source of harassment (*Cronin v. United Service Stations,* 1992). Also added to the growing list of potential harassers are customers and clients (*Priest v. Rotary,* 1986), suppliers and vendors, and even instances when passers-by caused actionable harassment *(EEOC v. Sage Realty Corp.,* 1981).

Naturally, hostile environment sexual harassment is established by satisfying a series of legal proofs, the first three of which are the same as for quid pro quo sexual harassment. The fourth proof is met when the alleged victim demonstrates that the conduct of a sexual nature was sufficiently severe or pervasive as to have the effect of unreasonably interfering with work performance, or by creating "an intimidating, hostile, or offensive working environment" (*Meritor,* 1986, p. 65). In some rare instances, a single incident of sexual behavior could be sufficiently severe to meet these criterion, hence establishing the severity criterion. The courts and the EEOC have long contended that a single incident of physical assault *(Moylan v. Maries County,* 1986), physical

contact with intimate body areas, or, in some special instances, verbal abuse can result in creating an immediate hostile environment (Equal Employment Opportunity Commission, 2000). For example, if an employee grabbed the intimate body part of a coworker, this single incident would be sufficient to establish hostile environment sexual harassment. Virtually any incident involving sexual assaults would also satisfy this condition.

In most instances, however, the isolated conduct does not rise to the level of severity to establish actionable sexual harassment in a single incident. Most often, the complaining party must demonstrate that the harassment was of sufficient severity and occurred frequently enough over a period of time to create an abusive work environment. Still, it is not sufficient merely to show that the conduct in question offended the victim; rather, it must be shown that the discriminatory conduct was severe and pervasive enough to create an objectively hostile or abusive working environment (*Harris v. Forklift Systems, Inc.,* 1993; *Butler v. Ysleta Independent School,* 1998; *Wallace v. Texas Tech Univ.,* 1996; *Blout v. Sterling Healthcare Group, Inc.,* 1996). Examples of sufficiently severe or abusive work environments would be those that:

1. affect the psychological well being of the victim (*Phillips v. Smalley Maintenance Service,* 1983, p. 1529);
2. interfere with the victim's work performance (*Meritor,* 1986, p. 63);
3. result in a constructive discharge (*Young v. Southwestern Savings and Loan Assoc.,* 1975, p. 144). A constructive discharge occurs when job conditions have become so unpleasant that a reasonable person would have felt compelled to resign (*Bourque v. Powell Electrical Manufacturing,* 1980); and/or
4. alter the conditions of [the victim's] employment and create an abusive

working environment. (*Jones v. Flagship International*, 1986, pp. 719–720).

These are not mutually exclusive criteria. Any one, or a combination of them, would demonstrate a hostile environment sexual harassment claim. Since 1993, the Supreme Court rejected the requirement that hostile environment claims could be substantiated only by demonstrating that the complaining party's psychological well-being had been adversely affected (*Harris v. Forklift Systems, Inc.*, 1993). Though documented psychological harm would clearly establish a hostile environment harm, it is not the only means of doing so. Some incidents are not sufficiently severe of and by themselves to create a hostile environment, but compounded over time (and occurring on a fairly regular basis) they could result in establishing one of the previously outlined outcomes.

The problem confronting HR managers is discerning when the frequency of the unwelcomed conduct reaches the level of actionable hostile environment sexual harassment. There is, unfortunately, no clearly objective means of doing this. In attempting to answer this question, any party investigating a sexual harassment complaint must consider all of the circumstances surrounding the alleged harassment. Factors used to make such determinations may include the frequency of the discriminatory conduct, its severity, whether it is physically threatening or humiliating, and whether it unreasonably interferes with an employee's work performance (*Harris*, 1993, p. 23). The effect on the employee's psychological well-being is, of course, relevant to determining whether the plaintiff actually found the environment abusive. In establishing actionable sexual harassment, the mere utterance of an epithet that simply engenders offensive feelings or amounts to normal job stress is neither sufficiently severe nor pervasive to violate Title VII (*Trujillo v. University of Colo. Health Sciences Ctr.*, 1998, p. 1214; *DeAnge-*

lis v. El Paso Municipal Police Officer's Ass'n, 1995, p. 594). Simple teasing, offhand comments, and isolated incidents, unless extremely serious, normally does not arise to the level of an actionable discrimination claim (*Faragher v. City of Boca Raton*, 1998, p. 783). Additionally, incidental or occasional sexual comments, discourtesy, or rudeness does not establish discriminatory changes in the terms and conditions of a worker's employment (*Nash v. Electrospace Systems, Inc.*, 1993, p. 404).

However, the guidance of the courts remains elusive and, when confronted with increasing exposure to liability, many employers have reacted to this ambiguity by banning any form of sexual behavior in the workplace. Having addressed the nature of actionable sexual harassment, we will now examine some of the more recent developments in its evolutionary progress.

SAME-SEX SEXUAL HARASSMENT

Remember the third proof, the one which is necessary to establish the connection between the unwelcomed conduct and unlawful discrimination on the basis of sex. In essence, the third proof that states "but for the victim's sex" she (or he) would not have been subjected to the harassment in question (*Bundy v. Jackson*, 1981, p. 942). What is critical to any sexual harassment claim is this requirement for the complaining party to demonstrate that she (or he) was treated differently because of her or his sex. In other words, had the victim been of a different sex, he or she would not have been targeted for the unwelcomed sexual behavior. This means that a female employee becomes the object of harassment from a heterosexual male supervisor because she is a female. Had she been a male, the heterosexual male supervisor would not have made her the object of unwelcomed sexual behavior. If the treatment is not differentiated based on sex, there is no Title VII claim.

Several federal decisions have applied this line of reasoning to same-sex harassment (*McWilliams v. Fairfax County Board of Supervisors,* 1996; *Joyner v. AAA Cooper Transportation,* 1983; *Wright v. Methodist Youth Services,* 1981). In each of these cases, a homosexual male supervisor would make sexual advances toward male employees. The homosexual male supervisor would not have been interested in female employees. Hence, males were targets of this behavior only because they were males. The connection with Title VII was made because the male victims were subjected to different treatment in the workplace that female employees were not subjected to. Clearly, their sex was the main reason they were harassed. However, one federal circuit, the Fifth, did not interpret Title VII as prohibiting harassment by individuals of the same sex, and hence barred all same-sex harassment claims (*Giddens v. Shell Oil Co.,* 1993).

In the *Oncale v. Sundowners Offshore, Inc.* (1998) decision, the Supreme Court made it extremely clear that Title VII's prohibition on sexual harassment protects men as well as women.

Title VII prohibits "discriminat[ion] . . . because of . . . sex" in the "terms" or "conditions" of employment. Our holding that this includes sexual harassment must extend to sexual harassment of any kind that meets the statutory requirements . . . The critical issue, Title VII's text indicates, is whether members of one sex are exposed to disadvantageous terms or conditions of employment to which members of the other sex are not exposed. (*Oncale,* 1998, p. 79)

The impetus for the Supreme Court's ruling in Oncale arose from a series of events involving a male employee of Sundowner Offshore Services on a Chevron oil platform in the Gulf of Mexico, Joseph Oncale. Three members of the eight-man crew to which the complaining party was assigned

were alleged to have forcibly subjected him to sex-related, humiliating actions. Among these actions were physically assaulting Oncale in a sexual manner in the presence of the rest of the crew. One of his coworkers even threatened to rape him. When Oncale complained of his treatment to supervisory personnel, they took no action. The organization's safety compliance clerk went as far as to tell Oncale that two of the same employees who were harassing Oncale had also "picked [on] him all the time too." Oncale also alleged that the safety compliance clerk even called him a name suggesting homosexuality (*Oncale,* 1998, p. 77). When the complaining party received no support for his complaint he quit, stating that he felt compelled to leave because "I felt that if I didn't leave my job, that I would be raped or forced to have sex" (*Oncale,* 1998, p. 71) .

Oncale then filed a complaint in the United States District Court for the Eastern District of Louisiana against his employer on the grounds that he was discriminated against in his employment because of his sex. The district court relied on a previous ruling by the Fifth Circuit (*Garcia v. Elf Atochem North America,* 1994, pp. 451–452), which followed the established pattern of ruling that same-sex sexual harassment was not actionable under Title VII. Consequently, the district court, following the Fifth Circuit's precedent, held that "Mr. Oncale, a male, has no cause of action under Title VII for harassment by male coworkers." Not surprisingly when Oncale appealed the district court decision to the Fifth Circuit, he lost his appeal (*Oncale,* 1996). Oncale then appealed his case to the United States Supreme Court.

Oncale and Harassment Based on Sexual Preference

It is important to dispel the impression that the *Oncale* ruling gives Title VII protection to employees based on sexual preference. The federal courts have long held that there is no protection on the basis of effeminacy (*Smith v. Liberty Mutual Insurance Co.,* 1978), homosexuality (*Polly v. Houston Lighting & Power Co.,* 1993; *Ulane v. Eastern Airlines,* 1984; *DeSantis v. Pacific Telephone & Telegraph Co.,* 1979), or transsexuality (*Sommens v. Budget Marketing, Inc.,* 1982; *Holloway v. Arthur Andersen & Co.,* 1977; *Voyles v. Ralph K. Davies Medical Center,* 1975). Though the Supreme Court has ruled in *Oncale* that workers are protected from unwelcomed conduct from homosexual supervisors, the Court has not ruled that homosexuals are protected under Title VII from harassment specifically directed toward homosexual conduct. To understand this line of reasoning, assume a homosexual female manager demands sexual favors from a homosexual female subordinate; this would be conduct actionable under Title VII. The homosexual female employee was treated differently because of her sex. The male subordinates could not have been the objects of the homosexual female supervisor because she would not have had any sexual attraction to them. The third proof for establishing actionable sexual harassment has been met. It is the homosexual female worker's *sex* that made her the object of the supervisor's unwelcomed advances, not her sexual preference.

However, if the same homosexual female employee was being verbally and physically harassed by her supervisor or coworkers because of her homosexuality (her sexual preference or orientation), this would not be actionable under Title VII (*Hamner v. St. Vincent Hospital and Health Care Center,* 2000). Thus, Title VII protects workers against discrimination based on sex, not sexual orientation or preference. This does not mean that harassment based on sexual preference may not be actionable under statutes other than Title VII, it merely means that sexual preference is not protected under federal equal employment opportunity law.

At the time of this writing, nine states (California, Connecticut, Hawaii, Massachusetts, Minnesota, New Jersey, Rhode Island, Vermont, and Wisconsin) and the District of Columbia have enacted statutes or ordinances that prohibit harassment of homosexuals and transsexuals [California Government Code, § 12920 (2000); Connecticut General Statues, §§ 4a-81 *et. seq.* (1999); District of Columbia Code, § 1-2501 (1999); Hawaii Revised Statutes, § 378-2 (1999); Massachusetts Annotated Laws, Ch. 151B, § 4 (2000); Minnesota Statutes, § 363.03 (1999); New Jersey Statutes, § 10:5-4 (2000); Rhode Island General Laws, 1956, § 28-57 (1999); Vermont Statutes Annotated, Title 21, § 495 (2000); and Wisconsin Statutes, § 111.31 (1999)]. Hence, in these states, overt discrimination on the basis of sexual preference in certain work settings could be litigated under these laws.

Perhaps the most significant consequence of *Oncale* on organizations is that every time an employee makes a complaint that a coworker of the same-sex is "harassing" him [or her], the employer should feel obligated to conduct a thorough investigation. Under same-sex harassment, the employer would risk liability (as in an opposite-sex sexual harassment complaint) if the complaint was later shown to have substance. Previous federal rulings have held the employer liable for sexual harassment when it has failed to take immediate and appropriate action designed to prevent the harassment from recurring (*Katz v. Dole,* 1983; *Barrett v. Omaha National Bank,* 1984). If heterosexual-on-heterosexual harassment is actionable, then same-sex harassment would be analyzed under the same standard.

Heterosexual-on-Heterosexual Same-Sex Harassment

One issue that is still unresolved is whether heterosexual-on-heterosexual, same-sex sexual harassment is an actionable Title VII complaint. HR professionals and managers are encouraged to wait for developments in this area. Theoretically, one way in which this form of sexual harassment could occur is if a female supervisor has a preference for male subordinates and creates a hostile work environment for female employees with the intention of driving them out of the workplace. The same would be true in instances where male supervisors were purposefully harassing male employees in order to maintain predominantly female workforces. In either instance, the harassment is based on the victim's sex rather than the supervisor's sex.

Equal Opportunity Harassers

One of the more peculiar developments in sexual harassment to emerge after the *Oncale* (1998) decision is the "equal opportunity harasser." What happens in the instance when the alleged harasser is bisexual? The *Oncale* (1998) decision went to great lengths explaining the necessity of demonstrating that one sex is treated differently from the other. What would happen if both sexes are treated equally to unwelcomed sexual behavior?

This very situation was postulated while sexual harassment was still in its formative years. As sexual harassment theory was developing in the late 1970s and early 1980s, several early federal court decisions theorized that a bisexual supervisor could not violate Title VII. This conclusion was drawn because, from a Title VII perspective, a bisexual treats either sex the same, or more accurately, both sexes equally. The insistence upon sexual favors would not constitute sex discrimination because the bisexual's propositions apply to males and females alike (*Barnes v. Costle,* 1977, p. 990 n. 55; *Henson v. City of Dundee,* 1982, p. 905).

This decision had previously overturned a ruling that began to move actionable sexual harassment from the realm of different treatment to that of unwelcomeness of the behavior. In *Doe v. City of Belleville, Ill.*

(1997), the Seventh Circuit concluded that, "sexual harassment cases differ because the discriminatory nature of the charged conduct speaks for itself. The main issue in sexual harassment cases is not whether the employer harassed the employee on the basis of her gender, but whether the claimed harassment affected the terms, conditions, or privileges of the plaintiff's employment, as Title VII uses those words." That decision also offered the observation that Title VII did not require that sexual harassment be motivated by attraction, only that it be "because of sex," that it was often motivated by issues of power and control on the part of the harasser, issues not necessarily related to sexual preference (*Doe v. City of Belleville, Ill.,* 1997, p. 588). *Holman* (2000) clearly refutes this contention by returning sexual harassment to Title VII's prohibition on different treatment based on sex.

What had been theory nearly two decades ago recently became a fact when a husband and wife each filed separate sexual harassment complaints against their supervisor for requesting sexual favors and then retaliating against them when they refused (*Holman v. State of Indiana,* 1998). Using the aforementioned logic, both the District Court and the Appellate Court dismissed the Title VII complaint because "both the husband and wife had been subjected to the *same* treatment" (*Holman v. State of Indiana and Indiana DOT,* 2000). Citing *Oncale* (1998, p. 80), the Court of Appeals for the Seventh Circuit concluded that the prohibitions contained in Title VII only protect members of one sex from being "exposed to disadvantageous conditions of employment to which members of the other sex are not exposed." Based upon this rationale, a bisexual supervisor could not commit actionable sexual harassment. This case squarely focuses HR managers' attention to the realization that it is not merely the behavior that is important, but also whether the behavior is directed towards only members of one sex.

STRICTER LIABILITY FOR HARASSMENT COMMITTED BY SUPERVISORS

In two 1998 rulings, *Faragher v. City of Boca Raton* and *Burlington Industries, Inc. v. Ellerth,* the Supreme Court of the United States imposed a more demanding level of liability on employers for hostile environment sexual harassment when it is committed by supervisory and managerial personnel. As a result of these decisions there is now a more rigid national standard for employer liability arising from hostile work environments. There is now an important distinction based upon the status of the harasser, and that status determines whether the organization is held to a standard of direct liability or indirect liability. The Supreme Court's conclusion is that in instances involving sexual harassment by a supervisor, the appropriate standard to be applied is the more onerous indirect liability—whether quid pro quo or hostile environment (*Faragher v. City of Boca Raton,* 1998; *Burlington Industries, Inc. v. Ellerth,* 1998).

In *Burlington Industries,* a female salesperson in a two-person office was allegedly subjected to constant sexual harassment by her vice president who repeatedly made boorish and offensive remarks and gestures of a sexual nature. On three separate occasions the vice president made comments that could be interpreted as threats to deny the employee tangible job benefits; however, none of these threats were ever carried out. The employee, who was aware of the company's anti-sexual harassment policy, did not inform anyone of the vice president's conduct. On her own she sought and received a right-to-sue letter from the Equal Employment Opportunity Commission (EEOC) and filed suit in federal district court for actionable sexual harassment. The District Court ruled in favor of the company, holding that while the vice president's conduct, as described by Ellerth, was sufficiently severe and pervasive enough to create a hostile work environment, the company should not be liable for the vice president's conduct because it had not known about the conduct. The logic applied was, how could the company take corrective action if it was unaware of behavior that needed correction? The company had an anti-harassment policy which the victim chose not to use.

When appealed to the United States Court of Appeals for the Seventh Circuit, that court reversed the District Court's decision with respect to the employer's liability. The Seventh Circuit concluded that the harassment, since it involved a member of management, contained elements of quid pro quo sexual harassment and thus demanded a stricter level of liability. It was now the employer who appealed the case to the Supreme Court.

In *Faragher,* a female lifeguard for the City of Boca Raton, Florida, filed suit in federal district court alleging that two of her immediate male supervisors had sexually harassed her. Because the two supervisors who harassed her were agents of the city and because their unwelcomed sexual conduct had created a hostile work environment, the city should be held responsible for nominal damages. Like the employee in *Burlington Industries,* this employee failed to initiate action under the organization's anti-harassment policy. The District Court concluded that the harassment was pervasive enough to support an inference that the city knew or should have known of the harassment and was, therefore, liable (*Faragher v. City of Boca Raton,* 1994, p. 1563–1564). This time United States Court of Appeals for the Eleventh Circuit, hearing the case *en banc,* reversed the lower court's ruling against the city on the grounds that the supervisors who harassed Faragher were acting outside the scope of their employment. Furthermore, the city, which had an anti-harassment policy, had no knowledge of the harassment's occurrence and was precluded from taking corrective action (*Faragher v. City of Boca Raton*, 1997, p. 1544). The complaining party appealed this decision to the Supreme Court.

Direct v. Indirect Liability

The Supreme Court heard both of these cases and from them established new requirements for determining employer liability for sexual harassment. Employers are held to a standard of direct liability unless they can carry an affirmative defense, which we will discuss later. In order to fully appreciate the impact of holding employers to a standard of indirect liability, it is best to distinguish it from the less rigorous standard of direct liability. For an employer to be directly liable for the hostile environment sexual harassment committed by one of its employees, the employer either had to know, or should have known, that the harassment was occurring and then failed to take immediate and appropriate corrective action (*Katz v. Dole*, 1983; *Barrett v. Omaha National Bank*, 1984). The employers would be liable for the harassment only had the victims reported the harassment under the anti-harassment policy, and the employers failed to take any action.

In comparison, indirect liability (sometimes aptly referred to as strict liability) holds the employer liable for the wrongful actions of its employees regardless of whether or not the employer knew, or should have known, of the sexual harassment. An employer is likely to be held indirectly responsible for the sexual harassment of one of its supervisory personnel when the following conditions are met (*Faragher v. City of Boca Raton*, 1998, p. 1536):

1. *The unlawful harassment occurred within the scope of the supervisor's employment.* The employer is always liable when the supervisor was instructed or required by the employer to create a sexually hostile environment. In a hostile environment setting, any instruction (explicit or implicit) from the employer to "run off" an employee because of that employee's sex is sufficient to establish this condition. When a supervisor is acting under the instructions of the employer, he or she is acting within the scope of employment. If he or she is harassing an employee in the absence of such instruction, he or she is acting outside of the scope of employment.

2. *The supervisory personnel, though acting outside the scope of their employment, were aided in accomplishing the harassment by the existence of the agency relationship.* Essentially, the supervisor uses his or her authority provided by the organization—the authority specifically delegated to that position to make employment decisions—to pressure the employee to submit to the harassment (*Sparks v. Pilot Freight Carriers, Inc.*, 1989, pp. 1559–1560). For example, the supervisor may threaten the employee with termination, no raises, or no promotion if she (or he) refuses his advances.

In quid pro quo harassment, holding the employer to the stricter liability (indirect liability) for the actions of its supervisory personnel has long been the practice in most of the federal circuits. Since the supervisor used his (or her) actual authority to control the employee's benefits to extort sexual favors from the employee, the supervisor's harassment was facilitated by the employer's delegation of such authority (*Miller v. Bank of America*, 1979).

The legal problem posed by the application of indirect liability to hostile environment claims is that, technically, employers will always be punished for quid pro quo harassment regardless of whether or not any tangible job benefits are affected. Thus, the distinction between the two forms of harassment would be erased. The practical problem for employers is that there is little that they can do to insulate themselves from liability once a complaint has been made involving managerial personnel. Currently, under direct liability, employers may avoid liability by taking immediate and appropriate corrective action. Indirect liability would make this pointless, or at least create a greater incentive to cover up, rather than rectify, the sexual harassment incident.

The Affirmative Defense

Ostensibly, an employer is indirectly liable for all actionable discrimination caused by a supervisor. Had the Supreme Court left its decision at this point, employers would be held strictly liable for the action of supervisors, and nothing the employer could do would enable him or her to avoid the legal consequences. However, the Supreme Court added an affirmative defense to avoid this particular situation, and to encourage sensible implementation of Title VII, by giving employers an incentive to prevent and eliminate harassment and by requiring employees to take advantage of the preventive or remedial action (*Faragher*, 1998, p. 732). As a consequence, the Supreme Court will permit the employer to escape liability provided that two criteria are first satisfied: (1) the employer exercised reasonable care to prevent and promptly correct any sexually harassing behavior, and (2) the complaining party unreasonably failed to take advantage of any preventive or corrective opportunities provided by the employer or to otherwise avoid harm (*Burlington Industries*, 1998, p. 765; *Faragher*, 1998. p. 780).

In order to demonstrate that the employer exercised *reasonable care to prevent* sexual harassment, it is absolutely essential that the employer has a sexual harassment policy and has disseminated it to all employees. The Supreme Court's guidance on this matter is:

While proof that an employer had promulgated an anti-harassment policy with complaint procedure is not necessary in every instance as a matter of law, the need for a stated policy suitable to employment circumstances may appropriately be addressed in any case when litigating the first element of the defense. (*Burlington Industries*, 1998, p. 765)

As a matter of practicality, organizations without sexual harassment policies will find themselves hard-pressed to sustain the first criterion. Employers should further note that, at a minimum, these policies should contain the following (Robinson, Franklin, & Frink, 1993):

- A statement that sexual harassment will not be tolerated.
- A definition of sexual harassment.
- Examples of conduct and behavior that could constitute sexual harassment, including both quid pro quo and hostile environment forms.
- A choice of channels for reporting sexual harassment. This provides the employee an option if one of the company officials in the complaint procedure is the alleged harasser or has close ties to the harasser.
- Information on how the organization will handle the complaint to include conducting a thorough investigation and maintaining confidentiality.
- A statement that the organization will take appropriate corrective action to remedy any violation of the policy

Furthermore, no policy by itself will insulate an employer (Robinson et al., 1993). All members of the organization must be aware of the policy's complaint procedures; to be effective, it must be disseminated. It is advisable to create and maintain some documentation that each employee has been familiarized with the policy and how (and where) to file a complaint. A document attesting to this fact would go a long way in establishing that the employer was earnest in preventing sexual harassment and that the employee had been made fully aware of internal means of resolving misconduct. Because these new standards of liability affect only supervisory personnel, it is recommended that these personnel be trained in their obligations under company policies regarding sexual harassment. A record of supervisory training should be maintained, as should documention that rank-and-file employees were made aware of anti-harassment policies. Again, this would provide evidence that the employer was exercising reasonable care in preventing sexual harassment.

The second criterion, the complaining party *unreasonably failed* to avail herself (or himself) of the company's preventive or corrective policies, appears to address the issue of employer notification. The basic premise is that a victim has a duty "to use such means as are reasonable under the circumstances to avoid or minimize the damages"(*Ford Motor Co. v. EEOC,* 1982, p. 231, n 15) that result from violations of Title VII. The dilemma is determining when a complaining party has *unreasonable failure* to use the company's anti-harassment complaint procedure. The problem with federal courts is that terms such as "reasonable" and "unreasonable" are sufficiently flexible to allow for broad interpretation in subsequent litigation. It is hoped, though, that by providing evidence that the company had a viable complaint/notification procedure, the alleged victim was aware of the means to report the harassment and failure to utilize this mechanism was done strictly at the victim's own volition. This would be particularly true if the employer's policy made provision for filing a complaint without exposing the victim to undue risk and had a clearly delineated mechanism for investigating and resolving such complaints.

Any failure on the part of the victim to use these procedures would go a long way in satisfying the second criterion. The Supreme Court has placed a greater burden on the complaining party to notify the employer of alleged sexual harassment when the employer has provided a viable anti-harassment mechanism. This occurred in *Slattery v. HCA Wesley Rehabilitation Hosp., Inc.* (2000) when a Federal District Court concluded that "the hospital ha[d] a well-defined anti-harassment policy and conflict resolution procedure; that the policy commits the hospital to a workplace free of harassment; that the policy provides a comprehensive conflict resolution procedure; and that the policy encourages prompt reporting of all workplace complaints or concerns to the employee's supervisor or the human resources department" (*Slattery,* 2000, pp. 1229–1230). In this instance, the hospital was able to meet the affirmative defense because it had a formal policy, the policy was disseminated, and the employee failed to avail herself of the policy.

As a final word on the affirmative defense, the reader is cautioned that it applies exclusively to hostile environment sexual harassment attributed to supervisors (*Burlington Industries,* 1998, p. 761). The affirmative defense cannot be applied in quid pro quo sexual harassment (*Faragher,* 1998, p. 808). In instances where supervisory personnel threatened the employee with loss (or gain) of tangible job benefits, no affirmative defense is permitted to extenuate the employer's liability.

Ramifications

The first, and obvious, result of the *Faragher* and *Burlington Industries* decisions will likely be increased sexual harassment litigation. Increasing the risk of being found liable in supervisor-initiated hostile work environments will only serve to fuel the already rapidly rising litigation in this area. Just as the *Meritor* decision sparked an increase in hostile environment litigation, *Faragher* and *Burlington Industries* may be expected to do the same.

Additionally, the regulatory costs to businesses will increase as organizational resources are diverted from more productive uses to litigation deterrence. Costs will be experienced in increased record keeping as well as in increased training expenses. An increase in human resources staffs, especially for larger organizations, can be anticipated as more compliance specialists and trainers are added. Further, by holding employers to a stricter standard of liability, there is now a very real incentive for increased employee monitoring and surveillance in the workplace. This can be accomplished by narrower spans of control or through the increased use of technology.

An unfortunate consequence of the two rulings may be a less-than-evenhanded treatment of supervisors accused of hostile environment. An incentive exists to rapidly, and perhaps ruthlessly, eradicate the source of harassment. Thus the emphasis is on strict policies and prompt action, not due process. As a result, procedural justice may outweigh distributive justice.

Employers are encouraged to conduct thorough investigations before imposing disciplinary action. Otherwise, less scrupulous employees may use the policy as a means of removing supervisory personnel that they abhor.

Mitigating Liability for Quid Pro Quo Harassment

As mentioned earlier, *Faragher* and *Burlington Industries* provide for an affirmative defense only in instances of hostile environment sexual harassment. There are no such provisions when the sexual harassment is of the quid pro quo type. The case of *Kolstad v. American Dental Association* (1999) may offer some relief to an employer for imputing liability in the punitive damages context. Though not addressing sexual harassment, *Kolstad* did address the circumstance in which punitive damages may be awarded under Title VII for intentional discrimination. Sexual harassment is an intentional Title VII violation subject to punitive and compensatory damages (see Table 3-2).

As the *Kolstad* Court noted, "Holding employers liable for punitive damages when they engage in good faith efforts to comply with Title VII, however, is in some tension with the very principles underlying common law limitations on vicarious liability for punitive damages—that it is improper ordinarily to award punitive damages against one who himself is personally innocent and therefore liable only vicariously" (*Kolstad,*

TABLE 3-2 Maximum Awards for Compensatory and Punitive Damages	
Size of Employer's Workforce	*Maximum Combined Punitive and Compensatory Damages per Complaining Party*
15–200	$50,000
201–300	$100,000
301–500	$200,000
>500	$300,000

Source: 29 U.S.C. §1981a.

1999, p. 544). Where an employer has undertaken a good faith effort to comply with Title VII, the Supreme Court had previously concluded that "the institution of a written sexual harassment policy goes a long way toward dispelling any claim about an employer's 'reckless' or 'malicious' state of mind" (*Harris*, 1993, pp. 983–984).

With regard to sexual harassment, " . . . Title VII is designed to encourage the creation of anti-harassment policies and effective grievance mechanisms" (*Burlington Industries*, 1998, p. 764). The Court has clearly indicated that the purpose underlying Title VII is to encourage employers to adopt antidiscrimination policies and educate their personnel on their Title VII responsibilities. However, if employers were held liable in every instance when a supervisor callously disregarded their desires and policies, employers would have little incentive to implement such policies. Whether or not an organization had a policy and a procedure for enforcing it the outcome would be the same—strict liability. Where is the reward for achieving Title VII's purposes when conscientious employers are punished along with negligent ones? Clearly, this is counter to the Court's interpretation of Title VII's intent.

In *Kolstad*, the Supreme Court required the complaining party to meet four standards. First, the complaining party must show the employer acted with malice or reckless indifference to his or her Title VII rights (*Kolstad*, 1999, p. 536). This would be demonstrated by showing that the employer discriminated against the employee with the knowledge that he or she might be violating federal law (*EEOC v. Wal-Mart Stores, Inc.*, 1999, p. 12). Second, the complaining party must show the supervisor representing the employer committed the violation. Third, the complaining party must show the supervisor was working within the scope of his or

her employment. Finally, the complaining party must show the supervisor's action was not contrary to the employer's good faith efforts to comply with Title VII (*Kolstad*, 1999, p. 544).

Under *Kolstad*, an employer may not be able to avoid all liability for quid pro quo sexual harassment of a superior, but it may avoid punitive liability. Previously, the Supreme Court had concluded that it may be necessary to determine whether an employer had been making good faith efforts to enforce an antidiscrimination policy before determining damages (*EEOC v. Wal-Mart*, 1999). Though the employer may be vicariously liable for the harassment of an employee serving in a managerial capacity, the employer's good faith efforts may mitigate the damages.

CONCLUSION

There have been substantial changes in the interpretation of sexual harassment since the beginning of the last decade. The most notable change, in terms of human resources management costs, involves stricter liability standards for harassment committed by managerial personnel. Federal court rulings have now made it absolutely essential that organizations develop viable anti-harassment policies. No affirmative defense can be mounted in the absence of such policies.

Although anti-harassment policies are a necessary condition for establishing an employer's good faith effort to maintain a harassment-free workplace, they are not sufficient to do so by themselves. For employers to clearly demonstrate their good faith efforts, they must disseminate anti-harassment policies to employees and consistently enforce such policies. Most importantly, the dissemination and enforcement must be documented. In litigation, it is not so much what you have done as much as it is what you can prove you have done. This means that more emphasis will be placed on documenting that employees were aware of organizational policies and reporting procedures. It also means better documentation of in-house investigations.

Finally, organizations must take all allegations of sexual harassment seriously. Failure to investigate a complaint that later proves to have merit would impair the employer's affirmative defense. This especially may be true of same-sex allegations, which can be expected to increase and will have to be handled in the same serious manner as opposite-sex harassment complaints. Due to the development of case law in the late 1990s, employers may find themselves dealing with types of sexual harassment complaints they have never dealt with before. ∎

REFERENCES

Barnes v. Costle, 561 F.2d 983 (D.C. Cir. 1977).

Barrett v. Omaha National Bank, 726 F.2d 424 (8th Cir. 1984).

Blout v. Sterling Healthcare Group, Inc., 934 F.Supp. 1365 (S.D. Fla. 1996).

Bourque v. Powell Electrical Manufacturing, 617 F.2d 61 (5th Cir. 1980).

Bundy v. Jackson, 641 F.2d 934 (D.C. Cir. 1981).

Burlington Industries, Inc. v. Ellerth, 524 U.S. 742 (1998).

Butler v. Ysleta Independent School Dist., 161 F.3d 263 (5th Cir. 1998).

California Government Code, § 12920 (2000).

Capaci v. Katz Besthoff, 1976 U.S. Dist. LEXIS 13827 (E.D.La. 1976).

Civil Rights Act of 1964, 42 U.S.C. § 2000e *et. seq.* (2000).

Connecticut General Statues, §§ 4a-81 *et. seq.* (1999).

Corne v. Baush and Lomb, Inc., 390 F.Supp. 161 (D.Ariz. 1975).

Cronin v. United Service Stations, 809 F.Supp. (M.D.Ala. 1992).

DeAngelis v. El Paso Municipal Police Officer's Ass'n, 51 F.3d 591 (5th Cir. 1995).

DeSantis v. Pacific Telephone & Telegraph Co., 608 F.2d 327 (9th Cir. 1979).

Doe v. City of Belleville, Ill., 119 F.3d 563 (7th Cir. 1997).

District of Columbia Code, § 1-2501 (1999).

EEOC v. Sage Realty Corp., 507 F.Supp. 599 (S.D.N.Y. 1981).

EEOC v. Wal-Mart Stores, Inc., 1999 U.S. App. LEXIS 29858 (November 15, 1999).

Faragher v. City of Boca Raton, 864 F.Supp 1552 (S.D.Fla. 1994).

Faragher v. City of Boca Raton, 111 F.3d 1530 (11th Cir. 1997).

Faragher v. City of Boca Raton, 524 U.S. 775 (1998).

Ford Motor Co. v. EEOC, 458 U.S. 219 (1982).

Garcia v. Elf Atochem North America, 28 F.3d 446 (5th Cir. 1994).

Giddens v. Shell Oil Co., 12 F.3d 208 (5th Cir. 1993) (unpublished).

Hamner v. St. Vincent Hosp. & Health Care Ctr., Inc., 224 F.3d 701 (7th Cir. 2000).

Hardin v. Carlson, 1978 U.S. Dist. LEXIS (S.D.N.Y. 1978).

Harris v. Forklift Systems, Inc., 510 U.S. 17 (1993).

Hawaii Revised Statutes § 378-2 (1999).

Heelan v. Johns-Manville Corp., 451 F.Supp. 1382 (D.Colo. 1978).

Henson v. City of Dundee, 682 F.2d 897 (11th Cir. 1982).

Holman v. State of Indiana, 24 F.Supp. 909 (N.D. In. 1998).

Holman v. State of Indiana and Indiana DOT, 211 F.3d 399 (7th Cir. 2000).

Holloway v. Arthur Andersen & Co., 566 F.2d 659 (9th Cir. 1977).

Jones v. Flagship International, 793 F.2d 714 (5th Cir. 1986).

Joyner v. AAA Cooper Transportation, 597 F.Supp. 537 (M.D. Ala. 1983).

Katz v. Dole, 709 F.2d 251 (4th Cir. 1983).

Kolstad v. American Dental Association, 527 U.S. 526 (1999).

Massachusetts Annotated Laws, Ch. 151B, § 4 (2000).

McWilliams v. Fairfax County Board of Supervisors, 72 F.3d 1191 (4th Cir. 1996).

Meritor Savings Bank FSB v. Vinson, 477 U.S. 57 (1986).

Miller v. Bank of America, 418 F.Supp. 233 (N.D.Cal. 1976) rev'd 600 F.2d 211 (9th Cir. 1979).

Minnesota Statutes, § 363.03 (1999).

Moylan v. Maries County, 792 F.2d 746 (8th Cir. 1986).

Mumford v. James T. Barnes & Co., 441 F.Supp. 459 (E.D.Mich. 1977).

Nash v. Electrospace Systems, Inc., 9 F.3d 401 (5th Cir. 1993).

New Jersey Statutes, § 10:5-4 (2000).

Oncale v. Sundowners Offshore Services, Inc., 83 F.3d 118 (5th Cir. 1996).

Oncale v. Sundowners Offshore Services, Inc., 523 U.S. 75 (1998).

Phillips v. Smalley Maintenance Service, 711 F.2d 1524 (11th Cir. 1983).

Polly v. Houston Lighting & Power Co., 825 F.Supp 135 (S.D. Tex. 1993).

Priest v. Rotary, 634 F. Supp. 571 (N.D.Cal. 1986).

Rhode Island General Laws, 1956, § 28-57 (1999).

Robinson, R. K., Franklin, G. M., & Frink, R. L. (1993). Sexual harassment at work: Issues and answers for health care administrators. *Hospital & Health Services Administration*, 38 (2), 167–180.

Rogers v. EEOC, 454 F.2d 234 (5th Cir. 1971), *cert. denial* 406 U.S. 957 (1972).

Slattery v. HCA Wesley Rehabilitation Hosp., Inc., 83 F.Supp. 2d 1224 (D. Kan. 2000).

Smith v. Liberty Mutual Insurance Co., 569 F.2d 325 (5th Cir. 1978).

Sommens v. Budget Marketing, Inc., 667 F.2d 748 (8th Cir. 1982).

Sparks v. Pilot Freight Carriers, Inc., 830 F.2d 1554 (11th Cir. 1989).

Tomkins v. Public Serv. Elec. & Gas Co., 568 F.2d 1044 (3d Cir. 1977).

Trujillo v. University of Colo. Health Sciences Ctr., 157 F.3d 1211 (10th Cir. 1998).

Ulane v. Eastern Airlines, 742 F.2d 1081 (7th Cir. 1984), *cert. denied* 471 U.S. 1017 (1985).

U.S. Equal Employment Opportunity Commission (2000). *Guidelines on Sex Discrimination.* 29 C.F.R. § 1604.11.

U.S. Equal Employment Opportunity Commission (2001). Sexual Harassment Changes. Available online at www.eeoc.gov/stats/harass.html.

Vermont Statutes Annotated, Title 21, § 495 (2000).

Voyles v. Ralph K. Davies Medical Center, 403 F.Supp 456 (N.D. Cal. 1975), *aff'd mem.* 570 F.2d 354 (9th Cir. 1978).

Wallace v. Texas Tech Univ., 80 F.3d 1042 (5th Cir. 1996).

Williams v. Saxbe, 413 F.Supp. 654 (1976).

Wisconsin Statutes, § 111.31 (1999).

Wright v. Methodist Youth Services, Inc., 511. F. Supp 307 (N.D. Ill. 1981).

Young v. Southwestern Savings and Loan Assoc., 509 F.2d 140, 144 (5th Cir. 1975).

CHAPTER

4

THE LABOR MARKET AND THE CHANGING WORKFORCE

The workforce consists of all people who are working, looking for work, or serving in the armed forces. The number of individuals in the workforce has grown dramatically over the last few decades. This increase can be attributed to the growing numbers of women and minority group members who have recently been incorporated into the workforce. The workforce will continue to expand with higher than average growth in the participation rates for the African-American, Hispanic, and Asian populations. Further, workers are both living and working longer. The U.S. workforce is aging. A number of organizations (e.g., McDonald's, Wal-Mart) have engaged in hiring seniors. This is both a sensible and a socially responsible action.

As the population becomes more diverse, organizations are becoming more interested in developing a workforce that more accurately mirrors the population. Diversity is an asset. Inclusive hiring strategies will facilitate the expansion of a quality workforce. During the 1970s and 1980s, affirmative action was seen as the way to include all individuals in the workforce. The 1990s and 2000s have seen the realization that diversity is a valued workforce trait. Organizations are convinced that diversity will increase the knowledge, creativity, innovativeness, and competency base of the workforce.

The changing workforce has dictated additional emphasis in the strategies of human resources programs. Selection of a workforce has always been driven by the choice of those who best fit in with organizational objectives. The most effective strategy with our evolving workforce is to enlist the most competent and diverse population in order to increase coverage of potential and ideas. This shift toward diversity will necessitate greater sensitivity on the part of managers. The results of increasing diversity have thus far been quite positive. We predict that these positive outcomes will only increase.

The article by Bhawuk, Podsiadlowski, Graf, and Triandis emphasizes that organizations must continue to search for ways of managing the new workplace. Organizations need to meet the challenge of managing diversity, not just protect themselves from a legal standpoint. These differences, according to the authors, provide opportunities, not problems. The other articles in this section confront different workforce issues. Allen and Renn look at the issue of telecommuting. Telecommuting surfaces a much different set of problems for human resources managers. The authors recommend strategies for managing those workers who work in this fashion. Wheeler, Buckley, and Halbesleben address an area of the workforce that has been misunderstood by many. Are contingent workers a plus or a minus for an organization? The answer is not straightforward but the issue is not going away. In fact, the use of contingent workers promises to increase in the future.

READINGS

CORPORATE STRATEGIES FOR MANAGING DIVERSITY IN THE GLOBAL WORKPLACE

Dharm P. S. Bhawuk, Astrid Podsiadlowski, Jennifer Graf, and Harry C. Triandis

Diversity is a state of heterogeneity in societies and organizations; that is, people are different from each other with respect to many demographic variables as well as cultural heritage. For example, Japan, Korea, and Germany are homogeneous societies where people speak one language, are largely descendents of one stock of people, and eat similar food. On the other hand, Singapore, India, and the United States are diverse societies where people speak many languages, are descendents of more than one stock of people, and eat different indigenous foods. With globalization of business and extensive growth of international travel, diversity has become an important subject for business and human resources management.

Researchers and practitioners use the label of diversity to cover a gamut of cultural and demographic differences that people bring to the workplace (Bhawuk, 2000; Jackson & Alvarez, 1992). Although the notion of diversity has gained currency with both academics and practitioners, there is not a commonly accepted definition. Some people see the concept of diversity as referring to any group of people other than white males. Others use diversity to indicate people of color. Still others define diversity as demographic characteristics such as age, gender, years of education, ethnicity, national origin, work status, and so forth. The underlying theme in all these definitions is difference between individuals or groups of people.

Bhawuk (2000) proposed that differences can be classified as objective and verifiable (e.g., race, gender, age, disability, and some aspects of profession and economy-based lifestyle), and subjective and subtle (e.g., attitudes, beliefs, values, and some aspects of profession and economy-based lifestyle). He proposed that jobs and professions have both objective (engineers and accountants perform different tasks) and subjective (engineers and accountants have a different conceptualization of how organizations work or should work) differences. For example, Heller (1969) found that American managers in finance and accounting were more autocratic than those in purchasing and sales, who were in turn more autocratic than those in personnel and less specialized jobs. This finding lends support to the idea that professions have both objective and subjective differences. Similarly, an economy-based lifestyle also offers objective (e.g., where people live, work, take vacation, and so forth) and subjective (e.g., conceptualization of money as frivolous versus frugal spending, conceptualization of education as public versus private schools, and so forth) differences.

We examine the issues that managers face today in these diverse workplaces. We begin by tracing the changes taking place globally that are leading to an increase in diversity in the society and the workplace. We then present a conceptual framework for understanding diversity by examining the meaning of culture, race, ethnicity, and nationality. We also examine the ways in which cultural differences can be operationalized, and discuss the consequences of intercultural interactions. We conclude this section by examining two opposite philosophies of dealing with diversities, the melting pot and multiculturalism. In the next section, we examine some of the major differences between the so-called mainstream and other ethnic groups such as Asian-, African-, Hispanic-Americans. Finally, we discuss the reasons U.S. corporations are concerned with diversity, and the emerging strategies that are adopted by some of them.

GLOBAL CHANGES LEADING TO DIVERSITY

The workplace worldwide is becoming increasingly more diverse. With women entering the workplace in droves, the workplace is becoming less masculine. Women made up 31 and 11 percent of the workforce in the United States and Japan, respectively, in 1955, whereas in 2000 they represented 66 and 41 percent, respectively (Fullerton, 2001; Hunter, 1993; "Human Rights," 2000). The United Nations Population Commission also considers the feminization of labor migration, particularly the Asian labor migration, a notable trend. According to the Commission, with life expectancy increasing, there is "global graying." The aging population is changing the human social composition in that while we might have had ten workers for one retired person in the past, we are likely to have two workers per retiree in the future. Also, organizations are forced to hire older people due to the graying population, and have to deal with the special needs of these employees. For example, Italy's current population of 57 million is projected to decline to 41 million in 50 years, during which time the population of people over 65 would rise from 18 to 35 percent. Similar patterns exist in other industrialized countries such as Spain and Germany. Finally, with increasing globalization and migration, the workplace is becoming more culturally heterogeneous both in developing and developed countries.

In economically developed countries, the increase in diversity in the workplace is particularly noteworthy. The reasons are many. Perhaps the most important reason is that the populations in industrialized countries are reaching a plateau, whereas populations in developing countries are growing rather rapidly, leading to a migration of people from developing to developed economies. For example, the population growth in Japan, Italy, France, the United Kingdom, and Germany has been small, 2 to 4 percent between 1991 and 2001, whereas the population growth in China, Brazil, Mexico, Indonesia, and India in the same period has been 9 to 16 percent. Thus there is a natural tendency for migration from the developing to the developed countries. The United States provides a strong case of this pattern, especially with its open national immigration policy. It is interesting to note that though the natural growth in U.S. population has been low, in the 1990s the population growth in the United States was 9 percent.

The world's poorest countries are the least equipped to handle the economic, nutritional, housing, and environmental needs of their growing populations. This population pressure will bring continued urban growth, high rates of laborforce growth, degradation of land and water resources, increased deforestation, scarcity of food, and increased rates of infectious diseases. Desjarles, Elsberg, Good, and Kleinman (1995) believe that such tainted living conditions may force the "environmental" impoverished into more prosperous regions. The United Nations expects 20 percent of the world population to become environmental refugees by the year

2020 (George, 1993). This is another reason to expect diversity globally.

There are already 150 million people living outside their home countries. Thus migration from developing to industrialized countries is likely to accelerate. This migration will be driven by the need of the migrants to improve their standard of living, and the requirements of the people of industrialized countries to obtain services that only migrants are willing to provide ("A Refugee," 2001; George, 1993). In addition, professionals from industrialized countries will increasingly interact with the workers of developing countries because of the globalization of world business. E-commerce, the Internet, telecommunications, mass transportation, and interconnected international economies provide a global context for daily human life. For example, Germany has loosened its governmental regulations to pass out work permits for engineers from countries such as India and Indonesia.

Refugees constitute a significant part of migration, and according to the United Nations High Commissioner for Refugees, there were 12 million refugees in December 1999 who had left their native country for other destinations, 1.2 million asylum seekers, and 2.5 million refugees who returned home ("A Refugee," 2001). There are 1 million refugees from Myanmar, formerly Burma, who are taking shelter in Thailand. Similarly, in the 1970s, and 1980s, about 1.3 million boat people migrated from Vietnam to the United States. According to the United Nations refugee convention, people who leave their homeland for a "well-founded fear of being persecuted for reasons of race, religion, nationality, membership in a particular social group or political opinion" are granted asylum by countries they visit. Under the UN convention such people are protected from being forced back to their home country (i.e., "refoulement"). Refugees often enter the lower end of social structure, and are more amenable to assimilate. However, their as-

similation still poses many challenges to organizations in particular and societies in general.

Refugees are not the only people who migrate. There is also an increase in the number of professionals migrating from developing to developed countries. The shortage of computer programmers and other information technology professionals in recent years has forced the United States, Germany, Japan, and other industrialized countries to further open their doors to immigrants from all over the world. For example, the need to solve the Y2K problem alone saw hundreds of thousands of Indian software experts move to different countries. Usually these professionals enter the middle or upper middle class segment of society and are likely to preserve their native culture, creating a need for everybody to deal with cultural differences.

The design-production-distribution processes of the twenty-first century will involve extreme diversity. For example, product design may occur in Germany, financing may be obtained from Japan, execution of the plans might be directed from the United States, clerical work performed in Nepal, manufacturing work done in China, and the distribution may include a universalist salesforce. The interfaces among those activities will require highly diverse workplaces. In developed countries the shift from manufacturing to service and information economies will also require that the salesforce be as diverse as the populations of customers. These global trends have significant implications for organizations.

For organizations, globalization means not only having subsidiaries in many countries, but also establishing many strategic alliances through transnational mergers and acquisitions. Coordination and cooperation between organizations across different cultures is becoming more routine. People with diverse cultural backgrounds are required to work together and cooperate on a personal level. Project teams, work groups, departments, and top management teams have heterogeneous compositions. Cross-cultural interactions are increasing within and across organizations. Multinational teamwork is growing in significance in research and development teams. Experts in information technology are recruited worldwide. Companies have started programs to attract the most qualified people in other countries for local hiring.

A CONCEPTUAL FRAMEWORK FOR UNDERSTANDING DIVERSITY

To understand issues resulting from diversity in the workplace, it is important to understand how culture shapes our social behavior. To facilitate this, we present a cultural framework for understanding diversity. Culture is to society what memory is to individuals (Kluckhohn, 1954). It consists of ways of perceiving, thinking, and deciding that have worked in the past and have become institutionalized in standard operating procedures, customs, scripts, and unstated assumptions that guide behavior. Culture consists of both objective (tools, roads) and subjective (concepts, beliefs, attitudes, norms, roles, and values) elements (Triandis, 1972). Culture is adaptive and functional, and allows a group of people who speak the same language to develop shared beliefs, attitudes, norms, roles, and values through transmission from generation to generation. Members of a culture have a common language so as to communicate the ideas that are later shared, and live during the same time period in areas that are geographically close enough to make communication possible. Thus, *language, time, and place* are three criteria that can be used to identify a culture (Triandis, 1994). Moynihan, (1993, p. 72) estimated that there are about 10,000 cultures and 6,170 distinct languages in the world. Given that there are fewer than 200 members of the United Nations, clearly, most nations are multicultural.

Having defined culture, it is easier to define race, ethnicity, and nationality. Race is not a scientific category, but a social one. People respond differently to members of the same physical type; that is, race such as caucasians, negroids, or mongoloids. People of the same descent (i.e., descending from particular ancestors) or lineage are said to have the same ethnicity (Brislin, 1988). Therefore, there are many ethnic groups within each race. Nationality refers to affiliation to a nation state, and in terms of culture, race, and ethnicity often means little, because in most countries there are people of many races and ethnic backgrounds. Race, ethnicity, living in the same neighborhood, same gender, age, and so on provide opportunities to develop similar subjective cultures (e.g., concepts, beliefs, attitudes, norms, roles, and values), reflected in similar attitudes and the like.

Operationalizing Culture

Cultures differ among themselves along three dimensions: complexity versus simplicity, tightness versus looseness, and hierarchy versus equality (Triandis, 1994). These constructs are discussed first, and then a summary dimension—individualism and collectivism—that is useful in understanding cultural differences is described.

Complexity Versus Simplicity The more there is role differentiation, stratification, and affluence in a culture, the more complex that culture is. Information societies are very complex, and the big seven economies of the world provide examples of complex societies. In complex societies social behavior is based on exchanges (e.g., on profit and loss). Behavior in public settings has many of these attributes. The market provides a good metaphor of such relationships.

Folk societies (e.g., nomadic tribes, hunters and gatherers) are usually less complex in social organization, less economically developed, and are characterized by simplicity. Every member of the society knows most other members, and much behavior occurs in private settings. The family is the best metaphor of such relationships.

Tightness Versus Looseness   The more homogeneous and isolated the culture is, the more agreement there is about the elements of subjective culture (e.g., clarity of norms), and thus the more definitively the norms can be imposed on members. The behavior of members of such cultures is tightly regulated. Even small deviations from "proper" behavior are punished. For example, Japan is a tight culture, and if one arrives even two minutes late for an appointment, there will be negative consequences.

In cultures that have evolved at the confluence of two or more unique cultures, or those that have a more heterogeneous population, norms are imposed only if there is a major deviation from accepted behavior patterns. These cultures show looseness (as opposed to tightness). Thailand and the United States are examples of such cultures. In Thailand, an employee may simply walk away from a job without explanation and not be punished.

Hierarchy Versus Equality   The extent to which people behave differently toward those at the top and bottom of the social structure, relative to the way they behave toward people at their own level, indicates the presence of hierarchy. Cultures vary on this dimension. Some societies are more hierarchical than others; for example, in Japan, one cannot speak correctly without knowing the relative rank of the other person and oneself. In other societies, such as Iceland and Israel, status differences are downplayed and equality is stressed. These cultures are less hierarchical.

A Summary Dimension   Collectivism and individualism are contrasts that summarize the dimensions. Maximum collectivism

occurs in simple, family-type relationships, in tight cultures, and where there is considerable emphasis on hierarchy. Maximum individualism occurs in complex societies that have market-type relationships, are loose, and favor equality.

Because a particular culture can be anywhere on the three basic dimensions, the final attributes of a culture involve some mixture of these dimensions. For example, Japan is complex, tight, and hierarchical. Thus it is somewhat collectivist, but not extremely. Many folk societies are simple, tight, and equal. That makes them very collectivist. But there are folk societies with simple, tight, and hierarchical profiles. The United States is complex (with emphasis on public relations), loose, and moderate in hierarchy. Thus collectivism and individualism are complex dimensions, which can be analyzed into the three basic dimensions of complexity, tightness, and hierarchies.

In collectivist cultures, the self is defined as an aspect of the collective (e.g., the family, caste, tribe, work group, village, or country). Each culture has its own profile of the relative importance of each collective. In individualistic cultures, the self is independent of groups (Bhawuk, 2001; Markus & Kitayama, 1991). In collectivist cultures people pursue their in-group goals, are norm driven, and are relational in their social exchanges, whereas in individualist cultures people pursue their self goals; are attitude, value, and belief driven; and are rational in their social exchanges (Bhawuk, 2001; Triandis, 1995).

Consequences of Intercultural Interactions

Each culture emerges in its own ecology, in ways that favor adjustment to that ecology (Berry, 1967, 1976). The experiences that people have in particular ecologies result in unique ways of perceiving their social environment (Triandis, 1972). Their level of adaptation (Helson, 1964) in making judgments depends on their experiences. For example, if a person has experienced wealth, that person has a level of adaptation concerning compensation that is much higher than a person who has experienced poverty.

When cultures come in contact with one another, the location of the cultures on the four dimensions is a factor that determines, in part, the cultural distance between them. Other barriers to good relationships are differences in economic status, language, and the past history of intergroup conflict. The more different the cultures are on these dimensions, the more distant they are from each other.

Most humans are ethnocentric; that is, they judge other cultures as good to the extent they are similar to their own culture. That is inevitable, because we all grow up in specific cultures and view those cultures as providing the only "correct" answers to the problems of existence (Triandis, 1994). As we encounter other cultures, we may become less ethnocentric, but it is only if we reject our own culture that we can become non-ethnocentric, and that is relatively rare.

When people from different cultures work together, their ethnocentrism will result in misunderstandings and low levels of interpersonal attraction. The greater the cultural distance, the lower may be the rewards experienced from working together. If the behavior of others in the workplace does not make sense, because people do not make sufficiently similar attributions, one experiences a loss of control. Such loss of control results in depression (Langer, 1983), culture shock (Oberg, 1960), and dislike of the other culture's members.

People from cultures that are very distant face more difficulty interacting with and adjusting to each other, and are more likely to experience communication breakdowns when they come in contact (Triandis, Kurowski, & Gelfand, 1994). However, people from cultures with smaller cultural distance may also be confronted with major

communication problems, as they do not expect each other to have different basic assumptions and they may be even less aware of their own and the others' cultural backgrounds. Many studies have shown that Germans experienced more misunderstandings working with Americans than working with Japanese, despite the perceived similarities between the two "Western cultures" and the perceived differences between the eastern and western cultures in working styles, attitudes, and so forth (Friday, 1989; Schroll-Machl, 1996).

The more intergroup interactions (i.e., emphasizing their membership in groups), the more cultural differences are emphasized. If they become interpersonal (i.e., paying attention only to the personal attributes of the other and ignoring the cultural aspects of the other's behavior) it is possible to like the member in spite of the cultural distance (Tajfel, 1982). However, there are some necessary conditions: Contact has to lead to the perception of similarity. This can be achieved if there is no history of conflict between the two cultures, the person knows enough about the other culture to anticipate the culturally determined behaviors of the other person, the person knows the other's language, they have common friends, and they have common superordinate goals (Triandis et al., 1994).

If these conditions do not exist, there is usually considerable social distance, which increases the more insecure and anxious the perceiver is (Triandis & Triandis, 1960). If there is conflict, stereotyping becomes very negative (Avigdor, 1953) and interpersonal attraction is low or negative. However, if these conditions do exist there can be attraction toward the other, little negative stereotyping, and little social distance. We think that, despite the history of conflict between certain groups, other factors such as common organizational goals, having common friends, learning the other's language, spending time together, interacting frequently, and so forth can lead to the perception of similarity in the workplace, and improve the effectiveness of interpersonal interactions.

Two Conflicting Philosophies

Two approaches have been proposed to deal with diversity on the societal level. First, there is the melting pot conception (Zangwill, 1914), which argues that the best country has a single homogeneous culture. People of different cultures are encouraged to surrender their differences in favor of a "mainstream" language, norm, work ethic, and so forth (i.e., one culture). The United States is an example of the melting pot philosophy in which people of different European descent adopted English as their language. Since the United States was a British colony, English, the language of the empire, was readily adopted by non-English-speaking immigrants coming to the United States. The melting pot model evolved in the United States in this historic context. When people in Germany expect migrants from Turkey and other countries to assimilate by accepting the German language and culture, they are also following this model. Other countries maintain homogeneity by shutting out people who are different from their own. For example, Japan has refused to receive migrants on the grounds that they will reduce the quality of life in that society.

It has been argued by Brewer (1991) that each human strives for "optimal distinctiveness," which is a balance between the forces toward assimilation and merging with groups, and differentiation from groups. The optimal point depends on the culture. This is a finding that has important implications for diversity management in that it can be predicted that people are unlikely to totally assimilate, as is assumed in the melting pot philosophy.

Second, there is the multiculturalism conception, which assumes that each cultural group can preserve much of its original culture, without interfering with the smooth functioning of the society. Canada has an official multicultural policy. The multiculturalism viewpoint requires that each individual understand the viewpoints of members of other cultures, and learn to make attributions concerning the causes of behavior of members of the other culture that are more or less like the attributes that these members make in explaining their own behavior (Triandis, 1975).

The multiculturalism conception best characterizes the society in Hawaii, which is the most multicultural state in the United States, and offers an example of what is to come elsewhere given globalization. The population in Hawaii includes 12 major groups (in order of decreasing size): Whites, Japanese, Filipinos, Native Hawaiians, Chinese, Portuguese, African-Americans, Koreans, Okinawans, Puerto Ricans, Samoans, and Vietnamese. When the world was divided along cultural lines, Fuchs (1961) thought that Hawaii offered ". . . a promise for the entire nation and indeed the world, that people of different races and creeds can live together, enriching each other, in harmony and democracy." The basis of this multicultural model is that each cultural group can preserve its original culture and still function in a larger society (Okamura, 1998). Such a model requires that each individual understand the viewpoints of other cultures and make similar attributions concerning the causes of behavior.

Results from the 2000 census shows that in Hawaii there are 42 percent Whites, 23 percent Asian-American, 9 percent Hispanics, and 2 percent African-Americans. Interestingly, 24 percent of the Hawaiian population can be called multiracial as they have a mixed cultural background. This makes Hawaii unique with a comparatively low 2 percent multiracial population nationwide. The laborforce rates as estimated by the Hawaii State Department of Labor in 1998 almost mirror the resident population. Resident population rates are White, 33.4 percent; Japanese, 22.2 percent; Filipino, 15.2 percent; Hawaiian, 12.5 percent; Chinese, 6.2 percent; African-American, 2.5 percent; American Indian, Eskimo, Aleutian, 0.5 percent; and other 7.5 percent (1990). Civilian labor rates are White, 31.6 percent; Japanese, 22.8 percent; Filipino, 15.4 percent; Hawaiian, 10.4 percent; Chinese, 5.5 percent; Korean, 2.2 percent; other Asian or Pacific Islander, 2.8 percent; African-American, 1.3 percent; American Indian, Eskimo, Aleutian, .48 percent; other, 1.4 percent; and Hispanic, 6.12 percent. About 67 percent of Hawaii's laborforce is from a minority group and 47 percent are women (U.S. Department of Labor, 2001).

The current diversity movement in the United States is moving away from the melting pot metaphor to the multiculturalism metaphor, or what can be termed the "Salad Bowl" metaphor, where every ingredient in a salad bowl retains its distinctive quality, and the distinctive qualities add to each other. Clearly, Hawaii may be the vanguard of a demographic shift that may transform the world (i.e., one which sees itself as a "salad bowl"), where each ingredient has its own unique characteristic but is part of something larger to result in positive multiculturalism.

It should be noted that apartheid, where one group of people is given preferential treatment over another, is not discussed here. After the fall of this ideology in South Africa, this method has been globally discarded as a nonviable approach to diversity. However, what is happening to Indians in Fiji, or the Gypsies in the Czech Republic, should constantly remind us that apartheid is still to be dealt with actively in our global workplace.

ISSUES FACING VARIOUS GROUPS IN THE WORKPLACE

Diversity in society is usually reflected in the workplace. According to the latest census, in the year 2000 African-Americans and Hispanics made up 12 and 10.7 percent of the U.S. population, respectively, which is an increase of 21 percent for the African-American population and of 54 percent for the Hispanic population (U.S. Census Bureau, 2000). Asian-Americans show the largest increase (71 percent) since the 1990 census, and they will also become an increasingly important part of the U.S. workforce. Such demographic changes are and will be reflected in the current demographic composition of the U.S. workforce and in the years to come.

According to the Department of Labor, the current U.S. workforce is comprised of 11.9 percent African-Americans and 10.9 percent Hispanics. In the year 2000, women and minorities constituted 54.7 percent of the U.S. workforce (38.1 percent Caucasian, 11.3 percent African-American, and 10.7 percent Hispanic). Also, 22.6 percent of workers were aged 50 or older. Women and minorities are projected to rise to 61.8 percent for the year 2006. Then 69.4 percent of the new entrants shall be women and minorities, and Asian-Americans are projected to comprise 4.9 percent of the workforce in the year 2006 (U.S. Department of Labor, 1998).

According to the projections from the U.S. Department of Labor, by the year 2006, only a minority of the new entries into the U.S. workforce will be white males (30.6 percent). Women and minorities increasingly make up the workforce, with 66.4 percent having entered the workforce between 1986 and 1996—a figure which is still on the rise with

69.4 percent of the new entrants for the year 2006 (U.S. Department of Labor, 1998). It has also been projected that by the year 2050, the face of America will be 52 percent White, 25 percent Hispanic, 14 percent African-American, 8 percent Asian/Pacific islander, and 1 percent American Indian (the numbers today are 72.7, 11, 12, 3.6, and 0.7 percent, respectively. The number of African-Americans in the workforce will double and the number of Hispanics will triple. Thus, if projections are accurate, organizations in the future will operate with more diverse groups.

As discussed earlier, the demographic composition of the resident population as well as of the workforce has been changing, and despite many women and minorities entering the workforce there are signs of stratification and inequality for certain groups on both societal and organizational levels worldwide. The concentration of men and women in occupations and jobs are different, which frequently implies financial degradation of certain occupations and functions. This leads not only to horizontal segregation in occupations and functions but also to vertical segregation in organizational hierarchy. Both forms of segregation correlate with a differential allocation of status, power, and income and are linked with inferior status for women and ethnic minorities (Aschatz, Allmendinger, & Hinz, 2000). We examine the issues these specific groups face in the workplace today.

Diversity Due to Sex Difference

Women constitute almost half of the workforce now. Their problems include the glass ceiling; unequal allocation of benefits and pay; inequality; sexual harassment; and a lack of role models and mentors, job opportunities, and career advancement. According to the U.S. Department of Labor, women held just 30.5 percent of management positions in the nation last year, although they represent nearly half of the workforce. *For-tune* magazine's *Fortune* 500 list of leading American corporations includes just two female CEOs. Thus the so-called glass ceiling effect, reflecting nonpromotion to higher managerial ranks, is still prevalent. A recent study found that women in Hawaii are even less likely to work in managerial and professional specialty occupations than mainland women (Villani, 2001). Hawaii ranked 49th in the nation for the proportion of women employed in these areas. It should be noted that although Hawaii appears to be a model for racial harmony, it is hardly any better when it comes to gender issues.

Pay remains another key issue, with women earning 72 cents for every dollar earned by men in the United States in 1999. The National Committee on Pay Equity found that women in management and administrative positions earned 64.6 percent of men's salaries. In Hawaii, women did better on pay, and earned about 84 percent of the male standard in 1997.

Issues of inequality are reported worldwide, and a variety of reasons can be found. Kanter (1977) talked of "homosocial reproduction," which means the tendency of promoting and judging people positively if they are perceived to have similar attributes compared to the dominant majority. Because white males still represent the dominant majority, systems and criteria of performance evaluations, applicant interviews, appraisals, or task assignments are developed, implemented, and practiced to suit the needs of this group, which naturally leaves women at a disadvantage. There is also evidence that there is a hierarchy of inequality in which white males are on top, white women are next, minority males rank third, and minority women are last. Part of the difficulty for women is the absence of suitable mentors. They are often confronted with old-boy networks that exclude them from important information.

Another important issue facing women is sexual harassment, which is a topic that could use a whole chapter. It is important to note that the threshold for its perception is lower for women than for men. With the passage of the reasonable woman's perspective in case law, we have made some progress toward delivering justice to victims of sexual harassment. However, counting the number of cases that are filed every year, it is clear that this problem is going to remain a dominant workplace issue.

It is interesting to note that there are global similarities and differences on the issues dealing with workplace segregation by sex. For example, in a recent study Aschatz, Allmendinger, and Hinz (2000) found that horizontal and vertical sex segregation at the organizational level is similar in the United States and Germany. In core jobs, 85 percent of surveyed U.S. establishments employed either exclusively women or exclusively men. This applies to about 79 percent of surveyed organizations in Germany. Gender-balanced positions, however, are only taken by employees in 9 percent of organizations in the U.S. sample, and in 11 percent of organizations in the German sample. In managerial positions, 87 percent of the surveyed organizations in the United States and 89 percent in Germany employ exclusively women or exclusively men in high-ranked jobs. Neither the overall higher percentage of managerial positions (more favorable opportunity structure) in U.S. firms nor the more favorable institutional framing of gender equality lead to more sex-integrated employment.

Flexible on-the-job training also has not helped much. Instead, the higher inclusion of American women in top-ranked positions leads to a considerably higher proportion of organizations that exclusively fill their managerial positions with women (35 percent of all organizations in the United States versus 12 percent in Germany). So, despite similarities, there is one clear difference: In Germany, managerial positions are overwhelmingly dominated by males. In the United States, organizations in the nonprofit sector are least segregated—in core as well as in managerial jobs. On the other hand, in Germany, women dominate the core jobs and men control managerial positions in the nonprofit sector, but in the public sector organizations are substantially less segregated. The authors hold the EEO policies in the United States accountable for these differences as they are targeted at small and large organizations alike.

Diversity Due to Ethnicity

It should be noted that the demographic distribution of ethnic groups varies across nations and is unique to a country; it even varies within regions of any one country. Major issues facing ethnic minorities are discrimination, availability of fewer opportunities for career advancement, lack of role models and mentors, and negative stereotypes. As with women, selection processes and tendencies towards homogeneity impede selection, promotion, integration, and advancement. Tsui and O'Reilly (1989) showed that African-American subordinates were assessed to be less effective and were less liked by their superiors than their white counterparts. Cox and Nkomo (1990) found that objective criteria are used more when evaluating the performance of subordinates of the same color, whereas subjective criteria prevail when assessing people of another color.

Limitations of space preclude a fuller coverage of the way significant U.S. populations differ. A more complete discussion can be found in Triandis et al. (1994). Each relationship (e.g., African-Asian Americans, African-Latin Americans, etc.) is different and must be studied separately and examined in detail. We only touch on some of the main ways in which these populations differ from the mainstream.

African-Americans   This group is the largest minority group in the United States, and like most other groups, it is very hetero-geneous. Despite the historical importance of this group, research is limited. For example, in the area of organizational behavior, Cox and Nkomo (1990) found that during 1964 to 1989 there were only 201 papers published that dealt with race relations. Years of struggle have not made life easier for African-Americans in corporate America, and they continue to face racial discrimination in hiring (Kirschenman & Neckerman, 1991), although it is more subtle today than in the past. Research shows that they still face many kinds of "exclusionary barriers" in corporations at different stages of selection and promotion (Braddock & McPartland, 1987), and they often face negative stereotypes, solo status, and tokenism (Pettigrew & Martin, 1987).

Hispanics This, too, is a heterogeneous group, coming from different countries, and under the influence of Iberian, African, and American-Indian cultural patterns in different mixtures. Though many people use the terms Latino and Hispanic interchangeably, it is a good practice to choose the word that the target group is comfortable with. The term *Hispanic* is derived from the Latin word *Hispania,* and it is generally used to describe people who trace their origins to Spain and the Spanish-speaking Latin American countries. It could even be argued that Hispanic is a category invented by the U.S. Census Bureau. *Latino* is considered a more inclusive term, which encompasses Native Americans, Africans, Asians, Brazilians, and Haitians. Many Latinos like to distance themselves from Spain and its history of conquest, colonialism, and slavery, and thus find the term Latino closer to their identity.

According to the U.S. Census Bureau, 61.2 percent of the Hispanics are Mexicans, 12.1 percent are Puerto Ricans, 6 percent are Central Americans (Salvadorians, 1.1 percent; Guatemalans, 20.3 percent; Nicaraguans, 15.3 percent; Hondurans, 9.9 percent; Panamanians, 7 percent; Costa Ricans, 4.3 percent; and others 2.1 percent), 4.8 percent are Cubans, 4.7 percent are South Americans (Colombians, 33.2 percent; Ecuadorians, 15.1 percent; Peruvians, 13.8 percent; Argentineans, 8.7 percent; Chileans, 5.5 percent; and others 11.7 percent), 4.4 percent are Spaniards, 2.4 percent are Dominicans, and others are 3.9 percent. It should be noted that though we often associate Hispanics with recent immigration waves, Latinos actually have long ancestral links to the United States. Latino settlements date back to the 1500s, evidenced by the names of cities such as St. Augustine, San Antonio, Santa Fe, and Los Angeles. Also, with the acquisition of Florida in 1819, and the annexation of Puerto Rico in 1848 and 1898, respectively, people living in these regions became U.S. citizens. One apparently common element among Latinos is that they are collectivists of the family and have high expectations that other people will treat them well, not criticize them, and will try to be *simpatico* (e.g., nice, pleasant, and non-critical) when interacting with them (Triandis, Marin, Lisansky, & Betancourt, 1984). Thus, they feel that mainstream Americans behave quite inappropriately, because they do not try to be *simpatico.*

Asian-Americans These are a very heterogeneous group, but they tend to be more collectivist and less assertive than the mainstream. They pay more attention to the context of social behavior than do mainstream Americans, who tend to depend entirely on the content of verbal exchanges. This can result in misunderstandings.

Diversity Due to Disability

Often when one thinks about diversity issues, one thinks of race, gender, and ethnicity. Disability is just beginning to be recognized as a type of diversity. This may be due to the fact the Americans with Disability

Act (ADA) was passed only recently, in 1990. Because individuals with disabilities are not an internally homogenous minority group, culturally based models are inadequate for characterizing and analyzing the workplace needs of those with disabilities. Like cultural minorities, individuals with disabilities often are targets of prejudice and misconceptions, find the workplace inhospitable, face discriminatory hiring practice, and receive lower wages. Cultural models do not work in this special case, because individuals with disabilities do not have common experiences in the workplace or in the larger community. They are not a group that shares traditional customs and norms, and there are a variety of reasons for impairment. Thus disability is a continuum, not a category, and depends on the context (Roberts, 1996).

ADA defines disability as a physical or mental impairment that "substantially limits" one or more major life activities. It is a form of diversity management required by law that asks for "reasonable accommodation," which allows the covered individual to perform "essential functions" of the job. It is comprehensive, and puts demands on employers. The disabled have fewer opportunities for employment, and when they are hired they face lack of accommodation, which leads them to leave the workplace. The attitudes evoked by this group, such as anxiety and the inability to handle the ambiguity of the social situation, is one of the issues emerging from research with this group.

To effectively integrate disabled employees in organizations, we must look at both the organizational level and the individual level. Beyond accommodations, organizations must adopt a broad-based definition of disability, ignore the issue of potential fault or personal responsibility for the impairment, and approach such diversity with flexibility and creativity and have efforts that dispel general misconceptions about disability. Those who require accommodation at the individual level and those

coworkers who may be affected by the implementation of an accommodation must be able to give input. Explicit mechanisms must exist for revisiting accommodations that are not effective or have become obsolete. The nature of disability is more insistent on attention to the individual and recognition of the contribution of culture and context to how a problem is defined than with most other sources of diversity.

Diversity Due to Age

By 2005, American workforce will include 27 million people between the ages of 50 and 59, compared with 20 million in 1997. The number of workers over 65 has edged up during the past decade, from 3 million to 3.8 million, and it is predicted to rise to 4.3 million by 2005. In the meantime, the number of workers aged 25 to 44 is falling. The median age of the workforce will be over 40 by 2005; it was 34.7 in 1979. It is predicted that by 2025 the whole of America will be as gray as Florida, the country's retirement home.

Older employees can be more hardworking, loyal, and flexible. People over 65 have half as many accidents at work as their younger and more careless colleagues. However, there are also costs associated with elderly workers. A more elderly workforce is likely to cost more in pay and benefits, workplace safety, and employee mobility. Once workers reach about age 42, the cost of their health care coverage starts to rise dramatically. Older workers save about three times as much as younger ones in their pension plans; if a company matches contributions, as many do, they again face higher costs. They are much more fragile in that older workers take longer to recover and are more likely to die of job-related injuries. Therefore, many jobs may have to be redesigned if they are to be done by older people. American companies are used to having a mobile workforce that can be sent just about anywhere. As workers get older, however, they put down firmer roots, and are not amenable to transfers.

Other management challenges may have to do with career paths. Despite some delayering and horizontal management, most U.S. businesses are still pyramid-shaped; the longer you stay, the higher you rise. As baby boomers age, they will create increasingly top-heavy structures. And in most firms, both pay and holidays also tend to go up with seniority, increasing the cost to the organization with the aging of the population.

Diversity Due to Sexual Orientation

Sexual orientation in the workplace has become a critical issue in human resources management. Some of the issues facing gays and lesbians in the workplace include lack of tolerance due to various negative stereotypes and the right to "reciprocal beneficiaries" similar to spousal benefits. Gays insist on fairly managed workplaces, and are requesting health care coverage for significant others.

Gays are becoming open about their sexuality, and what once was a big issue in the early 1990s—whether to be open about their sexual orientation—may soon become a nonissue. The Netherlands has become the first nation to recognize same-sex marriages with full equal rights. Though many other nations allow gays to register as partners and some allow them the term *marriage,* the Dutch legislation is groundbreaking in that it eliminates all references to gender in laws governing matrimony and adoption. The law eliminates legal ambiguities on inheritance, pension rights, taxes, and divorce. Dutch dictionaries will be amended, and marriage will refer to any two people. The general acceptance of diversity in sexual orientation can be seen in public surveys in the Netherlands, which show that 75 percent of the population supported this legislation. News of lesbians and gay couples getting married in the Netherlands is likely to slowly but surely change people's attitudes around the globe, and people will be able to openly identify their sexual orientation without fear of adverse impact on their life and careers. For now, though, this legislation does not allow foreign nationals to get married in the Netherlands, and it does not allow Dutch gays to adopt children from other countries.

Gays and lesbians are not covered under federal civil rights laws in the United States. However, legal developments are expanding the rights of gays to be free of hostile work environments and to share fully in the U.S. promise of equal employment opportunity. Business attitudes are also changing, and public opinion polls indicate strong support for nondiscrimination for all in the workplace. Domestic partner benefits are a crucial step towards equal pay for equal work, especially since benefits can be up to 40 percent of one's overall compensation.

Considering the diversity of populations present in the United States, and knowing that the United States adopted the melting pot philosophy to assimilate its diverse population both in the society and in the workplace, a natural question to ask is, why are U.S. corporations changing their way of handling human resources? What has led the corporate world into the diversity movement? These questions are addressed in the next section.

Diversity Management in U.S. Corporations

Bhawuk (2000) and Bhawuk and Triandis (1996) studied the diversity management strategies of some large U.S. multinational firms. They carried out the study in two steps. First, they studied archival information from internal reports and printed documents of these companies, and then they conducted structured qualitative interviews with the HR managers of these organizations. They found that U.S. corporations invested in diversity management for a number of reasons, and developed some unique diversity management strategies in the last decade.

Reasons for Managing Diversity

Many companies have been sued for discrimination; the sexual harassment charges brought against Mitsubishi is an example of a high-profile case that people often remember. Organizations are forced to deal with such lawsuits because of the punitive damages that juries award victims of discrimination. For example, Coca-Cola started to tie top managers' pay to new goals for diversity and established an office of diversity after eight employees filed suits claiming discriminations. Besides such reactive approaches, corporations are also developing many proactive strategies.

The following are some of the reasons offered by organizations for involving themselves in diversity management (Bhawuk, 2000; Bhawuk & Triandis, 1996):

- To retain the best talent necessary to remain competitive.
- To improve community and public support for the company's business agenda.
- To recruit and employ talented women and minorities in the company.
- To present themselves in the best possible way as a socially conscious organization committed to diversity and justice.
- To position the company as a diversity management leader in the marketplace for customers, vendors, potential employees, and shareholders.
- To meet the diverse needs of the growing ethnic segments of the U.S. market.
- To attract a more diverse clientele.
- To show commitment to the principles and practices of equal opportunity.
- To address the legal requirements associated with Title VII of the Civil Rights Act of 1964, disabled workers (American with Disability Act or ADA), sexual harassment, etc.
- To increase the performance of individuals, teams, and organizations.

It is clear that organizations want to hire the most talented people as well as retain the people they hire. Because women and minorities will constitute the largest portion of people entering the workforce 10 years from now, it is important for organizations to lure them into their folds. It is felt that if organizations do not have a fair representation of minorities and women in management, they may not be able to attract them. Also, customers, vendors, and shareholders may ostracize such organizations. It is also clear that Title VII, ADA, and other legal requirements are still a driving force for organizations to attend to the diversity issues. The cost of litigation related to sexual harassment, ADA, promotion, etc., are so exorbitant that organizations are better off addressing these issues proactively. The emerging strategies adopted by many U.S. corporations in managing their diversity efforts is discussed next.

Emerging Diversity Strategies

Organizations function in different environments, which forces them to adopt different approaches to diversity management. Also, they have different needs, which result in different policies. Bhawuk and Triandis (1996) proposed that organizations can be classified on a continuum from "not doing anything" to "having a full-blown diversity strategy," with most falling in the middle, carrying out only awareness training programs or mandatory AA/EEO activities. Those organizations that have developed a strategy for diversity management approach the issues from more than one perspective. Their approach could be considered an inclusive approach that includes AA/EEO activities, awareness and other training programs, and more. Therefore, the points on the continuum are not exclusive of each other; instead, they are more like evolutionary phases of organizations going through different styles of diversity management. It is likely that most organizations will fall somewhere on this continuum. We now discuss these phases of organizational development and the associated diversity strategies, which are critical for carrying out effective human resources management.

Phase 1: Basic Diversity Strategy   In the early phase of learning to deal with diversity in the workplace, organizations start with activities that enable them to deal with the Affirmative Action (AA) and Equal Employment Opportunity (EEO) legislations. Title VII of the Civil Rights Act of 1964 prohibits employment discrimination on the basis of race, color, religion, national origin, and sex. There was no mention of sexual harassment in the law or its legislative history. However, following court rulings (e.g., *William v. Saxbe*, 1976; *Barnes v. Costle*, 1977) and the 1980 guidelines from the Equal Employment Opportunity Commission (EEOC), the agency that enforces Title VII, sexual harassment is interpreted as sexual discrimination under Title VII.

Every organization has to deal with AA/EEO at some level. Organizations that are involved in mandatory AA/EEO activities are sensitive to Title VII rights of employees and make an effort to avoid lawsuits. Organizations that are limited to these activities consider dealing with minorities a legal aspect or a cost of doing business. Most organizations have gone through this phase and those who have no diversity programs may still fall in this category, since AA/EEO cannot be avoided.

All organizations disseminate legal information to managers and supervisors who are responsible for selection, training, promotion, and so forth (i.e., the areas that are affected by AA/EEO). Currently, this is an important human resources function. Sexual harassment and the Americans with Disabilities Act are prominent topics of current discussion.

A limitation of doing only what is required by law is that white employees feel rejected in the course of implementing AA/EEO activities. Even if organizations are not able to identify the benefits of diversity policies and do not have a pressing need for diversity activities, they often feel a need for an awareness program, which allows the inclusion of the white majority.

Phase 2: Individual Employee Awareness Diversity Strategy   When organizations realize that there is value in expanding their AA/EEO activities to exploit the benefits of diversity, they usually start conducting diversity awareness programs for their managers and salaried employees. However, these programs are usually not extended to grassroots workers. Awareness programs can be classified into three categories.

First, there are organizations that use diversity films to increase employee awareness of diversity issues. Some popular films used are *Valuing Diversity* (by Griggs Productions Inc.), *Harness the Rainbow* (by Determan Marketing Corporation), and *Bridges: Skills for Managing a Diverse Work Force* (By BNA Communications). Usually, a discussion session follows the films. This type of program is easy to conduct and relatively inexpensive. Internal human resources experts usually facilitate these discussion sessions.

Second, most organizations invite experts in the area of diversity to conduct group discussions. Each expert has his or her own approach to handling diversity, which they promote in their discussion programs (Lynch, 1997). It is difficult to estimate the effectiveness of these programs since they are of short duration and usually do not (and cannot due to time limitation) use a behavior modification approach.

Third, many organizations have one-, two-, or three-day awareness training programs that aim at giving managers and other employees skills to build effective culturally diverse teams. These training programs usually focus on topics such as cultural and gender differences, stereotypes, socialization processes, differences in communication styles, legal aspects of AA/EEO, and so forth. Again, group discussion led by experts is the popular mode for doing this, but experiential exercises like Bafa-Bafa (Shirts, 1973), Albatross (Gochenour, 1977), and so forth are also used. Also, discussions are seldom led by offering theoretical explanations for differences in behavior or misunderstandings that take place in the work place. We believe a theory driven approach would improve building intercultural communication skills (Bhawuk, 2001, 1990).

We think HR managers and diversity trainers have a lot to learn from the rich cross-cultural training literature. There are numerous methods of intercultural training (Bhawuk, 1990 for a succinct summary for practitioners) and among the most important responses to dealing with diversity is to use them. Following is a brief description of the main types of training; interested readers are directed to a review by Bhawuk and Brislin (2000).

Self-Insight   Understanding how culture influences one's own behavior can be accomplished by interacting with actors who have been trained to behave in the opposite way from the way members of one's own culture behave. Discussions that follow viewing the trainee's reactions to these interactions can clarify the meaning of culture and elucidate how it influences behavior. This can be particularly useful to bring about awareness of ethnic differences in work ethics, interpersonal interaction styles, approaches to handling the conflict, and so forth, so as to motivate employees to improve their interpersonal skills.

Attribution Training   This method (called a culture assimilator) consists of working through a programmed learning curriculum that is constituted by episodes of social interaction (critical incidents) involving members of one's own and other cultures. After reading or viewing each episode, the trainee makes judgments about the causes of the behavior of the member of the other culture. Each judgment is followed by feedback that criticizes or supports it. This training helps the trainee in making attributions that match the attributions that members of the other culture make when viewing the same episodes.

Culture assimilators are the most extensively researched intercultural training method and are appropriate for diversity training (Bhawuk & Brislin, 2000). Culture assimilators are available for training people to interact with African-Americans (Triandis, 1976) and Hispanics (Albert, 1983; Tolbert, 1990). Considering the effectiveness of this method, it would be worthwhile to develop assimilators to train people to deal with the issues of differences in sexual orientation, age, and so forth. This method should also be effective in training people to reduce sexual harassment in the workplace.

Behavior Modification   This method provides feedback while the person is behaving in role-playing situations toward members of other cultures. When the trainee's behavior is inappropriate (e.g., offensive to members of the other culture) the feedback directs the trainee to substitute behaviors that are considered desirable in the other culture. This method is likely to be effective in training people to prevent sexual harassment in the workplace, since new acceptable behaviors replace old unacceptable behaviors. Diversity managers and professionals have yet to take advantage of this method.

Diversity training programs seem to be more effective when they focus on particular issues, such as sexual harassment or dealing with the disabled, rather than when they discuss abstract ideas, such as stereotypes and communication styles. When training is issue-focused, both the negative and the suggested replacement behaviors can be identified and discussed. For example, sexually harassing behaviors can be classified into verbal, physical, and visual categories, and an example of unacceptable and acceptable behaviors in each category can be offered and discussed. Similarly, in a program focusing on dealing with disabilities, it is easy to point out how people inadvertently stereotype by using phrases such as "John, a hard-working retarded person," (this suggests that disabled people are not hardworking). The concreteness of the behaviors helps people shape their own behaviors in the workplace.

Evaluation of diversity programs is done mostly by qualitative methods. A human resources manager commented that investment in diversity programs is like investment in advertisement, one does not know what is useful and what is not. Feedback from participants is still the most prevalent evaluation method. However, opinion surveys and focus group analyses are also used.

Phase 3: Fully Developed Diversity Strategy
Those organizations that have a fully developed diversity strategy usually are found to have experimented with diversity for at least three years, and begin to integrate various interventions into an organization-wide general framework. Thus, diversity management ceases to be isolated as the specialty of an HR section, and is integrated in daily business activities. This does not mean that these companies have achieved their long-term desired organizational diversity goals. Indeed, it would be quite some time before they can fully realize their diversity objectives. Organizations with a fully developed

diversity strategy typically commit significant resources in order to deal systematically with diversity. In what follows, two unique diversity strategies, developed by organizations identified by Bhawuk and Triandis (1996), are discussed.

An Integrated Diversity Strategy   This approach integrates the formal efforts of the organization at both the corporate and business unit levels with the informal efforts of employees at the grassroots level. At the corporate level a diverse (both demographically and functionally) employee panel is formed that monitors and oversees diversity activities. This corporate body is known by various names such as "Chairman's Affirmative Action Committee," "Diversity Forum," "Corporate Diversity Advisory Council," "Corporate EEO Committee," or "Pluralism Council." This panel usually has 15 to 20 people and includes the vice president of human resources or diversity, and a representative sample of line and staff managers. In other words, the corporate level diversity forum is modeled after a diverse organization and conceptually drives the diversity activities.

At the business unit level, the impact of diversity issues on various business activities is analyzed, and diversity policies are integrated with daily business activities in coordination with the diversity forum and advocacy groups. At the grassroots level, employees form advocacy panels, which are independent, informal organizations of various minority groups within the company, that provide information about the issues that concern them. The advocacy groups are used to feed diversity issues and concerns experienced by employees in the organization to both the diversity forum and the business units. The diversity forum, advocacy groups, and business units generally act in tandem; each communicating and sharing information with the other, both as dyads and triads. This arrangement is represented pictorially in Figure 4-1.

The diversity forum usually serves the following objectives:

- It facilitates sustained attention on diversity issues.
- It increases senior management's awareness and sensitivity about the diversity issues.
- It examines the impact of new HR policies on various groups of employees.
- It shares information about both successful and unsuccessful diversity programs.
- It discusses urgent concerns related to diversity.

When organizations take this approach, solving diversity problems is the task of business units; the forum is only a platform for the discussion of issues and the development of policies. The corporate office provides broad strategies, policies, and training resources, but the business units are accountable for managing diversity. It appears that organizations are concerned that diversity may become a staff function and hence lose some impetus, so they make efforts to delegate the handling of diversity issues to the business units, thus treating diversity strictly as a business issue. Similarly, advocacy groups are sources of information and channels of communication of diversity measures to both the forum and the business units; not an agency that implements diversity efforts. These groups also help organizations to network and communicate effectively with the minority organizations and interest groups in the community.

Xerox Corporation provides a good example of how diversity strategy evolves in an organization over the years. At Xerox, diversity management began and continues as an extension of the values of the founders of the company. The company focused on the African-American population following the civil rights movement and the resulting legislation in the 1960s; in the 1970s the focus was broadened to include women and other minorities. Currently, Xerox has expanded its coverage to other groups such as those with nontraditional sexual orientations and disabilities. Thus, Xerox provides an example of a company that has moved from "not doing anything" to "dealing with affirmative

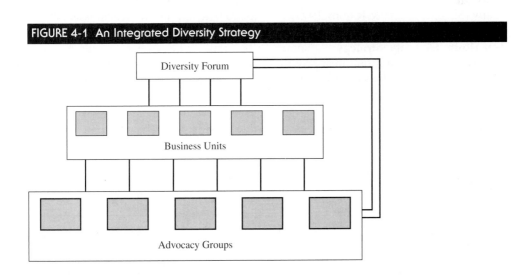

FIGURE 4-1 An Integrated Diversity Strategy

action" to "developing an integrated strategy" (called the balanced workforce) that covers all aspects of diversity. The stated goal of this strategy is to achieve and maintain equitable representation of all employee groups. Managers have been held accountable for balancing their groups and they are evaluated in this area on performance reviews. Through its aggressive measures, Xerox was able to achieve a nearly balanced workforce in the 1990s. However, they could not achieve parity for women in the highest two grades of the organization, and it should be noted that no goals were set for persons with disabilities and nontraditional sexual orientation. Caucus groups, though not an official part of the company, are crucial in helping manage diversity. Xerox has succeeded in creating one of the most diverse workforces in the United States by going beyond sensitivity training to include skill building, career planning, and performance appraisal systems for balanced workforce goals. They also are emphasizing work and family issues to meet the different needs of individuals and families. Xerox is an example that organizational change is a long-term process that requires vigilance and support on many levels of the company (Sessa, Jackson, & Rapini, 1995).

A Top-Down Diversity Strategy   Some organizations reject the bottom-up approach in favor of the top-down diversity strategy. In these organizations the champion of diversity

management is the CEO. This strategy takes a "changing corporate culture" or "organizational development" approach to managing diversity. The belief is that since the workforce is diverse, management also should be diverse. If management is diverse, it is hoped that there will be fewer problems handling a diverse workforce. In this approach, diversity management is operationalized through succession planning and the focus is on breaking the "glass ceiling." This strategy is pictorially represented in Figure 4-2.

In this approach, the corporate office is responsible for formulating the strategy, which is communicated to the business units (BUs). The first leg of the diversity efforts involves the CEO communicating "management accountability" (i.e., the CEO tells the presidents of the BUs what is to be done, why it is to be done, and how the presidents are accountable). In formulating the strategy, the CEO is assisted by the vice president of diversity. The BU presidents are accountable for "internal readiness." They are responsible for finding out where the barriers to diversity are in their units, what strategy is needed to eliminate those barriers, how the presidents should communicate this to others in their units, and how they can make it clear that it is a strategic and not a tactical issue. In short, the presidents are responsible for preparing their units to be ready to handle diversity issues effectively by breaking the glass ceiling.

The third leg of this strategy involves managing "community relations." Organiza-

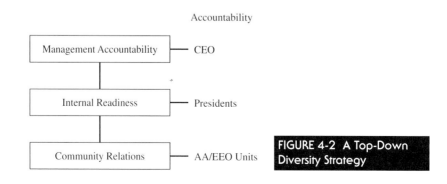

FIGURE 4-2 A Top-Down Diversity Strategy

tions strive to build a strong partnership with community organizations such as the Urban League for Blacks, La Raza, Catalyst (women's advocacy), and so forth. This allows organizations to gain the confidence of different communities. Each BU has an EEO/AA unit and the vice president of diversity meets with them twice a year. This is called the Chairman's AA Committee and it helps keep the communication lines active between the corporate office and the BUs.

The business units and the presidents of these units are made accountable for the implementation of the diversity efforts including the reaching of parity goals. Annual and long-term goals are given to the BU presidents. Since there are not many minority individuals at the vice-president level, the goal of promoting at least a certain number of women and minority individuals (e.g., say, three women and two minority individuals) to the position of vice president each year is set. The BU presidents are responsible for identifying, from among minorities, capable individuals, including women (and white men), who can become VPs, and then groom them to take that position in about three years.

It is important to note that the increase in vice presidents should not be limited to the traditional areas of human resources management, but should also include important and critical functional areas. For director, manager, and beginner positions, the goal of matching the national census (i.e., to have, in specific functional areas, as many managers and directors as the average national percentage of that ethnic group) is considered reasonable.

Massachusetts Institute of Technology (MIT) offers an example of the typical—reactive and top-down—approach to diversity management. In March 1999, MIT released a document called "A Study on the Status of Women Faculty in Science at MIT," which reported on gender discrimination against female faculty members in its School of Sci-

ence. This document was compiled by a group of 15 tenured women faculty beginning five years previous to the release of this report. This group later created a committee, which found that most of the female faculty in the school had received lower salaries and fewer resources than their male counterparts and had been excluded from significant roles in their departments. Upon learning of the results of the study, Dean Birgeneau took prompt action to make things more equitable. First, he redistributed the benefits that are signs of respect for faculty members. Female professors were asked to join committees involved in hiring new faculty members and the dean helped to recruit new female faculty. These efforts lead to the overarching goal of increasing the number of female faculty members in science. Tenured women also found this increased support from the university as making their research more fruitful.

Upon publication of this report, much attention was given to MIT's handling of gender discrimination as a model for other institutions. While it had changed the situation for some women in science at MIT, questions have been raised about whether or not significant changes have come at the department level or only from above, and how permanent changes can be made. Perhaps this model will begin the process to true equality in the workplace.

In Germany, on the behest of a board member responsible for personnel, one of the largest insurance companies decided to examine gender issues in the organization. They commissioned an academic team to find ways to attract and retain qualified women, better integrate women at all levels and in all functions in the company, and why women are not represented in senior management levels. This team was charged to analyze employees' personnel data, trace their career development, evaluate personnel selection procedures, and validate personnel development measures, performance ratings, and employee interviews. The objective was to better integrate women in the company in the next three years. This clearly is a top-down strategy, though the result of the investigations may lead to an integrated strategy later on. Signs of such an integrated strategy can be found in the development of a diversity forum, which includes members from the project team as well as some external consultants. Also, an advocacy group of women who convey issues and concern of employees and provide information directly to the board of directors was established. This advocacy group led to the creation of a company-specific child care facility, which is not common in Germany. Germany has no legal provisions comparable to the American Civil Rights Act of 1964. Thus this company has moved toward a gender-balanced workforce proactively, starting with the board of directors' conviction, and would develop similar policies for other groups in the future to avoid negative reactions from them.

One of the consequences of diversity management is that organizations in the United States are becoming sensitive to the use of languages other than English in the workplace. Knowledge of another language, especially Spanish, is considered an advantage, especially by organizations that have high frequencies of interaction with Spanish-speaking clients. Some organizations have even started communicating to Filipino, Chinese, and Japanese customers in their languages. Neither organizations nor other units of the society are paying enough attention to the consequences of using more than one language in business activities. Such tolerance for other nonnative languages in the workplace is likely to emerge globally, especially in countries like Japan, Korea, Germany, and so forth.

CONCLUSION

To summarize, organizations are becoming aware of diversity, and are concerned about finding ways of managing the new work-

place. Organizations are more willing than they were in the past to accept minority organizations and interest groups, both within the organization and out in the community. They frequently communicate with them to deal with diversity issues. Also, they are clearly concerned about the "glass-ceiling" phenomena and are finding ways of grooming women and minorities for promotion to middle- and upper-management positions. EEO/AA is still an important consideration for doing business in the United States, and diversity management provides the umbrella under which these issues can be handled beyond legal requirements. However, the major thrust of diversity management is on the acceptance of demographic and ethnic differences, and very little attention is paid to focusing on similarities.

Most human resources specialists recommend open communication in diversity management. Therefore, it seems diversity issues are forcing management to become more participatory, at least, with respect to human resources management practices. One wonders if there was a lack of open communication in U.S. organizations in the past. If so, diversity is making a definite contribution by promoting participatory management in organizations.

Diversity needs to be dealt with at three levels. On an individual level, interactions can be improved by sensitivity-focused tools and valuing differences. On a group level, diverse teams have to be established and supervised, giving them time and opportunities for contact to work out common procedures and goals. On the organizational level, the focus should be on establishing structure (e.g., diversity committees, employee resource groups, or networking with community and minority organizations; Bhawuk, 2000).

What makes a successful program? An indicator of success seems to be commitment to inclusion of diversity management as part of the organization's culture and business strategy. Also, top management support is of critical importance to achieve diversity benchmarks. Diversity programs that are evaluated and those where managers are held accountable also seem to have more success.

Will organizations develop a comprehensive strategy along the lines discussed here, or will they only meet the challenges of the diverse workforce halfway by merely protecting themselves from lawsuits? Will a multicultural society emerge in the end, or will the melting pot be victorious? We are confident that the foundation of a society that will be just and open to differences is being laid, and that U.S. corporations are taking a lead in finding ways to manage people with differences in their objective (demographic variables) and subjective (attitude, norms, values, beliefs, etc.) cultures. Diversity management is a critical global issue, and it provides businesses an opportunity to show that they are socially responsible. ■

REFERENCES

Aschatz, J., Allmendinger, J., & Hinz, T. (2000). *Sex segregation in organizations: A comparison of Germany and the U.S.* Paper presented at the ASA 2000 Meeting in Washington.

Albert, R. D. (1983). *The Hispanic culture assimilator.* Department of Education, University of Minnesota.

Avigdor, R. (1953). Edudes experimentales de la genese des stereotypes. *Cahiers Inernationaux de Sociologie, 5,* 154–168.

Berry, J. W. (1967) Independence and conformity in subsistence level societies. *Journal of Personality and Social Psychology, 7,* 415–418.

Berry, J. W. (1976). *Human ecology and cognitive style.* Beverly Hills: Sage.

Bhawuk, D. P. S. (1990). Cross-cultural orientation programs. In R. W. Brislin (Ed.), *Applied cross-cultural psychology.* Beverly Hills: Sage Publications.

Bhawuk, D. P. S. (2000). *Integration research and practice: Toward a theory of diversity management.* Paper presented at the Academy of Management, 60th Annual National Meeting, Toronto.

Bhawuk, D. P. S. (2001). Evolution of culture assimilators: Toward theory-based assimilators. *International Journal of Intercultural Relations, 25* (2), 141–163.

Bhawuk, D. P. S., & Brislin, R. W. (2000). Cross-cultural training: A review. *Applied Psychology: An International Review, 49* (1), 162–191.

Bhawuk, D. P. S., & Triandis, H. C. (1996). Diversity in the workplace: Emerging corporate strategies. In G. R. Ferris & M. R. Buckley (Eds.), *Human resource management: Perspectives, context, functions and outcomes* (3rd ed.). Upper Saddle River, NJ: Prentice Hall.

Braddock, J. H. II, & McPartland, J. M. (1987) How minorities continue to be excluded from equal employment opportunities: Research on labor market and institutional barriers. *Journal of Social Issues, 43* (1), 5–39.

Brewer, M. B. (1991). The social self: On being the same and different at the same time. *Personality and Social Psychology Bulletin, 17,* 475–485.

Brislin, R. W. (1988). Increasing awareness of class, ethnicity, culture, and race by expanding on students' own experiences. In I. Cohen (Ed.), *The G. Stanley Hall Lecture Series* (Vol. 8, 137–180). Washington, D.C.: American Psychological Association.

Cox, T., & Nkomo, S. (1990) Invisible men and women: A status report on race as a variable in organizational behavior research. *Journal of Organizational Behavior, 11,* 419–431.

Desjarles, R., Elsberg, L., Good, B., & Kleinman, A. (1995). *World mental health: Problems and priorities in low income countries.* New York, NY: Oxford University Press.

Friday, R. A. (1989). Contrasts in discussion behaviors of German and American managers. *International Journal of Intercultural Relations, 13,* 429–446.

Fuchs, L. (1961). *Hawaii Pono.* Honolulu, HI: University of Hawaii Press.

Fullerton, Howard N. (2001). Labor force participation: 75 years of change, 1950–1998 and 1998 to 2025. Online article.

George, S. (1993). One-third in, two-thirds out. *New Perspectives Quarterly, 10,* 53–55.

Gochenour, T. (1977). The owl and the albatross. In D. Batchelder & E. G. Warner (Eds.), *Beyond experience.* Brattleboro, VT: Experiment Press.

Helson, H. (1964). *Adaptation level theory.* New York: Harper and Row.

Heller, F. A. (1969). *Managerial decision making.* London: Human Resources Center, Tavistock Institute of Human Relations.

"Human Rights." (2000, June 26). Human Rights in Japan. Bureau of East Asian and Pacific Affairs. U.S. Department of State.

Hunter, Janet (1993). *Japanese women working.* London: Routledge.

Jackson, S. E., & Alvarez, E. B. (1992). Working through diversity as a strategic imperative. In S. E. Jackson & Associates (Eds.), *Diversity in the work place: Human resources initiatives* (13–36). New York: Guilford Press.

Kanter, R. M. (1977). *Men and women of the corporation.* New York: Basic Books.

Kirschenman, J., & Neckerman, K. M. (1991). "We'd love to hire them, but . . .": The meaning of race for employers. In I. C. Jencks & P. E. Peterson (Eds.), *The urban underclass* (201–231). Washington, D.C.: Brookings Institution.

Kluckhohn, C. (1954). Culture and behavior. In G. Lindzey (Ed.), *Handbook of social psychology* (Vol. 2, 921–976). Cambridge, MA: Addison-Wesley.

Langer, E. J. (1983). *The psychology of control.* Beverly Hills: Sage.

Lynch, F. R. (1997). *The diversity machine.* New York, NY: Free Press.

Markus, H., & Kitayama, S. (1991). Culture and self: Implications for cognition, emotion and motivation. *Psychological Review, 98,* 224–253.

Moynihan, D. P. (1993). *Pandaemonimum.* Oxford, U.K.: Oxford University Press.

Oberg, K. (1960). Culture shock: Adjustment to new cultural environments. *Practical Anthropology, 7,* 177–182.

Okamura, J. Y. (1998). The illusion of paradise: Privileging multiculturalism in Hawaii. In D. C. Gladney (Ed.), *Making majorities: Constituting the Nation in Japan, Korea, China, Malaysia, Fiji, Turkey, and the United States* (264–284).

Pettigrew, T. F., & Martin, J. (1987). Shaping the organizational context for Black American inclusion. *Journal of Social Issues, 43* (1), 41–78.

Podsiadlowski, A. (1994) *Training interkultureller Kompetenz. Effektivitätssteigerung in Projektgruppen mit deutschen und amerikanischen Teilnehmern in einem multinationalen Unternehmen.* München: unpublished master's thesis.

"A Refugee." (2001, March 3). When is a refugee not a refugee? *The Economist.*

Roberts, K. (1996). Managing disability-based diversity. In E. E. Kossek & S. A. Lobel (Eds.), *Managing diversity: Human resource strategies for transforming the workplace* (310–331) Cambridge, MA: Blackwell Publishers.

Schroll-Machl, S. (1996). Kulturbedingte Unterschiede im Problemlöseprozeß bei deutsch-amerikanischen Arbeitsgruppen. In A. Thomas (Hrsg.), *Psychologie interkulturellen Handelns* (S. 383–409) Göttingen: Hogrefe.

Sessa, V., Jackson, S., & Rapini, D. (1995). Work force diversity: The good, the bad and the reality. In G. R. Ferris, S. D. Rosen, & D. T. Barnum (Eds.), *Handbook of human resource management* (263–281). Cambridge, MA: Blackwell Publishers.

Shirts, G. (1973). *BAFA-FAFA: A cross-cultural simulation.* Del Mar, CA: Simile 11.

Tajfel, H. (1982). *Social identity and intergroup relations.* New York: Cambridge University Press.

Tolbert, A. S. S. (1990). *Venezuelan culture assimilator: Incidents designed for training U.S. professionals conducting business in Venezuela.* Unpublished doctoral dissertation, University of Minnesota.

Triandis, H. C. (1972). *The analysis of subjective culture.* New York: Wiley.

Triandis, H. C. (1975). Cultural training, cognitive complexity, and interpersonal attitudes. In

R. W. Brislin, S. Bochner, and W. J. Lonner (Eds.), *Cross-cultural perspectives on learning.* Beverly Hills: Sage.

Triandis, H. C. (1976). *Variations in black and white perceptions of the social environment.* Urbana: University of Illinois Press.

Triandis, H. C. (1994). *Culture and social behavior.* New York: McGraw-Hill.

Triandis, H. C. (1995). *Individualsm and collectivism.* Boulder, CO: Westview Press.

Triandis, H. C., & Triandis, L. M. (1960). Race, social class, religion, and nationality as determinants of social distance. *Journal of Abnormal and Social Psychology, 61,* 110–118.

Triandis, H. C., Kurowski, L., & Gelfand, M. J. (1994) Workplace diversity. In H. C. Triandis, M. Dunnette, & L. Hough (Eds.), *Handbook of industrial and organizational psychology* (2nd ed.). Palo Alto, CA: Consulting Psychologists Press.

Triandis, H. C., Marin, G., Lisansky, J., & Betancourt, H. (1984). *Simpatica* as a cultural script

of Hispanics. *Journal of Personality and Social Psychology, 47,* 1363–1375.

Tsui, A., & O'Reilly, C. (1989). Beyond simple demographic effects: The importance of relational demography in superior-subordinates dyads. *Academy of Management Journal, 32,* 402–423.

U.S. Census Bureau (2000). *Census 2000.* Washington, D.C.

U.S. Department of Labor (1998). Employment outlook 1996–2006: A summary of BLS projections. *Bureau of Labor Statistics, Bulletin 2502, Feb. 1998.* Washington, D.C.

U.S. Department of Labor. Employment and earnings. *Burea of Labor Statistics. Vol. 48 (1), Jan. 2001.* Washington, D.C.

Villani, S. (2001, March). Breaking through. *Island Business.* Honolulu, HI.

Zangwill, I. (1914). *The melting pot: Drama in four acts.* New York: Macmillan.

TELECOMMUTING: UNDERSTANDING AND MANAGING REMOTE WORKERS

David G. Allen
Robert W. Renn

The Wall Street Journal recently reported that about 19 million Americans now telecommute (February 6, 2001). In addition, over 50 percent of U.S. companies have telecommuting programs (McCune, 1998). *Telecommuting* is an alternative work arrangement facilitated by telecommunications technology that allows employees to work physically away from their employer's premises (Feldman & Gainey, 1997; O'Mahony & Barley, 1999).

Growth in this work arrangement is due to the increasing power, availability, and affordability of telecommunications technology, as well as pressure from employees, organizations, and society. Employees, especially high-tech, engineering, marketing, and other professionals, are demanding greater flexibility and work-family balance. Employers see opportunities to reduce overhead costs, tap underutilized labor sources, and make current employees more satisfied and productive. Also, societal pressure to reduce traffic congestion, air pollution, and fuel consumption continues to gain momentum.

As more companies and employees become involved in telecommuting, researchers and managers need to understand the effects of this relatively new working arrangement on the work perceptions and behaviors of telecommuters. For example, are telecommuters likely to be more satisfied and productive? Does telecommuting lead to employee isolation and reduced commitment to the organization? How can managers motivate and monitor employees from a distance? Are some individuals better suited for telecommuting than others? How can telecommuting arrangements be designed to maximize the potential benefits and minimize the potential drawbacks of this work arrangement? Although organizational research on these questions is just beginning to emerge, it is beginning to provide insights into these important issues.

In this article we draw from organizational theory and research to explain how telecommuting alters the way people work and the impact these changes can have on job performance, work-family conflict, and organizational attachment. In exploring these issues, we organize our discussion around three broad ways telecommuting affects the work experience. First, telecommuting requires an adjustment to a new working arrangement that presents telecommuters with more autonomy, and also exposes them to greater potential for distractions from family and friends during working hours. Each of these changes has implications for telecommuters' job performance. Second, telecommuting simultaneously provides greater flexibility to manage work and nonwork demands, while also blurring the distinctions between work time and space and family time and space. Thus, telecommuting modifies employees' work and family experience. Third, telecommuting physically removes the individual from the workplace and surrounding social context. This change has implications for telecommuters' identification with and at-tachment to the organization. Before elaborating on these issues, we will first examine telecommuting arrangements.

NOT ALL TELECOMMUTING IS CREATED EQUAL

Telecommuting needs to be differentiated from other work arrangements in which individuals work away from a traditional office setting. Workers who run businesses from their home or who happen to live at their work site (e.g. farmers) are not considered telecommuters because there is no commute trip to eliminate, reduce, or shift. Also, although the terms telecommuting and telework are often used interchangeably, telework is defined as using telecommunications technology to conduct business at a distance; thus it includes using faxes, e-mail, cellular phones, and ordinary phone calls from any location, such as from the car on the way to work. Telecommuting is a subset of telework that involves using telecommunications technology to work outside the office in lieu of traveling to the traditional office and to allow greater flexibility to employees.

Further, although a simple view of telecommuters classifies them as workers who work almost entirely with computers, who telecommute full-time, and who work from home, this classification fails to capture the full complexity of telecommuting. A review of the available literature and analysis of the work practices of several large companies with extensive telecommuting experience reveals that telecommuting designs in practice differ along a number of important dimensions. For example, only a fraction of telecommuters do so full-time; most do so part-time. Many telecommuters work part of the day in the office and part out of the office. Such telecommuters do not eliminate commute trips; they shift them to off-peak hours much like employees working on flex-time. In some cases, telecommuters' work does not require use of a computer. Further, telecommuting need not occur only at home. Telecenters, where equipment and supplies are located in small satellite offices, are a growing telecommuting option. In this case, commutes are reduced, though not eliminated.

Drawing from our review and earlier work by Feldman and Gainey (1997), we identify six important facets of telecommuting: (1) percentage of work time spent telecommuting, (2) relative amount of telecommuting in various locations, (3) flexibility of telecommuting scheduling, (4) formalization of policies, (5) extent of electronic performance monitoring, and (6) attributions about the underlying motivation for adopting telecommuting.

Percentage of Work Time Spent Telecommuting

Few individuals are full-time telecommuters. Instead, the amount of time spent telecommuting may range from as little as a few hours per week to full-time telecommuters who rarely, if ever, visit the office. Individuals who work a great deal out of the office are likely to have different experiences than those who do so only a few hours. For instance, greater time spent telecommuting should increase flexibility and autonomy, but may reduce feelings of inclusion and social support, as well as the quantity and quality of communications with others.

Relative Amount of Telecommuting in Various Locations

Telecommuters may work part of the time in the office, part at home, part from alternate work sites such as telecenters, or any combination of locations. Telecommuting from home is a different experience than doing so from a telecenter or satellite office. Depending on its location, telecommuting from a satellite office should still shift, reduce, or eliminate stressful commutes, and may also avoid some types of conflicts and distractions possible when working at home, such as dependent children, household chores, and lack of separation between work and home. On the other hand, telecommuting from a satellite center may not provide as much flexibility or increased ability to balance work and family as telecommuting from home.

Flexibility of Telecommuting Scheduling

Telecommuters differ in terms of the flexibility of their schedules, or the control they have over when and from where they will work. Some telecommuters are required to work certain hours at the office and certain hours from another location, such as home. Others may have core hours during which they must be in the office or must be at home. However, during other times, the employee decides from where to work. Still others have complete flexibility in scheduling the timing and location of work. Telecommuters with greater scheduling flexibility should experience more control and autonomy, and may also perceive that they are better able to balance work and family demands.

Formalization of Policies

There are a host of potential policy issues associated with a telecommuting arrangement, such as communication guidelines, equipment ownership, frequency, and location. Yet there is evidence that organizations vary in the extent to which they provide formal policies regulating the arrangement. One survey indicates that 80 percent of respondent companies lacked formal telecommuting policies, while others provided extensive documentation of specific policies (Farrah & Dagen, 1993). Although this is likely to change as telecommuting becomes a more established work arrangement, the detail and rigidity of such policies will vary. More formal policies should mitigate ambiguity or uncertainty about role expectations, but may also reduce perceived flexibility or autonomy.

Extent of Electronic Performance Monitoring

Management of telecommuters also varies in the extent of electronic performance monitoring that occurs. Concerns about managing and trusting individuals who are not physically present and the possibility of shirking are often cited as barriers to telecommuting arrangements. Thus the evaluation of telecommuters' job performance is an important issue. For telecommuters in professional jobs, evaluation is often based on objectives and results; however, for clerical, data entry, and other nonprofessional telecommuting jobs, an alternative is to closely monitor the amount of time spent at the computer or logged into a system, even to the extent of monitoring keystrokes. Differences in electronic monitoring should result in different experiences in terms of flexibility and control.

Attributions About the Underlying Motivation for Adopting Telecommuting

The assumption is often made that telecommuting is a boon to the telecommuter. However, there are clear differences in the reasons why organizations allow or require telecommuting and these reasons affect the ways in which telecommuting arrangements are implemented. Telecommuters who make more positive attributions about these motivations are likely to have different experiences than those who make less positive ones.

For example, telecommuting arrangements may be initiated for reasons including saving overhead costs, legal compliance, environmental concerns, increasing productivity, greater staffing flexibility, allowing employees greater flexibility, helping employees meet nonwork responsibilities, etc. These underlying adoption motivations may vary in the extent to which they are intended to benefit the telecommuter versus the organization. Although telecommuting may be intended to benefit the employee and company, the experiences of a lower-level data entry worker required to begin telecommuting to save office space are likely to be quite different from those of a manager allowed to telecommute to help accommodate family responsibilities. Underlying adoption motivations more explicitly intended to benefit the telecommuter should result in more positive experiences and outcomes. In the upcoming sections, we will use these telecommuting facets to explain and reveal telecommuting's effects on job performance, work-family conflict, and organizational attachment.

TELECOMMUTING AND JOB PERFORMANCE

Telecommuting has the potential to increase employee productivity, largely because of reduced distractions and commute time. However, telecommuting's effects on job performance will certainly be determined by how well an employee adjusts to this new working arrangement, how a telecommuter uses the increased autonomy, and a telecommuter's personal characteristics.

As they adjust to telecommuting, employees may experience confusion about how to perform their new jobs and job responsibilities that, in turn, temporarily compromises their job performance. Telecommuting is a technological change and an alternative way of designing work. Although a telecommuter's general job responsibilities and tasks may remain fundamentally similar, the work environment and the ways in which they accomplish work may change, perhaps drastically, as a function of telecommuting.

For instance, telecommuters may have to work with unfamiliar technologies, establish and maintain their own safe working environment, lose social contact with co-workers and supervisors, and exercise self-discipline to accomplish work without guidance. Telecommuters may also receive less job-related information from experienced coworkers and supervisors and may not receive as much performance feedback from supervisors as on-site employees because they are physically and psychologically removed from the workplace. Consequently, telecommuters may experience ambiguity about job responsibilities, goals, and the permissible means for accomplishing them that, in turn, forces them to relearn how to best plan, organize, and control their work. The inability to rely on tried and true methods of working successfully may also lower telecommuters' task-related self-confidence, a condition likely to hamper work performance (Bandura, 1986; Jackson & Schuler, 1985; Katz & Kahn, 1978).

Managers have several options for preventing telecommuters from experiencing temporary or even prolonged confusion while adjusting to new working conditions. Formal telecommuting policies and procedures lessen ambiguity by providing guidelines for performing work and for establishing safe and efficient workspaces (Jackson & Schuler, 1985). Unfortunately, statistics indicate that the majority of telecommuters work for companies with fewer than 100 employees, companies that likely do not have job descriptions much less formal telecommuting policies (Greenberg & Baron, 2000). Managers can also carefully monitor telecommuters during the adjustment period and provide assistance for those having difficulty with learning the norms and roles needed to function effectively as telecommuters. In this respect, more frequent communication and performance feedback as well as empathic listening would be expected to clarify expectations and reassure telecommuters during the transition period. To help telecommuters develop a sense of team spirit, even though they work in isolation, managers could socialize new telecommuters as a group. Going through the same training experiences and

facing the same upcoming challenges facilitates a sense of camaraderie and helpful supportive relationships that new telecommuters can draw assurance from during the early days of telecommuting (Johns & Saks, 2001). Finally, telecommuters may go through a transition period where they start with a few hours of telecommuting and then work up to full-time telecommuting.

How employees use the increased autonomy telecommuting provides also influences their job performance. The degree of autonomy various telecommuting arrangements provide differ widely, both in terms of flexibility of scheduling and the policies and procedures regulating the work arrangement. While formal telecommuting policies and procedures may mitigate ambiguity, they may also restrict autonomy and the telecommuter's perceptions of personal control over when and how to work. Despite these variations in job design, as compared with traditional on-site working arrangements, telecommuting should still provide enhanced freedom and flexibility because of the ability to eliminate or shift commutes and to determine how to work, as well as the scheduling of when and from where to work.

While research indicates that greater control over one's work and work environment can enhance work quantity and quality, some telecommuters report difficulty adjusting to the lack of structure this work arrangement creates (Wells, 1997). To prepare employees for the increased autonomy and the lack of structure that accompanies telecommuting, companies could provide telecommuters with self-management training (see article by Renn & Himel in chapter 15). This type of training would teach telecommuters how to better structure their work and set and achieve work goals without external control. Studies clearly indicate that teaching individuals to observe and record their own behavior, set personal improvement goals, and evaluate and reward their own accomplishments enhances job performance, as well as a variety of other work behaviors (Frayne & Geringer, 2000).

Personal characteristics will also affect telecommuters' job performance. For example, telecommuters are physically and psychologically removed from an organization and its members. Thus they work in greater isolation and have less social contact with other employees than on-site employees. Consequently, individuals with low needs for affiliation may perform better in telecommuting jobs than those with high needs for affiliation. According to McClelland (1985), individuals with high affiliation needs desire friendly relationships with others and should perform better in jobs that match this need, such as customer service and training and development. Because telecommuting minimizes face-to-face contact with coworkers and managers, employees' desire for frequent and positive relationships with others may go unmet, and their work motivation and performance may reflect this deprivation.

Telecommuters have greater control over their own work than do regular employees. Because they have more work-related discretion, telecommuters who are conscientious about their work may perform better than those who rank low on this trait. Conscientiousness is an individual difference that represents the extent to which an individual is careful, scrupulous, and persevering (Barrick & Mount, 1991; George & Jones, 1999). Greater latitude allows telecommuters more opportunity to shirk work responsibilities without sanctions, and some telecommuters may find it difficult to remain focused on work if they are not being monitored. Thus, a telecommuter's conscientiousness may explain whether he or she is more likely to use the freedom to set challenging work goals and structure the workday so as to enrich job performance or to drag his or her feet on work assignments.

Lastly, telecommuters' locus of control may also influence how well they perform in less structured working environments. Locus of control is a trait that reflects one's beliefs about who or what controls the events in our lives (Rotter, 1966). *Internals,* or individuals with an internal locus of control, believe that they control their own destiny. By contrast, *externals* attribute the events in their lives to luck, fate, or chance. Studies have revealed many differences in the work attitudes and behaviors of internal versus external employees; however, one difference in particular is relevant to telecommuting (Renn & Vandenberg, 1991). Internals are more independent than externals and perform better than externals on less structured complex tasks. In addition, externals prefer structured working conditions and directive supervision. These differences suggest that telecommuters with an internal locus of control may adapt better, be more satisfied with, and perform better than external telecommuters in a job where they essentially plan, organize and control their own work.

To recap, the relationship between telecommuting and job performance is complex and likely depends on telecommuter preparation, training, adjustment, management, and personality. Additionally, telecommuting may benefit employees by aiding them in managing work and nonwork responsibilities.

TELECOMMUTING AND WORK-FAMILY CONFLICT

Despite more organizations adopting family-friendly policies, employees continue to report experiencing stress from trying to balance work and family responsibilities (George & Jones, 1999). An important potential benefit of telecommuting is the ability to reduce work-family conflict by allowing employees to better balance these competing responsibilities. However, there is some research that suggests that telecommuting may actually increase the potential for work-family conflict (Eagle, Miles, &

Icenogle, 1997). Because telecommuting shifts work at least partially out of the office and often into the home, it affects the boundaries between work and nonwork roles, particularly with regard to work and family (Ashforth, Kreiner, & Fugate, 2000). The unique nature of telecommuting simultaneously provides greater control over the extent to which work and family concerns spill over into each other while also increasing the extent to which the two spheres overlap.

Work-family conflict occurs when the demands of the work role intrude into the family role and vice versa (Pleck, Staines, & Lang, 1980). Spillover theory (Shamir, 1992; Zedeck, 1992) suggests that the amount of control an individual has over the interactions between roles determines whether the spillover between roles is positive or negative. Thus, providing telecommuters greater flexibility over the scheduling of the timing and location of work should result in positive spillover and reduce work-family conflict.

At the same time, though, telecommuting from home can increase the extent to which work and family roles interact, blurring the distinctions between the two, and potentially leading to increased work-family conflict. This is particularly true to the extent the telecommuter has dependent care responsibilities in the home. Thus telecommuters with access to alternative satellite work locations outside the home may benefit from increased flexibility while being less susceptible to work-family conflict.

Alternatively, if circumstances favor telecommuting from the home, telecommuters can be trained to more effectively manage the boundaries between work and family. Setting up a workspace with barriers to interruptions (e.g. an office with a door that can be closed) and ground rules for acceptable and unacceptable interruptions are methods of managing such boundaries. To the extent that telecommuters can more effectively manage these boundaries, they should experience less work-family conflict.

Further, even though telecommuting may present telecommuters with many distractions during working hours, to the extent that these interruptions are reduced, managed, or ignored they should not negatively affect a telecommuter's job performance. Research indicates that individuals differ in their ability to ignore or screen out distractions and this personal characteristic might play an important role in managing work-at-home arrangements. High stimulus screeners are individuals who can block out distractions while working, whereas low stimulus screeners have a more difficult time ignoring outside distractions. Telecommuters who are high stimulus screeners may thus outperform low stimulus screeners in settings where work and family interruptions are commonplace. As explained by Oldham, Cummings, & Zhou (1995), high stimulus screeners are able to cope more effectively with unwanted distractions and interruptions created by the physical context where work is performed.

Although telecommuting certainly has the potential to make employees more productive and better able to manage work-family conflict, such arrangements are not without concerns. One primary concern is the extent to which remote workers will feel that they are a part of the organization and become attached and committed to the organization's success.

TELECOMMUTING AND ORGANIZATIONAL ATTACHMENT

As noted earlier, telecommuting physically removes the telecommuter from the traditional workplace. Such an arrangement may benefit both the telecommuter and the organization through increased flexibility and reduced commuting time. However, there is concern about whether an employee removed from the workplace will continue to identify with and be attached to the organization. A widely expressed concern of employees regarding telecommuting is that they will feel isolated from the workplace and from social contacts at work (Handy & Mokhtarian, 1995). Such separation from coworkers, work culture, and managers will affect telecommuters' organizational attachment through social identity processes, social support, and perceived organizational support.

Social and Personal Identity

Individuals define who they are through the groups to which they belong, and they infuse their group memberships with special meanings. Thus the groups with which one identifies (e.g., company, occupation, sex, race, favorite sports team, family, etc.) influence perceptions of the self and one's place in the world (Hogg & Terry, 2000). As the degree of separation between telecommuters and their company increases, telecommuters will likely spend less time with their work groups and have less exposure to organizational values, meanings, and standards. Less exposure to coworkers and organization culture may cause telecommuters to lose sight of their position in work groups, departments, and the larger social domain of the organization (Hogg & Mullin, 1999). In other words, telecommuters lose contact with those who provide them with a significant part of their social identity.

This may drive telecommuters to seek new groups with whom to identify, to assimilate themselves, and to derive self-esteem (Hogg & Terry, 2000), and may also affect organizational commitment, an attitude or orientation that attaches the identity of a person to an organization (Sheldon, 1971). As opposed to an employee who works on company premises, a telecommuter's ability to identify with the organization may be weakened by the physical and psychological barriers that separate the individual from the organization and its groups. Due to lack of exposure to an organization's context and its groups, telecommuters may become victims of a blurred social identity with specific groups within the organization, and thus struggle to maintain an attachment with the organization.

For this reason it is in the organization's interests to limit the amount of time individuals may telecommute, and to require periodic visits to the office. Managers may also require attendance at other organization functions designed to promote interaction (e.g., parties), and may also be able to offset some of the effects of isolation through frequent rich communication with telecommuters. In addition to telecommuters visiting company premises, managers may venture out and hold progress meetings with individual telecommuters or groups of telecommuters at a telecommuter's home office.

Social Support

Social experiences play a large part in individuals' attachment to an organization. Because we are susceptible to social influence, our coworkers can strongly influence our commitment to an organization by expressing their dependence on us (Salancik, 1977). In addition, the more individuals are integrated into the social fabric of an organization, the greater the likelihood that individuals will develop a strong linkage with the organization (Mowday, Porter, & Steers, 1982).

The frequency and location of telecommuting are likely to affect telecommuters' integration into an organization's social network and perceptions of social support. There is some evidence that extensive computer and Internet use may displace social activities and the maintenance of strong social ties (Kraut, Patterson, Lundmark, Kiesler, Mukopadhyay, & Scherlis, 1998). Similar effects may also occur from extensive telecommuting. Unfortunately, the physical separation telecommuters experience acts as a barrier to interactions with others, reducing face-to-face interactions and frequency of communication with supervisors and coworkers. While videoconferencing may mitigate some of the negative effects of physical separation, individuals who work outside the traditional office are likely to feel less social support from both supervisors and coworkers. Individuals who telecommute from a satellite center are likely to have more interactions with coworkers and perhaps experience greater inclusion in workplace norms and culture than individuals who telecommute from home.

How can managers maintain telecommuters' place in the organization's society, and thus their attachment to the organization? They could require periodic interactions with other organizational members at weekly meetings. They could assign telecommuters to projects with on-site employees and ask that some of the project work be done on company premises. Managers could also train supervisors and coworkers on the role and importance of communication in maintaining telecommuters' connection with the organization. Finally, managers will need to express their and the organization's care and concern for telecommuters' well being.

Perceived Organizational Support

Telecommuting may also affect organizational commitment through perceived organizational support (POS). When employees perceive the organization cares about them, they feel obligated to reciprocate through loyalty and by engaging in behaviors that support organizational goals (Wayne, Shore, & Liden, 1997).

Policies and practices, especially discretionary ones, that express concern for employees enhance POS. Employees who perceive the driving forces behind telecommuting (i.e., adoption motivation) as primarily serving the organization—for example, lower overhead costs and legal compliance—may interpret telecommuting as a sign that the organization does not value

their well-being as much as when the organization provided a pleasant on-site work space. In addition, employees who are forced to telecommute may interpret the decision as an indication that the organization doesn't care about their future careers with the organization. The negative impact that telecommuting may have on career advancement is a primary concern of telecommuters (Perlow, 1997).

On the other hand, employees who believe that the forces motivating telecommuting stem from the desire to help employees avoid stressful commutes, provide greater schedule flexibility, and allow more time to meet nonwork responsibilities may surmise that telecommuting is an action by an organization that cares about their well-being. At the same time, telecommuters who are given a great deal of discretion in managing their work processes will likely perceive that the organization both trusts them and cares about them. Allowing telecommuters to design their own schedules and not shackling them with extremely restrictive rules and monitoring should increase perceived organizational support. Extremely limited flexibility or restrictive rules, policies, and monitoring, on the other hand, might reduce these perceptions. Thus, organizations need to carefully manage telecommuter perceptions of the adoption of telecommuting work arrangements. Managers must also consider the trade-offs involved in closely monitoring and controlling telecommuters' work and performance, and consider allowing telecommuters flexibility in setting their work schedules, within limits.

CONCLUSION

The question of whether telecommuting is a good or bad way of designing work is probably moot: pressures from employees, organizations, and society are likely to continue the trend towards increased telecommuting. The important questions then become what are the effects of designing work to include telecommuting, and how can we design and manage telecommuting arrangements to take advantage of the potential benefits while minimizing the potential drawbacks? Knowing whether the potentially harmful effects on attitudes and behaviors of the dark side of telecommuting will mitigate, overwhelm, or be overwhelmed by the more positive effects requires further empirical evidence. However, our analysis of current research and theory suggests the recommendations expressed in this paper should contribute to the effective management of telecommuters and other remote workers. ■

REFERENCES

Ashforth, B. E., Kreiner, G. E., & Fugate, M. (2000). All in a day's work: Boundaries and micro role transitions. *Academy of Management Review, 25*, 472–491.

Bandura, A. (1986). *Social foundations of thought and action: A social cognitive view.* Upper Saddle River, NJ: Prentice Hall.

Barrick, M. R., & Mount, M. K. (1991). The big five personality dimensions and job performance: A meta-analysis. *Personnel Psychology, 44*, 1–26.

Eagle, B. W., Miles, E. W., & Icenogle, M. L. (1997). Interrole conflicts and the permeability of work and family domains: Are there gender differences? *Journal of Vocational Behavior, 50*, 168–184.

Farrah, B. J., & Dagen, C. D. (1993). Telecommuting policies that work. *HRMagazine*, 64–71.

Feldman, D. C., & Gainey, T. W. (1997). Patterns of telecommuting and their consequences: Framing the research agenda. *Human Resource Management Review, 7*, 369–388.

Frayne, C., & Geringer, M. (2000). Self-management training for improving job performance: A field experiment involving salespeople. *Journal of Applied Psychology, 85*, 361–372.

George, J. M., & Jones, G. R. (1999). *Understanding and managing organizational behavior.* Reading. MA: Addison-Wesley.

Greenberg, J., & Baron, R. A. (2000). *Behavior in organizations: Understanding and managing the human side of work.* Upper Saddle River, NJ: Prentice Hall.

Handy, S. L., & Mokhtarian, P. L. (1995). Planning for telecommuting: Measurement and policy issues. *Journal of the American Planning Association, 61*, 99–111.

Hogg, M. A., & Mullin, B. A. (1999). Joining groups to reduce uncertainty: Subjective uncertainty reduction and group identification. In D. Abrams & M. A. Hogg (Eds.), *Social identity and social cognition* (249–279). Oxford: Blackwell.

Hogg, M. A., & Terry, D. J. (2000). Social identity and self-categorization processes in organizational contexts. *Academy of Management Review, 25*, 121–140.

Jackson, S. E., & Schuler, R. S. (1985). A meta-analysis and conceptual critique of research on role ambiguity and role conflict in work settings. *Organizational Behavior and Human Decision Processes, 36*, 16–78.

Johns, G., & Saks, A. M. (2001). *Organizational behavior: Understanding and managing life at work.* Toronto: Addison-Wesley Longman.

Katz, D., & Kahn, R. L. (1978). *The social psychology of organizations.* New York: Wiley.

Kraut, R., Patterson, M., Lundmark, V., Kiesler, S., Mukopadhyay, T., & Scherlis, W. (1998). Internet parodox: A social technology that reduces social involvement and psychological well-being? *American Psychologist, 53*, 1017–1031.

McClelland, D. C. (1985). *Human motivation.* Glenview, IL: Scott, Foresman.

McCune, J. C. (1998). Telecommunicating revisited. *Management Review, 87*, 10.

Mowday, R. T., Porter, L. W., & Steers, R. M. (1982). *Employee-organization linkages: The psychology of commitment, absenteeism, and turnover.* New York: Academic Press.

Oldham, G. R., Cummings, A., & Zhou, J. (1995). The spatial configuration of organizations. *Research in Personnel and Human Resources Management, 13*, 1–37.

O'Mahony, S., & Barley, S. R. (1999). Do digital communications affect work and organization? The state of our knowledge. In R. Sutton & B. Staw (Eds.), *Research in Organizational Behavior* (vol. 21, 125–162). Greenwich, CT: JAI Press.

Perlow, L. (1997). *Finding time: How corporations, individuals, and families can benefit from new work practices.* New York: Cornell Univesity.

Pleck, J. H., Staines, G. L., & Lang, L. (1980). Conflict between work and family life. *Monthly Labor Review, 103,* 29–32.

Renn, R. W., & Vandenberg, R. J. (1991). Differences in employee attitudes and behaviors based on Rotter's (1966) internal-external locus of control: Are they all valid? *Human Relations, 44,* 1161–1178.

Rotter, J. B. (1966). Generalized expectancies for internal versus external reinforcement. *Psychological Monographs, 80* (1, Whole no. 609).

Salancik, G. R. (1977). Commitment and the control of organizational behavior and belief. In B. M. Staw and G. R. Salancik (Eds.), *New Directions in Organizational Behavior.* Chicago: St. Clair Press.

Shamir, B. (1992). Home: The perfect workplace? In S. Zedeck (Ed.), *Work, families, and organizations* (272–311), San Francisco: Jossey-Bass Publishers.

Sheldon, M. E. (1971). Investments and involvements as mechanisms of producing commitment to the organization. *Administrative Science Quarterly, 16,* 142–150.

Wayne, S. J., Shore, L. M., & Liden, R. C. (1997). Perceived organizational support and leader-member exchange: A social exchange perspective. *Academy of Management Journal, 40,* 82–111.

Wells, S. (1997). For stay-home workers speed bumps on the telecommute. *New York Times.* Availible online at www.nytimes.com.

Zedeck, S. (1992). *Work, family, and organizations.* San Francisco: Jossey-Bass.

THE BASICS OF THE CONTINGENT WORKFORCE

Anthony R. Wheeler
M. Ronald Buckley
Jonathon R. B. Halbesleben

With the growth of the contingent workforce in the economies of industrialized nations, our understanding of the contingent workforce and of the individuals working as a part of the contingent workforce has grown considerably. Within organizations, the use of contingent workers acts as a vital human resources strategy, which allows organizations increased flexibility when responding to changes in the market. For individuals working in the contingent workforce, the impact is not quite as clear. As we enter the new millenium, our inclusion in a global economy ensures that organizations will continue to rely on the contingent workforce to remain responsive to the dynamic nature of a fast-paced, consumer-oriented business environment. This article serves three main purposes: (1) to introduce you to the contingent workforce as organizations use it, (2) to introduce you to the individual who works in the contingent workforce and the impact of contingent work on the individual, and (3) to discuss the future of the contingent workforce, for both the organization and for the individuals involved.

INTRODUCTION TO THE CONTINGENT WORKFORCE

Prior to beginning our conversation about the contingent workforce, we must first define what we mean by "the contingent workforce." The contingent workforce includes a variety of employment contracts, some long-term and some short-term. For the purposes of this article, we will use the definition of the contingent workforce as including part-time workers, contract workers, employee leasing, job-sharing, domestic day work, and third-party employees (which we traditionally think of as a temporary employee who works through an agency). Each of these employment contracts can vary in length and should be used to fit the needs of the organization that uses them.

As of the end of the last century, the contingent workforce as an industry was a very lucrative industry. In 1998, temporary employment agencies alone reported over $50 billion in revenues (National Association of Temporary and Staffing Services, 1999). With the increased use of computer networks, companies specializing in staffing information technology contract workers as network administrators, computer help-desk specialists, and other assorted IT-related jobs, the contingent workforce probably generates more than $50 billion to our nation's and the world's economy (NATSS, 1999). As organizations continue to strive for maximum efficiency, maximum flexibility, and maximum responsiveness, organizations must use the assets of the contingent workforce as a strategy to meet organization goals.

Companies use contingent workers for a myriad of reasons, most of which aid in the attainment of corporate goals. Historically,

we have thought of the contingent workforce as temporary employees that work for an agency (Rogers, 1995). Organizations establish a contract with these temporary employment agencies in order to provide fill-in or stand-by labor for when someone calls in sick or is on vacation. Historically, this service was provided for mostly administrative or clerical jobs. When the secretary called in sick, a replacement could be found within minutes. Typically, these assignments lasted from a couple of hours to a couple of weeks. The temporary employment agency does not always have to send the same temporary employee to the job from day to day. As long as a capable employee filled the vacant position each day, all parties felt satisfied. We must note, however, that temporary employment is only one facet of the contingent workforce (Polivka & Nardone, 1989). Instead of using a temporary employment agency for the purpose of temporarily filling clerical positions, some organizations turned to part-time workers to fill the void.

Technically, the United States Department of Labor considers part-time employment any job in which the incumbent works at least 20 hours per week but less than 40 hours per week (United States Department of Labor, 2001). Typically, organizations are not required by law to provide benefits (i.e., health care, retirement, vacation, sick leave, etc.) to part-time employees. Some organizations staff positions with part-time employees on a rotation, where multiple part-time employees staff a single position and work a combined 40-hour workweek. The organization loses no productivity and reduces expenses by not having to pay overhead on the position.

As organizations realized the benefits of these agreements, they sought to expand the use of the contingent workforce into other parts of the organization. In the global economy of the twenty-first century, organizations typically focus on "core competencies" that are critical to the well-being of the organization. For a public relations and marketing firm, any positions that are not value-added to the attainment of corporate goals become a financial burden to the company. In the case of the PR and marketing firm, any positions directly related to public relations and marketing are critical to the performance of the company. The firm may then view other jobs, such as human resources, MIS, or administrative jobs as noncritical functions within the organization. This does not mean that these functions hold no importance to the functioning of the firm, but it may mean that the company should not directly employ all workers in these jobs. Therefore, the organization may choose to outsource or contract out some of these positions to a company that specializes in doing those jobs. In the case of our PR and marketing firm, they may enter into an agreement with an IT firm that specializes in network administration to run the PR firm's Web site and internal network. The IT staffing firm would then provide employees called "contract employees" or "consultants" to work on-site, at the PR firm, to staff those jobs. The IT staffing firm would also assume the responsibility of providing benefits to those workers; thus, our PR firm would reduce its payroll expenditures and reduce the amount of overhead costs associated with providing benefits to those employees (anywhere between 15 to 30 percent of total compensation costs).

With this strategy of focusing on core competencies by eliminating non-value-added positions within the organization, the corporate world saw an explosion in the use of contingent workers and an explosion in the number of companies offering expertise in contingent workforce services. An organization sees numerous benefits to using this strategy. As mentioned earlier, organizations can reduce overhead costs associated with paying benefits (Golden & Appelbaum, 1992). Organizations can also reduce the costs associated with recruiting, staffing,

and human resources management by using various types of contingent relationships (Golden & Appelbaum, 1992). Instead of conducting a job search, interviewing candidates, training new employees, and socializing new employees, an organization can bring in a contract worker, who has been screened and trained by an outside firm, to perform the job required.

Aside from reducing payroll, benefits, recruiting, and training costs, the use of contingent workers allows an organization more flexibility and responsiveness. Organizations must be able to respond to the market in which they compete, and they must be able to respond to changes in the market as quickly as possible. Let us return to our example of a PR and marketing firm. Ten years ago, our firm worked primarily in print, such as magazines and newspapers. Their account representatives established business contacts through repeat customers and through customer referrals. With the advent of the Internet, their business cycle increased rapidly. Customers required new outlets of exposure and wanted it done quickly. Our PR firm decides to use the Internet as its main vehicle to more efficient operations, yet no one within the organization has the technical expertise to establish their new mode of PR and marketing. The firm has stand-alone personal computers, but does not have a network. The firm has two choices. The first choice is to conduct a job search for a person(s) who has the required expertise and buy the computer equipment needed. The second choice is to conduct a search for an IT firm that specializes in installing, maintaining, and supporting networks and Web sites, including providing the employees needed to perform the work. Conducting the job search could take months, while outsourcing the function could take as few as a couple of weeks to complete. Obviously, the traditional way of recruiting, selecting, and training does not lend itself easily to a rapidly changing business environment. Using the contingent workforce allows for rapid, yet efficient, acclimation to changes in the business environment. Using the contingent workforce also allows for rapid adaptation to new product or service lines, should an organization decide to enter a new product market.

Many companies and organizations also use contingent employment to meet peak-cycle demands (Galup, Saunders, Nelson, & Cerveny, 1997). The department store industry uses contract workers during the winter holiday season, where they have a peak demand for their services. Typically, department stores will hire a large amount of contract workers to maintain inventory, to help with sales, and even to act as Santa Claus. The contract employees will begin their employment with the store as the store begins to gear up for the oncoming season. They will work through the holiday season, and then end their contract with the department store. While they work at the department store during the peak season, they will receive only their wages; but they can be guaranteed at least a 40-hour workweek. In many cases, they will work more than 40 hours per week and will receive overtime pay for work beyond 40 hours per week. Another area we see this peak-cycle staffing strategy is in local, state, and federal government agencies. The United States Department of Interior hires thousands of summer-only contract workers to maintain national parks, monuments, and museums during peak tourism season (United States Department of Labor, 2001). These contract workers act as tour guides, box office attendants, or lawn maintenance employees. At the end of the summer, the workers must find another means of earning wages. The Census Bureau also used contingent workers to canvass neighborhoods across the country to complete the 2000 Census Report (United States Department of Labor, 2001). This strategy allows organizations to meet peak consumer demands very efficiently, without blowing a hole in their budget.

IMPLICATIONS OF THE CONTINGENT WORKFORCE

The use of the contingent workforce does not come without limitations or implications. Primarily, organizations should utilize a mix of both permanent and contingent employees. Some organizations that rely too heavily on contingent employees experience decreased organizational communication, whereby organizational goals are not communicated between permanent and contingent employees (Sias, Kramer, & Jenkins, 1997). Because employees tend to cluster with others similar to themselves, organizations might encounter situations where the two groups seldom, if ever, directly communicate. This reduces organizational communication, and can harm the efficiency and productivity of an organization. Conversely, an organization that sparingly uses contingent employees runs the risk of isolating those employees from others in the work process. In essence, the excluded employee becomes invisible, both physically and socially (Rogers, 1995). This, too, can harm the efficiency and productivity of an organization.

Organizations that have a unionized workforce may encounter resistance from its permanent employees if the organization decides to utilize contingent employees, especially in jobs traditionally held by union members (Paul & Townsend, 1998). Unions perceive the use of contingent employees as a means of not paying wage rates established through union collective bargaining agreements. In a related situation, a Fortune 500 software company recently lost a legal ruling made by the Labor Relations Board. The board ruled that the organization could not hire long-term temporary software developers solely to avoid paying those employees benefits or including them in corporate profit-sharing plans (Swoboda, 2000). The board is currently seeking to establish rules governing the use of contingent employees with regards to offering benefits.

Most importantly, organizations should only use contingent workers when and where it makes most sense. Utilizing the contingent workforce only to cut costs serves to undermine the utility and flexibility of the contingent workforce. By simply using contingent workers as a strategy to cut costs, an organization may experience resentment and dissatisfaction from its permanent employees; moreover, the organization will incur costs associated with employee dissatisfaction, such as increased absenteeism, decreased productivity, and increased turnover. Organizations should utilize the contingent workforce only if it enhances the productivity of the organization or if it supports the strategic goals of an organization. Our PR and marketing firm would be ill-advised to use contingent employees in vital or core positions within the company, such as marketing specialists, account managers, or graphic designers.

EXPERIENCE OF THE CONTINGENT WORKER

Up to this point, we have spoken only about how organizations utilize contingent employees to enhance the flexibility of organizations to respond to changes in the business environment. Unfortunately, we know little about the impact of being a member of the contingent workforce. Earlier, we defined the term "contingent employment," which included employment situations such as part-time employment, contract employment, various types of consulting, and employees working for a temporary employment agency. We must note that people enter into the contingent workforce for various reasons, mostly personal ones.

In the historical sense of contingent employment, a typical employee would probably be a female filling some type of clerical or administrative position (Henson, 1996). Moreover, the earliest form of the contingent employee, the part-time employee, would also most likely be a female filling a clerical or administrative position. Many women happily entered these types of employment situations in order to supplement her spouse's income, without compromising her "traditional" role of raising children. This same employment situation also provided great opportunities to women attempting to re-enter the workforce after giving birth or raising children. For these women, part-time or temporary employment enabled them to develop new skills or retrain skills needed to succeed in corporations. The contingent workforce provided a mechanism for reentry into organizations after a period of absence from the corporate world. This classic situation represents a "win-win" situation for both the employer and the employee; however, this classic situation of the contingent workforce is no longer as prevalent.

While the temporary employment industry continues to employ a disproportionate number of women, mostly in the same types of clerical and administrative jobs, it would be inaccurate to describe the current contingent workforce as being dominated by one sex. However, a mentality or stereotype continues to exist regarding the contingent worker (Rogers, 1995). Because the growth of the contingent workforce, mostly through part-time and temporary employees, coincided with the mass entrance of women into the business environment, some people continue to believe that being a contingent worker means you are a woman working in an administrative position. Furthermore, because women occupied mostly administrative, lower-paying jobs during the growth of the contingent workforce, the stereotype continues to exist that contingent jobs are low-paying jobs. While we hope this stereotype erodes, little research exists that examines if this stereotype has diminished.

The result of this stereotype, and the resulting negative attitude, about contingent workers lingers in modern companies (Rogers, 1995; Henson, 1996). Many members of the contingent workforce, specifically temporary and part-time employees, come away from their employment experiences feeling bitter. Much of what we know about the contingent workforce comes directly from the reports of these employees (Rogers, 1995; Henson, 1996). Needless to say, the picture they paint about contingent employment experiences does not reflect positively on the organizations that use contingent employees. Again, little research exists that examines if attitudes toward contingent employment have changed.

Contingent workers typically report being physically and socially isolated, not only from the permanent employees working around them on the job, but also from other contingent employees. Contingent workers report that they seldom receive feedback from their on-site supervisors (see the Halbesleben, Buckley, & Wheeler article in chapter 6), and the feedback they do receive comes unsolicited (Galup et al., 1997). Many contingent employees believe that the permanent employees they work with hold negative attitudes toward them. Because contingent employees historically have worked in administrative or clerical positions, some permanent employees may believe that contingent employees are not capable of filling positions aside from the low-level administrative or clerical jobs. Many permanent employees also resist forming relationships with contingent employees due to the brevity of the contingent employee's assignment with the organization.

For consultants or contract employees, permanent employees may resist forming relationships due to the belief that the con-

sultants or contract employees represent competition for their own jobs (Galup et al., 1997). Because contingent employees typically work for a third-party organization, some permanent employees view them as outsiders. Further stressing this belief is that organizations usually bring in contingent employees to perform jobs that cannot be done by the existing staff, or the organization in the past handled these jobs in-house but currently outsources the functions to increase flexibility. The organization owns some of the responsibility for fostering this "outsider" view of contingent employees by using the appearance of cost cutting as the reason for using contingent employees. If the organization effectively communicates the strategies and goals behind the use of contingent employees, the use of contingent workers may not result in the labeling of contingent workers as "outsiders."

We should now address the long-held belief that contingent workers receive less pay for their work than do permanent employees. We can examine this issue in two ways. The first view of examining contingent workers' pay looks solely at the pay per hour of work received by the contingent worker. From this view, contingent employees, especially consultants and contractors, earn higher wages per hour than do permanent employees performing the same job (NATSS, 1999). For a part-time employee or a temporary employee, this may or may not hold true. Depending on the terms of the contract established between the part-time employee or the contract established between the temporary agency providing the service and the organization using the service, the wage earned by the contingent employee varies. The National Association of Temporary and Staffing Services (NATSS) reported on their 1998 survey of temporary employees that the average wage earned per hour by a temporary employee working in an administrative capacity was more than $10 per hour. In most cases, however, contingent employees do not receive benefits as a part of their pay.

This aspect of employee compensation, the lack of benefits received, is the second way to examine contingent employee pay. Again, consultants and contract workers differ from part-time and temporary employees. In either case, the organization where the contingent employee works on-site holds no responsibility for covering the cost of benefits to the contingent workers. If the contingent employee receives benefits as a part of their total compensation, the company that they directly work for, as opposed to the company they work on-site for, generally covers those costs. Many consultants or contract workers, if they work for a larger consulting or contracting firm, receive benefits. If the consultants or contract workers are self-employed, they must cover their own benefit costs. Similarly, temporary employees have not historically received benefits as a part of their total compensation. Today, however, many temporary employment agencies do offer benefits to temporary employees based upon the length of time the temporary employee has worked through the agency (NATSS, 1999). For the part-time employees, federal and state laws do not require companies to pay benefits to those individuals who work less than 40 hours per week. The authors must note, however, that these employment laws and employment practices of not paying benefits are undergoing change. As mentioned earlier, a landmark labor case recently mandated that companies could not hire long-term contingent employees solely to avoid paying benefits. This ruling may alter many established practices regarding pay and the contingent workforce.

Until this point we have made little mention of why an individual would want to work in the contingent workforce. We noted that, historically, women used the contingent workforce as a means to earn supplemental family income, develop new or little used skills, or to gain entrance or reentry in the workforce. While some people may continue to seek contingent employment for the same reason, a shift has occurred in the reasons as to why an individual would enter the contingent workforce (Wheeler & Buckley, 2001).

Individuals employed through a temporary employment agency, which now staff jobs including administrative, IT, HR, and health care (such as nurses), may seek contingent employment for several reasons. Some individuals use contingent employment as a means to earn a paycheck when looking for new job (i.e., when layoffs occur), and many recent college graduates use contingent employment as a way to enter the workforce (Feldman, Doerpinghaus, & Turnley, 1994). Many people also use contingent employment to "test drive" jobs or companies. In this instance, an individual can work in an occupation or for a company to see if they enjoy the work or the company. The experience provides the employee with a form of a realistic job preview, and they can move on to a different job or a different company until they find a suitable job.

Another recent trend is for organizations to "test-drive" employees, using contingent employment in the same way as employees might (Paul & Townsend, 1998). In this instance, an organization will bring in a contingent worker for a probationary period. If the worker performs to an acceptable level, the organization will hire the employee as a permanent employee. If the worker fails to perform adequately, the organization can simply bring in a new employee without having to conduct another job search. This allows organizations to reduce recruiting and human resources costs, without compromising productivity.

Several people also use the contingent workforce because it simply fits their lifestyle (Wheeler & Buckley, 2001). These people may not want to work for one company in one job. They may enjoy the flexibility that contingent work provides. Many contingent employees can set their own schedules, work the number of hours in a day or week that they wish, and work in the jobs or for the companies for which they want to work. It appears that this type of contingent employee enjoys the bouncing from one job to the next, and it appears that the lack of social relationships or social identity created through work does not affect them as it might other people. Consultants and contractors may view their work in similar ways.

The consultant or contract worker also has a choice in the type of job and type of company for which they work. Normally, contract workers and consultants possess highly specialized, highly coveted skills (Galup et al., 1997). Organizations are willing to pay high wages to these members of the contingent workforce because these workers possess expertise that might not be found within most organizations. Sometimes you may find organizations comprised of contingent employees with specialized business expertise. While employees at these organizations may not have the flexibility of accepting work based on personal preference, the organizations they work for normally pay high wages to attract qualified workers. These organizations also establish good relationships with companies that use their contingent workers; thus they develop repeat customers and develop solid reputations within an industry. The consultant or contract worker that is self-employed enjoys great flexibility in whom they work with and where and when they will work. For the independent consultant or contractor, contingent employment is almost always a "win-win" situation.

THE FUTURE OF THE CONTINGENT WORKFORCE

So far we have discussed what the contingent workforce is, why organizations use contingent employees and the impact of using them, and why individuals enter the contingent workforce and what the impact is on those who choose to enter it. We should now examine the future of the contingent workforce, for both the organizations using it and for the individuals working within it. No end to the use of contingent employees appears in sight. Moreover, we should expect a greater reliance upon the contingent workforce in the future.

The roots of the contingent workforce began with part-time and temporary employees working mostly in clerical and administrative jobs. As our economy melds into a global economy, with increased emphasis on efficiency, technology, and customer service, we will see an expansion of the contingent workforce into all occupations in all industries. In the temporary employment industry, we have seen a shift in the services offered to organizations. Temporary employment agencies staff and recruit almost any kind of company or any kind of job imaginable. From administrative (the bedrock of the industry) to human resources positions, to information management and technology positions, to health care positions, temporary employment agencies can staff an organization's needs. An entire sub-industry within the temporary employment industry solely staffs manual and blue-collar jobs. These jobs range from certified electricians and masons to day laborers and construction workers. These temporary agencies usually pay their workers at the end of each day and can usually staff an entire construction site for an unlimited period of time. Although labor unions typically resist the use of contingent workers in these areas, organizations will continue to utilize these contingent employees as a means of finding qualified workers without paying union-bargained rates for their services.

With the boom in information technology, we should also expect continued use of contingent employees, especially contract and consulting workers. Although temporary employment agencies also fill these positions, companies that rely upon technical expertise in very specialized fields do not mind paying high wages for the services a contractor or consultant can provide. In fact, many temporary employment agencies, consulting firms, and contracting firms that specialize in IT and MIS act as a recruiting and selection source for companies seeking talented workers. An entire industry of recruiting for IT and MIS jobs has sprung up surrounding the use of contingent employees.

It is also worth noting that as managed health care grips the medical industry, we will see heavy reliance upon contingent employees to fill vital positions in this industry. Managed health care companies seek to drive down the costs related to medical service without compromising the quality of the service provided. Managed health care firms have begun to hire contract or temporary nurses to staff positions within their network of health care providers. By eliminating the costs associated with hiring permanently employed nurses, managed health care firms can hire certified and competent nurses at a fraction of the cost of hiring a permanently employed nurse. The savings associated with this type of hiring practice are then passed on to the consumer. While many people disagree with this method health care, due to fears of malpractice, we should expect to see an increased use of the contingent workforce in this industry.

We will continue to see organizations using contract workers to meet peak-cycle demands. As organizations continue to respond to the demands of their customers or consumers, especially in service-oriented industries, we will see the organizations staffing to meet the peak production demands using contract employees. When the demand for production subsides, organizations can terminate the employee contract and use permanent employees to meet the average production demand. When demand increases, organizations can simply rehire the contract workers to meet production demands. The organization will be able to maintain this staffing cycle easily, efficiently, and cost effectively.

As more workers enter the contingent workforce, we should expect to see the negative stereotype associated with contingent employment slowly change into a more positive view. As contingent employment becomes more prevalent in organizations and more accepted as an effective strategy for adapting to change and increasing productivity, many people will see the utility of the contingent employee. While some may view contingent workers as competition or imitation workers, others may see the expertise that many contingent workers possess. In fact, we may see an increase in employees opting to work as contingent employees. In the temporary employment industry, we may have already begun to see the shift in attitudes toward temporary employment. As more people enter temporary employment and dispel the stereotype that temporary employees are unskilled, unintelligent, and unworthy of our attention, we have seen an increase in the acceptance of these workers. As mentioned earlier, with contingent workforce firms beginning to grant benefits to contingent workers, the total compensation of contingent employees will increase.

CONCLUSIONS

In conclusion, we have discussed numerous uses and implications of the contingent workforce. From its roots of employing administrative and clerical positions, the contingent workforce has grown to encompass almost every job in any industry that one can imagine. We have also discussed the contingent workforce as it moves from a traditionally female-dominated endeavor to an evenly mixed endeavor for both males and females. As more organizations rely on contingent workers to perform technical and demanding jobs, we can expect to see a more positive regard for contingent employment. In the past, this may not have always been the case, and we examined how this negative view of contingent employees has affected their performance. Because organizations and individuals within organizations are more familiar with the contingent workforce, we should expect the contingent workforce to become more mainstream in the global business community. ■

REFERENCES

Feldman, D. C., Doerpinghaus, H. I., & Turnley, W. H. (1994). Managing temporary workers: A permanent HRM challenge. *Organizational Dynamics, 13* (2), 49–62.

Galup, S., Saunders, C., Nelson, R. E., & Cerveny, R. (1997). The use of temporary staff and managers in a local government environment. *Communication Research, 24* (6), 698–730.

Golden, L., & Appelbaum, E. (1992). What was driving the 1982–1988 boom in temporary employment?: Preference of workers or decisions and power of employers. *American Journal of Economic and Sociology, 51* (4), 473–493.

Henson, K. D. (1996). *Just a temp: The disenfranchised worker.* Philadelphia, PA: Temple University Press.

National Association of Temporary and Staffing Services. (1999). *Who are temporary workers?: You may be surprised to learn.* Available online at www.natss.org.

Paul, R. J., & Townsend, J. B. (1998). Managing the contingent workforce—Gaining the advantages, avoiding the pitfalls. *Employee Responsibilities and Rights Journal, 11* (4), 239–252.

Polivka, A., & Nardone, T. (1989, December). On the definition of contingent work. *Monthly Labor Review,* 9–16.

Rogers, J. K. (1995). Just a temp: Experience and structure of alienation in temporary clerical employment. *Work and Occupations, 22* (2), 137–166.

Sias, P. M., Kramer, M. W., & Jenkins, E. (1997). A comparison of the communication behaviors of temporary employees and new hires. *Communication Research, 24* (6), 731–754.

Swoboda, F. (2000, August 31). Temporary workers win benefits ruling. *Washington Post,* A01.

United States Department of Labor. (2001). Available online at www.usdl.gov.

Wheeler, A. R., & Buckley, M. R. (2001). Examining the motivation process of temporary employees: A holistic model and research framework. *Journal of Managerial Psychology, 15* (6). In press.

PART III

FUNCTIONS OF HUMAN RESOURCES MANAGEMENT

There are myriad activities with which human resources professionals need to be concerned. Managers confront and address these tasks on an ongoing basis. The effectiveness with which these tasks are accomplished can be translated directly into human resources effectiveness. Although many of these tasks are considered mundane and pedestrian, failure to accomplish them may result in great ineffectiveness from an organizational standpoint. Part III is concerned with the building blocks of organizational success that are the basis of the human resources functions. Successful managers cannot afford to ignore these foundations of human resources.

To reduce the impact of a dynamic environment on the human resources function, organizations need to collect information that will reduce ambiguity and facilitate the planning and staffing process. The articles in Chapter 5 are concerned with those issues that take an individual from outside the organization and yield an organization member. Once an individual is inside an organization, effective performance must be facilitated and evaluated, as is suggested in the articles in Chapter 6. The articles in Chapter 7 are concerned with the compensation process. Developing an optimal compensation system is a difficult but necessary task for an organization. It must be able to both attract external applicants and retain internal employees. A current topic that has received much attention is life-long learning, also known as employee training and development. The articles in Chapter 8 address this issue. Our employees need to be developed at work. This advantages both the employee and the organization. These articles outline ways in which this development can take place.

CHAPTER

5

HUMAN RESOURCES PLANNING AND STAFFING

Personnel and human resources management is often viewed as a series of activities designed to process people into, through, and out of organizations. In this view, the first activity is human resources planning. Human resources planning seeks to determine the number and kinds of people the organization needs now and may need in the foreseeable future and seeks ways to satisfy those needs—perhaps even to anticipate them. With the growing interest in strategic human resources management and its link to strategic business planning, we will probably see attempts at more systematic human resources planning in the future.

The link between human resources planning and strategic business planning is important because, in the development of an informed forecast of the firm's human resources needs, it is necessary to have input concerning the direction the organization will be taking in the future: whether growth or decline is projected, what types of skills will be required, and so forth. It is also important to consider the current and potential availability or supply of human resources skills in the organization and the marketplace. Organizations establish human resources information systems to help keep track of such matters. Timely and accurate human resources information may, for example, enable an organization to postpone or implement a variety of recruitment and training activities or to capitalize on the availability of a given mix of skills to pursue a new venture.

Within a broader, more integrated view of the personnel function, career planning and development activities in organizations represent a logical component of human resources planning. Making sure that the right people with the right skills are at the right place at the right time is quite consistent with helping people plan their careers in organizations and establishing routes to take and time frames to meet.

The process of entry into the organization involves both recruitment and selection. Recruitment concerns itself with attracting as large a qualified pool of candidates as possible to apply for the organization's available openings. Selection involves making the fine distinctions necessary to better match job requirements with personal skills and abilities.

A number of personnel screening tools aid the organizations' entry process. Despite its recognized lack of objectivity and validity, nearly every organization employs the interview in some phase of the entry process. Because it is unlikely that we will see a decline in the use of the interview, we need new ways to make it a more effective decision making tool. Conducting multiple interviews or a structured interview, or using the interview only for evaluating the characteristics that it is good at measuring, might lead to improvement. Other selection devices include a personnel test, reference checks, weighted application blanks, and simulations or work samples.

The articles in this chapter are an eclectic mix. The first article, by Fenner and Renn, addresses the issues of how organizations can retain individuals in the information technology profession. Beu and Buckley look at the interview process. This is one of the first points of contact between the individual and the organization. This article is written from the perspective of the candidate in the interview process. If you will conduct an interview, or just be interviewed at some time in your future, you will glean important information from this article. Mumford, Manley, and Halbesleben suggest that using background data can be useful in the selection, recruitment, and development of individuals at work. They provide numerous suggestions concerning how this may be accomplished. Veres, Sims, Locklear, Jackson, and O'Leary present a primer on job analysis, a technique that serves as the basic building block of many of the functions in the human resources management process. In the last article, Higgins discusses the notion of fit and how that notion has become an important issue in the staffing process. "Fit" has always been an interesting concept—everyone knows what it is, but few can adequately define it.

READINGS

CONTINGENT VERSUS REGULAR INFORMATION TECHNOLOGY PROFESSIONALS: INSIGHTS ON RETENTION FROM SOCIAL IDENTITY THEORY

Grant H. Fenner
Robert W. Renn

The Internet and the information revolution are changing the face of business in the twenty-first century. In addition, leveraging information technology effectively is vital to corporate success in a global marketplace where customers demand quick service, high quality, and value (Daft, 2001). Not surprisingly, companies are investing a great deal of money and time recruiting, training, orienting, and retaining information technology (IT) workers. These costly and highly sought after workers, however, have one of the highest annual turnover rates in today's organizations. Managers suggest that turnover rates among IT professionals ranging from a low of 15 percent to a high of 30 percent per annum are typical (Alexander, 1998; Callas, 1998; Duffy, 1998; Fryer, 2000). A survey conducted by Deloitte & Touche in 1998 revealed that 30 percent of responding chief information officers experienced higher turnover than the industry average of 20 percent for these technical positions (Callas, 1998).

We interviewed managers of a Fortune 500 firm located in the Southeast and learned that not only did this organization lose many of its IT workers to other organizations, but that a significant number of its regular IT employees quit in order to become contingent workers (Fenner & Renn,

1999). Contingent workers are employees who lack a long-term career relationship with an employer and are often referred to as consultants or contract workers. A personal communication with Zeff-Geber (1999) revealed that managers of an organization undergoing a software conversion expressed fears that core team members might be lost to contingent work during a 1996–1997 project. As it turned out, the organization lost nine regular employees to the contracting firm, with a number of these people becoming independent contractors themselves shortly thereafter. These findings suggest that IT workers are not just quitting and going to work for other companies as regular employees, but that a significant number leave secure jobs for contingent work.

Because IT employees are becoming increasingly critical to corporate success and because of the expensive direct and indirect costs of losing these valued employees, managers need to understand the causes of IT worker turnover, especially when contingent work is involved. Unfortunately, traditional views of the turnover process shed little light on why IT employees leave permanent jobs for contingent work, because these frameworks apply to regular or permanent employees who depart for alternative jobs. In fact, work groups that include part-time, temporary, and contingent workers are often excluded from turnover studies because they fail to fit the standard turnover model (Hulin, Roznowski, & Hachiya, 1985). In this article, we provide an explanation for the quitting behaviors of regular IT employees who exchange their careers for contingent work. We begin by exploring the rapid growth of contingent work in U.S. business.

A GROWING CONTINGENT WORKFORCE

The U.S. workforce has undergone a transformation in the last 20 years as a new class or category of worker has emerged in increasing numbers. This new type of worker has been referred to by a variety of names: temporary worker, consultant, and independent contractor. We will use the term *contingent worker* to describe those workers who fall outside the boundary of regular or conventional career employment. This term, coined in 1985 by Audrie Freedman, describes a management strategy calling for the hiring of workers when there is a specific and immediate need for their services (Hershey, 1995; Plovika & Stewart, 1996). Nollen & Axel (1996) offer a more comprehensive definition of contingent workers and the jobs they hold, describing them as follows:

> . . . people who have little or no attachment to the company at which they work. Whether they work, when they work, and how much they work depends upon the company's need for them. They have neither an explicit or implicit contract for continuing employment. Their work is contingent on the work to be done according to the company's call. (p. 7)

In 1995, the Bureau of Labor Statistics reported that contingent workers made up 12.6 million or 10 percent of the U.S. workforce (Cohany, 1998). The jobs contingent

workers perform no longer consist of only clerical or unskilled day jobs. Instead, these newly emerging contingent jobs include skilled shop employment and professional positions, such as those found in heath care, academics, engineering, software programming and even in senior management (Allen & Sienko, 1997; Caudron, 1994; Matusic & Hill, 1998; Rousseau, 1995; Thompson, 1997; and Zeff-Geber, 1999).

The rapid expansion of contingent work is due to a combination of corporate forces and employee needs. From a corporate perspective, use of contingent workers represents a strategy to reduce costs and increase flexibility; contingent workers rarely receive benefits, and they can be hired or released with no long-term commitment or consequence. In addition, corporate downsizings and restructurings have forced out many regular full-time employees who then reluctantly or even involuntarily take contingent work (Nollen & Axel, 1996; Van Horn-Christopher, 1996; Van Dyne & Ang, 1999).

Contingent work is also expanding because more employees are attracted to jobs with reduced hours and flexible schedules. This kind of work is appealing to people with competing obligations at home, such as caring for younger children or an elderly family member (Kallenberg & Schmidt, 1997; Larson, 1996; Van Dyne & Ang, 1999; Victor, 1989). Lastly, contingent jobs are attractive to those families looking for a secondary or supplementary source of income and whose primary wage earner's employer provides fringe benefits. Next we turn our attention to a specific segment of the contingent workforce, the contingent technical professional.

FROM REGULAR IT WORKER TO CTP

According to the Bureau's statistics previously mentioned, about 800,000 of the 12.6 million contingent jobs surveyed consisted of contractor positions, a group of contingent jobs that includes workers referred to as contingent technical professionals (CTPs) (Zeff-Gerber, 1999). Although smaller in size in comparison to other contingent job classifications, CTPs represent one of the most rapidly growing sectors of contingent work. This population of contract workers increased 24 percent from 1995 to 1997, and is expected to grow by an impressive 123 percent between the years 1996 and 2006 (Melchiomo, 1999).

Contingent technical professionals are individuals who engage purposefully in temporary or contingent work and who possess expertise in fields such as engineering, manufacturing technology and design, and computer design and programming. These contingent workers commonly refer to themselves as consultants as opposed to contractors, despite the fact that they are commonly involved in "doing" as much as they are in "advising" (Zeff-Geber, 1999). Contingent technical professionals frequently work for a firm that provides their services to other client organizations under contract; they often work at a physical facility owned by the client organization and typically work with one client organization at a time (Cohany, 1998). Although college graduates may seek entry-level jobs as CTPs to gain work experience that may lead to permanent positions, the ranks of CTPs are increasingly being filled by regular full-time IT workers who leave secure jobs for contracting work.

Our research indicates that traditional turnover frameworks cannot explain the behaviors and decisions of regular IT workers who opt for contingent professional work. Traditional turnover models offer a satisfactory explanation for the quitting behaviors of regular technical professions who leave the organization for regular jobs at other organizations (cf. Mobley, 1977; Mobley, Griffeth, Hand & Meglino, 1979). However, these models do not explain why regular employees with secure careers quit for what is commonly regarded as less attractive contingent work. Although the work of CTPs may provide attractive gross earnings, this type of contingent work also offers greater uncertainty, little or no job security, few if any fringe benefits, and larger demands on personal time. It also commonly requires extensive travel.

Furthermore, traditional turnover frameworks rely upon a person leaving a job because of low job satisfaction and establishing one's intention to leave as a foregoing condition for quitting one's job (Lee, Mitchell, Holtom, McDaniel & Hill, 1999). The Lee & Mitchell (1994) unfolding model of voluntary turnover suggests that environmental events representing system shocks can lead otherwise satisfied employees to reevaluate their present jobs and consider alternative job opportunities. The end result is that relatively satisfied employees might quit and take alternative jobs that promise to be more satisfying.

In the interviews we conducted (Fenner & Renn, 1999) and in the personal conversations with Zeff-Geber (1999), the large-scale loss of regular IT workers to contingent work did not occur until a significant event occurred in the work environment. Specifically, the IT professionals who left full-time positions for contingent jobs worked for companies undergoing a major software conversion that required hiring specially trained and knowledgeable consultants who facilitated the software conversion process and transferred operating knowledge to existing core employees. Thus we have looked beyond traditional turnover models for an explanation for the actions of full-time IT employees who leave their secure jobs for contingent work. Our explanation for this particular type of turnover is grounded in social identity theory and the unfolding model of turnover (Hogg & Terry, 2000; Lee & Mitchell, 1994).

INFLUENCES OF SOCIAL IDENTITY ON IT WORKER'S DECISION TO LEAVE

Social identity theory (SIT) describes the forces that motivate individuals toward group membership and explains why individuals find some groups attractive and others unattractive. It also sheds light on the motivating properties of group membership and how group membership affects individuals' attitudes and behaviors. With SIT managers can gain an understanding of how employees define who and what they are through the skills they hold, their work groups, and their employing organization. More specifically, SIT provides managers insight into why full-time IT workers may consider contingent work because of their conflicting roles as IT professionals, members of an IT department, and as constituents of a larger and more abstract organization.

Social Identity and Redefinition of Oneself

Organizations are composed of many groups embedded within a network of relationships separated by differences in power, status, and prestige (Hogg & Terry, 2000). It is from membership in one or more of these work groups that individuals derive much of their social identity. Social identity refers to our awareness of belonging to specific social groups, how our self-concept is defined by group membership, and the value we attach to membership in these groups (Tajfel, 1972).

Social identity differs from personal identity. Personal identity refers to definitions of our self-concept based on comparisons with other individuals. By contrast, social identity refers to how we define ourselves through membership in valued groups. Social psychologists suggest that our membership in work organizations, departments, and groups greatly influences our social identity. Indeed, these experts argue that

for some individuals professional and organizational identities are more important for defining who and what they are than the identities they attach to gender, age, and race (Hogg & Terry, 2000).

Ingroups and outgroups clarify individuals' social identity. Ingroups are groups that individuals claim membership in, and outgroups are groups to which individuals do not claim membership. Ingroups and outgroups represent social categories that partition individuals into discrete units. Individuals categorize themselves into ingroups and outgroups along several dimensions, including families, gender, race, and religion, as well as work organizations, functional specialization, and skill levels. It is important to note that individuals are capable of self-categorizing into more than one of these groups at a time. Social psychologists have found that cognitively partitioning oneself and others into ingroups and outgroups accentuates perceived similarities and differences between groups, and influences individuals to show preferences for ingroups over outgroups. In addition, studies also indicate that self-categorizing oneself into ingroups produces conforming behavior, stereotyping, and increased cooperation (Hogg & Terry, 2000).

Individuals are motivated to identify with ingroups for social identity purposes, because doing so can reduce uncertainty and because individuals derive self-esteem and validation from ingroups. Individuals often experience uncertainty about their beliefs about themselves and the world because these beliefs are subjective and lack objective reference points. Subjective uncertainty presents a threat to individuals' ability to control their destiny and serves to motivate behavior designed to mitigate its effects (Hogg & Mullin, 1999). To reduce subjective uncertainty, individuals seek and derive validation for their beliefs from similar others or, more specifically, members of ingroups. By contrast, individuals expect to disagree with outgroups and do not use outgroups as sources of uncertainty reduction or social reference points.

Individuals also derive a positive self-identity and enhanced self-esteem through ingroup memberships. Indeed, social psychologists find that individuals' self-esteem is enriched by the success and achievements of ingroups, even when the individuals had no role in the groups' success (Cialdini, Borden, Thorne, Walker, Freeman, & Sloan, 1976). While external threats to individuals' self-esteem can strengthen the importance of membership in particular ingroups, Kramer (1991) argues that the nature of ingroup identification is not static and that ingroup identification may shift from one group to another as the situation dictates from the individual's perspective.

Optimal Distinctiveness

Optimal distinctiveness refers to the individual's need for inclusion and distinctiveness, that is, the dual motives of identifying with a larger group and distinguishing oneself from others and being seen as an individual. Brewer (1991) suggests that groups that are exclusive, as opposed to highly inclusive, foster greater attachment and identification because they better satisfy the need for inclusion and distinctiveness. Independent of self-esteem needs, optimal distinctiveness motivates individuals to select a social identity that achieves the most desirable level of distinctiveness for a particular person (Sherman, Hamilton, & Lewis, 1999).

An example of the strength of being distinctive recently made the headlines with the U.S. Army's planned adoption of the black beret as part of the standard uniform for all U.S. Army service personnel. In the past, the beret was the exclusive military issue provided solely to the members of Special Forces. Its distribution to all Army personnel weakens the distinctiveness of being a member of the Green Berets.

Therefore, despite adopting multiple identities from membership in a profession, functional department, or organization, the need for optimal distinctiveness suggests that individuals will not assign equal value to membership in each ingroup. That is, people face a conflict or identity crisis such that they may feel obliged to depersonalize their identity by aligning themselves with larger departmental or organizational groups in contrast to individualizing their identity at the professional level predicated on their possession of requisite skills. This choice will depend upon the distinctiveness that either group's membership is capable of offering and if the benefits of membership are desirable or relevant at a particular point in time.

In summary, social identity theory sensitizes managers to the importance of carefully monitoring the effects of introducing contingent IT workers into the workplace on regular IT workers' social identities, self-esteem, and ingroup/outgroup dynamics. Doing so may threaten regular IT workers' self-esteem because contingent IT workers are typically highly skilled, respected, and well paid, and thus may be viewed as more prestigious and successful than regular IT employee groups. Because of the perceived high status and success attributed to them, contingent IT worker groups may attract regular IT workers to seek membership in their group rather than being discriminated against as outgroups. Indeed, social psychologists have found that individuals identify more strongly with groups that are successful and have high status than with low-status, unsuccessful groups (Ellemers, van Kippenberg, de Vries, & Wilke, 1988). Successful groups offer members greater self-esteem building qualities, and workers may shift favored ingroup membership in order to reinstill lost or threatened self-esteem.

In addition, a worker is not limited to membership in any one group and may consider himself or herself to be a member of several groups at one time. Hence, it is possible for IT workers to view themselves as members of local software programming work groups, as members of professional organizations, and as company employees simultaneously. Lastly, workers are engaged in constant conflict between individual and group identification targets predicated on the distinctiveness and desirability associated with self-definition. It is now important to determine how these theories contribute to an understanding of IT worker turnover by exploring the Lee & Mitchell (1994) unfolding model of voluntary turnover.

THE TURNOVER MODEL

According to SIT, the inordinately high turnover among IT workers does not rest solely with worker dissatisfaction and the availability of job alternatives in a tight labor market. In this section, we offer a rationale describing how IT worker turnover rates are positively skewed by the quitting behaviors of workers who leave their regular jobs for contingent work in spite of remaining satisfied with their jobs. The Lee & Mitchell (1994) unfolding model of voluntary turnover illustrates how even satisfied employees leave their jobs in the wake of a significant shock or environmental event.

The unfolding model of turnover includes four major themes. First, an employee experiences an event or shock that sharpens his or her awareness of the work situation. Examples of shocks include layoff announcements, unsolicited job offers, death of a loved one, or a coworker quitting.

Second, this shock is followed by the employee's search in memory for a similar experience or script that describes how best to respond to the shock. For instance, a memory of layoffs at another employer might reveal that feelings of personal guilt accompanied the dismissal of friends and coworkers and that leaving that organization was the only way of escaping these negative feelings. Based on this memory, the employee may

leave the present employer that is laying off its employees without further consideration or the presence of job alternatives.

Third, in the absence of a memory that scripts a response or if the script is not followed, the employee evaluates whether the situation surrounding the event runs contrary to personal values, goals, and activities directed towards goal attainment. The previously mentioned company layoff may demonstrate to the employee that (a) the firm lacks loyalty to its people, which is inconsistent with the person's value system; (b) future career paths may be blocked by the elimination of positions held by those who lost their jobs; and/or (c) one's work load and tasks might increase, making it difficult to demonstrate the superior job performance required to earn the next promotion or pay raise that had been hoped for before the layoff was announced.

Finally, the presence of this shock and the employee's perceptions that the present conditions conflict with his or her personal beliefs may lead to resentment, which motivates the employee to begin comparing alternative jobs to these same values, goals, and goal-directed activities in search of a better fit. Upon determining that a better fit exists, the employee quits an otherwise satisfactory job for one offering greater satisfaction. The analysis of these four themes present in job situations contributes to the unfolding model's ability to more accurately predict the quitting behaviors of employees than traditional turnover models (Lee, Mitchell, Wise, & Fireman, 1996).

This view also suggests that people tend to follow one of four separate unfolding decision paths when they voluntarily quit a job. For our purposes, we will focus our attention on decision path 3, describing an employee's response to a shock, search for clues contained in their memory that describe the best response to the shock, comparison of personal belief systems to the circumstances surrounding the shock, and the potential for resentment resulting from a lack of fit between the employee's personal belief systems and the present job situation following a system shock.

Decision Path 3 Leading to Worker Turnover

A shock is defined as an environmental event of significance that occurs somewhere in an employee's surroundings. Furthermore, this shock may be labeled in one of three ways. First, a firm that makes a layoff announcement may produce a shock that is viewed negatively by its employees. Second, a shock can be viewed in a neutral manner as in the case of a firm announcing to its employees that it is preparing to embark upon a software conversion project in order to improve its information processing abilities. Third, this shock can also be viewed positively as in the case of an employee who receives an unsolicited job offer from another organization.

Lee, et al. (1999) suggests that these shocks may be expected or unexpected and be personal in nature, such as the death of a loved one or marital problems versus an organizationally inspired event such as introducing contingent workers into the workforce. System shocks like these prompt a worker to pause and search their memory for cues suggesting how similar events in the past affected them and how best to respond.

When a worker recalls a past occurrence that resembles the present shock and his or her experience has suggested that quitting is the best response to the event, it is reasonable to expect the worker to follow this cue and quit the organization for work elsewhere. In the absence of a script where no clear-cut action plan for the worker exists or in the event the script is not adopted, the system shock encourages the employee to begin reassessing his or her attachment to the organization. This evaluation process occurs in the presence of some option such as an unsolicited job offer or the realization that alternative forms of employment exist in

their profession, such as those jobs held by the CTPs recently introduced into the work environment (Lee, et al., 1996).

The evaluation process involves a worker's assessment of the system shock and the immediate circumstances surrounding his or her existing employment to determine the degree of fit existing between the organization and the worker's personal values, goals, and pathways leading to goal attainment. If the circumstances surrounding a system shock match the employee's belief systems or self-image, he or she would not be motivated to search for alternatives. On the other hand, if this same comparison suggests a mismatch between an employee's personal belief system and the circumstances surrounding a system shock, resentment or disaffection is likely to occur, prompting the employee to begin analyzing alternatives for an improved fit with his or her self-concept. A series of rational evaluations of job alternatives unfolds and concludes with the selection of an alternative that survived the final screening. The employee ultimately selects the job alternative capable of producing the greatest gratification.

It is interesting to note at this point how earlier turnover models commonly accepted the premise that quitting one's job for alternative employment meant assuming a position with another firm. What these turnover theories fail to acknowledge is the plausibility of a worker leaving his or her current job for an entrepreneurial startup, returning to school to continue an unfinished education, or exchanging a regular career position for a contingent job (Lee, et al., 1999). A blending of SIT with the unfolding model of voluntary turnover enables us to better grasp how this might occur.

BLENDING SIT AND THE UNFOLDING MODEL IN THE IT WORKPLACE

Information technology workers, like other employees in an organization, will maintain any number of identities based on ingroup membership. For instance, the skills learned in school and further developed in the workplace may have contributed to an employee assuming a professional identity. In addition, the socialization efforts performed by a firm early in the employee's career may have engendered this firm's desire for the employee to assume a stronger organizational identity. Finally, it is probable that another ingroup may be formed at the functional work group level and be comprised of those people with similar skills and work orientation with whom one works with on a day-to-day basis.

The Presence of a System Shock

An initial system shock capable of setting the wheels of turnover in motion in the IT workplace can take many different forms. Examples of possible shocks revealed earlier dealt with an organization's announcement of a major software conversion project or the introduction by the firm of CTPs into the various workgroups to offer training and assistance towards facilitating a successful conversion process. It is clear these environmental events are organizationally inspired, but whether they are expected or unexpected will be determined in part by the quality of the organization's communication channels. The more information that is transmitted through formal channels, the less likely a shock will be unexpected—as in the case of learning about a conversion project through the grapevine or happening upon CTPs without knowing why they are present. Whether employees will consider these events positive, neutral, or negative will depend in part upon their frame of reference, but neither could be considered as abhorrent as a massive layoff or as positive as a promotion or an unsolicited job offer. Conversely, a regular IT employee who learns that a CTP earns an hourly wage rate upwards of 100 percent more than himself or herself may likely perceive this shock negatively.

Searching for a Script

This system shock sets off a search by the regular IT worker in his or her memory for similar events that may have occurred in the past and that are capable of offering behavioral cues. If the memory probe reveals that conversion projects or the presence of contingent workers led to unpleasant consequences in the past, the IT worker will leave the organization in search of regular work elsewhere. On the other hand, the absence of a suitable script for the worker to enact directs the worker to begin the process of evaluating the fit of his or her identity and belief systems with the organizational characteristics pertinent to the shock as well as to other likely job alternatives.

Evaluation of Confidence and Esteem-Building Alternatives

The period of evaluation produces an atmosphere ripe for exploring how SIT influences an IT worker's job behavior. In addition to the introduction of CTPs into the workforce being perceived as a system shock, their presence additionally introduces a new group of workers with which the regular IT worker will categorize as either an ingroup or outgroup. Should the IT worker's evaluation of the shock and the attending situation determine that they are congruent with their self-concept, then the employee does not quit and simply proceeds to the next challenge. The absence of a fit between prevailing conditions and the employee's belief systems will produce worker resentment and initiate a process of evaluating alternatives. As a result, the employee may begin to evaluate the attractiveness of specific ingroup membership as well as alternatives to one's existing job.

The absence of a script following the IT worker's memory search may additionally mean that there are no ready-made rules that the worker can call upon that are capable of serving as a guide or action plan to follow.

The inability of a worker to call upon past experience to offer current direction may lead to subjective uncertainty. The presence of uncertainty holds important consequences for the organization, because it motivates people to gravitate towards ingroups that are a source of similar others whom, in turn, help clarify one's social identity, offer behavioral guidance, and become a proverbial "anchor in the storm" of uncertainty.

Organizational identity and the value given to organizational membership may be undermined by perceptions of the IT worker who assigns responsibility to the organization for the uncertainty they feel. After all, from the IT worker's point of view, it was the organization that announced a need for a software conversion or which sanctioned the introduction of contingent professionals into the worker's world in the first place. Recognizing that the desirability of ingroup membership is subject to change as environmental conditions change, IT workers may likely redefine their preferred identity from the broader organizational level to other identification alternatives in order to achieve an improved fit. As an example, the worker may now determine that viewing oneself as a company employee first and all other things second no longer holds the attractiveness it once did. The IT worker, in search for uncertainty avoidance, self-validation, and clarification of one's identity, may seek out "similar others," such as those found in more specific functional work groups or even at the professional skill level personified by CTPs.

During this unfolding process of evaluating alternatives, the regular IT worker may additionally be attracted to the self-esteem enhancing attributes characterized by close association with the CTPs who may have earlier been defined as members of an outgroup. After all, these contingent workers are bringing to the organization unique skills that are not distributed equally among the regular workers. The early successes achieved by the CTPs in furthering the organization's attainment of its goals and objectives may serve to reverse the group's status and strengthen the importance of group membership by self-esteem seeking IT employees.

The Value of Being Distinctively Different

Despite the attractiveness of ingroup membership in more than one group, the partiality held for exclusive membership with a group of CTPs may hold more appeal as time passes for certain employees. Although initially conceived of as an outgroup, the CTPs' maverick nature as a "hired gun" with the capacity of making meaningful contributions towards the attainment of organizational and work unit outcomes may motivate a regular employee to want to identify with and be associated with this newly transfigured ingroup.

The Quit Decision

In the final analysis, IT workers may have determined that realigning their own social identity with that of a CTP represents a superior vocation to that held as a regular IT worker. The choice for some may be as simple as asking, "Why should I remain dependent upon a larger organization whom I find more difficult to identify with when I can (1) rely upon my own professional skills to overcome uncertainty, (2) improve my own image of myself, (3) feel special or unique from the maddening crowd of less distinct regular workers, and (4) get paid more for my efforts?"

When the decision to quit is made, it has not been the result of the much simpler conception of an employee's job dissatisfaction. To the contrary, the employee who has left a regular job for contingent work may have been satisfied with his or her regular job. However, in light of the influences imposed by SIT and the nuances present in the unfolding model of turnover, the employee may have found that identification with the role of CTP to simply be more attractive or more satisfying than the role present in the regular job.

MANAGERIAL IMPLICATIONS

Quit rates among regular IT workers in organizations undergoing significant technical conversions have been suggested by some IT managers to be a problem that is real and which negatively impacts their organization. Surely, factors such as compensation and job satisfaction will influence an employee's voluntary quit decision. However, the theories that have been introduced here suggest that voluntary quit decisions can be a result of a more complicated process deeply rooted in an employee's own self-evaluation and social identity.

Managers can contribute to lowering turnover rates by focusing on anticipated events such as software conversion projects or the introduction of contingent workers into the workplace as being potential system shocks to their employees. This awareness offers the manager an opportunity to take advantage of existing communication channels to clearly articulate the company's message to affected employees well in advance of an organizational change and how it will impact its workers. The desired effect is reducing the impact of an organizational and tactical change in order to minimize uncertainty and maintain the worker's identification with and loyalty to the company and its vision for the future.

Additionally, managers can use their communication skills to more effectively convey to their regular IT workers that in spite of the greater gross earnings received by CTPs, significant drawbacks exist with contingent work. Managers should stress the clearly defined career paths and ready access to fringe benefits associated with regular work while simultaneously emphasizing the lack of job security, requirements for travel, and the demands on one's personal time commonly associated with contingent work. The time spent identifying the differences between the two kinds of work with one's regular workers additionally helps these employees to better differentiate the two contrasting work groups of regular versus contingent workers. The desired outcome is for the regular IT worker to more clearly appreciate the advantages of ingroup membership as a regular employee at the organizational level and to more objectively compare this employment to contingent work.

Lastly, recognition that an employee's response to an organizational event may produce disaffection and enact evaluation of alternatives suggests that managers must remain cognizant of those factors that influence the employee's need to preserve or enhance self-esteem. Brockner (1988) suggests that an employee's self-esteem can be jeopardized if a firm extends help or assistance to workers that imply they are incompetent or dependent. Recognizing this, those actions that managers can take to instill competence, feelings of importance, and control by their workers will help avert threats to their self-esteem. It may even be suggested that regular workers be offered participation in the decision to bring CTPs into the organization in the first place. In so doing, they will be more inclined to own the decision, be aware of all the ramifications such as disparity in pay well in advance, and be less inclined to perceive their presence as an environmental shock. ■

REFERENCES

Alexander, S. (1998). Managing IT turnover. *Infoworld, 20,* 85–86.

Allen, P., & Sienko, P. (1997, June 22). A comparison of contingent and core worker's perceptions of their jobs' characteristics and motivational properties. *SAM Advanced Management Journal, 62,* 4.

Brewer, M. (1991). The social self: On being the same and different at the same time. *Personality and Social Psychology Bulletin, 17,* 475–482.

Brockner, J. (1988). *Self-Esteem at Work.* Lexington, MA: Lexington Books.

Callas, E. (1998). Getting at the heart of the IT turnover puzzle. *Health Management Technology, 19,* 41–42.

Caudron, S. (1994, July). Contingent work force spurs HR planning. *Personnel Journal, 73,* 52.

Cialdini, R. B., Borden, R. J., Thorne, A., Walker, M. R., Freeman, S., & Sloan, L. R. (1976). Basking in reflected glory: Three (football) field studies. *Journal of Personality and Social Psychology, 34:* 366–374.

Cohany, S. (1998). Workers in alternative employment arrangements: A second look. *Monthly Labor Review, 121,* 3. (Infotrac Search Bank Article A54007785).

Daft, R. L. (2001). *Organization Theory and Design* (7th ed.). Cincinnati, OH: South-Western College Publishing.

Duffy, M. (1998). Keeping 'em down on Wall Street. *Wall Street & Technology, 16,* S8–S9.

Ellemers, N., van Kippenberg, A., de Vries, N., & Wilke, H. (1992). Social identification and permeability of group boundaries. *European Journal of Social Psychology, 18:* 497–513.

Fenner, G., & Renn, R. (1999). *Understanding turnover among information technology employees: Structured interviews with IT managers of a Fortune 500 firm.* Working paper. The University of Memphis, Memphis, TN.

Fryer, Bronwyn (2000). IT departments face high staff turnover. *Information Week, 675,* 104.

Hershey, R. (1995, August 19) Survey finds 6 million fewer that thought, in temporary jobs. *The New York Times,* 31.

Hogg, M., & Mullin, B. (1999). Joining groups to reduce uncertainty: Subjective uncertainty reduction and group identification. In Abrams & Hogg (Eds.), *Social Identity and Social Cognition* (249–279). Oxford, U.K.: Blackwell.

Hogg, M., & Terry, D. (2000). Social identity and self categorization processes in organizational contexts. *Academy of Management Review, 25,* 121–140.

Hulin, C., Roznowski, M., & Hachiya, D. (1985). Alternative opportunities and withdrawal decisions: Empirical and theoretical discrepancies and an integration. *Psychological Bulletin, 97,* 233–250.

Kallenberg, A., & Schmidt, K. (1997) Contingent employment in organizations. In A. L. Kallenberg, D. Knoke, P. Marsden, & J. Spaeth (Eds.), *Organizations in America: Analyzing Their Structures and Human Resource Practices* (253–275). New York: Sage.

Kramer, R. (1991). Intergroup relations and organizational dilemmas: The role of categorization process. In L. Cummings and B. Staw (Eds.), *Research in Organizational Behavior* (14, 191–207). Greenwich, CT: JAI Press.

Larson, J. (1996, February). Temps are here to stay. *American Demographics, 18,* 26. (Infotrac Search Bank Article A17966617).

Lee, T., & Mitchell, T. (1994). An alternative approach: The unfolding model of voluntary employee turnover. *Academy of Management Review, 19,* 51–89.

Lee, T., Mitchell, T., Holtom, B., McDaniel, L., & Hill, J. (1999). The unfolding model of voluntary turnover: A replication and extension. *The Academy of Mangement Journal, 42,* 450–462.

Lee, T., Mitchell, T., Wise, L., & Fireman, S. (1996). An unfolding model of voluntary employee turnover. *Academy of Management Journal, 39,* 5–36.

Matusik, S., & Hill, C. (1998). The utilization of contingent work, knowledge creation, and competitive advantage. *Academy of Management Review, 23,* 680–697.

Melchiomo, R. (1999). The changing work force: Managerial, professional, and technical workers in the personnel supply industry. *Occupational Outlook Quarterly, 43,* 24. (Infotrac Search Bank Article A54153027).

Mobley, W. (1977). Intermediate linkages in the relationships between job satisfaction and employee turnover. *Journal of Applied Psychology, 62,* 237–240.

Mobley, W., Griffeth, R., Hand, H., & Meglino, B. (1979). Review and conceptual analysis of the employee turnover process. *Psychological Bulletin, 86,* 493–522.

Nollen, S., & Axel, H. (1996). *Managing Contingent Workers.* New York: American Management.

Plovika, A., & Stewart, J. (1996, October). Contingent and alternative work arrangements, defined. *Monthly Labor Review, 119,* 3.

Rousseau, D. (1995). *Psychological Contracts in Organizations.* Thousand Oaks, CA: Sage.

Sherman, S., Hamilton, D., & Lewis, A. (1999). Perceived entitativity and the social identity value of group memberships. In D. Abrams and M. Hogg (Eds.), *Social Identity and Social Cognition* (80–110). Oxford, UK: Blackwell.

Tajfel, H. (1972). Experiments in a vacuum. In J. Israel and H. Tajfel (Eds.) *The Context of Social Psychology: A Critical Assessment.* London: Academic Press.

Thompson, J. (1997, November 21). The contingent workforce: The solution to the paradoxes of the new economy. *Strategy & Leadership, 25,* 44.

Van Dyne, L., & Ang, S. (1999). Organizational citizenship behavior of contingent workers in Singapore. *Academy of Management Journal, 41,* 692–703.

Van Horn-Christopher, D. (1996). Will employee meltdown mean a "contingent" workforce? *Business Forum, 21,* 11. (Infotrac Search Bank Article A19104304).

Victor, K. (1989, July 15). How long is temporary? *The National Journal, 21,* 1804.

Zeff-Geber, Sara (1999). Independent contractors: The impact of perceived fair treatment on measures of commitment, organizational citizenship behavior, and intent to stay. Unpublished manuscript presented at the 1999 Academy of Management Conference.

INTERVIEW RESEARCH APPLIED TO CANDIDATES

Danielle S. Beu
M. Ronald Buckley

INTRODUCTION

There has been a great deal of research on the selection interview during the past 100 years. The structure, validity, reliability, and predictive power of the interview have been investigated, analyzed, and reexamined through the eyes of myriad researchers. Scholars in management, psychology, sociology, and public administration, as well as field practitioners, have been responsible for the evolution of the interview process and have paved the way for new and creative ideas pertaining to interview research and practice. Over the past century, the interview has been criticized, praised, structured, enlarged, tested, recorded, and analyzed. Through all of this, the interview has remained the most popular and widely used selection tool in the selection process.

As research has evolved, so too has the practice of interviewing. More attention is being paid to finding a candidate with a specific set of skills who can adapt as job requirements change, not just finding a likable person. Academic research, as well as practice, has resulted in an overall trend toward a more scientific selection process, although there continues to be many different styles of interviewing. This article was written with this in mind—we attempt to use interview research to aid the candidate in his or her job search. As a candidate goes from interview to interview, it is difficult to know what to expect. Will the interview be friendly or stressful? Will it be by one interviewer or many? Will the interviewer ask inappropriate questions? Will the answers be scored or will the interviewer just come to a general conclusion? By understanding the research to date, the candidate can prepare effectively for any type of interview.

WHY DO EMPLOYERS USE INTERVIEWS?

The interview as part of the selection process has been researched extensively over the past 100 years (Buckley, Norris, & Wiese, 1998). It is one of many tools used to attract and select competent and productive employees. Employers hope to select a candidate who creates the best match with the requirements of the job believed to lead to successful performance. Unlike other selection tools, the interview is heavily influenced by the judgment of the interviewer and is subject to a variety of personal and political agendas (Eder & Harris, 1999). Thus, a great deal of the early research focused on the validity of the interview—is this tool truly useful in selecting successful employees?

In 1915, Scott challenged the effectiveness of the interview, after a study showed

that interviewers' abilities to identify successful applicants were problematic (Eder, Kacmar, & Ferris, 1989). Further evidence from a study by Hollingsworth (1922) found that the rankings given by evaluators of a pool of candidates showed great variability. Some candidates' rankings even ranged from the very best to the very worst. The effectiveness of the interview was challenged again by Moss in his 1931 study about the ability of interviewers to predict the success or failure of medical school students. When the students' actual performances were compared with the predictions from the interviews, the results showed that 33 percent of the students who failed would have been eliminated—that's the good news. However, it also found that 23 percent of the students who received average grades of 85 percent or higher would have been eliminated— that's the bad news. In 1947, Dunlap and Wantman found that interviews were little better than chance in predicting flight school success. Newman, Bobbitt, and Cameron (1946) reported similar findings. The interview's contribution to the selection process was also questioned in 1946. Conrad and Satter (1946) found that test scores alone predicted the success of naval candidates into the Electricians' Mates School better than test scores combined with interview information. A review by Wagner (1949) of empirical results found that the overall validities of the interview ranged from −.20 to .85.

Based on these disappointing results, a number of researchers turned to the question of why the interview appeared to lack consistent validity. One source that was examined was the interviewer. It was found that interviewers developed a stereotype of an ideal candidate and then sought to match the candidates interviewed to that stereotype. Another stream of research showed that interviewers made judgments about a candidate's honesty in an interview, but had difficulty explaining how they reached those judgments (Maier & Thurber, 1968). In fact, those who only listened to or read the transcripts of the interview did a better job of identifying deception than those who saw and listened to the interview. A well-cited study found that interviewers make their decision during the first few minutes of the interview based on appearance and the application form (Springbett, 1958). In 1965, Ulrich & Trumbo suggested that the complexity of information exchanges and the decision-making processes within the interview may partially explain why the interview lacked strong validities. Because of the limitations on time and information, they argued that interviewers should limit their ratings to a single trait. This research showed that the decision-making capabilities of the interviewer were susceptible to a number of influences.

The 1970s saw research on the effects of verbal and visual cues, such as eye contact, smiling, posture, interpersonal distance, and body orientation (Washburn & Hakel, 1973). Those who maintained more eye contact, smiled more, faced the interviewer, sat upright, and leaned forward received more positive results than those who did not. Wexley, Yukl, Kovacs, and Sanders (1972), among others, found that the order in which candidates interviewed affected decision making (the contrast effect). The late 1970s experienced a focus on the cognitive information processing of the interviewer. This research examined information acquisition and encoding to storage and memory retrieval in order to delineate the variety of information processing errors that undermine interview validity (Ilgen & Feldman, 1983; Schmitt, 1976). Zedeck, Tziner, and Middlestadt (1983) found that despite interviewer training, interviewers continued to use only a limited number of rating criteria (application materials) to reach their decisions. Finally, in 1988, Eder and Buckley proposed an interactionist perspective to the interview, suggesting that both the interview context (situation) and the interviewer information search efforts (person) affect decision making during an interview.

The research clearly showed that interviewers are poor decision makers and information processors and that the interview's validity is questionable. Based on this research, we ask again: "Why do employers use interviews?" As Wagner (1949) so eloquently stated:

> The interview remains popular as a selection procedure despite its questionable reliability. Even if the interview were thoroughly repudiated, it probably would not be abandoned; there seems to be a certain human curiosity which can be satisfied in no other way than by seeing a man in the flesh. (p. 42)

With this understanding, researchers decided to focus on making a better mousetrap—they worked to improve the reliability and validity of the interview.

INTERVIEW STYLES

Degree of Structure

For the most part, research that questioned the usefulness of the interview examined unstructured interviews. These interviews are generally casual, with the interviewer unprepared and the questions unplanned—often based on interviewer hunches or "pet questions." Questions may be very open-ended, subjective, and general ("Tell me about yourself"), they may be obtuse ("If you were an animal, what type would you be, and why?"), or they may be highly speculative ("Where do you see yourself in 5 years?"). The interviewer makes a relatively quick and final evaluation of the candidate. The unstructured interview is still the most common form of interview in actual interview practice (Eder & Harris, 1999; Heneman, Judge, & Heneman, 2000). However, researchers continue to demonstrate that this type of interview has low reliability and validity and why.

In an unstructured interview, interviewers rate each candidate using different factors and different hiring standards. They also differ in the degree to which their actual selection criteria match their intended criteria (Graves & Karen, 1996). The candidate's physical appearance, including facial attractiveness, use of cosmetics, type of attire, and weight have been shown to affect interviewers' decisions (Pingatore, Dugoni, Tindale, & Spring, 1994). Additionally, nonverbal cues such as eye contact and smiling have been found to be related to interview ratings (Burnett & Motowidlo, 1998). The unstructured interview has been labeled the "search for negative evidence" because negative information receives so much more weight than positive information (Rowe, 1989). It has been shown that information gathered before the interview, or during the first few minutes of the interview, may guide the interviewer's line of questions (Dougherty, Turban, & Callender, 1994). Interviewers with positive first impressions sell the candidates on the company more and do more recruiting. A similar-to-me bias appears to affect the interviewers, in that candidates who are similar to the interviewer tend to receive higher ratings (Prewett-Livingston, Feild, Veres, & Lewis, 1996). Finally, the information-processing capabilities of the interviewers makes accurate recall of pertinent information difficult (Carlson, Thayer, Mayfield, & Peterson, 1971). Due to these problems with the unstructured interview, researchers began to look at other types of interviews that may be more effective.

Since unstructured interviews did not appear to be helping companies select the best employees for the job, perhaps structure would improve validity. Structured interviews are frequently characterized by the use of the same questions across interviews, detailed rating scales, multiple interviewers per candidate, extensive interviewer train-

ing, notetaking during the interview, and consensus processes after the interview. In the 1930s, researchers began to favor standardized interview formats (Adams & Smeltzer, 1936; Hovland & Wonderlic, 1939). Since that time, a number of researchers have reiterated that structured interviews are much more valid than unstructured interviews (Conway, Goodman, & Jako, 1995; Huffcutt & Arthur, 1994; Janz, 1982; Latham & Saari, 1984; Latham, Saari, Pursell, & Campion, 1980; Lowry, 1994; McDaniel, 1985; McDaniel, Whetzel, Schmidt, & Maurer, 1994; Orpen, 1985; Weekley & Gier, 1987; Wiesner & Cronshaw, 1988).

A review of the literature by Campion, Palmer, and Campion (1997) identified 15 components of structure: (1) base questions on a job analysis; (2) ask the exact same questions of each candidate; (3) limit prompting, follow-up questioning and elaboration on questions; (4) use better types of questions (situational, behavioral, background, job knowledge as opposed to opinions and attitudes, goals and aspirations, self-descriptions, and self-evaluations); (5) use longer interviews or a larger number of questions; (6) control ancillary information such as application forms, resumes, test scores, recommendations, etc.; (7) do not allow questions from the candidate until after the interview; (8) rate each answer during the interview and rate multiple scales at the end of the interview; (9) use detailed, anchored rating scales; (10) take detailed notes; (11) use multiple interviewers; (12) use the same interviewer(s) across all candidates; (13) do not discuss candidates or answers between interviews; (14) provide extensive interviewer training; and (15) use statistical rather than clinical predictions. Regarding content, the use of job analysis, asking the same questions, and asking better types of questions appear more important than other components. Regarding evaluation, rating each answer during the interview, using anchored scales, and interviewer training appear more important. Among those components that are less important, limiting prompting, longer interviews, control of ancillary information, and forbidding questions from candidates have the greatest potential negative effects in terms of reactions from the candidates. Some research shows that multiple interviewers increases validity (Dreher, Ash, & Hancock, 1988; Pulakos & Schmitt, 1995). However, Pulakos, Schmitt, Whitney, and Smith (1996) suggest that in a structured interview situation, multiple interviewers are not necessary because this does not add incremental validity. Additionally, panel interviews may be stressful for candidates (Campion, Palmer, & Campion, 1997). Required notetaking and forbidding discussion among interviewers may be resented by the interviewers. However, Burnett, Fan, Motowidlo, and Degroot's (1998) results indicate that when interviewers voluntarily took notes during the interview, notetakers made more valid ratings than nonnotetakers. Because interviewers recognize the need for trade-offs between psychometric properties and user reactions, candidates can expect a range of structure in their interviews.

Constructs Assessed

Researchers have examined what the interview is truly good at measuring. According to Eder and Harris (1999), the interviewers are trying to determine the candidate's reliability; knowledge, skills, and abilities (KSAs); values, and motivation. Interviewers want to know that the candidate will abide by the basic rules and policies of the job and the organization—in other words, be reliable. The values of the candidate include preferences for work environment and organizational culture, as well as candidate attitudes. Interviewers are also interested in the types of rewards that will motivate the candidate.

Evidence suggests that appearance, manners, likability, sociability, attitudes, outside interests and hobbies, forcefulness, decisiveness, oral communication skills, manner of self-preservation, and disagreeable mannerisms could all be observed and rated in an interview (Charters, 1927; Dunlap & Wantman, 1947; Holt, 1958; Zedeck, Tziner, & Middlestadt, 1983). Schneider and Schmitt (1986) concluded that interviews were best at assessing motivation or affinity for a particular job, with the understanding that motivation does not always coincide with productivity. However, researchers also found that certain qualities such as dependability, honesty, persistence, and loyalty could not be ascertained during the interview process (Charters, 1927). Researchers concluded that interviews based on overt behaviors were more valid than those that focused on less observable applicant characteristics (Buckley & Eder, 1988; Charters, 1927; Latham, Saari, Pursell, & Campion, 1980).

Types of Questions

It is the interviewer's job to ask the appropriate questions to assess the desired constructs. What questions need to be asked to determine the candidate's KSAs, reliability, values, and motivation (Eder & Harris, 1999)? Questions pertaining to the candidate's educational, training, and work experience background are generally used to assess KSAs. Some work experience questions, such as "why did you leave your last job?" may also assess the candidate's reliability. Interviewers may assess the candidate's reliability and motivation by asking questions about potential work schedules (e.g., overtime, weekends, graveyard), or potential adverse working conditions (e.g., heavy travel, chemical exposure). All of the standard inquiries into candidate self-descriptions and opinions are trait-based questions. They are intended to shed light on each of the four constructs, however, the research does not show that they accurately predict job performance.

Low validity of trait-based questions led researchers to examine behaviorally oriented questions that are job related. Behaviorally oriented questions include experience-based and situational questions. Experience-based questions are past oriented in that they ask candidates to relate what they have done in past jobs or other life experiences to skills that are relevant to the job. On the other hand, situational questions ask candidates to imagine a set of circumstances and then indicate how they would respond—they are future oriented. McDaniel, Whetzel, Schmidt, and Maurer (1994) suggest that situational interviews are more valid than job-related interviews and that job-related interviews are more valid than psychological-based interviews. Pulakos and Schmitt (1995) compared the validity of two different types of structured behavioral interview questions that were written for a single set of job-relevant dimensions identified through a job analysis and found that experience-based questions were more valid than situational questions with respect to predictions of performance. Because interviews that do not measure relevant job behaviors are less valid than interviews that are (Arvey, Miller, Gould, & Burch, 1987), behaviorally oriented questions are based on a careful job analysis to determine the desired job-related behaviors that lead to successful performance.

In 1929, O'Rourke developed the first situational, structured interview based on job-relevant information with anchored scales for evaluation. Sixty years later, after numerous studies, researchers suggested that using structure, questions based on job analysis, rater training, notetaking during the interview, panels of interviewers, and behaviorally anchored rating scales to evaluate the interviewees' answers all play a role in the improvement of interview reliability and validity (Campion, Pursell, & Brown, 1988). Nevertheless, interviews are far from standardized and the candidate will probably

not know what type of interview to expect. If all this research has yet to make it into common management practice, then what real value does it have for the candidate?

RESEARCH APPLIED TO CANDIDATES

Research on the interview is extremely valuable to candidates precisely because the candidate does not know what interview style to expect. By understanding the different degrees of interview structure, constructs, and question types, the candidate can prepare for the most valid interview style—the structured behaviorally oriented interview. Providing specific examples of behaviors performed gives evidence of the candidate's job-related skills. The candidate can communicate his or her skills honestly and effectively, thereby providing the interviewer with true qualifications and diminishing any biases. In order for the candidates to reach this point, they need to be familiar with the types of interviewers they are likely to encounter.

Interviewer Types

The candidate will encounter a wide variety of experiences because each interview situation and each interviewer will be different. On one extreme is the interviewer that relies strictly on instinct (Green, 1996). This interviewer uses an unstructured style, relying on intuition and unknown subjective criteria to attempt to discover personal characteristics, such as impressions, personality traits, and emotions. When the interview is over, this person evaluates the candidate on an overall impression. One step removed from the instinctual interviewer is the one that makes the candidate feel like a colleague. This is an unstructured interview that focuses on job-related issues. The interview begins, and because there is no prepared list of questions, just seems to flow naturally based on the candidate's responses and the interviewer's job knowledge. The casualness of the conversation makes the candidate feel as though the interviewer just wants to get to know him or her better. However, the candidate must be aware that the interviewer is using rapport to gather information. The collegial interviewer is interested in the candidate's values, and during the course of the interview the candidate may lose focus and reveal important details that may otherwise never come out.

Just as unstructured interviews can focus on the candidate as a person or on the candidate's job experience and job skills, so can structured interviews. Dunn, Mount, Barrick, and Ones (1995) suggest that interviewers can effectively use information about the personality characteristics of candidates to make hiring decisions. Armed with this knowledge, an interviewer can use a structured format with the goal of measuring key personality characteristics (Green, 1996). In combination with personality testing, this method can be effective with a trained interviewer. However, untrained interviewers may use the information gathered to incorrectly stereotype a candidate. Questions about unstructured interviews and those that look at personality characteristics leads us to the most valid interview—the structured, behaviorally oriented interview. If a candidate effectively prepares for this type of interview, he or she will have the capacity to be effective in any type of interview. In behaviorally oriented interviews, the candidate is asked for information about past events. If the candidate can talk at length about a specific instance that represents a desired behavior, the interviewer can better assess those skills. By understanding that an interviewer is taking notes to be more accurate, the candidate will not be intimidated by this practice. If the candidate is well-prepared, he or she can confidently respond to a variety of questions from a panel of interviewers. In other words,

knowledge and preparation are the keys to a structured, behaviorally oriented interview, and this knowledge and preparation will allow the candidate to perform well under any interview circumstance.

Preparing for the Interview

This article has given the candidate knowledge of the types of interviews and interviewers to expect. Now it is time to use this information to prepare for the interview. Candidates must be able to present a summary of their qualifications in a concise, enthusiastic, and poised manner (*USA Today,* 2000). This being the case, the candidate needs to perform a self-evaluation because it is difficult to convey information that is unknown. Based on the interviewer types discussed, candidates should be able to answer questions about the overall impressions they generate, the values they hold, their dominant personality characteristics, and what they can do (Green, 1996). By relating their impressions, values, personality characteristics, and past behaviors to their skills, they can describe to an interviewer specifically what they can do on the job.

Built on the belief that past performance is the best predictor of future success, many interviewers are asking behavioral-type questions. The interviewer believes that he or she can tell much more about a candidate's attitudes, work habits, and skills by hearing them describe real actions taken in real circumstances. If an interviewer prepares by reviewing the job description to determine a job's required skills and traits and asks for specific examples that demonstrate those characteristics, the candidate should go through a similar process. The candidate should ask for a job description from the employer prior to coming for the interview and develop a list of experiences that cover the skills and characteristics required for the position. This information can be used to prepare honest and accurate statements that show the match between the candidate's skills and the benefits those skills can generate for the company. During an interview, specific examples are more likely to influence the interviewer than generalities. Therefore, the candidate should prepare examples that provide a detailed description of the situation, any constraints on action, exactly what was done, a description of the results attributed to those actions, and an evaluation of the skills desired (Green, 1996). This way, when an interviewer asks the candidate about a skill, the candidate can substantiate that particular technical or performance skill with a clear, detailed example that shows he or she is qualified for the job.

The process of interview preparation suggested here is not an easy task for anyone, but the candidate's personality characteristics may actually show the type of preparation he or she will employ. Research has shown that extraversion (sociable vs. introverted), openness to experience (intellectual curiosity vs. preference for routine), and conscientiousness were positively related to the use of social sources to prepare for interviews (Caldwell & Burger, 1998). Social sources include faculty, relatives, friends, an incumbent at the potential employer, or someone in a similar job (or company). Candidates can use these social sources to find out specific information about the organization and the job. At the organizational level, candidates can attempt to identify the employer's problems that they can help solve. At the job level, they can determine what constitutes high, medium, and low performance, which will assist them in coming up with specific examples from social, school, and work experiences to demonstrate how they can benefit the organization. Research has shown that the use of social sources for preparation for initial interviews was positively related to the likelihood of re-

ceiving follow-up interviews and job offers (Caldwell & Burger, 1998). Additionally, conscientiousness was positively related to the use of nonsocial preparation, such as reading material from the Career Center, magazines, newspapers, and/or company releases. The results suggest that personality is related to candidate success during an interview through actions taken prior to the interview process. Additionally, two studies indicated that those high in communication apprehension avoided thinking about interviews and avoided preparing for interviews (Ayres, Keereetaweep, Chen, & Edwards, 1998). This research shows that who we are as individuals affects the outcomes of our job searches by affecting the way we prepare for the interview. With this knowledge, candidates can overcome tendencies that will prevent them from being successful.

Interviewer–Candidate Interaction

Success in an interview depends on the interaction between the interviewer and the candidate. Research suggests that the top characteristics used to select candidates for a second interview are (1) interpersonal skills, (2) compatibility with the firm, (3) oral communication skills, (4) enthusiasm, (5) maturity, (6) ethical standards, (7) selfstarter evidence, and (8) leadership evidence. Six of the top eight criteria are items that can be demonstrated through interviewer–candidate interaction. One of the strongest predictors of interviewers' evaluations and recommendations is their subjective impressions of candidates' interview performance (Dipboye, 1992). In studies that have examined both paper credentials, such as GPA or prior work experience, and subjective impressions of candidate performance, subjective impressions explained substantially more variance in hiring recommendations. Perceived candidate similarity with the interviewer, interpersonal attraction, and candidates' demonstrated leadership and goal orientation all predicted interviewers' ratings (Gilmore & Ferris, 1989). These findings suggest that applicants who promote interpersonal attraction or highlight their motivation and competence are more likely to receive positive evaluations from interviewers.

Interviewers attend to what candidates say and what they do, therefore, many popular job-hunting guides recommend the use of impression management tactics to influence interviewers' evaluations. Baron (1986) reasoned that candidates are very aware of the significant influence of the interview on hiring decisions, and have adjusted their behaviors accordingly. They attempt to enhance their ability to convey a positive impression to interviewers. The candidates in his study were instructed to act in a specific way during their interviews, either exhibiting positive nonverbal cues, such as smiling and making eye contact, or not exhibiting such behaviors. Some were also instructed to wear perfume during their interviews. Those who exhibited positive nonverbal cues and wore perfume were rated lower by male evaluators because the candidates appeared to be trying too hard. However, female evaluators gave applicants high ratings if they exhibited positive nonverbal cues, regardless of whether they were wearing perfume. Gilmore and Ferris (1989) suggested that interviewers for technical jobs may be influenced less by candidate impression management tactics and more by candidate credentials. Argyle (1988) argued that nonverbal behavior, although capable of manipulation, is actually less controllable than verbal behavior. Thus, although naturally occurring nonverbal cues have been shown to influence hiring decisions, perhaps intentional nonverbal cues will not lead to the intended results.

Many researchers have expressed concern over the ability of candidates to create a falsely positive impression with interviewers (Anderson, 1992; Baron, 1989; Dipboye, 1992; Gilmore & Ferris, 1989; Snyder & Copeland, 1989). They argue that impression management is an influential bias, which may undermine the validity of outcome decisions. Self-monitoring is one tactic of impression management that may allow a candidate to create a more positive image of himself or herself to the interviewer (Snyder & Gangestad, 1986). It has been suggested that individuals high in self-monitoring are able to regulate their expressive self-presentation in order to achieve desired public appearances. They are highly responsive to social and interpersonal cues of situationally appropriate behavior. Individuals who are low in self-monitoring do not have a concern for appropriate self-presentation and may not pick up on social cues. Thus, they may be unable to modify their self-presentations to create desired impressions. Anderson, Silvester, Cunningham-Snell, and Haddleton (1999) found that self-monitoring ability did not appear to be related to interviewer evaluations of candidate suitability. This study also found that interviewer ratings of candidate personality were strongly associated with overall outcome decisions. Recruiters in this study rated candidates more favorably who they perceived to be interesting, strong, mature, dominant, active, enthusiastic, and relaxed. This may suggest that interviews are often used as social interaction "tests" of candidate personality. However, self-monitoring as an impression management tactic was generally uncorrelated with the positiveness of recruiter impressions of candidate's personality, although it is interesting to note that high self-monitoring candidates were perceived as being more interesting by interviewers. If impression management tactics have little impact on interviewers, then perhaps candidates would be better off concentrating on actions that improve their employability (Stevens & Kristof, 1995).

Once again, let's turn to the research to examine impression management—exactly what it is, how to engage in it, as well as when to engage in it. Impression management is "conscious or unconscious attempts to control the images that are projected in . . . social interactions" (Schlenker, 1980, p. 6). According to Schneider (1981), impression management can take many forms, including verbal statements, nonverbal or expressive behaviors, modifications of one's personal appearance, and integrated behavior patterns, such as giving favors. Verbal impression management tactics may be classified as assertive (e.g., ingratiation tactics or self-promotion) or defensive (e.g., excuses or justifications) (Stevens & Kristof, 1995). Ingratiation tactics can take the forms of other enhancement or opinion conformity. Because people like those who like them and who are similar to them, these tactics may work. However, ingratiation can also backfire if the interviewer is aware that the candidate is using these tactics. On the other hand, self-promotion refers to positive statements about oneself, one's past experiences, and one's future aspirations in order to elicit specific character attributions (Godfrey, Jones, & Lord, 1986). Self-promoters may also claim responsibility for positive events, claim that the event for which they were responsible was more positive than it initially appeared, or describe how they overcame obstacles while pursuing goals (Stevens & Kristof, 1995). In an unstructured interview that focuses on getting acquainted, the candidates tend to use more assertive, rather than defensive, impression management tactics. Unstructured interviews also lend themselves to a greater variety of tactics, which may be another reason for their low validity. In interviews that focus on job qualifications, candidates use more self-promotion impression management tactics. This study showed that higher levels of tactic use were associated with more positive outcomes.

In preparing for the behaviorally oriented interview, candidates should compose several specific examples. Research shows that stories, when accompanied by self-promotion tactics, help document or prove candidates' claims to a strong work ethic, competence, confidence, interpersonal skills, goal orientation, adaptability, leadership skills, etc. (Green, 1996; Stevens & Kristof, 1995). Candidates can discuss positive outcomes on jobs or class projects, success in persuading others who were difficult to persuade, or overcoming difficulties in a job or school work. These stories, when well-constructed and well-delivered, may help candidates stand out from the crowd by serving as a memory trigger for the interviewer.

Candidates also need to be able to answer questions for negative information. A skilled interviewer will ask the candidate for examples of times when the candidate was not effective. Candidate attributions are potential clues to the candidate's likely motivation in future work situations. Weiner (1986) suggests that individuals who explain failure in terms of unstable, internal, or controllable causes will demonstrate higher levels of motivation in future situations that are similar because they believe that the failure is not permanent and is open to influence. Silvester (1997) showed that successful candidates made relatively more personal and stable attributions when explaining previous negative events than less successful candidates. While the majority of attributions for all negative events produced by candidates were unstable and universal, the results suggest that more successful candidates are less defensive and more willing to describe certain negative outcomes as ongoing and personal. It appears that interviewers are less likely to approve of candidates who consistently externalize responsibility for negative events. By attributing negative events to external, uncontrollable, and unstable causes, the candidate fails to convey the impression that he or she learned anything from the situation and will therefore make the same mistake again in the future. Also, if the candidate blames others for negative events, this may be an unpopular strategy among colleagues. Therefore, candidates should demonstrate that they were able to recognize the mistake (hopefully before others did), take action to remedy it, and learn from the experience. They may then go on to describe a positive event demonstrating that they did, indeed, learn from the prior mistake.

Nonverbal behaviors accompany both assertive and defensive verbal impression management tactics. These behaviors include bodily movements, such as eye contact, smiling, and leaning forward. Research has shown that although nonverbal behaviors tend to occur spontaneously, most adults can regulate this behavior for self-presentation purposes (DePaulo, 1992). Personality characteristics that are relevant to managerial effectiveness—extraversion, conscientiousness, and agreeableness—have been linked to nonverbal cues (Barrick & Mount, 1991). Smiling, eye contact and gaze, spatial proximity, rapid body movement, and physical attractiveness are related to extraversion (Albright, Kenny, & Malloy, 1988; Argyle, 1988; Borkenau & Liebler, 1992; Kenny, Horner, Kashy, & Chu; 1992). Conscientiousness has been related to relaxed posture and aspects of dress, or appearance (Albright, et al., 1988; Borkenau & Liebler, 1992; Kenny, et al., 1992). Smiling, hand movements, and rapid body movement are associated with agreeableness (Borkenau & Liebler, 1992; Kenny, et al., 1992). Thus, candidates who demonstrate more of these nonverbal cues should be perceived as having more of these personality characteristics associated with managerial effectiveness. Parsons and Liden (1984) reported that frequent eye contact and smiling do elicit positive responses. However, candidates need to make sure this behavior is natural because interviewers do not ap-

preciate feeling like they are being manipulated. Additionally, the benefits of nonverbal behavior may be restricted in an interview to situations in which candidates provide appropriate, informative verbal responses (Burnett & Motowidlo, 1988; Rasmussen, 1984). Obviously, nonverbal behavior is important and the candidate needs to use it to his or her advantage. Appropriate nonverbal behaviors will not get the candidate a job, but inappropriate behaviors will cause the candidate to lose one.

CONCLUSION

Anyone who is searching for a job will experience an interview. Even though the interview has been criticized for poor reliability and validity, it continues to be the most common selection tool. Valid interviews, as part of the selection process, are important because firms that are better able to achieve a match with the individuals they hire receive many advantages. Proper selection can save the time and money associated with recruiting, selecting, and training due to high turnover. It can also enhance morale, decrease insecurity, and increase job satisfaction among employees. Many employers have benefited from the research generated by academicians. This article attempted to show the candidates that research can also benefit them.

Candidates who understand interview structure, the constructs interviewers assess, and the types of questions interviewers ask can effectively prepare for any interview. During the self-exploration stage of preparation, candidates can discover or rediscover their strengths and weaknesses. Knowledge of the best methods of preparation will provide tools for success to any candidate. By preparing specific examples that demonstrate their skills, candidates can vividly show their potential employer how they can contribute to the organization. Knowledge of what an interviewer is looking for in a candidate, as well as how he or she may try to elicit that information, will provide the candidate information on how to respond verbally. Additionally, preparation provides the candidates with a positive outlook and confidence, which will manifest itself in nonverbal behaviors. To conclude, research allows interviewing to be a positive experience by creating knowledgeable and prepared candidates. ■

REFERENCES

———. (2000). Initial minutes of job interviews are critical. *USA Today, 128,* 8.

Adams, C. R., & Smeltzer, C. H. (1936). The scientific construction of an interviewing chart. *Personnel, 13,* 3–8.

Albright, L., Kenny, D. A., & Malloy, T. A. (1988). Consensus in personality judgments at zero acquaintance. *Journal of Personality and Social Psychology, 55,* 387–395.

Anderson, N. R. (1992). Eight decades of employment interview research: A retrospective metareview and prospective commentary. *European Work and Organizational Psychologist, 2,* 1–32.

Anderson, N., Silvester, J., Cunningham-Snell, N., & Haddleton, E. (1999). Relationships between candidate self-monitoring, perceived personality, and selection interview outcomes. *Human Relations, 52* (9), 1115–1131.

Argyle, M. (1988). *Bodily Communication,* 2nd Edition. London: Methuen and Co.

Arvey, R. D., Miller, H. E., Gould, R., & Burch, P. (1987). Interview validity for selecting sales clerks. *Personnel Psychology, 40,* 1–12.

Ayres, J., Keereetaweep, T., Chen, P., & Edwards, P. A. (1998). Communication apprehension and employment interviews. *Communication Education, 47* (1), 1–17.

Baron, R. A. (1986). Self-presentation in job interviews: When there can be "too much of a good thing." *Journal of Applied Psychology, 16,* 16–28.

Baron, R. A. (1989). Impression management by applicants during employment interviews: The "too much of a good thing" effect. In R. W. Eder and G. R. Ferris (Eds.), *The Employment Interview: Theory, Research, and Practice.* Newbury Park: Sage.

Barrick, M. R., & Mount, M. K. (1991). The big five personality dimensions and job performance: A recta-analysis. *Personnel Psychology, 44,* 1–26.

Borkenau, P., & Liebler, A. (1992). Trait inferences: Sources of validity at zero acquaintance. *Journal of Personality and Social Psychology, 62,* 645–657.

Buckley, M. R., & Eder, R. W. (1988). B. M. Springbett and the notion of the "snap decision" in the interview. *Journal of Management, 14,* 59–67.

Buckley, M. R., Norris, A. C., & Wiese, D. S. (1998). A brief history of the selection interview: May the next 100 years be more fruitful. *Journal of Management History, 6,* 113–126.

Burnett, J. R., Fan, C., Motowidlo, S. J., & Degroot, T. (1998). Interview notes and validity. *Personnel Psychology, 51* (2), 375–397.

Burnett, J. R., & Motowidlo, S. J. (1998). Relation between different sources of information in the structured selection interview. *Personnel Psychology, 51,* 963–980.

Caldwell, D. F., & Burger, J. M. (1998). Personality characteristics of job applicants and success in screening interviews. *Personnel Psychology, 51* (1), 119–137.

Campion, M. A., Palmer, D. K., & Campion, J. E. (1997). A review of structure in the selection interview. *Personnel Psychology, 50* (3), 655–704.

Campion, M. A., Pursell, E. D., & Brown, B. K. (1988). Structured interviewing: Raising the psychometric properties of the employment interview. *Personnel Psychology, 41,* 25–42.

Carlson, R. E., Thayer, P. W., Mayfield, E. C., & Peterson, D. A. (1971). Improvements in the selection interview. *Personnel Journal, 50,* 268–275.

Charters, W. W. (1927). The discovery of executive talent. *Annual Convention Series,* American Management Association, 69, 10–13.

Conrad, H. S., & Satter, G. A. (1946). *The use of test scores and quality classification ratings in predicting success in Electricians' Mates School* (OSRD No. 133290). Washington D.C.: U.S. Department of Commerce.

Conway, J. M., Goodman, D. F., & Jako, R. A. (1995). A meta-analysis of interrater and internal consistency reliability of selection interviews. *Journal of Applied Psychology, 80,* 565–579.

DePaulo, B. M. (1992). Nonverbal behavior and self-presentation. *Psychological Bulletin, 111,* 203–243.

Dipboye, R. L. (1992). *Selection interviews: Process perspectives.* Cincinnati, OH: South-Western Publishing.

Dougherty, T. W., Turban, D. B., & Callender, J. C. (1994). Confirming first impressions in the employment interview: A field study of interviewer behavior. *Journal of Applied Psychology, 79,* 659–665.

Dreher, C. W., Ash, R. A., & Hancock, P. (1988). The role of the traditional research design in underestimating the validity of the employment interview. *Personnel Psychology, 41,* 315–327.

Dunlap, J. W., & Wantman, M. J. (1947). *An investigation of the interview as a technique for selecting aircraft pilots.* (Report No. 50308). Washington, D.C.: U.S. Department of Commerce.

Dunn, W. S., Mount, M. K., Barrick, M. R., & Ones, D. S. (1995). Relative importance of personality and general mental ability in managers' judgments of applicant qualifications. *Journal of Applied Psychology, 80,* 500–509.

Eder, R. W., & Buckley, M. R. (1988). The employment interview: An interactionist perspective. In G. R. Ferris and K. M. Rowland (Eds.), *Research in Personnel and Human Resources Management* (Vol. 6, 75–107). Greenwich, CT: JAI.

Eder, R. W., & Harris, M. M. (1999). Employment interview research: Historical update and introduction. In R. W. Eder and M. M. Harris (Eds.), *The Employment Interview Handbook.* Thousand Oaks, CA: Sage.

Eder, R. W., Kacmar, K. M., & Ferris, G. R. (1989). Employment interview research: History and synthesis. In R. W. Eder and G. R. Ferris (Eds.), *The Employment Interview: Theory, Research, and Practice* (17–31). London: Sage.

Gilmore, D. C., & Ferris, G. R. (1989). The effects of applicant impression management tactics on interviewer judgments. *Human Relations, 15,* 557–564.

Godfrey, D. K., Jones, E. E., & Lord, C. G. (1986). Self-promotion is not ingratiating. *Journal of Personality and Social Psychology, 50,* 106–115.

Graves, L. M., & Karen, R. J. (1996). The employment selection interview: A fresh look at an old problem. *Human Resource Management, 35,* 163–180.

Graves, L. M., & Powell, G. N. (1988). An investigation of sex discrimination in recruiters' evaluations of actual applicants. *Journal of Applied Psychology, 73,* 20–29.

Green, P. C. (1996). *Get hired! Winning strategies to ace the interview.* Austin, TX: Bard Books.

Heneman, H. G., Judge, T. A., & Heneman, R. L. (2000). *Staffing Organizations.* Middleton, WI: Irwin McGraw-Hill.

Hollingsworth, H. L. (1922). *Judging Human Character.* New York: D. Appleton.

Holt, R. R. (1958). Clinical and statistical prediction: A reformulation and some new data. *Journal of Abnormal and Social Psychology, 56,* 1–12.

Hovland, C. I., & Wonderlic, E. F. (1939). Prediction of industrial success from a standardized interview. *Journal of Applied Psychology, 23,* 537–546.

Huffcutt, A. I., & Arthur, W. (1994). Hunter and Hunter revisited: Interview validity for entry-level jobs. *Journal of Applied Psychology, 79,* 184–190.

Ilgen, D. R., & Feldman, J. M. (1983). Performance appraisal: A process focus. In L. L. Cummings and B. M. Staw (Eds.), *Research in Organizational Behavior* (Vol. 5, 141–197). Greenwich, CT: JAI.

Imada, A. S., & Hakel, M. D. (1977). Influence of nonverbal communication and rater proximity on impression and decisions in simulated employment interviews. *Journal of Applied Psychology, 62,* 295–300.

Janz, J. T. (1982). Initial comparisons of patterned behavior description interviews versus unstructured interviews. *Journal of Applied Psychology, 67,* 577–580.

Kenny, D. A., Horner, C., Kashy, D. A., & Chu, L. (1992). Consensus at zero acquaintance: Republican, behavioral cues, and stability. *Journal of Personality and Social Psychology, 62,* 88–97.

Latham, G. P., & Saari, L. M. (1984). Do people do what they say? Further studies on the situational interview. *Journal of Applied Psychology, 69,* 569–573.

Latham, G. P., Saari, L. M., Pursell, E. D., & Campion, M. A. (1980). The situational interview. *Journal of Applied Psychology, 65,* 442–431.

Lowry, P. E. (1994). The structured interview: An alternative to the assessment center? *Public Personnel Management, 23,* 201–216.

Maier, N. R., & Thurber, J. A. (1968). Accuracy of judgments of deception when an interview is watched, heard, and read. *Personnel Psychology, 21*(1): 23–30.

McDaniel, M. A. (1985). *A meta-analysis of the validity of training and experience ratings in personnel selection* (OSP-85-1). Washington, D.C.: U.S. Office of Personnel Management, Office of Staffing Policy, Examining Policy Analysis Division.

McDaniel, M. A., Whetzel, D. L., Schmidt, F. L., & Maurer, S. D. (1994). The validity of employment interviews: A comprehensive review and meta-analysis. *Journal of Applied Psychology, 79,* 599–616.

Newman, S. H., Bobbitt, J. M., & Cameron, D. C. (1946). The reliability of the interviewing method in an officer candidate evaluation program. *American Psychologist, 1,* 103–109.

O'Rourke, L. J. (1929). Measuring judgment and resourcefulness. *Personnel Journal, 7,* 427–440.

Orpen, C. (1985). Patterned behavior description interviews versus unstructured interviews: A comparative validity study. *Journal of Applied Psychology, 70,* 774–776.

Parsons, C. K., & Liden, R. C. (1984). Interviewer perceptions of applicant qualifications: A multivariate field study of demographic characteristics and nonverbal cues. *Journal of Applied Psychology, 69,* 557–568.

Pingatore, R., Dugoni, B. L., Tindale, R. S., & Spring, B. (1994). Bias against overweight job applicants in a simulated employment interview. *Journal of Applied Psychology, 79,* 909–917.

Prewett-Livingston, A. J., Feild, H. S., Veres, J. G., & Lewis, P. M. (1996). Effects of race on interview ratings in a situational panel interview. *Journal of Applied Psychology, 81,* 178–186.

Pulakos, E. D., & Schmitt, N. (1995). Experience-based and situational interview questions: Studies of validity. *Personnel Psychology, 48* (2), 289–309.

Pulakos, E. D., Schmitt, N., Whitney, D., & Smith, M. (1996). Individual differences in interviewer ratings: The impact of standardization, consensus discussion, and sampling error on the validity of a structured interview. *Personnel Psychology, 49* (1), 85–104.

Rasmussen, K. G., Jr. (1984). Nonverbal behavior, verbal behavior, resume credentials, and selection interview outcomes. *Journal of Applied Psychology, 69,* 551–556.

Rowe, P. M. (1989). Unfavorable information and interview decisions. In R. W. Eder and G. R. Ferris (Eds.), *The Employment Interview: Theory, Research, and Practice* (77–89). London: Sage.

Schlenker, B. R. (1980). *Impression management: The self-concept, social identity, and interpersonal relations.* Monterey, CA: Brooks/Cole.

Schmitt, N. (1976). Social and situational determinants of interview decisions: Implications for the employment interview. *Personnel Psychology, 29,* 79–101.

Schneider, D. J. (1981). Tactical self-presentations: Toward a broader conception. In J. T. Tedeschi (Ed.), *Impression Management Theory and Social Psychological Research* (23–40). New York: Academic Press.

Schneider, B., & Schmitt, N. (1986). *Staffing organizations.* Glenview, IL: Scott, Foresman.

Scott, W. D. (1915). Scientific selection of salesmen. *Advertising and Selling Magazine, 5,* 5–6ff.

Silvester, J. (1997). Spoken attributions and candidate success in graduate recruitment interviews. *Journal of Occupational and Organizational Psychology, 70* (1), 61–73.

Snyder, M., & Copeland, J. (1989). Self-monitoring processes in organizational settings. In R. A. Giacalone and P. Rosenfeld (Eds.), *Impression Management in the Organization.* Hillsdale, NJ: Erlbaum.

Snyder, M., & Gangestad, S. (1986). On the nature of self-monitoring: Matters of assessment, matters of validity. *Journal of Personality and Social Psychology, 51,* 125–139.

Springbett, B. M. (1958). Factors affecting the final decision in the employment interview. *Canadian Journal of Psychology, 12,* 13–22.

Stevens, C. K., & Kristof, A. L. (1995). Making the right impression: A field study of applicant impression management during job interviews. *Journal of Applied Psychology, 80* (5), 587–606.

Ulrich, L. D., & Trumbo, D. (1965). The selection interview since 1949. *Psychological Bulletin, 63,* 100–116.

Wagner, R. F. (1949). The employment interview: A critical summary. *Personnel Psychology, 2,* 17–46.

Washburn, P. V., & Hakel, M. D. (1973). Visual cues and verbal content as influences on impressions formed after simulated employment interviews. *Journal of Applied Psychology, 58,* 137–141.

Weekley, J. A., & Gier, J. A. (1987). Reliability and validity of the situational interview for a sales position. *Journal of Applied Psychology, 72,* 484–487.

Weiner, B. (1986). *An Attributional Theory of Motivation and Emotion.* New York: Springer-Verlag.

Wexley, K. N., Yukl, G. A., Kovacs, S. Z., & Sanders, R. E. (1972). Importance of contrast effects in employment interviews. *Journal of Applied Psychology, 56,* 45–48.

Wiesner, W. H., & Cronshaw, S. F. (1988). The moderating impact of interview format and degree of structure on interview validity. *The Journal of Occupational Psychology, 61,* 275–290.

Zedeck, S., Tziner, A., & Middlestadt, S. E. (1983). Interviewer validity and reliability: An individual analysis approach. *Personnel Psychology, 36,* 355–370.

BACKGROUND DATA: APPLICATIONS IN RECRUITMENT, SELECTION, AND DEVELOPMENT

Michael D. Mumford
Gregory A. Manley
Jonathon R. B. Halbesleben

When you want to get to know someone, you ask questions. You might ask the person where they grew up, how many brothers and sisters they had, how much they liked their college courses, or how they found their last job. All of these questions, in one way or another, ask people to describe their past life history. We use this information to draw conclusions about this person—whether we like them, whether we would ask them to a party, or whether we would work with them on a project. Essentially, background data measures represent a formalization of these questions about people's day-to-day lives. Put more technically, background data measures present a set of structured questions where people are asked to describe behavior and experiences occurring earlier in their lives (Hesketh, 1999; Mumford & Owens, 1982, 1987).

In this article we will examine the nature of background data measures and their applications in human resources management. We will begin by examining the psychological principles that make background data measures such useful predictors of people's future (Mael, 1991; Mumford, Stokes, & Owens, 1990). We will then examine various types of background data questions and the procedures used in developing these questions (e.g., Clifton, Mumford, & Baughman, 1999; Owens, 1976). Subsequently, we will examine the application of background data measures in three arenas. We will begin by considering the application of background data measures in personnel selection (e.g., Hunter & Hunter, 1982; Nickels, 1994; Reilly & Chao, 1982). Although background data measures are most commonly used in personnel selection, those measures might be used to address a number of other problems in human resources management. In this article we will consider two of these alternative applications. More specifically, we will examine the potential applications of background data measures in recruitment (Brush & Owens, 1979) and career development (Owens & Schoenfeldt, 1979).

THE PSYCHOLOGY OF BACKGROUND DATA

In some ways, people are naïve psychologists. Our naïve psychology tells us that to understand a person, we must know something about where that person comes from. A key question confronting students of background data, however, is exactly what type of information is provided by people's answers to these life history questions. Broadly speaking, four major theories have been proposed that might be used to explain the value of the information provided by people's answers to background data questions. These theoretical models of background data include (1) the social constraints model, (2) the self-concept model, (3) the motivational model, and (4) the adaptation or ecology model. All of these models, in one way or another, try to explain how people's past behavior and experiences shape their future.

The first theory of background data was the social constraints theory. This theory, in its simplest form, holds that people will behave in the future as they have in the past due to learning and social constraints (Owens, 1976). A more elaborate version of social constraints theory, however, may be traced to scholars such as Havinghurst (1953) and Owens and Schoenfeldt (1979). In their view, people's life history occurs within a social system and the experiences people have in this social system condition the experiences they have and the opportunities available, thereby shaping the person's future behavior (Muchinsky, 1994). More directly, we assume that a person who grew up in New York, attended Columbia Law, and has two children will exhibit certain behaviors as a function of these experiences and the constraints these experiences place on likely behavior. Thus, we would not expect a person with this background to become a logger or remain long on a job in Montana.

In contrast to the social constraints model, which assumes that external forces shape life history, the second model, the self-concept model, assumes that internal forces, specifically the individual's identify or self-concept, shape how people will behave in the future (Mael, 1991). In self-concept theory, people are held to actively create a positive image of themselves, and their future lives, behaving in such a way as to maximize consistency with this idealized image (Mumford, Snell, & Reiter-Palmon, 1994). Accordingly, people recall and report life experiences in terms of this self-image while reacting to new situations based on this self-image (Handel, 1987). Thus, if I conceive of myself as an executive, I will seek out and create situations where I can lead, seeing as significant those events relevant to my movement into executive positions.

A third theory of background data stresses the importance of motivation, values, and personality in shaping the life course (Allworth & Hesketh, 1999; Mumford & Owens, 1982; Tenopyr, 1994). Essentially, this motivational model holds that any life involves choices, and people's past behavior and experiences, along with their future behavior and experiences, are a function of the factors that influence the choices people make. Typically, these choices are held to be determined by stable, enduring characteristics of the individual involving the personality, motives, values, and beliefs. Thus, if I spend much of my leisure time reading, I will, in the future, be more likely to go on to graduate school due to the value I place in intellectual activities.

The fourth and final theory, the adaptation or ecology model (Mumford, Stokes, & Owens, 1990), holds that the relationship between past and future behavior derives from people's active, conscious attempts to adapt to a dynamic environment. This model holds that people choose to enter situations based on their motives, beliefs, and values, as well as cognitive appraisals of the opportunities provided by a situation. After they enter a situation, exposure to this situation and subsequent development will provide knowledge of the situation and the skills needed to exploit similar situations in the future. These knowledges and skills will, in turn, influence subsequent choices, self-image, and values leading to the emergence of coherent patterns of behavior throughout the life course. Some key support for this model has been provided by Reiter-Palmon, Mumford, and Threlfall (1998), who have shown that people are better able to solve problems, specifically day-to-day problems, that are consistent with their prior pattern of life

experiences. Thus, if you enjoyed science courses in high school, I might expect you to take more science courses, and get better grades in these courses, in college.

DEVELOPING BACKGROUND DATA QUESTIONS

These theories examining how past behavior is related to future behavior are noteworthy because they influence the approaches people use to develop background data questions. An illustration of application of the ecology model in the development of background data items may be found in Mumford, Costanza, Connelly, and Johnson (1996). They developed background data questions by first specifying the key attributes likely to underlie performance in a certain situation or class of situations. For senior executives, one might argue that individualized consideration and planning skills are of critical importance. Next they sought to identify situations occurring earlier in people's lives where they might have an opportunity to develop or express these skills. For example, in the case of individualized consideration, one might examine situations involving the counseling of a poor-performing member of a team or helping a friend cope with personal problems. Next, background data questions are written focusing on people's behavior and experiences in these situations that examine performance attributes, such as individualized consideration with respect to (1) situational exposure, (2) situational choice, (3) behavior in situations, (4) reactions to the situation, (5) others' reactions to behavior in a situation, and (6) the outcomes of behavior in the situation.

Typically, in applying this approach, an attempt is made to develop a number (10 to 20) of questions that might capture each of the targeted performance capacities. The resulting items are then reviewed by a panel of experts for clarity, appropriateness of the situation, relevance of the item to the targeted performance capacity, the potential for faking, and discretion or whether the question reflects something the individual did rather than something done to them. Within this approach one may develop direct questions, examining behavior and experiences in situations similar to the job situation, or indirect questions, examining behavior and experiences in situations that are rather different in superficial content than the job situation. Table 5-1 provides some illustrative direct and indirect items for two performance capacities, individualized consideration and planning.

Another approach to the development of background data questions has been proposed by Russell, Mattson, Devlin, and Atwater (1990). The approach they suggest is based on the identity or self-concept model. Here a sample of people working on the job is obtained, typically including 15 to 25 successful and 15 to 25 less successful people.

These people are then asked to write a series of essays intended to reveal how they conceive of themselves and their behavior in certain performance situations. Thus, an essay question might ask "Please describe your most important accomplishment at work." "Describe a time where you had to work under a high pressure deadline." or "Think of the highest performing people you know on your job and describe the work and nonwork experiences that contributed to their performance."

A content analyses of the resulting essays is then used to identify common themes appearing in people's descriptions of their past behaviors and experiences. The themes emerging in these essays are then used to develop background data items by identifying the experiences and behaviors that seem to differentiate high and low performers. Table 5-2 illustrates some items resulting from one application of this approach where the intent was to distinguish successful and unsuccessful leaders.

TABLE 5-1   Examples of Direct and Indirect Items for Individualized Consideration and Planning

Individualized Consideration	*Planning*
Indirect	*Indirect*
How often do your friends come to you for advice about personal problems?	Have you typically kept a list of chores to be done around the house?
How easy is it for you to recognize changes in someone's mood?	In college, did you plan time away from distractions to finish your reading assignments?
Have you been able to remember birthdays of friends and relatives?	How often were you asked to organize the activities of clubs you belonged to?
Direct	*Direct*
How often have you worked overtime to help a coworker finish a project?	How much time do you spend thinking about a task before starting work?
How often do you thank support staff for their work on a proposal?	How often are you asked to organize meetings at work?
How often have you thought about a person's career goals before assigning them to a task?	How often have you been the one to point out negative consequences of implementing a proposal?

TABLE 5-2	General Items Distinguishing Successful and Unsuccessful Leaders

1. How have you tried to handle unexpected deadlines?
   a. Worked substantially longer hours.
   b. Gotten other people to help out.
   c. Asked for an extension.
   d. Did what I could in the time allotted.
2. What did you do when trying to correct a subordinate who was having difficulty getting along with other team members?
   a. Asked them to talk to other members of the team.
   b. Tried to assign them to another team.
   c. Asked another team member to coach them.
   d. Talked to your supervisor about the problem.

3. What approach did you use when planning group activities?
   a. Worked with the more experienced group members to develop a plan.
   b. Asked the group as a whole to come up with a plan.
   c. Provided the group with an outline of the plan and its goals.
   d. Developed the plan on your own.
4. When providing a group with feedback about its performance, how did you give the feedback?
   a. Delivered the bad news directly.
   b. Prepared a few members of the group to receive the bad news.
   c. Talked first about the things the group had done well.
   d. Tried to avoid delivering the news.
   e. Asked someone else to give the news.

Both these approaches provide viable frameworks for the development of background data questions. For example, Mumford, Costanza, Connelly, and Johnson (1996) report that application of their procedures yield scales evidencing good reliability, producing internal consistency coefficients in the .70s, and good validity, yielding criterion-related validity coefficients in the mid .30s across a range of performance measures including managerial assessment, training performance, and decision making. Along similar lines, Russell, Mattson, Devlin, and Atwater (1990) have shown that essay techniques yield items capable of predicting leadership performance.

Although both these techniques appear to provide viable frameworks for the development of background data items, they do display some noteworthy differences. The techniques proposed by Mumford, Costanza, Connelly, and Johnson (1996) organize item generation around psychological constructs. Thus, items can be scaled with respect to a construct (e.g., grouping together all items that measure achievement

motivation) and validation occurs by correlating total scale scores with the criteria of interest. The techniques suggested by Russell, Mattson, Devlin, and Atwater (1990) tend to produce a number of loosely linked items. When there is no a priori framework for organizing background data items, items are scaled using a technique referred to as empirical keying (Hogan, 1994; Owens, 1976). In empirical keying, items, or item response options, are weighted based on their ability to predict the criterion measure of interest. Although both these techniques yield similar results (Reiter-Palmon & Connelly, 2000), the construct-based approach is preferred when adequate criteria cannot be obtained and well-designed criterion-related validation studies cannot be conducted.

CHARACTERISTICS OF GOOD QUESTIONS

To this point we have examined the procedures commonly used in the development and scaling of background data questions. At this juncture, before proceeding to the applications of background data measures, it would seem germane to briefly consider what we know about the characteristics of "good" and "bad" background data questions. The characteristics of background data have been studied from three perspectives: (1) the structure and framing of questions, (2) the characteristics of questions that contribute to accurate reporting, and (3) the characteristics of questions that promote the use of background data in personnel selection.

With regard to the structure and framing of questions, more effective background data measures examine prior behaviors and experiences across a range of situations (Mumford, 1999). Typically, viable items try to examine situations most people in the population under consideration would have been exposed to earlier in their lives, focusing on recent situational exposure rather than events that occurred many years ago. In addition to these situational characteristics, responses to the questions are typically framed in a 5 to 7 point multiple choice format where response options are graded along a continuum. Additionally, items are commonly structured to provide an escape clause. Owens (1976) has shown that items evidencing these characteristics typically yield high reliability. Table 5-3 provides an illustration of some of the response formats commonly applied to developing background data items.

Although the content of items and response options are an important characteristic of background data questions, one must remember that responses to background data questions rely on someone's autobiographical memory (Asher, 1972). Recently, Clifton, Mumford, and Baughman (1999) examined the characteristics of background data questions that resulted in more accurate and consistent recall of prior experiences. They found that the accuracy and consistency of recall improved when background data questions focused on (1) event

summaries, (2) goal relevant events, (3) event organizers, and (4) salient events. Table 5-4 provides some examples of "good" and "poor" items falling in each of these categories. When items display good recall characteristics, people can respond to these questions in an accurate fashion that, in fact, reflects their prior life history (McCrae & Costa, 1988; Roberts, Block, & Block, 1978; Schaffer, Saunders, & Owens, 1986).

When background data questions are to be applied, certain requirements of the intended application may make some types of items more desirable than others. Because one of the most common applications of background data is in personnel selection, a number of scholars (Asher, 1972; Mael, 1991; Mumford & Whetzel, 1997) have sought to identify the characteristics of background data questions that promote their use in personnel selection. Broadly speaking, good items for use in personnel selection focus on the individual in a fair and objective fashion. Thus, items that are potentially verifiable and job relevant where the behavior at hand is under the individual's control are preferred. By the same token items that are restrictive, in that not all people would have been exposed to the situation, socially desirable, stereotypical, or loaded should be avoided. Table 5-5 presents some examples of "good" and "bad" items with respect to each of these characteristics.

BACKGROUND DATA IN PERSONNEL SELECTION

As previously noted, the most common application of background data measures is in the area of personnel selection. In personnel selection, one of two general models is commonly applied in assessing people's capabilities. The first approach, a maximal performance approach, appraises people's capacities to do the work under optimal conditions. The ability tests commonly used in

TABLE 5-3   Item Formats

1. *Binary items*
   Have you found your life to be pleasant and satisfying?
   a. Yes
   b. No

2. *Continuum, single choice*
   What is your weight?
   a. 132 or under
   b. 133–155
   c. 156–175
   d. 176–195
   e. Over 195

3. *Noncontinuum, single choice*
   What was your marital status at college graduation?
   a. Single
   b. Married, no children
   c. Married, one or more children
   d. Widowed
   e. Separated or divorced

4. *Noncontinuum, multiple choice*
   Circle each of the following from which you have ever suffered:
   a. Allergies
   b. Asthma
   c. High blood pressure
   d. Ulcers
   e. Headaches
   f. Gastrointestinal upsets
   g. Arthritis

5. *Noncontinuum plus escape option*
   When have you been most likely to have a headache?
   a. When I've strained my eyes
   b. When I haven't eaten on schedule
   c. When I've been under tension
   d. January 1
   e. Never have headaches

6. *Continuum plus escape option*
   What was your length of service in your most recent full-time job?
   a. Less than 6 months
   b. 6 months to 1 year
   c. 1 to 2 years
   d. More than 5 years
   e. No previous full-time job

7. *Common stem, multiple continua*
   Over the past five years, how much have you enjoyed each of the following? (Use continuum 1 to 4 at right below.)
   a. Loafing or watching TV
   b. Reading
   c. Constructive hobbies
   d. Home improvement
   e. Outdoor recreation
   f. Music, art, or dramatics, etc.

   1. Very much
   2. Some
   3. Very little
   4. Not at all

TABLE 5-4   Examples of Background Data Items That Encourage Good and Poor Levels of Recall

Item Types	*Good Recall*	*Poor Recall*
Event summaries	How often were you able to improve your grades in a class when you did poorly on the first test?	How much did you improve your grade on your algebra test?
Goal relevant	How often have you been angry with someone who took advantage of a coworker?	How often have you been angry?
Event organizers	When meeting new people, how easy is it for you to introduce yourself?	How easy is it for you to introduce yourself?
Relevant events	How difficult was it for you to learn calculus in college?	How difficult was it for you to learn addition in elementary school?

TABLE 5-5 Examples of Appropriate and Inappropriate Items That Address Selection on Issues

Faking Issues	Appropriate Items	Inappropriate Items
Restrictive	How many of the following activities have you participated in during the last year? 1. Sky diving 2. Scuba diving/snorkeling 3. Hiking 4. Camping	How often have you been scuba diving in the past year?
Social stereotyping	How important has it been for you to have coworkers who showed an interest in your projects?	How often have you enjoyed working with women who were very nurturing?
Controllability	When choosing houses or apartments, how likely are you to look in uncrowded suburbs or in the country?	What was the size of the town in which you grew up?
Job relevance	How many days per week do you typically stay late to finish something at work?	How many times per month do you go to church?
Verifiable	What was your average pay raise over the last five years?	Are you typically seen as a better performer than your peers?
Social desirability	How often have you gone out of your way to spend time with unpopular colleagues?	How important has it been for you to be friends with your coworkers?
Loaded	How often have you continued to put in extra time on a project to compensate for mistakes made by management?	How hard have you worked on assignments?

personnel selection provide one illustration of this maximal performance approach. The second approach, a typical performance approach, appraises people with respect to their day-to-day expression of these performance capacities. Background data measures, like interviews, provide an assessment of typical performance capacities.

In fact, background data measures have become a favored alternative to other measures of typical performance for a rather straightforward reason. Quite simply, well-developed background data measures have been found to be highly effective predictors of job performance across a range of settings and criteria. Typically, well-developed background data scales yield validity coefficients in the .30s to .40s when used to predict per-

formance (Mumford & Stokes, 1992). These observations lead Hunter and Hunter (1982), Mumford and Stokes (1992), and Reilly and Chao (1982) to conclude that background data measures are the best available alternative to tests of cognitive abilities for use in personnel selection.

A number of other considerations recommend the routine use of background data in personnel selection. To begin, background data measures provide an unusually flexible assessment format because they can be used to assess virtually any characteristic manifest in people's life history. As a result, characteristics that cannot be easily assessed using other types of measures can often be assessed through background data. In one study along these lines, Mumford, Connelly, Helton,

Mowry, and Osburn (in press) showed that background data scales can be developed to assess characteristics, such as negative life themes and power motives, related to unethical behavior. In still another study, Allworth and Hesketh (1999) developed background data scales to assess people's ability to cope with change-measuring attributes such as experience of change, positive coping, and negative coping. They found that these scales produced a multiple correlation of .35 when used to predict measures of adaptation to a changing job environment.

The Allworth and Hesketh (1999) study is also noteworthy because it indicates that background data consistently adds to the prediction of performance obtained from more traditional measures of cognitive ability. Somewhat more compelling evidence for the incremental validity of background data measures has been provided by Stokes, Searcy, and Toth (1998). They developed background data scales using a variation on the procedures suggested by Mumford, Costanza, Connelly, and Johnson (1996). When these scales were added to a well-developed battery of cognitive ability measures, use of background data was again found to result in significant gains in prediction. These findings have led many scholars to conclude that most selection systems should include a cognitive component, intended to assess maximal performance potential, and a set of background measures, intended to assess typical performance.

The incremental validity of background data is noteworthy in part, however, because it suggests that the use of background data, in conjunction with cognitive ability tests, will reduce adverse impact. It has long been known that background data measures evidence substantially less adverse impact with respect to disadvantaged populations than cognitive ability tests (Mumford & Stokes, 1992; Reilly & Chao, 1982). This reduced adverse impact occurs because background data measures implicitly assess individuals *within* the context of their life space, thereby controlling for differences in economic opportunity. Cognitive ability, or maximal performance, tests compare individuals *across* environments, thereby resulting in higher adverse impact. As a result of these differential adverse impact rates, background data measures are often included in selection batteries as a way of reducing adverse impact without sacrificing the validity of the resulting selection system.

The final attraction of background data in personnel selection is its utility (Mitchell, 1994). Background data measures allow a great deal of information to be acquired about job applicants at a relatively low cost when these measures are compared to ability tests, interviews, and assessment centers. In comparison to these techniques, background data measures cost less to develop, less to administer, and less to score and maintain. When the low cost of background data is considered in light of the validity of the resulting measures, their low adverse impact, and the likely gains in overall prediction vis-à-vis more traditional selection strategies, it is little wonder that background data has become one of the techniques most commonly applied in personnel selection.

BACKGROUND DATA IN RECRUITMENT

The success of background data measures as a selection technique has, in one sense, become something of a liability. The success of background data in selection has led us to lose sight of the many other potential applications of background data in human resources management. One area where background data has shown great promise is in the area of recruitment—specifically in identifying the sources of viable workers.

Initial studies examining the potential applications of background data in recruitment began more than 40 years ago. In one study along these lines, Chaney and Owens

(1964) attempted to identify the antecedents of entry into sales, research, and general engineering positions. They developed background data items examining high school and college experiences using the social constraints model of background data. They found that sales engineers differed from research and general engineers with respect to engagement in social activities (e.g., fraternity membership), athletic activities (e.g., involvement in varsity sports), and leadership activities (e.g., class president).

Information of this sort is clearly useful for recruiters because it provides markers of attraction to a job. In fact, a variety of studies have examined the relationship between background data and vocational interests. Studies by Eberhardt and Muchinsky (1984); Mumford and Owens (1982); Neiner and Owens (1985); and Rounds, Davis, and Lofquist (1979) indicate that background data is related both to interest in certain jobs and the kind of reinforcers people are looking for in various jobs. Given these findings, one way background data measures might be applied is by developing questions examining different activities, goals, and pursuits. These questions might be administered to new hires and the questions that differentiate high- and low-tenure groups could be used to provide recruiters with interview guidelines.

Another way background data measures might be applied in recruitment has been suggested by Russell (Personal Communication-2001). He examined a background data item pool being used by a large federal agency. Included in this item pool were questions examining the source of information by which people found the job, such as radio advertisements, newspaper advertisements, etc. Comparison of successful, long-term workers with respect to their answers to these questions permitted identification of more and less successful sources of recruits. Along similar lines, Nickels and Mumford (1988) used background data

questions focusing on prior employment sites to identify the optimal recruits for sales positions in a large home supply chain.

BACKGROUND DATA IN EMPLOYEE DEVELOPMENT

Another potential application of background data measures may be found in the area of career development. Although background data questions are commonly framed to capture behavior and experiences occurring prior to employment, there is no reason why questions cannot be developed to examine behavior and experiences occurring after employment or entry into an occupational field. Comparison of more and less successful workers with respect to career progress may, in turn, be used to draw conclusions about the kind of experiences likely to prove beneficial to people at different points in their careers.

In one recent study along these lines, Mumford, Marks, Connelly, Zaccaro, and Reiter-Palmon (2000) examined the career development experiences contributing to leadership performance in a sample of army officers. They developed a series of 52 background data questions examining exposure to significant career development experiences such as mentoring (e.g., participated in discussions with senior officers), networking (e.g., discussed work problems with peers), and career intellectual involvement (e.g., read military history), among others. In addition, an assignments characteristics inventory was developed examining exposure to assignments calling for mentoring and developing others, long-term strategic planning, discretionary decision making, teamwork, etc.

Army officers, ranging in grade and experience from second lieutenant to full colonel, were asked to complete these two background data inventories along with a series of measures examining leadership skills and performance in leadership positions. A series of correlational analyses were conducted examining the relationship between the career development questions and skill growth as these officers moved from junior to mid-level, and mid-level to more senior leadership positions. It was found that experiences involving mentoring and developing others, discretionary decision making, strategic planning, complex problem solving, and boundary spanning, along with advanced professional training and self-development activities, contributed to the acquisition of leadership skills, and better leader performance, across these officers' careers.

These findings, of course, provide some potential guidelines for the kind of career experiences that might be used to develop leaders. Other studies by Anastasi and Schaefer (1969) and Morrison, Owens, Glennon, and Albright (1962) have examined the kind of career development experiences contributing to creativity and innovation. Taken as a whole, these studies indicate that background data questions may provide an important source of information guiding the design of career development systems.

CONCLUSIONS

These observations about the applications of background data in career development and recruitment bring us to our first conclusion. Although background data has most commonly been applied in the selection arena, it appears that background data may be used to address a host of questions in human resources management. In this article, we have focused on the potential application of background data in recruitment and career development. It is possible, however, that background data might play a role in a number of other human resources initiatives, including staffing system design, team construction, and compensation (Mumford, Stokes, & Owens, 1990).

Although background data might be used to address a variety of questions confronting human resources managers, its primary application has been in personnel selection. The literature we reviewed earlier indicates that background data measures are not only effective predictors of job performance but that they provide a useful supplement to more traditional selection techniques, resulting in improved prediction and a reduction in adverse impact. Moreover, they allow us to consider a wider range of characteristics in personnel selection at a relatively low cost, thereby permitting a more comprehensive assessment of candidates.

The range and success of background data applications is, of course, a reflection of the fundamental nature of the questions being asked and the problems confronting us in human resources management. Almost by definition, human resources management issues involve people. People do not arrive at their jobs and begin life anew. Instead, their experiences on the job are a function of their prior life history (Howe, 1982). By allowing us to examine people's life history in a systematic fashion, background data measures provide a key piece of descriptive information needed in many, if not all, human resources interventions. ■

REFERENCES

Allworth, E., & Hesketh, B. (1999). Construct-oriented biodata: Capturing change-related and contexually relevant future performance. *International Journal of Selection and Assessment, 7,* 97–111.

Anastasi, A., & Schaefer, C. E. (1969). Biographical correlates of artistic and literary creativity in adolescent girls. *Journal of Applied Psychology, 54,* 462–469.

Asher, E. S. (1972). The biographical item: Can it be improved? *Personnel Psychology, 25,* 251–269.

Brush, D. H., & Owens, W. A. (1979). Implementation and evaluation of an assessment classification model for manpower utilization. *Personnel Psychology, 32,* 369–383.

Chaney, F. B., & Owens, W. A. (1964). Life-history antecedents of sales, research, and general engineering interests. *Journal of Applied Psychology, 48,* 101–105.

Clifton, T. C., Mumford, M. D., & Baughman, W. A. (1999). Background data and autobiographical memory: Effects of item types and task characteristics. *International Journal of Selection and Assessment, 7,* 57–71.

Eberhardt, B. J., & Muchinsky, P. M. (1984). Structural validation of Holland's hexagonal model: Vocational classification through the use of background data. *Journal of Applied Psychology, 67,* 138–145.

Handel, A. (1987). Personal theories about life span development of one's self in autobiographical self-presentations of adults. *Human Development, 30,* 83–95.

Havinghurst, R. (1953). *Human Development and Education.* New York: Longman.

Hesketh, B. (1999). Introduction to the International Journal of Selection and Assessment Special Issue on biodata. *International Journal of Selection and Assessment, 7,* 55–56.

Hogan, J. B. (1994). Empirical keying of background data measures. In G. S. Stokes, M. D. Mumford, and W. A. Owens (Eds.), *Biodata Handbook: Theory Research and Use of Biographical Information in Selection and Performance Prediction* (69–108). Palo Alto, CA: Consulting Psychologists Press.

Howe, M. J. (1982). Biographical evidence and the development of outstanding individuals. *American Psychologist, 37,* 1071–1081.

Hunter, J. E., & Hunter, R. F. (1982). Validity and utility of alternative predictors of job performance. *Psychological Bulletin, 96,* 72–98.

Mael, F. A. (1991). A conceptual rationale for the domain and attributes of biodata items. *Personnel Psychology, 44,* 763–792.

McCrae, R. R., & Costa, P. T. (1988). Recalled parent-child relations and adult personality. *Journal of Personality, 56,* 417–433.

Mitchell, T. W. (1994). The utility of biodata. In G. S. Stokes, M. D. Mumford, and W. A. Owens (Eds.), *Biodata Handbook: Theory, Research, and Use of Biographical Information in Selection and Performance Prediction* (485–516). Palo Alto, CA: Consulting Psychologist Press.

Morrison, R. F., Owens, W. A., Glennon, J. R., & Albright, L. E. (1962). Factored life history antecedents of industrial research performance. *Journal of Applied Psychology, 46,* 281–284.

Muchinsky, P. M. (1994). The influence of life history experiences on vocational interests and choices. In G. S. Stokes, M. D. Mumford, and W. A. Owens (Eds.), *The Biodata Handbook: Theory, Research, and Use of Background Data in Selection and Performance Prediction* (535–554). Palo Alto, CA: Consulting Psychologists Press.

Mumford, M. D. (1999). Construct validity and background data: Issues, abuses, and future directions. *Human Resource Management Review, 9,* 117–145.

Mumford, M. D., Connelly, M. S., Helton, W. B., Mowry, J. R., & Osburn, H. K. (in press). On the construct validity of intelligence tests: Individual and situational factors. *International Journal of Selection and Assessment.*

Mumford, M. D., Costanza, D. P., Connelly, M. S., & Johnson, J. P. (1996). Item generation procedures and background data scales: Implications for construct and criterion-related validity. *Personnel Psychology, 49,* 361–398.

Mumford, M. D., Marks, M. A., Connelly, M. S., Zaccaro, S. J., & Reiter-Palmon, R. (2000). Development of leadership skills: Experience and timing. *Leadership Quarterly, 11,* 87–114.

Mumford, M. D., & Owens, W. A. (1982). Life history and vocational interests. *Journal of Vocational Behavior, 21,* 330–348.

Mumford, M. D., & Owens, W. A. (1987). Methodology review: Principles, procedures, and findings in the application of background data measures. *Applied Psychological Measurement, 11,* 1–31.

Mumford, M. D., Snell, A. F., & Reiter-Palmon, R. (1994). Personality and background data: Life history and self-concepts in an ecological system. In G. S. Stokes, M. D. Mumford, and W. A. Owens (Eds.), *The Biodata Handbook: Theory, Research and Use of Background Data in Selection and Performance Prediction* (583–625). Palo Alto, CA: Consulting Psychologists Press.

Mumford, M. D., & Stokes, G. S. (1992). Developmental determinants of individual action: Theory and practice in applying background data measures. In M. D. Dunnette and L. M. Hough (Eds.), *Handbook of Industrial and Organizational Psychology* (2nd Ed.) (61–138). Palo Alto, CA: Consulting Psychologists Press.

Mumford, M. D., Stokes, G. S., & Owens, W. A. (1990). *Patterns of Life Adaptation: The Ecology of Human Individuality.* Hillsdale, NJ: Erlbaum.

Mumford, M. D., & Whetzel, D. L. (1997). Background data. In D. L. Whetzel and G. R. Wheaton (Eds.), *Applied Measurement Methods in Industrial Psychology* (207–240). Palo Alto, CA: Consulting Psychologists Press.

Neiner, A. G., & Owens, W. A. (1985). Using biodata to predict job choice among college graduates. *Journal of Applied Psychology, 70,* 127–136.

Nickels, B. J. (1994). The nature of biodata. In G. S. Stokes, M. D. Mumford, and W. A. Owens (Eds.), *The Biodata Handbook: Theory, Research, and Use of Background Data in Selection and Performance Prediction* (1–16). Palo Alto, CA: Consulting Psychologists Press.

Nickels, B. J., & Mumford, M. D. (1988). *Selecting Sales and Cashiers at Home Depot: Validation of a Background Data Inventory.* Atlanta, GA: Georgia Institute of Technology.

Owens, W. A. (1976). Background data. In M. D. Dunnette (Ed.), *Handbook of Industrial and Organizational Psychology* (619–651). Chicago, IL: Rand-McNally.

Owens, W. A., & Schoenfeldt, L. F. (1979). Toward a classification of persons. *Journal of Applied Psychology, 64,* 569–607.

Reilly, R. R., & Chao, G. T. (1982). Validity and fairness of some alternative employee selection procedures. *Personnel Psychology, 35,* 1–62.

Reiter-Palmon, R., & Connelly, M. S. (2000). Item selection counts: A comparison of empirical keying and rational scale validities in theory-based and non-theory based item pools. *Journal of Applied Psychology, 85,* 143–151.

Reiter-Palmon, R., Mumford, M. D., & Threlfall, K. V. (1998). Solving everyday problems creatively: The role of problem construction and personality type. *Creativity Research Journal, 11,* 187–198.

Roberts, K. V., Block, J., & Block, J. E. (1978). Relationship between personality and life history. *Journal of Personality, 46,* 223–242.

Rounds, J. B., Davis, R. V., & Lofquist, L. (1979). Measurement of person-environment fit and prediction of satisfaction in theory of work adjustment. *Journal of Vocational Behavior, 31,* 297–318.

Russell, C. J., Mattson, J. A., Devlin, S. E., & Atwater, D. (1990). Predictive validity of biodata items generated from retrospective life experience essays. *Journal of Applied Psychology, 75,* 511–523.

Shaffer, G. S., Saunders, V., & Owens, W. A. (1986). Additional evidence for the accuracy of biographical information: Long-term retest and observer ratings. *Personnel Psychology, 39,* 791–809.

Stokes, G. S., Searcy, C. A., & Toth, C. S. (1998, April). *Is it rational to be empirical? An in depth look at an unresolved issue.* Paper presented at the 13th Annual Conference of the Society for Industrial and Organizational Psychology, Dallas, Texas.

Tenopyr, M. L. (1994). Big five, structural modeling, and item response theory. In G. S. Stokes, M. D. Mumford, and W. A. Owens (Eds.), *Biodata Handbook: Theory, Research, and Use of Background Data in Selection and Performance Prediction* (519–554). Palo Alto, CA: Consulting Psychologists Press.

JOB ANALYSIS: YESTERDAY, TODAY, AND TOMORROW

John G. Veres III
Ronald R. Sims
Toni S. Locklear
Applied Psychological Techniques, Incorporated
Katherine A. Jackson
Ryan S. O'Leary

JOB ANALYSIS: YESTERDAY, TODAY, AND TOMORROW

Gatewood and Feild (2001) observed that there are probably as many different definitions of job analysis as there are writings on the topic. They suggested a definition that views job analysis as "a purposeful, systematic process for collecting information on the important work-related aspects of a job" (p. 285). Others have characterized job analysis as the collection and analysis of just about any type of job-related information by almost any method for any purpose (Tiffin & McCormick, 1965). One researcher has given us a definition bordering on the metaphysical, characterizing job analysis as a way to analyze reality (Levine, 1983). We prefer a definition that views job analysis as a systematic process for collecting, analyzing, and interpreting job-related information.

THE NATURE OF JOB ANALYSIS

Part of the problem in defining job analysis stems from a difficulty with the term *job.* Most people seem to mean something fairly specific when they talk about a job. Ordinarily, *the* job means what people do on a day-to-day basis; the thing that results in a paycheck. Although the terms *job* and *position* are often used interchangeably, experts in human resources management (HRM) do not use the terms in the same way. The duties a given individual performs are described as a *position* (Prien & Ronan, 1971). Position has been defined as a "group of related job functions performed by a single person . . . because each position is staffed by an unique person, it is different from any other position, even those bearing the same job title in the organization" (Lopez, 1988, p. 881). Thus, if there are two persons operating word processing equipment, there are two positions (one for each person) but just one job (word processing operator). A job can then be defined as "a group of positions whose functions are so similar that their satisfactory performance requires an identical set of incumbent traits" (Lopez, 1988, p. 881). It is important to make this distinction because, to understand what is meant by job analysis, we must first understand that HRM specialists are talking about groups of positions whenever they use the term *job;* rarely are they talking about what one person does.

When we use the term *analysis,* most of us mean the separation of a whole into its component parts with the intent to examine and interpret those parts. Similarly, HRM specialists describe what is done in a job analysis as breaking down the component parts of a job so that we can achieve some better understanding of it. Bemis, Belenky, and Soder (1983) describe job analysis as "a systematic procedure for gathering, documenting and analyzing information about three basic categories of a job: job content, job requirements, and the context in which the job is performed" (pp. 1–2).

Job content identifies and describes the activities of the job or what workers actually do on the job. Depending upon the particular job analysis method used, descriptions of job content may range from general statements of job activities through detailed descriptions of duties and tasks, or from more detailed statements of the steps or elements involved in a particular process to descriptions of motions needed to perform an activity. When gathering information about tasks, the job analyst seeks to determine what the worker does, the purpose of the action, and the tools, equipment, or machinery used in the process. The analyst may also gather additional information about tasks, such as their relative importance, the expected performance levels, and the type of training, if any, needed by a new worker in order to perform the tasks satisfactorily.

In the past, *job (or worker) requirements* have included factors such as years of education and experience, degrees, licenses, and so forth—credentials assumed to be evidence that an individual possesses the qualifications needed for successful job performance. A more modern view of job requirements identifies the knowledge, skills, abilities, and physical and other characteristics that a person must possess for effective job performance in a particular situation or context.

Job context refers to the conditions under which work is performed and the demands such work imposes on workers. Specific types of job context information typically identified during a job analysis includes factors such as its purpose, the degree of accountability or responsibility of the employee, the availability of guidelines, the extent of supervision received and/or exercised, the potential consequences of error, and the physical demands and working conditions of the job.

This short description is but one of many attempts to categorize the component parts of a job. Job analysis may be thought of as a process that attempts to reduce to words the things that people do in the world of work (Ash, 1988). The components into which the job is divided and the words that serve as labels for those components vary from one job analysis system to another. There are many different ways of analyzing jobs and many different uses for the information resulting from job analyses. As we shall see in the following sections, many researchers have adopted a variety of approaches for structuring information about jobs. Before we describe these approaches, it is important to think about why we should worry about conducting job analyses in the first place.

WHY CONDUCT JOB ANALYSIS?

Two major forces have contributed to the need to conduct job analyses: conducting human resources planning on a continuous basis in response to competition, and equal employment opportunity concerns (Holley & Jennings, 1983). Employers in the United States, faced with increased foreign and domestic competition, must engage in human resources planning on a near-continuous basis while simultaneously trying to ensure that their employees are working efficiently. New technology, shifts in labor demand, and improved work methods, for example, can each alter an organization's human resources needs. As a result of these changing needs, the way workers perform their jobs may change. Jobs that have changed in response to new technology create a somewhat different problem. Employers must find individuals with the requisite knowledge, skills, and abilities to adequately perform the activities required. Effective HRM planning allows adjustments and refinements to be made, transforming an organization's workforce to meet the projected future needs of the organization.

Job analysis is the most basic building block of HRM. The set of jobs employees perform in an organization provide the vehicle for coordinating and linking the various activities necessary to achieve its overall mission. Job analysis is such an important activity to HRM that it has been called the building block of everything that personnel does (Cascio, 1991). Almost every HRM program requires some type of information gleaned from job analysis.

Perhaps the single largest contributor to the increasing use of job analysis techniques is equal employment opportunity legislation. Title VII of the Civil Rights Act of 1964, as amended; the Equal Pay Act of 1963; the Age Discrimination in Employment Act of 1967, as amended; the Americans with Disabilities Act of 1990; and other laws passed over the last 35 years have dramatically increased the use of job analysis, making it an integral part of establishing the job-relatedness of employment practices. The large number of court cases involving allegations of employment discrimination has been highly instrumental in enhancing the importance of job analysis. As a judge noted in an employment test validation case:

> The cornerstone of the construction of a content valid examination [an examination based on qualifications really needed in the job] is the job analysis. Without such an analysis to single out the critical knowledge, skills, and abilities required by the job, their importance to each other, and the level of proficiency demanded as to each attribute, a test constructor is aiming in the dark and can only hope to achieve job-relatedness by blind luck. (*Kirkland v. New York Department of Corrections*, 1974)

In 1978 the federal agencies charged with enforcing equal employment opportunity laws issued the Uniform Guidelines on Employee Selection Procedures (Equal Employment Opportunity Commission, Civil Service Commission, Department of Labor, & Department of Justice, 1978), which confirm the place of job analysis as a fundamental prerequisite for proving employment practices to be free of discrimination (Holley & Jennings, 1983). The courts have worked to define further the role of job analysis in demonstrating job-relatedness. Thompson and Thompson (1982) reviewed a number of employment discrimination lawsuits to determine the criteria the federal courts use in assessing job analysis in the context of selection tests. The following were among their conclusions:

- Expert job analysts must perform the job analysis.
- The results of the analysis should be reduced to written form.
- The job analysis process employed must be described in detail.
- Data should be collected from a variety of sources.

- Information on tasks performed must be included in the job analysis.
- Knowledge, skills, and abilities should be clearly specified and must be operationally defined in terms of work.

More recently, Buckner (1989) reviewed 185 court cases from 1979 through 1987 dealing with hiring, promotion, reclassification, and training issues. Among her findings for content-related validation (job-relatedness) studies were that courts generally ruled for employers when the following conditions existed:

- Job content was well-defined.
- Work behaviors were defined in behavioral terms.
- KSAs (knowledge, skills, and abilities) were operationally defined.
- Subject matter experts (i.e., incumbents and/or supervisors) rated KSA importance.

These findings, taken together with the Thompson and Thompson (1982) results and the language in the federal Uniform Guidelines, present a clear picture of the importance of job analysis in this context. The passage of the Americans with Disabilities Act in 1990, discussed later in more detail, focused even more attention on job analysis outcomes. So long as equal employment opportunity laws remain on the books, job analysis is here to stay.

THE MAJOR USES AND IMPORTANCE OF JOB ANALYSIS INFORMATION

As noted previously, the information gained through job analysis is of utmost importance; it has great value to the organization as a whole and particularly to HRM specialists and line managers. HRM researchers have identified a number of specific uses of job analysis information, including descriptions, job specifications, job classification, job evaluations, job design (Bemis et al., 1983), recruitment, selection, performance appraisal, training and development, job evaluation, career planning, work redesign, and HRM planning (Wright & Wexley, 1985).

Job Description　　A job description is an account of the duties and activities associated with a particular job. Its purpose is to identify a job, define that job within established limits, and describe its content (Gael, 1988b). The job description concentrates on describing the job as it is currently being performed. While the format for job descriptions vary somewhat, most job descriptions contain sections that include the job name, a brief summary description of the job, a listing of job duties and responsibilities, and an explanation of organizational relationships pertinent to the job. Job descriptions have a number of important uses, including development of job specifications, workforce planning and recruitment, orientation of new employees, and development of performance appraisal systems.

Job Specifications　　Job specifications describe the characteristics needed to perform the job activities identified in the job description. They focus on the individuals doing the job rather than on the work itself. Job specifications may include information regarding the KSAs or the competency, educational, and experience qualifications the incumbent must possess to perform the job. A job specification may be prepared as a separate document or, as is more often the case, as the concluding section of a job description. It is important to note that accurate job specifications identify what KSAs a person needs to do the job, not necessarily what qualifications the current employee possesses. Job specifications allow HRM specialists to identify persons with the skills they seek and help target efforts to recruit them.

Job Classification   Classification involves grouping similar positions into job classes and grouping comparable job classes into job families. There are several good reasons to group jobs. One is simplicity. If HRM specialists (and managers) had to deal with each position individually, the sheer volume of paperwork would be overwhelming. Grouping positions into job classifications allows HRM specialists to deal with personnel functions at a more general level. One of the HRM functions that can be handled at this level is pay. Individuals employed in a particular job classification typically receive salaries within the pay range established for that classification.

Job Evaluation   HRM specialists often mention job classification and job evaluation in the same breath. The process of job evaluation involves assessing the relative dollar value of each job to the organization to set up internally equitable pay structures. There are two basic approaches to job evaluation, both of which rely heavily on job analysis data. One approach involves comparing the target organization's pay practices to those of other organizations. This approach is often referred to as the market pricing method. To apply this method, we must be sure that our jobs are indeed analogous to the ones selected for comparison. Job analysis information on both jobs assures us that they are comparable. The second approach involves rating jobs on the basis of factors that indicate the relative worth of different jobs within the organization. This approach has been called the factor comparison or point factor method. Assessing the relative worth of jobs means analyzing them on a common set of criteria such as know-how, problem solving, accountability, working conditions, and complexity (Hay & Purves, 1954; U.S. Civil Service Commission, 1977). The factors selected for comparison may vary, but job analysis remains a foundation for job evaluation.

Job Design   The goal of job design is simplifying, enriching, enlarging, or otherwise changing jobs to make the efforts of each employee better fit together with jobs performed by other workers. In recent years, an important aim for job design has been to provide individuals meaningful work that fits effectively into the flow of the organization. Changing one job can make the overall system work more efficiently.

From the organization's viewpoint, jobs, as performed, must lead to efficient operations, quality products, and well-maintained equipment. From the workers' viewpoint, jobs must be meaningful and challenging, provide feedback on performance, and call on their decision making skills (Davis & Wacker, 1988). HRM specialists design jobs that attempt to meet the needs of both employers and employees.

Human Resources Management Planning
Job analysis provides fundamental input to the HRM planning process by helping planners understand exactly what kinds of work must be performed. Through a process of job analysis, managers can identify and define the kinds of general work and specific jobs that the organization will be relying on in the future (Greer, 1995). This planning process requires accurate information about the levels of skill required in various jobs to ensure that enough individuals are available in the organization to meet the HRM needs of the strategic plan (Walker, 1992).

Recruitment   The job analysis specifies the staffing required to complete the job duties. Job analysis can help the HRM specialist generate a higher quality pool of job applicants by making it easy to describe a job in newspaper ads in a way that more precisely targets qualified job applicants. Job analysis also helps recruiters screen job applicants because it defines the task, duties, and responsibilities that comprise the job.

Selection   To identify the applicants most qualified for a job, it is first necessary to determine the tasks that will be performed by the individual hired and the knowledge, skills, and abilities the individual must have to perform the job effectively. This information is gained through job analysis (Gatewood and Feild, 2001). An organization's managers or HRM specialists use the job analysis information to identify or develop appropriate selection devices (e.g., interview questions, tests). As will be noted later in this article, EEO guidelines clearly require a sound and comprehensive job analysis to validate recruiting and selection criteria.

Performance Appraisal   Through job analysis, the organization can identify the behaviors and results that distinguish effective performance from ineffective performance (Murphy and Cleveland, 1991). Information obtained from a job analysis can be used to develop performance appraisal forms that list the jobs tasks or behaviors and specify the expected performance. It is imperative that performance appraisal standards used to judge employee performance for purposes of promotion, rewards, discipline, or layoff be job related.

Compensation   Job analysis is an essential basis for making decisions about compensation. Job analysis information is used to determine job content for internal comparisons of responsibilities or relative worth of contributions. In a typical pay structure, jobs that require mastery of more complex skills or that have greater levels of responsibility pay more than jobs that require only basic skills or have low amounts of responsibility. Job analysis also may be used to make external comparisons with the compensation paid by competing employers.

Training and Development   Organizations use job analysis information to assess training needs and to develop and evaluate training programs. Almost every employee

hired by an organization will require some training in his or her job. By comparing the KSAs that employees bring to the job with those that are identified by job analysis, managers can identify employees' skill gaps and then identify or develop training programs to address these gaps. Some training programs may be more extensive than others, but all require the trainer to have identified the tasks performed in the job to ensure that the training will prepare individuals to perform the job effectively (Goldstein, 1993).

Career Planning   Career planning entails matching an individual's skills and aspirations with opportunities that are or may become available in the organization. This matching process requires those in charge of career planning to identify the skill requirements of the various jobs. This allows them to guide individuals into jobs in which they will succeed and be satisfied.

COLLECTING JOB ANALYSIS DATA

As mentioned previously, job analysis is a systematic process for collecting, analyzing, and interpreting information about the job content, work method and approach, expected outcome, and KSAs needed to perform the job. A useful job analysis outcome is dependent on identifying good sources of data and using effective techniques to collect those data.

Sources of Data

Most methods of job analysis require that a knowledgeable person describe what goes on in the job or make a series of judgments about specific activities required to do the job. A job analyst may gather information from documents such as technical manuals, organization studies, and training materials as well as consult with job incumbents, supervisors, managers, engineers, and technical experts. The term *job agent* is generally used to refer to an individual who provides or collects the desired job information. In addition, the term *subject matter expert* (SME) is sometimes used to refer to a job agent who is familiar with the target job or possesses special expertise that is relevant to job activities. Each of the sources sees the jobs from a different perspective, and associated with each source are different advantages and disadvantages. There are three classes of job agents typically employed to collect job analysis information: (1) job analysts, (2) job incumbents, and (3) job supervisors (McCormick, 1979).

Job Analysts   The individuals who collect, analyze, and interpret job data are generally referred to as job analysts. Job analysts are specially trained individuals whose mission is to collect and process job information. In many instances, outside consultants or members of the organization's HRM function take on the role of job analyst. Sims and Veres (1985) and Siegel (1987) have emphasized the importance of training job analysts and made specific recommendations on a desired curriculum. Formally trained job analysts should require less orientation to the job under study and less time to analyze it because they are already well-versed in the method of job analysis being used (Gatewood & Feild, 2001) and are likely to provide more objective, reliable, and accurate job data. Furthermore, trained analysts are more likely to appreciate fully the legal issues associated with conducting job analysis. However, there are some drawbacks associated with their use as job agents, particularly if they fail to seek information from other individuals who are closely tied to the job. Certain nuances and subtleties of a job may escape job analysts because they are less familiar with specific jobs than are incumbents or supervisors. Job analysts may rely on preexisting stereotypes of job content, particularly when they have prior experience with particular jobs or

when commonly held jobs are studied (Harvey, 1991).

Job Incumbents   An employee who performs a job is often best able to detail "what is *actually* done, rather than what should be done" (Gatewood & Feild, 2001, p. 293). In addition, involving incumbents in the job analysis process may increase their acceptance of any work changes stemming from the results of the analysis. When large numbers of employees are available, the job analyst has the opportunity to obtain differing perspectives on a given job. However, it should be noted that there are problems associated with this source of job analysis information. Incumbents may not have the verbal skills needed to convey their impressions to job analysts in written or oral form. Even if they do have the communication skills to relay the information, incumbents may paint an inflated picture of their jobs if they believe it beneficial to do so (McCormick, 1979; Smith & Hakel, 1979).

Job Supervisors   Individuals who supervise incumbents performing the job under study can provide accurate job data because they observe the work being performed. Gatewood and Feild (2001) note that supervisory assessments assume that supervisors have worked closely enough with incumbents to possess "complete information about employees' jobs" (p. 294), an assumption that may not be correct. Researchers have observed a tendency for supervisors to describe subordinates' jobs on the basis of what *should* be done rather than what has been done in actuality (Sparks, 1979, 1981). Despite this limitation, supervisors can provide the analyst with an additional perspective on a given job. This can be important particularly when incumbents have limited verbal skills. Further, supervisors may be in a better position to describe what tasks should be included in the job, and what tasks could be included if the job is to be redesigned (Schneider & Konz, 1989).

Cornelius (1988) reviewed the research pertaining to the choice of job agent and summarized the literature as follows:

1. Supervisors and subordinates agree more about the tasks performed than they do about the personal characteristics necessary for job performance.
2. Incumbents and supervisors may provide higher ratings than analysts on job elements that are high in social desirability.
3. Supervisors and incumbents attach different meanings to various descriptions of work and may organize work activities differently.
4. Trained observers (i.e., job analysts) can give similar estimates of job characteristics.

Cornelius recommends that supervisors and subordinates be used to collect data on job activities and that trained job analysts be used to collect data regarding the knowledge, skills, abilities, or other characteristics necessary to perform the job. Moreover, he suggests that the tendency of supervisors and incumbents to inflate their ratings of job characteristics high in social desirability prohibits their use as job agents in situations where job analysis data will be used in certain decisions (for example, salary decisions).

Although job incumbents and supervisors are typically the prime source of job analysis data, a good analyst will consult with multiple sources to collect the information he or she needs to understand the job in question and to complete the job analysis (Bemis et al., 1983). In choosing the sources of job data, a job analyst should be familiar with the research on the optimum source for obtaining job data.

Data Collection Techniques

Numerous techniques exist for collecting job information. HRM specialists tend to prefer different approaches for different types of jobs. For example, a job with substantial physical demands requires different data collection techniques than a job that requires primarily mental abilities. Techniques for collecting data include background research, job performance, site observations, individual and group interviews, job analysis questionnaires, and employee diary/logs.

Background Research A review of job-relevant documents should be the first step in any job analysis process. The analyst should review the job analysis literature to identify previous job analyses or studies of the job in question. This initial research serves to familiarize the analyst with the data collection and analytic techniques used by others, the problems they encountered, and their results (Gatewood & Feild, 2001). The review of the professional literature should be followed by an examination of organization documents such as existing job descriptions, technical manuals, training materials, organization charts, and previous job analyses.

Job Performance Performing the job may be an effective data collection technique when the job involves primarily either psychomotor skills or physical operations that can be learned readily. For some jobs, there is no source of data that can provide the type of information that could be obtained by performing it. For example, equipment operation that demands hand-eye coordination or fine motor skills may require performing the task for full understanding. Generally, however, because of safety concerns, task complexity, or time constraints, it is more efficient to rely on observation or interview techniques than to expend effort in training an analyst to perform the job.

Site Observations Visiting incumbents at their work sites allows the job analyst to observe the specifics of task performance and determine the degree to which tasks are interrelated. Direct observation familiarizes the job analyst with the materials and equipment used on the job, the conditions under which work is performed, and the factors that trigger the performance of a given task. Observation is usually not as useful when the job primarily entails unobservable mental activity (lawyer, design engineer) or important activities that occur only occasionally, such as a nurse who handles emergencies. Additionally, employees frequently change their routine when an analyst is watching, reducing the usefulness of the information gained during the observation.

Individual and Group Interviews   The interview is probably the most commonly used technique for collecting job data (Cascio, 1991; Van De Voort & Stalder, 1988). The job analyst questions experienced job incumbents or supervisors to determine the tasks that are performed on the job as well as the requirements workers must meet to carry out those tasks. In the group interview technique, several subject matter experts are convened to discuss the job in question. Typically, job incumbents or supervisors serve as subject matter experts. However, technical experts (such as design engineers or top management) are used to identify tasks when a new job is being created or an existing one updated. Like individual interviews, group sessions may be structured or unstructured. Typically, the job analyst directs the session and imposes structure upon the discussion to elicit the necessary information in the desired format.

Interviews are difficult to standardize—different interviewers may ask different questions and the same interviewer might unintentionally ask different questions of different respondents. There is also a real possibility that the information provided by the respondent will be unintentionally distorted by the interviewer. The interview method can also be quite time-consuming, especially if the interviewer talks with two or three employees doing each job. Finally, the

costs of interviewing can be very high, especially if group interviews are not practical.

Questionnaires   A questionnaire presents a list of items that are assumed to be job-related and asks subject matter experts to rate each item on its relevance to the job under study. SMEs identify, among the tasks listed on the inventory, the ones that job incumbents perform, and they rate each task on factors such as the importance to successful job performance and the frequency with which the task is performed. In addition, some questionnaires also require SMEs to identify the KSAs required for the job and to rate discrete KSAs on factors such as their importance to acceptable job performance and the extent to which their possession distinguishes between superior and adequate job performance. A commercially available questionnaire may be used, or one may be tailored to fit the job of interest. The items on tailor-made questionnaires can be developed on the basis of information derived from background research, job performance, site observations, individual interviews, or group interviews.

A major disadvantage of the questionnaire method is the possibility that either the respondent or the job analyst will misinterpret the information. Also, questionnaires can be time-consuming and expensive to develop. Further, the questionnaire method assumes that employees can accurately analyze and communicate information about their jobs. For these reasons, the questionnaire method is usually combined with interviews and observations to clarify and verify the questionnaire information.

Employee Diaries or Logs   One drawback of observations, interviews, and questionnaires is that the information that they yield is likely to be dependent on the time it happens to be collected. Whatever is most salient at the time of the interview is most likely to find its way into the job and organizational analysis results. Diaries/logs offer one solution to this problem. A diary/log asks employees to keep a diary/log or list of what they do during the day. For every activity the employee engages in, the employee records the activity (along with the time) in a log. The employee might, of course, try to exaggerate some activities and underplay others. However, the detailed, chronological nature of the log tends to mediate against this. If job incumbents and supervisors keep a diary over a period of several weeks, the results are less likely to be biased by the timing of the analysis.

A concern about this approach is that it may be burdensome for employees to complete an accurate log, especially because many employees are too busy to record accurate diary entries. Employees sometimes perceive this approach as creating needless documentation that detracts from the performance of their work. Additionally, this approach is not appropriate for some jobs if the communication skills of the incumbents is not at the level necessary to document activities in writing or the activities on the job do not allow any distraction from the job for any period of time. However, if a diary is accurate, it is useful when analyzing jobs that do not lend themselves to direct observation as for a manager, an engineer, an outside salesperson, or a scientist.

JOB ANALYSIS METHODS

There are various methods for analyzing jobs, and it is very difficult to identify "one best way." In this section we shall discuss a number of techniques available for analyzing jobs. All of these techniques can yield information useful in completing HRM tasks such as redesigning work, developing performance measures, planning for training programs, and setting pay levels. Job analysts commonly combine methods of data collection to achieve a comprehensive picture of the job under study. Most approaches to job analysis mix and match various job data sources and data collection techniques.

A variety of systems have evolved for conducting job analyses and collecting job-related information, and several systems for classifying job analysis methodology have been suggested (e.g., Harvey, 1991). We have adopted the approach most commonly encountered; focusing on the distinction between *work-oriented* and *worker-oriented* methods. Work-oriented job analysis focuses on a description of the work activities performed on a job. Emphasis is on what is accomplished, including a description of the tasks undertaken and the products or outcomes of those tasks. Other names for this approach include *task-oriented* and *activity-based* job analysis.

Worker-oriented analyses tend to examine the attributes or characteristics the worker must possess to perform job tasks. The primary products of work-oriented methods are the KSAs and other characteristics required for effective job performance. A worker-oriented analysis of a secretarial position might generate worker characteristics such as "skill in typing" or "knowledge of the organization's filing system." Until recently, worker-oriented approaches dominated the field to the extent that one writer, in a 1976 publication, described worker-oriented methods as "conventional job analysis procedures" (McCormick, 1976, p. 654). Before we discuss the relative pros and cons of each approach, it may be beneficial to describe examples of each in a bit more detail.

Work-Oriented Approaches

Functional Job Analysis Functional job analysis (FJA) (Fine & Wiley, 1971) provides an approach that takes into consideration the organization, its people, and its work. The FJA approach employs three data collection techniques, including a review by trained analysts of background and reference materials, interviews with employees and their supervisors, and on-site observations of employees. From this data collection, the purpose, goals, and objectives of the organization are identified by the job analyst and top management. Once analysts have gained an understanding of the organization's work system, they develop task statements in consultation with SMEs. To ensure validity and reliability, analysts edit the task statements with the guidance of incumbents, supervisors, and other SMEs. From the task statements, worker functions are identified, primarily through inferences made by analysts. Finally, FJA attempts to place the individual job clearly in the context of the whole organization by focusing on the results of task performance and the way those results contribute to the attainment of organizational goals and objectives. Because FJA provides a method for assessing the level of each task by describing the employee's required level of involvement with other factors on the job, Fine, Holt, and Hutchinson (1974) recommended it for a broad range of applications. The two most prominent features of FJA are its formal task statements and worker function scales.

One advantage of FJA is that the results produce a quantitative score for each job, allowing jobs to be arranged for compensation or other HRM purposes. Another advantage of the FJA method is that it analyzes each task separately, which results in a detailed picture of the job and makes the method more applicable for organizational purposes. However, FJA is not particularly useful for job classification or evaluation unless combined with other techniques.

Critical Incidents Technique Developed by John Flanagan (1954), the critical incidents technique (CIT) relies on information from supervisors and others who are in a position to observe job behavior. Supervisors are asked to identify and classify those behaviors that result in effective or ineffective

job performance (critical incidents). Critical incidents include a high level of behavioral detail, focusing on the action of the worker, the context in which the behavior occurs, and the consequences of the behavior. This level of specificity makes CIT very useful in performance appraisal. Perhaps the best way to understand the CIT approach is to examine a critical incident for the job of firefighter (Bownas & Bernardin, 1988):

> The firefighter studied two units of the "Red Book" during his daily training period for two weeks. At the end of the period, he couldn't perform the tasks outlined in the manuals, and he couldn't answer sample questions on the content. Because he hadn't picked up these skills, he could only be assigned as a helper to another firefighter at a fire scene. (p. 1123)

This example illustrates the characteristics of a good critical incident. It is specific, its focus is on observable behaviors, and the context in which the behavior occurred is described. Finally, it identifies the consequences of the firefighter's behavior.

CIT has been used for training and job design (Bownas & Bernardin, 1988) and in the development of structured oral interviews (Gatewood & Feild, 2001). One limitation of CIT is that it does not identify the common, routine behaviors performed on jobs. This limitation in Flanagan's approach can be eliminated easily by extending the CIT procedure to include statements concerning average performance and thus provides a better overall view of job behaviors (Zedeck, Jackson, & Adelman, 1980).

Comprehensive Occupational Data Analysis Program The task inventory/comprehensive occupational data analysis program (TI/CODAP) developed by Christal (1974) for application at Air Force installations consists of two basic components: a task inventory and a computer analysis package. This questionnaire requires subject matter experts to make judgments about the tasks constituting their job. A task is defined as a meaningful unit of work that can be readily identified by the employee. Task statements for the inventory are constructed by supervisors, incumbents, and other job experts. Job incumbents rate the tasks on a "relative time spent" scale and on other scales as deemed appropriate or applicable. The task inventory also collects background information such as work experience, education, race, sex, and use of equipment or tools as demanded by the job. These ratings are then analyzed through a series of interactive computer programs that organize the job information in a variety of forms.

CODAP programs perform a number of important HRM functions, including describing work performed by individuals or groups, comparing work performed by specified groups, empirically identifying jobs in an occupational area, and analyzing task characteristics (Christal & Weissmuller, 1988). The programs can be used for group job descriptions and individual position descriptions, classification, and evaluation. Other programs allow for job classification and evaluation. Christal and Weissmuller note that TI/CODAP has been applied to problems ranging from the study of job satisfaction to the fulfillment of equal employment opportunity requirements and even to the identification of job hazards. Although task inventories like the TI/CODAP might indirectly suggest the types of KSAs and other characteristics people might need to perform the job, these KSAs do not come directly out of the process. Thus, other approaches that do put the focus squarely on the people requirement associated with jobs were developed (e.g., worker-oriented approaches).

Worker-Oriented Approaches

Position Analysis Questionnaire   The position analysis questionnaire (PAQ) is a very structured job analysis questionnaire that contains 194 different items (such as *written materials*), each of which represents a basic element that may or may not play an important role in the job. Designed by E. J. McCormick (McCormick, Jeanneret, & Mecham, 1972), the PAQ seeks to determine the degree to which the different items, or job elements, are involved in performing a particular job. The 194 PAQ items are organized into six sections:

1. Information input—Where and how a worker gets information needed to perform the job.
2. Mental processes—Reasoning, decision making, planning, and information-processing activities involved in performing the job.
3. Work output—The physical activities, tools, and devices used by the worker to perform the job.
4. Relationships with other persons—The relationship with other people required in performing the job.
5. Job context—The physical and social contexts where the work is performed.
6. Other characteristics—The activities, conditions, and characteristics other than those previously described that are relevant to the job.

The PAQ is completed by a job analyst, a person who should already be acquainted with the particular job to be analyzed. The analyst then rates the item on six scales: extent of use, amount of time, importance to the job, possibility of occurrence, applicability, and special code (special rating scales used with a particular item).

The advantage of the PAQ is that it provides a quantitative score or profile of any job in terms of how that job rates on five basic job activities: (1) having decision-making/communication/social responsibilities, (2) performing skilled activities, (3) being physically active, (4) operating vehicles/equipment, and (5) processing information. The PAQ's real strength is in classifying jobs. It allows the assignment of a quantitative score to each job based on its decision-making, skilled activities, physical activity, vehicle/equipment operation, and information-processing characteristics. These results can be used to compare jobs relative to one another and to assign pay levels for each job (Smith and Hakel, 1979; Butler & Harvey, 1988).

While the PAQ has been used extensively for personnel selection, job classification, and job evaluation, its use in performance appraisal and training systems is limited. The worker-oriented PAQ items make analyzing a wide variety of jobs easier, but they also make it difficult to translate PAQ scores directly into specific performance standards or training content. Other shortcomings of the PAQ are that the instrument itself is relatively complex and an employee must have a reading level of a college graduate to be able to complete it. Therefore, PAQ executives recommend that only trained experts complete the questionnaire, as opposed to using job incumbents or supervisors for this purpose. Further, although the PAQ is supposed to be applicable to most jobs, there is reason to believe that it is less useful for describing higher level managerial jobs and white-collar jobs (DeNisi, Cornelius, & Blencoe, 1987).

Job Element Method   The job element method, developed by Primoff (1975), represents a unique approach to job analysis in that its focus is on worker characteristics rather than on job activities. The job element method identifies skills, knowledge, inclinations, and other characteristics of employees in a particular job classification. This method typically relies not on job analysts to gather information but rather on a group of approximately six job incumbents, supervisors, or both who are familiar enough with the job under study to easily recognize characteristics of superior workers (Feild & Gatewood, 1989). These factors are organized into the

following six broad categories of job elements (Primoff, 1975, p. 2):

- a knowledge, such as knowledge of accounting principles;
- a skill, such as skill with woodworking tools;
- an ability, such as ability to manage a program;
- a willingness, such as willingness to do simple tasks repetitively;
- an interest, such as an interest in learning new techniques; or
- a personal characteristic, such as reliability or dependability.

Once the job elements have been identified, the subject matter experts generate a corresponding list of subelements for each element. For example, having identified "knowledge of mathematics" as an element, SMEs might more clearly define the parameters of that knowledge by including "knowledge of addition of fractions" as a subelement. Subject matter experts then rate the job elements and subelements along a series of dimensions that are designed to measure the correlation between success on the job and possession of each job element. Through this correlation, the job element method attempts to identify the worker characteristics that should result in superior job performance.

Primoff originally intended the job element method be used in conducting job element rating sessions, preparing selection devices based on rating results, and testing and refining selection measures (Primoff, 1975). However, a drawback associated with this method was its inability to satisfy the federal Uniform Guidelines' requirements for content validation, in that it did not place the necessary focus on work behaviors. Later, however, Primoff began work to integrate the job element method with FJA and CIT to meet content validity requirements (Bemis et al., 1983).

Other Approaches

The distinction between work- and worker-oriented approaches to job analysis became blurred as personnel consultants and human resource managers recognized the utility of collecting both types of information (Guion, 1978; McCormick, 1979; Prien, 1977). This development led to recommendations for the use of multiple job analysis systems, and new systems were developed in attempts to meet a variety of HRM needs. These so-called multimethod approaches employ data collection techniques that obtain both work- and worker-oriented information.

IMES Variants   An early attempt to incorporate both work- and worker-oriented job analysis data, the Iowa merit employment system (IMES) is a systematic multi-step process designed to aid in the development of content-valid selection devices (Menne, McCarthy, & Menne, 1976). IMES emphasizes the use of a group interview in which supervisors and incumbents work jointly to identify relevant job content. First, job tasks are identified. These tasks are then expanded into a standardized form that answers the following questions: (1) What is the action being performed? (2) To whom or what is the action directed? (3) Why is the action being performed? (4) How is the action done?

Once job tasks have been defined as formal task statements, the knowledge, skills, abilities, and personal characteristics (KSAPCs) needed to perform each of the job tasks are identified. Incumbents and supervisors then rate task statements on dimensions such as importance, time spent, and necessity at entry. The KSAPCs arising from the aforementioned group interview are also rated for their importance and linked to job tasks. The data provided by these ratings are analyzed, and a picture of the job task and job knowledge domain is obtained. Among the variants of the basic IMES approach are the Alabama merit system method (Elliott, Boyles, Hill, Palmer, Thomas, & Veres, 1980) and integrated job analysis (Buckley, 1986).

Behavioral Consistency Method   Schmidt, Caplan, Bemis, Dewir, Dunn, and Antone (1979) developed the behavioral consistency method to identify competencies workers needed to perform mid-level government, professional, and managerial jobs. The method has since been used to identify competencies in private sector managerial and blue-collar jobs. Two basic principles underlie the behavioral consistency approach: (1) applicants should be evaluated only on dimensions that clearly differentiate between superior and minimally acceptable performers, and (2) these dimensions must be determined through consultation with individuals who have known and observed superior and marginal performers. The behavioral consistency method involves four major components: (1) the identification and description of job activities and tasks; (2) the identification of knowledge, abilities, skills, and other characteristics (KASOs) needed to perform the work; (3) the rating of KASOs by subject matter experts; and (4) the analysis of these ratings to evaluate KASOs.

Job agents independently rate each KASO on six scales: (1) importance in preventing job failure, (2) percentage of current workers who meet minimum performance standards, (3) necessity for all positions, (4) usefulness in differentiating between superior and minimally acceptable workers, (5) extent of variability in the applicant pool, and (6) ratings for sub-specialties. The behavioral consistency method represents a significant breakthrough in reviewing the appropriateness of applicant qualifications. Its use has been limited primarily to this application.

VERJAS   A successor to the behavioral consistency method is the versatile job analysis system (VERJAS) developed by Bemis, Belenky, and Soder (1983). VERJAS extends some of the principles underlying the behaviorial consistency method to a wider variety of applications including job design, classification and evaluation, recruitment, selection, training, and performance appraisal. A VERJAS job description contains a list of duties, tasks, task ratings for importance and for needed training, job context descriptions, and competencies needed for the job. As noted by Bemis et al. (1983), "VERJAS is composed of procedures utilized in other job analysis methods integrated into a single system to meet management's total job analysis needs. The system is a job analysis melting pot in both origin and use" (p. 61). The detailed operational definitions of competencies and clear linkage of competencies back to important job tasks are two appealing features of VERJAS. As a hybrid system, VERJAS provides a wealth of practical information that can be used for many purposes. When using this approach, Bemis et al. (1983) suggest adhering to the following guidelines:

1. *Identify duties.* The first step in VERJAS is to identify the duties or functions of the job. Most jobs have three to seven duties.
2. *Identify tasks.* The next stage is to identify the tasks associated with each duty. A task is defined as "an activity a worker performs to create a product or a service that they will use in performing another task or that someone else will use" (p. 62). The task statements should describe the:

a. Action
b. Object of the action
c. Purpose or expected output of the action
d. Machines, tools, equipment, manuals, laws, rules, and other work aids used to accomplish the activity

3. *Evaluate tasks.* Each task statement must then be evaluated on four scales: performance at entry, training mode, importance level, and reason for important/critical ratings.
4. *Evaluate job context.* The next step is to analyze the context of the job: its scope, effect, and environment.
5. *Evaluate worker competencies (worker requirements).* The final step of VERJAS is to record the needed worker competencies. There are two types of competencies: basic and special. Basic competencies are those a worker needs to perform the job at a minimally acceptable level. Special competencies are those needed for superior performance. These are the competencies possessed by only the best workers.

These five steps also typify other multimethod approaches to job analysis, including guidelines-oriented job analysis (Biddle, 1976), the health services mobility study method (Gilpatrick, 1977), and integrated job analysis (Buckley, 1980).

Evaluation of Traditional Methods

Several factors have given rise to an increased preference for multimethod approaches to job analysis. Veres, Lahey, and Buckley (1987) enumerate some of the factors contributing to a rise in multimethod approaches, including level of task specificity, communicability, and the Uniform Guidelines' requirements. The Guidelines require that a validity study used to support a selection procedure include a job analysis that generates the "important work behavior(s) required for successful performance" (p. 38302). As worker-oriented techniques do not collect work behaviors, these techniques clearly do not conform to the Guidelines. The Guidelines define a selection procedure as "any measure, combination of measures, or procedure used as a basis for *any* employment decision" (Equal Employment Opportunity Commission et al., 1978, p. 38308). Given this definition, the Guidelines cover any measure or procedure that is used as the basis for a personnel decision. Thus, HRM professionals must consider the approach to job analysis that is used to construct each procedure.

The courts have supported the Guidelines by endorsing a multimethod approach to job analysis. Courts have determined that a job analysis without task-oriented information does not comply with regulatory guidance and Title VII (Thompson & Thompson, 1982). They have also required demonstration of the ties between work behaviors (or tasks) and their companion KSAs *(United States v. State of New York*, 1979)—a goal that can be achieved only when both types of job information are collected.

Research on job analysis in this realm has been restricted largely to job analysts' evaluation of method effectiveness. Levine, Ash, Hall, and Sistrunk (1983) gathered evaluations on seven commonly employed job analysis methods. These evaluations were obtained by means of a questionnaire containing items regarding the effectiveness and practicality of each method. Ninety-three experienced job analysts completed the questionnaire. The researchers' findings produced no clear "winner" overall. However, some particular systems were found to be superior for a given application.

The effectiveness ratings revealed that the experienced job analysts preferred TI/CODAP and FJA for constructing job descriptions. For purposes of job classification, TI/CODAP, FJA, and the PAQ were rated highest, whereas the CIT was rated significantly lower than the other methods. The PAQ, FJA, and TI/CODAP were also rated highest for job evaluation. For job design purposes, TI/CODAP and FJA were rated higher than other methods. If the purpose of the job analysis is to develop a performance appraisal instrument, the recommended method is CIT. Only work- and worker-oriented methods were assessed in the 1983 study; no multimethod systems were considered.

Most experts agree that the choice of a job analysis method depends upon the purposes to be served by the data and the practicality for particular organizations. Because research provides no definitive guidance on what system to use, the Guidelines' requirements and court opinions merit considerable weight. The most definitive findings from the research on the relative effectiveness of the various methods is that multiple methods of job analysis should be used whenever possible. For example, a quantitative approach such as the PAQ should probably be augmented by a qualitative approach such as the CIT, which can provide more specific information about jobs than what typically can be derived from the quantitative method. As mentioned previously, legal considerations would seem to favor multimethod approaches. Also, a number of researchers have advanced conceptual and measurement-oriented arguments for adopting multimethod approaches to job analysis (Guion, 1978; Prien, 1977). Others have argued that multimethod approaches should be preferred on more pragmatic grounds (Veres et al., 1987).

Which Method Should Job Analysts Use?

As noted previously, certain methods seem to be better suited to a given situation than others (Levine, Ash, Hall, & Sistrunk, 1983). In the absence of a strong theoretical reason why one method should be superior to another, many organizations base their choice on their current needs. There are several factors that may be used to assess job analysis methods (Levine, Ash, Hall, & Sistrunk, 1983). Some criteria that serve as the basis for assessments are presented in Table 5-6. Although these criteria can be helpful in comparing different methods, identifying the best method depends on the particular objectives of the organization, as well as on cost limitations and other factors governing the project.

The final consideration listed in Table 5-6 is particularly important. This criterion is so pervasive that it is impacted, in part, by many of the others. Purpose, for example, is an important consideration not only for maximizing the utility of the job analysis, but also for legal reasons. An organization must make it clear why a job analysis is being conducted and choose a method of analysis relevant for that purpose.

RECENT AND FUTURE TRENDS IN JOB ANALYSIS

Up until about 1970, the different job analysis approaches focused primarily on a single type of information (Prien & Ronan, 1971). However, over the past 30 years, there has been growing recognition in the job analysis camp that multiple forms of information are needed, as evidenced by the number of multidomain approaches available (e.g., Drauden & Peterson, 1974; Lopez, Kesselman, & Lopez, 1981; Prien, Goldstein, & Macey, 1987). Clearly, job analysis researchers have recognized the need to modify and improve on the tools they use. This challenge continues as the business environment is characterized by incredible competition and change (Hamel & Prahalad, 1994). In response to changes in the world of work, there is a growing concern that traditional job analysis procedures may not play a central role in the new HRM environment. In this context we shall examine recent trends in job analysis and look into the crystal ball

to see what may be on the horizon for job analysis. This is the focus of the remainder of this article as we highlight recent trends in job analysis and offer our view of future job analytic trends.

Recent Trends in Job Analysis

As noted previously, the passage of the Americans with Disabilities Act (ADA) has placed new demands on organizations and HRM specialists, increasing the emphasis on job analysis, job descriptions, and job specifications. Certain physical ability requirements long taken for granted, such as normal vision and hearing, can be applied only if an employer can document that an employee needs them to perform "essential job functions." The identification of the essential functions themselves must rely on a thorough task-oriented or multimethod job analysis. The linkage between essential functions and requisite knowledge, skills, mental abilities, and physical abilities can best be accomplished via a multimethod job analysis process. Obviously, job analysis methods that do not capture information salient to the essentiality of job functions and underlying mental and physical abilities fail to protect employers from ADA-related law suits.

To comply with ADA requirements, employers should conduct analyses to identify the essential functions and formulate job descriptions to facilitate compliance with the law. The law itself doesn't require written job descriptions, but when the EEOC investigates an employer's compliance with ADA, written job descriptions are one of the first documents they ask to see. Written job descriptions may provide evidence, although not conclusive, of the job's "essential functions" and serve as baselines for performance reviews. It's important, therefore, that written job descriptions be accurate and correspond to the current requirements of the job (Harris, 1998).

The need to produce ADA-sensitive job specifications has created renewed interest

	TABLE 5-6	Criteria for Assessing Job Analysis Methods

Number	Criterion	Definition
1	Purposes served	Can the data collected be used for a variety of purposes?
2	Versatility	Can a method be used to analyze many different jobs?
3	Standardization	Does a method provide data that can be easily compared to data collected by other methods?
4	User acceptance	Do users of the method accept it as a reasonable way to collect job data?
5	Training required	How much training is needed before individuals can use it to collect data in the organization?
6	Sample size	How large a sampling of information source is needed before an adequate picture of the job can be obtained?
7	Off the shelf	Can the method be used directly off the shelf, or must considerable development work be done to tailor it for use in a particular organization?
8	Reliability	Does the method produce reliable data?
9	Time to complete	How long does it take to analyze a job using the method?
10	Cost	How much does the method cost to implement and use?
11	Legal defensibility	Will this method provide sufficient evidence to support HR practices built upon the job analysis results?

in the Fleishman Job Analysis System (F-JAS) (Fleishman & Reilly, 1992). The F-JAS is an approach to job analysis that has been researched and refined for a number of years and is based on a taxonomy of human abilities (Fleishman & Quaintance, 1984). F-JAS currently consists of 72 scales, consisting of a definition of the ability to be rated; the difference between the ability to be rated on the scale and other, similar abilities; a behaviorally anchored rating scale; and the definition of the highest and lowest levels of the ability. The inclusion of cognitive, psychomotor, physical, and sensory/perceptual F-JAS scales can help analysts identify cognitive and physical aspects of work that are used to perform essential job functions. When F-JAS scales are linked to essential job functions, the analyst can use this information to determine abilities that are and are not essential to the job. Identification of requisite mental and physical abilities can indicate abilities that are likely to require consideration in the making of reasonable accommodations.

A second trend in job analysis is the growing interest in focusing on the competencies that individuals need in order to perform jobs, rather than on the tasks, duties, and responsibilities composing a job. As Lawler (1994) suggests, instead of thinking of an individual performing a job that is relatively stable and can be written into a typical job description, it may be more relevant to focus on the individual's competencies used to perform the job. Competencies are basic characteristics that can be linked to enhanced performance by individuals or teams of individuals. Unlike the traditional approach to analyzing jobs, which identifies the tasks, duties, knowledge, and skills associated with a job, the competency approach considers how the knowledge and skills are used. The approach also attempts to identify the hidden factors that are often critical to superior performance. For instance, many supervisors talk about employees' attitudes, but they have difficulty identifying what they mean by attitude. The competency approach uses some methodologies to help supervisors identify examples of what they mean by attitude and how those factors affect performance.

The competency approach affects HRM activities (Pritchard, 1997), particularly those of selection and placement, HR development, compensation, and performance management. It focuses on linking business strategies to individual performance efforts. It also encourages employees to develop competencies that may be used in diverse work situations, rather than being boxed into a job. This approach can be a useful tool for employee development. Employees can develop capabilities useful throughout the organization as it changes and evolves. The increased interest in the competency approach to job analysis is most evident with the recently completed work of the Society for Industrial and Organizational Psychology (SIOP) commissioned task force to investigate and review the practice of competency modeling. The findings of this task force highlight the increased value of integrating competency approaches and traditional approaches to job analysis in ways that add value and contribute to organizational success (Shippmann et al., 2000).

The *Dictionary of Occupational Titles* (DOT) (U.S. Department of Labor, Employment & Training Administration, 1977) is in the process of being replaced by the U.S. Department of Labor's new job analysis service entitled the *Occupational Information Network,* also know as O*NET. O*NET, first released to the public in the fall of 1998, has a function similar to that of DOT—"to provide a comprehensive database system for collecting, organizing, describing and disseminating data on job characteristics and worker attributes." O*NET can be accessed online at www.doleta.gov/programs/onet. O*NET better captures the role of advanced technologies and the increasing importance of service-based jobs. This new framework describes jobs as having six content areas: experience requirements, worker requirements, worker characteristics, occupation characteristics, occupation specific, occupation requirements.

Like DOT, O*NET is intended to be a resource for employees, but an added objective of O*NET is to serve as a resource for anyone who seeks to make informed employment decisions. People can get facts about occupations and jobs by visiting O*NET's homepage and searching the database. O*NET is quick, and it's essentially free. Furthermore, the job descriptions available through O*NET are based on hundreds of observations.

The Changing Nature of Jobs

Increasingly there is an understanding that the nature of jobs and work is changing so much that the concept of a "job" may be obsolete for many of today's employees. For example, in some high-technology organizations employees shift from project to project and work in cross-functional project teams. The focus in these organizations is less on performing specific tasks and duties and more on fulfilling responsibilities and attaining results. Therefore, the basis for recruiting, selecting, and compensating these individuals is their competence and skills, not what they do (Nelson, 1997). Even the job of managers changes in such situations, for they must serve their project teams as facilitators, gatherers of resources, and removers of roadblocks.

However, in many organizations that use lower-skilled employees, traditional jobs continue to exist. Job analysis researchers can study these jobs and their work consequences with relative ease because of the repetitiveness of the work and the limited number of tasks each employee performs. Analyzing the two types of jobs (i.e., lower skilled and highly technical) requires different approaches. Many of the traditional processes associated with identifying job descriptions are still relevant with the lower-skilled, task-based jobs. However, for more and more of today's fast-moving organizations, a job description is becoming an obsolete concept.

As evidenced by the discussion thus far, the term *job* has taken on new forms as has the utility of job analysis. Writers have recently stated that the more fluid and changeable nature of modern organizations brings into question the very logic of job analysis (Cardy and Dobbins, 1992). William Bridges, in his 1995 book, *Job Shift*, suggests that jobs "are artificial units superimposed on this field. They are patches of responsibility that, all together, were supposed to cover the work that needs to be done" (Bridges, 1995, p. 1).

Clearly, in many organizations today, jobs are becoming amorphous, more difficult to define. In other words, the trend is toward *de-jobbing* many organizations. De-jobbing is ultimately a result of the changes taking place in business today. Organizations need to grapple with revolutionary forces—accelerating product and technological change, political instability, globalized competition, deregulation, demographic changes, and trends toward the information age and a service society. Forces like these have dramatically increased the need for organizations to be responsive and capable of competing in a global marketplace. The new organizational approaches are undermining the traditional notions of the job as a well-defined and clearly delineated set of responsibilities. Here are a few examples.

Instead of traditional pyramid-shaped organizations with seven or more management layers, flat, less hierarchical organizations with just three or four levels are becoming more prevalent. Many organizations have already drastically cut their management layers. As the remaining managers are left with more people reporting to them, they can supervise them less, so the jobs of direct reports end up bigger in terms of both breadth and depth of responsibilities.

A boundary-less organization seeks to eliminate the chain of command, have limitless spans of control, and replace departments with empowered teams. The ultimate goal is to eliminate the boundaries that typically separate organizational functions (like production and sales) and reduce hierarchical levels. The focus is on defining the job at hand in terms of the overall best interests of the organization, thereby further shifting or de-jobbing the organization. Any boundaries that exist between jobs are "constantly shifting, resulting in enhanced need for very general capacities, abilities, and skills" (Schmidt, 1993, p. 500). This implies that recent trends toward specificity of KSAs to achieve content validity (Goldstein, Zedeck, & Schneider, 1993) may be limited to job analyses conducted on certain jobs or for specific purposes (e.g., as the basis of test development).

The Future of Job Analysis: A Strategic View

The business environment today is increasingly characterized by incredible competition and change (Hamel & Prahalad, 1994). And, as noted previously, organizations are responding in various ways. Accompanying these changes has been a growing concern that traditional job analysis procedures may be unable to play a central role in the new HRM environment (Barnes-Nelson, 1996). Traditional job analysis techniques force boundaries to be drawn between jobs, making these techniques inconsistent with the trend toward increased sharing of responsibilities across jobs and across levels in the organization (Morgan & Smith, 1996; Carson & Stewart, 1996). Today, the issue seems to be one of how we can better use our current job analysis methods in a dynamic work environment rather than simply doing away with detailed job analysis altogether (Mitchell & Driskill, 1998).

One response to changing work conditions is strategic job analysis, which utilizes standard job analysis methodology to look at the future requirements of a job (Schneider & Konz, 1989). In a future-oriented job analysis the emphasis shifts from *descriptions* of the present to *prescriptions* about what the future should be like. Organizations today are concerned with how they can get flexibility without employee resistance, while also satisfying employees' needs for comfort. The goal includes shifting employee's attention from thinking only about doing "my job" to thinking about doing whatever is necessary to accomplish the organization's work (Bridges, 1995). Corresponding to this, some HRM professionals have argued that the term *work analysis,* discussed earlier in this article, be used in place of the term *job analysis* (Jackson & Schuler, 2000). This shift from a focus on "the job" to "the work" is almost inevitable in organizations where work is organized around teams instead of individuals. Because the self-managed team as a whole is assigned duties and can organize the team's work any way they wish, asking individuals about the work of the team may be much more useful than asking them to describe their "individual jobs" (Mohrman, Cohen, & Mohrman, 1995).

CONCLUSIONS

We have attempted to convey a general idea of the practice of job analysis. As evidenced by the large number of studies cited in this article, much has been done in the way of job analysis research and application. However, at least one cautionary note bears repeating from our earlier paper (Veres, Locklear, & Sims, 1988). This concern is the effect of external influences on the practice of job analysis.

Job analysis research has been conducted for some 85 years, beginning with Hugo Munsterberg's (1913) study of street-car operators. Progress has not been steady, however. Many of the accomplishments reported in these pages have occurred in the last 25 years. The federal courts have mandated that any personnel action that adversely affects minorities or women demonstrate its job-relatedness. Job analysis has become the primary vehicle for making that demonstration. Although HRM specialists would like to assume smug self-satisfaction about milestones attained in job analysis research, external forces have worked to and will increasingly continue to shape us, perhaps more than we have acted to shape them.

Job analysis research has unquestionably come a long way. Sidney Gael's (1988a) substantial work, *The Job Analysis Handbook for Business, Industry, and Government,* is a testament to the scope of job analysis research performed over the last three-quarters of a century. Harvey's (1991) chapter in the *Handbook of Industrial and Organizational Psychology* chronicles decades of research in the area and lays out a roadmap for future research. The enormous breadth of the research reported in these two handbooks can be taken as an indication that job analysis is indeed a fundamental starting point for human resources management. More recently, one need only look at the work of the Job Analysis and Competency Modeling Task Force (Shippmann, Ash, Carr, Hesketh, Pearlman, Battista, Eyde, Kehoe, Prien, & Sanchez, 2000) to see how job analysis researchers are moving forward in their efforts to demonstrate the value of job analyses in achieving organizational effectiveness and success. As May (1996) notes, job analysis may be most useful in a work world that does not include jobs, because the information it provides may enable more effective design and management of work processes. We agree with May that:

Job analysis information is the raw material that is essential to build new work processes and create efficiencies that cannot emerge any other way. This much-maligned tool holds great promise for the future of organizations if we seize the opportunity that presents itself. (p. 100)

The question is: Will job analysis research and its resulting tools keep pace with the de-

mands of an ever changing world of work? That world will provide many opportunities for job analytic research to play an important role in helping organizations meet the demands for constant change and development in an increasingly competitive environment. We think, and hope so! ■

REFERENCES

Ash, R. A. (1988). Job analysis in the world of work. In S. Gael (Ed.), *The Job Analysis Handbook for Business, Industry, and Government* (Vol. 1, 3–13). New York: Wiley.

Barnes-Nelson, J. (1996). The boundaryless organization: Implications for job analysis, recruitment, and selection. *Human Resource Planning, 20,* 39–49.

Bemis, B. E., Belenky, A. H., & Soder, D. A. (1983). *Job analysis: An effective management tool.* Washington, DC: Bureau of National Affairs.

Biddle, R. E. (1976). *Guidelines-oriented job analysis manual.* Sacramento, CA: Biddle & Associates.

Bownas, D. A., & Bernardin, H. J. (1988). Critical incident technique. In S. Gael (Ed.), *The Job Analysis Handbook for Business, Industry, and Government* (Vol. 2, 1120–1137). New York: Wiley.

Bridges, W. (1995). *Job shift: How to prosper in a workplace without jobs.* St. Leonards, Australia: Allen & Unwin.

Buckley, R. (1980). *Integrated job analysis* (2nd ed.). Los Angeles: Psychological Services, Inc.

Buckley, R. (1986). *Integrated job analysis and selection.* Glendale, CA: Psychological Services, Inc.

Buckner, K. E. (1989). A review and empirical analysis of court standards for employee selection. Unpublished doctoral dissertation, Auburn University, Auburn, AL.

Butler, S., & Harvey, R. J. (1988, Winter). A comparison of holistic versus decomposed rating of Position Analysis Questionnaire work dimensions. *Personnel Psychology,* 761–772.

Cardy, B., & Dobbins, G. (1992). Job analysis in a dynamic environment. *Human Resources Division News, 16* (1), 4.

Carson, K. P., & Stewart, G. L. (1996). Job analysis and the sociotechnical approach to quality: A critical examination. *Journal of Quality Management,* 49–64.

Cascio, W. (1991). *Applied psychology in personnel management* (4th ed.). Upper Saddle River, NJ: Prentice Hall.

Christal, R. E. (1974). *The United States Air Force occupational research project.* Lackland Air Force Base, TX: Air Human Resources Laboratory.

Christal, R. E., & Weissmuller, J. J. (1988). Job-task inventory analysis. In S. Gael (Ed.), *The Job Analysis Handbook for Business, Industry, and Government* (Vol. 2, 1036–1050). New York: Wiley.

Cornelius, E. T. (1988). Practical findings from job analysis research. In S. Gael (Ed.), *The Job Analysis Handbook for Business, Industry, and Government* (Vol. 1, 48–68). New York: Wiley.

Davis, L. E., & Wacker, G. J. (1988). Job design. In S. Gael (Ed.), *The Job Analysis Handbook for Business, Industry, and Government* (Vol. 1, 157–172). New York: Wiley.

DeNisi, A., Cornelius, E., & Blencoe, A. (1987). A further investigation of common knowledge effects on job analysis ratings: On the applicability of the PAQ for all jobs. *Journal of Applied Psychology, 72,* 262–268.

Drauden, G. M., & Peterson, N. G. (1974). *A domain sampling approach to job analysis.* St. Paul, MN.: State of Minnesota Personnel Department.

Elliott, R. H., Boyles, W. R., Hill, J. B., Palmer, C., Thomas, P., & Veres, J. G. (1980). *Content oriented personnel selection procedures—A training manual.* Montgomery, AL: Auburn University at Montgomery, Center for Government and Public Affairs.

Equal Employment Opportunity Commission, Civil Service Commission, Department of Labor, & Department of Justice. (1978). Adoption by four agencies of uniform guidelines on employee selection procedures. *Federal Register, 43,* 38290–38315.

Feild, H. S., & Gatewood, R. D. (1989). Development of a selection interview: A job content strategy. In R. W. Eder and G. R. Ferris (Eds.), *The Employment Interview: Theory, Research, and Practice.* Beverly Hills, CA: Sage.

Fine, S. A., Holt, A. M., & Hutchinson, M. F. (1974). *Functional job analysis: How to standardize task statements.* Kalamazoo, MI: W. E. Upjohn Institute for Employment Research.

Fine, S. A., & Wiley, W. W. (1971). *An introduction to functional job analysis: A scaling of selected tasks from the social welfare field.* Kalamazoo, MI: W. E. Upjohn Institute for Employment Research.

Flanagan, J. C. (1954). The critical incident technique. *Psychological Bulletin, 51,* 327–358.

Fleishman, E. A., & Quaintance, M. K. (1984). *Taxonomies of human performance: The description of human tasks.* Orlando, FL: Academic Press.

Fleishman, E. A., & Reilly, M. E. (1992). *Handbook of human abilities.* Palo Alto, CA: Consulting Psychologists Press, Inc.

Gael, S. (Ed.) (1988a). *The job analysis handbook for business, industry, and government* (Vols. 1–2). New York: Wiley.

Gael, S. (1988b). Job descriptions. In S. Gael (Ed.), *The Job Analysis Handbook for Business, Industry, and Government* (Vol. 1, 71–89). New York: Wiley.

Gatewood, R. D., & Feild, H. S. (2001). *Human resource selection* (5th ed.). Hinsdale, IL: Dryden.

Gilpatrick, E. (1977). *The health services mobility study method of task analysis and curriculum design basic tools: Concepts, task identification, skill scales and knowledge system.* Springfield, VA: National Technical Information Service.

Goldstein, I. L. (1993). *Training in organizations* (3rd Ed.). Pacific Grove, CA: Brooks/Cole.

Goldstein, I. L., Zedeck, S., & Schneider, B. (1993). An exploration of the job analysis–content validity process. In N. Schmitt and W. C. Borman (Eds.), *Personnel Selection in Organizations* (3–32). San Francisco: Jossey-Bass.

Greer, C. R. (1995). *Strategy and human resources.* Upper Saddle River, N.J.: Prentice Hall.

Guion, R. M. (1978). Scoring of content domain sample: The problem of fairness. *Journal of Applied Psychology, 63,* 499–506.

Hamel, G., & Prahalad, C. K. (1994). *Competing for the future.* Boston: Harvard Business School Press.

Harris, M. (1998). Practice network: ADA and I-O psychology. *The Industrial-Organizational Psychologist, 36* (1), 33–37.

Harvey, R. J. (1991). Job analysis. In M. Dunnette and L. M. Hough (Eds.), *Handbook of Industrial and Organizational Psychology* (71–163). Palo Alto, CA: Consulting Psychologists Press.

Hay, E. N., & Purves, D. (1954). A new method of job evaluation: The guide chart–profile method. *Personnel, 31* (7), 72–80.

Holley, W. M., & Jennings, K. M. (1983). *Personnel management: Functions and issues.* Chicago: Dryden.

Jackson, S. E., & Schuler, R. S. (2000). *Managing human resources: A partnership perspective.* Cincinnati, OH: South-Western.

Kirkland v. New York Department of Corrections, 374 F. Supp. 1361 (S. D. NY 1974).

Lawler, E. E. (1994). From job-based to competency-based organization. *Journal of Organizational Behavior, 15,* 3–15.

Levine, E. L. (1983). *Everything you always wanted to know about job analysis and more: A job analysis primer.* Tampa, FL: Mariner.

Levine, E. L., Ash, R. A., Hall, H., & Sistrunk, F. (1983). Evaluation of job analysis methods by experienced job analysts. *Academy of Management Journal, 26,* 339–348.

Lopez, F. M. (1988). Threshold traits analysis system. In S. Gael (Ed.), *The Job Analysis Handbook for Business, Industry, and Government* (Vol. 2, 880–901). New York: Wiley.

Lopez, F. M., Kesselman, G. A., & Lopez, F. E. (1981). An empirical test of a trait-oriented job analysis technique. *Personnel Psychology, 34,* 479–502.

May, K. E. (1996). Work in the 21st century: Implications for job analysis. *The Industrial-Organizational Psychologist, 33,* 98–100.

McCormick, E. J. (1976). Job and task analysis. In M. Dunnette (Ed.), *Handbook of Industrial and Organizational Psychology.* Chicago: Rand McNally.

McCormick, E. J. (1979). *Job analysis: Methods and applications.* New York: American Management Association.

McCormick, E. J., Jeanneret, P. R., & Mecham, R. C. (1972). A study of job characteristics and job dimensions as based on the Position Analysis Questionnaire (PAQ). *Journal of Applied Psychology, 56,* 347–368.

Menne, J. W., McCarthy, W., & Menne, J. (1976). A systems approach to the content validation of employee selection procedures. *Public Personnel Management, 5,* 387–396.

Mitchell, J. L., & Driskill, W. (1998). Military job analysis: A historical perspective. *Military Psychologist, 8* (3), 119–142.

Morgan, R. B., & Smith, J. E. (1996). *Staffing the new workplace: Selecting and promoting quality improvement.* Milwaukee: ASQC Quality Press.

Morhman, S. A., Cohen, S. G., & Mohrman, A. M., Jr. (1995). *Designing team-based organizations: New forms for knowledge work.* San Francisco: Jossey-Bass.

Munsterberg, H. (1913). *Psychology and industrial efficiency.* Boston: Houghton Mifflin.

Murphy, K., & Cleveland, J. (1991). *Performance appraisal: An organizational perspective.* Boston: Allyn & Bacon.

Nelson, J. B. (1997). The boundary-less organization: Implications for job analysis. *Human Resource Planning, 20,* 39–50.

Prien, E. P. (1977). The function of job analysis in content validation. *Personnel Psychology, 30,* 167–174.

Prien, E. P., Goldstein, I. L., & Macey, W. H. (1987). Multidomain job analysis: Procedures and applications. *Training and Development Journal, 41,* 68–73.

Prien, E. P., & Ronan, W. W. (1971). Job analyses: A review of research findings. *Personnel Psychology, 24,* 371–396.

Primoff, E. S. (1975). *How to prepare and conduct job element examinations.* Washington, DC: U.S. Civil Service Commission, Personnel Research and Development Center.

Pritchard, K. H. (1997). Introduction to competencies, White Paper, Society for Human Resource Management. Available online at www.shrm.org/whitepapers.

Schmidt, F. L. (1993). Personnel psychology at the cutting edge. In N. Schmitt and W. Borman (Eds.). *Personnel Selection in Organizations* (497–515). San Francisco: Jossey-Bass.

Schmidt, F. L., Caplan, J. R., Bemis, S. E., Dewir, R., Dunn, L., & Antone, L. (1979). *The behavioral consistency method of unassembled examining.* Washington, DC: U.S. Office of Personnel Management.

Schneider, B., and Konz, A. M. (1989). Strategic job analysis. *Human Resource Management, 28,* 51–63.

Shippman, J. S., Ash, R. A., Carr, L., Hesketh, B., Pearlman, K., Battista, M., Eyde, L. D., Kehoe, J., Prien, E. P., & Sanchez, J. I. (2000). The practice of competency modeling. *Personnel Psychology, 53* (3), 703–719.

Siegel, G. B. (1987). Education and training for the job analyst. *Personnel, 64* (7), 68–73.

Sims, R. R., & Veres, J. G. (1985). A practical program for training job analysts. *Public Personnel Management, 14,* 131–137.

Smith, J. E., & Hakel, M. D. (1979). Convergence among data sources, response bias, and reliability and validity of a structured job analysis questionnaire. *Personnel Psychology, 32,* 677–692.

Sparks, P. (1979). *Job analysts under the new Uniform Guidelines.* Houston, TX: Exxon Corporation, Personnel Research.

Sparks, P. (1981). Job analysis. In K. Rowland and G. Ferris (Eds.), *Personnel Management* (78–100). Boston: Allyn and Bacon.

Thompson, D. E., & Thompson, T. A. (1982). Court standards for job analysis in test validation. *Personnel Psychology, 35,* 865–874.

Tiffin, J., & McCormick, E. J. (1965). *Industrial psychology.* Upper Saddle River, NJ: Prentice Hall.

U.S. Civil Service Commission. (1977). *Instructions for the factor evaluation system.* Washington, DC: US. Government Printing Office.

U.S. Department of Labor, Employment and Training Administration. (1977). *Dictionary of occupational titles* (4th ed.). Washington, DC: U.S. Government Printing Office.

United States v. State of New York, 82 FRD 2 (D. C. NY 1978) decon merits, 475 F. Supp 1103 (D. C. NY 1979).

Van De Voort, D. M., & Stalder, B. K. (1988). Organizing for job analysis. In S. Gael (Ed.), *The Job Analysis Handbook for Business, Industry, and Government* (Vol. 1, 315–328). New York: Wiley.

Veres, J. G., Lahey, M. A., & Buckley, R. (1987). A practical rationale for using multimethod job analyses. *Public Personnel Management, 16*, 153–157.

Veres, J. G., Locklear, T. S., & Sims, R. R. (1988). Organizational entry. In G. R. Ferris, K. M. Rowland, and M. R. Buckley (Eds.), *Human Resource Management* (79–103). Boston: Allyn and Bacon.

Walker, J. (1992). *Human resource strategy.* New York: McGraw-Hill.

Wright, P., & Wexley, K. (1985, May). How to choose the kind of job analysis you really need. *Personnel,* 51–55.

Zedeck, S., Jackson, S. J., & Adelman, A. (1980). *Selection procedures reference manual.* Berkely, CA: University of California.

THE EMERGENCE OF PERSON-ORGANIZATION FIT IN ORGANIZATIONAL STAFFING PROCESSES

Chad A. Higgins

The process of staffing an organization is both challenging and exhilarating—challenging in the sense that we often must evaluate numerous applicants for a limited number of jobs (or, at other times, not enough applicants for too many jobs), and exhilarating because the people we ultimately choose to fill those positions can have a significant impact on the future success of the organization. As a result, it is important that great care be taken in designing and implementing a staffing process that enables us to select the most qualified applicants to become members of our organizations. One important step in designing such a staffing process is determining what criteria will be used to evaluate potential employees.

The purpose of this article is to examine one criterion that has become increasingly important in the staffing processes of many organizations. That criterion is person-organization (P-O) fit. Research has shown that hiring people who are a good fit with the organization can produce benefits for both parties. For example, hiring based on P-O fit can result in higher levels of employee job performance (Tziner, 1987), a greater tendency of employees to exhibit organizational citizenship behaviors (O'Reilly & Chatman, 1986), higher levels of employee satisfaction (Bretz & Judge, 1994), greater organizational commitment (Chatman, 1991), and lower levels of work-related stress (Matteson & Ivancevich, 1982). Despite the many benefits that can result from staffing processes have not always included P-O fit as a selection criterion. It has been only in the past decade that P-O fit has emerged as an important part of the new model of staffing.

In order to understand the new staffing model, this article explores traditional staffing processes, the emerging use of P-O fit in organizational staffing, and the role of P-O fit as both a dependent and independent variable in the new staffing model. In addition, I examine the P-O fit construct in detail, discuss the impact of interpersonal influence behaviors on perceptions of fit in the employment interview, and provide a discussion of future research needed to more fully understand the role of fit in the staffing process. In so doing, I hope to provide a better understanding of the current model of organizational staffing as well as stimulate further thought and research into the implications P-O fit has on staffing decisions and processes.

STAFFING PROCESSES: FROM PAST TO PRESENT

Traditional staffing processes focused on matching applicants' knowledge, skills, and abilities to the requirements of the job in question. Evolving from scientific management, early staffing processes focused almost exclusively on physical attributes of the applicants: size, strength, and/or flexibility. However, over time, other individual differences entered into staffing decisions.

One of the greatest advancements in organizational staffing occurred when general mental ability (also known as intelligence) emerged as a valuable tool for predicting the future job performance of applicants. In the 1980s, Schmidt, Hunter, and colleagues provided another boost to staffing research when they argued that tests of general mental ability not only were valid predictors of job performance, but were valid predictors across many types of jobs and in many dif-

ferent situations (Hunter & Hunter, 1984; Schmidt & Hunter, 1981). Prior to this groundbreaking research, staffing practitioners believed that each new job or situation required the validation of a new set of selection procedures. This, obviously, was quite costly and time consuming. Based on Schmidt and Hunter's work it became apparent that individual differences, such as general mental ability, could be used to select individuals for a wide variety of jobs.

In the late 1980s and early 1990s personality traits such as conscientiousness and emotional stability were identified as other valid individual difference criteria that organizations could use to select individuals who were likely to perform well on the job. Barrick and Mount (1991) and Mount and Barrick (1995) found that measures of conscientiousness were particularly good predictors of job performance and, as with general mental ability, the predictive validity of conscientiousness held across a wide variety of jobs.

It is clear that traditional staffing processes were designed to match applicants with a particular job by evaluating certain applicant attributes (e.g., strength, intelligence, and conscientiousness) that were likely to lead to successful job performance. One interesting similarity among all of these applicant attributes is that each one can be determined objectively through paper and pencil tests. Yet these types of tests are not the most common component of most organizational staffing processes. The most commonly used tool in organizational staffing processes is the employment interview. Despite somewhat limited reliability and validity, 85 to 90 percent of all organizations use the employment interview as part of their staffing process (Bell, 1992).

One might question why organizations would use a device as subjective as the employment interview to evaluate applicant attributes that may be more accurately assessed through objective testing. The answer seems to lie in a shift in the criteria organizations use to select employees. Rather than focusing exclusively on the fit between an applicant and a specific job, many organizations have begun to select applicants based on something more than the extent to which they fit a particular job. Many organizations have broadened their selection criteria to include an assessment of the degree to which characteristics of the person match similar characteristics of the organization. This match is known as P-O fit (Kristof, 1996), and this is the basis for organizations' continued reliance on the employment interview as a primary means of evaluating applicants.

RECENT DEVELOPMENTS IN ORGANIZATIONAL STAFFING

The preceding discussion suggests that we have entered a new stage in the development of organizational staffing processes. It is a stage wherein hiring individuals for a particular job has become less important than hiring individuals who fit the organization as a whole. It is a stage that is being driven by the need for organizations to be flexible, to have the ability to respond quickly to changes in the environment, and the need for employees who are able to function effectively in a variety of capacities.

Because of the complexities and constant change faced by employees in the current business environment, several researchers have suggested that organizations should move away from the traditional approach to staffing, and instead select employees based on broader attributes that are not easily acquired through training and that generalize to a number of different jobs (Behling, 1998; Pfeffer & Veiga, 1999).

Although the suggestions by Behling, Pfeffer and Veiga were made quite recently, it is not the first time someone has suggested that employees should be hired with a focus on how they will fit within the scope of the entire organization. In 1991, Bowen, Ledford, and Nathan suggested that such a shift in staffing philosophy was likely to occur and, in fact, was beginning to occur. It seems that now, 10 years later, the prophetic words of Bowen et al. (1991) have been realized. Many firms have begun to look for employees who fit with the broader organization and, as a result, P-O fit has become a central component in the staffing processes in these organizations.

THE PERSON-ORGANIZATION FIT CONSTRUCT

Before further exploring the role of P-O fit in organizational staffing processes, it is important to understand the construct of P-O fit. In general, fit is the compatibility between two components. A number of different types of fit have been identified, including person-environment (P-E) fit, person-group (P-G) fit, person-job (P-J) fit, and, of course, P-O fit. Although each of these types of fit has similarities and differences, the most obvious difference is the entity to which the person is compared (e.g., the environment, organization, group, or job). When applied specifically to the staffing process, most of the attention has focused on P-J fit and P-O fit. Although P-J fit is a crucial component of the traditional staffing process and remains an important part of the new model of staffing, it has been extensively reviewed elsewhere (see Edwards, 1991) and will not be discussed in great detail here. Rather, the focus of the current article is on P-O fit.

P-O fit can be defined as the compatibility between specific individual attributes and comparable organizational attributes. Although this definition is fairly straightforward, there are several issues that make the construct of P-O fit more than simple compatibility. Three issues that apply directly to the role of P-O fit in the staffing process are discussed next. For a more complete review of P-O fit, please see the seminal work of Kristof (1996), which discusses these and other issues in greater detail.

The first issue that complicates the P-O fit construct is how one conceptualizes compatibility, or fit. Fit can be conceptualized as either supplementary or complementary. Supplementary fit exists when one party has attributes that are similar to attributes of another party. For example, when an applicant desires to continue learning once he or she begins a job and an organization encourages its employees to take part in continuing education programs, supplementary fit exists because both parties have a desire to see continuous learning occur. Complementary fit occurs when one party adds a missing piece to the party or to the environment to make the other party or the environment whole (Kristof, 1996; Muchinsky & Monahan, 1987). Complementary fit occurs if an applicant is skilled at Web page development and the organization is seeking someone to establish their presence on the Internet. In this instance, the applicant brings a skill to the organization that was previously missing, thus making the organization whole. Although both conceptualizations of fit have relevance to the staffing process, it is supplementary fit that has been the focus of most studies of P-O fit (e.g., Adkins, Russell, & Werbel, 1994; Cable & Judge, 1997; Chatman, 1991).

The second issue that provides a more complete understanding of P-O fit is the manner in which P-O fit is operationalized. The most common operationalization of P-O fit is the congruence between individual values and organizational values (e.g., Adkins et al., 1994; Chatman, 1989, 1991; O'Reilly, Chatman, & Caldwell, 1991). The basis for using values as a means of operationalizing P-O fit stems from the fact that values are enduring beliefs that guide indi-

viduals' attitudes, judgments, and behaviors (Chatman, 1989; Rokeach, 1973). As a result, by basing judgments of fit on the congruence between applicant and organizational values, organizations can expect applicants with high levels of P-O fit to behave in accordance with the norms and desires of the organization.

Another means of operationalizing P-O fit is to examine the congruence of individual and organizational personality traits. As early as 1991, researchers suggested effective staffing processes should include a screening of applicant personality attributes in order to determine which applicants' personalities would most closely match the culture of the organization (Bowen et al., 1991). Later, work by Schneider, Smith, Taylor, and Fleenor (1998) provided evidence that organizations do appear to use assessments of applicant personality as part of their hiring processes. In their study, Schneider et al. found that managers within organizations share more personality similarities than do managers who work in different organizations. This suggests that organizations do hire individuals based, in part, on the extent to which their personality matches that of other employees within the organization and, as a result, the homogeneity of managerial personalities is greater within organizations than across organizations.

Whereas the preceding findings indicate that personality traits are examined by many organizations as part of the staffing process, these findings, on their own, do not necessarily mean that recruiters use personality as a means of evaluating P-O fit. However, a final piece of evidence provided by Kristof-Brown (2000) solidifies the argument that applicant personality traits are an integral part of P-O fit assessments. In a study of 31 recruiters from four consulting companies, every recruiter reported using applicant personality characteristics as an indicator of P-O fit. In fact, results of this study suggest that the two operationalizations of P-O fit mentioned previously, values congruence and personality congruence, are the two most common means used by recruiters to assess P-O fit.

Regardless of the way in which P-O fit is operationalized, a third factor that impacts the role of P-O fit in the staffing process is measurement. P-O fit can be measured either directly or indirectly. Direct measures of P-O fit are typically obtained by asking interviewers whether they *perceive* the applicant to be a good fit with the organization. Thus, direct measures of P-O fit are based on an individual's perception of P-O fit, regardless of whether there is an actual, or objective, fit between the individual and the organization. In order to determine whether actual P-O fit exists, we often rely on indirect measures. Indirect measures typically consist of independent assessments of individual characteristics and organizational characteristics. For example, indirect measures of fit may be determined by having an applicant complete a survey about his or her values and having an organizational recruiter complete a survey designed to assess the values of his or her organization. These independent assessments then are objectively compared to determine the degree to which P-O fit exists. This type of measurement reflects actual, rather than perceived, P-O fit because respondents are not asked to implicitly judge P-O fit.

As you can see, P-O fit is more than just a simple match between two parties. It can involve different types of matching (supplementary or complementary), different characteristics can be used as indicators of fit (values or personality), and fit can be measured in different ways (directly or indirectly). Despite these complicating factors, P-O fit has clearly become an important part of the staffing process. As a result, it is important to examine the effect P-O fit's emergence has had on specific selection methods used in organizational staffing processes.

P-O FIT AND THE EMPLOYMENT INTERVIEW

Perhaps no single selection method has been as widely criticized and, at the same time, as widely used as the employment interview. On the one hand, employment interviews have been criticized as having only low levels of reliability and validity. Although studies by McDaniel, Whetzel, Schmidt, and Maurer (1994) and Huffcutt and Arthur (1994) found that structured interviews and situational interviews can result in more acceptable levels of validity, many people still subscribe to the belief that even structured interviews are little more than "orally administered cognitive ability test[s]." (Campion, Pursell, & Brown, 1988, p. 36) Just as the interview has its drawbacks from an organizational standpoint, many job seekers also argue that the interview should be eliminated from the staffing process. One of the most stressful and anxiety-inducing elements of the job search process is the employment interview. Nearly anyone who has ever interviewed for a job is familiar with the stress and nervousness induced by the mere thought of having to face a recruiter in an employment interview in an effort to obtain a job. Thus, it can be argued from both the organization side and the applicant side that there are legitimate reasons for eliminating the employment interview from the staffing process.

On the other hand, as noted earlier, the employment interview continues to be one of the most popular and commonly used selection tools. In fact, many organizations will not consider hiring an individual without first interviewing him or her, even if the interview is informal and does little more than provide an opportunity for the two parties to introduce themselves to one another. Likewise, many applicants have become so accustomed to the employment interview being a major part of any job search that they are wary of joining an organization that does not use an employment interview as part of the hiring process. This unwavering devotion to a seemingly undesirable method of selecting employees has come under fire many times in the past 50 years. Yet, until recently, there had been no empirical explanation for organizations' affection for the employment interview. In the past decade, however, it has become abundantly clear that the basis of organizations' continued reliance on the interview most likely lies in their search for P-O fit.

When asked what it is they are looking for in an applicant, recruiters often report that fit plays an important role in their hiring decisions. Although some basic applicant characteristics—such as leadership, motivation, and enthusiasm—are desirable in every applicant, research by Rynes and Gerhart (1990) has found that recruiters' P-O fit judgments are distinguishable from such assessments of general employability. In addition, Cable and Judge (1977) reported that recruiters' judgments of P-O fit were strongly related to their own hiring recommendations and to organizations' hiring decisions. This evidence supports the notion that recruiters do use assessments of P-O fit in making staffing decisions. However, this doesn't explain why recruiters rely on the employment interview to assess P-O fit rather than some other selection tool. To fully understand why the employment interview plays such an important role in assessing P-O fit, we must look at the elements recruiters use to assess P-O fit and how those elements may manifest themselves in the employment interview.

Although research has proposed a number of different characteristics that might be used to form P-O fit judgments (e.g., goals, KSAs, values), research by Kristof-Brown (2000) indicates that individuals' values and personality are the two most important factors in recruiters' evaluations of P-O fit. At the most basic level, these characteristics are major determinants of individuals' behaviors and responses to environmental stimuli. Our values and personality traits help determine how we interact with others and how we behave in a given situation. As a result, our values and personalities play an important role in our interpersonal interactions. Because the employment interview has a strong interpersonal component and is the one selection method that allows a recruiter to experience an applicant's interpersonal skills firsthand, the employment interview easily lends itself to the assessment of P-O fit.

Through the employment interview, recruiters have the opportunity to interact with applicants to determine whether they possess values and personality characteristics that are similar to those desired by, and present in, the organization. Although applicant values and personality can be assessed objectively through pencil-and-paper tests, the employment interview provides a much richer setting that allows recruiters to assess for themselves the degree to which an applicant fits with the organization. In support of this argument, recent research by Cable and Judge (1997) found that recruiters' subjective assessments of P-O fit made during employment interviews are much stronger predictors of organizational hiring decisions than are objective measures of P-O fit that are obtained through pencil-and-paper tests. As such, it seems that the employment interview is indeed an important means for organizations to assess P-O fit.

EFFECTS OF INTERPERSONAL INFLUENCE ON FIT

It is an often unstated, yet well-understood fact, that applicants have a strong incentive to actively manage the impressions that organizational recruiters form of them. By managing impressions correctly, a candidate may increase his or her chances of receiving a positive evaluation from an interviewer. In fact, one study found that impression management tactics had a more powerful effect on interviewer judgments than did objective qualifications for the job (Gilmore & Ferris, 1989). There are a number of reasons why the employment interview is susceptible to applicant use of impression management tactics. There is also evidence that these tactics, when used successfully in the employment interview, can effect recruiters' perceptions of P-O fit.

First, several characteristics of the employment interview make it a suitable environment for the use of impression management tactics. Researchers have suggested that when an individual's ability to achieve a goal is highly dependent on another party, and when that individual has a strong desire to reach the goal, the individual is motivated to engage in efforts to manage the impressions others form of them (Leary & Kowalski, 1990). In the employment interview, one of the applicant's goals typically is to receive a job offer. A job offer is normally strongly desired by the applicant and in order to achieve that goal the applicant is highly dependent on the interviewer's judgments and impressions of the applicant's ability to do the job and be a good member of the organization. As such, the applicant should be motivated to manage the impressions the interviewer forms. In addition to the motivational forces present in the employment interview, the ambiguity and uncertainty found in the employment interview also encourage the use of impression management tactics (Ferris, Russ, & Fandt, 1989). When ambiguity and uncertainty are prevalent in a situation, the opportunity arises for one party to manage the perceptions and impressions that are created in that situation. In the employment interview, for example, because the inter-

viewer often does not have an extensive knowledge of the applicant's background, the applicant is afforded the opportunity to determine what information he or she will disclose and the manner in which that information will be conveyed. By managing the flow of information in measured and deliberate ways, the applicant can control the impressions that are formed of him or her. As this discussion suggests, the employment interview provides the motivation and the opportunity for applicants to actively manage impressions. The question then becomes, if applicants do manage impressions in the interview do those efforts affect interview outcomes, including perceptions of P-O fit? Recent research suggests the answer is yes.

For example, research by Stevens and Kristof (1995) suggests that not only do applicants use impression management tactics during employment interviews, but those tactics have significant effects on interview outcomes. Specifically, Stevens and Kristof reported that applicant impression management tactics were significantly related to interviewer evaluations of applicant suitability, likelihood of organizational pursuit of the applicant, and site visits and job offers received by the applicant. In addition, as noted earlier, Gilmore and Ferris (1989) found that impression management tactics may have a stronger effect on interviewer judgments than even objective qualifications. Finally, the author of the current article recently conducted a study that examined the effects of self-promotion and ingratiation on interviewer perceptions of fit. Results of that study suggest that, although both tactics are correlated with perceived fit, the use of ingratiation has a much stronger effect on fit perceptions (Higgins, 2001). Combined with previous research on the role of impression management in the employment interview, it is clear that applicants who engage in impression management tactics are able to influence interview outcomes, including perceptions of P-O fit.

THE ROLE OF P-O FIT IN THE ORGANIZATIONAL STAFFING PROCESS

As discussed at the beginning of this article, the traditional means of selecting employees consisted of matching applicant KSAs to the requirements of the job in an effort to select those applicants who had the best chance of achieving high levels of job performance. This basic staffing model held true until the 1990s. In the last decade, however, many organizations, in an attempts to maintain or even improve employee job performance in increasingly complex environments, have broadened their staffing criteria to include an examination of the match between applicant characteristics, such as values and personality, and comparable attributes of the organization. The addition of P-O fit to the staffing model has had broad implications for the staffing process and has resulted in a new model of organizational staffing. This new model is presented in Figure 5-1 and is discussed below.

To begin, the basic elements of organizational staffing processes remain. Organizations are still interested in hiring individuals who possess the KSAs necessary to perform the job for which they are hired. This focus on P-J fit is represented on the right side of the new staffing model. As the model indicates, P-J fit is determined by a comparison of applicant knowledge, skills, and abilities with the requirements of the job in question. The greater the extent to which applicants' KSAs match the job requirements, the higher the degree of P-J fit. However, the model also suggests that applicant influence behaviors will affect the assessment of P-J fit. Just as the author's own research has found that applicant influence behaviors affect perceptions of fit, research by Kristof-Brown, Barrick, and Franke (in press) suggests that applicant influence behaviors also affect perceptions of P-J fit. In a

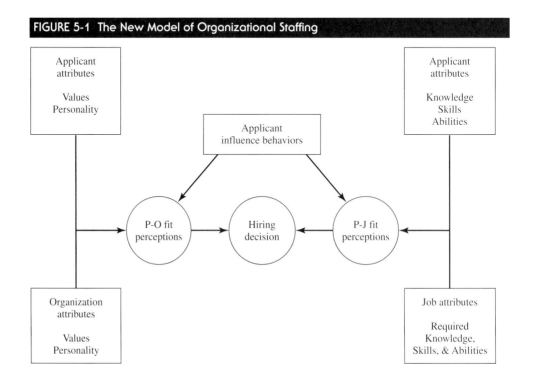

FIGURE 5-1 The New Model of Organizational Staffing

study of 72 applicants participating in mock interviews, Kristof-Brown, et al. found that applicant influence behaviors, and self-promotion in particular, had significant effects on perceived P-J fit. As a result, applicant influence behaviors are expected to affect perceptions of P-J fit in the new staffing model.

The left side of Figure 5-1 illustrates the expanded portion of the staffing model. Here we see that the comparison of applicant values and personality to organizational values and the predominant personality traits found in the organization results in interviewers' perception of P-O fit. Also, just as applicant influence behaviors are expected to affect P-J fit, applicant influence behaviors are also expected to affect perceptions of P-O fit. As discussed earlier, ingratiation in particular is likely to impact interviewers perceptions of P-O fit.

The new staffing model depicted here is designed only to illustrate the expanded criteria used by many of today's most successful organizations. As such, it is a rather simplistic model that does not fully capture the complexities of the staffing process, and does not attempt to do so. For example, this model does not include the effects of environmental factors, such as labor supply and economic conditions, which will likely affect the extent to which organizations depend on P-O fit relative to P-J fit in making hiring decisions. To illustrate, in an extremely tight labor market, organizations may be forced to hire anyone who meets the basic requirements of the job without regard to their fit with the organization. Although this is certainly not the ideal, in many cases, it is the unfortunate reality. Furthermore, this model does not include organizational factors that may determine the extent to which P-O fit is, or can be, included in the staffing process. For example, an organization with a weak organizational culture and few guiding values may be hard-pressed to determine P-O fit because of an inability to accurately as-

sess the organizational side of the equation. If P-O fit cannot be determined, it is obviously quite difficult to make it a part of any staffing decision.

FUTURE RESEARCH

Though our understanding of P-O fit has advanced greatly in the past decade, there is still much we do not know. For example, much of the existing research on P-O fit in the employment interview is focused on the initial interview. The typical sample has included students taking part in mock interviews or interviewing with employers through a campus placement office. Although these studies have contributed greatly to our current understanding of P-O fit, they have ignored the role that P-O fit may have at later stages of the staffing process. It is possible that P-O fit, though known to be important in the early stages of the interview process, may become even more important during second interviews and/or site visits. It can be argued that the initial interview is used simply to screen out applicants who don't meet the job requirements (i.e., who lack P-J fit) and later interviews are used to determine which of the remaining applicants would best fit the organization. Future research that examines this possibility would greatly enhance our current understanding of the role of P-O fit in the staffing process.

Another issue that has not been fully explored is whether high levels of P-O fit are desirable in every situation. It seems certain that organizations benefit from high levels of P-O fit in many situations, but are there situations in which lower levels of P-O fit might be better for the organization? In one of the few articles examining this issue, Powell (1998) argues that the importance of achieving high levels of P-O fit is, in fact, more important in some situations than in others. For example, Powell suggests that organizations should strive for fit when they compete in an industry that is expected to be in a state of equilibrium for the foreseeable future, when they are in the early stages of the organizational life cycle, and when the organization has a low degree of customer contact. However, Powell recommends that organizations search for more diversity when they exist in a turbulent, rapidly changing environment, when they are in later stages of the organizational life cycle, and when the organization has a high degree of customer contact. In situations with these latter attributes, greater diversity within the organization's workforce in terms of personality and values may allow the organization to respond to changes more quickly and to handle a greater variety of situations because there exists a greater variety of employee attributes on which to draw.

On the other hand, Candice Carpenter, co-founder and chairman of iVillage Inc., has suggested that, in terms of both skills and temperament, "At the beginning, you need more diversity than you can imagine . . . But as critical as diversity is at the beginning, once you start to scale, you want the opposite: a team of minds that think alike" (McCauley & Canabou, 2001, p. 87). This suggests that high levels of fit are more important at later stages of the organizational life cycle and may actually be detrimental in the early days of the organization. Although Powell and Carpenter's suggestions seem to contradict one another, they also both appear to be valid arguments. Future research is necessary in order to determine which, if either, of these arguments applies to today's organizations.

One final issue that has received scant research attention is the role of P-O fit in non-American organizations. Although we recognize that P-O fit plays an important role in the staffing processes of many American firms, we know very little about the role of P-O fit in the staffing processes of non-American firms. It is quite possible that so-cietal norms and cultural expectations in other countries affect the importance placed on P-O fit by organizations based in those countries. For example, in collectivist societies, such as Japan, a heavy emphasis is placed on relationships. As such, one might expect P-O fit, with its emphasis on interpersonal relationships, to have an even more significant role in the staffing processes of organizations that operate in collectivist societies than it does in organizations operating in individualistic societies.

In fact, anecdotal evidence suggests that some Japanese organizations focus on P-O fit almost at the exclusion of P-J fit. This seems to hold true even when these firms have operations located in the United States. For example, Klein (1992) notes that at Japan-based Nissan Motor Manufacturing Corp. U.S.A., an automotive engine manufacturer with operations in the United States, one of the most important qualifications recruiters look for in an applicant is a cooperative attitude. In addition, Klein notes that some human resources executives have suggested that Japanese firms prefer to hire individuals with a team orientation and who are committed to their company over those individuals who have experience. The fact that applicant values, such as teamwork and loyalty, are emphasized more than job-relevant experience suggests that P-O fit does have a significant role in the staffing processes of at least some Japanese firms.

Although the anecdotal evidence just presented suggests that P-O fit is used in the staffing processes of firms based outside of the United States, current research on P-O fit has been limited almost exclusively to North American samples. As a result, definitive conclusions cannot be made about the global importance of P-O fit in the staffing process. Because globalization is occurring at an ever-quickening pace, it is important that we examine the role of P-O fit in the staffing processes around the world.

CONCLUSION

In the past decade, researchers and practitioners alike have come to recognize the importance of P-O fit in organizational staffing processes. We have developed a better understanding of the construct of P-O fit, found the search for P-O fit to be a plausible explanation for the continued use of the employment interview, and begun to understand the expanded role that P-O fit plays in the organizational staffing process. At the same time, there are a number of questions about P-O fit that remain unanswered. With organizations continuing to change and the environments in which they operate continuing to become more and more volatile, it seems likely that the importance of P-O fit will continue to grow in the next 10 years. It is my hope that this growth in the decade ahead will encourage others to take a closer look at P-O fit and help develop an even better understanding of the role of P-O fit in organizational staffing processes. ■

REFERENCES

Adkins, C. L., Russell, C. J., & Werbel, J. D. (1994). Judgments of fit in the selection process: The role of work value congruence. *Personnel Psychology, 47,* 605–623.

Barrick, M. R., & Mount, M. K. (1991). The big five personality dimensions and job performance. *Personnel Psychology, 44,* 1–26.

Behling, O. (1998). Employee section: Will intelligence and conscientiousness do the job? *Academy of Management Executive, 12,* 77–86.

Bell, A. H. (1992). *Extraviewing: Innovative ways to hire the best.* Homewood, IL: Business One Irwin.

Bowen, D. E., Ledford, G. E., & Nathan, B. R. (1991). Hiring for the organization, not the job. *Academy of Management Executive, 5,* 35–51.

Bretz, R. D., Jr, & Judge, T. A. (1994). Person-organization fit and the theory of work adjustment: Implications for satisfaction, tenure, and career success. *Journal of Vocational Behavior, 44,* 32–54.

Cable, D. M., & Judge, T. A. (1997). Interviewers' perceptions of person-organization fit and organizational selection decisions. *Journal of Applied Psychology, 82,* 546–561.

Campion, M. A., Pursell, E. D., & Brown, B. K. (1988). Structured interviewing: Raising the psychometric properties of the employment interview. *Journal of Applied Psychology, 41,* 25–42.

Chatman, J. A. (1989). Improving interactional organizational research: A model of person-organization fit. *Academy of Management Review, 14,* 333–349.

Chatman, J. A. (1991). Matching people and organizations: Selection and socialization in public accounting firms. *Administrative Science Quarterly, 36,* 459–484.

Edwards, J. R. (1991). Person-job fit: A conceptual integration, literature review, and methodological critique. *International Review of Industrial and Organizational Psychology, 6,* 283–357.

Ferris, G. R., Russ, G. S., & Fandt, P. M. (1989). Politics in organizations. In R. A. Giacalone and P. Rosenfeld (Eds.), *Impression Management in the Organization* (143–170). Hillsdale, NJ: Lawrence Erlbaum.

Gilmore, D. C. & Ferris, G. R. (1989). The effects of applicant impression management tactics on interviewer judgments. *Journal of Management, 15,* 557–564.

Higgins, C. A. (2001). The effect of applicant influence tactics on recruiter perceptions of fit. Unpublished doctoral dissertation, University of Iowa, Iowa City.

Huffcut, A. I., & Arthur, W., Jr. (1994). Hunter and Hunter (1994) revisited: Interview validity for entry-level jobs. *Journal of Applied Psychology, 79,* 184–190.

Hunter, J. E., & Hunter, R. F. (1984). Validity and utility of alternative predictors of job performance. *Psychological Bulletin, 96,* 72–95.

Klein, E. (1992). The U.S./Japanese HR culture clash. *Personnel Journal, 71*, 30–37.

Kristof, A. L. (1996). Person-organization fit: An integrative review of its conceptualizations, measurement, and implications. *Personnel Psychology, 49*, 1–49.

Kristof-Brown, A., Barrick, M. R., & Franke, M. (in press). Applicant impression management: Dispositional influences and consequences for recruiter perceptions of fit and similarity. *Journal of Management.*

Kristof-Brown, A. L. (2000). Perceived applicant fit: Distinguishing between recruiters' perceptions of person-job and person-organization fit. *Personnel Psychology, 53*, 643–671.

Leary, M. R., & Kowalski, R. M. (1990) Impression management: A literature review and two-component model. *Psychological Bulletin, 107*, 34–47.

Matteson, M. T., & Ivancevich, J. M. (1982). Type A and B behavior patterns and health symptoms: Examining individual and organizational fit. *Journal of Occupational Medicine, 24*, 585–589.

McCauley, L., & Canabou, C. (2001, February). Unit of one. In A. M. Webber and W. C. Taylor (Eds.), *Fast Company, 43*, 85–95.

McDaniel, M. A., Whetzel, D. L., Schmidt, F. L., & Maurer, S. D. (1994). The validity of employment interviews: A comprehensive review and meta-analysis. *Journal of Applied Psychology, 79*, 599–616.

Mount, M. K., & Barrick, M. R. (1995). The big five personality dimensions: Implications for research and practice in human resource management. *Research in Personnel and Human Resources Management, 13*, 153–200.

Muchinsky, P. M., & Monahan, C. J. (1987). What is person-environment congruence? Supplementary versus complementary models of fit. *Journal of Vocational Behavior, 31*, 268–277.

O'Reilly, C. A., III, & Chatman, J. (1986). Organization commitment and psychological attachment: The effects of compliance, identification and internalization on prosocial behavior. *Journal of Applied Psychology, 71*, 492–499.

O'Reilly, C. A., Chatman, J., & Caldwell, D. F. (1991). People and organizational culture: A profile comparison approach to assessing person-organization fit. *Academy of Management Journal, 34*, 487–516.

Pfeffer, J., & Veiga, J. F. (1999). Putting people first for organizational success. *Academy of Management Executive, 13*, 37–48.

Powell, G. N. (1998). Reinforcing and extending today's organizations: The simultaneous pursuit of person-organization fit and diversity. *Organizational Dynamics, 26*, 50–61.

Rokeach, M. (1973). *The nature of human values.* New York: Free Press.

Rynes, S., & Gerhart, B. (1990). Interviewer assessments of applicant "fit": An exploratory investigation. *Personnel Psychology, 43*, 13–35.

Schmidt, F. L., & Hunter, J. E. (1981). The future of criterion-related validity. *Personnel Psychology, 33*, 41–60.

Schneider, B., Smith, D. B., Taylor, S., & Fleenor, J. (1998). Personality and organizations: A test of the homogeneity of personality hypothesis. *Journal of Applied Psychology, 83*, 462–470.

Stevens, C. K., & Kristof, A. L. (1995). Making the right impression: A field study of applicant impression management during job interviews. *Journal of Applied Psychology, 80*, 587–606.

Tziner, A. (1987). Congruency issue retested using Fineman's achievement climate notion. *Journal of Social Behavior and Personality, 2*, 63–78.

CHAPTER

6

PERFORMANCE EVALUATION AND MANAGEMENT

Following the completion of organizational entry activities, the need soon arises to evaluate work performance to satisfy the organization's efforts to monitor and improve effectiveness and to give employees feedback about how well they are doing. Organizations' concerns about productivity have sparked interest in performance appraisal as an organizational control mechanism that, if used properly, can constructively influence future work performance. Furthermore, recent legislation has forced careful examination of performance appraisal and employee feedback as evidence to support internal administrative or termination decisions.

Historically, approaches to solving performance appraisal problems focused on issues of instrumentation or scale development and procedures. It was hoped that, through these means, better results would be achieved. More recently, the emphasis has shifted from the technical issues to the process issues or the dynamics of the supervisor-subordinate relationship in the work setting. The focus on process, as well as concerns with ensuring procedural justice, have highlighted the usefulness of incorporating self-appraisals along with supervisor appraisals of subordinates' performance. This additional source of input frequently enhances perceptions of fairness on the part of subordinates and increases the validity of the resulting evaluations. Such shared feedback on past performance also facilitates the establishment of jointly owned and often more challenging goals for the future.

In the first article, Halbesleben, Buckley, and Wheeler explore a number of the problems that occur in the performance management process and suggestions for managers who encounter these problems. In addition, they have outlined some new issues that may have an influence on this process. The Villanova, Austin, and Bernardin article outlines the continuing-to-evolve legal issues surrounding performance management systems. The next article, by Bernardin and Villanova, takes a prescriptive approach to performance management. They insist that the process can be improved by implementing three prescriptions, and we agree. In the last article in this chapter, Davis and Fedor discuss the difficulties in giving feedback in organizations. They point out that conflicts may develop due to disparate interpretations, different feedback styles, and diverse individual variables.

READINGS

OVERLOOKED AND EMERGING ISSUES IN PERFORMANCE APPRAISAL

Jonathon R. B. Halbesleben
M. Ronald Buckley
Anthony R. Wheeler

With the vast amount of performance appraisal research to sift through, a student of management might feel like there is nothing that could have possibly been overlooked. However, with the dynamic nature of contemporary organizations, the need for new performance appraisal research is at an all-time high.

In this article, we will discuss a number of issues in the performance appraisal literature that have either been generally overlooked or are becoming more important as the performance landscape changes in organizations. We will begin with a look at the political motives that can significantly influence the performance appraisal system. We will use politics as a springboard into the more specific issue of pluralistic ignorance, a social comparison process that can undermine the process of and influence the reactions to performance appraisal. This will lead us into a discussion of the general effect of managers toward the appraisal process and how this may lead managers to undermine the appraisal system.

The second part of the article will address a number of issues that are becoming more important as the employee mix in organizations changes. We will begin by examining the increased utilization of contingent workers and the implications of this move for performance appraisal systems. We will then turn to the work team literature, exploring the use of performance appraisal in such contexts. We will conclude with the increased focus on customer feedback and how it relates to performance appraisal administration.

POLITICS IN PERFORMANCE APPRAISAL

In a number of respects, it is unfair to call politics in performance appraisal an overlooked issue, as there is a great body of established research that addresses this issue. However, one could argue that despite the work that has been done, little of this research has translated into actual changes in performance appraisal administration in organizations. Furthermore, despite the body of literature that exists that demonstrates how politics can have an important impact on performance appraisal, very few studies take into account politics as a situational factor when interpreting the findings. In this section we will discuss attempts by managers to change their performance ratings in order to satisfy some personal motive. In some cases these conscious changes in appraisals will benefit the employee that is rated; at other times it may result in unnecessarily deflated ratings.

A goal of many organizations today is to seek a competitive advantage by increasing the commitment of their workforce. However, as Ferris and Kacmar (1992) have suggested, one of the ways to reduce organizational commitment is by increasing perceptions of politics in the organization. Many of these perceptions may be attributed to the performance appraisal process, despite our relative lack of understanding about how politics influences the formulation of performance ratings (Tziner, Latham, Price, & Haccoun, 1996).

In general, much of the performance appraisal error research has focused on unintentional errors committed by raters (Bernardin & Villanova, 1986). In fact, many of the models of the performance rating process assume that raters try to rate their subordinates accurately, but are limited in their ability to do so (Tziner et al., 1996). However, this is not a universally accepted assumption. Cleveland and Murphy (1992) proposed a model of performance appraisal that treated it as a goal-directed behavior, one in which the goals may be linked to outcomes that benefit the manager as well as the employee. Furthermore, a number of studies have detected deliberate alterations to ratings in order to satisfy a variety of managerial motives; we turn to these studies next.

Longenecker and his associates (Gioia & Longenecker, 1994; Longenecker, 1984; Longenecker & Ludwig, 1990; Longenecker, Sims, & Gioia, 1987) have written a series of papers on the political behavior managers engage in when conducting performance appraisals. They found a number of interesting (and perhaps disturbing) patterns. In general, they have found that managers realize that the performance appraisal process holds some utility for the manager (Longenecker, 1984). In other words, managers realize that there are a number of ways in which they can use the appraisal process to their advantage. As such, in some cases it is to the advantage of the supervisor to inflate ratings, and at other times it is more advantageous to deflate performance ratings.

Using qualitative data from interviews with 60 managers, Longenecker, Sims, and Gioia (1987) found that managers tend to inflate ratings in order to maximize the likelihood of a merit increase for the subordinate, to avoid making themselves look back, to avoid tainting the employee's personnel record, to avoid confrontation, to account for accelerated performance toward the end of the rating period, and to promote a subordinate "up and out" of the department when he or she simply does not fit in or get along well with the manager. It is interesting to note that in a number of cases, the ratings were inflated primarily in order to benefit the manager, *not* the employee (although the employee may have experienced some benefit as a result of the manager's motive).

Longenecker, Sims, and Gioia (1987) also found that while it is far less common, managers occasionally deflate performance ratings. The managers provided a variety of reasons for consciously deflating the ratings, including spurring a subordinate to better performance through the shock of a low rating, teaching an employee a lesson, trying to get an employee to consider leaving the organization, or trying to build up a record of poor performance that will assist in the legal justification for terminating the employee. With the rise in wrongful termination lawsuits over the past decade or so, the final reason for deflating ratings has become even more important.

It is clear that the manager's motives can have a direct impact on the employee's performance review, perhaps to the point that the actual performance of the employee is irrelevant. Human resources managers must recognize these trends when making decisions based on performance ratings.

Implications for Research and Practice

While researchers have begun to closely investigate the implications of politics in performance appraisal, there are a number of areas that have not yet been explored. For example, more work is needed to establish the link between business strategy (particularly if employee commitment is an aspect of strategy) and managerial performance rating behaviors. Furthermore, more work is needed to look at how political rating behaviors influence overall perceptions of politics in the organization. The perceptions of politics model proposed by Ferris and Kacmar may be a viable framework to utilize in order to investigate some of these issues. Furthermore, the Questionnaire of Political Considerations in Performance Appraisal (QPCPA) developed by Tziner and his colleagues (1996) holds some promise for addressing some of these issues through measurement.

With regard to practice, it is clear that managers are explicitly influencing ratings. Organizations need to consider how this political influence influences overall firm performance and how rating inaccuracy might fit into the overall corporate strategy. If these changes in performance ratings in order to satisfy managerial motives are problematic, researchers and practitioners need to develop techniques that reduce the negative influence of inaccurate ratings. Also, as noted earlier, human resources managers must be cognizant of intentional bias when making important human resources decisions based on performance ratings.

In this section we have discussed very explicit forms of bias in performance ratings, focusing primarily on behaviors managers engage in to consciously alter performance ratings to their advantage. In the next section, we will discuss a more implicit form of bias where managers change their rating style in order to fit in with a misperceived organizational norm.

PLURALISTIC IGNORANCE IN PERFORMANCE APPRAISAL

An additional situational variable that can be as important as politics is inadvertent causes of error in performance appraisal.

The concept of halo errors, similar-to-me errors, and others are well-established in the performance appraisal literature and have been important topics of study for a number of decades. However, this literature often fails to consider how a manager might use the perceptions of rating standards of other managers to determine their own. Halbesleben and Buckley (2001) have developed a model of pluralistic ignorance in performance appraisal that predicts how a manager might react if the performance standards or procedures they use for performance appraisal are perceived to be different from the majority of other managers in his or her firm (see Figure 6-1). Note that the emphasis is placed on whether or not the perception of differences exists, not whether or not those differences exist in reality.

The model focuses primarily on the social comparison phenomenon of pluralistic ignorance. Pluralistic ignorance occurs when an individual holds a belief but mistakenly perceives that the majority of his or her peers hold the opposite belief (Allport, 1924). There are many examples of pluralistic ignorance that have been well-documented in a variety of fields. A common example is one that is likely to be familiar to many students. During a very difficult college lecture (perhaps in your HRM class), a student does not understand something that has been presented. He or she is unsure whether to ask a question, so he or she looks around at the others in the classroom to determine the extent to which his or her classmates understand the material. He or she does this discreetly, in order to look as though he or she understands the lecture fully. Since no one else has asked a question, and it appears (at least to the student in question) that everyone else understands the material, the student decides not to ask the question for fear that he or she would look less intelligent. If everyone understood the material, this would not be a very interesting situation, and would certainly not be considered a social

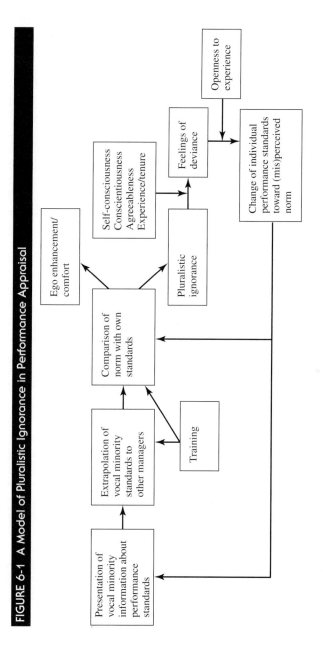

FIGURE 6-1 A Model of Pluralistic Ignorance in Performance Appraisal

comparison error. However, what is more likely to occur is that there are a large number of students in that situation during the lecture, and they cannot accurately judge the understanding of their peers because their peers, as well as themselves, are trying not to show their misunderstanding. As a result, there is a large contingent of students who do not understand the material presented, but because they think everyone else understands the material, they do not ask any questions about it. What is troubling is that this may occur numerous times during a lecture and during a semester, and the result is significantly reduced understanding of course material—a problem that might have been rectified much earlier had the misperception not occurred.

The phenomenon of pluralistic ignorance has been applied in many areas, but has seen little application to the work setting (with the notable exceptions of Buckley, Harvey, & Beu, 2000, and Sallot, Cameron, & Lariscy, 1998). The Halbesleben and Buckley (2001) model is an attempt to apply pluralistic ignorance to the performance appraisal process. The model begins with the presentation of performance standard information from a vocal minority and extrapolation of that vocal minority information to other managers. Recent work has suggested that people may mistakenly base their opinions of others on a small group of individuals who are vocal about their opinions (Halbesleben, Sauer, & Buckley, 2001). This suggests that managers may overhear a manager (or small group of managers) discussing what performance criteria are important to him or her and may assume that those standards are also important to the other managers at the firm. This extrapolation will create an "organizational norm" of performance standards.

The next step in the Halbesleben and Buckley (2001) model is a comparison with the manager's own standards. The resulting outcome will determine whether or not the manager is actually experiencing pluralistic ignorance. If the perceived organizational standards are consistent with the manager's standards, the result is ego-enhancement and comfort because the manager appears (in his or her own mind) to fit in with the other managers in the firm. On the other hand, if the comparison reveals inconsistencies between the organizational standards and the manager's individual standards, the result may be pluralistic ignorance, the mistaken belief that one's opinions are opposite of the majority of his or her peers.

It has been suggested in the pluralistic ignorance literature that pluralistic ignorance can lead to feelings of deviance (Miller & Prentice, 1994) and may eventually lead to a change in opinion toward the misperceived social norm (Miller & Prentice, 1994), in this case resulting in the manager adopting new standards of performance that are consistent with his or her view of the organizational norm. While there has been little research investigating the relationship between pluralistic ignorance and its consequences, Halbesleben and Buckley (2001) have suggested a number of potential moderators of those relationships, including self-consciousness, conscientiousness, agreeableness, experience, tenure, fear of embarrassment, and openness to experience.

The final important aspect of the model is the comparison of the new standards with the perception of organizational standards. In this sense, the model is somewhat iterative, as each time the employee adopts new standards to rectify perceived discrepancies, there is a new comparison with the (mis)perceived organizational standard. Again, this may results in ego-enhancement or pluralistic ignorance, depending on the outcome of the comparison.

Since the presentation of a model can be rather abstract, we will present an example of how the Halbesleben and Buckley (2001) model might play out in practice. Consider Jennifer, a new sales manager at a firm that specializes in audio/visual equipment. She has worked in the audio/visual industry for a number of years, and has an idea about what (in her mind) will lead to high performance of a salesperson. While taking a break to get a soda, she overhears another manager complaining about how his employees consistently arrive at work late in the morning. Another manager in the room agrees that it is a problem with her employees and that it may be causing their overall sales to decrease. From this conversation, Jennifer determines that punctuality must be important to all of the managers at her firm and is an important aspect of the performance of the organization. She begins to think about her own standards of performance, and realizes that she never really considers punctuality when she completes her performance reviews.

Because she is a rather new manager and seeks to fit in with the other managers of the firm, Jennifer feels guilty for not considering punctuality in her reviews. She decides that in the future, she will keep track of what time her employees arrive at work in order to include that in her ratings. She thinks about how this relates to the standards of the other managers of her firm, and is comforted now that her standards are similar to theirs.

Note that the situation described in this situation is not necessarily problematic, particularly if the managers in Jennifer's organization all really feel that punctuality is important. However, problems exist when other managers do not actually agree that punctuality is an important aspect of performance. For example, while the managers who originally discussed punctuality as a problem might have been annoyed that their employees have not been arriving on time, that does not necessarily mean that they consider punctuality in their ratings of employee performance. As a result, Jennifer may have adopted an aspect of performance that is not actually part of the organizational standard at all.

Certainly, many would argue considering punctuality when others do not is not going to lead to the downfall of organizations. However, if the described situation occurs frequently, and in a number of managers, it could lead to the development of a wide variety of idiosyncratic standards of performance that are not actually related to the business strategy of the organization. This is where pluralistic ignorance leads to real problems, in situations where the standards that managers use to determine performance ratings are inconsistent with each other and are inconsistent with the objectives of the organization.

Implications for Research and Practice

While the model presented by Halbesleben and Buckley (2001) appears to hold some promise with regard to explaining the relationship between pluralistic ignorance and the performance appraisal process, it is important to note that there have not been any empirical studies to support the model to this point. Clearly, it is important that researchers make an effort to test the relationships proposed by the model in a systematic fashion in order to determine the true nature of the influence of pluralistic ignorance in the process.

With regard to practice, it is important for managers to realize the influence of misperceptions of organizational standards of performance on their own ratings. Research in pluralistic ignorance (Schroeder & Prentice, 1998) has suggested that by asking victims of pluralistic ignorance to discuss their opinions and how pluralistic ignorance might influence their opinions, levels of pluralistic ignorance can be reduced, both in the short-term and long-term. There appears to be a relationship between this kind of training and frame-of-reference training in performance appraisal: By exposing people to group misperceptions, the development of a common frame-of-reference is developed among those involved, which may facilitate the accuracy of managerial appraisals. A recent review has suggested that frame-of-reference training has had the best track record of any performance rater training system available (Bernardin, Buckley, Tyler, & Wiese, 2000). Researchers and managers should investigate the relationship between pluralistic ignorance and frame-of-reference training and the potential benefits of combining the two techniques.

In the previous two sections, we focused on overlooked variables in the rating process. We will now change course a bit, and consider the performance (and appraisal of that performance) of two groups of employees that are becoming more important to organizations today: contingent workers and customers.

PERFORMANCE APPRAISAL FOR THE CONTINGENT WORKFORCE

The use of contingent workers has increased dramatically over the past two decades; one recent survey estimated that 90 percent of employers use temporary workers (Golden & Applebaum, 1992). Further, the temporary work industry has grown to be a $50 billion per year industry (National Association of Temporary and Staffing Services, 1999). Contingent workers are often used as a mechanism for flexibility in staffing that allows the organization to concentrate on its core competency (see Wheeler, Buckley, & Halbesleben in Chapter 4 of this text for more information about the basic nature of contingent work).

With such a large impact on organizations, one may wonder what techniques exist to give feedback to this important group of employees. Very little research attention has been given to the appraisal of contingent workers' performance and its link to positive changes in performance. In this section, we discuss some possible reasons why performance appraisal of contingent workers

has been largely overlooked, implications for the lack of performance feedback given to contingent workers, and some potential avenues for research in this area.

One might argue that contingent workers have the ultimate performance appraisal—they are asked to do more work or not asked to return to work. While this is one form of performance feedback, one might liken it to the feedback that a permanent worker receives by not being fired each day. Researchers are unlikely to consider this sort of feedback adequate for development of new skills and increased performance. And while this sort of feedback may be significantly valued (and expectancy theorists might argue that there is a positive valence associated with a contingent worker being asked back to work), most would argue that such feedback has its limits with regard to motivation.

One potential explanation for the lack of performance feedback in contingent workers is a classic problem in the performance literature: There is not a clear definition of performance criteria for contingent workers. Most would argue that without reasonable criteria, it is not meaningful to attempt to measure performance in the context of contingent workers. At issue here is the level of expected performance, especially compared to permanent workers. Performance is often conceptualized as including two components, task performance (the actual implementation of the responsibilities of the job) and contextual performance (contributions to organizational performance that are not specifically task related) (Borman & Motowidlo, 1993). It is difficult to argue that contingent workers would have an adequate opportunity to exhibit contextual performance, particularly if they have a short-term assignment. In some cases, it may not even be reasonable to expect that a contingent worker has all of the knowledge necessary to engage in acceptable task performance (for example, in jobs that are related to common positions, but require a number of unique tasks that are not commonly performed across industries).

This difficulty in defining the task and contextual performance leads researchers looking for other options. Recently, van Dyne and Ang (1998) investigated the relationship between contingent work and organizational citizenship behaviors. They found that when contingent workers felt some commitment to their organization and felt good about their psychological contract with the organization, they engaged in organizational citizenship behaviors. In fact, the relationship between commitment and contracts was stronger for the contingent workers than it was for a sample of permanent workers in the same organization. These findings offer some promise in using organizational citizenship behaviors to help define performance in contingent workers; however, this idea brings with it as many questions as it does answers. For example, is it really fair to base performance on organizational citizenship behaviors, which, by definition, are actions that the employee engages in that they are not expected to engage in? Furthermore, is it fair to use organizational citizenship behavior to define performance in situations where employees are not committed to the organization or feel uncomfortable with their psychological contract because they are not treated well by their host organization? Finally, which is more important to the contingent/temporary worker, the psychological contract with the temporary work firm or the contract with the host firm (Hulin & Glomb, 1999)? These are issues that will have to be considered further in order to adequately assess the contribution of organizational citizenship behaviors in performance of contingent workers.

The problem of performance definition is further compounded by the difficulty in comparing the performance of contingent workers to that of permanent workers. This comparison might not be meaningful, particularly if the jobs that contingent workers fill differ significantly from those of permanent employees (Hulin & Glomb, 1999). An interesting consideration is the definition of job tasks for contingent and permanent workers. It was noted that contingent workers might not have as much to offer as far as task and contextual performance are concerned. On the other hand, the tasks of contingent workers are typically much more clearly defined. Contingent workers typically are given a set of tasks to do and are expected to simply work through those tasks to the best of their ability. On the other hand, permanent workers are asked to complete job tasks along with other, less efficient tasks such as meetings, office politics, or even training the contingent workers. This distinction is reflected by a recent finding by the Bureau of Labor Statistics that temporary workers produce the equivalent of two more hours per day of work than permanent workers in the same firm (Caudron, 1994). From this, it would appear that contingent workers are actually much more productive but, in effect, it might be the same as comparing apples to oranges because the tasks of each group are defined differently.

Considering the difficulties inherent in offering performance feedback to contingent workers, one might question the value of attempts to offer feedback to this particular group of employees. To address this question, we will discuss how organizations use contingent workers and how this relates to the organization's performance. Many organizations now use contingent workers on a temp-to-hire basis. This allows both the organization and the employee to engage in a "test drive" prior to the permanent hiring of the employee. Clearly, if an organization is interested in hiring a temporary worker for a permanent position, they could benefit a great deal by offering performance feedback to the worker before he or she is actually a permanent worker. This may aid in the development of task and contextual performance even earlier for that worker, which in turn will benefit the organization.

A number of organizations rely heavily on large numbers of contingent workers who perform many important, although peripheral, functions within the organization. It seems almost laughable that organizations would allow such a large part of their workforce to continue to work without any sort of systematic feedback. They would never consider such a practice if the workers were all permanent, yet the relatively short contract with many contingent workers makes them "exempt" from feedback. These practices apply to organizations that regularly employ large numbers of contingent (perhaps temporary or part-time) employees for a relatively sustained amount of time (for example, department stores that hire large numbers of workers to help out during the holiday season).

Implications for Research and Practice

The previous discussion leads to a number of important directions for both research and practice. First, it is important to work toward the establishment of a definition of performance for contingent workers. This is an important issue in performance appraisal generally; however, the lack of any reasonable definition of contingent worker performance is a great hindrance in the literature on this emerging group. Furthermore, attempts must be made to understand the relationship between motivation and performance in contingent workers. While there has been some work in this area (cf., Wheeler & Buckley, in press; Wheeler, Buckley, & Halbesleben, Chapter 4 in this text), there is a need to continue to establish this relationship.

The previous statements suggest that researchers should rush out to study contingent workers and their characteristics. This may not be as easy as it sounds. Because, by defini-

tion, the tenure of contingent workers is often temporary, data collection in such groups may be a significant hurdle (Hulin & Glomb, 1999). Although this work may be filled with tedium, we hope that researchers will meticulously address the issues of importance in the performance of contingent workers.

As for managers working with contingent workers, it is important to realize the importance of offering job-related feedback when possible. The use of performance appraisal and feedback may pose some administrative difficulty, but may actually be more important for the development of contingent worker performance than it is for permanent workers. There certainly are exceptional situations where performance feedback may not be worth the time. For example, offering a 30-minute feedback interview to an employee who is merely filling in for an ill administrative assistant for the day is probably not worth the time it would take to offer the feedback. However, in cases where the worker may benefit from meaningful feedback (perhaps because they will be returning for another assignment), the feedback should be offered, even if it is just a few comments at the end the day about how they could do a better job.

We would like to switch gears now to discuss a type of worker that may be even more "contingent" or "temporary" than contingent workers: customers. It seems that their performance is also rather inadequately defined, to the detriment of organizations.

APPRAISING THE PERFORMANCE OF CUSTOMERS AS EMPLOYEES

In reality, customers often do a great deal of meaningful work for organizations. For instance, think about the times when you have put gas in your car and have paid at the pump. You pumped the gas yourself, swiped the credit card, and perhaps washed your own windows. At fast-food restaurants, you go up to the counter to order (as opposed to having someone come to your table), you carry your products to the dining area, you get your own refills, and you clean up your garbage. One may wonder, "Am I getting paid for all of this work?" Generally, customers are paid with lower prices (fast food compared to a full-service restaurant) or faster service. With the increasing amount of work that is done by customers, one may wonder what can be done to encourage customers to perform at high levels—in effect, to be better employees of the organization.

The idea that customers are a form of employee has been largely overlooked in the literature (with the notable exceptions of Bowen, 1986, and Mills & Morris, 1986), in part because this has been a quickly increasing phenomenon over the past couple of decades. However, in light of the remarkable increase in the use of customers as employees, organizations might benefit from a better understanding about how human resources management practices might apply to this important group.

Prior to discussing the more specific application of performance appraisal of customers, it is necessary to define the conditions under which a customer is considered an employee. A customer may be considered an employee if he or she engages in behavior that would either not normally be considered common for a customer in that situation or would not be expected at other venues in a similar situation. In other words, simply paying for goods and services would not be considered "employee" action; however, swiping your own credit card would be. Additionally, cleaning up your food at a fast-food restaurant is an action that is not taken at other food venues and, as such, would be considered employee actions.

One reason why organizations may be reluctant to provide meaningful performance feedback to customers is a concern that incorrect implementation of such feedback may result in a significant loss in customer retention. This fear is somewhat justified given the tremendous link between customer service and customer satisfaction and retention. Organizations are cognizant to the often delicate service needs of customers, particularly in markets where competition is significant.

Clearly, it would be silly to suggest that organizations implement the same performance feedback system for a customer that is used for employees. First, there would be no quicker way to see the previously mentioned concerns materialized than to offer significant amounts of negative feedback to customers. While polite correction may be acceptable to many customers, a detailed description of their performance shortcomings would almost surely turn off even the most loyal customers.

A second important consideration is the frequency of customer return rate and the number of organizational outlets. If return customers are infrequent, investing time and resources on feedback to customers may not be feasible. While it may be frustrating when home or car buyers are not adequately prepared for the tasks at hand, the frequency of such consumption is low enough that it may not be worthwhile to spend extraordinary amounts of time "training" these customers. Additionally, as the number of outlets or venues is fewer, the benefit of providing feedback to customers declines. Providing feedback to customers of a small-town diner with only one location is far less useful than providing feedback to customers of a nationwide fast-food chain.

A final issue of consideration to organizations that deal with customer coproduction is the relationship between permanent employees of the organization and the customers. The employees dealing with the coproducing customers are responsible for coaching ("training") the customers so that they do the job correctly (Schneider & Bowen, 1995). This may mean that the performance of the customer is somewhat out of his or her control, and has moved partially to the employees of the organization. As such, there may some greater difficulty in offering feedback, particularly if the customer feels that his or her performance was beyond his or her control.

Implications for Research and Practice

Many of the issues for research are similar for customers as they were with contingent workers. First, it is important that attempts be made to further define performance in coproducing customers and examine that performance in relationship with existing employees (although, for a good start, see Bowen & Waldman, 1999). It would also be beneficial to consider individual differences in receptiveness to feedback between individual customers. Researchers may be wise to consider models of employee receptiveness to performance feedback as a starting point, as there appears to be some potential for application to a customer population. Finally, it would be useful to tie some of the developed concepts of customer performance into current theories of motivation, in particular, equity and expectancy theories.

The authors recognize that customers can be a rather delicate group to conduct research with, which may result in some difficulty in development and testing of the concepts presented in this section of the article. The use of customer surveys and focus groups (particularly if tied to rewards from the organization conducting or hosting the research) may offer a viable starting point.

For managers of organizations that utilize coproducing customers, it is important they recognize the need for this group of "partial employees" to receive feedback.

Just as employees need some direction, customers will also need some direction in order to effectively complete the tasks that the organization would like them to. While there has been a focus on customer service in organizations for a number of years now, this idea will become even more important as more organizations attempt to utilize the services of their customers.

CONCLUSIONS

In this article, we have discussed a number of important issues in performance appraisal research that either have been generally overlooked in the literature or are becoming more important as business practices evolve. We have addressed the implications of both deliberate and inadvertent bias in performance ratings, with suggestions that may help guide research in practice in the field. We have also discussed the implementation of feedback to two groups of employees who are often overlooked, contingent workers and customers.

It is our hope that students of human resources management can take the ideas presented in this article and use them as a springboard for their own research. We further hope that students who become managers will understand the impact of the issues discussed, and develop proactive solutions for the problems that they create. Finally, we hope that in future discussions of the issues presented, the term "overlooked" will no longer be appropriate, as researchers and practitioners will have taken the opportunity to investigate these concepts more fully. ■

REFERENCES

Allport, F. H. (1924). *Social Psychology.* Boston: Houghton-Mifflin.

Bernardin, H. J., Buckley, M. R., Tyler, C. L., & Wiese, D. S. (2000). A reconsideration of strategies in rater training. In G. R. Ferris (Ed.), *Research in Personnel and Human Resources Management* (Vol. 18). Stamford, CT: JAI Press.

Bernardin, H. J., & Villanova, P. (1986). Performance appraisal. In E. Locke (Ed.), *Generalizing from Laboratory to Field Studies.* (43–62). Lexington Books: Lexington, MA:

Borman, W. C., & Motowidlo, S. J. (1993). Expanding the criterion domain to include elements of contextual performance. In N. Schmitt and W. C. Borman (Eds.), *Personnel Selection in Organizations.* San Francisco, CA: Jossey-Bass.

Bowen, D. E. (1986). Managing customers as human resources. *Human Resource Management, 25,* 371–384.

Bowen, D. E., & Waldman, D. A. (1999). Customer-driven employee performance. In D. R. Illgen and E. D. Pulakos (Eds.), *The Changing Nature of Performance: Implications for Staffing, Motivation, and Development.* San Francisco, CA: Jossey-Bass.

Buckley, M. R., Harvey, M. G., & Beu, D. S. (2000). The role of pluralistic ignorance in the perception of unethical behavior. *Journal of Business Ethics, 23,* 353–364.

Caudron, S. (1994). Contingent workforce spurs HR planning. *Personnel Journal, 73,* 52–60.

Cleveland, J. N., & Murphy, K. R. (1992). Analyzing performance appraisal as a goal-directed behavior. In G. R. Ferris (Ed.), *Research in Personnel and Human Resources Management* (Vol. 10). Stamford, CT: JAI Press.

Ferris, G. R., & Kacmar, K. M. (1992). Perceptions of organizational politics. *Journal of Management, 18,* 93–116.

Gioia, D. A., & Longenecker, C. O. (1994). Delving into the dark side: The politics of executive appraisal. *Organizational Dynamics, 22,* 47–58.

Golden, L., & Applebaum, E. (1992). What was driving the 1982–88 boom in temporary employment? Preferences of workers or decisions and powers of employers. *American Journal of Economics and Sociology, 4,* 473–493.

Halbesleben, J. R., & Buckley, M. R. (2001). Pluralistic ignorance: An overlooked variable in the performance appraisal process. Paper under review at the Southern Management Association.

Halbesleben, J. R., Sauer, N. S., & Buckley, M. R. (2001). Pluralistic ignorance in jury decision-making: Implications for the vocal minority hypothesis. Paper presented at the 19th Annual Oklahoma Psychological Society Spring Research Conference, Oklahoma City, OK.

Hulin, C. L., & Glomb, T. M. (1999). Contingent employees: Individual and organizational considerations. In D. R. Illgen and E. D. Pulakos (Eds.), *The Changing Nature of Performance: Implications for Staffing, Motivation, and Development.* San Francisco, CA: Jossey-Bass.

Longenecker, C. O. (1984). Executive cognition and affect in performance appraisal: A qualitative study. Unpublished doctoral dissertation, Pennsylvania State University.

Longenecker, C. O., & Ludwig, D. (1990). Ethical dilemmas in performance appraisal revisited. *Journal of Business Ethics, 9,* 961–969.

Longenecker, C. O., Sims, H. P., & Gioia, D. A. (1987). Behind the mask: The politics of employee appraisal. *Academy of Management Executive, 1,* 183–193.

Miller, D. T., & Prentice, D. A. (1994). Collective errors and errors about the collective. *Personality and Social Psychology Bulletin, 20,* 541–550.

Mills, P. K., & Morris, J. H. (1986). Clients as "partial employees" of service organizations: Role development in client participation. *Academy of Management Review, 11,* 726–735.

National Association of Temporary and Staffing Services. (1999). *Who are temporary workers?: You may be surprised to learn.* Available online at www.natss.org.

Sallot, L. M., Cameron, G. T., & Lariscy, R. A. W. (1998). Pluralistic ignorance and professional standards: Underestimating professionalism in our peers in public relations. *Public Relations Review, 24,* 1–20.

Schnieder, B., & Bowen, D. E. (1995). *Winning the service game.* Boston: Harvard Business School Press.

Schroeder, C. M., & Prentice, D. A. (1998). Exposing pluralistic ignorance to reduce alcohol use among college students. *Journal of Applied Social Psychology, 28,* 2150–2180.

Tziner, A., Latham, G. P., Price, B. S., & Haccoun, R. (1996). Development and validation of a questionnaire for measuring perceived political considerations in performance appraisal. *Journal of Organizational Behavior, 17,* 179–190.

van Dyne, L., & Ang, S. (1998). Organizational citizenship behavior of contingent workers in Singapore. *Academy of Management Journal, 41*, 692–703.

Wheeler, A. R., & Buckley, M. R. (in press). Examining the motivation process of temporary employees: A holistic model and research framework. *Journal of Managerial Psychology, 15*.

LEGAL REQUIREMENTS AND TECHNICAL GUIDELINES INVOLVED IN PERFORMANCE MANAGEMENT SYSTEMS

Peter Villanova
James T. Austin
H. John Bernardin

INTRODUCTION

This article presents material on developing and defending systems for measuring performance in organizations. The concept of performance appraisal (PA) traditionally occupies a central role in human resources management (Austin & Villanova, 1992; Ferris, Rosen, & Barnum, 1995). This centrality exists for several reasons. Several stakeholder groups use information on individual job performance. Organizations use performance data to validate selection decisions and as a predictor of future performance for subsequent compensation or promotion decisions. Among those decisions are layoffs, promotions, discharge, merit pay, or some combination (Martin, Bartol, & Kehoe, 2000). Importantly, it also happens that the practice of PA is a source of controversy and litigation (Bowman, 1999).

Recent changes in the conceptualization and practice of performance appraisal have also captured a fair amount of attention and further propelled PA onto the center stage among human resources management functions (Taylor & Pierce, 1999; Bernardin, Hagan, Kane, & Villanova, 1998).

Contemporary thinking regarding the practice of performance assessment in organizations has expanded beyond the traditional confines of performance measurement to embrace a more proactive management of performance (Banks & May, 1999). Performance management is the moniker in vogue today to describe this more holistic and continuous process to maintain and foster individual performance. In addition to performance measurement practices, performance management (PM) includes a host of ancillary performance support activities such as feedback, coaching, and wider constituent participation in the design and implementation of the system. Also, whereas the traditional performance appraisal was often a discrete annual event with very little to do with day-to-day workplace concerns, PM is an ongoing process that involves employees on a continuous basis. Because performance management is more akin to a cycle of assessment and employee development, there may be more opportunities for illegal bias to intrude. Consistent with the more future-oriented perspective of PM, we also adopt a more proactive stance in this article than we have in the past. That is, we focus on the potential legal implications for practices more so than case law.

Because PM is also a somewhat unwieldy creature, possessing numerous features and requiring multiple sources of support and widespread participation, we also must cast a somewhat wider net than we have in the past. The breadth of PM is especially apparent as the recent decade has witnessed increasingly diverse PM practices such as team appraisal (Reilly & McGourty, 1998), customer appraisal (Bernardin, 1992; Villanova, 1992), and multisource (aka 360-degree) appraisal (Bracken & Timmreck, 2001; Fletcher & Baldry, 1999). As such, the potential legal risks of the practice are correspondingly broader, but so too are the opportunities to deter instances of employee disaffection with appraisals. Our purpose is to expand the discussion of potential legal implications to PM practices while providing a review of established legal precedents and guidelines for defensible PM systems. Before proceeding to a more detailed discussion of PM and recent court cases relevant to PM processes, we provide an introduction to the basic terminology necessary to understand the legal environment, case law, executive orders, and legislation relevant to adjudicating cases involving appraisal data. We also follow this section with a review of the professional and technical standards that serve as guides for effective PM system administration and that offer some modicum of protection against allegations of illegal discrimination. Finally, once we have discussed recent cases in the context of PM, we conclude with recommendations to improve the defensibility of PM systems.

THE LEGAL ENVIRONMENT OF ORGANIZATIONS

The legal environment within which contemporary organizations operate is a complex one that evolves as social pressure leads to the passage of legislation, decisions concerning the legislation are rendered by courts, executive agencies interpret and implement those laws and decisions, and managerial responses are enacted (Ledvinka & Scarpello, 1991). Although the legislation itself may seem quite straightforward, its judicial interpretation and the subsequent application of those interpretations complicates matters (Arvey & Faley, 1988; Bixby, Beck-Dudley, & Cihon, 2001; Cascio, 1998). There has been an expansion of both equal employment legislation and litigation over the past 35 years. Title VII of the 1964 Civil Rights Act (1964 CRA) prohibits employment discrimination based on race, color, sex, religion, or national origin. The Age Discrimination in Employment Act (ADEA; 1967, 1978) forbids discrimination against workers above age 40. And the Americans with Disabilities Act (ADA; 1990) protects people with mental and physical disabilities. Through recent amendments to Title VII, contained in the Civil Rights Act of 1991, Congress attempted to respond to a perceived erosion of the previous legislation brought about by Supreme Court decisions rendered in the late 1980s.

> As legislation has broadened, the focus of litigation has also expanded because multiple selection decisions are made affecting members throughout their tenure with an organization. Thus, the focus of equal employment litigation has evolved beyond organizational entry decisions to encompass selection decisions at later stages. Such expansion makes sense within a career and systems perspective on personnel and human resource management in which a decision to hire is the first in a series of personnel decisions (Cascio, 1998).

Legal Requirements: Legislation and Executive Orders

The five-member Equal Employment Opportunity Commission (EEOC) and its staff is the federal agency that oversees and enforces Title VII, the ADEA, and the ADA. Title VII and the ADA (as of July 1994) apply to all organizations that employ more than 15 employees. The ADEA applies to firms with 20 or more employees. Recent figures on the scope of work of the EEOC are provided by Martin, et al. (2000), who cite 77,000 employment discrimination claims during 1999. As of May 2001 there are over 30,000 claims awaiting resolution.

The EEOC has little statutory power to enforce legislation. Rather, it must turn to the courts for relief. When it receives complaints of discrimination, the EEOC uses a three-step procedure of investigation, conciliation, and litigation. Investigation involves gathering information about the complaint. Subsequently, the EEOC attempts to resolve complaints by conciliatory mediation between the complainant and the organization. The number of successful resolutions achieved through the EEOC mediation program increased 50 percent in fiscal year 2000 (7,438) as compared to those of fiscal year 1999. If conciliation fails, the EEOC is vested with the authority to file suit in federal district court against private sector employers on behalf of individuals (e.g., EEOC v. Sandia Corporation, 1980). Even where the EEOC declines to file suit, individuals can sue on their own after conciliation efforts have failed.

The EEOC also collects and disseminates information on equal employment opportunity through its annual EEO-1 form, which must be completed by most organizations. In addition, the EEOC sponsors outreach, education, and technical assistance programs. Nearly 3,000 such events occurred in 2000. There are also state laws on fair employment practices, but these vary by state. Such laws are also subsumed by the Constitution, which establishes federal law as paramount. Table 6-1 presents a summary of the relevant laws regulating employment discrimination.

Presidential executive orders (EOs) are a second broad means of combating discrimination. Executive orders are rules, regulations, policies, or orders issued by the President that relate to the operation of the federal government. Within that sphere, they carry the force of law. The most important order dealing with employment discrimination is EO:11246, first issued by President Johnson, and reissued by every subsequent president. It applies principally to federal contractors and subcontractors, but this is a deceptively large number of organizations, including almost all large educational institutions, manufacturers of military equipment, and organizations that sell products and/or render services to the federal government. EO:11246 prohibits employment discrimination by federal contractors. An additional component of EO:11246 is its requirement for affirmative action (AA). AA goes beyond the notion of nondiscrimination or equal employment opportunity in that it requires employers to take active steps to ensure that the underutilized women and minorities are identified and actively recruited by organizations; AA is a social force emphasizing the "righting of past wrongs" against minority groups (Ledvinka, 1995). Nonetheless, there are changes in the environment. Sackett, Schmitt, Ellingson, and Kabin (2001), for example, reviewed alternative selection methods for what they described as a post-affirmative action era. Their rationale for that description was the recent Supreme Court decisions that they assert altered the terrain of this area. The Office of Federal Contract Compliance Programs recently issued a final rule on affirmative action that reflects this new environment.

President Roosevelt issued the first nondiscrimination order in 1941; EO:8802

TABLE 6-1 Major Federal Laws Regulating Employment Discrimination		
Law	*Date*	*Relevance*
Equal Pay Act	(1963)	Prohibits sex discrimination in pay practices
Civil Rights Act	(1964)	Prohibits discriminatory employment practices against five protected groups
Age Discrimination in Employment Act	(1967)	Extends Title VII protection to workers age 40+
Equal Employment Opportunity Act	(1972)	Extends Title VII of 1964 CRA to public and private sector firms
Rehabilitation Act	(1973)	Prohibits discrimination against mental/physically handicapped individuals
Americans with Disabilities Act	(1990)	Prohibits discrimination against the disabled and promotes affirmative efforts at "reasonable accommodation"
Civil Rights Act	(1991)	Restores evidentiary burdens established in *Griggs* but also requires plaintiffs to identify specific mechanism responsible for discrimination

prohibited discrimination by defense contractors on the basis of race, creed, color, or national origin, but not sex. In 1961 President Kennedy issued EO:10925, which formed the basis for subsequent orders by President Johnson in that it was the first to use the term "affirmative action." President Johnson's EO:11246 was largely similar to EO:10925 with the notable exception that it empowered individual federal agencies to impose sanctions and penalties prior to court action (Gutman, 1993). EO:11246 also established the Office of Federal Contract Compliance Programs (OFCCP) in the Department of Labor as the relevant enforcement agency, but did not yet include gender-based discrimination. This oversight was remedied by EO:11375. Executive Order 11478 (1969) changed the first part of EO:11246 to apply to federal government employment and established the Office of Personnel Management (OPM) as the supervisory agency. In addition, EO:11478 prohibited discrimina-

tion based on age and disability. Because the different federal agencies were inconsistent in their enforcement of EO:11246, in 1978 President Carter issued EO:12086, which recognized the OFCCP as the sole authority for enforcing EO:11246.

Dispute Resolution

Individuals who consider themselves wronged in a discriminatory manner may elect to use either state or EEOC channels to obtain relief. Some individuals use both mechanisms. After exhausting the EEOC's conciliatory procedures, individuals may file suit in either the federal or the state court systems. Two higher levels in both federal and state judicial systems are the courts of appeal and the Supreme Courts. The state court system is thus modeled on the federal system. In such cases the employee is termed the plaintiff and the employer the defendant. Several important legal concepts involved in such cases include (1) burden of proof and its shifts between plaintiff and defendant during legal proceedings, (2) disparate impact and disparate treatment legal models, and (3) business necessity and job relatedness.

Burden of proof refers to the evidentiary tasks of plaintiffs (employees) and defendants (organizations). Disparate treatment and disparate (adverse) impact are the two theories used by the courts when considering Title VII cases. *Disparate treatment* is the most frequently used theory because it defines discrimination as the use of personal characteristics (e.g., sex, race), expressly prohibited by law, as a basis for treating people differently in any personnel action. *McDonnell Douglas Corporation v. Green* (1973) and *Texas Department of Community Affairs v. Burdine* (1981) are the two leading Supreme Court cases that detail what a plaintiff must prove to win a disparate treatment case (the latter served to clarify the former). Such cases develop in three stages. The first stage requires the plaintiff to establish a prima facie (i.e., possibly rebuttable) case of discrimination. This is done by proving four elements: (1) that the plaintiff is a member of a protected group; (2) that the plaintiff was qualified for, and interested in, the position; (3) that an unfavorable personnel action was taken (e.g., the plaintiff was not hired, not promoted, or was terminated); and (4) that others with similar qualifications were not treated unfavorably. Corbett (1998) provides a silver anniversary review of the *McDonnell Douglas* criteria. He argues strongly for retaining these four criteria, which if met move the case to the second stage. Here, the defendant must produce evidence of a legitimate, nondiscriminatory reason for the personnel action. Note that the defendant's burden is merely to produce evidence and not to prove that its evidence is true. The burden of proof remains, at all times, with the plaintiff. If the defendant provides a legitimate, nondiscriminatory explanation for the action, then

in the third stage of the case the plaintiff is given an opportunity to prove that the explanation is false and is merely a pretext or cover-up for discriminatory motives.

The evidentiary burden for plaintiffs in disparate treatment cases is more onerous than in disparate impact cases. For example, in disparate treatment cases, the plaintiff must establish that the defendant *intended* to discriminate on the basis of a personal characteristic proscribed by Title VII. Thus, disparate treatment refers to "motivated" or intentional discrimination; whereas disparate impact involves "unmotivated" or unintentional discrimination. The concept of intention plays a major role in the judicial system. Another major distinction between the two is that disparate impact was supposed to be applicable to "facially neutral" or objective devices only. Furthermore, the plaintiff, in establishing a prima facie case, did not have to show that the discrimination was intentional. On the other hand, disparate treatment involves the presentation of evidence that intentional discrimination was present, certainly a much heavier burden for the plaintiff.

Disparate impact involves unlawful discriminatory employment practices that unequally impact groups of individuals as a function of sex, race, age, color, religion, or national origin. Such "adverse" impact on groups of individuals is illegal if the employment practice is not job related. *Griggs v. Duke Power Co.* (1971) established the evidentiary burdens of plaintiffs and defendants in a disparate impact case. First, the plaintiff must demonstrate that a statistical disparity exists between protected class members (e.g., blacks, females) and the majority class (white males) with respect to the number of individuals hired for a job versus those who applied. This disparity usually involves a comparison of selection ratios of the two classes. Prima facie evidence for adverse impact is said to exist when the selection ratio (i.e., the number of applicants hired divided by the total number of applicants) of the protected class members is less than 80 percent that of the majority class members. Once this evidence is established, the defense receives the burden of demonstrating that the selection instrument used, say a cognitive ability test or interview, is job related or was adopted due to business necessity. If in fact the selection device is demonstrably job related, then the plaintiff has the burden of showing that less discriminatory, equally valid alternatives to achievement of the employer's goals were available.

Business necessity and job relatedness are the two permissible defenses for the use of a selection device that has adverse impact. The two terms mean different things and are often confused (Hills, 1980). *Business necessity* refers to the right of business organizations to make personnel decisions based on business conditions. For example, in *Coburn v. Pan American World Airways* (1982) there was a reduction in force mandated by economic conditions. In the eyes of the courts, such business decisions are best left to the organization, because courts are not qualified to judge whether conditions warrant the reduction. However, having decided to make reductions, it is incumbent on the organization to make fair and nondiscriminatory decisions (cf. *Nicholson v. Western Electric Co.*, 1982). *Job relatedness*, on the other hand, refers to whether a decision-making device is related to job performance. Standards for job relatedness in the case of selection tests were stated clearly by the Supreme Court in *Griggs v. Duke Power Co.* (1971) and have been since elaborated. Guion (1998) and Schmitt and Chan (1999) present current treatments of validation that balance rigor and relevance.

Basically, establishing job relatedness requires evidence that one's score on a selection test has a observable relationship with job performance. Although the statistical methods of formal validation are equally applicable to objective (e.g., intelligence tests) and subjective selection tests (interviews, performance appraisals), formal validation may not be required for a successful defense of informal standards (e.g., arrest records, credit information) (Gutman, 1993). Wingate and Thornton (2000) review statistical methods for employment discrimination (cf. Connolly & Peterson, 1997). One of the features of their treatment is an examination of statistics used in cases filed under Title VII and ADEA.

Technical and Professional Standards

In addition to legislation, three sets of professional-technical standards cover all selection devices, in principle including both objective and subjective performance appraisals. Each takes a slightly different perspective. The *Principles for the Validation and Use of Personnel Selection Procedures* (hereafter *Principles;* Society for Industrial and Organizational Psychology, 1987) are guidelines for organizations that best incorporate recent research in personnel psychology. The recently revised *Standards for Educational and Psychological Testing* (hereafter *Standards;* American Educational Research Association, American Psychological Association, & National Council on Measurement in Education, 1999), on the other hand, are relevant to the general development and evaluation of general assessment instruments for applied (educational, mental health, and organizational settings) and basic research purposes. Camara (2000) discusses the implications of these guidelines for test practices and extensions to PM. A third set of standards is the *Uniform Guidelines on Employee Selection Procedures* (hereafter *Guidelines;* Equal Employment Opportunity Commission, Department of Labor, Department of Justice, & Civil Service Commission, 1978). The *Guidelines* and *Standards* were recognized by the courts as influential in several early Supreme Court decisions (*Griggs v. Duke Power Co.*, 1971; *Albemarle Paper Co. v. Moody*, 1975).

Professionals and personnel workers depend heavily on these standards for guidance.

For performance appraisals, which comprise a primary source of data on employees after entry into an organization, criterion validation involves correlating appraisals by different raters or with independent measures of job performance (i.e., work samples). If appraisal data are used to support promotion decisions, a stronger strategy would involve correlating these performance appraisal ratings with subsequent performance at the higher-level position. Demonstrations of content-oriented scale development might consist of demonstrating linkages between behaviors rated in the appraisal device and behaviors judged to be important for task performance on the basis of job analyses. A construct validation strategy is possible and may be called for in specific instances (Austin, Villanova, Kane, & Bernardin, 1991; James, 1973). One means of implementing this strategy is to develop and evaluate models of job performance; another is to combine criterion and content validation evidence in a series of studies. In certain situations, courts have permitted the results of other studies, expert testimony, and the organization's prior successful experience with the challenged device to establish job relatedness. We do not mean to imply that organizations typically validate their performance appraisal systems; most do not. However, in the future it may be a sound practice to do so for legal defensibility. This practice would be especially valuable if the results of appraisals are used to make personnel decisions, for example, layoffs or terminations necessitated by downsizing.

The 1991 Civil Rights Act

As we mentioned earlier, the 1991 Civil Rights Act was passed largely in response to recent Supreme Court decisions that upset established precedents regarding evidentiary burdens of plaintiffs and defendants es-tablished in *Griggs* (1971). Some important provisions of the 1991 CRA follow.

First, it reinstated the evidentiary burdens first established in *Griggs* (viz. plaintiffs must first establish a prima facie case and then defendants must *persuade* the Court of the test's job relatedness or business necessity).

Second, the prima facie burden on plaintiffs was made more specific. That is, the plaintiff must disaggregate the data to identify the specific employment practice responsible for the disparate impact. In the event that the elements of the organization's decision-making process are not separable, the entire decision-making process may be treated as a single employment practice. However, determination of whether a decision-making process can be disaggregated is left to the discretion of the courts.

Third, it let stand the Court's decision to allow the use of a disparate impact strategy in instances where subjective practices are at issue. Thus, promotion decisions, often based on performance appraisal data are also amenable to statistical comparisons using the 4/5ths rule in order to establish a prima facie case.

Fourth, contrary to *Burdine*, an unlawful employment practice is established when a worker demonstrates that race, color, religion, sex, or national origin was a motivating factor for any employment practice, even when other (job-related) factors also motivated the decision.

Fifth, it provides plaintiffs in disparate treatment cases access to jury trials and offers winning plaintiffs the possibility of compensatory and punitive damage awards (adjusted for size of organization). Thus, the liability risks to employers associated with disparate treatment have been enhanced substantially. (*Congressional Quarterly*, 1991)

Also of potential significance was the tone of the Court regarding the *Guidelines* in the *Watson v. Fort Worth Bank & Trust* (1998) case. In a footnote, the *Watson* plurality noted that the 4/5ths rule, endorsed by the *Guidelines,* has been criticized on technical grounds and has proved to be only a rule of thumb for the courts. It is unclear as yet whether this commentary will ultimately be translated into benefits for plaintiffs or defendants. The plurality in *Watson* further stated that formal validation studies may not be required of defendants, particularly in the case of subjective practices; the *Watson* minority concurred on this point. According to Landy (1989), because defendants need only present a business justification as their defense, there is likely to be a decrease in the importance of the *Guidelines,* while the importance of the *Principles, Standards* and case law will likely increase. Regardless, the fact that plaintiffs are provided an opportunity to attack the employer's business justification defense with their own validation studies will likely serve to motivate employers' continued adherence to one of the primary sets of professional-technical standards.

A third reference to the *Guidelines,* specifically its requirement that employers maintain adequate records documenting the individual components of their selection systems, was made by the *Wards Cove* majority (*Wards Cove Packing Company v. Atonio,* 1989), and codified by the 1991 CRA. It is this reference that may create a substantial burden on employers (Kandel, 1989; Mitchell, 1990; Potter, 1989; Sharf, 1989). According to the *Watson* plurality, plaintiffs must disaggregate the data, especially when subjective and objective criteria are combined. Employers must therefore maintain disaggregated data on their subjective practices; this requirement may prove difficult (e.g., in the case of performance appraisal; Landy, 1989; Mitchell, 1990). However, a failure to provide plain-tiffs with such data under rules of discovery might leave employers with *no defense,* thus "forfeit[ing] any legal advantage gained through the *Wards Cove* decision" (Mitchell, 1990). Also, when disaggregation is not feasible, the courts may rule that the entire decision-making process is prone to defense (1991 CRA).

PERFORMANCE MANAGEMENT PRACTICES AND RECENT COURT CASES

In our view, performance management consists of four distinguishable components. *Performance measurement* is the foundation for an effective and fair PM system. This requires careful analysis of the job and the activities that comprise employee contributions to firm performance. *Standards setting* is a second step in PM as it requires the development and articulation of performance standards used to make judgments of performance suitability. The *appraisal process* includes a plethora of factors ranging from the rating format used to the administration of the appraisal system, including such seemingly mundane issues as scheduling of the appraisal, appraisal sources, and the role of raters and ratees in appraisal system development. Finally, the provision of performance feedback and the facilitation of performance goals are central to the *coaching and development* component of PM. We now illustrate how these are each relevant to the resolution of recent cases utilizing PM data.

Performance Measurement

Performance measurement involves identifying critical features of the job that are necessary to represent in a formal appraisal of job performance. Performance measurement systems in organizations vary on a host of features, including precisely which features of job performance will be subject to formal evaluation, the inclusion of external and internal customer criteria, and the extent to which judgment is required of appraisers. A problem arises in performance measurement because the choice of what work behaviors or work outcomes will be used to formally represent performance may be subject to a host of factors that make this a less than scientific decision (Austin & Villanova, 1992). Stakeholder coalitions may differ in what they view as valuable contributions and how different contributions may be weighted in arriving at a summary judgment. For example, appraisal systems may adjust overall performance ratings on the basis of seniority, suggesting that a powerful constituency may have exercised political influence to underscore the value of seniority to the organization. Or, more commonly, some job functions are omitted from the formal appraisal whereas others may be represented more than once so as to increase their impact on summary appraisals. Determining what samples of performance are to serve as formal criteria for basing an appraisal constitutes the initial catalyst for potential legal contests. Rater and ratee ambiguity as to what is defined as relevant job performance, or even disagreement as to what should "count" when assessing performance, can lead to disappointment, anger, and distrust with the process and the results it produces.

An arbitrator found in favor of the plaintiff when supervisors of *City of Indian Harbor Beach* (1994) supplemented performance ratings of police officers with subjective judgments of merit to determine merit pay increases. The arbitrator refused these subjective factors because they were not "reasonable, demonstrable, or objective" to substantiate their use in determining pay differentials. Similarly, the court found in favor of *Eldred* (*Eldred v. Consolidated Freightways*, 1995), a female dispatcher who was denied promotion based on her alleged lack of "aggressiveness" and for being too "soft" with drivers. Testimony in this case in-

cluded admission that the same male supervisor's "gut feeling" responsible for denying her promotion also failed to predict that the person selected for the promotion had performed the job poorly.

Numerous instances of litigation involve ambiguous and/or subjectively determined and unsubstantiated criteria applied to the assessment of employee performance (Malos, 1998). The emphasis placed on performance measurement by traditional appraisal systems is not unwarranted, but it is not sufficiently comprehensive to deter the occurrence of legal challenge.

Standards Setting

Quite simply, standards setting involves determining "how high we should set the bar." What instance of performance represents an "acceptable" or "satisfactory" level? This is a question that inevitably arises once an organization has decided what forms of contributions it decides to value. Not surprisingly, this also invites occasions of disagreement and conflict when the standards are considered ambiguous, unfair, unstable, or unevenly applied to all employees. The typical PM system utilizes relatively nonspecific benchmarks to describe levels of performance. Often the benchmarks are adjectives appearing as anchors on a rating scale that require the rater to interpret them on an individual basis (e.g., far exceeds requirements, meets requirements, sometimes fails to meet, frequently fails to meet). Obviously such "standards" are ambiguous and idiosyncratic. From the perspective of ratees, such standards may be perceived as invitations to capricious rating behavior.

A significant problem with standards in organizations is reflected in part by the levels of performance ratings employees receive (Bretz, Milkovich, & Read, 1992). Students recognize leniency in ratings as "grade inflation"—that is, being rated at a level of performance that is higher than one actually deserves. In organizations this is a real problem because leniency reduces the amount of merit money that could be allocated to recognize true excellence in performance, undermines trust in the appraisal process, and provides false diagnostic information to the organization (cf. Kane, Bernardin, Villanova, & Peyrefitte, 1995). All this makes for a troublesome scenario that serves to fuel employee suspicions about the integrity of the PM process. While some component of leniency may be due to rater dispositions (such as personality differences; Bernardin, Cooke, & Villanova, 2000), a good portion may be attributable to the discomfort raters experience should they violate the common expectations of ratees to receive good ratings (Villanova, Bernardin, Dahmus, & Sims, 1993).

Leniency may serve as a signal of underlying problems with PM, and specifically the standards-setting component. Leniency becomes a problem because it also intimates that not all employees may be held equally accountable—the standards may vary from one ratee to another such that one receives very lenient ratings and another more stringent ratings. Organizations have sought ways to deal with this problem but none have been entirely successful. The need for controlling leniency is even more pressing as of the day this article was written because organizational mergers and acquisitions, downsizing, and increased competition have driven organizations to workforce reductions as an adaptive strategy. Just recently, First Union National Bank in Charlotte and Wachovia Bank in Winston-Salem have announced their intention to merge operations under the banner of Wachovia Bank. First Union intends to acquire Wachovia at a cost to its shareholders but also at a cost to some 5,500 banking employees in the state of North Carolina. Employees will be able to apply for positions within the new, larger bank. It's common in these instances for employers to base their retention decisions on both employee seniority and job performance. The problem that confronts many of

these organizations is that the decision to retain is complicated by the fact that almost every employee receives good performance ratings.

In response, some organizations have turned to rankings as a way of making clearer distinctions between employees. These take the form of simple rankings where each employee is compared to another in a work group, or they may be a forced distribution where a limited number of employees are assigned to specific performance categories. At General Electric, supervisors are asked to identify the top 20 percent and the bottom 10 percent of their managerial and professional employees this way. High-technology companies also use this method as it has become necessary to produce savings and reduce personnel due to the softening of demand for their products during the last year. Cisco intends to use a ranking system to lay off 5,000 employees in the next few months; Hewlett-Packard has such a ranking system already in place. Even more traditional large manufacturing organizations find the use of ranking systems attractive. Ford requires that only 10 percent of the automaker's 18,000 managers get "A" grades and 5 percent are required to receive "C"s. A manager receiving a second consecutive "C" can be fired for failing to meet performance expectations (Hymowitz, 2001). These ranking approaches are problematic because they tend to pit employees against each other and, in so doing, undermine cooperation and the sharing of resources— behaviors that are particularly essential for effective team functioning. Criticisms and other expressions of employee disaffection abound in Internet chat rooms where employees complain about being unfairly rated under such systems.

Such "rank and yank" systems are not invulnerable to unfair discrimination. Age, gender, and race stereotypes are not controlled for although across-the-board leniency is. Again, the problem isn't so much elevation of ratings, but selective elevation coupled with the potential for systematic downgrading of protected class members. Microsoft is the object of one such lawsuit that claims its ranking system led to predominantly white male managers ranking blacks and women lower than they deserved relative to their peers (Abelson, 2001).

The Appraisal Process

Courts have long recognized that poorly designed and implemented appraisal systems "are a ready mechanism for discrimination against Blacks much of which can be covertly concealed and, for that matter, not really known to management" (*Rowe v. General Motors Corporation*, 1972). Rating scales comprise the largest portion of operational performance appraisal systems (cf. Guion, 1998), but due to their subjective nature these scales may permit, conceal, and even facilitate illegal discrimination.

Appraisal process issues arise once the samples of performance have been selected as criteria and these criteria have had standards applied to them. The choice of the rating scale format (if any), the sources of appraisal data (who will be the raters?), and what specific administrative and support procedures will be used to buttress the system are those that characterize appraisal process decisions. Raters don't appear to have a strong preference for specific rating formats so long as they understand how to give an employee a good or bad rating. That is, the rating format is "transparent" to the rater. Nontransparent formats such as forced-choice and mixed standard scales often encounter rater resistance, as raters are hard-pressed to account for any low ratings. Raters and ratees both appear to prefer rating scales that require ratings on different aspects of performance to those that require only a single overall rating (Hedge & Teachout, 2000).

Although there are a host of problems with the use of ratings there isn't much to be gained by relying solely on objective criteria such as productivity and errors because these measures are not available for most jobs and also suffer their own share of problems (Austin, et al., 1991). Specifically, work output is not always attributable to one individual as compared to others. Nor is it always attributable to individual as opposed to situational factors (Bernardin, et al., 1998; Dobbins, Cardy, Facteau, & Miller, 1993). Also, objective criteria may suffer from the same deficiency and contamination problems that bias subjective ratings (Landy & Farr, 1983). A deficiency problem refers to elements of an ultimate criterion that are not included in the actual criterion. For example, sales may be a good measure of sales alone but not a good measure of how well the employee works as a member of the sales team. Contamination refers to irrelevant elements that are included in the actual measure. The great sales record of the employee might be due more to the market he was assigned as it is to his own efforts to produce sales. The poorer salesperson may have sold fewer goods simply because he was assigned an impoverished market, provided poorer sales training, or was refused necessary resources needed to pursue sales. Finally, judgment is involved in even the most objective criterion measures. For example, in the classification of absences or determination of what is "scrap," subjective evaluations are used extensively. Thus, illegal bias may still occur with low-judgment measures. Such discrepancies resulting from careless use of objective criteria can pose as much of a legal problem as misuse of subjective rating criteria.

In *Thomas v. IBM*, the court found in favor of the defendant because IBM's appraisal system maintained procedural components that minimized the possibility for bias and discrimination. A written performance plan, objective criteria, a required performance narrative, and independent review of the supervisor's rating were all cited as procedural aspects that enhanced the integrity of the appraisal. In *Eldred v. Consolidated Freightways* (1995), the absence of narratives to support the supervisor's "gut feeling" that Eldred was not qualified for promotion was cited as additional information to discredit the plaintiff's appraisal process. On the other hand, not all cases involving poor procedures result in plaintiff success if sufficient evidence does not exist to suggest that the defendant's job-related reasons for an adverse decision are questionable (*Kelly v. Drexel University*, 1995).

Procedures that utilize a variety of *bias suppression* features tend to fare better in general. Bias can be suppressed by holding raters accountable for their ratings, allowing employees an opportunity to appeal the ratings, and having the ratings reviewed by the rater's supervisor. Bias suppression can also take the form of employing multiple raters whereby the bias of any one rater may be partially offset by those of other, independent raters. Assuming raters don't all share the same biases, this suppression method is more statistical than psychological in its effect. The use of multiple raters also allows the organization to systematically study the rating behavior of raters and better identify potential sources of discrimination.

In fact, the use of multiple rater systems may be mandated as a redress for discrimination by the courts (Bernardin & Cascio, 1988). The Mobile, Alabama, police department was ordered to use multiple raters for each officer to be rated. In this instance, two of the five raters were to be selected by the person being rated. However, multiple rater systems are no panacea. In a case involving the use of appraisals for promotion, a common ratings form was passed from rater to rater whereby the ratings made by the second and third raters were done with knowledge of the first rater's ratings. The three ratings of the plaintiff were identical. The court, in the context of other evidence indicating that the first rater may be biased, con-

cluded that the rating process was not an objective measure of the plaintiff's ability and that the lack of independent ratings nullified the incremental objectivity in the multiple rating process (*Loiseau v. Department of Human Resources*, 1983). Obviously, the key here is to use independent raters.

Coaching and Development

Yet another component of PM that distinguishes it from traditional appraisal is an emphasis on performance improvement and employee development. The use of appraisal data is often characterized as serving a summative or formative purpose. A summative rating purpose is one in which the performance ratings are used to make administrative decisions about employees such as merit pay, promotion, and termination. A formative use of appraisal data is focused exclusively on employee development in that they serve a diagnostic purpose to identify employee strengths and weaknesses. These two purposes are often at odds and their separation has been advocated for nearly 40 years. However, the primary purpose for most PM systems remains an administrative one where the ratings are used to make career decisions about people.

Coaching employees for improved performance cannot be done effectively without carefully developed performance criteria, precise standards, or a comprehensive appraisal process. In addition, coaching entails providing employees with timely and useful information about their performance and participating with the employee in developing strategies to remedy current performance deficiencies (Kirkpatrick, 1982). Developmental purposes of appraisal are usually better in this respect; recommendations of how to improve performance are less likely to be perceived as threatening to the ratee and so don't place the rater in the position of having to resolve potential social conflict. The use of performance data for administrative purposes shouldn't preclude frequent feedback to ratees and it does enhance the defensibility of decisions based on this information. One clear advantage of providing intermittent performance feedback is that it avoids surprising ratees who subsequently receive lower performance ratings.

The *Collins v. James River Paper Company* (1993) case illustrates the advantages that accrue to an employer when ratees are given frequent, documented feedback within a supportive coaching environment. Collins was a 56-year-old male employed as a division controller who alleged that his termination was motivated by age discrimination. However, his poor performance had been carefully documented in specific behavioral terms by three different supervisors over the course of a three-year period. There were also a number of follow-up reviews between Collins and his supervisors in addition to the formal annual appraisal meetings. In each of these instances Collin's performance was reviewed in detail and he was provided with specific objectives that he repeatedly failed to meet. The court's summary judgment in favor of the defendant concluded that there was no evidence of age discrimination. Rather, the setting of specific performance standard, ample feedback to the employee about his deteriorating performance, behavioral documentation of his failure to meet objectives, and the opportunity for the employee to avoid negative sanctions by improving performance all spoke in favor of the defendant's treatment of the employee.

RECOMMENDATIONS FOR PERFORMANCE MANAGEMENT SYSTEMS

Professional practice concerning the design and operation of PM systems evolves from several sources, including societal pressures, personnel research, and consensus among researchers and practitioners on applications of performance appraisal. Table 6-2 provides a summary of selected reviews dating back to 1980, a date selected because it closely followed the adoption of the Uniform Guidelines.

Specific prescriptive guidelines for performance appraisal systems have been provided by Burchett and DeMeuse (1985), Ashe and McRae (1985), Bernardin and Beatty (1984), Barrett and Kernan (1987), and Malos (1998). Based on previous court decisions and professional guidelines, these recommendations suggest that the successful defense of performance appraisal systems is most likely when the following features are incorporated in PM systems.

Criteria are developed from documented job analyses. In *Wade v. Mississippi Cooperative Extension Service* (1974), the court ruled that the performance appraisals used for promotion decisions were not based on the results of a job analysis and that appraisal of performance using a trait-based rating scale without reference to job analysis data was a suspect practice. On this point, there is clear consensus among members of the professional community; a formal job analysis must be conducted as a prerequisite for the development of valid performance appraisal criteria. As a result of this decision, the organization was obligated to employ qualified minorities in large numbers within a prescribed period of time.

In several other instances, practices inconsistent with professional standards were cited by the court decisions as reasons for defendant culpability. Several cases have underscored the importance of job analysis information in the choice and development of performance criteria (*Wade v. Mississippi Cooperative Extension Service*, 1974; *Albemarle Paper Co. v. Moody*, 1975; *Patterson v. American Tobacco Company*, 1978). Also, in the case of *Carpenter v. Stephen F. Austin State University* (1983), the court held that updated job analyses were required in order to ascertain whether significant changes may have occurred in the job (changes had occurred). At present the best strategy is to

TABLE 6-2	Selected Narrative and Quantitative Reviews of Performance Appraisal System Defensibility, 1980–2000		
1980	Lubben, Thompson, & Klassen	Review of legal implications of PA (start of a cottage industry!!) 1. HR managers need to reassess adequacy of existing PA systems, ensuring that they are defensible against charges of discrimination 2. Significant cases brought before the courts regarding PA systems, certain conclusions emerged as to what would constitute a defensible appraisal system 3. Strategic options: validation of challenged PA system or adoption of a subjective quota system for making a variety of decisions for any basic HR system 4. Concludes importance of making overall appraisal process as formal, standard, and objective as possible (consider subjective supervisory ratings as only one component of the overall evaluation process)	Narrative
1981	Cascio & Bernardin	Reviewed PA legal defensibility using prescriptions 1. Presented eight prescriptions for organizations 2. Summarized case law at appellate & Supreme Court level	Narrative
1981	Kleiman & Durham	Reviewed PA in promotion litigation 1. Reviewed 23 Title VII court cases 2. Topics: adverse impact determination, adjudication strategy, and evidence to justify the performance appraisal procedures	Narrative
1982	Feild & Holley	Analyzed case outcomes in terms of PA system characteristics (discriminant analysis) 1. Reviewed 66 cases/decisions in terms of 13 PA characteristics (63 in FEP series) 2. Reviewed history of quantitative case analyses (cf. Nagel & Neef, 1979): content analysis 3. Benefits in design of PA systems and litigation (plaintiffs and defendants) 4. 5/13 significant: organizational type, written instructions, PA system, JA, and ratee review 5. Concludes that organizational practices lag professional standards/guidelines	Quantitative
1985	Burchett & DeMeuse	Reviewed PA and law	
1985	Ashe & McRae	Reviewed legal issues of PA for 1980–1985 (Title VII & ADEA) 1. Fairness is critical 2. Key features: formality, subjectivity, challenge to PA, organizational level, and purpose of PA (RIF or termination)	Narrative

TABLE 6-2 (*continued*)

1986	Martin, Bartol, & Levine	Reviewed legal implications of PA using McDonnell Douglas standard 1. Sampled cases 2. Promotion actions hardest to defend. General strategies: (a) Show the employee had performance shortcomings. (b) Show that the applicant failed to acquire the necessary credentials. (c) Show that the employee performed poorly when given duties associated with a higher level job. (d) Show that the applicant had inferior qualifications to those of the employee promoted. 3. Discharges focus on capability to function in current position 4. Layoffs and merit pay briefly discussed	Narrative
1987	Barrett & Kernan	Reviewed use of PA for terminations since *Brito v. Zia* (1973) case 1. Professional views of case examined and criticized in light of professional practice and subsequent case law 2. Major issues distilled from the review of cases 3. Implications and recommendations for personnel practices presented	Narrative
1987	Koys	Reviewed across states to identify judicial philosophies and to determine which states have accepted or rejected exceptions to employment at-will 1. Frequent legal arguments against employment at-will are public policy violations, breaches of implied contracts in manuals, and torts of outrageous emotional distress 2. Need for consistency on issue is highlighted	Narrative
1990	Miller, Kaspin, & Schuster	Reviewed PA implications for ADEA cases 1. Cases consisted of 53 federal ADEA cases (PA evidence central to case) 2. Discriminant analysis suggests that the employer most likely to be successful when employee younger (particularly 40–49) 3. PA system characteristics previously found to be significantly related to outcomes not supported in these decisions 4. Study results go against research that concluded that successful defendants tended to have formal appraisal systems based on JA and characterized by behavior-oriented questions, specific written instructions, and feedback to employees 5. HR action dictates proof required to substantiate nondiscriminatory decision	Quantitative

TABLE 6-2 *(continued)*

1991	Martin & Bartol	Updated Martin, et al. (1986)	Narrative
		1. Establishing pretext for the employer's action often important for plaintiff	
		2. Successful strategies to defend failure to promote are: (a) Employee exhibited major performance shortcomings. (b) Qualifications of selected person > plaintiff. (c) Promotion sought not realistically available.	
		3. Successful defenses and legitimate business reasons for a discharge include a chronic pattern of unsatisfactory performance and deterioration of performance.	
		4. Employers generally able to support actions when PA documentation available	
1997	Werner & Bolino	Analyzed appellate court decisions in terms of accuracy, fairness, and validation	Quantitative
		1. Sample: 295 cases from 1980–1995; multivariate LOGIT analyses used	
		2. Decision outcome predicted by job analysis, written instructions, employee review of results, and rater agreement	
		3. Decision outcome NOT predicted by appraisal frequency and PA content (trait vs. behaviors or results), which had been expected	
		4. In this sample, fairness and due proces most salient, accuracy issues important, and validation virtually ignored	
1998	Malos	Reviewed PA system from legal and design perspectives	Narrative
		1. PA and employment relationship (post-organization entry, not prior); Table 1 summarizes legal principles and laws related to PA	
		2. Specific PA processes and liability (Title VII, ADEA, ADA, tort)	
		3. Substantive and procedural PA dichtomy applied to defensibility of legal employment decisions	
		4. Emerging legal issues in PA (flex job designs, security/privacy, and workplace violence)	
1998	Werner	Reviewed appellate decisions using secondary analysis (Werner & Bolino, 1997)	Quantitative
		1. Compared judicial circuits using plaintiff/defendant frequencies	
		2. Concluded that different intervals demonstrated shifts (1980–1988, 1989–1995)	
2000	Martin, Bartol, & Kehoe	Legal ramifications of PA: A growing problem	Narrative
		1. Involved in layoffs, promotions, discharge, merit pay, or a combination of actions	
		2. Emphasizes layoffs because of increasing filings (given mergers/acquisitions), uses successful and unsuccessful defenses to organize each HR decision (layoffs, etc.)	
		3. Evaluations of job performance should be based on PA systems that incorporate concerns for organizational justice and fairness	

follow the guidelines derived from previous court cases by Thompson and Thompson (1982). Nonetheless, those guidelines are dated and in need of revision and updating, perhaps using a framework similar to the one used by Sparks (1988).

Performance standards are communicated to employees in writing. This seems so obvious that one would wonder whether an organization that failed to communicate performance expectations to an employee could even remain in business. In fact, one of the world's largest organizations, General Motors, lost a case because it was found to base promotion decisions on standards not clearly communicated to employees (*Rowe v. General Motors Corporation*, 1972). And more recently, the *Collins* case illustrated how timely and detailed communication can enhance the defensibility of a PM system.

Employee performance is recognized as variable across job dimensions and thus each dimension is rated separately (although overall ratings are not forbidden). The use of a single overall rating of effectiveness (e.g., *Bigby v. City of Chicago*, 1984) or a ranking of employees on a similar global standard is not acceptable to the courts. Generally, court decisions have characterized such rating systems as "vague and inadequate" and "subject to racial bias" (*Albemarle Paper Co. v. Moody*, 1975; *Watkins v. Scott Paper Company*, 1976). In *Bigby*, raters first provided a global rating of subordinates' performance and then completed subscale ratings that were required to average to the global ratings. The courts require that separate dimension ratings be combined through some formal weighting system to arrive at a summary score (e.g., *Allen v. City of Mobile*, 1978). Note also that both raters and ratees prefer rating scales that require ratings for separate dimensions of performance (Hedge & Teachout, 2000).

Subjective ratings reflect judgments of job-related behavior and are supported by objective criteria. The courts prefer perfor-

mance appraisals that focus on job-related behavior rather than global trait descriptions. In *Brito v. Zia Co.*, (1973) the 10th Circuit Court of Appeals ruled that subjective performance appraisals were used as tests and should be evaluated using similar standards. Banks and Roberson (1985) advocated that individuals involved in the development, supervision, and administration of performance appraisals regard themselves as test developers. The concept is that a good test should be content valid, have a standardized scoring procedure, and minimize susceptibility to contaminating effects. This idea is directly generalizable to the evaluation of performance appraisal effectiveness. However, use of an advanced or carefully developed appraisal instrument does not ensure a decision favorable to the defendant. As noted by Nathan and Cascio (1986, p. 17), "It is possible that in the presence of severe adverse impact a judge would rule against an employer regardless of what type of rating scale used."

A mechanism for employee appeal is available. In *EEOC v. E.I. du Pont de Nemours & Co.* (1978), the court was favorably impressed with the appeals mechanism that allowed employees to seek redress at multiple levels of the organization. Including a formal appeals process also might convey to raters that performance appraisal is considered an important component of their supervisory role. Also, it might make raters more reluctant to deliberately manipulate ratings to satisfy their own political agenda. In a related vein, employees should have the opportunity to review and make comments, written or verbal, about their appraisal before it becomes final. While this step should be provided whether or not a formal appeals mechanism is available, it can also be the first step in any formal appeals process. Appeal and review mechanisms provide voice to those rated, enhancing fairness. Such factors were influential in Werner and Bolino (1997) quantitative analysis of appellate decisions, while validation was virtually ignored.

One appraiser is never given absolute authority in determining a personnel action. This prescription involves two aspects: (1) provision for higher management review and (2) use of multiple raters. Some higher level of management, perhaps the rater's own manager, should review all performance appraisals before they become final. Not only does this practice enable management to detect particular cases or patterns of ratings that indicate illegal bias, it also helps to assure consistency in use of formats, performance dimensions, and criteria among raters.

The use of multiple raters is becoming more popular as many firms move toward team-based management systems. Use of multiple raters reduces the influence of idiosyncratic rating policies on personnel decisions. However, to implement this prescription faithfully, an additional requirement must be invoked. Namely, raters should complete their evaluations *independently* of each other. That is, sharing ratings to arrive at a consensus is not an acceptable way of offsetting the bias of a single rater (*Loiseau v. Department of Human Resources,* 1983).

All information bearing on a personnel decision is documented in writing. The need to provide thorough documentation to support personnel decisions is of central importance to the defense of a performance appraisal system. For example, in *Marquez v. Omaha District Office of Ford Motor Company* (1971), the court ruled that the organization had not provided sufficient documentation of its reasons for removing an employee from a promotion list. Mr. Marquez maintained an excellent and promotable performance record for 15 years with the company. Mr. Marquez was never promoted and, for no apparent reason, his name was removed from the company promotion list. Similarly, in *Turner v. State Highway Commission of Missouri* (1982) and the *Collins* (1993) case, the court ruled in favor

of a defendant who was able to produce documented instances of inadequate performance. Documentation appears especially important in instances where performance appraisals are used for termination and promotion decisions (cf. Martin, Bartol, & Levine, 1986).

Without exception, courts condemn informal performance evaluation practices with minimal documentation (Ashe & McRae, 1985). In *Martinez v. El Paso County* (1983), the defendant organization asserted that a male clerical worker was fired for lack of adequate typing skills. The plaintiff alleged the company had discriminated against him on the basis of sex since a clearly superior female typist had been retained (Ashe & McRae, 1985). The organization could offer scant empirical support for the decision to terminate on the basis of poor performance. And, somewhat unbelievably, the defendant argued that the absence of documented performance appraisals could not be used as evidence suggesting discriminatory practices because all employees were evaluated in the same way.

A major change in employment discrimination litigation is the 1991 CRA requirement that plaintiffs disaggregate the defendant's overall system to show specific discriminatory impact. So that organizations may defend against lawsuits, it will be necessary to maintain records that permit fine-grained analyses of components of the selection process. As an example, suppose that an organization uses ratings of past performance and two other predictors for promotion to first-line supervisor status. If there is evidence of disparate impact, the 1991 CRA requires the plaintiff to demonstrate to a court which of the components is responsible for the disparate impact. Documentation should also serve the dual purpose of establishing a systematic formal appraisal system that is equally applied to all incumbents performing the same job and provide data regarding how the system operates. With respect to the latter, the documentation can be used as data for conducting performance appraisal system diagnostics. For example, this information may facilitate identification of rater bias due to gender or race differences between raters and ratees. Organizations that undertake such fine-tuning or tweaking demonstrate their concern with the accuracy and fairness of the system.

Supervisors are instructed and/or given training in the use of the appraisal instrument. Formal training of raters in the observation and rating of performance is acknowledged by both professionals and the courts to be a desirable characteristic of PA systems (Burchett & DeMeuse, 1985). Research indicates that providing a common frame of reference for raters helps to increase accuracy, although increasing observational skills and identifying idiosyncratic raters should receive greater attention (Bernardin, Buckley, Tyler, & Wiese, 2000). In the absence of a formal rater training program, an organization must, at the least, provide written instructions to raters for using the rating scale for evaluation of personnel. Instructions on use of the rating scale are considered a necessary prerequisite, not a guarantee, to systematic, unbiased appraisals.

CONCLUSION

PM is essential to decision makers who need performance data in order to adequately monitor organizational effectiveness and develop or implement policies in response to organizational performance. This information is particularly critical for making decisions that have become increasingly common among contemporary organizations. We have emphasized that PM systems with features that best correspond to meeting technical and professional standards are better positioned to defend themselves against allegations of illegal discrimination. However, simple adherence to professional standards does not in and of itself guarantee a favorable court decision. The key may be a distinction between the *design* and the *actual operation* of PM systems. Recall that the courts' task is to decide whether unlawful discrimination in employment practices has occurred in a specific instance, not whether the appraisal system was designed according to technical standards. It takes only one supervisor who violates the rights of an employee under Title VII to cast doubt on the entire system.

One angle to pursue in defending performance measurement systems is to adhere to codified legal requirements. Yet there is a complementary focus based on literature that discusses individual perceptions of organizational justice (Folger & Cropanzano, 1998). Two dimensions of justice perceptions within this framework are distributive and procedural (Greenberg, 1987). A question of distributive justice is said to be relevant when the issue concerns the fairness of the ends achieved. In the context of performance appraisal, distributive justice involves the levels of ratings assigned and the distribution of any outcomes that are linked to the ratings. Procedural justice issues revolve around questions pertaining to the fairness of the procedures (i.e., means) employed to attain distributive outcomes. In performance appraisal, this can include, for example, the extent to which members are allowed to participate in the development of performance criteria (Cawley, Keeping, & Levy, 1998), have an opportunity to submit self-appraisals as part of the overall evaluation (Atwater, 1998), and are entitled to submit appeals in cases where they disagree with supervisory ratings (Greenberg, 1990). The importance of these procedural components should be apparent to the reader as they mirror several of the prescriptions we outlined earlier. In addition, including these procedural characteristics is also consistent with the contemporary ethos that places a premium on employee empowerment.

Adherence to professional and technical guidelines alone cannot prevent lawsuits, because a lawsuit alleges discriminatory behavior on the part of individual supervisors or the organization. However, we hope that it is obvious that PM systems that stress objectivity and accountability will tend to be better for these concerns. Tendencies for individual raters to behave in a discriminatory manner are reduced when organizations adopt strong normative standards in favor of fair employment and back up these norms with procedures that regulate appraiser behaviors throughout the process. ∎

REFERENCES

Abelson, R. (2001, March 19). Employees sue over ranking systems. *New York Times News Service.*

Albemarle Paper Co. v. Moody, 422 U.S. 405 (1975).

Allen v. City of Mobile, 464 F. Supp. 433 (1978).

American Educational Research Association, American Psychological Association, and National Council on Measurement in Education. (1999). *Standards for educational and psychological testing.* Washington, DC: American Educational Research Association.

Arvey, R. D., & Faley, R. H. (1988). *Fairness in selecting employees* (2nd ed). Reading, MA: Addison-Wesley.

Ashe, R. L., & McRae, G. S. (1985). Performance evaluations go to court in the 1980's. *Mercer Law Review, 36,* 887–905.

Atwater, L. E. (1998). The advantages and pitfalls of self-assessment in organizations. In A. I. Karut & A. K. Korman (Eds.), *Evolving Practices in Human Resource Management* (331–369). San Francisco: Jossey-Bass.

Austin, J. T., & Villanova, P. (1992). The criterion problem 1917–1992. *Journal of Applied Psychology, 78,* 836–874.

Austin, J. T., Villanova, P., Kane, J. S., & Bernardin, H. J. (1991). Construct validation of performance measures: Definitional issues, development, and evaluation of indicators. In G. R. Ferris and K. M. Rowland (Eds.), *Research in Personnel and Human Resources Management* (Vol. 9, 159–233). Greenwich, CT: JAI Press.

Banks, C. G., & May, K. E. (1999). Performance management: The real glue in organizations. In A. I. Karut and A. K. Korman (Eds.), *Evolving Practices in Human Resource Management* (118–145). San Francisco: Jossey-Bass.

Banks, C. G., & Roberson, L. (1985). Performance appraisers as test developers. *Academy of Management Review, 10,* 128–142.

Barrett, G. V., & Kernan, M. C. (1987). Performance appraisal and terminations: A review of court decisions since *Brito v. Zia* with implications for personnel practices. *Personnel Psychology, 40,* 489–503.

Bernardin, H. J. (1992). The "analytic" framework for customer-based performance content development and appraisal. *Human Resource Management Review, 2,* 81–102.

Bernardin, H. J., & Beatty, R. W. (1984). *Performance appraisal: Assessing human behavior at work.* Boston: Kent.

Bernardin, H. J., Buckley, M. R., Tyler, C. L., & Wiese, D. S. (2000). A reconsideration of strategies in rater training. In G. R. Ferris and K. M. Rowland (Eds.), *Research in Personnel and Human Resources Management, 18,* 221–274.

Bernardin, H. J., & Cascio, W. F. (1988). Performance appraisal and the law. In R. Schuler and S. Youngblood (Eds.) *Readings in Personnel/ Human Resources,* 248–252. St. Paul: West Publishing Co.

Bernardin, H. J., Cooke, D. K., & Villanova, P. (2000). Conscientiousness and agreeableness as predictors of rating leniency. *Journal of Applied Psychology, 85,* 232–236.

Bernardin, H. J., Hagan, C. M., Kane, J. S., & Villanova, P. (1998). Effective performance management: A focus on precision, customers, and situational constraints. In J. W. Smither (Ed.),

Performance Appraisal: State of the Art in Practice (3–48). San Francisco, CA: Jossey-Bass.

Bigby v. City of Chicago, 38 FEP 844 (1984).

Bixby, M., Beck-Dudley, C., & Cihon, P. (2001). *The legal environment of business.* Upper Saddle River, NJ: Prentice Hall.

Bowman, J. S. (1999). Performance appraisal: Verisimilitude trumps veracity. *Public Personnel Management, 28,* 557–594.

Bracken, D. W., & Timmreck, C. W. (Eds.). (2001). *The handbook of multisource feedback: The comprehensive resource for designing and implementing MSF processes.* San Francisco, CA: Jossey-Bass.

Bretz, R. D., Milkovich, G. T., & Read, W. (1992). The current state of performance appraisal research and practice: Concerns, directions, and implications. *Journal of Management, 18,* 321–352.

Brito v. Zia Co., 478 F.2d 1200 (1973).

Burchett, S. R., & DeMeuse, K. P. (1985). Performance appraisal and the law. *Personnel, 62,* 29–37.

Camara, W. (2000, September). Implications of the revised testing standards for personnel testing practice. Presentation to Personnel Testing Council of Southern California.

Carpenter v. Stephen F. Austin State University, 706 F.2d 6708 (1983).

Cascio, W. F. (1998). *Applied psychology in personnel management* (5th ed). Upper Saddle River, NJ: Prentice Hall.

Cascio, W. F., & Bernardin, H. J. (1981). Implications of performance appraisal litigation for personnel decisions. *Personnel Psychology, 34,* 211–226.

Cawley, B. D., Keeping, L. M., & Levy, P. E. (1998). Participation in the performance appraisal process and employee reactions: A meta-analytic review of field investigations. *Journal of Applied Psychology, 83,* 615–633.

City of Indian Harbor Beach, 103 LA 634, 637 (1994).

Coburn v. Pan American World Airways, 32 FEP 722 (1982).

Collins v. James River Paper Company, CIV Action No. 91–30245-F, D. Mass. (1993).

Congressional Quarterly (Volume 47, 1991). *Compromise civil rights bill passed,* 251–261.

Connolly, W. B., & Peterson, D. W. (1997). *Use of statistics in equal employment litigation.* New York: Law Journal Seminars Press.

Corbett, W. R. (1998). Of babies, bathwater, and throwing out proof structures: It is not time to jettison *McDonnell Douglas. Employee Rights and Employment Policy Journal, 2,* 361–379.

Dobbins, G. H., Cardy, R. L., Facteau, J. D., & Miller, J. S. (1993). Implications of situational constraints on performance evaluation and performance management. *Human Resource Management Review, 3,* 105–128.

Eldred vs. Consolidated Freightways, 71 FEP Cases 33; D. Mass. (1995).

Equal Employment Opportunity Commission v. E.I. du Pont de Nemours & Co., 445 F. Supp. 223, (1978).

Equal Employment Opportunity Commission v. Sandia Corporation, 23 FEP 810 (1980).

Feild, H. S., & Holley, W. H. (1982). The relationship of performance appraisal system characteristics to verdicts in selected employment discrimination cases. *Academy of Management Journal, 25,* 392–405.

Ferris, G. R., Rosen, S. D., & Barnum, D. T. (1995). *Handbook of human resource management* (462–493). London, England: Blackwell.

Final Rule, Government Contractors Affirmative Action Requirements (2000, November 13). *Federal Register, 165* (219), 68022–68047.

Fletcher, C., & Baldry, C. (1999). Multi-source feedback systems: A research perspective. In C. L. Cooper and I. T. Robertson (Eds.), *International Review of Industrial and Organizational Psychology 1999* (Vol. 14, 149–193). Chichester, England: Wiley.

Folger, R., & Cropanzano, R. (1998). *Organizational justice and human resource management.* Thousand Oaks, CA: Sage.

Greenberg, J. (1987). Using diaries to promote procedural justice in performance appraisals. *Social Justice Research, 1,* 219–234.

Greenberg, J. (1990). Organizational justice: Yesterday, today, and tomorrow. *Journal of Management, 16,* 399–432.

Griggs v. Duke Power Co., 401 U.S. 424 (1971).

Guion, R. M. (1998). Assessment, measurement, and prediction for personnel decisions. Mahwah, NJ: Erlbaum.

Gutman, A. (1993). *EEO law and personnel practices.* Newbury Park, CA: Sage.

Hedge, J. W., & Teachout, M. S. (2000). Exploring the concept of acceptability as a criterion for evaluating performance measures. *Group and Organization Management, 24,* 22–44.

Hills, F. S. (1980, March). Job relatedness vs. adverse impact in personnel decision making. *Personnel Journal, 229,* 211–215.

Hymowitz, C. (May 15, 2001). Ranking systems gain popularity but have many staffers riled. *The Wall Street Journal,* B1.

James, L. R. (1973). Criterion models and construct validity for criteria. *Psychological Bulletin, 80,* 75–83.

Kandel, W. L. (1989). Current developments in employment litigation: *Atonio* and *Betts.* *Employee Relations Law Journal, 15,* 267–272.

Kane, J. S., Bernardin, H. J., Villanova, P., & Peyrefitte, J. (1995). The stability of rater leniency: Three studies. *Academy of Management Journal, 38,* 1036–1051.

Kelly v. Drexel University, 5 AD Cases 1101, E.D. Pa. (1995).

Kirkpatrick, D. L. (1982). *How to improve performance through appraisal and coaching.* New York: Amacom.

Kleiman, L.S., & Durham, R. L. (1981). Performance appraisal, promotion, and the courts. *Personnel Psychology, 34,* 103–121.

Koys, D. (1987). State Court disparity on employment at will. *Personnel Psychology, 40,* 565–578.

Landy, F. J. (1989, September). *Implications of recent Supreme Court rulings on employment practices.* Presentation to the Metropolitan New York Association for Applied Psychology, New York, NY.

Landy, F. J., & Farr, J. (1983). *Performance measurement.* New York: Academic Press.

Ledvinka, J. (1995). Government regulation of human resources. In A. Howard (Ed.), *The Changing Nature of Work* (67–86). San Francisco, CA: Jossey-Bass.

Ledvinka, J., & Scarpello, V. G. (1991). *Federal regulation of personnel and human resource management* (2nd ed). Boston: PWS-Kent.

Loiseau v. Department of Human Resources, 567 F. Supp. 1211 (1983).

Lubben, G. L., Thompson, D. E., & Klassen, C. R. (1980, May-June). Performance appraisal: The legal implications of Title VII. *Personnel,* 11–21.

Malos, S. B. (1998). Current legal issues in performance appraisal. In J.W. Smither (Ed.), *Performance Appraisal: State of the Art in Practice* (244–277). San Francisco, CA: Jossey-Bass.

Marquez v. Omaha District Office of Ford Motor Company, 440 F.2d 1157 (1971).

Martin, D. C., & Bartol, K. M. (1991). The legal ramifications of performance appraisal: An update. *Employee Relations Law Journal, 17,* 257–286.

Martin, D. C., Bartol, K. M., & Kehoe, P. E. (2000). The legal ramifications of performance appraisal: The growing significance. *Public Personnel Management, 29,* 379–406.

Martin, D. C., Bartol, K. M., & Levine, M. J. (1986). The legal ramifications of performance appraisal. *Employee Relations Law Journal, 12,* 370–396.

Martinez v. El Paso County, 710 F.2d 1102 (1983).

McDonnell Douglas Corporation v. Green, 411 U.S. 792 (1973).

Miller, C. S., Kaspin, J. A., & Schuster, M. H. (1990). The impact of performance appraisal methods on Age Discrimination in Employment Act cases. *Personnel Psychology, 43,* 555–578.

Mitchell, T. W. (1990). In the wake of *Wards Cove.* *MetroNews, 2,* 2–4.

Nathan, B. R., & Cascio, W. F. (1986). Introduction: Technical & legal standards. In R. A. Berk (Ed.), *Performance Assessment: Methods & Applications* (1–50). Baltimore: Johns Hopkins Press.

Nicholson v. Western Electric Co., 555 F. Supp. 3 (1982).

Patterson v. American Tobacco Company, 586 F.2d 300 (1978).

Potter, E. E. (1989). Supreme Court's *Wards Cove Packing* decision redefines the adverse impact theory under Title VII. *The Industrial-Organizational Psychologist, 27,* 25–31.

Reilly, R. R., & McGourty, J. (1998). Performance appraisal in team settings. In J.W. Smither (Ed.), *Performance Appraisal: State of the Art in Practice* (244–277). San Francisco, CA: Jossey-Bass.

Rowe v. General Motors Corporation, 457 F.2d 348 (1972).

Sackett, P. R., Schmitt, N., Ellingson, J., & Kabin, M. B. (2001). High-stakes testing in employment, credentialing, and higher education: Prospects in a post-affirmative action world. *American Psychologist, 56,* 302–318.

Schmitt, N., & Chan, D. (1999). Personnel selection: A theoretical approach. Thousand Oaks, CA: Sage.

Sharf, J. C. (1989, October). Practical solutions to real problems in the use of assessment. Paper presented at the National Assessment Conference, Minneapolis, MN.

Society for Industrial and Organizational Psychology. (1987). *Principles for the validation and use of personnel selection procedures* (3rd ed.). College Park, MD: University of Maryland Press.

Sparks, C. P. (1988). Legal basis for job analysis. In S. Gael (Ed.), *The Job Analysis Handbook for Business, Industry, and Government* (37–47). New York: Wiley.

Taylor, P. J., & Pierce, J. L. (1999). Effects of introducing a performance management system on employees' subsequent attitudes and effort. *Public Personnel Management, 28,* 423–452.

Texas Department of Community Affairs v. Burdine, 450 U.S. 248 (1981).

Thomas vs IBM, 48 F. 3d 478, 484 (10th Cir. 1995).

Thompson, D. E., & Thompson, T. A. (1982). Court standards for job analysis in test validation. *Personnel Psychology, 35,* 865–874.

Turner v. State Highway Commission of Missouri, 31 EPD 33, 352 (1982).

Uniform Guidelines on Employee Selection Procedures. (1978). *Federal Register, 43,* 38290–38315.

Villanova, P. (1992). A customer-based model for developing job performance criteria. *Human Resource Management Review, 2,* 103–114.

Villanova, P., Bernardin, H. J., Dahmus, S. A., & Sims, R. (1993). Rater leniency and performance appraisal discomfort. *Educational and Psychological Measurement, 53,* 789–799.

Wade v. Mississippi Cooperative Extension Service, 372 F. Supp. 126 (1974).

Wards Cove Packing Company v. Atonio, 109 S.Ct. 2115 (1989).

Watkins v. Scott Paper Company, 503 F.2d 159 (1976).

Watson v. Fort Worth Bank & Trust, 108 S.Ct. 2777 (1988).

Werner, J. M. (1998). Employment discrimination cases in U.S. Courts of Appeals: A brief commentary on Mollica. *Employee Rights and Employment Policy Journal, 2,* 255–265.

Werner, J. M., & Bolino, M. C. (1997). Explaining U.S. courts of appeals decisions involving performance appraisal: Accuracy, fairness, and validation. *Personnel Psychology, 50,* 1–24.

Wingate, P. H., & Thornton, G. C., III (2000). Statistics and employment discrimination law: An interdisciplinary review. *Research in Personnel and Human Resources Management, 19,* 295–337.

A TRINITY OF PRESCRIPTIONS FOR PERFORMANCE MANAGEMENT SYSTEMS

H. John Bernardin
Peter Villanova

INTRODUCTION

That great American philosopher Woody Allen captured the way many people feel about performance appraisal. In his Notes to Graduates, Allen (1980) proclaims that: "More than any other time in our history, mankind faces a crossroads. One path leads to utter despair and hopelessness. The other to total extinction. Let us pray that we have the wisdom to choose correctly."

This is how a lot of people feel about performance appraisal. Those who do appraisals, are appraised, or administer over performance management systems are generally not happy with this most problematic of HR functions. One Digital Equipment manager may have summed it up best when he said "I'd rather kick bricks with my bare feet than do performance appraisals."

Many surveys underscore the pessimism and dissatisfaction with performance management and appraisal. The Conference Board recently found that 90 percent of HR administrators felt that their performance appraisal systems needed reform (Grensing-Pophal, 2001).

It would not be a stretch for us to proclaim that the majority of individuals who participate in the performance management process believe that the process is a resounding failure. The Society of Human Resource Management concluded that over 90 percent of performance appraisal systems are unsuccessful, and a 1993 survey by Development Dimensions Incorporated found that most employers expressed "overwhelming" dissatisfaction with their performance management (PM) systems (Smith, Hornsby, & Shirmeyer, 1996).

Perhaps as a result of all this dissatisfaction, some practitioners argue that formal performance appraisal is not an effective tool for any purpose and particularly not if the primary objective is performance improvement. At least one survey reports an increase in the use of nontraditional appraisal approaches, such as appraisal-by-exception-only, or nonstandardized, narrative reviews (Smith, et al., 1996). For example, SAS, a software firm headquartered in North Carolina, eliminated formal performance appraisal in 1997 and reports that their new informal system has worked very well.

Among the theories presented to explain the disappointing results with appraisal is that the systems are too complicated. Grensing-Pophal (2001) argues that "giving an employee bad news during a performance review is tough enough. So why make the job any tougher by saddling managers with complicated appraisal systems?" Indeed, managers tend to resist appraisal systems they view as too time-consuming (they almost never really view them as too "complicated"). Other writers on the subject indict the disconnect between what is evaluated in performance appraisals and the real and critical "vital signs" of the organization. For example, Arthur Anderson principal Steven Hronec (1993) argues persuasively that "most companies just don't measure the right things the right way" (p.4).

The negative sentiment has become so great that consultants have engineered a name change in the hopes of generating more support for their intervention. The term "performance management" (PM) is the contemporary term that recognizes the many features of a performance appraisal system. PM refers to performance measurement, performance standards, performance appraisal, and performance coaching and development. We will use the term PM throughout this text because we strongly support the notion that appraisal is but one aspect of an effective system no matter what the purpose is for this critical HR function.

We have a more optimistic perspective on PM and propose that when certain features of a system are adopted, PM has the potential to significantly improve organizational effectiveness and is more likely to accomplish any of the objectives of the system. Our view is that few organizations adhere to these features and that the absence of these PM features is responsible for the dissatisfaction echoed by the survey respondents described. We are reminded of Richard Wagner's humble words after completing his incomparable opera "The Ring of the Nibelung." Wagner said: "There are those of us, artists and strong men in other ways, who for our own ease, so that we may do that which we have to do with conviction and strength, must be unwaveringly supported, never questioned, set above all other persons, given everything. All is clear if one understands this." With regard to what is to follow, think of us in that light. We propose that the effects of PM systems will be more positive if and when certain prescriptions are followed, which practitioners have generally not heeded.

We provide three major prescriptions in this chapter. These are (1) Define performance as precisely as you can for individuals and work units in the context of the organization's mission; (2) Use internal and external customers to derive performance definitions and measure performance; and (3) Incorporate the measurement of con-

straints of performance into the formal PM system. We will offer a number of additional recommendations under each of these prescriptions that should improve the effectiveness of any organization's PM system.

A growing body of research supports these prescriptions. Also, our prescriptions are compatible with the findings regarding the legal implications of performance appraisal discussed in the previous article in this book. Table 6-3 presents a summary of our prescriptions and underlying recommendations. We believe they are just what the doctor ordered in terms of increasing the satisfaction with and, more importantly, the effectiveness of PM systems.

PRESCRIPTION 1: DEFINE PERFORMANCE AS PRECISELY AS YOU CAN FOR INDIVIDUALS AND WORK UNITS IN THE CONTEXT OF THE ORGANIZATION'S MISSION

Marlon Brando once predicted, "I'm going to be as big as Orson Wells." Has he achieved his goal? We believe that precision in both defining and in measuring performance is critical to effective performance management. Surprisingly, and this is where that notion of keeping it simple confuses things, most organizations do an awful job of defining actual performance and few make much of an attempt to tie these definitions into mission statements for the organization or the unit. Hronec (1993) tells the story of his visit to a CEO's office and the prominent display of the company's mission all over the premises. The mission stated that "This organization provides products and services which consistently meet or exceed standards set by our customers, on time and at the lowest cost" (Hronec, 1993, p. 4). But when Hronec investigated whether the CEO was collecting data to assess the extent to which this mission was accomplished, he found little evidence that such assessments were being collected. Hronec convinced the CEO

TABLE 6-3 Prescriptions

PRESCRIPTION #1. Define performance as precisely as you can for individuals and work units in the context of the organization's mission. Distinguish between the measurement of performance and the causes of performance. Measure the performance first, then diagnose the causes. **Put Specific Criteria in Goals, Objectives, and Standards.**

PRESCRIPTION #2. Use internal and external customers to derive performance definitions and measure performance. The major qualification for including a particular rating source to provide both performance definitions and performance measurement is whether that source is the recipient of important products or services from the person to be appraised and whether this information is unique enough to be collected. **Customers should provide the specific definitions of the performance outcome.**

PRESCRIPTION #3. Incorporate the measurement of constraints of performance into the formal PM system. A spreadsheet matrix should be prepared with the rows made up of the performance dimensions and the columns listing all potential constraints on performance. The appraisal meeting should focus on the discrepant cells as well as those where there is agreement on a constraint.

that if "goals such as cost, quality, and time are important enough to be in the mission statement of an organization, then there ought to be a way of determining whether these goals are being achieved." (1993, p. 3,4). We couldn't agree more. This seems so simple yet most organizations make little attempt to measure the extent to which they have accomplished the goals of their mission statement. Effective performance measurement should include the identification of the critical features of the job that relate to organizational success.

Yet performance measurement is often a more complicated process in actual practice because the choices of what aspects of performance are to serve as formal criteria for administrative purposes is often one of contention between different constituencies (see the article by Villanova, Austin, & Bernardin in this chapter). The decision as to what samples of performance are selected to serve as criteria is a product determined by their availability, measurement cost, and user acceptance. Uncontaminated outcome measures of performance may not be available, though we argue that often not enough effort is devoted to developing appropriate outcomes. Sometimes different

measures of performance may pose significant costs. Small firms may wish to obtain precise outcome data on a variety of performance outcomes but the technology to monitor and interpret the data may be beyond their financial capabilities. Finally, performance outcome measures do not go unchallenged as perfect measures. Users may balk at the use of certain measures because they may be deficient, contaminated, or because they personally do not excel on that specific measure.

Distinguish Between the Measurement of Performance and the Causes of Performance

One of the problems with the measurement of performance is clearly distinguishing between the causes or correlates of performance and actual performance. For example, among the "elements of a good appraisal," according to a staff writer for *HR Magazine* (Joinson, 2001), is a "list of specific competencies or skills being measured." (p. 39). We define performance as the record of *outcomes* produced on a *specified job function* or activity during a *specified time period* (Bernardin & Beatty, 1984). Within this definition, performance on a job as a whole would be equal to the sum (or average) of performance on critical or essential job functions. Unfortunately, many so-called performance appraisal programs still focus on a person's skills, traits, or competencies, rather than on a person's performance.

Many writers on the subject seem to confuse the measurement of actual performance with the measurement of these causes and correlates of performance. For example, the American Management Association includes self-confidence, positive regard, self-control, spontaneity, stamina, and adaptability of critical managerial performance competencies (Parry, 1996). While AMA may now call these competencies, they used to be called traits. Almost all appraisal scholars have condemned the use of traits as a basis for performance appraisal. They correctly point out the legal and psychometric problems related to their use. Our criticism is more basic: The measurement of competencies, traits, skills, abilities, and knowledge may be important measurements, they're just not measures of performance.

The extent to which performers possess such traits or competencies may be useful information in a program of performance diagnosis. But their measurement is not synonymous with the measurement of performance. PM should first focus on *the record of* outcomes that the person (or persons) actually achieved on the job. The recent trend toward competency assessment seems to have further clouded this distinction. Competency assessment involves identifying abilities and skills relevant to multiple jobs. The idea is that these traits may contribute to performance at different levels of the organization, from entry-level positions to senior management. The idea is appealing and increasingly popular among organizations because it appears to simplify complex processes such as selection, performance appraisal, and training by explaining success as being attributable to some core set of competencies (Shippmann, et al., 2000). Also, competency assessment seems more consistent with the increasingly popular "academy culture" in organizations that fosters learning and continuous improvement to leverage human resources as a competitive advantage. Yet the word "competency" has no universally accepted definition beyond that used by the person with whom one is speaking (Zemke, 1982).

Put simply, our advice is measure the performance first, then diagnose the causes. We can measure LA Laker Shaquille O'Neal's fine motor skills, the size of his hands, his height, and his work ethic. But his foul shooting performance is 42 percent and that is one element of his performance that directly impacts on the team's ability to implement a winning strategy. Detroit Lions running back John Henry Johnson was once reputed to have said "I'm not going to bust my ass for no extra two or three yards." This quote may indicate a motivational problem with John Henry. But John Henry's rushing performance was 4.6 yards per carry and that may explain why the Lions really didn't come down too hard on John Henry for his self-assessment of "motivational" problems.

In the workplace, we need something analogous to that foul shooting percentage or rushing average before we start theorizing about the underlying causes of the performance. One of the myths regarding PM is that analogous performance measures are rare in the real world; measures such as Shaq's foul shooting percentage or Tiger Woods' per-round average are not available for most jobs. In fact, Bernardin, Hagan, and Hennessey (2001) found that important outcome measures such as these are available for most public-sector jobs.

Using our definition of performance and using customers to derive the criteria and assess the outcomes, we believe the work world can be more like the sports world and yield clear measures of work performance. Once we get the performance level established, we can start to theorize about the causes of the performance level. One example of a study that supports the importance of precision in measurement showed that companies which used more precise definitions of performance linked to corporate objectives had higher profits, higher stock value, and significantly greater gains in financial performance (McDonald & Smith, 1995). A case study from Merck, the pharmaceutical giant, also found increased return on assets after the company had installed a PM system with precise measures of performance tied to the mission statement (Murphy, 1993). A recent study found greater specificity in individual performance standards and the extent of their connection to unit objectives was related to the likelihood of exceeding those objectives (Bernardin, Hagan, & Hennessey, 2001).

Behaviors versus Outcomes

Our view is that outcomes must be the critical component of a PM system, that the definitions of "outcomes" should be derived from critical internal and external *customers* (discussed later in this section), and that outcomes can be defined and measured for virtually any job.

Bernardin (1992) borrowed a quote from a Digital Equipment Corporation manager: "If the behaviors don't produce a result which is useful to the boss, the behaviors don't count." While we strongly disagree with the focus on "the boss" instead of "the customer," we agree that the basic sentiment is a realistic and appropriate one for the measurement of performance.

Among the companies that embrace this conceptualization of performance "outcomes," which are then combined with hard, countable results related to business objectives, are Ritz-Carlton Hotels, Pizza Hut, Burger King, Jaguar Cars, Office Depot, Monsanto, and Blockbuster Video. These organizations combine customer satisfaction data with countable results to derive a composite performance score for individuals, work units, stores, districts, and even regions (Bernardin, 1992).

When outcomes are not available or the use of technology and statistical corrections becomes prohibitive because of financial or user acceptance costs, behaviors may serve as substitutes when they are clearly responsible for producing desired results. There may also be instances when behaviors are necessary to measure because the "form" of service delivery may have significant consequences in themselves beyond meeting outcome objectives. Soliciting clients or closing a sale in conformance with company policy may be a behavior organizations value as much as the number of sales or total sales revenue. Behaviors can (and should) be a part of any definition of performance as long as a consequence or outcome can be theoretically linked to the behavior, be measured, and be important to a customer.

Put Specific Criteria in Goals, Objectives, and Standards

Once an organization clearly identifies what it means by "performance" in terms of functions and outcomes, it must approach its measurement with similar concerns about specificity. This is what we mean by the standards-setting component of PM. Surveys indicate that the majority of companies use some form of standards-based or management-by-objectives PM systems (e.g., Bretz, Milkovich, & Read, 1992). Yet even when an organization identifies and defines an objective or standard, Bernardin, Hagan, and Hennessey (2001) found that fewer than 25 percent of performance standards written for managers had a moderate (or greater) level of specificity in the definition of the outcome that defined performance. As a result, raters and ratees often disagreed over exactly what constituted a level of performance or whether a standard had been met (or exceeded).

This disagreement between the rater and the ratee often leads to the failure of the PM system, no matter what its purpose. Research shows that the greater the specificity in the definition of performance standards, goals, objectives, or any criteria, the more likely that the purposes for the measurement process are accomplished (Bernardin, et al., 1998; Schrader & Steiner, 1996).

Performance standards have been defined as levels of performance that correspond to predesignated levels of effectiveness (Bernardin & Beatty, 1984). As such, they convey critical information that affects all appraisal participants. From a rater's point of view, standards form the frame of reference within which to judge a ratee's performance. Depending on the nature of the standards, this comparison can range from a simple matching process involving a determination of whether someone did or did not meet the objective to a more complex integration process in which a rater assigns values to each performance element, then combines them to arrive at an overall evaluation (Murphy & Cleveland, 1991). Whatever the method, the values assigned should be linked to meeting or exceeding customer requirements and meeting business objectives.

From a ratee's point of view, performance standards are an important communication mechanism through which employees decipher what is expected of them (Bobko & Colella, 1994). From an organization's point of view, performance standards are a key factor in creating a job-content foundation for an appraisal process. As such, standards can be a key linking pin that aligns employee efforts with organizational strategies, goals, and objectives. Our review of both PM literature and real-world practices indicates that there is little operational distinction among the terms "performance benchmarks," "standards," "goals," or "objectives." In fact, considering the position they occupy within PM systems, we

believe that these terms are essentially interchangeable (Bernardin, Hagan, Kane, & Villanova, 1998). What is not interchangeable is the content of the standards across different jobs and even across different organizations where employees may perform the same functions but where the organizations subscribe to different cultural imperatives that influence both the form and level of standards.

Thus it is no surprise that discussions about appraisal include the assertion that clear, specific performance standards, rather than ambiguous standards or no standards, will improve the overall accuracy or effectiveness of an appraisal process. Aside from the direct potential performance enhancement effects that clear and specific standards provide, they also serve an important "bias-suppression" effect that may not only reduce instances of employee grievance but also promote perceptions of fairness with the PM system (Greenberg, 1986).

Several management theories have been built on the core assumption that clear, unambiguous expectations or standards are an important element of effectiveness. Bobko and Colella (1994) provide an extensive review of this literature. From goal-setting research, they cite evidence to support the following contentions: (a) that performance standards directly influence an individual's self-set goals, (b) that an individual's personal goals regulate actions, and (c) that those aspiring to achieve difficult, specific goals perform better than those who work towards easy, vague, or no goals. Similarly, feedback theory research suggests that specific information concerning one's performance positively influences future effectiveness (Tubbs, 1986).

To summarize, precision in the definition of performance and in setting performance standards is critical in creating and sustaining an effective PM system. The research relevant to this proposition from a variety of research trails is compelling. As a foundation for rater assessments, standards, goals, or objectives focus rater attention on already established performance criteria and limit the opportunity for extraneous, irrelevant factors to contaminate raters' judgments.

PRESCRIPTION 2: USE INTERNAL AND EXTERNAL CUSTOMERS TO DERIVE PERFORMANCE DEFINITIONS AND MEASURE PERFORMANCE

Regardless of the purpose for the PM system, a growing number of writers advocate the incorporation of a multisource or 360-degree rating system (Bracken, Timmreck, & Church, 2001). Unlike traditional "top-down" appraisal where the supervisor provides the formal appraisal, multisource appraisal ideally involves at least a sample of external customers, peers, subordinates, and supervisors. This is a very popular approach to appraisal for managers.

There are three major reasons to incorporate multisource appraisal into a PM system: (1) There is a clear legal signal that when more than one rater participates in an appraisal, the resultant personnel decision is more defensible in court and less likely to be challenged through any judicial process (Bernardin & Tyler, 2001); (2) There is growing evidence that the rating a person receives is to a significant extent a consequence of the particular rater and his or her attitudes, dispositions, and characteristics (Bernardin, Cooke, & Villanova, 2000; Kane, Bernardin, Villanova, & Peyrifitte, 1995; Kozlowski, Chao, & Morrison, 1998; Villanova, Bernardin, Dahmas, & Sims, 1993). The use of more than one rater will at least dilute and randomize the effects of individual rater proclivities. Multisource appraisal is a more valid and comprehensive picture of a performance; and (3) Multisource appraisal has greater potential to actually change behavior and improve performance.

Performers tend to perceive multisource appraisal as less biased, fairer, less political, and more accurate. They are more likely to change their behavior after consistent multisource feedback than feedback from a single source (Bracken, Timmreck, Fleenor, & Summers, 2001). Supervisors also welcome multisource appraisal, as they no longer occupy the singular role and responsibility of rating employees. In a sense, multisource appraisal deflects some of the potential conflict that may ensue over poor ratings to other agents involved in the process so that the supervisor is not the focal cause of disappointing ratee expectations.

So who should participate in this multisource process? There are certainly a number of options (self, subordinates, peers, superiors, clients, customers). We prefer to look at "multisource" as multi-customer, including both internal and external customers. Internal customers may be fellow members of a work team, production system, department, or could even be employees in different departments that somehow make use of products or employ the services of fellow employees (Bernardin, 1992). External customers include end users of the product or service but may also include some broader conceptualization of "customer" to include the specific industry or societal members. For example, the recall of Firestone tires not only impacted the individuals who directly purchased the tires but also the auto industry, Firestone's reputation, and other tire manufacturers, as well as its relationship with Ford Motor Company.

The major qualification for including a particular rating source to provide both performance definitions and performance measurement is whether that source is the recipient of important products or services from the person to be appraised and whether this information is unique enough to be collected. If the answer to this question is "yes," and it is practically feasible, an effort should be made to first use that source to derive precise performance definitions and then later to gather appraisal data on how the performer's products or services compared to the definitions. As we discussed under Prescription 1, these definitions can be called standards, goals, objectives, expectations, or requirements. Whatever they are called, they should come from the major customers who are the recipients of the performers' work outcomes.

Customers Should Provide the Specific Definitions of the Performance Outcome

How do these customers participate in the derivation of precise performance definitions? For example, the "quality" of an outcome is almost always considered a vital aspect of value for assessing performance on any major functional area. But customers should define quality. Consider the case of a new law firm associate who must draft a brief for a partner who will then work on the brief before it is submitted to a client's legal team. The brief written by the associate is one outcome, the quality of which should be assessed by the partner, the critical internal customer. The partner may define quality as the "brief was submitted in such perfect condition that I had to make absolutely no changes to the draft before submitting it to the client." Of course, the external customer should have the final say in assessing the quality of the brief and will undoubtedly assess the cost of the brief as well. (We will return to conflicts between "customers" later.)

Are subordinates ever recipients of a manager's or supervisor's products or services? Absolutely. Managers and supervisors are supposed to be facilitating the accomplishment of unit or individual goals. Subordinates can assess the extent to which supervisors have provided that facilitation. In academic settings, for example, department chairs are often responsible for help-

ing department faculty to conduct research and teach. Department chairs can and should be formally evaluated by the faculty on the extent to which this facilitation has been accomplished. Faculty are sometimes in the best position to judge how well the chair is doing certain parts of the job. The same argument applies to the assessment of K-12 principals, and retail managers and assistant managers. A growing percentage of organizations now use formal upward appraisal systems as one source of information about managerial behavior (Atwater, Roush, & Fischthal, 1995; London & Smither, 1995). Table 6-4 presents a summary of the steps involved for deriving definitions of outcomes from the customer perspective (adapted from Bernardin, 1992, and Villanova, 1992).

Although the importance of external customer data has been advocated as a part of multisource PM systems, external customers are not usually a part of the formal systems. Edwards and Ewen (1996) indicate that customer feedback provides valuable information to an organization as an input to the production process, as a presence in the quality control area, as an opportunity to increase understanding about what customers value, and as information on which to base future product or service development.

Some organizations make direct links between customer satisfaction data and internal customer appraisals. The Ritz-Carlton has followed this model, not only linking specific items on their customer satisfaction instrument with the factors defining their PM system for internal customers, but also using a performance weighting system based on the predictive value of each item for overall customer satisfaction. The PM data are then linked to bonus points in the compensation system. Interim Temporary Employment Services links responses from their annual Customer Satisfaction Measurement Program to specific performance standards for Interim managers assigned to

TABLE 6-4 Steps in the Development of Customer-Based Outcome Measures

1. In the context of business unit performance data, benchmark data, customer-based research, and unit-level objectives, identify the products or services necessary to achieve the goals related to the requirements of the external customers. This can be achieved through customer surveys, focus-group discussions, and other user responses to product/service features.

2. Collect data on internal customer requirements and determine relationships with external customer requirements from Step 1. Develop priority list/importance weights for internal job functions based on importance for meeting external customer requirements. Data collection will yield customer-based PM criteria.

3. Consult with work unit on the products required based on unit level goals from Steps 1 and 2. The product specifications should be derived from customer-based research, i.e., customers determine the job specifications in terms of quantity, timeliness, and especially quality.

4. Supervisors and subordinates consider potential constraints on attainment of required outcomes. Management attends to constraints that can be eliminated and analyzes organizational structure/job design characteristics in the context of customer demands (See Bernardin, 1989).

particular industrial segments. Their managerial pay-for-performance system is then tied to an assessment of performance relative to these standards. Harley-Davidson developed a customer satisfaction instrument for retailers selling its product and then linked the satisfaction data with managerial process improvement assessments.

Many companies now tie PM criteria to the results of evaluations from so-called professional "customers" or "mystery shoppers." This approach is very popular in the retail, fast-food, and banking industries. Typically, this process involves contracting with an organization to provide "anonymous" individuals who periodically shop the store, evaluating and reporting about the experience from a customer's viewpoint. Mystery shoppers usually review a predetermined menu of variables for each store they shop, based on criteria established by the organization. At the Limited and the GAP, for example, mystery shoppers follow a script in order to test the extent to which store employees adhere to their training regarding customer interactions. At Burger King, shoppers purchase particular foods, use the restroom, and may make a complaint. Store

employees get a grade on the visit and can earn valuable prizes for their efforts.

The use of mystery shopping has become so popular that, in 1994, one contractor reported a professional shopping staff of 8,800 and a business that was growing at the rate of 50 percent per year (Helliker, 1994). Other organizations, including Neiman Marcus, Hyatt Hotels, Hertz Auto Rentals, Barney's New York, and Revco Drug Stores have had extensive experience using mystery shoppers to obtain customer-based information.

One corporate example of linking managerial PM criteria to mystery shopper data is Office Depot. Their mystery shopping data is converted into a Customer Satisfaction Index (CSI) that includes customer complaints. The CSI is then compiled and reported to each store manager once a month. The data, aggregated across the year, becomes a key determinant of each manager's annual appraisal, bonus, base salary increase, and objectives for the next appraisal cycle.

Hauser, Simester, and Wernerfelt (1996) suggest that an internal customer focus is a logical next step once an organization implements an external customer feedback process. There are three advantages to this approach. First, an internal customer focus may better align internal supplier objectives with firm objectives, because they sometimes conflict. Second, especially when technical skills are involved, the internal customer may be in the best position to accurately appraise the effectiveness of specific outcomes and also to better report on what specific functions contribute to the satisfaction of external satisfaction criteria (Villanova, 1992). Third, internal customer appraisal may drive a consistent, customer-focused cultural norm throughout the entire organization. This is important if the focus on customers becomes blurred the deeper into the organization one ventures.

The Metropolitan Life Insurance Company of New York determined that only 25 percent of its employees were engaged in directly servicing customers while the remaining 75 percent provided support functions related to servicing customer needs (Zeithaml, Parasuraman, & Berry, 1990). The use of internal customer appraisal in this type of situation may drive a customer-driven culture deeper into the firm (Hauser, et al., 1996) and buttress the view that an organization is a collection of upstream-downstream, value adding, customer-focused activities.

Our emphasis on developing a PM system that includes an internal customer focus is consistent with Deming's first prescription for successful performance appraisal: Organizations must clearly and consistently communicate the firm's mission or constancy of purpose (Deming, 1986). What better way to do this than through institutionalizing the customer perspective inside the organization?

Internal customers are also invaluable for the appraisal of *contextual performance* (Borman & Motowidlo, 1993). *Contextual performance* includes work behaviors that have "added value to the firm" above and beyond the technical core of performance. These may include being compliant with or-ganizational policies, spontaneously offering suggestions for improving work processes, taking the initiative to repair broken machinery, maintaining good coworker relationships, assisting coworkers, and providing mentoring for younger workers.

These types of behaviors are also referred to as organizational citizenship behaviors (Findley, Giles, & Mossholder, 2000). Accordingly, a good organizational citizen is an employee who contributes beyond the formal role expectations of a job as might be detailed in a job description. Such employees are positively disposed to take on alternative job assignments, respond cheerfully to requests for assistance from others, are interpersonally tactful, arrive to work on time, and may often stay later than required to complete a task. These are contributions to organizational success that may not be formally recognized by the PM system (i.e., do not serve as criteria for decision making) but that have been repeatedly shown to influence supervisors' ratings of subordinate performance just the same (Borman, White, & Dorsey, 1995).

The need to formally recognize contextual contributions to overall performance arises for three reasons:

1. Contextual performance operates to either support or inhibit technical production and can facilitate its translation into individual-, group-, and system-level outcomes;

2. Omission of legitimate components of the contextual performance domain places the rater in a compromised position; and,

3. Significant contributions to individual, group, and system performance may go unrecognized and unrewarded, making them less frequent over time but no less essential.

Although contextual performance may contribute in its own right to individual effectiveness by enhancing an individual's leadership position or by developing additional skills that improve efficiency, the value of contextual performance is more often in the way of supporting the organizational, social, and psychological environment that surrounds the technical core of production behavior.

One important implication of contextual performance is that it serves a system maintenance function (Dobbins, Cardy, Facteau, & Miller, 1993; Murphy & Cleveland, 1991). Just as situational leadership theories posit that a leader's directive and task-centered behaviors function best when leader-member relations are positive and the position power of the leader is strong (Hersey & Blanchard, 1988), contextual performance facilitates the translation of productive effort into productive results. In this way, contextual performance can be construed as a resource variable much like those described by Peters and O'Connor (1980) in the framework of situational constraints. In the absence of a supportive work context, it may be that much more difficult to translate productive behavior into results or to even engage in productive behaviors. In such a case, the absence of contextual performance may actually serve as a situational constraint that inhibits the translation of work-directed effort into performance outcomes (Dobbins, et al., 1993; Peters & O'Connor, 1980) or may even discourage an individual to expend productive effort in the first place by eroding self-efficacy perceptions and lowering aspiration level (cf. Villanova, 1996).

The failure to recognize contextual performance in a PM system will result in the inevitable criterion contamination that characterizes supervisory ratings of work performance. In a study that presaged the current emphasis placed on contextual performance, Grey and Kipnis (1976) demonstrated that supervisory ratings of performance for compliant workers were contingent on the proportion of noncompliant workers in the rater's work group; as the proportion of noncompliant workers in a group increased, so did the ratings given to compliant workers by their supervisors.

Research has established that extra-role behaviors (viz. contextual performance) account for as much, if not more, of the variance in supervisory ratings of performance as do actual production records (MacKenzie, et al., 1991) or technical performance (Borman & Motowidlo, 1993). Perhaps it isn't surprising that managers rate the performance of more compliant and helpful workers higher than what they deserve if based solely on their actual production. It is likely that the contextual contributions of these workers promotes managers' leadership position in the group, allows them to delegate more group maintenance functions to others, and provides a wealth of expertise that may be used to enhance managers' positions among their peers. Omitting contextual performance from the formal criterion domain of a performance appraisal system places the manager in a quandary. In the first place, performance ratings that are influenced by contextual considerations but that aren't substantiated by the production data open the door to accusations of bias and favoritism. On the other hand, if managers rate their more compliant and dedicated subordinates solely on the basis of their technical performance, they may extinguish behaviors that promote their own leadership position in the group.

Incorporating contextual contributions to system effectiveness remains a challenge, and it may, along with aggregated values in formal criteria adopted by organizations, be among the most significant contemporary frontiers in criterion development. Villanova (1992) describes a methodology for linking customer criteria with the performance of different work functions. Essentially, the process entails having customers detail the criteria that they value and then finding correspondence between the satisfaction of these customer requirements and the specific activities workers perform on their jobs. The idea is to estimate the relative impact and scope of job functions for satisfying different customer values.

Extension of this methodology to contextual performance may be one way to integrate contextual performance contributions into a customer-based criterion system. For example, several of the behavior and result measures described by Borman and Motowidlo (1993) could be subsumed within the model we presented for Prescription 1. If performance is defined at a more specific task or activity level, contextual performance could be (and should be) represented in the description of the activity combined with one or more specific outcome measures. Such a representation should be easily accomplished as constructs are derived with an internal customer focus and multi-rater systems are employed which include peer and subordinate assessments.

Broadly construed, we could think of ratees as customers of the appraisal system. That is, the system designed to hold them accountable for their contributions to the organization may also be viewed as responsible for shepherding their performance, and as such the system can be subject to evaluation on the basis of how well it meets user objectives. Later, we conclude the article with some observations that support this more universal depiction of customers and the role of ratee participation in designing the appraisal system to which they are subject.

To summarize, then, we believe that the subject of customer appraisal—both internal and external—holds great promise for organizations and PM systems. The strong trend toward multi-rater systems is compatible with the conceptualization of defining performance from the perspective of internal (e.g., peers, subordinates) and external customers (e.g., mystery shoppers, real customers). Research should focus on conditions under which customer feedback provides particular advantage; the processes associated with collecting valid, reliable, useful information; and the effectiveness of various HR interventions designed to respond to such feedback or appraisal results.

PRESCRIPTION 3: INCORPORATE THE MEASUREMENT OF CONSTRAINTS OF PERFORMANCE INTO THE FORMAL PM SYSTEM

Our third prescription concerns the role of situational constraints in moderating organizational effectiveness and methods that could formally consider, account for, and (hopefully) reduce such constraints. Research indicates that raters and ratees often disagree on the extent to which situational constraints have affected performance (Bernardin, Hagan, Kane, & Villanova, 1998). This disagreement translates into dysfunctional reactions to the PM system and may have a great deal to do with the dissatisfaction voiced from all perspectives. One major goal of a PM system is to eliminate or reduce the effects of situational constraints on performance, real or imagined, and to facilitate maximal performance. One of the ultimate objectives for PM is to improve organizational performance. A focus on and elimination of performance constraints should help accomplish this objective.

Situational Influences on Performance

Circumstances beyond a performer's control can have the effect of either facilitating or constraining the level of performance achieved. While there are certainly situational facilitators that boost performance, constraints on performance are of the greater interest because they tend to account for a great deal of the disagreement between raters and ratees—disagreements that often translate into costly, deleterious effects for the PM system and the organization (Dobbins, et al., 1993). The consequences of ratings contaminated by situational constraints are profound. Circumstances beyond a performer's control can have the effect of either facilitating or constraining the level of performance achieved. Moreover, raters' knowledge of situational constraints makes them more capable of fulfilling the coaching and development function of performance management. Any good coach should be able to suggest ways to remove obstacles to performance and certainly should be aware of the obstacles that exist. After all, the persons rated are also customers of the appraisal system in which they are imbedded. A performance management perspective maintains that subordinates hold a reasonable expectation that a review process should suggest methods of improvement and not just serve as a summary account of their accomplishments and failings.

This approach is also compatible with the conceptualization of the supervisor or manager as a potential facilitator of the work unit's performance. Traditional appraisal is often not sufficiently remedial in that it emphasizes an account of what was achieved in the past. However, an appraisal system more consistent with the performance management perspective we emphasize would apply a more "diagnostic" analysis to the assessment of employee and situational factors that account for performance. Although this seems intuitive, in practice appraisal has too often focused on accounting for past objectives while simultaneously being employed to assess training needs without a careful inventory of the factors that support or undermine performance, both dispositional and situational (Leat & Lovell, 1997). A systems view of performance determinants would maintain that performance stems from multiple, potentially interacting factors that need to be inventoried on a person-task-organization unit of analysis if meaningful conclusions of training needs are to result (Bramley, 1989).

Possible situational constraints include lack of equipment and training, turnover of key personnel, poor management or co-workers, faulty selection procedures, lack of cooperation among work units, material and supply shortages, economic cycles, government regulation, court rulings, and even the weather. The proponents of the Total Quality Movement emphasize the extent to which situational influences, or what they call system factors, constrain performance (e.g., Masterson & Taylor, 1996; Waldman, 1994). Indeed, the father of TQM, W. Edwards Deming (1986), has claimed that such situational factors account for 94 percent of the variance in performance, 90 percent of which is the result of "common causes" that are beyond the control of the performer.

Whether real or illusory, a majority of workers from one survey felt that factors beyond their control had a "significant impact" on their own performance. A majority also maintained that their supervisors do not adequately understand the deleterious impact of these factors (Bernardin, 1992). Perceptions of the impact of constraints may also explain discrepancies in self versus supervisory performance evaluations (Bernardin, 1989). Formal or informal, all of us do self-appraisals. Most of us compare these appraisals to those made by our supervisors and others.

Not only do discrepancies in self versus supervisory evaluations have an effect on subsequent worker behavior, these discrepancies are also related to very costly grievance and appeal processes when evaluations are tied to important personnel decisions such as merit pay, selection, promotions, discharges, etc. Thus, regardless of whether we are talking about employee motivation, turnover, group cohesion, or monetary costs, the effects of discrepancies in self versus supervisory evaluations on the PM system can be great (Cardy & Dobbins, 1994).

Research on attribution theory may provide an explanation for these discrepancies.

The actor/observer bias is the tendency for actors to attribute less than perfect performance to factors that were beyond their control whereas observers tend to attribute the same outcomes to stable personal characteristics such as ability or motivation. Workers doing poorly on the job often have a different perspective on a problem than does the supervisor, particularly when the supervisor has never performed the work. In attempting to explain inadequate performance, the worker may point to various external constraints on his or her performance such as lack of supplies, unpredictable workload, troublesome coworkers, ambiguous job assignment, etc. The supervisor very often disagrees with employees on the extent to which different factors constrained their performance (Zuckerman, 1979). The supervisor is often convinced that the worker lacks some enduring quality such as aptitude or motivation. The supervisor is also less likely to be cognizant of contextual performance factors that constrain individual performance.

A 1995 *Detroit News* "report card" on the Detroit Red Wings provides a nice illustration of the actor/observer bias. After the Red Wings were swept four straight games by the New Jersey Devils for hockey's Stanley Cup, a *News* reporter gave Red Wing Ray Sheppard an "F" for his performance. The reporter theorized that Sheppard lacked "motivation or desire" in the Cup final but did allow that "granted, he had a broken wrist." Just maybe Mr. Sheppard, and for that matter any other person who has actually played hockey, may have placed a little more weight on the broken wrist and a little less on his motivation.

This type of disagreement over attributions may not only be at the root of the self versus supervisory differences, it may also be a key element in the employee's motivation regarding future performance. Abundant empirical evidence supports the contention that perceived work constraints reduce aspiration levels (e.g., Phillips & Freedman, 1984; Villanova, 1996). Disagreement on why goals were not achieved may result in lower goal commitment to future goals or outright abandonment of supervisor-assigned goals. This is particularly likely in instances where a worker had previously enjoyed considerable latitude over the setting of goals and who now faces closer scrutiny of and less control over the goals that are established (cf. Austin, 1989). The potential erosion of goal commitment to assigned or participatively set goals is likely to be acute when the shift in goal setting from one of personal control to one of greater supervisory control is perceived by the worker as a response to previous failure that is misattributed by the supervisor. Procedures, which serve to reduce the differential attributions of performance, should also reduce differences in self versus supervisory performance evaluations and consequently increase commitment to negotiated or assigned goals. In addition, the procedures will focus attention on these critical external factors that, if either real or illusory, should be a major concern for PM system effectiveness.

This orientation can also give managers and supervisors, charged with achieving results, an appropriate perspective on their jobs. Attending to real constraints on unit performance should be a major focus of any manager's job. Most organizations use PM systems that tacitly allow raters to add or subtract "fudge factors" to adjust for situational influences. This informal correction fails to control for potentially wide differences between raters in their recognition of, and willingness to adjust for, such influences and makes such judgments prone to allegations of unfairness.

Bernardin (1989) argues for explicit rating by supervisors of factors that may facilitate or impede performance so that adjustments to ratings, if made, are documented in an employee's work record. Recognizing that performance management is a two-way street, Dobbins, et al. (1993) also champion this approach for the purpose of not only providing a more accurate record of employee performance but also as a record of management's response or lack of response to correct constraints that are addressable through management intervention. Thus, the accountability feature of including a descriptive record of constraints works both ways.

Attributional Training

Bernardin (1989) introduced attributional training to focus the attention of the supervisor and subordinates on the perceived effects of constraints on specific dimensions or elements of performance. One assumption of attributional training is that some type of behavior-based or results-based PM system is in place. The approach is also appropriate for appraisal systems that call for individualized or group performance standards, goals, or objectives. Indeed, attributional training is even more essential for both accurate accounting of performance and training needs analysis in these instances where performance is more complexly determined.

A spreadsheet matrix should be prepared with the rows made up of the performance dimensions and the columns listing all potential constraints on performance (Bernardin, et al., 1998, p. 38–39; Peters & O'Connor, 1980; Phillips & Freedman, 1984; Villanova & Roman, 1993). The supervisor and a subordinate are asked to independently consider and rate the subordinate's maximum potential for performance on each dimension and the extent to which any of the constraints may have deterred this potential. The rater is asked to write a specific example (if one can be retrieved) for each relevant combination dimension/constraint.

Most cells of the matrix should be empty because the constraints are inapplicable to the job. Participants should be encouraged to write specific examples of how a given constraint affected a given performance dimension. The supervisor and the subordinate then exchange their completed matrices and are given an opportunity to study them (the supervisor may also want to verify some of the subordinate's information).

The appraisal meeting should focus on the discrepant cells as well as those where there is agreement on a constraint. The supervisors should allow the subordinates an opportunity to fully explain any of the cells the subordinates have selected that the supervisors do not regard as relevant. The discussion should concentrate on specifically how and how often a constraint affected performance on a given performance dimension. This phase in the training should end with an agreement that certain cells are a legitimate and significant problem to which time and effort for correction should be committed.

The final and most important phase of the discussion is future-oriented. The supervisor and subordinate should now concentrate on what each can do to limit or eliminate the relevant constraints. For example, where feasible, the supervisor should commit to attending to those constraints for which he or she is responsible or of which he or she can investigate. For example, the subordinate may attribute problems due to shortages of certain supplies. The supervisor could then investigate the supply problem and, if significant, take action to alleviate it.

The final phase of attributional training should be based strictly on the timetable for investigating specific constraints on performance. The supervisor and subordinate should meet pursuant to the dates established for dealing with each constraint. This approach will focus the meeting on only the relevant constraints and the extent to which their impact has been reduced by the supervisor or subordinate's actions. Such an approach meets the requirements for timely and specific feedback and should be far less traumatic than an annual or semiannual meeting that covers a plethora of topics. Once the dimension $\times$ constraint matrix is completed the first time, the entire process should be relatively painless for the supervisors and subordinates. The matrix can then be incorporated into normal work and planning and review procedures.

Research on the effects of attributional training showed reduced discrepancies between self versus supervisory appraisals and increased overall performance for the work unit (Bernardin, et al., 1998). In addition, one year subsequent to the training, ratees who had participated indicated that fewer constraints had hindered their performance. Even if this finding is merely illusory, it nonetheless has positive implications for the efficacy of a PM system because these same people also perceived relatively stronger connections between their performances and desired personal outcomes. In addition, this formal consideration of situational constraints also enhanced perceptions of fairness and due process for the PM system, an important ancillary benefit.

CONCLUSION

Some 20 years ago, Bernardin & Beatty (1984) compiled a list of appraisal factors thought to influence employee attitudes and performance. However, only recently has systematic research on user acceptability of the appraisal process and the system in which it is imbedded become a fixture in the appraisal literature (e.g., Findley, et al., 2000; Hedge & Teachout, 2000). This research has shown that appraisals that require a rater to rate specific dimensions as opposed to providing just an overall rating tends to be more acceptable to both raters and ratees (Hedge & Teachout, 2000), supporting our admonishment earlier for the use of more specific criteria. Both instrumental ratee participation in the appraisal (through participation in the design of the system or providing self-ratings, for example) and expressive participation (through the solicitation of their reactions to the appraisal) positively influence ratees' satisfaction and motivation (Cawley, Keeping, & Levy, 1998). Conceptualizing ratees as customers of the appraisal process contribute to an awareness that it is beneficial to design processes with the intention of enhancing ratees' responsiveness to appraisal system feedback. The results of the Hedge and Teachout survey also show that bias suppression in the form of minimizing the impact of situational constraints on performance leads to greater user acceptability of the performance appraisal process, again underscoring the importance of situational constraints on employee performance accounts.

Contextual performance not only has implications for performance management but is also subject to influence from the performance management system. For example, Findley, et al. (2000) found that appraisal process (e.g., standard setting, employee input, supervisor observation) and system factors (e.g., employee opportunity to challenge ratings, knowledge of the system, multiple sources of data) both contribute uniquely to employee extra-role contributions (i.e., contextual performance). Employees who acknowledged the presence of these factors in their appraisal system also tended to evidence higher levels of these extra-role behaviors.

Considering the accumulating evidence of the current transformation in appraisal practices, we believe human resources management practices will be better served when they adopt the prescriptions we described in this article to buttress their appraisal system. Only when ratees are provided specific feedback about their performance, in the context of the situation in which it occurs, and when it is based on legitimate job-relevant organizational effectiveness criteria will a performance management system have the necessary legs to support an ambitious human resources agenda in today's complex world. ∎

REFERENCES

Allen, W. (1980). *Side effects.* New York: Random House, 57.

Atwater, L., Roush, P., & Fischthal, A. (1995). The influence of upward feedback on self- and follower ratings of leadership. *Personnel Psychology, 48,* 35–60.

Austin, J. T. (1989). Effects on shifts in goal origin on goal acceptance and attainment. *Organizational Behavior and Human Decision Processes, 46,* 315–335.

Bernardin, H. J. (1989). Increasing the accuracy of performance measurement: A proposed solution to erroneous attributions. *Human Resource Planning, 12,* 239–250.

Bernardin, H. J. (1992). The "analytic" framework for customer-based performance content development and appraisal. *Human Resource Management Review, 2,* 81–102.

Bernardin, H. J., & Beatty, R. W. (1984). *Performance appraisal: Assessing human behavior at work.* Boston: Kent-Wadsworth.

Bernardin, H. J., Cooke, D. K., & Villanova, P. J. (2000). Conscientiousness and agreeableness as predictors of rating leniency. *Journal of Applied Psychology, 85,* 232–236.

Bernardin, H. J., Hagan, C. M., & Hennessey, H. (2001). The effects of criterion specificity on performance measurement effectiveness. Unpublished manuscript.

Bernardin, H. J., Hagan, C., Kane, J. S., & Villanova, P. (1998). Effective performance management: A focus on precision in measurement, customers and situational constraints. In J. Smither (Ed.) *Performance management: The state of the art.* San Francisco: Jossey-Bass, 3–48.

Bernardin, H. J. & Tyler, C. L. (2001). Legal and ethical issues in multisource feedback. In D. W. Bracken, C. W. Timmreck, & A.H. Church (Eds.). *The handbook of multisource feedback.* San Francisco: Jossey-Bass, 447–462.

Bobko, P., & Colella, A. (1994). Employee reactions to performance standards: A review and research propositions. *Personnel Psychology, 47,* 1–36.

Borman, W. C., & Motowidlo, S. J. (1993). Expanding the criterion domain to include elements of contextual performance. In N. Schmitt and W. C. Borman (Eds.), *Personnel Selection in Organizations* (71–98). San Francisco: Jossey-Bass.

Borman, W. C., White, L. A., & Dorsey, D. W. (1995). Effects of ratee task performance and interpersonal factors on supervisor and peer performance ratings. *Journal of Applied Psychology, 80,* 168–177.

Bracken, D. W., Timmreck, C. W., & Church, A. H. (Eds.) (2001). *The handbook of multisource feedback.* San Francisco: Jossey-Bass.

Bramley, P. (1989). Effective training. *Journal of European Industrial Training, 13,* 2–33.

Bretz, R. D., Jr., Milkovich, G. T., & Read, W. (1992). The current state of performance appraisal research and practice: Concerns, directions, and implications. *Journal of Management, 18,* 321–352.

Cardy, R. L., & Dobbins, G. H. (1994). *Performance appraisal: Alternative perspectives.* Cincinnati, OH: South-Western Publishing Co.

Cawley, B. D., Keeping, L. M., & Levy, P. E. (1998). Participation in the performance appraisal process and employee reactions: A meta-analytic review of field investigations. *Journal of Applied Psychology, 83,* 615–633.

Deming, W. E. (1986). *Out of the crisis.* Cambridge, MA: Massachusetts Institute of Technology, Center for Advanced Engineering Study.

Dobbins, G. H., Cardy, R. L., Facteau, J. D., & Miller, J. S. (1993). Implications of situational constraints on performance evaluation and performance management. *Human Resource Management Review, 3,* 105–128.

Edwards, M. R., & Ewen, A. J. (1996). *360-degree feedback: The powerful new model for employee assessment and performance improvement.* New York: AMACOM.

Findley, H. M., Giles, W. F., & Mossholder, K. W. (2000). Performance appraisal process and system facets: Relationships with contextual performance. *Journal of Applied Psychology, 85,* 634–640.

Greenberg, J. (1986). Determinants of perceived fairness of performance evaluations. *Journal of Applied Psychology, 71,* 2, 340–342.

Grensing-Pophal, L. (2001). Motivate managers to review performance. *HR Magazine, 46,* 44–49.

Grey, R. J., & Kipnis, D. (1976). Untangling the performance appraisal dilemma. *Journal of Applied Psychology, 61,* 329–335.

Hauser, J. R., Simester, D. I., & Wernerfelt, B. (1996, August). Internal customers and internal suppliers. *Journal of Marketing Research,* 276–280.

Hedge, J. W., & Teachout, M. S. (2000). Exploring the concept of acceptability as a criterion for evaluating performance measures. *Group and Organization Management, 24,* 22–44.

Helliker, K. (1994, November 30). Smile: That cranky shopper may be a store spy. *The Wall Street Journal,* B1.

Hersey, P., & Blanchard, K. H. (1988). *Management of organizational behavior: Utilizing human resources.* (5th ed.) Englewood Cliffs, NJ: Prentice Hall.

Hronec, S. M. (1993). *Vital signs: Using quality, time and cost performance measures to chart your company's future.* New York: American Management Association.

Joinson, C. (2001). Making sure employees measure up. *HR Magazine, 46,* 36–43.

Kane, J. S., Bernardin, H. J., Villanova, P. J., & Peyrefitte, J. (1995). The stability of rater leniency: Three studies. *Academy of Management Journal, 38,* 1036–1051.

Kozlowski, S. W., Chao, G. T., & Morrison, R. F. (1998). Games raters play: Politics, strategies, and impression management in performance appraisal. In J. Smither (Ed.) *Performance management: The state of the art.* San Francisco: Jossey-Bass, 163–208.

Leat, M. J., & Lovell, M. J. (1997). Training needs analysis: Weaknesses in the conventional approach. *Journal of European Industrial Training, 21,* 143–152.

London, M., & Smither, J. W. (1995). Can multi-source feedback change perceptions of goal accomplishment, self-evaluations, and performance-related outcomes? Theory-based applications and directions for research. *Personnel Psychology, 48,* 803–839.

MacKenzie, S. B., Podsakoff, P. M., & Fetter, R. (1991). *Organizational Behavior and Human Decision Processes, 50,* 123–150.

Masterson, S. S., & Taylor, M. Susan. (1996). Total quality management and performance appraisal: *Journal of Quality Management, 1,* 67–89.

McDonald, D., & Smith, A. (1995). A proven connection: Performance management and business results. *Compensation & Benefits Review, 27* (1), 59–64.

Murphy, K. J. (1993, spring). Performance measurement and appraisal: Merck tries to motivate managers to do it right. *Employee Relations Today,* 47–62.

Murphy, K. R., & Cleveland, J. M. (1991). *Performance appraisal: An organizational perspective.* Boston, MA: Allyn & Bacon.

Organ, D. W. (1988). *Organizational citizenship behavior: The good soldier syndrome.* Lexington, MA: Lexington Books.

Parry, S. B. (1996, July). The quest for competencies. *Training,* 48–53.

Peters, L. H., & O'Connor, E. J. (1980). Situational constraints and work outcomes: The influence of a frequently overlooked construct. *Academy of Management Review, 5,* 391–397.

Phillips, J. S., & Freedman, S. M. (1984). Situational performance constraints and task characteristics: Their relationship to motivation and satisfaction. *Journal of Management, 10,* 321–331.

Podsakoff, P. M., Ahearne, M., & MacKenzie, S. B. (1997). Organizational citizenship behavior and the quantity and quality of work group performance. *Journal of Applied Psychology, 82* (2), 262–270.

Schrader, B. W., & Steiner, D. D. (1996). Common comparison standards: An approach to improving agreement between self and supervisory performance ratings. *Journal of Applied Psychology, 81* (6), 813–820.

Shippmann, J. S., Ash, R. A., Battista, M., Carr, L., Eyde, L. D., Hesketh, B., Kehoe, J., Pearlman, K., Prien, E. P., & Sanchez, J. I. (2000). The practice of competency modeling. *Personnel Psychology, 53,* 703–740.

Smith, B., Hornsby, J. S., & Shirmeyer, R. (1996, summer). Current trends in performance appraisal: An examination of managerial practice. *Sam Advanced Management Journal,* 10–15.

Smither, J., London, M., Vasilopoulos, N., Reilly, R. R., Millsap, R. E., & Salvemini, N. (1995). An examination of the effects of an upward feedback program over time. *Personnel Psychology, 48,* 1–34.

Tubbs, M. (1986). Goal setting: A meta-analytic examination of the empirical evidence. *Journal of Applied Psychology, 71,* 474–483.

Villanova, P. (1992). A customer-based model for developing job performance criteria. *Human Resource Management Review, 2,* 103–114.

Villanova, P. (1996). Predictive validity of situational constraints in general versus specific performance domains. *Journal of Applied Psychology, 81,* 532–547.

Villanova, P., Bernardin, H. J., Dahmus, S., & Sims, R. (1993). Rater leniency and performance appraisal discomfort. *Educational and Psychological Measurement, 53,* 789–799.

Villanova, P., & Roman, M. A. (1993). A meta-analytic review of situational constraints and work-related outcomes: Alternative approaches to conceptualization. *Human Resource Management Review, 3,* 147–175.

Waldman, D. A. (1994). The contributions of total quality management to a theory of work performance. *Academy of Management Review, 19,* 510–536.

Zeithaml, V. A., Parasuraman, A., & Berry, L. L. (1990). *Delivering quality service: Balancing customer perspectives and expectations.* New York: The Free Press.

Zemke, R. (1982). Job competencies: Can they help you design better training? *Training, 19,* 28–31.

Zuckerman, M. (1979). Attribution of success and failure revisited: The motivational bias is alive and well in attribution theory. *Journal of Personality, 47,* 245–287.

THE PROMISE AND PERIL OF GIVING NEGATIVE FEEDBACK

Walter D. Davis
Donald B. Fedor

INTRODUCTION

Practicing managers, as well as management scholars, have recognized the crucial role of feedback in motivating workers. In management circles, feedback is often referred to as "The Breakfast of Champions" because it is a critical component of job design, goal setting, and behavior management. Accordingly, a great deal of attention has been devoted to discussions regarding how feedback should best be delivered. Furthermore, understanding how individuals respond to feedback remains critical in designing feedback systems, especially as organizations look to institute quality initiatives and encourage greater self-management by their employees. As organizations look to redirect employee efforts, it is often necessary to provide negative feedback with the expectation that the recipients of this feedback will expend efforts to improve the performance in question.

Employees often use information about their performance to correct inappropriate behaviors and to recognize areas for possible improvement. Besides having positive effects on performance, feedback can increase job satisfaction and alleviate stress arising from feelings of uncertainty. Feedback can also help employees establish a realistic idea of what is expected of them and how well they are meeting these expectations. However, even with all of these positive qualities attributed to feedback, supervisors are often reluctant to give it, especially when it is negative, with the result that employees often feel "in the dark" about what they are doing and how well they are doing it.

In this article, we outline some of the issues that arise when a supervisor gives negative feedback to a subordinate. First, we discuss reasons why a supervisor might give negative feedback. The motives for giving such feedback are not as simple as they might appear. Next, we discuss the process that an employee goes through in understanding negative feedback and deciding how to respond to it. Then, we discuss some of the ways in which subordinates might actually respond to negative feedback. Unfortunately, most of the problems associated with performance feedback tend to occur when feedback is seen as negative. Not only do managers tend to avoid giving negative feedback, but recipients often fail to respond to negative feedback with efforts to improve performance. Based on our discussion of how employees respond to negative feedback and the process by which these responses may occur, we discuss factors that may affect how employees respond to negative feedback. Finally, we offer some guidelines for delivering such feedback.

PURPOSES OF NEGATIVE FEEDBACK

In order to understand the various reasons why a supervisor might deliver negative feedback to a subordinate, it is first necessary to make a distinction between *outcome* feedback and *process* feedback. Outcome feedback is information regarding the level of performance in relation to some performance standard or goal. In the case of negative feedback, outcome feedback points to some discrepancy between actual performance and some desired level of performance. Process feedback is information regarding the way in which someone performed a task, and often includes a comparison with a preferred or optimal way of performing a task. Process feedback may be necessary for the recipient to determine how or why performance is or is not up to some performance standard (the goal). Such feedback helps individuals determine whether or not changes in task strategies will be necessary. Managers may decide to give more of one kind of feedback than another. This can depend on the motivation for delivering the feedback or expectations of how the recipient might respond. For example, a sales manager may tell a salesperson that he or she has not met his sales quota for the current month (outcome feedback) and then follow this information with some suggestions for developing more client leads or getting more orders from existing clients (process feedback). In the case of negative feedback, process feedback is likely to include information about how the subordinate has done a task incorrectly.

There are a number of reasons why a supervisor may decide to deliver negative feedback. First, the supervisor may want to *motivate* the subordinate to exert more effort. In this case, outcome feedback is necessary to alert the subordinate that performance is substandard or that goals are unmet. Assuming that an individual actually wants to achieve a goal, discrepancies between actual and desired performance tend to motivate individuals to exert greater effort toward goal attainment. This is because goal achievement typically leads to some reward or, at the least, the avoidance of some negative sanction.

Second, a supervisor may want to *teach* a subordinate the necessary knowledge and skills needed to perform better. In the short-term, the focus of attention may be on correcting performance on the task at hand. In the long-term, the supervisor's focus may be on developing an employee's knowledge and skills in such a way that he or she is prepared to tackle more sophisticated duties in the future. In either case, process feedback that provides information about what a subordinate has done incorrectly and how the task or project should be performed is likely to be even more important than outcome feedback that merely points out the fact that performance was not up to the expected level.

Third, a supervisor may want to deliver negative feedback in order to *justify a decision*. Often these decisions will center around administrative issues such as pay, promotion, or even discharge. A manager who decides that a subordinate does not deserve a pay raise or promotion, or does deserve to be discharged, must somehow justify this decision. Often this justification will take the form of negative outcome feedback that indicates that performance is not up to standard.

Finally, a manager may deliver negative feedback in order to *deflect blame*. When a manager's unit in the organization is not performing well, he may not be willing to take the blame for this failure himself. Instead, he may want to attribute the failure to the shortcomings of his subordinates. The manager may want to deflect blame in order to protect himself from the negative consequences of poor unit performance, or simply to protect his own ego. Further, providing negative feedback can be an attempt to demonstrate that the "problem" is being dealt with since steps are being taken.

THE PROCESS OF UNDERSTANDING NEGATIVE FEEDBACK

Before an employee can respond to negative feedback, he or she must (1) accurately perceive it, and (2) understand it. Our later discussion of factors affecting responses to negative feedback will suggest actions a supervisor can take to ensure that negative feedback is accurately perceived. Our focus here is on the process by which employees understand, or "make sense" of such feedback. This "sense-making" process often finds the recipient of negative feedback asking two distinct but related questions. First, the recipient may ask "Why is my supervisor giving me negative feedback"? Then, assuming the recipient actually agrees with the feedback, he or she may ask, "What was the cause(s) of my poor performance"?

Our interest in this article centers on the question of what happens when a supervisor finds it appropriate to give negative feedback in order to *motivate* greater effort or *teach* needed skills and knowledge for the purpose of performance improvement. Surely we prefer to think that when a supervisor gives negative feedback, it is for the purpose of encouraging and developing better employees. However, the other potential motives for delivering negative feedback cannot be overlooked, and when employees receive negative feedback they will usually try to determine the motive(s) behind it. These judgments, which we will refer to as causal attributions, play a large role in determining a recipient's ultimate response to feedback. An employee who believes the supervisor is giving negative feedback for the purpose of motivating and teaching may be more receptive to the feedback and much more likely to respond appropriately. In contrast, if the employee believes the supervisor is trying to justify some adverse employment decision (e.g., demotion, termination, no pay raise) or deflect blame, he or she may focus more attention to defending himself or herself against these adverse actions.

Even if a subordinate trusts the supervisor's motives for delivering the feedback, and accepts as fact that performance was not up to standard, he or she must still make some attribution regarding the cause of the substandard performance. Poor performance can be a result of (1) lack of effort; (2) lack of needed knowledge, skills, or abilities; (3) an overly difficult task; or (4) some other uncontrollable force (e.g., a sluggish economy causes a salesperson to miss quota). If an employee accepts that poor performance is due to lack of effort, then he or she also may see a clear path to improved performance: simply work harder. On the other hand, an attribution of poor performance to lack of skill or some uncontrollable force may lead to a much different reaction to negative feedback: simply give up. Most people won't expend much effort toward a goal if they don't think they have control over those things that are necessary for goal achievement.

To complicate the matter, supervisors and subordinates often have different perceptions regarding the real cause(s) of poor performance. While subordinates may be aware of obstacles getting in the way of good performance (e.g., a lack of resources), supervisors often see a subordinate who is failing to get the job done. In this case, the supervisor may incorrectly attribute the poor performance to lack of effort, and deliver feedback that essentially says, "You're not trying hard enough." Such feedback may only discourage an already frustrated employee. This suggests that before a supervisor delivers negative feedback, some information gathering is often advisable. Ascertaining the true cause of poor performance is important if the supervisor is to deliver feedback that the subordinate can understand, accept, and respond to appropriately.

POSSIBLE REACTIONS TO FEEDBACK

Before we tackle the issue of what influences responses to feedback, it is appropriate to first discuss the types of responses feedback can engender. As most managers know, these responses can cover a broad range. In the case of negative feedback from the supervisor, expected employee responses can range from constructive (i.e., taking steps to correct the problem) to nonconstructive. The response that is probably most desired by the supervisor is to *attempt to improve performance.* Such attempts may include exerting greater effort or changing task strategies. A number of questions are likely to enter the mind of the feedback recipient when deciding whether to attempt performance improvement. These questions include: Will increased effort or a new task strategy actually lead to performance improvement? Will any gains in performance actually lead to desired outcomes (e.g., rewards, avoiding punishment)? Do I even have any control over whether or not performance improves or rewards are obtained? Following negative outcome feedback, these questions often remain unanswered. Years of scientific research (and a reasonable amount of common sense) tell us that unless these questions are answered affirmatively, individuals are not likely to invest much effort toward performance improvement. Given that negative feedback isn't always followed by performance improvement, it is necessary to examine other potential responses and why they may occur.

A second potential response to negative feedback is to *actively monitor one's own performance.* In most jobs, employees are not solely dependent on supervisors or other people for feedback. It is possible for individuals to observe their own performance and compare their judgments of their own performance to some performance standard (outcome feedback), as well as try to ascertain why performance is possibly substandard (process feedback). More experienced employees, with higher levels of job relevant knowledge, are more likely to successfully monitor their own performance. Active performance monitoring by a subordinate may be a good way to gain a better understanding of the job, may motivate higher levels of effort, and may free the supervisor of the burden of constantly observing subordinate behavior. However,

such monitoring might also lead to resistance on the part of the recipient. This would occur when the recipient decides, after further monitoring, that he or she believes the feedback is inaccurate (this response is discussed in greater detail below).

A third potential response to negative feedback is to *seek additional feedback* in order to better understand the feedback and determine how best to respond. The situation in which the recipient actively seeks feedback from the source is a commonly overlooked aspect of the feedback process. In such a case, the employee may solicit the supervisor's impressions of a project or some other work activity. Where close supervision doesn't exist or where management has implicitly adopted the "let sleeping dogs lie" approach to feedback, an employee may only receive feedback that he or she actively seeks. Although generally viewed as a positive employee attribute, feedback-seeking behavior (FSB) raises another set of issues for the source. FSB may be a response to negative feedback as the recipient seeks feedback to (1) try to better understand how his or her performance was judged to be inappropriate, (2) gather information about how to improve performance, or (3) try to understand what the consequences of substandard performance may be.

Furthermore, an employee may seek feedback as a way to manipulate a supervisor's response to poor performance. That is, the person may ask for either positive or negative feedback in hopes of earning credit for successful endeavors or avoiding blame for failures. Negative feedback may be solicited if the employee expects that the supervisor will eventually lose patience with lackluster performance and provide more negative feedback at a later time. This short-circuiting of the negative feedback process may lead to a less severe reaction from the supervisor.

This points to *impression management* as a fourth potential response to negative feedback. Although impression management may take the form of feedback seeking (as just discussed), it may also take on other forms. An employee may try to convince the supervisor that performance is not really as bad as it appears. In other words, he or she may argue that the supervisor's assessment of performance is inaccurate. But even if the subordinate accepts the feedback as accurate, he or she may try to manage impressions regarding the *reasons* for the poor performance. While the supervisor's feedback may focus on a lack of effort or skill, a subordinate may argue that the real reason for poor performance is lack of resources, an overly difficult task assignment, or just plain bad luck (e.g., a recession causes decreased sales). The key point here is that most people are reluctant to accept the fact that they are to blame for poor performance, and even if they do accept the blame, they are often motivated to protect themselves from negative consequences by managing impressions.

Another potential response is *retaliation against the source of the feedback* (e.g., the supervisor). In this case, an employee can be hurt emotionally, place some or all of the blame on the supervisor, withhold future cooperation, complain to others such as coworkers or personnel representatives, or perhaps even charge harassment and file a formal grievance. Unfortunately, criticism of employee performance in the form of negative feedback may render the supervisor vulnerable to counterattack or may negatively affect the supervisor's relationship with the employee or the entire work group.

Finally, the recipient of negative feedback may decide to simply *ignore the feedback*. In this case, the recipient has decided that no response is warranted. There are a number of reasons why this response may occur. First, as noted earlier, recipients must first perceive and understand feedback before they can respond to it. It is possible for a supervisor to deliver what he or she believes to be negative feedback, when in fact the recipient doesn't see the feedback as negative. In this event, from the standpoint of the recipient, no response is necessary. Second, even if the feedback is perceived and understood as negative, the recipient may simply not believe that the feedback is correct. This may be especially likely when the recipient has little or no respect for the supervisor. Third, the recipient may not believe that poor performance will have sufficiently negative consequences to warrant a correction. If there is no perceived connection between poor performance and bad outcomes, why bother improving?

FACTORS AFFECTING RESPONSES TO NEGATIVE FEEDBACK

A number of factors can influence which response(s) the recipient chooses to enact. This is based on the fact that feedback is not simply a piece of objective information given by the supervisor to a recipient. It is an event that occurs between the two parties in the context of a relationship, the recipient's perception of his or her own performance, other recent feedback events, and the broader organizational environment. Thus, feedback can be viewed by the recipient as information, a reward, a punishment, or a justification for some decision made by the supervisor. While there are a tremendous number of things that can affect feedback recipient responses, we are going to highlight four of them. These are as follows: (1) supervisor credibility and power, (2) the specificity of the feedback, (3) the frequency of feedback, and (4) the availability of alternative sources of feedback.

Credibility and Power

The feedback source possesses certain qualities as perceived by the recipient that can significantly influence feedback responses. For example, some supervisors serve as wonderful role models or have valuable information they can share and thus are judged to have high credibility. Others have the power to require compliance or make their subordinates' lives miserable. What has been found is that the more "positive" forms of supervisor power (role modeling, expertise) tend to engender productive responses on the part of subordinates following corrective feedback. In other words, supervisors with high referent power (seen as positive role models) or high expert power (seen as having valued expertise) tend to be seen as credible sources of feedback and subordinates will often try to improve their performance following feedback from them. Also, such sources are often perceived to be good people to go to for additional performance-related information. This is because the subordinates tend to see them as approachable and having information that will be useful.

In contrast, supervisors seen as having primarily authority granted by the organization (high legitimate power) or the ability to punish (high coercive power) do not engender such responses. Instead, subordinates will often comply with the supervisor's demands, but not try to go beyond this mere compliance. Therefore, actual performance improvement, over the long run, often will not occur when corrective feedback is delivered by those with simply legitimate or punishment-related power. When it comes to feedback seeking, subordinates will tend to avoid these supervisors. One might think that it would be prudent to seek feedback from those with high coercive power, but current research indicates that this "logical" response is overridden by the desire to avoid such people. So even if the supervisor has valuable information to share, subordinates will tend not to avail themselves of it.

Specificity

The specificity of the feedback makes a real difference. For instance, telling someone that he or she is a poor worker is quite dif-

ferent from explaining that the person failed to complete two of the last three assignments or that the rejection rate for his or her product has been running 12 percent above the standard set for the department. Very general feedback does not supply much useful information. The more specific the feedback is in relation to goals, standards, or actual outcomes, the less recipients will tend to take the feedback as statements about them, and the more it will be perceived as useful performance-related input.

Here again, we need to provide one qualifier. As noted, specific feedback is almost always preferable over nonspecific feedback. However, if a task calls for creativity, supervisors need to be careful about the kinds of specific feedback given. For example, if an employee is trying to work out a more efficient process for manufacturing an item, then certain types of feedback, such as exactly what alternatives one should consider, might be detrimental to the final outcome.

Timing and Frequency

The timing and frequency of feedback can have an impact on its effectiveness. For example, if a supervisor lets two weeks pass before evaluating an employee's performance on a particular project, some of the impact will certainly be lost. The employee will have to try to remember all the pertinent details. For jobs that continue to change, this memory exercise can be difficult. If the employee did not perform well, the time lag may unfairly obstruct efforts to improve as his or her attention has shifted to other tasks. Further, this can raise the issue concerning the supervisor's motives for giving the feedback. As noted earlier, feedback recipients naturally consider the reasons why feedback is being provided. The longer the time lag, the more likely the recipient is to feel that there is something else going on that has caused the feedback to be given. As a result, the feedback can be more easily dismissed as not being job relevant.

Although fairly immediate feedback is usually preferable, we need to alert the reader to the fact that there are situations where providing feedback too quickly can be dysfunctional. On complex tasks, where employees are trying to figure out the processes that are linked to successful performance, providing corrective feedback as soon as the employee encounters difficulty can make them less self-reliant. In other words, the employee does not get the benefit of puzzling through the options and incorrect responses to fully learn how to perform a task.

The appropriate frequency of feedback is a difficult issue to address because feedback has something of a dual personality. On one hand, feedback contains useful information. On the other hand, feedback can represent a form of control. To see how this works, put yourself in the place of an employee who has just been given a new assignment. Your supervisor first shows you how to do the task and then stops by frequently to point out any mistakes you are making. Within a couple of days you begin to feel comfortable with what you are expected to do and how to do it. But how would you feel if your supervisor continued to come around and tell you how your performance could be improved? If you are like most people, the initial feedback would be welcomed, especially if the new assignment is relatively challenging. However, after a while the value of the information would decrease, while the perception of superfluous criticism and intrusion would increase. The proper frequency of feedback really depends on how much information the employee desires (this will be different for different individuals), how often a product is completed or service provided, and the point at which evaluation or adjustment is appropriate or necessary. Therefore, feedback should be frequent enough to supply relevant information without exerting undue control over the recipient.

Alternative Sources of Feedback

Although our discussion has focused on the supervisor as the source of feedback, there are many alternative sources. These include the employee's coworkers, clients or customers, other representatives of the organization, the job itself, and even the employee. When it comes to these alternative sources, supervisors who see a need to deliver negative feedback to subordinates should remember two important facts. First, these alternative sources may contradict the supervisor, offering different assessments of the quality of performance and the reasons for it. Second, subordinates may see these alternative sources as having higher credibility. In the following discussion, we argue that an effective supervisor will actually leverage off of the higher credibility of alternative sources in order to effectively deliver the message that performance improvement is needed.

Some feedback sources have direct contact with the recipient, and no one else is needed to pass along the performance information. Such sources would be providing *unmediated* feedback. It is not channeled through any source that could interpret or evaluate it. In other words, unmediated feedback is received directly from the job, from oneself, or from a customer or client. In contrast, feedback about job performance received from other sources, such as the supervisor or coworkers, is considered *mediated* feedback. For example, a customer complaining directly to an employee about a problem (i.e., unmediated feedback) and the supervisor passing along a complaint from a customer can be two quite different situations. The supervisor may over- or understate the gravity of the problem. The employee must try to determine from the supervisor's feedback what will satisfy the customer and worry about how the customer's complaint will affect the supervisor's evaluation of the employee.

Before we look at the differences between unmediated and mediated feedback and consider why they might have different effects on an employee, we should note that these forms of feedback are not as independent as they might appear. For instance, a supervisor may decide to have the employee chart his or her own progress on a project or to allow direct contact between employee and customer. In this way the supervisor is influencing what information the employee uses from an unmediated source and thus may be able to affect the results without having direct involvement in the feedback process. This tactic may be especially useful if the supervisor needs to convince the employee that performance is substandard and that performance improvement is needed. The employee may doubt the feedback if it is mediated and trust the negative feedback more if it is unmediated (or from other mediated sources such as coworkers).

As a general rule, the greater the distance between the recipient and the source of the feedback, the less credible the source appears. In other words, one's coworkers would tend to be seen as more credible than the personnel department as a source of feedback. Moreover, sources of unmediated feedback, such as the job or oneself, are often perceived as more valid than sources of mediated feedback, especially as employees gain additional job experience. Therefore, falling behind on one's job is an indisputable signal that something is wrong because the job cannot have malicious intent and its expertise and reliability are not in question.

In reading this you may have noticed a problem that organizations face in providing performance feedback. The agent most often responsible for providing feedback (the supervisor) is often viewed as having less credibility than the job, the employee, or the employee's coworkers. As a result, the organization relies on a source with only a moderate level of ability to influence behavior. For this reason, a supervisor might be more effective by influencing the sources of unmediated, such as specific, organizationally important aspects of the job, rather than by providing feedback directly. Indeed, current approaches to job design/redesign often focus on providing feedback from sources other than the supervisor, such as the job itself when enriched jobs are designed, or from coworkers when a team-based approach is initiated. An organization can use this method of providing feedback to improve the quality of employee work life and to give employees more involvement in decision making.

RECOMMENDATIONS AND IMPLICATIONS

The intent of this article is not to discourage organizations or managers from administering negative feedback because it is often an extremely important management tool. Instead, the point is that managers should use feedback wisely to reap the possible benefits. A supervisor can give feedback that has all the right qualities (i.e., it is constructive, specific, and immediate) and still not realize the desired effects. As we pointed out earlier, this can be due to a number of things such as the power of the supervisor or the attributions made by the recipient for why the negative feedback is being given.

The feedback process becomes complex as recipients interpret the feedback and combine it with other information. It may be discounted because of contextual factors (e.g., organizational rumors pertaining to the reason the feedback is given) or because it is discrepant with information from other sources. Therefore, simply giving feedback may not be enough. The source may need to explore with the recipient the latter's perceptions of the intentions behind the feedback and how it fits with other performance information. Some of the most effective feedback directs the recipient to other sources, such as important characteristics of the job. Performance feedback that one generates for oneself (unmediated feedback) may be more credible than feedback that is mediated through other sources.

Moreover, we cannot forget that sources may hesitate to give feedback when they anticipate negative responses. Supervisors can be helped to understand that there are sources other than themselves for feedback on employee performance. The most important thing that supervisors might do, in terms of feedback, is to structure situations whereby the recipients generate the feedback for themselves or feel comfortable requesting the feedback they need or desire. In the former case, this can be done in a number of ways. It may take training employees on how to better interpret the available feedback they have at hand or it may necessitate setting up new systems whereby they get the feedback directly. For example, in a service organization, it may mean having the employees review feedback or complaints from customers before these get forwarded to the supervisor. Further, the supervisor might then have the employees summarize the results and make recommendations for dealing with any problems.

There are several means by which supervisors can enhance their own value as a feedback resource. The first is to work at developing positive relationships with subordinates and to be a good role model. Research has consistently pointed to the fact that referent power is one of the best bases from which to direct employees. This may be especially true when the employees are professionals. Second, supervisors would do well to maintain certain areas of expertise that are seen as valuable by subordinates. We should point out that this is not necessarily technical knowledge. Depending upon their training and backgrounds, subordinates may need the supervisor's organizational knowledge more than they need concrete "how to" skills.

Further, it would be advisable to lessen the use of official or punishment-based power in conjunction with negative feedback. There is a growing body of knowledge that continues to show that, over the long run, these might not serve supervisors well when it comes to motivating their employees. Corrective feedback should be given informally and immediately. It should not be restricted to the context of a formal performance appraisal where the focus of attention is likely to be on adverse employment-related decisions regarding compensation, discipline, and discharge. Although a supervisor may find it necessary to deliver negative feedback during a formal performance appraisal in order to justify such decisions, one should not expect this feedback alone to be sufficient for teaching and motivating performance improvement.

In addition, the feedback provider needs to think about coupling important process feedback with the negative outcome feedback. Here again, we need to signal that timing can be especially important. If one's subordinate has just learned that his or her performance is below some appropriate level or standard, there will be an emotional reaction. Process feedback offered at the same time may not be well attended to or understood. It may take the recipient of the feedback a few days before he or she is ready for the details. When in doubt, it is best to ask the potential recipient what he or she needs and when. People are not perfect judges of their own emotions or needs, but it is still usually better than guessing.

CONCLUSION

The implication for management training is that there is no simple formula for effective employee feedback. Merely instructing managers to give specific and timely feedback is not always adequate. Managers must learn to analyze feedback environments, determine the credibility of different feedback sources available to employees, and check employees' perceptions of the feedback. Only then can managers make informed decisions about how to intervene in the feedback process. ■

REFERENCES

Ashford, S. J. (1995). The feedback environment: An exploratory study of cue use. *Journal of Organizational Behavior, 14,* 201–224.

Baron, R. A. (1990). Counteracting the effects of destructive criticism: The relative efficacy of four interventions. *Journal of Applied Psychology, 75,* 235–245.

Baron, R. A. (1993). Criticism (informal negative feedback) as a source of perceived unfairness in organizations: Effects, mechanisms, and countermeasures. In R. Cropanzano (Ed.), *Justice in the Workplace: Approaching Fairness in Human Resource Management* (155–170). Hillsdale, NJ: Lawrence Erlbaum Associates.

Cusella, L. P. (1987). Feedback, motivation, and performance. In F. M. Jablin, L. L. Putnam, K. H. Roberts, & L. W. Porter (Eds.), *Handbook of Organizational Communication* (624–678). Newbury Park, CA: Sage.

Fedor, D. B. (1991). Recipient responses to performance feedback: A proposed model and its implications. In G. R. Ferris and K. M. Rowland (Eds.), *Research in Personnel and Human Resources Management* (Vol. 9, 73–120). Greenwich, Conn.: JAI Press.

Fisher, C. D. (1979). Transmission of positive and negative feedback to subordinates: A laboratory investigation. *Journal of Applied Psychology, 64,* 533–540.

Herold, D. M., & Parsons, C. K. (1985). Assessing the feedback environment in work organizations: Development of the job feedback survey. *Journal of Applied Psychology, 70,* 290–305.

Ilgen, D. R., Fisher, C. D., & Taylor, M. S. (1979). Consequences of individual feedback on behavior in organizations. *Journal of Applied Psychology, 64,* 349–371.

Kluger, A. N., & DeNisi, A. (1996). The effects of feedback interventions on performance: A historical review, meta-analysis and a preliminary feedback intervention theory. *Psychological Bulletin, 119,* 254–284.

Sternthal, B., Phillips, L. W., and Dholakia, R. (1978). The persuasive effect of source credibility: A situational analysis. *Public Opinion Quarterly, 33,* 285–314.

Sweeney, P. D., & Wells, L. E. (1990). Reactions to feedback about performance: A test of three competing models. *Journal of Applied Social Psychology, 20,* 818–834.

Tang, T., & Sarsfield-Baldwin, L. (1991). The effects of self-esteem, task label, and performance feedback on goal setting, certainty, and attribution. *Journal of Psychology, 125,* 413–418.

VandeWalle, D., & Cummings, L. L. (1997). A test of the influence of goal orientation on the feedback-seeking process. *Journal of Applied Psychology, 82,* 390–400.

7

COMPENSATION AND REWARD SYSTEMS

Pay, in the form of wages and salaries and a wide range of legally required and agreed-upon benefits, collectively represents the means by which employees are financially compensated for joining organizations, staying in them, and accomplishing certain levels of work performance. The compensation activity in personnel management, therefore, is a key people-processing activity, which begins with the planning that occurs before people enter organizations and continues until their exit and beyond. For a good many organizations, the compensation provided employees can account for as much as 50 percent of total cash flow. For others it can account for an even higher percentage, especially if the organization's product or service system is labor intensive.

In addition to the equal employment opportunity laws—especially Title VII of the Civil Rights Act of 1964 and its amendment, the Pregnancy Discrimination Act of 1978, and the Age Discrimination in Employment Act of 1967—the legal environment in which the compensation activity is conducted is bounded by several other major pieces of federal legislation. The most basic of these is the Fair Labor Standards Act (FLSA) of 1938 and its amendments, including the Equal Pay Act of 1963, which contains provisions for minimum wage, overtime, and equal pay. Federal legislation also supports the Old Age, Survivors, Disability, and Health Insurance Program (OASDHI) and a number of legally required benefits associated with that program, such as Social Security and unemployment insurance. Another major piece of federal legislation is the Employment Retirement Income Security Act (ERISA) of 1974, which regulates the pension programs of employers and includes requirements regarding vesting, accrued benefits, funding, and so forth. Finally, the Revenue Act of 1978, the Economic Recovery Tax Act (ERTA) of 1981, and other tax laws define, as part of the Internal Revenue Code, the taxable or nontaxable status of benefits.

Organizations, in this context, must make their compensation systems both attractive and equitable to current and prospective employees. Information regarding the external labor market, often supplied through industry or area wage surveys, is necessary for determining an appropriate pay structure in making individual wage and salary decisions within that structure. Also necessary is information regarding the internal labor market. Again, is the compensation system attractive? Is it equitable? A variety of job evaluation methods are available for establishing pay grades and ranges for jobs on the basis of their relative worth to the organization. Attempting to make and then maintain a balance between the compensation demands of the marketplace and the compensation demands of employees is not an easy task. The task is further compounded by the rather subjective nature of the performance appraisal process (discussed in Chapter 6), which should be a primary source of information for making compensation decisions.

The first article (Lawler) is a nice summary and extension of the proper use of compensation with the evolving workforce. Lawler suggests a number of ways in which pay systems can fulfill their potential of facilitating organizational performance. Benson and Hornsby delve into the controversy over executive compensation. Executives are compensated at a rate that, in comparison with other industrialized nations, is disproportional to the wage paid to shop floor workers. In the last article, Benson and Scroggins present an overall picture of the compensation process, outlining the issues that continue to be problematic in organizations.

READINGS

PAY STRATEGY: NEW THINKING FOR THE NEW MILLENNIUM

Edward E. Lawler III

It is time for new thinking, new practices, and more strategic direction in the pay systems of organizations. The simple fact is that organizations, the business environment, and individuals are changing at a rate that is much faster than the rate of change with respect to the way organizations design and manage pay systems. There are a number of reasons for this. Pay practices are clearly hard to change. Pay system change is complex, in part because many individuals and organizations are comfortable with their existing pay practices and find it difficult to leave them behind. But this is not a sufficient reason to accept a slow rate of change and misaligned pay systems. It is simply too important to have a pay system that supports an organization's business strategy and contributes to organizational effectiveness.

All too often a misaligned pay strategy not only fails to add value, it produces high costs in the compensation area as well as inappropriate and misdirected behavior. Thus, organizations that fail to adapt their pay systems to today's business challenges operate with a significant handicap and at a tremendous disadvantage.

It is beyond the scope of this article to go into detail with respect to the major societal and business changes that have implications for pay system change. But it is worth highlighting some of the key ones in order to underline the amount of change that has occurred.

More and more products and services are competing globally and this has led to much greater competition. Organizations increasingly need to operate globally—moving products and people across national boundaries in seamless ways. In order to be successful, organizations increasingly have to get their products to market more quickly and improve their customer service. The Internet is creating new sales channels and changing the way information is distributed and managed within organizations.

In order to be competitive, organizations increasingly have to operate with lateral processes that are supported by advanced information technology systems. Increasingly, work in a number of areas requires advanced knowledge and skills.

Organizations can no longer afford extensive hierarchies with command and control management structures. More and more individuals do not have stable work activities that can be described as jobs. Instead, they have roles and general areas of responsibility that they flexibly perform. Individuals no longer have a traditional loyalty contract with organizations. Instead, they have a temporary relationship in which they try to maximize their rewards while adding to their skills and capabilities. Because individuals don't see companies being loyal to them, they are not loyal to their employers and are increasingly willing to change jobs when better opportunities present themselves.

Key technical and management skills frequently have more demand than supply and as a result, certain individuals become "hot talent" and enjoy considerable leverage in negotiating for their working conditions. The workforces of many organizations are becoming more diverse and as a result, there are large, individual differences in what their employees want from work and how they want to be treated by reward systems. Individuals increasingly work in teams and are collectively responsible for producing products and services.

There is no reason to believe that business will return to the way work was done when most of the current pay practices used by organizations were developed and fine-tuned. If anything, with the increased development of e-business and the Internet, the rate of change is likely to accelerate. The explosive growth of the Internet, for example, is likely to lead to greater globalization. Employee mobility and workforce diversity will continue to increase. We are likely to see more cases of "hot talent," and the growth of businesses in which knowledge development is the key to organizational success.

The challenge, and it is a significant one, is to develop pay systems that fit the way organizations, individuals, and society are changing and to change pay systems at the speed of business. No single pay system or set of pay practices is likely to provide the answer to how organizations should alter their pay systems. I do believe, however, that there are three major strategic positions that organizations should take with respect to pay systems that will allow them to develop pay practices that will be effective in the future. These three strategic approaches are described below.

PAY THE PERSON

Historically, the pay systems of most large organizations have been based on jobs and job evaluation technology. This approach made sense in a world in which individuals had stable duties and the market value of individuals was largely determined by the way

in which their jobs were designed and managed. In a world in which individuals do not have traditional jobs and are often able to add considerable value because of their high levels of knowledge and skill, it is very dangerous and misleading to pay them according to job worth rather than their individual worth. It ignores the difference-making value that is added by people with high levels of knowledge and performance. It also fails to encourage individuals to develop the right skills and knowledge.

Increasingly, human capital is the key capital for an organization. Human capital must earn a fair return or like any other capital it will search for a higher rate of return and it will frequently find it. Thus, organizations must be sure that their people are paid according to their market value. Pricing the job that they are doing at the moment is simply not a good enough way to value individuals. They must be valued for the knowledge, skills, and competencies that they have. This evaluation must take into account not just the internal labor market within their organization, but the external labor market as well. Indeed, it must primarily take into account the external labor market. Placing too much focus on the internal labor market runs the great risk of either underpaying highly valued individuals or overpaying individuals who do not have the knowledge and skills that the most valuable employees have.

Developing an approach that pays individuals according to their market value requires a pay system which measures the knowledge, skills, and competencies of individuals and prices them in the external market. At this time, the technology to do this is admittedly still under development and in a rudimentary form, but organizations still can begin to pay individuals according to their market value. They often can get a good idea of the market value of their key individuals simply by monitoring the actual hiring transactions that go on in the labor market. This, of course, is a far different approach from the traditional one of looking at salary survey data in order to gain information about what individuals doing particular jobs are paid.

Perhaps the greatest challenge in paying individuals for their skills, knowledge, and competencies is developing good measures of them. Too often organizations that have tried to measure them have chosen to measure the degree to which individuals possess very generic competencies, such as leadership ability and communication ability. They have not written specific knowledge and skill descriptions for the roles that individuals need to perform and then developed measures of whether individuals have these specific skills and knowledge. As a result, they have not developed systems that are particularly good at rewarding individuals for developing the kinds of technical and business knowledge that individuals need in order to perform effectively.

I believe that in the future we will increasingly see organizations develop detailed, intranet-based descriptions of the kind of knowledge and skills individuals need to be effective in their roles. They will also have skill and knowledge profiles of their employees available on the intranet. These person descriptions will be supported by measures of skill and knowledge mastery and used as a basis for the market pricing of individuals, the assignment of work, and the development of individuals.

By tying increases in pay to the development of the skills and knowledge that is called for in person descriptions, organizations will be able to accomplish two very important objectives. First, they will have a positive effect in motivating individuals to learn the skills and knowledge they need to perform in their current role, and second, they will raise the pay of individuals as they become more valuable in the external labor market. These two outcomes are clearly key to developing pay systems that create learning organizations and organizations that develop and retain valuable human capital.

REWARDING EXCELLENCE

There are a number of reasons why an intense focus on paying for performance is appropriate. It is an important way to attract and retain top performers and it is a potentially powerful motivator that can be a partial substitute for a traditional loyalty employment relationship.

The research literature on pay has for decades shown that although pay can be an effective motivator, often it is not. A few theorists have argued that, in fact, pay cannot be a motivator, but the research evidence does not support this view. Instead, it argues that pay motivates behavior when there is a clear relationship between a significant amount of pay and behavior, but it goes on to argue that often because of poor plan designs, pay winds up motivating dysfunctional behavior as well as functional behavior. It also has conclusively established that the traditional approach to pay for performance—merit pay—is generally a failure. It is a failure for numerous reasons, including the fact that it is often based on poor measures and it usually delivers such small changes in compensation that it has no motivational impact. Further, it fails to pay good performers highly enough to retain them in a hot job market.

Perhaps the most important thing that we have learned from the research on pay for performance is that there is no silver bullet. No single plan fits all organizations nor is pay for performance an accomplishable objective in all organizations. Nevertheless, pay for performance needs to be an important part of most organizations' reward systems. The type of pay for performance that is utilized needs to very much reflect the strategy, structure, business processes, and management style of the organization.

The pay for performance approach of an organization needs to effectively translate its business strategy into measures that can be used for reward system purposes and it needs to fit the characteristics of the organization's structure with respect to coordination and integration. It is unlikely that any one pay for performance plan or approach will be able to accomplish all the objectives that the reward system needs to accomplish. Thus, an effective pay for performance system for an organization is likely to have multiple pay for performance plans.

Individual pay for performance systems accomplish different objectives than do team and organization-wide pay for performance systems. Bonus systems have different impacts than do stock-based plans. Thus, organizations need to carefully design a combination of pay for performance plans that covers all the objectives they need to accomplish with their plans.

The point has already been made that merit pay increases are poor motivators. Part of the problem with them is that they create an annuity payment which employees receive as long as they are employed regardless of their future performance. This ties up a considerable amount of an organization's payroll in an inflexible base pay commitment. One of the major effects of this is that few salary dollars are left to reward present performance. Thus, one key recommendation is that in the future, organizations should rely on variable pay plans in order to reward performance.

Every organization needs to carefully consider the use of stock. Stock ownership and stock options are powerful ways to reward performance. They can be given to individuals based on performance and, of course, their value changes as an organization's performance changes. They do suffer from one major weakness, however. The line of sight from an individual's behavior to the value of stock is often poor, thus for many members of an organization they may not have a powerful, motivational impact. Nonetheless, when organizations are trying to integrate everyone toward a common set of goals and a mission, broad-based stock plans can be quite useful because they give everyone a common fate. Stock option plans also can be a powerful way to retain individuals if they require individuals to remain with an organization in order to exercise them.

One of the most difficult decisions in pay system design concerns whether to reward individuals, groups, business units, or the organization as a whole. Plans that reward individuals clearly accomplish different objectives than plans that reward the organization as a whole. The former are a much more powerful motivator of individual behavior. Plans that reward the organization as a whole are good at integrating individuals and encouraging them to understand the business and develop effective lateral relationships, but poor at directly motivating individuals. Team bonus plans can be extremely powerful in motivating team performance and cause individuals to work together to accomplish the team's goals and objectives. On the other hand, they do little to encourage teams to work together.

Given the different impacts of individual, team, and business-based pay for performance plans, they may all have a place in a single organization's approach to paying for performance. For example, individuals may be paid based on their individual performance, their team's performance, as well as on their businesses' performance. This makes good sense in situations where individual performance can be measured; individuals are part of a team whose performance is well measured, and the organization is practicing employee involvement in a way that encourages individuals to understand the business and participate in decisions affecting the entire organization. Under this set of conditions, it makes sense for an organization to have three different types of pay for performance plans.

If individual performance is not measurable because highly interdependent teams are used and the major focus should be on team performance, a system that rewards team performance and organizational performance may be most appropriate. Finally, in situations where individual performance is all that counts and the organization does not practice employee involvement, an individual pay for performance system that is highly leveraged with variable pay may be all that is appropriate.

Given the trends in organization design toward lateral organizations, employee involvement roles, rather than jobs, and the lack of loyalty, it is possible to make some general statements about what pay for performance approaches are likely to become more popular. Clearly broad-based stock plans are likely to become much more popular. They fit the idea of employee involvement and they support the development of lateral thinking in organizations. They also do not require the kind of individual performance metrics that are difficult to collect in a role-based organization. Team-based pay for performance plans are also likely to become much more popular. The increasing use of teams and the difficulty in measuring individual performance makes this particularly likely. Team-based cash bonus plans have the potential to develop a good line of sight and can be a direct motivator of individual performance.

The use of profit-sharing plans and plans which pay bonuses based on business unit and operating unit performance is also likely to increase significantly. Particularly in small business units and in operating units such as plants, they have the potential to create a reasonably strong line of sight, and research on gainsharing and goalsharing suggests that they therefore can be quite effective motivators. With education and employee involvement, a reasonable line of sight can often be developed so that individuals see how their performance impacts performance measures and therefore the bonus that they receive. Particularly if the bonus offered is of a significant size it can be an effective motivator of performance.

The loser is individual pay for performance. Not just merit pay, which has already been dismissed, but variable individual pay. It simply does not fit as well in lateral team-based organizations as does team- and organization-based pay for performance.

When the practice of paying individuals for their skills and knowledge is combined with a system which rewards performance, organizations can use pay systems as an effective substitute for loyalty. The pay system can encourage people to develop the skills the organization needs to have and it can motivate them to stay with the organization. It can also motivate them to perform well. Thus, it can do much more than the loyalty system, because seniority-based loyalty systems are primarily effective at encouraging individuals to stay with an organization. Because loyalty systems do not reward skill development or performance effectiveness, they do not motivate individuals to improve their skills or perform effectively. Thus they fail to do a good job at developing the human capital of an organization and retaining the most valuable employees.

INDIVIDUALIZING THE PAY SYSTEM

Traditionally the pay programs of organizations have adopted a one-size-fits-all approach to rewards. Individuals are given little choice with respect to how they are rewarded and what rewards they receive. The differences that exist within organizations are usually the result of the type of work individuals do rather than their needs and desires. This approach generally fits a homogeneous workforce but does not fit a diverse workforce. With a diverse workforce it runs a tremendous risk of giving individuals rewards that they do not value while failing to reward them with things that they value highly. This can obviously have negative consequences for both the attraction and retention of individuals as well as for motivation.

The obvious alternative to a one-size-fits-all reward system is one that gives individuals a significant amount of choice. In the United States, some organizations have taken one step in this direction with the installation of cafeteria or flexible benefit plans, but in most cases it is a small step. Individuals are given little choice and, as a result, these plans are not very effective. With a diverse workforce it may make sense to give individuals a considerable amount of choice in the reward packages that they are offered. This can include individuals being given options with respect to working simply for cash, having extensive benefit packages, and even choosing the type of pay for performance system that they are covered by. The advantages of greater flexibility include tailoring rewards to employee preferences and thus greater effectiveness in attracting and retaining a diverse workforce. The potential negative of this approach is that it may create too diverse a workforce for a company that wants to establish a strong unified culture.

Because the reward system is a powerful tool for attracting and retaining individuals, a one-size-fits-all reward system tends to lead to a homogenous internal population of employees. This can be a real negative if it leads to not enough individuals wanting to work for an organization and/or a homogenous culture that lacks adaptability and flexibility, as well as the ability to understand diverse markets. On the other hand, it can be a positive if the organization has a very specialized niche and the kind of performance capabilities that it needs are best developed by having an internally homogenous workforce.

Organizations need to think through the consequences of having a diverse versus a homogenous workforce and then pick the reward profile that fits the degree and type of diversity they desire. Given that many organizations are moving towards a more diverse workforce and becoming more global, it is likely that organizations will increasingly choose to have flexibility and individualization in their reward system. This simply makes sense with respect to optimizing the impact of the dollars organizations spend, particularly organizations which are dealing with diverse markets and multiple national cultures.

CREATING THE STRATEGIC REWARD SYSTEM

What should the pay systems of organizations look like in the future? Based on how organizations are changing and the impact of reward systems, I have suggested that three strategic thrusts are appropriate:

- Person-based pay should be used to reward individuals for their skills, knowledge, and competencies relative to their external market value.
- Multiple pay for performance approaches should be used, with variable pay and stock as rewards.
- Reward systems should be individualized to fit the characteristics of individuals that an organization wishes to attract and retain. In most cases, this can best be done by allowing individuals a choice in the rewards that they receive.

Although these strategic thrusts are widely applicable, they clearly do not fit all situations and they are only the first step in developing an actual reward system for an organization. The next step is to develop actual pay practices that follow them and fit with the management style, structure, and strategy of the organization. This step involves developing a good understanding of the business strategy, the appropriate measures of organizational effectiveness, and of course, an understanding of the kinds of relationships and communication patterns that are needed in order for an organization's structure to be effective. In short, the three approaches are the basic building blocks upon which an effective pay system can be built for tomorrow's organizations. ■

THE VIEW FROM THE TOP:
THE CONTROVERSIES OVER EXECUTIVE PAY

Philip G. Benson
Jeffrey S. Hornsby

> *The identity of all classes of labor is one thing on which capitalist and communist doctrine wholly agree. The president of the corporation is pleased to think that his handsomely appointed office is the scene of the same kind of toil as the assembly line and that only the greater demands in talent and intensity justify his wage differential. The communist office-holder cannot afford to have it supposed that his labor differs in any significant respect from that of the comrade at the lathe or on the collective farm with whom he is ideologically one. In both societies it serves the democratic conscience of the more favored groups to identify themselves with those who do hard physical labor. A lurking sense of guilt over a more pleasant, agreeable, and remunerative life can often be assuaged by the observation 'I am a worker too' or, more audaciously, by the statement that 'mental labor is far more taxing than physical labor'. Since the man who does physical labor is intellectually disqualified from comparing his toil with that of the brainworker, the proposition is uniquely unassailable.*
>
> —John Kenneth Galbraith (1958)

In calendar year 1999, Jack Welch, the CEO of General Electric, earned $577.3 million, when unexercised stock options are included. In the same year, and again including all components of pay, Sanford Weill, CEO of Citigroup, earned $228.5 million, Lawrence Bossidy of Honeywell International earned $183.7 million, and Douglas Ivester of Coca-Cola Company earned $188 million. These figures have prompted the largest labor organization in the United States, the AFL-CIO, to list them on their Web page, along with rather critical commentary on the reasonableness of such pay when compared to the performance of the firms in question. Likewise, other popular sources have been critical of executive pay, including the Web site for Graef Crystal, a former consultant for executive compensation plans and now a major critic of the practices he once helped to establish. (These Web sites can be found at www.aflcio.org/paywatch/index.htm and www.bloomberg.com/columns/ respectively). Also, the Friday, April 6 edition of *USA Today* compared the nation's highest paid executives to current sport stars such as Alex Rodriquez. The article discusses the similarities in salaries as well as the criticism sport stars and CEOs receive for high salaries. Under mounting criticism for receiving high performance bonuses when the value of company stock has decreased greatly, Hewlett Packard's Carly Fiorina gave up $1 million of her annual bonus compensation. The article cites other firms such as McDonalds, Spring, AT&T, and Bank of America as other targets for reducing CEO pay.

Clearly, many people have become concerned over the levels of executive pay, and such criticisms can be especially harsh. Not only are corporate executives highly paid, the pattern suggests that this is especially true in the United States. Consider the figures when executive pay levels in the United States are compared to the levels found in other industrialized countries (Anonymous, 2000). In the United States, CEOs of Standard & Poor's 500 leading firms on average earn about 475 times more than the typical workers in their firms, whereas in Europe the figure is from about 11 to 24 times as much. Clearly, executives in general earn very high levels of compensation, and this is especially true in the United States.

Part of the concern over high levels of executive pay is the rate at which these salaries have increased, not just the levels of pay that have been attained. For example, critics (e.g., Blumenthal, 2000) have pointed out that from 1990 to 1999, top executive pay increased 535 percent, whereas the profitability of the firms on average increased 116 percent. In addition, the pay of the typical American worker increased only 32 percent in the same time frame. If the average workers' pay had increased as fast as the pay of corporate CEOs, the average American worker would today be earning $114,035, but the actual figure for workers is instead only $23,753.

How is it that such high salaries are set? Are they reasonable? What kinds of justification is there for such extreme levels of pay? Does payment of such extreme salaries give a return to the organization that justifies the cost, and do such pay policies help to align executive behaviors and goals with the overall goals of the employing organization? Over the last decade or two, these issues have seen increasing controversy, and strong arguments have been made on both sides of the issue. It is the nature of this controversy that will be reviewed here.

Before reviewing the specific methods (and controversies) applicable to this issue, first we will discuss the theoretical background to CEO pay. By initially discussing these issues, perhaps the reason such pay practices are commonplace will be more clear.

AGENCY THEORY AND THEORETICAL VIEWS OF CEO PAY

In recent decades, HR scholars have increasingly turned to agency theory as a way of describing pay practices in general, and especially the pay given to executives (Eisenhardt, 1989). Agency theory is largely derived from the work of economists, and general discussions can be found in such texts (e.g., see Mas Colell, Whinston, & Green, 1995; Milgrom & Roberts, 1992). The theory has also seen increasing use in management, and has important implications when applied to HR issues such as executive pay.

Essentially, this view says that firms have principals and agents, and that aligning the goals of both is often difficult. Principals "own" the firm, but in all but the smallest of firms (sole proprietorships with no employees) the principal must hire others to help in running the enterprise. These employees are "agents" of the owner, and the essential problem is to recognize that they have goals and desires that are sometimes not consistent with the desires of the principal.

At a formal, mathematical level agency theory can be both very complex, and may be a less-than-perfect description of reality.

However, as a general description of economic interactions, certain key points emerge that are useful in understanding the behavior of employees and the policies of their employers. First, the theory assumes that an agent is averse to effort, and would prefer to be paid without exerting any more effort than absolutely necessary. In addition, the agent is assumed to be risk averse, and in an employment relationship, the agent realizes that some aspects of performance are really not within his or her control. Thus from an agent's perspective it would be best to be paid for the hours actually worked, because this would require the least effort, and would also "smooth over" any random fluctuations in output that are beyond the employee's control. The principal, however, would like to encourage effort on the part of the employee, and would like to eliminate risk by controlling the cost of any goods produced. This can be done by paying the worker for the actual units produced, rather than for the time spent on performing work tasks regardless of output.

This model is fine for discussion of work output that is easily measurable, such as would be found in units produced in a manufacturing context. However, when executive pay is considered, the outputs are not clearly measurable, and coming up with incentive approaches is not as easily done. The primary question is how to bring the concept of "risk" into the pay of CEOs and other top executives. In recent decades, the general approach has been to increase the "at-risk" element of executive pay, and to give executives an interest in the firm's overall success. This is best seen in an increase in the use of such compensation strategies as the use of stock options and other ownership plans; in this way, the executive becomes a stockholder, and this in turn increases the degree to which the CEO's interests are aligned with the interests of the stockholders in gen-

eral. More will be said about these kinds of compensation plans later in this article.

In many regards, the pay given to corporate executives tends to parallel the pay of "superstars" in general. Such individuals are paid far higher salaries than others in their industry, and usually the justification for such high pay is the notion of limited supplies of people with the skills needed to perform at that level (Rosen, 1983). In this view, extremely high salaries are given because the demand for such rare talent far exceeds the number of people available with the requisite ability to perform at the level required. In addition, very high salaries can be given to such individuals to indicate their value, either to the highly paid individuals themselves, or to signal value to other firms (Baron & Kreps, 1999). In short, even though the salaries given to CEOs and other executives may seem very high, there are theoretical reasons why such pay is given; however, these reasons have not eliminated criticism of such practices, and it is clear that many people find such rates of pay to be difficult to justify. What, then, are the ways we pay executives, and how do these pay forms relate to the organization's goals and objectives?

FORMS OF CEO PAY

In general, executive pay is considered to be comprised of four distinct components (Joyce, 1999). These include base salary, short-term incentives or bonuses, long-term incentives or stock plans, and perquisites. Although CEO pay can take any of these forms, increasingly the trend is to use variable pay for executives (Hanson, 2000a, 2000b). In general, variable pay or "at-risk" pay places far less emphasis on salary, and far more emphasis on items that reward the executive only under certain circumstances. Thus in the last decade we have seen CEO pay that has a much smaller proportion in base pay, and a much greater portion in such things as stock options and incentives.

Considerations in CEO Base Pay

Base pay is what we think of as "the pay-check," the amount of money that is given for some unit of time. In the United States, a base pay rate in excess of $1 million is not unusual for the CEOs of large corporations, and yet this amount is only a small portion of the total pay given such individuals. Because many individuals have been critical of such high pay, in 1993 Congress passed the Omnibus Budget Reconciliation Act, which includes a provision to limit the amount of executive pay that can be deducted for corporate taxes; this amount was limited to $1 million for the top five executives in a corporation, but does provide for increases beyond that limit if certain conditions are met, including shareholder approval. Thus limits on base pay are still rather high and not really limited, and the fact is that executives get much of their pay through other mechanisms regardless, so the limits have little impact. Indeed, one can argue that the law ironically suggests that top executive pay be $1 million, setting a minimum for such pay rather than setting a maximum (Henderson, 2000).

Performance Bonuses and Short-Term Incentives

Much of the pay given to CEOs is in the form of incentive pay, and these incentives can be either short-term or long-term in orientation. Short-term incentives include additions to pay that are given in a current operating year (Henderson, 2000); these are becoming increasingly popular as a form of at-risk pay for all levels of the organization, not just for executives. In recent years, the trend is for executive pay to emphasize more bonuses and less base pay (Hansen, 2000a, 2000b).

Long-Term Incentives

We also pay incentives to executives, where the time frame emphasized is much longer in scope. Long-term incentives are supposed to motivate strategic thinking based on a longer, at least three- to five-year, time frame. A variety of practices can be mentioned here.

Stock Ownership   One particular issue is the use of company equity, or stock holdings, as a means of aligning executive interests with the interests of the shareholders. In the framework of agency theory, discussed earlier, this makes tremendous sense as a way of motivating executives to further the interests of the owners of the firm (i.e., the stockholders). One approach is to simply require executives to own some minimum amount of stock in the company. By making them stockholders, it can be assumed that they will take on some of the interests of stockholders in general. However, most ownership plans are far more complex, and involve a variety of ways to encourage the executives to take a keen interest in the performance of the company. One such way is to give stock in lieu of cash bonuses. Companies that are not publicly traded may offer a phantom stock plan where the executive is given shares of stock based on the current assessed value of the company. Upon retirement or leaving the company, this "stock" can be cashed in and will be valued based on the value of the firm at the time the phantom shares are turned in to the company.

Stock Options   Stock options entitle executives to purchase company stock in the future at a predetermined price. The price of the stock is usually based on the current selling price of the stock the day the options are issued. The executive can then exercise the options and purchase the stock when the price of the stock has appreciated. Again, this incentive approach is viable under agency theory because it causes the employee to take an interest in the long-term value of the company. Stock options are seen as very positive to executives because Internal Revenue Service regulations require taxes to be paid on the capital gains only when the stock is actually sold by the executive. In order to moderate the taxes paid on gains when selling stock, many firms now offer their executives nonstatutory or discount stock option plans (Martocchio, 2001). These plans offer options at a discounted rate to the current share price. The executive pays taxes on the amount of the discount up front and thereby moderates the taxes paid in the future when the options are exercised.

Recently, many executives have realized that their current stock options are essentially worthless. Many organizations have seen a great decline in share value during years 2000 and 2001. This devaluation in the compensation package to many talented executives has caused the company to increase the number of options provided when the stock prices are depressed. This increase in options should pay off once stock prices increase over time. Other firms are simply revaluing the price of exercising the options to reflect the current stock price. Firms engaging is this practice should explore the tax consequences before implementing such a program.

Supplemental Retirement Plans Supplemental retirement plans are designed to provide additional compensation to executives and not violate the "qualified status" of the company's regular retirement plan. Qualified plans provide current-year tax benefits to employers and allows employees to accrue retirement savings with pretax dollars. However, IRS regulations require qualified plans to be nondiscriminatory in that they do not favor more highly paid employees. Most qualified plans then would not provide a highly paid executive enough in-

come replacement. Supplemental retirement plans can make up the difference. In these plans, the employer invests for the employee, usually in the form of a life insurance policy or a trust account. The executive gains access to the funds upon retirement.

Executive Benefits and Perquisites A longstanding means of compensating executives has been through the use of special benefits, called perquisites or "perks." These can take many forms, and historically were very advantageous from an income tax standpoint. However, over years the IRS has increasingly restricted the tax advantages of perks, but many are still in use. Today, most perks are viewed as a form of income and taxed at the executive's current tax rate. Some common perks include use of a company jet or car, spousal travel, low interest loans, legal and financial services, parking, an entertainment allowance, and club memberships.

One controversial form of perk is the use of "golden parachutes" for top executives in corporations. As the rate of corporate mergers and acquisitions escalated in the last few decades, these have grown substantially in popularity (Thompson, 1999, 2000). Essentially, these provide benefits to executives if their firm is acquired or merged, and pay substantial financial benefits to those individuals who lose their job due to the new corporate structuring.

Golden parachutes are in practice quite variable, and can take many forms. Commonly, the executive's base pay can be continued after the takeover (and subsequent release of the executive from employment), and sometimes may continue for several years. Also, benefits may be continued, and any bonuses that would have been given may also be mandated as part of the package. Another common requirement is to mandate that all stock options become immediately vested; this has an interesting implication. To take over a company requires that current stockholders agree to the bargain, and for this reason there is usually a favorable outcome for stockholders. This in turn will typically cause a run-up in the price of the acquired company's stock, which makes stock options a very attractive form of compensation, at least in the short term.

It is typical that relatively few executives are eligible for the golden parachutes that are given, but even so, the costs can be substantial. This in turn makes the value of the takeover less to the acquiring company, and in turn this discourages hostile acquisitions of firms. In spite of these additional costs, however, the pace of mergers and acquisitions has continued to increase.

EXPLAINING THE NEED FOR HIGH COMPENSATION PACKAGES

Many explanations can be provided for why executive compensation has grown to the amounts cited earlier in this article. Two explanations offered here include the understanding of the employee motivational process and the executive agent acting with a mercenary agenda.

Motivation and Executive Compensation

The Porter and Lawler (1968) model of motivation is a well-received approach to understanding individual motivation and can be applied to the executive pay process. Porter and Lawler's (1968) Integrative Model of Motivation incorporates important elements of Adam's (1965) Equity Theory of Motivation and Vroom's (1964) Expectancy Theory of Motivation. Based on this model, effort to performance relationships are made by both the company and the executive. An executive's attraction to a specific position is based on how much the executive values the rewards, in this case the total compensation package offered, as well as the social/psychological rewards that the employment provides, and any other

rewards the executive values. Once the individual takes the position, his or her motivation to continue is contingent upon comparisons made between actual rewards and expected rewards. Also, in order to offer and to continue to provide such high compensation packages to executives, management must believe that strategic and managerial actions will lead to specific outcomes achieved by the firm, such as increased innovative behaviors, and increased sales, profit, and/or market share. Therefore, two important compensation activities must be implemented to attract and retain talented executives and to justify high compensation packages.

First, accurate market pricing through market surveys must be conducted to determine the market value of the position. Firms in the same industry and firms who hire similar individuals with similar qualifications should be surveyed to determine the market price for the executive position. Offering a salary package below market value would create a low value to the employee and reduce his or her motivation to take the position. Second, performance standards should be developed to provide benchmarks for merit pay increases. Often standards such as gain in share value, market share, and other growth indicators are utilized. The problem is that often these benchmarks are hard to tie directly to executive performance.

Agent Executive as Mercenary Operative

Milkovich and Newman (1999) paint a dim picture of top executives. They claim that they may "blatantly manipulate" the system to increase wages in any circumstance. Three scenarios for increasing wages are provided. First, if the CEO is really underpaid, a consultant is utilized to survey the "true" competitors of the company. The consultant, based on the survey results, reports to the board of directors that the CEO is underpaid and recommends an amount to be market-competitive. Second, if the CEO is not underpaid and the firm is doing well, a consultant is hired to conduct a salary survey. Under these circumstances, the consultant is provided with firms to survey. These firms are selected based on the high salaries paid to executives. The skewed survey report will again suggest the CEO is underpaid and deserves a raise. Third and finally, if the CEO is not underpaid but the firm is doing poorly, a consultant is hired to identify ways to keep key talent from going to competitors during tough financial times. No effort to identify the causes for poor firm performance are studied. The consultant makes recommendations to increase wages to avoid the loss of the key talent.

The second two methods of using a consultant cause executive salaries to be inflated. However, many compensation experts blame this result on the seeding of company boards with peers, other firm's CEOs. In colloquial terms it is the proverbial "I'll scratch your back if you scratch mine." Boards use the faulty data to justify pay increases due to business necessity and not political payback.

RECOMMENDATIONS FOR MANAGING EXECUTIVE PAY PRACTICES

As stated at the beginning of this article, CEO compensation is under increasing scrutiny because of its growth relative to other employee groups. In fact, executive compensation has grown despite the financial setbacks experienced by most firms in the early 2000s. Several practices can be recommended to ensure that executive pay, especially CEO pay, is fair and equitable and is high enough to ensure the attraction of talent but not too high to fly in the face of efficiency and fairness to employees and company stockholders. First, watchdog organizations, especially those financed by concerned stockholders, play a viable role by

ensuring that bylaws and regulations are followed when developing and implementing executive compensation plans. These organizations can draw attention to outrageous compensation rates and initiate activity to reduce compensation packages to reflect economic reality. Second, improved board governance and selection procedures would allow the selection of board members who are not politically in the pocket of the chief executive. Conflict of interest clauses should be made clear and be rigidly followed. Third, systematic procedures for conducting accurate market surveys should be implemented. A true random sampling of competitors should be conducted to determine the real price of the executive position. Fourth, and related to the previous suggestion, consultants should adhere to ethical guidelines for the profession. Perhaps the ethical code provided by the Society for Human Resource Management (SHRM) for human resources professionals could be followed. Finally, improved performance management for senior executives is necessary. Practical performance standards should be delineated and adhered to during the evaluation period. Pay raises, bonuses, and other forms of compensation should be based on meeting and/or exceeding these standards.

In summary, it is not the intent of the authors to generalize the belief that all CEOs and other senior executives are overpaid or have purely mercenary intentions. Many, in light of their experience and firm performance under command, are paid fairly. In these cases, one must turn to motivation theory to understand the need to offer marketable salaries and provide raises, bonuses, etc., to continue to reinforce desired behavior. It is not unreasonable to demand a higher salary than what the executive is currently paid to make a job change. The companies themselves must also receive something in return for such high compensation. Paying high compensation rates must also be reinforced by achieving desired organizational objectives that are clearly stated and understood by the employee. However, many CEOs are overpaid. Implementing the recommendations made here may help stem the tide of rising compensation and develop a more fair and equitable mechanism for distributing the rewards of work. ■

REFERENCES

Adams, J. S. (1965). Inequity in social exchange. In Leonard Berkowitz (Ed.), *Advances in experimental social psychology*, New York: Academic Press.

Anonymous (2000, September 30). Economic indicators: Executive pay. *The Economist, 110*.

Baron, J. N., & Kreps, D. M. (1999). *Strategic human resources: Frameworks for general managers*. New York: John Wiley & Sons.

Blumenthal, R. G. (2000, September 4). The pay gap between workers and chiefs looks like a chasm. *Barron's, 80* (36), 10.

Eisenhardt, K. M. (1989). Agency theory: An assessment and review. *Academy of Management Review, 14* (x), 57–74.

Galbraith, J. K. (1958). *The affluent society*. Boston: Houghton Mifflin Company.

Hansen, F. (2000a). Currents in compensation and benefits. *Compensation and Benefits Review, 32* (5), 6–14.

Hansen, F. (2000b). Currents in compensation and benefits. *Compensation and Benefits Review, 32* (6), 6–13.

Henderson, R. I. (2000). *Compensation management in a knowledge-based world* (8th ed.). Upper Saddle River, NJ: Prentice Hall.

Joyce, W. B. (1999). Executive bonuses: Determination and payment. *Journal of Compensation and Benefits, 14* (4) 59–62.

Martocchio, J. J. (2001). *Strategic compensation: A human resource management approach*. Upper Saddle River, NJ: Prentice Hall.

Mas Colell, A., Whinston, M. D., & Green, J. R. (1995). *Microeconomic theory*. New York: Oxford University Press.

Milgrom, P., & Roberts, D. J. (1992). *Economics*. Upper Saddle River, NJ: Prentice Hall.

Milkovich, G. T., & Newman, M. (1999). *Compensation*. Boston: Irwin McGraw-Hill.

Porter, L. W., & Lawler, E. L., III. (1968). *Managerial attitudes and performance*. Homewood, IL: Richard D. Irwin, Inc.

Rosen, S. (1983). The economics of superstars. *American Scholar, 52* (4), 449–460.

Strauss, Gary (2001, April 6). CEO paychecks: Fair or not? *USA Today*.

Thompson, R. W. (1999). Golden parachutes are on the rise. *HRMagazine, 44* (9), 10.

Thompson, R. W. (2000). Golden parachutes soar in active merger climate. *HRMagazine, 45* (1), 10.

Vroom, V. H. 1964. *Work and Motivation*. New York: John Wiley.

EMPLOYEE COMPENSATION SYSTEMS AND HR STRATEGY: ISSUES AND PERSPECTIVES

Philip G. Benson
Wesley A. Scroggins

Over many decades, the management of human resources has required attention to the manner in which employees are compensated for their work efforts. Professionals in wage and salary administration paid special attention to issues such as job evaluation (the process of determining pay levels for different kinds of jobs in the same organization), wage and salary surveys (the process by which employers determine the competitiveness of pay levels compared to other organizations in the relevant labor market), and the role of merit and seniority in setting wages for specific employees in comparison to other workers doing the same kind of work within the organization. Additionally, the effective management of employee pay systems required substantial attention to the legal environment of HR, as numerous laws exist that limit the practice of salary administration.

Recently, the approach taken toward compensation management has taken a somewhat different direction. As with HR management in general, the notable shift has been toward a model that emphasizes strategic concerns in pay administration. Such a strategic approach still requires the organization to attend to issues such as the pay for specific jobs in the organization, monitoring the pay levels of other employers competing for employees in the same labor market, the bases of pay increases for specific employees, and the legal implications of HR practices. However, a strategic approach puts a different interpretation on some of these activities, and certainly has implications for the way we tie all of these activities together. What we'll review here is the nature of strategic HR management, and the way this impacts practice and theory in the management of organizational compensation systems.

WHAT IS A STRATEGIC APPROACH?

Managing the HR function from a strategic perspective requires a holistic approach to organizational functioning. For example, Baron and Kreps (1999) have strongly suggested that HR policies and procedures cannot be considered piecemeal, but instead are based in broad and powerful social, psychological, and economic forces, and unless the HR functions are made to fit together, the practices will end up in conflict with each other. Very different policies and procedures can be made to work in various settings, but the consistency of the "HR whole" is critical to consider.

The holistic approach to strategic HR management has been demonstrated by Hackett and McDermott (1999) in the context of administration of compensation systems in organizations. They show that a piecemeal approach to implementing compensation programs not only can fail to make the organization more effective, it may actually have negative effects, such that the firm would have been better off not to make changes at all. Poorly implemented compensation plans can have an effect that is contrary to the stated strategic goals of the organization.

Dreher and Dougherty (2002) have described a strategic model for human resources management, and have developed their model around the different components within HR functions. They have analyzed reward systems as having the following dimensions.

Pay Level

Should the firm pay the average for a particular job classification, pay more than other employers, or pay less than the market? These are also known as meet, lead, or lag market policies, and employers must fit somewhere into the economy in this regard. The correct policy for a given firm is dependent on many other HR considerations and the nature of the firm in question. The policy selected can have a major impact on organizational costs, the ability to attract and retain employees, and the satisfaction level of employees in the organization; all of these in turn can relate to overall firm strategies and the effectiveness of the firm in attaining its broader goals and objectives.

Pay Structure

What should be the relationships among pay levels for different kinds of jobs within a given firm? Very few firms have only one kind of worker, and it has been assumed that different kinds of work should receive different levels of pay. Many organizations are moving away from the notion of "paying the job" and have changed to an approach of skill-based (or competency-based) pay. In a system of this sort, employees are rewarded (through higher salaries) for learning new skills and adding to their capabilities, not for being promoted into a higher-level job that has a larger salary assigned to it. This approach is consistent with an emphasis on employee growth and development, and works well for firms in highly dynamic product markets where employee flexibility and adaptability is desirable.

Pay at Risk

Firms have increasingly emphasized "risk" in pay practices in recent years, but the choice is still dependent on the nature of the organization and its overall strategy. At-risk pay is administered in a way that increases are not guaranteed and, most importantly, the increases in pay tend to be given as a one-time increment, not as an add-on to an employee's base pay. In this way, a "good year" for an employee will be rewarded, but only once; in contrast, building it into the employee's base will ensure that the increment will continue to be given for as many years as the employee remains with the firm, regardless of future performance levels. A wide variety of plans can be used to increase the "at-risk" component of pay, and the appropriateness of any of these methods again depends on the nature of the firm in question and its overall strategies and goals.

Performance-Contingent Pay

Often, performance-contingent pay (or merit pay) is also administered at risk, but the two dimensions of pay strategy have slightly different implications, and may not always be tied in practice. To make pay contingent on performance is to pay people for their successes, in contrast to a seniority system that simply increases pay for time continued on the job. However, use of merit pay also assumes that performance differences are measurable, and that the system used by the organization is indeed perceived as fair by employees. If not, the system will not function to motivate desired behaviors.

In addition to these dimensions, Dreher and Dougherty (2002) show that these aspects of pay systems interact not only with each other but with other components of the HR system, and in fact reflect the overall organization. Staffing issues, career planning, benefits, advancement opportunities, training methods, and other such HR functions all form a coherent picture of the HR management function within an organization. We will return to issues of alignment of HR practices later in this article.

THE NEED FOR A STRATEGIC APPROACH

Much of the shift to a more strategic approach has been predicated by a fundamental change in the nature of modern organizations and in the work that is done in those organizations. For example, Heneman, Ledford, and Gresham (2000) have discussed in detail the nature of work as we enter the twenty-first century, and have shown that traditional compensation practices are not always a good fit to the modern organization. Significantly, in recent years the modern workplace has seen changes in the nature of the employment relationship, in technology, in business strategy, in organizational structures, and in job design; all of these have potential impacts on the design and administration of organizational pay systems.

Work relationships are increasingly nonpermanent in nature (Valletta, 1999; Williams & Ferris, 2000) and this impacts the employment relationship in both institutional and psychological ways (Heneman, et al., 2000). Roehling, Cavanaugh, Moynihan, and Boswell (2000) have reviewed the nature of the employment relationship and, although some inconsistencies emerge in the literature, the fundamental change that is most apparent is the trend toward employers being expected to provide support through developmental opportunities, employees being responsible for their own development of skills, and a declining emphasis on traditional views of job security and employee loyalty.

Williams and Ferris (2000) point out that some of these changes have strategic implications in HR. With the decline in an employment model based on the exchange of loyalty for job security, and the growth of a model based on the employee providing skills in exchange for opportunities to learn and thus develop even greater skills, employees have the potential to actually gain power in the employment relationship. Specifically, the newer employment relationship makes the employees a key variable in the organization's ability to develop a strategic competitive advantage over other firms.

In the framework of strategic HR, this means that employees become a source of unique organizational competitiveness. To the extent that human resources provide sustained competitive advantage for the employer, those resources have potential strategic value to the firm (Barney, 1991). More specifically, Barney and Wright (1998) have suggested that resources which provide strategic advantage can be characterized as having value, rareness, imperfect imitability, and organization.

Consider the role of the human resources in an organization from this perspective. The value of the human organization is reflected in knowledge and skills possessed by individuals, in cooperation or communication patterns that have developed among individuals or groups, and in relationships that develop over time among organizational members and with individuals external to the organization. All of these factors can be resources that are valuable organizational assets, especially when they meet the criteria for core competencies and function as a means of competitive advantage for the organization possessing them. Employee knowledge and skill have received considerable attention in recent years as organizations recognize the importance of knowledge and learning for competitive advantage. This is evident in the emphasis on continuous learning in many organizations today (Noe & Ford, 1992). Employees are motivated to actively participate in the learning process to develop knowledge and skills the organization values and believes are important for competitive advantage. If organizational members possess knowledge or skill that is rare and differentiates them from employees in competitor organizations, then these members, and the knowledge and skill they possess, are of value to the organization and provide the organization with competitive advantage.

Cooperation, communication, and relationships among organizational members and others external to the organization can also provide value and be a source of sustained competitive advantage. This is especially true when the nature of the cooperation, communication, and relationships is unique and difficult to imitate. Many resources possessed by organizations that are likely to function as sources of sustained competitive advantage are likely to be those that involve social processes among the organization's human resources. Social processes among organizational members are often hard to imitate. They are often rooted in unique historical conditions, are path dependent and causally ambiguous and, therefore, very difficult to imitate by organizations that do not have the same history. Furthermore, they are often socially complex and are difficult for other organizations to develop and manage (Barney, 1991). Unique forms of cooperation, communication, and relationships among organizational members and between these members and key individuals external to the organization are valuable to the extent that they facilitate the accomplishment of goals and objectives that are beyond the ability of competitor organizations. They will serve as sources of sustained advantage to the extent they are rooted in the history of the organization, and are causally ambiguous and complex, so that they cannot be easily imitated or substituted by competitors.

Strategically, human resources practices such as compensation should be used to reinforce behaviors valuable to the organization. Compensation practices could become a core competency in and of themselves, being rare and imperfectly imitable and valuable. More often, however, compensation practices will be used to reinforce the more difficult to imitate factors previously discussed that may function as core competencies and sources of sustained competitive advantage. Compensation structures and policies need to be aligned with strategy so that compensation practices reinforce employee behaviors and attitudes that lead to the development of the valued core competencies necessary for strategic advantage (Barney & Wright, 1998; Becker, Huselid, Pickus, & Spratt, 1997). Compensation mixes and levels should be competitive so that the organization is able to attract and retain highly skilled workers and motivate these workers to engage in continuous learning and skill development. If cooperation, relationships between organizational members, or customer relationships are the factors around which core competencies exist or are to be developed, then the compensation system should reinforce and reward behaviors and attitudes that facilitate cooperation and interpersonal relationships. An organization's human resources can be a source of value and sustained competitive advantage and the organization's HR practices, including compensation practices, must be used to create this value.

STRATEGIC PAY AND THE CONSISTENCY OF ORGANIZATIONAL HR PRACTICES

In the literature on strategic management, issues of fit have long been recognized. Recently, these have been discussed in the context of strategic management of HR; in particular this has emphasized the distinction between internal alignment and external alignment. Discussions by Barney and Wright (1998) and Becker and Huselid (1998) have been especially good examples of this approach.

Internal or horizontal alignment refers to the alignment of various human resources practices and policies that complement each other and consistently convey valued organizational behaviors. External or vertical fit refers to the alignment of the human resources system with the mission, goals, and objectives of the organization and the degree to which behaviors produced by the human resources system are appropriate for the implementation of the organization's strategy. Our focus will be primarily on the issues related to internal fit and the alignment of various human resources practices.

Barney and Wright (1998) argue that sustained competitive advantage results from human resources systems more than from single human resources practices. Aspects of human resources that are valuable, rare, and inimitable will be sources of competitive advantage only if the organization is prepared to use these resources. Organization of the firm focuses attention on systems instead of single HR practices used in isolation. This requires a shift in traditional thinking about functional areas of HR management. Instead of considering HR subfunctions (recruitment, selection, training, performance assessment, and compensation) in isolation, each of the organization's HR subfunctions needs to be viewed as an interrelated part of an interdependent HR system. It is the interrelatedness of the system that will create competitive advantage because the complex interactions among the parts can be very difficult, if not impossible, to imitate.

Research indicates that HR practices are more effective when they are internally aligned with other HR practices in a system (Huselid & Becker, 1995; Lado & Wilson, 1994; MacDuffie, 1995; Wright & McMahan, 1992). Huselid and Becker, in a study involving more than 1,500 companies, found that the combination of lead-market compensation policies with performance management programs had a 50 percent larger effect than the effects of the two policies considered independently. They believe this effect is due to the synergistic effects that result from the subtle interactions between the various components when they are combined into a system. They call these subtle interactions and unintended consequences "powerful connections" and believe that these add value to the organization when the economic returns from the HR system as a whole are greater than the sum of the individual HR subfunctions. Management's objective should be to develop systems of practices that create synergistic effects, rather than focusing upon individual practices in isolation. This is accomplished by aligning each of the HR functions in such a way that there is a high level of internal fit and each of the functions are reinforcing the same attitudes and behaviors, and focusing employees' attention on common organizational goals and objectives. This means that when considering HR system components (selection, training, compensation), each is evaluated and considered within the context of the other components of the system. When individual components are aligned with each other it increases the likelihood that the system will provide value to the organization by giving competitive advantage. If individual HR practices are not aligned with each other, these individual practices can be in conflict with each other, with the greater HR system, and with the overall organizational strategy, and have the potential of diminishing value and competitive advantage.

Consistency as an issue for strategic management of human resources has been further discussed by Baron and Kreps (1999), who consider several further distinctions among measures of internal alignment or consistency. First, there is the issue of having various HR policies and practices that are in agreement with each other, what has been referred to as single-employee consistency. The essential issue here is that one employee should not feel that various components of the HR function are in conflict, such that HR practices need to attain some degree of alignment. Pay practices have a substantial impact on employee attitudes (Heneman & Judge, 2000), employee attraction and retention (Barber & Betz, 2000), and employee motivation (Bartol & Locke, 2000), and thus it is critical that compensation plans augment other HR functions. Baron and Kreps (1999) also discuss the issue of among-employee consistency, and suggest that the treatment given to one employee must be the same as that given to other, similarly situated employees. Issues of among-employee consistency go far beyond the issues of strategic HR, but clearly there are strategic impacts on the firm. Finally, Baron and Kreps also discuss issues of temporal consistency or continuity. This requires policy makers to consider how employees are treated over time, and to recognize that certain kinds of stability are desirable from an employee's perspective. Although the environment of modern organizations can be far more fluid than that of past eras, it is still desirable to have some degree of predictability in organizational management. We will address each of these forms of consistency in more detail.

Single-Employee Consistency

Single-employee consistency is necessary to ensure that the employee does not feel that the organization is sending "mixed messages" and creating ambiguity in terms of expectations for the employee. This is especially true for managing employee behaviors that are robust or intractable, and resistant to change. For such behaviors, multiple policies and practices, consistent with each other and supportive of the desired behavior, are needed to adequately encourage the necessary behavioral outcomes. Dreher and Dougherty (2002) point out in particular that properly aligned HR policies and practices create the HR function as a coherent whole, and show that congruent HR prac-

tices provide a firm with distinct competitive advantages. To integrate HR systems requires firms to (1) focus multiple and powerful forces on employee behaviors of interest; (2) ensure that staffing, reward, and development practices do not conflict; and (3) ensure that varied HR practices are mutually supportive.

Among-Employee Consistency

The issues of among-employee consistency suggest that each employee should be treated in a manner consistent with the treatment accorded other workers in the same firm. This is especially obvious in the literature on organizational justice, and the great emphasis given to issues of fairness in treatment of employees (Folger & Greenberg, 1985).

Research has identified two types of justice or fairness that are important to employees: distributive justice and procedural justice (Cropanzano & Folger, 1996). Both of these can be impacted by issues of among-employee consistency. Distributive justice refers to the perceived fairness of outcomes. For example, the perceived fairness of the amount of compensation given for performance is a distributive justice issue. Procedural justice refers to the perceived fairness of the process and procedures used to make decisions about employees. The process or manner by which management decides on the amount of compensation for performance is an issue of procedural justice (Mathis & Jackson, 2000). When HR policies and practices result in different outcomes for similarly situated employees or in the differential treatment of certain organizational members, employees' perception of distributive and procedural justice are often negatively impacted.

A number of factors that have been found to impact perceptions of distributive and procedural justice. Distributive justice is affected by perceptions of equity between an employee's outcome/input ratio and the outcome/input ratio of similarly situated others. For instance, if a high-performing employee receives the same pay raise as a low-performing employee, inequity is likely to be perceived and perceptions of distributive justice violated. In this case, there are true performance differences between the employees, but the organization does not recognize the differences and outcomes for the employees are the same. Likewise, two employees may have similar performance records and one receive a significantly greater pay increase than the other. In this case it is also likely that perceptions of distributive justice will be violated (Mowday, 1996). In both cases the ratio of outcomes to inputs is perceived to be different for an employee in relation to other organizational members. The implication for compensation practices is that high levels of both internal and external equity need to exist for organizational members to perceive outcomes as distributively fair. If internal or external equity do not characterize the compensation system, it is likely that employees will have negative perceptions of distributive justice regarding organizational outcomes.

Numerous factors have also been identified that affect employee perceptions of procedural justice. Research suggests that employees are more likely to consider procedures as just and fair when those procedures are applied consistently and without personal bias when the opinions of affected employees are solicited and taken into account, when they are made with as much accurate information as possible, and when they are subject to modification if needed (Folger & Greenberg, 1985). All HR practices, including compensation policies, should consider these factors when developing and implementing policies and practices that affect organizational members. When the processes by which managers make personal decisions are characterized by these factors it is more likely that employees will perceive the processes to be procedurally just and the more likely it is that the procedures and resultant outcomes will be acceptable to employees. In the context of compensation, managers must apply pay policies consistently across time and employees; consider employees' opinions regarding compensation types and amounts; collect as much job-related information as possible regarding job evaluation, market rates, and employee performance; and be willing to modify procedures within reason if they are not acceptable to employees. A failure to give consideration to factors that can make processes and procedures more positive may result in violations of organizational members' perceptions of procedural justice.

Temporal Consistency

In this regard, an organization's HR policies and procedures should be in some sense predictable, showing coherence from one point in time to another. Again, assuming that HR practices form an organized pattern and are not "piecemeal," an employee should be able to infer likely organizational positions on issues that have not been previously addressed. In addition, rules should be stable within reason, and employees should be able to trust the organization's future stance on issues based on their past experiences.

In compensation, a long-standing issue has been the controversy over the use of piece-rate pay systems, and this controversy is not likely to be resolved soon (e.g., see Wilson, 1992). In this approach, employees are paid for the units they actually produce, and not for the time they spend in production of those goods or services. For many decades, an issue of concern has been the view of employees that management cannot be trusted, and that working harder will not lead to greater income (for higher production), but rather will lead to changes in the piece rate so that employees will merely be working harder for the same pay. Whether or not this actually occurs is immaterial, as long as employees perceive that this will be the likely outcome of increased effort. Indeed, not only does the use of a piece-rate system presuppose a degree of trust between management and labor, but it is possible that instituting a piece-rate system can actually cause a deterioration in labor-management relations (Wilson, 1992).

TYING COMPENSATION STRATEGY TO THE OVERALL STRATEGY OF THE FIRM

The pattern of HR activities needs to be internally consistent and patterned, but compensation policies also must reflect the larger organizational strategy. This is important for various reasons, and can be achieved in multiple ways. For example, Dreher and Dougherty (2002) have proposed a model of strategic HR systems that describes the interconnections among various components of a firm. In this model, the firm's overall business strategy and the technology of production are direct causes of certain organizational design options, and lead to certain work processes. These organizational designs and work methods/processes in turn lead to specific behavioral and role requirements for employees, and it is these behaviors that must be the focus of HR system design. Further, Schuler and Jackson (1987) have expanded on the types of employee role behaviors that can impact competitive strategies of firms.

Consider the following issues suggested by Schuler and Jackson (1987). Employee role requirements can vary in many dimensions, such as the need for employees with repetitive predictable behavior versus the need for employees who are creative and innovative, the need for very cooperative behavior among employees versus the need for employees who are autonomous and independent, the need for high versus low risk

taking by employees, the need for a short-term focus by employees versus the need for a long-term focus, a high versus low concern for quality, a high versus low concern for quantity, a high concern for process versus a concern for outcomes, or the need for high versus low involvement in the job or organization. Using these and other dimensions, Schuler and Jackson point out that the overall strategy of the firm can determine the kind of employee role behaviors that are demanded. For example, a firm with a strategy of innovation would require behaviors that include an emphasis on creativity, a longer-term focus, a requirement for cooperative and interdependent behavior, a moderate concern for quality and quantity, and a greater degree of risk taking. Using Dreher and Dougherty's (2002) dimensions of HR practice, especially as regards compensation, it would seem that the firm should consider a pay policy that leads the market (to ensure the ability to hire and retain the best workers), the use of performance-based pay at the team level (to encourage positive interactions among coworkers), a reduced emphasis on at-risk pay (to encourage innovative thinking and risk taking by employees), and little emphasis on seniority-based pay (to encourage high performance). In short, the "best" compensation practices are to be determined on a case-by-case basis, and no single pay strategy should be held out as a panacea for all organizations.

CONCLUSION

Pay in the modern organization is a complex responsibility for the HR professional, and requires greater innovative thinking than at any previous time in the history of the field. As we enter the twenty-first century, the demands on wage and salary professionals will continue to increase.

At one time, an emphasis on the technical aspects of wage and salary administration was sufficient for the practicing HR manager. An HR manager was expected to provide technical and administrative support, and to make sure that HR activities were done in a conscientious and timely manner, while being as fair to employees as possible. In the new era of HR, this is not enough; while technical adequacy is still of critical importance, the modern wage and salary administrator needs to move into the role of a strategic partner, and needs to see how HR practices can have positive impacts on the long-term success of the firm. ■

REFERENCES

Barber, A. E., & Betz, R. D., Jr. (2000). Compensation, attraction, and retention. In S. L. Rynes and B. Gerhart (Eds.), *Compensation in Organizations: Current Research and Practice.* San Francisco: Jossey-Bass.

Barney, J. (1991). Firm resources and sustained competitive advantage. *Journal of Management, 17* (1), 99–120.

Barney, J., & Wright, P. M. (1998). On becoming a strategic partner: The role of human resources in gaining competitive advantage. *Human Resource Management, 37* (1), 31–46.

Baron, J. N., & Kreps, D. M. (1999). *Strategic human resources: Frameworks for general managers.* New York: John Wiley & Sons, Inc.

Bartol, K. M., & Locke, E. A. (2000). Incentives and motivation. In S. L. Rynes and B. Gerhart (Eds.), *Compensation in Organizations: Current Research and Practice.* San Francisco: Jossey-Bass.

Becker, B. E., & Huselid, M. A. (1998). High performance work systems and firm performance: A synthesis of research and managerial implications. In K. Rowland and G. Ferris (Eds.), *Research in Personnel and Human Resources Management* (Vol. 16). Greenwich, CT: JAI Press.

Becker, B. E., Huselid, M. A., Pickus. P. S., & Spratt, M. F. (1997). HR as a source of shareholder value: Research and recommendations. *Human Resource Management, 36* (1), 39–47.

Cropanzano, R., & Folger, R. (1996). Procedural justice and worker motivation. In R. M. Steers, L. W. Porter, and G. A. Bigley (Eds.), *Motivation and Leadership at Work* (6th ed., 72–83). New York: McGraw-Hill.

Dreher, G. F., & Dougherty, T. W. (2002). *Human resource strategy: A behavioral perspective for the general manager.* Boston: McGraw-Hill.

Folger, R., & Greenberg, J. (1985). Procedural justice: An interpretive analysis of personnel systems. In K. Rowland and G. Ferris (Eds.), *Research in Personnel and Human Resources Management* (Vol. 3, 141–183). Greenwich, CT: JAI Press.

Hackett, T. J., & McDermott, D. G. (1999). Integrating compensation strategies: A holistic approach to compensation design. *Compensation and Benefits Review, 31* (5), 36–43.

Heneman, H. G., III, & Judge, T. A. (2000). Compensation attitudes. In S. L. Rynes and B. Gerhart (Eds.), *Compensation in Organizations: Current Research and Practice.* San Francisco: Jossey-Bass.

Heneman, R. L., Ledford, G. E., Jr., & Gresham, M. T. (2000). The changing nature of work and its effects on compensation design and delivery. In S. L. Rynes and B. Gerhart (Eds.), *Compensation in Organizations: Current Research and Practice.* San Fransisco: Jossey-Bass.

Huselid, M. A., & Becker, B. E. (1995). High performance work systems and organizational performance. Paper presented at the 1995 Academy of Management Annual conference, Vancouver, BC.

Lado, A., & Wilson, M. (1994). Human resource systems and sustained competitive advantage: A competency-based perspective. *Academy of Management Review, 19,* 699–727.

MacDuffie, J. (1995). Human resource bundles and manufacturing performance: Organizational logic and flexible production systems in the world auto industry. *Industrial and Labor Relations Review, 49,* 197–221.

Mathis, R. L., & Jackson, J. H. (2000). *Human resource management* (9th ed.). Cincinnati: South-Western College Publishing.

Mowday, R. T. (1996). Equity predictions of behavior in organizations. In R. M. Steers, L. W. Porter, and G. A. Bigley (Eds.), *Motivation and Leadership at Work* (6th ed., 53–71). New York: McGraw-Hill.

Noe, R. A., & Ford, K. J. (1992). Emerging issues and new directions for training research. In K. M. Rowlands and G. R. Ferris (Eds.), *Research in Personnel and Human Resources Management* (Vol. 10), Greenwich, CT: JAI Press.

Roehling, M. V., Cavanaugh, M. A., Moynihan, L. M., & Boswell, W. R. (2000). The nature of the new employment relationship: A content analysis of the practitioner and academic literatures. *Human Resource Management, 39* (4), 305–320.

Schuler, R. S., & Jackson, S. E. (1987). Linking competitive strategies with human resource management practices. *Academy of Management Executive, 9* (3), 207–219.

Valletta, R. G. (1999). Declining job security. *Journal of Labor Economics, 17* (4), S170–S197.

Williams, S. L., & Ferris, G. R. (2000). The changing nature of the employment relationship: Reclaiming values in the workplace. *National Productivity Review, 20* (1), 25–30.

Wilson, T. (1992, March–April). Is it time to eliminate the piece rate incentive system? *Compensation and Benefits Review, 24* (2), 43–49.

Wright, P. M., & McMahan, G. C. (1992). Alternative theoretical perspectives for strategic human resource management. *Journal of Management, 18*, 295–320.

8

HUMAN RESOURCES DEVELOPMENT

The training and development of human resources is an important activity in organizations. The outcomes of any of the previous activities (e.g., recruitment and selection, performance appraisal) may indicate need for improvements in work performance, updates in job knowledge, modifications of existing skills and abilities, or a new awareness of and response to changing environmental conditions. Training and development, in its many aspects, is used by organizations and employees to advance their individual and collective self-interests.

Estimates suggest that U.S. organizations spend more than $200 billion a year on the planning and implementation of all types of training and development programs, ranging from technical skill training to management development. With an investment of this magnitude, one would expect organizations to have a good deal of evidence concerning the benefits of those programs. However, the contrary is true: In most organizations the quality of the evaluation component of training and development has been seriously neglected. Organizations are fairly conscientious in their efforts to determine training and development needs and to design the content, structure, and techniques of programs to meet those needs, but few if any systematic efforts are exerted in program evaluation. Much program evaluation today is limited to collecting the subjective reactions of program participants rather than evaluating the longer-term, more objective measures of change in behavior. But, with an increasing focus on accountability and strategic human resources management, we will very likely see more careful attention paid to program evaluation in the future.

The first article, by Zenger, Ulrich, and Smallwood, takes the approach that people can be developed into leaders. Perrewe, Young, and Blass discuss the important concept of mentoring in organizations. Their interesting twist is that we must realize that the mentoring process occurs in a political atmosphere. Political forces that operate in an organization influence human resources development. Gilmore's article on executive coaching outlines an approach whereby executive talent can be developed in an organization through a relatively long-term relationship between organization, individual, and consultant. The Martinez article focuses on women and what is necessary to train them for positions of leadership in organizations. The final article, by Dubois, addresses the evolution of one's career and those competencies necessary for success in the future.

THE NEW LEADERSHIP DEVELOPMENT

Jack Zenger
Dave Ulrich
Norm Smallwood

Here are some of our own experiences that illustrate several concerns about past leadership development programs:

- "My first experience with leadership development was as a graduate student. The university offered a program called 'Skill Practice in Supervision.' I was a graduate assistant, responsible for the administration of the program, and in time I became a staff member running some of the sessions. In this program, we never talked about skill, there was never any practice, and supervisory challenges were never addressed. It was pure sensitivity training. People liked it, but later research showed no lasting behavior change came from it."
- "A *Fortune* 500 company hired a group of prestigious consultants and academicians to conduct a leadership development program, and I felt honored to be in the group. A great deal of effort was directed at making the presentations relevant to the company. The faculty and facilities were top-drawer. The participants rated those as well as the food, handouts, and support staff. Virtually every element of the program was scrutinized.

   "But what was striking was the total unwillingness to evaluate whether the participants had learned anything or whether they'd applied what they learned. It was clear that the client didn't care whether the program produced any results; the only concern was how the participants felt about the program. Unfortunately, that seems to be the rule, not the exception."
- "I was working with a firm that initiated a major executive development program for senior people at the corporate and operating company level. The bill exceeded $2 million per year, not calculating any participant time off the job. At the end of the second year, I asked the director what changes he could see as a result. He smiled and said, 'I can't see one thing that has changed. Nothing.'"

The disparate experiences we described have some things in common, and they illustrate some of the flaws in current leadership development. Everyone running those programs was doing what seemed best at the time. They used the latest teaching and learning methods. They wanted to make a difference in the lives of the participants. The executives from the client companies that sponsored the activities believed in the importance of developing their key people. They willingly spent money and gave participants time off from work. The immediate results were some new ideas, a broadened perspective, new ways of framing problems, and some new tools.

The ultimate outcomes of those programs also had much in common. There was no evidence of permanent improvement or that the participants were better leaders in the end—and that, ostensibly, was the purpose for which the programs were given.

RADICAL REMEDIES

The fundamental problem in leadership development isn't the lack of executive support or ample expenditure. It is, instead, the huge disparity between what is being spent and the return from that investment in contrast to what the return could be if leadership development were done more effectively.

As practitioners who have seen a number of approaches to leadership development, we propose some radical remedies.

Clarify the Business Purpose and Desired Outcomes   Organizations often embark on leadership development because they "ought to be doing something to develop their leaders." So, with the best of intentions, they initiate a major effort. What's usually missing is a clearly stated business objective for the outcome. Absent clarity about the business purpose, it's impossible to evaluate the effectiveness of an activity. That does not have to be the case. Here are some business purposes that leadership development could target:

- Produce measurable gains in the productivity of an organization's knowledge workers.
- Solve a thorny company problem in supply chain management.
- Implement an important company initiative, such as greater diversity, more innovation, or better retention.
- Introduce a new strategic direction, such as moving the organization toward globalization through acquisitions and strategic alliances.
- Help the organization be first or faster to market with new products or services.

- Increase the market value of a publicly traded company by increasing its management equity.

Any one of those business objectives removes the related activity from the realm of doing it because you "ought to" and ties it to a business outcome. If your development programs have a clear business case, your organization's leaders are more likely to support those programs, and that support will be sustained over a longer period of time. We predict that participants will be less inclined to skip sessions because they can identify with the business purpose.

Put Leadership Development into an Organizational Context   A description of a highly regarded and popular executive development program reads: *The focus of this program is thus on the leader as an individual . . . on the personal dimension of leadership. It recognizes that leadership is primarily a process of human interaction and that to improve it, a leader must begin with objective self-awareness.*

That statement further illustrates some of our concerns about many leadership development activities. The emphasis is placed on the individual, devoid of any organizational context. Yet, we know people who are skillful leaders on a football field but not effective in leading a business team. A person who is a brilliant leader of a small group of technicians can be ineffective trying to convince a board of directors to take a new direction in research. And we know an executive who was extremely successful in one organization but failed after moving to another.

We don't think it's possible to separate effective leadership from an organization and its mission. The nature of that organization, including its norms, culture, values, history, work processes, and systems can't be ignored. They make up the stage on which the leadership drama is played, and that stage has a large bearing on the success of the leader.

Viewing leadership primarily as a process of human interaction is, we fear, a bit like saying that being a great surgeon is primarily the skill of making and suturing incisions. Those are the observable actions of a surgeon, but they are the front-end diagnosis of the reason to operate and omit the knowledge of physiology and anatomy required. We argue that any definition of leadership should include results, not just the method or process of human interaction. Developing a clear vision isn't necessarily done through human interaction, though a vision is well recognized as an important element of leadership.

We think it's a mistake for a leadership program to make self-awareness the ultimate goal and to ignore organizational awareness. If self-awareness is the basic key to being a good leader, then psychotherapists should be our best leaders. That hasn't proven to be true in most cases.

Further, organizations are constantly changing and creating new demands on leaders. Companies are becoming streamlined, with integrated processes, more employee involvement, and increased emphasis on teams and shared leadership. Hierarchies are flattening, organizations are becoming boundary-less. The workforce has changed from a population of factory workers to one of white-collar and knowledge workers. But though factory workers are about 50 times more productive than they were in the 1880s, knowledge workers seem not to have made improvements in productivity. In fact, Peter Drucker has said that most knowledge workers are less productive than they were in 1929. New challenges change the demands on the people who lead organizations.

The strategy of an organization should be the foundation of any leadership development effort. The vision of where the organization is going is paramount, and any effective development program must help leaders be clear about and articulate that vision to everyone. In every activity, the leaders must be crystal clear about the desired end-state.

That all suggests that the most effective leadership development takes place inside an organization rather than elsewhere. Does that mean that public programs provide no value? Certainly not. But the payoff from such programs is the contact with leaders from other organizations, the exposure to seminal thinkers, and the fresh perspectives from being away from the organization. Public programs can have enormous educational value, but they tend to have little impact on a leader's ability to produce better results—and that's ultimately what leadership and leadership development are about.

Start at the Top

People in an organization pay close attention to what the people at the top do. Every effective leadership development program must have the full endorsement of senior-level managers, who have to be good examples of whatever is being taught in the program. It's imperative to have the entire top team go through whatever program is planned. If not, there is the invariable question: "If this is so important, how come the top brass hasn't been through it?" Or, "This is good stuff. It's too bad the top execs don't know about it."

In fact, it's even more powerful when senior executives serve as instructors. Think of Jack Welch's legendary visits to Crotonville. He'd get into the pit with GE executives and interact one-on-one. We know of many senior executives who routinely spend a day or an evening with every leadership development group. Intel CEO Andy Grove taught sessions in the company's supervisory development programs for many years. When people asked how he could afford to take the time, he'd reply, "Where can I have more leverage in shaping the future of Intel?"

Begin with Results, Back into Attributes

Leadership development programs have traditionally operated on the hope that if they could increase executives' competencies and knowledge, that would over time enable them to produce better results on the job.

For example, a General Motors director of personnel development said, "In our experience, [leadership development] has to do with getting people to reflect on and reexamine things they have come to believe about themselves, the organization, and other people in the organization. It's those beliefs and assumptions that drive their current behavior."

But the link between what took place in most leadership development programs and participants' performance on the job was tenuous. The organizers of such programs hoped that the participants would build that bridge, but the research hasn't confirmed that it ever happened.

We believe it's far more powerful to start at the other end. Begin with results: "What does this leader need to accomplish in the next six months, as seen by those above, alongside, and below?" "What outcomes—balanced among the interests of employees, customers, the organization, and investors—should be produced?"

Any leadership development effort ought to produce leaders who are more skilled at recruiting and hiring people, and who instill enthusiasm for the organization and its mission in everyone working there. Leaders should develop the capability and the commitment of the workforce. They should improve the loyalty of the customer base. They should produce results that enhance financial performance. They should leave behind a more robust, stronger organization than the one they inherited.

In other words, leaders should produce measurable results. That's what leadership development is about. It's not about making a leader a better person or providing new bodies of knowledge. Those are only vehicles to reach results.

The main point we seek to drive home is to stop hoping for results that might occur as we build competencies, knowledge, or someone's character. That's the wrong place to start. By starting with results, there's a much greater likelihood that participants will develop missing competencies, acquire needed knowledge, and behave as better role models—plus achieve the results the organization requires. Why? Because they'll see more clearly the link between results and the attributes required to obtain vital outcomes.

In most leadership programs, far too much time and attention have been placed on analysis and diagnosis; too little have been spent on implementation. Leadership is all about action. Without skillful implementation, no amount of analysis or planning is of any value.

Rather than select people on the basis of their competencies, a more effective approach is to look into a person's past to see what he or she has done. Someone who was captain of the soccer team, student body officer, or debate team captain or who began their own business is more likely to succeed as a leader later in life. Such people have a habit of producing results. They're comfortable being in the spotlight and taking responsibility for outcomes. They like to make a difference and achieve.

Build Scoreboards for Results

How hard would athletes play if no score was kept? The scoreboard motivates them to focus and perform with intensity, and it links to people's natural desire to do their best and excel.

Many leadership development programs have encouraged each participant to leave with a defined series of actions to undertake. We strongly applaud them and advocate the next logical step. Though it's valuable to have a list of to-do's, leaders need to leave a program with ways to measure progress in selected areas.

For example, the examples on page 336 under "Clarify the business purpose and desired outcomes" lend themselves to measurement: the effectiveness of a diversity initiative, better employee retention, progress to globalization, more management equity. The latter can be measured by comparing stock price as a multiple of EBIT, compared to other firms. In the 1960s, 85 percent of the value of a firm's stock was based on earnings. Now, that number has declined to 55 percent. The remaining 45 percent is made up of intangibles, of which 40 percent, our colleague Tom Lawson says, is attributable to the public perception of what a firm and its stock are worth. The lesson would be that Crotonvilles ultimately pay off in an increased market value.

Without scorecards, a leadership development activity might be an enjoyable exercise, but neither the company nor the executives can expect much in the way of outcome. We suspect that leads people to perform short of their true capacity.

Link Competencies to Results

Competencies will make the most sense to participants if they can see the link clearly between a competency and the organization's desired results. Then, the competency has a purpose.

For example: There has been much discussion about the competency of coaching as an important leadership skill. But why? We believe that coaching behavior translates into some clear business benefits. Leaders who coach

- create more loyalty, which results in higher retention of workers
- communicate an expectation of continual improvement that results in ever-improving performance and productivity
- are better informed about organizational problems and issues, because

people come to them more readily (and the leader experiences fewer surprises)
- create a work climate of open, direct, candid communication (and a culture in which problems are resolved quickly, there's less turf protection, and people are inclined to share information).

Every competency statement should be followed by the words *so that* and a list of business benefits, outcomes, or results—whatever term you want to use—produced by that competency. Better yet, leaders should know how the people with whom they work view the leaders' competencies. In what areas are they strong? What needs shoring up? That information is of enormous value to leaders in laying out their self-development plans.

In years past, it was popular to discuss the difference between leadership and management. It often boiled down to leadership being about inspiring and motivating people, while management had to do with numbers, budgets, structures, processes, and financial performance. Many of us found that distinction artificial and concluded that most people in key positions in any organization have to be both leader and manager. We prefer to see the coming together of those dimensions as the necessary characteristics of a true leader.

A true leader must raise the bar on what results an organization expects and must help the people inside seek loftier goals. True leaders help people perform better than they would have if the leaders hadn't been there. That happens when a leader sees a far greater potential and doesn't shrink from asking people to achieve it.

Change the Learning Methodologies

Traditionally, leadership development programs have included a variety of learning methods. The most prominent:

- lectures
- case studies

- discussion groups
- reading assignments
- simulations.

A few programs have added physically challenging experiences such as whitewater rafting or mountain climbing to teach teamwork, improve interpersonal relations, and build self-awareness.

Here's what we believe the most effective leadership development programs in the future will do:

- Spend time planning in detail what participants need to do differently on returning to their jobs.
- Create measurements that will be used when participants return to work.
- Offer tailored skill-building activities targeted specifically to an individual's needs, based on personalized data collection such as 360-degree feedback.
- Provide engaging and realistic simulations that let participants experience the consequences of their decisions in compressed time.
- Provide examples and stories from respected, seasoned leaders inside the firm that explain how things are best accomplished inside the organization. (For example, the U.S. Marines have senior officers meet with aspiring officers to describe how they secured an enemy vessel with minimal advance preparation.)
- Create action-learning projects in which participants tackle real and important issues the organization faces and in which they take some role in implementing their recommendations. (A recent *Business Week* article describes Siemens's management education programs as executive teams solving problems that in times past would've been given to outside consulting firms. Siemens estimates that it has saved approximately $11 million in one year.)

- Provide mechanisms for follow-up and tools for holding people accountable.

That transition follows several principles that we suggest should guide all developmental activities:

- Use practical, concrete content, not academic or theoretical.
- Structure job-related activities rather than those irrelevant to the real work of the organization, regardless of their excitement or entertainment value.
- Use involving, emotionally engaging, action-oriented learning methods and activities.
- Create ongoing activities and short sessions rather than long, one-time events.
- Focus on implementation skills instead of stopping at problem-solving and decision-making skills.
- Emphasize learning that can be immediately applied instead of distant applications.
- Generate accountability on the part of participants.
- Develop feedback mechanisms from peers, staff, and people higher in the organization.
- Use the most respected, talented executives of the organization in the learning processes. Let them coach the aspiring leaders.
- Group participants from the same organizational level. They'll be more comfortable and will face similar issues.

Transform Leadership Development from an Event into a Process

Leadership programs have traditionally been one- or two-week events. In participants' minds, when the event was over, leadership development for the year was over. The most effective leadership development programs in the future will transform an event into a process that lasts a participant's entire career.

In lieu of a two-week session, we strongly favor three- to five-day sessions spaced over 18 to 24 months. Between formal sessions, other learning mechanisms can occur. Formalized sessions are valuable because they shield participants from their jobs. Because people are working longer hours and everyone's pace has quickened, there's a need for formal programs to temporarily protect participants from the pressures of work. However, formal sessions should be viewed as punctuation marks, not the text.

In the intervening times, online or telephone coaching can be useful, as are buddy groups. In addition, a series of e-mail messages can maintain participants connection. There should be a constant review of the metrics showing results, including periodic reminders of the commitment and the changes that were agreed to.

Create Accountability

Missing from most leadership development programs is accountability. Most rely on smile sheets and shy away from tests or measures, fearful of hurting participants' self-esteem or alienating an important client. But leadership is about accepting responsibility and accountability. If participants in a leadership development activity believe that after the final day there will be no measurement of what was covered and that no one will ever ask what they've done about it, it's highly likely that nothing will change.

If, on the other hand, participants know that 12 to 18 months later the same 360-degree survey will be repeated and they'll be sitting with their bosses to review their progress, they're more likely take the program seriously.

The measurements we propose are not to compare one executive to another. We don't advocate a forced ranking process that can diminish people's self-esteem. Instead, we advocate measures that show leaders their personal improvement.

If specific results have been defined in the context of a leadership development process and there are measurements of those results, then participants are more likely to take sustained action.

Ultimately, leadership is about change; it's usually not required for maintaining the status quo. Leadership is essential, however, if you want to move an organization in a new direction or to a higher level of performance. Leaders are accountable for producing such changes and for keeping their organization moving forward.

Help Leaders Transform Complexity into Simplicity and See the Big Picture   In the flood of information coming at leaders, they must learn to simplify. Proctor & Gamble has the long tradition that no memo can be more than one page. The discipline of distilling a complex issue into a one-page memo is a way to practice the necessary skill of simplifying. The Marines encourage boiling down a complex decision to three alternatives and no more. Each alternative can be explored, and one is decided on.

Some executive development programs seem to want to make sure leaders understand how complex every decision is and how many variables there are. That's commendable as an educational exercise, but for practical purposes there needs to be less complexity.

One of the big-picture perspectives that leaders must maintain is keeping their organization balanced between the interests of stockholders, customers, employees, and the public. It means balancing the need to take care of the people inside and the need to produce results in a time crunch, often with a lack of appropriate resources. It means balancing the need for greater innovation with the need to have reasonable controls and coordination. It means balancing growth and change with the need for predictability and control. It also means balancing autonomy and self-control with the need for crisp direction and well-defined roles and responsibilities. It's important to step back and take a birds-eye view.

Create Realistic, Pressured Situations in Which to Learn, Fail, and Try Again

To apply Robert Bjork's metaphor, it's one thing to learn to fire a rifle while birds are chirping, the sun is shining, and you're lying on a soft, clean mat aiming at a target that doesn't move. It's quite another to fire a rifle while you sit in mud with the thundering noise of tanks and mortars and someone a few yards away firing at you. The new leadership development should prepare people to perform in realistic, pressured situations.

Many business decisions must be made quickly, without all of the necessary information. The Marine Corps trains leaders to plan a mission at lightning speed. For example, one exercise has the leader plan a complex mission in just six hours. That's a powerful way to learn decision making and how to execute a complex plan in a pressured situation.

Train Everyone to Lead

Thirty years ago, Scott Myers wrote *Every Employee a Manager*. The book argued that organizations would function best if we treated every employee as a manager. Since then, other people have extrapolated Myers's idea to mean leadership development at every level of an organization. Most people would agree, we think, that there are differences between what top executives do and what people on the firing lines do. But there's also a good deal of similarity.

Jon Katzenbach and Jason Santamari, in their *Harvard Business Review* article "Firing Up the Frontline," describe how the Marine Corps trains everyone to lead. It invests in everyone to learn leadership skills, not just the senior officers or "best and brightest." The Marine Corps's remarkable accomplishments are at least partly attributable to training all members at all levels.

Katzenback and Santamari point out that several private-sector organizations operate with that same philosophy with positive results, such as Southwest Airlines.

We believe that many, if not most, high-performing organizations in the future will adopt the philosophy of "everyone a leader" and will invest accordingly. But we repeat an earlier caveat: It's not enough to just develop people one at a time. Unless there's a line of sight to business results, people won't know how to contribute their best.

Nothing's more important to the future of all institutions, private and public, than their ability to find and develop strong leaders. We're experiencing a growing shortage. It's estimated that 40 percent of new managers fail in the first 18 months. Roughly 70 percent of companies are going outside to hire executives, including the CEO. People running leadership development programs are often caught in a paradox: They want to produce change, but many of their colleagues want them to preserve the status quo. For staff people, the rewards for success can pale in comparison to the punishments for failure. So, there's a tendency to not take risks and limit activities and thus cut down on the number of targets for criticism. A colleague, Marshall Goldsmith, observes that some HRD people are quite satisfied if leadership programs simply please the participants. Real change can be messy. Executives who receive bad feedback can become upset and then be upset with the HRD people who initiated the program.

Nevertheless, we see people who are working successfully to bring about change and who take risks they believe will benefit their organizations. We believe there's a new era emerging for leadership development. In the past, we've thought of it as a process for developing one leader at a time, with the focus on the individual. In the future, companies will align their leaders to organizational outcomes and *then* determine what skills are needed to deliver on those explicit results.

What we propose is in its embryonic stage. We're just learning how to develop and deploy effective measures of leadership. The links between corporate culture, leadership, and organizational performance are getting clearer all of the time. Part of what has held us back has been not having the right tools and techniques to make it happen.

What we suggest will most certainly not be the last word on this complex sub-ject. But if an organization were to follow the recommendations, we believe their success in leadership development would be greatly enhanced. In fact, it should then be possible to calculate a clear and spectacular return on their investment in leadership development. ■

MENTORING WITHIN THE POLITICAL ARENA

Pamela L. Perrewé
Angela M. Young
F. R. Blass

Mentoring remains an important issue to organizations as a mechanism for improving socialization and communication (Mullen, 1994), job satisfaction and organizational commitment (Hunt & Michael, 1983; Kram, 1985), and perceptions of organizational justice (Scandura, 1997). For individuals, mentoring can be an effective career development tool and a means to develop a social support network (Kram & Isabella, 1985; Fenalson & Beehr, 1994). However, to benefit from mentoring, organizational leaders and employees must have a firm understanding of the mentoring process, factors relevant to mentoring relationships, and benefits and risks of mentoring or being mentored. Moreover, success in career advancement often depends upon a keen sense of an organization's politics. The predominant view of mentoring is one of career enhancement, with less attention given to the importance of mentoring as a tool to develop the political acumen needed to excel in organizations. This paper explores the research on mentoring and extends current perspectives by conceptualizing the mentor-ing process as a conduit for the development of organizational political skill.

MENTORING

The traditional definition of mentoring characterizes the relationship between two individuals with different levels of expertise, for example, the expert and novice (Kram, 1985). The individual with less experience, the protégé, typically seeks support related to career development while the more experienced mentor provides guidance and encouragement. Definitions of mentoring have been broadened to include mentors at all skill levels and organizational ranks, inside or outside a protégé's organization. In fact, in 1997, Eby published a typology of mentorship that included expert, peer, intra-organizational, and inter-organizational mentors. Eby's expanded topology illustrates the breadth of mentoring relationships and suggests the importance of this organizational relationship, in all its possible forms, as a mechanism for social support (Kram & Isabella, 1985) and career development (Hunt & Michael, 1983; Kram, 1985; Noe, 1988).

THE MENTORING PROCESS

The process of initiating, developing, and maintaining mentoring relationships will differ depending upon a number of factors, including the purpose and form of the mentoring relationship. Two main forms of mentoring, formal and informal, are developed typically to enhance socialization and success in an organization, but the formality of the mentoring relationship makes a profound impact on the relationship development and outcomes (Chao, Walz, & Gardner, 1992; Kram, 1985; Ragins & Cotton, 1999).

Formal and Informal Mentoring

Formal relationships are those that are formed by organizational leaders. They typically have a defined duration and purpose. For example, mentoring programs used in socializing or training new managers are typically formal programs. In formal programs, mentors and protégés are assigned to work together, and the relationship has a specific purpose defined by the organization. Informal mentorships are formed spontaneously by either the mentor or protégé and take on a purpose defined by each partner. Informal mentorships tend to last longer than formal relationships and informal mentorships are associated with greater career-enhancing benefits for protégés (Ragins & Cotton, 1999). Although formal mentorships typically last only as long as required by the mentoring program, mentors and protégés may develop a strong bond and a formal relationship can transform into an informal mentorship.

Recent research (Ragins, Cotton, & Miller, 2000) suggests that employees in highly satisfying mentoring relationships (both formal and informal) report more positive job and career attitudes than non-mentored employees. Interestingly, this same study found that individuals in only marginally satisfying mentoring relationships had similar job and career attitudes as those who were not mentored. In other words, the presence of a mentor does not guarantee positive work attitudes.

Stages of Development

Formal and informal mentorships are comprised of several specific behaviors and progress through several stages of development. Kram (1985) interviewed 18 mentor-protégé pairs and identified several common themes regarding mentoring relationships. Based on previous research and her own findings, Kram defined two basic groups of mentoring support: career support functions and psychosocial support functions. Career support functions relate to such behaviors as providing protection, visibility, and coaching to a protégé. Psychosocial support deals with the more emotional side of the relationship and includes counseling, friendship, and acceptance. Role modeling, once included in the category of psychosocial support (Kram, 1985), has been found to be distinct from career and psychosocial support, and in most current mentoring research is considered as a third and separate dimension of support (Scandura & Ragins, 1993). Role modeling takes place when protégés observe, perceive, and adopt personal and professional behaviors of the mentor.

Role modeling, career, and social support are provided as the relationship progresses through several phases beginning with initiation and ending with a redefinition of the relationship (Kram, 1985). With each new stage of development, the expectations and behaviors of mentors and protégés, and outcomes of the relationship, change (Chao, et al., 1992). According to Kram (1985), the mentor and protégé develop an understanding of one another in the initiation phase and then enter a more productive and focused stage of cultivation.

After the protégé accumulates experience and perhaps seeks different opportunities and more independence, the relationship moves into the separation phase. Finally, a redefinition takes place in which the mentor and protégé accept the change in the relationship, perhaps defining a new collegial relationship or friendship.

Mentoring from an Exchange Perspective

Although the predominant view of mentoring is that support behaviors are exclusive to mentors (i.e., mentors provide support), some researchers have suggested that mentoring should be viewed as an exchange (Auster, 1984; Young & Perrewé, 2000a; Scandura & Schriesheim, 1994). A social exchange perspective of mentoring is well-supported theoretically. In developing social exchange theory, Homans (1958) suggested that relationships could be viewed from the perspective of an exchange that is comprised of costs and benefits. Positive feelings that develop based on communicating, having contact with, or associating with another person are among the tangible benefits Homans referred to in defining social exchange. The negative feelings developed in a relationship or harmful outcomes of an association are costs of the exchange. According to Homans, when the benefits of being in a relationship outweigh the costs, the relationship is likely to continue. When costs exceed the benefits, the relationship will likely end.

Applying social exchange theory (Homans, 1958) to the mentoring relationship, we could say that the benefits of mentoring are those positive long-term outcomes of being a mentor or protégé such as career attainment, promotion, and personal and professional satisfaction (e.g., Hunt & Michael, 1983). However, looking even more closely at the mentoring relationship itself and applying social exchange to the day-to-day behaviors required in mentoring, we could say that the frequent exchange of

behaviors between a mentor and protégé also comprise costs and benefits of mentorship. This latter view is more closely associated with a social exchange perspective, and offers a more likely explanation for relationship success or failure.

The social exchange perspective, used by Young and Perrewé (2000a) to develop a comprehensive model of mentoring, included antecedent factors relevant to mentoring, behaviors of mentors and protégés, and outcomes of the mentoring process. According to the authors, although the mentor provides support, the protégé is more than just a passive recipient of the support. The protégé must also engage in productive relationship behaviors related to role modeling, career, and social support. Granted, there may be several behaviors that are unique to protégés or mentors, but Young and Perrewé contend that there are several role modeling, career, and social support behaviors that are shared and reciprocated by mentors and protégés, respectively. For example, a mentor may suggest a project to the protégé to encourage development of technical skills. In a healthy and productive relationship, the protégé, in turn, would respond to the mentor by considering or accepting the project. Moreover, the protégé may ask for suggestions about projects, guidance in developing skills, and so forth, but many of the requests of the protégé and suggestions by the mentor will focus on aspects of mentoring support (i.e., career support, social support, or role modeling).

Developing a successful mentoring exchange then, requires that mentors and protégés engage in enough behaviors related to career, social support, or role modeling to satisfy a mentoring partner (Young & Perrewé, 2000b). Too much or too little attention by the mentor, or lack of interest from the protégé, and a partner may find the relationship too costly. A mentor and protégé can develop a more successful exchange by working diligently to understand and satisfy a mentoring partner, but there are other factors that will impact the exchange. Next, factors influencing the mentoring process are examined in more detail.

FACTORS RELEVANT TO THE MENTORING PROCESS

Up to this point, we have focused on the behaviors and forms of mentoring relationships, and the process of exchange that takes place in a mentorship. There are, however, several other factors outside the mentoring function that influence the process.

Factors important to mentor relationship development are related to individual characteristics, environmental, and career and relationship factors. Many of these factors, such as individual characteristics, have been studied extensively (Aryee, Chay, & Chew, 1996; Fagenson, 1992; Kalbfleisch & Davies, 1993; Koberg, Boss, Chappell, & Ringer, 1994; Mullen, 1994; Turban & Dougherty, 1994). Other factors such as environmental characteristics, and career and relationship factors have been studied, but to a lesser extent (Allen, Poteet, & Burroughs, 1997; Kram, 1985). Interestingly, there have been more studies focusing on protégés than on mentors, and research focusing on mentor–protégé pairs is scarce (Fagenson-Eland, Marks, & Amendola, 1997). However, we do have knowledge about some factors that influence the development of the mentoring relationship, behaviors throughout the relationship, and outcomes of mentorships.

Individual Characteristics

What we know about individual characteristics, and the subsequent effect on mentoring, is that protégés report different levels of needs and dispositional qualities than do nonprotégés (Fagenson, 1992), and some individual characteristics are strongly related to protégé behaviors such as initiating or seeking mentorships (Turban & Dougherty,

1994). In 1992, Ellen Fagenson surveyed protégés and nonprotégés and found that protégés reported higher power and achievement needs than did nonprotégés. The relevance of this finding is that it provides some indication that perhaps individuals with high need for power and achievement use mentoring or value mentoring as a career development tool to satisfy certain needs. In another study on individual characteristics, Turban and Dougherty (1994) found that protégés most likely to initiate mentoring relationships had a high internal locus of control, high self-monitoring, and high emotional stability. Findings from Fagenson (1992) and Turban and Dougherty (1994) suggest that protégés who value mentoring or seek mentorships may differ, in terms of individual characteristics, from people who do not recognize the importance of mentoring in career development.

Demographic factors (e.g., gender, socioeconomic status) have also been the focus of some research, and findings are varied. Whitely, Dougherty, and Dreher (1992), for example, found that protégés from higher socioeconomic background received more mentoring support than other protégés. Another factor, gender, has received considerable attention by researchers. Some researchers have found that women tend to receive less career-related mentoring support than men, and women participate in fewer developmental relationships than men (Burke, 1984; Dreher & Cox, 1996; Koberg, et al., 1994). However, Burke (1984) also found that female protégés reported receiving greater amounts of social support, and Ragins and McFarlin (1990) found that female protégés used female mentors as role models more than protégés in other mentorships.

We know somewhat less about characteristics of mentors. Mentors have been described as self-confident, experienced individuals who hold power in organizations (Hunt & Michael, 1983). This makes sense given that mentoring is mainly a career development tool, and responsibilities of the mentor include protecting protégés and making certain that protégés are visible and known to influential others in the organization (Kram, 1985). Allen, Poteet, Russell, and Dobbins (1997) found that individuals who had a high intent to mentor others also reported having a high internal locus of control and strong desires for advancement in the organization, termed "upward striving" by the authors. Yet, Aryee, Chay, and Chew (1996) presented another finding related to individual characteristics of mentors. The authors found that mentors reported strong feelings of altruism, and speculated that this may explain why some people become mentors. In addition to individual characteristics such as needs and traits, demographic characteristics of mentors have been examined, but few differences have been found. For instance, despite a common view that women are not as willing as men to be mentors and that female mentors are not as prevalent, Ragins and Scandura (1994) found no evidence of a difference between male and female executives in their willingness to be mentors. In another study, researchers found no gender differences in individuals' intent to mentor others (Allen, Poteet, Russell, & Dobbins, 1997). Although most research has been focused on mentors or protégés, information about the interaction of characteristics between a mentor and protégé is also needed. In a rare study on mentor–protégé pairs, Kalbfleisch and Davies (1993) found that a protégé's communication competence and self-esteem were strongly related to a mentor's participation in the relationship.

In sum, the findings provide some evidence that people who become mentors and protégés possess certain qualities. Although we do not know the extent to which these characteristics drive a person to participate in mentoring, we may be reasonably confident that individual characteristics such as a desire for advancement and a high internal locus of control are among the many reasons why people elect to be mentors.

Environmental Factors

Individuals operate within a larger environment, and often select jobs, assignments, or relationships based on environmental factors such as available opportunities or rewards (Chatman, 1989). Kram (1985) stated that, in mentoring, the organization's processes and structure is an important influence on the frequency of and extent to which meaningful and productive relationships are formed and maintained. Environmental factors relevant to the mentoring process and proposed by researchers include opportunities for mentoring, rewards for mentors, and the organizational climate (Allen, Poteet, & Burroughs, 1997; Kram, 1985).

Opportunities for Mentoring   The methods of making opportunities for mentoring clear to organizational members depends upon the formality of the mentoring desired by organizational leaders. If a formal mentoring program is developed, then it is imperative that potential mentors and protégés have clear and well-defined information about opportunities and requirements for participating in mentoring (Kram, 1985). Informal mentoring is more spontaneous and essentially consists of the voluntary pairing of mentors and protégés. Given that informal mentoring occurs more naturally in organizations, organizational leaders may decide that encouraging this type of mentorship is worthwhile. To encourage informal mentoring, organizational leaders may develop some assistance in pairing interested mentors and protégés without defining a formal structure and purpose for the relationship.

Rewards   Just as perceived opportunities depend upon the formality desired in an organization, rewards for mentoring must be known. Organizations make it clear to employees whether or not mentoring is a useful endeavor by the direct and indirect rewards given to mentoring participants (Kram, 1985). In terms of more direct forms of reward, such as time and monetary compensation, organizations can send indisputable messages about the value of mentoring. More indirect forms of rewards such as faster promotion rates of those being mentored or status associated with being a mentor will also influence potential mentors and protégés to participate in mentoring (Kram, 1985). Because employees will interpret information from the environment, organizations should consciously define objectives of mentoring and purposefully support behaviors in line with those objectives.

Organizational Climate   Opportunities and rewards for mentoring are part of a greater organizational climate, and we know that an organization's climate influences mentoring. For example, Allen, Poteet, and Burroughs (1997) examined mentors' willingness to mentor others and determined that an organization's climate can help or hinder mentoring relationships. The authors found that a climate supportive of mentoring includes such practices as organizational support for learning and development, coworker support, and company training. Additionally, mentors identified competitive organizational environments and ambiguous performance expectations as factors that hindered the mentoring process.

Career and Relationship Factors

Most researchers agree that mentoring is predominantly a means to develop oneself professionally (Hunt & Michael, 1983; Kram, 1985; Noe, 1988; Russell & Eby, 1993; Zey, 1988). Ironically, mentoring has proven to be a useful method of enhancing career development, yet many behaviors and skills developed through working with a mentor are the very skills and behaviors needed to develop and maintain mentoring relationships. Factors relevant to both formal and informal relationships include attraction, attitude toward career and mentoring, and past mentoring experiences.

Mutual Attraction   Any relationship, whether personal or professional, formal or informal, is based on attraction (Bersheid, 1994). Elements of attraction in mentoring relationships are those elements that draw together potential mentors and protégés. The three dimensions of mentoring support—role modeling, career, and social support—require varied levels of contact between mentors and protégés. Role modeling, for example, requires that the mentor's behavior be known to the protégé. To give and receive career and social support, there must be close communication and more than a superficial understanding of each other. Mutual attraction, therefore, is a key aspect in allowing mentors and protégés to motivate themselves to engage in meaningful dialogue and frequent contact (Kram, 1985).

Little direct evidence exists regarding mutual attraction in mentoring relationships. However, early in mentoring research, Mertz, Welch, and Henderson (1987) identified four criteria that influence a mentor's attraction to a potential protégé. The authors labeled the criteria: fit, risk, predictability, and payoff. More recent research suggests that perceived similarity (Ensher & Murphy, 1997), power and influence held by a mentor (Ragins, Townsend, & Mattis, 1998), protégé ability, commitment to the relationship, and potential for success (Allen, Poteet, & Russell, 2000; Green & Bauer, 1995; Kram, 1985) are factors relevant to attraction. In examining the mentoring relationship as a career development tool, and the costs and benefits associated with being a mentor or protégé, we can speculate about many elements that would make a potential partner more or less mutually attractive. Knowing this aspect of the mentoring process helps us to shape our behavior to build more productive alliances as mentors and protégés.

Attitude Toward Mentoring   Mentoring is a fairly common term in organizations, and is certainly becoming widely recognized as an important organizational concept (Russell & Adams, 1997). Although the concept of mentoring is becoming more familiar, what it means to individuals in terms of career development or expectations of mentoring partners is likely to vary based on individual perceptions and experiences (Fagenson-Eland, Marks, & Amendola, 1997). Our attitude toward mentoring is, in turn, likely to influence the extent to which we seek new relationships and may change our expectations for future relationships (Fagenson-Eland, Marks, & Amendola, 1997). We know that individuals do indeed form attitudes about what mentoring is or can do for them. For example, in a study of female executives, Ragins, Townsend, and Mattis (1998) found that having an influential mentor and networking with influential colleagues ranked moderately high among advancement strategies identified by female executives. When we understand the value individuals place on workplace relationships, networking, and a person's attitude toward mentoring and career development, we can better understand why or why not individuals seek, initiate, or participate in mentoring.

Past Mentoring Experiences   Some of the most profound learning experiences develop through our experiences and influence future behavior (Levinson, Darrow, Klein, Levinson, & McKee, 1978). Kram (1985) noted that past experiences can greatly influence our future behavior or participation in mentoring, as did other researchers (Fagenson-Eland, Marks, & Amendola, 1997; Noe, 1988). In fact, past mentoring experiences influence the extent to which we are receptive to building future

relationships (Allen, Poteet, Russell, & Dobbins, 1997; Ragins & Cotton, 1993). It is imperative that mentors and protégés manage relationships carefully to develop healthy and productive experiences, as each mentoring experience will result in outcomes that affect our careers and alter future decisions and behaviors about mentoring. In addition, in training mentors and protégés, it would be advantageous to address concerns, issues, and experiences from past mentoring to ensure that the past does not unnecessarily and unproductively pervade current relationships.

THE BENEFITS AND RISKS OF MENTORING

Benefits associated with being a protégé have been researched extensively. Protégés have been found to experience higher levels of career attainment (Bahniuk, Dobos, & Hill, 1990; Kram, 1983; Turban & Dougherty, 1994), greater career mobility (Scandura, 1992), higher levels of early career success (Whitely, Dougherty, & Dreher, 1991), and greater feelings of work and career satisfaction (Kram, 1985). In addition, protégés have been found to receive more promotions (Whitely & Coetsier, 1993) and have higher perceptions of fairness or organizational justice (Scandura, 1997). The most powerful outcomes in terms of career advancement can still be found in those relationships that develop more informally and spontaneously (Ragins, et al., 2000; Ragins & Cotton, 1999). For example, Ragins and Cotton (1999) found that protégés in informal relationships reported receiving more career-enhancing mentoring support and higher salaries than protégés in formal relationships. Research findings leave little question about whether or not mentoring can enhance one's career; however, mentoring is not without its risks.

Some researchers caution that mentoring can have a destructive side, and unhealthy relationships may become unproductive and harmful (Burke & McKeen, 1997; Carden, 1990; Kram, 1985; Scandura, 1998). Keeping in mind the traditional sense of mentoring as a relationship between a more powerful and influential individual and a less experienced or new member of an organization, the harmful effects of unhealthy mentorships become obvious. There are points throughout the relationship in which mentors and protégés may be more vulnerable to unproductive behaviors. For example, the separation phase can often be a troubling time as mentors and protégés change their attitude toward each other as a result of the diminished need of the protégé (Kram, 1985). In addition, disagreements, conflicts, or conflict resolution styles can often result in resentment and frustration on the part of the protégé, and equally negative feelings by the mentor (Kalbfleisch, 1997; Kram, 1985).

Although benefits and risks to the protégé have been researched more extensively, mentoring has associated benefits and risks to mentors (Noe, 1988). However, there is little more than speculation about benefits and risks to mentors. For example, some researchers have suggested that mentors can revitalize an otherwise stable or stagnant career by mentoring others (Kram, 1985; Hunt & Michael, 1983). In addition, researchers have presented evidence that mentors feel a sense of satisfaction in helping others (Aryee, Chay, & Chew, 1996; Kram, 1985). Risks associated with being a mentor have been researched even less than benefits to mentors; however, risks to mentors have been alluded to in some research. Risks to mentors are often related to organizational issues such as workload and lack of organizational support (Kram, 1985), or individual issues related to potential of a protégé or risk in mentoring a protégé who fails (Horgan, 1989).

THE POLITICS OF MOVING UP IN THE ORGANIZATION

Reviewing some of the factors relevant to the mentoring process and the benefits and risks of mentoring, it is evident that many aspects of developing a mentoring relationship are of a political nature. The political aspects of mentoring can be found in the criteria related to mutual attraction. For example, the ability of a protégé's (Allen, et al., 2000) potential for success (Green & Bauer, 1995), and power and influence of a mentor (Ragins, Townsend, & Mattis, 1998) are factors of attraction mentioned by mentors or protégés. Protégés want mentors and mentoring relationships that will propel their careers, while mentors select protégés who will be successful.

The behaviors and outcomes associated with mentoring are also related to politics in the organization. The predominant function of mentorship is to provide role modeling, career, and social support, which are described with such terms as "protection," "sponsorship," and "visibility" (e.g., Kram, 1985). In fact, the mentor–protégé relationship has been referred to in terms of a *power-dependent dyad* (Auster, 1984; Hunt & Michael, 1983; Ragins, 1997). Career advancement requires more than technical skills. Indeed, a mentor's fear of a protégé who might fail (Horgan, 1989; Mertz, et al., 1987) or a protégé's fear of a mentor who misuses power and influence (Scandura, 1998) are sentiments that allude to the political nature associated with mentoring.

An examination of the mentoring exchange illustrates how politics is inherent in the outcomes associated with mentoring, and, at the same time, is a component of the mentoring process. Because many of the factors relevant to the mentoring process and its outcomes are strongly related to political behavior in organizations, it is clear that mentoring can be considered a complementing phenomenon to organizational politics. As more organizations encourage individuals to manage their own careers and career pathways begin to blur (Wayne, Liden, Kraimer, & Graf, 1999), mentoring relationships can be utilized to navigate through social structures to achieve career success (Rousseau, 1997). Specifically, we would like to propose that the mentoring process is an efficient means through which protégés can gain the necessary political skill for career success.

The Nature of Political Skill

Many subscribe to the belief that organizations are inherently political arenas where competing interest groups, scarce resources, coalition building, and the exercise of power and influence best characterize the work environment. We have to look no further than the language and labels that are in common use in organizations to see evidence of political undertones. Commonly used terms such as "yes-man" and "in-group" and phrases such as "it's not what you know, but who you know" imply that politics permeates the organizational climate. Furthermore, bookstore shelves are full of books that identify political influence tactics and behaviors and promise to make one effective at office politics. The implications are clear; to succeed and be effective in organizations, it seems that people must possess intuitive savvy concerning what behaviors to demonstrate in particular situations. Indeed, an extensive body of work now exists showing that employment decisions such as personnel selection, performance evaluation, and promotions tend to be quite political in nature.

However, what has been missing is an understanding of how the ability to exert influence in organizations is enhanced by, if not borne of, interpersonal style. If organizations functioned in a purely rational manner, then influence behaviors and tactics would be relegated to mere curious behavior. However, with the recognition that organizations are social enterprises follows the need to understand how influence is exerted. The style or manner of influence behaviors in organizations is a critical missing piece, and it represents a special type of social competency and astuteness we refer to as political skill.

Ferris, Perrewé, Anthony, and Gilmore (2000) defined political skill as an interpersonal style construct that combines social astuteness with the ability to relate well, and otherwise demonstrate situationally appropriate behavior in a disarmingly charming and engaging manner that inspires confidence, trust, sincerity, and genuineness. Political skill differs from other types of social skills in that political skill is specific to interactions aimed at achieving success in organizations. Clearly, many of these interactions may take place outside of organizational boundaries, such as at a wedding reception or birthday party, however, the underlying purpose remains unchanged; that is, to exert influence and gain personal success.

Just as the use of political skill is not limited to organizational boundaries, it is also not bound by "face-to-face" interactions. People high in political skill are able to express emotion in a genuine and convincing manner even through seemingly impersonal forms of communication such as e-mail or voice mail. Thus, we are not simply referring to the ability to be at the right place, at the right time, saying the right thing, or the clever ability to deliver and respond to certain nonverbal cues. Instead, political skill allows people to create synergy among all aspects of communication, even those so discrete they are subliminal. These behaviors transcend the obvious to project a set of interpersonal communiqués that result in personal and career advantage. We believe that mentoring relationships may be the primary arena for learning and honing political skill.

Mentoring and the Development of Political Skill

As organizations shift from a focus on organization to one of organizing, organizational activities become less programmed and more novel (Rousseau, 1997). Rousseau also argued that with this shift comes an erosion of the traditional external guides for behavior, thus creating internally and socially constructed guides that adapt to the more fluid boundaries of firms, inter-firm networks, and workgroups. As these socially constructed guides emphasize adaptation and learning, the dependence on mentoring as a method of indoctrination will become even more important in organizations. As new members in organizations seek to understand their organizational environment, they will invariably seek answers from more experienced members of the organization. This initiative to establish dialogue with seasoned members presents the first opportunity for establishing a mentoring relationship. Whether the initial relationship crystallizes into a mentoring relationship is due to factors such as individual characteristics, environmental factors, and career and relationship factors (Young & Perrewé, 2000a).

We suggest that one of the primary focuses of a mentoring relationship is the transference of political savvy. Mentors instruct protégés on office and firm politics, they help manage protégé image and visibility, and they can even influence promotion decisions. Mentors, operating from a stronger power base, can "run interference" for the protégé, clearing out potential obstacles in support of the protégé's progress. Mentors can tap the protégé into a vast network of relationship alliances to promote the protégé's visibility and progression. However, it is fundamentally a relationship based on exchange. Previous studies indicate that mentors will select protégés they believe can bring certain desirable traits and/or competencies to the relationship in order to bring greater rewards to the mentor (Allen, et al., 2000; Young & Perrewé, 2000b).

Ferris, Frink, Bhawuk, Zhou, and Gilmore (1996) proposed that protégés are apprentices who are shown "the ropes" and educated in the ways of the game within the organization. They suggest that mentoring is at the heart of this education process, and the political skills developed by the protégés may actually be the most critical set of skills that they acquire in their entire careers. They add that the information passed to protégés is in the form of organizational context, and that this conceptual context provides the necessary roadmap for the boundaries and the informal rules of the game. If privileged information and the development of political skill are only provided to chosen "insiders," then, what is the criteria for choosing a protégé?

Because the mentoring relationship is one of an exchange between the mentor and protégé, the mentor would likely enter into a mentoring relationship after assessing the protégé's potential for success. Because a mentoring relationship is likely to be a substantial investment of time and energy on the part of the mentor, the mentor must make a cost–benefit judgment when considering a protégé. Indeed, research suggests that protégé potential may be the single most probable characteristic of interest to a mentor (Allen, et al., 2000). To the degree a mentor is perceived as having the ability to recognize and develop talent, they attract not only a host of loyal followers, but also earn the respect and admiration of their peers and superiors (Scandura, Tejeda, Werther, & Lankau, 1996).

We contend that the protégé with social skills will be recognized as having the requisite skills for the development of political savvy. As these mentoring relationships develop, protégés are instructed in the ways of politics in the organization. As protégés become successful in the organization, their mentors gain status and extend their social networks, and protégés become privy to these expanded networks that better position them for success in the future. This relationship, which is regarded as mutually beneficial to both the mentor and the protégé (Young & Perrewé, 2000a), includes the refinement of social skill into political skill. Although there are numerous antecedents to mentoring, as previously discussed, we believe that protégés with identifiable social skills will be the most attractive to prospective mentors and, in turn, will be the most receptive to the development of political skill.

CONCLUSION

Mentoring is discussed as a mutually enhancing relationship where a more experienced member of an organization (i.e., the mentor) provides a new or less experienced member (i.e., the protégé) with professional and personal guidance. The research on important antecedents and consequences of mentoring is examined as well as the process of mentoring. Finally, mentoring is argued to be important in the development of protégés' political skill.

Because politics is an important aspect of social interaction within organizations, we see political skill as the leveraging of social capital that can be marshaled when needed to promote effectiveness in achieving one's goals. People high in political skill are quite pragmatic and shrewd when forming social connections, thus inspiring trust and confidence in others (Perrewé, Ferris, Frink, & Anthony, 2000). We argue that the mentoring process is a viable and reasonable vehicle by which these valuable political skills can be developed and refined. ■

REFERENCES

Allen, T. D., Poteet, M. L., & Burroughs, S. M. (1997). A field study of factors related to supervisors' willingness to mentor others. *Journal of Vocational Behavior, 50,* 1–22.

Allen, T. D., Poteet, M. L., & Russell, J. E. A. (2000). Protégé selection by mentors: What makes the difference? *Journal of Organizational Behavior, 21,* 271–282.

Allen, T. D., Poteet, M. L., Russell, J. E. A., & Dobbins, G. H. (1997). The mentor's perspective: A qualitative inquiry and future research agenda. *Journal of Vocational Behavior, 51,* 70–89.

Aryee, S., Chay, Y. W., & Chew, J. (1996). The motivation to mentor among managerial employees: An interactionist approach. *Group and Organization Management, 21,* 261–277.

Auster, D. (1984). Mentors and protégés: Power-dependent dyads. *Sociological Inquiry, 54,* 142–153.

Bahniuk, M., Dobos, J., & Hill, S. (1990). The impact of mentoring, collegial support, and information adequacy on career success: A replication. Handbook of replication research in the behavioral and social sciences [special issue.] *Journal of Social Behavior and Personality, 5,* 431–451.

Berscheid, E. (1994). Interpersonal relationships. *Annual Review of Psychology, 45,* 79–129.

Burke, R. J. (1984). Mentors in organizations. *Group and Organization Studies, 9,* 353–372.

Burke, R. J., & McKeen, C. A. (1997). Benefits of mentoring relationships among managerial and professional women: A cautionary tale. *Journal of Vocational Behavior, 51,* 43–57.

Carden, A. D. (1990). Mentoring and adult career development: The evolution of a theory. *The Counseling Psychologist, 18,* 275–299.

Chao, G. T., Walz, P., & Gardner, P. (1992). Formal and informal mentorships: A comparison on mentoring functions and contrast with non-mentored counterparts. *Personnel Psychology, 45,* 618–636.

Chatman, J. A. (1989). Improving interactional organizational research: A model of person-organization fit. *Academy of Management Review, 14,* 333–350.

Dreher, G. F., & Cox, T. H. (1996). Race, gender and opportunity: A study of compensation attainment and the establishment of mentoring relationships. *Journal of Applied Psychology, 81,* 297–308.

Eby, L. T. (1997). Alternative forms of mentoring in changing organizational environments: A conceptual extension of the mentoring literature. *Journal of Vocational Behavior, 51,* 125–144.

Ensher, E. A., & Murphy, S. E. (1997). Effects of race, gender, perceived similarity, and contact on mentor relationships. *Journal of Vocational Behavior, 50,* 460–481.

Fagenson, E. A. (1992). Mentoring—who needs it? A comparison of protégés' and nonprotégés' need for power, achievement, affiliation and autonomy. *Journal of Vocational Behavior, 41,* 48–60.

Fagenson-Eland, E. A., Marks, M. A., & Amendola, K. L. (1997). Perceptions of mentoring relationships. *Journal of Vocational Behavior, 51,* 29–42.

Fenalson, K., & Beehr, T. (1994). Social support and occupation stress: Effects of talking to others. *Journal of Organizational Behavior, 15,* 157–175.

Ferris, G. R., Frink, D. D., Bhawuk, D. P. S., Zhou, J., & Gilmore, D. C. (1996). Reactions of diverse groups to politics in the workplace. *Journal of Management, 22,* 23–44.

Ferris, G. R., Perrewé, P. L., Anthony, W. P., & Gilmore, D. C. (2000). Political skill at work. *Organizational Dynamics, 28,* 25–37.

Green, S. G., & Bauer, T. N. (1995). Supervisory mentoring by advisers: Relationships with doctoral student potential, productivity, and commitment. *Personnel Psychology, 48,* 537–561.

Homans, G. C. (1958). Social behavior as exchange. *American Journal of Sociology, 63,* 597–606.

Horgan, D. D. (1989). A cognitive learning perspective on women becoming expert managers. *Journal of Business and Psychology, 3,* 299–313.

Hunt, D., & Michael, C. (1983). Mentorship: A career training and development tool. *Academy of Management Review, 8,* 475–485.

Kalbfleisch, P. J. (1997). Appeasing the mentor. *Aggressive Behavior, 23,* 389–403.

Kalbfleisch, P. J., & Davies, A. (1993, Fall). An interpersonal model for participation in mentoring relationships. *Western Journal of Vocational Behavior, 57,* 399–415.

Koberg, C. S., Boss, R. W., Chappell, D., & Ringer, R. C. (1994). Correlates and consequences of protégé mentoring in a large hospital. *Group & Organization Management, 19,* 219–239.

Kram, K. E. (1983). Phases of the mentor relationship. *Administrative Science Quarterly, 26,* 608–625.

Kram, K. E. (1985). *Mentoring at Work.* Glenview, IL: Scott, Foresman and Company.

Kram, K. E., & Isabella, L. A. (1985). Mentoring alternatives: The role of peer relationships in career development. *Academy of Management Journal, 28,* 110–132.

Levinson, D. J., Darrow, C. N., Klein, E. B., Levinson, M. A., & McKee, B. (1978). *Seasons of a Man's Life.* New York: Knopf.

Mertz, N., Welch, O., & Henderson, J. (1987, November). *Why women aren't mentored.* Paper presented at the Annual Meeting of the American Educational Research Association, Portland, OR. (ERIC Document Reproduction Service No. ED292953).

Mullen, E. J. (1994). Framing the mentoring relationship in an information exchange. *Human Resource Management Review, 4,* 257–281.

Noe, R. A. (1988). An investigation of the determinants of successful assigned mentoring relationships. *Personnel Psychology, 41,* 457–479.

Perrewé, P. L., Ferris, G. R., Frink, D. D., & Anthony, W. P. (2000). Political skill: An antidote for workplace stressors. *Academy of Management Executive, 14,* 115–123.

Ragins, B. R. (1997). Antecedents of diversified mentoring relationships. *Journal of Vocational Behavior, 51,* 90–109.

Ragins, B. R., & Cotton, J. L. (1993). Gender and willingness to mentor. *Journal of Management, 19,* 97–111.

Ragins, B. R., & Cotton, J. L. (1999). Mentor functions and outcomes: A comparison of men and women in formal and informal mentoring relationships. *Journal of Applied Psychology, 84,* 529–549.

Ragins, B. R., Cotton, J. L., & Miller, J. S. (2000). Marginal mentoring: The effects of type of mentor, quality of relationship, and program design on work and career attitudes. *Academy of Management Journal, 43* (6), 1177–1194.

Ragins, B. R., & McFarlin, D. B. (1990). Perceptions of mentor roles in cross-gender mentoring relationships. *Journal of Vocational Behavior, 37,* 321–339.

Ragins, B. R., & Scandura, T. A. (1994). Gender differences in expected outcomes of mentoring relationships. *Academy of Management Journal, 37,* 957–971.

Ragins, B. R., Townsend, B., & Mattis, M. (1998). Gender gap in the executive suite: CEOs and female executives report on breaking the glass ceiling. *Academy of Management Executive, 12* (1), 28–42.

Rousseau, D. M. (1997). Organizational behavior in the new organizational era. *Annual Review of Psychology, 48,* 515–546.

Russell, J. E. A., & Adams, D. M. (1997). The changing nature of mentoring in organizations: An introduction to the special issue on mentoring in organizations. *Journal of Vocational Behavior, 51,* 1–14.

Russell, J. E. A., & Eby, L. T. (1993). Career assessment strategies for women in management. *Journal of Career Assessment, 1,* 267–293.

Scandura, T. A. (1992). Mentorship and career mobility: An empirical investigation. *Journal of Organizational Behavior, 13,* 169–174.

Scandura, T. A. (1997). Mentoring and organizational justice: An empirical investigation. *Journal of Vocational Behavior, 51,* 58–69.

Scandura, T. A. (1998). Dysfunctional mentoring relationships and outcomes. *Journal of Management, 24,* 449–467.

Scandura, T. A., & Ragins, B. R. (1993). The effects of sex and gender role orientation on mentorship in male-dominated occupations. *Journal of Vocational Behavior, 43,* 251–265.

Scandura, T. A., & Schriesheim, C. A. (1994). Leader-member exchange and supervisor career mentoring as complementary constructs in leadership research. *Academy of Management Journal, 37,* 1588–1602.

Scandura, T. A., Tejeda, M. J., Werther, W. B., & Lankau, M. J. (1996). Perspectives on mentoring. *Leadership and Organization Development Journal, 17,* 50–56.

Turban, D. B., & Dougherty, T. W. (1994). Role of protégé personality in receipt of mentoring and career success. *Academy of Management Journal, 37,* 688–702.

Wayne, S. J., Liden, R. C., Kraimer, M. L., & Graf, I. K. (1999). The role of human capital, motivation and supervisor sponsorship in predicting career success. *Journal of Organizational Behavior, 20,* 577–595.

Whitely, W., & Coetsier, P. (1993). The relationship of career mentoring to early career outcomes. *Organization Studies, 14,* 419–441.

Whitely, W., Dougherty, T. W., & Dreher, G. F. (1991). Relationship of career mentoring and socioeconomic origin to managers' and professionals' early career progress. *Academy of Management Journal, 34,* 331–351.

Whitely, W., Dougherty, T. W., & Dreher, G. F. (1992). Correlates of career oriented mentoring for early career managers and professionals. *Journal of Organizational Behavior, 13,* 141–154.

Young, A. M., & Perrewé, P. L. (2000a). The exchange relationship between mentors and protégés: The development of a framework. *Human Resource Management Review, 10,* 177–209.

Young, A. M., & Perrewé, P. L. (2000b). What did you expect? An examination of career-related support and social support among mentors and protégés. *Journal of Management, 26,* 611–632.

Zey, M. G. (1988, January). A mentor for all reasons. *Personnel Journal, 67,* 46–51.

EXECUTIVE COACHING

David C. Gilmore

While there may be some exceptions to the rule, most successful business executives gain considerable experience and repeatedly demonstrate success before they are given the responsibility of managing a major business unit or entire organization. Is this simply a conspiracy to promote more experienced and older individuals into high-paying jobs, or do these people have some unique skills? If we assume that they do have some unique skills, how do they learn them? Is it simply year after year of grinding one's way through an organizational hierarchy to the top, or are there some "smart" ways to develop the skills necessary for success at the top?

When new managers join an organization, they typically are provided training to assist them in performing the functions of their job. The training may be a mix of technical and soft skill training because performing the lower-level manager's job involves both technical mastery of the business (e.g., whether it be production, accounting, or marketing), and managing people issues in that particular technical area. Assuming that the lower-level manager is successful, additional training assists the person in taking on increasing responsibility, which eventually may involve cross-functional assignments and/or more strategic challenges. In addition to simply learning by doing the job, managers develop their skills in these roles by participating in internal and external training programs, by receiving feedback from more senior managers who can review their work at critical stages, and sometimes by working with mentors who can provide additional guidance and feedback. Over time, managers integrate those experiences and modify the way

that they manage others. If the feedback, training, and mentoring have been good and the manager changes his or her behavior in appropriate directions, then the manager will likely be successful and receive more challenging assignments.

Organizations hire, train, and develop managers with a goal of building a highly competent group of people that can aggressively and successfully lead the organization to long-term success. Well-managed organizations systematically evaluate the talent pool of managers and provide managers with increasingly challenging assignments, ultimately resulting in the development of a group of senior-level executives who can provide strategic leadership. Development of this executive talent takes time, takes careful planning to give people the right developmental experiences, and requires that people be guided, coached, and changed in the process. Guiding and coaching managers through this process requires that people be given individual attention and opportunities to find new ways of behaving in the new roles. Ultimately, the organization expects that highly capable managers will be developed through this process, and that these managers will then be able to guide the organization. If the organization is unable to develop a managerial talent pool in this way, then it will have to resort to recruiting managers/executives from other organizations. Either way the managers have developed their skills through job assignments, feedback, and coaching that has occurred throughout their careers.

For lower-level managers, much of the feedback and coaching comes from their immediate work group and from their managers. As one moves up the hierarchy, managers encounter qualitatively different challenges than faced at lower levels, and the availability of feedback changes. At high levels in an organization, challenges faced by executives are likely to be more strategic in nature, may involve cross-functional teams, may have more political implications, and may deal more with external environmental factors. Additionally at these higher levels, there is less agreement on what the correct solutions are, resulting in much less concrete feedback. At higher levels, managers contend with uncharted territory and wrestle with more strategic decisions that involve more unknowns. The larger scope of the projects at senior levels necessarily involves more unknowns in terms of technology, people, government regulation, competitors, and so forth. Coping with uncertain environments is what senior managers and executives are expected to do, and oftentimes they are left mostly to their own devices. Who do these executives turn to for advice, to help in solving a problem, or to help the executive develop a skill that will improve his or her performance? Enter the executive coach.

WHAT IS EXECUTIVE COACHING?

Kilburg (2000) defines executive coaching as a "helping relationship formed between a client who has managerial authority and responsibility in an organization and a consultant who uses a wide variety of behavioral techniques and methods to assist the client to achieve a mutually identified set of goals. . . ." (pp. 65–67). The focus of executive coaching is usually on themes such as being more strategic and learning to delegate to subordinates, managing upward, managing conflict, emotional competence, influencing others without formal authority, learning how to coach and develop subordinates, and building coalitions. Witherspoon and White (1996) note that executive coaching focuses on executive skills such as "political savvy, strategic agility, and vision and purpose"

(p. 127). Thus, working more effectively with and through others, becoming more effective in sensitive interpersonal interactions, and moving the organization in strategic ways seem to dominate executive coaching.

PROCESS OF EXECUTIVE COACHING

Executive coaching is a process that depends heavily upon the relationship between the two parties and usually is long-term. Once the coach and the executive are matched up, the coach determines how the executive is functioning in the present position. After a detailed conversation with the executive, the coach gathers data through interviews with people with whom the executive works (e.g., peers, subordinates, and boss), 360-degree feedback measures, and/or psychological instruments (Kiel, Rimmer, Williams, & Doyle, 1996). After integrating this information into an assessment of the executive, the coach provides feedback to the executive. This feedback, once validated by the executive, becomes the basis for understanding the present situation (How am I doing?), and helps target the areas that need improvement (What needs to be changed?). Once the executive has determined his or her needs, then desirable changes can be contemplated, and goals can be set. From this point, each executive coaching situation is unique because it is tailored to the individual executive's needs.

Once the focus or goals of the coaching experience have been clarified, written down, and agreed to explicitly by the coach and the executive, the two decide upon a process (method) that can address each goal. Frequently, a formal contract is developed that specifies the parameters of the coaching and includes the frequency and duration of contact, cost, and expectations for both the coach and the executive. Most coaching contracts are long-term (e.g., 12 months) to ensure commitment from both parties, and implicitly recognizes that change is not a quick process. Ideally, executive coaching is done at the executive's workplace, involves a few hours to a few days per month, and likely continues for months or years. For example, Kiel, et al. suggest one day per month during the first year, and a half-day per month during the second year of a coaching relationship. Diedrich (1996) recommends that executive coaching should be done for a contractual period of at least 12 months, and advises those coaching assignments of less than 6 months' duration be avoided. There do not appear to be any quick fixes when developing subtle changes in executive behavior.

Executive coaching is not therapy, but relies heavily upon a partnership between the coach and executive. The coach helps the executive identify issues that are now affecting or may affect performance in the executive role, works with the executive to develop new behaviors, and provides ongoing feedback to develop the subtle changes in behavior that can enhance the executive's effectiveness. As Witherspoon and White (1996) note, "coaching is more personal and individualized than other forms of organized learning . . ." (p. 127).

For example, how does an executive deal with a superior who is micromanaging him or her? The executive and the coach might explore alternative strategies that the executive might use to alter a more powerful superior's behavior in this politically sensitive situation. After considering various alternatives and evaluating likely consequences, the executive can choose a way to approach this situation. Then, the coach would likely suggest that the executive and coach role-play a meeting between the executive and the micromanaging superior. At the conclusion of the role-play, which could be videotaped, the coach provides feedback on what was said, how it was said, and the impact of the meeting. By such behavioral rehearsal/feedback, the executive can experiment with new behaviors, gets feedback from the coach, and learns to alter behavior in subtle ways that can dramatically change the impact upon others. There is no guarantee that the executive will alter the superior's micromanaging behavior, but the approach is likely to be better thought out, the behavior rehearsed, and feedback has been provided by an independent observer before the "real" interaction occurs.

NEED FOR EXECUTIVE COACHING

Executive coaching is alluring because of its individualized attention and the close working relationship that is developed between the coach and the executive. Doesn't everyone want such an arrangement? A "personal trainer" paid for by the organization to help the executive in managing his or her work and career is a very nice benefit. However, coaching is expensive and organizations invariably ask the question about the need for such an expensive "perk." What can executive coaching do?

Executive coaching is appealing because it can accelerate the learning process of executives. If organizations simply wait for nature to take its course and let some people fail and some succeed at top-level management, the potential cost could be great. Assume that an organization promotes a person into a senior-level management or executive position, and gives that person responsibility for a division that has 200 employees. Obviously, this will be a new job for the executive and he or she will make some mistakes. If the executive receives some support (e.g., coaching, mentoring, etc.) and minimizes the mistakes that could have been made, much can be gained. If little support is provided, the person may fail. What is the cost of a failed executive? His or her mistakes directly affect the people in their own operation and indirectly affect people in other parts of the organization, customers, and suppliers. If turnover increases, if strategic opportunities are missed, and if customers are lost due to failures in senior management, the costs of rectifying the problem are far greater than what executive coaching might cost. Trial and error learning can be very costly, and can have pervasive negative impact when done at the senior leadership level in an organization.

An additional cost of executive failure is the personal loss to the failed executive. The harm done to the individual executive's psyche is difficult to price, but certainly is "expensive" personally and professionally. Additionally, the organization has some sunk cost in the person's development (e.g., the cost of training the person over the years) to that point, and loses it if the failed executive ultimately leaves to "pursue other business interests." Thach and Heinselman (1999) suggest that the return on investment in an executive coaching situation is often very great, particularly when the salary level of executives is considered. Lindemann (2001) estimated an average return on investment for executive coaching of 5.7 (i.e., ROI = 5.7 times the investment cost).

Although the need to provide coaching can be justified by looking at what can go wrong without it, the other side of the argument is also compelling. How much better could an executive be with a little more support? It is difficult to put an exact figure on the "potential benefits" of coaching, but when one considers the cost of failure there certainly must be an equivalent benefit from an executive being better than average in job performance. Increased profits or productivity of an organization are obvious benefits that could accrue from good executive coaching. Executive coaching can also accelerate the learning curve for an individual who is being groomed for senior management. Assume that, if left to his or her own devices, it would take the average "fast track" manager 10 years to learn through trial and error what is necessary for promotion into a senior position, but with executive coaching that learning curve could be cut to

eight years. By fast tracking the executive and supporting him or her with a coach, both the individual manager and the organization benefit. Schmidt, Hunter, and Pearlman (1982) and Cascio (1998) offer methods for costing the impact of various training programs in dollar terms, and executive coaching appears to be a good investment.

Thus, executive coaching can help managers enhance their learning and avoid mistakes that can affect the bottom-line, speed up the promotional process of managers who are being coached, and enhance strategic opportunities for the organization's long-term survival.

FORMS OF EXECUTIVE COACHING

There are a number of activities that could be included in executive coaching. When a coach and an executive have a private meeting, coaching probably has occurred. While not an exhaustive list, some of the methods employed by executive coaches are listed below:

1. Role play
2. Behavioral modeling
3. Videotaping/feedback
4. Brainstorming
5. Writing in a journal/reflecting/discussion with coach
6. Discussions

These methods can focus on a number of issues that executives need to face, sometimes with little prior experience and a lack of meaningful feedback. The issues that executives could need help with is nearly endless, but some examples may illustrate the far-reaching nature of executive coaching:

1. Managing upward
2. Conflict management
3. How to fire or lay off an employee
4. Becoming more strategic
5. Public speaking
6. How to conduct a meeting

7. Balancing personal/work life
8. Gaining political support from a peer
9. Negotiating a contract
10. Communication skills

No matter what methods are used or what the issues are, the coach provides advice and confidential feedback to the executive so that he or she can develop the needed skills in a safe environment.

THE EXECUTIVE'S ROLE IN THE DEVELOPMENT OF NEW SKILLS

When an executive coach works with an executive on developing new skills, the executive is responsible for his or her own learning. The coaching process is a joint venture in which the executive takes responsibility for developing skills. The coach helps, guides, challenges, and provides feedback, but the executive must try out the new behavior, solicit feedback from others, and work toward the desired goal. The executive is an active participant in the learning process and sets goals, initiates the new behavior, and then solicits feedback and evaluates the effectiveness of new ways of behaving. The coach can help, support, model, and provide feedback, but the executive drives the process.

ADVANTAGES AND DISADVANTAGES OF COACHING

Hall, Otazo, and Hollenbeck (1999) maintain that many programs help executives determine where they might need help in improving their job performance, whether it be 360-degree feedback, morale surveys, or off-site training. However, as Hall, et al. point out, knowing what was wrong was good, but executives really need help in making changes in real time on their jobs. Executive coaching provides the individual attention and safety needed to wrestle with new ways of behaving.

Clearly, coaching is geared to the individual needs of the executive and focuses on job-related issues. The "surroundings" for the coaching session are the same as for the performance of the new skill, making it appear more realistic and job related. Executive coaching provides immediate feedback to the executive so that immediate corrections can be made. Some other advantages are purely logistical. The coaching usually is accomplished in the executive's workplace, and therefore no travel time by the executive is required and the coaching can fit right into the executive's schedule. Coaching involves active learning, provides immediate feedback, is done in the job setting, and is tailored to individual needs. Theoretically and practically executive coaching is a good training process.

Of course, executive coaching is not a panacea—it has some potential weaknesses. First, coaching is expensive because it involves one-on-one training and executive coaches do charge for their services. Second, some executive/coach matches are not perfect, and the executive does not always receive what was expected. A third possible flaw in this process is that the goals pursued in coaching may not always coincide with the organization's goals. For example, it may be desirable for the executive to develop better self-presentation skills that may then be utilized in finding a new job with a different organization. Or coaching may focus on getting more work/leisure balance in the executive's life that may ultimately result in an early retirement.

As coaching becomes a more common practice in organizations, executives may perceive it is an organizational "passage rite" that must be completed before moving up the hierarchy. Whether needed or not, executives may seek out a formal coaching relationship to further verify that he or she is ready for the next assignment. This could become an expensive "ticket that must be punched" before one is qualified for a promotion, particularly if the coaching is not focused on relevant goals.

WHEN DOES SOMEONE NEED EXECUTIVE COACHING?

While it is tempting to say that everyone could benefit from executive coaching, organizations are going to restrict its use to those who need it the most because it is costly and takes time away from the immediate job. There are some instances, however, where it appears that coaching is particularly critical:

1. *New Job*—When an individual has recently taken on a new responsibility he or she may be faced with multiple challenges. Having a confidential relationship with an executive coach enables the executive to explore options, get feedback on potential strategies, and to experiment with new behaviors.

2. *Unique Job*—People who have a one-of-a-kind job may have a difficult time learning from others unless they turn to people outside their organization. Professional organizations often fill part of need for individuals who can share experiences with their professional peers and learn from that experience. However, if proprietary issues are involved, outsiders can be of little help. Also, if the executive needs to explore strategic issues, it would be imprudent to engage peers in other organizations.

3. *Unique Skill Needed*—Individuals who have needs for a one-of-a-kind skill cannot turn to their organization's training function and ask that a training program be created to meet one person's need. If one or only a few people need that particular skill, an organization cannot efficiently build a training program for one or a few trainees. An individual coach is likely the answer.

4. *Try New Behavior*—When any individual executive wants to try out a new behavior, having the support, feedback, and counsel of a coach is very desirable. What may be difficult to do in a business context may be much easier if it has been talked about, practiced, and shaped in a safe environment with a coach.

5. *No Mentors Available*—While mentoring may be an excellent method for developing some skills in people; there are situations in which mentors will not work very well. For example, when mentors do not possess and cannot train the desired skill, mentoring will not work. There is little to be gained by teaching executives bad behaviors. Another instance where mentoring may not be feasible is when the executives who have the desired skills may not have the time available to mentor or may not be particularly effective in coaching others. Mentoring is also ill-advised when the executive does not want to expose all of his or her "weaknesses" to someone who may later influence their career. Obviously, executive coaches provide some of the same kind of support that a mentor would, but have the added advantage of being someone outside the organization who is unequivocally working for the executive. Judge and Crowell (1997) suggest that an executive should have a mentor to provide inside-the-organization perspective and a coach to provide outside objectivity.

6. *Difficult Feedback*—When an executive needs to receive difficult feedback, it may be delivered best by an outsider who is not connected to the organization. Feedback from an insider, no matter how well intended and delivered, may have long-term impact on either or both the sender and the receiver. Difficult feedback from a member of the organization can forever undermine the executive's confidence or can alter a critical working relationship. As Hall, et al. (1999) point out, top-level executives

receive little undistorted feedback. The external coach is bound by confidentiality, and difficult feedback from the coach clearly is only trying to help the executive improve. Defensiveness is minimized with an external coach.

7. *Political Considerations*—The political climate inside an organization may make it difficult for an executive to talk with insiders about a sensitive issue, particularly if there is an in-group/out-group mentality. An independent outsider may be preferred to the inside mentor who also may be enmeshed in the very political environment that the executive is encountering. An external executive coach can provide counsel and support, as well as a possibly more objective view to the situation.

WHAT TO LOOK FOR IN AN EXECUTIVE COACH

When an executive decides that an executive coach is needed, then a search/selection process begins. What should one look for in an executive coach and where are they to be found? Executive coaches almost all have one thing in common—they have experience. The experience that a potential coach can offer can come from a variety of different areas, each offering a slightly different perspective. It appears that executive coaches can be classified into four general prototypes based upon their primary background: business executive, organization development/trainer, clinical/counseling psychologist, or industrial/organizational psychologist.

The business executive type of executive coach has a wealth of practical business experience and likely has had academic training in general business, has managed successfully in a variety of situations, and now has decided to help others by becoming an executive coach. This type of coach is typically well-grounded in business, but may not offer anything more than another manager's advice. If this type of coach is answering the question, "What do you think I ought to do?" very often, then there is a real likelihood of the manager becoming dependent upon the coach. This type of coach may help in solving short-term business problems, but may not focus on the long-term development of the executive or on the more psychological/philosophical aspects of a coaching relationship. The risk with this type of coach is that the executive may become dependent upon the coach for business advice, instead of learning new and more effective ways of solving problems.

The second type of coach that is common comes from an organizational development/trainer background. This type of coach has developed and delivered training to managers and naturally gravitates into leadership development. This type of coach generally has a good perspective on skills needed by executives, on how to train those skills, and a good feel for how those skills fit into the staffing needs of an organization. This type of coach may have a long list of desired new behaviors that could be taught, which may or may not help the executive in his or her daily work. This type of coach may not have much operational experience to support their perspective.

The third type of coach is one who comes from a background of doing talk therapy with people, such as in clinical or counseling settings. The skills used in therapy are very transferable to some aspects of executive coaching. Reflecting feelings, probing for underlying meaning in communication, interpreting psychological instruments, and exploring human relationships can be used in helping executives learn how to deal more effectively with others. In fact, one of the better books on the subject of executive coaching (Kilburg, 2000) uses psychodynamic models to frame much of the discussion of what executive coaches do. Care must be taken that executive coaching does not become an organizationally sanctioned form of therapy. Many executives want the help and support that a coach can offer, but do not desire or need therapy. It can be a fine line of distinction between the two services.

Finally, the fourth type of executive coach is the industrial/organizational psychologist who has strong research skills and a good theoretical understanding of how organizations affect people. This type of coach likely has a good understanding of the psychological instruments and 360-degree feedback tools used in executive coaching, and has other psychological training to support executive coaching. Typically this coach's business experience has been in a staff function, and he or she may suffer from not having been "in the trenches" of operating a business.

Each of the four prototype executive coaches offers unique facets to the coaching process. Ideally a coach who possesses all of the positive characteristics and avoids the pitfalls would be the best choice. Finding a good fit is critical since coaching is such an individualized interaction between the coach and the executive.

EVALUATING THE EFFECTIVENESS OF EXECUTIVE COACHING

As with any training activity, evaluating the effectiveness of executive coaching is important so that organizations can determine how well it works and if the costs are justified by the benefits of the program. Because executive coaching is a relatively new technique, not much evaluative research has been conducted. A notable exception is a study conducted by Olivero, Bane, & Kopelman (1997) in which they were able to compare the impact of a weeklong classroom-based management skills program and coaching. In this research, coaching was used to support and follow up the in-classroom training program. These authors found that the classroom training increased the managers' productivity by 22 percent, and that coaching increased productivity by 88 percent. This research demonstrates that coaching can significantly impact individual and organizational effectiveness. As more executives experience coaching and more research is conducted on the coaching process, our understanding will increase. Nevertheless, executive coaching is becoming an integral part in the development of executive talent in organizations.

EXECUTIVE COACHING IN THE FUTURE

As executive coaching becomes more entrenched in the corporate culture and more experience is gained with this new procedure, we will all come to understand it better and experimentation will occur. Variants will appear. Instead of face-to-face meetings, coaching can be done over the telephone or by videoconferencing. Instead of paying external executive coaches, organizations may use internal human resources people as coaches, even though confidentiality may be compromised. Cost-conscious organizations may adopt a "managed care" perspective for executive coaching and only based upon a demonstrated need may authorize a particular treatment, for example, no more than five one-hour sessions with an executive coach. What are now open-ended coaching relationships may be constrained by costs in the future. Also, credentialing of executive coaches may become a way to ensure some minimal background of training and experience before entry into this type of work. The "potential consumer" may take some solace in knowing that a prospective coach has some minimal level of competence in a somewhat nebulous enterprise. Related to this point is that the ethical conditions and the "contract" that exists between a coach and an executive may need some clarification, particularly since a third party (organization) usually pays for the service. Finally, as more research is conducted on executive coaching, we may find that particular forms, methods, or strategies of coaching are more effective than others are, and executive coaching models may develop. Today's individualized rela- tionship, which appears to have more art than science as its basis, will likely become a more scientific endeavor in the future. ■

REFERENCES

Cascio, W. F. (1998). *Applied psychology in human resource management,* 5th ed. Upper Saddle River, NJ: Prentice Hall.

Diedrich, R. C. (1996). An iterative approach to executive coaching. *Consulting Psychology Journal: Practice and Research, 48* (2), 61–66.

Hall, D. T., Otazo, K. L., & Hollenbeck, G. P. (1999). Behind closed doors: What really happens in executive coaching. *Organizational Dynamics, 27* (3), 39–54.

Judge, T., & Cowell, J. (1997). The brave new world of executive coaching. *Business Horizons, 40* (4), 71–78.

Kiel, F., Rimmer, E., Williams, K., & Doyle, M. (1996). Coaching at the top. *Consulting Psychology Journal: Practice and Research, 48* (2), 67–77.

Kilburg, R. R. (2000). *Executive coaching: Developing managerial wisdom in a world of chaos.* Washington: American Psychological Association.

Lindemann, M. (2001, April). *Maximizing the impact of executive coaching.* Symposium conducted at the meeting of the Society for Industrial and Organizational Psychology, San Diego, CA.

Olivero, G., Bane, K. D., & Kopelman, R. E. (1997). Executive coaching as a transfer of training tool: Effects on productivity in a public agency. *Public Personnel Management, 26,* 461–470.

Schmidt, F. L., Hunter, J. E., & Pearlman, K. (1982). Assessing the economic impact of personnel programs on productivity. *Personnel Psychology, 35,* 333–347.

Thach, L., & Heinselman, T. (1999). Executive coaching defined. *Training & Development, 53* (3), 34–40.

Witherspoon, R., & White, R. P. (1996). Executive coaching: A continuum of roles. *Consulting Psychology Journal: Practice and Research, 48* (2), 124–133.

PREPARED FOR THE FUTURE

Michelle Martinez

Women make up 46 percent of the U.S. labor force, yet only 10 percent of all corporate officers are women. Among the companies in the *Fortune* 500, only one has a woman CEO.

The day will soon come, however, when companies will have no choice but to promote women into top positions, simply because there will not be enough Caucasian males to fill the available jobs. But many of the most talented women in the workforce are turning their backs on corporate America.

When a woman manager leaves the corporate ranks, many organizations assume she is giving up paid work altogether. However, when Catalyst, a research organization that conducts confidential studies for companies, asked several thousand women why they left their positions, the answers were striking: The women Catalyst surveyed were either moving to companies that provide a more level playing field, or starting their own businesses.

"Most women don't want to fit into a male-dominated company mold," explains Judy Rosener, professor at the University of California. Irvine, and author of *America's Competitive Secret: Utilizing Women as a Management Strategy.* Many of the successful ones leave.

"If leaders could see that human capital can convert to money, we could convince people that they would be better served by breaking the glass ceiling," explains Rosener, who believes that attitudes will not change until people at the top understand that such change is in their economic interest. "We need to tie human resources to human capital and look at it as a commodity, something to maximize."

LEVELING THE FIELD

That's exactly how George C. Harvey, former CEO of Pitney Bowes in Stamford, Connecticut, saw it back in the early 1980s. At that time, the company began recruiting more women into its sales force. Impressed with their performance and contributions to the bottom line, Harvey set out to reward and advance them.

Harvey's philosophy, says Johnna G. Torsone, Pitney Bowes's vice president of personnel, had nothing to do with affirmative action, but everything to do with performance. When the company eliminated institutional barriers, women as well as minorities were able to perform at their maximum level, improving company-wide performance and ultimately increasing profits.

"He took tough stands when it wasn't the popular thing to do," recalls Torsone. "He set the example by appointing women into nontraditional positions, such as running factories. As the senior leader of the company, he made some pretty bold moves. People were furious with him, but he did it because he believed in it."

Over the years, Pitney Bowes has embraced and enhanced Harvey's mission of recognizing all people for their accomplishments. Resource groups made up of women and minority employees at all job levels once served as advisors to senior management. Now that structure has been "taken to another level," says Torsone. "Called the corporate diversity task force, its mission is to set a vision for the organization, ensuring that we are attentive to diversity in a broader sense."

Because Pitney Bowes' goal is integrating diversity into every segment of the business, each of its eight business units are required to develop objectives against the company's diversity plan. The financial services division provides a good example of how that strategy works: Key employees developed a model of what diversity should look like in each unit. Then, the president of the financial services group challenged those employees to "prove that such an environment is better than what we are working in." The business unit employees used the model to brainstorm revenue-generating ideas, and the 10 best ideas were implemented.

"The units that have been most successful have integrated diversity thoroughly into the business environment," says Torsone. "They develop the best products because everyone can bring their thoughts to the table, offering different points of view."

ESTABLISHING FEEDER GROUPS

According to Catalyst's *1996 Census of Women Corporate Officers and Top Earners,* of the 978 women with vice president–level titles, only 271 (28 percent) held positions dealing directly with profit-and-loss responsibilities—the type of experience needed for very senior positions.

"For any organization willing to create a level playing field, the challenge is to have a diverse group of high performers that can feed into the line or 'pipeline' positions," says Torsone, who adds that this is an area targeted for improvement at Pitney Bowes. "Establishing feeder groups really brings us back to planning how to develop, assess, and train employees."

Of course, employers can attempt to raid other employers of their talent to create feeder groups of talented women, but most organizations that are committed to advancing women and minorities try to develop their own talent.

Knight-Ridder Inc.—a *Fortune* 500 communications company headquartered in Miami—lives that philosophy. "If we raid other companies, then we are not adding to the pool of top-flight women in the corporate ranks around the country," explains Rebecca Baybrook-Heckenbach, assistant vice president of human resources.

To develop their own talent, employers often have to take a grass-roots approach to establishing feeder groups that include women. "If you are running a consulting firm in environmental engineering, find out from the Department of Labor if the percentage of women in this industry job category is more than 30 percent. Then, focus on finding, recruiting, and selecting those people," advises Baybrook-Heckenbach. "If there are less than 30 percent women, start investing in women through internship programs at colleges or local high schools and make your workplace attractive to them."

But Meredith B. Fischer, vice president of communications, marketing, and future strategy and one of four women at Pitney Bowes who holds a corporate officer position, cautions that some companies, in an effort to "do the right thing," have gotten away from more equitable selection processes.

"I was employed in the oil industry at the time when women were being promoted for affirmative action reasons. Bunches of women were being promoted without regard to their skills, and it caused a weak link in the team chain," recalls Fischer. "I was promoted around the same time, and felt I was part of this group of women who were at a deficit and poorly

trained." She eventually left the oil company to join Pitney Bowes.

Baybrook-Heckenbach agrees that merely finding women to fill the feeder positions is not enough. "The most important issue you will have to focus on is mentoring them once you have them," she says.

IDENTIFYING HIGH PERFORMERS

As part of a corporate mentoring program at Knight-Ridder's corporate level, a handful of senior executives target a diverse list of employees for growth, and create annual development plans. "We stay in contact with the individual assigned to us and ensure that we hold ourselves accountable for these people developing and growing in their careers," explains group member Mary Jean Connors, senior vice president of human resources.

The mentoring or coaching process goes much deeper at Knight-Ridder; the corporation strives to identify high performers at various levels, a process that involves the managers who oversee the multiple business units. "We have a long tradition of identifying potential leaders and ensuring there is diversity in that group," says Connors.

"Every year, corporate executives visit the various units. We sit with key leaders and talk about our people as corporate assets, taking into account the leadership competencies we have developed," she says. "All individuals—no matter where they are located or what they do—are measured on these competencies. We talk about what managers, the corporation, or individuals might do to strengthen development and work experiences."

Knight-Ridder uses assessments as a tool to help individual employees realize their goals, Connors says. Pitney Bowes has also used many assessment tools with people in the past three years, according to Torsone.

Baybrook-Heckenbach believes organizations are responsible for two things: "Being as clear as possible about what it takes to get top jobs and offering opportunities for employees to contribute in meaningful ways."

"For me, there have been a dozen men and women who have been very beneficial in helping me see what I have to contribute," she explains. "The one thing I found is that women will ask for help more directly than men, so there is more networking. And when women ask for help, the relationship that forms tends to be more lasting."

Juanita Cox Burton, a former executive with U.S. West, feels she was lucky that her former boss was a good mentor, placing her in "growth experience" situations. "He put me in situations where I was visible and had to take risks," she says, recalling a training project he assigned. Her task was to train high-level employees (directors and above) in selling methods that would take into account the market and the competition.

"It was a scary thought for me to be training a group of men—the majority of them with a lot of marketing experience—in the new way," says Burton. "Here I was, a person that may have been perceived as not having the credibility. Fortunately, I had run a small business before, I decided to take the task on because it was high exposure."

FOCUSED LEADERSHIP PROGRAMS

Specialized leadership programs for women have become popular in the past several years. Now an entrepreneur whose business focuses on leadership development for women, Burton points out that "no one teaches politics for women." She says her programs help women and people of color develop confidence, self-esteem, and leadership styles they can be comfortable with.

"We talk about why women sometimes don't understand office politics," says Burton, citing as an example the woman whose good idea is not heard or acknowledged by the group at a business meeting. "Yet 10 minutes later, a man will say the same thing

and everyone in the room will say what a good idea it is."

Burton believes women have difficulty communicating effectively in business settings because corporations are built on a military model and based on competition. "Men understand those things because of the environment in which most of them grew up—win-or-lose types of situations," she says. "As women, we don't often have the win-lose mind-set. We understand there is a goal and we try to work to meet it."

There are several reasons employers have begun sending women with high potential to programs like Burton's or those in the women's leadership program developed by the Center for Creative Leadership (CCL). These types of specialized programs not only help women develop in their individual careers, but can also make them enthusiastic about networking with and perhaps mentoring other women colleagues. Many believe that the more open developmental environment of these programs allows women to talk freely.

"Employers are investing in the development of women because they recognize women are a significant part of the workforce and they need them," says CCL's Sara King, director of open enrollment. CCL's women-only program focuses on trends in organizations and the issues women are facing, in addition to extensive personal assessment. "We look at political behavior and how to navigate and behave in a collaborative way," says King.

Like all CCL programs, the women's leadership program involves homework. The assignment is designed to tie senior executives at the company sponsoring a woman to her developmental experience. Before arriving at the program site, each participant must interview one of her company's senior executives, asking about the major challenges facing the organization. After completing the CCL program, the women go back to the executives and discuss the ways they can help their companies meet the challenges identified in the interviews.

"It's a chance for them to promote themselves and volunteer to work on something outside the scope of their job," explains King, who believes that the exercise helps prepare women to take on broader roles, including line responsibilities.

But leadership programs tailored specifically to women's needs are not appropriate for every organization. Knight-Ridder and Pitney Bowes do not send women to such programs, perhaps because both organizations have extensive in-house leadership development programs.

"Leadership transcends gender," says Baybrook-Heckenbach. "Women need to deal with all kinds of people and work with them in business." Knight-Ridder tries to make its programs as diverse as possible, ensuring that there are women in each group so people don't feel isolated by gender.

KEYS TO LEADERSHIP

In her book, *America's Competitive Secret*, Rosener describes the career path of Raydean Acevedo. As one of the few women in sales, Acevedo got tired of trying to fit into the traditional male-dominated culture. She left the corporate world to join the ranks of women entrepreneurs and is now the owner and CEO of Research Management Consultants Inc., a multi-million dollar company providing services in research, training, information systems, and environmental engineering to commercial firms and government agencies. Because her former employer did not value—or did not know how to value—this talented woman's contributions, it lost a potential leader.

Women and men need the same thing to advance and become leaders—opportunity in an open and accepting work environment. In companies where women have earned the positions that allow their voices to be heard, the dialogues about meeting business challenges and finding better ways to do work have been enhanced. At Pitney Bowes and Knight-Ridder, the contributions of diverse views and opinions have resulted in well-conceived, best-selling products.

HOW GENDER CHANGES THE PROMOTION PROCESS

In its study, "Managerial Promotion: The Dynamics for Men and Women," the Center for Creative Leadership (CCL) analyzed the promotion decisions in three *Fortune* 500 manufacturing companies. The study highlights how the promotion decision process can undermine women's advancement, even in organizations known for their progressive work on diversity issues.

CCL studied the promotions of 13 Caucasian women (average age: 37) and 16 Caucasian men (average age: 38) to middle and upper management. A promotion was defined as a change in job level with a commensurate increase in responsibility and pay. For each promotion decision, researchers interviewed the person promoted, the promoting supervisor's supervisor, and a knowledgeable HR representative.

CCL discovered more commonalities than differences between the women and men. For example, all the promotions were based on the combination of proven competencies and the potential for development. For both groups, credentials, experience, track record, skills, work ethic, ability to work on a team, interpersonal skills, and growth potential were frequently mentioned.

The differences involved subjective features of the process. A major difference was found in what caused executives to have confidence in a candidate.

Decision makers asked about promoting men mentioned having a high level of comfort with the candidate in 75 percent of the cases. Asked about one male candidate, the supervisor commented, "I feel very comfortable with him. I know his strengths and weaknesses. I know how he is going to behave. Our relationship is an effective one. I know I can count on it being stable and consistent throughout time."

Decision makers expressed confidence in women candidates differently. Comfort level was mentioned only 23 percent of the time. Instead, confidence in women candidates was described in terms of personal strength. Supervisors said the women candidates demonstrated a willingness to take risks and accept responsibility. One woman in the study was described as a risk-taker with "fire in her belly," willing to challenge past practices and ideas.

Familiarity with the components of the new job also played a different role in the promotions of the male and female candidates. A tendency to promote women to jobs they were already familiar with was evidenced by the degree to which continuity—an intimate knowledge of part of the new job—was mentioned as a reason for promotion. Continuity was important for 38 percent of the promotions of women, but only 6 percent of the promotions of men.

One woman's supervisor explained that although the woman had been well-prepared for a higher level job for some time, he didn't promote her until a position became available in the plant where she was currently working. He thought it would be easier for her to handle the new responsibilities if working with people she knew.

Continuity was important to this supervisor because he believed women have to work harder than men to establish credibility with their coworkers. As a result, he thought it would be easier for the woman to succeed in a new job in a location where she already had credibility. But, the woman felt restricted by having to wait for the right opportunity to open up. She would have preferred to take a similar opportunity sooner, in a different location.

THE 7 STAGES OF ONE'S CAREER

David D. Dubois

Our "career work" (as I call it) progresses (although not necessarily in an orderly way) through a series of stages in which we take certain actions that we hope will lead us to life and work satisfaction. The term *career work,* as it is used here, is the process of determining what one's path or journey through life will be, how that journey should or will be made, and how to manage the demands of one's life and work along the way. At each stage (detailed later), what we attend to is driven by our value systems— cultural, work, personal, and interpersonal.

In order for people to do their career work (or any other work for that matter) effectively, they must possess and appropriately use a wide variety of competencies. A competency is any personal characteristic that underlies successful performance of any type. A competency can be a skill, body of knowledge, way of thinking, motive, or social role. People perform tasks in order to achieve a result or an output; they use their competencies to perform tasks.

Virtually all of the competencies people use to succeed in their overall career work also can be used to complete their day-to-day work. So, organizations are wise to invest in helping their employees to acquire and use critical career work competencies correctly.

The important questions:

- What is the business environment that influences people's career work and organizational success?
- What is the meaning of the term *career work?*
- What seven-stage process can people use to master their career work?
- What are the 20 career work competencies that people need for success?

- How can leaders support employees' achievement of career work to their mutual benefit?

THE BUSINESS ENVIRONMENT

Organizations throughout the world exist because they produce outputs that their customers or constituents value and want. What they produce is a direct result of work completed by their employees or volunteer workers.

Workers and their organizations share a symbiotic relationship: No organization means no workers; no workers, no organization. In that sense, employees' career work is a joint responsibility of workers and their organizations if both are to succeed. That delicate relationship must reach and maintain a state of harmonious balance if workers and organizations are to prosper. However, the balance is more frequently impaired by internal and external factors as follows.

Multicultural   The workforce is becoming increasingly multinational. People from a variety of cultures working side-by-side have national and culturally specific memories as well as ties with family and friends who are oftentimes thousands of miles away. That puts intense pressure on workers to be tolerant of each other's customs, language difficulties, and concerns about distant family and friends—all of which are compounded by the pressure to perform their jobs well every day. In such an environment, how can one's career work receive adequate attention?

Economic Gaps   The economic disparity among workers is widening between the haves and the have-nots. That causes tension among differing people who must work collaboratively for organizational success. Who is looking after the career-work needs of the have-nots and maybe some of the haves?

The Age Gap

The American work population is aging. The challenges that people confront in their daily lives as they age require accommodation in the workplace if organizations are to benefit from veteran workers' refined competencies. That's a new requirement that many organizations are only beginning to recognize and act on.

Younger workers may have to accommodate older ones (or others) who might have diminished hearing, vision, or physical stamina. Younger workers must also sometimes be helped to recognize and avail themselves of the experience and wisdom of older workers, sometimes as mentors.

A good question: What help do veteran workers receive as they pursue their career work?

New Family Structures

Some societies, such as in the United States, are experiencing changes in the traditional nuclear family, including the rise of single parents. As a consequence, some workers are having to accommodate less traditional beliefs regarding family structures and relationships in order to have harmonious, productive work relationships. Both groups of workers—traditional and less traditional—require help in achieving their career work. Are organizations providing that help?

It's recognized worldwide that there's a shortage of qualified workers. Organizations will increasingly find it necessary to improve and extend their employee training and performance improvement programs to close the competency gaps.

Broad differences in workers' educational development and achievements have profound effects on workers' effectiveness and their organizations' ability to produce the expected outputs or results, at the required level of quality. Organizations are searching for ways to enhance workers' learning while maintaining adequate productivity. Does career work receive adequate educational attention?

The rapid and never-ending deployment of technology in organizations has occurred faster than workers have been able to master the use of technology for productivity improvements. There are several reasons for that. One is workers' predictable resistance to change, even when they know that the change will ultimately be to their benefit and the organization's.

Two, work units must often maintain dual work systems until automated conversions are installed, tested, and made fully operational. That's labor-intensive and time-consuming, and it places severe demands on workers to do double work. In turn, that affects overall productivity and causes worker overload and frustration.

Three, changes in computer operating systems and production software require workers to upgrade their competencies with each new product release. The training is typically given while employees are on the job and are also still expected to do work and produce results.

Four, information technology has provided new global opportunities in the way business is conducted. Skilled knowledge workers are a must for organization success. International endeavors force organizations to cope with multiple languages and ways of communicating. That requires workers to acquire and use new competencies in languages and managing diversity. The development and use of such new competencies might or might not be consistent with people's career work.

A persistent wave of mergers and acquisitions and the outsourcing of products and services have opened new business markets. The benefits include a wider customer base and improved products and services, research and development capabilities, and financial stability. But product and service branding to enhance customer recognition brings its own set of requirements and challenges.

Workers in such environments must be competent in addressing and managing change, while maintaining their productivity and achieving their organizations' work requirements—despite chaotic change and disruptive work conditions.

Organizations and their workers are facing unprecedented demands to achieve and maintain productivity while pursuing their personal career work. Those complex issues challenge companies as they aim to be profitable and meet the needs of customers. The demands also create challenges for workers as they try to be successful in their daily work, while pursuing their career work.

THE SEVEN STAGES

The word *career* has broad meaning to people. In its most universal sense, career can be defined as a person's chosen path or journey through life. As one progresses on the journey, he or she fulfills many roles: parent, caregiver, worker, friend, partner.

Career work suggests that people progress, either formally or informally, through these development stages:

1. Exploration
2. Personal assessment
3. Analysis
4. Decision making
5. Planning
6. Implementation or development
7. Life-work management.

A person's progression through the stages is seldom linear because predictable and unpredictable life factors can occur at any time and in many ways. So, it's important the model not be viewed or applied rigidly.

Stage 1: Exploration

This stage includes a person's earliest recollection of "what I want to be when I grow up" and the revisions on that dream as the person commits to his or her career work. This stage is usually heavily affected by spoken and unspoken messages that people receive from family or significant others regarding what their life path or journey should be. The messages are usually from a person's elders about their desire for the type of work the person should do, where he or she should live, and spiritual dimensions and lifestyle such as choice of a partner, number of children, and so forth.

When someone begins career work formally, he or she usually has already had a variety of occupations (such as nurse or chef) and life or work roles (such as student or homemaker). And people have typically already considered a variety of subject matter areas, such as chemistry, mathematics, or nutrition for their life's journey. Some people, however, might arrive at this stage of career work with no options in mind. They can now take formal actions such as information interviewing, reading, and Internet research or informal actions such as brainstorming or talking with friends to determine their initial options.

Stage 2: Personal Assessment

At this stage, people bring with them a list of potential life and work options. The activities of this stage help people assess and understand their competency strengths; personality traits; abilities; interests; learning-style, work-style, and work-environment preferences; and personal, interpersonal, work, and cultural values.

At this stage, people usually receive detailed information from having completed formal or informal appraisal instruments, checklists, simulations, interviews, and so forth. Obtaining that information through online systems is effective and efficient. The output contains highly specific information about a person, including the effect of his or her value systems on personal preferences. People can use that appraisal information to revise the options they developed in the exploration stage.

Stage 3: Analysis

This stage involves analyzing information from stage 2, the personal assessment stage. It's rare that the life and work options determined in stage 1, exploration, survived stage 2 in their original form.

Once someone completes the personal assessment stage, he or she better understands the information from that stage of their career work, which includes assessing the circumstances of their lives or lives of significant others that might affect their future career work. During the analysis stage, people break down that information and trace the smaller parts to past, present, or future cause-and-effect relationships so they can be understood in a more profound and holistic way.

At this and the remaining stages of career work, the importance of a person's personal, interpersonal, work, and cultural values again becomes apparent in setting life and work goals. The values affect what will or will not be included in a person's life journey or career. People's values help them determine what's important in their lives and what's worthy of their attention and energy. One's cultural values are a particularly powerful influence.

Table 8-1 illustrates a special case in which a person examines his or her cultural, personal, interpersonal, and work values before attending to remaining information that should be included in career work goal setting. The table implies that people sort out their values through a process of awareness, analysis, and understanding. The outcomes are the primary drivers of the career work goal setting. For certain people, values are equally or more important to their ca-

reer work than are their competencies, interests, abilities, and the like.

The analysis results are expressed as a set of tentative or candidate career work goals. People use those goals during the next stage of career work, decision making.

TABLE 8-1 The First Consideration
Considerations of Career Work Goals
Values • cultural • personal • work • interpersonal
Goals • competencies • interests • abilities
Based on the individual's awareness, analysis, and understanding.

Stage 4: Decision Making

The candidate career work goals defined during the analysis stage are now reviewed and subjected to a decision-making process of the person's choice. He or she must decide which goals to pursue and over what time period. The person evaluates how important the pursuit of each goal is and approximate time for achieving each goal. Once those decisions are made, he or she can choose all or a few of the possible goals to pursue.

This is a delicate stage of career work because the outputs must be grounded in reality to the greatest degree possible, if they aren't realistic, people are likely to experience frustration or disappointment later on. That could cause them to be discouraged, which could lead to abandoning any further effort. Thus, the decision-making process should result in a set of realistic career work goals, given the information available at the time.

Stage 5: Planning

At this stage, people define how they will achieve each of their goals. They write a plan similar to a detailed project management plan: Each goal becomes a career work project. In the plan for each goal, people identify

- tasks they must complete to achieve each goal
- approximate time to complete each of the tasks
- order in which the tasks will be completed
- other people who might have a role in achieving each task.
- target date for completing each task.
- expected outcomes once goals are met.

As people formulate their plans, they might discover that their goals are not compatible or that some goals should be modified to make them more consistent. It's essential to make those adjustments at this stage rather than later and that people know how to obtain the necessary resources.

Stage 6: Implementation and/or Development

Here, people execute a project plan. This stage is often referred to as "working your plan." The order of work depends on the complexity of each goal and whether there are dependent relationships among the goals. You might be able to accomplish some goals simultaneously, others sequentially.

Stage 7: Life-Work Management

As a person achieves each goal, it becomes part of his or her life-work management stage. It's here that people reap the rewards of achieving their goals. That requires people to maintain successful performance of the work resulting from goal achievement (for example, successful performance as a manager, partner, or laborer). Additionally, they must maintain balance among all of life's elements while they pursue their re-

maining goals or they cope with unanticipated challenges, such as having to care for an ill family member or becoming a parent. Such events can occur at any stage of career work and can present the greatest challenge of any stage.

People usually find themselves recycling through prior stages of their career work as they achieve, modify, discard, or rework their goals, or as life or work circumstances surface that require changes to their paths.

THE KEY COMPETENCIES

Completing career work successfully—which means completing the journey through life successfully—requires that people have and use, in appropriate ways, certain competencies. Recall that a competency is any personal characteristic that underlies successful performance. A personal characteristic is not a competency unless it can be shown to contribute to successful performance. Although completing some life tasks requires the use of only one competency, it's more common that people have to use several competencies in conjunction.

Here are some key competencies people can use for success in their career work:

Achievement Orientation

People with this competency tend to be action-oriented in order to continuously enhance their life and work circumstances or work performance and personal satisfaction.

Analysis

An understanding of career-work information or situations by breaking down the factors and tracing pieces to cause-and-effect relationships.

Assessment

People complete assessment or appraisal activities and receive and review information regarding their interests, preferences, capabilities, competencies, prior achievements, values, personality factors, and so forth for completing their career work.

Awareness

Being conscious or informed of key information, circumstances, and other factors that can affect the successful completion of one's career work.

Change Management

The ability to manage predictable and unpredictable changes affecting the achievement of one's career work.

Computer Literacy and Facility

The ability to use a personal computer and hardware or software applications, and to retrieve or send information on the Internet, that will help achieve one's career work.

Decision Making

Being able to identify and apply a preferred decision-making model or process to help make career work decisions.

Exploration

Identifying life and work concerns, possibilities, options, values, interests, or achievements as an initial stage of career work.

Goal Setting

Defining realistic life or work goals and making a personal commitment to achieve them.

Information Identification/Collection

Getting key information for achieving career work.

Interpersonal Skills

A desire to understand other people whether as individuals or groups and to demonstrate to observers an accurate perception and comprehension of other people's unspoken or partially communicated feelings, concerns, or thoughts.

Networking

The ability to build relationships that promote a flow of information useful to career work.

Oral Communication

The clear expression of ideas or thoughts or the ability to listen effectively and respond so that the speaker feels understood.

Perseverance.

Demonstrating in a positive way resolute and persistent thoughts, feelings, and actions relative to the achievement of career work.

Conflict Resolution

The ability to use conflict-resolution techniques effectively during the pursuit of career work.

Planning

Identifying the necessary steps or actions for achieving career work and listing the steps in the logical or optimal order for their completion.

Résumé and Portfolio Development

The identification of critical elements and the ability to organize and format them attractively and easily readable, towards achieving career work.

Self-Management

Demonstrating one's comprehension and effective use of such techniques as adopting and maintaining a positive mindset, expressing gratitude, and managing emotions while pursuing achievement of career work.

Strategic Thinking

Identifying and understanding work environment trends, changes, opportunities, threats, strengths, and weaknesses that can affect achievement of career work, and identifying appropriate responses.

Written Communication

The ability to communicate effectively one's thoughts, feelings, and other information in written form so that other people grasp their meaning.

As you read each competency, did you note its usefulness for completing career work successfully? Career work is about living one's life meaningfully, as you understand and want it to be. The competencies are aligned with the requirements for successful living.

Two questions remain: What can organizations do to help employees achieve their career work? How can people make progress in achieving their career work in their organizations?

CAREER WORK IN ORGANIZATIONS

Work in organizations can be complex and intense, and how work is performed changes as worldwide business, political, or economic conditions change. To meet those challenges, organizations must attract and retain competent workers who invest in their organizations. To do that, workers must see a future in the energy they expend. That's an employee retention issue. But an organization's leaders and employees must do their part for their mutual benefit.

Leaders must

- gain an understanding of career work and its mutual importance to employee and organizational success
- recognize that career work is a continuous lifelong process that everyone, including leaders, can't escape if they want to have a meaningful and productive life
- understand career work as a key element of employee satisfaction and retention, giving those continuous attention through climate surveys and targeted organization-wide actions

that support all employees' career work
- see that providing opportunities for workers to acquire and use career work competencies enhances the pool of worker competencies available to the organization for achieving business objectives—a win-win situation.

Initiatives that leaders can take:

- Create and make competency development and application opportunities available to employees through enhanced job assignments, job rotations, external assignments, and so forth.
- Implement the use of succession planning programs open to all employees who aspire to roles or positions in the system.
- Offer a formal career work facilitation program as a line function and make its services available to all employees; staff the function with well-trained and experienced career-development facilitators.
- Establish innovative and customized job competency development and application opportunities to improve employee competencies needed by the organization and that also support employees' career work.
- Provide financial support to employees so that they can take advantage of external competency development opportunities.
- Support or sponsor informal competency development activities such as lunchtime seminars, learning circles, and similar activities.
- Make it a high priority to keep employees informed of planned change and help them align their career work with new or different opportunities that might become available as a result of the change.

What should employees do to make progress in completing their career work?

Here are several suggestions:

- Accept full responsibility for doing one's own career work.
- Use the seven-stage model as a roadmap for completing career work.
- Use community resources such as libraries, job banks, organizations, career centers, and universities.

Employees must express their interests and intentions to management or to other people in the organization who have a leadership role or information influence. When a work opportunity becomes available that an employee believes will help achieve his or her career work, the employee must let other people know of his or her interest. Employees should also volunteer for new or different assignments that are consistent with their career work.

Employees should consider taking a lateral assignment as a way to broaden their competency base and functional or technical capabilities. They should even consider taking a demotion if that will place them on a more direct path to completing their career work.

Get on the Internet where there are plenty of free or inexpensive life and work resources. Leave the organization if that will help you pursue your career work in a more productive and meaningful way. Consider, if only temporarily, being self-employed.

There are no easy solutions or gimmicks for completing one's career work. It is the difficult work of living successfully. But take heart and realize that you're not alone in your journey, and there can be many blessings along the way.

THE INTERNAL CONTEXT OF HUMAN RESOURCES MANAGEMENT

J ust as the external environment has an impact upon what occurs in an organization, a number of internal factors have an impact upon the management of human resources. Internal factors range from the work environment to the individuals who make up that environment to work policies to work stress and health-related issues. Internal and external factors interact, in a relatively unpredictable fashion, and result in potentially unintended organizational consequences. The articles in Part IV reflect the internal issues that may have an effect upon organizational outcomes.

Chapter 9 includes articles that are concerned with the labor relations process. The relationship between labor and management is more than just a unionization issue. It is important to note that this evolving process continues to call out for novel approaches to workplace harmony. There remains a need to develop strategies whereby workplace conflict can be both resolved and beneficial. The articles in Chapter 10 are an attempt to capture the changing nature of the workplace. Values at work have changed. Is work the centralized focus of individuals? These articles are an attempt to provide some insight on this issue. Chapter 11 contains a series of articles that focus upon the culture of an organization and the tangible outcome associated with that culture. We believe the issue of spirituality in the workplace is one that merits much discussion. In the final chapter (Chapter 12), there are articles concerning employee health and safety. These issues have been and will continue to be of paramount importance. Furthermore, in recent years, the boundaries of health and safety have been expanded to include not only physical health, but psychological well being as well.

CHAPTER

9

LABOR RELATIONS IN CONTEMPORARY WORK ENVIRONMENTS

A consensus prevails that labor-management relations in the United States are changing—rather dramatically, some believe. For example, the percentage of unionized employees in the nonfarm workforce dropped from a high of nearly 33 percent in 1950 to 19 percent in 1985, and is predicted to decline further. But this still means that approximately one out of every five employees today is a union member, with the ratio of unionized to nonunionized employees much higher in such industries as auto manufacturing, mining, steel, construction, food retailing, air transport, and trucking. Those responsible for the personnel function in unionized organizations, therefore, whether they are directly or indirectly involved with labor-management relations, should become familiar with current trends in the labor movement, the reasons employees want unions, the ways union campaigns are conducted, the implications of concession bargaining for the employee-employer relationship, and the strategies that organizations might follow in the labor relations area.

Although the labor movement is now in a period of declining size and strength, unions and the underlying philosophies of unionization will probably continue to affect the field of personnel and human resources management. Unions and threats of unionization have played a significant role in the development and elaboration of several human resources activities, especially compensation and safety and health. Nonunionized organizations have in many instances modified their personnel policies and practices to discourage unionization.

Labor-management relations are affected by numerous federal laws and court decisions. The most important federal laws are the National Labor Relations (Wagner) Act of 1935 and its two amendments, the Labor-Management Relations (Taft-Hartley) Act of 1947 and the Labor-Management Reporting and Disclosure (Landrum-Griffin) Act of 1959. Each piece of legislation has a somewhat different focus. The Wagner Act encourages unionization, specifies a number of unfair employer labor practices, and establishes the National Labor Relations Board to enforce its provisions. The Taft-Hartley Act, enacted in response to union growth and a series of major strikes and boycotts during the years following the passage of the Wagner Act, seeks to achieve a balance of power more favorable to employers by specifying a number of unfair union practices in such areas as union membership, bargaining requirements, strikes, and boycotts. The primary purpose of the Landrum-Griffin Act is to prevent corruption and abuses of power by union leaders.

The article by Devinatz and Howard predicts the future of unionization in an economy that has undergone much change in the past decades. The decade of the 2000s promises to be much different than the 1950s or the 1990s. Will union density further erode? Time will inform us, but these authors have a good idea about what might occur. The next article, by Blanchard, suggests a number of different options for resolving the inevitable conflict that happens at work. Conflict will occur—we just have to learn to manage it and direct it toward individual and organizational benefits.

READINGS

THE FUTURE OF UNIONS
IN A CHANGING ECONOMY

Victor G. Devinatz
Jack L. Howard

Over the past century, the U.S. economy has gone through dramatic changes. In the late nineteenth and early twentieth century, the shift occurred from an agrarian-based economy to an industrial-based economy to a service-based economy. Through these transformations, unions have engaged in a variety of struggles, some of which continue today. Even though unions experienced their greatest strength from the 1940s through the 1960s, there still exist some sectors of the economy where unions are much needed. Based on an examination of where unions have come from, along with changes in the economy, the external environment, and unions themselves, we suggest that not only are unions needed, but that certain opportunities exist where unions could benefit particular sectors of the labor force not currently represented by unions. In this article, we specifically examine the historical strongholds of unions, as well as the changing economy and the external environment and the opportunities it presents for unions. A brief discussion of how unions have confronted these changes and the new directions that unions should consider are discussed, given the dynamic external environment.

HISTORICAL STRONGHOLDS OF UNIONS

In the United States, craft unions first formed in the late eighteenth century. These unions were local organizations, because only local labor and product markets existed at this time. Although these unions operated in a hostile legal environment, these unions enjoyed some success well into the mid-nineteenth century when an attempt to create a federation of unions occurred. In 1869 the Knights of Labor was formed, which sought to improve working conditions for a wide variety of workers, including both skilled and unskilled laborers. This federation failed, however, because it did not adequately address the needs of any one of its constituents, which included both employees and employers. Too many union members found that little was gained with their association with the Knights of Labor.

At about the time of the organization of the Knights of Labor, product markets began to take on a more national orientation in the United States due to improvements in the nation's transportation system, including the nascent presence of the transcontinental railroad. Local craft unions began to join together and created national unions by the latter decades of the nineteenth century. These national unions formed the American Federation of Labor (AFL), which was founded in 1886. Unlike the Knights of Labor, the AFL organized only skilled workers and refused to organize women and immigrant workers.

In the late nineteenth and early twentieth centuries, the AFL unions organized within the craft industries were successful in limiting the supply of skilled workers and in commanding higher wages. However, one of the biggest problems faced by these unions was that they were not legally recognized, and employers could and did take actions against workers and unions that today would not be considered legal (e.g., Olson & Howard, 1995).

As manufacturing companies expanded and utilized more unskilled labor by the beginning of the twentieth century, the Industrial Workers of the World (IWW), formed in 1905, attempted to organize both skilled and unskilled workers. Claiming that employers and workers had nothing in common, the IWW utilized a variety of direct-action tactics on the shop floor to organize all workers, including women, immigrant, and African-American workers—groups that traditionally had been ignored by the AFL unions. Although successful in leading a number of important strikes, the IWW refused to sign contracts, believing that such instruments restricted the types of actions that workers could carry out on the shop floor. Although the peak of the organization's strength was during the 1910s, the IWW's opposition to U.S. involvement in World War I resulted in federal government repression of the union, thus severely weakening it.

However, the World War I period proved to be beneficial for the AFL unions. Due to the federal government's concern that production not be interrupted during the war, the War Labor Board and the War Industries Board granted major concessions to these unions, such as the eight-hour work day—a demand the AFL unions had been fighting for during the past three decades. Thus, at the end of the war period, the AFL unions had been reinvigorated through state intervention and were flourishing.

During the 1920s, the AFL unions were on the defensive due to a number of factors. Employer implementation of scientific management and Fordism in the manufacturing industries led to the deskilling of craft

jobs and contributed to the subsequent weakening of the AFL unions. Some employers launched all-out assaults and did everything in their power to break these unions. Other employers established company unions—a type of employee representation plan organized and controlled by the company—as a substitute for AFL union representation. By the end of the decade, on the eve of the depression, the AFL had been severely weakened.

The 1930s saw a revival of the U.S. trade union movement. In an attempt to revive the flagging economy, the National Industrial Recovery Act (NIRA) was passed in 1933, which provided, among other things, legal protection both for the organizing of unions and collective bargaining for a majority of private sector workers. When the codes of fair competition outlined under the NIRA were declared unconstitutional in 1935, the passage of the National Labor Relations Act (NLRA), also known as the Wagner Act, that same year extended federal protection for collective bargaining activities first outlined under the NIRA. Although it has been amended by the Taft-Hartley Act (1947) and the Landrum-Griffin Act (1959), the NLRA continues to protect a large number of private sector workers today.

In the same year that the NLRA was passed, internal strife occurred at the AFL convention over the federation's organizing strategy. Several union leaders, including the United Mineworkers president, John L. Lewis, believed that the main way to effectively organize these workers was to focus on the organizing of industrial unions—that is, all workers in a facility, regardless of occupation and skill level, would be organized into a single union—as opposed to the craft unions' strategy of organizing only the skilled workers in the workplace. When nine unions walked out of the 1935 AFL convention, they formed the Committee for Industrial Organization (CIO) and revived industrial unionism in the United States.

Two years later, the split from the AFL was formalized, with the creation of the Congress of Industrial Organizations (CIO).

With the passage of the NLRA and the birth of the CIO, union growth was tremendous. Because the economy was still largely based on manufacturing, both AFL and CIO unions focused on organizing workers in the major industries at this time, often competing against each other in union certification elections. These industries included, but were not limited to, the steel, automotive, and rubber industries. Using innovative tactics such as the sit-down strike or plant occupation, first pioneered by the IWW two decades earlier, the industrial unions of the CIO began to increase in numbers, as these workers flocked to these vibrant and militant organizations after the occurrence of successful collective actions. From 1936 to 1938, the wave of sit-down strikes was especially effective given the fact that employers could not replace strikers, and therefore suffered a loss of business and productivity. Because of these tactics, heavy manufacturing became a primary stronghold for unions through the late 1970s.

Once a union was organized in a particular firm and experienced success at increasing wages and benefits for its members, these gains were passed on to other workers in unionized firms within the same industry through pattern bargaining. Unions in industries such as the auto and steel industry used pattern bargaining by targeting a particular employer to develop what the union would perceive to be a strong or good contract. Once that contract was signed, they would open negotiations with another major employer in the same industry, attempting to develop a contract similar to the first agreement. This tactic was highly successful from the late 1940s through the early 1980s in retaining union strength and in taking wages out of competition.

Pattern bargaining not only worked within an industry, but also was effective between industries, as news of the gains made by one union in an industry encouraged unions in other industries to seek comparable contracts. Additionally, this benefited nonunion workers, as employers were more likely to increase wages and provide better working conditions in an attempt to avoid the threat of the organizing of their workforce. Unions, however, still maintained higher wages and superior benefits to their nonunion counterparts.

Due to the increasing power and success of unions from 1935 to 1946, the Taft-Hartley Act was passed in 1947, amending the NLRA. Referred to as the "slave labor act" by unions and union supporters, this piece of legislation placed severe limitations on union activity at the peak of organized labor's power. Among the Act's restrictions were the prohibition of closed shops, secondary boycotts, and organizational strikes, making it more difficult to organize unions and increase membership.

Foreign policy and political disputes among the CIO unions in the late 1940s led to the expulsion of 11 radical unions from the federation in 1949 and 1950. This maneuver paved the way for the AFL-CIO merger in 1955, which provided a variety of benefits to the union movement. A no-raiding agreement among all affiliated unions in the AFL-CIO was implemented, and the resources of the two organizations were combined for more effective attempts at organizing, political, and educational actions. It was hoped that this merger would help counter the loss of power imposed by the Taft-Hartley Act and would lead to greater organizational and political success for unions.

In spite of the passage of the Taft-Hartley Act, industrial and craft unions continued to increase in size, propelling labor unions into many firms and homes, with unions representing nearly 36 percent of the private sector workforce in 1953. Growth continued for private sector union membership, with the number of members topping out at nearly 17 million in 1970 (Troy, 1986). While union membership increased from 1953 to 1970, the workforce expanded at a faster rate. As a result, union density actually dropped, a trend that continues today.

THE CHANGING EXTERNAL ENVIRONMENT'S EFFECTS ON UNIONS

The economy of the United States has changed significantly since the early twentieth century. As the industrial economy grew, so did union membership, albeit in a fluctuating and uneven manner. However, since the 1950s, when white-collar workers first outnumbered blue-collar workers, the economy has continued to shift to the service sector (Ivancevich, Lorenzi, Skinner, & Crosby, 1994). Since union strongholds were found primarily in the manufacturing, transportation, and mining industries, union density began diminishing at this time.

A second aspect of the changing economy involves how manufacturing and industrial operations are currently conducted. Over the past few decades, employment in individual manufacturing and industrial operations has dropped, although total employment has remained stable. Due to a variety of causes, these operations are conducted with fewer employees. First, organizations have focused on efficiency, utilizing fewer employees to generate the same or greater levels of production. Second, the use of technology, such as computer-aided manufacturing, allows organizations to use robotics to manufacture products, resulting in the need for a lower number of workers. Additionally, the fewer employees in these settings have different skills and abilities, and may not be the same type of employee who once sought out union representation.

Another closely related factor is that the workforce in the United States has continued to grow. This has contributed to the continuing decline in union density, since in-

creases in union membership have not proportionately matched the growth of the workforce at large. While the number of manufacturing and industrial jobs have diminished, service sector employment has expanded rapidly, encompassing a wide diversity of jobs from the highly skilled software development jobs found in Silicon Valley to the plethora of unskilled jobs such as janitors and cashiers. This has further contributed to the decline in union density.

Service sector work is not necessarily confined to the traditional office or factory as was the majority of work performed in the first half of the twentieth century. At the beginning of the twenty-first century, workers employed in many service industries are sent out to a wide variety of locations to conduct business. This has changed the nature of work for service employees, as well as how unions need to approach the organization of these workers.

With dramatic improvements in technology, more and more service sector jobs can be conducted across multiple settings. Information technology easily allows workers to take tremendous amounts of information and work with them in nice, neat, and small packages. Because the labor market has tightened over the past decade and recent developments in information technology permit work to be done away from a traditional worksite, employers have been increasingly flexible in allowing employees to work off-site. This is a dramatic change, making it difficult for unions to pinpoint who works for which employer, as well as when the worker might actually be working.

Demographic changes in the workforce represent another key transformation in the economy. As stated earlier, unions focused their efforts on the manufacturing and industrial sectors of the economy, which offered high wages and were dominated by white males. The workers entering the labor force today are quite diverse, and white males are clearly not the majority of new entrants. Women and minority groups traditionally have not identified themselves with unions in the same manner as white males, which may be another cause for the decline in union density.

A final change in the external environment concerns the federal government's hard-nosed approach to dealing with labor during the 1980s, which began with Reagan's firing of the air traffic controllers during the PATCO strike in 1981. In addition, National Labor Relations Board decisions during this decade indicated that the federal government approached both public and private sector labor unions in a more aggressive manner.

UNION RESPONSES TO ENVIRONMENTAL CHANGE

Some have argued that unions have been slow to respond to environmental changes, but the evidence suggests otherwise. One of the earliest responses was a push for employee involvement (Bluestone & Bluestone, 1992), which first originated with the United Auto Workers (UAW) in the early 1970s. In the face of a dynamic external environment, unions have worked with management and have devoted significant time and effort to becoming more involved in quality and efficiency issues to improve the production process. In addition, unions have worked closely with management in order to resolve issues of common concern to both parties, such as those including organizational survival, the implementation of employee assistance programs, and increasing workplace safety.

One of the ways in which unions have responded to environmental change is to aggressively organize public sector employees. Based on executive orders that were established in the 1960s, federal employees were first given the legal right to organize and form unions (Cihon & Castagnera, 1993). This eventually led to the establishment of the Civil Service Reform Act in 1978, formalizing employment law for U.S. public sector employees and leading to a rapid increase in public sector union membership. Several states established similar legislation, further assisting public sector union growth. Today, unions represent nearly 40 percent of all public sector workers, a union density rate more than four times higher than that of the private sector. Additionally, public sector union members comprise more than 40 percent of total union members. Unions have embraced this opportunity, and appear to have experienced considerable success in this arena. The growth in this sector has helped to partially offset the decline found in private sector union membership.

However, there are a number of obstacles currently confronting public sector unions. With the dismantling of the welfare state in the United States, there has been an ideological shift among an increasing number of citizens who are openly contesting the amount of taxes that they are required to pay. In many communities, referenda have been passed that place limits on the ability of schools and municipalities to increase taxes to continue their operations. This adversely affects public sector unions, since when there is no increase in budgets, many areas must be cut as other costs continue to rise. Wage increases might be limited in some instances, while jobs might be lost in others.

Another factor that has affected public sector unions is the continuing threat of the privatization of traditional public sector services. The outsourcing of these jobs occurs in order to lower the costs of these services, as private sector companies may be able to provide them more inexpensively. Government agencies do not simply hand over their operations and employees in these cases. Rather, the rights to provide the service are handed over, and the public sector union may be negatively impacted because private sector firms assuming these responsibilities use their own workers. In many cases, these providers do not have unionized employees. The net effect for public sector unions is a loss of union members.

One way in which unions have responded to the challenge created by environmental change is the creation of a new type of membership, namely associate membership (Jarley & Fiorito, 1990). This type of membership is drastically different from traditional union membership, where a union organizes a work site and provides collective bargaining services to increase membership. Instead of being represented at the bargaining table, workers from a variety of workplaces become members in order to gain access to a variety of benefits and services, such as group health insurance and life insurance. This allows unions to have contact with pro-union workers in nonunion workplaces, which could lead to the launching of union organizing drives in the future.

Another major environmental change confronting unions is the continuing wave of mergers and acquisitions among employers. In response, some unions have merged as a defensive strategy due to the increasing concentration of capital. Although this does not increase union density, these union mergers help to minimize the losses and consolidate resources associated with this evolving business environment.

These environmental challenges have also led unions to attempt to transform the dynamics of the organizing process. In the mid-1980s, the AFL-CIO considered the idea of using professional union organizers. These organizers would be educated on the process of union organizing and would be employed by specific unions to attempt to organize workers at various locations. In 1989, the AFL-CIO offered its first Union Organizing Institute, where potential professional organizers were intensively trained, provided with organizing internships and apprenticeships and, shortly thereafter, were hired by affiliated unions.

Union organizing has also changed with respect to the labor organizations targeting workers in new jurisdictions and industries. For example, in the 1980s and 1990s, the United Auto Workers expanded their organizing to include clerical workers at insurance companies and teaching/research assistants at colleges and universities. This led to the transformation of industrial unions into general unions (Devinatz, 1993) and represents a step forward for the union movement.

It was not until the AFL-CIO came under the leadership of John Sweeney, Richard Trumka, and Linda Chavez-Thompson in 1995 that the federation began to commit additional resources to union organizing. Compared with the administrations of the previous four decades, the new leadership team offered specific plans for dealing with decreasing union density, declining real wages and living standards, corporate restructuring and the elimination of jobs, capital flight, decreasing political influence, deindustrialization, and globalization (Eisenscher, 1999). These leaders understood the necessity of adopting a different orientation and new tactics if the federation and their affiliated unions were to continue to survive.

One of the major undertakings of the new administration was the establishment of an Organizing Department within the AFL-CIO (Herman, 1998). Additionally, the federation committed financial resources to organize nontraditional groups of workers and sectors of the economy. For example, women, minorities, and immigrants—groups that were traditionally ignored by unions affiliated with the AFL-CIO—were targeted segments for unionization. While the AFL-CIO committed more of its budget to organizing, obtaining these resources required cooperation from individual unions. Unions were required to jointly commit funds in order to obtain AFL-CIO financial support, a major departure from the past.

Another new direction embarked on by the AFL-CIO was the effort made to organize low-wage workers. By focusing on low-wage jobs, the new leadership indicated to the public that it was interested in helping all workers, not just high-wage workers found in the traditional union strongholds of the auto, steel, and rubber industries. Additionally, broader initiatives, such as the "Union Summer" campaign of 1996, brought 1,000 young workers into union organizing campaigns, voter registration drives, and political campaigns over a three-week period.

NEW ORGANIZING OPPORTUNITIES FOR U.S. TRADE UNIONS

Even with the AFL-CIO's increased emphasis on organizing activity, union density declined from 13.9 percent at the end of 1999 to 13.5 percent at the end of 2000. Private sector union density dropped from 9.5 percent to 9.0 percent over this same time frame, with public sector union density remaining at a relatively healthy rate of 37.5 percent. In spite of the recent efforts put forth by the AFL-CIO, union density continues to fall. While unions and the federation have taken positive steps to reverse the status quo, progress has been painstakingly slow. One area of opportunity for unions is to target groups of employees that have not been aggressively courted before.

Professional Employees

Although many people believe that unions are only beneficial to blue-collar employees, at the turn of the twenty-first century, white-collar employees are experiencing many of the same types of problems at work that traditionally have confronted blue-collar workers (Devinatz, 2000). Such pressures led the American Medical Association in 1999 to endorse collective bargaining for medical doctors in an attempt to halt the continuing decline in power exercised by physicians in the medical industry. As the service sector in the U.S. economy continues to expand at a rapid rate, higher numbers of professional employees at all levels and in a variety of industries will comprise a growing portion of the nation's labor force.

There are two major reasons why the time might be ripe for an attempt at the unionization of large numbers of professional employees. First, a greater number of professional employees, including medical doctors, lawyers, and engineers, are salaried employees and have little control over their incomes and working conditions. Second, a foundation of professionalism is the presence of work autonomy, which has disappeared or been severely eroded in many professions. For example, many physicians who work for health maintenance organizations must make health care decisions based on cost factors and may be required to examine a certain quota of patients each day. Unions representing these doctors can begin to restore democracy and autonomy in the workplace. With respect to lawyers, many will never have their own practice; most must devote 60 hours a week to their chosen profession in order to have a small chance to obtain partner status at a medium or large-sized law firm. Only one in twenty will be successful in achieving this status (Aronowitz, 1998).

Unions have been successful in organizing professional employees in a number of industries such as acting, nursing, and teaching, although the dominant view that still exists among professional employees is that the presence of unionism and professionalism are fundamentally incompatible. Specifically, professional employees typically believe that unionism undermines professional values, including the opportunity for such employees to engage in organizational decision making in a collegial environment, a compensation system based on meritorious performance, and the ability of professional employees to carry out their duties in an independent manner. The evidence, however, suggests that unionism and professionalism are compatible. In addition to covering wages, benefits, and working conditions, professional employee contracts also contain provisions protecting these employees' professional values and interests, as well as economic and job security issues that are unique to professional employees (Rabban, 1991).

Contingent Employees

Contingent employees can be defined as working at jobs in which the individual possesses neither an explicit nor an implicit contract for long-term employment. These employees engage in part-time jobs, contracted and subcontracted employment, day labor, on-call employment, and temporary work. According to the Bureau of Labor Statistics, approximately one-third of the U. S. labor force, or 40 million workers, can be categorized as temporary or contingent employees.

With the tremendous growth of employees provided by staffing agencies, which increased to three million employees from 1989 to 1997, this type of contingent employee was explicitly defined as being employed by the agency as opposed to the place of employment where the employee works. Because of the nature of this employment relationship, a new category of contingent employees, referred to as "perma-temps," emerged who worked for long periods of time for a single employer. Although perma-temps often work side by side and do the exact same work as full-time employees, they often do not receive the same benefits as full-time employees, which may include health insurance, paid vacations, and pension plans (Human Rights Watch, 2000).

For example, the following situation confronts approximately 6,000 employees working at Microsoft Corporation, including high-tech computer programmers who formed an organization, the Washington Alliance of Technology Workers (WashTech). Affiliated with the Communication Workers of America, WashTech initiated a union organizing drive in early 1998. Although it has achieved some minor concessions from Microsoft, it may ultimately take years of hard work before the campaign reaches fruition (Human Rights Watch, 2000). Besides being active in recruiting employees to the organization, WashTech has engaged in a variety of what it calls "collective action" tactics including lobbying, letter writing, exerting public pressure, and organizing employee-protest actions (DeBare, 1999).

Because the rapidly expanding high-tech industry depends heavily on the use of contingent employees, there have been other preliminary unionization attempts in this industry. In Silicon Valley, such organizing has taken the form of an effort called the Working Partnership's Temporary Workers Project. The project includes the establishment of a temporary workers' association, outlining a code of conduct for employers and setting up their own temporary agency called Together@Work, which would provide increased compensation and health benefits for contingent employees that for-profit agencies have failed to provide (Kotkin, 1999). In addition to organizing Together@Work in Silicon Valley, the South Bay Labor Council of the AFL-CIO has established another nonprofit temporary agency called Solutions at Work (DeBare, 1999).

Another group of contingent employees that is ripe for organization are workfare employees who have come into existence with the abolition of the six-decades-old federal program, Aid to Families with Dependent Children (AFDC), in 1996. With the primary responsibility of welfare programs now assigned to the individual states and requirements imposed that recipients work a specified number of hours per week in public employment to receive their benefits, this group of employees desperately needs union representation to protect their rights on the job. However, the major obstacle to the unionization of these employees is that the law, at this time, does not provide them with collective bargaining rights. For example, although there was overwhelming support for collective bargaining representation among New York City's workfare employees in the late 1990s, the city was not required, by law, to either recognize or to negotiate with these employees.

Immigrant Employees

Although the AFL largely refused to organize immigrant workers from the time of its formation in 1886 through the early years of the depression in the mid-1930s, the active and aggressive organization of unskilled Eastern and Western European immigrant workers in basic industry by the CIO unions from the mid-1930s through the end of the World War II period led to a revival and to a stable and thriving U.S. labor movement by the mid-twentieth century. As we enter the twenty-first century, immigrant employees, largely from non-European countries, are one of the keys to the future revival of U.S. trade unions.

Based on a report issued by the Federal Reserve Bank of Dallas, in excess of one million people immigrate to the U.S. each year. Of this number, 850,000 are granted permanent residence status while some 250,000 are undocumented. According to the report, if this rate of immigration remains constant, a little more than half of the U.S. population growth between 1995 and 2025 will result from the new immigrants and their U.S.-born children. With respect to labor force growth rates, half of this growth, approximately 16.5 million workers, will come from this post-1995 immigration base. If this im-

migration ended, the number of employees in the U.S. labor force would start to decrease after 2015 (Amaya, 2000).

Although the AFL-CIO was a strong supporter of the Immigration Reform and Control Act (IRCA) at the time of its passage in 1986, on February 16, 2000, the AFL-CIO reversed its position on U.S. immigration policy. At its winter meeting in New Orleans, the labor federation's executive council argued that U.S. immigration policy is "broken and needs to be fixed." Additionally, the AFL-CIO called for the outright repeal of IRCA and for granting amnesty to six million undocumented workers currently living in the U.S. (Greenhouse, 2000).

Realizing that undocumented workers were exploited by employers and that IRCA had not been effective in preventing employers from hiring them, the federation realized that this legislation was undermining the rights of all workers to organize. Specifically, with the AFL-CIO attempting to organize hundreds of thousands of immigrants laboring in farms, hotels, meatpacking, construction, and other industries within the past few years, the federation saw that employers would threaten to terminate undocumented workers who supported unions. Employers would even go as far as to call in immigration officials to deport undocumented workers to thwart unionization drives (Greenhouse, 2000)

THE WITHERING AWAY OF THE STRIKE?

Strike activity on the part of U.S. unions hit a record low in 1999, after nearly two decades of diminished strike activity. For example, in bargaining units representing 1,000 or more employees, there were only 17 reported work stoppages involving 73,000 employees in 1999, a dramatic decrease from an average of nearly 270 strikes (and more than 1.3 million employees) per year from 1971 through 1980 in these large bargaining units. Experts attribute the paucity of strikes in the U.S. in recent years to globalization and changes in technology that undermine job security. Unions and union members fear that strikes may lead to employers moving work to nonunion domestic factories or to factories located outside the country (Holley, Jennings, & Wolters, 2001).

Even with decreased strike activity in recent years, strikes have still been effective when they have been utilized in a strategic manner. For example, UAW local unions conducted strikes against General Motors (GM) from 1994 through 1997, focusing on increasing plant staffing levels, limiting subcontracting, and resolving plant and safety issue disputes. These strikes were particularly successful because they exploited the inherent weakness in GM's just-in-time parts delivery system. Because of the company's integrated and lean production system, each of these local strikes was effective in shutting down production in most of GM's assembly plants and in achieving the local unions' demands within a relatively short period of time (Moody, 1997).

Even at the national level, the Teamsters Union conducted a strike against the United Parcel Service (UPS) that resulted in an unambiguous victory for the U.S. labor movement. After six months of an educational campaign in which the union presented its case for substantial increases for the thousands of part-time UPS employees, who made between $9 and $11 per hour, and the demand that the company create 10,000 new full-time jobs, the Teamsters struck on August 4, 1997. With strike support of $10 million per week promised by the AFL-CIO and with the Teamsters conducting a successful public relations campaign in which the union won three-quarters of the public to its side, UPS was placed in a defensive position. Furthermore, with company losses mounting to $60 million within two weeks of the strike's commencement, UPS granted the Teamsters' demands, promising to create 20,000 full-time jobs contingent upon the continued presence of satisfactory economic conditions (Aronowitz, 1998).

THE EFFECTS OF GLOBALIZATION

The effects of globalization provide new challenges to the AFL-CIO and its affiliated unions. For example, the passage of the North American Free Trade Agreement (NAFTA) in 1993 has accelerated the loss of domestic manufacturing and industrial jobs and is an indicator of the power that transnational corporations (TNCs) have in shifting capital throughout the world with relative ease. Because of this, U.S. trade unions have been forced to establish links with their foreign counterparts on issues of common concern so as to have the ability to protect U.S. employees.

To illustrate this point, NAFTA has led to a number of U.S. trade unions engaging in cross-border organizing with both Mexican and Canadian trade unions. The Communication Workers of America (CWA) became involved in a joint solidarity campaign with the Canadian Auto Workers and the Communications, Energy, and Power (CEP) workers of Canada in order to support a strike at a New Jersey Northern Telecom facility. Northern Telecom, a company based in Canada that manufactures telecommunications equipment, was shifting work out of Canada into the United States, while decertifying the unions at these facilities. This alliance eventually grew to include 11 unions in eight nations. In addition, the CWA has formed an enduring relationship with the Telecommunications Union of Mexico (STRM) and the CEP in attempts to organize Mexican workers employed at Sprint into the CWA and to force Sprint to recognize the STRM as the collective bargaining representative of the workers in a joint venture between Telmex and Sprint (Moody, 1997).

The United Electrical Workers (UE) and the Mexican Authentic Labor Front (FAT) established a "strategic organizing alliance" to organize factories in metal and electrical industries in both the United States and Mexico. With the help of the UE, the FAT was able to successfully organize a number of plants in these industries in central Mexico. At this same time, the FAT aided the UE in its successful organizing campaign of Mexican immigrant workers at the Aluminum Casting & Engineering Company in Milwaukee (Moody, 1997).

Because of the expected expansion and continuing penetration of TNCs into more areas throughout the world, in order to successfully organize and negotiate with such organizations, U.S. trade unions may feel the necessity to become increasingly involved in the 14 international trade secretariats (ITSs) that can be described as "worldwide federations of affiliated national unions in specific industries." Examples of ITSs include the International Metalworkers' Federation (IMF), the Postal, Telegraph and Telephone International (PTTI), the International Union of Food and Allied Workers (IUF), the Public Service International (PSI), and the International Federation of Chemical, Energy, Mine and General Workers' Unions (ICEM).

The major activities of the ITSs is to disseminate information and provide leadership training, support, and coordination of collective bargaining activities to national affiliates that operate within internationalized industries. Most ITSs have industrial departments for focusing on specific industries and a number have set up world corporate councils for dealing with individual TNCs. Although the ITSs have conducted effective solidarity and pressure campaigns against a number of TNCs, no ITS has been involved in organizing strike actions across nations (Moody, 1997).

THE FUTURE OF U.S. LABOR-MANAGEMENT COOPERATION EFFORTS

Because of increased global competition in a number of industries, employers and unions have embarked on a variety of labor-management cooperation programs with increasing frequency beginning in the 1980s through the present. Employers offered unions an increasing role in the participation in the management of the firm. These labor-management cooperation programs appeared in various forms such as total quality management programs, quality circles, quality of work life programs, employee involvement, and joint labor-management committees. A form of labor-management cooperation with respect to contract negotiation is mutual gains bargaining (MGB), in which the two parties attempt to move beyond the adversarial approach of traditional collective bargaining negotiations. MGB involves the union and management participating in problem-solving behaviors by emphasizing fair proposals based on objective (neutral) criteria, the open and honest sharing of information with respect to negotiating priorities, and focusing on the parties' shared interests in arriving at a mutually beneficial agreement.

A number of these cooperative efforts have been recognized as bringing mutual benefits to both the employer and the union, such as the establishment of joint union-management study teams by the Amalgamated Clothing and Textile Workers Union (now UNITE!) and the Rochester-based Xerox corporation. This cooperative program was initiated in the early 1980s when Xerox discovered that its market share in copiers had been cut in half from 82 to 41 percent. The study teams created were engaged in multiple activities. The union became involved in strategic human resources planning, the plant was redesigned, a top-down total quality management program was implemented, various forms of employee participation and autonomous work groups were created, the outsourcing of work was examined, and a no-layoff policy was put into effect (Holley & Jennings, 1997).

Benefits derived from these efforts included reductions in cost levels, employee hours lost, and employee defect levels. In addition, there were more timely deliveries and a higher net return from employee hours worked. Because of these changes, by 1993 the firm was in the process of regaining its market share. Union manufacturing jobs at the company increased from 2,600 in the early 1980s to 4,100 in 1993 (Holley & Jennings, 1997).

Two additional labor-management cooperation efforts that have been considered to be successful include the programs established by the UAW and the New United Motor Manufacturing Inc. (NUMMI), a joint venture between GM and Toyota, in Fremont, California, and the UAW and GM's efforts at the Saturn plant in Spring Hill, Tennessee. These two cooperative efforts, as well as other successful relationships, have five programmatic elements in common: (1) involvement of the company's CEO, the union, and front-line supervisors in the program; (2) mutual trust; (3) clear program objectives that are achieved through joint problem solving between the two parties; (4) continual communication between the union and management; and (5) an openness with regards to experimentation and innovation (Holley & Jennings, 1997).

With respect to the first characteristic, it is important that there is active support for the cooperation program from the highest to the lowest managerial levels of the organization as well as the union as an institution. Often, front-line supervisors feel threatened because they may perceive that cooperation programs empower employees and undermine their authority within the organization. These supervisors must be reassured by top-level management that they have an important role to play in the success of both the organization and the cooperation program. In addition, the union must be made to feel comfortable that participation in the program will not undermine its unique role as the employees' collective bargaining representative.

The second characteristic, the existence of mutual trust among the two parties, is an essential ingredient, although it takes significant time and effort to develop and nourish, especially if there has been an adversarial collective bargaining relationship between the two parties in the past. Working on a joint issue of mutual benefit to the two parties, such as the initiation of a safety program, is a good first step towards building this mutual trust. This means that neither the union nor management should agree just to agree with the other side, but both parties should work together on issues of common concern as a way to develop and nurture this mutual trust.

The presence of the third characteristic, establishing clear objectives, is essential for guiding the cooperation program. Without these, significant amounts of time and resources may be devoted by both the union and management without achieving measurable gains that are needed to justify this effort. Clear objectives need to be established early in the program so that both parties have confidence that the effort will achieve their mutual needs.

Concerning the fourth characteristic, because the two parties will be working in a more intimate situation, both formal and informal communication between the union and the management is even more crucial than in the absence of such programs. Both sides need to be open and able to listen to what the other side is saying, and to consider problems from their counterpart's point of view.

Finally, in terms of the fifth characteristic, the union and management should strive to be flexible in considering a wide variety of ideas while working together in this cooperation program. In their search for innovative solutions to problems, ideas should be considered from a variety of perspectives and no proposal should be immediately rejected until each proposal has been carefully examined for its feasibility.

With respect to MGB, a study of the characteristics and outcomes of the implementation of MGB in the labor relations arena indicates that successful MGB outcomes can emerge in spite of a pride relationship characterized by poor relations and minimal trust between the union and management. Successful MGB outcomes also appear to depend upon prior training of the union and management in MGB principles and the use of facilitators in the negotiation process. Finally, the implementation of MGB can lead to the establishment of labor-management committees designed to resolve problems on an ongoing basis (Devinatz, 1998).

The implementation of such cooperative programs, however, can be problematic at times. If the relationship between the union and the employer has been conflictual and hostile, the union will be unlikely to want to participate in any type of labor-management cooperation program until there is an improvement in the underlying relationship between the two parties. Research evidence indicates that even in companies that have developed cooperative relationships with their unions, managers do not believe that unions should be allowed to have any type of decision-making input within their firms (Perline & Sexton, 1994).

Perline and Sexton's (1994) research gets to the heart of the criticism of labor-management cooperation programs from some unions' and critics' viewpoint: employ-

ers often desire union participation in cooperative programs in order to achieve the employers' agenda, rather than on an agenda worked out and decided jointly between the two parties. This illustrates the importance of establishing both mutual trust and clear objectives when pursuing labor-management cooperation, if the union is to agree to its involvement. In addition, such participation can have negative effects for the unions as an institution. For example, in a study entitled *Jointness at GM: Company Unionism in the 21st Century,* Leary and Menaker (1994) demonstrated that the structure of joint union-management committees replicates the company structure and ties more of the union structure to that of the firm. Since more decisions concerning union policy and practice are actually made by these committees, union democracy is eroded with rank-and-file union members having a diminished role in making internal union decisions. Thus, when participating in cooperation programs, unions need to be cautious so that they can maintain their distinct identity separate from the employer.

If employers and unions are sincere in demonstrating their commitment to establishing mutually beneficial labor-management cooperation programs, then they should implement the following "good faith" guidelines, or ground rules, when constructing such programs. The employer and the union should negotiate "a sunset clause" for all cooperation programs so that none of these participation structures is independent or lasts beyond the existence of the collective bargaining agreement. In addition, both parties may want to specify certain dates during each contractual period for reassessing the cooperation program. During the operation of these cooperation programs, the employer should allow the union to have their own planning time prior to any joint meetings with management. In addition, during joint union-management meetings, the union and the management participants should have the right to adjourn the meeting at any point in time and be allowed to caucus among themselves. Finally, employers should allow the union to have the exclusive right in the selection of its facilitators, permit the union to communicate what is going on in the participation program to all union members, and allow the union to terminate its participation in the program if the union feels that it is not obtaining the promised mutual benefits (Parker & Slaughter, 1997).

As a concluding point, we believe that in order for labor-management cooperation programs to be successful and beneficial for the union as well as management, a prerequisite is that unions must have equal power to management and that the collective bargaining relationship between the two parties is not undermined through participation in the program. Such goals can more easily be obtained through the reinvigoration of the union as an institution, and through the construction of alliances with other constituencies as detailed next.

THE WAY OUT OF THE IMPASSE?

With continued pressure on union resources, the wave of union mergers that occurred in the late 1980s and 1990s (Chaison, 1996) will likely continue in the first decade of the twenty-first century as unions combine to consolidate their treasuries and staffs in organizing attempts, collective bargaining activities, and political campaigns in order to combat increasing international agglomerations of capital. However, the revival of the U.S. trade union movement does not merely depend on quantitative changes in union density, collective bargaining power, and political influence, but qualitative changes as well. For unions to successfully embark on a path of encouraging increased cooperation with management, and to obtain benefits from such participation, it is necessary that rank-and-file union

members take a more active role in the regeneration of the unions.

Although unions have begun to use the newest information technologies (e-mail, the Internet, etc.) in their union-organizing efforts, contract negotiation/administration, and solidarity efforts (Shostak, 1999), the future of the U.S. labor movement clearly rests with the reinvigoration of rank and file union members. This requires that union officials and staff become more involved with educating union members to take more responsibility with respect to union-organizing efforts, negotiations, and political campaigns. The purpose of this is not only for increasing democracy within unions, which is a desirable goal in and of itself, but to build stronger unions through obtaining increasing member commitment to labor organization.

Finally, for unions to succeed in the twenty-first century, unions must be able and willing to link up with other constituencies present within the communities in which they operate. The building of labor-community alliances serves two purposes. In the first place, it helps unions achieve their goals and secondly, it forces unions to expand their concerns beyond the work site, occupation, and industry to include the communities' interests. Many of the interests of the unions and communities do, in fact, intersect out of necessity. For example, both unions and communities are interested in retaining members' jobs. Unions see it as a necessity for retaining both union membership and collective bargaining power, while communities see the retention of these jobs as a way to ensure the economic health of their communities (Eisenscher, 1999). In fact, research involving U.S. public sector unions has demonstrated that the use of labor-community alliances have been particularly successful in the situation when these unions have conducted collective actions (Devinatz, 1996; Johnston, 1994).

The revival of the U.S. trade union movement in the twenty-first century is neither a foregone conclusion nor necessarily likely, although it is certainly possible and desirable. If union density continues to erode, this will have a negative effect not only on union workers but nonunion workers as well because no longer will nonunion employers feel that it is necessary to imitate union wages and working conditions. In the absence of a significant union "threat effect," employers will have more power to determine the terms and conditions of employment for both unionized and nonunion workers. Certain environmental factors which have led to the unions' decline are unfortunately beyond the institution's control. However, as mentioned in this article, there are things that can be done by the unions and the AFL-CIO in an attempt to turn around the labor movement in adapting to this dynamic environment. ∎

REFERENCES

Amaya, J. (2000, April 2). America needs a dialogue on immigration: Try reason, not rhetoric. *The Denver Post,* K-01.

Aronowitz, S. A. (1998). *From the ashes of the old: American labor and America's future.* New York: Houghton Mifflin Company.

Bluestone, B., & Bluestone, I. (1992). *Negotiating the future: A labor perspective on American business.* New York: Basic Books.

Chaison, G. N. (1996). *Union mergers in hard times: The view from five countries.* Ithaca, NY: Cornell University Press.

Cihon, P. J., & Castegnera, J. O. (1993). *Labor and employment law* (2nd ed.). Belmont, CA: Wadsworth Publishing Company.

DeBare, I. (1999, July 16). Organizing tech temps: Labor group seeks benefits, security for Microsoft permatemps. *The San Francisco Chronicle,* B1.

Devinatz, V. G. (1993). From industrial unionism to general unionism: A historical transformation? *Labor Law Journal, 44,* 252–256.

Devinatz, V. G. (1996). Testing the Johnston "public sector union strike success" hypothesis: A qualitative analysis. *Journal of Collective Negotiations in the Public Sector, 26,* 99–112.

Devinatz, V. G. (1998). What do we know about mutual gains bargaining among educators? *Journal of Collective Negotiations in the Public Sector, 27,* 79–91.

Devinatz, V. G. (2000, September 1). Office workers unite: Labor Day a holiday for white collars, too. *The Chicago Tribune,* Section 1, 23.

Eisenscher, M. (1999). Critical juncture: Unionism at the crossroads. In B. Nissen (Ed.), *Which Direction for Organized Labor? Essays on Organizing, Outreach, and Internal Transformations.* Detroit: Wayne State University Press.

Greenhouse, S. (2000, February 17). Labor urges amnesty for illegal immigrants. *The New York Times,* A26.

Herman, E. E. (1998). *Collective bargaining and labor relations* (4th ed.). Upper Saddle River, NJ: Prentice Hall, Inc.

Holley, W. H., & Jennings, K. M. (1997). *The labor relations process* (6th ed.). New York: The Dryden Press.

Holley, W. H., Jennings, K. M., & Wolters, R. S. (2001). *The labor relations process* (7th ed.). Fort Worth, TX: Harcourt College Publishers.

Human Rights Watch (2000). *Unfair advantage: Workers' freedom of association in the United States under international human rights standards.* New York: Human Rights Watch.

Ivancevich, J. M., Lorenzi, P., Skinner, S. J., & Crosby, P. B. (1994). *Management: Quality and competitiveness.* Burr Ridge, IL: Richard D. Irwin, Inc.

Jarley, P., & Fiorito, J. (1990). Associate membership: Unionism or consumerism? *Industrial and Labor Relations Review, 43,* 209–224.

Johnston, P. (1994). *Success while others fail: Social movement unionism and the public workplace.* Ithaca, NY: ILR Press.

Kotkin, J. (1999, September 26). Grass-roots business: Unions see fertile fields at lower end of high tech. *The New York Times,* Section 3, 4.

Leary, E., & Menaker, M. (1994). *Jointness at GM: Company unionism in the 21st century.* Woonsocket, RI: UAW New Directions Region 9A.

Moody, K. (1997). *Workers in a lean world: Unions in the international economy.* London: Verso.

Olson, B. A., & Howard, J. L. (1995). Armed elites confront labor: The Texas militia and the Houston strikes of 1880 and 1898. *Labor's Heritage, 7,* 52–63.

Parker, M., & Slaughter, J. (1997). Advancing unionism on the new terrain. In B. Nissen (Ed.), *Unions and Workplace Reorganization.* Detroit: Wayne State University Press.

Perline, M. M., & Sexton, E. A. (1994). Managerial perceptions of labor-management cooperation. *Industrial Relations, 33,* 377–385.

Rabban, D. M. (1991). Is unionism compatible with professionalism? *Industrial and Labor Relations Review, 45,* 97–112.

Shostak, A. B. (1999). *CyberUnion: Empowering labor through computer technology.* Armonk, NY: M.E. Sharpe.

Troy, L. (1986). The rise and fall of American trade unions: The labor movement from FDR to RR. In S. M. Lipset (Ed.), *Unions in Transition: Entering the Second Century.* San Francisco: ICS Press.

ASSESSING WORKPLACE CONFLICT RESOLUTION OPTIONS

Kirk Blackard

Some counterproductive conflict occurs in all organizations. Thoughtful managers must consider how much time, effort, and money they are investing in such conflict, and whether they are dealing with it as well as they can. If the organization does not already have a formal conflict resolution system, management should consider whether use of one would improve organization effectiveness and add economic value.

This article discusses factors management should consider when looking at the needs of its organization and available conflict resolution options to determine if a better approach is appropriate. It briefly reviews various options, outlines their potential benefits, and presents an approach for management to use in deciding whether it should adopt alternative dispute resolution (ADR) processes.

CONFLICT RESOLUTION OPTIONS

One option is for management to be essentially passive and allow the disputants (in conflict among employees) or the other party (in conflict between employees and management) to control the dispute resolution process. When this happens, a management with a firm position as to the substance of a dispute may nevertheless allow the employee or employees involved to determine the process through which it is resolved. For example, management might aggressively defend a decision or policy at the heart of a controversy, but nevertheless allow employee complainants to decide when to surface the dispute, whether to appeal a decision internally or externally, or whether to litigate. In such cases, management implicitly relegates decisions as to how conflicts will be resolved to the employees involved.

While delegating decisions to employees is often a positive management practice, allowing employee disputants to control the process for resolving conflicts they have raised has many pitfalls, particularly where their dispute is with management. Doing so allows decisions concerning the resolution process to be controlled by individuals who have interests that are different than those of the organization or other individuals in it, and who may not have the appropriate information, expertise, or resources to pursue creative or nontraditional approaches. Employees are likely to use processes that lead to substantive decisions based on who is "right" from a legal or policy viewpoint, or who has the power to coerce the other party to give in. Absent early concessions by one party or the other, litigation is the likely result.

Making decisions on the basis of rights and power may, on the surface, seem to favor management, which typically has more information, is in a better position to understand legal and policy issues, and has more power than employees. However, settlements that are decided by force or by a third party through litigation are frequently costly, rarely address the real interests of either party, and seldom truly resolve the underlying problems in a way that prevents recurrence or accomplishes a purpose beyond resolving the immediate dispute.

A wiser option is for management to have a strategy for managing conflict; a plan that is an alternative to employee-controlled processes that so often lead to costly litigation and further conflict. ADR, an umbrella term that covers a wide range of nonlitigious options, can be part of such a strategy. A management concerned about counterproductive conflict should consider its particular circumstances and use one or more practices from a wide range of ADR options. Three different strategies that demonstrate

increasing levels of planning, management/employee involvement, and cost can represent this range.

Level 1: Ad hoc alternative dispute resolution is a minimal approach in workplace conflict resolution. In this case, management encourages employees to surface conflict, perhaps through an open-door policy or "management by walking around," and may provide training in effective communication, active listening, or other such conflict avoidance practices on an as-needed basis. Management maintains an awareness of ADR options that avoid litigation and proposes their voluntary use after conflict surfaces. For example, when management in the normal course of events becomes aware of a counterproductive conflict, it might encourage use of a third party to facilitate problem solving. Or at later stages it might encourage mediation or arbitration in lieu of employees filing complaints with external agencies or resorting to litigation. This ad hoc approach provides alternatives that frequently are more effective and less risky for both parties than traditional approaches, and it can be used at a lower cost than more complex systems. However, it continues to allow employee disputants to unilaterally decide what process will be used to resolve their complaints.

Level 2: Dispute resolution policies, through which management spells out procedures for surfacing and dealing with conflict, are implemented before the fact and give management greater control over how disputes are resolved. Such policies may, for example, require employees to work through the chain of command, formalize an open-door policy, offer assistance from the human resources department, or provide for voluntary or condition-of-employment mediation and/or arbitration in resolving disputes. They emphasize providing employees a simple, understandable procedure for resolving disputes in a fair, cost-effective manner. While such dispute resolution policies do little to minimize the occurrences or severity of conflict, they allow disputes to easily surface and make the process for resolving them more predictable, less risky, and usually less costly. Development and implementation of such policies require both effort and cost, as they must be carefully crafted and properly administered, particularly if mediation or arbitration is to be a condition of employment. However, since such policies usually rely on employees to take the initiative and contemplate only a reactive role from management, the effort and cost associated with their ongoing administration is minimal.

Level 3: Conflict resolution systems are implemented before the fact in an active effort to reduce incidents of counterproductive conflict, minimize their severity, and provide effective ways to resolve disputes that do occur. These systems may include various components, as appropriate for the particular organization, such as the following:

- Conflict management as a specific part of the organization's business and human resources strategy
- A clearly articulated policy that provides due process for all employees and a full understanding of appropriate ADR procedures
- A conflict management point person, committee, or department
- Ombuds (neutral members of the organization, from outside the normal chain of command) who provide confidential, informal assistance to employees in addressing workplace issues
- Voluntary or condition of employment policies on mediation or arbitration
- Panels of external or internal third party neutrals
- Peer review panels that assist in resolving employee complaints

- Neutral fact-finding by a third party or parties to examine complaints and issue nonbinding reports
- Policies for compensating independent counsel or other cost sharing with employees who have complaints against the organization
- Conflict management/resolution education and training
- Feedback of appropriate, nonconfidential information to other management systems

Conflict resolution systems can substantially reduce the cost of counterproductive conflict and pay dividends to the organization, but developing, implementing, and maintaining them has a price. To insure optimum effectiveness, external assistance and a broad cross-section of employees should usually be involved in their development. Initial communication and training must be comprehensive and extended to all employees. And for optimal effectiveness, ongoing administration requires the attention of one or several employees, continuing training and education, frequent management attention, and out-of-pocket expense. Thus, a decision whether to use such a system must be guided by a careful balancing of the expected value against the projected cost.

SELECTING AN ADR APPROACH

A comprehensive conflict resolution system is the approach most likely to minimize the effect of counterproductive conflict in most workplaces. But is a comprehensive system cost-effective? Is ad hoc alternative dispute resolution or a simple dispute resolution policy all that is needed or that can be economically justified in a particular situation? Each case must be evaluated on its own merits, considering all the potential benefits of ADR and the capacity and need of the organization.

ADR Benefits

ADR processes are used to resolve disputes among employees or between employees and the organization. But thinking only in terms of resolving disputes fails to recognize some of the potential benefits of such processes and may cause management to forgo their use or implement a narrowly focused program that misses opportunities. To avoid such pitfalls, management should view ADR from a broad perspective. It should think in terms of a management process that will minimize the organizational cost of counterproductive conflict and contribute to organizational excellence.

A broad-based conflict resolution system can minimize the cost of conflict and contribute to organizational excellence in a number of ways. Some are concrete and easy to quantify, while others are more nebulous but nevertheless of real value. The most important are discussed below.

Reduces Litigation Cost   The most frequently discussed and easily quantifiable cost saving from effective conflict resolution is a reduction in litigation costs. ADR methods that surface and resolve disputes informally at an early stage and use mediation or arbitration when third party intervention is needed avoid much of the cost normally associated with litigation. Legal costs are likely to be reduced or nonexistent, and management time spent on each dispute is minimized. ADR processes such as mediation enhance the likelihood of mutually agreeable resolution, and arbitration is typically more predictable than litigation, with large judgments less likely than from a jury trial. More important, however, an effective dispute resolution system addresses root causes such as systems problems, cultural differences, lack of trust, or poor communications, and thereby reduces the number of disputes and the need for third party intervention in the future.

Minimizes Wasted Time and Effort   Counterproductive conflict takes time and energy away from constructive business endeavors. Those involved in a dispute think about it, worry about it, and spend time trying to do something about it. Supervisors and managers become involved when disputes are with management or when employees need help in resolving disputes among themselves. This involvement diverts management time, energy, and attention from leadership activities that should leverage the efforts of all employees, and therefore tends to multiply the cost of a dispute. An effective ADR system limits the occurrences of disputes and causes them to be handled in a more timely and efficient fashion, thereby reducing the time and effort wasted by both the disputants and others who must be involved.

Builds Trust in Management   Trust is an unwritten and usually unspoken contract that allows each party to a relationship to depend on the honesty, integrity, reliability, and justice of the others. Trust is necessary for an effective workforce, and its absence increases the cost of doing business by increasing adversarial activity and the costs associated with administering and enforcing policies, contracts, or laws to insure that transactions among people are executed as expected. An effective conflict resolution system helps build trust. Allowing employees to easily and inexpensively include a third party in a contest with management demonstrates management's willingness and ability to deliver on its commitments. Shifting the focus from power-based settlement to effective problem resolution helps the parties deal with the difference in power between management and employees. More importantly, providing an accessible, fair, easy-to-use conflict resolution system exposes management's vulnerabilities within a setting that is reasonably predictable and controlled, thereby demonstrating to employees that management trusts them.

Enhances Bottom-Up Communication Management frequently makes bad decisions because it fails to listen to employees. It talks to employees but does not elicit their input or hear what they say. An effective conflict resolution system improves bottom-up communication. Consistent with confidentiality obligations, relevant data from cases handled by the system are fed back to management. This feedback process provides management valuable information to discern patterns of behavior, trends, employee concerns, or other issues existing in the workforce. More importantly, an ADR system helps give employees the confidence to become involved and provide direct input, because they believe that any disputes that develop will be resolved fairly.

Supports Diversity Diversity of thought in the workforce is necessary for the creativity and innovation required for optimum organizational performance. An ADR system encourages such diversity by valuing the differences that make people unique and providing a mechanism for employees to work out their differences and manage their conflicting interests in a positive, respectful way. Such a system helps create a workplace where minorities and women prefer to work because they feel any discrimination or other inappropriate treatment will be dealt with quickly and fairly.

Fosters Cultural Change Effective companies must change faster than the environment around them in order to stay ahead of a predictable business cycle of growth followed by decline. This means they must change their fundamental corporate culture from time to time, often at the peak of their success. An effective conflict management system can surface problems, exhibit trends, and provide management with early warning of developing issues and the need for fundamental cultural change. If such a system is not in place, implementing one can represent the first step toward increased openness, more employee involvement, or other fundamental changes that may be necessary for broad cultural transformation.

Capacity and Need

The potential benefits of ADR provide the context against which management must consider its needs and decide whether a conflict resolution process is likely to add value. Three fundamental questions are important when addressing such issues.

1. *Is the organization large enough to justify a conflict resolution system?* The answer depends on the level of conflict in the organization and the type of system being considered, and it involves assessment of potential benefit as compared to cost. In a small organization where the top decision maker manages the business through his or her direct personal relationship with employees, a formal conflict management system normally will not be used enough to offset the cost and pay dividends. In addition, a conflict management system could actually hurt organizational performance by imposing a potential barrier between management and employees, limiting direct communication, and impeding more direct resolution of conflicts. Thus, where a personal relationship drives the organization, management typically should follow good management practices, encourage employees to resolve their own disputes, and adopt an ad hoc approach to ADR, using only processes that are appropriate for individual cases when they arise.

    The conclusion may be different, however, where the organization is large enough that the top decision maker does not have direct contact with all employees, and instead must manage through levels of supervision, policies, and systems. In larger organizations, a more comprehensive conflict resolution system may be a cost-effective way to improve communication, surface conflict at an early stage, and resolve it in mutually beneficial ways. When this threshold has been met, management should consider a simple dispute resolution policy or a broader conflict management system as appropriate.

2. *What is appropriate for the organization's culture?* The conflict management process is really a subsystem that is a working part of a larger management system. It is connected to other parts, and it influences and is influenced by them. Its interconnectedness is facilitated by feedback loops through which a change in how conflict is managed influences other parts of the larger management system, which then change in ways that loop back to influence how conflict is managed. Thus, for a conflict management process to be effective, it must "fit" with other parts of the management system. This fit must be founded on a common purpose, similar values, and complementary practices.

An effective conflict resolution process must embody characteristics of a collaborative, involved workplace. For example, it must be based on and encourage trust, be open and facilitate a free flow of information while at the same time respecting the confidentiality of employees, and involve employees and empower them to resolve many of their own issues. A conflict management system will not be effective unless it is part of a broader workplace system with similar characteristics. If the conflict resolution system transmits or receives influences that are fundamentally inconsistent with other systems, both management and employees will be confused and the system may create conflict rather than manage it. Even

when individual disputes are resolved, the broad, systemic improvements that make a conflict management system cost-effective are not likely to occur. Thus, a comprehensive conflict management system should not be implemented unless it fits the existing corporate culture or is part of a plan to transform the culture so there will be a fit.

3. *Does the level of conflict justify a conflict management system?* Comprehensive conflict management systems take time and commitment, and they cost money to develop, implement, and maintain. Both costs and benefits are difficult to quantify, and management often faces a chicken/egg dilemma: it cannot assess the cost/benefit relationship without understanding the details of a system for its situation—but it is reluctant to incur the cost and distraction of a detailed needs analysis and preliminary design unless it expects the value to exceed the cost. A logical starting point for dealing with this dilemma is to do a preliminary screen of business need as a prerequisite for further action.

Organizations can do an initial screen of their need for better conflict management by assessing the significance of the following potential concerns:

- Challenges to management actions or policies
- Disputes between employees or groups
- Employee disputes with external stakeholders
- Disputes with major organizational impact
- Employee disciplinary actions
- Employee time involved with conflict issues
- Management time devoted to conflict issues

- Dissatisfaction after conflict settlement
- Recurrence of similar conflicts
- Antagonistic dealings with labor leaders
- Complaints filed with external agencies
- Litigation handling costs
- Settlement/judgment costs

The preliminary assessment should be done by a small number of informed managers, supervisors, and employees working either individually or in a group. The status of each potential issue should be considered separately and described as one of the following: (a) Not an issue, (b) Occasional concern, or (c) Excessive.

Drawing conclusions from the descriptions is not a science. However, if the consensus is that all factors are "not an issue," maintaining good management practices and using ad hoc approaches as appropriate to resolve disputes is probably the best approach. If, on the other hand, there is "occasional concern" about a large number of factors or even one or a few are considered "excessive," further action is suggested. This action should include more extensive organizational diagnosis, a preliminary system design, an estimate of the expected cost and benefit of such a system, and a decision as to whether or not to go forward.

CONCLUSION

ADR presents organizations with a number of options for managing conflict. In selecting among those options, management should balance potential costs against potential benefits. In doing so, it should take a broad view of what a conflict management system can contribute to organizational excellence and consider the organization's capacity and need for such a system. A preliminary screen of potential areas of concern provides a starting point for future awareness and discussion. As with many other areas of human resources management, considering new models for old problems is essential.

CHAPTER

10

RIGHTS, RESPONSIBILITIES, VALUES, AND ETHICS

The personal relationship between an individual and an organization has undergone considerable change. Individuals want to be able to buy into the values of an organization. There have been many changes made in order to capitalize on this evolving relationship.

Allowing employees to participate in organizational decision making has a number of positive ancillary benefits. Participation can help subordinates understand the circumstances surrounding and required by a decision. This is normal adult behavior that satisfies individual needs for autonomy and achievement. Cooperative social and work interactions, a goal of human resources programs, are facilitated when participation is allowed. In fact, many behavioral scientists believe that participation will result in better decisions to the extent that the talents and skills of the entire group are tapped. This belief has been operationalized as a move toward "empowering" people in organizations—sharing power with organization members.

Is empowerment an effective strategy? Is it right for all organizations? From a human resources perspective, the correct answer is that it all depends upon a number of related issues. The articles in this chapter are aimed at elucidating the important issues surrounding the question of whether empowerment is right for a particular organization.

Another current issue is accountability. Accountability is the management philosophy that all individuals are liable or accountable for how well they use the legitimate authority vested in them by an organization. Have people lived up to their responsibilities and their duties to perform the activities assigned to them? If individuals fail on the tasks for which they are accountable, some punitive action should result. By the same token, success should bring desired rewards.

In the context of human resources, accountability refers to the notion of responsibility for either effective or ineffective human resources programs. Where does this responsibility reside? The question is not necessarily straightforward. Can outcomes be dissociated from environments and attributed solely to those charged with implementation? Probably not! Accountability is a complex issue.

The first article in this chapter, by Williams and Ferris, outlines how the employment relationship for an individual has changed from "loyalty for job security" to an "adult to adult" relationship. People want more out of work than just compensation. The authors believe that individuals want to work where they can integrate their values and beliefs with similar organizational values and beliefs. In the next article, Douglas defines empowerment and outlines those boundary conditions necessary for empowerment to

405

make a positive contribution to an organization. He suggests that empowerment can work and influence the bottom line.

Have you ever tried to find an accountable person in an organization? In the last article in this chapter, Mero and Frink outline the importance of developing accountability in human resources systems. When people are aware that they will have to justify an action, they have a tendency to more fully grasp the implications of their level of performance. Accountability is important from both an internal and an external standpoint, and by both managers and employees. The authors believe it is an important variable and we would agree.

READINGS

THE CHANGING NATURE OF THE EMPLOYMENT RELATIONSHIP: RECLAIMING VALUES IN THE WORKPLACE

Sandra L. Williams
Gerald R. Ferris

Most organizational leaders readily talk about delivering value to attract and retain customers. Increasingly, however, many of them are also talking about setting values to attract and retain employees.

No longer reserved for discussions around the family dinner table or in a Sunday school classroom, values lie at the foundation of the mission and business strategy of some of the most competitive firms. Today, their leaders are finding that shared values are the essential glue that can hold an organization together.

At Corning Inc., for example, clearly articulating and standing beside certain fixed organizational values has resulted in increased individual flexibility and empowerment and enabled the company to improve product quality, reduce errors, attract and retain skilled workers, and foster an atmosphere steeped in concern for personal needs and lifelong learning. Corning articulates seven core values, with all of them resting on valuing the individual, who is viewed as being critical to the company's competitive advantage. According to chairman James R. Houghton, the only way to remain competitive and to attract the best talent is to "value the individual."

Tom Chappel, president and co-founder of Tom's of Maine, a personal care products company, suggests that identifying core organizational values is imperative for staying on track with the organization's mission. Identifying employee-generated beliefs and values provides Tom's of Maine with a distinctive organizational identify, which not only prevents inconsistent product or market developments, but forces honesty and the admission of mistakes, ultimately improving customer loyalty.

Discerning core organizational values and communicating guiding values to employee members can have positive effects. For example:

- Frequent and overt discussion of guiding values allows for a more collective application of energy, thereby leading to greater organizational effectiveness.
- Activities that engage in developing or supporting the core shared values unite an organization.
- Communities of workers create sustainable results, and these communities can adapt to change because they are challenged and committed to what they care about.
- Conducting business around shared values results in improved teamwork and collaboration, thereby enhancing creativity among staff members, and promoting a strengthened sense of ethics.

Thus, the individual need to find personal fulfillment in balancing work as a journey toward personal wholeness expands viewpoints, enlarging possibilities and releasing capabilities. All these enhance the organization's flexibility, productivity, and adaptability, ensuring its success in today's global marketplace.

THE FALL OF AN ECONOMIC MODEL LEADS TO AN EMPHASIS ON VALUES

Twentieth-century science and its revised ideas on order and interconnectivity throughout the universe have dramatically altered viewpoints about human relations and organizational structure. Organizations are increasingly viewed as networks of individual relationships, and this notion is influencing old models about hierarchy and control in the corporate workplace. Externally, companies are changing their practices and relationships with clients, vendors, service providers, and the public, viewing them as interactive components of an entire system. Internally, corporations are revising relationships with individual employees, teams of employees, subcontractor groups, managers, and executives.

At the same time, individuals are also rethinking their employment relationship and their reasons why they work where they do. Continuous organizational change, coupled with the now-recognized resource value of the knowledge-rich worker, is leading individuals to reexamine the purpose of their work and the function of work within their lives. The reasons why individuals join specific organizations are being reassessed. A movement toward engagement based on ethics and values is emerging, and the implications for individuals and organizations that share values are extraordinarily powerful.

Industrial-era precepts about buying, selling, and producing emphasized conspicuous consumption, cut-throat competition, personal identity related to social position

or material possessions, and individual autonomy. This industrial economic model no longer holds true in today's interactive global market, which emphasize shared usage, business partnering, identity related to knowledge and capabilities, and team responsibilities. The new economic model relies on a constant exchange of information, customized product and delivery mechanisms, shared knowledge, and creativity. The old management model that called for planning, organization, and control because resources were scarce no longer works.

Likewise, the historic loyalty-for-job-security model of the employment relationship and the perceived need for a management practice that controlled or ordered that relationship is changing. The growing sophistication and technological expertise of the information worker is shifting the employer-employee relationship because workers now own the strategic competitive advantage for most organizations—knowledge and adaptability. This power shift—away from the organization and toward the employee as a knowledge worker—forces a new perspective on human resources. The organization now must view its employees as investments to which to add value rather than as a corporate asset from which to extract value. Similarly, the old employee perspective that one must do what one has to do to build a successful career in one organization is being replaced by a new belief in building personal, portable skills for a career of learning across several entities.

Sensing the power shift, the current workforce is demanding new relationships with employers, and looking for places to build skills, but also seeking to identify places where information is shared and communication is open. This results in a wholly different philosophy of work, one that recognizes the value of each individual for the contribution he or she makes and where the individual looks for personal worth beyond the economics of employment. It involves a fundamental change in perspectives where individuals, now responsible for their own learning and personal growth, are forcing a move away from the former paternalistic model of controlled employment toward an adult-to-adult model of employment by choice.

A TRUST AND COMMITMENT MELTDOWN

The prolonged period of reengineering, restructuring, and downsizing in which many organizations engaged during the 1980s and 1990s significantly destabilized the historic employer–employee relationship. Having been broadly implemented by employers, the downsizings had long-term negative effects on employee morale. Employment ties with huge numbers of workers were suddenly and unexpectedly severed, frequently resulting in increased workloads for those who were retained. Further, many organizations revamped their policies and structures without considering the underlying psychological contract embedded in the old employment model. The employer-employee relationship was traumatized to such an extent that such factors as honesty, trust, and good faith were undermined. Trust levels were not only negatively affected, but entirely eroded in many organizations.

Throughout today's organizations, the long-held values of trust-assuredness in the employer's integrity and behavior have become a debilitating casualty of the strategies and methods that leaders deployed for short-term financial resource reasons. A study conducted in 1996 and 1997 by Manchester Consulting of Bala Cynwyd, Pennsylvania, indicated that trust levels had declined at 75 percent of the 215 workplaces surveyed.

Although companies have been warned of the competitive disadvantage they face by losing trust and commitment among their workers, few have taken proactive steps to improve morale with any lasting result. Furthermore, recent evidence indicates that employee cynicism has increased directly as a result of the broad failure of managers to deliver on prior promises that had inflated employee hopes and expectations. The resulting low morale now affects the entire spectrum of the workforce. As mistrust grows, full capabilities are going underutilized at all levels within organizations, and leaders have lost the confidence of their subordinates. Additionally, distrustful workers are less committed and ultimately less productive than those who do trust their leaders.

Thus, the broken employment and social contract has made the traditional trust-based relationship both nonviable and nonrenewable for employers and employees alike. Concurrently, having less confidence in leaders and organizations, people are less secure in their workplaces.

Because of the lack of trust and the nearly constant pace of change, today's organizations are highly unpredictable. With many systems and organizations lacking stability, individuals have begun to look inwardly for reasons of employment engagement. Tired of living compartmentalized, disconnected lives, individuals are beginning to bring together the personal, social, and spiritual sides of themselves in one endeavor. Individuals are moving further away from the dependency that was characteristic of employees in the paternalistic employment model and toward a view of work as a part, but not the primary focus, of each person's own journey toward wholeness. They are recognizing that the human being is composed of more than economic aspirations, and is more than just a worker or an economic unit.

Unencumbered by the loyalties of past industrial-era practices, individuals are now able to reexamine the meaning of work and the value of the workplace. A sociological study of thousands of public opinion surveys revealed that 10 percent of all adults—some 20 million people—are seeking new ways of living, consistent with new ways of thinking about their lives and roles. A new movement, underscoring the importance of self-management and the pursuit of higher ideals in relation to one's work, is emerging. Individuals have started to practice bringing one's whole self to work, and consultants such as Steven Covey and Peter Block encourage the reacknowledgement of personal values throughout one's home, community, and worklife. This intersection of work with the individual seemingly is tied to one's core values, an innate sense of wisdom, and a commitment to be of service.

TAKING ADVANTAGE OF THE VALUE OPPORTUNITY

Advances in science, technology, psychology, and sociology are becoming increasingly interrelated and overlapping in impact. The ability of an enterprise to operate independently, separated from the community in which it resides or the aspirations of its members, is diminishing rapidly. Those organizations that persist in this approach are following a roadmap to failure.

To be successful, organizations must recognize the trend toward value discernment and employee engagement that is emerging in both academic research and in the work environment itself. Although formal research on value alignment is limited, it teaches profound lessons. If the benchmarks of the new global economy now include increased underemployment, individuals pursuing multiple jobs in search of learning, personal growth, and service, it is certain that the innate desire to align who one is with the values of the workplace will only grow. What matters at work is what the employing organization values, in both its words and its actions.

While organizations have been slow to discern or reveal underlying values and beliefs, those that have focused on values, naming and clearly upholding those that they

hold dear, are experiencing a new sense of vibrancy and enhanced morale. Following the distrust and diminished loyalty that resulted from the breaking of the old employment contract, organizational leaders must examine values to effectively utilize their only remaining competitive resource in their changing environments: a truly motivated and engaged workforce.

Business organizations are finding various ways of motivating and bonding their workforce through the power of values. A few organizations are beginning to define and communicate their core values, sometimes by allowing employees to develop a set of belief statements, so that everyone understands the standards to which they are aligning themselves. Others connect organizational vision and organizational values, or encourage open, honest discussions of values at the most senior executive levels as a critical means to reconnect an organization's purpose and performance. The objective of these organizational reviews is not to curtail strategic plans and business goals, but to infuse them with an ethical conscience and a values orientation.

It is becoming incumbent upon organizations to spend time developing a value base for the organization so that when caught in a dilemma or needing direction, a foundation for individual reference will already exist. Values constitute a philosophical position about what the organization thinks is important; they are the bedrock truths to which the organization holds. Different values also serve to identify and define organizational culture and personality and, thus, differentiate institutions. Honesty, respect, and integrity are values that business entities are trying to incorporate in their systems.

Determining organizational values is not only an opportunity for competitive advantage; it is becoming a necessity. For individual employees to progress, the guiding values of the organization must be known and communicated clearly to the workforce. Although many organizations do work on their vision, mission, and values, those that do so in a very deliberate, regular, and explicit way are creating an advantage over their competition. They are perceived as being much more capable of gaining the commitment and creativity of their employees and loyalty from their customers.

WHICH VALUES AND WHY

Values can be defined as the underlying precepts or principles that lead to an esteemed standard of character. However, determining specific values to uphold is a very individualistic process, and each person likely has his or her own methods for identifying and incorporating them. Individuals are beginning to discern core values critical to their personal sense of wholeness and to integrate these with work. But which ones are core values?

In 1996, the High-Tor Alliance, a New York research and consulting firm, studied the practice of spiritual and contemplative disciplines by individuals in several organizations. The study identified service as among the most often mentioned values of respondents, whether for the individual or a group. A central premise to the theme of organizational stewardship centers on the growing concept of service without control or compliance.

Other key values practiced by individuals at work were found to include integrity, congruence, and honesty. Positive relations among coworkers was also viewed as a value. According to research conducted by the University of Chicago's social psychology department, which surveyed 17 million employees in 40 countries about their values, people value eight behaviors. The top two are treat others with uncompromising truth, and lavish trust on associates.

A lack of integrity was identified by Manchester Consulting as the greatest depleter of trust within an organization.

Clearly, integrity (based on trust), honesty (based in truth), and service (without control) are important values for individuals.

PERSONAL VALUES AND ORGANIZATIONAL CHOICE

In many organizations, employees have begun to identify a value gap—the chasm between the values companies espouse and what they practice. The High-Tor Alliance study participants clearly emphasized the importance for individuals to operate at work in a manner that is guided by their deepest values. Nearly 80 percent of the respondents identified their day-to-day work as "completely" or "mostly" a path of personal development. They view work and the workplace as an opportunity to practice their personal values. Additionally, nine out of ten respondents indicated that they chose to work in organizations whose values were congruent with their personal values.

Perhaps because of the resurgence of wholeness as a social and scientific concept, and possibly fueled by continued signals of insecurity and misdirection from organizations, there appears to be a personal examination taking place on the part of individuals who, having recognized the value gap in prior organizational associations, may be searching to align themselves with groups committed to similar personal values in current and future work associations.

With the decline of such traditional societal bonds as the extended family, the neighborhood, the small town, and the church or synagogue, employees are bringing their social and spiritual needs to the workplace in a new way. Since the time spent at the workplace is increasingly the only time individuals group together willingly, the workplace is becoming the setting for greater personal exchange of values and behavioral validation. Many individuals are learning that one can hold onto one's personal core values and still participate in a successful, profit-making venture. They are now seeking opportunities to share those core values within their groups. Some individuals are looking for work that touches the soul, stirs the imagination, and corresponds with a bedrock of personal identity. These same individuals want to bring their best to work only if they can involve their entire selves. This involvement includes feeling free to talk about issues of passion, and to explore shared views and values. Opportunities for shared discussion increasingly occur during work hours, when people group for extended periods of time.

Thus, rather than being the locus of an economic livelihood, the workplace is emerging as one of the critical environments for the integration of values that people want to incorporate in their personal, non-work lives. Within our organizations and institutions, a deep longing for personal development, a new sense of community, and meaning is being expressed.

These same organizations, however, have acted haphazardly in determining collective values except for the heavily weighted profit values of the past. Yet, top talent is in short supply in today's labor market, which increases the competition for intellectual capital and puts pressure on an organization's retention capabilities. Not only attracting, but retaining, top talent significantly affects an organization's ability to maximize creativity, innovation, and flexibility. Companies today have to be concerned about employee needs, interests, and values, or these talented individuals will simply go to work elsewhere. Some organizations are beginning to discuss value-centered corporate purposes, perhaps having recognized that in dealing with constant economic change, neither the latest tactics nor the old methods work. Companies are learning that they need to reclaim core values just to survive in a wave of increased employee turnover and environmental change. This necessitates a clarification about which values and principles really matter to the organization and why.

Corporate business is beginning to realize that to ensure its own survival it must create workplaces that are nurturing and healing. Mark A. Lies, II, senior partner with the international corporate law firm of Seyfarth, Shaw, Fairweather and Geraldson, notes of his client companies, "Business firms around the world are recognizing a need to provide a sense of community for their employees, as much as they need to provide a paycheck, in order for employees to remain motivated and productively engaged." Additionally, organizations that engage in covenantal employment relationships, characterized by mutual trust, open-ended communication, and shared values, are more likely to have employees who display citizenship behavior and remain engaged. Change-focused and adaptive organizations need to determine their hard core group values now, and communicate and exemplify those values constantly to tap this innate desire of the twenty-first century workforce for personal fulfillment across life's spectrums. The power of an energetic, united, and value-sustained workforce, a membership of self-aligned whole selves, is probably unlimited in its productive potential and creative beyond imagination. Time will determine the strength of this power, but no organization can afford to ignore it and hope to survive. ■

EMPLOYEE EMPOWERMENT IN ORGANIZATIONS TODAY

Ceasar Douglas

Today, organizations are making abundant changes to cope with a highly turbulent external environment. The competitive demands and complex environments have led organizations and managers to call for greater employee involvement. Evolving expectations now placed on all employees warrants a closer look to determine the effect of empowerment on the organization, managers, and employees.

The challenge of empowerment raises major issues. For employees and managers, the new demands are more complicated and difficult, and many appear impossible given the current trends for organizations (downsizing, outsourcing, etc.). For organizations, the problem is no longer one of quality of work life—the traditional issue. Now the problem centers on organization culture and the changing nature of the employment relationship companies have with their employees. Organizations and their membership recognize the importance of empowerment, and realize that it often is no longer optional.

This article briefly explores the concept of empowerment and examines what makes it a necessity in contemporary organizational environments. It then focuses on what makes empowerment difficult and what needs to be done to improve the empowerment process.

AN OVERVIEW OF EMPOWERMENT

Empowerment is a management concept that has received much attention and varied reviews, but what does it mean? Is empowerment just another way of increasing employee involvement, or is it a process for redesigning the organization? This section attempts to develop a clearer understanding of empowerment and its effects on organizations and their members.

Foundation Issues

The foundation of empowerment can be traced to Emerson's view of power, where power is seen as the product of a social relationship that resides implicitly in the other's dependency (Emerson, 1962). From Emerson's perspective, two things seem obvious: the social nature of power and the requisite condition of dependency. Based on the first condition, empowerment implies some level of interaction between the power holder and the recipient. It is safe to say that the quality of this interaction will affect the success of the empowerment process. Also, if power results from one's dependence on another, then to empower means to shift or reduce dependence. Typically, an employee depends on a manager for information and resources, but as the empowerment process begins, this relationship should change. A fully empowered employee would have access to the necessary information and resources, and the manager would depend on the employee for the outputs and progress reporting from work activities. The success of this scenario rests on the transition of power from the manager to the employee. To successfully empower employees, managers must establish a social relationship that aids in the transfer of power to employees.

Organizational Issues

In the late 1980s, in an effort to generate a higher form of employee participation, employee empowerment became the focus of many organizations. Building on job enrichment and employee involvement programs, empowerment programs were designed to grant employees the authority to make changes without asking permission (Ford & Fottler, 1995). Initially, empowerment was viewed as an organizational intervention where top managers insisted that lower-level employees take on greater responsibility and decision-making authority. In many respects, this action represents a necessary first step; however, it fails to embrace the necessary subsequent steps. Top management actions convey the importance of empowerment, but the actual empowerment process begins at lower levels within the organization. To accommodate the empowerment process, department and first-line managers must modify work assignments and provide encouragement, and front-line employees need to accept new responsibility and agree to participate in a new capacity. To be successful, empowerment requires not only willing participants, but also the completion of complementary activities across organizational levels.

Individual Issues

As an individual employee, empowerment is seen as a form of intrinsic motivation directed toward a persons' work (Spreitzer, 1996). Employees seeking to be empowered take an active orientation toward work, and they see their job as a source of personal growth and development.

How does the individual employee seeking empowerment gain the opportunity to affect his or her work environment? To begin this process, we need jobs tailored with broad responsibilities and lower managerial support. Lower-level managers are critical to the empowerment process be-

cause they are needed to create the participative environment. Although upper management provides the initial directive, it is up to the first-line managers to modify the existing climate and give access to the necessary information and resources, and thus implement the empowerment process.

In summary, empowerment stems from the social relationship between the power holder and a dependent individual. The empowerment process within an organization generally begins as a top-down initiative, identifying the need for greater employee participation and decision making. However, actual empowerment does not occur until individuals are willing to assume greater responsibility, and front-line managers take steps to facilitate the process.

So what exactly is empowerment? Empowerment is a process consisting of a set of job-related activities designed to increase organizational effectiveness that requires (a) motivated workers with the skill and desire to take on additional responsibility, and (b) managers willing to share power and facilitate employee development. This view of empowerment takes a hybrid approach, combining the management (business practices) and psychological (motivational) approaches. Before turning to what makes empowerment a challenging process, we discuss why empowerment is essential for organizations today.

WHY IS EMPOWERMENT NECESSARY TODAY?

Faced with unrelenting complexity in their external environments, organizations must develop new structures and activities to deal with this complicated landscape. This requires managers to engage in practices that aid firms in adapting to new challenges. In short, firms must develop the ability to quickly process information and make decisions. To do so requires a highly involved and empowered workforce.

Organization Structure

Structure is viewed as the ultimate constraint within organizations (Brass, 1984). As the structure changes, access and control of resources changes, and organizational roles change. Structural change represents the firm's response to the changes in the business environment. Organizations seek flatter structures that enable firms to respond quickly to business demands. Bringing flexibility to the organization to help speed decision making and communication has become a priority. Consequently, this has escalated the interest in structures that improve flexibility through the use of empowerment.

The organization structure is salient in determining the need for greater employee empowerment, and a decade of downsizing has restructured many organizations. Today, organizations are designed with fewer managers and employees who must be more productive and face greater competition. With fewer employees and managers, the concepts of well-structured jobs with limited responsibility and command-and-control management are quickly fading. Because of the managers' wider span-of-control, we now rely on more self-management by employees who have taken on more responsibility.

The paradigm currently evolving within organizations that are striving to gain greater long-term flexibility features significant structural and functional change. These firms veer from the traditional hierarchal structure to a more flexible approach using teams and jobs with broad responsibilities. Indeed, adapting to a new structure requires not only new skills, but also new attitudes and culture.

American Standard is an example of one company that has adopted a more flexible structure. American Standard dismantled its hierarchy and has organized all employees (managers and workers) into process teams (Deutsch, 1999). Each team is responsible for every aspect of producing a product, from staffing to accounts receivable. The new approach generated demand for additional training. Thus, as a second step, American Standard introduced a new position coach to focus on employee development and training. The team structure placed some individuals where they had to make decisions in areas beyond their expertise, and as a result they needed additional training. The employee's coach would then provide or arrange for training. American Standard, through the use of empowered teams and coaches, streamlined operations and greatly improved customer service.

Programs

Solutions to the challenge of remaining competitive, even in the face of today's dynamic environment, begin with understanding the importance of product/service quality and customer service. Organizations uniformly view product/service quality and customer service as priorities, and both activities depend heavily on employee empowerment.

Product/Service Quality   Increasingly, organizations have realized the importance of product and service quality. More specifically, total quality management (TQM) has had a clear impact on management practices. TQM can be described as a comprehensive way to improve total organization performance and quality. Along with TQM came the notion that organizations needed greater participation from each employee to make the new system work.

TQM removes hierarchal distinctions to engage employees in activities centered on continuous improvement. Organizations that adopt TQM are flatter, information oriented, and invest heavily in training to give employees more autonomy and responsibility (Hackman & Wageman, 1995). Importantly, TQM provides employees both the ability and opportunity to participate in decision-making activities.

The University of Michigan Hospitals, for example, adopted TQM as a way to become the provider of choice in southeast Michigan. Executive director John Forsyth believed that TQM would create a motivated and empowered workforce (Jones, George, & Hill, 2000). Teams were established to address workflow and service quality issues. As a result, the hospital made valuable improvements in areas ranging from accounts receivable to pharmacy administration. The University of Michigan Hospitals embraced TQM and credited it for increasing work effort and developing good attitudes. Importantly, employee empowerment played a major role in the success of this intervention.

Customer Service   Another important activity for organizations is to find ways to make the firm more responsive to customer needs. Organizations must compete for customers with their products and services, so responsiveness to customers' needs is vital. Service organizations depend entirely on their employees to produce high-quality service at a reasonable cost. The most straightforward way to do this is to limit or reduce the number of individuals needed to take appropriate action. Nordstrom's, a Seattle-based retailer, believes that empowerment is a key to customer service, and supports this with Employee Rule #1: Use your good judgment in all situations. There will be no additional rules (Pfeffer, Hatano, & Santalainen, 1995). This rule encourages efficient decision making and relies heavily on employee empowerment.

Also, the success of many manufacturing firms depends on their ability to satisfy the changing demands of customers. To improve customer service, manufacturing firms are implementing techniques such as flexible manufacturing and just-in-time systems. These advanced manufacturing systems rely heavily on empowered workers to make timely decisions with limited supervision.

Federal-Mogul, a manufacturer of safety lighting systems, dismantled its production line and replaced it with a modular production process. The new system features empowered teams that are responsible for inventory control, product quality, scheduling, and customer satisfaction. The idea is to streamline the production process by making employees responsible for a greater range of activities, and move many of the decision-making activities closer to the customer. The modular production process gives Federal-Mogul flexibility that allows for better customer service.

As an outgrowth of the new competitive environment, TQM and improved customer service are now mainstay activities within many organizations. The main thrust of these activities involves employees working to identify quality and operational factors that impact success. It is clear that empowered employees have more responsibility than employees in the past. However, the shift to greater empowerment is no accident; it has served to accelerate improvement in product and service quality, making firms more competitive.

WHAT MAKES EMPOWERMENT DIFFICULT?

Many organizations have embraced the idea that empowerment improves effectiveness and employee commitment. Empowerment is difficult to implement, however, because greater involvement necessitates change. Difficulties associated with empowerment stem from three issues: control over and commitment to work processes, organization culture, and individual acceptance of empowerment. To better understand the problems linked to the empowerment process, these issues are discussed further in the following sections.

Control/Commitment

In an ideal situation, as empowerment develops, we witness a movement from managerial control to systems guided by employee commitment. Managers often struggle with the concept of losing control over employees as they relinquish control over work processes (Forrester, 2000). Also, the results of downsizing have left many managers fearful that their empowering activities will eventually lead to their own obsolescence. On the other hand, employees struggle with commitment because of the changing nature of the work relationship. In an environment where layoffs, plant closings, and the use of temporary workers are commonplace, employees no longer equate improved productivity with job security. Employees see a change in the psychological contract and in the very nature of the employment relationship, which makes the empowerment process difficult.

For the firm to achieve greater employee empowerment, a degree of mutual trust is needed to aid the transition from command and control to ownership and commitment. Many managers fail to realize that empowerment represents a form of trust developed through sharing responsibilities with employees, and many employees are leery of taking ownership and responsibility (Dobbs, 1996).

Once entrusted with new responsibilities, the job will serve as a new source of control. Sam Walton, founder and former CEO of Wal-Mart, sums up the importance of this relationship in stating that " the best control comes from not controlling" (Thompson, 1998). Empowerment is a way of increasing control without controlling. Needless to say, getting managers to give up control and employees to accept new responsibilities is a daunting task. Managers and employees alike must have trust in the process and in each other.

Trust is an essential part of the empowerment process. No matter how much they agree on the importance of empowerment, employees and managers could not get beyond the concepts, taking on more responsibility and giving up control, without some

level of mutual trust. The managers' trust in the employees is derived from the belief that employees are competent and will perform consistently. On the other hand, employees' trust is closely linked to managers' integrity and openness. The bottom line is that managers need to feel that the employees are capable and reliable, and employees must feel that the managers are accessible and honest. The absence of trust between managers and employees will make empowerment a short-lived process.

Moving to empowerment requires a shift in responsibilities: Employees must understand the importance of commitment and managers must embrace the idea of giving up control, which is a challenge for both. After seeing what is required of both parties, how do we get the process started? We view trust as the catalyst for the empowerment process. A degree of trust is necessary to start the process; without trust, empowerment is a risky proposition.

Organization Culture

The essence of organization culture can be described as the norms, beliefs, values, and practices of an organization that function as a control system. More specifically, culture determines the use of power that ultimately affects the empowerment process.

Like other forms of employee involvement, empowerment is difficult to achieve without a change in employee behavior. To successfully empower employees, organizations may find it necessary to reassess the underlying values and practices that contribute to the culture. Additionally, managers' and employees' beliefs on delegation of authority, access to information, and risk taking are products of the culture and will shape the empowerment process.

Overall, organization culture can aid or obstruct change that is requisite to the empowerment process. Flexible cultures can make a difference, as Herman Miller demonstrated by empowering employees to establish an "adaptable relational" organization structure in response to a changing business environment. At Herman Miller, employees were empowered with greater access to information and decision-making authority to improve productivity and customer service. The organization culture at Herman Miller has always favored employee participation; however, during this redesign process, employees saw more room for creativity and greater participation.

The lesson is that a flexible organization culture can support the empowerment process. In Herman Miller's case, the organization culture paved the way to greater employee empowerment and a more responsive organization. Organizations with rigid cultures would struggle and probably fail to gain the advantages of employee empowerment.

Individual Acceptance

Empowerment tends to stretch individual capacity. Employees are expected to accept additional job-related responsibilities, and managers are expected to facilitate employee development at the expense of their own power base, which can cause managers to resist empowerment. Therefore, the success of empowerment is dependent on its acceptance by both individual employees and managers as an opportunity and not a threat.

Why does an individual employee want to be empowered? To begin answering this question, we must make an assessment of the individual. An empowered employee will take an active orientation toward his or her job responsibilities that is linked to an internal motivation to satisfy a need (Spreitzer, 1996). Typically, employee needs will vary from job growth (which may be satisfied by a wider range of responsibilities) to additional compensation. The only certainty surrounding employee willingness to accept empowerment is that the chance of acceptance improves when the empowerment decision is made at the individual employee level. To increase the likelihood of success,

more time must be taken to discover if and why employees want to be empowered. Only then will employees feel committed to the process, and organizations benefit fully from their empowerment.

At the individual level, the empowering manager is most important to this process. Essentially, the empowerment process begins with a manager sharing his or her power with an employee. Many organizations view empowerment as an organizational or departmental process, failing to acknowledge the source of the power that is passed along to the employees. Moreover, this blanket approach to empowerment fails to engage managers at the individual level, leading to the loss of their much-needed support.

In no other organizational intervention is managerial support more important than in the empowerment process. Indeed, many studies showcase firms that have successfully empowered lower-level employees (e.g., Wal-Mart, Southwest Airlines). However, absent from these studies are recounts of the contributions made by lower-level managers in support of the empowerment process.

Beyond the basic talk of managerial support, there are two areas that require special effort from lower-level managers to ensure success for the empowerment process. Managers must provide access to information and promote employee development.

The sharing of information is crucial to the empowerment process. Providing broad access to information can reduce the knowledge gap between managers and employees (Kanter, 1986). When employees are well informed they are more committed and exhibit higher productivity. Managers are reluctant to share information because it is a source of power and control. By not freely sharing information, managers may gain a sense of security, but they also stall the empowerment process.

Promoting employee development is a vital activity that can and should be supported by the organization; however, it cannot become a required activity. Similar to the mentoring process, promoting employee development requires a relationship between the manager and the newly empowered worker. The primary goal is to give appropriate levels of contact and support aimed at increasing employee efficacy (Forrester, 2000). We must realize that moving from making suggestions to making changes without asking permission is risky for many employees. However, contact with a supportive manager may speed employee development and the empowerment process. Unfortunately, when the empowerment process starts at the organizational or departmental level, the significance of this developmental activity is often overlooked. Overall, the developmental relationship between managers and employees only serves to strengthen the likelihood of success for the empowerment process.

In summary, what makes empowerment difficult? Several factors contribute to the problems many organizations experience. In this section, we have identified three issues that organizations must consider as they begin the empowerment process:

1. *Focus on the transition from managerial control to employee commitment.* In the movement to empowerment, managers must relinquish control and employees must increase commitment to work processes. Both managers and employees will discover that through these steps, a level of mutual trust is needed to smooth the process. As this grows, managers and employees will become more comfortable with the idea of shared responsibility, and the empowerment process will develop. Also, organizations should try to establish a means for tracking how managers and employees work in these areas. As an example, look for changes in the level of employee involvement in decision making and planning, or the amount of time spent by managers monitoring employee work activities.

2. *Examine the organization's culture.* The organization's "personality" will greatly affect the transition to greater power sharing. Recall that culture reflects the underlying values and beliefs of the organization. The culture provides a framework within which other activities must fit. Organizations with flexible cultures will enjoy more success with employee empowerment than those with rigid cultures.

3. *Recognize the importance of individual acceptance.* Empowerment is best viewed as a dyadic power exchange occurring between managers and employees. Managers must willingly take steps to promote employee development, and employees must take ownership of work processes. Viewing empowerment as an aggregate process, occurring at the organization or department level, serves only to delay or reduce its effectiveness.

WHAT CAN BE DONE TO IMPROVE THE EMPOWERMENT PROCESS?

How can we improve the empowerment process? The issues discussed so far provide some answers to help meet the challenge facing organizations in their attempts to increase employee empowerment. With the increased emphasis on customer service, quality, and organizational responsiveness, the demand for empowered employees will only grow. To accommodate this trend, organizations will need to focus on practices that have an effect on the empowerment process. In particular, we feel that through leadership, and the selection and training processes organizations can achieve greater success with this troublesome process.

Leadership

From our prior discussion, it is obvious that a strong link exists between leadership and empowerment. This process presents an opportunity for managers to exercise leadership skills by sharing power and influence with employees. But managers must also remember that empowerment works best when it is viewed as a dyadic process.

To understand the value of leadership to the empowerment process, one must understand the essence of empowerment. Empowerment is more than employees performing a new set of activities; it also involves increasing employees' commitment, which requires managers to use a varied approach to leadership based on individual needs.

So how can managers use leadership to improve the empowerment process? Effective leaders will make investments in the empowerment process with the following:

1. *Provide vision.* This is most important for top managers; remember that empowerment may conflict with the existing culture and require considerable change. Top managers will need to communicate where they see the organization heading, and why empowerment is needed.

2. *Provide positive support and words of encouragement.* These will help build employee confidence and trust. Through the empowerment process, employees may gain responsibility over everyday activities. However, with limited experience in this capacity employees lack much-needed confidence, and leader support is essential. Also, trust develops when leaders are supportive and provide encouragement.

3. *Highlight exemplar behavior.* Making employees aware of those who have successfully made the transition may give others the belief that they too can be successful.

4. *Recognize incremental success.* Employees, because of risk aversion, may take on new responsibilities in a step-like manner, seeking reinforcement to guide

future actions. In this case, leaders must understand the importance of their feedback and be prepared to recognize incremental progress.

5. *Share power based on individual needs and ability.* It is counterproductive to assume that all employees want and can handle similar levels of responsibility. To utilize empowerment to its fullest, leaders must differentiate levels of responsibility among employees based on ability and internal motivation.

Organizational effectiveness depends on power sharing, where leadership has a pivotal role. Our argument suggests that there is no best approach to empowerment; managers must adjust their approach to the needs and abilities of their employees. The value in this message is that success with empowerment is not likely to come from a generic approach. Initially, empowerment is a time-consuming process, but if you are successful, the benefits will outweigh the costs.

Selection and Training

For empowerment to be successful, selection and training programs must be supportive of the requirements for empowered employees. The objective is to create a good fit between new hires and the organization, and to give existing employees the requisite knowledge and skills.

Selection   Without the right people, the empowerment process faces an uphill battle. Organizations need people with willingness to assume decision-making responsibility (i.e., be a truly "value-added employee"), not just follow instructions. The selection process should screen on attributes unlikely to change through training. Empowerment works best when employees have the internal motivation to grow with the job, a characteristic that is rarely a product of training.

Organizations may also benefit from the use of realistic job previews to help select individuals for empowered positions. Because these positions may require that employees assume a wide range of activities and responsibility, the realistic preview is needed to give a clear and accurate view. Steps taken in the selection process can help individuals and organizations make informed choices about whether a good match exists, which are issues vital to the empowerment process.

Training   Skills and knowledge have considerable bearing on the job performance of empowered workers. Organizations can fail to gain the full potential advantage of empowerment if workers do not have the needed skills. When lacking the necessary skills, workers tend to perform poorly, or avoid the challenge of new activities truncating the empowerment process.

In the empowerment process, training serves a dual purpose. The first is to provide job-related skills and knowledge. The second is to increases employee commitment by making employees feel important. The more valuable employees are made to feel, the more they view themselves as part of the organization, which may result in greater buy-in to the empowerment process.

CONCLUSION

Empowerment is achievable, but not without special efforts in several key areas. First, a level of trust must develop between empowering managers and employees. Next, managers must become leaders, sharing power and being supportive of employees as they accept greater responsibility. Although it is tempting to try to empower all workers with the same approach, these efforts are unlikely to succeed; this process works best at the dyadic level. Organizations must also understand the impact of culture: If it is not open and receptive to change, it will make empowerment difficult to achieve. Empowerment works best in a climate that stresses trust, encouragement, and has strong leadership to provide a clear organizational vision. ■

REFERENCES

Brass, D. J. (1984). Being in the right place: A structural analysis of individual influence in an organization. *Administrative Science Quarterly, 29*, 518–539.

Deutsch, C. H. (1999, May 7). A new kind of whistle-blower: Company refines principles of coaching and team work. *The New York Times*, C1–C2.

Dobbs, J. H. (1996). The empowerment environment. In G. R. Ferris (Ed.), *Human Resources Management: Perspectives, Context, and Outcomes* (3rd ed.). Upper Saddle River, NJ: Prentice Hall.

Emerson, R. M. (1962). Power-dependence relations. *American Sociological Review, 27*, 31–41.

Ford, R. C., & Fottler, M. D. (1995). Empowerment: A matter of degree. *Academy of Management Executive, 9* (3), 21–28.

Forrester, R. (2000). Empowerment: Rejuvenating a potent idea. *Academy of Management Executive, 14* (3), 67–80.

Hackman, J. R., & Wageman, R. (1995). Total quality management: Empirical, conceptual, and practical issues. *Administrative Science Quarterly, 40*, 309–339.

Jones, G. R., George, J. M., & Hill, C. W. (2000). *Contemporary management*, 2nd ed., Boston: Irwin McGraw-Hill.

Kanter, R. M. (1986). The new workforce meets the changing workplace: Strains, dilemmas, and contradictions in an attempt to implement participative and entrepreneurial management. *Human Resource Management, 25*, 515–538.

Pfeffer, J., Hatano, T., & Santalainen, T. (1995). Producing sustainable competitive advantage through the effective management of people. *Academy of Management Executive, 9* (1), 55–72.

Spreitzer, G. M. (1996). Social structural characteristics of psychological empowerment. *Academy of Management Journal, 39*, 483–504.

Thompson, K. R. (1998). Confronting the paradoxes in a total quality environment. *Organizational Dynamics, 26* (Winter), 62–72.

ACCOUNTABILITY IN ORGANIZATIONS AND HUMAN RESOURCES MANAGEMENT

Neal P. Mero
Dwight D. Frink

The concept of accountability has become an important term in the American lexicon. Within the realm of American politics, constituents talk of holding their political representatives accountable for their legislation (or lack of legislation). Politicians talk about holding criminals more accountable for their actions. In education, recent efforts towards educational reform at all levels have led to a call for holding educators at all levels accountable for student learning (Kearns, 1998). Even President George W. Bush has made increasing the accountability of school systems for the education of their students a central plank of his education plan.

Within the business environment, there is also a call for increasing the accountability of corporations and their management. Externally, the focus of accountability is on holding corporate leaders accountable for the decisions they make, the ethical behavior of their organizational members, and the safety of their products for consumers. One recent example typifies the high stakes involved in increased accountability of organizations and their leaders. Bridgestone/Firestone Tire Company is facing increasing scrutiny through legislative and judicial processes into their handling of a problem with the Firestone ATX model tires mostly fitted on Ford Explorers. *USA Today* reports that between 1989 and 1995, Bridgestone/

Firestone received 57 complaints about their ATX tires. However, in 1998 and 1999, 720 complaints were received and some of these complaints were associated with claims that the failure of these tires resulted in the deaths of up to 165 motorists. The increasing public pressure led Bridgestone/Firestone Tire to recall some 6.5 million Firestone tires. In addition, the public's desire that someone be held accountable led to the resignation of Bridgestone/Firestone Tire's CEO Masatoshi Ono shortly after the recall.

Accountability within organizations is also an increasingly important issue. Returning to the Bridgestone/Firestone example, how accountable is the manager of the tire plant where the tires were made for the higher than expected tire failure? How about the employees who gathered the raw materials from which the tires were made or the actual workers on the assembly line? Some would argue that each of these individuals or groups should be accountable for the outcome. The Bridgestone/Firestone situation is but the most recent example where consumer and safety groups have called for increasing accountability of organizations and their members.

Accountability is viewed by some as a panacea for all organizational problems. That assumption seems to be the motivation for calls to increase the accountability of individuals and organizations in all walks of life. If so, then increasing accountability should lead to improved individual and organizational performance. However, research into accountability as a human resources management strategy has found that accountability can improve, impair, or have no effect on performance (Lerner & Tetlock, 1999).

Accountability linkages in organizational relationships have critical implications for managing human resources. This article focuses on those linkages. It is important to remember that because people are agents of their own actions, that is, that they bear responsibility for what they do, accountability is a prerequisite for any viable social system. In other words, for any social system to function, there must be a means to bind people to the norms and expectations to maintain social order. Otherwise, we could never enforce rules of any kind.

In this article, we review the notion of accountability in human resources management systems by first defining accountability as it is used in research on organizations. We then consider the mechanisms through which organizations increase the accountability of organizational members, and we consider the implications of increasing accountability to improve the performance of an organization's human resources.

DEFINITION AND NATURE OF ACCOUNTABILITY

So, what is this concept called accountability that seems to be so important? In organizational settings, accountability means that somebody or some entity wants the individual, group, or organization to answer for what they did or said, and bear the consequences of their actions. Thus, accountability can be defined as being answerable for one's actions or decisions (Tetlock, 1992). Tetlock suggests that accountability can be viewed as the glue that connects the actions of individuals, groups, or organizations to the social structure that surrounds them. When individuals are held accountable for their decisions, by having to justify those decisions to others, they adopt a decision strategy that helps them prepare for that justification. Accountability then becomes an influential part of the decision context. In other words, accountability is the organizational mechanism that links our decisions, actions, and other behaviors to those around us.

Increasing accountability in an organizational context initially seems a simple concept. However, this seemingly simple concept has several important underlying issues. The first concerns how aware an individual is of his or her accountabilities. There are two questions related to this issue. One is the degree to which one perceives, or is aware of, the accountabilities that are in place. The second is the degree to which one understands the nature and implications of those accountabilities. That is to say, do they think that they might be held accountable, and what do they think that might mean in that particular circumstance? The second issue concerns the salience of the accountabilities to a specific individual (how much do they consider it?). A third issue relates to the valence of the accountability (or its relative importance to the indivdual). A fourth issue concerns the constituencies, or audiences, to which one feels accountable; that is, who are they and what do they want (and by the way, can we skirt the issue?). This issue also has several facets, including the number of persons we are accountable to, number of things we are accountable for, status of the people to whom we feel accountable, and so forth. We examine these in more detail later.

The following example demonstrates how accountability is thought to work. President Bush wants to increase the accountability of individual schools by linking the apportionments of federal money to the performance of students within the school. In other words, school administrators and teachers would be accountable for the performance of their students. If the students do well on a measure of academic performance preferred by the federal government, then additional federal funds will be provided. If they don't meet performance standards, then those funds would be removed and the parents of the students would be provided a voucher that would allow them to choose a different school.

One question you could ask is how accountability is different from responsibility. Responsibility can be viewed as a necessary but not sufficient condition of accountability. Within organizations, a person is responsible for an outcome when it can be considered that through their organizational role, organization rules or policies, or some set of events they can be "connected" to a set of outcomes. We consider a person accountable for those same outcomes when they have the additional requirement of having to explain or justify the outcomes. The distinction between the two concepts is more important than it would first appear. Let's say you are working with a customer on a large order and you have scheduled an appointment to meet with that customer on Tuesday at 9:00 A.M. However, you inadvertently mark the appointment for Wednesday at 9:00 A.M. On Wednesday, when you call on the customer, you find out that she chose a different supplier because she was concerned that the fact that you missed the appointment may indicate something about the overall reliability of the company you represent. From your organization's perspective you are responsible for losing the customer, however, someone within the organization may not hold you accountable for what happened. Your supervisor may be unaware of what happened, or may just choose to not confront you with the situation.

In addition to showing the difference between responsibility and accountability, this example also reveals some interesting aspects about the nature of accountability. First, in organizational contexts individuals can be accountable to a wide variety of audiences. While you may not have been required to account for losing the customer account to your supervisor in the previous example, you certainly would have had to explain your actions to the customer. One can quickly realize that in traditional organizational settings, organizational members may be accountable to multiple constituents, including their supervisors, other leaders higher in the organizational structure, or other members of the organization in specialized roles, such as quality control, accounting departments, and legal staff. We can also be accountable to peers and coworkers, subordinates, customers, and other members of the general public to whom we have to explain our behavior. This latter group includes those in formal or official positions, such as political constituencies, the general public, specific communities, business partners, or co-investors.

In addition to being accountable to numerous constituents, accountability systems in modern organizations may lead to an individual being accountable for numerous and sometimes competing outcomes. Let's consider an example of a CEO managing a business in an economic recession. That CEO would be accountable to shareholders for organizational performance as measured by maximizing shareholder wealth; in other words, the outcome desired by shareholders is to minimize the loss of stock value. That same CEO is also accountable to the firm's employees who would certainly want their jobs protected, even though this may result in poorer financial performance of an organization.

The nature of accountability is that individuals at all levels of an organization are accountable to numerous constituencies and for varied and competing outcomes. The net effect is that accountability is a pervasive part of our organizational lives, as we are required to justify actions and decisions to others within our social context. Understanding how individuals respond to accountability is a fundamentally important issue in managing an organization's human resources.

WHY ARE ACCOUNTABILITY SYSTEMS SO IMPORTANT?

So why are we so interested in understanding the influences of accountability in our human resource management systems? One reason for the interest in accountability is not just because people generally want to hear an explanation for why a certain person made a particular decision or behaved in a particular way. Specifically, it is because we are beginning to understand that when we make someone aware that they will have to justify an action, that requirement will influence the subsequent behavior of organizational members in ways that are important for organizational leaders to understand. Consider the example of holding educators responsible for their students' performance. President Bush assumes that the pressure created by that requirement will force administrators and teachers to act in a way that will optimize the education provided to students and, as a result, students will perform better.

Should we conclude then that if we simply tell people what constitutes desired behavior, and put in place appropriate monitoring devices with appropriate rewards and punishments, functional organizational behavior is sure to follow? It is rather obvious that it is not that simple. People have conflicting interests, goals, and personal characteristics, and any one accountability system cannot elicit appropriate behavior for all people in all situations. Nor is the development of an accountability system necessarily straightforward.

Unfortunately, as stated in the introduction, academic researchers have concluded that accountability in organizations is not nec-essarily a panacea. Research has found that accountability is related to improved performance in some cases, poorer performance in others, and in some situations accountability appears to have no effect on performance. As a result, to better understand why accountability can have these widely varying effects, we need to consider how HR systems can influence accountability.

HOW DO HUMAN RESOURCE SYSTEMS INFLUENCE ACCOUNTABILITY?

So how do human resource systems influence accountability in organizations? There are many ways organizations do this, and it is usually through their formal and informal systems of behavioral control. In general, we assume that people respond to accountability partly because of the direct cost or benefit that is at stake for compliance or noncompliance. In other words, accountability systems are organizational control systems, which is to say that they constrain or motivate desired behavior. Motivation theories propose that people are motivated to choose one course of action over another for the purpose of achieving desirable outcomes and avoiding undesirable outcomes. The viability of an accountability system's ability to influence behavior is contingent on the perceived positive or negative impact of compliance or noncompliance. The difference between accountability systems and motivation systems is that accountability is a more abstract concept that is not directly concerned with motivating employees, but with establishing a system of potential constraints on behavior through the potential requirement of answerability that should result in organizationally preferred behaviors.

Additionally, accountability adds another factor to the motivation equation. While motivation theories generally address a direct action-outcome relationship, accountability systems require organizational members to anticipate the reaction(s) of the evaluator(s). Thus, accountability influences behavioral choices people make, not just in terms of the direct benefits to them but also choices to elicit specific, usually positive, responses from the evaluator(s). It suggests our behaviors and decisions are not so simplistic as motivation theories might indicate. In principle, however, there is a substantial overlap in the implications for design and implementation. Accountability systems also work because they make behavior more visible.

An appropriate question to ask at this point is how an HR system can motivate "dysfunctional" organizational behaviors. The answer comes from a careful look at what often happens in practice as a result of an organization's accountability systems. In the military, there is an old saying that "it is not what's *expected*, it is what's *inspected*." In practice, there appears to be some truth to this statement as it applies to accountability systems. Through a variety of systems such as statements of mission, visions, and goals; incentive programs; or performance monitoring systems, organizations and their leaders try to influence the behavior of members. However, sometimes what we hope for in terms of the behaviors we desire are not the behaviors motivated by our organizational control systems. Organizations want us to work harder and smarter in our organizations, but they often have difficulty measuring how productive we are, so instead they measure things such as how often we are absent for work or report late. This sets up the situation that Steve Kerr calls "the folly of rewarding A while hoping for B" (Kerr, 1995). Kerr points out that our HR control systems often run counter to organizational objectives.

This discussion suggests that the fundamental problem can be found in our human resources systems. There is often a disconnect between what we as managers want from our employees and what we actually

encourage through these control systems. In others, when we get behaviors we didn't really want, we should focus on the influence that HR systems may have in motivating the "wrong" behavior. From the perspective of the employee, human resources management systems should answer three questions. First, "For what am I accountable?" second, "What are the standards of performance?" and third, "To whom am I accountable?" The first two questions are usually communicated to organization members through the HR accountability system and are discussed in the next section. The third question is discussed later.

HR SYSTEMS AND ACCOUNTABILITY

HR systems communicate to organizational members information about what the organization values and, as a result, the things for which individuals are accountable. The key systems we will consider are compensation and incentives systems, the performance appraisal system, and the influence of informal systems that result from the organization's culture. Each of these systems is key to inducing accountability. We begin our look at HR accountability systems with a discussion of the role of compensation and incentive systems.

Compensation and Incentive Systems

It is important to understand the relationship between incentives and accountability because incentive alignment systems and how they are monitored are critical aspects of how people work in a formal, structured supervisor–subordinate working relationship. The relationship between the two is reciprocal. Perceptions of accountability should be strengthened when incentive systems are in place, and incentive systems should be more effective when accountability is present. Moreover, for incentive alignment to be successful, the inducements must be consequential (i.e., highly valued), and must be linked to a justification requirement that increases accountability. Doing so should make accountability mechanisms associated with the incentives more salient to organizational members. In other words, the greater the consequence, the more accountability is expected to influence attitudes and behaviors (Cummings & Anton, 1990; Frink & Klimoski, 1998; Mitchell, 1993).

As we begin the discussion of incentives, we should point out that incentives can be both positive and negative. Sanctions are the incentives or penalties that are administered for improper behavior or decisions. For either incentives or sanctions to influence performance, the individual must believe that there is a clear link between the behavior and receipt of the incentive or sanction. This linkage is the essence of an accountability system. For example, if the organization has a system for holding a member accountable for customer service, yet the individual who will be called to answer does not believe that inattention to customers will make a significant difference in a later performance appraisal, then accountability will decrease or possibly disappear altogether. This in turn diminishes the effectiveness of the incentive system. Similarly, if accountability is espoused within the organization, yet there are no mechanisms that link incentives or sanctions to inappropriate outcomes, then perceived accountability will not become salient and the desired behaviors will not be demonstrated. Therefore, the effectiveness of incentive systems, as a form of organizational sanction, must be strongly linked to accountability.

Another important feature of compensation as an accountability mechanism is, as previously mentioned, a clear linkage between the performance evaluation and compensation systems. The essence of incentive and compensation programs as a part of accountability systems is that they enhance the importance of the accounting to the individual. In other words, it increases the stakes. Incentives can focus the individual on the task at hand, and make outcomes that are important for the organization more important for the individual. But the highest levels of accountability will be achieved when there are direct linkages between performance and compensation. This notion emphasizes the role of performance evaluations for organizational accountability systems. Although performance evaluations are clearly accountability mechanisms in their own right, the interplay between numerous mechanisms provides a synergy that can be taken advantage of to construct vital and effective systems.

One outcome of an effective HR system is that it links compensation systems to strategic organizational objectives. This integrated, systematic approach is interesting not only in how it influences employee performance, but also in how it increases the stakes for HR managers to develop effective HR systems. In other words, it can make HR managers and compensation policy decision makers more accountable for the effectiveness of the overall compensation system. Thus, those to whom employees are accountable are accountable themselves for the advancement of the organizations.

The overall practice of linking performance to incentives through an accountability system is not without its problems. In the early 1990s, Sears developed a strategic objective of cutting costs by $600 million with the goal of making all employees accountable for profits. For employees working in Sears Tire and Auto Centers, this goal translated into an accountability system making managers accountable for higher quotas and reinforcing the quotas with a commission-based incentive system. Clearly, the linkage of incentives as a mechanism to enhance accountability was effective in increasing the pressure on employees. However, one negative side effect was that the pressure created by being accountable to create increased revenue led to some employees encouraging customers to make unneeded repairs. The California Consumer Affairs Division discovered that, in 34 out of 38 cases, Sears had charged for unneeded repairs at an average of $235 per repair (Kelly & Schine, 1992).

Before we leave the discussion of incentives, we need to briefly discuss a related topic that is often used to integrate incentive programs with performance evaluation programs. Incentive systems are often linked to specific goals (e.g., as in the Sears example). In and of themselves, goals can communicate priorities. However, unless goals are linked to some form of accounting, they are usually less effective. Many firms have instituted management by objectives systems (MBOs) or other goal-setting and review systems to try to link accountability and compensation to specific, measurable outcomes. These programs, while varying in effectiveness, often enhance accountability because they link performance to outcomes and require (through an incentive or monitoring system) an accounting for whether the goals were achieved and why. This type of a system certainly doesn't guarantee an effective accountability system, but it does provide a context where accountability strongly influences behavior.

Performance Appraisal and Other Monitoring Systems

Similar to the effects of incentives on behavior, monitoring to increase accountability can influence behavior. Monitoring systems also provide information to employees about what is valued by the organization. Of interest, of course, is that they equally provide information on behaviors that are not monitored. Monitoring systems can also make behavior more visible so that it can be evaluated. As stated earlier, visibility increases the pressure to justify and increases the influence on behavior. A useful point to note is that increasing visibility can be uncomfortable, distasteful, or objection-

able to employees. Research indicates that people dislike intense scrutiny or close monitoring and react negatively to it, creating a dysfunctional accountability mechanism. As a result, we should note that monitoring can have negative implications for performance.

There are several issues relating to accountability that must be considered in any discussion of a performance appraisal system. A comprehensive performance appraisal system can form a psychological contract between the employee and the organization that becomes part of the basis for the employees' perceptions about organizational justice or fairness (Cummings & Anton, 1990). As the stakes of the performance appraisal system increase, the supervisor, as well as the organization itself, has the onus for fair evaluations based on appropriate and useful performance criteria, and for ensuring the linkage between the evaluation and any resulting outcomes is maintained. One potential way of improving performance evaluations is to use multiple sources of information, such as supervisors, peers, self, subordinates, and clients or customers. This approach will add to the accuracy of the evaluations in most cases. Of course, it also makes ratees accountable for their performance to more individuals.

Another potential way to enhance the usefulness of accountability systems is to evaluate outcomes as well as behaviors. There are advantages to both. Evaluation of behavior helps address the criterion problem (i.e., the spectrum of performance measurement challenges associated with determining exactly what to measure and how to measure it), yet is not always satisfactory in linking behaviors to results. Compared to behavior-oriented evaluations, results-oriented evaluation tends to be less detailed and often a less valid as a means of assessing an individual's contributions. Of course, to improve the effectiveness of performance appraisal systems, it might be appropriate to hold the evaluators (i.e., who are the agents of accountability) accountable as well. Mero and Motowidlo (1994) found that accountability has the potential of improving the accuracy of performance appraisal systems.

A closer look at the potentially ambiguous and political nature of performance evaluations (Ferris & Judge, 1991) further underscores the importance of accountability in the process. Two potentially biasing conditions in the performance evaluation process are subjectivity and affectivity. Subjectivity permits individual rater discretion, often based on unpredictable factors, and affectivity may unfairly color performance evaluation decisions. Accountability mechanisms may be able to mitigate the biasing effects of these conditions by clarifying standards and evaluating the rater according to those standards. Two of the means for holding raters accountable are (1) to include the rating process in the supervisor's own performance evaluation, and (2) to provide a feedback system to the employee. Klimoski and Inks (1990) conducted an interesting study that illustrates how accountability might influence performance evaluations, sometimes in unintended ways. They found raters modifying their ratings in the direction of the ratees' expected ratings. They suggested, however, that ratings might be distorted when face-to-face feedback to the employee is expected. They further proposed that ratings might be distorted in two different ways: by amount of distortion, and by direction of distortion. It seems possible that, if distortions are predicable and in the same direction, the ratings could be relatively more accurate because fewer, instead of several, irrelevant factors area at play. Of course, distortions that are random, not monitored, or misunderstood could hardly be useful or appropriate. Two implications from this particular point are that we need to know much more about these issues, and that the type of accountability mechanisms employed need to be carefully selected and implemented to match the purpose and method of the evaluation system. For example, Martell and Borg (1993) found ratings to be less variable when a panel of evaluators rated the individuals. The question then remains regarding the accuracy and validity of the restricted-range evaluations, and whether these evaluations were more or less useful to the particular organizational context.

As with incentives, performance appraisal aspects of accountability systems have potential negative effects. Research suggests that monitoring may lead to negative feelings by the individual (Frink & Klimoski, 1998), erode flexibility (Weick, 1987), and encourage commitment to a failed course of action (Staw & Ross, 1987). This may happen when the evaluation system over-specifies individual behavior. For example, if the performance evaluation system specifies exactly what should be done, when it should be done, and how it should be done, one could view that as a strong accountability system because it provided specific information about what an individual is accountable for, and is part of a mechanism that forces the "accounting." However, it is easy to see how a system such as this could be viewed as demotivational. A highly structured system such as this one would diminish individual autonomy and flexibility, which would in turn negatively influence employees' attitudes and could diminish how effectively they perform their job. It also presumes that the HR manager or supervisor who developed the evaluation system knows the "best way" to accomplish the task. This certainly erodes individual flexibility and would inhibit a person from looking for more efficient and effective ways of accomplishing a task. In addition, it is evident that people who work in highly structured and controlled environments are the most susceptible to negative stress effects, such as burnout and physical problems.

Finally, a well-developed performance monitoring system makes an individual's behavior more public, and this may have some unintended negative consequences. Research into escalating commitment has found that individuals who pursue a course of action that is visible to others often feel the need to pursue that course of action to "save face." This leads to what is called escalation of commitment. In this case, because accountability systems often make individual behavior more public, this can lead to another area where dysfunctional behaviors occur.

In summary, people can be characterized as information seekers, and often the information they seek concerns their performance in relation to some standard. Incorporation of feedback mechanisms such as a performance appraisal system is an essential aspect of human resources development, and can be highly motivating. Feedback systems are one type of accountability mechanism that is useful to consider in the implementation of accountability systems.

Organization Culture

A discussion of accountability systems would be incomplete without a discussion of other ways organizations influence accountability. The culture of an organization is a fundamentally important influence on an individual's relationship with the organization. Culture can be described as the values, rites, rituals, and heroes associated with an organization (Deal & Kennedy, 1982). These four components of culture may partially define the context in which individuals, who face the pressure of accountability, search for cues as to how to react to an accountability system.

One way in which culture can influence accountability is by cultural aversions to different decision characteristics such as the acceptance of risk. For example, Deal and Kennedy (1982) developed a typology of culture that considered, among other factors, the type of risks that are typically as-

sumed in organization. According to the authors, "macho" and "bet your company" cultures are ones where corporate decisions are regularly very risky and market feedback is the key criteria for decision making. Within these contexts you would expect that under conditions of accountability, individuals would make decisions consistent with the views suggested by the prevailing culture; that is, decisions that reflect the willingness to accept higher risk. In fact, in one study, participants made riskier bets when they assumed their evaluator was not risk averse (Weigold & Schlenker, 1991).

Culture can influence responses to accountability in the way it provides feedback about one's identity. Within organizational settings, a person's organizational identity is preserved by their conformance with the rules and norms that they are taught are appropriate. Research has found that rather than relying on their personal expectations that their behavior would be followed by a certain outcome, individuals often use others as a source of information about appropriate behavior (Miller & Grush, 1988). This suggests that people are not only rational (as is suggested by incentives and monitoring influences on accountability), but also social, and consider what important others think they should do as guides for developing attitudes and displaying behavior. The implication is that cultural norms provide not only important cues about appropriate behavior, but also influence expectations about accounting for that behavior. These cues take on increasing importance when incentive alignment and monitoring systems provide vague criterion for performance.

Incentives and compensation systems, performance monitoring/appraisal systems, and cultural aspects all are important components of accountability systems. Each of these systems provides important cues about what an individual is accountable for, and the standards by which they will be judged. In combination, these systems also increase the importance of accountability in an organization.

THE ROLE OF THE AUDIENCE IN ACCOUNTABILITY SYSTEMS

One other important question exists for our discussion of accountability systems, and that is to consider the question of "To whom am I accountable?" In other words, what is the role of the audience in terms of an accountability system? The importance of the audience of the accounting cannot be overstated. Tetlock (1992) suggested and found support for the premise that, when an individual is made accountable for an outcome, knowledge of the views or preferences of the audience influences how the individual will respond. The audience then plays a powerful role in the accountability relationship because they represent the social influence that provides the cues that influence accountability response.

Let's briefly discuss how that influence may occur in a context where a product manager is made accountable for an important decision, for example, choosing whether to pursue new product line A, B, or C. An important premise of accountability systems is that they place pressure on the individual to develop a strategy that will put them in an optimum position to defend (account for) their decision. One important variable in the strategy chosen is whether the product manager is aware of the opinions or attitudes of those to whom the decision is to be justified. Let's say that in discussions, the product manager becomes aware that his boss, the vice president of marketing, prefers product B. Tetlock (1985) argued, and there is significant support for the argument, that the decision maker will make the choice that he or she believes will be more acceptable to the audience. In other words, it is the choice that would be easiest to justify. In this case, the suggestion is that accountability mechanisms can lead individuals to make decisions based on the criterion of what is easiest to justify rather than what is the optimum decision. Many would argue that it is probably an expedient political tactic to agree with your boss. Unfortunately, it may be a factor that leads to ineffective decisions and dysfunctional behavior in response to an accountability system.

Accountability to an audience with unknown views will also affect the decision processes of individuals, but in a different way. In this case, the product manager may not have any knowledge of preferences held by the person to whom he or she is accountable. In this case, the objective would be to make a decision that is rational and justifiable. The product manager would then use a strategy that is more carefully considered and is justified by the best available information or data. This would allow him or her to appear highly rational in response to the justification requirement.

There are other aspects of the audience that may influence an individual's response to accountability, and three seem particularly relevant: (1) the number of constituencies that form the audience, (2) the influence of the audience, and (3) the authority of the audience

Number of Constituencies

As discussed earlier, in organizational contexts the audience to whom a person may feel accountable may be quite diverse. These audiences could include employees, important customers, political elements within the community, key regulatory agencies, and so forth. The net effect is that a common organizational condition may be one of accountability to numerous and not necessarily similar audiences. This condition of *diffused accountability* will probably minimize the effect an audience would have on the accountability system. In this case, any required justification can be readily explained in terms of the audience's desires that most closely align with the individual decision maker.

Influence and Authority of the Audience

Another consideration about the audience is that all audiences to whom you may have to account for your behavior are not the same. For instance, an important customer may exert significant influence over an agent because of the need to maintain a strong relationship (i.e., access to required resources). Again, the political nature of the individual directly supports the linkage between the influence of a key constituent and the response to accountability. Organizational authority should also be related to how an individual reacts to accountability. This authority manifests itself in control of performance evaluation mechanisms, reward and punishment power, and control over other key personnel decisions (e.g., promotion and termination). Anxiety about having to account for a decision should be heightened when the stakes are high for the employees (i.e., their personal risk increases). This situation is amplified when the employee must account to someone with authority. In addition, accountability mechanism will be more powerful when evaluator authority and influence is higher.

The role of the audience is a central issue in discussions of accountability systems. In most organizational decisions, there are multiple constituencies to which the individuals feel accountable. Because of the factors previously discussed, some audiences can overshadow other more important audiences. The important issue is that HR managers must not only consider "what" employees are accountable for but also "to whom" they are accountable.

DESIGN ISSUES FOR ACCOUNTABILITY SYSTEMS

In this section, we examine broader issues of design relative to implementing an effective accountability system. There are numerous considerations for implementing effective accountability systems. First, the effectiveness of accountability systems may be a function of the structure of certain organizations or particular jobs within an organization. Second, implementing accountability systems, as with implementing any significant organizational intervention, requires a basic understanding of issues related to organizational change. One of the most fundamentally important change issues HR managers face is the tendency for employees to resist any type of change. Often, people have become comfortable with the status quo and they resist experiencing anxiety about the personal implications a change like implementing an accountability system might have. In this section, we discuss both the structural issues related to implementing accountability systems as well as dealing with employee resistance to change.

Workplace Structure

In designing accountability systems, the structure of the organization and the type of work engaged in are all-important considerations. For example, firms are increasingly implementing team-based and "empowerment" initiatives that have a significant effect on the organization's structure. If the focus is on severing the tight individual-level controls in favor of group-level controls, how should accountability mechanisms (e.g., performance evaluations, reporting structures, discipline systems, quality control, goal-setting and management systems, and so forth) be adjusted to maintain accountability at the individual level while pursuing teamwork or autonomy?

Performance-based evaluations permit integration of team outputs with individual evaluations, and also allow evaluation of one's autonomous contributions without violating that autonomy via close behavioral monitoring or control. Another method that may be useful for accountability in these environments is the use of multiple levels of goal setting. If the firm uses an MBO or other goal-setting system, goals can be established for multiple levels of the organization, thereby providing a means of accountability for actions and decisions that not only make the individual look good, but have organizational benefits as well. As discussed earlier, goal-setting systems provide a unique type of accountability system in that the objectives can be explicitly tailored to provide for the development of the individual, as well as the organization. The systems can also provide a follow-up, or accountability, mechanism to measure performance against the standards set by the goals. Use of this measurement against standards also provides a way to tightly link compensation or incentives to performance.

The concept of accountability juxtaposes two very different issues when viewed as a part of the organization's structure. On the one hand, limited monitoring and accountability systems lend themselves to an environment characterized by trust, flexibility, and autonomy, or a rather loosely coupled organizational environment. On the other hand, there is another environment characterized by monitoring, verification, and control, or a tightly coupled organization. Because it is unlikely that either extreme is optimal, useful accountability systems should seek a balance point between these two paradigms of organizational environments. As President Ronald Reagan stated concerning the relationship between the United States and the former Soviet Union, "Trust, but verify." The balance point, or area, will not necessarily be similar across situations, but elements from both perspectives are useful.

A second structural consideration in the implementation of accountability systems deals with the reality that organizations are extremely complex, with oft-competing objectives. In light of that, all aspects of both organizational and normative reward systems should be analyzed to ensure commonality of purpose, and reinforcement of

appropriate means-end relationships. Organizational goals can be different from the individual goals, and a successful accountability system may rest on recognizing and addressing those differences.

Resistance to Accountability Systems

As mentioned earlier, people have a tendency to resist encroachment on the areas over which they have discretion. It may also be argued that people in general attempt to enlarge the sphere over which they have discretion or autonomy. Feelings that we may be held accountable for actions or decisions reduce the discretion we may feel is available. At the very least, accountability constrains the viable options we have. There also is a likelihood that people tend to attempt to reduce uncertainty in their surroundings, or environment, and one means to do this is to secure entitlements or claim rights. These situations characterize those in which accountability mechanisms may be resisted the most. Specifically, situations involving entitlements, autonomy, or ambiguity are likely to be those where accountability is resisted.

In order to impose accountability in those situations, special attention is needed to ascertain appropriate means-ends relationships to include a serious consideration of how we measure and standardize these. Some examples of these types of environments include educational institutions, research and development departments, and entitlement positions. These instances are characterized by either an unclear relationship between efforts and outcomes, or weak linkages between outputs and rewards or sanctions. This issue has become a major concern of educators in response to President Bush's plan to increase the accountability in our school systems. A major challenge of such a system is to develop clear but fair criteria for determining what constitutes effective performance for a school system. Is it scores on standardized tests? If so, what tests and how valid are these tests? Is it graduation rates? If so, couldn't educators improve graduation rates by simply reducing the standards required for a student to graduate? Surely that is not the objective of President Bush's plan. Until criterion are more clearly articulated, there is likely to be significant resistance from many educators. From the perspective of overcoming resistance to change, accountability mechanisms can serve to reduce ambiguity if standards are clear and consistently applied. In such instances, the relationships between what one does and the outcomes from those efforts are clarified, and evaluation criteria are explicit and well understood, thus eliminating uncertainty and resistance.

That there are alternative potential outcomes indicates that accountability systems are necessarily complex, and must be considered as such. Employee resistance may be a sign that the accountability system needs to be clarified.

ORGANIZATION-LEVEL ISSUES OF ACCOUNTABILITY

The previous sections have considered accountability on the level of an individual acting within an organization's accountability system. However, in addition to considering that accountability has significant influence on behavior within the organization, no discussion of accountability would be complete without some consideration of the effects of accountability at the organization and group level, and in relation to an organization's external environment. This considers issues such as the design of a CEO's compensation package as a means of making him or her more accountable to external shareholders or others with a stake in the organization's performance. We also consider the relationship between accountability and organizations in terms of a long-term or short-term focus.

As discussed earlier, U.S. businesses are under continual calls to be accountable from various quarters. These calls are in response to perceptions about the status of business and its dealings with the environment in which it operates. Examples of some of the major areas that are of concern include CEO compensation, business policy (short-term vs. long-term focus), employee management, and environmental issues. In the Bridgestone/Firestone example provided at the beginning of this article, it is clear that the CEO was held accountable for the overall safety of the company's product and, as a result, felt pressure to resign. For organizational leaders, the accountability to external constituents can be a significant factor.

CEO Compensation

CEO salaries are spiraling, currently at an average of about 70 times the income of the average worker for CEOs of major corporations. Executives in the United States are the highest paid globally, even though some U.S. firms are losing ground in terms of profits and market share. The real concern is not the dollar value of these salaries, but the unchecked power sought and wielded by these CEOs. The system fosters a situation in which executives rigidly resist efforts to curb their discretion in establishing their own compensation packages, as this represents not only an encroachment on their personal finances, but also an encroachment on the prerogative they enjoy in their position. After all, CEOs have typically worked very hard for many years to "earn" that prerogative. This condition has its roots in the independent and individualistic nature of American culture, but is permitted, and perhaps even exacerbated, by the absence of accountability at the top.

This area of accountability in human resources management has received more press than any other (Crystal, 1991; Gomez-Mejia & Balkin, 1992). These authors suggest that the CEO compensation system is a paramount example of what can happen when there are no constraints other than token self-justification to a board or committee, which has a vested interest in justifying the salary structure rather than monitoring it as the members are likely CEOs themselves. A common method for establishing CEO salaries is for the CEO to hire a salary consultant who makes a market-based recommendation to the CEO, who includes the recommendation in a report to the board of directors. The common rationale for the level of salary is that, in order to be competitive, the firm must have the very best leadership, and if the recommended (and inflated) salary is not paid, the CEO will leave for a better offer. Note that this rationale is very clearly separated from any performance or other measurable criteria. If the firm is doing poorly, they need a "savior" and must pay a premium for that "savior." If the firm is doing well, they need to pay a premium in order to (1) reward the leader, (2) maintain the high image appropriate for success, and (3) ensure continued success. Monks and Minow (1991) recommend stockholder groups becoming active in the calling of both the CEOs and the corporate system to account for what some perceive to be excessive and detrimental compensation practices.

Short-Term Versus Long-Term Focus

A second issue when dealing with accountability at the organizational level is the tendency to adopt a short-term perspective regarding both the development of human resources as well as the overall indicators of corporate success, such as profits. The Competitiveness Policy Council chastised U.S. business in general for their short-term emphasis, stating, "The first, and perhaps most fundamental, problem is America's proclivity to think and act with a short-term horizon." While most any party would agree that a short-term perspective is myopic and ultimately damaging to an organization's future well being, nevertheless the short-term per-

spective dominates U.S. business decisions and systems.

One reason suggested for this condition, as well as a prescription for addressing it, is related to the mechanisms of accountability under which the decision makers operate. Management is historically evaluated by quarterly performance by the requirements and publications of federal agencies, such as the Securities and Exchange Commission, and media, such as financial publications. In order to receive evaluations that please investors, management is enticed to act in terms of short-term interests. These short-term pressures, as well as an individual's own tendency to consider immediate results, tend to produce similar short-term approaches to dealing with human resources policy.

Employee Management

Internal to the organization but outside of traditional accountability systems is an organization's overall relationship with its employees. Historically, the paradigm that operated was the old master-servant relationship, where the employer owned the employee for the amount of time for which that employee was paid. While feelings of belonging to an organization are potentially useful to both sides, viewing employees as a commodity that can be purchased and discarded without consideration of the implications of the differences between human resources and other resources is dysfunctional in general.

One of the fundamental objectives of the union movement is to be able to impose an accountability system regarding the organization's human resources. Additionally, Title VII of the Civil Rights Act, the Age Discrimination in Employment Act, and the Americans with Disabilities Act serve as examples of efforts by the government to impose accountability for employment practices in response to failures to self-monitor. Because businesses did not accept the viability of the society and community as agencies to which they were accountable, mechanisms were imposed via regulatory agencies to impact organizational policy regarding human resources.

Environmental Issues

Over the past two decades, firms have been cited for environmental abuses, and the issue continues. Environmental activists claim that timber cutters, for example, are devastating timber resources in the Northwest beyond repair, indicating that the loggers are unaccountable to any viable entity with environmental interests. The timber producers, on the other hand, claim that they are leaving plantings of more trees than they are harvesting, and the forests that replace those harvested are more productive and healthier. Some would argue that timber producers would be less sensitive to any need for environmental protection if there not for environmental groups calling for their increased accountability.

Even where organizations can be held accountable by means of the legal or regulatory systems, the legendary sluggishness of bureaucratic systems has the effect of leaving organizations largely unaccountable, especially in the short term, for much of what may be questionable practices. For example, a chemical firm in Northwest Florida has been repeatedly accused by local residents of polluting a stream used for discharge of wastewater, a charge that they consistently deny. Local agencies were unable to find conclusive evidence that the plant was the sole culprit, and the plant found itself essentially unaccountable for wastewater discharge.

FAILED ACCOUNTABILITY SYSTEMS: THE CASE OF THE HUBBLE SPACE TELESCOPE

The United States spent $1.5 billion on the Hubble Space Telescope in eager anticipation of unlocking more secrets of the uni-

verse. The disappointment was global when it was discovered that the telescope could not work to standard because the eight-foot main mirror was made wrong, and it could not focus as well as hoped. How could this $350 million part, the heart of the telescope, be wrong? How was it possible for an error of that type to slip through the host of engineers and craftsmen building the mirror, as well as the project administrators at NASA? This situation can be cast in terms of failed accountability mechanisms. The following discussion is based on the article by Capers and Lipton (1993), who offer insights as to how the mirror project failed to meet standards.

First, the contractor, under intense competitive pressure, and in response to information from NASA, "low-balled" the price, expecting additional funds to be available later. This put intense financial strain on the entire project and, as a result, individuals in different parts of the organization had divided accountabilities. One loyalty was to the mirror quality, and another was to the "bottom line." There were also intense time pressures for completion, which exacerbated the division of loyalties as to what individuals were accountable for. The information from NASA indicated that additional funding would be available for unforeseen technological difficulties, but the agency later backed away from this commitment, and no agency personnel were accountable for this situation.

The time and money pressures mounted as the project continued, as did management's concerns with financial issues. The result was normal scientific rigor was deemphasized in favor of saving cost—another accountability failure. Accountability for the quality of the product was replaced with accountability for the schedule, and quality measures were overlooked.

In the midst of this confusion, people were contending with a shift in management style at the contracting firm as they had shifted to a matrix-structure. In a matrix structure, workers have two or more bosses, their department supervisor and their project supervisor; this type of dual accountability can have offsetting effects and lead to confusion and perhaps the diffused accountability discussed earlier.

NASA had accountability problems as well. On the heels of the Challenger disaster, where safety was a dominant issue, they were desperate to reestablish their credibility and viability. In so doing, it seems the emphasis shifted from substance to form, and the quality issues with the mirror were stuck in the middle. The quality engineer sent by NASA to oversee the project was explicitly told to ignore mirror quality and focus on safety issues, because another group was to oversee the quality issues. Not only did no one oversee quality, there were only three NASA engineers on site at the plant, as opposed to the 20 that were involved with the building of the Saturn V booster rockets some years earlier. It is notable that of the thousands of parts in the telescope, the mirror is the only one that has no NASA official's signature for quality.

Compounding the problem, the NASA headquarters at the Marshall Space Flight Center was headed by an individual who had a notorious dislike for bad news, and so was given little. This same problem was criticized in the Challenger investigation. This highlights the fact that accountability can be normative, occurring in the context of social or informal systems, as well as structural, occurring in the context of the organization's formal systems. Stein and Kanter's (1993) analysis of the situation is summed up by stating that "the culprit becomes a system under such pressure to perform that mistakes are encouraged, constructive actions undercut, and information withheld" (p. 59).

Thus it seems that a noble scientific endeavor with high aspirations went awry because of problems with accountability. In some cases accountability was ignored, in some cases overlooked, in some cases too narrow, in some cases confounded, and in some cases it was normatively driven rather than purpose driven. There were two organizations involved, and questions about who bore responsibility for the mirror problems—the contractor or NASA. For the contractor, there were five key issues. First, financial pressures focused accountability on costs. In so doing, quality checks and production monitoring suffered. Second, time pressures focused accountability on progress toward a tight deadline, which impinged on accountability for quality. A third issue the contractor faced concerned the nature of their relationship with NASA. The contractor's agents believed that NASA promised additional funding for cost increases. Unfortunately, they did not "get it in writing," and NASA could not be held accountable for failing to fulfill these expectations.

The fourth issue the contractor faced was a change to a matrix organizational structure. Matrix organizations are highly susceptible to accountability breakdowns for two primary reasons, both of which are rooted in the dual chain of command. One is that having two "bosses" inherently dilutes accountability because employees must balance their responsiveness between the two, because there may be inconsistencies between the expectations communicated by the two supervisors, and because employees can play one against the other with statements like "But so-and-so told me to stick with this instead." The other reason is that blurring the lines of authority and dividing supervisory responsibilities allows potential for things to fall through the cracks (as happened in this story). Thus, the two reasons rest on whether the domains of supervisor responsibility overlap or fail to adequately complement one another. Finally, the fifth issue for the contractor was that the cumulative effect of these conditions was to sacrifice scientific rigor and quality assurance.

That is to say that the various diversions and undermining of accountability resulted in an accountability collapse on perhaps the key factor in building the mirror.

From NASA's perspective, there were three key issues concerning accountability. First, given NASA's public image problems during those years, an underlying emphasis on legitimacy shifted the focus of accountabilities to the program's image rather than substance and rigor. Simply put, people generally quit asking about quality and technical factors and instead asked image-related questions. Remember the military adage about what's inspected over what's expected. A second issue for NASA concerned the division of responsibilities. Their understaffed engineering group was charged with production schedule oversight. But with no one being assigned responsibility for quality, there simply was no accountability for it.

The third issue for NASA was the social norm that emerged in response to a leader's strong personality. The tradeoffs between delivering bad news to an executive with a strong distaste for it versus keeping quiet with a very low and distant probability of serious implications for silence predictably resulted in ignoring serious concerns. Again, the perceptions and the norms surrounding our accountabilities may be the most important factor in the effects that accountability has. In this case, control mechanisms were never engaged because nobody pushed the issue, again, predictably so.

A follow-up analysis of the whole debacle turned up the source of the error, and it is almost amusing in its simplicity except for the devastating career and personal costs that some individuals paid. As it turns out, when the equipment for grinding the mirror was being assembled, one piece appeared to not align properly. Someone simply added about fifteen cents worth of cheap steel washers to fill a gap, which in turn set the grinding mechanism a slight fraction of an inch too low. The measuring devices were not calibrated to detect that margin, and the mirror was perfectly shaped—to the wrong specifications.

CONCLUSION

In this article, we have provided an overview of the concept of accountability, described how it might work, and highlighted the role of HR systems in influencing organizational accountability. The case of the Hubble Space Telescope illustrates the systemic nature of accountability in influencing individual and group behavior. Our hope is that you understand the critical nature of accountability in organizations and understand how the complexity of accountability systems can lead to both functional and dysfunctional organizational behaviors. It is the latter effect, the unintended negative consequences of accountability, that is a significant challenge for any manager dealing with an organization's human resources management system. ■

REFERENCES

Capers, R. A., & Lipton, E. (1993). Hubble error: Time, money, and millionths of an inch. *Academy of Management Executive, 7,* 41–57.

Crystal, G. S. (1991). *In search of excess: The overcompensation of American executives.* New York: W. W. Norton.

Cummings, L. L., & Anton, R. J. (1990). The logical and appreciative dimensions of accountability. In S. Sivastva, D. Cooperrider and Associates

(Eds.), *Appreciative Management and Leadership* (257–286). San Francisco: Jossey-Bass.

Deal, T. E., & Kennedy, A. A. (1982). *Corporate cultures: The rites and rituals of corporate life.* Reading, MA: Addison-Wesley.

Ferris, G. R., & Judge, T. A. (1991). Personnel/human resources management: A political influence perspective. *Journal of Management, 17,* 447–488.

Frink, D., & Klimoski, R. (1998). Toward a theory of accountability in organizations and human resources management. In G. R. Ferris (Ed.), *Research in Personnel and Human Resources Management* (Vol. 16, 1–51). Greenwich, CT: JAI Press.

Gomez-Mejia, L. R., & Balkin, D. B. (1992). *Compensation, organizational strategy, and firm performance.* Cincinnati, OH: South-Western Publishing Co.

Kearns, K. P. (1998). Institutional accountability in higher education: A strategic approach. *Public Policy & Management Review, 22* (2), 140–156.

Kelly, K., & Schine, E. (1992, June 29). How did Sears blow this gasket? *Business Week,* 8.

Kerr, S. (1995). On the folly of rewarding A, while hoping for B. *Academy of Management Executive, 9,* 7–15.

Klimoski, R., & Inks, L. (1990). Accountability forces in performance appraisal. *Organizational Behavior and Human Decision Processes, 45,* 194–208.

Lerner, J. S., & Tetlock, P. E. (1999). Accounting for the effects of accountability. *Psychological Bulletin, 125,* 255–275.

Martell, R. F., & Borg, M. R. (1993). A comparison of the behavioral rating accuracy of groups and individuals. *Journal of Applied Psychology, 78,* 43–50.

Mero, N. P., & Motowidlo, S. J. (1994). Effects of rater accountability on the accuracy and the favorability of performance ratings. *Journal of Applied Psychology, 80,* 517–524.

Miller, L., & Grush, J. (1988). Improving predictions in expectancy theory research: Effects of personality, expectancies, and norms. *Academy of Management Journal, 31,* 107–122.

Mitchell, T. R. (1993). Leadership, values, and accountability. In M. M. Chemers and R. Ayman (Eds.), *Leadership Theory and Research: Perspectives and Directions* (109–136). San Diego, CA: Academic Press.

Monks, R. A. G., & Minow, N. (1991). *Power and accountability.* New York: HarperCollins.

Staw, B. M., & Ross, J. (1987, March–April). Knowing when to pull the plug. *Harvard Business Review,* 68–74.

Stein, B. A., & Kanter, R. M. (1993). Why good people do bad things: A retrospective on the Hubble fiasco. *Academy of Management Executive, 7,* 58–62.

Tetlock, P. E. (1985). Accountability: The neglected social context of judgement and choice. In B. M. Staw and L.L. Cummings (Eds.), *Research in Organizational Behavior* (Vol. 7, 297–332). Greenwich, CT: JAI Press.

Tetlock, P. E. (1992) The impact of accountability and judgment and choice: Toward a social contingency model. In M. P. Zanna (Ed.), *Advances in Experimental Social Psychology* (Vol. 25, 331–377). New York: Academic Press.

Weick, K. E. (1987). Perspectives on action in organizations. In J. W. Lorsch (Ed.), *Handbook of Organization Behavior* (10–28). Upper Saddle River, NJ: Prentice Hall.

Weigold, M. F., & Schlenker, B. R. (1991). Accountability and risk taking. *Personality and Social Psychology Bulletin, 17,* 25–29.

11
ORGANIZATION CULTURE AND CHANGE

There are many surveys that tout "The 100 best companies to work for" or "The best companies in the country." These are basically assessments of the culture of an organization. Again and again we are told that culture is an important variable in an organization. Cultures are believed to help individuals cope with the uncertainty and ambiguity that naturally occurs in organizations. The article by Bowen is an attempt to shed some light on the ways in which human resources professionals can best participate in building, maintaining, and changing the culture of an organization. His article serves as a primer for a human resources person—basically, and everything you wanted to know about culture. The remaining two articles in this chapter are concerned with the notion of spirituality in the workplace. Spirituality at work encompasses more than just religion. The idea is that since work encompasses so much of a person's life, organization practices can contribute much to personal growth. The article by Burack expresses his agenda for a return to a more humanistic approach to work. Work must be changed so that it means something to individuals—people matter; integrity is sought by people; trust, faith, and justice should be established as a foundation for work. Organizations should jointly meet individual and organization needs.

READINGS

ORGANIZATIONAL CULTURE, CHANGE, AND HUMAN RESOURCES

Michael G. Bowen

"You don't need a weatherman to know which way the wind blows."
— BOB DYLAN

A recent *Fortune* magazine cover story entitled "The 100 Best Companies to Work For" (Levering & Moskowitz, 2001, p. 148) states that the current business environment can be characterized as a "pitched battle for talent. There are just more jobs than people, especially in firms . . . that need highly skilled people." The article also poses the question "How do the best companies maintain their leading edge in such a competitive environment?" *Fortune*'s answer lies in one word: culture. Quoting Patricia Brown of First Tennessee Bank, "Nice perks may help somewhat in recruiting, but to keep people here we've got to demonstrate that we offer a culture where they are respected and treated as adults, one that shows people that we really do care about them" (Levering & Moskowitz, 2001, p. 150).

As the *Fortune* article so clearly illustrates, the concept of culture has become an increasingly important factor in the management of today's organizations. This is particularly so now, as each day (as of this writing, April 2001) more businesses announce layoffs and cutbacks—perhaps signals of a tightening in the nation's labor markets—and many already stressed-out work environments are producing growing numbers of burnout and motivation problems (Maslach, 1999; Moore, 2001; Saad, 1999).

The purpose of this article is to offer a dynamic perspective on organizational culture, and then, by way of a few short case examples and a newly offered change management paradigm, shed some light on ways today's human resources (HR) professional can best participate in building, maintaining, or changing an organization's culture.

ORGANIZATIONAL CULTURE

There are at least as many slants on the definition of the term "organizational culture" as there are writers on the subject. Virtually all published definitions, however, suggest that culture is a complex set and pattern of assumptions, beliefs, formal and informal operating rules and policies, norms, values, and behavioral artifacts (e.g., language, jargon, stories, symbols, myths, ceremonies, and rituals) that develop within an organization (see: Deal & Kennedy, 1982; Goffee & Jones, 1998; Morgan, 1997; Hofstede, 1997; Smircich, 1983). An organization's culture is its heart and soul. It is its shared understanding of how things are, how things get done, why things get done, and what the ground rules are. Its shared meanings and symbols facilitate everyone's interpretations and understandings of how to act within an organization. It can be, as *Fortune* magazine suggests, the reason that employees are attracted to work at a business, and it is what new hires work so hard to learn about and understand when they first arrive at their new job. It is also itself a subculture, being part of, and deriving many of its key values from, the larger societal culture (Pauchant & Mitroff, 1992). Furthermore, there is a tendency for organizational cultures to have their own subcultures (Goffee & Jones, 1998). Often, these subcultures are specific to departments or work units and can be a cause of synergies or problems when the various subunits of an organization attempt to work together.

BACKGROUND

The idea that a business (or other) organization's culture might be an important factor in its effectiveness has been around since the early 1930s. Despite significant work in the 1930s, 1940s, and 1950s on norms, values, and culture by management writers such as Chester Barnard (1938), Phillip Selznick (1948), and Elliot Jaques (1952), the concept of culture was generally viewed as too "soft," and as such an impractical theoretical and academic pursuit rather than an important and necessary factor in managing an organization (Cavaleri & Obloj, 1993).

Culture began to enter the mainstream of managerial thought, however, in the early 1980s. This was for two main reasons. First, there was then a strong interest in understanding the relatively sudden and phenomenal economic success of Japanese firms worldwide, as Japan had become a true economic superpower by the late 1970s. Although there were many explanations proposed for this success, probably the most visible and accepted explanation for the rising market power of the Japanese firms came from then Stanford University professor William Ouchi. A student of Japanese versus American business practice, Ouchi's *Theory Z* (Ouchi, 1981) suggested that the reason was in the Japanese cultural tendency to involve organization members in decision making about matters that affected

them. Such participation and employee involvement were keys to the Japanese practice of developing a shared set of values throughout a firm. According to Ouchi, the shared values in Japanese businesses served as a guide for employee understanding of how things work in the organization, and as a template for behavior and decision making (see also Pascale & Athos, 1981).

A second, and related, reason for the interest in corporate culture during the early 1980s was the concurrent poor performance of U.S. firms relative to the influx of Japanese competition after the Arab oil embargo against the United States in 1974. This "problem" prompted many managers and management experts to take a serious look at how Japanese firms were able to compete so well in the U.S. against American businesses. Whereas Japanese firms had in the 1950s and 1960s been subject to some derision in the U.S. for poor product quality (the term *Made in Japan* was commonly used pejoratively), many of those same firms were now being hailed as business exemplars. What investigators found was that the Japanese firms had followed the ideas of American business consultants W. Edwards Deming and Joseph Juran on quality management in transforming their operations. By doing so, Japanese companies demonstrated that a fundamental change in management philosophy might be necessary for American businesses to be able to compete in a more global economy. Consequently, so-called "soft" business practices that had been underemphasized or dismissed as trivial in the United States, such as a primary emphasis on understanding and serving the customer, worker participation and empowerment, work "families," shared values, and culture, were now being described as the prescription for excellent performance (see Imai, 1986).

The result of this call for a change in managerial mindset in the United States created feelings of great concern in the American business community. This was true particularly in some who believed that U.S. businesses had been left behind by "better managed" foreign companies, which were unencumbered by the bureaucratic constraints on decision making and action so common in U.S. firms. At the same time, however, there was also a growing reactive sense in the United States that the Japanese success stories were due to (1) unfair trade practices (e.g., high tariffs on U.S. imports into Japan versus no tariffs on Japanese imports into the United States); (2) the fact that the Japanese transformation was, after all, directed in large part by U.S. consultants—even though few firms in the United States had, at that time, listened to those consultants' advice; and (3) that the roots and essences of successful management practices could be found in U.S. firms as well. Indeed, Deal and Kennedy's (1982) book, which coined the term "corporate culture," together with the perhaps even more influential *In Search of Excellence* (Peters & Waterman, 1982), offered welcome antidotes to criticisms of U.S. management in those days by demonstrating that Japan was not the only nation capable of producing companies that could compete in the worldwide business arena. Describing the U.S. companies that their research had identified as "excellent" performers, Peters and Waterman wrote: "The excellent companies seem to have developed cultures that have incorporated the values and practices of the great leaders and thus those shared values can be seen to survive for decades after the passing of the original guru. . . . it appears that the real role of the chief executive is to manage the values of the organization" (Peters & Waterman, 1982, p. 26).

These ideas, and the business practices they spawned, took the United States by storm in the 1980s and helped many U.S. businesses change the way they managed themselves. It was hoped that in doing so, U.S. firms would regain their competitive advantages and reassume their domination in the global marketplace.

As a result, the trial and acceptance of these "new" best business practices by U.S. businesses has led to an increasing emphasis on the "softer" side of managing; an emphasis that is still evolving today. The material offered in current discussions of new models of leadership (e.g., Block, 1993; DePree, 1992; Greenleaf, 1991; O'Neil, 1993; O'Toole, 1995; Spears, 1995, 1998), organizational change and change management (e.g., Belasco & Stayer, 1993; Kanter, 1985, 2001; Manz & Sims, 1993; Peters, 1987, 1992), systems' thinking and system dynamics (e.g., Richardson, 1991; Sterman, 2000; Wheatley, 1992), quality management and business process reengineering (e.g., Deming, 1986; Dobyns & Crawford-Mason, 1991; Juran, 1992; Hammer & Champy, 1993), self-discovery and improvement, emotional intelligence, and spirituality in management (Goleman, 1995; Peck, 1993; Whyte, 1994), and business ethics (e.g., Jackall, 1988; O'Toole, 1993; Walton, 1988; Williams & Houck, 1992) all have been evoked in this ongoing conversation.

WHERE CULTURE COMES FROM

If culture is manageable and experienced through the organization's shared and unshared values; spoken and unspoken assumptions; myths, histories, and rituals; and formal and informal policies and procedures; then it can be argued that organizational leadership plays the preeminent role in the creation, maintenance, and changing of that culture. In support of this claim, business history is filled with interesting and informative examples of how the leaders and founders of many well-known businesses left an indelible imprint on their organization's culture and performance. Such individuals as McDonalds' Ray Kroc, whose obsession with quality, service, cleanliness, and value still influences the actions of virtually every employee; Johnson & Johnson's General Robert Wood Johnson, whose "credo" has had a profound influence on corporate behavior throughout the company's history, including its highly regarded and well publicized handling of the "Tylenol" case; Ford Motor Company's Henry Ford, who is credited with first adapting assembly-line technologies to the production of automobiles, his philanthropy, and for his often heavy-handed paternalism; and Southwest Airlines' Herb Kelleher, who brought an ethic of unparalleled customer service and fun to his company; are just a very few examples of this.

Nevertheless, certainly not all cultures in all companies form under the direction of a strong founder or leader. Undoubtedly, most organizations' cultures develop on their own as a function of the development of the organization's system (Forrester, 1968; Sterman, 2000) without a strong focus or direction from leadership. For example, management experts such as W. Edwards Deming (1986) and Jay Forrester (1968) argue that approximately 85 to 90 percent of the behavior exhibited within an organization is produced by the system: the formal and informal reward structure, policies, and behavioral norms of that organization. If an organization muddles along over time without strong leadership, focus, direction, and a shared sense of values, so does its culture.

Goffee and Jones' (1998, pp. 34–37) discussion of the life cycle of corporate cultures is also informative on this point, as they argue that many, but not all, companies tend to go through a predictable pattern of cultural changes. For example, Goffee and Jones write that companies often start out as *communal*, given their small size and the fact that the owner(s)/founder(s) are around to instill their sense of high energy, vision, and commitment. Startup ventures often work as close-knit teams in a work environment characterized by a strong sense of mission, excitement, and adventure. Often the fight for survival develops a deep sense of community among organization members "which rarely stops when the business day is over" (Goffee & Jones, 1998, p. 35). But, as Goffee and Jones point out, no culture lasts forever. "Leaders change, as do products, competitors, or whole industries. In other words, the environment changes, and the cultural response with it" (Goffee & Jones, 1998, p. 35). Cultures at this stage can also change because the organization has grown too large (i.e., the communal spirit is difficult to maintain in groups larger than 50), managerial reporting relationships have increased, and organizational roles have begun to differentiate, meaning that the organization has probably begun to employ different types of people who may not share the same values, goals, or views about what is important to the business. What tends to emerge next, according to Goffee & Jones, is a *networked* culture, where "a lot of things happen because of relationships" (Goffee & Jones, 1998, p. 35). Whereas in the previous stage employees tended to see themselves as a single group (i.e., David) at war with some larger competitor(s) (i.e., Goliath) in the outside world, employees tend to form subgroups that socialize mainly within their subgroups in a networked culture. The organization-wide sense of shared goals has been lost.

According to Goffee and Jones (1998), at some point (i.e., after several years or perhaps decades) the networked culture can backfire. In such conditions, a *mercenary* stage can occur if complacency has set in—particularly should Goliath have been slain. Here "poor performance is too often tolerated, and consensus building too often gives way to compromise solutions. Usually, an unexpected and harsh competitive assault pushes networked companies into the *mercenary* mode. Simply to survive, the company is forced to fire lousy, fair, and even some 'pretty good' employees, whether they are well liked or not, and rivet its attention on business goals and performance standards" (Goffee & Jones, 1998, p. 35). Such managerial changes can bring about stability and a renewed interest in sociability among the organization's members that might even return to a healthy version of the networked culture or even a communal culture. On the other hand, the rearranged culture might so damage trust and loyalty that a negatively *fragmented* culture can form, where people barely speak to each other let alone carry on productive conversations such as ones dealing with how to better serve customers.

As stated earlier, Goffee and Jones' research shows that not all firms proceed through the life cycle described. "Some (businesses) start in *mercenary* or even *fragmented* cultures and stay there ad infinitum. . . . And for most, it is not possible to languish in the *fragmented* quadrant. Some bounce back into one of the other three quadrants (i.e., cultures), often due to the efforts of senior management. Some go bust. Others are acquired and then, very often, the cycle begins again" (Goffee & Jones, 1998, pp. 36–37). Goffee and Jones' research also is very clear in stating that any culture is bad only inasmuch as it does not fit the needs and opportunities facing the organization in its competitive environment.

CORPORATE CULTURE AND CHANGE MANAGEMENT: TWO EXAMPLES

To tie this discussion of organization culture to effective human resources management practice today, two short case examples are presented. The first case describes the cultural transformation at Johnsonville Foods, Inc., a maker and wholesaler of sausage products headquartered in Sheboygan, Wisconsin. The second case reports on the current culture change efforts at the Hewlett-Packard Company being led by CEO Carly Fiorini. Each case is then discussed to illustrate how the human resources function might be used to create, reinforce, or change an organization's culture in order to enhance its competitive capabilities.

Johnsonville Foods, Inc.[1]

Even with sales growing at a vigorous 20 percent per year, and his company earning a healthy profit, Johnsonville (www.johnson ville.com/) CEO Ralph Stayer was still unhappy. Although 1981 sales had been strong, Stayer wanted more. He wanted his employees to be as excited about the business as he was.

There were other reasons for his concerns, too: Stayer was particularly worried about the competition. His company was a regional producer of sausage products (the current year's sales—1982—would reach $15 million) that would not be able to compete with any of the larger national firms that might suddenly become predatory. Of greater concern, however, was the fact that he had come to believe that workers at Johnsonville had become bored, careless, and mistake prone, resulting not only in poorer quality product being shipped, but also in lots of wasted materials, time, and money. No one seemed to care. No one took responsibility for their jobs or seemed concerned with the company's welfare. Working at Johnsonville was just that, work! Stayer decided to find a way to change the company, to make it more competitive, and to make it a place where people indeed cared and took responsibility for their work and the company's welfare.

Thus believing that there was a huge gap between what the company was and what it could be, he first tried every flavor-of-the-month management fad he could find, and

[1]This mini case is based upon information contained in the following sources: Belasco & Stayer, 1993; Mullins, 1998; Roberts, 1986, 1992; Schneff, 1990; Stayer, 1990; and the company Web site.

watched as each failed. He then administered an employee-attitude survey, which showed that worker morale was about at the national average for companies of Johnsonville's size. This led him to think that perhaps he needed to take a hard look within himself for the source of the problem. He soon believed he'd found it there. The survey, which he at first tried hard to believe was invalid, told him that his employees saw their jobs only as a means to their personal ends. He wanted his employees instead to be able to commit their efforts to company goals, but the survey indicated that they saw little or nothing to commit to. This led him to the realization that since *he* controlled virtually all of the decision making at the company, *he* had to change before the company, or anyone else working there, could. Moreover, if employees were acting on the basis that they had no stake in the company and no power to make decisions and control their actions, perhaps the answer was for *him* to give up control and make *them* responsible.

What happened next amounted to a series of learning experiments conducted in the attempt to increase employee involvement and commitment to the business. In one such experiment, for example, Stayer, acting on instinct, ordered that employees were—from then on—responsible for making their own decisions. This action proved to be a failure. As Stayer later came to understand: "No one had asked for more responsibility; I forced it down their throats. They were good soldiers, and they did their best, but I had trained them to expect me to solve their problems. I had nurtured their inability by expecting them to be incapable; now they met my expectations with an inability to make decisions unless they knew which decisions I wanted them to make" (Stayer, 1990, p. 68). What Stayer learned from this experiment is that managers cannot give responsibility away in an organization. In order for such a cultural transformation to take place, employees have to *demand* such responsibilities. "The goal was not so much a state of shared responsibility, as an environment where people insist on being responsible," says Stayer (1990, p. 69).

During these years, Stayer gained other insights about changing the culture of his company. These included ideas that the work context (i.e., the language, symbols, and set of worker expectations as manifest by his organization's systems and structures) was key to making cultural change successful and lasting. He learned that to generate credibility in a change effort the most visible systems possible should be changed first. At Johnsonville, this amounted to (1) getting workers to taste and approve the quality of the sausage that was being shipped to customers, and (2) redesigning the compensation and employee promotion systems to make it in every employee's best interests that everyone at Johnsonville never stop learning and improving their skills and knowledge, to make the company better.

In addition, to promote the company's learning process, workers are encouraged to actively use their access to company financial and other information, and are rewarded not only for their own learning and professional development but also for their contributions to others' learning and development. Furthermore, an employee self-management system has developed where workers handle most of the jobs traditionally held by management. At Johnsonville, functional departments were eliminated (including HR, whose members remain as a resource for worker teams that perform most of the traditional HR activities), and managers are coaches, mentors, and facilitators who aid worker teams that manage their jobs and continue to develop the system that controls most aspects of organizational life there.

Now, in 2001, after years of overcoming many difficult obstacles and challenges, backsliding, and false starts in their change efforts, Johnsonville stands as a healthy and profitable company (in 1998, sales exceeded $200 million). The company's culture has been altered from one with an unhappy, un-committed, uninvolved workforce, to one where employees relish their responsibilities for and role in the corporation's success. Key corporate values, developed by workers, customers, and the larger community, consist of *Integrity* (adhering to your values), *Commitment* (heart and drive), *Innovation* (changing the playing field), *Teamwork* (together everyone achieves more), and *Continuous Learning* (learning to be great). It is a company that is not perfect, knows that it is not, and that seemingly acts on the idea that perfection is an unattainable and moving target. It is a company whose key goal is to never stop learning and growing.

Hewlett-Packard Co.[2]

A long-time member of the *Fortune* 500 list of America's largest business enterprises (currently #19 on the list), Hewlett-Packard (HP) is the #2 computer company worldwide, behind IBM. Regarded as one of the best managed and most admired companies on the planet, HP (www.hp.com) currently manufactures computers and imaging and printing peripherals, and develops software and computer-related services for customers worldwide.

The company has come a long way since Bill Hewlett and David Packard founded it in a one-room garage in Palo Alto, California, in 1938. True management pioneers (see: www.hp.com/hpinfo/news room/hewlett/fathers.htm), Hewlett and Packard founded HP with the belief that their new company's culture would be a key factor in the business's success. They thus established, from the outset, a unique way their employees would work together, organizing all interactions at the company around a set of five core values: (1) respect

for the individual, (2) contribution to the customer and the community, (3) integrity, (4) teamwork, and (5) innovation. These five values became known as the "HP way," and over the many years of HP's success and growth, provided a meaningful and visible guide for behavior and strategy at the firm.

Since 1999, under the leadership of new CEO Carly Fiorina, HP has begun reinventing itself as an Internet specialist, providing Web hardware, software, and support services in the world marketplace. HP's current vision is to help build a customer driven, networked world in which people can communicate easily—any time and anywhere—and to position itself as the only computer vendor that will be able to offer the integrated set of computer hardware, infrastructure solutions, and e-services to make this happen.

The current restructuring process began in 1999 when, under Fiorina's guidance, the company began to focus on its then spiraling out-of-control costs. Because of a slowdown in sales for HP's core products and her conviction that the business environment was fundamentally changing, Fiorina believed she had no choice but to undertake what some have called "a radical and bold management experiment" to move the company successfully into the future. "We looked in the mirror and saw a great company that was becoming a failure," says Fiorina. "This is the vision Bill and Dave would have had if they were sitting here today" (Burrows, 2001, p. 72).

So, to meet tomorrow's challenges head-on, Fiorina worked quickly (i.e., too quickly in some analysts' views) to completely restructure HP's historically decentralized confederation of autonomous product units. First, Fiorina challenged each of the then 83 business unit leaders to justify why HP should continue to invest in their businesses. Those unit heads that succeeded

---

[2]This mini-case is based on information contained in the following sources: Axelrod, 2001, Boyle, 2001; Burrows, 2001; Seybold, 2001; Stedman, 2001; Zachary, 2000; and the HP Web site.

in doing so were given six weeks to revamp the company's overall advertising and marketing plans and to relaunch the HP brand. She then set a tough 20 percent growth target for the company that needed to be reached by the year 2002. With this goal came a challenge: If executives could show her a different way to reach the 20 percent growth target than by the proposed radical corporate restructuring, she would postpone her plan. "Five weeks later, the best alternative was a plan for 16 percent growth. The restructuring would start by year end" (Burrows, 2001, pp. 77–78).

The result is a new organization, reduced from 83 to six business units, including three "back end" or manufacturing business (product generation) organizations, and three "front end" or sales (customer-facing) organizations. Fiorina believes that this new organizational structure will promote better collaboration throughout the organization. Among other things, this means allowing sales and marketing executives greater access to engineers and designers. What's more, Fiorina sees the improved communication inherent in these cross-company initiatives as a better way to get products designed and built that will solve customers' problems. The intent has thus been to reconstruct HP around customer satisfaction and loyalty, resulting in long-term business relationships built upon HP's ability to listen and respond to customers' needs.

To better take HP into the future, Fiorina also decided it was essential to reassess and update the "HP way." With the aim of "Preserving the best from the past—and reinventing the rest" (www.jobs.hp.com/Navigation/information.asp?link=whywork#benefits), the company has now reformulated the long-standing set of values as "the Rules of the Garage," which are targeted at "letting people take personal responsibility within a 'sharing' environment." In Fiorina's words, "These Rules of the Garage signify a new way of engaging with each other—our

customers, partners, shareholders, and with each other. I believe these rules represent the essence of who we are and how we'll work together in the future." (www.hp.com/ghp/features/invent/rules.html). This set of updated and future oriented corporate values is shown in Table 11-1.

As part of the restructuring and new set of corporate values, Fiorina, with the aid of outside consultants (in contrast to the old HP way of pushing strategy down to the managers most involved with the business), has also put together a multiyear strategic plan for returning the company to its former glory. In addition, Fiorina has named a nine-person executive Strategy Council that meets monthly to allocate resources, set priorities, and offer her advice on acquisitions and partnerships.

What all of this suggests is that throughout her tenure as HP's CEO, Fiorina's managerial style has been quite different than what many long-timers at HP had become used to. Tending to immerse herself in operating details, she has placed much of the burden for decision making at HP on her own shoulders. "The people dealing with Carly directly feel very empowered, but everyone else is running around saying, 'What do we do now?' says one HP manager" (Burrows, 2001, p. 73). Perhaps even more telling is a statement made by previous CEO Lewis Platt, "Bill and Dave did not feel they had to make every decision" (Burrows, 2001, p. 80).

The results of the restructuring, now almost two years into the process, are at best mixed. On the plus side, one group leader offers an example of how things are changing at HP: "We were like a refugee camp. We had five different organizations, we were located on one site, and we had to transform ourselves into an integrated manufacturing organization while facing a changing and uncertain market. We worked at the same company but spoke different languages. . . . To redesign the organization, the unit held

TABLE 11-1   HP's Rules of the Garage
✔ Believe you can change the world.
✔ Work quickly, keep tools unlocked, work whenever.
✔ Know when to work alone, and when to work together.
✔ Share—tools, ideas. Trust your colleagues.
✔ No politics. No bureaucracy. (These are ridiculous in a garage.)
✔ The customer defines a job well done.
✔ Radical ideas are not bad ideas.
✔ Invent different ways of working.
✔ Make a contribution every day. If it doesn't contribute, it doesn't leave the garage.
✔ Believe that together we can do anything.
✔ Invent.

Source: www.hp.com/ghp/features/invent/rules.html.

five large group sessions involving nearly everyone. During these conferences, people built connections that allowed new levels of coordination and cooperation. People began to see a need for change and became connected around a common purpose—creating a new organization that could effectively meet industry challenges. As a result, the refugee camp was transformed into an efficient, collaborative, customer-focused organization." (Axelrod, 2001, p. 54).

On the minus side, a redesigned sales commission structure, intended to reinvigorate HP's sales force, has produced increased sales but mostly for low-margin products that have done little to help meet financial goals. As a result, further layoffs and cost-cutting measures have been announced (Stedman, 2001). An even bigger problem, however, may be with the organization's new structure. HP executives, now overwhelmed with responsibilities for managing many products or services instead of one or a few in the former organization, might be more prone to miss details on any particular product that might keep the product competitive.

For her part, Fiorina, who returned $625,000 in bonus money given her by the board of directors last year, takes exception to claims that the restructuring is not going

well. "This is a multiyear effort," she says. "I always would have characterized Year Two as harder than Year One because this is when the change really gets binding. I actually think our fourth-quarter miss (profit projection) and the current slowing economy are galvanizing us" (Burrows, 2001, p. 73). Says another HP leader, new chief technology officer Rich DeMillo, "I have an almost religious belief that if you assemble the right people and give them the right resources, the ideas will bubble and important things will happen," DeMillo says. "And when you walk down the halls here, you hear it: The ideas are bubbling." (www.hp.com/hpinfo/newsroom/feature_stories/demillo.htm).

CHANGING CORPORATE CULTURE: SOME LESSONS, AND A MODEL

Both the Johnsonville and HP cases confirm the experience of consultants and organization development specialists that changing any established corporate culture is a long-term, difficult, and never-ending endeavor (e.g., Cory, 2001). There are no manuals and no quick answers or fixes for such efforts; even though Johnsonville is relatively much further along in their process, one would expect that both Johnsonville and HP will proceed in the face of significant challenges to becoming and maintaining the type of organizations they aspire to be. Furthermore, in general, the culture change process is probably best described as one of trial and error in the midst of the usual organizational tragedies, comedies, loves, hates, wars, peace, reason, and emotional discharges (Frost, Mitchell, & Nord, 1992). One key to success is the ability of participants to sense when any particular course of action might not be expected to produce desired results, and to try another strategy. This, of course, is far easier said than done.

The two cases also show why any serious attempt at changing corporate culture is doomed to failure without the total support and commitment of the organization's top leadership. Again, as practitioners and consultants have found, top leadership brings necessary initiative, vision, credibility, and reassurance to the process, without which the effort will more than likely founder and die. In addition, the importance of success(es) as the process proceeds, or at least the reassurance and promise of successful outcomes, cannot be overemphasized. To obtain the best chance for change processes to succeed, the organization must demonstrate at each stage of the process there is some hope that the changes are, or might be, putting the company on the right track. Certainly, poor results will weaken or pose significant challenges for leaders who, like Stayer and Fiorina, attempt major culture transformations (see Staw & Ross, 1980). This may be particularly true for HP's Fiorina, who, at this writing, is attempting to alter her company's culture in the midst of reduced revenue forecasts and analysts' doubts resulting from the current economic slowdown in the United States and Europe.

To add additional insights to our discussion of the cases and HR practice, a model of change management proposed by noted management consultant and systems thinker,

Robert Axelrod (2001), is given here. Axelrod offers this model based on his, and many others', observations that change efforts too often end in failure and cynicism, and his belief that one reason for this might be that current best-practice paradigm for initiating and conducting organizational change efforts (i.e., the "parallel organization paradigm," see Table 11-2, and also Haines, 2000, pp. 84–85) is seriously flawed. This is because: (1) in setting up a parallel or mini-organization operating within and alongside the larger organization to lead and manage the change effort, leaders/participants often fail to include enough of the organization in the process; (2) change efforts often are developed by consultants and/or managers, rather than by workers attempting to facilitate change from within the organization; this leads to resistance to change caused by the development of *defensive routines* (Argyris, 1990) in participants and those affected by the changes; (3) the process fails to include outside stakeholders in the process; and (4) change management too often concentrates on process improvements at the expense of cultural issues (Axelrod, 2001, pp. 48–49).

Consequently, Axelrod (2001, pp. 50–56) offers the following four principles of change management. Each will now be described and used as a basis for discussion of cultural change processes at Johnsonville and HP.

1. Widen the Circle of Involvement

In direct opposition to the recommendations of the traditional best-practice model, this means including a critical mass of "hundreds, even thousands, of employees" (Axelrod, 2001, p. 51) in a change process, including lower-level employees, customers, and suppliers (at least 20 to 40 percent employee involvement, or enough to ensure that the ideas are adopted by the whole organization) from the beginning of the process.

At Johnsonville, a much smaller company than HP, managers learned through an

TABLE 11-2 The Parallel Organization Model of Change Management

The typical parallel organization is composed of:

- A *sponsor group* of senior leaders who initiate the process, cheerlead the effort, and provide the funding.
- A *steering committee* that represents a cross-section of people from all levels and functions who manage the change process.
- One or more *design groups* that develop the specific changes.

Together these teams function alongside the regular organization to plan, manage, accelerate, and reduce barriers to change. The promise of the parallel organization is based on the following assumptions:

- A diversity of members on the teams, along with key decision makers, provides a way to overcome red tape and is the most efficient governance structure for the change process.
- Teams populated with "the best and the brightest" ensure high-quality solutions.
- Cross-functional and multilevel membership breaks down silos and guarantees solutions that favor the total organization.
- The team members' cooperation will be transmitted throughout the organization.
- The teams' consensus decision making ensures both high-quality solutions and members' buy-in.
- The teams' cross-functional and cross-hierarchical nature ensures that members will believe they were represented in the process.
- The teams' credibility ensures that organization members will readily accept their ideas.

Source: R. H. Axelrod. (2001). Why change management needs changing. *Reflections: The SoL Journal, 2,* 47–48.

extended sequence of trial and error that the desired change could not take place, and that the system is dysfunctional, unless every employee is involved in and committed to the process. At HP, it is clear that not everyone is involved in planning many of the changes occurring there, although they may be working towards building the necessary critical mass of involvement in the process. It is also clear, however, that there is a small top-level executive staff planning much of the change effort and passing down orders through the command structure, and that in many cases decision making has become more centralized—at least temporarily so.

2. Connect People to Each Other and Ideas

Leaders need to facilitate communication with and between coworkers. How? First, by bringing people together to discuss what they want and need to change in the company and for themselves, and what they are doing that has purpose and meaning for them. Second, by being sure to honor the past and present to create the future. These include the organization's folklore, and individuals' personal stories about what brought them to the company and why they stay. Third, by listening until you feel you cannot stand it, and then listening some more; by listening with understanding and empathy; by working for understanding, not agreement; and lastly, by making the whole system visible to everyone, and allowing people to learn what happens in other departments and throughout the organization.

At Johnsonville in 1982, when CEO Stayer initiated what was just the latest in a series of organizational change efforts, there was little reason to believe that this attempt would end up differently. What was different this time, however, is that he had realized his management style and expectations were fundamentally in conflict with the new vision for the company. Over the ensuing years Johnsonville *learned* its way through the culture change process, coming to the point where worker teams and management listen to each others' inputs and jointly discuss and solve company problems as necessary. Johnsonville has also learned that if workers are to assume the roles in decision making and self-managing that are expected of them, they need access and control of all information necessary for them to do so. Consequently, all (financial and nonfinancial) information is shared so that learning will occur and the company can develop on the strength of the entire company's best efforts.

To initiate the change process at HP, CEO Fiorina held "Coffee with Carly" discussion sessions with top business unit executives in 20 countries to boost morale and convince them of the urgency to meet the competitive challenges ahead. Corporate management then orchestrated changes to the organizational structure, rewrote the "HP way"—keeping visible and meaningful ties to the company's past—and cut costs to ready the organization for the future. Yet while it is clear that HP does not inform (it does have an Internet-based information system) or encourage responsibility and decision making throughout the organization to the full extent Johnsonville does, at least not yet, the new "rules of the garage" do champion the desire to operate in such a manner. For example, the company seems to have a more centralized decision structure than before, and many people apparently feel that they are less empowered than before, although the new set of espoused company values include worker empowerment, collaboration, risk taking, and thinking out of the box. This situation may be temporary,

however, as the tradeoffs inherent in making such radical changes so quickly—to meet financial considerations and market conditions—may be overwhelming the longer-term progress towards realizing HP's new value set. Another difference may certainly rest in the somewhat larger challenge HP faces in conducting the change process in a company with operations so geographically dispersed around the globe (e.g., Zachary, 2000, p. 2).

3. Create Communities for Action

Leaders must form a community, or a group of people willing to work together to achieve a common goal, that truly cares about achieving desired organizational outcomes and cares about every member's involvement. This is done by involving a critical mass of people at the beginning of the process and when important decisions are made. Also, there is the need to create a focus on the future that will maintain attention on new possibilities the group's energies can create, and to generate a learning environment where people learn and discover together. Culture change is a difficult trial and error process, and people solving their own problems is a positive factor in everyone becoming more likely to commit themselves to the decided upon course of action.

At both Johnsonville and HP, the goals of the culture change efforts are essentially the same: to encourage the absolute best from each and every individual; to work together; to learn together; and to create a better, more competitive, business organization. Although Johnsonville is further along in the community building process, HP has also demonstrated their long-term commitment to creating the type of organization and processes that value the contributions of individuals working alone when appropriate, and from group synergies.

4. Embrace Democratic Principles

Because it has become apparent to most leaders that authoritarian approaches to change will not work, many are creating organizations that embrace democratic principles. Such principles include "equity and fairness," which suggest that everyone has an equal responsibility to contribute to a successful outcome; "maximum sharing of information," where everyone can know what is happening in the internal and external environments; "freedom and autonomy," by which an appropriate balance is struck between the freedom and autonomy to act on one's own, and, the restrictions necessary to maintain control and focus; and "open decision making processes," in which leaders encourage and promote input from everyone who has a stake in the outcome.

Again, while the activities at Johnsonville seem geared to meeting the principles outlined earlier, HP, espousing such principles in their "rules of the garage," seems to be working towards the goal of becoming more democratic. It is still too early in the cultural transformation process, and the competitive pressures on the company may be too great at this time, to expect more than the organization can now offer. It will take determined top-level leadership and focused efforts throughout the organization for HP to reach its goals in the years ahead.

CHANGE MANAGEMENT AND THE HUMAN RESOURCES FUNCTION

As this article has described thus far, HR functions (i.e., whether designed and administered solely by HR professionals or using HR people as consultants to employee teams) are integral parts of the change processes at Johnsonville and HP. To clarify and elaborate this point, the following examples from Johnsonville and HP are organized around sets of related HR functions and suggest how HR professionals might best contribute to organizational culture change efforts.

Recruiting, Compensation, Employee Development, Training, and Personnel

Before the changes occurred at Johnsonville in the 1980s, workers were brought into the company by traditional HR means. The HR department was responsible for recruitment, hiring, determining compensation for, and training new workers. As the company moved towards an employee self-management model, these functions were assimilated into workers' roles and the HR department dissolved as that staff function assumed a consultative role within the company. Now, Johnsonville's HR experts advise workers in decisions about how and when to hire new team members, work with member teams to design training programs, administer the worker-management generated pay structure (i.e., rate plus profit-based bonuses, with pay raises depending on how much workers have "grown" in the past period), and handle the work necessary to keep the company in compliance with federal and state laws and regulations.

Additionally, in the Johnsonville and HP cases "hypocrisies" between the company values being espoused and realities within the workplace became apparent as part of the learning process during cultural transformation. In general, therefore, any company undertaking a cultural transition, such as from an individual-based pay and promotion system to one based on achieving profit goals and individuals' contributions as learners, needs to be carefully and continuously checked for inconsistencies and mixed signals. So too, espoused company goals for employee responsibility and decision making must be matched by policies that indeed support those goals. Professional HR experts should thus provide the guidance necessary, as integral participants in the strategic planning process, to ensure that the system is not operating at cross-purposes. Systems that do present such mixed signals understandably are more likely to fail, and will increase the level of worker stress in an organization.

Because change efforts can thus bring about increased stress, it is necessary to note that worker stress is caused by two different kinds of conditions in organizations. The first is that referred to earlier, where companies give hypocritical mixed signals (e.g., requiring or espousing effective team performance, yet financially rewarding individual achievement), behavior that can be remedied by bringing goals and policies into proper alignment. A second type of worker stress, however, is generated by the real or perceived threats to individuals and organizations inherent in achieving goals, change efforts, and more generically, the nature of competitive, uncertain, and equivocal decision situations. With the intensity of the competitive business environment today, and the fact that there are no ready-made or "correct" answers to strategic problems (Bowen, 1987), decision makers are going to feel stress about whether their choices will produce desired outcomes. The task for HR professionals in this, again, is to ensure that behavior supporting corporate values is encouraged. If, for example, the organization's leadership encourages risk taking (as at Johnsonville, HP, and many other companies), and that value is supported throughout the company culture, stress on decision makers is still very real, but minimized. In such work environments, decision makers can at least have some measure of confidence that the organization understands the game. If an organization's leadership demands positive results from decision makers *or else*, the stress level of decision makers is greater, but acceptable if the "*or else*" is con-

sistent with the organization's culture, is well understood beforehand, and is administered fairly in everyone's eyes. This, perhaps, describes the situation at HP in 1999 when CEO Fiorina issued the challenge to her troops that if they could propose an alternative strategy that could meet the desired 20 percent return rate, she would postpone her plan to radically restructure the company. They could not, and the restructuring began.

With regard to company hiring activities, HR professionals must be careful to ensure that the individuals hired, trained, and promoted in their organizations fit well with the culture and goals of the organization. Who is hired, rewarded, and promoted can have a dramatic effect on the corporate culture through the quantity and quality of their talents, insights, attitudes, and ideas. Regardless of the nature of the company's culture, however, some individuals will thrive, and some will not. At both Johnsonville and HP, some individuals fit, and some do not. Those that do are more likely to participate actively and productively in the organization. Those that do not will need to be replaced, or they will remain in the organization as unproductive and unhappy noncontributors. That is why the selection process is so critical, and it is the HR professional's responsibility to either recruit or help to recruit and identify those individuals who will thrive in their organization.

Finally, at Johnsonville, continuous learning, one of the company's core values, is about improving their products, services, processes, and relationships. Continuous learning there is comprised of two key components: member development (they call workers "members") and continuous improvement. In programs created by HR staff and members together, and directed and sometimes taught by the HR professionals on staff, these components require each member to commit to learning and self-development activities to benefit themselves and the company. Development activities consist, in part, of opportunities to grow by assuming additional or other positions, and company-sponsored courses and training sessions members need to carry out their responsibilities.

Appraisal, Organizational Design, and Communications

As can be seen or inferred in the two cases, employee appraisal, development, and organization design are key elements in the ongoing cultural change processes. For example, Johnsonville's culture has developed to where workers expect a key role in the appraisal process, both in determining the criteria against which their performance is compared and the rewards that accrue for performing well. There, in light of the understanding that product quality is key to the organization's success, members test and approve product before it is shipped to customers. Members are also now responsible for improving the quality of their work life. To be able to do this, the information and tools members need to address the issues that arise are made available to them. At Johnsonville, the company's organizational structure has thus been redesigned and flattened by members' (not managements') creation of a culture that shifts responsibilities for problem solving and strategy to those who "own" the problems. All of these activities have reflected Stayer's understanding early in the process that, in the final analysis, he, as CEO, doesn't "really manage people. They manage themselves." (Stayer, 1990, p. 72)

At HP, CEO Fiorina's goal to make customer experience management a core business process is supported by the fact that the entire organization is being restructured around listening and responding to customer needs. Additionally, her decision to place two senior-level executives in charge of "owning" the customer experience, thus elevating the importance of the customer experience

to the top-strategic level at HP, indicates very clearly just how serious the company is about changing. To support the initiative lower in the organization, HP is now using customer satisfaction and loyalty measurements to determine executive bonuses.

Furthermore, the vice president and director of human resources at HP, Susan Bowick, has worldwide responsibility for all HR activities. Listed among her responsibilities are partnering with the Executive Council charged with reinventing HP, the design and implementation of integrated strategic change, staffing, diversity, education, compensation, benefits, and personnel systems. Because of her strategic position in the change process, attempts are thus certainly underway to align the appraisal system and reward structure throughout the company for all employees with the new corporate structure and goals. In addition, although HP is still more centralized than Johnsonville at this time, HP is employing cutting-edge Web technology to inform, instruct, and promote better communication throughout the company. For example, HP has created a "Total Customer Experience Activists Network" composed of 200 employees from around the world. This network holds virtual meetings every month to discuss ways of improving the total experience for HP's business customers and spread best practices through HP. Further, much of HP's HR practice is moving online utilizing enterprise software. This allows employees and managers to find needed information, fill out forms, and perform many basic HR functions without the necessity of working through HR personnel.

CONCLUSIONS AND THOUGHTS ABOUT THE FUTURE

The Johnsonville and HP cases, as representative of stories at many, but certainly not all, business organizations, show how HR professionals need to become an integral part of culture change processes. This point needs to be emphasized because too often HR departments can become isolated from business realities. Such isolation often occurs simply because in many organizations the HR department and staff were not hired to be strategic thinkers. Most CEOs don't ask their HR teams to do anything more than the paperwork necessary to make things run smoothly and avoid lawsuits. Although this might indicate a problem with top leaders' perspectives, a part of this problem might also be that many HR people see the employee as their sole customer. Even though this is understandable, it is not a strategic point of view. To command attention, and so that they can assume their proper strategic role in company planning processes, the focus of some HR professionals may thus need to shift upward and outward. In this way, they will be better able to offer organizational leaders the perspective, counsel, and expertise they need.

Furthermore, with the societal trend towards more democratic workplaces (e.g., increasing worker self-management) and the outsourcing of key administrative functions, the HR function may need to adapt to a role as consultants to empowered workers, as at Johnsonville. Indeed, some of the current discussion on HR Web sites questions whether large HR departments are becoming obsolete as workers assume more management responsibilities (as at Johnsonville and HP), as well as with the development of human resources management information system software (e.g., SAP, PeopleSoft, HRVantage) and the many specialty HR

software products and Web technologies on the market. These programs and technologies can, and in many cases already do, help companies recruit, disseminate information and corporate communications, train, educate, collaborate, and perform other basic HR functions from individuals' desktops. Such technologies are changing the cultures of many organizations by restructuring the way that organizations manage internal relationships and relationships with external stakeholders. Because all of these hold the promise of adding significant value to business operations, particularly in tough times, HR professionals must adapt aggressively and proactively in their organizations.

This article began with reports from a recent *Fortune* magazine cover story stating that corporate adoption of an organizational culture in which employees are respected and treated like adults is a significant component of business success. Despite this, and the already considerable movement towards developing that type of culture in U.S. workplaces, there are also widespread reports of workplaces where high stress levels are debilitating and destructive to individuals, and are adversely affecting firms' abilities to compete. Too often, perhaps, change efforts are begun with the best of intentions but end in failure and fad-of-the-month–bred cynicism. In efforts to change an organization's culture, the role and expertise of HR professionals—as agents and positive forces in both the strategic and critical people aspects of the change process—have never been more important. ■

REFERENCES

Argyris, C. (1990). *Overcoming organizational defenses: Facilitating organizational learning.* Needham Heights, MA: Allyn & Bacon.

Axelrod, R. H. (2001). Why change management needs changing. *Reflections: The SoL Journal, 2,* 46–57.

Barnard, C. (1938). *The functions of the executive.* Cambridge, MA: Harvard University Press.

Belasco, J. A., & Stayer, R. C. (1993) *Flight of the buffalo: Soaring to excellence, learning to let employees lead.* New York: Warner Books.

Block, P. (1993). *Stewardship: Choosing service over self-interest.* San Francisco: Berrett-Koehler.

Bowen, M. G. (1987). The escalation phenomenon reconsidered: Decision dilemmas or decision errors? *Academy of Management Review, 12,* 55–66.

Boyle, M. (2001, January 8). How the workplace was won. *Fortune,* 148–168.

Burrows, P. (2001, February 19). The radical: Carly Fiorina's bold management experiment at HP. *Business Week,* 70–80.

Cavaleri, S., & Obloj, K. (1993). Management systems: A global perspective. Belmont, CA: Wadsworth Publishing Company.

Cory, D. (2001, December/January). A pioneer on the next frontier: An interview with Jay Forrester. *The Systems Thinker, 11* (10), 1–5.

Deal, T., & Kennedy, A. (1982). *Corporate cultures: The rites and rituals of corporate life.* Reading, MA: Addison-Wesley.

Deming, W. E. (1986). *Out of the crisis.* Cambridge, MA: MIT Center for Advanced Engineering Study.

DePree, M. (1992). *Leadership jazz.* New York: Currency/Doubleday.

Dobyns, L., & Crawford-Mason, C. (1991). *Quality or else: The revolution in world business.* New York: Houghton Mifflin.

Forrester, J. W. (1968). *Principles of systems.* Cambridge, MA: MIT Press.

Frost, P. J., Mitchell, V., & Nord, W. R. (1992). *Organizational reality: Reports from the firing line,* 4th edition. New York: HarperCollins.

Goffee, R., & Jones, G. (1998). *The character of a corporation: How your company's culture can make or break your business.* New York: HarperBusiness.

Goleman, D. (1995). *Emotional intelligence: Why it can matter more than IQ.* New York: Bantam Books.

Greenleaf, R. K. (1991). *Servant leadership: A journey into the nature of legitimate power and greatness.* New York: Paulist Press.

Haines, S. G. (2000). *The systems thinking approach to strategic planning and management.* Boca Raton: St. Lucie Press.

Hammer, M., & Champy, J. (1993). *Reengineering the corporation: A manifesto for business revolution.* New York: HarperBusiness.

Hofstede, G. (1997). *Culture and organizations: Software for the mind.* New York: McGraw-Hill.

Imai, M. (1986). *Kaizen: The key to Japan's competitive success.* New York: Random House.

Jackall, R. (1988). *Moral mazes: The world of corporate managers.* New York: Oxford University Press.

Jacques, E. (1952). *The changing culture of a factory.* Hinsdale, IL: Dryden Press.

Juran, J. M. (1992). *Juran on quality by design.* New York: The Free Press.

Kanter, R. M. (1985). *The change masters: Innovation and entrepreneurship in the modern corporation.* New York: Simon & Schuster.

Kanter, R. M. (2001). *Evolve: Succeeding in the digital culture of tomorrow.* Cambridge, MA: Harvard Business School Press.

Levering, R. & Moskowitz, M. (2001, January 8). The 100 best companies to work for. *Fortune,* 148–168.

Manz, C. C., & Sims, H. P. (1993). *Business without bosses: How self-managing teams are building high-performing companies.* New York: John Wiley.

Maslach, C. (1999, September 1). Take this job and . . . love it! (6 ways to beat burnout). *Psychology Today.*

Moore, D. W. (2001, February 15). Many Americans feel anxious about their jobs. *Poll Releases,* The Gallup Organization.

Morgan, G. (1997). *Images of organization,* 2nd edition. Newbury Park, CA: Sage Publications.

Mullins, R. (1998, April 17). Johnsonville workers test sausage, management. *The Business Journal of Milwaukee.*

O'Neil, J. R. (1993). *The paradox of success: A book of renewal for leaders.* New York: G. P. Putnam & Sons.

O'Toole, J. (1993). *The executive's compass: Business and the good society.* New York: Oxford University Press.

O'Toole, J. (1995). *Leading change: Overcoming the ideology of comfort and the tyranny of custom.* San Francisco: Jossey-Bass.

Ouchi, W. G. (1981). *Theory Z: How American management can meet the Japanese challenge.* Reading, MA: Addison-Wesley.

Pascale, R., & Athos, A. (1981). *The art of Japanese management.* New York: Simon & Schuster.

Pauchant, T. C., & Mitroff, I. I. (1992). *Transforming the crisis-prone organization.* San Francisco: Jossey-Bass.

Peck, M. S. (1993). *A world waiting to be born: Civility rediscovered.* New York: Bantam Books.

Peters, T. J. (1987). *Thriving on chaos: Handbook for a management revolution.* New York: Harper & Row.

Peters, T. J. (1992). *Liberation management: Necessary disorganization for the nanosecond nineties.* New York: Alfred A. Knopf.

Peters, T. J., & Waterman, R. H. (1982). *In search of excellence: Lessons from America's best-run companies.* New York: Warner Books.

Richardson, G. P. (1991). *Feedback thought in social science and systems theory.* Philadelphia: Univ. of Pennsylvania Press.

Roberts, M. J. (1986). *Johnsonville Sausage Co. (A), Case #9-387-103.* Cambridge, MA: Harvard Business School.

Roberts, M. J. (1992). *Johnsonville Sausage Co. (B), Case #9-393-063.* Cambridge, MA: Harvard Business School.

Saad, L. (1999, September 3). American workers generally satisfied, but indicate their jobs leave much to be desired. *Poll Releases,* The Gallup Organization.

Schneff, J. (1990, November). Managing the journey. *Inc.,* 45–54.

Selznick, P. (1948, February 13). Foundations of the theory of organization. *American Sociological Review,* 25–35.

Seybold, P. (2001). *The customer revolution: How to thrive when customers are in control.* New York: Crown Business Publishers.

Smircich, L. (1983). Concepts of culture and organizational analysis. *Administrative Science Quarterly, 28,* 339–358.

Spears, L. C. (1995). *Reflections on leadership.* New York: John Wiley & Sons.

Spears, L. C. (1998). *Insights on leadership.* New York: John Wiley & Sons.

Staw, B. M. & Ross, J. (1980). Commitment in an experimenting society: An experiment on the attributions of leadership in administrative scenarios. *Journal of Applied Psychology, 65,* 249–260.

Stayer, R. (1990, November–December). How I learned to let my workers lead. *Harvard Business Review,* 66–83.

Stedman, C. (2001, April 18). HP warns of another weak quarter, moves to cut more jobs. *Computerworld.com.*

Sterman, J. (2000). *Business dynamics: Systems thinking and modeling for a complex world.* Boston: Irwin McGraw-Hill.

Walton, C. (1988). *The moral manager.* New York: HarperBusiness.

Wheatley, M. J. (1992). *Leadership and the new science.* San Francisco: Berrett-Koehler Publishers.

Whyte, D. (1994). *The heart aroused: Poetry and preservation of the soul in corporate America.* New York: Currency/Doubleday.

Williams, O. F., & Houck, J. W. (1992). *A virtuous life in business: Stories of courage and integrity in the corporate world.* Boston: Rowman & Littlefield.

Zachary, G. P. (2000, July). Mighty is the mongrel. *Fast Company* (www.fastcompany.com/online/36/mongrel.html).

SPIRITUALITY IN THE WORKPLACE

Elmer H. Burack

INTRODUCTION

This article focuses on newer work life and organizational culture arrangements that improve the human experience and thereby help to achieve longer term enterprise stability, growth, and profitability. Relational terms such as credibility, trust, wisdom, and ethics are used to describe these approaches. These discussions are based on the writer's years of research and corporate experiences as well as thoughtful analyses, examples, and discussions of other social scientists.

Current progress in defining and creating a more hospitable work life environment and enriching human experience is too frequently taken to mean soft or devious management or a thinly veiled attempt at a religious renaissance in Corporate America. The former is wrong and the latter point valid only in a very general sense. In truth some commonly used terms and descriptive titles use meanings, values, and experiences from quite different contexts. Some examples include "spirituality," "soulfulness," "rediscovering the soul," and "managing with love." I suspect that it will be some years yet before these terms gain general usage in business. Regardless, they are used in this article, albeit selectively.

Bases for this article's approach to workplace spirituality represent the initial discussions. Next, a diverse group of organization application examples suggest the broad utility of these approaches. Since some readers are likely to be interested in various of the theoretical models and concepts underlying these discussions, the following section provides several "wiring" diagrams or models and a brief explanation of these. The final section includes some of my speculations as to possible future directions.

For article purposes, the following concepts of spirituality in the workplace will be used:

- Spiritual growth and advancement of the human experience involve mental growth—problem solving and individual learning will often be the main vehicles of individual development.
- Spiritual growth reflects the gratification of individual needs, especially "belonging" and those of a higher order such as a sense of achievement. The individual's context for these is broad, encompassing work-family connections and workplace settings.
- Spirituality in the workplace is communicated and reinforced through the institution's leaders, organizational culture, policies, and work design, among other factors. Sensitivity to and interest in the person (employee) must be common to all approaches.

WORKPLACE SPIRITUALITY: WHY THE INTEREST?

The fast-growing interest in and durability of workplace spirituality stems largely from two mainstream business developments. One is termed the "economic-technological imperative" and the other is simply described as "people-centered management." The foundation for the latter approach will be described as "Theory YZ" in recognition of two of its early contributors.

The economic-technological imperative has been a part of the business scene from the very beginning. Economic or technological considerations in the past were the major driving forces for introducing major changes that led to new economies of scale or higher productivity. More recently, the scenario would be as follows. "Downsizing and re-engineering are now a way of life for us. However, we seem to be confronted with decreasing economic returns and competition has caught up and now are doing similar things in a technological driven environment. We concluded that it is people who now will make the difference." Their numbers are growing fast, albeit, their commitment to people-centered approaches is more tenuous. Ford Motor Company is an outstanding example of a firm that made a complete turnaround in favor of people-centered approaches (Burack, 1993). Now in force for some two decades, its people-driven approaches are viewed as the main contributing factor to their outstanding performance in the highly competitive automotive industry according to a recent *Wall Street Journal* article (July 16, 1998, p. A1).

The people-centered premise served as the central foundation for what to date has been quite a different group of firms. This organizing principle drove workplace practices, policies, process, and culture. Some business owners and founders such as those at Hewlett-Packard and Fel-Pro were committed to these practices from their beginnings or shortly thereafter.

THEORY YZ AND THE SPIRITUAL LEGACY: A PERSONAL VIEW

I believe that the world we live in is governed by various physical and spiritual "laws." Airplane flight, cellular biology, and the essential goodness of many people are examples of things I do not fully understand. But I do not have to because they are there and they work and form an essential part of our lives (Marcic, 1997, pp. 2–44). Also, after years of research and consultive experi-

ences, I have concluded that growing numbers of organizations are moving towards work arrangements that are described in this article as "spiritual." This is quite a generalization so let me be more specific.

- Some companies have been people oriented and quite profitable for many years. They thoughtfully balanced various business and work dimensions to achieve high productivity and profitability (Vaill, 1989). Some were built on people-centered principles from their beginning. The critical elements balanced were physical (e.g., equipment, pay, and safety), intellectual (e.g., leveraging available knowledge and capabilities, learning, and planning), emotional (e.g., interpersonal relationships and communications, teaming, feedback, and emotional development), volitional (e.g., willingness to change and good adaptability to new demands or conditions), and spiritual (e.g., concern with ethics, empathy for people, justice and individual dignity). These dimensions are highly interdependent and must be dynamically balanced for enterprise success in response to fast-changing circumstances (Marcic, 1997, pp. 31–43).

- Some companies were managing with "spirituality" from their founding. Others were drawn to this organizational and managerial mode at a relatively early point in their history. In more recent years, increasing numbers have been drawn towards these approaches based on much more pragmatic considerations: Their version of theory X (people as work instruments, centralized direction, etc.) did not work any more; technology, process re-engineering, and restructuring still did not do "it"; or more generally, all of the accoutrements of high efficiency were installed including individual empowerment, but authenticity and trust were still missing.

- Many companies have been rated in national surveys as among the "best places to work" and are also good to highly successful long-term profit performers (Burack & Mathys, 1998).

- Some companies, perhaps a relatively large number, are still anchored to Theory X. I believe that these will continue to thin out in numbers as more and better alternatives appear and employees increasingly exercise their employment preferences for whom they are willing to make a high performance commitment (Burack, 1993; Meyer & Allen, 1997).

A NEW ROLE FOR SPIRITUALITY IN THE WORKPLACE

Newer organization types are emerging that are much flatter than classical pyramidal structures and which emphasize increasingly empowered and collaborative employment relationships. Personal contacts among employees and between employees and managers are often brief, transitory, or even nonexistent (Shaw, 1997). Trust, a belief that those on whom we depend meet our positive expectations of them (Shaw, 1997, p. 21), assumes a new and critical role. A new employment relations compact is being defined between workers and management. The rapid reinvention of organizational form and function has been driven directly by widespread downsizing and more generally a fast-changing competitive environment of global dimensions.

The newer work environments place a premium on employee qualities best described as conscientiousness. They are called on to do much more problem solving, adapt quickly and learn rapidly, often work longer hours, and gain newer capabilities derived largely from job-related experiences (Behling, 1998, pp. 82–84). Unfortunately,

employee respect and confidence in management is being eroded based on data from the International Research Corporation as reported in *Business Week* (June 28, 1998, p. 72). Distrust has grown (Shaw, 1997, p. XI).

Distrust leads to unclear performance targets and generally disrupts critical organizational communications, processes, and relationships. Advice giving is avoided and internal communications viewed suspiciously. Relationships and communications become more perfunctory and people cooperate by the rule book, necessitating extensive negotiation and perhaps coercion. The promise of a learning organization is dimmed and fast response to environmental change suffers (Shaw, 1997, pp. 11–14).

SPIRITUALITY AND WORK: A CONTEMPORARY VIEW

The traditional notion of spirituality has been enlarged much beyond its anchorage in religious traditions. Transformations in religious and philosophical thought over the millennia have led to numerous applications in worklife and organizational settings. M. Scott Peck (1980) makes no distinction between mind and spirit; thus the process of achieving spiritual growth is "one and the same" as achieving mental growth (Peck, 1980, p. 11). Life takes on meaning through the process of meeting and solving problems (Peck, 1980, p. 11). Because work comprises so much a part of everyone's life, organization practices can contribute greatly to spiritual (mental) growth. For example, problem-solving processes that call forth creativity or challenge conventional thought patterns, or which lead to workable or new solutions, result in additional learning and thus we experience spiritual growth.

There are other important ideas related to spirituality that have come to define a modern idea of spirituality in the workplace. One dispirited leader, seeking something more than a good bottom line, discovered his soul and learned how to be kind to his spirit and that of the organization. In the book *Leading with Soul* (Bolman & Deal, 1995) typical prescriptions include developing more hospitable work spaces, rendering services to both the organization and community, and facilitating in the workplace — while strengthening organizational objectives and performance (Conger, 1997). Dorothy Marcic (1997) reinforced the idea that successful businesses may in part contribute to their financial success by facilitating the realization of "spiritual values" in organization life. She provides numerous examples that are compelling and underscore the importance of "spiritual" analysis and thinking in the work setting.

Abraham Maslow's (1962) widely acknowledged work on motivation systematically delineated higher states of mental health and possibilities for individual accomplishment. Implicit within his theorizing is the notion that organizations can assist people in achieving their possibilities become instrumental to their own improved economic bottom line. Maslow argues that all people operate out of an "inborn hierarchy of needs." Creating the culture and organization for gratifying lower order needs — physical, safety, and belonging — is in itself an accomplishment. Even in the downsizing era of the 1990s, an important degree of security is provided to people who have been helped to develop transferable skills and for whom thoughtful counseling has been provided. At the same time, when these lower order needs are satisfied, the person is in a position to move to higher order needs where selflessness, loyalty, and public-spiritedness increasingly manifest themselves. Perhaps only a small minority will achieve their higher order possibilities, but the needs hierarchy does suggest another tangible path for enlarging upon spirituality in the workplace. This approach is also likely to open doors to unprecedented levels of work and enterprise accomplishment. Other

work-design avenues to achieving higher levels of individual motivation (for performance) via self-realization of individual needs are beyond the scope of this article. However, two important points need to be made regarding spirituality approaches described here before proceeding further.

Ultimately the individual and a sense of spirituality at "true work" comes from one's own being (Fox, 1994). In this view, goodness and being are interchangeable (p. 81). In the last analysis, it is the person who takes on the expression of spirituality, albeit, the organization culture or environment is conducive to this process. When the inner self connects to one's work, work and the inner self seem to know no limits; the highest level of work is spiritual "because it challenges the limits of being and stretches for the . . . spiritual horizon" (Fox, 1994, p. 82).

The other point concerns the organization's economic imperatives. In the spirituality approaches described here, profitability is seen as a key but not sole outcome of business activity. Even in wholly owned private businesses, where more latitude exists for the leader/owner, spirituality thinking is viewed as a way to help ensure long-run profitability, bolster shorter run returns, and establish a more harmonious tone in the organization.

THE REINVENTION OF ORGANIZATIONS—FOCUS ON WORKLIFE AND SPIRITUALITY

Dramatic environmental changes underway for better than a decade have drastically altered the business setting and thus led to radical shifts in organizational structure, process, and focus. Globalization, competition, diversity, aging populations, and environmental pollution are among the widely acknowledged factors. These developments have led to a reinvention of organizations involving architecture (systems and processes), job/works, life features, and the focus of decision making (Burack, 1993). Human resources roles and relationships have taken on new importance (step 3), which are people centered and built on empowerment and team-centered activity (Ulrich, 1998; Jaffe, Scott, & Tobe, 1997). Leadership has assumed a new and critical role in these reinvented business settings. Credibility of the leader's actions, organizational policies, and far-flung business practices assume new importance in bottom-line results (Kouzes & Posner, 1993). The newer systems, fast-changing conditions, the people dependency of empowerment and team oriented activities, and increased work demands place a new premium on gaining employee commitment (Conger, 1989; Meyer & Allen, 1997; Schuster, 1998; Wood & Bandura, 1989).

The scope and complexity of organizing and managing the new systems rests importantly on the quality of past relationships and the type of organizational culture created. Leadership's actions and organizational practices will be reviewed in the light of managerial and leadership acumen displayed (e.g., in decision making, innovation); and adherence to core values, ethics, and integrity. Leadership will be expected to foster individual and group learning, and shape on a newer basis for employment relationships under greatly changed environment conditions. Creating and reinforcing a sense of spirituality in the workplace are necessary accomplishments for achieving a unified whole. For the purposes of this paper, these approaches are based on Theory YZ. This "theory" reflects the contributions of Douglas McGregor (1960: Theory X and Theory Y) and Bill Ouchi (1980: Theory Z). The critical elements of "theory YZ" include:

- Recognition of the worth and value of people—pursuing an employee-centered management approach.
- Desire to create high integrity work climates.

- Establishing a foundation of trust, faith, justice, respect, and love (Marcic, 1997).
- Fostering organizations that jointly meet ownership's economic and individual needs.

Needless to say, where the quality of relationships has been poor, management faces a daunting task in establishing or restoring a trustful climate (Defoore & Renesch, 1995; Shaw, 1997).

A final point concerns the hoped for outcomes of applying a Theory YZ approach to create a sense of workplace spirituality. Perhaps these are most easily thought of as concerned with four different but highly interrelated outcomes:

1. Leadership and the organization—demonstrated concern for employees, respect for others, consistency of actions, and demonstrated acumen.
2. Employees—conscientious (e.g., quality, cooperation) continuing skill and knowledge advancement, adaptability and high sustained performances.
3. External (strategic constituents)—quality, consistency, environmentally aware, and a responsible community member.
4. Mutual—trust and shared responsibilities for joint benefits.

ORGANIZATION DEMOGRAPHICS, CULTURE, AND WORKPLACE SPIRITUALITY

The particular features of workplace spirituality are shaped by the organization's defining vision of its worklife and what it is all about. These are influenced importantly by such key factors as work, technology, competition, organization size, and other basic features of structure and process. Thus, for example, a spirituality dimension such as worker opportunities to identify with and shape their work varies greatly in specifics for engineering units in comparison with production units. Differences would also rise because of size—enterprises of 100 employees versus, say, 10,000 employees. The above notwithstanding, organization culture embodies the values, beliefs, and attitudes of the enterprise's defining vision. It encompasses the entire organization. Organization culture becomes the "biblical mobile ark" of what is stood for, the presence of which is felt throughout the organization. The litmus test of functionality becomes the extent to which the espoused values, beliefs, and attitudes are reasonably enacted in workplace design, communications, and interpersonal relationships. Ongoing indications of workplace spirituality are then registered by the employee's sense of credibility, trust, and personal fulfillment opportunities regarding enterprise leaders, managers, and work associates. Some short corporate case summaries follow that help to illustrate this rather complex picture. Details of designing for workplace spirituality are presented in a concluding section.

Hewlett-Packard and the H-P Way

H-P's presence among the small circle of "most esteemed" companies in the United States largely reflects the entrepreneurial spirit and vision of its founders Bill Hewlett and Dave Packard. Prior to 1970, H-P was a highly successful manufacturer of precision measuring instruments. In the decades following, it reinvented itself completely to become a world-class computer leader in the 1990s. However, in the decades after its founding (1939), the H-P way (its culture) continued to provide an overarching presence shaping workplace attitudes, relationships, compensation systems, communications, and employee initiatives and fulfillment opportunities. The founders erected a management by objectives framework that incorporated both long- and short-term goals and permitted a highly decentralized management style. This facilitated many autonomous employee opportu-

nities. Highlights of H-P's culture and its enactment are presented in Table 11-3.

The items listed under "General guidelines" provided direction for organization design and the fleshing out of relationships and workplace policies. The "H-P way" set out mutual understanding and respect as basic to its cooperative relationships and achieving and sustaining leadership in creative products and manufacture. These understandings came to characterize its operations. H-P became one of the first organizations to introduce flextime, which represented top management's vote of confidence in its employees and recognition of widely differing individual needs rather than a "one style fits all" approach.

A final point regarding the H-P way concerns their employment and staffing policies in periods of financial adversity or business downturns. Temporary economic downturns were handled through attrition and shortened work weeks (shared by all). Longer term business downturns were handled through early retirements, buyouts, and attrition. Downsizing was easily the most severe threat in terms of numbers affected and threatened loss of one's livelihood. When confronted with the need to downsize in the early 1990s, the numbers affected were substantially reduced because of long-term human resources planning and staffing approaches.

Tom's of Maine

Organizations with less than 250 employees and often under 100 employees are far more characteristic of U.S. companies and thus more open for spirituality opportunities in the workplace. Tom's of Maine provides a highly interesting and informative scenario because it provides one of the few documented examples of "the middle way," living its values and being successful financially (Chappell, 1994). Here the "middle way" is the Buddhist notion—a special type of "balance." This is an organization that is perhaps

TABLE 11-3	Hewlett-Packard's Corporate Culture—A Foundation for Workplace Spirituality
Niche	Product and manufacturing innovation in the measurement and computer fields
General guidelines and management style	Trust and mutual respect serve as basic building blocks
	Link employee compensation and performance to corporate success
	Get best people
	Seek/develop will-to-win people and teams
	Avoid command and control organization
	Shirt-sleeve informality (first name)
	Continuing learning and renewal
	Enactment responsibility—at lowest level proximate to customer
	Maintaining a sense of small organization, regardless of size
	Be a good corporate citizen
	Tomorrow's returns follow from today's inputs
	"Open door" managerial accessibility
	Management by walking around (MBWA)
	Attention to detail basic to quality
Relationships	Mutual understanding and respect
	Personal two-way communications to back up written communications
	Personal contacts, management by walking around
	Leadership is earned, not enacted
	Build cooperation and shared sense of purpose
Worklife policies	Flexible time
	Organization-wide performance bonuses versus individual incentives
	Establish mutually agreed on objectives that are specific and measurable
	Person builds own security through contributions and performance
Nourishment for the individual's spirit	Setting own worktime within "flextime" boundaries and reflecting personal needs and situation
	Recognition for creative accomplishment and performance
	Sense of being in charge of own destiny
	Working in an environment where people can do their best, realize their potential, and be recognized for their achievements

Source: Based in part on Packard (1995).

best described as living paradoxically. This means combining reflection and action; being severe but strong; connecting reflection and action; and communicating faith, integrity, honesty and passion to people and its products while sustaining a healthy regard for making money. The value of Tom's experience to the tens of thousands of other small(er) firms (and large ones too!) is the fact that its mission evolved over a long ges-

tation period. Initially it was a typical entrepreneurial start-up by a husband and wife team. It sold various personal care household products featuring environmentally friendly, natural ingredients. The leaders' preoccupation with survival and growth largely resulted in bottling up personal and strongly held values as these might become an integral part of the business. Put another way, creating, manufacturing, marketing, and distributing a unique family of products was highly demanding—and not surprisingly they fell much short of creating an organization that evidenced these values. For more than four years, Tom Chappell relentlessly pursued the challenge of fully identifying their passionately held values and beliefs and then achieving an organization design, policies, and relationships that fully represented these—while becoming financially sound and achieving an enviable bottom line. His process of self discovering included a four-year stint at Harvard's Divinity School. His "sabbatical" and change process included numerous give-and-take sessions and retreats involving their board, senior managers, employees, friends, and various professionals.

Central to their eventual success was the role of leadership. Tom, as the president and main stockholder, had the faith and the strong convictions and passions needed to carry them through many trial and error episodes and traumatic experiences and head-to-head encounters with possessors of conventional wisdom and believers in command and control tactics. The essence of the company, its "soul," was to be found in its core belief and values structure. Highlights of these included:

- mind and spirit can work together for market share;
- one can do well (economically) by doing good;
- an enterprise can be socially responsible and environmentally sensitive and still make a (good) profit;
- heart and head have to be united in ways that meet the need of the company and the person;
- corporate identity is found in the quality of relationships in their main constituencies;
- people have a high capacity for creativity and excellence and it is an organization's responsibility to unlock

these for the benefit of the enterprise and person; and
- products can be conceived and marketed that embody the company's core values.

Achieving these values and beliefs meant that they had to create an organization staff with people who espoused these and a willingness to grow. A high level of individual competence would be necessary to achieve these but the people in turn had to have confidence in the leadership's acumen; they had to experience this new leadership model and examples of support that would make success for the individual and business realistic. One example of corporate actions supporting employee confidence and trust was the recall of some 400,000 units of product at a critical period in their growth—because the product was not as good as it should be.

Management's credibility and trust was established over an extended time period through numerous actions. A representative group of these included child care facilities, a viable retirement plan, placing fruit snacks out in the plant, and picnics and other employee get-togethers. Additional company actions included tithing 10 percent of profits for worthy charities and providing for employees to take 5 percent off on company time for worthy community and charitable work projects. Tom's of Maine is an outstanding example of a company that chose to do good. They created a morally and socially responsible company that also was profitable.

The Ford Motor Company Experience

Over 20 years ago, the Ford Motor Company "discovered" downsizing in order to survive. By the early 1980s they had accumulated financial losses of almost $3 billion and had reduced their North American workplace by several hundred thousand (Burack, 1993, Chapter 6). The (radical) reinvention of the company, requiring some

10 to 15 years, witnessed a complete scraping of a "Theory X" management style. This "X" style dated back to the early years of the century and reflected the philosophy of (the senior) Henry Ford. "Theory X," the view of people as essentially nonthinking tools requiring much direction and close control, was gradually replaced with a newer vision of human resources potential. This was considered as a work in process that took years to work out because of its scope uniqueness and customized fit to Ford circumstances. This concept, critical to the process of reinventing the company, rested squarely on two key assumptions:

1. Corporate credibility with workers and the consuming public had to be addressed and progress achieved before survival, let alone future growth, was assured.
2. Long-term business success would be the consequence of consistent progress as measured by two "bottom lines"—one financial and the other people.

Trustful relationships between the management and the workers (and the union), a key achievement in their attaining high performance, required meeting the antecedent condition of credibility.

Their new vision of worklife and employment relationships represented a new social-psychological contract. It was truly a work in progress because few functional models existed and there were none which even approximated the scale and the radical changes that eventually took place.

CONCLUSIONS AND IMPLICATIONS

There is no question in my mind that profound changes are taking shape in the workplace and that spirituality will be one of the main themes. The critical ingredients for accelerating and sustaining change are now in place: a critical mass of solid scholarship and research; widespread, numerous, and growing writings divided among scholarly and popular publications; expressed needs by individuals; and last but not least, an even widening proof of top executives and owners who are convinced of the merits of these approaches. More and more managers will be seeking information to guide interval design and change initiations. ∎

REFERENCES

Behling, O. (1998). Employee selection: Will intelligence and conscientiousness do the job? *Academy of Management Executive, 12* (1), 77–86.

Bolman, L. G., & Deal, T. E. (1995). *Leading with soul.* San Francisco, CA: Jossey-Bass.

Burack, E. H. (1993). *Corporate resurgence and the new employment relationships.* Westport, CT: Quorum.

Burack, E. H., & Mathys, N. (1998). Employee oriented cultures and performance. Working Paper, University of Illinois at Chicago, College of Business Administration, Chicago, IL.

Chappell, T. (1994). *The soul of a business: Managing for profit and the consumer good.* New York, NY: Bantam-DoubleDay.

Conger, J. A. (1989). Leadership: The art of empowering others. *Academy of Management Executive, 3* (1), 17–34.

Conger, J. A. (Ed.). (1997). *Spirit at work.* San Francisco, CA: Jossey-Bass.

Defoore, B., & Renesch, J. (Eds.). (1995). *Rediscovering the soul of a business: A renaissance of values.* San Francisco, CA: Sterling & Stone.

Fox, M. (1994). *The reinvention of work: A new vision of livelihood for our time.* New York, NY: HarperCollins.

Jaffe, D. T., Scott, C. D. and Tobe, G. R. (1997). *Rekindling commitment.* San Francisco, CA: Jossey-Bass.

Kouzes, J. M., & Posner, B. Z. (1993). *Credibility: How leaders gain and lose it, why people demand it.* San Francisco, CA: Jossey-Bass.

Marcic, D. (1997). *Managing with the wisdom of love.* San Francisco, CA: Josey-Bass.

Maslow, A. (1962). *Toward a psychology of being.* Princeton, NJ: Van Nostrand.

McGregor, D. (1960). *The human side of enterprise.* New York, NY: McGraw-Hill.

Meyer J. P., & Allen, N. J. (1997). *Commitment in the workplace: Theory, research and application.* Thousand Oaks, CA: Sage.

Ouchi, B. (1980). *Theory Z.* New York, NY: Doubleday.

Packard, D. (1995). *The H-P way.* New York, NY: Harper-Collins.

Peck, M. S. (1980). *The road less traveled.* New York, NY: Simon & Schuster, Touchstone.

Schuster, F. (1998). *Employee-centered management: A strategy for high commitment and involvement.* Westport, CT: Quorum

Shaw, R. (1997). *Trust in the balance.* San Francisco, CA: Jossey-Bass.

Ulrich, D. (1998). *Human resource champions: The next agenda for adding value and delivering results.* San Francisco, CA: Jossey-Bass.

Vaill, P. (1989). *Managing as a performing art: New ideas for a world of chaotic change.* San Francisco, CA: Jossey-Bass.

Wood, R. E., & Bandura, A. (1989). Impact of conceptions of ability in self-regulation mechanisms and complex decision-making. *Journal of Personality and Social Psychology, 56,* 407–415.

12

WORK ENVIRONMENT STRESSORS, SUPPORT, SAFETY, AND HEALTH

P hysical and psychological components of the work environment may result for some employees in excessive job stress, poor performance, and the breakdown of social relationships within and outside the workplace. Certain employees may experience even more serious outcomes, such as alcoholism, drug abuse, permanent handicap, or death. A major piece of federal legislation designed to remove or reduce such physical and psychological hazards is the Occupational Safety and Health Act (OSHA) of 1970. Although opinions regarding the effectiveness of OSHA are mixed, it certainly has increased awareness of the importance of protecting employees.

In addition to environmental stressors related to safety issues, other workplace issues contribute to stress. One example is sexual harassment. An individual experiencing sexual harassment at work is in a hostile working environment. Legal protection against sexual harassment is still evolving, with the Supreme Court taking up the issue of psychological damage to a person who claims harassment. The Court decided that the individual alleging harassment need not demonstrate psychological damage. According to this finding, sexual harassment has occurred if a hostile working environment has been created; the plaintiff does not have the burden of demonstrating that he or she has experienced psychological damage.

Many organizations have attempted to develop effective employee assistance programs to combat the stress associated with juggling work and personal concerns and to demonstrate their support for their workers. This is a controversial area: A number of experts think that organizations have no right to become involved with nonwork-related concerns of employees. Organizations have become involved in employee assistance programs for other than altruistic reasons. Such programs have been shown to be related to the development of a more effectively functioning organization.

In the first article, Zellars addresses those issues that are associated with job stress and the outcomes of job stress. This is an important issue as many negative job outcomes are tied to stress, for example, burnout and stress-related disabilities. The next article, by Kiewitz and Hochwarter, is concerned with the increasing problem of violence at work. Numerous examples of workplace violence and aggression have been reported in the popular press. This article will assist the reader in noticing those variables that may be associated with this problem. The third article, by Thacker, presents the issue of sexual harassment as more of an interpersonal issue, not as the legal issue presented in the readings in Chapter 3. She writes from the perspective of the recipient of sexual harassment and attempts to explain the reactions of those who experience such harassment. In the last article, Stollak describes the stakes and stakeholders associated with employee assistance programs (EAPs). The benefits of EAPs are discussed in relation to each of the involved constituencies.

READINGS

THE THREE "C'S" OF JOB STRESS: CAUSES, CONSEQUENCES, AND COPING

Kelly L. Zellars

In the 1980s, it was popular to blame work stress on rocky economic times, downsizing, mergers, and a general distrust of management. Despite the economic boom of the 1990s, individuals continue to report high levels of job stress; some have suggested that work-related stress is reaching epidemic proportions (Marino, 1997). A survey of 700 American workers found that 79 percent felt that 1995 was one of the most stressful years ever, and that work was the primary cause of that stress (*HR Focus*, 1996). Surveys of managers report that 88 percent are experiencing elevated levels of stress (Tilson, 1997), and most report feeling more stress now than in the past (Cohen, 1997).

Numerous studies in the psychological and medical literature support a relationship between stress and negative outcomes (for reviews, see Kahn & Byosiere, 1992; Matteson & Ivanevich, 1987), and the estimated financial costs associated with job stress are staggering. The costs of workers' compensation claims in 1982 were $20 billion; in 1990, the costs rose to $60 billion (Bordwin, 1996). Stress-related disability claims are the most rapidly growing form of occupational illness within the workers' compensation system (King, 1995). Finally, information cited in Karasek and Theorell (1990) suggests that the total costs of stress to U.S. companies resulting from absenteeism, reduced productivity, compensation suits, health insurance claims, and direct medical expenses exceeds $150 billion annually. In short, work stress continues to plague workers, and organizations are seeing mounting costs.

CAUSES OF JOB STRESS

It is difficult to identify all of the sources of stress and the exact conditions under which job stress will occur. Individuals within the same organization and position may experience and/or perceive environmental stimuli differently. Job stress generally refers to the physiological and psychological reactions of individuals to conditions encountered at work. Investigators have referred to these conditions as "stressors" and the responses as "strains" (Ganster & Schaubroeck, 1991). Years of research and numerous studies have identified a wide variety of job and organizational stressors, including long hours, high work loads, conflicting or ambiguous demands, fast pace, strict deadlines, job insecurity, interpersonal conflict, shiftwork, organizational politics, and harsh or controlling supervisory styles. In general, workers in jobs in which a greater number of these stressors are present report higher levels of work stress.

Research has established several organizational and individual factors that affect the likelihood that an organizational member will experience job stress. Among the most researched and salient antecedents to job stress are organizational role stressors, work/family conflict, and individual differences.

Organizational Role Stressors

Since the early work of Kahn, Qoldw, Quinn, Snoek, and Rosenthal (1964), the antecedents and consequences of role stress have been central to the study of occupational stress. As a result, much of this research has focused on role ambiguity and role conflict. Role ambiguity refers to the unpredictability of performance consequences as well as unclear information regarding expected role behaviors. Conversely, role conflict refers to incongruent expectations, and it can occur both between roles (e.g., employee role and family role) as well as within roles (e.g., trying to fulfill expectations for two supervisors whose requests are incompatible). Research has shown role ambiguity and conflict to be linked with a number of dysfunctional outcomes, including uncertainty, job dissatisfaction, psychological strain, intentions to leave the organization (Jackson, 1983; Schaubroeck, Cotton, & Jennings, 1989), and burnout (Jackson, Turner, & Brief, 1987; Zellars & Perrewé, in press).

Work/Family Conflict

Research examining the conflict between work and family roles has increased dramatically, which is partially due to the changing and evolving nature of balancing work and family responsibilities (Kinnunen & Mauno, 1998). During the past two decades, work environments have seen an increase in dual-income couples (Zedeck, 1992), single-parent families (Zedeck, 1992), and individuals involved in the care of elderly parents (Goodstein, 1994).

Work/family conflict is a form of inter-role conflict in which one role interferes with the other role (Greenhaus & Beutell, 1985). Work/family conflict has been conceptualized as a two-dimensional construct (e.g., Frone, 2000; Frone, Russell, & Cooper, 1992; Frone, Yardley, & Markel, 1997; Netemeyer, Boles, & McMurrian, 1996), where work interferes with family (work-to-family conflict) and family interferes with work (family-to-work conflict).

Women's increased role in the workplace and the fact that the life expectancy for individuals has increased have created a caregiver role for many employees that include both children and aging parents. Over the past decade, research has focused on evaluating the extent to which this caregiving role affects the work and family interface. Not surprisingly, research has found that family-related absence from work is more common among women, the traditional family caregivers, than it is among men (Vanden Heuvel, 1997).

Work-family conflict has been associated with a number of dysfunctional outcomes, including general work withdrawal behaviors (Kirchmeyer & Cohen, 1999; Thomas & Ganster, 1995), decreased family and occupational well-being (Kinnunen & Mauno, 1998), psychological costs and physical complaints (Frone, 2000; Frone, Russell, & Cooper, 1992), and job and life dissatisfaction (Netemeyer, Boles, & McMurian, 1996; Kossek & Ozeki, 1998; Perrewé, Hochwarter, & Kiewitz, 1999).

Given these demographic changes in the workforce and in the population as a whole, the impact of caregiver roles on work/family conflict is a more salient topic than ever. These changes will create a large group of employees "sandwiched" in caregiving roles. These individuals will be simultaneously fulfilling caregiving roles for both children and elderly parents. Therefore, many organizational researchers argue that the study of job stress stemming from work/family conflict should include the role of caregiver for both children and aging family members (Buffardi, Smith, O'Brien, & Erdwins, 1999; Chapman, Ingersoll-Dayton, & Neal, 1994). Over the course of the next 20 years, the elderly population will significantly increase due to the aging of the "baby-boomer generation." The aging of this segment of the population, coupled with the dual-career household, will ensure that a larger number of employees will continue to balance work demands and roles as caregiver to an elderly parent.

Individual Differences

Personality characteristics and dispositional differences have also been examined as possible contributors to the experience of work stress. The work of Lazarus and Folkman (1984) has largely influenced the proposition that personality variables influence the stress-strain relationship. They argue that the degree of fit of the person to his or her environment is a significant determinant of the amount of stress experienced.

Watson, David, and Suls (1999) argue that the personality traits of neuroticism and extraversion need to become a central focus within stress and coping research, and research substantiates that neuroticism and extraversion have significant influences on the experience of job burnout (e.g., Zellars, Perrewé, & Hochwarter, 2000). Three of the most well researched personality dimensions regarding job stress are neuroticism, extraversion, and hardiness.

Neuroticism Neuroticism, or negative affect, is probably the most frequently examined personality characteristic in the job stress literature (Cooper, 2000). Individuals high in negative affectivity (NA) report pervasive feelings of anxiety, fear, or depression (Tellegen, 1982; Watson & Pennebaker, 1989). The link between high NA and greater levels of stress has been attributed to a variety of causes: the tendency of high NA individuals to enact more stressful situations (Depue & Monroe, 1986), cope less effectively (Bolger, 1990), generate more negative interpretations of ambiguous stimuli (Watson & Clark, 1984), or simply overreport stressors and strains because they selectively focus on negative aspects of situa-

tions (Brief, Butcher, George, Robinson, & Webster, 1988). Regardless of the underlying reasons, over time, workers higher in NA report greater levels of work-related stress. The role of negative affectivity in job stress research as substance or bias, and how researchers should measure or control for its effects, are the subjects of ongoing debate (Spector, Zapf, Chen, & Frese, 2000; Payne, 2000; Judge, Erez, & Thorsen, 2000).

Extraversion Individuals high in extraversion or, as some call it, positive affectivity (PA), exhibit a positive sense of well-being and also perceive stimuli, think, and behave in a manner that encourages positive emotions (George, 1992). Their inherent optimistic outlook likely provides high extraverts a stronger sense of well-being about themselves and others. Evidence suggests that individuals who have a strong sense of well-being are less likely to experience work exhaustion and perform better (Wright & Cropanzano, 1998, 2000). Further, the positive thinking and actions (George, 1992) taken by extraverts likely contribute to actually getting more done, thereby increasing one's actual personal accomplishments. In general, those who are more extraverted and have more optimistic outlooks are less likely to experience negative effects from a stressful work environment.

Hardiness Hardiness refers to the dispositional tendency to find meaning in stressful events or challenges (Kobasa, 1979; Kobasa, Maddi, & Kahn, 1982) and therefore exhibit fewer symptoms when under stress (Kobasa, 1979). Recent research (Britt, Adler, & Bartone, 2001) suggests that soldiers engaged in peacekeeping missions who are higher in hardiness were able to derive greater meaning in their work and subsequently derive benefits from a stressful experience. Future research is needed to examine how employers can help workers derive greater meaning from their work and thereby alleviate some of the strain experienced under stressful working conditions.

Looking at other individual differences, some researchers have examined self-beliefs in the stressor-strain relationship. In general, these studies suggest that positive self-perceptions can ameliorate the effects of stressors. For example, Jex and Bliese (1999) found that among army soldiers, self-efficacy (i.e., beliefs that one can successfully perform a specific task) affected the relationship between stressors and strain. Specifically, soldiers with strong self-efficacy reacted less negatively, in terms of psychological and physical strain, to long work hours and high work overload.

A common thread underlying both the individual difference and the environmental streams of stress literature is the notion that there is a mismatch of the individual to the demands of the situation. In the environmental approach, the conditions of the job (e.g., fast pace, high demands) are viewed as the culprit overwhelming the skills of the individual. In the personality approach, the culprit lies within the individual in that the individual doubts his or her capability to succeed in the current situation. Looking to the environment is a more objective approach, whereas examining personality characteristics or self-beliefs places importance on the individual's subjective perception of the situation. Both approaches result in defining a mismatch of the individual to the situation.

CONSEQUENCES OF JOB STRESS

The consequences of experienced job stress can have an impact on the organization as well as the employee. Although a comprehensive examination of the consequences of stress is beyond the scope of this article, I discuss several of the most commonly examined outcomes. Specifically, I discuss individual and organizational performance, job satisfaction, organizational withdrawal, and employee well-being. I conclude this section with a brief discussion about the assumed stressor-strain relationship.

Individual Performance

Nearly a century ago, Yerkes and Dodson (1908) proposed that excessive levels of stress were associated with decreased performance in an inverted U-shaped relationship. In this view, known as the Yerkes-Dodson Law, stress initially can arouse or motivate an individual, thus improving performance. As stress increases, an optimal point is reached and then performance begins to deteriorate, as arousal becomes too great. Unfortunately, few studies have been conducted outside the laboratory to test the inverted U-shaped relationship.

Several meta-analyses (e.g., Jackson & Schuler, 1985; Abramis, 1994; Tubre, Sifferman, & Collins, 1996) have examined the impact of role stressors (role ambiguity, role conflict) and performance. In summary, the evidence suggests the relationship between job stressors and performance is not very strong. However, Jex (1996) argues that conclusions are premature for several reasons. First, there is considerable error in measuring job performance. Many of the studies have been conducted in the laboratory and in field studies, and performance has almost always been assessed subjectively and correlated with reports of stress by the same respondents. Such percept-percept correlations are weak evidence. Contrast such studies with one using objective measures of stress and multiple measures of both objective and subjective performance. In the latter study, excessive demands were found to be associated with reduced performance among military cadets (Westman & Eden, 1992).

Second, there is considerable variation in the relationship between the specific stressor examined and performance. Finally, in some situations, even a small effect may have considerable implications for the individual, the client, and the organization. Consider, for example, the potential implications of even small errors occurring because a surgeon is working under a great deal of stress.

The relationship between job stress and performance is complex. In many cases, the relationship may be indirect (i.e., mediating factors), such that job stressors influence moods or cognitive processes which in turn affect performance. Alternatively, the relationship may be the result of an interaction of characteristics of the person and situation constraints.

Organization Performance

The vast majority of studies examining job stress and performance have focused on the individual level of performance. However, a few studies suggest that organizations with higher levels of stress may incur some performance decrements. Today's organizations are leaner than in the past, and often performance depends on teamwork. Some studies suggest that stressors lead to a reduction in cooperative behavior (Bliese & Halverson, 1996; Ostroff, 1992), thus impairing group performance. Hospitals in which employees reported higher levels of stress reported a greater number of malpractice claims (Jones, Barge, Steffy, Fay, Kunz, & Wuebker, 1988) compared to hospitals with lower stress levels. More recently, Ryan, Schmit, and Johnson (1996) reported that branches of a finance company reporting higher levels of stress had lower levels of customer satisfaction, more delinquent accounts, and a higher rate of turnover. Although it appears that stress levels may impact some dimensions of performance, the studies remain few in number. Clearly, more research is needed at the organization level.

Job Satisfaction, Absenteeism, and Withdrawal

It is widely accepted among researchers that increased levels of stress are associated with decreased job satisfaction and greater ab-
senteeism. Numerous studies have demonstrated a consistent link between role ambiguity and higher levels of job dissatisfaction, mental strain, and intentions to leave an organization (e.g., Beehr, 1976; Jackson, 1983; Schaubroeck, Cotton, & Jennings, 1989). Using these findings, researchers have turned to examining the intervening processes. For example, findings indicate that supervisors can influence the degree of role stress and uncertainty that their subordinates experience, which in turn influences levels of satisfaction and turnover intentions (O'Driscoll & Beehr, 1994). Individual differences also continue to be investigated. For example, while in general work overload is negatively associated with job satisfaction and positively associated with psychological strain, recent findings indicate that individuals with higher self-efficacy (a stronger belief in one's abilities to succeed) reacted less negatively in terms of psychological and physical strain to long work hours and work overload (Jex & Bliese, 1999). These individuals also reported higher job satisfaction.

Employee Well-Being

Stress is widely recognized as a daily problem that can threaten individual well-being. Workload has been associated with lower self-esteem and various physical and psychological problems (Glowinski & Cooper, 1986; Rydstedt, Johansson, & Evan, 1998). Relationships at work have also been examined as a potential source of stress. Mistrust of coworkers is related to low job satisfaction and poor psychological well-being (see Cooper & Cartwright, 1994). Workplace jealousy and envy have been blamed for extreme outcomes such as workplace violence and harassment (Vecchio, 1995). The impact of the home-work interface has also been examined. Managing the links between home and work is a large source of stress for many employees and the "spillover stress" has been associated with emotional exhaustion and job satisfaction

(Boles, Johnston, & Hair, 1997). In their review of stress research, Ganster and Schaubroeck (1991) failed to find a strong relationship between specific work experiences and physical or mental disorders. However, they conclude that the indirect evidence from occupational studies showing differences in health and mortality are not easily explained by other factors. Further, they argue that within-subject studies indicate a work stress affect arising from the causal effect of work experiences on physiological and emotional responses.

Clarifying the Stressor-Strain Relationship

Much of the early literature appears to assume that all work-related stressors generated consistent negative outcomes for the person or the organization. However, during the last decade, researchers have begun to suggest that the relationship between stress and work outcomes is less direct than previously assumed. For example, studies have failed to find a significant relationship between self-reported work stress and job search (Bretz, Boudreau, & Judge, 1994) and job satisfaction and intentions to quit (Leong, Furnham, & Cooper, 1996). Although private sector executives perceived more stress than civil servants, they reported fewer stress outcomes, such as job dissatisfaction and mental and physical health problems (Bogg & Cooper, 1995). Such findings have led to new inquiries into what causes stress to generate negative outcomes or fail to generate negative outcomes.

Self-reported stress associated with some stressors may result in negative outcomes whereas other stressors may result in positive outcomes such as a competitive edge or source of positive change (Marino, 1997; Merlman, 1997). Cavanaugh, Boswell, Roehling, and Boudreau (2000) recently examined the potential outcomes of different types of stressors, labeling some as "chal-lenge-related stressors" and others as "hindrance-related stressors." Such efforts are consistent with the managerial development literature which reports that executives, although recognizing some job demands to be pressure-laden and stressful, also derive rewarding experiences from their work (McCall, Lombardo, & Morrison, 1988). Researchers have only recently begun to examine the relationship between positive affect and stressful situations, and how positive affect influences coping processes (Folkman & Moskowitz, 2000).

WAYS OF COPING WITH JOB STRESS

It should be clear that there are numerous sources of job stress as well as some negative personal and organizational consequences. This next section examines ways organizations can help employees to cope with job stress as well as ways in which individuals can cope with stress. First, organizational programs aimed at stress reduction are discussed. Next, I discuss employee control, individual coping, and social support as means for employees to cope with stressors.

Organizational Efforts

Organizations have attempted to help their employees cope with job stress through stress management programs, job rotation, mandatory breaks and vacations, and a variety of wellness programs. Eliminating or reducing stressors that are intrinsic to the nature of the job include ergonomic solutions, task/workplace redesign, increased staffing, and role clarification. Organization-directed strategies have shown some measure of success in reducing stress levels (Cooper & Cartwright, 1994). A more recent approach to reducing job stress can be found in the growing number of organizations that have adopted family-supportive work programs. One of the most popular family-friendly organizational approaches is providing for flexible work hours.

Schedule Flexibility   Organizational research has demonstrated that organizational programs that provide employees with alternatives to the traditional workweek can be beneficial. Flexible work schedules have been found to reduce absenteeism (Dalton & Mesch, 1990) and increase productivity and job satisfaction (Baltes, Briggs, Huff, Wright, & Neuman, 1999). Further, Thomas and Ganster (1995) found schedule flexibility regarding work arrangements gave employees greater control over work and family matters, thereby helping employees manage the often-conflicting demands of work and family.

Interestingly, Kossek and Ozeki (1998) found that organizational policies initiated to help employees meet family responsibilities have not generally had the desired impact of reducing levels of strain. Clearly, additional research into the costs and benefits of family-supportive work policies is needed. Because it is doubtful that any formal program can help employees unless management supports it, one promising area of research that could increase the effectiveness of family-supportive policies is the organizational support for these policies.

Managerial Support   When organizations formally adopt family-supportive programs, some managers may not be supportive. Interestingly, many organizations have adopted family-friendly policies, but the implementation of these programs is determined on a case-by-case basis, giving discretion to the managers. Although many alternative work arrangements may result from employees negotiating individually with their managers on an as-need basis (Scandura & Lankau, 1997), not all managers may support these programs.

Only a few studies have examined the role of the supportive manager when adopting family-friendly work policies. Powell and Mainiero (1999) concluded that permission to have an alternative work arrangement is often based on the manager's previous personal experiences and beliefs. Thomas and Ganster (1995) found that perceptions of managerial support were linked to lower levels of work/family conflict and psychological and physiological strain. Finally, Carlson and Perrewé (1999) concluded that the quality of the relationship employees have with their supervisors, coworkers, and subordinates reduces the perceived stressors that lead to work/family conflict. Although research is still needed in this area, it does appear that management support for family-supportive programs is a prerequisite to program effectiveness.

Perceived Control

The stress literature discusses a variety of factors that impact the severity of negative consequences of stress. Two factors receiving a great deal of attention have been perceptions of control and the individual's ability to cope. Researchers have long recognized individuals' attempts to adapt to their environments. In a process he described as the General Adaptation Syndrome (GAS), Selye (1976) was among the first to posit that under stress, an individual senses alarm, resistance, and either flees or adapts to a situation. Fleeing the perceived source of stress likely occurs when the individual fails to perceive the ability to alter the situation. Alternatively, perceived control allows for an individual to respond to the environment; that is, assert oneself in such a way as to alter the conditions causing the strain.

In his decision latitude model, Karasek (1979) proposed that job demands and job control vary independently in the work environment. In his model, job demands are the psychological stressors (e.g., too much to do, conflicting demands). Job decision latitude has two components: the workers' authority to make decisions on the job and the variety of skills needed for the job. The central argument of the model is jobs that are simultaneously high in demands and low in latitude (i.e., low control) produce the greatest strain (Karasek & Theorell, 1990). Numerous researchers have examined the impact of a variety of demands and varying levels of control, and Karasek's model has been subjected to critical reviews. Consistent results have not always been reported (Spector, 1998). Nevertheless, two recent studies from epidemiological literature suggest that the role of demands and control warrant further investigation. For example, Marmot, Bosma, Hemingway, Brunner, and Stansfeld (1997) reported that civil servant workers at the lower grade levels (clerical and office support staff) reported significantly higher rates of coronary heart disease. After examining standard coronary risk factors, the researchers concluded that the psychosocial work environment was a significant factor in the health of workers. Theorell, Tsutsumi, Hallquist, and Reuterwall (1998) also reported that job demands and decreases in control significantly predicted myocardial infarctions. Consistent results were reported earlier by Fox, Dwyer, and Ganster (1993). Testing the demands-control model in a hospital setting, Fox and her colleagues found that the interaction of workload demands (both objective and subjective) and perceived control predicted physiological measures of strain (e.g., neuroendocrine arousal or salivary cortisol). Moreover, they found the interaction predicted carryover effects on blood pressure several hours after the workday had ended.

Some researchers have proposed that empirical studies failing to demonstrate the predicted interaction of high job demands and low job control have failed to correctly conceptualize the control dimension or include important individual characteristics. In their study of Dutch nurses, de Rijk, Le Blanc, Shaufeli, and DeJonge (1998) used a more focused measure of job control and two potential moderators: active coping and need for control. Their results indicated that active coping moderated the interaction between job demands and job control. Earlier, Ferris, Frink, Gilmore, and Kacmar (1994) found that it was an understanding of organizational politics that moderated the politics-strain relationship. In a recent review of the control literature, Terry and Jimmieson (1999) concluded that high levels of control were directly associated with a variety of positive outcomes, including decreased anxiety and depression (Carayon, 1993; Mullarkey, Jackson, Wall, Wilson, & Grey-Taylor, 1997), greater job satisfaction (Tetrick & LaRocco, 1987), and improved job performance (Greenberger, Strasser, Cummings, & Dunham, 1989). In the context of workplace violence, Schat and Kelloway (2000) reported that perceptions of control are associated with reduced fear and enhanced emotional well-being. From this brief review, it is apparent that a great deal of work continues to be done to investigate the measurement and impact of job control on stress-related outcomes and significant factors altering the control-strain relationship.

Individual Coping

Individuals differ as to their perceptions of and reactions to job stressors. Although I have already discussed individual personality, individuals also differ in the way they cope with job stress. First, individuals may differ in the way they perceive or appraise the stressful situation. Second, individuals may have specific skills, such as organizational political skill, that can reduce the negative impact of job stress.

Appraisal Lazarus and his colleagues (Lazarus, 1981, 1991; Lazarus & Folkman, 1984) have strongly influenced research efforts that examine the extent to which problems or hassles impact the feelings of individuals (i.e., experience anger, frustration, sadness). Instead of simply looking at environmental causes of stress, Lazarus and his colleagues suggest that strain results when a person feels unable to adequately cope with an identified threat. In other words, not every potential stressor becomes a source of strain for an individual. In the appraisal model, individuals assess whether events have implications for their well-being. Those deemed to be irrelevant have no bearing on well-being. Events that potentially affect well-being trigger a secondary appraisal in which individuals determine the adequacy of their coping resources. In numerous studies, styles of coping fall into one of two categories: emotion focused (sometimes referred to as avoidant coping) or problem focused, or instrumental coping. Emotion-coping efforts focus on improving the feelings experienced and problem-coping efforts focus on altering the source of the stress. For example, running five miles after work may make one feel better after a long day at the office (emotion focused). Making a priority list or asking for additional help (i.e., problem focused) may alter the source of the felt stress. There is some evidence that escapist coping efforts are associated with greater job burnout (Leiter, 1991).

Political Skill   Political skill can be viewed as an interpersonal style that combines social awareness with the ability to communicate well (Ferris, Perrewé, Anthony, & Gilmore, 2000). People who practice this skill behave in a disarmingly charming and engaging manner that inspires confidence, trust, sincerity, and genuineness. People who are high on political skill are at their best in interpersonal interactions and thrive in social situations where working with and through others is requisite to job and work unit success (Ferris, et al., 2000).

Perrewé and colleagues see the use of political skill as reducing stress for employees in two ways (Perrewé, Ferris, Frink, & Anthony, 2000). First, political skill is conceptualized as directly reducing employees' perceptions of organizational stressors.

Specifically, if employees possess political skill, they are less likely to perceive their environment as stressful. Research has found that concerns about self-presentation and managing impressions can lead to social anxiety with potential health risks. Employees high in political skill are more confident about their ability to control images, impressions, and interactions at work, thus they are less likely to perceive their situation as stressful. When employees do not perceive their organizational environment as stressful, they are less likely to experience psychological and physiological strain.

Second, political skill is argued to act as a buffer between perceived stressors and strain (Perrewé, et al., 2000). Even when employees perceive their environment as stressful, political skill can be used as a coping mechanism to reduce the negative effects of stressors on strain. The important role of coping with stress has been well documented, demonstrating among other things that the tendency to cope by dealing actively with the problem is associated with improved mental and sometimes physical health. Further, political skill can help employees feel more in control of their environment. Hence, political skill can be viewed as a coping mechanism that can (a) lessen the negative impact of stressors, and (b) serve as an antidote to work stressors.

Social Support

Social support is another stream of research that has examined how individuals cope with and adapt to challenges. Social relationships may increase an individual's confidence to face stressful situations or, alternatively, may provide the information one needs to solve a stressful problem. Evidence suggests that individuals with more social support experience less strain and greater well-being (e.g., Cohen & Wills, 1985). In retail environments, employees' perceptions of coworker involvement and supervisory support were associated with reduced job stress (Babin & Boles, 1996), and workers in high strain jobs accompanied by high social support reported lower health care costs than workers in low strain conditions (Manning, Jackson, & Fusilier, 1996). The authors of this latter study propose that some stress, if coupled with social support, may result in a healthy level of arousal. The researchers conclude that social support may be the key to the individual's interpretation of strains as "eustress" rather than "distress."

Recently, Vermeulen and Mustard (2000) found that in a large cross-section of job types, the combined effect of low social support and high job strain (low control and high demands) was associated with the greatest increase in distress. Nevertheless, the relationship between support and strain needs further clarification. The exact nature of the support-strain relationship (antecedent, mediator, or moderator) continues to be debated as well as the importance of the source and content of support. In a series of studies, Beehr and his colleagues have investigated the content of social support, identifying three types of affective communications among workers: nonwork-related, negative work-related, and positive work-related communications. Results indicate the content of social support expressed as conversations among coworkers appears to significantly influence the outcomes (e.g., Beehr, King, & King, 1990; Fenlason & Beehr, 1994). Sources of support (work, family) have also been shown to differentially affect job and family satisfaction (Parasuraman, Greenhaus, & Granrose, 1992).

The level of perceived social support has been linked to an individual's coping style. Individuals with supportive family networks tend to use more active, problem-focused coping strategies as compared to individuals with less social support who are more likely to engage in avoidant coping strategies (Billings & Moos, 1982; Holahan & Moos, 1987). In related research, investigators continue to examine the role of personality in the seeking or receiving of social support (e.g., Collins & DiPaula, 1997) and in choosing a coping style (e.g., Watson, David, & Suls, 1999). For example, in nonwork situations, extraversion has been linked to support receipt and perceptions of support (Lakey & Dickinson, 1994). Conversely, hostility has been linked to having few supportive relationships. Further work is needed to investigate how personality characteristics impact the receipt of support and the type of support used in the workplace.

I close this article with a brief discussion of two relatively new areas of job stress research that warrant further investigation: organizational justice and injustice and stress among entrepreneurs. Finally, because longitudinal studies of job stress remain rare but critical to our fuller understanding of job stress, I briefly describe two recent longitudinal studies in the hope that they will encourage others to continue such efforts.

NEW TOPICS AND LONGITUDINAL EFFORTS

Organizational Justice and Injustice

Early on, Adams and Freedman (1976) recognized that an individual's reactions to perceived inequity could include damaged self-esteem if the inequity is deemed to be personal or intentional. Lind and Tyler (1988) proposed that psychological distress arises from being denied a voice in decisions that affect oneself. A few recent studies have found relationships between injustice and relatively mild manifestations of discomfort (Gilliland, 1994; Koper, Van Knipperberg, Bouhuijs, Vermunt, & Wilke, 1993; Tyler, Degoey, & Smith, 1996), but very little work has been done that examines the links between organizational injustice and chronic work stress. In their review of the justice literature, Brockner and Wiesenfeld (1996) point out the researchers have examined a variety of outcomes arising from perceived injustices. Attitudinal outcomes include organizational commitment, satisfaction, and intentions to turnover. Behavioral outcomes include citizenship behavior and performance levels. Cropanzano, Weiss, Suckow, and Grandey (1999) point out that noticeably absent is consideration of emotional outcomes. The authors propose that more research is needed to examine the discrete emotional responses to perceived injustices. Outlining links between equity theory, justice theory, appraisal theory, and research in emotions, the authors offer some new insights into the potential links between perceived injustices and workplace stress. Using vignettes and lab studies, the researchers examined the impact of perceived fairness of outcomes and procedures on discrete emotions (anger, guilt, happiness, and pride). As expected, students reported the highest anger when the outcome was unfavorable and the procedures biased against them. Surprisingly, students reported high levels of pride when they earned a favorable outcome through an unfair process. The authors argue that past justice research has deemphasized the cognitive processes by which justice decisions are made and emotion theories have ignored judgments of ethicality. Clearly, as an initial study into the links between perceived justice and emotions, including those emotions typically accompanying a stressful experience (e.g., anger, frustration), the work of Cropanzano and his colleagues have opened up new avenues in stress research. If outcomes are more important than procedures in predicting levels of stress, what can organizations do to alleviate stress in times of limited allocation of resources?

In related research, subordinates whose supervisors exhibited more abusive behavior reported greater psychological distress, and those with less job mobility experienced the greatest levels of distress (Tepper, 2000). Seeking and obtaining a new job can be deemed an instrumental form of coping in the Lazarus model, and obviously employees with more job opportunities will perceive more means to alter their current situations (i.e., perceive greater control). Interactional justice reflects the interpersonal dimensions of fairness (Bies, 2000) such as being treated with respect, honesty, or sensitivity to one's personal needs. Tepper's results suggested that interactional justice is a better predictor of psychological distress than the more frequently studied procedural justice. In addition, Tepper proposes, interactional justice appears to play an important role in explaining how work-related experiences affect employees' lives away from work. In related research integrating stress and coping theory (Lazarus & Launier, 1978) with justice theory, Tepper (in press) recently reported that the relationships between procedural justice and psychological distress were stronger when distributive justice was lower.

Job Stress Among Entrepreneurs

Relative to nonowners, little research has examined the stress process among owners. This is somewhat surprising because studies have shown that owners and nonowners differ in working conditions (e.g., hours) and perceived control (Eden, 1975; Naughton, 1987), independence (Chay, 1993), and nonwork satisfaction (Jamal, 1997). Results comparing physical and mental health of owners and nonowners are mixed (e.g, Eden, 1975; Lewin-Epstein & Yuchtman-Yaar, 1991). Recently, Tetrick and her colleagues (Tetrick, Slack, DaSilva, & Sinclair, 2000) have continued to explore the work experiences of entrepreneurs. In a comparison of owners and nonowners, they reported that although owners reported less social support from work-related sources, they reported less exhaustion and greater job satisfaction and professional satisfaction than nonowners. Ownership and social support from work-related sources moderated the relationship between exhaustion and job satisfaction. Future research is needed to examine the means by which ownership and the resulting level of control can offset the negative effects of strain. If owners rely on less social support at work than nonowners (i.e., employees), what are other key factors in alleviating their strain? Such studies appear especially important given the number of small businesses starting up and failing in recent years.

Longitudinal Studies

Although theoretical models describe how the stressor-strain relationship unfolds over time (e.g., Frese & Zapf, 1988), there are still only few empirical longitudinal studies (Zapf, Dormann, & Frese, 1996). One exception is the ambitious study conducted by Garst, Frese, and Molenaar (2000). Using latent growth curve models, the researchers examined both stressors and strains in six waves over five years. Among their findings are that both short-term and long-term effects of stressors occur; there are meaningful differences in stressors for an individual detected across a five-year period; and for some stressors, the strain effects were quite high and specific.

Spector, Chen, and O'Connell (2000) have also recently reported the results of a longitudinal stress study. Previous research most often assumes job stressors in general lead to job strains in general. The researchers found that although workload was associated with frustration or anxiety, it failed to significantly predict job satisfaction or physical symptoms. Their results suggest that more attention needs to be given to how specific stressors are related to specific strains over longer time periods.

Clearly, the studies cited in this article indicate that researchers and organizations continue to be interested in job stress, both the causes and consequences, as well as factors that ameliorate its effects. Future researchers are likely to continue seeking clarification of the person-job fit and misfits that result in strain, turnover, or even workplace violence. ■

REFERENCES

Abramis, D. J. (1994). Work role ambiguity, job satisfaction, and job performance: Meta-analysis and review. *Psychological Reports, 75,* 1411–1433.

Adams, J. S., & Freedman, S. (1976). Equity theory revisited: Comments and annotated bibliography. In L. Berkowitz and E. Walster (Eds.), *Advances in Experimental Social Psychology* (Vol. 9, 43–90). New York: Academic Press.

Babin, B. J., & Boles, J. S. (1996). The effects of perceived coworker involvement and supervisor support on service provider role stress, performance and job satisfaction. *Journal of Retailing, 72,* 57–75.

Baltes, B. B., Briggs, T. E., Huff, J. W., Wright, J. A., & Neuman, G. A. (1999). Flexible and compressed workweek schedules: A meta-analysis of their effects on work-related criteria. *Journal of Applied Psychology, 84,* 496–513.

Beehr, T. A. (1976). Perceived situational moderators of the relationship between subjective role ambiguity and role strain. *Journal of Applied Psychology, 61,* 35–40.

Beehr, T. A., King, L. A., & King, D. W. (1990). Social support and occupational stress: Talking to supervisors. *Journal of Vocational Behavior, 36,* 61–81.

Bies, R. J. (2000). Interactional (in)justice: The sacred and the profane. In J. Greenberg and R. Cropanzano (Eds.), *Advances in Organizational Justice.* Lexington, MA: New Lexington Press.

Billings, A. G., & Moos, R. H. (1982). Work stress and the stress-buffering roles of work and family resources. *Journal of Occupational Behavior, 3,* 215–232.

Bliese, P. D., & Halverson, R. R. (1996). Individual and nomothetic models of job stress: An examination of work hours, cohesion, and well-being. *Journal of Applied Social Psychology, 26,* 1171–1189.

Bogg, J., & Cooper, C. (1995). Job satisfaction, mental health, and occupational stress among senior civil servants. *Human Relations, 48,* 324–341.

Boles, J. S., Johnston, M. W., & Hair, J. F., Jr. (1997). Role stress, work-family conflict and emotional exhaustion: Inter-relationships and effects on some work-related consequences. *Journal of Personal-Selling and Sales-Management, 17,* 17–28.

Bolger, N. (1990). Coping as a personality process: A prospective study. *Journal of Personality and Social Psychology, 59,* 525–537.

Bordwin, M. (1996). Overwork: The cause of your next workers' comp claim? *Management Review, 85,* 50–52.

Bretz, R. D., Boudreau, J. W., & Judge, T. A. (1994). Job search behavior of employed managers. *Personnel Psychology, 47,* 275–301.

Britt, T. W., Adler, A. B., & Bartone, P. T. (2001). Deriving benefits from stressful events: The role of engagement in meaningful work and hardiness. *Journal of Occupational Health Psychology, 6,* 53–63.

Brockner, J., & Wiesenfeld, B. M. (1996). An integrative framework for explaining reactions to decisions: Interactive effects of outcomes and procedures. *Psychological Bulletin, 120,* 189–208.

Buffardi, L. C., Smith, J. L., O'Brien, A. S., & Erdwins, C. J. (1999). The impact of dependent-care responsibility and gender on work attitudes. *Journal of Occupational Health Psychology, 4,* 356–367.

Carayon, P. (1993). A longitudinal test of Karasek's Job Strain Model among office workers. *Work and Stress, 7,* 299–314.

Carlson, D. S., & Perrewé, P. L. (1999). The role of social support in the stressor-strain relationship: An examination of work-family conflict. *Journal of Management, 25,* 513–540.

Cavanaugh, M. C., Boswell, W. R., Roehling, M. V., & Boudreau, J. W. (2000). An empirical examination of self-reported work stress among U.S. managers. *Journal of Applied Psychology, 85,* 65–74.

Chapman, N. J., Ingersoll-Dayton, B., & Neal, M. B. (1994). Balancing the multiple roles of work and caregiving for children, adults, and elders. In G. P. Keita and J. J. Hurrell, Jr. (Eds.), *Job Stress in a Changing Workforce: Investigating Gender, Diversity, and Family Issues* (283–300). Washington, DC: American Psychological Association.

Chay, Y. W. (1993). Social support, individual differences, and well-being: A study of small business entrepreneurs and employees. *Journal of Occupational and Organizational Psychology, 66,* 285–302.

Cohen, A. (1997). Facing pressure. *Sales and Marketing Management, 149,* 30–38.

Cohen, S., & Wills, T. A. (1985). Stress, social support, and the buffering hypothesis. *Psychological Bulletin, 98,* 310–357.

Collins, R. L., & DiPaula, A. (1997). Personality and the provision of support: Emotions felt and signaled. In G. R. Pierce, and B. Lakey (Eds.), *Sourcebook of Social Support and Personality* (429–443). New York: Plenum Press.

Cooper, C. L. (2000). Introduction: A discussion about the role of negative affectivity in job stress research. *Journal of Organizational Behavior, 21,* 77.

Cooper, C. L., & Cartwright, S. (1994). Healthy mind, healthy organizations—A proactive approach to occupational stress. *Human Relations, 47,* 455–471.

Cropanzano, R., Weiss, H. M., Suckow, K., & Grandey, A. A. (1999). Doing justice to workplace emotion. Paper presented at the 1999 meeting of the Society for Industrial and Organizational Psychology, Atlanta, GA.

Dalton, D. R., & Mesch, D. J. (1990). The impact of flexible scheduling on employee attendance and turnover. *Administrative Science Quarterly, 35,* 370–387.

Depue, R. A., & Monroe, S. M. (1986). Conceptualization and measurement of human disorder in life stress research: The problem of chronic disturbance. *Psychological Bulletin, 99,* 36–51.

de Rijk, A. E., Le Blanc, P. M., Shaufeli, W. B., & DeJonge, J. (1998). Active coping and need for control as moderators of the job demand-control model. *Journal of Occupational and Organizational Psychology, 71,* 1–18.

Eden, D. (1975). Organizational membership vs self-employment: Another blow to the American dream. *Organizational Behavior and Human Performance, 13,* 79–94.

Fenlason, K. J., & Beehr, T. A. (1994). Social support and occupational stress: Effects of talking to others. *Journal of Organizational Behavior, 15,* 157–175.

Ferris, G. R., Frink, D. D., Gilmore, D. C., & Kacmar, K. M. (1994). Understanding as an antidote for the dysfunctional consequences of organizational politics as a stressor. *Journal of Applied Social Psychology, 24,* 1204–1220.

Ferris, G. R., Perrewé, P. L., Anthony, W. P., & Gilmore, D. C. (2000). Political skill at work. *Organizational Dynamics, 28,* 25–37.

Folkman, S., & Moskowitz, J. T. (2000). Positive affect and the other side of coping. *American Psychologist, 55,* 647–654.

Fox, M. L., Dwyer, D. J., & Ganster, D. C. (1993). Effects of stressful job demands and control on physiological and attitudinal outcomes in a hospital setting. *Academy of Management Journal, 36,* 289–318.

Frese, M., & Zapf, D. (1988). Methodological issues in the study of work stress: Objective vs. subjective measurement of work stress and the question of longitudinal studies. In C. L. Cooper and R. Payne (Eds.), *Causes, Coping, and Consequences of Stress at Work* (375–410). Chichester, England: Wiley.

Frone, M. (2000). Work-family conflict and employee psychiatric disorders: The National Comorbidity Survey. *Journal of Applied Psychology, 85,* 888–895.

Frone, M. R., Russell, M., & Cooper, M. L. (1992). Antecedents and outcomes of work-family conflict: Testing a model of the work-family interface. *Journal of Applied Psychology, 77,* 65–75.

Frone, M. R., Yardley, J. K., & Markel, K. S. (1997). Developing and testing an integrative model of the work-family interface. *Journal of Vocational Behavior, 50,* 145–167.

Ganster, D. C., & Schaubroeck, J. (1991). Work stress and employee health. *Journal of Management, 17,* 235–271.

Garst, H., Frese, M., & Molenaar, P. C. (2000). The temporal factor of change in stressor-strain relationships: A growth curve model on a longitudinal study in East Germany. *Journal of Applied Psychology, 85,* 417–438.

George, J. M. (1992). Feeling good—doing good: A conceptual analysis of the mood at work-organizational spontaneity relationship. *Psychological Bulletin, 18,* 185–213.

Gilliland, S. W. (1994). Effects of procedural and distributive justice on reactions to a selection system. *Journal of Applied Psychology, 79,* 691–701.

Glowinski, S. P., & Cooper, C. L. (1986). Managers and professionals in business/industrial settings: The research evidence. *Journal of Organizational Behavior Management, 8,* 177–193.

Goodstein, J. (1994). Institutional pressures and strategic management responsiveness: Involvement in work-family issues. *Academy of Management Journal, 27,* 350–383.

Greenberger, D. B., Strasser, S., Cummings, L. L., & Dunham, R. B. (1989). The impact of personal control on performance and satisfaction. *Organizational Behavior and Human Decision Processes, 43,* 29–51.

Greenhaus, J. H., & Beutell, N. J. (1985). Sources of conflict between work and family roles. *Academy of Management Review, 10,* 76–88.

Holahan, C. J., & Moos, R. H. (1987). Personal and contextual determinants of coping strategies. *Journal of Personality and Social Psychology, 52,* 946–955.

HR Focus (1996, May 12). Speaking of stress. . . .

Jackson, S. E. (1983). Participation in decision making as a strategy for reducing job-related strain. *Journal of Applied Psychology, 68,* 3–193.

Jackson, S. E., & Schuler, R. S. (1985). A meta-analysis and conceptual critique on role ambiguity and role conflict in work settings. *Organizational Behavior and Human Decision Processes, 36,* 16–78.

Jackson, S. E, Turner, J. A., & Brief, A. P. (1987). Correlates of burnout among public service lawyers. *Journal of Occupational Behavior, 8,* 339–349.

Jamal, M. (1997, October). Job stress, satisfaction, and mental health: An empirical examination of self-employed and non-self-employed Canadians. *Journal of Small Business Management,* 48–57.

Jex, S. M. (1996). *Stress and job performance.* Thousand Oaks, CA: Sage Publications.

Jex, S. M., & Bliese, P. D. (1999). Efficacy beliefs as a moderator of the impact of work-related stressors: A multi-level study. *Journal of Applied Psychology, 84*, 349–361.

Jones, J. W., Barge, B. N., Steffy, B. D., Fay, L. M., Kunz, L. K., and Wuebker, L. J. (1998). Stress and medical malpractice: Organizational risk assessment and intervention. *Journal of Applied Psychology, 73*, 727–735.

Judge, T., Erez, A., & Thorsen, C. J. (2000). Why negative affectivity (and self-deception) should be included in job stress research: Bathing the baby with the bath water. *Journal of Organizational Behavior, 21*, 101–111.

Kahn, R. L., & Byosiere, P. (1992). Stress in organizations. In M. D. Dunnette and L. M. Hugh (Eds.), *Handbook of Industrial and Organizational Psychology* (2nd edition, Vol. 3, 571–650). Palo Alto, CA: Consulting Psychologists Press, Inc.

Kahn, R. L., Qoldw, S. M., Quinn, R. P., Snoek, J. D., & Rosenthal, R. A. (1964). *Organizational stress: Studies in role conflict and ambiguity.* New York: Wiley.

Karasek, R. (1979). Job demands, job decision latitude, and mental strain: Implications for job redesign. *Administrative Science Quarterly, 24*, 285–311.

Karasek, R., & Theorell, T. (1990). *Healthy work: Stress, productivity, and the reconstruction of working life.* New York: Basic Books.

King, P. M. (1995). The psychosocial work environment: Implications for workplace safety and health. *Professional Safety, 40*, 36–39.

Kinnunen, U., & Mauno, S. (1998). Antecedents and outcomes of work-family conflict among employed women and men in Finland. *Human Relations, 51*, 157–177.

Kirchmeyer, C., & Cohen, A. (1999). Different strategies for managing the work/non-work interface: A test for unique pathways to work outcomes. *Work and Stress, 13*, 59–73.

Kobasa, S. C. (1979). Stressful life events, personality, and health: An inquiry into hardiness. *Journal of Personality and Social Psychology, 37*, 1–11.

Kobasa, S. C., Maddi, S. R., & Kahn, S. (1982). Hardiness and health: A prospective study. *Journal of Personality and Social Psychology, 42*, 168–177.

Koper, G., Van Knipperberg, D., Bouhuijs, F., Vermunt, R., & Wilke, H. (1993). Procedural fairness and self-esteem. *European Journal of Social Psychology, 23*, 313–325.

Kossek, E., & Ozeki, C. (1998). Work-family conflict, policies, and the job-life satisfaction relationship: A review and directions for organizational behavior-human resources research. *Journal of Applied Psychology, 83*, 139–149.

Lakey, B., & Dickinson, L. G. (1994). Antecedents of perceived support: Is perceived family environment generalized to new social relationships? *Cognitive Therapy and Research. 18*, 39–53.

Lazarus, R. S. (1981). The stress and coping paradigm. In C. Eisdorfer, D. Cohen, A. Kleinman, and P. Maxim (Eds.), *Models for Clinical Psychology* (177–214). New York: Spectrum.

Lazarus, R. S. (1991). Cognition and motivation in emotion. *American Psychologist, 46*, 352–367.

Lazarus, R. S., & Folkman, S. (1984). *Stress, coping, and adaptation.* New York: Springer.

Lazarus, R. S., & Launier, R. (1978). Stress-related transactions between person and environment. *Perspectives in Interactional Psychology, 287*–327.

Leong, C. S., Furnham, A., & Cooper, C. L. (1996). The moderating effect of organizational commitment on the occupational stress outcome relationship. *Human Relations, 49*, 1345–1363.

Leiter, M. P. (1991). Coping patterns as predictors of burnout: The function of control and escapist coping patterns. *Journal of Organizational Behavior, 12*, 123–144.

Lewin-Epstein, N., & Yuchtman-Yaar, E. (1991). Health risks of self-employment. *Work and Occupations, 18*, 291–312.

Lind, E. A., & Tyler, T. R. (1988). *The social psychology of procedural justice.* New York: Plenum.

Manning, M. R., Jackson, C. N., & Fusilier, M. R. (1996). Occupational stress, social support, and the costs of health care. *Academy of Management Journal, 39*, 738–750.

Marino, S. (1997). The stress epidemic. *Industry Week, 246*, 14.

Marmot, M. G., Bosma, H., Hemingway, H., Brunner, E., & Stansfeld, S. (1997). Contribution of job control and other risk factors to social variations in coronary heart disease incidence. *The Lancet, 350,* 235–239.

Matteson, M. T., & Ivanevich, J. M. (1987). *Controlling work stress: Effective human resource and management strategies.* San Francisco, CA: Jossey-Bass Publishers.

McCall, M. W., Jr., Lombardo, M. M., & Morrison, A. M. (1988). *The lessons of experience: How successful executives develop on the job.* Lexington, MA: Lexington Books.

Merlman, D. (1997). Stressed. *Forbes, 159,* 20–21.

Mullarkey, S., Jackson, P. R., Wall, T. D., Wilson, J. R., & Grey-Taylor, S. M. (1997). The impact of technology characteristics and job control on worker mental health. *Journal of Organizational Behavior, 18,* 471–489.

Naughton, T. J. (1987). Quality of working life and the self-employed manager. *Journal of Small Business, 11,* 33–40.

Netemeyer, R. G., Boles, J. S., & McMurrian, R. (1996). Development and validation of work-family conflict and family-work conflict scales. *Journal of Applied Psychology, 81,* 400–410.

O'Driscoll, M. P., & Beehr, T. A. (1994). Supervisor behaviors, role stressors, and uncertainty as predictors of personal outcomes for subordinates. *Journal of Organizational Behavior, 15,* 141–155.

Ostroff, C. (1992). The relationship between satisfaction, attitudes, and job performance: An organizational level analysis. *Journal of Applied Psychology, 77,* 963–974.

Parasuraman, S., Greenhaus, J. H., & Granrose, C. S. (1992). Role stressors, social support and well-being among two-career couples. *Journal of Organizational Behavior, 13,* 339–356.

Payne, R. L. (2000). Comments on "Why negative affectivity should not be controlled in job stress research: Don't throw out the baby with the bath water." *Journal of Organizational Behavior, 21,* 97–99.

Perrewé, P. L., Ferris, G. R., Frink, D.D., & Anthony, W. P. (2000). Political skill: An antidote for workplace stressors. *Academy of Management Executive, 14,* 115–123.

Perrewé, P. L., Hochwarter, W. A., & Kiewitz, C. (1999). Value attainment: An explanation for the negative effects of work-family conflict on job and life satisfaction. *Journal of Occupational Health Psychology, 4,* 318–326.

Powell, G. N., & Mainiero, L. A. (1999). Managerial decision making regarding alternative work arrangements. *Journal of Occupational and Organizational Psychology, 72,* 41–56.

Ryan, A. M., Schmit, M. J., & Johnson, R. (1996). Attitudes and effectiveness: Examining relations at an organizational level. *Personnel Psychology, 49,* 853–882.

Rydstedt, L. W., Johansson, G., & Evan, G. W. (1998). A longitudinal study of workload, health and well-being among male and female urban bus drivers. *Journal of Occupational Organizational Psychology, 71,* 35–45.

Scandura, T. A., & Lankau, M. J. (1997). *The effects of flexible work hours on organizational commitment: A matched sample investigation of female and male executives.* Presented at the Academy of Management Meeting, Atlanta, GA.

Schat, A. C., & Kelloway, E. K. (2000). Effects of perceived control on the outcomes of workplace aggression and violence. *Journal of Occupational Health Psychology, 5,* 386–402.

Schaubroeck, J., Cotton, J. L., & Jennings, K. R. (1989). Antecedents and consequences of role stress: A covariance structure analysis. *Journal of Organizational Behavior, 10,* 35–58.

Selye, H. (1976). *The stress of life,* 2nd edition. New York: McGraw-Hill.

Spector, P. E. (1998). A control theory of the job stress process. In C. L. Cooper (Ed.), *Theories of Organizational Stress* (153–169). New York: Oxford University Press.

Spector, P. E., Chen, P. Y., & O'Connell, B. J. (2000). A longitudinal study of relations between job stressors and job strains while controlling for prior negative affectivity and strains. *Journal of Applied Psychology, 85,* 211–218.

Spector, P., Zapf, D., Chen, P. Y., & Frese, M. (2000). Why negative affectivity should not be controlled in job stress research: Don't throw out the babe with the bath water. *Journal of Organizational Behavior, 21,* 79–95.

Tellegen, A. (1982). *Brief manual for the differential personality questionnaire.* Unpublished manuscript, University of Minnesota, Minneapolis.

Tepper, B. J. (2000). Consequences of abusive supervision. *Academy of Management Journal, 43,* 179–190.

Tepper, B. J. (in press). Health consequences of organizational injustice: Tests of main and interactive effects. *Organizational Behavior and Human Decision Processes.*

Terry, D. J., & Jimmieson, N. L. (1999). Work control and employee well-being: A decade review. In C. L. Cooper and I. T. Roberston (Eds.), *International Review of Industrial and Organizational Psychology* (Vol.14, 95–148). Chichester, England: Wiley.

Tetrick, L., & LaRocco, L. M. (1987). Understanding, prediction, and control as moderators of the relationships between perceived stress, satisfaction, and psychological well-being. *Journal of Applied Psychology, 72,* 538–539.

Tetrick, L., Slack, K. L., DaSilva, N., & Sinclair, R. P. (2000). A comparison of the stress-strain process for business owners and nonowners: Differences in job demands, emotional exhaustion, satisfaction, and social support. *Journal of Occupational Health Psychology, 5,* 464–476.

Theorell, T., Tsutsumi, A., Hallquist, J., & Reuterwall, C. (1998). Decision latitude, job strain, and myocardial infarction: A study of working men in Stockholm. *American Journal of Public Health, 88,* 382–388.

Thomas, L., & Ganster, D. (1995). Impact of family-supportive work variables on work-family conflict and strain: A control perspective. *Journal of Applied Psychology, 80,* 6–15.

Tubre, T. C., Sifferman, J. J., & Collins, J. M. (1996). *Jackson and Schuler revisited: A meta-analytic review of the relationship between role stress and job performance.* Paper presented at the annual meeting of the Society for Industrial and Organizational Psychology, San Diego, CA.

Tyler, T. R., Degoey, P., & Smith, H. (1996). Understanding why the justice of group procedures matters: A test of the psychological dynamics of the group-value model. *Journal of Personality and Social Psychology, 70,* 913–931.

Vanden Heuvel, A. (1997). Absence because of family responsibilities: An examination of explanatory factors. *Journal of Family and Economic Issues, 18,* 273–297.

Vecchio, R. P. (1995). It's not easy being green: Jealousy and envy in the workplace. *Research in Personnel and Human Resources Management, 13,* 201–244.

Vermeulen, M., & Mustard, C. (2000). Gender differences in job strain, social support at work, and psychological distress. *Journal of Occupational Health Psychology, 5,* 428–440.

Watson, D., & Clark, L. A. (1984). Negative affectivity: The disposition to experience aversive emotional states. *Psychological Bulletin, 96,* 465–490.

Watson, D., David, J. P., & Suls, J. (1999). Personality, affectivity, and coping. In C. R. Snyder (Ed.), *Coping: The Psychology of What Works* (119–140). Oxford, England: Oxford University Press.

Watson, D., & Pennebaker, J. W. (1989). Health complaints, stress, and distress: Exploring the central role of negative affectivity. *Psychological Review, 96,* 234–254.

Westman, M., & Eden, D. (1992). Excessive role demand and subsequent performance. *Journal of Organizational Behavior, 13,* 519–529.

Wright, T. A., & Cropanzano, R. (1998). Emotional exhaustion as a predictor of job performance and voluntary turnover. *Journal of Applied Psychology, 83,* 486–493.

Wright, T. A., & Cropanzano, R. (2000). Psychological well-being and job satisfaction as predictors of job performance. *Journal of Occupational Health Psychology, 5,* 84–94.

Yerkes, R. M., & Dodson, J. D. (1908). The relation of strength of stimulus to rapidity of habit formation. *Journal of Comparative Neurological Psychology, 18,* 459–482.

Zapf, D., Dormann, C., & Frese, M. (1996). Longitudinal studies in organizational stress research: A review of the literature with reference to methodological issues. *Journal of Occupational Health Psychology, 1,* 145–169.

Zellars, K. L., & Perrewé, P. L. (in press). Affective personality and the content of emotional social support: Coping in organizations. *Journal of Applied Psychology.*

Zedeck, S. (1992). Introduction: Exploring the domain of work and family concerns. In S. Zedeck (Ed.), *Work, Families, and Organizations* (1–32). San Francisco: Jossey-Bass.

Zellars, K. L., Perrewé, P. L., & Hochwarter, W. A. (2000). Burnout in healthcare: The role of the five factors of personality. *Journal of Applied Social Psychology, 30,* 1570–1598.

AGGRESSION AND VIOLENCE IN THE WORKPLACE

Christian Kiewitz
Wayne A. Hochwarter

INTRODUCTION

Workplace violence is a specific form of aggression that involves physical assault on a victim at work or on duty. Violence of this type can take many forms, including homicide, rape, robbery, and simple and aggravated assault. According to experts, instances of aggression at work are on the rise and pose a substantial problem for human resources personnel and their organizations. Because workplace aggression is pervasive and will persist in the future, it is critical that human resources managers understand the magnitude of the problem and take the necessary actions to protect their employer, employees, and other involved parties.

In this article, we explore some of the many facets of workplace aggression while highlighting scope, nature, causes, outcomes, and measures for prevention. Our focus is on aggressive behavior that targets both current and former coworkers and employers. Our major contention is that human resources managers need to take preventive steps against aggression to intervene early to avoid escalations of workplace conflict. We begin this article by considering the costs of workplace aggression for organizations and their members.

WORKPLACE AGGRESSION: WHY WE SHOULD CARE

Notwithstanding the inherent ethical responsibilities, managing the issue of workplace aggression and violence is critical for improving performance and productivity (Allcorn, 1994), quality of work life (Fisher & Ashkanasy, 2000), and the mental health of organizational members (Glomb & Hulin, 1997). It is clear that the failure to understand these phenomena has the potential to be extremely costly for both employers and their employees (Chappell & Martino, 2000). Most seriously, workplace aggression may cause psychological damage (Barling, 1996; Fitness, 2000) and may even cost human lives. One example is a case involving an employee of the U.S. Department of Agriculture who got so angry in a meeting about work schedules that he shot and killed three coworkers (Caudron, 1998). Such incidents not only lead to a loss of organizational reputation (as is the case with the U.S. Postal Service; Bensimon, 1994) but also result in substantial financial losses. According to a study by liability experts, juries typically award $2.2 million for a workplace-related death and $1.8 million for a rape (Weisberg, 1994). A recent example is a 1999 ruling by a North Carolina jury awarding $7.9 million to the families of two workers killed at a tool distribution center in 1995. Both workers had become victims of a violence-prone employee who had been fired from his job. The jury found the center's management negligent in ignoring the killer's threats of retaliation and in failing to protect the two men (Jackson, 1999).

An often cited number in this context is based on a 1993 study by the National Safe Workplace Institute, which estimated the cost of all incidents of workplace violence for U.S. organizations at $4.2 billion annually (Bensimon, 1994). A 1994 study by the Workplace Violence Research Institute, however, showed that the annual loss due to workplace violence may be closer to $36 billion (Kaufer & Mattman, 1998). The authors of the latter study argued that the dramatic difference in estimated costs "proved that an incident of workplace violence has a far-reaching financial impact on an organization, when all the cost factors are considered" (p. 2). They repeated the study in 1995, again defining incidents of workplace violence as including threats, acts of harassment, aggravated assaults, rapes, or fatalities. This time, the estimated costs amounted to $35.4 billion.

From this discussion, it is evident that workplace aggression and violence are costly in psychological and financial terms for both employers and employees. These facts not only justify, but also obligate, human resources professionals to pay closer attention to the problem. We continue our discussion by clarifying (a) misconceptions about the issue and (b) the meaning of the terms workplace aggression and workplace violence.

MISCONCEPTIONS ABOUT WORKPLACE AGGRESSION

In all likelihood, it is a combination of distorted media portrayals, "common sense" assumptions, and a lack of scientific research that is responsible for the existence of many misconceptions about aggression and violence in the workplace (cf., Baron, Neuman, & Geddes, 1999; Bulatao & VandenBos, 1996). In the following section, we consider some of the more rampant ones.

Misconception #1: Workplace Violence Equals Homicide

A cursory look at recent newspaper stories seems to confirm the impression that workplace violence is about disgruntled employees going "postal." For example:

- A nursing assistant, who resented having been fired, killed two nursing home executives as they were leaving the building. The angry assistant fired multiple gunshots at them, including an "execution-style" shot to the head of one executive (Wessel, 2001).
- A software engineer accused of "methodically" executing seven coworkers was enraged that his employer planned to turn over some of his wages to the IRS (Morrison, 2000, p. 3A).
- A Xerox worker, who was obviously disgruntled about being laid off, shot and killed seven coworkers in Hawaii (Sterngold, 1999).
- A Connecticut lottery employee, angered at not receiving a promotion, shot and killed four supervisors and then himself (Felton, 1998).

Although such cases certainly make the headlines, they are not representative of the vast majority of violent acts in the workplace (Baron & Neuman, 1996; NIOSH, 1997). According to the U.S. Department of Justice, homicides accounted for "only" 1,000 of the more than two million violent victimizations that U.S. residents experienced each year while at work or on duty between 1992 and 1996 (Warchol, 1998). During the same time, U.S. employees suffered an estimated average of 1.5 million simple assaults (i.e., attack without a weapon resulting either in no, minor, or undetermined injury), 396,000 aggravated assaults, 84,000 robberies, and 51,000 rapes and other sexual assaults in the workplace each year. In other words, homicides constitute less than 1 percent (i.e., 0.05 percent) of all violent incidents at work. Yet the news media leave us with the impression that workplace aggression typically culminates "in bloodshed" (Costello, 2001, p. B1; also see Baron, et al., 1999; Bulatao & VandenBos, 1996).

Misconception #2: Most Perpetrators of Workplace Homicides Are Disgruntled Employees

Surpassed only by vehicle accidents, workplace homicide continues to be the second leading cause of job-related deaths in the United States (for data see Jenkins, 1996b; OSHA, 1999). However, the primary motive in the majority of cases (85 percent) was robbery. Disputes among coworkers and with customers and clients accounted for only about 10 percent of all job-related homicides (OSHA, 1999). In other words, strangers committing robbery are much more lethal than disgruntled employees assaulting coworkers.

Misconception #3: It Did/Does/Will Not Happen in My Organization

Aggression is pervasive in today's work environments (Fitness, 2000; Neuman & Baron, 1998; VandenBos & Bulatao, 1996). In fact, it has become a global problem that transcends the boundaries of work settings, occupational groups, and countries (Chappell & Martino, 2000). Even more noteworthy is the fact that experts recently noted an increase in the number and severity of confrontations among U.S. workers (cf., Costello, 2001; Newton, 2001).

Misconception #4: Workplace Aggression Is a Male Problem

Workplace violence involves women as both targets and perpetrators (Kirsta, 1994). For example, the violent nursing assistant featured in the first newspaper story is a woman (Wessel, 2001). Although women commit extremely violent acts at work less frequently than do men (Neuman & Baron, 1998), it is instructive to consider general research on female aggression (Baron & Richardson, 1994). For instance, although men are typically more aggressive than women in unprovoked situations, the genders are equally aggressive when provoked (Bettencourt & Miller, 1996). Moreover, whereas women are less likely to employ overt, direct aggression (e.g., physical assault), they are more likely to engage in covert, indirect aggression (e.g., telling lies behind the target's back; Baron & Richardson, 1994). These research findings suggest that female employees might engage in acts of workplace aggression more often than one would think. It is just that their acts tend to be less violent and overt and therefore less obvious to others. This notion is supported by recent findings from research on *workplace bullying* (i.e., harm-intending behavior directed at coworkers), which indicates that there might be no gender differences between men and women acting as bullies (Rayner & Hoel, 1997).

To date, management research has neglected the issue of female aggression at work. Sadly, it is likely that we will see more women engaging in workplace violence in the future (Kinney, 1995; Kirsta, 1994). This increase is related to the fact that women's aggression is greatly determined by their gender roles (Eagly & Steffen, 1986), and that recent changes in gender roles have made aggressive behavior more acceptable to women. At the same time, one must not forget that many women suffer from workplace violence. Homicide is actually the leading cause of death for women at work (Chappell & Martino, 2000; Jenkins, 1996a). Further, approximately 260,000 women annually become victims of workplace rapes, beatings, and other forms of violence at work. Despite these facts, "there's this perception that violence is a male problem," deplores Dr. Sharon Harlan from the Center for Women in Government (Associated Press, 1998).

Misconception #5: Workplace Aggression Is a Passing Problem

We have already mentioned that workplace aggression has become an omnipresent, global problem. Unfortunately, it appears that it will not lessen in the near future. As management researchers have found a link between workplace aggression and work-related stress (e.g., Barling, 1996; Chen & Spector, 1992), it is worrisome that current commentators on the state of the U.S. workplace noted a general increase in job stress (Hymowitz & Silverman, 2001). This situation might contribute at least in part to the current increase of less-than-violent conflicts at work, as exemplified in stress-related incidents of "desk rage" (Costello, 2001). Indeed, workplace consultants estimate that "low- to medium-caliber altercations have increased 'tenfold'" in recent times (Newton, 2001, p. 1D). It thus seems that workplace aggression is a problem that will stay with us in the near, if not distant, future.

Misconceptions: Summary

The previous discussion shows that workplace aggression and violence is about much more than disgruntled, male employees killing coworkers. Workplace aggression is a complex problem that takes on many forms, ranging from hostile remarks to physical assault. It requires the attention of human resources personnel because it is pervasive, persistent, and costly for both employees and organizations (Barling, 1996; Chappell & Martino, 2000; Vanden-Bos & Bulatao, 1996).

Given the vast scope and complexity of the topic, the following discussion focuses on workplace aggression that is targeted at both current and former coworkers and/or employers. From a HRM perspective, such a focus is appropriate because it is here where (a) human resources management can make the biggest difference in preventing and responding to workplace violence (cf., Neuman & Baron, 1998; O'Leary-Kelly, Griffin, & Glew, 1996), and (b) considerable, yet not readily apparent, liabilities arise for employers (e.g., Braverman, 1999).

DEFINING WORKPLACE AGGRESSION AND VIOLENCE

The above clarifications beg the question of how these misconceptions came about in the first place. Among others, much of the confusion stems from the fact that the precise meaning of the term *workplace violence* is often unclear and that neither the media nor researchers use the term in a consistent manner. For example, is the 1993 bombing of the New York World Trade Center by terrorists a case of workplace violence? Although some would answer the question "yes" (e.g., Kinney, 1995), most management researchers would deny it (e.g., Neuman & Baron, 1998; O'Leary-Kelly, et al., 1996). Being able to define workplace aggression and workplace violence will help human resources managers gain more clarity about the issue.

What do we mean when we say *workplace violence* or *workplace aggression?* As noted previously, researchers do not agree on any single definition, nor do they use the same terms when referring to aggression and violence in the workplace (Neuman & Baron, 1998). Instead, they may speak of *antisocial behavior in organizations* (Giacalone &

Greenberg, 1997), *deviant workplace behaviors* (Robinson & Bennett, 1995), *mobbing* or *bullying at work* (Zapf, 1999), *organization-motivated aggression* (O'Leary-Kelly, et al., 1996), and so on (discussion in Beugré, 1998). The existence of such an assortment of different labels reflects the fact that there is disagreement about how broadly one should define workplace aggression and violence (Bulatao & VandenBos, 1996). Some management researchers take a more narrow perspective by concentrating on just a few aspects of the issue. An example is work on organization-motivated aggression, which involves only aggression instigated by some factor within a given organization (O'Leary-Kelly, et al., 1996). Other scholars are more comprehensive in that they forgo references to the likely cause(s) of aggression and simply include all deviant behaviors that employees exhibit at work (e.g., Robinson & Bennett, 1995).

In returning to our question about the 1993 bombing of the World Trade Center, the reader may note that most management researchers do not account for acts of terrorism in their writings (exception in Van Fleet & Van Fleet, 1998). Instead, they—and we—focus on current and former employees as (potential) perpetrators. Accordingly, we define workplace violence as a severe form of workplace aggression, the latter denoting all "efforts by individuals to harm others with whom they work, or have worked, or the organizations in which they are presently, or were previously, employed" (Neuman & Baron, 1998, p. 395). The term workplace violence is then reserved for behaviors that involve physical assault (e.g., homicide, rape, robbery, aggravated and simple assault; Bulatao & VandenBos, 1996). However, in order to simplify our writing and because laypeople—as opposed to researchers (Baron & Richardson, 1994)—often use the terms aggression and violence interchangeably, we use the broader term *workplace aggression* to refer to both workplace aggression and workplace violence from this point forward.

FORMS OF WORKPLACE AGGRESSION

A news reporter recently noted that "workplace violence culminating in bloodshed . . . gets the most publicity, but far more common are the shouting matches and fights that don't make the evening news" (Costello, 2001, p. B1). Indeed, an interesting question for human resources managers concerns the forms of workplace aggression that they can expect to encounter on the job. Recent research on the frequency and nature of workplace aggression found that three forms prevail in the workplace, namely (1) expressions of hostility, (2) obstructionism, and (3) overt aggression (Baron, et al., 1999; Neuman & Baron, 1998). Accordingly, *expressions of hostility* primarily involve verbal or symbolic aggression such as spreading rumors, sexually harassing with words, acting in a condescending manner, making obscene gestures, giving dirty looks, leaving the work area when the target enters, and so on. *Obstructionism* refers to behavior that impedes a victim's ability to perform on the job or interferes with an organization's goals and objectives. Most of these behaviors involve passive aggression in the form of withholding some needed resources or actions. Examples are the failure to return e-mails or phone calls, causing others to delay action on important matters, missing or showing up late for meetings run by the victim, blocking the victim's work, or refusing to provide needed equipment. Finally, *overt aggression* involves violent behaviors (e.g., physical assault) and aggressive actions such as threats of physical violence, theft of personal or organizational property, sabotage, destruction, and so on.

In accordance with the data presented above, recent research suggests that both obstructionism and expressions of hostility are widespread forms of aggression in the workplace and are both more frequent than acts of overt aggression (Baron, et al., 1999; Cortina, Magley, Williams, & Langhout, 2001). The results of one study also showed that participants rated expressions of hostility as occurring more frequently than instances of obstructionism (Baron, et al., 1999). This is surprising because obstructionism is a form of passive-aggressive behavior that enables perpetrators to minimize the danger to themselves (especially if the victim has authority over the perpetrator; Neuman & Baron, 1998). Indeed, the covert nature of obstructionism makes it difficult for human resources personnel to track such behaviors. Yet it is important to address this issue because, although expressions of hostility and obstructionism might not cause physical harm to employees, such behaviors constitute extreme work stressors that have the potential to lead to more extreme acts of aggression (Allcorn, 1994; Neuman & Baron, 1998; Zapf, 1999). Moreover, both experiencing and witnessing workplace aggression take a toll on employees and are likely to impede their functioning and ultimately that of the organization (Barling, 1996). Consequently, human resources personnel should pay attention to even minor incidents of workplace aggression to safeguard against loss of resources. However, preventing such behavior from occurring in the first place seems more desirable than having to cope with its possible escalations (Andersson & Pearson, 1999; Goldstein, 1999). Therefore, we discuss the process and causes of workplace aggression in the next section.

WORKPLACE AGGRESSION IS A PROCESS INVOLVING MANY CAUSES

Workplace aggression often involves a process that develops over time, and in which the aggressive act itself is only the cul-

mination of a series of problems, conflicts, and failures (Baron & Neuman, 1996; Fein, Vossekuil, & Holden, 1995; Goldstein, 1999; Zillmann, 1994). An example of such a process is the research on the spiraling effect of incivility in the workplace, which demonstrates just how easily minor conflicts can turn into workplace aggression (Andersson & Pearson, 1999). Workplace incivility involves low-intensity deviant behaviors that violate workplace norms for mutual respect, such as being rude or discourteous. An incremental exchange of such behaviors can build up to a situation in which perceived wrongdoing and subsequent aggression escalate into a spiral of grim conflict. In other words, aggressive behaviors that are less intense in nature become an initial step in an upward conflict spiral that culminates in the use of severe aggression: "One person mocks another; the second responds with an obscene insult. The first shoves; the second hits. And the conflict escalates" (Andersson & Pearson, 1999, p. 458).

The previous depiction shows why it is imperative for human resources personnel to intervene as early as possible in workplace conflicts (cf., Goldstein, 1999). Early interventions may be particularly critical for the prevention of severe acts of workplace violence, as they may prevent individuals from becoming too highly agitated (e.g., being extremely angry). This point is important because highly agitated individuals are posited to be less receptive to rational thoughts and dialogue, and are less likely to consider the consequences of their actions (Zillmann, 1988, 1994). Indeed, data compiled by the Bureau of Labor Statistics suggests that anger plays a significant role in many cases of homicides (cf., Kinney, 1995). Moreover, thoughts formed under extreme anger may play a decisive role in those severe incidents of workplace violence where individuals aggressed a long time after the anger-evoking event occurred (cf., Bryant & Zillmann, 1979). Specifically, research "has shown that intensely felt anger may instigate retaliatory intentions, and that these intentions may be executed 'in cold blood' long after recovery from acute anger" (Zillmann, 1994, p. 56).

Another reason why early conflict intervention is noteworthy rests with the understanding that experiencing or witnessing unsanctioned incivility or aggression may undermine norms of civil behavior in organizations (Andersson & Pearson, 1999). If aggression at work goes unpunished employees may gain the impression that such behavior is acceptable, which in turn may result in more aggression. Social learning theory (Bandura, 1973, 1986) explains this process in that individuals who obtain positive outcomes from their aggressive acts are more likely (i.e., they learn) to use aggression in the future. Moreover, others may imitate (model) the perpetrator's aggressive behavior if they perceive it to be successful (Bandura, 1986; O'Leary-Kelly, et al., 1996).

We now shift our attention from the process of workplace aggression toward specific causes and discuss various factors related to aggression at work.

POTENTIAL CAUSES OF WORKPLACE AGGRESSION

Extrapolating from management research and the human aggression literature, it is safe to conclude that there is no singular cause of workplace aggression (cf., Baron & Richardson, 1994; Martinko & Zellars, 1998). Instead, workplace aggression and violence are multifaceted phenomena that emerge from a complex interplay among various factors, such as characteristics of the perpetrator(s), victim(s), situation, organization, and even the societal environment (Aquino, Grover, Bradfield, & Allen, 1999; Beugré, 1998; Braverman, 1999; Neuman & Baron, 1998). Unfortunately, the sheer number of risk factors and their possible interactions make the prediction of workplace

aggression excruciatingly difficult (Chappell & Martino, 2000).

These circumstances pose a considerable challenge for HR professionals who want to tackle the issue of workplace aggression. Where does one start? One strategy is to structure the problem by conceiving of workplace aggression as the outcome of an interaction, more precisely, an interaction among factors at different levels. As such, workplace aggression typically involves (1) an aggressing individual or group, and (2) a situational condition that (a) triggers the aggression, and (b) occurs in a setting that facilitates, permits, or at least does not stop the aggression from transpiring (Neuman & Baron, 1998; Beugré, 1998; Fein, et al., 1995; Zapf, 1999). By examining which factors may play a role at each level and their possible interactions, HR managers will gain a more comprehensive understanding of workplace aggression issues (cf., Beugré, 1998). We next discuss some of the factors that may be of importance for many organizations.

Situational Factors

Situational factors that make workplace aggression more likely to occur typically involve stressful conditions in both the physical and psychological environment (Baron, 1994; Mack, Shannon, Quick, & Quick, 1998; Neuman & Baron, 1998). For example, adverse conditions in the physical environment such as heat, noise, poor air quality, and crowding have been shown to negatively influence people's attitudes and behaviors by triggering aggressive thoughts and feelings (Anderson, Bushman, & Groom, 1997; Beugré, 1998). Moreover, stressful changes in the work environment such as layoffs, downsizing, reengineering, restructuring, and the increased diversity of the workforce may result in heightened tensions and interpersonal conflicts (Baron & Neuman, 1996; Bensimon, 1994; Chappell &

Martino, 2000; Neuman & Baron, 1998). Such changes tend to be very taxing on employees' resources, which in turn makes the occurrence of aggression at work more likely because employees have less resources to cope with other stressors (cf., Hobfoll, 1989). Good HRM practices have the capability of making a significant difference by helping to properly manage stressful transitions and by working toward the reduction of general and specific work stressors (Boye & Jones, 1997; Braverman, 1999).

Further conditions that might facilitate workplace aggression pertain to an organization's climate and culture, especially those that "reward" aggression. One example are organizations with a strong oppositional culture that reinforces aggressive employee behavior by rewarding conflict and negativism (Cooke & Lafferty, 1989; Cooke & Szumal, 1993). Because an organization's culture communicates normative beliefs and behavioral expectations, such oppositional cultures encourage employees to gain status by taking a confrontational and critical stance toward others (Cooke & Szumal, 1993).

Another example is the creation of a hostile work environment, which results from a work culture or climate that is punitive toward people of a different gender (DeNisi & Griffin, 2001). This is not only problematic in view of potential lawsuits but may also lead to a consistent decline in victims' job satisfaction and psychological health. Moreover, hostile work environments foster recurring aggression because an organization's tolerance of sexually harassing behaviors is linked to the recurrence of both indirect and direct sexual harassment (Glomb, Richman, Hulin, Drasgow, Schneider, & Fitzgerald, 1997). In a similar vein, there is evidence that a work group's stance toward aggression may facilitate subsequent aggressive behavior. A recent study with the telling title "Monkey see, monkey do" found that antisocial behavior of work groups fosters antisocial behavior of individuals (Robinson & O'Leary-Kelly, 1998). Specifically, the group's aggressive behaviors serve as role models for individual members, which in turn makes it more likely that they will also behave aggressively (Bandura, 1973). The pressure of work groups on an individual's behavior in this regard is often considerable (cf., Barker, 1993), as groups may express dissatisfaction with coworkers that engage in less antisocial behavior than other group members (Robinson & O'Leary-Kelly, 1998).

HR managers should be aware of the fact that organizational cultures and climates, and their respective norms, values, and role models, play a significant role in the deterrence or facilitation of workplace aggression (Neuman & Baron, 1998; O'Leary-Kelly, et al., 1996; Pearson, 1998; Robinson & O'Leary-Kelly, 1998). One effective way to reduce aggressive employee behavior is to modify the organizational climate, which involves changing employees' shared perceptions of their organizational environment (Boye & Jones, 1997; Neuman & Baron, 1998). Best results are obtained when organizational climate modifications address employees' perceptions and motivations, instead of simply attempting to decrease opportunities to engage in aggressive behavior (Boye & Jones, 1997). Some of the suggestions made by researchers to this effect include setting examples through leadership in honesty and integrity, reducing job stress, enriching employees' jobs, providing fair compensation, adopting and communicating a policy regarding workplace aggression, consistently punishing aggressive behavior, and treating employees in a fair manner and with trust, respect, and dignity (review in Boye & Jones, 1997).

The last recommendation brings us to the issue of organizational justice, which is concerned with employee perceptions of fairness at work (Greenberg, 1990b). Importantly, the perceived fairness of outcomes, procedures, and social interactions has been shown to have a strong influence on how employees react to, think, and feel about work-related issues (Greenberg, 1990b), and whether they will engage in workplace aggression (Baron, et al., 1999; Greenberg & Alge, 1998). Perceptions of unfairness not only reduce employees' efforts to go beyond the call of duty (Moorman, 1991), but also result in a wide scope of negative and aggressive behaviors ranging from theft (Greenberg, 1990a) to retaliatory behaviors (Skarlicki & Folger, 1997). Fairness and respect for employees should therefore be a guiding principle in implementing organizational change and prevention programs targeting workplace aggression (Kinney, 1995; Neuman & Baron, 1998).

In addition, HR managers might want to pay attention to how an organization has implemented and handles key HR functions that deal with the allocation of scarce resources. In many organizations, key HR functions such as staffing, evaluation, and rewards are influenced by organizational politics and impression management tactics (Ferris & Judge, 1991; Ferris & King, 1996). If employees perceive that key HR functions are handled in an unfair manner, it is more likely that they will react with aggressive acts (Folger & Cropanzano, 1998). Similarly, the likelihood of future aggression at work increases if an employee's aggressive behavior (e.g., delaying somebody's work to make oneself look better) is rewarded by the organization (e.g., pay raise).

Individual Factors

Several personality characteristics increase the likelihood that an employee will engage in workplace aggression (e.g., Beugré, 1998; Chappell & Martino, 2000; Neuman & Baron, 1998). One group of risk factors pertains to the employee's past experiences and involves such aspects as a person's history of violence, substance abuse, and mental health problems (Chappell & Martino, 2000). For example, individuals who grew up in families that employed aggression to resolve conflicts are more likely to use aggressive behavior to the same end in their adult lives, and thus at work (cf., Dodge, Bates, & Pettit, 1990; Huesmann, Eron, Lefkowitz, & Walder, 1984). It is important that HR managers pay attention to an employee's biography because one of the best predictors for future behavior is a person's past behavior, and doing so will help to avoid instances of negligent hiring, retention, or supervision. For example, in accord with the Occupational Safety and Health Act of 1970 (OSHA), HR managers may find it fruitful to demonstrate reasonable diligence in ensuring that future employees do not pose a danger to others in the workplace, so as to safeguard against negligent hiring (Braverman, 1999; Chappell & Martino, 2000).

Another group of risk factors is related to personality characteristics, such as exhibiting a hostile attribution bias, Type-A behavior, and high negative affectivity. *Negative affectivity,* along with positive affectivity, represents one of the two major dimensions of emotional experience (Watson & Tellegen, 1985). Individuals high on negative affectivity are more likely to experience discomfort at all times and across situations, even in the absence of overt stress, as they dwell on the negative side of themselves and the world (Watson & Clark, 1984). *Hostile attribution bias* refers to an individual's tendency to perceive hostile intent in others' actions, even when such intent is lacking (Dodge & Coie, 1987). Unsurprisingly, employees with a high hostile attribution bias rarely give others the benefit of the doubt (Folger & Baron, 1996). *Type-A behavior* is a behavioral pattern found in "those individuals who are engaged in a relatively chronic struggle to obtain an unlimited number of poorly defined things from their environment in the shortest period of time, and, if necessary, against the opposing efforts of other things or persons in their same environment" (Friedman & Rosenman, 1971, p. 302). At work, Type-A individuals are often known for their excessive drive and job involvement, impatience, and hostility (Friedman, 1992).

One can easily imagine how these characteristics increase the likelihood of someone becoming aggressive in a given situation. For example, individuals with a high hostile attribution bias have been found to readily respond to interpersonal challenges with the arousal of negative affects such as anger (Suarez, Kuhn, Schanberg, Williams, & Zimmermann, 1998). Employees with such a bias are thus more prone to misinterpret even a harmless question from a colleague as a threat and respond aggressively (cf., Dill, Anderson, Anderson, & Deuser, 1997). Similarly, research shows that the more pronounced the Type-A behavioral pattern is in a person, the higher the frequency of engaging in acts of workplace aggression and being the victim of such acts (Baron, et al., 1999).

Despite the importance of these personality characteristics, it is important to reiterate that aggressive, or any other, behavior always involves both individual and situational aspects (Barling, 1996; Baron & Richardson, 1994). Hence, there are certain work situations that enhance the potential for aggression in individuals with combative predispositions. For example, a person with a high hostile attribution bias may react to instances of organizational unfairness more aggressively because he or she perceives malice in others' actions (Beugré, 1998). In a similar vein, "the combination of negative work conditions and the Type-A behavior pattern may be especially deadly where workplace aggression is concerned" (Baron, et al., 1999, p. 293).

Given all the individual and situational factors that may lead to workplace aggression, one can not help but wonder why aggression at work (especially severe forms) is actually not more commonplace. After all, many employees may possess, at least in part,

the characteristics we described, and those employees may encounter unfair, hostile, and provoking situations at work every day. Yet, why is it that most Americans do not aggress under such circumstances? The answer has to do with the fact that our social behavior is regulated by self-control processes (Bandura, 1986), which give individuals the capacity to prevent themselves from responding in a certain way (Baumeister & Heatherton, 1996). For example, our self-control enables us to refrain from lashing out at someone who has provoked us. In turn, a majority of "aggression occurs when people fail to exert control over their feelings and responses" (Baumeister & Boden, 1998, p. 128).

If we accept the self-control argument, then what is it that pushes employees "over the edge?" One important part of the answer is work stress, because it depletes individuals' resources for coping with other stressors and thus makes them more vulnerable for responding to taxing circumstances with aggression (for details see Baumeister & Boden, 1998). It is noteworthy that all the factors discussed are potential stressors that might raise employees' stress levels, and thus increase the potential for workplace aggression (Berkowitz, 1998; Chen & Spector, 1992; Mack, et al., 1998). Indeed, workplace consultants think that heightened levels of work stress are responsible for the recent increase in workplace aggression (e.g., Albrecht, 1997; Braverman, 1999; Kinney, 1995). These sentiments are echoed in the HR trade press and the news media (Costello, 2001; Hymowitz & Silverman, 2001). For example, a writer for *Workforce* magazine concluded from interviews with HR professionals that "workplace grumbling rises" and that "firms were experiencing increased hostility" (Flynn, 1998, p. 27). Likewise, a recent survey indicated that "10 percent of Americans say they work in an atmosphere in which physical violence has occurred because of stress" (Newton, 2001, p. 1D). To this effect, HR personnel would make an important contribution in striving for a reduction of general and specific stressors in the workplace (Boye & Jones, 1997; Braverman, 1999). This fact brings us to our next discussion concerning measures to prevent workplace aggression.

PREVENTION

Human resources professionals have at their disposal a variety of means which, if employed properly, can serve to reduce the likelihood that violent behavior will surface in their organization. Some more useful strategies are outlined next (for further information see Braverman, 1999; Chappell & Martino, 2000; Neuman & Baron, 1998; Nicoletti & Spooner, 1996; VandenBos & Bulatao, 1996).

Policies and Procedures

Similar to statements regarding sexual harassment, organizations need to develop formal policies that establish a lack of tolerance for aggression at work (Paetzold, 1998). In addition to defining workplace aggression and violence, the policy should also address reporting channels and sanctions against those who take part in these acts at work. This policy should be applied uniformly for all instances of workplace aggression. Sample policies are featured in Braverman (1999), VandenBos and Bulatao (1996), and on the Internet site of the Occupational Safety and Health Administration (www. osha.gov). A list of published guidelines regarding workplace aggression can be found in Chappell & Martino (2000).

Screening and Selection

Organizations should conduct thorough background checks to ensure that problem employees are not hired (Braverman, 1999; Kinney, 1995; Neuman & Baron, 1998). The evidence is clear that those who are prone to violence at work are often repeat offenders (cf., Baumeister & Boden, 1998). Although

privacy laws may make the collection of this form of data problematic (Paetzold, 1998), the consequences of not doing so greatly outweigh the initial effort needed to ensure that the organization is not staffed with employees who are likely to repeat past offenses (Kinney, 1995). In addition to background checks, the organization may find it useful to employ psychological tests that may identify problematic individuals (cf., Braverman, 1999). HR professionals are strongly advised to conduct these and other inquiries in accordance with relevant laws, such as the Americans with Disabilities Act (ADA). From a legal standpoint, workplace aggression is a "minefield" (Kinney, 1995, p. 199), where erroneous actions may result in costly litigation (Paetzold, 1998). Soliciting counsel from legal experts is thus advisable. However, hiring an individual who has the capacity to adversely affect the organizational landscape is never a good idea, even in a tight labor market.

Training

While all employees will benefit from training efforts, supervisors especially need to be trained in all areas that deal directly with workplace aggression (Chappell & Martino, 2000; Neuman & Baron, 1998; Paetzold, 1998). For example, managers need to be able to identify potentially violent individuals and situations. Moreover, managers need to be trained to diffuse situations that arise while at work before irritations turn into violence. It is when individuals feel that management is untrustworthy and there are few mechanisms for airing grievances that aggression has the potential to materialize (e.g., Greenberg & Alge, 1998). To this effect, supervisors should strive to develop a climate of open communication and mutual trust. Finally, managers need to be given the authority to discipline those who act aggressively at work. Again, it is important to treat employees with respect and dignity, even when disciplinary actions have to be taken.

Often, meetings or hearings are scheduled for offenders to discuss certain situations for which they may have been responsible. Although all individuals should have their "day in court," sometimes removing the perpetrator from the situation is the best option. However, HR professionals should proceed with caution when terminating or laying off employees (Kinney, 1995). Fairness should be paramount, as *"no one ever took revenge simply for being fired.* Employees who become threatening always talk about *the way they were made to feel* in the process of losing their job" (emphasis in original text; Braverman, 1999, p. 130).

Work Stress and Employee Well-Being

The relationship between work stress and aggression has been well documented (e.g., Mack, et al., 1998). Hence, it is imperative that as many stressors be removed from the immediate work environment as possible (Braverman, 1999). In addition to minimizing stress at work, organizations will be well-served to provide employees the tools to control as many work stressors as possible. For example, something as simple as giving employees more autonomy may help reduce work ambiguity and overload, and hence limit much of the agitation that comes from immediate job demands. Furthermore, organizations should furnish employees with ample resources to cope with unavoidable work stress, for example, by implementing specific employee assistance programs (EAPs).

In a similar vein, organizations need to take all employee complaints seriously. A concern not deemed critical by the supervisor (i.e., "my office is too cool") may be extremely important to the employee. Damage to the employee-organization relationship can take two forms if management does not deal with concerns in a timely and effective manner. First, the problem will persist (i.e., "it's still too cold in here"). Second, the employee may perceive that the organization does not have concern for his or her well-being (i.e., "they don't even care enough to turn down the air conditioning"). Either case may serve as an agitator for violent behavior.

Organizational Justice

Finally, promoting fairness would likely neutralize much of the anger at work (Allcorn, 1994). Injustice has been posited to have a strong, direct relationship with aggressive behavior in past research (Greenberg & Alge, 1998). When individuals see that processes (e.g., a grievance hearing) or outcomes (e.g., a promotion or raise) are not based on a norm of equity that is performance-related, they may find it in their best interest to "tip the scales" in their behalf. These tactics may range from relatively innocuous strategies such as impression management to more pestilent forms such as theft, sabotage, or violence (e.g., Skarlicki & Folger, 1997).

CONCLUSION

We end this article by reiterating that workplace aggression is a serious problem that HR professionals cannot afford to ignore. The complexity of the topic is challenging and precludes resorting to "quick fixes" or "program of the month" approaches. Instead, HR professionals need to develop long-term strategies that target workplace aggression and implement them in a fair yet stringent and thorough manner. To this effect, we hope that the reader finds this article a helpful resource. ∎

REFERENCES

Albrecht, S. (1997). *Fear and violence on the job. Prevention solutions for the dangerous workplace.* Durham, NC: Carolina Academic Press.

Allcorn, S. (1994). *Anger in the workplace: Understanding the causes of aggression and violence.* Westport, CT: Quorum Books.

Anderson, C. A., Bushman, B. J., & Groom, R. W. (1997). Hot years and serious and deadly assault: Empirical tests of the heat hypothesis. *Journal of Personality and Social Psychology, 73,* 1213–1223.

Andersson, L. M., & Pearson, C. M. (1999). Tit for tat? The spiraling effect of incivility in the workplace. *Academy of Management Review, 24,* 452–471.

Aquino, K., Grover, S. L., Bradfield, M., & Allen, D. G. (1999). The effects of negative affectivity, hierarchical status, and self-determination on workplace victimization. *Academy of Management Journal, 42,* 260–272.

Associated Press. (1998, July 25). Women don't escape workplace violence, study says. *USA Today* Available online at www.usatoday.com [accessed October 16, 1998].

Bandura, A. (1973). *Aggression: A social learning analysis.* Upper Saddle River, NJ: Prentice Hall.

Bandura, A. (1983). Psychological mechanisms of aggression. In R. G. Geen and E. I. Donnerstein (Eds.), *Aggression: Empirical and Theoretical Reviews* (Vol. 1, 1–40). New York: Academic Press.

Bandura, A. (1986). *Social foundations of thought and action: A social cognitive theory.* Upper Saddle River, NJ: Prentice Hall.

Barker, J. R. (1993). Tightening the iron cage: Concertive control in self-managing teams. *Administrative Science Quarterly, 38,* 408–437.

Barling, J. (1996). The prediction, experience, and consequences of workplace violence. In G. R. VandenBos and E. Q. Bulatao (Eds.), *Violence on the Job. Identifying Risks and Developing Solutions* (29–49). Washington, DC: American Psychological Association.

Baron, R. A. (1994). The physical environment of work settings: Effects on task performance, interpersonal relations, and job satisfaction. In B. M. Staw and L. L. Cummings (Eds.), *Research in Organizational Behavior* (Vol. 16, 1–46). Greenwich, CT: JAI Press.

Baron, R. A., & Neuman, J. H. (1996). Workplace violence and workplace aggression: Evidence on their relative frequency and potential causes. *Aggressive Behavior, 22,* 161–173.

Baron, R. A., Neuman, J. H., & Geddes, D. (1999). Social and personal determinants of workplace aggression: Evidence for the impact of perceived injustice and the Type A behavior pattern. *Aggressive Behavior, 25,* 281–296.

Baron, R. A., & Richardson, D. R. (1994). *Human aggression,* 2nd edition. New York: Plenum.

Baumeister, R. F., & Boden, J. M. (1998). Aggression and the self: High self-esteem, low self-control, and ego threat. In R. G. Geen and E. Donnerstein (Eds.), *Human Aggression: Theories, Research, and Implications for Social Policy* (111–137). San Diego, CA: Academic Press.

Baumeister, R. F., & Heatherton, T. F. (1996). Self-regulation failure: An overview. *Psychological Inquiry, 7,* 1–15.

Bensimon, H. F. (1994, January). Violence in the workplace. *Training and Development Journal, 27*–32.

Berkowitz, L. (1998). Affective aggression: The role of stress, pain, and negative affect. In R. G. Geen and E. Donnerstein (Eds.), *Human Aggression: Theories, Research, and Implications for Social Policy* (49–72). San Diego, CA: Academic Press.

Bettencourt, B. A., & Miller, N. (1996). Gender differences in aggression as a function of provocation: A meta-analysis. *Psychological Bulletin, 119,* 422–447.

Beugré, C. D. (1998). Understanding organizational insider-perpetrated workplace aggression: An integrative model. In P. A. Bamberger and W. J. Sonnenstuhl (Eds.), *Research in the Sociology of Organizations, Vol. 15: Deviance in and of Organizations* (163–196). Stamford, CT: JAI Press.

Boye, M. W., & Jones, J. W. (1997). Organizational culture and employee counterproductivity. In R. A. Giacalone and J. Greenberg (Eds.), *Antisocial Behavior in Organizations.* Thousand Oaks, CA: Sage.

Braverman, M. (1999). *Preventing workplace violence. A guide for employers and practitioners.* Thousand Oaks, CA: Sage.

Bryant, J., & Zillmann, D. (1979). Effect of intensification of annoyance through unrelated residual excitation on substantially delayed hostile behavior. *Journal of Experimental Social Psychology, 15,* 470–480.

Bulatao, E. Q., & VandenBos, G. R. (1996). Workplace violence: Its scope and the issues. In G. R.

VandenBos and E. Q. Bulatao (Eds.), *Violence on the Job. Identifying Risks and Developing Solutions* (1–23). Washington, DC: American Psychological Association.

Caudron, S. (1998, August). Target HR. *Workforce.* 44–52.

Chappell, D., & Martino, V. D. (2000). *Violence at work,* 2nd edition. Geneva, Switzerland: International Labour Office.

Chen, P. Y., & Spector, P. E. (1992). Relationships of work stressors with aggression, withdrawal, theft and substance use: An exploratory study. *Journal of Occupational and Organizational Psychology, 65,* 177–184.

Cooke, R. A., & Lafferty, J. C. (1989). *Level V: Organizational Culture Inventory.* Plymouth, MI: Human Synergistics.

Cooke, R. A., & Szumal, J. L. (1993). Measuring normative beliefs and shared behavioral expectations in organizations: The reliability and validity of the Organizational Culture Inventory. *Psychological Reports, 72,* 1299–1330.

Cortina, L. M., Magley, V. J., Williams, J. H., & Langhout, R. D. (2001). Incivility in the workplace: Incidence and impact. *Journal of Occupational Health Psychology, 6,* 64–80.

Costello, D. (2001, January 16). Incidents of "desk rage" disrupt America's offices. *The Wall Street Journal,* B1, B4.

DeNisi, A. S., & Griffin, R. W. (2001). *Human resource management.* Boston: Houghton Mifflin.

Dill, K. E., Anderson, C. A., Anderson, K. B., & Deuser, W. E. (1997). Effects of aggressive personality on social expectations and social perceptions. *Journal of Research in Personality, 31,* 272–292.

Dodge, K. A., Bates, J. E., & Pettit, G. S. (1990). Mechanisms in the cycle of violence. *Science, 250,* 1678–1683.

Dodge, K. A., & Coie, J. D. (1987). Social information-processing factors in reactive and proactive aggression in children's peer groups. *Journal of Personality and Social Psychology, 53,* 1146–1158.

Eagly, A. H., & Steffen, V. J. (1986). Gender and aggressive behavior: A meta-analytic review of the social psychological literature. *Psychological Bulletin, 100,* 309–330.

Fein, R. A., Vossekuil, B., & Holden, G. A. (1995). *Threat assessment: An approach to prevent targeted violence* (Research in Action, NCJ 155000). Washington, DC: National Institute of Justice (U.S. Department of Justice, Office of Justice Programs).

Felton, B. (1998, March 15). Dealing with anger at work. *The Tuscaloosa News,* 1E, 4E.

Ferris, G. R., & Judge, T. A. (1991). Personnel/human resource management: A political influence perspective. *Journal of Management, 17,* 447–488.

Ferris, G. R., & King, T. R. (1996). Politics in human resources decisions: A walk on the dark side. *Organizational Dynamics, 20,* 59–71.

Fisher, C. D., & Ashkanasy, N. M. (2000). The emerging role of emotions in work life: An introduction. *Journal of Organizational Behavior, 21,* 123–129.

Fitness, J. (2000). Anger in the workplace: An emotion script approach to anger episodes between workers and their superiors, coworkers and subordinates. *Journal of Organizational Behavior, 21,* 147–162.

Flynn, G. (1998, September). Why employees are so angry. *Workforce,* 26–30, 32.

Folger, R., & Baron, R. A. (1996). Violence and hostility at work: A model of reactions to perceived injustice. In G. R. VandenBos and E. Q. Bulatao (Eds.), *Violence on the Job. Identifying Risks and Developing Solutions* (51–85). Washington, DC: American Psychological Association.

Folger, R., & Cropanzano, R. (1998). *Organizational justice and human resource management.* Thousand Oaks, CA: Sage.

Friedman, H. S. (Ed.). (1992). *Hostility, coping, and health.* Washington, DC: American Psychological Association.

Friedman, M., & Rosenman, R. H. (1971). Type A behavior pattern: Its association with coronary heart disease. *Annual Clinical Research, 3,* 300–312.

Giacalone, R. A., & Greenberg, J. (1997). *Antisocial behavior in organizations.* Thousand Oaks, CA: Sage.

Glomb, T. M., & Hulin, C. L. (1997). Anger and gender effects in observed supervisor-subordinate dyadic interactions. *Organizational*

Behavior and Human Decision Processes, 72, 281–307.

Glomb, T. M., Richman, W. L., Hulin, C. L., Drasgow, F., Schneider, K. T., & Fitzgerald, L. F. (1997). Ambient sexual harassment: An integrated model of antecedents and consequences. *Organizational Behavior and Human Decision Processes, 71,* 309–328.

Goldstein, A. P. (1999). *Low-level aggression: First steps on the ladder to violence.* Champaign, IL: Research Press.

Greenberg, J. (1990a). Employee theft as a reaction to underpayment inequity: The hidden cost of pay cuts. *Journal of Applied Psychology, 75* (5), 561–568.

Greenberg, J. (1990b). Organizational justice: Yesterday, today, and tomorrow. *Journal of Management, 16,* 399–432.

Greenberg, J., & Alge, B. J. (1998). Aggressive reactions to workplace injustice. In R. W. Griffin, A. M. O'Leary-Kelly, and J. M. Collins (Eds.), *Dysfunctional Behavior in Organizations: Part A. Violent and Deviant Behavior* (83–117). Stamford, CT: JAI Press.

Hobfoll, S. E. (1989). Conservation of resources: A new attempt at conceptualizing stress. *American Psychologist, 44,* 513–524.

Huesmann, L. R., Eron, L. D., Lefkowitz, M. M., & Walder, L. O. (1984). Stability of aggression over time and generations. *Developmental Psychology, 20,* 1120–1134.

Hymowitz, C., & Silverman, R. E. (2001, January 16). Can workplace stress get worse? *The Wall Street Journal,* B1, B4.

Jackson, M. (1999, August 2). Companies wake up to violence in workplace. *The Tuscaloosa News,* 9A.

Jenkins, E. L. (1996a). *Violence in the workplace. Risk factors and prevention strategies* (National Institute for Occupational Safety and Health (NIOSH), Publication No. 96–100). Washington, DC: U.S. Government Printing Office.

Jenkins, E. L. (1996b). Workplace homicide: Industries and occupations at high risk. *Occupational Medicine: State of the Art Reviews, 11,* 219–225.

Kaufer, S., & Mattman, J. W. (1998, April 3). The Cost of Workplace Violence to American Businesses. *Workplace Violence Research Institute*

[Internet document (Adobe Acrobat)]. Available online at www.workviolence.com/articles/articles.htm [accessed November 3, 1999].

Kinney, J. A. (1995). *Violence at work: How to make your company safer for employees & customers.* Upper Saddle River, NJ: Prentice Hall.

Kirsta, A. (1994). *Deadlier than the male.* London: HarperCollins.

Mack, D. A., Shannon, C., Quick, J. D., & Quick, J. C. (1998). Stress and the preventive management of workplace violence. In R. W. Griffin, A. M. O'Leary-Kelly, and J. M. Collins (Eds.), *Dysfunctional Behavior in Organizations: Part A. Violent and Deviant Behavior* (119–141). Stamford, CT: JAI Press.

Martinko, M. J., & Zellars, K. L. (1998). Toward a theory of workplace violence and aggression: A cognitive appraisal perspective. In R. W. Griffin, A. M. O'Leary-Kelly, and J. M. Collins (Eds.), *Dysfunctional Behavior in Organizations: Part A. Violent and Deviant Behavior* (1–42). Stamford, CT: JAI Press.

Moorman, R. H. (1991). Relationship between organizational justice and organizational citizenship behaviors: Do fairness perceptions influence employee citizenship? *Journal of Applied Psychology, 76,* 845–855.

Morrison, B. (2000, December 28). Office massacre called "methodical." *USA Today,* 3A.

Neuman, J. H., & Baron, R. A. (1998). Workplace violence and workplace aggression: Evidence concerning specific forms, potential causes, and preferred targets. *Journal of Management, 24,* 391–419.

Newton, B. D. (2001, February 4). Work altercations on the rise. *Tuscaloosa News,* 1D, 4D.

Nicoletti, J., & Spooner, K. (1996). Violence in the workplace: Responses and intervention strategies. In G. R. VandenBos and E. Q. Bulatao (Eds.), *Violence on the Job. Identifying Risks and Developing Solutions* (267–282). Washington, DC: American Psychological Association.

NIOSH. (1997, August 12). NIOSH Fact Sheet: Violence in the workplace (Document #705002). *National Institute for Occupational Safety and Health.* Available online at www.cdc.gov/niosh/violfs.html [accessed April 15, 2000].

O'Leary-Kelly, A. M., Griffin, R. W., & Glew, D. J. (1996). Organization-motivated aggression: A research framework. *Academy of Management Review, 21,* 225–253.

OSHA. (1999, August 18). OSHA Priorities—Workplace Violence. *Occupational Safety and Health Administration.* Available online at www.osha.gov/oshinfo/priorities/violence.html [accessed January 21, 2000].

Paetzold, R. L. (1998). Workplace violence and employer liability. In R. W. Griffin, A. M. O'Leary-Kelly, and J. M. Collins (Eds.), *Dysfunctional Behavior in Organizations: Part A. Violent and Deviant Behavior* (143–164). Stamford, CT: JAI Press.

Pearson, C. M. (1998). Organizations as targets and triggers of aggression and violence: Framing rational explanations for dramatic organizational deviance. In P. A. Bamberger and W. J. Sonnenstuhl (Eds.), *Research in the Sociology of Organizations, Vol. 15: Deviance in and of Organizations* (197–223). Stamford, CT: JAI Press.

Rayner, C., & Hoel, H. (1997). A summary review of literature relating to workplace bullying. *Journal of Community and Applied Social Psychology, 7,* 181–191.

Robinson, S. L., & Bennett, R. J. (1995). A typology of deviant workplace behaviors: A multidimensional scaling study. *Academy of Management Journal, 38,* 555–572.

Robinson, S. L., & O'Leary-Kelly, A. M. (1998). Monkey see, monkey do: The influence of work groups on the antisocial behavior of employees. *Academy of Management Journal, 41,* 658–672.

Skarlicki, D. P., & Folger, R. (1997). Retaliation in the workplace: The roles of distributive, procedural, and interactional justice. *Journal of Applied Psychology, 82,* 434–443.

Sterngold, J. (1999, November 3rd). Man opens fire in Hawaii office, killing 7. *New York Times,* A1, A14.

Suarez, E. C., Kuhn, C. M., Schanberg, S. M., Williams, R. B., Jr., & Zimmermann, E. A. (1998). Neuroendocrine, cardiovascular, and emotional responses of hostile men: The role of interpersonal challenge. *Psychosomatic Medicine, 60,* 78–88.

Van Fleet, E. W., & Van Fleet, D. D. (1998). Terrorism and the workplace: Concepts and recommendations. In R. W. Griffin, A. M. O'Leary-Kelly, and J. M. Collins (Eds.), *Dysfunctional Behavior in Organizations: Part A. Violent and Deviant Behavior* (165–201). Stamford, CT: JAI Press.

VandenBos, G. R., & Bulatao, E. Q. (Eds.). (1996). *Violence on the job. Identifying risks and developing solutions.* Washington, DC: American Psychological Association.

Warchol, G. (1998, July 28). National Crime Victimization Survey. Workplace violence, 1992–96 (Report No. NCJ-168634). *Bureau of Justice Statistics* (revised version). Available online at www.ojp.usdoj.gov/bjs/abstract/wv96.htm [accessed January 21, 2001].

Watson, D., & Clark, L. A. (1984). Negative affectivity: The disposition to experience aversive emotional states. *Psychological Bulletin, 96,* 465–490.

Watson, D., & Tellegen, A. (1985). Toward a consensual structure of mood. *Psychological Bulletin, 98,* 219–235.

Weisberg, D. (1994, March). Preparing for the unthinkable. *Management Review,* 58–61.

Wessel, K. (2001, February 9). Harris guilty of murder. *The Courier-Journal.* Available online at www.courier-journal.com/localnews/2001/02/09/ky_harris.html#top.

Zapf, D. (1999). Organisational, work group related and personal causes of mobbing/bullying at work. *International Journal of Manpower, 20* (1/2), 70–85.

Zillmann, D. (1988). Cognition-excitation interdependencies in aggressive behavior. *Aggressive Behavior, 14,* 51–64.

Zillmann, D. (1994). Cognition-excitation interdependencies in the escalation of anger and angry aggression. In M. Potegal and J. F. Knutson (Eds.), *The Dynamics of Aggression: Biological and Social Processes in Dyads and Groups* (45–71). Hillsdale, NJ: Erlbaum.

SEXUAL HARASSMENT IN THE WORKPLACE: WHAT WE KNOW AND WHAT WE WISH WE KNEW

Rebecca A. Thacker

The issue of sexual harassment in the workplace is one that presents many challenges. As a source of stress, sexual harassment must be near the top of the list—for managers making good faith efforts to comply with anti-discrimination laws, for those individuals wrongly accused, and for those who suffer legitimately from unwanted sexual attention. In *Meritor Savings Bank, FSB v. Vinson* (1986), the Supreme Court provided a definition of sexual harassment that is dual in nature: (1) the conditioning of benefits (e.g., promotions, pay raises) upon the receipt of sexual favors, or quid pro quo harassment, and (2) behaviors that create an offensive or hostile working environment (e.g., touching, multiple comments, and sexual jokes). The Supreme Court further admonished organizations to define and communicate sexual harassment prevention policies on sexual harassment that include an internal complaint procedure.

While we acknowledge that organizations are legally required to take proactive steps to prevent sexual harassment in the workplace, we have also come to understand that sexual harassment as an organizational phenomenon requires a broader definition, an acknowledgement of the complexity of the underlying dynamics surrounding it. Indeed, although organizations have designed complaint procedures and have informed employees of their zero tolerance policy, the problem has not disappeared. Sources have variously reported that approximately 50 percent of women have reported experiencing sexual harassment (cf., Fitzgerald &

Shullman, 1993; United States Merit Systems Protection Board [USMSPB], 1982, 1988). The Society for Human Resource Management reports from survey data an increase in the number of sexual harassment complaints every year between 1995 and 1998 (reported in Bland & Stalcup, 2001). And in a widely publicized case, Mitsubishi agreed to a payout of $34 million to 350 women assembly-line workers, who had allegedly been subjected to numerous incidents of sexual harassment by coworkers (Wilmsen, 1998).

In recent years, research has broadened our understanding of the multidimensional nature of sexual harassment as a workplace phenomenon. Early research concentrated on target response. Antecedents, outcomes, and consequences have also received attention. However, the largest gap in our understanding is in the area of the accused harassers, although recent scholarly discussion (O'Leary-Kelly, Paetzold, & Griffin, 2000) has begun to delve into this largely unresearched component of sexual harassment. Organizations are now better equipped to address sexual harassment in the workplace, and thus reduce the stress that it creates.

THE PROCESS OF SEXUAL HARASSMENT

Descriptive studies have indicated gender-based differences in sexual harassment complaints. The majority of accused harassers are male, and the majority of the targets of sexual harassment are female (Tangri, Burt, & Johnson, 1982; Terpstra & Cook, 1985; USMSPB, 1982, 1988). Males who exhibit sexually harassing behaviors are more likely to be perceived as sexual harassers than are women who exhibit the same behaviors (Gutek, Morasch, & Cohen, 1983; Reilly, Carpenter, Dull, & Bartlett, 1982). Also, females are more likely than males to view the same set of social-sexual behaviors as sexually harassing (Thacker & Gohmann, 1993). Consequently, sexual harassment is often characterized as a male-initiated phenomenon. Although cases of female harassers and same-gender harassers exist, sexual harassment targets are typically female.

Sexual harassment often carries with it an element of force and unwanted attention. Furthermore, sexual harassment frequently involves coercion (Thacker & Ferris, 1991); that is, the harasser often has the potential to inflict damage upon the target. Sexual harassment involves coercive behavior if the following conditions are met: (1) The harasser has the potential to inflict damage upon the target; (2) a threat to do damage to the target is implied, and the target recognizes the existence of the threat; and (3) the threat is enforced if the target does not comply.

A harasser may have coercive potential because of the harasser's control over promotions, raises, working conditions, or performance evaluations. The threat is either implied or explicitly stated (e.g., receipt of sexual favors in return for a raise, implying that the raise will not be given without the sexual favor). The harasser has not only the legitimate power to carry out the threat but also the power to follow through if the target refuses to comply. When the harasser is unwilling to challenge the harasser's power for fear of the consequences, the harasser's behavior is reinforced. If the target fails to file a complaint against the harasser, then the mere existence of an internal complaint procedure is useless as a deterrent.

By the same token, if the complaint procedure fails to address the underlying systemic problems that create the perception among accused harassers that sexually harassing behaviors are acceptable, the complaint procedure is less than optimal in its effect. This is particularly so when the harasser may have no formal authority over the target, but the target is dependent upon the harasser in some way. For example, the harasser may have a specific body of knowledge, expertise, critical information, or necessary support for the target to do his or her job effectively. Although a formal reporting relationship does not exist, the target is nonetheless dependent upon the harasser. In effect, those with expertise or critical information can threaten to withhold information important to effective job performance if noncompliance or complaints about the harasser's behavior result. Again, fear of the consequences may prevent the target from reporting the harasser's behavior. And the consequences are sometimes severe—job loss, psychological distress, and unpleasant working conditions, all major stressors (Terpstra & Cook, 1985; USMSPB, 1982, 1988).

From a variety of perspectives, then, the presence of organizational complaint policies may do little to extinguish sexual harassment and the stress that results. Evidence suggests that ignoring sexual harassment or complying with it can have the effect of reinforcing the harassment (Silverman, 1976). This is apparently what happened at the Mitsubishi Motor plant in Illinois, where employees reportedly complained frequently about being subjected to various sexually harassing behaviors (e.g., touching, lewd remarks, sexual jokes). Eventually one of the employees quit her job and the EEOC filed a complaint against Mitsubishi (Novak, 1998). Managers who pay lip service to sexual harassment prevention by publishing a complaint procedure, but who consciously or subtly reinforce a culture that promotes sexual harassment, are sending positive reinforcement to those who might want to engage in sexually harassing behaviors. One of the important elements in sexual harassment prevention, then, is an understanding of targets' responses to sexual harassment.

TARGET RESPONSES TO SEXUAL HARASSMENT

We have a great deal of information about target response to sexual harassment. Two conceptual models describing the behavior of sexual harassment targets have been suggested: (1) the confrontational response and (2) the passive, acquiescent response (Thacker, 1992a). Confrontation is based on reactance theory, which suggests that individuals become motivationally aroused when behavioral freedom is threatened (Brehm, 1966, 1972). Passive and acquiescent behavior is based on learned helplessness (Seligman, 1974). Learned helplessness rests on the notion that, regardless of a person's actions or behaviors, unpleasant outcomes are unavoidable.

Typical organizational policies concerning sexual harassment may neglect to provide an effective relief mechanism for targets responding with passive, acquiescent behaviors. On the other hand, typical sexual harassment policies do provide a mechanism for targets who respond with confrontational behaviors. In a way, organizations may in fact contribute to workplace stress for targets who are reluctant or incapable of responding with confrontational behaviors, as they fail to acknowledge the needs of the more passive, acquiescent target in their complaint procedure.

The Confrontation Model

The confrontation model is based on reactance theory. Reactance is a "motivational state directed toward the reestablishment of the free behaviors which have been eliminated or threatened with elimination" (Brehm, 1966, p. 9). Sexual harassment is an infringement upon personal freedom because it limits individuals' freedom to act as they desire. In some cases individuals must comply with the sexual harassment to avoid a negative occurrence such as termination, demotion, distasteful remarks, and so forth.

In effect, the issue is one of personal control. Attempts to regain lost control are forms of reactance. A variety of methods exist by which individuals can attempt to restore lost control; one of these is direct confrontation of the source of the problem (Brehm, 1966). For example, a target of sexual harassment may exhibit reactance behavior by actively (i.e., verbally) refusing to comply with the harasser. Similarly, another example of reactance behavior is threatening to complain about the sexual harasser's behavior to a supervisor or another person of higher authority.

To experience reactance, individuals must feel an increased amount of self-direction, perceiving that they can do what they want in directing their own actions and behaviors (Brehm, 1966). Refusing to comply with a sexual harasser's demands and threatening to complain about the harasser's behavior are indications that the target wants to control his or her working environment by removing obstacles that hamper ability to do so. Those who respond in this fashion and are extremely stressed about the sexual attention are likely to invoke the organization's complaint procedures, or file a lawsuit (Knapp, Faley, Ekeberg, & Dubois, 1997). For these individuals, the organization can help to alleviate their stress by communicating the complaint procedure available.

The Passive, Acquiescent Model

For those individuals who respond passively to sexual harassment, mere communication of the organization's complaint procedure will be ineffective as a stress relief mechanism. Individuals experiencing feelings of learned helplessness perceive that, despite their efforts, unpleasant or dissatisfying outcomes cannot be averted (Overmier & Seligman, 1967; Seligman, 1974). When the harasser has authority over the target or when the harasser is at a higher organizational level, the target may experience feelings of helplessness.

Particularly when the target of the unwanted sexual attention complains to various members of management, and complaints are ignored, the organization unwittingly contributes to the likelihood of stress in the workplace. Targets recognize that others' attempts to get organizational relief are disregarded (for a recent example of this, see a write-up of the Mitsubishi sexual harassment case by Novak in the *Chicago Sun-Times,* 1998). Knapp, et al. (1997) describe this response as "self-focused" and suggest further that individuals with this type of response are unlikely to request support for remedying their problem. Evidence from a massive study in the federal government also indicated that targets displaying passive, acquiescent behaviors are not likely to report or complain about incidents of harassment to appropriate authorities (USMSPB, 1982).

For organizations, this is indeed a problem. Helplessness behavior, over time, tends to reinforce individuals' beliefs that they are helpless, thus reducing perceived control over their environment and increasing their stress. Ultimately, inability to affect the behavior of harassers serves to create the perception that targets cannot control other job-related outcomes. Needless to say, this can lead to increased levels of stress and detrimental consequences for both the individual and the organization.

Moreover, even the most enlightened organizational policy will not deal effectively with passive targets. In the worst case scenario, the passive target decides to quit the job and go to an attorney or an outside agency, such as the EEOC. Outside attention to its sexual harassment problem eventually cost Mitsubishi $34 million. Nonetheless, even the most enlightened organizational policy will not deal effectively with passive targets.

Steps could be taken to help targets become comfortable with displaying confrontational behaviors and using the organizational complaint procedure. For example, training that includes role playing of passive, then confrontational, responses might go far to increase the comfort level with the more effective confrontational response. Organizations can also send a strong signal that sexual harassment will not be tolerated. Quick, tactful, fair investigation followed by whatever discipline called for by the prevention policy, even if the harasser is a higher level employee, can send the appropriate message.

DEALING WITH SEXUAL HARASSMENT IN THE WORKPLACE: A THREE-PRONGED APPROACH

The three prongs of an effective sexual harassment prevention policy are organizational communication about sexual harassment, active involvement of employees as a means of preventing sexual harassment, and proactive organizational responses to sexual harassment complaints.

Organizational Communication

The organization should communicate a prevention policy with an explicit statement that sexual harassment will not be condoned and that the organization is committed to eradicating sexual harassment. Most important, the policy should be communicated to all levels of the organization. As part of the communication process, whether through information sessions or in written form, the two different forms of sexual harassment should be explained.

A step-by-step procedure for voicing a complaint should be detailed in the prevention policy. Organizations looking for ideas about how to craft their policy could follow the lines of traditional grievance procedures. Once the target is directed to the appropriate person for dealing with work-related complaints in the organization, the investigating party would be instructed to gather evidence from both the target and the accused harasser, with corroborating testimony from witnesses where feasible.

A time frame for investigation and resolution should be established. As a result of its sexual harassment problems, Mitsubishi was required to state in its policy that it would investigate harassment complaints within a 3-week period (*New York Times,* 1998). Dissatisfaction with resolution of the complaint, on the part of either the target or the accused harasser, should also have an outlet. That is, either party to the complaint should have recourse to some higher authority in the organization, such as the senior human resources management official.

A sexual harassment complaint procedure should not name the employee's supervisor as the party with whom the complaint is initially registered. Supervisors are sometimes the very persons against whom sexual harassment complaints are filed. Complainants should be referred initially to an objective third party, such as a human resources manager or an organizational ombudsman. Organizations might also want to consider stating the penalties that would be imposed upon proven sexual harassers.

Employee Involvement

Employee training at all organizational levels concerning the behaviors that constitute sexual harassment is a necessary ingredient for sexual harassment prevention. Seventy-six percent of the respondents in the 1988 U.S. Merit Systems Protection Board survey indicated their belief that training employees would lead to a reduction in the frequency with which sexual harassment occurred. Training employees not only has the advantage of alerting potential harassers to the type of behaviors that will not be condoned but also removes any confusion about the behaviors the organization will find problematic.

Sexual harassment prevention training fits nicely into traditional supervisory and management training and development programs. All nonmanagerial and nonadministrative personnel should also be informed about the types of behavior that constitute sexual harassment. Training should go further than simply defining sexual harassment behaviors. Because some targets display passive, acquiescent behaviors, employee involvement should be targeted toward making potential targets comfortable with displaying confrontational behaviors such as refusal and complaint.

Role-playing may be one method of dealing with targets' reluctance to display confrontational behaviors (Thacker, 1992b). Providing employees the opportunity to act out responses to sexual harassment scenarios may remove some of the fear associated with confrontation in uncomfortable situations. Once employees have the opportunity to respond in a nonthreatening atmosphere, they may be more comfortable with exhibiting confrontational behaviors that were previously sources of discomfort.

Explaining the consequences of passive acceptance of sexual harassment might also help to induce confrontational behaviors, rather than passive acceptance or helplessness behaviors. Impressing upon employees the long-term consequences of failing to confront sexual harassers, and openly acknowledging passive response as a source of stress, may help to induce confrontational behaviors.

Proactive Response to Sexual Harassment Complaints

The organization should be explicit about the necessity for prompt objective investigation of sexual harassment complaints. Persons responsible for conducting the investigation should be identified (e.g., the human resources manager, staff ombudsman). The objectivity of the investigating parties should be without dispute. A description of the penalties or disciplinary action that will be taken against proven sexual harassers should be included. The organization could treat sexual harassment in the same way that other types of unacceptable performance are treated.

Supporting the written policy with visible action seems to be critical to legitimizing the organization's stated intent to eradicate sexual harassment. Without visible commitment and follow-through, those intent on sexually harassing others may perceive that they will suffer few, if any, adverse consequences. By the same token, targets who might think about invoking the organization's complaint procedure might be hesitant, fearful of retaliation. Furthermore, some research lends support to the notion that targets who complain but fail to realize a satisfactory outcome experience increased levels of stress (Long, Kahn, & Schutz, 1992). Indeed, not only will stress levels increase for those who suffer from unwanted sexual attention, but for future targets as well, as they see the only internal mechanism for complaint fail to achieve its desired result.

THE GAPS IN OUR UNDERSTANDING OF SEXUAL HARASSMENT AS A WORKPLACE PHENOMENON

Perhaps the most pressing need in our framework of understanding is a study of accused harassers. The tone that permeates much of the sexual harassment literature is one of targets vs. perpetrator. Legal guidance forces such an interpretation; that is, sexual harassment is in the eye of the beholder, regardless of the intent of the harasser. However, those labeled sexual harassers are painted with a broad and unflattering brush. Only recently has necessary

attention been given to this issue (O'Leary-Kelly, Paetzold, & Griffin, 2000).

O'Leary-Kelly, et al. (2000) make a useful distinction for future research purposes. They make the assumption that sexual harassers choose behaviors that will assist them in meeting their goal of sexually harassing the chosen target(s); thus, they assign intent to the sexual harasser. Yet, for some who are accused of sexual harassment, intent to harass is not part of their behavioral motivation. Perhaps their motives were misconstrued or misunderstood. Indeed, we learned from the 1988 USMSPB survey that disagreement over the behaviors that constitute sexual harassment is not uncommon. Or, in the worst case scenario, the accused harasser was a target of retaliation as a disgruntled coworker or subordinate used the complaint procedure to try to land the accused harasser into serious trouble.

How do organizations cope with this possibility? One suggestion is to provide an investigative route outside the normal internal channels, say, a formal mediator. A strongly worded statement that false or malicious accusations will not be condoned and will be handled as a disciplinary matter should also be communicated. Recent Supreme Court cases and some federal court cases suggest that employers who communicate the company's internal complaint procedure and ensure that no retaliatory measures are taken against complaining employees remove much of the company's liability that was previously associated with sexual harassment in their workplaces. The flip side of that coin is that employees who fail to use the internal complaint procedure now have reduced chances to prevail should they decide to sue their employer for sexual harassment. This is a major change in the burden of proof for employers.

Some attention is being given to the psychological and work-related consequences for those accused of harassment, with concern expressed that the accused not feel alienated, ostracized, or overly stressed by the investigative process—rehabilitation should be the goal (Bland & Stalcup, 2001). The message is that more research attention should be given to the accused harasser side of the sexual harassment equation.

For example, are there systematic personality differences between those accused of harassment and the nonaccused? Are there systematic differences in perceptions (of the accused harasser) of the culture, structure, strategy, or human resources management policies of those organizations in which sexual harassment complaints are filed vs. those who are not accused of sexual harassment? Greater understanding of the accused harasser's motivation and behavior are important if organizations are to do a proper job of addressing sexual harassment in the workplace and reducing the number of complaints.

A major issue continues to be the type of organization from which much of the data to this point have been collected. Much of the data have been collected from public sector organizations. Public sector data may in fact have systematic biases that distort the conclusions, and raise generalizability questions for the private, for-profit sector. For example, it is conceivable that, due to governmental emphasis on regulation, governmental entities and publicly funded entities such as universities are more likely to emphasize sexual harassment as forbidden activity, creating a "thou shalt not" mentality, as opposed to a "work it out within the company" mindset. The former encourages punitive action, the latter a more collaborative approach. Does this have a bearing upon the results? Perhaps. But until private for-profit firms allow researchers into their organization to investigate, something that they are legitimately reluctant to do for privacy reasons, we have unanswered questions.

Although we have learned much about the phenomenon of sexual harassment in the workplace and its effects on the target and the accused harasser, we have much more to learn. Until then, organizations have useful information upon which to base a good faith effort to eradicate sexual harassment from their workplace. ■

REFERENCES

Bland, T. S., & Stalcup, S. S. (2001). Managing harassment. *Human Resource Management, 40,* 51–61.

Brehm, J. W. (1966). *A theory of psychological reactance.* New York: Academic Press.

Brehm, J. W. (1972). *Responses to loss of freedom: A theory of psychological reactance.* Morristown, NJ: General Learning Press.

Fitzgerald, L.F., & Shullman, S. L. (1993). Sexual harassment: A research analysis and agenda for the 1990s. *Journal of Vocational Behavior, 42,* 5–27.

Gutek, B. A., Morasch, B., & Cohen, A. (1983). Interpreting social-sexual behavior in a work setting. *Journal of Vocational Behavior, 22,* 30–48.

Knapp, D. E., Faley, R. H., Ekeberg, S. E., & Dubois, C. L. (1997). Determinants of target responses to sexual harassment: A conceptual framework. *Academy of Management Review, 22,* 687–729.

Long, B. C., Kahn, S. E., & Schutz, R. W. (1992). Causal model of stress and coping: Women in management. *Journal of Counseling Psychology, 39,* 227–239.

Meritor Savings Bank, FSB v. Vinson (106 S.Ct. 2399, 1986).

New York Times. (1998, June 25). Mitsubishi Harassment Settlement Approved. D20.

Novak, T. (1998, June 12). Mitsubishi settlement sets record. *Chicago Sun-Times.* 1.

O'Leary-Kelly, A. M., Paetzold, R. L., & Griffin, R. W. (2000). Sexual harassment as aggressive behavior: An actor-based perspective. *Academy of Management Review, 25,* 372–388.

Overmier, J. B., & Seligman, M. E. P. (1967). Effects of inescapable shock upon subsequent escape and avoidance learning. *Journal of Comparative and Physiological Psychology, 63,* 28–33.

Reilly, T., Carpenter, S. Dull, V., & Bartlett, K. (1982). The factorial survey technique: An approach to defining sexual harassment on campus. *Journal of Social Issues, 38,* 99–110.

Seligman, M. E. P. (1974). Depression and learned helplessness. In R. J. Friedman and M. M. Katz (Eds.), *The Psychology of Depression: Contemporary Theory and Research* (83–113). Washington, DC: Winston-Wiley.

Silverman, D. (1976). Sexual harassment: Working women's dilemma. *Quest: A Feminist Quarterly, 3,* 15–24.

Tangri, S., Burt, M., & Johnson, L. (1982). Sexual harassment at work: Three explanatory models. *Journal of Social Issues, 38,* 33–54.

Terpstra, D., & Cook, S. (1985). Complainant characteristics and reported behaviors and consequences associated with formal sexual harassment charges. *Personnel Psychology, 38,* 559–574.

Thacker, R. A. (1992a). A descriptive study of behavioral responses of sexual harassment targets: Implications for control theory. *Employee Responsibilities & Rights Journal, 5,* 155–171.

Thacker, R. A. (1992b). Preventing sexual harassment in the workplace. *Training and Development Journal, 46,* 50–53.

Thacker, R. A., & Ferris, G. R. (1991). Understanding sexual harassment in the workplace: The influence of power and politics within the dyadic interaction of harasser and target. *Human Resource Management Review, 1,* 23–27.

Thacker, R. A., & Gohmann, S. F. (1993). Male/female differences in perceptions and effects of hostile environment sexual harassment: "Reasonable" assumptions? *Public Personnel Management, 22,* 461–473.

United States Merit Systems Protection Board. (1982). *Sexual harassment in the federal workplace: Is it a problem?* Washington, DC: U.S. Government Printing Office.

United States Merit Systems Protection Board. (1988). *Sexual harassment in the federal government: An update.* Washington, DC: U.S. Government Printing Office.

Wilmsen, S. (1998). Mitsubishi to pay $34m in harassment suit. *The Boston Globe,* A1.

A MULTIPLE CONSTITUENCY VIEW OF EMPLOYEE ASSISTANCE PROGRAMS

Matthew J. Stollak

Employee assistance programs (EAPs) have made significant inroads into the hearts and minds of U.S. businesses and corporations. Nearly 100 percent of *Fortune* 500 companies and over 10,000 companies in general offer some form of aid to their workers. Even in smaller firms, there has been a great interest in EAPs. The Research Triangle Institute, in their National Survey of Worksites and Employee Assistance Programs, found that 33 percent of all private work sites with 50 or more full-time employees had EAPs in 1993. The prevalence rate increased to 39 percent by 1995, and approximately 10 percent of those work sites without EAPs were considering starting programs (Hartwell, Steele, & French, 1996).

In an era where organizations have undergone monumental changes, from downsizing and restructuring to mergers and acquisitions, smaller workforces are being asked to do at least as much if not more, while being held accountable for the results. With layoffs increasing, stress levels of employees are rising as well. Thus, EAPs are more crucial today than ever before.

The significance of EAPs for business operation has not gone unnoticed as numerous journals (*EAP Digest, Employee Assistance Quarterly*) and textbooks (Dickman, Challenger, Emener, & Hutchison, *Employee Assistance Programs: A Basic Text,* 1988; Oher, *Employee Assistance Handbook,* 1999) have been published. Diversity in the sizes and types of EAPs, however, makes it difficult to establish the cost of operating an employee assistance program.

As the title of this book suggests, we are concerned with the perspectives, context, functions, and outcomes of human resources management (HRM). But with whose perspectives are we concerned? Under what context? What are the functions? What are the resulting outcomes? As with any organizational subunit, various constituents have varied needs. A given constituent group may have a unique "perspective" on what activities the organizational subunit performs and what the group wants from that subunit. The EAP, as one relevant organizational subunit of human resources management, has a number of constituents with whom it must interact.

This article examines the different constituent perspectives on the EAP. First I define the nature and design of EAPs. Then I focus on the multiple constituency approach, with special emphasis on the constituents of the EAP. Finally I present implications for managing human resources.

WHAT IS AN EAP?

Employee assistance programs have been broadly defined as "mechanisms that provide the workplace with systematic means for dealing with personal problems that affect employees' job performance" (Blum & Bennett, 1990, p. 43). *Personal problems* refers to "the abuse of alcohol and drugs, psychiatric disorders, marital and family

problems, and, to a limited extent, financial and legal difficulties" (Blum & Roman, 1989, p. 259).

Employee assistance programs have become increasingly broad in the scope of services that they offer. Holosko and Feit (1988) identify four stages or "generations" of programs that have emerged in the short history of EAPs. The first stage of EAPs, known as occupational alcohol programs, focused purely on the problems associated with alcohol. The second stage was marked by the expansion of EAP focus toward a broad range of behavioral problems that are related to job performance. In addition to addressing alcohol-related problems, program offerings expanded to cover all types of addiction counseling, marital and family intervention, and mental health services. Concurrent with expansion of EAP activities was expansion into more diverse organizational settings—for example, educational institutions and health care.

The third-generation programs are referred to as the "new-wave" EAPs. Emphasis is on a more proactive and preventative approach that addresses issues relating to overall employee health, wellness, and lifestyle.

Finally, the fourth generation of programs may be called "case management" programs. While maintaining the types of services already described, the case management approach tailors services to meet the unique needs of individuals. In an effort to contain costs, employees are tracked and monitored as they are linked to specialized services both within and external to the work organization.

Employee assistance programs play a critical role in addressing workplace problems. A brief examination of these job performance problems confirms the importance of the EAP as a unit worthy of study. It is estimated that 20 percent of any workforce is affected by personal problems that impact job performance (Masi, 1992). A 1989 study by the National Institute of Drug

Abuse indicates that 12 percent of individuals in the workforce have alcohol- and drug-related problems, while 6 to 8 percent have emotional problems. The result is a 25 percent decrease in productivity and increased costs for a given organization. Such lost productivity costs are calculated to be $50.6 billion for alcohol and $26 billion for drugs (Masi, 1992). The Substance Abuse and Mental Health Services Administration, in a 1996 National Household Survey on Drug Abuse estimates that approximately 5 percent of the population experienced heavy alcohol use (i.e., five or more drinks per occasion on five or more days) during the past month. Fifteen percent experienced at least one occasion of "binge" drinking. Table 12-1 outlines the types of losses that are attributed to job performance problems. Clearly, EAPs are an important weapon for combating these workplace maladies.

THE MULTIPLE CONSTITUENCY APPROACH

An organization wants to know whether or not it is effective. Is our product targeting the right audience? How can we improve our performance? Are our customers satisfied? These are some questions businesses have consistently tried to address. Researchers have adopted a number of approaches, such as the systems model (Katz & Kahn, 1966; Yuchtman & Seashore, 1967), in trying to provide organizations with answers to such questions. The multiple constituency approach arose out of a sense of dissatisfaction with the available organizational effectiveness models. The primary concern of multiple constituency models revolves around the question: "Whose preferences should be satisfied through the distribution of the outcomes of organizational performance?" (Zammuto, 1984, p. 606).

The multiple constituency model of evaluation has been most developed in the work of Tsui (1984, 1987, 1990) on personnel departments. "Effectiveness," Tsui argues, "is defined from the perspectives of the constituencies, who also define the subunit's activities and its evaluation criteria" (1984, p. 188). The model of evaluation focuses on three dimensions: the constituencies of an organization, the activities an organizational

TABLE 12-1	Quantifiable and Qualitative Losses Resulting from Job Performance Problems	
Quantifiable Losses	*Qualitative Losses*
Absenteeism	Friction among workers
Utilization of health benefits	Damage to public image
Overtime pay	Poor decision making
Tardiness	Threat to public safety
Machine downtime	Threat to corporate security
Sick leave abuse	Trust in employee
Workers' compensation claims	Trust in employer
Disciplinary actions	
Disability payments	
Retraining	
Personnel turnover	
Productivity losses	

Source: Adapted from Masi, D. A. (1992). Employee assistance programs. In D. A. Masi (ed.), *The AMA handbook for developing employee assistance & counseling programs*, 3. New York: AMACOM.

department performs, and the criteria on which the department and the organization are evaluated.

Overview

The Constituencies   Tsui refers to a constituency as "a group of individuals holding similar preferences or interests pertaining to the activities of a focal organizational unit" (1990, p. 461). A constituent, then, is a single individual within a constituency or stakeholder group. Each organization has a number of constituencies with which it must contend. Some are specific, such as unions in a unionized firm. Most often, though, organizations face similar constituents—owners, managers, employees, and customers.

The Activities of a Department   For Tsui, the concern is with domain specification and taxonomy. What are the important activities that should be performed by a personnel department? Under what conditions will these activities change? What kinds of activities are perceived as effective? Do the types of personnel hired by an organization affect these activities? How many activities should be performed?

The Evaluation Criteria   How do we measure the performance of a personnel department and an organization? The multiple constituency model suggests that constituents define the criteria by which the department is measured. Both process and outcome criteria affect personnel actions only when they are considered in relation to multiple constituencies who assign weight to and help measure the criteria. The criteria that are chosen may affect constituency satisfaction.

The employee assistance program can be seen as an important part of the human resources function. Tsui's (1987) conceptual analysis notes that the operating level of a firm is composed of organizational units involved in the actual design of products. As the definition of an EAP implies, it, too, is involved in the delivery of services.

Who Are the Constituencies of the EAP?

Given this view of the multiple constituency model, it is important to know the constituencies that influence EAP operation.

The Steering Committee   The steering committee is responsible for planning the EAP in collaboration with management and other professional employees. Once the program is implemented, the steering committee assumes overall management of the program. Though it does not have case-by-case responsibility, the steering committee does offer input at the public policy level. Training and orientation programs are additional responsibilities (Battle, 1988; Wright, 1985).

The EAP Staff   EAPs have integrated service delivery, with counselors, trainers, and occupational social workers that provide assistance. The counselor typically offers a broad treatment service for a broad range of psychosocial problems. The counselor must stay abreast of company policies as well as advances in the field. Most of all, the counselor is the keeper of confidentiality of information.

The trainer collaborates with the counselor in providing orientation and training regarding the operation of the EAP. Although most of the training occurs during the implementation of the program, the trainer will often return to offer seminars in various areas of interest, such as AIDS, stress management, sexual harassment, and violence in the workplace.

EAP staff members are often found to be in conflict with regard to their specific role in the organization. "Should it be an assessment and referral (A&R) resource for workers with productivity deficiencies? Or should it serve as a group of counselors and therapists who provide treatment for individuals with mental health or substance abuse problems?" (Yandrick, 1998, p. 90).

Organizational Management This constituency comprises what is typically referred to as "top management": human resources managers, department heads, and executives—those at the top of the organizational hierarchy. It is often argued that top management support is necessary for policy implementation.

Supervisors Through constructive confrontation, supervisors are responsible for referring employees with deteriorating job performance to the EAP for help. It is expected that supervisors will undergo yearly training to remain sensitive to the latest changes in EAP technology.

Users of the Program Program users clearly influence the operation of the program because they are so closely tied to its performance. Some employees enter the EAP voluntarily, either through self-referral or at the suggestion of others. Other employees may be required, through disciplinary action, to enter the program or face job loss.

The Medical Department The medical department offers the program a number of supportive services, such as integrating EAP services into the overall health care delivery systems.

Unions Within unionized firms, labor's endorsement is often perceived as critical to the success of the EAP. Before the establishment of EAPs, it was often the union that provided assistance to troubled employees. As Tramm (1985) argues, the role of the union is, much like the EAP staff, a complex one:

> Is the union's primary function to protect the chemically dependent, including the alcoholic, from disciplinary action by management? Is it to act as watchdog for the chemically dependent's job while the sick individual participates in treatment? Or is it to sanction the "human contract" of labor-management rela-

tions—the possibilities for a relationship of total human concern—while management is more interested in issues of economy and production? (p. 95)

Family Members Although family members do not directly influence EAP and organizational operation, they are directly affected by the treatment given to the troubled employee as well as by organizational changes. An employee's drinking problem does not affect the employee alone, nor does organizational relocation or downsizing. Also, family members may encourage or discourage an employee's use of the program.

External Constituents Numerous external constituents also affect the operation of EAPs. The government, through legislation, affects the types of services and programs offered by companies. For example, the Federal Comprehensive Alcohol Abuse and Alcoholism Treatment and Rehabilitation Act of 1970 recognized alcoholism as a handicap that must be treated like any other disease, and the Drug-Free Workplace Act of 1988 required certain federal contractors to certify that they provide and maintain a drug-free workplace.

Insurance companies, through third-party payment, affect the development of community resource network strategies. If employees are referred outside of the company's EAP service provider to other community resources, treatment is generally covered by the company's or the union's insurance.

The general public, in a limited way, affects organizational provision of services. Employers are rapidly moving toward corporate social responsibility, an approach that "focuses on assisting corporations and businesses to make a commitment to the social and economic well-being of the communities in which they operate" (Gould & Smith, 1988, p. 12). This approach recognizes the fact that corporations have an indelible impact on the communities in which they reside. Adoption and implementation of EAP services is one way for corporations to show commitment to their communities.

PROGRAM DESIGN

Having identified the relevant constituencies, it is important to consider the activities and guiding policies of the EAP. In this section, I first consider six aspects of the EAP core technology. Next, I discuss eleven ingredients necessary for the success of EAPs. Finally, I review four components of EAPs.

The EAP Core Technology

In his important work on organizations, Thompson (1967) examines the role of the core technology. Thompson refers to the core technology as the central activities of an organization, which the organization tries to protect from environmental influences. Organizations must cope with uncertainty when dealing with both the internal and the external environments. Protecting one's technologies is key to reducing uncertainty. The concept of an organizational core technology has been extended to employee assistance programs. Roman and Blum (1985, 1988) have identified six aspects of an EAP core technology.

The first component of the EAP core technology is *the identification of employees' behavioral problems on the basis of job performance issues.* Emphasis is placed on the specific job-related stressors rather than the symptoms related to alcoholism or other problems. This component assumes that dysfunctional job-related behavior could be identified easily by supervisors.

The second component of an EAP core technology identified by Roman and Blum (1988) is *the provision of expert consultation to supervisors, managers, and union stewards on the appropriate steps to take in utilizing employee assistance policy and procedures.* Blum and Roman (1989) have delineated four functions of this type of assistance. First,

assistance facilitates the first component by equipping supervisors to distinguish between job-based problems and symptomatic ones. A second function is information processing: The EAP specialist distributes information about the way the system operates. A third function is the creation of linkages to other organizational policies. The final function of this component serves to diminish the "troubled supervisor" syndrome. Supervisors may experience conflict between the duties of serving the organization and trying to aid their subordinates (Yandrick, 1998). Educating supervisors can alleviate the pressures that may give rise to conflict.

The third component of the EAP core technology is *the availability and appropriate use of constructive confrontation.* Typically, an employee is faced simultaneously with "proof" of job performance deterioration and an EAP referral for improvement. Through confrontation an organization can demonstrate its positive attitude toward helping employees.

A fourth component is *the development of microlinkages with counseling, treatment, and other community resources.* This component focuses on the individual, determining what "fit" of community resources is available. If outside referrals are made, the EAP can provide case management and can control costs by demanding that outside sources be accountable for the efficiency and quality of their services. The success of microlinkages clearly depends on the EAP specialist's awareness of community services.

The fifth core component of EAP technology is *the creation and maintenance of macrolinkages between the work organization and counseling, treatment, and other community resources.* Whereas the fourth component focuses on the individual, emphasis here is on the service providers. This core component operates as a gatekeeper, balancing the needs of the client, the service provider, and the organization. Quality, accessibility, and accountability of referral sources are emphasized. Again, one must assume that service providers are in sufficient quantity in the surrounding area. Further, it has been argued that 4,000 to 6,000 employees are needed to create one viable EAP position (Featherston & Bednarek, 1981). On the other hand, 15 to 20 percent of the workforce needs some sort of help (Masi, 1992).

The sixth and final component of the core technology is *the centrality of the employee's substance abuse problems as the program focus with the most significant promise for producing recovery and genuine cost savings for the organization in terms of future performance and reduced benefit usage.* It is hoped that, through the adoption and implementation of employee assistance, the organization can effectively, successfully, and constructively address substance abuse problems (Blum & Bennett, 1990; Blum & Roman, 1989; Roman & Blum, 1985, 1988). At this time, however, this core component has been expanded to include the increasingly diverse number of services that EAPs are currently offering.

Ingredients for EAP Success

Given this core technology, researchers suggest that a number of elements be present for an EAP to be effective (Balgopal & Patchner, 1988; Dickman, 1988). Eleven "ingredients" are seen as critical. First, endorsements must be present. Employees will not view the program as legitimate unless there is active involvement from the highest level of the corporate structure. Second, if an organization is unionized, endorsement must come from labor. Third, a policy statement is needed. The intentions and philosophy of the program must be clearly stated. A fourth crucial ingredient is confidentiality. Employees seeking assistance for their problems must be secure in the knowledge that their problems will be kept in the strictest confidence. Fifth, training must be given to supervisors as well as union stewards. It is suggested that training occur at

least once a year. Sixth, financial coverage is critical to a successful EAP. "When employees are clear that participating in the EAP may cost them something but that it won't break them, they will be more apt to accept a referral or to refer themselves" (Balgopal & Patchner, p. 98). Professional personnel are a seventh element. The EAP coordinator as well as the EAP staff must have sufficient knowledge and expertise in employee assistance, as well as access to needed resources. Broad service components are an eighth element. The EAP must be able to respond to a wide variety of employee needs and problems. A ninth element is accessibility. Employees need to be able to gain access to EAP sites quickly and conveniently as well as in a confidential manner. The tenth element for EAP success is awareness. The EAP must market its attributes throughout the organization. Finally, the EAP must conduct program evaluation regularly to assess how it is meeting constituents' needs.

Components of the EAP

As EAPs have grown, so has knowledge concerning their operation. Certain common elements have arisen that typify the diverse programs that are offered. These elements have been outlined by the U.S. Department of Health and Human Services (1987) and can be grouped into four functions: policies and procedures, administrative functions, education and training, and evaluation.

First, most EAPs have written policy statements that make their purposes clear. The policy statement often reflects both management's and labor's attitudes toward the objectives of the program. Confidentiality rules are developed and laid out to specify how records are maintained, how long they are maintained, who has access to records, and what information is released to whom under what conditions. Further, written procedures outline the appropriate actions to take vis-à-vis individuals referred by management, the union, or coworkers. Procedures are also developed to govern use of the program by employees and their family members.

Second, a number of administrative functions concerning the EAP are established: its position in the organization, its physical location, its record-keeping system, the relationship of the EAP to medical and disability benefit plans, the appropriateness of malpractice/liability insurance, and the qualifications of EAP staff.

A third common function involves education and training. The focus is on communication about EAP services that are available to employees and their families, employee education concerning substance abuse and other recognized problem areas, training for supervisors and labor stewards in appropriate constructive confrontation, and orientation regarding the appropriate roles of management and union representatives.

A fourth function involves the development of files for use in reviewing outside programs and evaluating both the program and the progress of its clients. On an individual level, the EAP focuses on follow-up and after-care to assess employee improvement. On a macro level, the company communicates with and rates external referral sources, as well as evaluating overall EAP effectiveness through any number of methods, such as cost-benefit analysis or cost-effectiveness analysis.

REFERRALS

As we have seen, there is considerable variety in the services offered by EAPs. Yet how do users come in contact with the EAP to take advantage of those services? This section outlines particular routes to assistance and their impact on the various constituents.

Self-Referral

Employees (or sometimes members of their families) may use EAP services in confiden-

tiality for personal problems. In deciding to utilize the EAP, an individual typically goes through three stages. First, the person recognizes, through either self-reflection or interaction with others, that he or she has a problem and tries to manage it so that it does not disrupt work or family relationships. Second, the person realizes that he or she can no longer contain the problem and must take action. Finally, the person decides to contact the EAP or some other community resource.

Defining what constitutes self-referral has been troubling for EAP researchers. Often, employees who are believed to self-refer have actually been pressured by family members, supervisors, or peers to seek help (Sonnenstuhl, Staudenmeier, & Trice, 1988).

Supervisor Referral

When looking at the core technology of EAPs, supervisor recognition of deteriorating job performance and the ensuing constructive confrontation was critical. This job performance model, which arose from the Alcoholics Anonymous philosophy involving "hitting bottom" and the industrial and labor relations philosophy of fairness (Sonnenstuhl, et al., 1988), defines emotional problems in the context of the workplace, offers employees the opportunity to change their behavior, and prevents them from being unnecessarily rushed into treatment. Trice & Beyer (1984a) found that employees who experienced constructive confrontation combined with counseling showed greater improvement than those who experienced either one alone.

Peer Referral

Peer referral is most often seen in union-based EAPs. Union leaders are critical of the job performance model, arguing that union solidarity should shelter employees from the demands of employers. Instead, the union helps its members and protects them from being forced into treatment. Whereas the job performance model focuses on constructive confrontation, proof of job impairment, and coercive motivation to use the EAP, the peer referral model relies on intervention, deepening concern, and ongoing support (Molloy, 1985).

Medical Referral

Medical referrals constitute a small portion of the paths taken to employee assistance. A study of the Anheuser-Busch national EAP, for example, showed only 2 percent of referrals attributed to the medical department (Magruder, 1988). A medical referral is based on the identification of a medical symptom or group of symptoms related to a personal problem such as alcohol abuse. Referral to the EAP is viewed as part of the required treatment plan. The decision to utilize the EAP, however, is up to the employee.

Other Sources of Referral

As we have mentioned, other parties may push an employee toward assistance. Family members may want a troubled employee to seek help. A benefits or safety department may want an employee to visit the EAP. Even courts, especially in driving-under-the-influence cases, may refer employees to the EAP.

SERVICE DELIVERY SYSTEM OPTIONS

Just as each organization has its own unique operation and culture, EAPs assume different forms. Phillips and Older (1988) have identified six distinct models for the delivery of employee assistance services. Differences in EAP services often arise from variations in organizational size, the amount of organizational slack available for EAP services, and the willingness of upper management to provide such slack in support of those services. In this section I will examine the various types of EAPs that constituents may encounter. Each subsection describes the nature and operation of a particular

model and then outlines the various benefits and disadvantages of the model for several constituencies, primarily users of the EAP, EAP staff, supervisors, and organizational management.

Model 1—Internal Program

Several types of internal programs exist. They can be categorized as (1) programs providing assessment and referral services; (2) programs providing assessment, referral, and counseling services; and (3) internal programs located off site. Coordination of client activity occurs within the context of the work environment. Follow-up and feedback are coordinated by the treatment resource and designated EAP personnel. EAP staffing varies with the kind of service provided—programs that offer counseling, for example, need professional staff members with formal training.

Users of the Program   Users find the program advantageous in that it is visible and accessible. With the internal program commonly on-site, employees may be more familiar with the program and the services that it offers. Not surprisingly, EAP users viewed the EAP more positively that did nonusers (Harlow, 1998). However, on-site programs encounter the problem of confidentiality. Users may be reluctant to visit the EAP if others may observe them. Further, an internal program is less likely to be perceived as a benefit by employees. Also, positive views of the EAP were dependent on perceived support by other employees and the belief that the EAP would not negatively affect their career (Harlow, 1998)

EAP Staff   A number of advantages accrue for the EAP staff. An internal program offers a sense of ownership. Staff members believe they have greater say in what services are offered. As insiders, EAP staff feel they are better able to influence change within the organization. Being inside also improves knowledge of the organization and its culture. Internal EAPs can respond to and intervene in crises more rapidly than other types of programs. Finally, internal programs offer EAP staff the opportunity to improve communications within the organization.

Internal programs also have disadvantages for EAP staff. Only large organizations are able to front full-time staffs to oversee such programs. As a result, the staff may consist of a part-time person or persons, inadequately trained and with insufficient time to see all troubled employees when they need help. A limited staff is expected to fill numerous roles; skills and expertise will be limited as well. Burnout may result. Finally, as mentioned earlier, staff members may experience conflict between provider and organizational roles: Who is the EAP supposed to serve—the troubled employee or top management constraints?

Supervisors Supervisors like internal programs for the improved communications with EAP staff that may occur, as well as the familiarity with EAP operations. Supervisors thus view internal programs as more credible than other types of programs.

Organizational Management Given the high cost of providing a full-time staff, management is reluctant to adopt this type of program, especially in mid-size and smaller organizations. However, internal programs do afford greater control over the types of services that are offered and the staff that is hired. Organizational control also means greater commitment on the part of management. Upper management must have the ability to evaluate the skills and performance of EAP staff, and this is not always the case.

Model 2—Service Center Program

The service center program is an external, or contracted, EAP. An outside agency is responsible for its major functions. Service centers fall into two categories. One type provides treatment through third-party re-imbursement; the other is free-standing, referring employees to appropriate community treatment facilities. The service center also may offer assistance with organizational development and with the clinical functions of assessment, referral, follow-up, and feedback.

Users of the Program The advantage of the service center program lies in its ability to protect the confidentiality of clients better than an internal program can. Because the program is off site, employees may be less reluctant to use it. Service center programs often have more diverse staffs than internal programs and thus can serve a broader range of employees. The service center also allows for better identification of community resources.

Despite these advantages, employees may not be as familiar with EAP services and operations. The service center may present an accessibility problem for employees who do not have their own transportation. Being located off-site also limits the ability of EAP staff to respond immediately to crises. Also, treatment may be too narrow.

EAP Staff Because it needs to interact with a broad range of organizations, this type of EAP employs a more diverse staff. Staff members are better able to identify resources and maintain communication with professionals in the community.

Unfortunately, being external to an organization, staff may suffer from a lack of knowledge concerning the organizational environment and work culture. Communication with the contracting organization may be difficult, and EAP staff may have trouble relating to the work issues within the organization.

Supervisors Supervisors are less enthusiastic about service center programs. They are less accessible to EAP staff and are reluctant to deal with "outsiders." Without a meaningful EAP liaison, service center programs are less likely to be contacted. This perspective can be seen as a product of "social distance;" the extent to which the supervisor felt there was someone in the service center program who knew the work organization.

Organizational Management The service center is more suitable for small organizations because of the lower costs involved and the diversity of resources that are made available. Some managers prefer service center programs because they fear the liability of medical malpractice that may arise if company clinicians treat employees. Contracting out provides the opportunity to shift medical liability (Sonnenstuhl, 1986).

Model 3—Internal Program with Service Center Support

This model adopts the service center approach but recognizes the ability of professionals within the work organization to publicize the EAP, assist employees, and motivate them to utilize the services. Options for assistance are thus available within or outside the workplace; the service center simply serves as a support for the internal EAP.

Users of the Program For users the advantages of the program are similar to those of service center programs—assured confidentiality and greater staff expertise and skill. This approach, with accessibility, familiarity, and responsiveness to crises, does not share the disadvantages of the typical service center.

EAP Staff With service center support, EAP staff can call on a greater range of resources. However, the combination of in-house and external resources may engender communication difficulties around role definition.

Supervisors This approach resolves some of the skepticism that supervisors feel toward service centers. EAP staff are more accessible, and supervisors are more familiar with

EAP operation. However, if the approach is to be optimally utilized, an internal liaison must be present, or its advantages will be lost.

Organizational Management From management's standpoint, the major drawback is cost. Combining the internal program with service center support increases the cost of operating the program. Also, given potential difficulties with role definition, organizational management may find it difficult to hold someone accountable if problems arise.

Model 4—EAP Located in a Treatment or Social Service Agency

This type of EAP is offered at no cost, or through a contractual arrangement, by a treatment or social service agency within the community. This approach is often adopted because the necessary assessment and referral services are not available within the organization and no free-standing service center can be established. The EAP staff consists primarily of internal coordinators who facilitate training and referral, but treatment takes place off-site.

Users of the Program For program users in small towns or rural areas, this type of approach may be the only one capable of providing the needed resources. Because counseling takes place off-site, confidentiality is better protected.

EAP Staff As with other off-site approaches, understanding of and communication with the work organization are limited. However, staff members of local facilities may feel they have a vested interest in the success of the program; EAP staff will be more committed to making the program work.

Supervisors Again, supervisors will be less familiar with the operation of the EAP and may be more reluctant to make referrals. An EAP coordinator from the agency must work to encourage supervisor acceptance.

Organizational Management In this model treatment can often be provided under the company's existing medical coverage. Although this approach is less costly, it still carries the price tag of questions about the validity of the assessment or diagnostic service as well as the validity of the referral.

Model 5 — Union-Based EAP

In this model, the union at the union office or hiring hall provides services. The impetus for providing assistance comes from union coordinators. Employees are referred to as external treatment resources, and the company EAP coordinates follow-up. Depending on the contract, supervisors and management may refer union members to the EAP office.

Users of the Program For users who are union members, the EAP is seen as much more credible. Given the union dislike of constructive confrontation, the union may provide a "safer" haven. Confidentiality is more likely to be protected.

EAP Staff In the union setting, the EAP staff's skills and expertise may be limited. Staff may not have connections to community resources. However, in this setting there is no conflict between the duty to serve the organization and the duty to serve the employee. EAP staff can concentrate more fully on the employee without the concern for accountability to organizational management.

Supervisors Beyer, Trice, and Hunt (1981) found that supervisors in unionized facilities were more likely to apply government policies concerning alcoholism. This phenomenon may be attributed to familiarity with those policies. Supervisors in unionized facilities were well-informed about union support for those policies and were therefore more likely to invoke them.

Organizational Management Because the union bears the cost of implementing and administering the program, management incurs little cost. Given the adversarial relationship between management and labor, union-based EAPs are likely to be viewed with some suspicion. However, cooperation is more likely to be found between managers and lower-level union officers than between managers and higher-level officers; cooperation may be seen as political rather than empathetic (Trice & Beyer, 1984b).

Model 6 — Group Consortium

A consortium develops out of small organizations' need for service and typically constitutes the only source of assistance for members of those organizations in the realm of personal problems. Assistance is provided for members of a profession, such as lawyers or teachers. External treatment resources are utilized.

Users of the Program The consortium often is the only source of assistance available to its users. The unique nature of the clientele also promotes flexibility in service delivery. Programs are designed to meet the particular needs of members. Confidentiality remains a problem, however, and there is no off-site screening and referral.

EAP Staff EAP staff are better able to coordinate treatment and monitor follow-up to meet the specialized needs of the clientele. As in model 1 (the internal program model), there are improved knowledge and communication within the organization, yet targeting a specific clientele limits the types of resources utilized. Available and useful community resources may be ignored.

Supervisors As with model 1, the group consortium is internal and thus has more credibility with supervisors. Supervisors will be more familiar with the EAP process and staff.

Organizational Management The consortium approach is costly given the substantial staffing requirements. Further, a high degree of inter-organization and cooperation is needed if the program is to be effective. The complexity of policy making increases, and there is less individual input into system operation.

EVALUATION OF EAPS

Given the diverse interests involved in operating an EAP, evaluation is critical in determining whether the EAP is offering an "appropriate" array of services while being viewed as "effective" by the multiple constituencies.

Masi (1997) argues that evaluation can take a number of forms. First, for contracted-out EAPs, it is important to benchmark the client contract. This will help establish the standards to be met. Second, one must monitor the 800 number to take into account technological considerations and to ensure the EAP client is reaching a caring voice. Third, the physical facility should be observed to cover such things as office hours, accessibility, confidentiality, and record maintenance. Fourth, the management information system should be evaluated to check such issues as the percentage of successful referrals to EAPs. Fifth, the utilization rate should be checked. Sixth, terminology should be standardized so that everyone one is on the same page. Seventh, some form of feedback mechanism should be in place to gauge program recipient responses. Eighth, cost benefit/cost-effective analysis should be conducted. Finally, counselor credentials should be monitored.

French and Zarkin (1995) offer a four-fold approach to guide future EAP evaluation. First, a process description should be in place to understand the structure, operating environment, and goals of the EAP. Second, a cost analysis should take place to comprehensively identify and estimate the full range of EAP costs. Third, an outcomes analysis should be conducted to rigorously estimate the effectiveness of the EAP for groups of employees and the overall impact of the EAP on employee performance and workplace productivity. Finally, an economic evaluation would estimate cost-effectiveness ratios, dollar benefits, and net benefits of the EAP.

While evaluation is critical, an evaluation is often fraught with difficulties. What problems does the researcher face in attempting to evaluate EAPs? A California State University survey on the current status of cost savings in evaluation of EAPs identified major obstacles that affected eighty-two organizations responding to the nationwide survey. Unavailability of data and lack of time were cited by 43 percent of the respondents as the two major obstacles they encountered in conducting evaluations of their programs. Cost constraints, confidentiality concerns, and difficulty in designing an evaluation strategy were the other difficulties that were reported as most prevalent (Burton & Houts, 1990).

Organizations that attempt to conduct thorough EAP evaluations often meet with roadblocks regarding the data required for such an undertaking. Many companies simply do not have useful, retrievable information available for program evaluation. Often, records that are supposed to be kept by program staff and supervisors are in reality not maintained consistently. Because of privacy concerns, qualitative data regarding clients' views of services and the impact of the program on their work environment are seldom collected systematically (Balgopal & Patchner, 1988). The main source for such data is anecdotal writings, which also may not be kept on a regular basis. Often, however, the evaluation effort itself leads the organization to organize, systemize, and update EAP data systems, to the benefit of future program planning and service delivery (Holosko, 1988).

The question of who should be responsible for collecting data for evaluation purposes is an issue in itself. Often the use of outside consultants only reinforces concerns about confidentiality and privacy. Moreover, there is no guarantee that the EAP staff will cooperate fully with the outside consultants in obtaining the necessary data, as their commitment to the program evaluation may be less than firm (Balgopal & Patchner, 1988). On the other hand, if data collection is the responsibility of EAP staff, their lack of research skills may complicate the project; a considerable time investment might be needed for them to acquire the necessary skills. Further, the EAP staff may be wary about the evaluation outcome and concerned about what the results might reveal about the program.

Another problem plaguing evaluation attempts is the lack of a shared database that would allow different EAPs to obtain comparison information on treatment results, utilization rates, and cost-benefit issues. The lack of such information makes it difficult for organizations to compare in-house and externally contracted programs, broad and specialized EAPs, and job performance scales and to assess the general impact of these programs on the workplace (Bureau of National Affairs, 1987).

The issue of participant confidentiality is another major concern in EAP evaluation. The employee has already taken a difficult step in seeking assistance to deal with substance abuse, marital or family conflicts, or emotional problems. Compounding this difficulty with apprehensions about personal data being exposed in an evaluation process is likely to be extremely threatening. For their part, EAP staff may be extremely reluctant to share information that is protected by doctor-client privilege. All employees have the right to ask for help and to know their problems will be kept in the strictest confidence.

For sound evaluation, certain elements of the research design must be in place; this has not always been the case in past evaluations. The preferred design is an experimental one incorporating random assignment to both treatment and control groups (Balgopal & Patchner, 1988), as in the testing of new therapeutic drugs. Random assignment serves to draw samples that are representative of a known population and comparable to one another within sampling error limits. The use of a control group rules out extraneous factors that may affect the course of an experiment (Cook & Campbell, 1979). In EAP evaluation, ideally one would sample the population to obtain representative numbers of program users and nonusers. Unfortunately, use of that design would be both difficult and unethical in the context of an EAP. One cannot randomly assign some people to a control group while others are in an experimental group receiving services. Clearly, assigning an alcoholic to a control group would be unsafe as well as unethical. Further, because of confidentiality concerns, even a comparison group of non-EAP users cannot be incorporated into a research design because an individual in the comparison group might erroneously be perceived by a supervisor, fellow worker, or researcher as an EAP client.

If the measurement tool is to be considered reliable, it must be possible to conclude that the behavioral changes of a person in treatment result from participation in the EAP and are not due to factors other than the treatment program itself. As discussed earlier, some EAP clients seek treatment voluntarily, whereas supervisors, because of poor job performance, formally refer others. The nature of the selection process may influence findings in an EAP evaluation as outcomes may reflect factors in addition to the EAP itself (Tompkins, 1990).

Tompkins (1990) also points out that sample size may well be a problem in EAP evaluations. An evaluation will be valid only if it is based on a sample that represents the target population in terms of employee demographic characteristics. In addition, the sample must be large enough to represent the various types of individuals for whom the program was designed (Kurtz, Googins, & Howard, 1984). Companies may need to compare their experiences, and they can accomplish this only through cooperative research efforts.

Conducting an EAP evaluation is very costly and time-consuming. Often companies feel that spending $500,000 to evaluate a program that costs only $300,000 to run is not a wise business decision (Walsh & Egdahl, 1989). Follow-up studies for EAP clients, recommended to last from three to five years, are likewise extremely costly and time-consuming, yet they are essential for an accurate assessment of sustained behavioral change brought about by an EAP (Kurtz, et al., 1984).

The criteria that are ultimately chosen to evaluate the EAP must meet the needs of various constituencies within the organization. In addition, these measures must reflect the specific goals of the EAP being evaluated. Top management, the EAP staff, employees, and supervisors all have different points of view regarding the EAP and its evaluation. Straussner (1988) points out, in a discussion of EAPs in New York, that top management is often looking for ways to avoid unnecessary costs, whereas the EAP staff and employees are more concerned about the accessibility and confidentiality of the EAP. Supervisors can become an EAP's most important ally if positive experiences result from the referral of employees to the program (Googins, 1989).

It is fair to conclude that pressures to evaluate EAPs will continue as corporate decision making is driven by concern for the bottom line, the high costs of employee benefits, and increased competition in national and foreign markets. Currently, there are no firm answers concerning which methodologies should be used in company settings to assess employee assistance programs. Until such answers are available, many EAP managers will be under pressure to persuade senior managers as well as other constituents that their programs deserve ongoing company support and commitment.

IMPLICATIONS FOR HUMAN RESOURCES MANAGEMENT

Strategic human resources management focuses on the best way to fit human resources policies and practices to an organization's business objectives and operational requirements. The employee assistance program is an important function of HRM that has both short- and long-term implications for organizational success. Personal problems, such as substance abuse, may be related to a decline in personal and coworker safety and productivity or to an increase in absenteeism or even criminal behavior (Tompkins, 1990; Trice & Beyer, 1984b). Addressing personal problems through the offerings of an EAP can help shape a productive workforce, which is clearly essential if an organization is to remain competitive.

The necessity of identifying the multiple needs of diverse constituencies also has strong implications for HRM. One potential use of the multiple constituency approach concerns the control of resources. For an EAP or any other organizational subunit, adequate funding and staffing are clearly necessary. Perceived EAP effectiveness may affect the amount of resources that the EAP can negotiate. The multiple constituency approach may provide avenues the EAP can take to secure a favorable assessment from those wielding power over resources. An understanding of the nature of the constituencies may also help EAP managers from other organizational units, assistance that could in turn help meet the needs of those constituencies.

According to Blum and Roman (1989), the EAP is viewed as a human resources tool with substantial potential for reducing uncertainty. But as we have noted, the EAP alone will not have much impact on uncertainty. The absence of strong quantitative data makes it difficult to establish the relative effectiveness and success of EAPs. The multiple constituency approach, however, provides a useful framework to help EAP managers understand the conflicting constituent demands they encounter. By identifying the various services desired by the constituencies and the criteria by which the EAP is judged, managers can achieve a better fit with the organizational operation and culture.

CONCLUSION

I have examined the functions of the employee assistance program, the contexts in which it operates, the perspectives of its various constituencies, and the different outcomes that may occur with the use of the multiple constituency approach. Evaluation of EAPs has proven to be a daunting task. The continuing shifts in emphasis within EAPs, as well as the changing constraints both within and external to the organizational work environment, particularly in these times of economic turmoil, make the multiple constituency approach a critical tool for future human resources and EAP practices. ■

REFERENCES

Balgopal, P. R., & Patchner, M. A. (1988). Evaluating employee assistance programs: Obstacles, issues and strategies. In M. Holosko and M. D. Feit (Eds.), *Evaluation of Employee Assistance Programs* (95–106). New York: Haworth Press.

Battle, S. F. (1988). Issues to consider in planning employee assistance program evaluations. In M. Holosko and M. D. Feit (Eds.), *Evaluation of Employee Assistance Programs* (79–94). New York: Haworth Press.

Beyer, J. M., Trice, H. M., & Hunt, R. (1981). Impact of federal sector unions on supervisory use of personnel policies. *Industrial and Labor Relations Review, 33,* 212–232.

Blum, T. C., & Bennett, N. (1990). Employee assistance programs: Utilization and referral data, performance management, and prevention concepts. In P. M. Roman (Ed.), *Alcohol Problem Intervention in the Workplace* (143–162). New York: Quorum Books.

Blum, T. C., & Roman, P. M. (1985). The social transformation of alcoholism intervention. *Journal of Health and Social Behavior, 26,* 365–378.

Blum, T. C., & Roman, P. M. (1989). Employee assistance programs and human resource management. In G. Ferris and K. Rowland (Eds.), *Research in Personnel and Human Resource Management* (Vol. 7, 259–312). Greenwich, CT: JAI Press.

Bureau of National Affairs. (1987). *Employee assistance programs: Benefits, problems and prospects* (BNA Special Report). Rockville, MD: Author unknown.

Burton, G. & Houts, L. (1990). The current status of cost-savings evaluations in EAPs. Internal paper, California State University, Fresno.

Cook, T. D., & Campbell, D. T. (1979). *Quasi-experimentation: Design & analysis issues for field settings.* Boston: Houghton-Mifflin.

Dickman, J. F. (1988). Ingredients of an effective employee assistance program. In J. F. Dickman, B. R. Challenger, W. G. Emener, Jr., and W. S. Hutchison, Jr. (Eds.), *Employee Assistance Programs: A Basic Text* (110–121). Springfield, IL: Charles C. Thomas.

Featherston, H., & Bednarek, R. (1981). A positive demonstration of concern for employees. *Personnel Administrator, 26* (9), 43–47.

French, M. T. & Zarkin, G. A. (1995). A methodology for evaluating the costs and benefits of employee assistance programs. *Journal of Drug Issues, 25* (2), 451–471.

Googins, B. (1989). Revisiting the role of the supervisor in employee assistance programs. *Drugs in the workplace: Research and evaluation data* (NIDA Research Monograph 91). Washington, DC: National Institute on Drug Abuse.

Gould, G. M., & Smith, M. L. (1988). *Social work in the workplace.* New York: Springer.

Harlow, K. C. (1998). Employee attitudes toward an internal employee assistance program. *Journal of Employment Counseling, 35* (3), 141–151.

Hartwell, T. D., Steele, P., & French, M. T. (1996). Aiding troubled employees: The prevalence, cost, and characteristics of employee assistance programs in the United States. *American Journal of Public Health,* 804–811.

Holosko, M. (1988). Prerequisites for EAP evaluations: A case for more thoughtful evaluation planning. In M. Holosko and M. D. Feit (Eds.), *Evaluation of Employee Assistance Programs* (59–67). New York:Haworth.

Holosko, M. J., & Feit, M. D. (1988). Onward and upward. In M. Holosko and M. D. Feit (Eds.), *Evaluation of Employee Assistance Programs* (281–283). New York: Haworth.

Katz, D., & Kahn, R. L. (1966). *The social psychology of organizations.* New York: Wiley.

Kurtz, N. R., Googins, B., & Howard, W. C. (1984). Measuring the success of occupational alcoholism programs. *Journal of Studies on Alcohol, 45* (1): 33–45.

Magruder, D. W. (1988). A national employee assistance program: An example. In J. F. Dickman, B. R. Challenger, W. G. Emener, Jr., & W. S. Hutchison, Jr. (Eds.), *Employee Assistance Programs: A Basic Text* (139–148). Springfield, IL: Charles C. Thomas.

Masi, D. A. (1992). Employee assistance programs. In D. A. Masi (Ed.), *The AMA Handbook for Developing Employee Assistance and Counseling Programs.* New York: AMACOM.

Masi, D. A. (1997). Evaluating employee assistance programs. *Research on Social Work Practice, 7* (3), 378–391.

Molloy, D. J. (1985). Peer referral: A programmatic and administrative review. In S. H. Klarreich, J. L. Francek, and C. E. Moore (Eds.), *The Human Resources Management Handbook: Principles and Practice of Employee Assistance Programs* (102–110). New York: Praeger.

Oher, J. M. (1999). *The employee assistance handbook.* New York: John Wiley & Sons.

Phillips, D. A., & Older, H. J. (1988). Models of service delivery. In J. F. Dickman, B. R. Challenger, W. G. Emener, Jr., & W. S. Hutchison, Jr. (Eds.), *Employee Assistance Programs: A Basic Text* (133–138). Springfield, IL: Charles C. Thomas.

Roman, P. M., & Blum, T. C. (1985). Modes and levels of data management affecting the EAP practitioner. In S. H. Klarreich, J. L. Francek, and C. E. Moore (Eds.), *The Human Resources Management Handbook* (203–221). New York: Praeger.

Roman, P. M., & Blum, T. C. (1988). The core technology of employee assistance programs: A reaffirmation. *ALMACAN, 15,* 3–8.

Sonnenstuhl, W. J. (1986). *Inside an emotional health program: A field study of workplace assistance for troubled employees.* Ithaca, NY: ILR Press.

Sonnenstuhl, W. J., Staudenmeier, W. J., & Trice, H. M. (1988). Ideology and referral categories in employee assistance program research. *Journal of Applied Behavioral Science, 24* (4), 383–396.

Straussner, S. L. A. (1988). A comparison of in-house and contractual employee assistance programs. In M. Holosko and M. D. Feit (Eds.), *Evaluation of Employee Assistance Programs* (69–78). New York: Haworth Press.

Thompson, J. D. (1967). *Organizations in action.* New York: McGraw-Hill, Inc.

Tompkins, C. P. (1990). *Drug abuse among workers and employee assistance programs.* Paper presented at the NIDA Center for Drug Abuse Services Research Annual Advisory Committee Meeting.

Tramm, M. L. (1985). Union-based programs. In S. H. Klarreich, J. L. Francek, and C. E. Moore (Eds.), *The Human Resources Management Handbook* (pp. 95–101). New York: Praeger.

Trice, H. M., & Beyer, J. M. (1984a). Work-related outcomes of constructive confrontation strategies in job-based alcoholism programs. *Journal of Studies on Alcohol, 45,* 393–404.

Trice, H. M., & Beyer, J. M. (1984b). Employee assistance programs: Blending performance-oriented and humanitarian ideologies to assist emotionally disturbed employees. In J. R. Greenly (Ed.), *Research in Community and Mental Health* (Vol. 4, 245–297). Greenwich, CT: JAI Press.

Tsui, A. S. (1984). Personnel department effectiveness: A tripartite approach. *Industrial Relations, 23* (2), 184–197.

Tsui, A. S. (1987). Defining the activities and effectiveness of the human resource department. *Human Resource Management, 26* (1), 35–69.

Tsui, A. S. (1990). A multiple constituency model of effectiveness: An empirical examination at the human resource subunit level. *Administrative Science Quarterly, 35,* 458–483.

U.S. Department of Health and Human Services. (1987). *Standards for employee alcoholism and/or assistance programs.* Public Health Service, Alcohol, Drug Abuse, and Mental Health Administration. Washington, DC: National Institution on Drug Abuse.

Walsh, D. C., & Egdahl, R. H. (1989). Corporate perspective on work site wellness programs: A report on the seventh PEW fellows conference. *Journal of Occupational Medicine, 31*(6), 551–556.

Wright, D. A. (1985). Policy and procedures: The essential elements in an EAP. In S. H. Klarreich, J. L. Francek, and C. E. Moore (Eds.), *The Human Resources Management Handbook* (13–23). New York: Praeger.

Yandrick, R. M. (1998). The EAP struggle: Counselors or referrers? *HR Magazine,* 90–96.

Yuchtman, E., & Seashore, S. (1967). A system resource approach to organizational effectiveness. *American Sociological Review, 32,* 891–903.

Zammuto, R. F. (1984). A comparison of multiple constituency models of organizational effectiveness. *Academy of Management Review, 9* (4), 606–616.

OUTCOMES OF HUMAN RESOURCES MANAGEMENT

Successful implementation of a quality human resources program will usually result in a number of positive organizational outcomes. It is, however, sometimes difficult to determine a priori which interventions will be successful. Our intention in this part is to indicate those factors that will have significant effects upon the outcomes of human resources management programs—the bottom line. Human resources programs are costly. However, in a long-range view of the process, the costs will be returned in terms of effectiveness, productivity, and the satisfaction of individuals in an organization. Money can be wasted on human resources or invested in human resources. The implications are obvious: Preparing and implementing well-thought-out human resources programs will only improve the bottom line of organizational success.

The articles in Chapter 13 are concerned with employee attitudes. The way employees view their work, the way they are managed, and the organization itself all affect the way employees perform. Negative attitudes toward work-related factors or toward the organization can be quite dysfunctional. Have we as a society developed different work values from those of our predecessors? The articles in this chapter provide insight into this issue.

In some instances, the most effective decision is a separation decision. Employees may leave an organization voluntarily or involuntarily for a number of reasons. Chapter 14 is concerned with the separation process and emphasizes techniques for handing it in a legally defensible manner.

Chapter 15 is related to the assessment of the most important outcomes in human resources—performance and effectiveness. What must an organization do to maximize the effectiveness of the human resources management program? Much advice is offered pertaining to activities that are essential to human resources competitiveness from both a dollar cost perspective and a strategic perspective.

13 EMPLOYEE ATTITUDES

Work-related attitudes play an important role in organization performance. Individual's work-related attitudes often result from myriad interactions with factors related to human resources programs. Thus, human resources professionals are instrumental in determining, developing, and improving work-related attitudes. Those attitudes include attitudes toward the job itself; attitudes toward the context or setting in which the work is performed; and attitudes toward coworkers, subordinates, and supervisors. Although the ways in which attitudes affect performance are not easy to predict, they nonetheless do have some impact upon performance.

There have been many reports that work-related attitudes have become less positive over the last few decades. Two possibilities are associated with negative work attitudes: They may be a sign of significant underlying problems in an organization, and they may be a cause of some undesirable organizational outcomes in the future (absenteeism, poor performance). Because they are linked to a number of deleterious organizational outcomes, negative attitudes can be directly related to the organization's financial viability.

In the first article in this chapter, Wilkerson addresses the issue of organizational cynicism. We hear from the popular press that cynicism, in general, is on the increase. This article looks at cynicism from an organizational perspective and the outcomes associated with this variable. Organizational cynicism is a deeply ingrained attitude and influences what occurs at work, but recommendations are presented in order to deal with this problem. Most of us will experience what Clawson and Haskins have termed the career blues. They suggest ways in which supervisors can create a situation that minimizes our inevitable bouts with career blues.

READINGS

ORGANIZATIONAL CYNICISM AND ITS IMPACT ON HUMAN RESOURCES MANAGEMENT

James M. Wilkerson

The academic and popular business management presses have paid increasing attention to various forms of employee cynicism in the last several years. Both have noted that cynical employees have an interesting perspective on jobs, management, the organization, and work life in general. In generic terms, cynical employees are downright sardonic about these things, often displaying contempt for and distrust of them. Basically, the discourse to date has noted that the contemptuous mockery of others' motives and the expectation of the worst out of people that generally define cynicism are increasingly applied to organizational officials, coworkers, processes, and features (Andersson, 1996; Dean, Brandes, & Dharwadkar, 1998). Little of the academic work on employee cynicism has related the phenomenon specifically to human resources management (HRM) practices, however. This is unfortunate because employees are major stakeholders in HRM initiatives, and one must question whether and how employee cynicism might hinder the success of such initiatives. If employee cynicism makes HRM more difficult, then it behooves HRM professionals and researchers to better understand what leads to this phenomenon and what its effects might be, and then search for ways to decrease it. In response, this reading focuses on a specific kind of employee cynicism—organizational cynicism—and describes some ways in which organizational cynicism impacts HRM.

My intention here is not to completely review all relevant literature on employee cynicism. For detailed reviews, see Andersson (1996) and Dean, et al. (1998). Instead, I seek to give readers a practical overview of the topic, relate organizational cynicism to HRM, and then encourage readers to use the reference section as a starting point for further study. Specifically, I will discuss:

- What organizational cynicism is, including targets or objects of cynicism.
- What organizational cynicism is not.
- To what other phenomena organizational cynicism is related.
- How organizational cynicism relates to HRM and supervision.
- What can be done to lessen organizational cynicism.

DEFINITIONS, DISTINCTIONS, AND CORRELATES

Although one could argue that employee cynicism, sometimes under different labels and guises, has appeared in the organizational and management research literatures for decades (e.g., McKelvey, 1969), most trace the origin of more recent interest in employee cynicism to Donald Kanter and Philip Mirvis's national survey work in the late 1980s. Kanter and Mirvis (1989) noted a distinct cynicism pervading American workers' attitudes toward their employment experiences, a cynicism emanating from unmet expectations and related disillusionment.

This notion of unmet expectations and an accompanying negative attitude is also reflected in subsequent theorizing about employee cynicism (e.g., Andersson, 1996; Dean at al., 1998). These two elements—unmet expectations and attitude—are key to any discussion of employee cynicism. The idea of unmet expectations implicates cynicism's origins, and answering the question of "Expectations about what?" becomes pertinent to managers' efforts to abate employee cynicism. Conceiving of cynicism in attitudinal terms implicates different objects of cynicism, just as all attitudes generally relate to a fundamentally positive or negative evaluation of some object, person, issue, or event (Ajzen, 1994; Petty, 1995). Thus, when we contemplate employees' cynicism toward the organization as a specific object, the term "organizational cynicism" is an apt label in the sense of referring to this particular attitude.

Organizational cynicism is a negative attitude toward one's employing organization in general, and toward its procedures, processes, and management, that is based on a conviction that these elements generally work against the employee's best interests. This attitude is associated with sarcasm, private or anonymous complaining and criticism, disloyalty-induced withdrawal, and emotions such as contempt, disdain, disappointment, disgust, frustration, hopelessness, and pessimism (Andersson, 1996; Dean, et al., 1998; Wanous, Reichers, & Austin, 1994). Employees displaying organizational cynicism may assume their best interests are being sacrificed by self-serving executives and unfair policies for the company's interests or benefit, or they may assume that the company is headed to self-destruction, such that no party's interests are being served in the long run. Either way, cynical employees expect to come out on "the short end of the stick" in their organizational experiences. Borrowing from the definition of distrust (without equating distrust with cynicism), we can say that organizational cynicism is similarly defined in terms of "confident negative expectations" about undesirable features of organizational life (Lewicki, McAllister, & Bies, 1998).

Organizational cynicism is theoretically distinct from more stable personal characteristics and traits such as ongoing cynicism about life in general, negative affectivity (i.e., chronically bad mood marked by anxiety, contempt, irritability, and the like; Tellegen, 1985) and low self-efficacy (i.e., people's judgments of their own ability to execute actions and behave in ways necessary to attain a given type of performance; Bandura, 1986). It is also theoretically distinct from other work-relevant attitudes such as skepticism, distrust, organizational commitment, job satisfaction, learned helplessness, and alienation (Andersson, 1996; Dean, et al., 1998; Guastello, Rieke, Guastello, & Billings, 1992; McAllister, 1999; Reichers, Wanous, & Austin, 1997; Wanous, et al., 1994; Wanous, Reichers, & Austin, 2000). Further, organizational cynicism should not be confused with nonorganizationally focused cynicism featured in, for instance, articles regarding police officers' cynical coping styles (e.g., Violanti & Marshall, 1983) or articles regarding cynicism toward an occupation or work in general (e.g., Stern, Stone, Hopkins, & McMillion, 1990). Note the tenor and emotional nature of the comments in Table 13-1. These cynical comments, taken from recent employee opinion surveys that I have conducted in my consulting work, display the sarcasm, disappointment, disdain, and frustration that characterize many employees' cynical attitudes toward their organizations. Note, too, the implications of unmet expectations and a sense of betrayal or disappointment due to changed working conditions that are evident in some of the comments.

Andersson (1996) integrated various types of cynicism research and positioned employee cynicism as an outcome of psychological

TABLE 13-1   Comments from Recent Employee Opinion Surveys that Reflect Organizational Cynicism

Appreciate dedicated, loyal employees. Don't treat them like trash for the sake of progress. I was a unit head for 12 years, helped coworkers, and worked an average of 12 hours' overtime weekly, consecutively, for years getting home to my family at 8:10 P.M. Went the extra mile in everything I did. I was told by management, "Work hard and promotions are in the future for you." I loved my job, it was my priority. When changes occurred in the department, I was told, "You may not have a job, because that's progress, we have a company to run." They could have said to us that we have been loyal employees and they will do their best to make the transition as stressless as possible. But actually the department manager turns his head in the opposite direction that I am walking, like *I* did something to *him!* My life is actually the one torn apart, not knowing if I'll lose my house, car, etc., and he just ignores me like a stranger.

The management needs to focus on its employees. [Company], at one time, was a great place to work. During the past year, morale has taken a downhill course. I don't think morale can get any lower. Management needs to realize that low morale is eating away at the company like a cancer. The symptoms are an ever-increasing attrition rate, low productivity, poor work quality, and high absenteeism. Employees and their opinions were once valued. Changes were made based on sound business sense of the management. Now, management is walking around with blinders on; what they don't say is speaking louder than what they say. Ludicrous changes are being made, and no one cares enough to speak up.

A remark was made some time ago that [Company] resembled a 90-year-old man trying to act like a teenager. I think that picture explains a lot.

I have very mixed feelings about this company. . . . The regional service teams and positions on them still have major problems, in my opinion. Some of these are being addressed, but some seem to perpetuate themselves year after year. I also have watched many African-American people come to the department only to be treated with a subtle lack of respect and to leave as soon as possible. . . . I am actually quite disgusted by this company at times. I am also happy to stay at [Company], but I am always watchful, and do not trust that higher-level management really gives a damn about much more than profitability.

About 2 years ago, this work had more quality than it has now. Employees are being trained and trained to do more and more jobs such that the quality is not there. We are burnt out—fatigued— and our memories are being overloaded to get these many tasks done in the required time frame, which now is a total laugh. There is absolutely no morale and the "I don't care anymore" attitude is a common feeling shared by all. It's true but sad!! As a matter of fact, it's disgusting and it makes me angry that I used to love to come to work and now I fear it.

The stated reasons for [going public] never included the "real" reason, that upper management wanted to get rich with stock options. In fact, [Company] will probably fail and be bought by someone else within a few years. Upper management seems clueless in several respects: the pointless quality fad, which has been debunked by Dilbert, and the poor quality of our computer systems under the leadership of Willard. [Company] claims to not manage by earnings, but they do so every quarter.

The modern, 1990s "business casual" approach engenders only a surface image of inclusivity, while the reality remains that those who are most often and quickly rewarded and/or promoted are those who regularly and sincerely play the "corporate game" built on a foundation of white male "schmoozing" and sports metaphors devoid of any trust in genuine ability and commitment to welcoming diverse views and approaches. [Company] is particularly enmeshed in this environment— speeding toward the twenty-first century with both feet firmly planted in the 1970s in terms of attitudes toward current business trends, changing markets, internal morale and compensation, systems and equipment, etc. Top management is genuinely and generally viewed as oddly inept when decisive leadership is needed most—aging white males in business casual, playing golf, driving sports vehicles, and waiting for a buyout. Awfully hard for the "troops" to maintain enthusiasm given the caliber of our leadership and the complete lack of meaningful, honest communication among departments and divisions.

contract violation. A psychological contract exists when the organization has shaped an employee's beliefs, or otherwise created certain expectations, about the terms of an implicit exchange agreement between that employee and the organization. And when the employee experiences some kind of damage or harm that the contract was designed to avoid due to the organization's failure to keep its commitment, a psychological contract violation occurs (Rousseau, 1995). Relatedly, Andersson's (1996) model points to unmet expectations, betrayal at the hands of self-interested business executives, rigid application of management techniques, poor organizational communications and interpersonal treatment, managerial incompetence, layoff activity, and workplace barriers to voicing concerns as causes of organizational cynicism. The comments in Table 13-1 reflect a number of these factors.

Dean, et al. (1998) defined organizational cynicism in terms of the three components of attitudes, which are beliefs (e.g., assuming organizational unfairness and executives' harmful self-interest are linked), affect (negative emotions such as contempt, anger, and disgust), and behaviors (e.g., criticizing, using sarcastic humor, sneering) reflecting the attitude. Significantly, Dean, et al. (1998) distinguished organizational cynicism from trust, noting that organizational cynicism is more emotional than trust, does not require the interpersonal vulnerability that the trust construct requires as a precondition, and can be more experience-based than distrust (i.e., sometimes distrust is felt due to inexperience or unfamiliarity with the other party, whereas organizational cynicism develops as a result of disappointing organizational experiences). Andersson (1996) and Andersson and Bateman (1997) made similar arguments in conceiving of cynicism as distinct from distrust. They argued that trust is essentially a more limited concept of belief or expectancy, whereas cynicism entails both belief and affect.

Some studies, employing a variety of measures and similar definitions of organizational cynicism, have measured connections between it and trust in the organization (McAllister, 1999), employee skepticism about organizational and quality improvement efforts (Reichers, et al., 1997; Waldman, Lituchy, Gopalakrishnan, Laframboise, Galperin, & Kaltsounakis, 1998; Wanous, et al., 1994, 2000), sudden downsizing and poor organizational performance as antecedents (Andersson & Bateman, 1997), supervisors' reactions to upward feedback (Atwater, Waldman, Atwater, & Cartier, 2000), low intentions to perform organizational citizenship behaviors (Andersson & Bateman, 1997), emotion-focused or maladaptive coping (O'Connell, Holzman, & Armandi, 1986), and observers' reactions to workplace aggression (Wilkerson, 2001). Viewing this body of studies as a whole, one senses some tendency to use the "organizational cynicism" label even when actually focused on objects of cynical attitudes that are narrower than the organization as a whole. Also, one can detect some confounding of the cynical attitude with its potential causes, a condition that can raise questions about whether the researcher is measuring a cynical attitude or a judgment of the event or condition that engendered the cynicism (cf. Stone-Romero, 1994). It appears "organizational cynicism" has meant slightly different things to different researchers and this area of research has not yet demonstrated consensus regarding the construct, so students of this literature must take care to not get too bogged down in labels. What is important to remember about organizational cynicism is that it is derived from the employee's disappointing experiences with a variety of organizational features and work life events, and that it reflects a resulting negative evaluation of and expectancy about those organizational features and similar, future work life events. Thus cynicism can be both general and specific (Andersson, 1996), and have multiple foci (Dean, et al., 1998).

While employees may well have a cynical attitude toward the organization as a distinct entity, they are also likely to display cynicism toward more specific organizational elements. Hence, the definition I provided: a negative attitude toward one's employing organization in general, and toward its procedures, processes, and management, that is based on a conviction that these elements generally work against the employee's best interests. Any glance at cartoon comic strips, Internet sites, electronic newsletters, and movies showcasing employees' cynical attitudes suggests that cynicism applies to many aspects of work life, some as general as "the company" and some as specific as a particular business function or level of management. While it may be a bit messy, treating employee cynicism in terms of the attitude's various objects seems to be the most useful way to precisely target and measure cynicism's effects. Thus object-specific work on cynicism about organizational change (Wanous, et al., 1994, 2000), cynicism about company management (Wilkerson, 2001), and cynicism about coworkers and subordinates (Atwater, et al., 2000) is useful for a more fine-grained understanding of employee cynicism.

For instance, I have found different types of cynicism to be differentially related to reasons employees give for observed workplace aggression. Specifically, I found that cynicism about company management related more to a perception of workplace pressures causing workplace aggression, whereas organizational cynicism (i.e., cynicism about prospects for improvement in the workplace, proper rewards, quality of work life in the company, etc.) related more to a perception of prevention failure causing workplace aggression. Even the HRM function itself can become an object of employee cynicism. For instance, it is not uncommon to read comments in employee attitude

surveys that reflect cynicism about the HR department. This can be due to early expectations of help, support, or confidentiality from the HR department becoming replaced, after several unfulfilling interactions, with expectations of unhelpfulness or unreliability. See Table 13-2 for a few examples of such comments.

IMPACT ON HRM

Should HRM professionals, supervisors, and other managers be concerned about organizational cynicism in any particular way? Is it a phenomenon with specific effects in the organization, thus requiring specific managerial attention? Research on employee cynicism gives us reason to suspect that the attitude may pose real problems for organizations. However, the paucity of empirical research on organizational cynicism's links to employee behaviors and organizational outcomes does not help us to know for sure. This lack of research extends to the question of what measurable impact organizational cynicism has on HRM. The potential for meaningful links between organizational cynicism and HRM practices seems great since so many aspects of an employee's work life are either directly managed by the HR function or are strongly influenced by it. Relatedly, success or failure of many HRM initiatives hinges on the attitude-consistent behaviors of employees. For instance, efforts to boost employee participation in savings plans can be thwarted by negative attitudes toward income deferral and efforts to reduce workplace injuries may be hampered by lackadaisical attitudes toward safety. Behaviors consistent with organizational cynicism are not likely to be the kinds of behaviors HRM programs are designed to inspire.

In general, most HRM professionals and supervisors can attest to the difficulty of maintaining positive employee relations when employees display organizational cynicism, in part because the attitude predis-

TABLE 13-2	Comments from Recent Employee Opinion Surveys that Reflect Cynicism About HR

Sometimes I wonder how this company stays in business. Absolutely, positively each and every single time without fail that I deal with the internal departments of this company (HR, Payroll, Benefits, etc.), they get it wrong the first time, every time! There has never been an exception to this, and I have been here more than 18 years. . . . After all, their motto seems to be "We get it wrong the first time". . . . In conclusion: The benefits are great, if you can get HR to administer them correctly without extreme frustration on error factors. The pay is "just O.K." At least it's better than working in a restaurant. . . . After 18 years, I'm looking for another job, this place has been nothing but frustration.

Up until a year ago, I was extremely loyal. . . . All that changed last year when I needed to take a medical leave of absence. . . . Rather than notify me that I needed to provide documentation or return to work, it was only after I contacted [Company] to return to work that I was notified my leave was unapproved beyond the FMLA period. I was terminated not because there was no position available for me to return to, but because they considered me to have abandoned my job. I was in shock. . . . What I felt betrayed and extremely offended by was that the intangible considerations were not given more weight before they terminated for abandonment. I had been employed for 14 years at that time. I had perfect attendance the 2 years prior. My performance reviews were very positive. . . . Although eventually restored to my position, I feel betrayed by [Company]. I know that they do not value their employees. Statistics is all that matters to them. . . . Due to this experience, I will be leaving [Company] with bitterness. I understand that the other party involved has a different perspective, but they have yet to make it clear to me how their scale was tipped to conclude I abandoned my job. . . . Human Resources represents the climate of the company. They certainly didn't act in a conscientious manner.

Personnel policies communicated by our dreadful personnel department (the outstanding weak link at [Company]) are irrational, inconsistent, and often so unfair that this department has little respect from any section of the company.

Our human resources department is *useless.* They do not help you or get back to you in a timely manner.

Don't even think about going to the Human Resources Department; they just appease you, do nothing, and are unable to be objective when they are friends with the supervisor.

1. I would release the company from Human Resources' reach/grip. HR does not serve the employee at [Company]. 2. Scrap the performance review process as it now exists. 3. Demand that management communicate downward with staff and hold management accountable for this communication responsibility. 4. I'd ensure that *real* career paths are available at [Company]. 5. Institute employee reviews of management performance.

poses employees to find fault with the organization. Mirvis and Kanter (1992) held that cynicism influences employees' attributions (causal explanations) for workplace events. Thus it is likely that organizational cynicism relates to fairly strong attributions to the organization for work life frustrations and disappointment, especially when the cynical employee blames managerial decisions or organizational functioning for the events that created the frustrations and disappointment. Against this kind of backdrop, employee counseling can fall on deaf ears, nonfinancial recognition can generate unappreciative derision, formal disciplinary processes can become even more contentious than they typically are, and employee involvement initiatives can be met with smirking and apathy. The difficulty of fostering positive employee relations among cynical employees is made worse in that these employees may also perform poorly (Ferris, Arthur, Berkson, Kaplan, Harrell-Cook, & Frink, 1998) and be less productive (Anthony, Perrewé, & Kacmar, 1999), which only increases the likelihood that line management will, at some point, turn to the HR department for help in improving employee attitudes for productivity's sake. Besides having difficulty getting good productivity out of cynical employees, supervisors may find such employees display few organizational citizenship behaviors (OCBs), or the kinds of extra-role, "above and beyond" behaviors that employees are sometimes counted on for the sake of voluntarily helping and making incremental improvements (Organ, 1988). Andersson and Bateman (1997) found that cynicism was related to lower intentions to perform OCBs. A diminishment in OCBs not only makes the supervisor's work life harder, but may also signal ineffectiveness in HRM programs and practices that are expected to give rise to OCBs (Morrison, 1996; Werner, 2000).

Some anecdotal evidence from the field suggests that organizational cynicism may relate to HRM in specific ways. When HRM professionals were asked whether they and their managerial peers perceive a connection between organizational cynicism and performance or behavior issues, they cited effects such as employee resistance to new procedures, reduced morale, and absenteeism problems. Relatedly, when asked about the impact of employee cynicism on employee retention and employee relations efforts, HRM professionals said they find cynicism associated with higher likelihood of quitting, an increased need for conflict management in the organization, more employee grumbling and nitpicking about new programs or changes, and greater effort required of the HR function to offset the attitude's tendency to, as one professional put it, "make issues larger than they warrant" (i.e., employee skepticism over new e-mail and Internet policy).

Interestingly, some of these HRM professionals have also pointed out that organizational cynicism is contagious, especially in a lateral sense among peers. Thus employee cynicism can form in the way some other work attitudes form, via a process of taking cues from coworkers (Salancik & Pfeffer, 1978; Zalesny & Ford, 1990). One organization development professional cited this kind of social contagion when discussing sources of organizational cynicism, saying cynical attitudes "come from many places: sometimes the leadership (employees repeat what their leaders are saying behind closed doors), sometimes from functional groups that band together for survival's sake, sometimes from rumors, sometimes from the fear of the unknown. The key is that they seem to be contagious. If a number of influential individuals begin the cynical behavior it then starts to run rampant." One HR director associates the socialization effects of cynical veterans' contagious attitudes with the sudden onset of cynicism among junior employees, which he regards as a factor in turnover among employees with less than a year's service.

Other ways in which organizational cynicism and HRM are linked include this attitude's impact on aspirations for a career with one's employer, perceptions about managerial communications, and pay satisfaction. Cynicism relating to career aspirations appears to arise from, among other things, unfair or politicized internal promotion practices, the practice of hiring talent from the outside instead of developing and promoting from within, and frustration over being deemed unqualified for promotion due to a lack of formal education credentials. The effect is evident in employee survey comments, often quite sarcastic and bitter in emotional tone, suggesting that these antecedent factors make further efforts at career development futile and reflecting a conviction that these dissatisfying conditions will continue indefinitely. Thus the cynicism is liable to suppress job bidding behavior, thereby having a direct impact on the operation and success of the organization's internal job-posting practice. To the extent cynicism contributes to turnover as disillusioned employees seek more promising career venues, demands on the HRM function to conduct external recruiting and deal with retention problems are increased.

Cynicism relating to managerial communications and other "official" corporate communications stems from instances in which executives and managers have failed to "walk the talk" or have failed to share important information. The resulting cynicism is evident in employees' snide comments impugning the communications' honesty, credibility, or completeness. Thus cynicism's impact on future communications is felt as managers find themselves having to persuade more, or simply repeat the message more, to overcome the effects of cynical employees having ignored the original communication that they were convinced was either not worth their attention or not credible.

Causes of pay dissatisfaction are clearly evident in survey comments about external inequity in pay, unfairness in the form of pay raises that seem minuscule relative to the effort and work quality employees produce, pay range compression, and instances in which the HR department has failed to produce or effectively communicate credible wage/market survey data that justify wage rates. The resulting cynicism toward compensation practices is apparent in comments describing the organization as "cheap" and wage rates or salary structure as "ridiculous" and "insulting." (An example is an exit interviewee's observation: "The pay level was FUNNY. Four percent increase yearly, and that's with being rated ABOVE EXPECTATIONS! Why don't you just slap us in the face?!") Also, many comments reflecting disgust with pay issues simultaneously invoke notions of being unrecognized and unappreciated, possibly indicating that cynicism is also associated with a real personalizing of the issue beyond just a matter of budgets and market rates. In any case, cynicism about pay practices almost certainly makes the HR de-partment's compensation design and administration tasks more difficult.

These observations I have related are anecdotal, and need to be validated with more rigorous research if we are to better understand organizational cynicism's relationship with HRM. An example is Atwater, et al.'s (2000) recent study. They observed that cynical supervisors were less likely to respond constructively to upward performance feedback, a finding with serious implications for the success of 360-degree feedback programs that HRM professionals may implement. Other links between organizational cynicism and HRM-relevant outcomes are worthy of investigation. For instance, the way in which organizational cynicism makes employees expect negative experiences with organizational systems and managers might suggest that the attitude would predict less training achievement and transfer, particularly if the training relates to skills and behaviors that are dependent on a supportive organizational setting for successful application (Baldwin & Ford, 1988; Tracey, Tannenbaum, & Kavanagh, 1995). Employees high in organizational cynicism simply may not believe that a supportive training transfer climate exists, regardless of the workplace's objective features. As one HRM professional suggested, cynical employees are less likely to actively participate in training and less likely to believe in what is being trained to the extent they sense a disparity between training's prescriptions and organizational culture's reality. While a poor application environment in the work setting beyond the training room will tend to diminish successful training transfer for just about any employee, one might hypothesize that organizational cynicism in conjunction with a poor application environment will predict especially poor training transfer.

A relationship between cynicism and training transfer is but one possible way in which organizational cynicism can impact

HRM. Might we also expect the employee high in organizational cynicism to be less likely to refer job applicants to the organization? This outcome can pose problems for the organization's recruitment efforts. If cynical employees are less likely to value long-term employment with the company and less confident of the company's future performance, might they tend to participate less in voluntary benefit plans such as 401(k) plans, especially to the extent the employer's contribution to the plan is in the form of company stock? Are cynical employees weaker team players, more deviant with respect to organizational norms, and less motivated by performance incentives? If so, employee involvement initiatives may be expected to suffer accordingly. How readily can the HR department count on staffing new operations in different locations with existing employees if organizational cynicism diminishes employees' desire to accept transfer? These questions are all subject to empirical testing, and knowing their answers would help us more fully gauge the impact of organizational cynicism on HRM.

My final point about organizational cynicism's impact on HRM relates to innovation and change. Wanous, et al.'s (1994) initial work on what they called organizational cynicism led directly to their more specific work on cynicism about organizational change (Reichers, et al., 1997; Wanous, et al., 2000; cf. Waldman, et al., 1998). Not surprisingly, this work has shown that failures of past organizational change initiatives breed employee cynicism about future change efforts, and this cynicism about organizational change is inversely related to employees' motivation to expend effort in support of change and problem solving. These findings relate directly to conceptual work on HRM innovations, or newly adopted programs, policies, and practices that organizations implement, often through the HRM function, to influence employee attitudes, skills, motivation, and behaviors

(Kossek, 1987; Wolfe, 1995). Regarding HRM innovations, Kossek's (1987) observation that "if past efforts resulted in a negative experience for the social system, then skepticism and distrust are likely to arise in response to new programs" (p. 88) is wholly consistent with views on cynicism about organizational change and its antecedents. Aggregate organizational cynicism and cynicism about organizational change can pose a context constraint on HRM innovations that could diminish the effects of even the most powerful innovation champions and change agents, and result in limited diffusion of HRM innovations (Wolfe, 1995). This should be of concern to HRM professionals, for their ability to manage change is a dominant factor in whether their organizational peers and superiors, most of whom are their internal customers, view them as competent (Ulrich, Brockbank, Yeung, & Lake, 1995).

WHAT TO DO?

Just as empirical research on organizational cynicism's actual effects is scarce, so are empirical research on its causes and research-derived recommendations for its prevention or reduction. Thus managers cannot get very detailed intervention guidance from most of the existing literature. However, researchers have made a number of general recommendations that are worth noting. These recommendations take into account an understanding of how organizational cynicism develops, how it has various foci, and its expectational nature. Most fundamentally, we must remember that organizational cynicism is considered to be an acquired attitude (Andersson, 1996; Dean, et al., 1998; Wanous, et al., 2000). That is, organizational cynicism is a learned, experientially-based attitude, and is accordingly subject to change (Dean, et al., 1998). Interventions aimed at preventing or reducing organizational cynicism must address the experiences that shape the attitude and exploit the attitude's changeability. The following discussion on attitude change and organizational interventions is prefaced with the reminder that the impact of these changes should be explicitly measured so management can know for sure whether positive change is occurring (Burke, Coruzzi, & Church, 1996). Further, this measurement effort should be longitudinal. That is, management should measure organizational cynicism and its effects at least twice, once before the change effort begins and at least once after the change effort has been made and enough time has passed for employee attitudes and related outcomes to truly reflect the effects of the intervention. Also, the cynicism measures should precede the measures of cynicism's effects, if at all possible.

Employees who have become cynical about their organizations have experienced disappointing work life events to such a degree, either in quantity or in severity, that they have become convinced that this is just the way it is and likely will continue to be with their employer. They are accustomed to suffering some sort of loss or experiencing frustration in their interactions with the organization and its features, and they expect little different in future interactions. But if this negative attitude formed from specific experiences, it conceivably can be reversed, or at least reduced, by giving employees different experiences resolved against possibly different expectations of the way work life is supposed to be (Petty, 1995). This approach focuses on increasing the perceived likelihood of particularly desirable aspects of the organization. For instance, suppose we determine that employees consider HR department responsiveness, confidentiality, and policy change explanation to be particularly desirable. Combating cynicism about the HRM function or HR department then entails reducing the time it takes to respond to employee queries, increasing the confidentiality of employee matters, and doing a better job of explaining the rationale for and practical implications of policy changes. These things have to be done consistently and repeatedly such that their likelihood seems high to employees.

Similarly, most recommendations for addressing employee cynicism, found mainly in writings about organizational cynicism and cynicism about organizational change, focus on providing employees with new, convincing experiences to offset a disillusioning track record of past experiences. Reichers, et al. (1997) gave 10 recommendations for managing and minimizing cynicism about organizational change; some of them readily relate to other forms of employee cynicism, as well. Some of these recommendations include informing employees fully and in a timely manner of upcoming organizational changes; involving employees more in workplace decisions affecting them; openly acknowledging past managerial mistakes and concretely redressing them; publicizing successful organizational changes so as to convince employees that things can work out as planned; learning more about employees' views of change and the organization through open, two-way communication; and enhancing the credibility of change-related communications by using credible spokespersons, repetitive messaging, and logical appeals for support for change.

Regarding this latter point about credibility, Reichers, et al. (1997) noted that research on attitude change (e.g., Petty & Cacioppo, 1986) supports the suggested inverse relationship between credibility and cynicism about organizational change. Attitude change theories and research also seem to support the recommendation for more employee involvement in workplace decision making as a means of lowering organizational cynicism. Employee involvement in routine problem solving, and even in any intervention specifically undertaken to reduce cynicism, would likely have the effect of making the intervention and related new experiences more personally relevant to the involved employees. Personal relevance, in turn, relates to more thoughtful evaluation of the new organizational experiences and more persistent attitude change (Petty, 1995; Petty & Cacioppo, 1979). Because the objects of employees' cynical attitudes (e.g., the boss, organizational change processes, promotion and reward practices, etc.) affect these employees' work lives and are typically quite important to them, it is likely that organizational cynicism usually forms under conditions of high personal relevance. Thus managers should not underestimate the need for highly relevant, convincing new experiences and persuasion to create enduring, more positive attitudes in place of cynical attitudes that are, themselves, quite persistent. Leveraging the relevance-inducing effects of employee involvement is one way of obtaining this.

In addition to making a similar recommendation with respect to employee involvement, Mirvis and Kanter (1992) focused some of their recommendations on managing employees' expectations as a way of minimizing the disillusionment and disappointment that presage employee cynicism. They recommended that organizations diagnose and act on employees' unrealistic expectations, perceptions of unfairness in the reciprocal relationship between employer and employee, and views of specific ways in which managers are not "walking the talk." This relates somewhat to the question of "expectations about what?" that I raised earlier. Unless employers know what employees' expectations are, both generally and with reference to specific organizational attributes, they cannot fully understand how the organization's features and realities are out of line with employees' expectations. Because psychological contract violation is a likely cause of employee cynicism (Andersson, 1996), organizations should avoid creating unrealistic initial expectations of things such as pay, advancement, job security, managers' competence, interpersonal treatment,

etc., that, when inevitably unmet later, could lead to cynicism. Lofty promises could come from communications in recruiting, by bosses, and in company publications (Turnley & Feldman, 1999; Wanous, 1992), and each should be examined and adjusted so as to not create unrealistic expectations.

The reader will note that implementing some, if not most, of these recommendations is likely to involve the organization's HRM function. Thus, just as organizational cynicism can impact HRM, so can HRM impact organizational cynicism for better or for worse. This is consistent with Ferris, et al.'s (1998) model of the linkage between HRM and organizational effectiveness that indicates HRM practices and systems influence employee attitudes both directly and through organizational climate. Aspects of organizational climate drive cynicism to the extent employees' experiences convince them that managers will not be considerate or supportive and rewards will be more political than performance-based. Furthermore, the aspect of organizational climate relating to task support relates to organizational cynicism to the extent frustrations with bad technology, poor interdepartmental communications and cooperation, excessive work loads, etc., lead employees to cynically conclude that achieving excellent task performance is all but impossible in the organization. Obviously, the HRM function can contribute to these adverse climate conditions and attitudinal outcomes to the extent management development programs do not inspire better support and coaching from managers, formal reward and performance appraisal systems ignore employee performance variance, etc. (Ferris, et al., 1998).

As HRM professionals contemplate interventions, they would do well to bear in mind some factors that are likely to influence the links between intervention effects and organizational cynicism. For instance, intervention efforts targeted at nonmanagement employees may be especially difficult as the employee's job level and intervention effects may affect each other. Mirvis and Kanter (1992) found that blue-collar employees were more cynical than white-collar employees, and Andersson (1996) related this to employee cynicism, proposing that blue-collar employees were more likely to be cynical when subjected to psychological contract violation. Reichers, et al. (1997) noted that enthusiasm for organizational change initiatives seen in upper management ranks is not shared farther down in the organizational hierarchy, where the efforts may be seen as "necessary evils or as the incomprehensible actions of a top management group out of touch with day-to-day operations" (p. 48). Furthermore, the experiences supposedly giving rise to organizational cynicism strongly implicate managers' and executives' choices, decision making, and competencies (Andersson, 1996; Dean, et al., 1998; Wanous, et al., 1994, 2000). Thus, nonmanagement employees are likely to be particularly skeptical about interventions aimed at reducing their organizational cynicism.

Another factor that could affect whether intervention efforts are successful in reducing employee cynicism is organizational politics. Highly politicized work environments may be characteristic of what Mirvis and Kanter (1992) called "cynical companies," which are companies that "embody expedient, self-serving values, that support managers who engage in deceptive and exploitative practices, and that communicate in a one-sided, hyped-up, and disingenuous fashion to their employees" (p. 61). Aspects of this description (specifically, self-serving values and exploitative practices) mirror organizational elements that employees are likely to perceive as evidence of workplace politics (Ferris & Kacmar, 1992). To the extent organizational politics give cynical employees the sense that intervention sponsors and change agents are only pursuing their own self-interests in a way

typical of workplace politicians, intervention efforts aimed at reducing organizational cynicism may be especially difficult (Ferris et al., 1998).

Finally, note a practical concern about getting information from employees for the purpose of intervention planning. The HRM professional taking a first step toward dealing with organizational cynicism by seeking to gauge employees' expectations and disappointments may encounter some difficulty in getting cynical employees to speak up. True, some have speculated that workplace cynics can serve as "the voice of conscience for the organization" (Dean, et al., 1998, p. 347). And cynical layoff survivors that Mishra and Spreitzer (1998) called "carping critics" are presumed to actively employ voice, albeit in a destructive manner. However, these cynical employees may not be especially likely to voice concerns in any very public way. It may be more likely that organizational cynicism is related to quiet apathy and private grumbling amongst peers who share the attitude.

Hirschman (1970), Farrell (1983), and Withey and Cooper (1989) all conceived of voice as a constructive thing, a phenomenon characterized by approach behavior. On the other hand, employee cynicism is clearly a phenomenon more generally characterized by avoidance or withdrawal behavior. One would expect it to be associated with some kind of passive, emotion-focused coping, not with problem-focused coping like speaking up about problems or concerns (i.e., voicing). Conditions conducive to employee voice include job satisfaction, organizational commitment, a belief that improvement is possible, and low personal cost of voicing (Morrison & Milliken, 2000; Withey & Cooper, 1989). The cynical employee is not as likely to be satisfied with the job or committed to the organization, is typically convinced improvements are not forthcoming and the organization's situation is hopeless, and may not trust that speaking up is costless. This suggests that employee cynicism may, in fact, be negatively associated with voice.

I recently conducted a study employing two employee cynicism measures and two voice measures (Wilkerson, 2001). The results suggest that, if anything, employee cynicism is weakly and inversely correlated with voice (the more cynical employees are, the less they speak up about workplace problems). Thus, it may be that the workplace cynic's sarcasm and verbal criticism of the organization (Dean, et al., 1998; Mishra & Spreitzer, 1998) cannot be equated with complaining to anyone in any overt, problem-focused way. Organizational cynics often gripe a lot about the organization and managers, but not necessarily publicly. To the employee strong in cynicism about management, company managers and executives are self-serving nincompoops who likely cannot find ways to improve things. As a result, the cynical employee may actually be less likely to voice concerns to management. Managers must not be fooled into thinking that nothing is wrong or that cynicism is low simply because they are not hearing complaints. The silence may itself be a symptom of organizational cynicism. Anonymous participation in focus groups and attitude surveys conducted by neutral third parties may be necessary to get organizational cynics talking "for the record."

In conclusion, the bad news is that organizational cynicism is likely a deeply-ingrained attitude that is not easily changed. The good news is that organizational cynicism, in being an experientially derived and context-based attitude, is probably more manageable than some other kinds of employee attitudes and dispositions. Organizational managers can do very little to change employees' traits and dispositional tendencies toward cynicism and related characteristics such as pessimism, misanthropy, or an aversion to work in general. However, since organizational cynicism develops in response to workplace experiences, countervailing experiences may be able to reduce it. This is likely to be more fruitful than simply blaming employee cynicism on personality variables such as negative affectivity, which Wanous et al. (2000) have recently determined is a weak predictor of cynicism about organizational change relative to situational factors. Also, taking preventative steps to shape employees' initial expectations and provide acceptable climates for career development, supervisory behavior, rewards, etc., are both doable and likely easier than attempting to change cynical attitudes after they have formed. ∎

REFERENCES

Ajzen, I. (1994). Attitudes. In R. J. Corsini (Ed.), *Encyclopedia of Psychology* (2nd ed., 114–116). New York: Wiley.

Andersson, L. M. (1996). Employee cynicism: An examination using a contract violation framework. *Human Relations, 49,* 1395–1418.

Andersson, L. M. , & Bateman, T. S. (1997). Cynicism in the workplace: Some causes and effects. *Journal of Organizational Behavior, 18,* 449–469.

Anthony, W. P. , Perrewé, P. L. , & Kacmar, K. M. (1999). *Human resource management: A strategic approach* (3rd ed.). Fort Worth, TX: Harcourt Brace & Company.

Atwater, L. E. , Waldman, D. A. , Atwater, D., & Cartier, P. (2000). An upward feedback field experiment: Supervisors' cynicism, reactions, and commitment to subordinates. *Personnel Psychology, 53,* 275–297.

Baldwin, T. T., & Ford, J. K. (1988). Transfer of training: A review and directions for future research. *Personnel Psychology, 41,* 63–105.

Bandura, A. (1986). *Social foundations of thought and action: A social-cognitive theory.* Upper Saddle River, NJ: Prentice Hall.

Burke, W. W., Coruzzi, C. A., & Church, A. H. (1996). The organizational survey as an intervention for change. In A. I. Kraut (Ed.), *Organizational Surveys: Tools for Assessment and Change* (41–66). San Francisco: Jossey-Bass.

Dean, J. W., Brandes, P., & Dharwadkar, R. (1998). Organizational cynicism. *Academy of Management Review, 23,* 341–352.

Farrell, D. (1983). Exit, voice, loyalty, and neglect as responses to job dissatisfaction: A multidimensional scaling study. *Academy of Management Journal, 26,* 596–607.

Ferris, G. R., Arthur, M. M., Berkson, H. M., Kaplan, D. M., Harrell-Cook, G., & Frink, D. D. (1998). Toward a social context theory of the human resource management-organization effectiveness relationship. *Human Resource Management Review, 8,* 235–264.

Ferris, G. R., & Kacmar, K. M. (1992). Perceptions of organizational politics. *Journal of Management, 18,* 93–116.

Guastello, S. J., Rieke, M. L., Guastello, D. D., & Billings, S. W. (1992). A study of cynicism, personality, and work values. *Journal of Psychology, 126,* 37–48.

Hirschman, A. O. (1970). *Exit, voice, and loyalty: Responses to decline in firms, organizations, and states.* Cambridge, MA: Harvard University Press.

Kanter, D. L., & Mirvis, P. H. (1989). *The cynical Americans: Living and working in an age of discontent and disillusion.* San Francisco: Jossey-Bass.

Kossek, E. E. (1987). Human resources management innovation. *Human Resource Management, 26,* 71–92.

Lewicki, R. J., McAllister, D. J., & Bies, R. J. (1998). Trust and distrust: New relationships and realities. *Academy of Management Review, 23,* 438–458.

McAllister, D. J. (1999, August). Cynicism at work: The social dynamics of extreme distrust in organizations. Paper presented at the annual meeting of the Academy of Management, Chicago.

McKelvey, W. W. (1969). Expectational noncomplementarity and style of interaction between professional and organization. *Administrative Science Quarterly, 14,* 21–32.

Mirvis, P. H., & Kanter, D. L. (1992). Beyond demography: A psychographic profile of the workforce. *Human Resource Management, 30,* 45–68.

Mishra, A. K., & Spreitzer, G. M. (1998). Explaining how survivors respond to downsizing: The roles of trust, empowerment, justice, and work redesign. *Academy of Management Review, 23,* 567–588.

Morrison, E. W. (1996). Organizational citizenship behavior as a critical link between HRM practices and service quality. *Human Resource Management, 35,* 493–512.

Morrison, E. W., & Milliken, F. J. (2000). Organizational silence: A barrier to change and development in a pluralistic world. *Academy of Management Review, 25,* 706–725.

O'Connell, B. J., Holzman, H., & Armandi, B. R. (1986). Police cynicism and the modes of adaptation. *Journal of Police Science and Administration, 14,* 307–313.

Organ, D. W. (1988). *Organizational citizenship behavior: The good soldier syndrome.* Lexington, MA: Lexington Books.

Petty, R. E. (1995). Attitude change. In A. Tesser (Ed.), *Advanced social psychology* (195–255). New York: McGraw-Hill.

Petty, R. E., & Cacioppo, J. T. (1979). Issue-involvement can increase or decrease persuasion by enhancing message-relevant cognitive responses. *Journal of Personality and Social Psychology, 37,* 1915–1926.

Petty, R. E., & Cacioppo, J. T. (1986). *Communication and persuasion: Central and peripheral routes to attitude change.* New York: Springer-Verlag.

Reichers, A. E., Wanous, J. P., & Austin, J. T. (1997). Understanding and managing cynicism about organizational change. *Academy of Management Executive, 11* (1), 48–59.

Rousseau, D. M. (1995). *Psychological contracts in organizations: Understanding written and unwritten agreements.* Thousand Oaks, CA: Sage Publications.

Salancik, G. R., & Pfeffer, J. (1978). A social information processing approach to job attitudes and task design. *Administrative Science Quarterly, 23,* 224–253.

Stern, D., Stone, J. R., Hopkins, C., & McMillion, M. (1990). Quality of students' work experience and orientation toward work. *Youth & Society, 22,* 263–282.

Stone-Romero, E. F. (1994). Construct validity issues in organizational behavior research. In J. Greenberg (Ed.), *Organizational behavior: The state of the science* (pp. 155–179). Hillsdale, NJ: Erlbaum.

Tellegen, A. (1985). Structures of mood and personality and their relevance to assessing anxiety, with an emphasis on self-report. In A. H. Tuma & J. D. Maser (Eds.), *Anxiety and the Anxiety Disorders* (681–706). Hillsdale, NJ: Erlbaum.

Tracey, J. B., Tannenbaum, S. I., & Kavanagh, M. J. (1995). Applying trained skills on the job: The importance of the work environment. *Journal of Applied Psychology, 80,* 239–252.

Turnley, W. H., & Feldman, D. C. (1999). A discrepancy model of psychological contract violations. *Human Resource Management Review, 9,* 367–386.

Ulrich, D., Brockbank, W., Yeung, A. K., & Lake, D. G. (1995). Human resource competencies: An empirical assessment. *Human Resource Management, 34,* 473–495.

Violanti, J. M., & Marshall, J. R. (1983). The police stress process. *Journal of Police Science and Administration, 11,* 389–394.

Waldman, D. A., Lituchy, T., Gopalakrishnan, M., Laframboise, K., Galperin, B., & Kaltsounakis, Z. (1998). A qualitative analysis of leadership and quality improvement. *Leadership Quarterly, 9,* 177–201.

Wanous, J. P. (1992). *Organizational entry: Recruitment, selection, orientation, and socialization of newcomers* (2nd ed.). Reading, MA: Addison-Wesley.

Wanous, J. P., Reichers, A. E., & Austin, J. T. (1994). Organizational cynicism: An initial study. In D. P. Moore (Ed.), *Best Papers Proceedings of the 54th Annual Meeting of the Academy of Management* (269–273).

Wanous, J. P., Reichers, A. E., & Austin, J. T. (2000). Cynicism about organizational change: Measurement, antecedents, and correlates. *Group & Organization Management, 25,* 132–153.

Werner, J. M. (2000). Implications of OCB and contextual performance for human resource management. *Human Resource Management Review, 10,* 3–24.

Wilkerson, J. M. (2001). An attribution-centered model of observers' reactions to workplace aggression. Unpublished doctoral dissertation, Georgia Institute of Technology, Atlanta.

Withey, M. J., & Cooper, W. H. (1989). Predicting exit, voice, loyalty, and neglect. *Administrative Science Quarterly, 34,* 521–539.

Wolfe, R. A. (1995). Human resource management innovations: Determinants of their adoption and implementation. *Human Resource Management, 34,* 313–327.

Zalesny, M. D., & Ford, J. K. (1990). Extending the social information processing perspective: New links to attitudes, behaviors, and perceptions. *Organizational Behavior and Human Decision Processes, 47,* 205–246.

BEATING THE CAREER BLUES

James G. Clawson
Mark E. Haskins

> *All organizations now routinely say, "People are our greatest asset." Yet few*
> *practice what they preach, let alone truly believe it.[1]*
> —Peter Drucker

An upper-middle manager for a large corporation struggles to get out of bed and into his car for the commute to work and realizes he's felt this daily dread for months. A senior government official stares at the paperwork accumulated on his desk and wistfully remembers a time when he loved going to work. A tenured professor at a prestigious university tries to get psyched up for yet another class in yet another offering of her introductory course. The headmaster at a successful, growing private school shakes his head at his lengthy list of administrative responsibilities and wonders where his energy went. The drive-through-window sales person for a major fast-food chain mumbles into her microphone and never notices anything, including her customers, beyond the reach of her hand. A mother of four notes that she's finding more and more ways to stay away from the house and that the dishes and laundry are piling up higher and higher.

All of these people suffer from the career blues. They have lost their motivation for their chosen work and the pleasure they once derived from it. They have become, to varying degrees, disengaged from their work, and although they may partially recognize that fact, they feel lost and uncertain about what to do about it. Most of us get the career blues from time to time; that's one reason why we take vacations, to refresh and renew our energies. But if people allow the career blues to linger, if the blues become a habit, they and their organizations suffer.

People who languish in the career blues work well enough to get along, but don't find satisfaction or ways to excel in what they do. Their organizations risk the mediocre performance and the continuation of old routines that come from tolerating more and more people doing only good enough. These people have lost what management thought leader Charles Handy calls their "E-factors"—their energy, enthusiasm, excitement, effort, and excellence.[2] Researcher and consultant Manfred Kets de Vries has found that even "CEOs . . . experience the 'blues.'"[3]

People suffering the career blues and the people who manage them need a set of ideas that explains what is going on and what to do about it. Traditional motivation theory—including hierarchies of motivational potentialities, expectancy theory, and operant conditioning—are too narrow to identify and address career blues. Career theories like anchors, stages, and skills-demands fit models help in selecting careers, but do not provide insights nor give answers about what to do with the blues. Even adult development theories that describe psychological dilemmas, alternating seasons, or letting go, lack robustness to help people with the career blues, and the managers they work for.[4] This article brings together several conceptual perspectives and melds them with our practical experience to provide a useful approach for diagnosing and managing career blues.

In a world where competition in virtually every business is intensifying and where companies are delayering, downsizing, and reengineering in an attempt to establish and maintain a competitive advantage, just getting along at work puts an employee's job and employability at risk. A company with too many employees who are just getting along risks being passed by competitors with more engaged employees attuned to and desiring ways to excel. Many organizations that claim that people are their greatest asset nevertheless tolerate good-enough performance. They and their employees find themselves increasingly noncompetitive and eventually obsolete.

WHAT ARE THE CAREER BLUES?

The career blues are marked by a loss of enthusiasm for work, a loss of a sense of purpose in work, and an emotional flatness regarding work that affect the use of time and talents, energy and effort, and aspirations and attitude while at work. People suffering the blues have lost their desire to go to work, view work as drudgery, and have no clear sense of how work adds value to their lives. They are going through the motions at work, and are uninterested, unenthusiastic, and unengaged.

The opposite of the career blues is career engagement. People engaged with their careers are enthusiastic about their work, have a sense of satisfying purpose in what they are doing, and are able to draw on and continuously renew that sense. They effectively utilize most of their time, talent, and energy. They give an honest, focused effort in the pursuit of fulfilling personal aspirations. People engaged in their work enjoy it and invest in it.

Career blues and career engagement represent polar opposites of what we label the career resonance continuum (CRC). At a given point in time, a person might be anywhere along this continuum. However, some people reside regularly in one region or the other, more or less always engaged with or disengaged from their work. Others vacillate from region to region, depending on their home lives or their work assignments. Any movement toward the disengaged or blue end of the CRC is cause for review and reconsideration. Persistent dwelling at that end is reason to reevaluate work and career. How can one tell where a person is on the CRC?

DIAGNOSING THE CAREER BLUES

A useful framework for diagnosing the career blues is what we call TEA[2] accounts. We borrow this name from general ledger accounting practice, where T-accounts are used for displaying debits and credits, but use it to refer to the positive manifestations of six indicators of career engagement: time, talent, energy, effort, attitude, and aspiration. These six aspects provide a powerful way of assessing a person's engagement in work. Since there are two dimensions for each letter, we call this the TEA[2] Framework.

Time is the most fundamental resource people bring to their work. Showing up at work is a basic indicator of engagement. Organizations monitor time spent at work in various formal and informal ways: Wage earners punch in and out, professionals bill hours, and salaried employees call in when absent. Absenteeism can often provide an insight into an employee's commitment to the workplace. Yet the time spent at work does not give the whole engagement picture. One recent report indicated that Americans waste as much as two-thirds of their time at work.[5] They surf the Internet, daydream, shmooze, work on personal matters, and take extended breaks. This is time not spent thinking, doing, or concentrating in positive and purposeful work-related ways. The work-focus to work-presence ratio is a useful part of an overall career-engagement assessment.

The use of one's talents at work is also a measure of career engagement. Although talent is difficult to measure since it constantly evolves and develops, most people have a sense of how much of their talent is being applied at work. People may apply less talent because their jobs do not invite or require more. Others may consciously choose to apply themselves in a limited way. All these reasons can lead to career blues. People who are not invited to use their talents may feel underrecognized or undervalued. People who choose not to apply their talents are often bored, angry, lazy, distracted, or lacking the spark to become engaged in their work. Charles Handy speculates that people may learn to use only one-quarter of their talents during their lifetimes. The opportunity costs for people who use only a quarter of their talents, and the organizations that employ them, appear needlessly high and reducible.

Energy and effort reflect how time and talent are directed to work. Physical energy fuels muscular effort; mental energy fuels concentration and thinking; emotional energy fuels discipline, concentration, and dedication, which catalyze physical and mental energies; and energy-of-the-spirit fuels buoyancy, enthusiasm, confidence, and resourcefulness.[6] Like a call to arms, energy is what brings talent to the fore. In an age where leisure time is declining despite rising levels of personal disposable income,[7] one's level of personal energy is becoming an increasingly important career issue. Companies such as Compaq and Quaker Oats recognize the value of regular exercise plans for their employees and provide facilities and the encouragement to stay fit. The underlying premise is that healthy and fit employees have more energy and work better.

The recent rise of interest in spirituality in the workplace[8] reflects similar feelings about spiritual energy. A leading thoracic surgeon, who regularly works 100-hour weeks, emphasizes energy management as a central tenet of balancing work and family life.

Effort is how hard we try. Effort is the conscious, purposeful, dedicated focusing of time, talent, and energy to a situation, opportunity, or challenge. Energy is a precursor to effort. Without energy, people are not able to exert much effort, but with a strong energy foundation, people have the basis for trying hard. McClelland showed that people try harder when they perceive challenges that appropriately test their abilities.[9] Expectancy theory, however, suggests that unless people value the potential outcomes they will not work hard to make them happen.[10] People who consistently bring low energy to work and who consistently put forth little effort are probably afflicted with the career blues; they feel disengaged and see no need to try harder.

The third dimension of our TEA[2] framework highlights attitude and aspirations. Positive attitude involves a can-do frame of mind in which an employee approaches work with an upbeat, cheerful, confident, optimistic perspective. Negative attitude involves looking for why things will not work instead of how they can work. Negative attitude is critical of others, of conditions, and the context of work. Attitude has a huge effect on people's engagement with work. In the words of religious broadcaster and commentator Charles Swindoll: "Attitude is more important than the past, than education, than money, than circumstances, than failures, than successes, than what other people think or say or do. We cannot change the inevitable. The only thing we can do is play on the one string we have, and that is our attitude."

Aspirations are the conscious dreams and goals one has for work. If aspirations are absent, people languish, repeating their daily routines without any sense of forward motion or progress. Without aspirations, a person has no direction; any outcome is as good as any other. This is not to say that all aspirations are alike: Some employees aspire to wealth, others to make a contribution, or both. If one's work is decoupled from one's aspirations, if it is no more than a fate to which one is subjected in life in order to survive, one is vulnerable to the career blues.

Michael Novak, the author of *Business as a Calling,* asserts that people in business are "eager to mix their own identity with their work and their work with their identity."[11] The purpose of life, according to Freud, is *"arbeiten und lieben"* — to work and to love. As stated by Peter Block: "There is a longing in each of us to invest in things that matter, and to have the organizations in which we work be successful . . . our task is to create organizations we believe in."[12] Initially and naturally, people seek to find a large measure of identity in their work. If they cannot, they will experience an erosion of aspiration and energy and be caught in the career blues. A person's sense of self, including hopes and dreams, is not naturally decoupled from work. When hopes and dreams can, in significant ways, flourish at work, people become engaged. Without a sense that aspirations can be fulfilled at work, attitudes sour, energy declines, effort is withheld, talents remain untapped, and time is squandered.

USING THE TEA² FRAMEWORK

The six dimensions of the TEA² framework provide a means of assessing a person's level of career engagement. One might do this formally or informally, using the TEA² framework as a guide. A good starting point is to rate the proportion of each of the TEA² accounts devoted to work. This perspective assumes that each person has a whole po-

tentiality for each dimension. While this potentiality may in fact expand and contract depending on various factors, at any given time we can reflect on the proportion of that person's TEA² account utilization. The basic questions to ask are: What is this person's work-focus to work-presence ratio (time spent at work focused on work divided by time spent at work)? What proportion of this person's weekly time (168 hours) is devoted to work? (If 50 hours a week is the company standard, how does this person compare?) What proportion of this person's talents is utilized at work? What proportion of potential energy is applied to work? What proportion of effort? What proportion of this person's positive attitude potential is demonstrated at work? What proportion of this person's aspirations relate to work? These questions can be used in a conversation with a colleague or employee to reach a joint, reflective assessment of that person's career engagement. They can also be asked of oneself for a self-assessment.

Our view of these six dimensions is that they dynamically vary. If there were perfect sensors to measure them, they would probably exhibit constant fluctuations, similar to what we see with an automobile speedometer or a thermometer. Accordingly, these six dimensions can be arrayed side-by-side as dynamic columns in a bar chart as shown in Figure 13-1. At any given time, how much time and talent, energy and effort, and positive attitude and aspirations a person exhibits can be displayed on the bar chart. Again, if there were a continuous way to measure these, the columns would rise and fall from day to day and from week to week. Over time, if the columns were not regularly in the upper regions of the chart, the indicators would point to a need to pay closer attention to that person's career engagement.

No precise level of engagement signals the onset of the career blues, but we suggest that they've taken hold when a person is not at or above the 75 percent level in each of

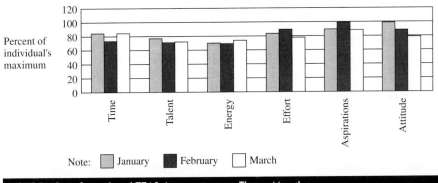

Percent of individual's maximum

Note: ▨ January   ◼ February   ☐ March

FIGURE 13-1 Sample of TEA² Accounts over Three Months

these measures on a regular basis. Employees operating at 50 percent of potential would seem to be insufficient for most employers. We doubt that employees can be at the 100 percent level for significant periods of time. If they were, they would probably begin to feel the effects of burnout. On the other hand, if a person's TEA² indicators are consistently below the three-quarter level, most observers would probably conclude that that person was significantly underutilizing his or her potential. Our logic and anecdotal evidence suggest an engaged employee exhibits percentages above 50 and below 100, over time.

FREQUENCY OF THE CAREER BLUES

If low levels of TEA² accounts continue for months, an employee is in danger of becoming unproductive, disengaged, and perhaps unwanted. Such people can be thought of as floating through life, wasting their time, talents atrophying, energy declining, expending little effort in any endeavor. As such a person's attitudes become cynical, aspirations dwindle, and life and work become unfulfilling, disengaging routines. The peaks and valleys of emotion, enthusiasm, and engagement have all flattened out into a featureless plain of boring experiences from which they learn nothing, reap no satisfaction, and connect with no one. Sometimes people can float for a month or two or maybe even more until they get fed up and begin searching for something better. Those who float long enough may find it is difficult to find release, and their performance declines.[13]

CLINICAL DEPRESSION

Are the career blues different from depression? Clinical depression has become a major health concern, and is largely underreported in the workplace. As a significant contributing factor to lost work productivity, time, and even suicide, clinical depression is a health factor to which executives and organizations need pay more attention. One management observer recently reported that in a large high-tech company, "20 percent of the IT department showed signs of clinical depression."[14] The article, "An Executive Guide to Workplace Depression," by Joseph Kline, Jr., and Lyle Sussman in this issue gives more insight on this challenging problem.

The career blues are not clinical depression; rather they represent a milder malaise in which one has lost one's sense of purpose in work. While the career blues may develop into depression, they are less severe and more easily dealt with.

Managing one's relationship to work can have a positive effect on the career blues, while clinical or biochemically based depressions need professional medical treatment.

WHAT'S THE TARGET?

If floating characterizes the career blues, what characterizes career engagement? A provocative and poignant way of typifying career engagement is resonance, or flow.[15] Athletes call it being in the zone, jazz musicians in the groove. Flow or resonance has several key features. First, time warps by either speeding up or slowing down. If it speeds up, you find yourself surprised at the end of the day how the time flew by unnoticed. If time slows down, things seem in slow motion and you feel you can easily keep ahead of them. Second, you focus intensely on the tasks, purposes, and goals at hand. Third, that focus is so intense that self-consciousness and concern about what others think of you disappear. Fourth, you perform at your highest level. You are doing things well, employing your peak capabilities. Fifth, work seems effortless. Without straining or even trying very hard, you are doing your best. Sixth, you find this high-level performance extraordinarily satisfying. You may feel a deep sense of connection with your work and environment. Seventh, when you have finished, you feel deeply satisfied, and more confident. As a result of this flow or resonant experience, you feel good about yourself, your contributions, and your work.

In dozens of conversations with groups of business managers at all levels and from all over the world, we have discovered that they talk about many different sources of resonance. Some talk about golf, swimming, running, and fishing. Others talk about reading, writing, doing calculus, performing experiments, and making handicrafts. Some refer to social events like leading meetings, public speaking, leading a project team, and captaining a sports team. Some speak of giving birth. Others will mention more seemingly mundane routines, like working on an assembly line. By definition, resonance is the state we are in when we lose track of time and our self-consciousness, and perform at our effortless best, with high internal reward. Almost everyone reports that resonant experiences are uplifting, satisfying, and purposefully directed. People with the career blues do not have this flow or resonance at work and perhaps have lost hope that they can.

Recent research shows athletes, surgeons, concert musicians, and corporate managers report similar experiences of resonance.[16] These world-class performers experience resonance as the result of a similar pattern of development. This common pattern consists of having personal aspirations relating to activities and feelings associated with them, investing in preparation to realize that dream, encountering obstacles, and overcoming those obstacles in a particular way by revisiting the dream. All were able to consciously recognize and recreate this cycle.

Dreams and aspirations are central to achieving one's potential. Dreams are interwoven combinations of feelings and activities that feed one another. Winning a gold medal is not the dream, but competing in a way to win and the feelings that accompany that effort is. To repeat: This is not a goal-oriented perspective, but a focus on the personal, internal experience during the activity. Of course, having a dream does not guarantee its realization. People who live their dreams prepare hard to make them come true. However, even with a dream and extensive preparation, most aspiring people encounter a variety of obstacles. When obstacles are allowed to block progress, dreams and aspirations remain distant. A distinguishing feature of many world-class performers is that they recognize the importance of revisiting their dreams. Rather than working or preparing out of duty, obligation, or necessity, world-class performers are able to mentally connect their daily efforts with their dream—and this mental discipline gives them a reservoir of energy and a positive attitude on which to call.

Of course, it is not possible to revisit a dream that did not exist in the first place. People without aspirations tend to float, reacting to the opportunities of life. While this approach can be very successful on some dimensions, it can be empty on others. We once explained this resonance model to an executive education group that included a senior executive who held marketing responsibility for most of North America in a major consumer products firm. Afterwards, he approached us excitedly and said: "For two decades, I've done well, been promoted, done well, been promoted again, and recently I've begun wondering, 'Why am I doing this?' Our discussion today gave me, for the first time in my life, a way of seeing what I need to work on and how to go about it!" Although he had become quite senior in his company and was successful by society's standards, he was experiencing the career blues, wondering where it was all headed. After learning about the concept of resonance, he left the program excited about the prospects of reengaging his dream and rethinking his work so that work would contribute to living his dream on a more regular basis.[17]

We believe that people get the career blues for one of three reasons: First, they have never experienced or found resonance and are unable to recognize or create it; second, they occasionally have resonance in nonwork activities, but cannot transfer it to their work; or third, they have had resonance at work, but lost it either because of burnout or a change in situation—sometimes even by being promoted.

Why would increasing engagement be good for an individual? Isn't it okay to be less than fully engaged at work and to spend your remaining time, talent, energy, efforts, attitudes, and aspirations on other things? We answer that it seems tragic for people to spend half their working hours only partially engaged.

People with the career blues often complain, making their attitudes and outlooks more poisonous, and irritating those around them. They do not like the sense of alienation that often results when others perceive their disengagement. Ultimately, they realize and lament the feeling of wasting their lives and their talents. Consider this recent research finding: "[People] wished to be able to express and develop their complete self at work [and] unless organizations learn how to harness the 'whole person' . . . , they will not be able to produce world-class products and services."[18] From an organization's perspective, benefits accrue by tapping and unleashing employees' greater potential. From an individual's perspective, alleviating the blues provides the hope for a richer, more fulfilling life.

HOW WE GET THE CAREER BLUES

Sadly, some people never find their resonance. They often float through life, moving from job to job or staying at the same job for decades, but finding no meaning or satisfaction. Perhaps they develop hobbies or avocations that occupy their time but these too, in the end, often are not satisfying. Sometimes they search for such short-term, escapist activities as drugs, alcohol, thrill-seeking stunts, or promiscuity. Hoping for a flow that does not occur, and looking for quick answers, these people are deep in the career blues.

Some people get fleeting glimpses of something outside their work that they enjoy, and begin shaping their lives around such outside interests as sports, camping, movies, or clubs. If they are unable or unwilling to bring this resonance to work, their work begins to suffer. Work becomes a second or third priority, and work-related learning, attentiveness, and focus wane and wither away.

Some people find resonance in their work, but in pursuing it, burn themselves out. Workaholism can be detrimental to health.[19] The Japanese have a word for this phenomenon, *karoushi,* or "working one's self to death." Workaholics at one level, have become addicted to flow and the personal euphoria it provides. They have lost their resonance by pursuing it too much.

The burnout on the other side of resonance can lead to various physiological health problems, including cardiovascular disease, chronic fatigue syndrome, and depression, conditions we also categorize as extensions of the career blues. It is important to note that workaholics are not resonating.[20] They have lost sight of their deep-seated, enduring dreams, and dream instead a false dream based on achievements or acquisitions.

Some organizations create work systems that discourage and inhibit career engagement. Wise managers examine and assess not only their own and their employees' career engagement, but also review their reward systems, decision-making systems, and work systems to see how these systems inhibit employees from experiencing high levels of career engagement on a regular basis.

HOW TO BEAT THE CAREER BLUES

We believe that a three-step process can help people move toward a personal state of career engagement wherein they not only perform at a higher level, but also enjoy the level of performance more.

Assess Your Career Emotional State

Daniel Goleman argues persuasively that there are many different kinds of intelligences, and that those with "emotional intelligence" are often more successful and internally satisfied than others.[21] He asserts that people with high emotional intelligence are able to recognize their own emotions, and manage those emotions in a way that avoids emotional hijackings of anger, fear, and depression. Many people have difficulty recognizing or acknowledging their own emotions. The ability to reflect, to become aware of one's emotions, particularly as they relate to career aspirations and daily work, is critical to managing the career blues.

Pausing regularly to reflect on one's level of engagement at work offers an opportunity to revisit one's dream. The following questions can help in assessing one's emotional state: How does your emotional state compare with those of the people around you at work? Do you dread Monday mornings and live for Friday evenings? Have you lost your enthusiasm for your work? Do you feel purposeful? Are you energized? Are you focused? Are you in synch with coworkers? If your answers to these questions suggest that you have the career blues, this recognition is the first step toward managing them.

Identify Resonance

The second step in managing the career blues is to think about times when you have felt energetic, harmonic, positive, and unusually successful. When were you performing at your best? When did time seem to fly by? What were you doing? What parts of that activity were enjoyable to you? How did you feel in those times? Those experiences may or may not have had anything to do with work. As you think about them, you may be able to identify a dream, a kind of feeling associated with the activity that defines how you want to experience life.[22] If you can identify this set of feelings, you can then begin to think about how to recreate similar experiences at work. It's a choice. Research suggests that with intent and practice, one can recreate these internal flow experiences in other activities.[23]

You may think that the areas that you resonate in do not, cannot, or should not relate to work. Ultimately, if that remains true, you are destined to do your best work outside of work. That is, unless we can bring resonance to work, we are stuck in what one of our colleagues calls "the condition of good enough."

One of the authors of this article had a mentor at a leading university who agreed to sit in on a class he taught. Afterward, the author was told: "You're boring!" After a moment of uncomfortable silence, the mentor continued: "I notice that you play basketball with the doctoral students. When you come back, you're emanating energy, barely touching the ground as you walk, and grinning from ear to ear. You've got to figure out how to play basketball in the classroom!" At first, the suggestion sounded ludicrous. On reflection, however, it became a powerful analogy for seeing work, the classroom, in a different light. The professor puts a topic in play, passes it off to a student who may drop the ball, pass it off, or score with a great insight; then the class discussion races off to another learning point. Back and forth it goes. And when it goes well, there is a grace, power, and rhythm to the experience that approximates the flow one feels in a real basketball game.

Identifying, recalling, and replicating your resonance involves discovering what experiences in life bring the greatest sense of satisfaction, achievement, and purposefulness while doing them. The resonance definition of a dream is not about collecting achievements: Ultimately these can be empty and unsatisfying. It is not about standing on the podium and receiving the medal. Rather it is about how you feel when playing the game. We often meet business people who enjoy golf. In conversations, they may speak with more energy, light in their eyes, and enthusiasm about golf than they do about their work. There is a sense that these people have given up hoping

for those kinds of feelings at work. Is that okay? Perhaps. But if those golfers could get such feelings at work, how much better would work be? How much more valuable would their contributions at work be?

Let's take this example and see how a business person might use it at work. Assume that, over the years, this person's job of managing insurance salespeople has become routine and unexciting. Yet this person eagerly anticipates playing golf on the weekends. Perhaps this person even makes golf clubs for the sheer joy of it. How can this person bring golf to work? A way to start is by determining how the office is like a familiar golf course. One has comfortable, pleasant routines as well as nurtured relationships with friends one confides in, gets real answers from, and truly partners with. At the beginning of the day, there's a tee-off. Each new round brings new challenges, even if it is the same course. Some days, the first shot is in the rough, others are in the middle of the fairway. When you mess up, you are faced with being creative and having to recover in order to carry on effectively. There are also opportunities to apply learning— for example, a lesson acquired from last week's session with the club pro. Sometimes, you use a driver (direct and strong instructions to a subordinate) and sometimes a wedge for a chip shot (modest suggestions in a meeting) that gets one closer to the hole. Sometimes, you get so close, you are left with a mere tap into the hole; others may even concede the putt (or an operational point in a meeting). Sometimes, you have to wait for the group in front of you. Sometimes, you get to play a captain's choice format where everyone's shot counts toward the team goal. At the end of the day, you count up your score. There were some good shots and some bad shots. Some days you play above your handicap, some days below. Highlighting and savoring these many aspects of a round of golf creates an overall feeling that the round was enjoyable, uplifting, and a prompt for tomorrow's round. This is true even though the round was not mistake-free and had a number of routine shots. With eyes, ears, attentions, and thoughts similarly attuned to the nuances of work, resonance is possible at work as golfer employees begin to see the golf-like aspects of what they do at work. Will it work with fishing? Quilting? Community service? Carving model duck decoys? We think so.

If a person can identify those experiences that create resonant feelings, then they can find ways to bring them to work. In essence, discovering resonance is finding one's most natural and satisfying synergies of time, talent, energy, effort, attitude, and aspiration. By choice, it is possible to recreate this experience on a regular basis.

Invest in a Capacity to Resonate

After assessing work-related reflections and identifying significant sources of resonance, it is important to begin to build the capacity to create resonant experiences at work. This necessitates setting some objectives of improving the ability to do at work what is satisfying in life. This may mean taking a class, reading new books, finding and talking with people who are good at what you want to do, and visiting new places. It may mean practicing new skills or focusing on different aspects of one's work. It means composing a work life, not just taking what a series of jobs hands out along the way.[24]

Investing in resonance also expands one's talents. People engaged in resonating pursuits dedicate time, energy, and effort, and cease to hoard, withhold, or misdirect these important personal development inputs. Their attitudes become positive, purposeful, engaged, and excited because aspirations are clear and reachable. The challenge for individuals is to realize their potential in life. The challenge for employers is to engage the resonant dimensions of their employees, and to create avenues for their pursuing them that are congruent with the organization's needs.

HOW TO MANAGE OTHERS OUT OF THE CAREER BLUES

Diagnose Career Engagement

We hope this article will provide a framework that managers and individuals can use to facilitate discussions about gaps between company needs and expectations and individual career goals and experience. Employers and employees who use a common framework and language will be better equipped to engage in discussions that are often ignored or handled poorly. The first step to helping others out of their career blues is to recognize the career blues and to help them see their presence. Begin by diagnosing an employee's career engagement using the TEA[2] dimensions. Remember that while you may be satisfied with their work, the real question is how much more they could be doing and how much better they could be doing it if they were truly resonating at work.

When workers exhibit an emotional flatness, a sign that the career blues may be at hand, many managers do nothing. They assume that people in low-level jobs, for instance, need not and cannot be motivated or fulfilled by their work. They assume that the professionalism of those in high-level positions will carry them through as it has in the past. Some employers even presume that people will work hard until they get the blues, then go to another job, thus allowing new energy to be hired at a lower salary. We believe that when a manager consistently observes low TEA[2] measures of an employee, that manager should initiate a career conversation that might include the following elements.

Discuss the TEA[2] Levels

As a conversation starter and as a cue to the ingredients for career engagement, share with the employee your perceived TEA[2] diagnosis. Ask if the employee thinks they are reasonable assessments. Revise the

TEA^2 charts if necessary, based on what you hear. Reassure the person that this is a conversation motivated by two interests, those of the employee and those of the company. Talk about the importance of resonance at work and how one can find it. Share stories about times when you both have felt resonance. In the context of your specific jobs, brainstorm ways to bring resonance to work for both of you. Your willingness to share your own stories with a colleague will make it easier for the employee to be open. Talk about your aspirations and how you see your work contributing to those aspirations and resonant feelings.

Emphasize the Need for High TEA^2 Levels

Discuss with the employee the importance of high TEA^2 levels for competing in today's environment. Compare the employee's discussion of aspirations and TEA^2 accounts with the general level of the TEA^2 accounts in his or her department. Solicit ideas and suggestions for raising the TEA^2 accounts in the department generally. This may mean that you as the leader or supervisor will need to reexamine your own TEA^2 accounts, in particular how your aspirations are met in the goals and mission of the organization, and how well you have been able to regularly experience such a mutually reinforcing flow.

Explore What Resonates for the Employee

We encourage you to leave the conversation open and to invite further discussions. Sometimes as people think about their aspirations in work, they evolve and become clearer. Sometimes such reflection leads to a conclusion to change jobs. More often than not, however, such a reflection does not require a new job, but leads to new foci, reordered priorities, and heightened sensitivities to the richly rewarding, but latent, subtleties of one's work.

The very fact of this conversation communicates to employees that you care about them, about their work, and about the match between the two. This is very different from demanding from them better work with higher engagement. Such demands are ultimately doomed to fail because they assume no causal links leading to high performance other than sheer willpower and/or determination. Unless managers understand what makes a particular person resonate, they are unlikely to be able to help that person perform at a sustainable higher level for any length of time.

We encourage managers to engage in three processes—awakening individuals to the potential of resonating at work; assisting them in bringing resonance to work; and aligning individuals and work—so that the clarity of personal and organizational aspirations and resonances emerge and people are better able to make decisions about how to work and what to work at. Managers should strive to facilitate employees' progression on the stairway from career blues to career engagement as shown in Figure 13-2.

After giving the employees some time to think about their dreams and what makes them resonate, managers can initiate another conversation to discuss these reflections and the skills and circumstances necessary to make resonance happen more often and for longer periods of time for them. In this conversation, focus on how the employee can begin to practice resonance at work. If you engage several employees in this kind of discussion, you begin to create a workplace that can become a strategic, competitive weapon. In essence, this is what is distinctive about startup, entrepreneurial companies: People know what resonates for them; organizational structures and systems allow people to pursue resonance with head, heart, and hands; individuals find pleasure and purpose in the myriad details and tasks that constitute each day and contribute to each accomplishment. On a larger scale, such are the hallmarks of the

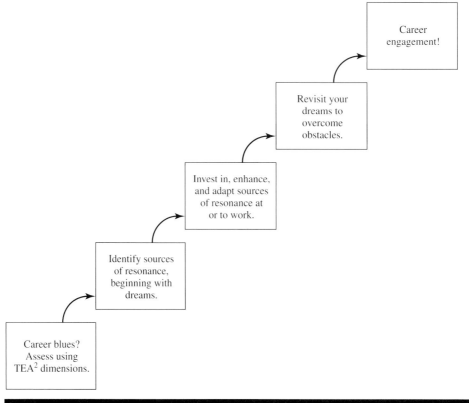

FIGURE 13-2 Beating the Career Blues

human resources management systems and culture at companies like Nordstrom, Southwest Airlines, and Wal-Mart.

Finally, managers should celebrate people who are resonating at work. When you begin to observe high levels of TEA^2 in employees, take the time to comment to them how much you enjoy working with them and the positive effect their high TEA^2 levels have on the department's work and on others. Encourage the sharing of aspirations, success stories, and career engagement stories. Make explicit commitments to provide avenues for pursuing aspirations, applying talents, renewing energies, and furthering relationships.

ENCOURAGING CAREER ENGAGEMENT

Quite bluntly, we observe far too many people who seem half-dead in their work. They perform listlessly and appear minimally motivated, unthinking, and disconnected. They steal time from employers by focusing most of their thoughts elsewhere; they bring to bear only a subset of their talents; their energy is low and their efforts marginal; their attitudes are negative. We believe these people have the career blues and are merely floating through their careers. We think there is much that managers can do to help themselves and their employees shake the career blues.

One way to address this situation is to assess an employee's level of career engagement by observing the proportion of time and talent, energy and effort, and positive attitude and aspirations he or she brings to work. Identifying the level in each of these TEA^2 accounts, over time, is a good first step in beginning to work with people to help them manage their own work experience. Most managers do this informally in their heads as they watch people. The assessment tool introduced here can help managers formalize their thinking about the career engagement of others. (See appendix.) A good next step is helping people to discover their area of resonance. This may take several conversations over some time as individuals reflect on what sorts of experiences create resonance for them and how they might replicate or create more of them at work. Fi-nally, managers who want to help people manage the career blues can initiate conversations in which they explore ways of investing in the capacity to reproduce resonance, and of aligning it with their work environment. The positive side of managing the career blues is managing one's career engagement. Ultimately, this is more than just having a positive attitude. It means finding one's resonance, investing in it, and making it happen on a regular basis. World-class performers do this. Companies that want to compete at world-class levels need to find ways for their people to do this. Leader-managers seeking to encourage world-class commitment and behavior in themselves and in their employees must be sensitive to the career blues phenomenon, and should be skilled in assessing it and conquering it. ∎

Appendix

A TEA^2 ACCOUNT DIAGNOSIS TOOL

Instructions: After observing another person or yourself for 2 weeks, make your assessment. You might then ask the person to self-rate, and use the two completed forms as a basis for a career-blues counseling session. Quarterly or yearly assessments of these TEA^2 accounts are then used to create the barometers illustrated in Figure 13-1.

Provide your best assessment of the percent of the time the person (yourself or another) behaves as described in the statement. (0 = never, 50 = half of the time, 100 = all of the time)

Statement	Percent of Time
Time	
1. Comes to work on time and leaves on time.	____
2. Time spent on work.	____
3. Purposeful and diligent at work.	____
4. Willing to work, when necessary, beyond normal working hours.	____
Talents	
5. Work-related talents improve.	____
6. Total talents applied at work.	____
7. Talks about work-related talents.	____
8. Discusses the lack of fit between perceived talents and the work requirements.	____

Energy

9. Behavior at work reflects high energy.   ____
10. Seems to gather energy from work.   ____
11. Meets work deadlines.   ____
12. Takes the lead.   ____

Effort

13. Puts forth greater effort than others.   ____
14. Resents or avoids situations that require extra effort.   ____
15. Looks for ways to help others.   ____
16. Exhibits curiosity and/or a dedication to continuous improvement.   ____

Attitude

17. Is upbeat and happy.   ____
18. Based on conversation, is glad to be at work.   ____
19. Eager to be at work.   ____
20. Conversations are positive, purposeful, and pleasant.   ____

Aspirations

21. Exhibits a sense of pride in work.   ____
22. Speaks of work as being more fulfilling than nonwork endeavors.   ____
23. Describes work and work goals as fulfilling and/or satisfying.   ____
24. Elevates and enriches others at work.   ____

Life's Dream

25. Purpose in life is clear.   ____
26. Seems to work toward a consistent goal in life.   ____
27. When things get difficult, can reconnect with life's dream and carry on.   ____
28. Behavior seems focused and connected to a central purpose.   ____

Note: The version of the instrument included here is an adaptation of the one we have used in our programs. This version is simpler in that there are no reverse-scored items—which may make it easier for someone to "game" the instrument. If you would like to see the original version in a packet that includes a short theory background, and instructions for scoring and interpreting, please contact the authors.

REFERENCES

[1]Drucker, P. (1992). The new society of organizations. *Harvard Business Review, 5*, 95–105.

[2]Handy, C. (1998). *The hungry spirit.* New York: Broadway Books.

[3]Kets de Vries, M. (1994). CEOs also have the blues. *European Management Journal, 12* (3), 259. See also Crosstalk: Edgar Schein and Manfred Kets de Vries on organizational therapy, *The Academy of Management Executive, 14* (1), 30–51.

[4]For more details on these various concepts and constructs, see: Maslow, A. (1970). *Motivation and personality.* New York: Harper & Row; Nadler, D. A., & Lawler, E. E. (1983). Motiva-

tion: A diagnostic approach. In J. R. Hackman, E. E. Lawler, and L. W. Porter (Eds.), *Perspectives on Behavior in Organizations.* New York: McGraw-Hill Book Co.; Levinson, D. J. (1978). *The seasons of a man's life.* New York: Alfred A. Knopf; Clawson, J. G., Kotter, J., Faux, V. & MacArthur, C. (1992). *Self assessment and career development.* Upper Saddle River, NJ: Prentice Hall; Dalton, G., Thompson, P., & Price, R. L. (1977). Four stages of engineering careers. *Organizational Dynamics, 1,* 19–42; Erikson, E. (1963). *Childhood and society.* New York: W. W. Norton & Co.; Schein, E. (1978). *Career dynamics.* Reading, MA: Addison Wesley; Skinner, B. F. (1971). *Beyond freedom and dignity*. New York: Alfred A. Knopf; and Viorst, J. (1986). *Necessary losses*. New York: Fawcett Books.

[5]See, for example, Gahten, R. (1999, May) The 37-second office. *Office Systems, 1,* 47.

[6]Buchholz, S., & Roth, T. (1987). *Creating the high-performance team*. New York: John Wiley & Sons, Inc.

[7]Schor, J. B. (1993). *The overworked American*. New York: Basic Books.

[8]Vaill, P. (1998). *Spirited leading and learning: Process wisdom for a new age*. San Francisco: Jossey-Bass; Conger, J. (1994). *Spirit at work: Discovering the spirituality to leadership*. San Francisco: Jossey-Bass; Cash, K. C., & Gray, G. R. (2000). A framework for accommodating religion and spirituality in the workplace. *The Academy of Management Executive, 14* (3) 124–133.

[9]McCleland, D. C. (1988). *Human motivation*. Cambridge, U.K.: Cambridge University Press.

[10]Lawler, E. E. (1994). *Motivation at work*. Cambridge, U.K.: Cambridge University Press.

[11]Novak, M. (1996). *Business as a calling*. New York: The Free Press.

[12]Block, P. (1996). *Stewardship: Choosing service over self-interest*. San Francisco: Berrett-Koehler Publishers.

[13]Kets de Vries, op. cit.

[14]Fitter, F. (1998, July 20). Singing the IT blues. *Computerworld,* 59.

[15]See Csikszentmihalyi, M. (1990). *Flow: The psychology of optimal experience*. New York: Harper & Row; Newburg, D. (1996, November/December), Always playing to win: The process of performance. *PC Magazine,* 19–20.

[16]See Newburg, op. cit. See also Clawson, J., & Newburg, D. (1999). Resonance, leadership and the purpose of life. In J. Clawson (Ed.). *Level Three Leadership*. Upper Saddle River, NJ: Prentice Hall.

[17]Although the terminology of "resonance" is not used, the vignettes presented in Salter, D. (1999, July/August) Enough is enough. *Fast Company,* 121–136, are indicative of one man's experience with introspection, values clarifying, and goal-directedness.

[18]Mitroff, I., & Denton, E. (1999, Summer). A study of spirituality in the workplace. *Sloan Management Review,* 83–92.

[19]For example, see Fassel, D. (1990). *Working ourselves to death and the rewards of recovery*. New York: Harper Books.

[20]Newburg, op. cit.

[21]Goleman, D. (1995). *Emotional intelligence*. New York: Bantam Books.

[22]Newburg, op. cit.

[23]Csikszentmihalyi, op. cit., and Newburg, op. cit.

[24]This terminology is central to the provocative work by Bateson, M. C. (1989). *Composing a life*. New York: Plume Books.

14 ORGANIZATIONAL EXIT

The final people-processing activity in personnel and human resources management is organizational exit, or the ways in which people voluntarily or involuntarily move out of organizations. The two most commonly discussed issues related to exit are absenteeism and turnover. They are among the most persistent problems in personnel management, and they represent major costs to many companies. However, a basic difference exists between the costs associated with these two phenomena. The costs and causes of absenteeism, whether personally or situationally determined, tend to remain with the organization. The costs and causes of turnover, on the other hand, sometimes leave the organization; this can prove to be advantageous, especially if the people who leave are poor performers and those who replace them bring new perspectives and talents. Decisions about absenteeism and turnover are ultimately made by employees and are, therefore, considered to be more voluntary than involuntary.

Other forms of organizational exit, in which representatives of the organization often directly initiate and control exit decisions and policies, are termination for cause (e.g., disobedience, insubordination), redundancy or incompatibility, and retirement. For the latter two forms of organizational exit, outplacement services are sometimes provided.

In the first article in this chapter, Nelson makes the important point that there is a need to be concerned for those who are downsized but that we should not overlook the needs of those who stay at work. Job survivors are a critical factor in the subsequent success of the company. This is a call to be concerned with their needs. Levinson and Wofford confront an important issue—individuals who retire from an organization need to develop a flexible outlook in order to be able to successfully transition into retirement.

READINGS

THE CARE OF THE UN-DOWNSIZED

Bob Nelson

By now, we all know the sad tale of downsizing: Apple Computer, down 1,300 jobs AT&T, down 78,000 managerial positions Kimberly-Clark, down 2,700 jobs. We could go on. Instead, let's ask whether layoffs are really needed to get organizations back on the right track. Maybe not.

According to a recent study by Watson Wyatt Worldwide, a pension and profit-sharing company located in Washington, D.C., only 46 percent of the companies surveyed met their expense-reduction goals after downsizing, less than 33 percent met profit objectives, and only 21 percent enhanced shareholders' return-on-investment.

In another study, the American Management Association found that fewer than half of the firms downsized since 1988 had increased their profits after layoffs; only one-third reported an increase in productivity. Worse, the study revealed that downsizing seems to beget more downsizing. Two-thirds of firms that cut jobs do it again the next year.

Kim Cameron, a University of Michigan professor and an expert in downsizing, sees layoffs as a quick fix that usually doesn't work. Cameron studied 30 auto-industry companies that had been through layoffs. "Only five or six had a marked increase in productivity," he says. "In all other cases, performance went down."

Downsizing, however, may not be the true culprit. The real problem is that many companies don't plan for downsizing. They just reduce head count, neglecting to figure out how they're going to move forward in their new "leaner and meaner" environments.

In such cases, the most important element of downsizing is ignored—the survivors. As downsizing analyst David Noer points out, "Survivors are left to fend for themselves, to somehow manage on their own."

FROM GUILT TO GROWTH

Downsizing is a traumatic experience—not only for terminated employees, but also for those who remain. Joel Brockner—a professor of management at Columbia University and an expert in survivor guilt—says, "When people react negatively to change—such as downsizing—it shows up in reduced productivity and low morale. The real cause is that people's self-esteem is threatened."

Ironically, survivors are perhaps the most critical factor in determining the future success of a downsized company. They are expected to assume additional workloads, work more efficiently, and adapt quickly to the new work environment in order to attain company goals.

Managers must anticipate survivors' reactions to downsizing and help them grow in spite of the situation. Management must find ways to help survivors cope with concerns that they might lose their jobs, with guilt about the termination of coworkers, and with resentment and burnout because of pressure to work harder.

Though the steps below aren't a panacea, they can help management channel its energies and efforts in the right direction.

Lead by Vision and Values, not Commands
In a downsized company, it's increasingly

THE MISCONCEPTIONS OF DOWNSIZING

Here are some common myths about downsizing:

- Downsizing occurs quickly and centers around a definitive event.
- Survivors are glad to still have jobs.
- Time heals all wounds.

- The weak people are the ones who leave.
- Survivors that seem to be OK really are.
- People take what management tells them at face value.

Source: Drake Beam Morin, New York.

---

difficult for management to tell employees exactly what they should be doing to be most effective in their jobs. That's because their jobs—and their work environment—are changing so fast. In fact, in many cases, employees are in the best position to know how to solve problems or serve their customers because they are closest to the situations.

It is more important for management to help employees focus on a larger vision of what is needed, emphasizing the strategies and values that will help make the vision attainable. For example, instead of telling people what to do (and risk being wrong), management should encourage workers to take the initiative when appropriate. Managers should meet regularly with employees to map goals and to seek ideas on how they can work together to meet the goals.

Managers and employees should agree on goals, both big and small. In addition, management should identify the kinds of rewards and recognition that motivate employees to try to attain goals. Having the end in sight and empowering employees to be creative and to develop their own skills and abilities can tap into a tremendous reserve of energy, ideas, and initiative.

Communicate More, Not Less During times of change and downsizing, communi-

cation should be uppermost. Surviving workers need to talk to managers and coworkers about their guilt, anger, and concerns. They also need information about what's going on in the company. Immediately following a downsizing, management should hold a companywide meeting to explain the reasons for layoffs, to outline the changes and their impact on survivors, to spell out the company's future, and to discuss what's needed from those employees who remain.

Management must communicate to employees what is expected of them in order to keep the company profitable and avoid more layoffs. Management should update employees regularly about the possibility of future layoffs. Never let employees read it first in the newspapers. Rumors must be addressed so that survivors understand what lies ahead.

Management must realize that it's impossible to "overcommunicate" with employees during turbulent times. That's when the quality and quantity of communications should be greater than usual. One reason is that more distortion occurs in a rapidly changing environment. The lines of communication that worked well in the past may be inadequate now. Past communication channels may be overloaded, too formal, or too slow to provide employees with information when they need it most.

To enhance communication, management may choose to experiment with new ways of talking with employees, including

- informal sessions between management and small groups
- message boards in the restrooms or lunchroom
- department visits by top managers
- electronic displays of announcements and updates
- chat sessions on the organization's intranet
- hotlines for employees' questions and concerns.

Some of the suggestions will work; some won't. By experimenting, an organization can discover what meets employees' needs best. In return for the efforts, survivors will respect and continue to serve the organization well.

Involve People Early On

Managing is what you do *with* people, not *to* them. To get the most from employees and obtain their commitment, start with them: who they are, what they want, and what they need. Then, build on that foundation by putting the best interests of employees first. Let them take part in decisions that affect their workloads and work environment. That can make them feel important and reassure them that they are truly making a contribution.

One way to involve employees in decision making is to let them assist with a downsizing. Noer recommends that employees be involved in preliminary discussions so they can help shape the criteria on who will go and who will stay: "If you can involve people in the process and give them options such as job-sharing or part-time work—you'll be better off." Then, layoff survivors are less likely to experience feelings of guilt and depression.

Another way to involve survivors in decision making is to have them help management determine how they all can work together in the leaner organization. After downsizing, peoples' roles and responsibilities will be new, and they may seem overwhelming. Involving employees in crucial decisions will help secure their commitment. They will have a better understanding of what is expected of them, and they will see how their support and hard work fit into the overall picture.

Involving employees in decisions also builds trust—vital to sparking their motivation and enthusiasm to do their best. By working through issues as a team, management is telling survivors, "We're in this together." The way employees are treated during stressful times of change says a lot about how they're regarded by management. Are they pawns in a game? Or, are they individuals to be treated with respect? Involving employees in decisions will demonstrate that even when times are rough, management has their best interests—and those of the company—in mind.

Recognize and Reward Performance

Many companies fail to recognize and reward the performance of survivors—thinking, perhaps, that they will be criticized for spending tight dollars foolishly. Nothing could be further from the truth.

After downsizing, management should recognize and reward performance that makes a difference. Employees feel ambiguous and unclear in times of flux, and they are likely to be skeptical about their future with the company. So that vital employees don't jump ship, they need to feel that their hard work and devotion are appreciated. Now, more than ever, management must reward them. Rewards and recognition go a long way to keeping employees motivated, satisfied, and committed.

Management should recognize employees for both their progress toward and

THE REALITIES OF DOWNSIZING

Here are some truisms about downsizing:

- When survivors are more involved in changes in the workplace, their reactions become less negative.
- The intensity of survivors' emotional reactions is proportionate to the speed of change.

- The longer an employee has been in a position, the greater his or her resistance to change.
- Though rewards and incentives may not lessen survivors' feelings of loss, they can motivate people and help them react positively to change.

Source: Drake Beam Morin, New York.

achievement of desired performance goals. It should show appreciation for small accomplishments as well as big ones. The recognition must be ongoing to reinforce employees' need to feel that they're doing a good job.

Moreover, the best forms of recognition typically have little or no cost.

Here are some suggestions for managers:

- Thank each employee personally or his or her hard work.
- Conduct morning chat sessions to update employees on the status of projects and to highlight desired performance by team members.
- Hold weekly team lunches so employees can share with coworkers and man-

agers their ideas on how things are going.
- Write about employees' accomplishments in the company newsletter. Circulate companywide bulletins of outstanding results.
- Institute and encourage an open-door policy—from lower-level workers to people at the top. Encourage employees to talk about their concerns and their ideas for new approaches.

Above all else, management must treat employees with trust and respect. Because survivors are likely to feel that their career paths are unclear, management must reassure them that it cares about them and their future with the company. ■

APPROACHING RETIREMENT AS THE FLEXIBILITY PHASE

Harry Levinson
Jerry C. Wolford

> *When Victor L. Lund, the chief executive of the American Stores Company,*
> *was told by his predecessor, Lennie Sam Skaggs, over a plate of eggs in 1992*
> *that Mr. Skaggs had personally chosen him to take the helm of the then*
> *troubled supermarket company, Mr. Lund knew he was taking on a big*
> *challenge. What he did not know was that one of the biggest problems he would*
> *face would be Mr. Skaggs himself.*
>
> —THE NEW YORK TIMES[1]

Conflicts between managers and their successors are not uncommon when the predecessor will not let go and interferes with the successor's dealings. There can be a variety of causes: An outgoing manager like Skaggs may have too much time on his hands. Or maybe he's trying to tweak management to move faster on getting its stock price up (it was $25.375 in January 1996; $40.875 on August 27, 1996). In the view of one analyst: "This seems to be just Sam rattling the cages and having a little fun." Skaggs had hired Goldman Sachs to advise him on what to do with his 18.3 percent stake in the company and filed documents with the Securities and Exchange Commission stating his intent to explore "alternatives" for the company's future. Continued the same analyst: "But smart investors can see there is a turnaround here, and so there seems to be a degree of irrationality at work." Indeed! Personal conflicts of the later work years can result in irrationality.

We refer to the executive's retirement years as that flexibility phase because of the many crucial options one must face. Freedoms of time, location, activities, and opportunities provide a flexibility that can enrich life. They can also add to the anxieties, stresses, and conflicts that often accompany uncertainties and choices. Our purpose is to understand the underlying stresses and emotions inherent in the flexibility phase, to explore steps in transitioning into retirement, and to share some insights into ways of smoothing the path into this phase of life. We draw on psychoanalytic theory, as well as on case studies of managers accumulated during many years of experience in consulting practice and interactions with managers.

SPECIAL ISSUES FOR MANAGERS NEARING RETIREMENT

How can we begin to understand such conflicts and what might be done to avoid or alleviate them? In order to answer that question we must begin with trying to grasp the complex situation of the senior executive and other managers. There are likely to be a growing number of such conflicts as life expectancy for males continues to rise. No doubt there will be similar problems for managerial women as their numbers increase.

As illustrated above, explanations for these conflicts may be speculative or clichés about generational conflict. Such explanations may describe, but they do not explain. Some facts are clear: Life expectancy for American males in 1900 was 47 years; in 1993, it was 76. Those who are now 65, on average, can expect to live until they are 81, and those turning 65 in the year 2040, until they are 85.[2] As Peter Drucker has observed, health for a person at 65 is as good today as it was at 55 in the 1920s. The average is likely to improve. In an information- and knowledge-based economy, many people will be able to continue to work into their later years. The legal age at which a person may be required to retire has been raised to 70, and even this limit is often not upheld by the courts. Given these figures, there is likely to be pressure to raise the limit even higher, especially since increasing numbers of prospective retirees indicate that they want to continue to work beyond 65 and larger numbers of prospective retirees indicate that they want to continue to work beyond 65 and larger numbers already do so. Even in high-level managerial ranks there are legendary examples like Armand Hammer of Occidental Petroleum Corporation and Royal Little of Textron Corporation, both of whom headed their respective companies until they died, Hammer at 91 and Little at 87. Peter Drucker, still widely respected as an innovative management thinker, was born in 1909. The retirement age chosen by managerial personnel in most companies continues to be near 65. Some companies, like IBM, have provisions for managers to choose earlier retirement. Yet the age at which most board members retire is 70.

Taken together, these factors suggest that men and women will be staying in managerial roles much longer. Corporate boards already lift the retirement boundaries when a CEO is still in the process of building an organization or, as in a family firm, where the CEO controls the board. We could even be approaching the Japanese practice of valuing age in chief executives for the purported wisdom it brings. We might even start asking, as a Japanese executive did at a seminar conducted by the first author: "How do you get rid of a CEO?"

The aging manager needs to guard against potential losses in several areas of functioning: diminished conceptual ability, obsolescence, rigidity, and dependency. People differ in the trajectories of their conceptual ability, or their capacity to deal with the complexity of the information they must process.[3] This is evident in the fact that some promising managerial candidates plateau (sometimes also because of poor interpersonal relations or lack of the knowledge needed for high-level roles), and that some highly successful corporate division presidents fail when they are promoted to head groups of such divisions. Although intelligence, as measured by intelligence tests, declines with age for most people up to 60, and tends to level off until age 69, it does not decline as rapidly among bright people.[4] However, subtle organic brain changes that impair judgment can begin in the mid-fifties.[5] Drucker did not have tongue in cheek when he said that senility in high places is one of the most degenerative diseases of an organization. Therefore, it probably would not be a good idea to raise the mandatory retirement age.

Aging carries with it the threat of obsolescence. Most people lose contact with various features of the environment as they age, simply because they narrow their social and occupational purviews. If they are in high-level managerial positions, they may lose touch with what goes on at lower levels in their organizations. Some tend not to keep in touch with the continuous shift in the way things are done, and complain about what appears to them as the strange vocabulary, outlandish dress, and atrocious manners of the young. These managers are concerned that cherished values are being lost. Worse still, they risk being out of touch with their competitive environments.[6]

People who lose touch with their changing social environments as they age tend to become more conservative, including those in managerial ranks. Evidence for this is provided by faculty members of advanced management programs, who note that some of the more senior middle managers who come to such programs seem not to want to learn anything new. Their conviction that they already know the program's content, and their refractoriness to the learning opportunity for which their companies are paying significant sums, reflects the narcissism of aging that protects people from the sense of potential helplessness that can accompany growing older.

In general, men become more dependent as they age, while women become more assertive. Thus, men, who are typically reluctant to lean on other men, want to lean more on their spouses, at a time when their wives want to become more active on their own. The concomitant declines in energy and mental sharpness can lead to a greater inward orientation, including reduced involvement with one's family and others.[7] This inward orientation may occur even by the mid-forties, well before the social losses of aging and the decline of social interaction are more common.

STRESSES AND EMOTIONAL RESPONSES BROUGHT BY THE LOSSES OF AGING

Losses associated with aging may take place gradually, like tiny pin pricks in a large balloon, gradually deflating one's ego and possibly leading to a deep-seated fear of retirement. Some successful managers try to cope by denying the prospect of retirement, especially those who have Type A personalities. For such intensely driven people, the unrelenting pursuit of success can be an enraged effort to cope with unconscious feelings of helpless dependency. To retire, to be out of action, is to lose that coping mechanism. Lee Iacocca says he has failed at retirement and misses the sense of challenge of his action-oriented career.

The fear of retirement has many facets of which prospective retirees should be aware. One is the fear of dropping out of sight, of no longer being where the action is, of not being in the game. Another is the loss of heroic posture, the sense of being somebody in an official position whose title defines one's place in society. A third facet is losing contact with the business or professional world about which one was knowledgeable, a fundamental context of one's life. Fourth is the concern about one's legacy and the perpetuation of organizational values to which one had dedicated oneself. Managers approaching retirement may experience some or all of these fears.

Other less obvious losses may be even more painful. The curmudgeonly literary critic, H. L. Mencken, remarked that people work in order to escape the depressing agony of contemplating life. Put more scientifically, our brains function continuously whether we are engaged in deliberate thought or not. As a result, we all experience a continuous flow of memory images or fantasies that, at more relaxed moments, we recognize as daydreams.[8] Many images refer repetitively to still unresolved emotional problems stemming from early childhood, with which we are still struggling mentally and which we try to keep out of our awareness. Concentrating our attention on something else, like work, is a common method for keeping these images at bay. That is why some people say they would go crazy if they did not work. That same heavy concentration can interfere with family life and inhibit social relationships, a problem that many young people who work long hours complain about. Some managers cherish the long hours because the intense involvement keeps them from having to supervise, direct, evaluate, and otherwise interact more closely with people outside work.

A decline in sexual potency, a withdrawal of libido, can result in the diminution of feelings of affection that temper the expression of feelings of aggression. This loss may result in greater irritability toward others and ambivalence toward those who are emotionally close. If we overcontrol anger to avoid offending others, we may turn it onto ourselves, resulting in feelings of depression. The depressive feelings are reflected in the recurrent complaint that the younger person does not care enough about the senior, nor about the corporation's external obligations or its employees. A former CEO of a service company complained bitterly to the first author that his successor failed to continue the charitable contributions and community leadership that had earned him and his company many plaudits, and that his successor was inconsiderate of longtime employees. When the successor wanted to shed these employees as superfluous or inadequate, the former CEO tried to have them rehired. In another instance, the head of an office supply company complained to the senior author about subordinates who were not as committed to the values and success of the organization as he was.

RIVALRY WITH THE SUCCESSOR AS RETIREMENT NEARS

The losses of aging may become more threatening when rivalry between the executive and the heir apparent intensifies as the time for retirement nears. Even in relatively flat organizations, managers have more power than those who report to them. Rivalry for power is inevitable. In cases where the retiring executives have built the business or a significant part of it, they may feel that their self-sacrificing effort is inadequately appreciated. This lack of appreciation can be manifested in the inattention from their recognized successors and others who no longer wish to inform them or consult them about important matters. These

feelings can exacerbate the elders' normal envy of younger individuals who have not only their futures before them, but also continuing influence within the organizations, thus stimulating feelings of jealousy, rivalry, and resentment.[9] Such feelings may be coupled with a fear and envy of the young people, who intimidate with their knowledge and self-confidence. They have not yet had salt in their wounds, as one senior executive put it.

All this may occur against an anomalous social context. In the course of human development, we grow from one psychological stage into another, each holding out the promise of continued evolution to more sophisticated behavior.[10] However, there is no social definition of that period beyond retirement, and no well-defined, characteristic set of behaviors outlining the transition into it. The transition out of it, which most people dread, is only too vividly clear. Some retirees find that to be aged is to be part of an unwanted generation. Betty Friedan contends that the mystique of age is much more deadly than what she called "the feminine mystique."[11] Although many welcome it, for most people who have no clear idea what to do, retirement can be the most difficult transition of life.

Just as children become disappointed when they discover their parents' imperfections, so lower-level managers must cope with similar feelings about those seniors whom they have held in esteem, from whom they have learned, and whose achievements they hope to emulate and exceed. If seniors are reluctant to yield their roles, juniors may feel that they are angry, rivalrous old fossils who should have passed on the batons a long time ago, but who just cannot let go. This is particularly likely for seniors who have built the organizations, especially if they have undertaken reorganizations or if the executives attempt to thwart prospective successors. The late Dr. Karl A. Menninger, a mentor of the first author, would eliminate a staff member's position or change the organization structure whenever the staff member rose in the esteem of the other staff to the point where they expected him to succeed the boss. Dr. Menninger wanted to keep the organization under family leadership.

Younger executives are often impatient to make their own marks. To differentiate themselves from their predecessors, they must make changes whether necessary or not. Sometimes drastic changes are indeed necessary because of rapidly changing competitive circumstances, even though the successor executive undertakes them with trepidation. This was the case when John F. Welch succeeded Reginald H. Jones at the General Electric Company. It was Welch who pointed out from his own experience: "When you're running an institution like this you're always scared at first. You're afraid you'll break it. People don't think about leaders this way, but it's true. Everyone who's running something goes home at night and wrestles with the same fear: 'Am I going to be the one who blows this place up?'"[12] That trepidation lies behind the facade of self-confidence of every successor. Wise executives anticipate the high cost of rivalry by mentoring the upward movement of their likely successors. When John W. Hanley was CEO of Monsanto, he paved the way for his successor, Richard J. Mahoney, by inviting him to high-level social affairs at his home and country club and by pushing him into community leadership roles.[13]

KEY STEPS TO SUCCESSFUL TRANSITION INTO THE FLEXIBILITY PHASE

Recognize the Complexities of the Transition

For a successful transition, both the executive and the successor must recognize that the process of retiring can be a painful and difficult phase of life. Therefore, the first step in dealing with the transition is for both parties to recognize the complexities discussed above. This is best done by talking with each other, preferably with the help of a psychologically trained consultant, who can help avoid the psychological shoals on which they might shatter their relationship, and who can help them temper their differences. It is frequently helpful for managers to learn that much of what they are struggling with is typical and not blameworthy. In one such situation, the first author counseled an executive over a five-year period about candidates to succeed him, and the candidate who was ultimately chosen later undertook his own separate consultation to better manage the transition with his predecessor. Both were pleased with the highly successful outcome.

Choose New Work and Life Activities

Seniors need to accept the fact that they must not retire from active work and life. As the late comedian George Burns asked: "Why should I retire? I'm doing the same things now that I've been doing all my life and I love it. The only time you should retire is if you find something you enjoy doing more than what you are doing now." Burns enunciated the two fundamental principles that apply to retirement: Continue what you enjoy doing and develop a parallel activity that can become even more enjoyable. There are many ways for managers to continue what they enjoyed in their work—becoming a consultant, helping embryonic organizations get started, moving into a government role, heading a smaller company in difficult straits, or joining a venture capital group.

When Harold Moore retired as managing director of the North Texas Contractors Association, he became active in arbitration and mediation work, which he was still enjoying at age 72. When one consultant lost his constituency because younger managers who did not know him were taking over in his client companies, the first author suggested that he and some of his retired peers might form a firm that would invest in small businesses. These investments would enable them to continue their relationships with the business world and be directly helpful to others. They accepted the suggestion and found the experience highly rewarding. Some managers have found that the Peace Corps, the Service Corps of Retired Executives, and the International Executive Service Program provide opportunities for continued contributions and travel that they could enjoy with their spouses. Others have found such activities to be devices to continue avoiding their spouses.

Often, however, managers whose work has been paramount do not have another consuming interest and do not know how to go about developing one. It is easier to do so if one has a cause. One high-level executive of a high-tech company, a loyal engineer alumnus of his university, became intensely committed to raising money for its engineering school. Another executive, dedicated to finding a cure for muscular dystrophy, became highly knowledgeable about that illness and became involved with the leading researchers in neurobiology. Others have invested themselves in community activities where their business knowledge enables them to strengthen museums, orchestras, schools, and similar local services that perennially need management help as well as financial resources. Those who do not have a commitment must create one. For example, like the executive of the high-tech company mentioned above, some people could find it stimulating to become knowledgeable about and supportive of their universities, departments, and professors who have areas of interest close to theirs. That may require an invitation from the university president or an academic dean. Prospective retirees cannot sit by and wait for others to create their opportunities for them. Carl Sloane, who headed a highly successful consulting firm, created such an opportunity for himself when he became a Harvard Business School professor.

Recognize and Deal with Loss

All change involves loss. No matter how desirable or advantageous the change, one loses familiar faces, characteristic patterns of daily routine and behavior, the support of colleagues and friends, and other sources of gratification. Anyone who has ever been promoted or transferred to a new site knows the sweet and sour nature of that experience. The less welcome the change, the more painful the losses.

Human beings are anchored in social networks. We have ties to friends, relatives, and others. We are anchored in intellectual networks—ideas, memories, values, religious beliefs—and in our characteristic stance toward the world around us. We see the world in certain idiosyncratic ways and act on the basis of these perceptions. We are anchored in physical networks: home, neighborhood, office, plant, community.

Change often uproots us from this psychologically nourishing and supportive soil; therefore, we may experience loss. In some cases, this loss results in feelings of sadness and depression.[14] Psychologically, we cry inside ourselves for what we have lost. But crying inside ourselves does not help much. In an effort to keep our feelings from showing, we may deny them even to ourselves. "It doesn't bother me," we say. "I should be able to manage my problems without becoming emotional," we may add. We keep a stiff upper lip. But fundamentally, we humans are emotional. Our limbic brainstems, the sources of sexual and aggressive drives, are the primitive powerhouses of behavior. When we overcontrol our emotions, we merely try to keep them buried. They do not disappear. This means we have to continue to overcontrol them, because as long as they are inside us, we remain afraid they will erupt. Therefore, we must devote energy to the controlling process, and such overcontrol inhibits spontaneity. The more effort we devote to controlling ourselves, the more stiff and cold we appear to others.

Not only can there be loss in separating from an organization, but also from giving up the activities and people with whom we have worked for many years, as well as the perquisites and supports. Frequently, there are multiple additional losses, such as the death of a friend. "It is natural that, as the years pass, we should increasingly consider our twilight," Pope John Paul wrote to his "elderly brothers and sisters."[15] He continued: "If nothing else, we are reminded of it by the very fact that the ranks of our family members, friends and acquaintances grow ever thinner."

So we need to express anger at our losses and disgorge the feelings of sadness. In short, we need to mourn. If we cannot mourn, then we are less able to adapt effectively to new situations, for we continue to live with underlying feelings of depression and anger. We still remain preoccupied with the past. Besides, chronic depression threatens physical health. Moving successfully from one stage of life to another requires a mechanism for mourning—someone to talk to early on about the prospective losses and concerns about the future. Doing the necessary grief work ideally involves time spent talking with one's spouse, with colleagues in the same situation, or with a professional counselor.

If there are colleagues in the same situation, it can be helpful to have a talking group, especially the year before retirement. For high-level executives, this may be done better in sessions away from their companies, with similar level executives in other companies. Alternatively, it may be done with one of a growing number of executive coaches. One needs ways of examining prospective plans out loud, of looking carefully at issues that one might not have seen clearly, and of examining options critically.

The executive group sessions should include spouses because the changes brought by retirement will have significance for them as well. They too must share the discussions and the planning, and have the opportunity to deal with their feelings, as well as those of the prospective retiree. They too must adapt. Sometimes, there will be special problems to be dealt with, like elderly parents or chronically ill children, and perhaps the impact of the choices of one partner on the work role of the other. If spouses are left in isolation, additional problems may occur. For example, the effects of isolation appear to be evidenced by reports of a growing number of homebound alcoholics. Some firms that do appliance maintenance in condominium communities report that their servicemen are sometimes called to repair appliances that are not broken. It may be that, for the price of an appliance repairman's time, a lonesome wife has someone to talk to while her husband is following his own interests.

Wives particularly welcome the opportunity to get their husbands to talk. Talking serves the purpose of mourning and is the stimulus to begin restitution activities. But some men have great difficulty talking about situations that precipitate intense feelings, even severe feelings of loss. For example, when an executive friend of the first author lost his wife in an airplane crash, the author called him and suggested that he talk with a professional colleague of his. "No," the executive said, "I'm a Stoic. I'm a stubborn old Dutchman." "That's what I am afraid of," Levinson replied. "We know from studies in England that there is a disproportionate death rate among widowers age 54 and older in the first six months after their spouses' deaths."

Fortunately, more of today's managers have learned to exercise, to watch what they eat, to temper their drinking, and to use consultants and facilitators. Increasingly, they are giving themselves permission to talk.

The transition process has an additional hazard: the ambivalence of close relationships. The closer we are to someone else, the more dependent we become on that person, and the more vulnerable we are to that person's behavior. The closer we are, the more easily we become angry and frustrated by the behavior of another whom we may not like or who rubs us the wrong way. In good marriages the partners learn to accept their differences and feelings of conflict. However, in transitional times, in moving from one phase of life to another, from one major activity to another, ambivalence is heightened because the usual boundaries of family and organization have been loosened. The prospective retiree should anticipate increased ambivalence and allow plenty of time to talk differences out.

Expecting that they will lose old friends and associates, people entering the flexibility phase should work at establishing new friends, counteracting the tendency toward constricting their social circles, and rebuilding sources of personal companionship. Helping others who are having difficulty turns the associations into a mutual support system.

Engage in Self-Assessment

In our mind's eye, we all have a picture of ourselves as we would like to be. This is our ego ideal.[16] This ideal view of self has many sources, but we are aware of only a few of them. Some of them we were never clear about, and others have become obscured by time. We do not have a fixed picture of that ideal, but can see its outlines if we look back on our life experiences and view them as an unfolding process, a pattern of our striving. We can get a sense of our direction, our values, those experiences that were highly gratifying, and those that were not. We can get another view of our ego ideal by the exercise of writing our own obituaries. What we want to have accomplished and the image that we want to present to others is what we are striving toward but never fully attain.

We also have a self-image, a picture of ourselves as we think we are now. The self-image may be more or less accurate. Since our ego ideals tend to be perfectionistic, there is always a gap between the ego ideal and the self-image. That gap leaves us feeling highly self-critical for not being as good as we think we should be. We are our own harshest critics.

To the degree that we are self-critical or angry with ourselves, we become depressed. Conversely, the closer we come to our ego ideals, the more elated we become. That gap, therefore, is the source of our ambition. The motivation for our striving is to narrow that gap. There is no motivation as powerful as the wish to like ourselves, and this occurs when we feel that we are moving toward our ego ideals.

In the retirement process, three problems arise from the ego ideal-self-image phenomenon. The first is that the ego ideal has a significantly irrational component. Not only do we strive for perfection, but our dreams and aspirations range far more widely than our ability to achieve them. We simply do not have the time or the resources to do all that we once thought possible. So we always have to make choices, to give up something. Coming into the retirement period means unequivocally that we must give up some wishes that have been important to us. Active people often say, as they regretfully settle for less than they had hoped for, "There was so much more I wanted to do." One academic colleague heaved a deep sigh as he discarded all the material he had been saving for a book that he now knew he would never write.

The second troublesome aspect of the ego ideal has to do with dependency. We are all born helpless in cognitive and physical abilities. We are all mortal. As we age, we can overcome our helplessness and mortality by acquiring skills and competencies, by achieving, and by having others depend on us. Managers who deny that they have strong dependency needs should consider the popularity of, indeed the demand for, executive employment contracts that afford protection against those on whom we are dependent. In our culture, to be independent and self-sufficient is the highest virtue. Yet aging means that, to varying degrees, we are likely to become more dependent, more helpless. Thus we must cope with the lowered self-image that aging can bring. We must also cope with our anger toward ourselves for being less adequate and less competent in some ways than we once were and still want to be.

The third negative aspect of the ego ideal phenomenon has to do with the rupture of the relationship with the organization where one has worked. Frequently, with that rupture comes significant loss of one's social status, power, income, use of certain skills and knowledge, perquisites, and one's place in an organizational structure. For all of their previous efforts and achievements, most people are less likely to be recognized for what they have done as the years pass. Newcomers do not know them. If they have been heroic, those who knew of their heroism are now likely to be gone or to be preoccupied with pursuing their own ego ideals. In his retirement, Fritz Roethlisberger, the late grand old man of human relations in the Harvard Business School, passed many students each day as he went to lunch in the faculty club. Yet few knew he was among them. We must come to terms with the fact that we may become less valued by those to whom we have given so much.

Recognize the Significant Psychological Meaning of This Stage

The psychoanalyst Erik H. Erikson described three major stages of adult life.[17] The last of these, the period from approximately age 55 on, he spoke of as the stage of integrity. At that time, he pointed out, people begin to draw their life experiences to a close and into an integrated whole. In doing so, they review the past and take leave of it. Looking back on their life experiences, they inevitably judge how well they have used their lives. If they are far from where they had hoped to be, they are likely to become depressed, even though such expectations might have been unrealistic. This is the psychological basis for the depression of old age or what technically is called involutional melancholia.

In the flexibility stage, we must come to terms with having already lived a large portion of our one and only life and accept the fruits of our efforts. Ideally, we should have acquired wisdom. We should have contributed something to society through the medium of our work and our families, and we should have left our mark in the lives of other people. Presumably, in the later years of our work, we have brought to bear our acquired wisdom and passed on that knowledge and experience to younger persons.[18]

Handling the Transitions

A person moving into the retirement period must deal with the experience of loss, with lowered self-image, with the feelings of growing helplessness, and with the issues of the integrity stage. He or she must handle the transitional disruptions, as well as the realities of that period of life. The person who does this well maintains a flexibility that enables the pursuit of a wide variety of pleasurable activities of his or her own choosing and pace. How does one go about doing that? We offer the following four rules of conduct that can guide a person through the process of moving into the retirement period.

Anticipate Change

Anticipation leads us to buy life insurance. It should also lead us to acquire psychological insurance. In the flexibility phase, most of us have a range of choices and anticipations about what we can do about our lot in life. We have already referred to the need to talk about our constricting life experience, about our sense of falling behind, about our increasing dependence, about the loss of friends and colleagues, about leaving our life's work and its environment, about growing impatience and irritability, about the sense of being passed by and being unwanted, about extending our present working horizons and developing new commitments, and about how to enjoy our grandchildren. In short, we need to talk about the need to mourn, to renew hope, to find pleasure, to give back, and to leave some indelible mark.

Expect Ambiguity

Before we leave our organizations and, perhaps, our communities, preparation and the expression of feelings that go with it counteract some of the potential feelings of anxiety and depression, of anger and frustration. These feelings can arise as we move from a situation that has been highly structured and in which we are well experienced, to a situation of considerable ambiguity and possibly unanticipated threat. Talking with friends or counselors may help us in examining our plans and in looking at dimensions and options that we may not have considered carefully. One manager, for example, wanted to start immediately on a book he had long promised himself he would write. He was brought up short when it was pointed out that he needed to supplement his retirement funding to meet his continuing financial obligations.

Take a Formal Leave

Knowing that we will lose our ties to the work organization, it is important to think of a formal goodbye or leave-taking process. Sometimes that is done by gradually cutting back on the time we work, sometimes by taking longer vacations, or by taking on more external responsibilities. Some executives depart abruptly to avoid the pain of parting or to elude the discomfort of emotional expressions of apprecia-

tion of their contributions. One petroleum company executive did just that: Rather than following advice to take his leave openly so as not to deprive his colleagues and subordinates of the need to say their goodbyes, he bolted to an around-the-world cruise. Even when one is glad to leave, smooth detachment is better than ripping up relationships. Besides, when one runs or hides, others are denied their right to mourn and to regret the departure. It is better to detach gradually and to mourn each detachment.

Let Go

Of course, it is natural to be reluctant to leave.[19] Executives who try to hang on make it difficult for others who are no longer certain of these executives' roles and what their formal relationships to them should be. Under such circumstances parting is not sweet sorrow. Reluctance to say goodbye may be a mask for the wish to stay, to deny that one is really leaving. One board chairman who refused to take his leave was signaling exactly that and continued to try to run the company through his successor. The successor quit. Another executive found it increasingly difficult to find CEO lunch partners, though still a member of the board. He also suffered from the loss of old friends who were dying off. When he busied himself with luncheon appointments with the managers who used to report to him, it did not sit too well with his successor.

Anticipating the flexibility phase as another in the life cycle, one can concentrate on the psychological work of adjustment the period may require. The tasks involve supporting one's self-image, meeting those unfulfilled demands of the ego ideal that can be fulfilled, and maintaining one's mastery of self and environment as long as possible. One must recognize that one is going through a crisis of normal development. Crisis means shock, surprise, dismay, anger, fear, threat. People who weather crises best not only anticipate them, but also have close relationships with other caring people. The highest suicide rate is among elderly single men.[20] Clearly, it is crucial that the laws of transition be applied effectively.

ACTION STEPS FOR RETIRING MANAGERS

What, in addition to developing new commitments and talking, are the action steps that a retiring executive should take? Since a fundamental issue is the need for a support system, that is a place to begin.

Recognize That the Environment Is Fundamental for Your Support System

A person must decide where to live in this new flexibility phase. One decision about this issue is whether to stay where the family is presently living or to retire to another community. Perhaps one prefers a change of climates. There may be certain kinds of activities to pursue. Being near friends or children may be important. Whatever the case, the location should provide maximum opportunity for flexibility in choosing activities and developing interests.

The prospective retiree and spouse should examine this situation together, preferably beginning in middle age. Simply put, some communities are not, by themselves, hospitable. To be accepted in them, people must create their own psychological settings. The newcomer must take the initiative. By the time they have reached retirement, couples who intend to retire to a new community should have already begun to establish roots there. Some do this by repeatedly going to the prospective new community on vacations, by establishing local contacts, by becoming involved in local political, social, and business activities, and

by beginning to develop work possibilities. Some do so by buying vacation homes, others by making trial moves. By establishing ties and supports in this new community, one has provided for oneself a place to hold on to when he or she must leave old relationships behind.

Develop Activities That Gratify Support Needs

Loneliness can be the curse of the aged. It is especially a problem for those executives whose careers have been the basis of their social relationships and activities. Almost everyone needs to be able to talk to others. However, once separated from old friends and relatives either by their moving, aging, or death, or one's own move, there is a great tendency not to replace those ties. It is more difficult to do so when one is a stranger in a new situation. To move into a new context where there are social mechanisms and devices for doing this makes life considerably easier, particularly when one is socially congenial. Some people do this by going to retirement communities, but many, especially those who want to maintain contact with people of all ages, feel that going to such a community is a withdrawal from reality, involving an acceptance of age segregation. Others develop a new context by being in settings where the nature of their work allows them to interact with others of various ages, and still others through churches, synagogues, mosques, temples, fraternal lodges, and various kinds of service organizations and community activities. There is a growing movement toward life-long learning programs, some developed by local colleges and some in which retirees teach each other, as at the Eckerd College in Florida. Retirees may also use their knowledge to enrich the cultures of their communities. A physician with a love for opera organized several operatic series in communities near his retirement home. A new community can provide the opportunity for one to continue to make use of one's skills and further one's interests. It should provide the stimulus for sampling and developing new skills and interests.

When one has not done the preliminary work on community location, then it must be done at the time of retirement. A person may lose several retirement years in searching for a new residence if the preliminary work was not done before retirement. This simply adds more burdens to a time of stress and ambiguity.

Contribute to the Development of Young People

For the prospective retiree who does not have children or grandchildren, or whose children are grown and gone, it may be important to help young people. Perhaps that may take the form of teaching skills, or finding a substitute grandson or granddaughter with whom one can maintain a continuing relationship or interest. This could be a gratifying way to have a stake in the development of a young person. Some retired physicians have helped undergraduate students with their papers on health care.

Do the Things You Always Wanted to Do

This may be anything from a long desired vacation trip, to undertaking a special task or project, to supporting a favored cause, or to championing a political issue. One should have the freedom to pick up some dream that was left behind and to follow up on it. One executive who had spent a professional lifetime in a staff function had always wanted to demonstrate to himself that he would have been a good line executive. He retired early and bought a small business which he ran with great pleasure.

A special interest or hobby can be an important medium for developing and sustaining ties to others. Some people do so with flowers or Japanese prints. One group

of former managers built and flew an airplane. It is astonishing to see the range and quality of artistic and craft skills that become visible in exhibitions of retirees' talents, many of which were developed after they retired.

Consider a Consulting Role

There are many advantages to being in a consulting role. Younger managers are more likely to employ an older consultant whom they do not see as competing for their jobs. Older managers may value retired executives as peers, perhaps also reluctant to trust younger people with less experience. Still others may value the continuity and stability they represent without having them tied to the organization permanently. When one executive in the plastics molding industry had built his company from a small struggling business to a large, highly profitable one, he retired from the company and began consulting. For one of his major clients, he evaluates four or five companies a year for their potential for acquisition.

For the retirees' part, many have great flexibility to come and go as they wish and to work at whatever they choose in whatever parts of the world they find themselves. The competencies retired executives carry with them constitute their portable skill bank. There are never enough people in any organization to solve all of the problems that have to be solved. The trick is to define a role for one's self, to define the problems that one is expert at solving, and to let prospective clients know of one's availability.

The flexibility phase requires a change in orientation in which we accept separation from our organizations. Retired executives must accept the reality that they now stand on their own independent feet, make their own choices, and follow their own directions outside the corporate world. They should fully accept the idea that they are dealing with their own lives, their own choices, and their own activities.

HOW ORGANIZATIONS CAN FACILITATE A SUCCESSOR'S ADAPTATION TO A MANAGER'S RETIREMENT

A fundamental task for every manager is to provide for his or her own succession.[21] The crucial factor in the adaptive process for the successor is patience. In psychology, the goal gradient hypothesis refers to the fact that the closer one gets to a goal, the greater the tension resulting from the urgency to attain the goal and the greater the extra effort required to control the impulse to act prematurely. Those who cannot control such an impulse risk losing their opportunity. One president of an insurance company became a former president when, with too much passion and vigor, he urged his chairman to leave. Another executive became inappropriately defensive about a delicate suggestion from his boss that his lawyer wife not attend a meeting that included spouses. The wife was a partner in a firm in litigation with a subsidiary of the corporation and company plans were to be discussed at the meeting. It takes years to build a trusting relationship, but often it takes only a trivial act or a slip of tongue to destroy it. It is a reasonable guess that candidates have undermined their chances when they are heard to speak of losing out because of politics, a plot, or nefarious motives. Sure, there are the proverbial incidences of the CEO's spouse who does not like the potential successor's spouse, but those influences are far fewer with increasing numbers of outside board members who usually make up the personnel committees.

If, however, a senior person does not give a junior colleague adequate and timely information about the latter's prospects, then the junior person is likely wiser to go elsewhere. Lower-level executives, too, must manage their own careers and should have their own counselors with whom to examine their options. These counselors may also help them to realize the degree to which their rivalrous feelings may get in the way. The opportunity to examine options and feelings should enable junior managers to maintain appropriate perspectives and to inhibit impulsive actions.

The continuing relationship with a retired predecessor requires careful attention. For all of the reasons above, retirement is a psychological bruise for many managers. No matter how much it may have been desired, separation can precipitate feelings of depression. Recovery from loss is made easier when others show that they care. In management relationships, this is advantageously done when junior executives continue to use retired seniors as mentors by occasional consultations. Sometimes the successors must take such radically different directions that the predecessors do not have much guidance to offer. In those circumstances, the successors can at least explain what is being done differently and why. Although predecessors may disagree with their successors' courses of action, their sensitivity has been considered.[22] It is easy for predecessors to experience changes as indictments of their regimes, especially if the changes have been announced with great public fanfare. Successors may also disdain or ignore their predecessors. One high-tech company CEO who did so found himself displaced when he learned, too late, that his predecessor still had significant influence on the corporate board. Taking a different perspective, one CEO makes sure his board members and those who report to him keep in touch with his predecessor so they can benefit from the senior's knowledge and wisdom.[23]

Many companies make excellent use of retirees who represent organizational memory and still have skills to contribute. Former executives can be helpful in representing the organization to some of its publics, chairing its charitable giving, and boosting internal morale with ambassadorial visits to work sites. Like all others who are accountable to the organization, they can function best and avoid misunderstanding when the successor gives them a well-defined task with clear focus, boundaries, and time limits. Where their relationship is close enough to do so, the successor may encourage the predecessor to talk about some of the feelings associated with retirement, in effect giving him or her psychological permission to do so. The shared feelings may help the successor to better prepare for future retirement.

With retirement comes flexibility: The freedom to make choices about new life endeavors, reordering of priorities, giving time to long-ignored interests, and acquiring new pursuits. Success in making the retirement transition begins with recognizing the complexities and opportunities that this phase of life affords. Social and emotional adjustments are important for dealing with the changes of this transition phase. These adjustments are augmented by social support of family, friends, and colleagues, and by interesting and valuable contributions to companies, the community, and individuals. These contributions may involve the investment of the retired executive's time, expertise, council, or financial resources. Opportunities for retired managers can be exciting and rewarding, but to be successfully taken advantage of, they require preparation and action. ■

REFERENCES

[1]*New York Times.* (1996, August 28). It's a clashing of the guard (old vs. new) at American Stores, D1.

[2]U.S. Senate, Select Committee on Aging, 1987–1988.

[3]Jaques, E., & Cason, K. (1994). *Human capability: A study of individual potential and its application.* Falls Church, VA: Cason Hall & Company.

[4]Schaie, K. W. (1979). The primary mental abilities in adulthood: An exploration in the development of psychometric intelligence. In P. B. Baltes and O. G. Brim, Jr. (Eds.) *Life-Span Development Behavior* (Vol. 2). New York: Academic Press; Horn, J. L. (1982). The theory of fluid and crystallized intelligence in relation to the concept of cognitive psychology and aging in adulthood. In F. I. M. Craik and S. Trehub (Eds.), *Aging and Cognitive Processes.* New York: Plenum.

[5]Perlmutter, M., & Hall, E. (1992). *Adult development and aging,* 2nd edition New York: John Wiley, 112.

[6]Tichy, N. M., & Cohen, E. (1997). *The leadership engine.* New York: Harper Business, 16.

[7]Neugarten, B. (1964). *Personality in middle and later life.* New York: Atherton Press.

[8]Vaillant, G. E. (1993). *The wisdom of the ego.* Cambridge: Harvard University Press, 338.

[9]Kets de Vries, M. (1988). The dark side of CEO succession. *Harvard Business Review, 88,* 56–60.

[10]Erikson, E. H. (1963). *Childhood and society,* 2nd edition. New York: W. W. Norton; Erikson, E. H., & Erikson, J. M. (1981). On generativity and identity: From a conversation with Erik and Joan Erickson. *Harvard Educational Review, 51,* 249–269; Erikson, E. H., & Hall, E. (1987). Erikson: The father of the identity crisis. In E. Hall (Ed.), *Growing and changing.* New York: Random House; Levinson, D. J., Darrow, C. N., Klein, E. B., Levinson, M. H., & McKee, B. (1978). *The season's of a man's life.* New York: Knopf.

[11]Friedan, B. (1984). *The feminine mystique.* New York: Dell Publishing Company; Friedan, B. (1993). *The fountain of age.* New York: Simon and Schuster.

[12]Tichy, N. M., & Sherman, S. (1993). *Control your destiny or someone else will.* New York: Doubleday/Currency.

[13]Levinson, H., & Rosenthal, S. (1984). *CEO: Corporate leadership in action.* New York: Basic Books.

[14]Lieberman, M. A. (1983). Social contexts of depression. In L. D. Breslau and M. R. Haug. (Eds.), *Depression and aging.* New York: Springer; Holahan, C. K., & Holahan, C. J. (1987). Self-efficacy, social support, and de-

pression in aging: A longitudinal analysis. *Journal of Gerontology, 42,* 65–68.

[15]*New York Times.* (1999, October 27), Pope describes his feelings in unusual letter to the aged, A5.

[16]Chasseguet-Smirgel, J. (1985). *The ego ideal.* W. W. Norton & Company.

[17]Erikson, op cit.; Erikson & Erikson, op. cit.; Erikson & Hall, op. cit.

[18]Wills, G. (1992). Enabling managerial growth and ownership succession. *Management Decision, 30,* 10–26.

[19]U.S. Bureau of the Census. (1990). *Statistical abstract of the United States,* 110th edition. Washington DC: U.S. Government Printing Office.

[20]Vancil, R. F. (1987). *Passing the baton.* Boston: Harvard Business School.

[21]Ciampa, D., & Watkins, M. (1999). The successor's dilemma. *Harvard Business Review, 77* (6), 160–168; Levinson, H. (1974). Don't choose your own successor. *Harvard Business Review, 52* (6), 53–62.

[22]Lamb, R. B. (1987). *Running American business: Top CEOs rethink their major decisions.* New York: Basic Books, 247–273; Sonnenfeld, J. (1986). Heroes in collision: Chief executive retirement and the parade of future leaders. *Human Resource Management, 25,* 305–333.

[23]Vancil, op. cit.

15 PERFORMANCE AND EFFECTIVENESS

Productivity in work organizations has become a prominent concern in this country. A growing number of organizations have become interested in determining what conditions in the work environment might contribute to their overall effectiveness. The key phrase in the discussion is "developing and maintaining competitiveness." Companies need to define and develop those factors that contribute to strategic competitiveness. We compete in a world economy; thus, we need to be aware of cutting-edge ideas for achieving and maintaining competitiveness.

Commensurate with the growing desire to enhance performance is the need to improve fiscal soundness through effective human resources programs. In these days of diminishing budgets, the functional areas of organizations, one of which is human resources management, are often required to justify their existence. This justification is frequently related to overall contribution to the bottom line. The administration of human resources certainly has an impact on organizational competitiveness and on the bottom line. With the increase in influence of the human resources department comes more responsibility for the overall effectiveness of the organization. We believe that human resources programs are up to the challenge. They can and do make a difference.

In the first article in this chapter, Galang makes an important case for the human resources department as a pivotal center in facilitating competitiveness. Many of the functions headquartered in the human resources area have the potential to add value to the bottom line of an organization. Perform these functions well and effectiveness results. The article by Renn and Himel makes an interesting point—we should move the primary responsibility for performance from the organizational to the individual. Their conclusion is that, due to the changing environment of work, there is a need for more self-management. Keiser takes a novel approach in the third article. The service sector of our economy has increased at a rapid pace, and what we know about managing employees in this sector has not kept up. Many of the human resources practices developed for other sectors do not transfer easily to the service sector. Attention to this detail may increase the performance of this sector. The last article in this chapter, by Zivnuska and Ferris, discusses the reciprocal influences of corporate reputation and organizational performance. Reputation influences organizational performance, which in turn influences human resources. Customers and employees notice whether organizations are true to their reputation.

READINGS

THE HUMAN RESOURCES DEPARTMENT: ITS ROLE IN FIRM COMPETITIVENESS

Maria Carmen Galang

Globalization, technological advancements, and demographic changes in the population have all contributed to making business environments increasingly complex and turbulent. Such an environment challenges firms to remain competitive. At the same time, and primarily because of these developments, firms can no longer rely on the traditional sources of competitive advantage (Pfeffer, 1995a, 1995b). It has become imperative for businesses to search for other means to maintain competitiveness. In this context, human resources have become relatively more important in providing the firm with competitive advantage.

The recognition of human resources as a sustainable source of competitive advantage has led to further refinement of this notion, through careful explanation of why and how it can be realized, and also in terms of empirical validation. However, despite this recognized importance of human resources for today's business organization, the human resources (HR) department, the individuals typically tasked with the responsibility of managing the firm's human resources, is under severe criticism (e.g., Galang, Elsik, & Russ, 1999; Stewart, 1996). Not everyone is convinced that the HR department has an essential part in creating this sustainable source of competitive advantage. Barney and Wright (1998), for example, write of a manager making a distinction between *little hr*, the human resources or the people that make up the organization, and *big HR*, referring to the human resources function,

with the value placed on the *little hr* and not on the *big HR*. Cognizant of these criticisms and the realization that human resources can be a source of competitive advantage for the firm, this article examines how the HR department can continue to have a role in the business striving for competitiveness. The prescriptions as to what this role or roles should be are presented, as well as some actual cases of transformations of the HR department. First, however, is a discussion of the notion of human resources as a source of competitive advantage for the firm.

HUMAN RESOURCES AS A SOURCE OF COMPETITIVE ADVANTAGE

Pfeffer (1995a, 1995b) argues that, relative to other traditional sources of competitive advantage (e.g., product and process technology, protected or regulated markets, access to financial resources, and economies of scale), human resources have now become an important source of sustainable competitive advantage. Using Barney's (1991) resource-based view of organizations, Barney and Wright (1998) and Wright, McMahan, and McWilliams (1994) further develop the arguments. To be a sustainable source of competitive advantage, that resource should meet all the criteria of value adding, rare, inimitable, and nonsubstitutable (Wright, et al., 1994), otherwise the resource in question can only provide competitive parity and not advantage, or might provide competitive advantage but only in the short term

(Barney & Wright, 1998). *Little hr* meet these criteria and are therefore potential sources of sustainable competitive advantage, but only when the *big HR* enables the knowledge, skills, and abilities of the *little hr* to be applied towards the firm's needs and objectives. It is the *big HR* that meets the fourth criteria of O (for organization) in Barney and Wright's (1998) VRIO framework. The arguments for *little hr* and *big HR* as sustainable sources of competitive advantage are summarized in Table 15-1.

Big HR creates the human capital, one of the three types of resources that Barney (1991) identifies as providing a firm with competitive advantage. On the other hand, without the *little hr*, there is nothing on which *big HR* can begin to develop the firm's needed human capital. Therefore, it is both the *little hr* and *big HR* that provide the firm with its sustainable competitive advantage.

Table 15-1 also points to two aspects that are central to this paper. First, individual HR practices by themselves are not rare, inimitable, or nonsubstitutable. However, as a system or package of practices that is embedded in the organizational context, it is much harder to imitate, and is rare (i.e., not many firms have managed to implement a cohesive and strategically contingent human resources management system). This package of interrelated practices that are also aligned with the organization's goals and strategies has been referred to as a high performance work system (HPWS), and is discussed in more detail later in this section.

The other key point in Table 15-1 is that the HR department is not a necessary player. While the activities falling under the HR function need to be performed in an organization, it need not be an HR department that does them. It is only an assumption that the HR function needs to be done by an internal HR department, supposedly because of its expertise in human behavior, compared to others in the organization. However, that expertise, one would argue, is also available outside the organization. Others also argue that whatever the HR department does, which they do quite ineffectively anyway (so the argument goes), can and should be done by others in the organization as well. The question of the role of the HR department in contributing to firm competitiveness is the main topic of this article, and the surrounding debate and issues with respect to this role are discussed in the next section.

One can point out the irony in organizational downsizing when the importance of human resources in firm competitiveness is being touted. An asset that is expendable can hardly be seen as one providing a source of competitive advantage. However, organizational downsizing does not disprove the value of human resources, but indicates the lack of understanding of how *little hr* can provide the firm with sustainable competitive advantage and the role that the *big HR* can play in this process, and the failure of the HR executives to explain this and take the necessary actions (Barney & Wright, 1998). It could also be that, instead of the lean and mean organizations hoped for, the round of massive downsizing that U.S. firms went through resulted in anorexic organizations of highly demoralized downsizing survivors, which are even in a worse position to compete. Firms now realize the need to focus attention on how the remaining human resources are managed, so that firms can benefit from having had to downsize their employment numbers in the previous decade (Kerr & Von Glinow, 1997).

A similar argument can be extended to the downsizing of HR departments. Like the rest of the organization, HR departments did not escape the directive from the top to cut costs. HR departments, which did not have any choice but to make use of whatever was left, turned the experience into an opportunity to become better at what they do. If they did not do so, then they faced the prospect of being totally eliminated from organizations. Hence began the transforma-

TABLE 15-1 Analysis of Human Resources as Sustainable Source of Competitive Advantage

Criteria	Little hr (people in the organization)	Big HR (human resources function)
Value adding	Because individuals differ in type and level of skill, and firms have different jobs that require different skills, there is variance in the contribution value of individuals.	The HR function can add value by ensuring that the right skills for the firm's requirements are acquired and mobilized, by decreasing costs (for example, becoming more efficient, or eliminating aspects that do not add value or create competitive disadvantage), or by helping to create revenues by differentiating the firm's product/service so that the firm can charge a premium price.
Rare	Skills needed by firms are normally distributed in the labor supply, and because the total talent pool is not unlimited, firms with more of the human capital pool gain this capital at the expense of other firms.	Although individual best practices can eventually diffuse to other firms, a system of interrelated HRM practices is much harder to implement, and therefore rarely found in practice.
Inimitable	It is difficult to identify which individual is responsible for the performance of the organization, and it is often the case that performance is not attributable to a single individual, but a group of individuals. Furthermore, people are relatively immobile because of the costs of leaving and transferring. Firms cannot expect that resources that add value can be freely purchased from the market, because those resources will be priced at the value to the firm.	Social complexity and causal ambiguity make it difficult to identify which practice or practices are responsible for good performance. History of interactions provides the firm with the ability to acquire and exploit particular firm resources, and develops a unique work culture and norms. Furthermore, if it is a system of HR practices, which create synergy within a given organizational context, and not just a single practice that accounts for good practice, then it becomes even harder to copy.
Nonsubstitutable	In the short term, other resources might provide competitive advantage, but only to the extent that those other resources are themselves value adding, rare, or inimitable.	The functions have to be performed, but whether it needs to be performed by the HR department is the question that is addressed by the need to transform.

Source: Based largely on Barney and Wright (1998), and Wright, McMahan, and McWilliams (1994). The point about the HR functions having to be performed but not necessarily by an internal HR department is based on Adams (1991) and Kerr and Von Glinow (1997).

tion of the HR department. This will be discussed in the next section.

Nonetheless, the recognition of importance of human resources management (HRM) for the firm is underscored by two studies that have looked at the effect of the firm's reputation in managing its human resources on its stock price. Chauvin and Guthrie (1994) and Hannon and Milkovich (1996) both found that after the annual announcement of best employers to work for, there was a statistically significant increase in the stock prices of the firms included in the list. There is therefore the common belief that, by managing its human resources well, the firm will become profitable and, therefore, warrant investment.

But what constitutes good HRM? Pfeffer (1995b) proposed the following thirteen practices: employment security, selectivity in recruitment, high wages, incentive pay, employee ownership, information sharing, participation and empowerment, self-managed teams, training and skill development, cross-utilization and cross-training, symbolic egalitarianism, wage compression, and promotion from within. He also points out, however, that what is important is that these practices need to be considered as a package of interrelated practices. One cannot just borrow a practice and apply it to an organization and expect to have the same positive results. Becker, Huselid, Pickus, and Spratt (1997) coined the terms *deadly combinations* and *powerful connections* to underscore the notion of systems thinking, which HR managers need to acquire in order to move into a new role: "*Deadly combinations* develop when firms adopt HRM policies and practices that might well make sense in isolation but when evaluated within the context of *other* HRM practices deployed throughout the firm are a recipe for disaster. . . . Alternatively, *powerful connections* reflect the presence of complementarities or synergies that can occur when economic returns from the 'whole' of the

HRM system adds up to more than the sum of its parts" (p. 43).

There is a growing literature examining the concept of HPWS (high performance work system), which has become the label applied to a set of HR practices that are internally coherent or integrated, and externally aligned with the business goals and objectives. Both internal and external fit are requirements for HRM to have a strategic impact on the organization, and therefore provide sustainable competitive advantage (e.g., Becker & Huselid, 1998; Dyer & Reeves, 1995).

In addition, Huselid and colleagues (Becker & Huselid, 1998; Delaney & Huselid, 1996; Huselid, 1995; Huselid & Becker, 1995, 1996, 1997; Huselid, Jackson, & Schuler, 1997; Huselid & Rau, 1997) have been collecting empirical evidence in support of the positive impact of HPWS on firm performance. Huselid (1995) estimated that firms will gain \$27,044 in sales per employee and \$18,641 in firm market value per employee from a one standard deviation increase in HPWS. This was from a cross-sectional study of 968 publicly held U.S. firms. Subsequent conservative estimates, taking into account measurement errors from either a cross-sectional or longitudinal study, placed the increase in firm market value per employee at \$14,350–\$17,275 (Huselid & Becker, 1996). In another sample of publicly held U.S. firms (n = 740), and using a broader measure of HPWS, Huselid and Becker (1995) estimated the gain in firm market value per employee at \$38,000–\$73,000. These dollar figures certainly are heartening to firms searching for sources of competitive advantage, as well as give support to the proposition that human resources can provide that advantage. Furthermore, Huselid and Becker (1995) observed a nonlinear relationship between HPWS and market value per employee, which was interpreted as providing further support to the competitive advantage argument (Becker & Huselid, 1998). Firms below the 20th percentile in terms of the level of HPWS are able to substantially gain market value until reaching that minimum threshold. At this point they become "part of the pack," meaning they have achieved competitive parity, but the HRM system only has smaller effects on firm performance. Only when firms reach the 60th percentile and above do they stand out from the rest: They have competitive advantage, and again gain substantially from the HRM system.

Another study evaluating the financial impact of HR practices is by Ostroff in 1995 (mentioned in Ulrich, 1997b). An overall quality of HR index was developed for each firm based on the aggregate ratings of all HR activities adopted by the firm. This index was then related to four financial measures: market/book value (market value of the firm based on stock price divided by firm's assets), productivity (dollar value of sales divided by number of employees), market value (stock price $\times$ outstanding shares), and sales. All four financial measures increased dramatically with the quality of HR practices.

The common feature in the studies cited here is that HR practices are investigated as a package, rather than as individual best practices. Thus there is often a composite index calculated from a set of practices that have been adopted by the firm, and it is this composite index that is subsequently related to organizational outcomes or antecedent conditions. Studies have also attempted to test whether the whole is greater than the individual parts (Whitfield & Poole, 1997).

One aspect of HPWS that has not fared as well in terms of empirical validation is that of external fit (Becker & Huselid, 1998; Dyer & Reeves, 1995). Theoretically, it makes sense that a set of HR practices that are internally coherent can only provide a sustainable source of competitive advantage if it is embedded in an organizational context because then it becomes difficult to im-

itate (Becker, & Huselid, 1998; Becker, et al., 1997). It is relatively rare, particularly because of the difficulty involved in implementing an entire cohesive system that works for the particular firm given the influences of different stakeholder groups (Galang, 1999). Becker and Huselid (1998) cited several studies that did not find strong and consistent support for the need for external fit. Similarly, Dyer and Reeves (1995) noted the contradictory results from different studies, but also that not much empirical studies have been done on the contingency perspective. On the other hand, there are studies that have found linkage between strategy and HR practices, and that this linkage had an impact on business performance (e.g., Ulrich, 1997b). One other example is Ostroff's study mentioned earlier.

The findings that HPWS has positive economic impact certainly helps the HR professional argue not only for his or her continued existence, but also for having more influence in the management of the organization. The concept of a high performance work system can provide the "powerful theoretical base, so that the myriad HR activities can become grounded in the business and integrated with one another" that Christensen (1997) attributes the lack of influence of the HR department to. His proposal for that needed simple theory reflects the essence of HPWS: Effective HRM has both external (providing the specific talent or competencies to build the organizational capabilities required of the organization's strategies) and internal (initiatives as being interrelated) fit. But while these studies provide proof of the impact of HRM on valued organization outcomes, the HR professional still needs to ensure that those benefits can be realized by his or her own organization.

What is not clear, from the empirical evidence of the positive impact of HPWS, however, is the set of practices that it encompasses. Unfortunately, not only do the different studies list different practices, but these studies also show contradictory effects from individual practices included in the set. For instance, Wood (1996) provided both conceptual arguments and empirical evidence on the incompatibility of incentive pay with high commitment management. To make it more complicated, Pucik (1997) also warned about ethnocentric HRM systems that might impede firms' efforts to globalize. There is still much to be desired in terms of what the package really looks like—and whether it is a question of more versus less, or a question of an entirely different set of practices, depending on organizational contingencies. One might argue that the package should not be the same for all firms, because the package, to provide a source of sustainable competitive advantage, should be inimitable, and inimitability comes from the social complexity and causal ambiguity that only a highly interrelated set of practices aligned with organizational contingencies creates. The jury is still out with respect to the contextual factors, including strategy, that relates to various types of packages. At this time, the answer for the HR professional is to propose those initiatives that are appropriate for the specific organizational requirements, while using the findings from the literature as to what some of those HR practices might be, and continuously monitor results.

The next question that arises is: Does the HR department still have a role in the firm's quest to remain competitive?

NEW ROLES, NEW COMPETENCIES?

Many firms seem to think that the HR department is not necessary. As Brenner (1996) reported, a 1995 Conference Board survey shows 58 percent of large U.S. corporations, across all industries, have downsized their HR departments by eliminating, automating, or outsourcing their functions. Nonetheless, the same report also shows that HR departments in these firms have not

completely disappeared, only that they have become much smaller, particularly the corporate HR group, and with a new role as a business partner to line managers. In fact, rather than it being a threat, downsizing has provided an opportunity for the HR department to move from somewhat of a supporting role in the organization to one that is more influential and strategically placed. Given less available resources and the need to prove their contribution (value added), HR departments needed to be more efficient and effective in performing their function. Outsourcing, far from being the evidence of the unnecessary role of HR departments, became part and parcel of this new role for HR departments, as it enables the use of expertise in a more economical way, and the focus on the more strategic issues facing the organization.

While the position of most HR people (both academics and practitioners) is one of transforming the role in order to remain useful (Ulrich 1997a), not everyone sees it that way. Rucci (1997), for instance, believes in the planned obsolescence of HR, or at least in the HR department's establishing that as a goal. By doing so, he argues, the HR department will concentrate on developing the HR profession's skills and mindset in all managers, which will then enable the organization to face the challenges and opportunities of a competitive business environment. Nonetheless, even if this goal does not lead to the complete elimination of the HR departments in organizations, Rucci (1997) believes that "it will certainly lead to more effective HR organizations, and it will at least prevent the eventual elimination of HR due to management frustration with its ineffectiveness. . . . Ironically, eliminating the need for the HR profession and its roles may be the most effective way of demonstrating HR's value" (p. 173).

Even among those who advocate transformation, there is not an agreement: On the one side are those who see the new role of the HR department as solely that of a strategic business partner; on the other side are those who see a need to balance the new role with traditional ones. Aside from being a strategic partner, there are three other roles for HR identified by Ulrich (1994; Conner & Ulrich, 1996) that many in the HR profession also acknowledge: employee champion, administrative expert, and change agent. These four roles differ in terms of focus (long term/strategic vs. short term/operational) and activities (people vs. process), and the traditional roles relate to the operational activities of an employee champion and administrative expert.

The role of a strategic business partner is seen as being narrow-minded and short-sighted by some. From an ethical perspective, it leads organizations to act too much out of self-interest, with little regard for employee and community interests (Ellig, 1997; Losey, 1997). In addition, because they rely more on employees' discretionary effort that comes from their commitment and loyalty, today's organizations all the more need to ensure that the traditional services are there for the employees to count on (Kerr & Von Glinow, 1997). Kochan (1997) maintains that HRM should attend to the "undercurrent of anxiety, insecurity, and perhaps even suppressed anger in the workforce" because of the changed implicit social contract that used to govern employment relations, which has resulted from pressure to remain competitive. All these fall within the HR department's more traditional roles.

For Ellig (1997) and Losey (1997), it is the role of employee advocate and strategic business partner that needs to be retained, because the administrative role can be reengineered, downsized, or outsourced. Information technology such as intranets—centralized service centers that can be accessed by 1-800 numbers—or external vendors can be utilized to perform the administrative functions of HRM. This frees up the time for the HR staff to focus on more

strategic concerns, as well as develop the skills and outlook that are often inconsistent with skills required for administrative responsibilities (Losey, 1997). Ulrich (1994) believes that "HR professionals must learn to deal with multiple, not single, roles. . . . To add value to increasingly complex business requires an ability to perform increasingly complex and, at times, paradoxical roles" (pp. 51–52). While he recognizes that each individual in the HR department may not have the competence for all four roles, he also urges that the aggregate of individuals comprising the department should.

Kochan (1997) also believes that the internally oriented focus of being a strategic business partner overlooks the classic market failure situation where a single firm does not have the capability or the motivation to solve many of today's most critical workplace problems. He suggests that HR professionals need the ability to "negotiate, build coalitions, and to solve problems with multiple internal and external interests and organizations including professionals in other firms, government, educational institutions, labor unions, and professional associations" (p. 124). The external focus is also stressed by Brockbank (1999) as it enables the HR department to be more strategically proactive by being able to link internal capability and external requirements.

Brockbank (1999), however, is clearly one HR professional who is in favor of being strategic over operational. Only by being strategic will HR be able to provide a competitive advantage for the firm. A study he cites supports this view. The University of Michigan, in three rounds of data gathering participated in by 20,000 individuals, found higher firm performance in both 1992 and 1997 as HR departments became more strategically focused and relatively less operational. This was in contrast with an earlier data gathering in 1988, where firm performance was high when HR departments were strongly and equally focused on both strategic and operational aspects. Similar results were found by Huselid, Jackson, and Schuler (1997). Data collected from 293 U.S. firms in 1991 and 1992 show significant relationships between measure of firm performance (employee productivity, cash flow, and market value) and strategic HRM effectiveness, but not with technical HRM. The shift towards more strategic activities was also observed by a mid-1990s study by McMahan, Mohrman, and Lawler (1996). Changes that had taken place in the HR function from the past five to seven years were reported by 130 large companies. All the changes observed were statistically significant. The largest increase in percentage of time spent was being a strategic business partner, from 10.3 to 22.2 percent. Development of HR service systems and practices also increased, from 14.3 to 18.6 percent. Maintaining records and auditing/controlling both decreased by about 7 percent, from 23.0 to 15.4 percent, and from 19.5 to 12.2 percent, respectively. However, most of the time spent was still in being a human resources service provider, although it decreased from 34.3 to 31.3 percent.

The more traditional, operationally oriented activities of the HR department may not provide competitive advantage, but if neglected may create competitive disadvantage (Barney & Wright, 1998; Brockbank, 1999). Huselid, et al. (1997) observe that the level of technical HRM effectiveness in their U.S. sample was on average higher than the level of strategic HRM effectiveness, suggesting that technical HRM activities are not sufficient to differentiate from competitors and therefore cannot be used to achieve competitive advantage. However, this conclusion, they note, is based on large U.S. firms, and may not hold for true when the levels of technical HRM are lower, such as in smaller U.S. firms, or in global environments. Nonetheless, they also believe that a moderate level of technical HRM provides the foundation for successfully implementing strategic HRM activities.

In summary, just as with the question of which practices constitute that set of practices that will lead to high performance (i.e., high performance work systems), the answer to what role the HR department should play perhaps is best addressed by the specific organization. The relative emphasis on each role, and which of the many activities that need to be undertaken can and should be retained within the organization or outsourced, depends on the organization itself. One of the critical factors to consider is the set of competencies that the HR staff already have that supports the needed roles, and whether these sets of competencies can be developed in the existing staff, or whether new staff with the requisite competencies can replace the existing staff. There are two major influential streams establishing the needed HR competencies: the University of Michigan studies, and the HR Planning Society's State-of-the-Art and Practices Studies.

In 1988 and in 1992, Ulrich, Brockbank, Yeung, and Lake (1995) surveyed HR professionals and their associates (such as clients or internal customers, peers, subordinates, or supervisors) in 109 firms. These included firms in *Fortune*'s list of most admired companies, the 50 largest U.S. employers, firms with relationships with the research team, firms outside the United States, and requests by firms to join the database, all in all representing a total of 1,500 businesses. The results reported were based on the responses of 1,928 HR participants and 12,689 associates, who rated the HR professional in terms of the listed 67 competencies in the three domains of knowledge of business, delivery of HR, and management of change processes, and in terms of their overall performance. Regression analysis showed that knowledge of business accounts for 18.8 percent of the overall performance of HR professionals, functional excellence or delivery of HR practices accounts for 23.3 percent, and management of change accounts for 41.2 percent. Over time, all percentages increased, particularly in knowledge of business, but management of change remained to be the most important in both years. The pattern was the same regardless of industry (except for the automotive industry where knowledge of business came second to management of change), the respondent's relationship to the HR professional, the hierarchical level of the HR professional, and size of the business.

Although Ulrich, et al. (1995) did not report in detail what competencies measured each of the three domains, an earlier published article listed specifics, based on that study combined with in-depth interviews of 50 executives from 10 major corporations: American Express, ALCOA, Baxter International, British Telecom, Hewlett-Packard, IBM, Intel, Johnson & Johnson, Levi Strauss & Co., and McKesson (Yeung, Brockbank, & Ulrich, 1994). These 10 firms were selected from a larger study of 25 corporations primarily on the basis of the prestige of their HR functions, the uniqueness of their HR practices, and their high performance level relative to their competitors in the industry. Yeung, et al. (1994) proposed four domains of competencies to include personal credibility to the three in Ulrich, et al. (1995) (see Table 15-2).

The list of competencies was later updated (Yeung, Woolcock, Sullivan, & the California Strategic Human Resource Partnership, 1996), incorporating findings from another set of in-depth interviews with senior HR executives in 10 companies: Apple Computer, Bay Networks, DFS Group Limited, Hewlett-Packard, International Paper, Kaiser Permanente Health Foundation, National Semiconductor, Oracle Corporation, Quantum Corporation, and Transamerica Corporation (see Table 15-2). These executives were asked about the competencies required of senior HR professionals at both

corporate and business-unit levels in the coming three to five years, and also strategies to effectively acquire or develop these new competencies. One other finding from this study is that competencies should be specific to the position, as there are HR generalists and specialists in corporate office, in business units, or in centers of expertise.

Another set of HR competencies comes from the yearly State-of-the-Art and Practice Study (SOTA/P) of the Human Resource Planning Society (see Table 15-3). Started in 1994, the highlights of these studies are published in the Society's journal, with the latest being the 1999 study (Wright, Dyer, & Takla, 1999). Unfortunately, only the 1995 and 1996 highlights provide specific lists of competencies expected from HR professionals (Eichinger & Ulrich, 1995; Eichinger, Ulrich, & The Human Resource Planning Society, 1997). Complete reports can however, be purchased from the Society.

These are all generic lists of HR competencies, which can serve as a starting point for firms to begin identifying the specific set of HR competencies that are relevant and critical for their respective situations.

Other Competencies: Measuring and Marketing

Part of the new expectations not only from HR but also from other functions in the organization is demonstrating the value contributed to the firm. Thus an important part of the transformation effort is measurement. Measurement also focuses attention on what needs to be delivered by the HR function (Ulrich, 1997b). Various measures can be and have been used, including the balanced scorecard—which takes into consideration the various interests of the three stakeholders (investors, customers and employees)—and the audit of the HR activities, the HR professionals, or the department itself (Ulrich, 1997b). The balanced scorecard enables the development of a systems view of how HRM affects the organization

TABLE 15-2 List of HR Competencies Identified by University of Michigan Studies	
Yeung, Brockbank, & Ulrich (1994)	*Yeung, Woolcock, Sullivan & the California Strategic Human Resource Partnership (1996)*
Business Mastery—general knowledge of finance, external customer needs and requirements, competitors, information technology, and other business processes	*Core* Business knowledge/acumen Customer orientation Effective communication Credibility and integrity Systemic perspective Negotiation and conflict resolution
HR Mastery—ability to design and deliver HR practices that are aligned with each other and closely linked to business objectives	*Leadership* Leadership skills and capability Leadership attributes Change advocacy
Change Mastery—interpersonal skills and influence management, problem-solving skills, and creativity	*HR Expertise* Knowledge of "best-in-class" HR practices Design and deliver HR services effectively (process management and improvement) Apply technology to HR Measure the effectiveness of HR practices
Personal Credibility—trust, building personal relationships, living the values of the firm, courage to stand up for own beliefs, to deliver both good and bad news, and to act in spite of resistance	*Consultation* Influencing skills Consulting skills (diagnosis, problem solving, contracting) Change facilitation and implementation (OD and OE skills) Collaboration and team building

Note: The original large-scale University of Michigan study (Ulrich, et al., 1995), which these two studies incorporated, identified three domains of competencies, namely knowledge of business, functional excellence or HR delivery, and change management. These domains, or the specific competencies under each, are not listed in any particular order.

(Pfeffer, 1997), and addresses the shortcomings of the current HPWS literature, which so far has primarily focused on the interests of the investor stakeholders. Aside from financial performance of the firm such as economic profitability or market value, other indicators could and should include customer commitment and retention, and employee satisfaction and competencies. The HR audit, on the other hand, assesses the value perceived by the internal customers of HR services, the resources spent on such services, and the effectiveness of the implementation of various programs and initiatives. Implementation effectiveness as perceived by internal customers has been shown to affect the impact of HPWS (Huselid & Becker, 1997).

Not all agree on the need to measure, however. Pfeffer (1997) lists a number of problems with HR measurements that should be heeded by the HR professional so that measuring is done in order to improve the impact of HRM on the critical performance aspects of individuals and organizations. These are (1) focusing on the measurable expenditure of resources, rather than on whether the resources are being spent wisely and effectively or not, often resulting in cutting for cutting's sake; (2) short-term perspective, when

TABLE 15-3 List of HR Competencies from the State-of-the-Art & Practice (SOTA/P) Studies

SOTA 95 (listed in order of frequency of mention)	*SOTA 96* (listed according to rank order)
Global operating skills	Personal credibility, integrity, and trust
Business and financial savvy	Business/industry savvy/acumen; a working understanding of the business proposition and the strategic intent of the organization
Strategic visioning, critical thinking, and problem-solving skills	Personal leadership presence and functional credibility with the internal customer
Ability to use information technology	Change management technology; leading organizational change initiatives using personal power, indirect influence, and facilitating skills; taking the lead on facilitating revolutionary change in the organization and in HR
Deep HR technology savvy	Analytical, conceptual, and critical thinking; problem-solving skills
Change management skills	Global HR/business strategic thinking and planning skills
Organization effectiveness	Political savvy; interpersonal skills Deep and working knowledge of the basic HR technologies; avoiding chasing fads, quick fixes, and benchmarked "me too's" that don't fit Organization design/effectiveness; TQM; process reengineering Financial analysis and process-costing skills

Source: Eichinger & Ulrich (1995); Eichinger, Ulrich, & The Human Resource Planning Society (1997).

effects of HR practices on organizational capability can only be seen in the long term; (3) absence of a systems focus that interrelates different factors affecting human resources effectiveness, thus allowing the measurement of critical indicators only; and (4) measuring what the HR function cannot influence. Apart from such technical pitfalls is the involvement of organizational politics in measurement, where the objective is to make the numbers look good for a particular person or interest group, even if these numbers are meaningless, or ultimately detrimental to human resources effectiveness.

Apart from these substantive changes in what HR professionals need to do, there is also the recognition of changing how HR professionals need to act; in other words, how to present or market themselves, and not just the programs or initiatives that they

are proposing. For instance, Brenner (1996) quotes consultant David Axson: "HR isn't used to selling its services. But marketing doesn't have to show a product will improve the bottom line in order to make it attractive. While bottom line is critical, HR must be more effective in selling the value-added component of its service. You have to have an appealing story and you have to be more proactive than HR has been in the past. Identify key players who are amenable to change, have them help design a solution, and they become the sales force" (p. 63). Hathcock (1996), as vice president of human resources for Siemens Rolm Communications Inc., wrote: "if [we] want to play in the frontlines and if we want value parity with other corporate functions, we must position ourselves as do other corporate functions (those big dogs again). For instance, we in human resources must stop referring to ourselves as a 'department' which smells of bureaucracy and administration. We are an *organization* just as is the engineering organization or the marketing organization. . . . If we want to be a fully integrated business partner, we need to act and look like a business partner" (p. 248). Ulrich and Eichinger (1998), in *HRMagazine,* wrote about HR with a professional attitude, that is, "acting with confident conviction . . . not arrogance, decisiveness not equivocation, risk taking and a bias for action not permission seeking and glad-handing" (pp. 157–158). They do warn, however, that "HR with an attitude—but without competence—is unwise bravado, unsupported by expertise and insight. Competence without an attitude leads to mediocre results. But the combination of attitude and competence transforms HR into a full profession" (p. 158). Galang and Ferris (1997), in a study of 242 U.S. organizations, found that symbolic actions by the HR department to portray its importance was indeed a strong predictor of its power or influence within the organization.

In summary, there are still unanswered questions (Ulrich 1997a) about the new roles and new competencies. Nonetheless, organizations have started to move constructively toward that new role, instead of merely being defensive against criticisms of its value. In fact, the following cases have defined what their new role is within the context of their own needs and requirements. Perhaps what lessons can be drawn from these organizations is not so much what those roles are, but rather the process of identifying what those roles are that their specific organizations require.

HOW HR DEPARTMENTS ARE TRANSFORMING THEMSELVES: SOME EXAMPLES

A few cases have been included in this article. There are certainly others that have been cited as good examples in the literature (see for example, Pfeffer 1995a; Becker & Huselid 1999). The cases selected here focus on an aspect of the transformation process, and hence contribute to an overall understanding of the process, rather than merely replicate the points of the other cases. Two of the cases, Continental Airlines and Mercantile Bancorporation, were direct results of Stewart's (1996) barbed criticism of HR departments, but elicited two different responses. Continental's case is offered as an example to refute the charges of worthlessness, and shows how the HR department can be an important partner in a business turnaround, and for Mercantile, it served to trigger a self-assessment. Pratt & Whitney is an example of how firms develop the competencies of their HR staff as a consequence of downsizing. Pratt & Whitney, as do Eastman Kodak and AT&T, provides a list of competencies, but Eastman Kodak and AT&T also describe the process by which they arrived at their sets of competencies. Both Eastman Kodak and AT&T identify different sets of competencies for different HR responsibilities or roles, which they themselves also identified. Mercantile, however, utilizes an existing framework on the different roles of the HR staff. AT&T further describes how they began to establish their competency model in the firm.

Continental Airlines

Continental Airlines' response to Stewart's criticism was to provide an example of HR's role as a strategic change agent (Carrig, 1997). Since 1978, Continental Airlines had operated at a loss and, in 1994, it was again almost bankrupt, having lost $650 million and a debt-to-equity ratio of nearly 30:1. Ten CEOs had come and gone in 10 years; the company's performance ranked last in every rating by the U.S. Department of Transportation (DOT); it had the highest lost-time and turnover rates in the industry. As Carrig (1997), HR vice president, described it, the work environment was hostile following years of contentious labor-management disputes, and management demonstrated a lack of vision, as the only clear focus was on costs.

By 1996, however, the company earned its greatest profit ever—$525 million on revenues of about $6.5 billion. Continental had become the 5th largest airline in the United States and the leading U.S. airline serving Mexico, Central America, and the Western Pacific, consistently ranking first or second in DOT's ratings for on-time performance and baggage handling. It was the first company ever to leap from last to first place in J.D. Power's Frequent Travel Satisfaction Survey for domestic long-distance flights. Employee satisfaction had improved; absenteeism and voluntary turnover had shrunk; and there were more applications for jobs with the company.

The turnaround began with the arrival of the new leadership team of Gordon M. Bethune (CEO) and Greg Brenneman (COO), who immediately devised a four-pronged strategy for change: (1) improve revenue and deliver a profit, primarily by downsizing and eliminating unprofitable services; (2) reduce the debt burden and free assets up to enable future growth; (3) improve service so that travelers would want to fly Continental, and employees would be proud of the company's product; and (4) create an environment of dignity and respect with the ultimate goal of employees feeling valued and enjoying coming to work. Carrig (1997) writes, "the human resource function was primarily involved in shaping and implementing ideas for achieving objectives three and four by reinventing work practices and communication practices throughout the company" (pp. 278–279). The HR practices that were introduced in support of this strategy for change included:

- Bonuses pegged to a highly visible and understandable performance measure to build commitment to reliable performance (DOT rankings for on-time performance). Results were immediate: Through 1995 and 1996 Continental was in the top tier of on-time performance. This, of course, came with realistic scheduling that eliminated many flights, and took into consideration the abilities and limitations of airport operations, flight operations, and maintenance. Together with profit sharing, performance-based compensation has become a significant incentive at Continental; total variable pay stood at zero in 1994 and is expected to surpass $65 million in 1996.

- Efforts to create an environment of dignity, respect, and empowerment: the firing of 36 vice presidents and replacing them with 21 new ones with track records at successful companies; an employee celebration at which the 800-page employee manual was burned in the parking lot of corporate headquarters, even before completing its replacement (1/10 of its size); a policy that no employees flying Continental were to be left stranded at the gate if the plane had even one empty seat; monthly employee meetings with the CEO, COO, and the HR vice president, with all levels of management required to lead similar forums for their work groups; introduction of technology that allows the automatic transfer of calls of employees inquiring about benefits and payroll to the right person; closing the corporate office first on Labor Day 1995, then in 1996 and Memorial Day 1996 with all executives and corporate employees travelling to Continental's 20 major airports to work alongside the field employees serving drinks, lifting bags, and helping passengers.

- Policies and activities directed toward creating the desired work climate: introduced performance standards and linked incentives to desired results, such as responsiveness (e.g., customer calls answered within 20 seconds) and number of completed sales by reservations agents, and gains in revenue from business travelers for the sales force; participation of all 3,000 managers in workshops on creating a winning work environment or leading performance through such skills as decision making and listening to employees; introduced communication tools, together with the Communications Department, such as daily news update, Gordon's voicemail, and so on; fun activities such as celebrations to honor employees with perfect attendance, including an employee lottery for seven Ford Explorers in Continental's colors; and bonus cheques for each board director six months early, taped under their seats during a recent conference.

Through outsourcing and reengineering, these results were delivered despite the 30 percent cut to the HR department's staff, bringing down the ratio to one HR employee for every 100 employees. Continental's HR department is now operating at far less than the industry average. The HR department has outsourced many functions to service providers with expertise and efficiencies in mostly routine areas, which enabled them to improve service as well as reduce costs. They have also started to involve their service providers in policy-related areas such as training and recruitment, eventually hoping to develop a more a strategic partnership in which the service provider participates in the organization's strategic planning, supporting the process by offering technical expertise and customizing services to meet their needs. In addition, they hope to refocus the HR people towards the business of running an airline; incorporate HR into departmental, divisional, and organizational strategy; and have HR staff with deep analytical and personal leadership skills, and business knowledge as well as HR knowledge and skill that traditionally have been valued (e.g., understanding of employee behavior).

Mercantile Bancorporation

Mercantile, a multi-bank holding company offering a full range of financial services, is headquartered in St. Louis with $31 billion in assets and 10,000 employees (Forbringer & Oeth, 1998). Operating then in five neighboring states, Mercantile has had more than 30 mergers and acquisitions since 1990. The growing number of employees created the need for HR to restructure. Forbringer and Oeth (1998), both vice presidents in HR, acknowledge that Stewart's criticism of HR departments led them to a self-assessment that eventually resulted in an ongoing development effort that includes identifying future HR initiatives. This self-assessment involved a search for best practices that have been shown to have a positive business impact, to provide the standard against which to measure themselves. However, these best practices also provided them with the direction to move forward. In particular, guided by Ulrich's four roles, they implemented the following initiatives.

Strategic partner

- Corporate-wide meetings of officers and directors to clarify the new organizational mission, in which HR's role was to conduct focus groups to determine the information that would be most helpful to the officers, and craft the messages delivered during these meetings. Feedback from the meetings suggested that the information provided did help in better understanding the new mission and its implications.
- Action forums or "work-out" sessions, wherein representatives of work groups gather at an offsite location for

three days to write proposals for suggested improvements to their team's assigned work issue in line with strategic objectives. The HR department monitors the management-approved projects throughout. A number of these sessions in a variety of settings has been conducted by the department. As these sessions also serve to assimilate acquired workers, this initiative is also an example of the change agent role.

- New testing policies and procedures aligned with the new mission, including new selection policies that clarified the desired competencies of employees. Improving selection procedures is an example of the administrative expert role, and establishing the desired employee competencies aligned with the organizational strategy is more strategic than operational, and hence is a strategic partner role activity.

Change agent

- Merger integration. HR is from the beginning a part of the due diligence team focusing primarily on the financial aspects of HR (e.g., compensation, payroll, and benefits). They eventually hope to establish a process that integrates acquisitions more quickly and effectively, involves HR earlier, and focuses on cultural and leadership aspects as well.

Administrative expert

- Installation of an applicant tracking/resume retrieval system (ATS) to scan resumes, automatically track EEO information, and transmit information to multiple users simultaneously. Planned enhancements from the system include online applications from numerous locations, a direct upload of new hire information into their HRIS for automated benefit enrollment of new employees, online personnel requisitions and transfers requests, an internal candidate pool for non-exempts, and the electronic routing and sharing of resumes and information about candidates throughout the entire company.

- Improvement of the performance appraisal system, specifically creating the form in various software packages and on e-mail to increase accessibility and usage. The HR department has also streamlined the performance management training sessions, conducting such training for intact work units. This way, HR is targeted to supporting a business unit's "just-in-time" strategy rather than merely providing training "just in case" it becomes useful.

Aside from these, some other initiatives that take a more strategic focus are under consideration: help identify, communicate, and support core cultural competencies; expand economic literacy within the organization; refine measurement systems that support strategy and culture, as well as establish more quantifiable measures of HR impact; expand corporate knowledge and capture collective wisdom by facilitating the development of learning alliances among employees, managers, and departments, such as mentoring programs, learning circles, study groups, cross-functional teams, and the creation of databases or e-mail discussion groups to share best practices within Mercantile; and help managers reengineer and redesign the organization and create a culture to support the change.

Pratt & Whitney

Pratt & Whitney makes airplane engines and parts and is headquartered in East Hartford, Connecticut (Laabs, 1995). After falling market share from 61 to 38 percent in the past decade, the engine maker is now second to General Electric in its field. The falling market share was the impetus for downsizing, which meant cutting its workforce by half, and reorganizing from 57 large, functional business units to eight product centers responsible for making what the company calls "charter parts." The HR department also cut its staff by 40 percent and decentralized its operations to the new product centers. Now, HR professionals report to line managers in each of the company's eight centers, rather than reporting to a large, corporate HR organization. The number of HR people in headquarters was reduced from 530 to 8, with a total of 250 in the entire Pratt & Whitney of about 30,000 employees.

The reorganization was a difficult transition for most of the remaining personnel managers. To help ease the transition, a human resources assessment-and-development center was created, in which the HR professionals could learn the skills needed in the new Pratt & Whitney (see Table 15-4). The center's purpose were to (1) broaden capable HR professionals, (2) help them become better business partners, (3) give them a strategic focus rather than a tactical focus, and (4) help them develop their financial and business acumen.

The development center wasn't new. Since 1984, Pratt & Whitney had sent supervisors and managers to the center for assessment; in 1988 they were sent for development, too. The year the company reorganized, however, was the first time it had sent any of its HR professionals, and the first time that the company had decided to send an entire functional group. Of the 250 people in HR, 50 of the company's top HR managers and leadership associates have been targeted to go through a formal, two-year development program. The rest of the organization's HR personnel are scheduled to complete various workshops on similar topics, although their interaction is limited to one to two days at a time.

The two-year program starts with an assessment of current competencies, with trained assessors helping to identify the degree to which they'll need to develop certain competencies, depending upon their current management level or the level to which they're aspiring. It is feedback in a nonthreatening environment, and the participants come up with an individual development plan based on 360-degree feedback that reflects two major management assets that they want to develop and two development needs. Managers carefully decide upon their development strategy before their supervisors see them. Then, over the next two years, managers work with their bosses on those development needs, usually involving on-the-job projects combined with formal training, which includes two case studies based on real problems the company recently faced (for example, a recent joint venture between the company and a firm based in Israel or a business startup problem). Because the cases involve business issues that affect human resources and the business, the training forces them to think as business people, build financial and business acumen, and to think in a broader, more long-term, forward-thinking manner.

Eastman Kodak Company

Like many other companies rethinking their human resources strategies and, simultaneously, the contribution and capacities of their human resources organizations, Eastman Kodak needed to specify competencies required of its HR staff (Blancero, Boroski, & Dyer, 1996). With the repeated waves of restructuring and cost-cutting as well as major workforce reductions, the HR organization (HRO) came under strong pressure to demonstrate added value to the businesses.

The Eastman Kodak (EK) case was selected because it describes in detail the methodology by which they identified the set of competencies that would be needed by their HR people. The previous case of Pratt & Whitney focused on developing the competencies they had identified. EK's compe-

TABLE 15-4	HR Core Competencies Identified by Selected Cases	
Pratt & Whitney ***(Laabs, 1995)***	***Eastman Kodak*** ***(Blancero, Boroski, & Dyer, 1996)***	***AT&T*** ***(Conner & Wirtenberg, 1993)***
• Leadership • Customer focus • Fostering empowerment • Developing organizational talent • Communication • Analysis • Judgment • Business acumen • Planning/project management • Financial acumen • Functional expertise • Flexibility • Managing and facilitating change	Six roles: • Competency practitioner • Strategist/generalist • Initiative leader • Operational support • Consultant • Organizational leader Core competencies: • Personal integrity >Ethics >Standards of quality >Good judgment • Ambition and drive >Results oriented >Initiative >Enthusiasm >Self-confidence • Team skills >Teamwork >Relationship building >Communication >Listening	• Accountability for business results >Results orientation >Strategic thinking >Business partner >Customer focus >Uses HR expertise • Self-image >Sees self as catalyst for change >Sees self as member of leadership team >Demonstrates self-confidence • Managing interpersonal relationships >Building information networks >Influencing others >Exhibiting interpersonal flexibility >Building and managing teams >Energizing and empowering others

tency model consisted of three components: (1) a relatively small number of core competencies applicable across the full range of HR roles, (2) an even smaller number of leverage competencies applicable to half or more (but not all) of the roles, and (3) a much larger number of competencies that are specific to particular roles.

The process of identifying the required competencies had three phases, and involved over 60 EK managers and professionals (line management and HR) from all of the company's major business groups. Phase 1 involved identifying, defining, and preparing the HRO vision statement, performance requirements, behavioral illustrations, and competencies through a participative, iterative process. The *vision statement* referred to partnering with line managers to develop integrated human resources strategies and systems to enhance organizational capability. The *performance requirements* were broad statements of expectations with respect to future HRO work, classified into four clusters derived from previous published studies: HR leadership, strategic planning, business operations, and organizational change and performance improvement. The participants were segmented into four groups, one for each cluster, and each group developed a draft list of performance requirements for its cluster. The group members, except for four designated leaders, then rotated to the next cluster, modifying the initial list. This process continued until each group had worked on all four clusters. The leaders remained with a single cluster throughout to explain the work done by the previous groups. Finally each group returned to its initial cluster and, with the leader's assistance, created a final list of performance requirements. A total of 26 performance requirements were identified. The *behavioral illustrations* were used to add substance to the performance requirements. During a two-day off-site workshop, participants working individually at networked personal computers generated examples of illustrative behaviors for the performance requirements. Then, in rotating groups again, the panelists assigned each behavioral illustration to a specific performance requirement at each specific level: basic, intermediate, or advanced. The participants then voted electronically on the appropriateness of each of the assignments, but final resolution was accomplished through small-group discussions. Finally, a list of *competencies*—the knowledge, skills, abilities, and other attributes required to perform desired future behaviors—was decided upon, based on previous research, both published and proprietary. The final list included 96 competencies grouped into eight categories: managerial, business, technical, interpersonal, cognitive/imaginative, influence style, organization, and personal.

Phase II identified and described the roles, or clusters of expected behavior patterns, through which HR work would be done. Roles were considered rather than positions or jobs, because roles are more flexible and durable and can be combined in various ways to constitute future positions. Six roles were identified (see Table 15-4), and specific performance requirements were assigned to each role, providing concrete behavioral anchors to illustrate basic, intermediate, and advanced levels of performance.

In Phase III, the 62 role advisors rated the competencies associated with the various roles, deriving competency profiles for each role. The questionnaire included a brief description of the role along with appropriate performance requirements and behavior anchors. Role by role, each competency was rated on an 8-point scale, ranging from unnecessary to essential. Some role advisors considered all six roles; others with less familiarity were given subsets. For each role, the 10 most essential competencies were used to construct a competency profile.

Three categories of competencies emerged. Eleven core competencies, rated as among the most essential across all six roles, were grouped into three clusters (see Table 15-4). A group of competencies, most important for three or four (but not all six roles), was called leverage competencies, because selecting for or developing them provides flexibility in making assignments involving multiple roles. These leverage competencies include influence, utilization of resources, customer awareness, creativity, questioning, and organizational astuteness. Finally, 33 competencies were identified as being role-specific, as they were judged essential for only one or two roles.

AT&T

HR's transformation started late in 1988 when AT&T itself began its transition from a strongly centralized company to an enterprise of some 20 relatively independent business units linked to common support divisions (Conner & Wirtenberg, 1993). At that time, a group of corporate HR professionals joined with members of the newly forming units to generate a new HR organization design. The position of HR leader for each business unit was established, reporting both to the president or division head of a business and to the senior VP of HR, to (1) collaborate with corporate HR professionals to begin shaping a business-focused direction for the 6,000-strong HR community and (2) partner directly with the business unit leaders in their strategic planning efforts, particularly when those efforts were people-related. In early 1991, corporate HR launched an initiative—HR professionalism—that would empower the HR community to contribute more strategically to the company's business goals. An HR professional development team was formed to direct this organizational change effort.

The first phase of the process involved identifying the competencies required of high-performance HR professionals. To accomplish this, the team consulted the "subject experts," HR's internal customers. Line managers who were already involving HR people in the business process were identified and in-depth interviews were conducted with a small group of these managers. Focus groups were also held with line managers, asking them about the business challenges and opportunities they were facing and anticipating, about their perceptions of the HR function, and the role they felt HR should play in the future. These customers pointed out the need for the HR organization and the business units to share accountability for leveraging the company's assets—financial, capital, and people—to meet AT&T's strategic business objectives in the most efficient and effective ways possible. That meant changing HR's traditional paradigm.

In addition to obtaining customer feedback, the team also (1) analyzed research studies, HR competency models, and best practices developed by professional associations and benchmark companies to validate these internal findings, and to discover other success skills and behaviors; (2) surveyed some 150 people in their HR community (a sample from all levels and the senior HR leadership team) about challenges they faced, and the training, education, and professional support that can be offered; and (3) interviewed a sample of 30 from the top 100 HR performers throughout the company identified by HR executives in order to develop a profile of the top performers.

The resulting competency model was called the High Performance Excellence Model, and the skills and behaviors associated with three success clusters are listed in

Table 15-4. Each cluster was segmented by scope of HR responsibility and sphere of influence, both vertically and horizontally, and three generic HR competency models were finally designated: HR leader (senior person in the business unit or division), HR function manager (responsible for a function or group of functions in corporate or business unit or division), and HR specialist (manages a single function and handles day-to-day issues). Although the competencies, by and large, remain the same among the HR models, the specific behavioral indicators of success often vary depending on the degree of responsibility and leadership required of the position.

Acceptance of the concept of HR professionalism by the HR community was recognized as essential; introducing it in a large, traditional culture was an important step, since enthusiastic support had to be built. The strategy included a 20-minute video featuring HR customers, a brochure with an introductory statement by the senior VP in HR, a two-day symposium, and an advisory council composed of 15 high-performing HR people to pre-test and pilot each of the HR professionalism components. The campaign started at the top with the HR leaders, who then introduced the program to their HR function managers and specialists, who were also given the opportunities to discuss the impact of HR Professionalism on their own development and career paths.

To complete the change process, the team tackled the question of institutionalizing next. Several activities were undertaken:

- A diagnostic tool that enables individual self-assessment as well as feedback from internal customers. A confidential report goes to the individual who then can attend a one-day workshop to develop an individual action plan. An organizational development plan can also be designed based on the information from the diagnostic tool.

- A recognition program for HR individuals who are models of HR professionalism, as well as for line managers who are models in managing the people side of their business.
- A self-paced written guide to teach people about the new competencies and to facilitate the design of individual action plans, which includes real-life success stories from top-performing AT&T HR practitioners.
- Business Partner Lecture Series, in which heads of business units present to HR professionals cutting-edge business issues and strategic challenges.
- Special Interest Forums, in which HR people from across levels and businesses learn about managing strategic HR issues more effectively.
- Other new performance measures and monitoring techniques—an ongoing survey process, in-depth interviews of business unit leaders and managers by HR leaders on the business unit's performance and HR's contributions, an internal electronic polling mechanism to track changes in the thinking and behavior of HR people, and information from applications to the recognition program that testify to the strategic contributions being made to the business by HR professionals.

Lessons from Other Cases

The study of Yeung, et al. (1994) of 10 major corporations identified the 10 most common tactics used in pursuing the three major agendas of reducing HR costs, enhancing the quality of HR services, and focusing on business objectives:

- shared services
- information system
- outsourcing
- reengineering HR processes in terms of shorter cycle times and quality output

- operating HR departments as profit centers where services are charged on a fee basis and where internal customers have a choice of using internal or external services
- redefining the relative roles and responsibilities of line managers and HR staff in people management
- facilitating the development of self-managed work teams
- providing consulting services instead of merely transactional activities
- increasing involvement in strategic planning sessions with line managers
- facilitating organizational change.

Becker and Huselid (1999) conducted in-depth case studies of how five leading firms—Herman Miller, Lucent, Praxair, Quantum, and Sears—actually manage their people to help provide a source of competitive advantage. From June to October 1997, they interviewed more than 60 senior executives, both HR and line, in these companies and examined background materials provided by each company. In summary, they have identified three elements of a *value-added* HR function:

- A business strategy that relies on people as a source of competitive advantage and management culture that embraces that belief.
- Operational excellence, a focus on client service for individual employees and managers, and delivery of these services at the lowest possible cost.
- HR managers that understand the human capital implications of business problems and can access or modify the HR system to solve those problems.

Becker and Huselid (1999) indicated that while necessary, each alone does not suffice to transform HR into a strategic partner in the organization. The first element requires strong support from the CEO and other line managers, which comes with a clear understanding of the underlying competencies needed to achieve the business strategy, and the HRM system that will develop those competencies. The second element stresses the necessity of performing the traditional HR activities, albeit with better quality and efficiency (cost and time-wise). The third element underscores the need for HR managers to develop new competencies for the new roles expected of them, including the ability to effectively balance these sometimes competing roles, and to develop supporting organizational structures and sufficient resources that will allow them to deliver the expected services.

IMPLICATIONS FOR MANAGEMENT PRACTICE

The cases discussed above indicate that HR departments can and should transform themselves in order to contribute to the firm's efforts to remain competitive. They also show that, to be successful, strong support from top management—particularly the CEO—is necessary. Indeed, there have been suggestions on how top management can provide this support, such as communicating to the entire organization the importance of both the *little hr* and the *big HR,* defining HR goals and holding the HR department accountable for results, and investing in HR initiatives including upgrading the competencies of the HR staff (Becker & Huselid, 1999; Ulrich 1998).

Whether the necessary support is provided depends on whether the CEO realizes the importance of human resources, the part that the organization's HR people can and must perform, and, most importantly, the extent of changes that will result from the new roles of the HR department (Beer, 1997). As Beer (1997) points out: "Many still judge the function by its effectiveness in delivering administrative services and keeping the company out of trouble with regulatory agencies. They are, therefore, unreceptive to radical ideas such as splitting off administrative and service functions and placing them within other administratively oriented corporate departments. CEOs further frustrate a transformation . . . when they expect HR executives to be their agents. This is often accompanied by an ambivalence about giving the HR function the freedom and power to confront deep cultural issues, particularly when these issues are connected to top management's own assumptions, values, and behavior. Yet . . . these issues are precisely the ones that must be confronted for a transformation to take place" (pp. 54–55).

Are there other factors and considerations involved in this transformation process? One can say that these prescriptions have been based on case studies of successful experiences. Are unsuccessful cases because of missing CEO support, or do other factors come into play, particularly those factors beyond the organization's control even? Bennett, Ketchen, and Schultz (1998) investigated 148 organizations representing different industries to determine both the antecedents to and consequences of integrating HRM with strategic decision making processes. Some of their findings are interesting. In terms of determinants, aside from whether top managers viewed employees as a strategic resource, integration between HRM and strategic decision making depended on the organization's strategy, but not an increase in organization size or labor market munificence. They also observed that highly integrated HR departments were evaluated as *less* effective by top managers, contrary to what was hypothesized. They interpreted this phenomena as a risk that HR managers face: Integration allows HR managers to have more input in the organization's overall direction, but it also raises expectations and accountability from HRM on outcomes for which they have little or no control. In terms of the consequences of the HRM strategic decision making integration, they did not find any significant association with sales per employee, perceived profitability, and voluntary turnover rate. At least two of these consequences, one should note, are organizational outcomes that are affected by factors external to the organization, precisely the situation that Pfeffer (1997) warned about in HR measurement. A study by Arthur (1994) also showed that the relationship between turnover and manufacturing performance of steel minimills (in this case, scrap rate and labor hours) was affected by the type of HR system that was implemented. Correlation was positive in a commitment HR system, while correlation was negative and insignificant in a control HR system. This suggests that firms gain economically from an HR system that centers on developing employee commitment only to the extent that it is able to reduce its turnover rate.

Finally, because of the forces that have made the business environment more competitive and complex, human resources, compared to other sources of competitive advantage, have become more important. This situation may shift, and it is always good management practice to keep tabs of developments that lead to a shift.

FUTURE RESEARCH

Blancero, et al. (1996) wrote of the competency model established by Eastman Kodak: "the acid test is whether or not they contribute significantly to improving the performance of future HR managers and professionals and, in turn, to business success" (p. 397). There does not seem to be an answer from the existing literature. What is more prevalent are case descriptions of the transformation process, but none that are follow-ups of these cases. Ulrich, et al. (1995) did some testing of this question, by comparing the change in overall HR compe-tence scores and competitiveness ratings given by either the general manager or senior finance executive in two time periods. Their study included 200 business units with data for 1988–1989 and 1991–1992. The change in overall HR competence was the difference in the average scores for all HR professionals and associates in the business (minimum of one HR professional and three associates and maximum of six HR professionals and all their associates). What they found was that as overall HR competency increased, there was also a small increase in competitiveness rating. They also compared competencies in each of the three domains: Competitiveness ratings increased extensively when HR professionals increased their business knowledge, in contrast to when business knowledge did not or when it decreased; management of change was also highly related to change in competitiveness; delivery of HR was less related. Two cautions were given by Ulrich, et al. (1995) in interpreting these observations: (1) direction of causality has not been established (that is, the alternative explanation that a more competitive business has more resources to invest in upgrading the HR function is also plausible), and, (2) business results are affected by many factors other than the competencies of HR professionals.

It has also been argued that for human resources to be a sustainable source of competitive advantage, firms need to implement at the very least a system of interrelated practices that lead to performance valued by the firm. This is because individual best practices, while adding value, may not be rare but are also easier to copy. However, there is still much to learn about which best practices when used in conjunction with each other will provide that synergy that is greater than the sum of its individual parts. In other words, which ones are *deadly combinations* and which ones are *powerful connections?* ∎

REFERENCES

Arthur, J. B. (1994). Effects of human resource systems on manufacturing performance and turnover. *Academy of Management Journal, 37*, 670–687.

Barney, J. B. (1991). Firm resources and sustained competitive advantage. *Journal of Management, 17*, 99–120.

Barney, J. B., & Wright, P. M. (1998). On becoming a strategic partner: The role of human resources in gaining competitive advantage. *Human Resource Management, 37*, 31–46.

Becker, B. E., & Huselid, M. A. (1998). High performance work systems and firm performance: A synthesis of research and managerial implications. In G. R. Ferris (Ed.), *Research in Personnel and Human Resources Management* (Vol. 16). Greenwich, CT: JAI Press.

Becker, B. E., & Huselid, M. A. (1999). Strategic human resource management in five leading firms. *Human Resource Management, 38*, 287–301.

Becker, B. E., Huselid, M. A., Pickus, P. S., & Spratt, M. F. (1997). HR as a source of shareholder value: Research and recommendations. *Human Resource Management, 36*, 39–47.

Beer, M. (1997). The transformation of the human resource function: Resolving the tension between a traditional administrative and a new strategic role. *Human Resource Management, 36*, 49–56.

Bennett, N., Ketchen Jr., D. J., & Schultz, E. B. (1998). An examination of factors associated with the integration of human resource management and strategic decision making. *Human Resource Management, 37*, 3–16.

Blancero, D., Boroski, J., & Dyer, L. (1996). Key competencies for a transformed human resource organization: Results of a field study. *Human Resource Management, 35*, 383–403.

Brenner, L. (1996, March). The disappearing HR department. *CFO*, 61–64.

Brockbank, W. (1999). If HR were really strategically proactive: Present and future directions in HR's contribution to competitive advantage. *Human Resource Management, 38*, 337–352.

Carrig, K. (1997). Reshaping human resources for the next century—Lessons from a high flying airline. *Human Resource Management, 36*, 277–289.

Chauvin, K. W., & Guthrie, J. P. (1994). Labor market reputation and the value of the firm. *Managerial and Decision Economics, 15*, 543–552.

Christensen, R. (1997). Where is HR? *Human Resource Management, 36*, 81–84.

Conner, J., & Ulrich, D. (1996). Human resource roles: Creating value, not rhetoric. *Human Resource Planning, 19*, 38–49.

Conner, J., & Wirtenberg, J. (1993). Managing the transformation of human resources work. *Human Resource Planning, 16*, 17–34.

Delaney, J. T., & Huselid, M. A. (1996). The impact of human resource management practices on performance in for-profit and nonprofit organizations. *Academy of Management Journal, 39*, 949–969.

Dyer, L., & Reeves, T. (1995). HR strategies and firm performance: What do we know and where do we need to go. *International Journal of Human Resource Management, 6*, 656–670.

Eichinger, R., & Ulrich, D. (1995). Are you future agile? *Human Resource Planning, 18*, 30–41.

Eichinger, R., Ulrich, D., & The Human Resource Planning Society (1997). It's de-ja future all over again: Are you getting ready? *Human Resource Planning, 20*, 50–61.

Ellig, B. R. (1997). Is the human resource function neglecting the employees? *Human Resource Management, 36*, 91–95.

Forbringer, L. R., & Oeth, C. (1998). Human resources at Mercantile Bancorporation, Inc.: A critical analysis. *Human Resource Management, 37*, 177–189.

Galang, M. C. (1999). Stakeholders in high-performance work systems. *International Journal of Human Resource Management, 10*, 287–305.

Galang, M. C., Elsik, W., & Russ, G. S. (1999). Legitimacy in human resources management. In G. R. Ferris (Ed.), *Research in Personnel and*

Human Resources Management (Vol. 17). Greenwich, CT: JAI Press.

Galang, M. C., & Ferris, G. R. (1997). Human resource department power and influence through symbolic action. *Human Relations, 50,* 1403–1426.

Hannon, J. M., & Milkovich, G. T. (1996). The effect of human resource reputation signals on share prices: An event study. *Human Resource Management, 35,* 405–424.

Hathcock, B. C. (1996). The new-breed approach to 21st century human resources. *Human Resource Management, 35,* 243–250.

Huselid, M. A. (1995). The impact of human resource management practices on turnover, productivity, and corporate financial performance. *Academy of Management Journal, 38,* 635–672.

Huselid, M. A., & Becker, B. E. (1995). The strategic impact of high performance work systems. Paper presented at the Academy of Management annual meetings, Vancouver, BC.

Huselid, M. A., & Becker, B. E. (1996). Methodological issues in cross-sectional and panel estimates of the human resource-firm performance link. *Industrial Relations, 35,* 400–422.

Huselid, M. A., & Becker, B. E. (1997). The impact of high performance work systems, implementation effectiveness, and alignment with strategy on shareholder wealth. Available online at www.rci.rutgers.edu/~huselid [accessed August 3, 2000].

Huselid, M. A., Jackson, S. E., & Schuler, R. S. (1997). Technical and strategic human resource management effectiveness as determinants of firm performance. *Academy of Management Journal, 40,* 171–188.

Huselid, M. A., & Rau, B. L. (1997). The determinants of high performance work systems: Cross-sectional and longitudinal analyses. Available online at www.rci.rutgers.edu/~huselid/bibliogr.html [accessed August 3, 2000].

Kerr, S., & Von Glinow, M. A. (1997). The future of HR: Plus ca change, plus c'est la meme chose. *Human Resource Management, 36,* 115–119.

Kochan, T. A. (1997). Rebalancing the role of human resources. *Human Resource Management, 36,* 121–127.

Laabs, J. J. (1995, August). Shrinking pains cause HR to redevelop talents. *Personnel Journal,* 78–82.

Losey, M. R. (1997). The future HR professional: Competency buttressed by advocacy and ethics. *Human Resource Management, 36,* 147–150.

McMahan, G. C., Mohrman, S. A., & Lawler III, E. E. (1996). The current practice of the human resource function. *Human Resource Planning, 19,* 11–13.

Pfeffer, J. (1995a). *Competitive advantage through people.* Boston, MA: Harvard Business School Press.

Pfeffer, J. (1995b). Producing sustainable competitive advantage through the effective management of people. *Academy of Management Executive, 9,* 55–72.

Pfeffer, J. (1997). Pitfalls on the road to measurement: The dangerous liaison of human resources with the ideas of accounting and finance. *Human Resource Management, 36,* 357–365.

Pucik, V. (1997). Human resources in the future: An obstacle or a champion of globalization? *Human Resource Management, 36,* 163–167.

Rucci, A. J. (1997). Should HR survive? A profession at the crossroads. *Human Resource Management, 36,* 169–173.

Stewart, T. A. (1996, January 15). Taking on the last bureaucracy. *Fortune,* 105–108.

Ulrich, D. (1994). HR partnerships: From rhetoric to results. In J. M. Rosow & J. V. Hickey (Eds.), *Strategic Partners for High Performance (Part 1 — The Partnership Paradigm for Competitive Advantage)* (45–60). Work in America Institute.

Ulrich, D. (1997a). HR of the future: Conclusions and observations. *Human Resource Management, 36,* 175–179.

Ulrich, D. (1997b). Measuring human resources: An overview of practice and a prescription for results. *Human Resource Management, 36,* 303–320.

Ulrich, D. (1998). A new mandate for human resources. *Harvard Business Review, 76,* 124–134.

Ulrich, D., Brockbank, W., Yeung, A. K., & Lake, D. G. (1995). Human resource competencies: An empirical assessment. *Human Resource Management, 34,* 473–495.

Ulrich, D., & Eichinger, R. W. (1998, June). HR with an attitude. *HRMagazine,* 155–160.

Whitfield, L., & Poole, M. (1997). Organizing employment for high performance: Theories, evidence and policy. *Organization Studies, 18,* 745–764.

Wood, S. (1996). High commitment management and pay systems. *Journal of Management Studies, 33,* 53–77.

Wright, P. M., Dyer, L., & Takla, M. G. (1999). What's next? Key findings from the 1999 State-of-the-Art & Practice Study. *Human Resource Planning, 22,* 12–20.

Wright, P. M., McMahan, G. C., & McWilliams, A. (1994). Human resources and sustained competitive advantage: A resource-based perspective. *International Journal of Human Resource Management, 5,* 301–326.

Yeung, A., Brockbank, W., & Ulrich, D. (1994). Lower cost, higher value: Human resource function in transformation. *Human Resource Planning, 17,* 1–16.

Yeung, A., Woolcock, P., Sullivan, J., & The California Strategic Human Resource Partnership (1996). Identifying and developing HR competencies for the future: Keys to sustaining the transformation of HR functions. *Human Resource Planning, 19,* 48–58.

SELF-MANAGEMENT IN CONTEMPORARY WORK ORGANIZATIONS: IMPLICATIONS FOR PERFORMANCE AND PERFORMANCE MANAGEMENT

Robert W. Renn
Bethany Himel

Today's organizations compete in volatile environments. Companies and positions are unstable. Organizations are downsizing, restructuring, and merging to be competitive in a global marketplace. In the 1980s, American companies eliminated 500,000 managerial and professional jobs, with an emphasis on dismantling the hierarchy of mid-level managers that dominated U.S. companies (Tsui and Ashford, 1994). This forced companies to find better ways of increasing productivity without adding managers (Castaneda, 1999).

As a result, jobs are more complex than in the past and increasingly incorporate responsibilities once reserved for managers. In the old industrialized economy, employees needed only their hands to accomplish their tasks. In contemporary organizations, employees assume more responsibility and have more freedom to work on their own. Employees must be able to adjust to change, make rapid decisions, and exercise self-discipline. Self-management is a way for employees to meet these challenges successfully.

Self-management involves using principles of learning to manage our own behavior. That is, individuals can learn to achieve goals with little or no external control by observing their own behavior, setting personal goals and comparing their behavior with those goals, and reinforcing themselves when personal goals are achieved. Self-management provides organizations with the advantage of employees being less dependent on control systems and more dependent on their own control mechanisms. When employee behavior is regulated internally rather than externally, it can be more effectively maintained (Castaneda, Kolenko, & Aldag, 1999).

In this article, we elaborate on self-management in contemporary work organizations. We first differentiate sources of management, and then we explain the self-management process. Next, we briefly review how to structure training programs in self-management, with an emphasis on this type of training's impact on job performance. Following training and performance issues, we discuss motivating self-managed employees.

SOURCES OF MANAGEMENT

Broadly speaking, there are two sources of managing behavior in organizations: internal sources and external sources. External sources include all outside forces around employees, from the coworker in the next cubicle to the assembly line that dictates how many widgets must be produced in a shift. Other examples include managers, rules, policies and procedures, job descriptions, performance evaluations, technology, compensation systems, and disciplinary practices. Rules and laws limit choices, and even tell employees how to function in organizations. Managers give employees raises for valued results. The rewards provide employees with cues about the "right" things to do. Employees work to achieve positive rewards and to avoid punishment. If employees disobey company policies or management's orders, they can face unpleasant disciplinary actions. These external factors influence what employees do every day, and "can shape our ultimate destiny in life" (Manz & Neck, 1999, p. 9).

Behavior in organizations can also be managed by internal sources. Internal sources reside within us, the inner self. This source recognizes every employee as his or her own individual, with unique characteristics and ways of thinking. It is based on self-determination or the recognition that our thoughts, feelings, and behaviors determine who we are and what we accomplish. The self makes decisions, sets goals, and works to control the environment. From this perspective, employees are not simply weather vanes constantly changing direction from the winds of organizational forces. Charles Manz calls this "a process of influencing oneself" (Manz & Neck 1999, p. 5). Every employee has to figure out his or her own way of doing things in order to succeed and excel. Employees do not do everything the same way or get the same results because they have different strengths and weaknesses. The shift of internal sources of control rests on the assumptions that employees actually know how they can do things to the greatest potential, and that they have the knowledge and power over themselves to accomplish valued organizational goals.

THE SELF-MANAGEMENT PROCESS

Self-management is "managing your whole life at work by contributing to the critical path and ensuring high job performance" (Kelley, 1998, p. 57). It is a process that can be used by anyone, not just extraordinary people. It allows average or ordinary individuals to become extremely effective. If you are organized, highly motivated, hard working, able to set realistic goals and meet them on schedule, you can be an effective and productive person. Good self-managers organize their time well, evaluate what they do, and try to make the right choices. Self-management encompasses several interdependent processes, including self-assessment, goal-setting, self-monitoring and self-evaluation, written contracts, and maintenance and relapse prevention.

Self-Assessment

Self-assessment is the first step in creating a self-imposed strategy to shift the source of goal achievement and improvement from external to internal control. It requires deciding which behaviors need modification and determining when, why, and under what conditions we use certain behaviors (Manz & Neck, 1999). Self-assessment starts by figuring out how our time is spent on a daily basis. Recording behaviors over a one- or two-week period is helpful in this regard. This provides a snapshot of how we are wasting time, when we are doing the not-so important tasks such as making too many trips to the water cooler. We can also use self-observation by noting another person's response or reaction to a particular task or action as a way of determining how to interact with the person, such as a boss or manager. This allows us to learn what things reinforce the other person's positive responses (Karoly & Kanfer, 1982).

To assist in self-assessment of work behaviors, employees need information about how well they have performed their tasks. By knowing what leads to desirable and undesirable behaviors, an employee can discover what needs to be changed and acquire cues on how to do this. One way employees can get corrective information is by actively seeking feedback from coworkers and managers (Ashford, 1986). Coworkers and managers may know what is right or wrong, and can sometimes see things differently or provide us with another perspective. Employees can also get ideas on what they need to improve upon by watching other successful employees. A self-managed employee must be able to take input from feedback and observing others and view it as meaningful criticisms, rather than personal attacks.

Goal-Setting

Self-managed employees set long-term and short-term goals for modifying behaviors in need of improvement identified in the self-assessment stage. Employees must recognize and link their long-term pursuits and short-term objectives. "Knowing what we value in life and what we want to accomplish allows us to set the goals" (Manz & Neck, 1999, p. 24). Having goals gives employees a purpose to work hard and achieve what they think is important. In order to establish a purpose and long-term goals, employees should answer three questions: Who am I? What am I meant to do here (in this job)? What am I trying to do with my life (job)? According to Manz & Neck, "Having purpose is the catalyst for organizing life" (1999, p. 27). And long-term goals are important for "orienting oneself and providing continuity across one's efforts" (Baumeister, Heatherton, & Tice 1994, p. 62).

Short-term goals and plans are couched within monthly and yearly goals and plans. Weekly planning allows employees to see their short-term goals and ways to accomplish these goals. Short-term goals, as noted by Bandura and Schrunk in (1981), give us a sense of "self-efficacy" because we are "frequently approaching and reaching these goals." They allow us to avoid discouragement that comes from seeing how difficult or far away one is from achieving the ultimate, long-term goals (Baumeister, Heatherton, & Tice, 1994, p. 62). To be effective, these goals should be specific, focused, and moderately difficult but attainable. If they are unrealistic, short-term goals can undermine self-confidence and performance.

Employees should write their goals down on paper. This provides them with a record of the goals, which can then be used as reminders of personal work-related goals and as references for evaluating their goal progress. Documenting goals does not mean they can't be changed. In fact, these goals may need to change if situations change, such as organizational or departmental priorities.

In developing long- and short-term goals, employees should keep in mind that changing behavior is a time-consuming and complicated effort. Employees should not force themselves to change too many behaviors at a time. In this vein, employees need to create work-related improvement goals, but only a couple at the same time. They, in conjunction with management, must decide which behaviors are the most important to change at that time, and only try to change a subset of those behaviors first.

Self-Monitoring and Self-Evaluation

Self-monitoring includes observing one's own behavior and maintaining a record of goal progress. Self-observation provides the information needed for self-evaluations. This must be accomplished to be able to reinforce the "good" or alter the "bad" behaviors through self-evaluation and self-reinforcement. Self-evaluation is a self-reinforcement strategy based on performance. Here, employees analyze the information they gathered and personally assess the effectiveness of their work efforts against short- and long-term goals.

Self-reinforcement is a "key if not the major theoretical and procedural component of most conceptualizations of self-management" (Karoly & Kanfer, 1982, p. 35). Self-rewards must be in place when employees accomplish short and long-term goals to give them a reason to do it again next time. Employees can reward themselves physically and mentally. They can give themselves something they want, such as dinner at a nice restaurant, a piece of clothing or jewelry, or a vacation weekend. These rewards positively reinforce goal achievement and increase employees' motivation to achieve desired behaviors in the future. Skinner explains that "one of the ways individuals control their behavior is by the administration of rewards to themselves without environmental restrictions and contingent upon certain behavior" (Karoly & Kanfer, 1982, p. 35).

Similarly, employees may need to apply self-correction. This could be eliminating a night out with friends, delaying a purchase of clothing or jewelry, or not taking a vacation weekend. However do not confuse purposeful self-correction with excessive self-criticism. "Habitual guilt and self-criticism can impair our motivation and creativity" (Manz & Neck, 1999, p. 32). Use caution with self-correction because punishment is not always an effective strategy for controlling behavior and may create negative emotions. For instance, punishment may hamper employees' ability to enjoy work by creating a discouraging atmosphere.

Besides physical rewards, cognitive strategies may be used in self-reinforcement. This deals with patterns of thinking which, in turn, influence behavior. Because we control our thought processes, cognitive strategies of self-reinforcement are relatively inexpensive to create and employ, take relatively little time to implement, and do not depend on someone else to be enjoyed. In comparison with physical rewards, mental incentives are an efficient technique for creating good feelings about staying on our critical path.

These can be natural rewards, such as those "derived from the task itself to generate constructive thinking and feeling about one's own efforts" (Manz & Sims 1989, p. 27). Most work can be enjoyed to some degree by seeking out natural rewards of the task, such as feelings of accomplishment and challenge. Three elements help promote constructive and positive thoughts and feelings about work: a sense of competence, self-control, and purpose. Self-rewarding activities make employees feel competent, providing a feeling of self-efficacy. Employees tend to enjoy activities they do well. Naturally enjoyable activities also make employees feel more self-controlling. People want to control their own destinies; it gives them a feeling of independence. The third feature of naturally rewarding activities is the ability to provide a sense of purpose. People yearn for a purpose and meaning in life, and some work activities provide these more than others, depending upon what's important in their own value system.

There are two ways of using natural rewards to aid self-management. First, build more naturally enjoyable features into tasks. Employees must find what aspects of their jobs they find naturally enjoyable and try to increase these as much as possible. This may be accomplished by recognizing that work may be done in several ways, and then choosing enjoyable courses of action. Jobs could also be organized so that intrinsically rewarding tasks are performed after less appealing tasks. In this way, the naturally enjoyable parts of a job serve as positive reinforcement for those less appealing aspects of one's work. By doing so, employees can build in natural rewards for their efforts.

A second way of finding natural rewards is for employees to concentrate on the way they think while they perform tasks. An employee can focus on the rewards expected from the work and be motivated by the future. Just as people develop behavioral patterns that become habitual, they can also develop habitual patterns of thinking. For example, employees may imagine the raise that they will get if they do something in particular and, thus, will be more motivated to do that task correctly to get that raise. Employees do not necessarily need to think of only tangible material rewards. They may also consider the importance of their jobs and the impact their jobs have on the organization, coworkers, and customers. Realizing that their job really makes a difference can be highly rewarding and motivating for some employees, especially those less concerned with extrinsic rewards than with the intrinsic benefits of their work.

Some tools to learn positive thinking patterns are managing beliefs, imagined experience, and self-talk. What a person believes can, and frequently does, happen.

When employees have difficulty with a particular task or certain situations, this difficulty can often be traced to particular beliefs, such as fear of speaking in front of people. But when used appropriately, these beliefs can serve as a catalyst for change (Manz & Sims, 1989). Change emanates from not allowing such beliefs to dominate and control behavior by replacing them with positive ones, thus eliminating one's fears. For example, an employee may have a fear of speaking in public that is grounded in a belief that the audience thinks critical thoughts about him or her while he or she is speaking. The employee can be taught to overcome the fear of public speaking by replacing those self-defeating thoughts with pleasant ones, such as thinking coworkers really want him or her to do well and are interested in what he or she has to say. By replacing negative thoughts with positive ones, the employee conquers the fear of speaking in public and experiences the satisfaction of personal growth and development.

Imagination is a second component of thought patterns. Mental images of likely outcomes can influence actions and orientations toward work. Dysfunctional mental images can undermine employees' confidence and contribute to failure. But employees are capable of changing these images to constructive images, just as they can change their beliefs. For example, employees can imagine giving perfect presentations before they happen or the new car they can buy with a raise.

Self-talk is the third component to thought patterns. It works by consciously reprogramming our unconscious mind through carefully crafted phrases. Although employees may not be consciously aware of it, unconscious counterproductive mental programming may be interfering with their success. For example, we often criticize ourselves internally by talking to ourselves in bad connotations if we mess up. For example, "You dummy! You can't do anything right!" But we can also use self-talk to reprogram our minds to our benefit by talking in a positive manner and using it to figure out what needs to be changed. Use a more constructive approach, such as "What went wrong? I know I can do better than that" (Manz & Sims, 1989). Furthermore, you can use more direct self-talk, such as "I am a capable person!" Eventually, your attitudes and behavior will align themselves with your new beliefs.

Written Contracts

Written contracts are documented agreements with ourselves specifying expectations, plans, and contingencies for the behavior to be changed. These contracts provide guidelines on how to go about the change, when it must be accomplished, and what the reward will be for doing it. Putting these agreements down on paper will increase employees' commitment to change and accomplishing goals by specifying the reinforcing conditions for meeting the goal, maintaining desired behaviors, and limiting relapse (Frayne & Geringer, 2000, p. 361).

For example, an employee may want to enhance his or her job performance through continuous learning. He or she would write this expectation in a journal, along with short-term objectives and plans for achieving continuous learning, a timeline for achieving this expectation, any situational conditions that may facilitate or impede achieving continuous learning, and the rewards to be administered if the expectation is met. In the journal, the employee may state in writing that he or she will attend two work-related educational conferences in the coming year, sketch out plans for the conferences to attend and when, and detail how to organize his or her work and personal time to be able to attend the conferences. The written contract would also specify situational conditions that affect the employee's

ability to attend the conferences, such as gaining approval from a superior and acquiring funding for the trips. Finally, the employee would describe the prize for following through and achieving continuous learning and applying it to his or her job. By writing such contracts, the employee will intensify his or her commitment to continuous learning, have a record of this expectation, and think through and more clearly understand the "whats, whens, and hows" of achieving this expectation.

Maintenance and Relapse Prevention

Maintenance of the actions discussed so far comes from education, training, and support designed to overcome problems in applying self-management techniques. Difficulties in applying self-management often can be traced to poorly constructed short- and long-term goals (i.e., not specific, attainable, etc.), establishing too many conflicting goals, inappropriate strategies for achieving the goals, self-administered reinforcements, and willpower. Thus, managers may need to provide employees advice and training targeted at improving competencies in one or more of these stages. Patience on the part of the manager and employee is vitally important because some or all of the self-management actions may be new for employees and cannot be accomplished overnight.

Supporting the development and application of self-management is not a sole enterprise. These steps need positive reinforcement from internal and external sources. Continuous feedback from managers via assessments and evaluations can be invaluable for maintenance of self-management processes. But these need to be different than traditional evaluations of a non-self-managed employee. Changing a work behavior is difficult. There are impulses and temptations along the way that give short-term satisfaction, such as talking with coworkers, leaving work early, and sleeping a few extra minutes and being late to work. Employees need coaching and support from their managers and coworkers rather than directive supervision in overcoming weaknesses in applying self-management techniques. Such support could be directed toward pointing out to employees any self-defeating behaviors, such as obstacles the employee may unknowingly be creating to his or her own goal achievement or over persistence to failing courses of action. Letting others know of your goals can also serve a supportive function. Encouragement from others can boost one's willpower, which is a large part of the prevention stage.

SELF-MANAGEMENT TRAINING AND PERFORMANCE

In this section, we discuss issues associated with training employees in self-management. We begin by discussing the key ingredients of self-management training, including modeling, guided participation, and shifting responsibility for self-management from external sources to internal sources. After laying out these ingredients, we provide examples of self-management training to improve attendance and job performance.

Modeling is essential for effective self-management training. Employees learn by observation, and they can evaluate their own performance by the standards of the others. Thus trainers should be good self-managers. They will serve as role models for employees. A trainer must practice behavioral and cognitive self-management; doing this in a visible and recognizable way will serve as a model for others (Manz & Sims, 1989). Once they learn self-management, employees then become role models from which other employees learn.

Guided participation is another key part of teaching self-management. This involves using guided questions to evoke self-management skills among the employees. For guided behavior to be effective, trainers must be sensitive to their own verbal behavior. Good questions for each category of self-management include the following: Self-assessment: "Do you know how well you are doing right now? How about keeping a record of how many times that happens?" Goal-setting: "How many will you shoot for? When do you want to have it finished? What will your target be?" Self-monitoring and self-evaluation: "How do you think you did? Are you pleased with the way it went?" Rehearsal: "Why don't we try it out? Let's practice that." (Manz & Sims, 1980, p. 365). The aim here is to give employees practice in the self-management behaviors by giving them guidance while learning.

Trainers also need to gradually shift responsibility for self-management from an external source to the employee. This includes the evaluative and reinforcement functions. In the beginning of training, trainers should reinforce self-management behaviors. But as training progresses, trainers should encourage employees to administer their own rewards for learning. In other words, as time goes by, reinforcement shifts from performance-related behaviors associated with the task to the process of self-management itself. From a manager's perspective, this means slowly relinquishing control over to employees who are learning self-management. The benefits for managers will come in the long run, because overall effectiveness of employees will be improved due to their increased abilities to regulate their own work-related activities. Managers will enjoy many benefits from these employees, such as more time spent working, more committed employees, an increase in innovative ideas, and a strength for progress that flows from working with more fully developed employees (Manz & Sims, 1989).

As employees become more capable of self-management, managers should use different patterns of reinforcement. Usually, managers reinforce specific performance-based behaviors, such as number of products sold. As the employee gains self-management behaviors, this will no longer be the best reward style. Instead, reinforcement needs to shift to the accomplishment of self-management itself. For example, managers can reward proper goal-setting and/or honest self-assessment.

Frayne and Latham (1987) developed and reported a self-management training program for attendance that included many of the above ingredients. The training encompassed the following components. For eight weeks, Frayne and Latham met with employees once a week in groups for one hour, followed by 30-minute one-on-one sessions. The sessions were structured around the steps of self-management discussed above. In the first week, the researchers simply explained the principles of self-management. For the second week, they concentrated on and taught self-assessment that, in this case, focused on attendance. The employees were asked to give reasons for using sick leave, and the reasons were written on the board and placed into categories. Sick leave was the focus because it accounted for almost 50 percent of the absenteeism for the company (Frayne & Geringer, 1994, p. 388). Here, employees were taught to develop a description of the problem behaviors, to identify the conditions that created and maintained the problem behaviors, and to identify coping techniques.

In week three, Frayne and Latham concentrated on goal-setting. They discussed the difference in distal and proximal goals and assisted employees in creating each type of goal. The distal goal was to increase attendance in a specified time period, and the proximal goals were the actual behaviors that the employees had to engage in to achieve the distal goal.

Self-monitoring was the central point of week four. The trainees were taught to record several things, such as their own at-

tendance and their reasons for missing work, and the steps that were taken to actually get to work. They recorded this information in charts and diaries. The researchers stressed the importance of daily feedback for motivational purposes, as well as the importance of accurate recording.

Self-evaluation and self-reinforcement were covered in week five. They identified reinforcements and punishments that could be self-administered due to accomplishing or failing to achieve proximal goals. The training emphasized that positive reinforcements needed to be powerful, but at the same time easy to do. The same was true with self-correction. It had to be easy to administer, but employees had to dislike the activity. Each employee created his or her own consequences and rewards that best fit them personally.

A review occurred in week six, and the trainees were asked to write a contract for themselves. Each wrote their goals, the time frame to accomplish them, the consequences, and the behaviors needed to accomplish the goals. Lastly, training in week seven concentrated on maintenance. They focused on how to avoid relapses, and planned for situations in which they might have missed work. They also discussed and developed strategies for dealing with particular troublesome situations. In the end, the employees who received self-management training attained significantly higher attendance than a control group who did not receive the training.

Studies also indicate that self-management can improve job performance. In a recent study, Frayne and Geringer (2000) demonstrated that self-management training produced significant increases in self-efficacy and beliefs about short- and long-term consequences of behavior. Moreover, the training improved both objective and subjective indicators of sales job performance, and sales performance continued to improve for a 12-month period after the training. Another study by Gist, Bavetta, and Stevens (1990) found that self-management trainees exhibited higher rates of skill generalization and higher overall performance levels on transferring training to a novel task than did trainees with only goal-setting training. Gist, Stevens, and Bavetta (1991) examined the effects of self-management to self-efficacy, a strong predictor of performance. They found that self-management training contributed to low and moderate self-efficacy trainees earning salaries comparable to those of high self-efficacy employees.

MOTIVATING SELF-MANAGED EMPLOYEES

To maximize the performance of employees trained in self-management, managers should pay close attention to reinforcement and work assignments. Self-management strategies and behaviors require reinforcement to be maintained. Although immediate external constraints or support may not be required, long-term reinforcement is necessary (Manz, 1986). In addition, the nature of a task can enhance or depress the positive effects of self-management of performance.

Manz and Neck (1999) suggest that those who oversee self-managed employees need to do three things: (1) Set a good example. Managers of these employees must have self-management skills, and must display them for employees to see. (2) Provide continual guidance by encouraging and instructing the employees in self-management skills. This can be as simple as asking the workers if they have set personal goals, and, if not, to work on them with the person. (3) Use reinforcement to stress the importance of tasks. Self-management must be encouraged and maintained by long-term consequences. For example, a runner trains

long hours and runs many miles through self-control. An employee may develop his or her self-management techniques to increase his or her performance. But there is reasoning behind all this. The runner wants to win a gold medal, and the employee is working for extrinsic (e.g., a raise) and intrinsic rewards (e.g., recognition). In the absence of these long-term reinforcements, self-managing behaviors will fade.

To reinforce self-management, managers can make suggestions for better ways of doing things and provide performance feedback. Some employees may find it difficult to deal with negative feedback because it reveals weaknesses. However, doing so is vital for performance improvement, thus managers need to encourage and reinforce accepting and learning from negative feedback by creating norms favoring such behaviors. Managers can also encourage employees to seek feedback from coworkers as well as managers. By paying attention to what is happening around them and asking coworkers for their assessments of work, self-managed employees can acquire additional performance feedback that can be used to set improvement goals that, in turn, contribute to higher performance (Renn & Fedor, in press).

The nature of the task or type of job also plays a role in the performance of self-managed employees. For instance, self-managed employees may perform time-sensitive jobs better than others. In these jobs, employees often don't have time to get help from mangers before they take action, and self-managed employees will be trained and prepared to make independent decisions and to execute appropriate actions. Similarly, jobs where mediocrity is tolerated may not be suited for self-managed employees (Tsui & Ashford, 1994). Organizations differ in the extent to which they test individual limits. Companies who test these limits are stressing a fight for survival, and will set up favorable conditions for self-managed employees. When employees have the opportunity to shirk without consequences, human nature allows them to take the easy way out, doing as little as possible without being caught or criticized. But if these employees had good role models, their managers showed that they were self-managers themselves and cared about their employers, this negative reaction would decrease and would better suit a self-managed employee.

CONCLUSION

Decreased levels of supervision, people working from the home (e.g., telecommuters), rising numbers of self-managed work teams, the increase in challenging jobs, and the growth in service and professional employment all create great opportunities and need for self-management. With this backdrop, managers must understand that self-management is a complex skill that requires training, reinforcement, and the right task. It also takes time, willpower, and coworker support. By following the recommendations provided by this article, managers should be well prepared to enhance the performance of self-managed employees. ■

REFERENCES

Ashford, S. J. (1986). Feedback seeking in individual adaptation: A resource perspective. *Academy of Management Journal, 29,* 465–487.

Bandura, A., & Shrunk, D. H. (1981). Cultivating competence, self-efficacy, and intrinsic interest through proximal self-motivation. *Journal of Personality and Social Psychology, 41,* 586–598.

Baumeister, R., Heatherton, T. & Tice, D. (1994). *Losing control: How and why people fail at self-regulation.* San Diego: Academic Press.

Castaneda, M., Kolenko, T. & Aldag, R. (1999). Self-management perceptions and practices: A structural equations analysis. *Journal of Organizational Behavior, 20,* 101–120.

Frayne, C., & Geringer, M. (2000). Self-management training for improving job performance: A field experiment involving salespeople. *Journal of Applied Psychology, 85,* 361–372.

Frayne, C. A., & Geringer, J. M. (1994). A social cognitive approach to examining joint venture general managers. *Group and Organization Management, 19,* 240–262.

Frayne, C., & Latham, G. (1987). Application of social learning to employ self-management of attendance. *Journal of Applied Psychology, 72,* 387–392.

Gist, M. E., Bavetta, A. G., & Stevens, C. K. (1990). Transfer training method: Its influence on skill generalization, skill repetition, and performance level. *Personnel Psychology, 43,* 501–523.

Gist, M. E., Stevens, C. K., & Bavetta, A. G. (1991). Effects of self-efficacy and post training intervention on the acquisition and maintenance of complex interpersonal skills. *Personnel Psychology, 44,* 837–861.

Karoly, P. & Kanfer, F. (Eds). (1982). *Self-management and behavior change: From theory to practice.* New York: Pergamon Press.

Kelley, R. E. (1998, May). How to manage your work life (and become a star). *Training and Development.* 57–60.

Manz, C. (1986). Self-leadership: Toward an expanded theory of self-influence processes in organizations. *Academy of Management Review, 11,* 585–600.

Manz, C., & Neck, C. (1999). *Mastering self-leadership: Empowering yourself for personal excellence,* 2nd Ed. Upper Saddle River, NJ: Prentice Hall.

Manz, C., & Sims, H. Jr. (1980). Self-management as a substitute for leadership: A social learning theory perspective. *Academy of Management Review, 5*, 361–367.

Manz, C., & Sims, H. Jr. (1989). *Super leadership: Leading others to lead themselves.* New York: Prentice Hall Press.

Renn, R. W., & Fedor, D. B. (In press). Development and field test of a feedback seeking, self-

efficacy, and goal-setting model of work performance. *Journal of Management.*

Tsui, A. & Ashford, S. (1994). Adaptive self-regulation: A process view of managerial effectiveness. *Journal of Management, 30*, 1.

HUMAN RESOURCES MANAGEMENT IN THE SERVICE SECTOR

John D. Keiser

The field of human resources management (HRM) continues to evolve, espousing new practices and theories to improve the management of organizational members. Historically, much of the field evolved in the manufacturing sector. After all, industrial engineers championed scientific management to increase manufacturing efficiency during the second industrial revolution, and the human relations school had its origins at Western Electric's Hawthorne telephone assembly plant. While the field has evolved, it has done so largely under the assumption that organizations are similar, and the managerial practices developed within the manufacturing sector are equally relevant to the service sectors. This is an unfortunate oversight for two reasons. First, because of a higher reliance on labor in the service industries, not to mention high employee and customer interaction, theories and practices developed with anonymous factory workers in mind fail to adequately address the special concerns of service industry workers. Secondly, the volume of HRM literature based on industry-sector assumptions far surpasses

service-sector HRM despite significant decreases in the industrial sector and enormous increases in the service sector (McNamee, 1998). Considering the size of the service sector and the distinctions separating it from the manufacturing sector, there has been only a limited focus on service industry–specific HRM (Lovelock, 1995).

The purpose of this article is to combine some of the existing themes of service quality and service HRM to present some special considerations for managing service organizations' human capital. The article is divided into seven sections. It begins with a presentation of some U.S. Census data documenting the scope of the services sectors and their reliance on labor. Next, it defines and explains concepts pertaining to "service value," which is necessary for understanding how the service sector is unique from other industries, and how the personal touch of service affects customers' perceptions of quality and satisfaction. The third section addresses the performance implications of establishing relationships with repeat customers. Next is a discussion of the role of frontline employees, and their importance to the service interaction. Then, the article focuses on the customer's role in service transaction, and how customers perform some of the labor for the organization. Assuming good service and high customer satisfaction, there is a reciprocated relationship known as the "Satisfaction Mirror," identified in the sixth section. Lastly is a discussion on the obstacles to high quality human resources management in the service sector.

SCOPE OF THE SERVICE SECTOR

The enormous growth and size of the service sector makes identifying its parameters difficult, but the Standard Industrial Classification Code offers some insight. Classification codes beginning with digits 7 and 8 constitute the services sector, identified by,

> establishments primarily engaged in providing a wide variety of services for individuals, business and government establishments, and other organizations. Hotels and other lodging places; establishments providing personal, business, repair, and amusement services; health, legal, engineering, and other professional services; educational institutions; membership organizations, and other miscellaneous services, are included. (U.S. Census, 2001)

However, the service industries category fails to include other services that have their own 2-digit categorization, such as transportation, communication, and utilities (SIC 41–49), wholesale trade (SIC 50–52), retail trade (SIC 52–59), and financial services (SIC 60–67). Based on census data, the service industries sector (SIC 7–8) alone outpaced all other sectors between 1992 and 1997 in the areas of new establishments and hiring. At $2.4 trillion dollars, the service industries constitute nearly 14 percent of GDP. However when combined with the other service sectors of transportation, com-

munication, utilities, wholesale, retail, and financial services, cumulatively, the service industries made up 72 percent of the GDP in 1997. Cumulatively, the service industries employed over 74 million paid workers, or approximately 75 percent, of the paid labor force that same year.

One reason why human resources management is so vital to service organizations is the high labor intensity of services. Again using census data, compared to all other major SIC categories, service industries have the highest labor costs in relation to sales. Payroll in the service industries accounts for over 37 percent of the total receipts, significantly more than mining with 12 percent, construction with 20 percent, or manufacturing with 15 percent. Despite the growth of the service sector, wages and salaries continue to lag behind other industries. Employees in the different service sectors earned an average of just over $26,000 in 1997, well behind employees in mining ($40,833), construction ($30,710), and manufacturing ($33,929) (U.S. Census, 2001).

From this data, one can arrive at several assumptions. First, the service sector is enormous, surpassing the manufacturing sector in terms of revenue and employment. Second, service industries rely more heavily on their employees as evidenced by the ratio of labor to sales. Third, earnings in the service sector are less than other sectors.

SERVICE VALUE

Services differ from other types of businesses for several reasons, the most obvious of which is that the customer receives little in terms of tangible product. Dry cleaners offer the service of cleaning laundry, but they do not provide the laundry itself. Another reason why service is different from the other industries is the level of personal interaction between the customer and the provider. Frontline service workers are the point of interface between the customer and the provider. Not only does this require the technical skills of the service, it also requires customer service skills. Emotional labor (Hochschild, 1979; Ashforth & Humphrey, 1993) or display rules (Rafaeli & Sutton, 1989) are the emotional signals frontline providers expend to psychologically accommodate customers and deliver compatible customer service.

Distinguishing the service and products industries is how customers value their purchases. When purchasing a product, customers simply consider the quality of the product in relation to its costs and cost of attainment. Services, on the other hand, are more complex. Customers must consider the quality of the results, or the actual service performed in relation to the access costs, but they must also consider the quality of the process, or the experience of obtaining the service (Kotler, 1967; Caveness & Manoochehri, 1993; Heskett, Jones, Loveman, Sasser, & Schlesinger, 1994; Heskett, Sasser, & Schlessinger, 1997). The quality of the process of the service is dependent on many things, including, but not limited to, the attractiveness of the surroundings and the convenience of the provider, but perhaps most important is the quality of the interaction between the customer and the service provider.

Another reason why the service sector deserves distinction from the industrial or manufacturing sector is because its intangibility (Sabolo, 1975) makes consumption simultaneous to the time of production (Sasser, 1976). Using a haircut as an example, the customer receives their haircut while the stylist cuts their hair. Producing uniform product for extended periods is not possible for service organizations, so their service has a greater uniqueness for each customer, thus making service outputs more unpredictable and multidimensional. This multidimensionality decreases the likelihood for tightly programmed or repetitive behaviors, increasing the possibility for in-consistencies and mistakes (Adam, Hershauer, & Ruch, 1981).

Maintaining service quality and consistency is especially difficult, particularly when one considers the high labor component of service provision. This suggests service providers require a different set of skills of their employees to accommodate the fluctuating demands of customers. As in other industries, quality movements such as total quality management or TQM have entered the lexicon of service, with service firms increasingly adopting the criteria for the Malcom Baldrige National Quality Award (Blodgett, 1999).

Although Baldrige Award levels of service are obtainable by only a few firms, there is a common set of attributes that distinguish "breakthrough" providers (Heskett, Sasser, & Hart, 1990) from the vast majority. Writers suggest that much of this distinction is determined not by operational procedures or policies but by employing individuals who have a "passion" (Schneider & Bowen, 1993) for providing superior service. This is consistent with advocates of the human capital school of thought who identify workers as the source of competitive advantage (Pfeffer, 1994) for sustained long-term success.

Managing for competence is challenging, but managing for levels of passion requires something more. In a study of highly successful service firms, Leonard Berry identifies "values-driven leadership" as the core component of reaching uncommonly high levels of service and success (Berry, 1999). Without shared values, he suggests, managers, workers, and even customers will not be as intrinsically motivated—or have the passion—to outperform competing providers.

Schneider and Bowen (1993) suggest that in order to achieve passionate levels of service quality, organizational cultures must go beyond a single-minded focus on quality. In addition, these firms must have a corporate culture directed to employee well-being. Without a culture of support for the workers' best interests, employees, especially frontline employees, will not be dedicated to exert the physical behaviors or emotional labor necessary for superior service.

ORGANIZATION PERFORMANCE AND REPEAT CUSTOMERS

Assuming customers receive positive value from the results and process of the interaction in relation to the cost of the service and the cost of obtaining said service (i.e., compared to other organizations offering similar services), it is logical to predict they will return for subsequent transactions. Repeat customers are the key to organization performance because they are more profitable than first-time customers (Heskett, Sasser, Schlesinger, 1997). First-time customers are expensive. It takes marketing and advertising to get them to visit for the first time, and their newness to the establishment makes them more difficult to serve. New customers need to learn the products and services of the establishment, which often requires time-consuming counseling by the salesperson or service representative. Anyone who has waited in line behind a first-time customer at a sophisticated coffee shop has experienced the time it takes for the counter help to explain the difference between a capuccino, espresso, latte, or au lait. A server can spend a considerable amount of time tutoring the new customer on the intricacies of ordering a relatively inexpensive beverage. As customers return, their knowledge of the process increases, and the time and effort it takes to serve them diminishes.

Repeat customers are not only easier to serve and are more profitable, they also willingly perform some of the work, such as advertising through word-of-mouth referrals and quality control by offering feedback.

This makes customer satisfaction particularly important (McCune, 1989), a concept we discuss in greater detail later in the article.

FRONTLINE EMPLOYEES

Interactions between the customer and the service organization typically occur with frontline employees; that is, the individuals who represent the company and determine the quality of the process experienced by the customer. In restaurants, these are typically servers; in retail stores, they're floor salespeople; and for airlines, they're the ticket agents and flight attendants. Collectively, these titles fall under the category of "customer service," occupations in which the main obligation is to see that customer needs are being met. In these and other service industries, these frontline positions are entry level with little, if any, supervisory authority. Ironically, these employees with the highest levels of interaction are, by nature of their organizational status, the employees with the least amount of experience, seniority, or discretion. Similarly, they are often among the lowest paid employees in the organization, and like many lower-wage jobs, experience higher levels of absenteeism and turnover.

Performing the operational tasks is just one component of a frontline worker's job. In order to be satisfied, customers have to perceive competence in the skills of the service provider (Mills, Chase, & Margulies, 1983). In other words, customers want to be confident they will receive the desired results of their service request. Yet operations and results are only part of the service transaction. There is also the process of the service encounter, which includes the interpersonal or customer service side of working. Emotional labor (Ashforth & Humphry, 1993) describes the mental work necessary to adequately handle the interpersonal transactions with customers. Considering the personality range of customers and the unpleasantness associated with difficult customers, emotional labor cannot be taken lightly. Customers also consider the provider's personality as part of the process, (Lin, Chiu, & Hsieh, 2001), so workers have to convey personalities that customers find attractive. Not only does this require a chameleon-like ability to adopt appropriate personalities, it also requires a keen sense of evaluating customers to determine which personality is appropriate. Because so much of the successful service depends on the process of the transaction, training frontline employees in customer service skills can be as paramount as training them in operational skills (Wehrenberg, 1987).

Due to their operational and customer-service skills, frontline employees most influence the process or experience of the service encounter, making them integral in the customers' determination of value. That these people are often the most entry-level in the organization begs the question, "How prepared are these people to serve the customers?"

Not every service company treats its frontline employees as low-end workers. Nordstrom, the department store chain out of Seattle, has a reputation for treating its salespeople superbly, preparing them with intensive training and rewarding them with a generous commission-based compensation plan. In return, the salespeople are legendary for their willingness to provide superb service, and customers are similarly loyal to the company (Pfeffer, 1994).

Generous compensation and competent training is not necessarily a panacea for outstanding service. Outstanding companies offer their frontline employees latitude, or discretion, to make autonomous decisions necessary to provide high levels of service (Rafiq & Ahmed, 1998). Often referred to as "empowerment," employee discretion and authority suggest employees can perform duties that are usually managerial in nature. Empowerment for frontline employees enhances customers' service encounters by giving employees more discretion in providing to special needs. In the event of service errors, empowerment allows frontline employees to correct mistakes, without requiring management approval.

Yet empowerment is more complicated than simply giving workers the green light to make decisions. Bowen and Lawler (1995) define empowerment as the product of power, information, knowledge, and rewards. In other words, they suggest empowered employees must be able to exercise their extra latitude in a manner benefiting both the customer and the organization. This requires awareness based on information and knowledge, and reinforcement based on rewards.

Certainly, the appropriate level of employee empowerment is dependent on other variables such as service difficulty and customer complexity. This explains why employees in fast food restaurants have seemingly little discretion. Their jobs have been reduced to a few simple tasks, and customer requests are based on pre-set menus rather than individual tastes.

Schlesinger and Heskett (1991) promote enfranchisement, a hybrid of empowerment and incentive pay, to encourage superior levels of service. This increases employee motivation markedly. Using a combination of intrinsic and extrinsic motivators, workers find the greater challenges more satisfying with the opportunity for higher income.

Empowerment makes sense, not only for employee satisfaction, but for customer satisfaction as well. When employees have little latitude to make decisions, they must forward questions or decisions to managers, forcing customers to wait. BancOne allows its branches more discretion than most other banks. Branches approve loan requests, which is more expedient than awaiting approval from headquarters (Heskett, Sasser, & Hart, 1990).

THE CUSTOMER'S ROLE

Because repeat patronage is the key to service for service organizations, it is imperative that service providers focus on maintaining relationships between themselves and their customers. Like any relationship, both sides have their roles in order to maintain a mutually satisfying relationship. As mentioned previously, satisfied customers perform some of the work of the organization, in the form of marketing, quality control, and simply aligning their own interests with that of the organization. Therefore, the more involved the customer, the greater the likelihood of higher service quality leading to a richer customer-organization relationship.

Retail food services have an especially long history of relying on customers to provide labor for the organization. When customers leave tips for servers they are, in essence, performing the dual role of performance evaluator and payroll administrator.

Conceptually, including the customer as part of the organization's labor force is not new. Writers as early as Barnard (1948) and Parsons (1956) have argued for customers to be included within organizational boundaries.

CUSTOMER-PROVIDER RECIPROCITY

When good service encourages repeat patronage, there's an escalating dynamic between the organization and its customers. Several writers (Schneider & Bowen, 1985; Heskett, Sasser, & Schlessinger, 1997) refer to this as the satisfaction mirror. Frontline employees are more familiar with the needs of repeat customers, resulting in superior service. Repeat customers become more comfortable with the organization and can

complain about problems when errors occur, or they can offer feedback to improve the quality of the service. In turn, employees can more effectively correct errors and improve service. Fewer errors reduce costs and increase value, while employees experience higher productivity. Customers receive better results and greater value, equating to greater satisfaction, and employees derive satisfaction from offering improved levels of service quality.

When working, the "mirror" cultivates a relationship between customers and frontline employees. The increased satisfaction of customers promotes repeat transactions, and the increased satisfaction of employees encourages workers to stay longer, reducing turnover. With a more experienced and skilled workforce, service organizations can provide better service, and the personal familiarity that occurs between repeat customers and frontline workers makes the service transaction more pleasant for both parties.

While the satisfaction "mirror" may sound like some sort of karmic exchange between customers and frontline employees, there is empirical evidence to support it. Companies as diverse as Chick-Fil-A restaurants, the Western European Money Center Bank, and Xerox document significant correlations between customer and employee satisfaction (Heskett, Sasser, & Schlessinger, 1997, p. 100). In addition, they document relationships between customer satisfaction and organization growth and profit in organizations such as Waste Management, Taco Bell, Swedbank, AT&T Travel, and Merry Maids (p. 31).

With documented relationships between customer satisfaction and employee satisfaction, it makes sense that service organizations would treat employees progressively, in ways to attract and retain the highly mobile service sector labor. Schneider and Bowen (1993) identify a relationship between customer attitudes on service and employee attitudes regarding human resources practices. When organization-customer relationships are the key to organizational performance, they argue that relationship management is paramount, and the frontline employees are the ones who manage the customer-organization relationships.

OBSTACLES TO GOOD HUMAN RESOURCES MANAGEMENT

Considering how labor intensive the service industries are, and how vital interpersonal transactions are in achieving customer satisfaction, it would seem the service industries would represent the state-of-the-art of human resources management. Yet that doesn't seem to be the case. Organizations such as those in the hospitality industries complain of the difficulty of finding and keeping good labor. Certainly low wages would explain part of the problem. Especially for workers with higher levels of education and skills, there's very little reason for them to go into the services industry when they can earn more in other sectors ("Where the jobs are," 1994).

High turnover is difficult for any industry, but it's especially a problem for the service organizations that try to establish relationships with the customers to develop repeat patronage. Heskett, Sasser, and Schlesinger (1997) identify the cycle of failure as the chain of events that occurs with low-skilled, low-wage jobs. These individuals get little support or training, and the organization suffers high rates of absenteeism and turnover. Chronically short-staffed operations cannot provide adequate levels of service, resulting in dissatisfied customers who prefer not to return. Not only is service quality compromised, high turnover among the frontline personnel discourages face-to-face familiarity of highly satisfying service encounters. Nor can the organization expect to learn customers' tastes when there is a revolving door of frontline workers.

There's another unanticipated consequence of high turnover. High turnover at the supervisory level increases the opportunity for promotion of lower-level workers or frontline workers. Although it's good for the promoted employees, the organization loses its most senior or capable customer service staff to promotions. Moreover, when the organization rewards their best workers with promotions away from the customers, it gives the signal that frontline customer service work is undesirable.

Promoting people away from the customers also systematically weakens the organizations' abilities to serve. Customer complaints first go to frontline service personnel. When the frontline employees are unable to handle the problems, which occurs in 25 percent of all errors, only a small handful (i.e., just 5 percent of dissatisfied customers) report their dissatisfaction to middle management. Of these, about 20 percent are still unsatisfied, and about half of them will complain to a higher level in the organization. (U.S. Office of Consumer Affairs, 1986). This complaint escalation pyramid nicely illustrates how little senior management hears of service errors through customer complaints. Less then 1 percent of customer complaints will go beyond middle management. That these people are typically the decision makers for the organization, it is remarkable how uninformed they are compared to their entry-level or frontline workers.

CONCLUSION

As the economy increasingly relies on the service sector to compensate for the shrinking manufacturing sector, it has become increasingly apparent that human resources theories and practices developed in the postwar, manufacturing economy do not transfer to all workplaces. The nature of service provision with its higher reliance on labor (especially frontline workers) and multiple skill sets required to provide adequate results and process during the service encounter suggests service sector HRM requires a higher complexity or sophistication. Unfortunately, this doesn't appear to be the case, as the service sector has earned its reputation for relying on low-skilled, low-wage workers.

This defies logic. When the demand for service labor increases in a labor market that's demographically shrinking, it would make more sense for employers to raise wages, and then manage workers to keep them productive and content to stay. Not only would this ensure a productive and committed workforce, it would provide the stability to establish long-term relationships with repeat customers, the key to profitability in the service industries. Unfortunately, to many organizations this doesn't make as much sense as cutting costs, and some organizations have shown a greater genius for finding low-wage workers than keeping highly skilled workers.

Organizations such as General Electric and British Airways have set up call centers for customer service personnel in places like Bangalore, India, where representatives answer phone inquiries from customers several thousand miles away (Landler, 2001). It's hard to imagine these individuals who have very little in common with their customers will be able to provide the kind of process-appealing service to encourage loyal patronage.

There are other aspects of service sector human resources management that defy conventional wisdom. It is difficult to imagine customers as employees, but due to the nature of the service industries, customers are the best-qualified individuals to offer quality control feedback or word-of-mouth marketing. Like key employees in any other industry, service organizations need to realize their value and keep them at all costs.

Similarly, key frontline employees are especially vital. When they have established relationships with valuable repeat customers, the organization risks losing loyal customers with the loss of every good frontline employee. Customers associate their transactions with individuals, not necessarily companies, so their loyalty can be directed to the individual provider, not the organization.

This is why successful service organizations manage their people differently than most organizations in other industries. They select people who have a passion for service; train them in operations to offer results, as well as in customer service to enhance the process; and empower them so that they can better serve their customers. These organizations also realize that their success is based on long-standing customer relationships, not necessarily with the organization, but with the frontline people who serve them. These workers are the companies' competitive advantage, and good companies recognize their value.

Beyond these distinguishing characteristics, managing people in the service industries is no different than in any other sector. The fundamentals of human resources management still hold true. Companies will need to find, retain, develop and motivate talented individuals to perform the work of the organization. That service organizations rely on their human capital more than other organizations, makes the management of these people even more vital. ∎

REFERENCES

Adam, E., Hershauer, J., & Ruch, W. (1981). Developing quality productivity ratios for public sector personnel services. *Public Productivity Review, 5,* 45–61.

Ashforth, B. E., and Humphrey R. H. (1993). Emotional labor in service roles: The influence of identity. *Academy of Management Review, 18* (1), 89–115.

Barnard, C. (1948). *Organizations and management.* Cambridge, MA: Harvard University Press.

Berry, L. (1999). *Discovering the soul of service: The nine drivers of sustainable business success.* New York: The Free Press.

Blodgett, N. (1999). Service organizations increasingly adopt Baldrige model. *Quality Progress, 32* (12) 74–76.

Bowen, D. E., & Lawler, E. E. (1995). Empowering service employees. *Sloan Management Review, 36* (4), 73, 84.

Caveness, J. P., & Manoochehri, G. H. (1993). Building quality into services. *SAM Advanced Management Journal, 58* (1), 4–9.

Heskett, J. L., Jones, J. O., Loveman, G. W., Sasser, Jr. W. E., & Schlesinger, L. A. (1994, March–April). Putting the service-profit chain to work. *Harvard Business Review,* 164–174.

Heskett, J. L., Sasser, Jr. W. E., & Hart, C. W. L. (1990). *Service breakthroughs: Changing the rules of the game.* New York: Free Press.

Heskett, J. L., Sasser, Jr., W. E., & Schlesinger, L. A. (1997). *The service profit chain.* New York: Free Press.

Hochschild, A. R. (1979). Emotion work, feeling rules, and social structure. *American Journal of Sociology, 85,* 551–575.

Kotler, P. (1967). *Marketing management, analysis, planning and control.* Upper Saddle River, NJ: Prentice Hall.

Landler, M. (2001). Hi, I'm in Bangalore (but I dare not tell). In *New York Times.* Available online at www.nytimes.com/2001/03/21/technology/21CALL.html.

Lin, N., Chiu, C., & Hsieh, Y. (2001). Investigating the relationship betweeen service providers' personality and customers' perceptions of service quality across gender. *Total Quality Management, 12* (1), 57.

Lovelock, C. H. (1995). Managing services: The human factor. In W. J. Glynn and J. G. Barnes (Eds.), *Understanding Services Management* (203–243). New York: John Wiley & Sons.

McCune, J. T. (1989) Customer satisfaction as a strategic weapon: The implications of performance management. *Human Resources Planning, 12* (3), 195–204.

McNamee, M. (1998, December 21). A tale of two job markets. *Business Week,* 38.

Mills, P. K., Chase, R. B., & Margulies, N. (1983). Motivating the client/employee system as a service production strategy. *Academy of Management Review, 8* (2), 301–310.

Parsons, T. (1956). Suggestions for a sociological approach to the theory of organizations. *Administrative Science Quarterly, 1,* 63–85.

Pfeffer, J. (1994). *Competitive advantage through people.* Boston: Harvard Business School Press.

Rafaeli, A., & Sutton, R. I. (1989). The expression of emotion in organizational life. In L. L. Cummings and B. M. Staw (Eds.), *Research in Organizational Behavior* (Vol. 11, 1–42). Greenwich, CT: JAI Press.

Rafiq, M., & Ahmed, P. K. (1998). A customer-oriented framework for empowering service employees. *The Journal of Services Marketing, 12,* (4/5), 379–396.

Sabolo, Y. (1975). *The service industries.* Geneva: International Labor Offices.

Sasser, E. (1976). Match supply and demand in service industries. *Harvard Business Review, 56* (2), 133–148.

Schlessinger, L. A., & Heskett, J. L. (1991). Enfranchisement of service workers. *California Management Review, 33* (4), 83–200.

Schneider, B., & Bowen D. E. (1985). New services design, development and implementation and the employee. In W. R. George and C. Marshall (Eds.), *New Services* (82–101). Chicago: The American Marketing Association.

Schneider, B., & Bowen, D. E. (1993). The service organization: Human resources management is crucial. *Organizational Dynamics, 21* (4), 39–53.

U.S. Census (2001). 1997 Economic census: Comparative statistics for United States (1987 SIC basis). Available online at www.census.gov/epcd/ec97sic/def/I.TXT.

U.S. Census (2001). 1997 Economic census: Comparative statistics for United States (1987 SIC basis). Available online at www.census.gov/epcd/ec97sic/E97SUSI.HTM.

U.S. Office of Consumer Affairs. (1986). Consumer complaint handling in America: An update study, part II. Washington DC: Technical Assistance Research Programs Institute.

Wehrenberg, S. B. (1987). Frontline interpersonal skills a must in today's service economy. *Personnel Journal, 66* (1) 115–118.

Where the jobs are: College graduates and job prospects. (1994, January/February). *Change, 26* (1), 33–37.

WALKING THE TALK: HUMAN RESOURCES AND CORPORATE REPUTATION

Suzanne Zivnuska
Gerald R. Ferris

> *Ben & Jerry's has carefully built up significant brand equity over the years, not only by providing innovative products but also by conducting business in a way that includes a concern for the community and establishes a personal relationship with our customers.*
>
> —PERRY D. ODAK, 2/23/1998

> *Much of the success of the Ben & Jerry's brand is based on its connections to basic human values, and it is our hope and expectation that Ben & Jerry's continues to engage in these critical, global economic and social missions.*
>
> —RICHARD GOLDSTEIN, 4/12/2000

Both of these statements, made more than two years apart, emphasize the importance of corporate reputation. In the first statement, Odak, prior CEO of Ben & Jerry's, implies that the success of Ben & Jerry's is due not only to traditional organizational tactics such as quality management, market creation, and organizational structure, but largely to how it is known to various publics, or its reputation. Odak's emphasis on corporate reputation apparently paid off. A mere two years later, on April 13, 2000, the company was sold to Unilever Foods, a multinational conglomerate, for $326 million—less than 1.5 times its impressive sales revenues ("Fat and Thin," 2000). At the time of the sale, Richard Goldstein, president of Unilever, reaffirmed the value of Ben & Jerry's reputation, not only acknowledging

its contribution to the ice cream maker's prior success, but pledging to uphold that reputation into the future.

So what exactly is this concept of organizational reputation? Reputation has proven difficult to define, shifting in name and explanation as often as a Rorschach inkblot. Reputation has been studied throughout the years under a variety of different disciplines and different names. For example, marketing professionals are concerned about corporate image, accountants and lawyers may assign value to a company's goodwill, and management specialists discuss reputation (Shenkar & Yuchtman-Yaar, 1997). All of these groups, however, are primarily concerned with the same thing: "How do various stakeholders view our organization?"

Organizations must create reputations that appeal to a wide variety of interest groups other than customers, from potential investors to their own employees, each of whom differ in respect to the degree to which they are involved with the organization (Williams & Moffitt, 1997). In some arenas, this wide variety of interest groups may represent a conflict of interest for organizations, as each stakeholder group is presumed to use different criteria when assessing an organization's reputation (Fombrun & Shanley, 1990; Shenkar & Yuchtman-Yaar, 1997). For instance, an organization may seek to establish a strong reputation with environmental groups who demand long-term earth-friendly practices, as well as with stockholders who demand maximum quarterly gains regardless of environmental concerns. A considerable amount of attention has therefore been granted to the competing demands of various stakeholder groups (Fombrun & Shanley, 1990; Shenkar & Yuchtman-Yaar, 1997).

This focus on competing demands, though interesting, actually may be misguided. In reality, fair human resources and management practices have been demonstrated to be the most important indicators of corporate reputation among multiple stakeholder groups (Ballen, 1992; Fombrun, 1996; Garbett, 1988; Koys, 1997; Riahi-Belkaoui & Pavlick, 1992). Therefore, rather than attempting to juggle multiple reputations at once, creating a consistent reputation for fair treatment of employees among stakeholders becomes a central concern (Koys, 1997). For instance, potential and current employees may use a company's reputation for fair treatment of employees as a key factor in decisions to join and remain with that organization (Shenkar & Yuchtman-Yaar, 1997). An organization with the reputation of treating its employees with fairness may therefore have less difficulty attracting and retaining employees than its competitors. Similarly, investors may be more inclined to financially support a

company with a reputation for fair human resources practices than another organization, as that reputation for fairness may be viewed as a signal of high quality management overall (Spence, 1974). This article, therefore, explores the role that HR policies and practices play in developing and maintaining a positive corporate reputation.

The exploration begins with a discussion of how and why human resources practices are important for building strong organizational reputations. Areas critical for building strong reputations within the realm of human resources are then discussed, with an eye to practical examples of both positive and negative reputations. Finally, practical recommendations for building a strong organizational reputation vis-á-vis HR policies and practices are presented.

WHY HUMAN RESOURCES?

Returning to our first example, Ben & Jerry's can help illuminate the relevance of HR policies and practices to an organization's overall reputation. At Ben & Jerry's, the mission statement is comprised of three component statements, one about their product, one about their economic goals, and one about their social commitment. The social commitment component specifically states the organization's commitment to "improving the quality of life of a broad community—local, national, and international" (Ben & Jerry's Statement of Mission, 2001). This mission statement projects an image of Ben & Jerry's that reflects a high degree of concern for quality of life and community interests, both of which are most directly served through the actions of progressive HR professionals. The mission statement continues to emphasize this value when it states that "underlying the mission of Ben & Jerry's is . . . a deep respect for individuals inside and outside the Company and for the communities of which they are a part" (Ben & Jerry's Statement of Mission, 2001).

Three key human resources management (HRM) goals have been studied in relation to corporate reputation (Koys, 1997). These three goals include the fair treatment of employees, the improvement of organizational performance, and legal compliance. Of these, the objective that has been empirically demonstrated to be related to reputation is the fair treatment of employees (Koys, 1997). Ben & Jerry's mission statement, a critical tool for signaling an organization's reputation (Spence, 1974), expands this HR objective and promotes it as a company-wide value, presumably also projecting an image that will reflect favorably on their reputation.

The link between strong HR practices, good reputations, and high financial performance holds true of even the top ten most well-regarded companies in the United States (Brown, 1999; Colvin, 2000a; Stewart, 1998). Several of the top ten best-regarded companies have also appeared on *Fortune*'s annual list of the top ten best companies to work for. Perhaps not coincidentally, these companies are also among the most profitable. Many have been ranked among the top creators of wealth for investors, and several also appear among the top companies in market capitalization among all U.S. corporations (Colvin, 2000a; Stewart, 1988). In contrast, none of the ten least admired companies made any of the other "top" lists. In fact, the ten least admired companies in the year 2000 averaged a negative total stock performance return in 1999, while the top ten averaged a positive total return (Colvin, 2000b). Although it is difficult to pinpoint which is cause and which is effect, it is clear that the link between HR, reputation, and profitability is impossible to ignore.

A lack of explicit interest in human resources issues may result in a poor reputation and lack of profitability. The airlines provide us with one example. The beginning of the new millennium has been characterized for the four largest carriers in the United States (United, American, Delta, and Northwest) by high tensions between top management and pilots, flight attendants, and mechanics. Employees were said to be so frustrated with management relations that deliberate sabotage of organizational operations may have occurred (Zuckerman, 2001). The resultant difficulties that these tensions caused have trickled down, disrupting normal operations and delaying flights at the inconvenience of passengers (Zuckerman, 2001). Specific topics at issue in the conflicts include traditional HR practices, including wages, pension plans, working conditions, and insurance (Draper, 2000a; Griffin, 2000).

The effects of these conflicts can be directly tied to the reputation of the airlines. In past years, for instance, employee-management conflicts at Delta were handled using a "gentleman's club," which allowed both sides to make small compromises and then walk away without damaging the company's image (Fonti, 2001). Pilots report that where there once was trust in management, now there is a "depth of bitterness" and feelings of betrayal (Fonti, 2001). As a result of these conflicts, Delta's productivity has suffered to the extent that in December 2000 the airline was last among major airlines in on-time arrivals and departures, which quickly spurred some business travelers to turn to other carriers (Fonti, 2001).

Similarly, a major consequence of labor-management conflict at United Airlines has led columnist Joe Brancatelli to label the airline a "national disgrace" (Huettel, 2000), where management does not know how to run a business or whose management team is "out of control" (Draper, 2000b). Passengers are then left to form their own conclusions about how these conflicts may impact their own travel plans and safety (Draper, 2000b). These statements demonstrate the extent to which conflicts over HR practices have tarnished United's reputation.

In contrast, Continental and Southwest have enjoyed positive labor relations, resulting in smooth operations, strong reputations, and high profits. Continental's success is largely attributed to their cultivation of the highest employee morale in the airline industry. Gordon Bethune, Continental's chairman, has dedicated himself during his tenure to making the airline an enjoyable place for its employees (Zuckerman, 2001).

Similarly, Southwest CEO Herb Kelleher emphasizes that the company's ranking as one of *Fortune*'s top ten best-regarded organizations is due to high productivity levels that are motivated by the "dedicated energy" of their employees (Woodyard, 2001). This employee energy may be largely due to the company's generous HR practices. A full 15 percent of Southwest's operating profits are earmarked for employee profit-sharing accounts, which are largely invested in the company's own stock. The profit-sharing plan is so successful that about 200 employees have actually become millionaires through it (Levering & Moskowitz, 2000; Woodyard, 2001).

This examination of the airline industry reveals the direct impact that HR practices have on corporate reputation, as well as consumer decision making—both for the better and for the worse. It is clear that maintaining positive management-employee relationships through fair policies and practices is critical for establishing and maintaining a strong reputation.

Too many corporations rely on slogans promoting employees as the most valuable organizational asset (Harrell-Cook & Ferris, 1997). Halcrow (2000, p. 37) even proudly claims that HR is "the custodian of what we understand more than ever to be our greatest assets: employees." Although in the best of worlds, this role of custodian is certainly the ideal, it is not always the reality. Strong reputations are not built on empty slogans. Rather, they are built on results. *Working Woman,* for example, bases their popular rating of the top 25 companies for women executives on hard data. Included in their ranking are board demographics; percentage of women at all managerial levels, including department heads and executive committee members; and number of women among the company's top five highest earners. Programs aimed at leadership development, mentoring, and networking, as well as evidence of a woman-friendly culture are also taken into account, but weighted at only 30 percent of the overall ranking.

A call for financial investments into the fair treatment of employees is admittedly a broad mandate. The rest of this article will address three specific areas where fair treatment may be particularly important. These areas include policies and practices related to diversity, family life, and work-life balance. In all three areas, it will be demonstrated that the key to a strong reputation relies not only on espousing these values but, more importantly, on proactively implementing them (Harrell-Cook & Ferris, 1997).

HUMAN RESOURCE PRACTICES AND REPUTATION

Although the existence of fair treatment policies is certainly a first step in creating a strong organizational reputation, it is the implementation of those policies that is truly the crux of a good reputation. When it comes to human resources, consistency between values and actions is at the very heart of the matter. An organization's relative consistency will be judged by a broad variety of stakeholders (Fombrun, 1996), and will to a large extent inform the reputation that develops as a result (Koys, 1997).

Three areas of HRM are of particular value to creating a positive reputation. Effectively managing ethnic diversity, creating women-friendly climates, and encouraging employees to achieve work-life balance are all ways in which an organization can actively implement its values and project a strong image.

Companies with a solid reputation for diversity management may wield a competitive advantage in the areas of employee recruitment and retention, thereby securing the best employees and reducing expensive turnover costs ("Female and Minority Candidates," 2001). This reputation must be earned by putting words into action. A 2001 WetFeet study of diversity and recruitment practices revealed that a key indicator of a company's commitment to diversity is the diversity of its workforce. Furthermore, a full third of respondents have used the lack of diversity as a criteria in eliminating potential employers ("Female and Minority Candidates," 2001). Therefore, rather than simply promoting a company's commitment to diversity, it is incumbent upon the organization to demonstrate this commitment by active improvement of its recruitment and promotion of diverse employees.

As with overall reputation, the link between a reputation for diversity and performance is clear. Minority-friendly employers tend to be top performers, generally beating the S&P 500 over the past three to five years (Colvin, 1999). Women-friendly organizations (Cleaver, 2000) regularly appear on *Fortune*'s most admired and most profitable lists. Organizations known to be good for minorities are often deluged with applicants and experience high levels of employee commitment and loyalty, stemming the tide of high turnover common in today's economy (Cleaver, 2001; Colvin, 1999). The key to reaping these benefits, then, is to create a reputation for diversity-friendly practices. Creating such a reputation requires consistency. It is difficult to build a reputation based on trendy benefit packages that include day care facilities, gyms, and time off when the organization's culture still supports 60-hour workweeks and emphasizes the importance of face time (Cleaver, 2000; Fishman, 2000a, b).

Wal-Mart is one example of a company with an excellent reputation for ethnic diversity. Wal-Mart was ranked among the top ten in *Fortune*'s recent survey of the best companies for ethnic minorities (Colvin, 1999), as well as appearing in the top ten of their annual most admired list two years in a row (Brown, 1999; Colvin, 2000a). With international expansion growing at the rate of a new outpost every week (Brown, 1999), Wal-Mart is considerably invested in ensuring that their employee profile matches their consumer base. Wal-Mart did not create a strong reputation for diversity simply by providing diversity awareness programs. Rather, the company is known inside and out as making an effort to implement and practice HR initiatives that make a real difference in terms of numbers. For instance, managerial bonuses are tied to the fulfillment of diversity goals, and minority applicants are regularly recruited from historically ethnic colleges and universities. In 1999, 25 percent of Wal-Mart's board of directors were minorities, almost half of their officials and managers were from minority backgrounds, almost a third of new hires were minorities, and they were the largest corporate employer of blacks and Hispanics in the United States (Colvin, 1999). In other words, Wal-Mart does more than create programs to enhance diversity in their corporation. They actively use those policies to change their workforce composition.

In direct contrast, the high-tech industry as a whole has been identified as severely lacking in effective diversity practices (Dreyfuss, 1999). Two exceptions include Sun Microsystems and Applied Materials. Perhaps not coincidentally, these two corporations also rank among the top five overall corporations in each of their industry groups (i.e., computer office equipment and electronics/semiconductors, respectively) (Brown, 1999). Despite these exceptions, Silicon Valley is under fire from a variety of minority leaders, including Jesse

Jackson, the NAACP, and the Urban League, for their reluctance to proactively improve industry diversity practices. Not only does the workforce in Silicon Valley not reflect the community's overall population (Angwin & Castaneda, 1998; Dreyfuss, 1999), in 1998 only 3 among 364 board members of 49 employers were of minority status. Furthermore, although there is strong Asian representation in the industry overall, reports suggest the presence of a glass ceiling effect that bars them from top corporate roles (Dreyfuss, 1999). The Valley's lack of a strong reputation in the area of diversity may result in measurable costs to the industry. Not only are labor markets going untapped in a time of high demand and low unemployment, the industry is vulnerable to severe legal sanctions. Diversity suits in the last 10 years have been known to cost companies up to $134 million dollars in settlement payments alone. Additionally, after such sanctions are paid, companies risk losing substantial market capitalization, as demonstrated by Texaco's drop of about half a billion dollars subsequent to diversity settlement payments made several years ago (Dreyfuss, 1999).

The good news for this industry is that many companies have been successful at turning negative reputations around. Several companies with weak reputations for diversity and even lawsuits within the last 10 years are now ranked among the best in the United States (Dreyfuss, 1999). Given the 7,000 Hispanics and blacks graduating each year in engineering, fair treatment practices in recruiting and hiring stand to make a substantial improvement to the high-tech industry's reputation slump.

Like ethnic diversity, gender equality is currently among the most salient components of effective HR efforts. Regular reports of the best companies for women, mothers, and families are relatively common in the popular press. According to *Fortune*, the 100 best companies to work for are typically 47 percent female and perform better financially than the S&P 500 (Levering & Moskowitz, 2000). In spite of the investment banking industry being male-dominated, Charles Schwab is ranked as the nation's second best company for women (Cleaver, 2000), as well as appearing in the top ten of *Fortune*'s list of the best companies to work for in the United States (Levering & Moskowitz, 2000). These rankings reflect both employee evaluations of their own companies, as well as indicators such as financial performance, number of women in management, and the actual results of women-friendly programs (Cleaver, 2000). More than a third of their employees are women, with a similar percentage of women acting as department and division heads. In fact, their management team is demographically a very close reflection of their overall workforce. Women at Schwab are actively prepared for new positions with anticipatory training and managerial mentoring. These strong HR results pay off for Schwab because they not only get excellent media publicity that helps to reinforce their reputation, they benefit in recruiting (they typically receive more than 17,000 applications yearly) and retaining committed employees. Furthermore, Schwab enjoyed high growth that created more than 3,000 new jobs in 1998 and 1999.

On the other hand, Mitsubishi Motoring Manufacturing of America Inc. learned the importance of having a strong reputation for women the hard way. In 1996, the company found itself in the difficult position of having to respond to an Equal Employment Opportunity Commission (EEOC) lawsuit affecting up to 500 women alleging that the company promoted a culture that was hostile towards women (Grimsley & Swoboda, 1996a). Mitsubishi responded to this lawsuit by refusing to admit any responsibility. The company went to court to get a gag order against the filing lawyer, staged a 3,000 person demonstration against the EEOC, and made several public statements vehemently denying the allegations (Grimsley & Swoboda, 1996b).

Their rationale for this public display was their explicit desire to preserve their reputation. The company's spokesman, Gary Schultz, stated that his goal was to clear the company's reputation (Grimsley & Swoboda, 1996b). The parent company's president, Minoru Makihara, expressed a fear that a lawsuit might damage the reputation of all the related Mitsubishi companies (Sugawara & Blustein, 1996).

These fears were realized when several organizations began to demand sanctions against the company just a few weeks after the lawsuit was filed. Several congresswomen joined in and publicly voiced their opposition to the company's position (Grimsley, 1996a). Subsequently, the National Organization for Women, the Rainbow Coalition, and Operation PUSH all called for a boycott of Mitsubishi products, expressing disappointment with the company's response to the allegations (Grimsley, 1996b).

As public outrage escalated, Mitsubishi changed its approach, hiring former Department of Labor Secretary Lynn Martin to investigate the company's workplace practices. This decision to take action was apparently meant to signal the company's commitment to providing a friendly, fair environment for women. Martin, along with an external team, was charged with the mission of examining workplace practices at the plant and making recommendations for change (Brown & Grimsley, 1996). Although the company persisted in its denial of the sexual harassment allegations in court, they implemented a comprehensive training program on sexual harassment for all plant employees (Grimsley, 1996c), and several months later issued a 34-point anti-harassment plan ("Legal Developments," 1996).

In this example, Mitsubishi was clearly aware of the importance that treating women fairly has on corporate reputation. The pattern of the company's response is an interesting illustration of the importance of consistency. Simply declaring that the allegations of a hostile environment for women were unfounded was not enough to satisfy the public. Instead, what was needed to preserve Mitsubishi's reputation was action consistent with their rhetoric, as was achieved by the independent audit and resulting recommendations.

The third HR component concerning fair treatment of employees is to support employees in their quest for work-life balance. The SAS Institute, a manufacturer of data analysis software, has dedicated their HR practices to this goal, and it pays off in terms of dollars saved and reputation. At the SAS Institute, fair treatment is integrated into every aspect of their strategic mission, particularly in terms of work-life balance. The standard workweek for SAS Institute employees is 35 hours, giving them ample time to actually enjoy the on-site gym, visit their children in the 700-child-capacity day care center, and take advantage of the on-site dentists and physicians. In this company, the gym is rarely empty, sweaty clothes are washed and returned overnight, and employees are encouraged to take their children to lunch in the employee cafeteria— high chairs are provided. In other words, not only does this company profess to value work-life balance, they take real steps to achieve this vision. Their policies all work together to create a corporate culture that is well-regarded in the public eye. It ranks among *Fortune*'s top ten best companies to work for (Levering & Moskowitz, 2000), boasts $870 million yearly in revenues, and receives approximately 200 applications for every job opening. Turnover at the SAS Institute is remarkably low in the software industry, at a maximum of 5 percent yearly. This low turnover is estimated to save the organization an impressive $75 million a year (Fishman, 2000a, b). Such well-integrated HR strategy does not emerge by the random addition of employee perks. The benefits at SAS are specifically implemented to work together as a full package, and each benefit must meet three requirements. They must be proven to fit with the company's culture, have a real impact on a significant number of employees and their families, and be cost accountable (Fishman, 2000b).

On the other hand, companies who do little to promote healthy work-life balance may suffer the consequences. Several years ago, Nike was known for unethical third-world child labor practices. As a direct result of this reputation, some of their market share dropped and their reputation suffered. After policy corrections were made, the company steadily regained their strong reputation and is now the most admired corporation in the apparel industry (Colvin, 2000b).

LOOKING TOWARD THE FUTURE

The message is clear: Companies with strong reputations, particularly those who are perceived as treating their employees fairly, come out on top when it comes to company performance and other financial indicators. Similarly, organizations with poor HR reputations tend to suffer in the marketplace. The conclusion? For organizations to be successful competitors in tomorrow's marketplace,

HR must be firmly established as a key driver of the organization's strategic mission (Harrell-Cook & Ferris, 1997).

Additionally, companies must not be complacent about the types of benefits that are offered. Not only must espoused values and practices be consistent, organizations must constantly rely on feedback and communication from their own employees as well as external groups in terms of being able to effectively meet HR needs. In the future, some areas of HR will assume more importance than they have in the past. Not only will the issues of diversity, women-friendly practices, and work-life balance continue to be critical to organizational success as the world market continues to grow and the pressure to do more with less heightens, workforce demographics will continue to change.

With the aging baby boomer population, organizations will need to provide entirely new lines of benefits aimed specifically at older workers. In just six years, the number of workers in the United States aged 34 and younger is expected to comprise only 36 percent of the workforce (Fandray, 2000). Furthermore, a recent American Association of Retired Persons (AARP) survey shows that a full 80 percent of baby boomers expect to continue working even after retirement (Fandray, 2000). More emphasis on readily accessible medical care, family-leave benefits, shortened days, and part-time options will all be demanded. Increasing physical accommodation for less mobile employees and other work assistance programs will demand exploration.

In the future, the very best companies—those that are most admired, most sought after as employers, and most profitable—will be those that are able to be flexible and progressive in treating their workers fairly. In other words, the companies at the top will be those who truly walk the talk of valuing their most important assets: their own employees. ■

REFERENCES

Angwin, J., & Castaneda, L. (1998, May 4). The digital divide: High-tech boom a bust for blacks, Latinos. *The San Francisco Chronicle*, p. A1.

Ballen, K. (1992). America's most admired corporations. *Fortune, 125* (3), 40–72.

Ben & Jerry's statement of mission. (2001). Available online at www.benjerry.com/mission.html.

Brown, E. (1999). America's most admired companies. *Fortune, 139* (4), 68–73.

Brown, W., & Grimsley, K. D. (1996, May 15). Former labor chief to head internal review at Mitsubishi: Lynn Martin to examine company's practices. *The Washington Post*, C01.

Colvin, G. (1999). The 50 best companies for Asians, Blacks, and Hispanics. *Fortune, 140* (2), 53–57.

Colvin, G. (2000a). America's most admired companies. *Fortune, 141* (4), 108–111.

Colvin, G. (2000b). Who's hot, who's not. *Fortune, 141* (4), 118.

Cleaver, J. (December 2000/January 2001). Top twenty-five companies for executive women. *Working Woman, 26*, 58.

Draper, H. (2000a, September 26). United bag handlers to strike: 85 contract employees plan to picket after pact rejected; other workers at DIA may follow suit. *Denver Rocky Mountain News*, 4A.

Draper, H. (2000b, December 3). Fasten belts, prepare for bickering: Canceled flights, delays likely through holidays as United fights union. *Denver Rocky Mountain News*, 1G.

Dreyfuss, J. (1999). Valley of denial: It's time for Silicon Valley to pull its head out of the microchips on the issue of diversity. *Fortune, 140* (2), 53–57.

Fandray, D. (2000, July). Gray matters. *Workforce*, 27–32.

Fat and thin. (2000, April 15). *The Economist*, 63–64.

Female and minority candidates look for diversity in executive management and staff when considering employment, according to Wetfeet study. (2001, February 6). *PR Newswire*.

Fishman, C. (2000a, March). Moving toward a more balanced work life. *Workforce*, 38–42.

Fishman, C. (2000b, March). Strategic benefits are meaningful, too. *Workforce*, 42.

Fombrun, C. J. (1996). *Reputation: Realizing value from the corporate image.* Boston, MA: Harvard Business School Press.

Fombrun, C., & Shanley, M. (1990). What's in a name? Reputation building and corporate strategy. *Academy of Management Journal, 33*, 233–258.

Fonti, N. (2001, February 25). For a company that has prided itself on its warm relationship with employees, heated pilot talks reflect a 'sea of change' for Delta. *The Atlanta Journal and Constitution*, 1P.

Garbett, T. F. (1988). *How to build a corporation's identity and project its image.* Lexington, MA: Lexington Books.

Griffin, G. (2000, November 4). Top United execs join talks with mechanics. *The Denver Post*, C1.

Grimsley, K. D. (1996a, May 2). Congresswomen fault Mitsubishi reply to EEOC: Automaker accused of retaliation. *The Washington Post*, D08.

Grimsley, K. D. (1996b, May 8). Jackson, NOW target Mitsubishi: Groups urge boycott of firm's products. *The Washington Post*, F03.

Grimsley, K. D. (1996c, July 17). Mitsubishi takes steps to reshape workplace: Employees to be trained to halt harassment. *The Washington Post*, F03.

Grimsley, K. D., & Swoboda, F. (1996a, April 19). Mitsubishi requests gag order: Firm says lawyer may prejudice jurors in harassment case. *The Washington Post*, D03.

Grimsley, K. D., & Swoboda, F. (1996b, April 20). Chicago EEOC braces for Mitsubishi protest. *The Washington Post*, D01.

Halcrow, A. (2000). Workforce optimus 2000. *Workforce, 79* (3), 37.

Harrell-Cook, G., & Ferris, G. R. (1997). Competing pressures for human resource investment. *Human Resource Management Review, 7*, 317–340.

Huettel, S. (2000, December 18). Goliath in the wings. *St. Petersburg Times*, Business 10.

Legal developments: Mitsubishi's sex suits bring resignations and a new "zero tolerance" model. (1996). *Compensation & Benefits Review, 29* (4), 9–10.

Levering, R., & Moskowitz, M. (2000). The 100 best companies to work for. *Fortune, 141* (1), 82–110.

Koys, D. J. (1997). Human resource management and *Fortune*'s corporate reputation survey. *Employee Responsibilities and Rights Journal, 10*, 93–101.

Riahi-Belkaoui, A., & Pavlik, E. L. (1992). *Accounting for corporate reputation*. Westport, CT: Quorum Books.

Shenkar, O., & Yuchtman-Yaar, E. (1997). Reputation, image, prestige, and goodwill: An interdisciplinary approach to organizational standing. *Human Relations, 50*, 1361–1381.

Spence, M. A. (1974). *Market signaling: Informational transfer in hiring and related screening processes.* Cambridge, MA: Harvard University Press.

Stewart, T. A. (1998). America's most admired companies. *Fortune, 137* (4), 70–73.

Sugawara, S., & Blustein, P. (1996, April 24). The Mitsubishi Suit: Hardball, hesitance. *The Washington Post*, F01.

Williams, S. L., & Moffitt, M. A. (1997). Corporate image as an impression formation process: Prioritizing personal, organizational, and environmental audience factors. *Journal of Public Relations Research, 9*, 237–258.

Woodyard, C. (2001, January 23). Fliers' discomfort linked to systems on 777's. *USA Today*, 1B.

Zuckerman, L. (2001, February 27). Happy skies of Continental: Satisfaction is up. Morale is up. So is profit. *The New York Times*, C1.

Index